CHURCHILL'S
WAR LAB

Also by Taylor Downing

Cold War (with Jeremy Isaacs)
Battle Stations (with Andrew Johnston)
Olympia
Civil War (with Maggie Millman)
The Troubles (as Editor)

CHURCHILL'S WAR LAB

CODE-BREAKERS, SCIENTISTS, AND THE MAVERICKS CHURCHILL LED TO VICTORY

Taylor Downing

THE OVERLOOK PRESS
NEW YORK

This edition published in paperback in the United States in 2012 by
The Overlook Press, Peter Mayer Publishers, Inc.

141 Wooster Street
New York, NY 10012
www.overlookpress.com

For bulk and special sales, please contact sales@overlookny.com

First published in Great Britain in 2010 by Little, Brown

Cataloging-in-Publication Data is available from the Library of Congress

Manufactured in the United States of America
ISBN 978-159020-851-9
2 4 6 8 10 9 7 5 3 1

For Anne
With thanks and for support

And for my Father
Who started my interest in all this

Contents

Introduction

A summer's day, 1886. The sunlight falls brightly across the nursery floor of a rather grand house in a smart street in London. Two boys are playing with their toy soldiers on the floor. The younger of the two plays in a desultory way. His heart is not in the game. His elder brother, on the other hand, is the very picture of concentration and seriousness. He moves his soldiers with utmost care and attention. He commands an army of nearly fifteen hundred troops. They are all perfectly painted in the colours of the British Army. Different regiments stand out clearly in their smart field uniforms. And they are properly organised into an infantry division with a cavalry brigade on the flank. There are artillery pieces as well: eighteen field artillery guns and a few heavy pieces for assaulting solid fortresses. The older boy has arranged his troops into a perfect formation of attack.

This afternoon the two boys' father comes to pay a visit. He is a very important man, a leading politician. Indeed, he has just been appointed Chancellor of the Exchequer in the Conservative government. Hence, he is always very busy and has little time for his sons; nevertheless, they adore him. On this occasion the father spends a full twenty minutes in the nursery, studying the impressive scene of an army ready to launch an assault upon its foe. At the end of his inspection, he asks his eldest son if he would like to go into the army when he grows up. Winston Churchill replies at once: yes, he would love to. It would be splendid to command a real army. After this day, the young Winston's education will be focused on getting him into the Royal Military College at Sandhurst, where he will learn the technical details of the profession of arms. The boy's obsession and fascination with his toy soldiers had, as he later wrote, 'turned the current' of his life. Winston Churchill would grow up to be a soldier.[1]

August 1898. The boy is now a distinguished young officer in one of the elite cavalry regiments of the British Army, the 4th Hussars. The only trouble is that the 4th Hussars are stationed in southern India. And there is no action in southern India. Seeking out the thrill of military combat, the twenty-three-year-old subaltern arranges a transfer to the army led by Sir Herbert Kitchener that is mounting an expedition into the Sudan. Churchill is temporarily enlisted with the 21st Lancers, who are part of this vast Anglo-Egyptian army of twenty-five thousand men that is slowly travelling down the west bank of the river Nile, teasing out an engagement with the Muslim Dervish army near Khartoum. He is enthralled by the magnificent sight of this advancing army with its five brigades, each of three or four infantry battalions, marching in open columns across the sandy desert, along with its artillery and transport, supported by a flotilla of grey gunboats sailing down the Nile. The 21st Lancers patrol the flank and scout ahead for the enemy.

On 1 September the Dervish army is sighted, fifty thousand strong, assembling in huge phalanxes. At dawn on the following day, battle ensues. Churchill watches the early stages of the battle from the top of a ridge while passing reports back to his commanding officers. As the sun slowly comes up he is exhilarated by the experience: 'Talk of Fun! Where will you beat this! On horseback, at daybreak, within shot of an advancing army, seeing everything and corresponding direct with Headquarters.'

The battle that follows sees a modern, well-equipped nineteenth-century army engage with a massed force of local tribesmen. The shells and bullets of British howitzers, Maxim guns and carbine rifles tear into the Dervish soldiers, creating huge, deadly swaths in their ranks. The result is a foregone conclusion. Within hours, the Anglo-Egyptian army wins a tremendous victory. But the Dervishes are tough, well-trained and highly motivated soldiers. Later that morning, as the 21st Lancers escort the infantry towards the enemy capital, they come under fire from their right flank. The trumpets and bugles sound the order first to 'Trot', then to 'Wheel Right', then to 'Charge', and the Lancers carry out a manoeuvre they have long trained for, a cavalry charge at full gallop and in close order against an enemy line. Churchill, leading his troop of some twenty-five men, rides right through the line of Dervish defenders, riflemen and spear carriers. But the line holds. Turning around on the other side, Churchill finds himself isolated and surrounded by ferocious Dervishes. He shoots at least three men at close range, rallies his troop and they regroup. Then they open rapid fire on the enemy, who cannot survive this enfilade. In twenty minutes the action is over. The Dervishes withdraw along a wadi, a sunken riverbed, carrying their wounded with them. Churchill is unscathed but counts his losses. His troop has done well, but his regiment of 310 officers and men has lost 5 officers and 65 men killed and wounded in just a few minutes.

Churchill has taken part in the last great cavalry charge in history, at the Battle of Omdurman. Noble and magnificent though it might have seemed, charging across the desert to the echo of hoofs and the clatter of reins, the officers with their swords raised, in reality the cavalry charge was a futile act on the fringes of the battle. It contributed nothing to the enemy's defeat and only inflicted losses of nearly one man in four on the 21st Lancers – far higher than those suffered by any other British unit that day. However, the event was covered with glory and the Lancers won three Victoria Crosses that morning. Churchill later described the battle in a way that encapsulates how many people saw wars on the fringes of the empire in the late nineteenth century: as good sport. He wrote, 'This kind of war was full of fascinating thrills . . . No one expected to be killed . . . [T]o the great mass of those who took part in the little wars of Britain in those vanished light-hearted days, this was only a sporting element in a splendid game.'[2]

Afternoon, 1 June 1944. A small group gathers in the Map Room located at the heart of the underground War Rooms, a top-secret bunker constructed for government leaders in what is called the Downing Street Annexe. The group discusses plans for the D-Day invasion, which everyone knows is now only a few days away. The King is at this briefing, along with his private secretary, Sir Alan Lascelles. The Prime Minister is also present, as well as a few top military figures. At the meeting the Prime Minister presses his desire to be present at the landings on the Normandy coast. He wants to be on board HMS *Belfast*, the flagship of the naval commander of the British fleet at this historic moment. It is agreed that there are risks associated with this: the ship could be bombed, hit by shells or struck by a mine. The largest amphibious landings in history will be taking place only a few thousand yards away.

The Prime Minister asks the King if he would like to be present also, and to lead his troops into battle, like monarchs in olden days. Lascelles is utterly horrified at the idea, feeling that neither the King nor the Prime Minister should put his life at such appalling risk. His face grows longer and longer. Eventually he speaks up and asks how the King would feel if he had to find a new prime minister during the middle of the D-Day landings. The Prime Minister dismisses this possibility, but the King argues that it is foolish of him knowingly to put himself in the face of such danger in what is a 'joy ride'. The Prime Minister replies that during the course of the war he has flown to the United States and the Middle East, and has crossed the Atlantic many times: sometimes he needs to take risks in order to carry out his duties.

The King leaves the meeting and returns to Windsor. On the following day, he resolves to instruct the Prime Minister not to witness the D-Day landings in person. He writes him a letter in which he claims: 'you will see very little, you will run a considerable risk, you will be inaccessible at a critical time when vital decisions might have to be taken; and however unobtrusive you may be, your mere presence on board is bound to be a heavy additional responsibility to the Admiral & Captain'. Later that day, the Prime Minister relents and reluctantly accepts the instruction of his sovereign not to travel to the battle-front.[3]

This story is again so typical of Winston Churchill. His generals and admirals are about to launch the long-awaited invasion of Europe. It has taken years to prepare for this moment. The assault on Fortress Europe will be one of the decisive moments of the Second World War, and one of its fiercest battles. And Churchill wants to be at the centre of it. He wants to witness the action. He wants to see the dawn bombardment, observe the landings, maybe even set foot on the beaches. He argues that leaders of men at times of war sometimes need 'the refreshment of adventure' and that his 'personal interest' is 'stimulated by

xiv   **Churchill's War Lab**

direct contact' with events. Although he offers the King the chance of being there too, in truth Churchill wants to lead the troops into battle himself. Just as he did at Omdurman. Just as he did when he laid out his toy soldiers as a boy.

Man and boy, soldiering and military history were part of Churchill's make-up, embedded in his DNA. For five years, from 1940 to 1945, he would oversee an extraordinary outpouring of radical new ideas and fabulous new inventions in a sequence of events rich with brilliant but wacky boffins, remarkable mavericks and frustrated war chiefs. This would be Churchill's War Lab.

War is the mother of invention. A cliché, but true.

And no war generated more incredible ideas, more technical advances and more scientific leaps than the Second World War.

In the cauldron of ideas that simmered throughout that conflict, new inventions ranged from jet engines to roll-on/roll-off ferries, from flying wings to floating tanks, from miniature radios to guided missiles. Winston Churchill immersed himself in the work of his engineers and inventors, his soldiers, sailors and airmen, imprinting his own personality on the machines that were created in his name. Like no other British prime minister at a time of war, Churchill relished military debate and immersed himself in the work of the code-breakers and scientific mavericks who were needed to get the best out of Britain's sometimes low-key war effort. As a result of his encouragement, these men and women would eventually have a real impact on the outcome of the war.

The Second World War was fought as much by scientists, or 'boffins', as they were often known, as by soldiers, sailors and airmen. New ways of thinking, of approaching and assessing a question in the science known as Operational Research were applied to challenges facing the RAF, the British Army and the

Royal Navy. Operational Research applied scientific method to solving problems ranging from finding the optimum setting for depth charges, to the search pattern aircraft should follow when hunting U-boats, to the most effective way of siting and firing anti-aircraft guns. A tiny device only a few centimetres long and invented at Birmingham University, the cavity magnetron, opened up revolutionary new possibilities for short-wave radar. This could be used to guide bombers to their targets and to track the conning tower of a U-boat from dozens of miles away. In many ways the cavity magnetron was a war-winning invention; certainly it was hailed as such by the Americans when it was first shown off in Washington. And, of course, harnessing the power of the atom in the massive Manhattan Project, which employed some 120,000 scientists and workers, was literally a war-winning discovery. Science would also help to crack the codes used in top-level enemy communications, and would help to guide shells towards aircraft in the skies. One leading scientist said during the war that 'there is hardly a phase of the national life with which scientists are not associated' and that you could 'hardly walk in any direction in this war without tumbling over a scientist'.[4]

Churchill took a keen interest in the application of science to the technology of war. It is the underlying contention of this book that his encouragement of science and of new ways of approaching military challenges was at the core of Britain's final victory in the long struggle of the Second World War. At one point the head of Bomber Command, Sir Arthur 'Bomber' Harris, remonstrated with Churchill about a new approach the Prime Minister was championing.

'Are we fighting this war with weapons or slide rules?' Harris asked.

Churchill replied, 'That's a good idea; let's try the slide rule for a change.'[5]

Churchill was a dynamo who generated energy (and heat) at the heart of government. Often his senior officers resented his interference. General 'Pug' Ismay repeatedly had to mediate in rows between the Prime Minister and his service chiefs. One intimate noted that, without this control on his actions, 'Winston would have been a Caligula or worse, and quite properly [would have] had his throat cut.' His involvement was not restricted to matters of grand strategy: although he always had strong views on these, he would also involve himself in detailed tactical battlefield questions. Within a few weeks of taking over at 10 Downing Street, a visitor was astonished to hear Churchill having a phone call with a local field commander, arguing whether the 'brigadier . . . at Boulogne nearly 100 miles away was doing the right thing in resisting the Germans at one end of a quay or the other'.[6]

Churchill could be petulant and sometimes even childish. He constantly felt frustrated by what he perceived as the lack of drive in the military leaders who reported to him. He thought it was his job to bring vim and vigour to their deliberations and new ideas to their thinking. Once he remarked that taking an admiral out and having him shot would do a great deal 'to encourage the others'. He said that one of his leading generals was more suited to running a golf club than an army of fighting men. At one point, his wife Clementine reluctantly wrote to him that 'there is a danger of your being generally disliked by your colleagues and subordinates because of your rough, sarcastic and over-bearing manner'. But the pace of work quickened when Churchill was around. And most of those forced to work with him accepted that there were more pluses than minuses in his leadership.

Churchill became Prime Minister on the evening of 10 May 1940. Earlier that same day Hitler had launched his armies against Holland, Belgium and France. That evening, as a mighty battle raged on continental Europe, Churchill might have been justified in feeling overawed, even overwhelmed, by the role he had just taken up. Instead, he sensed that his 'whole life had been a preparation for this hour and this trial', and felt exhilarated that he was, in his famous phrase, 'walking with destiny'.[7]

The first two chapters of this book look at the key elements of Churchill's early life that prepared him for leadership in May 1940. He served in several regiments of the British Army both as a young man and in the trenches in 1915–16. He had regularly come under fire in combat. As a politician, he was President of the Board of Trade, Home Secretary and Chancellor of the Exchequer, First Lord of the Admiralty at the beginning of both world wars, and Minister of Munitions at the end of the first. During his so-called 'wilderness years' in the 1930s he honed his ideas about history and what he called England's 'special destiny'. All of this helped to shape the man who became Prime Minister at the age of sixty-five in Britain's hour of crisis.

Chapters 3 and 4 look in detail at his leadership during the critical year when Britain stood largely alone, until first the Soviet Union and then the United States turned a European conflict into a world war. The next four chapters step out of the chronology to look thematically at Churchill's relationships with the scientists who played leading roles in the war, alongside his generals, his admirals and his air marshals. As we shall see, these scientists who advised him along with the military chiefs were core members of his War Lab. Chapter 9 picks up the chronology of the war at the beginning of 1943, as Churchill returns from the Casablanca Conference with President Roosevelt, and at the events that lead up to Operation Overlord, the invasion of Northern Europe. Chapter 10 looks at Churchill's role during the final year of the war, while the concluding chapter offers a brief assessment of his wartime leadership.

Every new book on Churchill has to justify its existence in the crowded market place of Churchilliana. This one has emerged out of years of making television programmes about the Second World War and meeting some of the key participants in that war. It comes from a realisation that, although the Allies certainly did not have a monopoly on good science and technology (far from it), the application of this scientific approach under Churchill's encouragement contributed significantly to their ultimate victory.

My father was a government defence scientist who had been recruited into the RAF straight out of university in 1942. He certainly regarded himself as a boffin, one of the 'backroom boys'. Looking back now, I suppose he left me with a lasting interest in the relationship between science, technology and war. So, *Churchill's War Lab* presents a new take on the remarkable years of Churchill's war leadership. It is partly about the technology of war, partly about how Churchill was forged into the sort of war leader he was, and partly about how he inspired the mavericks and innovators to go out and influence the course of the Second World War. Many of the characters who appear in this book deserve books of their own. But Churchill himself rightly occupies centre stage throughout.

Taylor Downing
October 2009

1

Preparation: The Army and the Navy

When Winston Churchill became Prime Minister in May 1940, to lead the British nation in a war for its survival, he knew more about military affairs and soldiering than any other wartime British premier. Much more than William Pitt the Younger and Spencer Perceval, who led Britain at the time of the Napoleonic Wars, when the country was threatened with invasion by Napoleon. More than Lord Palmerston, who was brought in to lead the government when the Crimean War broke out in 1854. More than Asquith and Lloyd George, who led Britain through the appalling sacrifices of the Great War. And certainly much more than recent British prime ministers who have taken the nation to war – Margaret Thatcher in the Falklands in 1982, John Major in the First Gulf War in 1991, Tony Blair in Iraq in 2003 and Gordon Brown, who inherited the war in Afghanistan. Churchill had trained as a soldier, had served in several regiments of the British Army, had considerable experience of coming under fire, had been captured and had escaped, had led men in battle, and had fought in the trenches in the First World

War. He had studied the fighting of wars and had written famous military histories. He had been in overall command of the Royal Navy in an era when Britannia unarguably ruled the waves. He had led a life that had been imbued with military matters. And he had loved it. It should not be surprising, then, that when he came to lead the nation in war he would run his government in a different way to any other war leader in history. This is that story. But first, it is necessary to see how his previous life was, as he later wrote, 'preparation for this hour and this trial'.

Winston Leonard Spencer Churchill was born on 30 November 1874 into the fringes of one of Britain's greatest aristocratic families. His ancestor, John Churchill, had led an army against France in the War of the Spanish Succession in the first decade of the eighteenth century. The victories he won established Britain on the European stage as a force to be reckoned with; and the riches heaped upon him by a grateful nation allowed him to build a vast estate centred on the magnificent Blenheim Palace, named after his greatest victory. Having been made the 1st Duke of Marlborough, John Churchill founded a dynasty. However, like many grandee families over the generations, the Churchills experienced ups and downs, with later dukes exhibiting profligacy, instability and particularly poor management of their lives and resources, resulting in a huge sale of art treasures to keep the family solvent.[1] Winston's father, Randolph Churchill, was the younger son of the 7th Duke of Marlborough, and he was already pursuing a promising political career at the time of his elder son's birth. He had followed the recent example of several scions of the English aristocracy and married an American heiress, the charming and beautiful Jennie Jerome, whose wealthy father was a stockbroker and part owner of the *New York Times*.

By the accident of being eight weeks premature, Winston was born at Blenheim Palace.[2] His parents were on a shooting party there and Jennie was riding in a pony carriage over rough ground when she went into labour. Winston's earliest years were spent in London and Dublin. As was the custom at this time, he was brought up largely by his nanny, Mrs Everest, to whom he became devoted. His mother, whom he later described as a 'fairy princess', was remote but caring. He wrote, 'She shone for me like the Evening Star.'[3] His father, who was rising through the ranks of the Conservative Party and seemed to have a dazzling political career ahead of him, was even more remote and showed no signs of tenderness, despite his son's adoration and love. Churchill later commented that he had only three or four intimate conversations with his father during his whole life. When he was seven, the young Winston was sent to a brutal primary school near Ascot where floggings with birch were common. He was almost certainly bullied there as well. He hated the school, and after two years was taken away and sent to a much gentler establishment in Brighton.

Churchill wrote about his youth in *My Early Life*, published in 1930 when he was in his mid-fifties. It is a wonderfully entertaining account of how a backward pupil finds a niche in life. Churchill displayed little academic ability in the narrow sense in which it was defined in the late Victorian public school system: that is, in classics and mathematics. His description of taking his entrance examination to Harrow perfectly captures the hopelessness he felt in the face of exams and conventional learning. He was unable to answer a single question in the Latin paper and remembers:

I wrote my name at the top of the page. I wrote down the number of the question '1'. After much reflection I put a bracket around it thus '(1)'. But thereafter I could not think of anything connected with it that was either relevant or true. Incidentally there arrived from nowhere in particular a blot and several smudges. I gazed for two whole hours at this sad spectacle: and then merciful ushers collected my piece of foolscap with all the others.[4]

From this slender indication of scholarship the headmaster of Harrow nevertheless offered the young Churchill a place at the exclusive school. It probably helped that his father was one of the most famous Tory politicians in Britain at the time.

Churchill was no star pupil at Harrow, but while he was hopeless at the conventional subjects, he had an extraordinary ability to learn by heart, once winning a prize for reciting twelve hundred lines of Macaulay's 'Lays of Ancient Rome' word perfectly. And although he failed to absorb much Latin or Greek, he did learn about the English language and how to write a sentence. He showed a particular interest in history and was skilled at writing essays in the subject (a talent that was not much respected then, as perhaps now). Having been obsessed with his toy soldiers, and disappointing his father because he did not have the ability to go on to become a lawyer, it was resolved that the young Winston should head for a career in the army. Unfortunately, once again the problem of the entrance examination loomed, this time to get into Sandhurst, where the young officers-to-be of the British Empire were trained. This time there was no favouritism to help a well-heeled son of one of Britain's finest families into the officer class. Winston had to get through the exams by himself, which included his old bugbear of mathematics. He failed the exams twice, then attended a crammer school in west London. On his third attempt he just scraped in – 95th out of 104 candidates. This was not high enough to qualify for the infantry, but the cavalry had lower standards and accepted him for a cadetship. At the age of eighteen, Winston Churchill was in the army at last.

Once at Sandhurst, Churchill's somewhat unpromising career took a completely new course. No longer handicapped by his lack of knowledge in Latin or mathematics, he began to enjoy courses in Tactics, Fortifications, Military Administration, Drill and Riding. He did well and soon stood out as good officer material and an excellent horseman. In December 1894 he succeeded in his final exams and passed out 20th in the list of 130. Then, with a little help from his mother and from the Marlborough family, he entered one of the most fashionable cavalry regiments, the 4th Hussars. They were smart, aristocratic and led by one of the leading officers in the British Army, a man who had close connections with the royal family. The only problem was that the salary of a young subaltern did not match the outgoings expected of an officer in this elite regiment, who had to provide his own uniform, run two horses and pay all of his mess bills. So any officer in the 4th Hussars, and indeed in most other cavalry regiments at the time, needed a private income. The bubble of Lord Randolph Churchill's career had burst when he resigned from the government in 1886 and, to his astonishment, was never asked back. Suffering from either syphilis or more probably some form of brain tumour, he experienced erratic mood swings and needed constant medical attention. By the time he died in 1895 he had used up all of his fortune. Winston's mother was left with barely enough to fund her own extravagant lifestyle, let alone those of her two sons. Consequently, money would be a problem for Churchill for some time to come, and the need to pay his own way partly determined his course of action over the following years.

Churchill threw himself into the life of his regiment. For an officer recruit this involved a round of activities at the Riding School, learning horsemanship; on the Barrack Square, learning cavalry manoeuvres; and in the mess, learning to be a true officer and a gentleman. At this point in the late Victorian era, the country had enjoyed many years of peace. Few officers below the rank of captain had seen any active service. It was Churchill's fear that he would serve dutifully for many years but not enjoy the thrill of combat. 'From very early youth I had brooded about soldiers and war,' he later wrote, 'and often I had imagined in dreams and day-dreams the sensations attendant upon being for the first time under fire. It seemed to my youthful mind that it must be a thrilling and immense experience to hear the whistle of bullets all round.'[5] So he now resolved to take full advantage of the perks of a young subaltern in a cavalry regiment, one of which was long holidays, and to put this matter right. In the winter of 1895, during his two-month break, instead of spending the time fox-hunting, as was usual for cavalry officers, Churchill and a fellow-officer travelled at their own expense to Cuba, where a war was raging between local rebels and the Spanish colonialists. With appropriate introductions from an old friend of Churchill's father, the two young officers were assigned to a mobile column of the Spanish Army marching into the jungle interior in search of rebels. They soon found them and a gunfight ensued in which the twenty-one-year-old Churchill came under fire for the first time. He found the whole experience exhilarating. But the mission was not a success. The Spanish forces deployed in conventional formation to assault the Cubans, who, adopting guerrilla tactics that would become much more familiar over the following hundred years, simply melted away into the jungle mists.

After a couple of weeks the column returned to base and Churchill and his friend sailed home. Today it seems incredible that a young army officer would pay his own passage halfway across the world to engage in combat, with all the risks of death or injury that entailed. But in the last decade of the Victorian era, before the futile horrors of the Great War, before the destruction of aerial bombing, and long before the nightmare of nuclear Armageddon came to haunt us, war was still seen as glamorous and romantic. Certainly Churchill saw it that way. And he was ambitious. The officers who had experience of warfare would probably be promoted more rapidly. Doubtless they would attract the awe and attention of fellow-officers. It also seems likely that Churchill was already looking ahead to a political career and wanted to notch up some worthwhile experience as a foundation for what would follow.

Soon after Churchill's return from Cuba, the 4th Hussars were sent to India. This was a regular posting for almost every unit in the British Army, and the Hussars were assigned to spend nine years in Bangalore in the south. For a young officer in an elite cavalry regiment, life on the India station in the heyday of the Raj could be very pleasant. Officers lived in spacious bungalows surrounded by neat gardens and were looked after by a butler and servants. There were a couple of hours of horse-riding drill from six o'clock each morning, then an hour or so in the stables, then nothing much through the heat of the day, until the officers started to play polo around 5 p.m. And each evening there were dinner and drinks in the mess. Churchill committed himself wholeheartedly to polo and soon developed into a fine player, despite sustaining a shoulder injury. But he rapidly realised that this leisurely officer's life was not enough for him. He needed something else.

Churchill was very aware that his earlier academic failings had forced him to miss out on a university education. So he decided he needed to catch up on his learning. In the many hours of his down time at Bangalore, he threw himself into a rigorous reading programme. His mother sent him crates of books which he devoured. He started with the eight volumes of Gibbon's *Decline and Fall of the Roman Empire*, which someone told him had been a favourite of his father, and the twelve volumes of Macaulay's *History of England*: 'fifty pages of Macaulay and twenty-five of Gibbon every day'. He then progressed to other classics of history and philosophy, from Socrates to Malthus and from Aristotle to Darwin and Adam Smith. He even asked his mother to send dozens of volumes of the *Annual Register*, a compendium of parliamentary debates and an official record of British public life. He read for four or five hours every day, for five or six months of the year. A mind that had not been accustomed to learning was suddenly soaking up ideas like a sponge. He loved the way the English language was used in these classics and was absorbed by the stories they related and the ideas they contained. And he stored away everything he discovered. His scholarly reading must have made him a very unusual figure among the other young cavalry officers of his regiment. But his enthusiasm for polo kept him in with his fellow-officers as a popular and sporting colleague.

Churchill longed for one of India's regular frontier wars in which he could seek further experience and possible fame. But in sleepy Bangalore all he had were his books, his polo and the daily round of regimental life. Then, in the spring of 1897, a dispute arose in the Swat Valley in Malakand on the North-West Frontier (now still an unruly quarter of northern Pakistan). Churchill was on leave in England but immediately raced back to India to try to be assigned to the field force that was setting out to teach the Muslim Pathan rebels a lesson. The commander cabled him: 'No vacancies; come as a correspondent; will try to fit you in.' Churchill rushed first to Bangalore, to get permission to join the field force, and then travelled for five days by train to the North-West Frontier. Meanwhile, back in London, his mother lobbied various editors and finally persuaded the *Daily Telegraph* to accept dispatches from her son at five pounds a column.

The Malakand Field Force was a unit typical of the British Raj. It consisted of regular British Army units on their tour of duty in the subcontinent, and units from the Indian Army, with British officers commanding native warrior-soldiers – Sikhs, Punjabis and others. Travelling with the force was a set of 'political officers' whose job it was to negotiate with the locals and enforce imperial rule. The field force's mission was to seek out the Pathan warriors and draw them into battle. On 16 September a small group was detached to go up the Mamund Valley. Churchill was advised that he might see some action here, so he joined the 35th Sikhs, who slowly marched their way up the valley, surrounded by mountains rising steeply to four or five thousand feet. At the top of the valley they reached a village. The troops were about to destroy the villagers' crops as a form of collective punishment when Churchill looked around and realised there were only four or five officers and about eighty Sikhs. The rest of the column was way behind them down the valley. At that moment, firing erupted and Churchill could see the glint of the swords of the Pathan tribesmen reflecting in the hot sun along the steep valley side. They had walked into a trap.

Churchill picked up a rifle and began to return fire. A British officer ordered the small force to withdraw down the valley. He was shot and killed only a few yards from Churchill. The Sikhs pulled back in some confusion and nearly broke one of the first rules of a frontier war: never leave the wounded behind at the mercy of an enemy who would probably hack them to pieces. But Churchill and a few of the Sikhs carried their wounded comrades down the valley, under constant harassment from groups of Pathan warriors. At one point a tribesman charged at Churchill, brandishing his sword. Churchill took out his revolver and fired. He missed, but the warrior withdrew hastily and hid behind a rock. Eventually, Churchill and his paltry force reached the rest of the company further down the valley, but the tribesmen were still in hot pursuit. Then came the reassuring sound of regular firing and the smart order 'Volley firing. Ready. Present' echoed across the valley. Another volley of rifle fire crashed out. A regular British Army unit, the East Kents, known as the Buffs, had arrived on the scene to save the day.

After further intense fighting, the numerically superior British and Indian troops finally took control of the valley. Over the next two weeks Churchill witnessed the systematic destruction of the Pathans' villages, the filling in of their wells, the burning of their crops and the smashing of their reservoirs in punishment. Such was the revenge of the British Empire. But for Churchill this combined Anglo-Indian expedition confirmed his belief in the Empire and his conviction that Britain had a mission to rule India. It was a belief he never gave up.

Churchill's dispatches in the *Daily Telegraph* were well received for their graphic and dramatic accounts. Encouraged by this, he wrote a book of the campaign which he sent back to London and his mother arranged for its publication. *The Malakand Field Force* was a great success, well reviewed and widely read. Even the Prince of Wales wrote to congratulate Churchill: 'Everyone is reading it, and I only hear it spoken of with praise.'[6] Churchill reflected that for a few months' hard work writing the book he had earned the equivalent of two years' pay as a cavalry officer. He was delighted with the praise and took on board the pecuniary lesson.

A year later another imperial sortie attracted Churchill's attention. Lord Salisbury's Conservative government had decided to send an army to the Sudan to teach the Khalifa and his Muslim Dervish army a lesson for the assault by his predecessor on Khartoum a decade earlier, which had cost the life of the British commander there, General Gordon. Sir Herbert

Kitchener assembled an expedition to march down the Nile into the Sudan and on to the Dervish capital. Churchill again tried to pull strings with influential people to get himself assigned to an expedition that offered even more dramatic imperial adventure than the North-West Frontier. However, despite much support for his placement, Kitchener refused to have Churchill in his expedition. There was clearly some hostility felt towards the young cavalry officer who always seemed to up sticks and leave his own regiment to be at the centre of the action. And many people did not like the idea of such a junior officer going into print and criticising his superiors. Even a telegram from the Prime Minister's office did not change Kitchener's mind. But Churchill was nothing if not persistent, and at the last minute the War Office assigned him to the 21st Lancers, who were to accompany the expedition south. Churchill embarked immediately for Cairo, where he joined the Lancers just as they were leaving. The border with the Sudan lay some fourteen hundred miles to the south. This time Churchill was contracted to supply letters to the *Morning Post* at fifteen pounds a column. His value was rising.

As we saw in the Introduction, Churchill marched with Kitchener's army down the left bank of the Nile, then acquitted himself bravely in the Battle of Omdurman. Just as on the North-West Frontier, he looked death in the face from frenzied tribesmen opposed to British rule and once again emerged without a scratch. Once this short engagement was over, 'the most dangerous 2 minutes I shall live to see', as he wrote to a fellow-officer, Churchill played no further role in the campaign.[7] Three hundred British troops died at Omdurman. But about ten thousand Dervishes were killed and another fifteen thousand were wounded. The wounded were left to die in the hot desert, and were offered no medical aid. Some were even murdered where they lay. Later, when British and Egyptian soldiers entered Khartoum, they desecrated the tomb of the Mahdi who had destroyed Gordon's army ten years before. His corpse was exhumed, decapitated and eventually taken to Cairo. Churchill was deeply shocked by this.

He returned home within days of the victory at Omdurman. The adventure was over. He briefly rejoined his regiment in Bangalore and helped them to win the Indian Polo Championship, despite a worsening of his shoulder injury. Then, having achieved his objectives of seeing action and commanding men under fire, he resigned his commission. The pace of regular army life was too slow for him and he wanted to move on. He returned to London to devote himself to writing and politics. Free to write without the limitations of being an army officer, he quickly finished another military book which told the story of the Sudan campaign, *The River War*. Published in two volumes and at 950 pages, this was as successful as his earlier work and helped to enhance his reputation. In *The River War* Churchill was outspoken in his criticism of Kitchener for failing to prevent the brutality of the army once the victory had been won. He was already beginning to work out his own philosophy of war, which involved being defiant in the face of defeat, resolute in the pursuit of battle, but magnanimous in victory. Kitchener's army had shown only barbarity after its triumph, and Churchill argued that this was not right. Unsurprisingly, the book won him few friends in military circles.

Back in London, Churchill decided it was time to launch his political career, and sounded out the Conservative Party.[8] The mixed reputation of his father preceded him and he was made a candidate for the tough working-class constituency of Oldham. The Lancashire cotton town faced a by-election in the summer of 1899. Churchill fought his first election campaign and lost. He felt disconsolate at his defeat. But, as ever in his remarkable life, unexpected events came to the rescue.

In October 1899, just as *The River War* was about to be published, war broke out with the Boers in South Africa. The quarrel between the ever-expanding British Empire and the Boer republics went back a long way. The Dutch settlers who had lived in southern Africa since the seventeenth century had been slowly migrating north from their old colony at the Cape. They were fiercely independent, strongly Calvinistic and had fought a succession of minor wars with their neighbours, the Zulus, as well as the British. What transformed a series of relatively petty arguments into something far more significant was the discovery of huge reserves of gold and diamonds in the Transvaal in the 1890s. Now that there were abundant natural resources to be exploited and fortunes to be made, the warlike Boers attacked British territory. For the first time in nearly half a century, Britain found itself at war with other white men. It was soon clear that this could escalate into a major imperial conflict.

Churchill once again felt the magnetic pull of war, and he negotiated a deal with the *Morning Post* to report from South Africa as a war correspondent. This time he commanded the princely fee of £250 per month plus all expenses, making him one of the highest-paid war reporters in South Africa. He sailed on the first available boat for Cape Town, travelling with the British commander-in-chief, General Redvers Buller, and his staff. Churchill's dispatches from South Africa would soon turn him into an international celebrity.

As with so many wars fought by Britain, the early stages of the Boer War went badly. The Boers showed themselves as skilled fighters, good horsemen and ingenious tacticians, and they had bought the latest weaponry, including magazine-loading rifles and modern artillery pieces. They laid siege to the British garrisons at Mafeking, Ladysmith and Kimberley, and in almost every head-on engagement they proved superior to the British forces. Churchill had to report one setback after another. In an attempt to be first with his story, he negotiated a trip on an armoured train from Durban to Estcourt. Then, on 15 November, the train ventured forth from Estcourt with two companies of infantrymen under the command of Captain Haldane, who asked Churchill to go along with them. The train moved cautiously into territory that had recently been raided by the Boers. On its way back it came under fire from a Boer raiding force and then ran into an ambush. The Boers had placed a heavy stone on the track and three coaches were derailed.

Churchill had only the status of a reporter, but so recently out of uniform and now finding himself and his companions under fire, he soon reverted to military mode. With Haldane's agreement, he spent about an hour trying to get the steam engine to push the derailed coaches out of the way. Throughout this time they were under continuous rifle and artillery fire. Four men were killed and about thirty wounded. Haldane wrote in his official report that Churchill 'with indomitable perseverance continued his difficult task'.[9] Eventually, Churchill managed to get the engine past the derailed coaches and it carried off the wounded men to the nearest town and safety. Churchill himself went just a few hundred yards and then left the locomotive to walk back to the scene of the ambush, where Haldane and the remaining soldiers were still exchanging fire with the Boers. He had not gone far when two Boer riflemen surrounded him and opened fire. Churchill ran back down the railway cutting with the riflemen shooting after him. 'Their bullets,' he later wrote, 'sucking to right and left, seemed to miss only by inches.'[10] He emerged from the cutting and headed for the cover of a river gorge, but was chased by a Boer horseman. With the Boer just forty yards behind, Churchill reached for his Mauser pistol. Later he said that, with his blood up, he would have killed the horseman. But his revolver was not there. He had taken it off earlier. The Boer aimed his rifle at Churchill who now had no alternative. He put his hands in the air and surrendered. Churchill was a prisoner.

All the men who had surrendered were rounded up like cattle and taken away. This action was typical of the many humiliations which the Boers inflicted on British forces at this stage of the war. The technically superior firepower of the armoured train had counted for nothing against a cleverly planned ambush by able fighters who had chosen their ground well and could soon overpower the British troops.

Churchill and the officers were taken to a school that had been requisitioned as a prisoner-of-war camp in Pretoria. When captured, Churchill had been unarmed and he had all his journalistic credentials on him. But the Boers realised they had a big catch in Winston Churchill and were unwilling to release him, despite his protests that he was an unarmed civilian. Churchill wrote formally to the Boer commander, demanding to be released. He claimed that he had at no time fired on Boer forces and had only been trying to evacuate the wounded. His appeals were ignored.

Churchill passed his twenty-fifth birthday in the POW camp. Thirty years later he wrote, 'I certainly hated every minute of my captivity more than I have ever hated any other period of my whole life.'[11] There is a photo of him at the camp in which he looks dejected and thoroughly peeved. When it seemed that his appeals to the Boers would fail, he began to plan an escape. He, Haldane and another prisoner who spoke some Dutch intended to climb over the hastily built prison fence and head east out of Boer territory into neutral Mozambique, travelling by night and resting up during the day. After several delays, on the night of 12 December Churchill made a dash for it while the guard was not looking. He clambered over the fence and into a neighbouring garden, where he waited in the shrubs for the others. But no one came. The guard was too watchful and the others could not make their escape. Churchill was on his own. He had some money in his pocket and some chocolate, but no map.

Unknown to Churchill, when his absence was discovered a huge hue and cry went up. Search parties were sent out to look for him. Posters were put up offering a reward of twenty-five pounds, 'dead or alive'. But he managed to hide on a train heading east through the night and the next morning he sheltered near a tiny station. He was safe for the moment, but knew that without food or help he would never be able to find his way the three hundred miles to Mozambique. There were guards on every bridge and at every station. He could not decide what was best. 'I stopped and sat down,' he later wrote, 'completely baffled, destitute of any idea what to do and where to turn.'[12] Finally, he took a huge risk and went up to the door of a house in a nearby kraal, or settlement, to ask for help. With extraordinary luck, he had picked the house of a British engineer who managed the local coal mine. The engineer knew that Churchill was a wanted man, but still he decided to help. He fed him and hid him in the mine for several days while he made a plan. With the support of three others (one of whom was from Oldham and so knew of Churchill's recent by-election campaign), the engineer then smuggled Churchill into the truck of a coal train heading east. Churchill eventually reached Lourenco Marques (now Maputo), where, covered in coal dust, he walked into the British Consulate and freedom.[13]

Churchill's escape brought him instant fame. It provided a brief moment of relief and celebration at a point when the war was going badly for the British. When Churchill arrived back in Durban on 23 December he was met by cheering crowds, who took over an hour to disperse. Three days later he met General

Buller, the commander of the British forces in Natal, who congratulated him wholeheartedly. Churchill had become a hero. And now he asked to enlist again in the fighting forces.

This posed a quandary for Buller, because the War Office had recently made it clear that serving officers could no longer write for the press and no journalists could fight in the regular army. But Buller was so keen to enlist Churchill with his fighting spirit that an exception was made and he was offered an unpaid commission in a local regiment, the South African Light Horse. He spent the rest of his time in South Africa with the unusual dual role of being both a fighting cavalry lieutenant and a war correspondent.

In the early months of 1900, Churchill witnessed some of the worst moments of the Boer War, including the aftermath of the fighting at the Tugela River and the battle at Spion Kop. For many days at a time he lived under constant shellfire and regular rifle fire. At one point, the feather in his hat was cut through by a bullet. At another, eight men around him were wounded by a shrapnel burst while Churchill was, yet again, unscathed. In April, he found himself alone, facing a group of Boer commandos, cut off and without a horse. At the last minute, a British scout rode up and Churchill leaped on his horse. They rode off together, but the horse was shot and died of its wounds. 'I don't think I have ever been so near destruction,' he wrote to his mother.[14]

These months of fighting and writing reports for the *Morning Post* helped to shape Churchill's view of war. He was fascinated by the commando tactics of the Boers, who attacked in small numbers, struck hard and then melted away into the countryside. This left Churchill with a lifelong respect for the use of small, well-trained forces that could hit the enemy with an impact out of all proportion to their numbers. This appealed to his romantic view of war and how it should be fought. He also later became firm friends with some of the Boer commanders, men like Louis Botha and Jan Christiaan Smuts.

On the other hand, although he continued to find the thrill of battle exhilarating, he was terribly moved by the death and mayhem he witnessed in South Africa. After the fighting on the Tugela River, he came across the dead bodies of two Boers: a man in his sixties who had been wounded in the leg and had bled to death; and alongside him a young boy of about seventeen, shot through the heart. A few hundred yards away were the corpses of two British soldiers, their heads smashed 'like egg shells'. Churchill wrote in the *Morning Post*: 'I have often seen dead men killed in war – thousands at Omdurman, scores elsewhere, black and white, but the Boer dead aroused the most painful emotions . . . Ah, horrible war, amazing medley of the glorious and squalid, the pitiful and the sublime.'[15]

Churchill also refined his views about the senior officers in the British Army. He felt they were not facing up to reality and were not using their troops effectively. He was amazed at how officers still ordered men into frontal attacks against troops who were able to employ the devastating firepower of their powerful modern rifles. There was no glory, only sacrifice, in this. He wrote in the *Morning Post*: 'We must face the facts. The individual Boer, mounted in suitable country, is worth from three to five regular soldiers. The power of modern rifles is so tremendous that frontal attacks must often be repulsed.'[16] He also felt that senior officers rarely showed enough aggressive spirit and too easily became depressed and almost fatalistic about the fact that the enemy would outperform them. This sense that British commanders needed to be more offensive-minded would return to worry Churchill again, forty years later.

In January 1900, Lord Roberts took command of the British Army in South Africa and Kitchener was sent from Khartoum as his chief of staff. With reinforcements of men and supplies arriving from Britain, the tide of war slowly turned against the Boers. Churchill wrote that the British now needed to show mercy to the Boers so as not to provoke a further phase of bitter warfare. His views were unpopular, going against the grain of jingoistic fervour that had been stirred up back home. Nevertheless, this was an important aspect of his concept of the morality of war – to be magnanimous in victory and to show goodwill in peace.

In May, the siege of Mafeking was relieved, prompting huge celebrations in Britain, and the creation of another new hero, Major Robert Baden-Powell, who had led the town's garrison through the dreadful hardships of the siege. In June, Churchill was present at the recapture of Pretoria, leading the troops that freed the remaining prisoners-of-war. Amid cheers, he tore down the Boer flag, replaced it with the Union Jack, and was reunited with many of those who had been captured with him six months before.

With the recapture of Pretoria and the relief of Mafeking, it seemed that the war had been won, and many people assumed it would soon be over. In fact, it dragged on for a further two years, with the Boers mounting a highly effective guerrilla war against the British right across southern Africa. Exasperated, the British, by now under Kitchener's command, did everything they could to destroy ground support for their guerrilla enemy. Farmsteads were destroyed, crops were burned and Boer citizens were rounded up and interned in what the British called 'concentration camps'. Tens of thousands of Boer women and children died in the overcrowded and unhealthy camps, leaving a lasting legacy of hatred towards British rule among the Afrikaner community.

Churchill returned to Britain in the summer of 1900 and immediately resumed his political career. The Conservative government of Lord Salisbury wanted to exploit the patriotism generated by the war and called a general election in the autumn. It became known as the 'Khaki Election'. Churchill once again stood in Oldham, where he was welcomed as a returning war hero by a crowd of ten thousand people. During the campaign, he was cheered wildly in speech after speech. In those days, general elections were not held on a single day, with the result announced the following morning. Instead, the election process could last anything up to five weeks. However, Oldham was one of the first constituencies to declare its result, and it returned two members. This time Churchill was elected as the second candidate by a narrow margin. This early victory in a working-class town gave a huge boost to the Conservative campaign, and Churchill was in great demand during the remaining weeks of voting. He addressed political rallies up and down the country, every night for four weeks, sharing the platform with many of the leading Conservatives of the day.

The triumphant Churchill, basking in the glory of his personal political success, then went on a whistle-stop lecture tour, using a magic lantern to tell the story of his experiences in the Boer War. Today, a young celebrity like the twenty-six-year-old Winston Churchill would probably go on a reality TV show. Then, public speaking was the way to become famous and to earn money. Churchill visited most of the big cities of Britain, captivating crowds of many thousands at a time, and often earning a hundred pounds or more for an evening lecture. The House of Commons, in which the Conservatives and Unionists enjoyed an increased majority, was due to meet in December, but the newly elected MP for Oldham chose to miss the opening of his first Parliament and instead continued his lecture tour in the United States and Canada. Here, even more money was on offer. After three lucrative months, Churchill had amassed about ten thousand pounds (roughly a million in today's money). He invested his earnings and had plenty to live on for years to come. The financial worries that had plagued him since he had joined the army were over and he was free to dedicate himself to his new political career. His military exploits had led to fame *and* fortune.

The young MP gradually began to build a new reputation for himself at Westminster. Fast-forwarding through his political career, which is not the subject of this study, Churchill never felt entirely comfortable within the Conservative Party. In particular, as a convinced free-trader, he disagreed with the Tory policy of tariff protection. In October 1903, he drafted a letter to a friend. It was never sent, but in it Churchill stated, 'I am an English Liberal. I hate the Tory Party, their men, their words and their methods.'[17] In May 1904, he took the highly unusual step of 'crossing the floor' of the House of Commons; that is, he left the Conservative benches and joined the Liberals. Many Tories never forgave him for this act of betrayal. And as the Conservative government was becoming unpopular, many others saw it as a purely opportunistic act, an attempt to seek office within a future Liberal government.

Sure enough, two years later, Sir Henry Campbell-Bannerman's Liberals won the general election. Churchill was elected as the Liberal MP for Manchester North West. With his fame and celebrity status, he was an obvious candidate for office and he duly became Under-Secretary of State at the Colonial Office. For two years he threw himself into his new role as a junior minister and oversaw the creation of self-governing states in the Transvaal and the Orange Free State, bringing the Boers into the British Empire and resolving the disputes in southern Africa. At one point he wrote six lengthy notes for the Colonial Office, outlining his plans for various other parts of the world. This prompted Sir Frances Hopwood, the senior

civil servant at the Colonial Office, to write, 'He is most tire-
some to deal with & will I fear give trouble – as his father did –
in any position to which he may be called. The restless energy,
uncontrollable desire for notoriety & the lack of moral perception make him an anxiety indeed.'[18] So Churchill was already
displaying the energy and drive that would characterise his
wartime leadership, but was still dismissed as an awkward
troublemaker by many in the establishment.

In the year 1908, two life-changing events took place. In
March, Churchill met Clementine Hozier at a dinner party. She
was ten years younger than him, and radiant. Churchill particularly liked her striking, mysterious eyes. He asked her if she
had read his recent biography of his father. She had not. Despite
this, Churchill became infatuated with Clementine and they
wrote and met regularly over the next few months. This was
not Churchill's first infatuation, there had been a small number
of society women who had previously attracted his attention.
But he was the first to admit that he was not a great romancer,
and found it difficult talking to young ladies. Clementine,
though, was different: she was serious-minded as well as beautiful; and, rarely for a girl of her class at the time, she had good
academic qualifications.[19] She liked his style, his wit and no
doubt his ambition, and when he proposed to her at Blenheim
Palace in August, she accepted. Churchill was delighted and the
two were married the following month.

Churchill loved 'Clemmie' intensely for the rest of his life and
he never strayed. She provided the support, homeliness and
large doses of good sense that he desperately needed. The
domestic life they began to build together was something new
for Churchill, who had endured a lonely childhood and since
Sandhurst had found most of his camaraderie in the male
worlds of the army and the House of Commons. Clemmie was
the ideal political wife. Despite long separations when Churchill

was away on business, they wrote lovingly to each other almost daily, and Churchill found Clemmie's support, always imbued with a great deal of common sense, a vital prop to both his emotional and his political life.[20]

While Churchill was courting Clemmie, Herbert Asquith replaced Campbell-Bannerman as Prime Minister. In the reshuffle that followed, Churchill was appointed President of the Board of Trade. So, aged just thirty-three, he became a member of the Cabinet. His star was rising quickly, along with that of another passionate and visionary politician, Chancellor of the Exchequer David Lloyd George. Asquith's government would become one of the greatest social-reforming administrations of the twentieth century, laying the foundations for the welfare state. Churchill was soon hard at work drafting legislation to create a minimum wage, to establish workers' rights to breaks for meals and refreshment (the much-loved British tea break became law in one of his reforms), and to create more than two hundred labour exchanges across the country to help the unemployed find work. Always keen to get into print, Churchill's next book was a compendium of his speeches on reform entitled *The People's Rights*.

In February 1910, Churchill was promoted again, this time to Home Secretary. He was now even more centrally placed to carry forward the Liberal agenda of improving conditions for working people. He also threw himself into prison reform and reduced the high numbers of young offenders in prison. But the tensions of Edwardian Britain were never far below the surface. There was the long-running and still unresolved issue of Home Rule for Ireland. Churchill was lukewarm in his support for Home Rule, even though it was official Liberal policy. British society was similarly divided over the issue of whether women should get the vote (there was still not universal suffrage for men, either). The suffragette movement eventually split, with one group resorting to violent protest in a bid to make its voice heard. The chant 'Votes for Women' echoed around Westminster. Churchill was not in favour. Clementine was, but was opposed to the violent tactics of the militants. As Home Secretary, Churchill approved the forced feeding of suffragettes who had gone on hunger strike in prison.

Along with this, Britain was hit by a series of increasingly damaging labour disputes, as working men and women began to exercise their political muscle. On Churchill's watch there was a series of strikes in the South Wales coal mines which led to local rioting and disturbances. Shops in the town of Tonypandy were looted and a local colliery attacked. In principle, Churchill was opposed to the use of the army to resolve domestic disputes, declaring in the House of Commons: 'It must be an object of public policy, to avoid collisions between troops and people engaged in industrial disputes.' However, he sent a squadron of cavalry to the Valleys and placed them on stand-by. The soldiers were never used, but Churchill was still widely condemned from all sides. The Conservatives accused him of being too soft on the rioters. The Labour Party, although still only small as a party at Westminster, was outraged that he had sent soldiers into an industrial problem. 'Remember Tonypandy!' was a cry heard against Churchill from the Left for many years to come.

These were all serious issues, but Asquith's administration faced its greatest crisis yet when the House of Lords rejected Lloyd George's reforming budget, known as the 'People's Budget'. In this, he proposed unemployment benefits and, most radically, Britain's first state pension. In order to pay for these, Lloyd George planned to increase taxation of the rich, including a new super-tax of six pence in the pound for those earning over five thousand pounds per year, along with rises in death duties and property taxes. The Conservatives were deeply opposed to this attempt to redistribute wealth, and used their substantial majority in the House of Lords to reject the budget. Asquith was outraged that the Lords could reject a money bill proposed by a democratically elected House of Commons, and a major constitutional crisis unfolded. Two general elections followed in 1910, the House of Lords finally gave in, and the budget was passed. But Asquith had not finished: he wanted to permanently restrict the power of the House of Lords and he persuaded King George V to agree in principle to the creation of 250 new Liberal peers if the Lords did not accept another piece of legislation, the Parliament Bill. In August, to avoid being swamped by the new peers, the Lords finally passed the bill by a tiny majority. The constitutional crisis was over. The People had won. Churchill, firmly committed to the side of the People, was viewed by the Conservatives as no less than a class traitor. They were now more hostile towards him than ever.

A totally different crisis also erupted in the summer of 1911 when the Germans sent a gunboat to Agadir in Morocco during a revolt against the Sultan. The French regarded Morocco as part of their sphere of influence in North Africa and were appalled at what they saw as aggressive German action. The British interpreted this piece of 'gunboat diplomacy' as an attempt to turn Agadir into a German port, a clear threat to the British naval base at Gibraltar, as well as a sign of Germany's ambition to rival the Royal Navy. The crisis was soon defused, but the Prime Minister decided that the Admiralty needed someone more assertive in charge. In October 1911, Asquith invited Churchill to visit him in Scotland. After a round of golf, the Prime Minister asked his Home Secretary quite abruptly if he would like to become First Lord of the Admiralty. Churchill later wrote that, after the crisis that summer, 'All my mind was full of the dangers of war. I accepted with alacrity.'[21] It was a few weeks before his thirty-seventh birthday. His new role would shape Churchill's career and his military thinking for years to come.

The Royal Navy, over which Churchill took civilian and political command in October 1911, was a mighty force that still ruled the waves. However, like many aspects of pre-Great War Britain, its supremacy was severely challenged by a series of weaknesses and fissures, some evident to contemporary observers, others less visible. A naval race had begun when Germany, traditionally a friend of Britain (the Kaiser was the nephew of King Edward VII), started to expand its fleet. British policy for almost a century was to possess a small, professional army but a vast navy that could defend British imperial and trading links around the world. The Royal Navy was intended to be as large as the next two most powerful navies combined. So when Germany started to build up her fleet this was taken as a major affront, an attempt to diminish Britain's authority in world affairs. Along with this rivalry came the development of an entirely new generation of fast-moving, turbine-powered, heavy steel-clad battleships called Dreadnoughts. This new class of super battleship left most of its predecessors obsolete. So, as the Germans began to build Dreadnoughts, the British government needed to do the same, at enormous expense, to maintain its supremacy. Earlier, in Cabinet, Churchill himself had opposed the cost of this in order to keep funds for his social reforms.

Once again, Churchill threw himself into a new challenge. Although he had served in the army and had written extensively about military campaigns, he knew relatively little about the navy. But he was eager to learn, and through long discussions with his chief naval advisers, the Sea Lords, along with extensive visits to naval bases and meetings with junior personnel, Churchill began to pick up knowledge of the intricacies of naval gunnery, the relative merits of different vessels, and the key elements in the complex organisation of the Royal Navy. The Admiralty at this time put at the disposal of the First Lord a 320-foot yacht, the *Enchantress*, with a crew of 196. Over the next two and half years, Churchill spent more than two hundred nights on board the yacht, witnessing reviews and generally trying to understand naval matters. In other words, he spent nearly one night of every four at sea.

One of Churchill's first tasks was to push through a major naval reform by creating a Naval War Staff. Indeed, he prepared a paper for the Cabinet on this subject within four days of his appointment. The Naval War Staff would be a central team of officers to look across the board at the threats facing Britain's sea power, and then establish ways of dealing with them. Its creation was based on reforms that had taken place five years earlier in the army at the War Office. The growing threat from German naval expansion made this reform a necessity, but it involved a level of strategic thinking that the Royal Navy was not used to. For the navy, promotion had always come after service at sea, and experience in the various ships of the line was the most favoured knowledge in Admiralty thinking. The First Sea Lord, Sir Arthur Wilson, the most senior naval officer, was deeply opposed to this change in naval tradition. He feared the creation of a new cadre of staff officers who might get to the top without devoting their lives to service at sea. Churchill soon removed Wilson and the Naval War Staff was created. Then, typically, Churchill himself wanted to be at the centre of this strategic review of naval threats and opportunities.

Fresh from his days as a social reformer, Churchill also wanted to improve the lot of the general sailor. He improved pay as well as facilities below decks and at shore establishments. And his 'Mates' Scheme' enabled ratings to be promoted to officer rank. Churchill wrote and communicated directly with officers below the rank it was regarded as appropriate for a First Lord to deal directly with. The Sea Lords deeply disapproved, but Churchill used it as a way to find out what junior officers were thinking and what they were concerned with, all of which he regarded as part of his remit.

He soon forgot his earlier opposition to the increased spending requirements of the navy. Alarmed by the growth of Germany's fleet, he speeded up the building programme of the mighty Dreadnoughts. In early 1912, he received Germany's new plan for naval construction. It projected huge growth, from the biggest new battleships to much smaller vessels, and a vast increase in naval personnel. Churchill calculated that at present growth rates the German Navy would one day deploy twenty-five battleships in the North Sea, whereas the Royal Navy would be able to put only twenty-two to sea. This would result in a substantial shift in the balance of power. It could not be allowed to happen. Churchill committed his energies to persuading his colleagues in Cabinet and throughout the nation of the urgent need to speed up the building of new Dreadnoughts. As he later put it: 'The Conservatives wanted six, the Liberals wanted four; we compromised on eight.'[22]

Churchill found many of his senior naval advisers rather stuffy, plodding and distinctly poor in analysis. The qualities that made a great naval captain were combative arrogance, the confidence to take risks and to be highly individualistic in the assessment of a situation and the leadership of men. But these were not the characteristics that made for good managers. Churchill later wrote of the senior admirals: 'They are so cocksure, insouciant and apathetic.'[23] Moreover, few senior naval men had the capacity to sit down and argue a case with an experienced debater like Churchill. They could not pull an argument to pieces and put it back together again. They often wilted under a concerted argumentative assault from Churchill, who thought them all the poorer for this. To be fair, of course, these were not the qualities that were judged to be admirable in naval circles.

One man who did delight Churchill was the retired admiral Sir John Fisher, who had been a controversial First Sea Lord from 1904 to 1910. He was ebullient, energetic and constantly looking for improvements, to find faster ships, deadlier weapons and better ways of doing things. It was Fisher who had overseen the introduction of the Dreadnoughts. He was a genuine eccentric even in the unusual circle of senior admirals, and Churchill took to him immediately. In many ways, the two men were alike. They both had an instinct to spot what was new and different. And each identified in the other a keen supporter of his own passionate beliefs. Fisher was soon encouraging Churchill in his reforms, and the two men enjoyed a close friendship. Inevitably, they argued, but this only strengthened their relationship. Churchill was keen for people to stand up to him and it was this that he missed in most of the senior admirals around him.

Another senior figure whom Churchill admired was Prince Louis of Battenberg, a cousin of the King. The royal family was close to the senior service. The recently crowned King George V had served in the navy and both of his sons, the future Edward VIII and George VI, were educated at the Royal Naval College. Churchill had a lively correspondence with the King about naval matters, especially the naming of new ships. For instance, the King vetoed the name *Oliver Cromwell* for a battleship, but Churchill got approval for his suggestion of *Iron Duke*. Churchill appointed Prince Louis as First Sea Lord in December 1912. He served Churchill and the navy well.

Churchill initiated several reforms in the years before the First World War. First, he gave great encouragement to the development of the Royal Naval Air Service. The Wright brothers had ushered in the era of powered flight only a few years earlier, in

1903. And the first flight did not take place in Britain until 1908, only three years before Churchill went to the Admiralty. But he was fascinated by this new activity, and although it is unrealistic to claim he spotted its full military potential at this stage, he certainly encouraged the navy to take up flying and to build a series of air stations. At this point, air power was seen simply as a form of reconnaissance, a potential extension of the 'eyes' of the navy to spot its enemy at sea. So keen did Churchill become that he asked some young naval pilots at their base at Eastchurch if they would teach him to fly. The pioneer aviators must have been astonished at the First Lord's enthusiasm, because flying was so dangerous that one flight in every five thousand resulted in a death. Nevertheless, Churchill persevered with his flying lessons throughout 1913, despite fierce opposition from his friends, his family and from his wife Clemmie. In December, after one of his instructors was killed in an accident, F.E. Smith, the politician and close friend of Churchill, wrote to him: 'Why do you do such a thing as fly repeatedly? Surely it is unfair to your family, your career and your friends.'[24] But Churchill's obstinate streak came through and he persisted with his flying lessons for another six months. Then, one of the planes he had flown crashed into the sea, killing the pilot who had been teaching Churchill only days earlier. Clemmie, who was five months pregnant with their third child, pleaded again with him to give up the deadly sport. This time he agreed and, despite nearly gaining his pilot's licence, reluctantly abandoned his flying lessons.

However, Churchill's commitment to naval flying only intensified. He made plans to draw civilian fliers into the navy. He named the type of aircraft that could land on water a 'seaplane' and ordered a hundred of them. He planned and budgeted for the building of five new air stations and for the provision of new flying facilities. And he was impressed by a flight he took in an airship over Chatham dockyard. Churchill's recurring fascination with the new attracted him to flying and drove him to push through these measures against an inherently conservative Admiralty establishment that just didn't get it.

The other major area of reform ushered in by Churchill at the Admiralty was the launch of another new class of battleship, the Queen Elizabeth. At twenty-five knots they were faster than anything that had gone before. They were armed with giant fifteen-inch guns, the largest in the navy. And, in a revolutionary step, they were powered by oil rather than coal. To support them, Churchill began a process of converting the whole navy to oil power, a massive transition that would take decades to complete and involved building oil storage depots around the world. Coal had been at the heart of Britain's industrial revolution and its supply was guaranteed for years to come, but oil was more efficient and lighter. As part of the transition, Churchill recognised the need to ensure that oil supplies would be secure well into the future. Consequently, in June 1914, in one of his most far-sighted acts, he persuaded the government and the House of Commons to take a 51 per cent stake in the Anglo Persian Oil Company (which later became British Petroleum). This marked several major shifts in long-term government thinking. First, it guaranteed the Royal Navy a plentiful supply of oil for the foreseeable future, enabling the transfer from coal to oil to proceed smoothly. Second, it marked a break from governmental laissez-faire policy towards business by creating a partly nationalised company dedicated to the provision of an essential raw material. For decades, the interests and investments of BP would be closely aligned to the interests of the British government, in marked contrast to the American oil giants that became huge private concerns. Third, the stake in Anglo Persian focused British attention on a region that had not been paramount in imperial thinking before: Persia (now Iran) and the Middle East. This would have major consequences over the next half century. It was one of the most radical steps taken by the pre-war government, and it is a sign of Churchill's achievement that, despite being so revolutionary, it was carried in the Commons overwhelmingly by 254 votes to 18.

Eleven days after the Commons voted to take the stake in Anglo Persian, a shot rang out in Sarajevo. This started the sequence of events that would lead Europe inexorably to war. But at the time few realised the importance of the assassination of Archduke Franz Ferdinand of Austria by a Serbian gunman, so great were the issues facing the British government. The Home Rule Act threatened to provoke civil war in Ireland. The Unionists in the North rallied behind their leader Sir Edward Carson. The Nationalists mobilised too, and groups of armed men marched openly in Belfast and Dublin. The suffragettes brought more violence to the streets of London. Labour disputes were causing real anxiety throughout the country. And the Cabinet was still arguing over the heavy expenditure demanded by the navy. When the Naval Estimates were finally agreed for the years 1914–15, Lloyd George passed a note to Churchill which read, 'Had there been any other Chancellor of the Exchequer your Naval Bill would have been cut by millions.' Churchill scribbled a reply: 'There would also have been another First Lord of the Admiralty! And who can say . . . that there would not have been another government?'[25]

By the end of July 1914, however, these issues were suddenly overshadowed by the extraordinary prospect of war between the nations of Europe. The Cabinet met on a hot, sultry Friday afternoon, 24 July, and spent several hours discussing the deadlock over Ulster. Then the Foreign Secretary, Sir Edward Grey, was handed a note which he immediately read out to his colleagues. It was the text of an ultimatum sent by Austria-Hungary to Serbia, and it was clearly phrased so that no self-respecting state could accept it. War suddenly looked likely.

But it took a while for the enormity of this document to sink in. Churchill later described how the border dispute in Ulster 'faded back into the mists and squalls of Ireland, and a strange light began immediately, but by perceptible gradations, to fall and grow upon the map of Europe'. He went straight to the Admiralty and immediately wrote down seventeen points which had to be attended to if war came. This piece of paper acted as a checklist for Admiralty officials over the next ten days.[26]

As the situation in the Balkans came to a head, the network of alliances that linked the nations of Europe divided the continent into two camps. If Austria declared war on Serbia, then Russia would come to Serbia's aid while Germany would support Austria. And if Germany went to war with Russia, France would come to Russia's aid. Knowing this, the German Army Command had devised a strategy known as the 'Schlieffen Plan'. This involved attacking France first and knocking it quickly out of the war, then turning to face Russia, which would be slower to mobilise. But the Schlieffen Plan necessitated passing across Belgian territory, which would draw Britain into the conflict because it had pledged to come to Belgium's aid in the event that it was invaded. As a result, within days, the whole of Europe slid helter-skelter into war.

Churchill was in his element. The Royal Navy's Home Fleet had gathered for its annual test mobilisation. The First Lord suggested that it should not disperse. Then he ordered the First Fleet to deploy from Portland on the south coast to the North Sea. This was tantamount to the fleet taking up its battle stations against Germany. Armed guards were put on naval supply depots and oil tanks.

At this moment, Clemmie was on holiday on the north Norfolk coast with their young family. Churchill, writing to her on 28 July, could not hide his excitement:

Everything tends towards catastrophe and collapse. I am interested, geared up and happy. Is it not horrible to be built like that? The preparations have a hideous fascination for me . . . We are putting the whole Navy into fighting trim . . . Everything is ready as it has never been before. And we are awake to the tip of our fingers. But war is the Unknown and the Unexpected . . . I feel sure however that if war comes we shall give them a good drubbing.[27]

On the evening of the following day, Germany declared war on Russia. Railways across Europe now started to move millions of men and thousands of tons of *matériel* in preparation for military activity. Churchill put the fleet on full mobilisation. Germany, as planned, prepared to launch its offensive against France and demanded right of passage through Belgium. Britain issued an ultimatum. On 4 August, as the German Army disregarded the ultimatum and crossed into Belgium, Britain declared war on Germany. At midnight, Churchill sent the order to all ships: 'Commence hostilities against Germany.' He rushed to 10 Downing Street where Lloyd George, who was already with Prime Minister Asquith, remembered his entrance thus: 'Winston dashed into the room, radiant, his face bright, his manner keen, one word pouring out on another how he was going to send telegrams to the Mediterranean, the North Sea and God knows where. You could see he was a really happy man.'[28]

Churchill was nearly forty. He had command of Britain's mighty navy at a time of major European war. And he was loving every minute of it.

2

Preparation: The War and
the Wilderness

Churchill saw the war when it came in August 1914 as an opportunity to prove he could be a great war leader. But he had what might be called a roller coaster of a war. He started in high regard at the Admiralty. And by 1918 he was much respected as one of the leading organisers of the military success that brought victory on the Western Front. But in between he suffered probably the biggest humiliation of his life, and he was closely associated with a failure that haunted him for many years. So deep was his depression at one point in the war that he thought he might never recover from the unpopularity he had generated.

At the beginning of the war, Lord Kitchener was appointed by Asquith as Secretary for War. As we have seen, Churchill had previously criticised elements of Kitchener's command in the Sudan campaign of 1898, but now the two men, in charge of the two military departments of state, worked closely and effectively together. At this stage, there was no War Cabinet and the government of war continued without dramatic change from the government of peace. Many people believed the war would be a short business, that it would all be 'over by Christmas'. Neither Kitchener nor Churchill shared this view. Kitchener appealed for a million men to join the army and his face adorned posters that went up across Britain. Hundreds of thousands of volunteers patriotically came forward to do their bit.

During the first few months of the war, the Royal Navy did not perform as well as everyone, and especially Churchill, had expected. Three elderly British cruisers were sunk by a German U-boat while on patrol off Dogger Bank on 22 September with the loss of nearly fifteen hundred men. And far away, along the Pacific coast of Chile, a German battle squadron under the command of Count von Spee sank two further British cruisers with similarly heavy loss of life. Before long, German surface vessels and submarines, U-boats, also began to sink merchant ships in large numbers. This was a challenge to the trade that Britain relied upon for its imports. And the equipment of the Royal Navy was found wanting. Mines sometimes failed to go off and torpedoes went too low in the water, passing harmlessly under the ship being targeted.

Churchill, however, soon committed himself to another campaign. The Germans had been turned back along the river Marne, only a few miles from Paris. The Schlieffen Plan and the strategy of knocking out France before attacking Russia had failed, so the German Army sought out a defensive line in the west. A 'race to the sea' began as both sides started to dig in and construct a network of trenches. Churchill wanted to prevent the Germans from occupying the Channel ports in Belgium, and he visited Dunkirk and Antwerp to encourage their garrisons to hold out. The army was too stretched to provide extra men for this and so Churchill committed naval troops and Royal Marines, who also came under Admiralty command.

Bizarrely, for a First Lord of the Admiralty who should have been running naval affairs from London, Churchill spent several days in Antwerp trying to rally the defence of the city. He became obsessed with the defence of Antwerp and on 5 October he wrote one of the strangest letters of his life to the Prime Minister. He offered to resign from the Admiralty and the government to take field command in Antwerp as an army general supervising the city's defence. Fortunately, Asquith rejected the resignation, but Churchill still stayed in Antwerp for another four days. The city surrendered the day after he left.

The incident is revealing. Maybe Churchill was overexcited by the reality of war. Probably his yearning for military command got the better of him. Perhaps he really thought that he could make a difference and turn the course of the war at this crucial point. But his actions certainly displayed a strange lack of judgement and at his relatively young age show that he could be unhinged by military events. The Conservative opposition leaders seized on the incident, which they regarded as near farcical, and Bonar Law thought it showed that Churchill had become mentally unbalanced. Clementine, too, felt for some years that her husband's sense of proportion had deserted him at Antwerp.

Back at the Admiralty, Churchill was faced with the decision of whom to appoint as the new First Sea Lord to replace Battenberg, who resigned in the face of unpopularity over his German origins. (Of course, these origins were shared by the royal family, who wisely changed their surname to the very British-sounding 'Windsor' later in the war. Battenberg himself changed his family name to Mountbatten, and his son would be one of Churchill's leading generals thirty years later.) Churchill wanted someone aggressive in spirit and decided to bring back the seventy-four-year-old Lord Fisher. It was not a good decision. Fisher proved unpredictable, irascible, and like many senior people of his age, impatient and crotchety when he did not get his way. Churchill remained a great admirer of the elderly Sea Lord, but their disagreements mounted, and Fisher would have a great impact on the next phase of Churchill's career.

Another development at the Admiralty that had a lasting effect upon Churchill was the rapid progress in code-breaking. Before the war, Naval Intelligence had largely been preoccupied with intercepting enemy cables. But wireless telegraphy spread rapidly in the years before 1914, and the German Navy now had the ability to communicate with its ships at sea by radio in code. Many routine instructions and orders were sent daily by this method. In a lucky break early in the war, the Russians captured a German naval code book and passed it on to the British. The Australians then captured another code book, used by the Germans in communications with their merchant ships. In November 1914, when a third code book was found in a sunken German destroyer, the Admiralty had all it needed to decipher messages between ships at sea and their commanders at home. Churchill already knew the value of breaking enemy codes from his experiences in the Boer War and had forged links with the world of spies and espionage before 1914, so he was excited by this development. A new unit was set up known as Room 40, named simply after the room in the Admiralty where it was located.[1]

Churchill became obsessed with the control of the high-grade intelligence that was intercepted and interpreted by the cryptographers in Room 40. Most of the messages sent by the Germans made little sense in themselves, but they could provide vital information when properly analysed and placed into context by intelligence experts. Churchill resisted this and delighted in reading the transcripts 'raw', as they were sent. And he permitted very limited distribution of the intelligence outside the Admiralty building. Even the Cabinet was not regularly informed of the decrypts. This made for confusion and a succession of blunders in the first six months of the war. In December 1914, when orders were intercepted that a German naval raiding party was to cross the North Sea and shell mainland Britain, Churchill and his leading advisers at the Admiralty decided to order a naval squadron to intercept the German vessels on their return. The Germans shelled Scarborough, Hartlepool and Whitby, killing or injuring some five hundred civilians, but the Royal Navy squadron missed them on their return in the fog. The press were outraged and demanded to know why the most powerful navy in the world had allowed Britain to be shelled from the sea. 'Where was the navy?' asked the Scarborough coroner. Instead of a great triumph caused by the interception of highly useful intelligence, it turned out to be a low point for Churchill who was blamed for the national humiliation.

In January 1915, more ciphers detailing German naval movements in the North Sea were intercepted. This time the Royal Navy was waiting for the German vessels at Dogger Bank. It was the first time two navies equipped with great Dreadnoughts had clashed at sea. Churchill described the excitement of following this action on the charts on the Admiralty's walls:

> There can be few purely mental exercises charged with more excitement than to follow, almost from minute to minute, the phases of a great naval action from the silent rooms of the Admiralty . . . Telegram succeeds telegram at a few minutes' interval as they are picked up and decoded . . . and out of these a picture always flickering and changing rises in the mind, and imagination strikes out around it at every stage flashes of hope or fear.[2]

The *Blücher*, one of the German warships, was sunk, there were no significant British losses, the German High Seas Fleet withdrew, and a great victory was proclaimed. In reality, the Royal Navy could have caused far more damage, but the commander thought there were U-boats in the vicinity and failed to press home his attack. The Admiralty had not passed on to him the intercepted message that said the nearest U-boat was forty miles away and well out of the action.

For Churchill, knowledge was power, and he relished the fact that just he and a tiny number of senior officials around him knew what the Germans were saying to each other at any given time. After he left the Admiralty, Room 40 grew and its work improved, and lessons were learned about the best distribution of the intelligence gained. But overall, British Naval Intelligence had a good war, and Churchill was proud of his role in helping to pioneer this. In the 1920s he wrote, 'Our Intelligence service has won and deserved world-wide fame. More than perhaps any other Power, we were successful in the war in penetrating the intentions of the enemy.'[3] And Churchill retained a fascination with code-breaking and the use of what became known as signals intelligence (SIGINT). This would play an even more important role in the next war.

By 1915, it seemed to Churchill that the war had settled into a battle of attrition on land and stalemate at sea. Many millions of men faced each other in a line running from Switzerland to the Channel, now called the Western Front. Machine guns, heavily constructed defensive positions and huge masses of barbed wire prevented either side from advancing. At sea, the Royal Navy had successfully blockaded much of the German Navy in its fortified harbours, from which it did not dare venture out. Churchill argued that torpedoes and mines were to ships at sea what barbed wire and the machine gun were to soldiers trying to advance on land. His whirlwind mind threw out a variety of ideas and innovations to address these problems. They would have a lasting effect on the future face of war.

Churchill was particularly worried about the U-boat menace. At that time the German submarines would use their torpedoes only against the biggest ships but would come to the surface and fire their deck guns to force smaller merchant vessels to surrender. Churchill encouraged the use of decoy ships, or 'Q-ships', which looked like cargo vessels and flew the Red Ensign, the Merchant Navy's flag. However, when a U-boat surfaced, the Q-ship's sailors, a Royal Navy crew in disguise, threw open various trap doors and shutters to reveal their guns and then engaged the U-boat. Although they enjoyed limited success in sinking U-boats, the Q-ships were the subject of many boy's-own tales of derring-do.[4]

While still at the Admiralty, Churchill also began the process of developing 'land ships', giant armoured vehicles with cater-pillar tracks that could advance through barbed wire under fire. He suggested to the War Office that the army should develop armoured tractors that could break the deadlock of trench warfare. His ideas were rejected as being 'not likely to lead to success'.[5] So, in February 1915, Churchill committed Admiralty funding to the design of these strange vehicles. They were built in great secrecy and were disguised as 'water tanks for Russia', soon shortened to 'tanks'. Later, the army took this programme over and eventually, and still somewhat reluctantly, launched a new era in warfare with the use of the armoured tank at the Battle of the Somme in September 1916. Many people later laid claim to have invented the tank, but a Royal Commission credited Churchill with the 'receptivity, courage and driving force' that turned the idea into an effective instrument of war.[6] For his part, Churchill would never forget that the army had obstructed an idea which he thought could provide a war-winning machine.

He was also concerned about Zeppelins, giant airships from which the Germans could drop bombs on mainland Britain. Churchill wanted to find a way to strike at the Zeppelins so he authorised bombing raids on the Zeppelin bases in Germany. Primitive aircraft of the Royal Naval Air Service launched the first tentative bombing raids on the Zeppelin sheds. Thus, through his encouragement of the art of deception at sea, the development of the tank on land and the beginning of a very primitive form of aerial bombing, Churchill had shown himself very much in support of radical new ideas for warfare, and especially anything that he thought might break the stalemate along the Western Front. He later wrote that the soldiers, sailors, airmen, civilians and inventors who came up with these new ideas 'were a class apart, outside the currents of orthodox opinion, and for them was reserved the long and thankless struggle to convert authority and to procure action'.[7] Churchill was already beginning to identify the need for a War Lab of people and new ideas twenty-five years before he would muster his own when he found himself in charge of another war effort.

At the Admiralty, Churchill also sought out strategies by which Britain might take the offensive. He explored the option of attacking Germany's northern coast in the Baltic, from where an army could drive on Berlin. Then he focused on attacking Turkey, which had come into the war as Germany's ally at the end of October 1914. Churchill tried to whip up Cabinet enthusiasm for a naval attack in the Dardanelles, the narrow channel that joined the Mediterranean with the Black Sea. The Turkish capital, Constantinople (now Istanbul), was only a few miles further north. Churchill talked ambitiously about sending a naval task force to bombard the forts of the Dardanelles and an army group to land at Gallipoli and march north to knock Turkey out of the war in a single blow. Kitchener supported the plan, but it required a level of coordination between the army and the navy that was way ahead of its time. And not much thought had been given in pre-war planning to amphibious operations to land men on beaches.

After several months of debate, the Dardanelles offensive began with a naval bombardment on the morning of 18 March 1915. On the first day, three British and one French battle-ship hit mines and sank. It was a dreadful start. From this day on naval commanders concluded that they could never again enter the 'narrows' of the Dardanelles or penetrate as far as Constantinople. So, on 25 April, soldiers were landed on the beaches at Gallipoli. Many were Australians and New Zealanders, in a newly arrived force known as the Anzacs. From day one of the campaign things here went wrong also. The Turks had built up their defences over the previous month, and the men who waded ashore under heavy machine-gun fire were able to take only a narrow bridgehead of land. The Turks proved far more effective soldiers than had been anticipated, and despite much bravery and heroism, the whole Gallipoli campaign was soon mired in a similar stalemate to that which characterised the Western Front.

In mid-May, the campaign ushered in a major political crisis. Fisher, the First Sea Lord, had been proving more and more difficult to work with, at times supporting the Dardanelles campaign, then opposing it. He offered to resign on several occasions, but then always carried on regardless. Then on 15 May, he walked out in a huff. He refused to see Churchill and announced he had left for Scotland. Churchill was aghast that anyone could just walk out at a time like this. But this time the resignation was final. This might not have precipitated a polit-ical crisis had it not coincided with a scandal on the Western Front, where it was revealed that the army was suffering from a major shortage of shells. Questions were now being asked about the ability of Asquith's government to manage the war. During several days of crisis meetings it was resolved that Asquith's Liberal government would be replaced by a Coalition government. Leading Conservatives agreed to join the Cabinet, but the price they demanded was the demotion of their old enemy, Churchill. Lloyd George became Minister of Munitions to sort out the shells crisis. Bonar Law, the Conservative leader, came into government as Minister of the Colonies and his fellow-Tory Arthur Balfour replaced Churchill at the Admiralty. Churchill himself pleaded with Asquith, 'I will accept any office – the lowest if you like that you care to offer me.'[8] He was given the relatively humble post of Chancellor of the Duchy of Lancaster, which he accepted because he could remain in the War Council, albeit in a non-executive position.

Churchill was shattered by this turn of events. He felt he had been made a scapegoat and was now unable to influence the course of military events just when the war needed someone with his abilities. The fighting in Gallipoli carried on until the end of 1915, when an evacuation was organised. It cost 140,000 Allied casualties, many of them Anzacs. Conservative enemies blamed Churchill for planning and orchestrating what became known as the 'Dardanelles fiasco'. In the House of Commons, they would shout 'Remember the Dardanelles!' when he got up to speak. With his departure from the Admiralty many observers thought that his political career was over. But there is no doubt that the humiliation was a political matter. The Conservatives had finally got their own back on this pushy, ambitious know-all who had betrayed them ten years before. As far as Great War military disasters were concerned, the Dardanelles campaign was no worse than many others. But Churchill had been made to pay the price for its failure. Although he remained in the War Council, from now on no one listened to his arguments or propositions. He was pretty well ignored.

For the next six months, and for the first time since entering government in 1908, Churchill found himself under-employed. With time on his hands, and unable to exercise his great passion for military affairs, he took up painting, which brought him some sort of solace. His correspondence with Clementine comes almost to a halt during this period – largely because he was at home much of the time and they had no need to write to each other. She provided great support, and he still had Cabinet meetings to attend along with his regular parliamentary duties. For many people, that would have been more than enough. But for Churchill it was a period of immense frustration and, along with the sense of grievance he felt, provoked a profound depression which he called his 'black dog'.

In the autumn he decided he needed to get away from Westminster for a bit and the next remarkable phase of his extraordinary life unfolded. He resigned from the government and took up a commission in the army, fulfilling his wish to command men in wartime. In November, he arrived in France and spent ten days with the Grenadier Guards, learning for the first time the realities of life in the trenches. He wrote home: 'Filth and rubbish everywhere, graves built into the defences & scattered about promiscuously, feet and clothing breaking through the soil, water and muck on all sides . . . the venomous whining & whirring of the bullets which pass overhead.' But he concluded: 'I have found happiness and content such as I have not known for many months.' Later that month he wrote: 'I am very happy here. I did not know what release from care meant. It is a blessed peace.'[9] In January, he was appointed lieutenant-colonel and for the next five months the man who had been President of the Board of Trade, Home Secretary and First Lord of the Admiralty commanded eight hundred men of the 6th Battalion of the Royal Scots Fusiliers on the Western Front. A friend from the Liberal Party, Archibald Sinclair, was made his deputy. Churchill's new unit was made up mostly of Scottish volunteers who had answered Kitchener's appeal at the beginning of the war. Many of the men were ex-miners, while the officers had been young professionals. They were initially sceptical of their eccentric commanding officer, who wore strange clothes and regularly received hampers of cheese, ham and pies from home. But he showed great interest in the welfare of his men and quickly won their respect and admiration. Morale improved soon after Churchill and Sinclair took command.

For the months he served in the trenches, his unit was stationed in grim, semi-waterlogged trenches around Ploegsteert, near the Belgian border. It was a relatively quiet period on this stretch of the Western Front and casualties were not great. But it was still a dangerous place to be. And just as in his previous combat experiences, Churchill did not hide from danger. Far from it. He seemed almost reckless at times. He surveyed the trenches daily, sometimes from no man's land. And his letters home reveal several near misses. On one occasion, he had just left a dugout when a shell landed there, killing one officer and wounding several others. He was frequently showered with debris after shells burst near by. Once, a piece of shrapnel big enough to have taken his hand off landed two inches from his wrist.

However, this period of intense soldiering proved a great fillip to Churchill. His daily letters to Clementine from the trenches are particularly intense. He had time to reflect on his political career so far, at one point writing: 'My conviction that the greatest of my work is still to come is strong within me: & I ride reposefully along the gale.' But there was also time for regret and frustration. Once, having seen a German aircraft above the trenches, he wrote: 'There is no excuse for our not having command of the air. If they had given me control of this service when I left the Admiralty, we should have supremacy today.' When he heard of the progress being made with the development of tanks, he wrote: '[H]ow powerless I am! Are they not fools not to use my mind – or knaves to wait for its destruction by some flying splinter.' On another occasion, when a shell landed close by, he mused: '20 yards more to the left & no more tangles to unravel, nor more anxieties to face, no more hatreds & injustices to encounter; joy of all my foes, relief of that old rogue, a good ending to a chequered life, a final gift – unvalued – to an ungrateful country.'[10]

For her part, Clementine was worried sick each day that her husband spent in the trenches. 'I live from day to day in suspense and anguish,' she wrote. 'At night when I lie down I say to myself "Thank goodness he is still alive".' But she went on giving him support and good advice about his political future. Once, back home on leave, he made a particularly ill-judged speech in Parliament and Clementine wrote: 'To be great one's actions must be able to be understood by simple people.'[11] It was wise advice and she would come back to it again: Churchill had to think about how others would interpret his actions and his behaviour.

After nearly five months with the Royal Scots, Churchill's battalion was withdrawn from the front line and was due to be merged with another that had suffered heavy losses. The forty-one-year-old Churchill took this moment to leave the army and return to political life. He had done his bit of soldiering and could feel justifiably proud of his active service, even though he had never had to lead his men over the top in one of the assaults so typical of the Western Front. He had been a popular and devoted commanding officer, and the Royal Scots were genuinely sad to see him leave. Fifty years later, they would provide a guard at his funeral.

Soon after Churchill returned to Westminster, Field Marshal Douglas Haig, the commander-in-chief of British forces in

France, launched his 'Big Push' along the river Somme. Churchill was lucky to be out of it. Almost twenty thousand British soldiers were killed and forty thousand wounded on the first day alone. And the battle dragged on for nearly five months, leaving a death toll of British, French and Germans running into several hundred thousand. Churchill was deeply opposed to such futile head-on attacks without an overall superiority in men or guns. And he said so powerfully in the Commons and in the press.

In December 1916, Lloyd George replaced Asquith as Prime Minister in a reconstituted Coalition government. He tried to bring Churchill back into the Cabinet, but the Conservatives still objected. However, in early 1917, an inquiry cleared Churchill of any blame in the Dardanelles campaign and he began to behave more like his old self again. His speeches in Parliament once more displayed his talents and his understanding of the nature of the war. Churchill's standing picked up and in July 1917, Lloyd George finally won the argument with his Conservative colleagues and brought Churchill back into the government, in the key role of Minister of Munitions (although still without a place in the central War Cabinet). It was two years since he had been forced to leave the Admiralty. Probably the worst two years of his life.

The Ministry of Munitions was one of the vast new departments of state that had been created during the war. Three million workers were involved in producing and supplying munitions. Churchill, as ever, immersed himself in his new task of spurring on the armaments factories, in order to deliver the most efficient supply of weapons and shells to the front. He went back and forth on countless trips to France, to see his French equivalent and to set up joint munitions programmes, and to visit the front line. The scene of military activity still exerted a magnetic pull on him. He made it clear to Haig that he thought the Germans could not be defeated on the Western Front. But that didn't stop the British commander from launching another futile offensive at Ypres in the summer and autumn of 1917. By its finish, it had led to even more slaughter and the loss of half a million men killed, wounded or missing.

In early 1918, Churchill began planning for the build-up of huge numbers of tanks and aircraft that he hoped would be used to mount a new style of offensive in 1919. He visited France on many occasions and was staying in a billet near the front line on the night of 20 March when he was awoken at 4.30 a.m. by the sound of a massive artillery barrage. It was the beginning of Germany's great offensive in the west to try to win the war. A few weeks earlier, Russia had signed a peace treaty with Germany in the aftermath of the Bolshevik Revolution, so Germany was now free to rush troops from the Eastern to the Western Front. And Germany had to hurry, because the Americans, who had entered the conflict the previous year but so far had not deployed many men, would soon be arriving in great numbers to tip the balance in the Allies' favour. Within weeks, the German offensive had rolled the Allied line back several miles. The Germans recaptured in a matter of days all the territory that had so painfully been won from them along the Somme in 1916. Haig prepared to withdraw to the Channel ports.

Lloyd George sent Churchill back to France to assess the situation. Churchill found Haig's headquarters lacking any sense of bustle or excitement despite the fact that a hundred thousand British soldiers had been killed or captured. In Paris, he was invited by the Prime Minister Georges Clemenceau to visit the front with him. He was more impressed by the determination of the French commanders, especially General Pétain and Marshal Foch, who was appointed commander-in-chief on the Western Front. The line never broke. So the

Germans were prevented from turning a breakthrough into a breakout.

Back at the Ministry of Munitions, Churchill slept in his office and worked literally day and night to deliver the ammunition and weapons needed to replace the losses in France, pushing and cajoling industry to increase its output to the limit. By the end of April, the British Army had replacements for every gun, tank and aircraft lost so far during the German offensive. Haig wrote in his diary, 'He has certainly improved the output of the munitions factories very greatly, and is full of energy in trying to release men for the army and replace them by substitutes.'[12]

By the summer of 1918, the German offensive, which had come within artillery range of Paris, slowly began to run out of steam. Churchill shuttled back and forth to and from France, visiting command posts and gathering information about munitions requirements. On 8 August the British Army launched a counter-attack with two thousand artillery pieces and 456 tanks. German commanders spoke of this as the 'black day' for their army. The tide of war at last began to turn. Over the next month, the British and French pushed the Germans relentlessly back in retreat. The static war now became a mobile war. Tanks were used in giant mechanised thrusts to punch their way through enemy lines. Rolling artillery barrages moved forward just in front of the advancing troops. Aircraft flew endless sorties in support of the troops on the ground. By sheer force of arms, the huge British Army (at the time the biggest ever to be sent into battle), along with the French, Canadians, Australians, New Zealanders and Americans, defeated the German Army in the field. In early November, the Germans sought an armistice. On 10 November, Churchill attended a Cabinet meeting to discuss peace terms, and at 11 a.m. the following day the guns finally fell silent. Churchill was in his office alone and heard people assembling in the streets outside. He saw Trafalgar Square fill with cheering crowds. Clementine, who was heavily pregnant with their fourth child, joined him and they went to Downing Street to congratulate Lloyd George. Churchill later wrote, 'Victory had come after all the hazards and heartbreaks in an absolute and unlimited form . . . All [the enemy's] armies and fleets were destroyed or subdued. In this Britain had borne a notable part, and done her best from first to last.'[13]

Churchill learned several lessons from the First World War that would prove invaluable when it came to leading the country in the Second. He reflected on many of these in his massive history of the war, *The World Crisis 1911–1918*, which he published in five volumes between 1923 and 1931.[14] Much of what he observed and wrote here became relevant in 1940. His suspicions of the limitations of admirals and generals hiding behind traditions and outdated custom and practice were confirmed. During the Boer War and the Great War, he felt that many military leaders lacked the necessary offensive spirit, and he would later be wary of this. Also, the failures he saw in the Great War confirmed his feeling that policy should clearly be set by politicians and then carried out by the military. He despaired at weak and indecisive political leadership and at any form of government organisation that did not allow clear, unambiguous decision-making to emerge. In wartime, political and military issues come together and Churchill felt that the Prime Minister should be intimately concerned with both setting and implementing military policy. He was also shocked by the fact that generals like Haig became such major public figures that they were virtually unremovable and could carry on with futile assaults despite opposition from their political masters. Churchill relished unorthodox thinking, whether inside the military or outside from civilian scientists or innovators. He thought the vast losses of the Great War were appalling, and avoidable. He would never rule over a government where human life was sacrificed so readily.

In the ten years that followed the end of the Great War, Churchill enjoyed a period of great activity, fame and considerable political success. This book is not the place to go through all the details, but some points have a bearing on his later story. In January 1919, Lloyd George appointed Churchill as Secretary for War and Air – a new position combining the traditional War Office responsibility for the army with responsibility for the growing field of aviation, both military and civil. This revived an enthusiasm in Churchill for flying, which he once again took up, having reluctantly given up lessons several years before. However, in July, he had a near-fatal accident at Croydon aerodrome just after taking off with his instructor. As his plane fell to earth Churchill thought, 'This is very like Death.' He was saved by his seat belt and was lucky to walk away from the wrecked plane, although his instructor was unconscious for some time. As before, Clementine and some of his friends pleaded with him to give up such a dangerous hobby. This time he did so for good, although his fascination with flying lasted for the rest of his life.

Churchill's first post-war political challenge was organising the process of demobilisation. Britain had nearly three and a half million men in arms at the end of the war and now most of them wanted to return home to resume civilian life as soon as possible. There was widespread discontent at how slowly this was being managed, and something resembling a mutiny took place near Calais. Haig suggested that the ringleaders should be shot. Churchill felt the whole issue was more in need of effective industrial-style organisation rather than military discipline and vetoed Haig's suggestion. Soon he came up with a fairer way to organise demobilisation, with the men who had been in military service the longest being the first to be demobbed, and the wounded given further priority. Within months, several million men had left the forces. The army rapidly made the transition to peacetime and a temporary boom in the economy helped men to find jobs when they got home.

A more tricky problem unfolded in Russia, where British troops were still stationed, supposedly to guard war supplies that had been sent there in 1917 and 1918, both during and after the revolution. Churchill was passionately opposed to communism, as were many members of the propertied classes in the West. He was also deeply upset by the treatment of the Russian aristocracy and especially of the deposed royal family, all of whom had been shot by the communists in 1918. Churchill was outraged at the atrocities committed by the Bolsheviks, who he said 'hop and caper like troops of ferocious baboons amid the ruins of cities and the corpses of their victims'. In contrast to many, he wanted to be magnanimous to the defeated Germans and to make war on the new communist regime, a policy he summed up as 'Kill the Bolshie, Kiss the Hun'.[15] In 1919, a civil war raged in Russia between so-called 'White' forces, who were opposed to the Bolsheviks, and the Red Army of the new regime. In London, the government wavered between committing British troops to the White cause and withdrawing its forces altogether. It was not an edifying spectacle and Churchill gained little credit from being in charge of the army at this time. At one point, Lloyd George told him to abandon his obsession with anti-communism, which, 'if you will forgive me for saying so, is upsetting your balance'.[16] Finally, as it became clear that the communist forces were about to defeat their opponents, British troops were ordered home. But Churchill would later be remembered by both the communist regime in Moscow and by the Left in Britain as the man who tried to strangle the Soviet Union at birth.

Much nearer to home, the problem of Ireland re-emerged, having been put under the carpet when war came. In 1921, the island was partitioned. The King opened a parliament for Northern Ireland and six of Ulster's nine counties retained their union with Britain. The status of the southern counties remained uncertain as all the elected Irish MPs were members of Sinn Féin who set up their own government in Dublin. Militants formed the Irish Republican Army and attacked the police and symbols of British rule in Ireland. In response, Churchill agreed to the establishment of the Auxiliaries to help maintain law and order. Better known as the Black and Tans, this mercenary group of ex-soldiers responded to terror with counter-terror and the situation degenerated into a vicious cycle of violence. Eventually, a truce was agreed; and in October 1921 two Irish leaders, Arthur Griffith and Michael Collins, led a delegation to London to negotiate the terms by which an independent state would be created. Churchill, who was by now Secretary for the Colonies, was one of the team of negotiators representing the British government. The negotiations went on for weeks. Churchill's total belief in the virtues of the British Empire made it difficult for him to comprehend why the Irish did not want to remain part of this great venture. And he was concerned that an independent Ireland might be a military backdoor that could be opened to Britain's enemies in a future war. The Irish delegation insisted that Ireland would remain neutral. Churchill was far from convinced. Despite their differences, however, Churchill took to Michael Collins, a soldier who had ordered acts of violence against the British. At one point, Collins told Churchill that there was a price on his head. Churchill responded by showing Collins a copy of the Boer poster that offered a reward for him, 'dead or alive'.

A treaty was finally agreed after a marathon session ended at three o'clock in the morning of 6 December. It fell to Churchill to sell the Irish Treaty to the House of Commons, where the majority of Conservatives regarded it as a betrayal of imperial rule. After Churchill gave one of his most brilliant parliamentary speeches, the Commons approved the treaty by 302 votes to 60. In Ireland, the treaty was rejected and a bloody civil war broke out, in which Michael Collins was killed. Churchill continued to work hard to negotiate a settlement between the Irish Free State and the Northern Ireland Unionists. His statesmanship did much to end this phase of the conflict and to restore his own reputation, partly healing the scar of the Dardanelles campaign.

As Secretary for the Colonies, Churchill also became involved in remapping the Middle East, a region that was becoming ever more significant in world affairs. At the outbreak of war, the area had been part of the Ottoman Empire. The British had made a series of promises to the Arabs in the Hejaz (now Saudi Arabia) that if they supported the Allies against the Turks, they would receive independence after the war. Simultaneously, British and French diplomats had negotiated a secret treaty in which they agreed to carve up the region after the war into their own spheres of influence. And in the Balfour Declaration of November 1917, Britain also promised that a Jewish 'national home' would be created in Palestine, as long as this did not harm the rights of the existing Arab population. These three conflicting promises were not only impossible to reconcile at the end of the war, but were to be the root of much trouble in the decades ahead.

In the last year of the war, Britain had enjoyed a considerable military victory when the army under General Allenby conquered the vast area of Palestine, Jordan and Syria. So, a British military administration was left in effective charge of much of the region after the war. Britain and France were granted various 'mandates' by the League of Nations to govern until such time as the local populations 'were able to stand alone'. Churchill was a great admirer of T.E. Lawrence, better known as Lawrence of Arabia, who had helped lead the Arabs in their revolt during the war. In March 1921, the two men led a substantial team on a tour of the region, and Churchill found himself playing the unlikely role of king-maker. At the Cairo Conference, he installed Emir Feisal, who had led the Arab revolt against the Turks alongside Lawrence, as ruler in Iraq. Moving on to Jerusalem, Churchill created a new entity to the east of the river Jordan called Transjordan and installed Feisal's brother, Abdullah, as ruler. (This royal dynasty still reigns in Jordan to this day.) While in Jerusalem, Churchill met separate delegations of Arabs and Jews. He overruled Arab objections to Jewish settlement on Palestinian land and wished the Zionists good luck in their quest to settle the land. He was excited by the idea of the Jews returning to Palestine and convinced that they would help develop the whole area. He would support the Zionist cause for the rest of his life and never appeared to understand Palestinian Arab objections to the loss of their land.

With the military budget pared right down, in these years Churchill helped the Royal Air Force to make the transition from war to peace. The RAF had been formed out of the alliance of the army's Royal Flying Corps and the Royal Navy's Air Service in 1918. But it struggled to find a role under Sir Hugh Trenchard. Churchill used it to quell potential uprisings in Somaliland and Iraq. For a fraction of the cost of sending in a large army troop, the RAF sent a few squadrons to bomb or machine-gun local rebels. The RAF policed sections of the Empire and survived, thankfully, to fight another day in very different circumstances.

In October 1922, Churchill fell ill and had his appendix removed. In those days, this was an operation that necessitated considerable rest and recuperation. While Churchill was recovering, Lloyd George's government fell and a general election was called. The electorate in Churchill's constituency of Dundee had changed dramatically following the granting of the vote to just about all men over twenty-one and women over thirty. As a tough working-class city, Dundee had also suffered in the economic downturn that followed the brief post-war recovery. Churchill could manage to visit his constituency only for the last few days of electioneering. He was in pain and unable to stand. He lost the election badly and went into a period of political exile. He had been a firm supporter of Lloyd George's coalition, but by now was not at all confident about his support for the Liberal Party, which seemed to be in terminal decline against the rise of the Labour Party. His defeat in the election prompted a witty comment that he was now left 'without an office, without a seat, without a party, and without an appendix'.[17]

In the hiatus that followed, Churchill for the second time in his political career changed sides. He returned to Parliament two years later as the Conservative MP for Epping in Essex, a constituency he would continue to represent for the next forty years. Maybe he had simply judged the age of the Liberal Party to be over, in which case he was proved right. He was also gently courted by the Conservatives, who felt his powerful oratory was needed on their side of the Commons. Added to this, his hostility to the socialism he believed the Labour Party would introduce encouraged him into the Conservative fold. After the third general election in as many years, in October 1924, Stanley Baldwin became Conservative Prime Minister and offered Churchill the position of Chancellor of the Exchequer. This was not only the second most important office of state, it was the post that Churchill's father had held nearly forty years before. He was thrilled, and served as Chancellor for the next five years.

Churchill's spell running the national economy is best remembered for his disastrous decision to return to the Gold Standard, which meant pegging the pound once again to the price of gold. 'The return to gold' was a mantra of 1920s politics and most advisers, including the Governor of the Bank of England and the mandarins at the Treasury, recommended it. The problem was that Churchill rejoined the Gold Standard at the pre-war level of parity. John Maynard Keynes, the finest economist of his generation, immediately denounced this decision and wrote a book entitled *The Economic Consequences of Mr Churchill*. He argued that sterling was now seriously overvalued, which would have dire effects on the economy by making exports overpriced. As a result, British industry would inevitably suffer. He correctly predicted that employers would try to cut wages and that unemployment would rise.

Churchill's five budgets as Chancellor are also interesting because he returned to the ideals of his reforming days by introducing a state-backed contributory pension scheme which would provide an income for men and women over the age of sixty-five. One recent historian has described this as a landmark piece of legislation affecting about fifteen million people and freeing many of them from dependence on the Poor Law.[18] On defence spending he adopted the Treasury line and introduced substantial cutbacks. (He conveniently forgot this when he called for rearmament ten years later.) Certainly, in the late 1920s, the prospect of war seemed remote. Germany was still recovering from its crushing military defeat and subsequent economic chaos. France and Italy were benign. The Soviet Union was inwardly focused. There were tensions in the Far East that prompted spending on a huge naval fortress in Singapore, but Churchill even trimmed the navy's budget. It would be several years before the Nazi Party began rearming Germany and posing a new threat to British security.

In May 1926, a long-standing dispute in the coal mines, where the owners wanted to reduce wages and increase hours, led to the nation's first and only general strike. Churchill was bullish in his opposition to the strikers throughout. He took charge of the *British Gazette*, the government's mouthpiece, which was still published while the rest of the press went on strike. For ten days he acted like a press baron, printing his own partisan views each morning. He also wanted the newly formed British Broadcasting Company (the forerunner of the British Broadcasting Corporation) to air the government line on the radio. Its general manager, John Reith, refused and insisted it must remain independent. But once the strike was over, Churchill took a conciliatory position, attacking the mine owners and supporting a minimum wage for the miners. Many of his men in the Scots Fusiliers had been miners and he felt for their plight.

During these busy and broadly contented years, Churchill's private and domestic life took on a form that would continue for many years to come. His income from book writing was considerable, and *The World Crisis* was well received. It has been described as a 'Mississippi of rhetoric, sweeping along with great narrative power though little interpretative depth'.[19] His journalism provided further steady income. These earnings, along with his ministerial salary, made him relatively rich. But he was profligate with his own, if not the nation's, money. He took long holidays in the south of France, where he regularly gambled and lost money in the casinos. He acquired a Rolls-Royce and employed a chauffeur. Meals were washed down with nothing but the finest champagne (vintage Pol Roger). He loved the finest Cuban cigars and smoked several every day. In 1922, he bought Chartwell Manor, a country house with about eighty acres of land, in a beautiful part of west Kent. It took two years to remove the dry rot and rebuild as Churchill wanted it and this cost a small fortune, but in 1924 Winston, Clementine and their four children were finally able to move in. (Their daughter Marigold had died of septicaemia in 1921, leaving Winston and Clementine distraught. Mary was born the following year.) The staff grew to eight house servants and three gardeners. Family life revolved around Winston and his needs and amusements. The large drawing room, with superb views across the Weald of Kent, became his pride and joy. Here, he would write, study and pontificate. He conversed with guests and held meetings with officials. Informal conferences on international finance were conducted here. In the grounds, Churchill drained ponds, built walls and gathered geese, swans and pets. Even feeding the birds was carried out like a military operation.[20]

At the dinner table, Churchill dominated conversation and guests sat wrapped in a torrent of wit, entertainment, history, politics and anecdote. Often it became a monologue. Only occasionally was Clemmie able to broaden the discussion to bring others into the debate. Churchill presided over his own court, and his courtiers became loyal friends for the next few decades. Professor Frederick Lindemann, an odd and very snobbish Oxford physicist, delighted Churchill by being able to reduce complex scientific ideas to accessible soundbites. Brendan Bracken, MP and businessman, amused Churchill with his witty and indiscreet descriptions of political friends and enemies. Lord Beaverbrook, the Canadian press baron, was a regular visitor and frequent commissioner of Churchill's words for the *Daily Express*. Churchill admired Beaverbrook as a driven man always doggedly determined to achieve what he set out to do. Churchill respected people who stood up to him and he argued furiously with some of his courtiers, especially Beaverbrook, but he never held a grudge and everything was always made up again in the morning. Clemmie put up with most of these friends: she genuinely liked very few, and disliked many. Along with the courtiers, Churchill's circle included the Bonham Carters, the Duff Coopers, the Sinclairs and other social equals who delighted in being in the presence of such a witty and important figure.

Churchill's flamboyant, larger-than-life personality, his energetic intervention in the business of other Cabinet members, and his support for the welfare of the working man might well have brought him into conflict with the Conservative leadership before long, as it had in the Edwardian era. But in May 1929 Baldwin was defeated in the general election and Ramsay MacDonald's Labour Party came to power. Churchill feared that a socialist revolution would follow, destroying everything that was good about Britain and her Empire.

In reality Churchill was falling out of sync with the times. He was out of line with most Conservatives as well as the Labour Party. The leading example of this was his dogged opposition to any sort of self-government for India. Churchill was still very much of a Victorian in his mindset about India. He believed the 'white dominions' of Canada, Australia, New Zealand and (at this time) South Africa were shining examples of cultural, political and linguistic solidarity, beacons illustrating the virtues of the British Empire. He just could not accept that non-whites would be able to achieve the same level of government as white men. In this he undoubtedly maintained the racist views on which the imperial project had grown and flourished. Some of his other concerns about a self-ruling India are of more relevance to our post-imperial view today. He was worried that there would be violence between Hindus and Muslims; and he predicted that the 'untouchables', the lowest Hindu caste, would be a minority totally left out of Indian society and would suffer far more than they did under the Raj. But more than anything, he felt that ceding power in India, the 'jewel in the crown' of the British Empire, would be the beginning of the end of the imperial venture. In this he was probably right.

For five years, Churchill argued against what became the Government of India Bill. When it finally went through Parliament in 1935, he had virtually no supporters left on his side. He was offensive towards Indians, especially Gandhi, whom he called 'a seditious Middle Temple lawyer now posing as a fakir'. And he insulted many of his parliamentary colleagues, including MacDonald, Baldwin, Sir Samuel Hoare, and Lord Halifax, who had been Viceroy in India. Once again, contemporaries suggested that he was unbalanced, unreliable and out of touch with the times. He was increasingly seen as out of date and old-fashioned. As one biographer has put it, his message sounded 'cracked and tinny, like a record played on an Edwardian phonograph'.[21]

This partly explains why, after ten 'good' years mostly in government, he was left out of office for the next decade, which became what he called his 'wilderness years'. And the mood of politics changed from the largely optimistic years of the 1920s to the slump, poverty and divisions of the 1930s. Politicians from across the spectrum called for disarmament and appeasement while Churchill was still pounding his drum as a warlord, making bellicose calls for action.

Increasingly, he turned to the past. His literary output was immense throughout the 1930s. He dictated most of what he wrote and kept at least one and sometimes two secretaries busy from breakfast until well after dinner. He would pace up and down and the prose poured out of him. In 1930, he wrote more than forty features for the press on a wide range of political and social topics. In the same year, he published a delightful, intimate account of his younger days, *My Early Life*. In 1931, the fifth and final volume of *The World Crisis*, on the war in the east, was published; and the following year a series of essays entitled

Thoughts and Adventures appeared. Then he began a substantial undertaking, a four-volume history of his ancestor the Duke of Marlborough, which was published from 1933 to 1938. He also had time to produce a series of biographical essays called *Great Contemporaries* in 1937. And during these years he began an even bigger project. In many ways, his *History of the English-Speaking Peoples* came to sum up his view of the white British Empire, conjoined with a history of the United States. This project was so vast that it was not completed until the 1950s, although Churchill earned a lot from the initial advances and he was still working on the first phase of the book when he was interrupted by events in 1939. These books and the journalism were vital in sustaining the income Churchill needed to support his extravagant lifestyle, maintain his family and keep up Chartwell. But they also define his view of the past and show how this shaped his attitude towards the present and the future.

The view of history that emerges from the millions of words in these books is fascinating and is the foundation stone of Churchill's belief in who the British are and what their role in history had been. Churchill did not work like a professional historian. He often started to write (or, rather, dictate) long before he had done much research. He knew the general thrust of his argument. This greatly shocked Maurice Ashley, his research assistant for the Duke of Marlborough biography. But Churchill was always keen to get the facts correct. He reportedly said, 'Give me the facts, Ashley, and I will twist them the way I want to suit my argument.'[22] His books were always very readable: like his speeches, they were akin to free-flowing rivers, full of great stories and vivid characters all borne along by the driving current of narrative. But the central arguments that emerge in his history were like religious dogma to Churchill. He believed passionately in the virtues of the institutions of British government, monarchy and Parliament, supported by the pillars of the great aristocratic families. Along with this went his trust in liberty and freedom as interpreted by the English governing class. He was a great believer in the Whig interpretation of history: that is, England (more so than Britain) had a special destiny among nations. This concept was forged out of centuries of conflict between barons and kings, the violence of the Civil War and the political experiment of Cromwell's Commonwealth before everything came good in the Glorious Revolution of 1688, which brought in the perfect combination of a permanent Parliament and a docile monarchy. England had then taken on the burden of overseas conquests and had set out to defeat continental tyrants. This was where the Duke of Marlborough came in, destroying the ambitions of Louis XIV to rule the continent. Britain (as it had now become) next went on to build an empire that was the most just that had ever been seen, and its people enjoyed the richest and freest democracy the world had ever known. This account largely ignored the process of industrialisation and the progress of science. These were acknowledged as being part of the British genius but were not of particular interest to Churchill in his histories. As long as the nation's political balance was maintained, Britain had a duty to stand up to tyranny and military rule whenever it threatened personal liberty.

This romantic but also very political interpretation of history underscored most of Churchill's political ideas, from his views on India and Ireland to his confidence in the Empire. It was central to his opposition to Bolshevism and socialism. It was behind his view of how Britain related to Europe. And it explains his earlier hostility to the Kaiser and to an aggressive Germany. For a man to whom conventional worship meant very little, these beliefs pretty well became Churchill's religion. And they would be at the heart of his appeal to the nation in 1940.[23]

Churchill had the time to develop and express these ideas throughout the 1930s. Although he hoped to be invited back into government when Stanley Baldwin returned to power in 1935, his unpopular stance over India prevented this. And so, with this world view very much on his mind, Churchill began to dwell on the next issue that would come to dominate his thinking and would then take over his life and bring his career to a peak – the rise of Nazi Germany.

As part of the research for his biography of the Duke of Marlborough, Churchill had visited Germany in the summer of 1932 to tour the battlefield at Blenheim, where his ancestor had won his greatest victory. Even then Churchill had been alarmed by the 'bands of sturdy Teutonic youths' he saw marching by. A meeting was actually arranged with the leader of the right-wing National Socialist Workers' Party, Adolf Hitler, in a Munich hotel. But Hitler failed to turn up. The following year, when Hitler and the Nazis were elected to power, Churchill was not immediately concerned. However, he was deeply shocked when Hitler banned all other political parties, and particularly when he outlawed Germany's Jews from the apparatus of the state, national, local and municipal.

By 1936, Churchill had started to focus ever more of his attention on what he saw happening in Germany. He deplored the growing persecution of the Jews and the bully-boy tactics of the Nazi thugs who intimidated, rounded up and murdered political opponents. He was also deeply worried by German rearmament, about which he started to receive evidence from an unusual source. Churchill had met Desmond Morton on the Western Front in 1916, and Morton was now a neighbour, living only a few miles from Chartwell. He was director of the government's Industrial Intelligence Unit, and so able to study first-hand secret reports on Germany's rearmament, which went against the terms of the Treaty of Versailles. Morton leaked some of these reports to Churchill, who then used the information in various articles and speeches. There is still debate over whether Morton acted with official sanction or purely on his own initiative.[24] But he certainly became a regular member of the Chartwell court, and Churchill acquired reliable evidence of Hitler's flouting of the Versailles Treaty and Germany's burgeoning arms industry. He was the first senior statesman in Europe to sound the alarm about the growing threat posed by a resurgent Nazi Germany.

Churchill's warnings fell on deaf, or at least covered, ears for some time. The general sense in Britain was that the Great War really had been 'the war to end all wars'. Its memory was still recent and painful. Hundreds of thousands of men had been lost, their names filling long lists on war memorials in every parish and in schools and workplaces across the land. In addition, hundreds of thousands had been physically maimed or psychologically scarred. Huge numbers had been shocked by the futility of the conflict, as is evident in the many anti-war memoirs that came out from the late 1920s onwards. And thousands of pacifists joined groups like the League of Nations Union and the Peace Pledge Union to protest at any form of rearmament. The policies of appeasement and disarmament were genuinely popular among the vast majority of the population, viewed as the best ways to maintain peace.

Yet Churchill was in no sense a warmonger. He had no wish to see a call to arms (although his fascination with warlike subjects remained), and he had long held that the Treaty of Versailles was unfair on the Germans and that they had good reason to reject some of it. Many in Britain felt the same, although very few in France agreed with this. But Churchill was the first to see that Hitler was a demonic leader who had to be stopped, who had to be stood up to. He instinctively knew that appeasing the German Chancellor would not bring his demands to an end and ensure peace; rather, it would encourage him to demand more. The only option was to rearm in order to deter him. Churchill argued that preparation for war was the best way to maintain peace when dealing with a dictator like Hitler.

As events unfolded, Churchill's lone voice and his predictions of an imminent catastrophe began to make more sense. He was particularly concerned by the growth of the German Air Force, the Luftwaffe. Another whistleblower, Ralph Wigram from the Foreign Office, passed him information about how the German aircraft factories were dramatically increasing output. With the predominant view at the time being 'the bomber will always get through', Churchill conjured up a terrifying vision of thousands of incendiary bombs being dropped on British cities and millions of people being killed as a consequence. Hitler and his Nazi cronies protested and denounced Churchill as a warmonger. But in 1935 Baldwin invited him to join a secret sub-committee on Air Defence Research. At the first meeting he attended, Churchill heard about successful tests that were being carried out in the use of radio waves to detect aircraft (see Chapter 5). He was interested but had no idea how significant this invention of radar, as it was later called, would prove to be.

In March 1936, Hitler remilitarised the Rhineland, territory that had been freed of German troops under the terms of the Versailles Treaty. We now know this was a critical moment for the German leader. He gambled that the British and French would not try to prevent him, but he did not yet have an army powerful enough to carry through the reoccupation if opposed. As it was, the British and French governments allowed him to go ahead. With great prescience, Churchill warned the Commons that Hitler would soon be in a position to invade France through Belgium and Holland, and that Britain's security was further endangered.

Throughout 1936, more visitors came to Chartwell with information about the inadequacies in Britain's air defences or with news of military unpreparedness. Many were serving officers: Squadron Leader Charles Torr Anderson reported how little was being done to train RAF pilots; Brigadier Percy Hobart brought details of deficiencies in the army's tank programme. All of these stories of British military weakness were in contrast to what Churchill heard about Germany's military growth. In truth, Britain *had* started to rearm, slowly and quietly, and within very limited budget parameters; and designers and manufacturers were working on plans for the next generation of planes and other machines of war. But they would not come into service until the end of the decade. Churchill was convinced it was too little, too late. More needed to be done, quickly. And he continued to say so, repeatedly, in public.

People were finally beginning to listen when in the winter of 1936–7 Churchill dropped to another low point in his yo-yoing career. His natural enthusiasm for the monarchy led him to support King Edward VIII in the abdication crisis that suddenly erupted in December. Churchill badly misjudged the mood of the country and he was shouted down in the House of Commons. It was a humiliating moment. He thought his career was finished. His 'black dog' depression returned and sometimes he could not even sleep at night. He also had financial worries and seriously considered selling Chartwell. It was saved for him by the generosity of one of Brendan Bracken's rich banker friends.

In May 1937, Baldwin resigned and Neville Chamberlain became Prime Minister. He pledged to continue the policy of appeasement while encouraging further minor rearmament. There was no way he would readmit Churchill to government. In February 1938, Sir Anthony Eden resigned as Foreign Secretary because he could no longer support the policy of appeasement. Churchill admired him for this but thought the future now looked grim. He told the Commons, 'I predict that the day will come when, at some point or other, you will have to make a stand, and I pray to God, when that day comes, that we may not find through an unwise policy, we have to make that stand alone.'[25]

In March 1938, Hitler announced the Anschluss, effectively a German takeover of Austria. Within twenty-four hours, thousands of Austrians who opposed Nazi rule were imprisoned or shot by the Gestapo. Churchill condemned Germany in the House of Commons and called for an alliance against further German aggression. This time many people rallied behind him. Harold Nicolson MP wrote in his diary, 'Winston makes the speech of his life'.[26] But, once again, the governments in London and Paris did nothing.

By now, the Luftwaffe had become far bigger than the RAF, and the Air Staff felt it could no longer guarantee the defence of Britain. But the Cabinet rejected plans to increase spending on RAF defences. Now it was the turn of the Minister for the Air, Lord Swinton, to resign. Churchill despaired further that his warnings were not being listened to.

During the summer of 1938, Hitler started demanding that the Sudetenland region of Czechoslovakia be incorporated into the growing German Reich. The area had a substantial Czech-German population. This prompted a major diplomatic crisis. Yet again the British and French governments decided they must let Hitler have his way. They did not consult the Czechoslovak government on the matter. In September, Prime Minister Chamberlain shuttled back and forth between Britain and Germany. Along with the French Foreign Minister, Edouard Daladier, Chamberlain ceded every point to Hitler. They believed him when he said that acquiring the Sudetenland was the end of his territorial ambitions. In Munich, at the end of a series of meetings, Chamberlain persuaded Hitler to sign a piece of paper which stated that he had no wish to make war on Britain. The Prime Minister returned to London a hero. At Croydon airport, he waved the piece of paper to cheering crowds. He said he had brought back 'peace in our time'.

Churchill took a different view. In Parliament, he told MPs:

> [W]e have sustained a defeat without a war . . . we have passed an awful milestone in our history, when the whole equilibrium of Europe has been deranged . . . do not suppose that this is the end. This is only the beginning of the reckoning. This is only the first sip, the first foretaste of a bitter cup which will be proffered to us year by year unless, by a supreme recovery of moral health and martial vigour, we rise again and take our stand for freedom as in olden time.[27]

In response, Chamberlain merely derided Churchill for his lack of judgement.

In March 1939, in blatant disregard of everything he had told Chamberlain six months earlier, Hitler's army occupied the rest of Czechoslovakia. Chamberlain's reputation and the Anglo-French policy of appeasement were now in tatters. Churchill had been proved right and the tide of events was at last beginning to flow in his direction. He seemed to be the right man to stand up to Hitler. As the government hastily drew up a treaty promising to defend Poland's integrity, a 'Bring Back Churchill' campaign started in the press. Even the Labour Party came round to thinking Churchill should be back in power.

Churchill didn't have long to wait. Towards the end of August, Germany signed a surprise pact with Stalin's Russia. The ideological enemies had become military allies. The way was clear for Hitler's next act. The House of Commons was recalled from its summer recess. On the last day of the month, Churchill was still immersed in his history writing. He confided to a friend: 'It is a relief in times like these to be able to escape into other centuries.'[28]

Events at the beginning of September 1939 brought to a climax the many years of appeasement. Churchill's dire predictions during his wilderness years had come to pass. On Friday the first of September the German Army invaded Poland. The British and French governments both issued ultimatums to Berlin that German forces must withdraw. They had finally drawn a line in the sand after years of letting Hitler get his way. Chamberlain at last recalled Churchill into the government. But then the Prime Minister hesitated. Churchill waited for more than twenty-four hours not knowing what position he would be offered.

At 11.15 a.m. on 3 September, Chamberlain made a radio broadcast to the nation from the Cabinet Room in 10 Downing Street. He told the British people that Hitler had ignored the government's ultimatum, and that Britain was 'once again at war with Germany'. The broadcast featured in many documentary films at the time and has appeared in countless television programmes since.[29] It powerfully captures the drama of the moment.

Later that day, Chamberlain formally offered Churchill the post of First Lord of the Admiralty in the newly formed War Cabinet. It was a moment of triumph for the sixty-four-year-old Churchill, who had spent more than ten years out of office and many thought had come to the end of his political career. Returning to government in any capacity would have been exciting, but returning to the Admiralty and the position he had very happily occupied between 1911 and 1915 was a special joy. When Churchill entered the Admiralty building at about six o'clock that evening, he went straight to the office he had worked in when war was declared in 1914. With its dark oak panelling, grand Grinling Gibbons carvings over the fireplace and large portrait of Nelson, it had changed little. Churchill asked, 'Where is the octagonal table?' His old table was soon produced. He also asked for the chart box he had used before, and the maps were soon hung up. 'These are the same charts I used in 1915!' he exclaimed with evident glee to the officer who would be his naval assistant.[30] Churchill's appointment was for him just reward for years of work calling upon the nation to be prepared for inevitable war with Nazi Germany. But in the mood created by the declaration of war it was a genuinely popular appointment. That evening a message went out to the fleet: 'Winston is Back'.[31]

The Second World War had begun, but nothing very much happened in Britain. At the time, the first few months were called the Bore War, and they later became known as the Phoney War. Most of the children who had been hastily evacuated over the weekend that war was declared returned home to anxious parents before the month was out. All of the action was taking place on the continent. The German Army invaded Poland from the west and succeeded in conquering the country in less than a month. At the same time, the Red Army invaded from the east. Poland ceased to exist. Hitler committed all of his armoured panzer units and most of his army to Poland, but the French, politically divided and worried about German reprisals, did nothing. They sat behind the mighty defensive wall known as the 'Maginot Line', which ran along France's border with Germany. One British general described it as a 'Battleship built on land'.[32] Meanwhile, the British assembled a small expeditionary force of nine divisions that crossed to the continent in October.

From his office in the Admiralty, Churchill threw himself into war planning. The Royal Navy was still a powerful force in

1939. There was a lot to command and a lot to organise. Once again, he faced a major challenge. He settled into a way of working that would become his style for the next few years of war. He kept everyone on their toes with a barrage of minutes or memos – dictated messages sent to his advisers and colleagues asking for information, cajoling, upbraiding or requesting action. Some were witty, some solemn. Like emails today, they could be misinterpreted by their recipients, as being more fierce or stern than they were intended to be. He sent several of these minutes every day, hundreds every month. Some related to high-level matters of strategy, such as how to deal with the German U-boat threat, or ideas for brand-new initiatives that needed to be explored. Others concerned the smallest details, like the specifics of dealing with mines. Today, Churchill would be known as a 'micro-manager'. No detail was too small to escape his attention or to avoid his fury if not attended to in a way he considered fit. This led to immense frustration and exhaustion among those who worked closely with him. But the Royal Navy, Britain's oldest and in many ways most conservative military service, was galvanised by the presence of this human dynamo in the Admiralty. One of his naval aides later described how 'He practically killed people by overwork, and at the same time inspired people to extreme devotion.' Kathleen Hill, who had joined him at Chartwell to take down dictation, went with him into government. She later recalled: 'When Winston was at the Admiralty, the place was buzzing with atmosphere, with electricity. When he was away, on tour, it was dead, dead, dead.'[33]

There were many issues to concern Churchill over the first few months of war. Getting the navy on to a war footing was at the top of the 'to-do' list. German undersea telephone cables to the outside world were cut on the very first day. A blockade of the German fleet had to be organised and enforced. And

Churchill insisted on the need to equip the Royal Navy with radar, which had not been done before the war as a cost-cutting measure.

Just like in 1914, things did not all go well. Part of the fleet was assembled at Scapa Flow, the vast anchorage in Orkney that had been used in the First World War. From here, the fleet could move out to intercept the German Navy if it tried to venture into the Atlantic. Prevailing wisdom was that this anchorage, the holiest of holies for the Royal Navy, was totally secure. But in the early hours of the morning of 14 October, a dark night with high tides and little moonlight, a U-boat managed to sail on the surface of a small channel, past the anti-submarine defences into Scapa Flow. Its commander looked around for the best target and fired four torpedoes at a huge First World War-era Dreadnought at anchorage that night. HMS *Royal Oak* went down in just eleven minutes and 810 men were lost, including an admiral and, horrifically, 150 boy sailors aged fifteen or sixteen who were sleeping on board. In the chaos that followed, the U-boat slipped back out of Scapa and returned to Germany. Its captain was fêted by Hitler in a triumphant parade down Unter den Linden in Berlin and he became one of the first German heroes of the war, launching the legend of the tough, daring U-boat menace that would haunt Churchill many times over the following years.

Churchill was always moved by losses at sea, and when he was told of the sinking of the *Royal Oak* it is reported that tears sprang to his eyes. As he wept he muttered, 'Poor fellows, poor fellows trapped in those black depths.'[34] The loss of this great old battleship from another era was a human tragedy, but it did not seriously affect the capability of the Royal Navy. However, it did lead to the repositioning of the fleet to Rosyth on the Firth of Forth. And typical of his concern for detail, Churchill followed every stage of the design and construction of the new sea defences that he ordered to be built at Scapa Flow. Fittingly, these later became known as the 'Churchill Barriers'.

The loss of the *Royal Oak* and concern about aerial reconnaissance photography of ships in anchorage or at sea prompted Churchill to look for an imaginative way of deceiving the enemy. This was the sort of challenge he relished. He called for the building of 'dummy' ships, constructed out of wood and canvas, which would look just like the real thing in the aerial photos taken by the enemy. He had encouraged something similar when First Lord during the First World War. Again, Churchill was obsessed with detail. When he observed one of the dummy ships on a later visit to Scapa he said no one would fall for it because there were no gulls flying above it, whereas real ships were always surrounded by seabirds. He ordered that scraps of food should be put out of the front and behind to ensure that gulls constantly circled the dummy ships.

In October, having defeated Poland, Hitler offered peace terms to Britain and France. Churchill argued forcefully to his colleagues in the War Cabinet to reject the approach. The *Daily Mirror* said it was Churchill's 'brilliant memorandum' that stiffened Chamberlain's proposed reply to Hitler. He also wanted the RAF to bomb the Ruhr industrial area, but this time he lost the argument in the War Cabinet. Some of his colleagues felt that such an action risked provoking Nazi reprisal bombings on England. The Secretary of State for Air even argued that bombing the Ruhr would not be appropriate because it was private property![35]

As the months passed, Churchill grew hungry for action, and increasingly frustrated at the negative and passive views in the rest of the War Cabinet. He came up with a plan to drop mines in the Rhine to destroy shipping in one of Germany's major transport arteries. This idea was opposed first by his Cabinet colleagues and later by the French. Then he spent much time developing a plan to attack Norway and Sweden in order to prevent Swedish iron ore from being exported to Germany. This would have struck a mortal blow to the German war economy. But the prevailing view was that Britain could not assault the integrity of neutral Norway and Sweden. Such lack of offensive spirit among his Cabinet colleagues, many of whom of course had been the leading appeasers throughout the 1930s, began to frustrate Churchill more and more.

After intense debate over many months, he finally persuaded the Cabinet of the need to mount a campaign against Norway. The date was repeatedly put back but was at last scheduled for mid-April 1940. The navy would mine Norwegian waters against German shipping and the army would seize the port of Narvik, from which much Swedish iron ore was exported. But Hitler beat Chamberlain's government to it. On 9 April he launched a daring invasion of Denmark and Norway in a combined naval and air operation, dropping airborne troops to capture key airfields – the first time this had been attempted.

The British and French governments were taken entirely by surprise. The earlier plan to land in the north at Narvik was switched at the last minute to a landing in Trondheim. This was then changed again to a pincer movement to the north and south of the city. Troops were landed hastily without artillery, anti-aircraft weapons and other essential equipment. The navy also failed to coordinate with the RAF, and in early May a rapid evacuation was ordered. The whole campaign was a horrible reminder of the fiasco in the Dardanelles in 1915. The Chief of the Imperial General Staff, General Edmund Ironside, chafed at the lack of clear direction of the campaign by his political masters and at the muddle that ensued. 'Always too late. Changing plans and nobody directing,' he wrote in his diary. '[V]ery upset at the thought of our incompetence.'[36] These were tough words from the nation's top soldier.

The Royal Navy lost several ships, including the aircraft carrier HMS *Glorious*, although the Germans also suffered major naval losses, including the battleship *Blücher*. Churchill was infuriated by the whole episode. He felt it revealed that the British war effort was badly led and lacked any coordinating body powerful enough to make key decisions and then ensure they were followed through. And he was not alone. A two-day debate in the House of Commons was turned by the Labour Opposition into a vote of censure. Many Tories turned against their own leaders, too. Leo Amery, an ex-Cabinet minister, pointed to the front bench and quoted the words Oliver Cromwell had once uttered in Parliament by saying: 'Depart, I say, and let us have done with you. In the name of God, go!'

Churchill was in a difficult position. He had argued for a campaign against Norway in the War Cabinet for six months. But as First Lord of the Admiralty he had overall responsibility for a campaign in which the Royal Navy had hardly excelled. He could suffer by being closely associated with its failure. But how could he denounce a government of which he was a senior member? He knew that he stood a good chance of taking over from the discredited Chamberlain. Churchill was associated in many people's minds with pursuing a more rigorous war policy. Chamberlain was still associated with the failed policies of the 1930s. Churchill had already received several approaches and suggestions that he should take over the reins of power.[37] On the other hand, if the government fell, he might fall with it. How could he help to bring down the government without bringing himself down with it?

At about ten o'clock on the evening of 8 May, Churchill rose to speak in the Commons to wind up the censure debate. He put on a fine parliamentary performance. Henry Channon MP wrote, 'One saw at once that he was in a bellicose mood, alive and enjoying himself, relishing the ironical position in which he found himself.'[38] Churchill did not betray Chamberlain, and he took full responsibility for the poor performance of the Royal Navy off the coast of Norway. But in a final blaze of oratory, he declared, 'let pre-war feuds die: let personal quarrels be forgotten, and let us keep our hatreds for the common enemy . . . At no time in the last war were we in greater peril than we are now and I urge the House strongly to deal with these matters.'[39] In the vote that followed, thirty-three Conservatives and other supporters voted with the Opposition and sixty abstained. Chamberlain's majority of 213 was reduced to 81. As the Prime Minister left the chamber, howls of 'Go! Go! Go! Go!' were directed at him.

Confronted by this humiliation, the following day Chamberlain decided that it was time to form a 'national government'. It was impossible to consider going to the people in a general election with the war at this critical stage. So the Prime Minister asked the Labour Party if they would join his government. Clement Attlee, the Labour leader, consulted with his colleagues, then made it clear that they would not join a Cabinet led by Chamberlain. So the question became: who could lead a government that would command the support of the Labour Party and the whole nation?

Later that day, Chamberlain called Lord Halifax, the Foreign Secretary, and Churchill to a meeting at 10 Downing Street. David Margesson, the Conservative Chief Whip, was also present. Halifax was Chamberlain's natural successor. He was urbane, aristocratic, an eminent Yorkshire landowner, maybe a little aloof, but many thought a natural leader. He was also admired for his sound judgement. Whereas Churchill was thought by many to be impetuous, untrustworthy, unpredictable and difficult to restrain. Furthermore, Halifax had the support of the King. However, Churchill was the one most associated with fighting the war rigorously.

According to Churchill, Chamberlain asked the two men whom he should recommend to the King to replace him after his own resignation. The King was almost certain to follow the advice of his departing Prime Minister. Many years later, in his wartime history, Churchill described what happened next:

> I have had many important interviews in my pubic life, and this was certainly the most important. Usually I talk a great deal, but on this occasion I was silent . . . As I remained silent a very long pause ensued. It certainly seemed longer than the two minutes which one observes in the commemoration of the Armistice.[40]

John Colville, later his private secretary, said that Churchill suspected a trap. If he proposed himself, he might be seen as too pushy. If he said he thought a peer could become Prime Minister, then Chamberlain might go for Halifax. So he stood with his back to Chamberlain, gazed out of the window towards Horse Guards Parade, and held his counsel.[41]

Eventually, according to Churchill, Halifax was the first to speak. He said that he felt he could not lead the nation in war from the House of Lords, that he would be in a hopeless position. He suggested Winston was a better choice. Churchill did not demur. Chamberlain took this as agreement to recommend the King should ask Churchill to become Prime Minister.

Churchill's account was written seven years after the event, and while making a splendid story out of the meeting no doubt has benefited from being recounted a few times. And it gets a few core fundamentals wrong, like the date of the meeting and who was there. On the other hand, Halifax's diary account of the same meeting, which was written that evening, makes no mention of any long pause. Halifax says that he felt an ache in his stomach at the thought of becoming Prime Minister at such a critical moment and so ruled himself out. He then claims that Churchill, 'with suitable expressions of regard and humility', eagerly accepted that he was the right man for the job.[42]

But that was still not the end of the matter. Chamberlain hesitated before going to the Palace to resign, so Churchill went back to the Admiralty. That evening, he had dinner with a few close colleagues and was described as being 'quiet and calm'. Later that night, his son Randolph telephoned from his army base to ask what was the latest news. Churchill replied, 'I think I shall be Prime Minister tomorrow.'[43]

3

Action This Day

What a difference a day makes. At 5.30 a.m. on 10 May 1940, Churchill was awoken in Admiralty House and told the news that German forces had launched an invasion of Holland and Belgium. Hitler's long-awaited and much-predicted attack upon the democracies of Western Europe had begun. The Phoney War was over. The real war was on.

Churchill was thrown into a round of urgent meetings as telegrams and messages poured in. The huge French Army was still stationed along the Maginot Line, the string of immensely powerful fortresses constructed along France's 250-mile border with Germany. Hitler simply bypassed this and threw his armies at neutral Holland and Belgium, bombing airfields and using airborne troops to capture key defensive positions. For the first few days, this was where the action was.

At eight that morning the War Cabinet met and authorised the sending of British troops to assist the Dutch and the Belgians. An hour later, Churchill was back at his desk in the Admiralty. The BBC had been broadcasting news of Hitler's invasion since seven o'clock and by now the entire country knew that a full-scale war crisis was on. But Chamberlain, having decided the previous day that a national government must be created, wavered again. He spoke with friends and said that maybe a change of government should be delayed until the battle on the continent was over, perhaps now was not the time for a change of leadership in Britain. Wiser colleagues, like Sir Kingsley Wood, a senior figure in the Conservative Party, spoke with Chamberlain and insisted the crisis made it even more important that he form a national government. Still Chamberlain hesitated.

The War Cabinet met again at 11.30 a.m. Ministers were beginning to feel that if a change of government were coming, it should happen sooner rather than later. But the overwhelming military business of the day crowded out any political debate. The news from Belgium was not good. Reports suggested that German airborne troops had seized a key fortress in a daring dawn raid.

In the late afternoon, the War Cabinet met for the third time that day. It heard that German infantry and tanks were now pouring into Belgium near Liège. Finally, the Prime Minister spoke up and told members that he intended to resign that evening and that a national government should be formed urgently. Chamberlain had at last accepted the inevitable and was about to bow out, despite the alarming news from across the Channel. He did not tell the Cabinet whom he would be recommending as his successor.

In accordance with tradition, Chamberlain went straight to Buckingham Palace to hand in his resignation to George VI. The King expressed his preference for Halifax as 'the obvious man' to become Prime Minister. When Chamberlain said Halifax had ruled himself out, the King knew that only 'one person . . . had the confidence of the country, & that was Winston'. Chamberlain agreed and left.

At about 6 p.m., Churchill was summoned to meet the King. No crowds had gathered as everyone was preoccupied with the news from Belgium, so Churchill slipped quietly into the Palace. According to his account, at this supreme moment in the nation's history, the King joked for a moment and asked, 'I suppose you don't know why I have sent for you.' Churchill responded wryly, 'Sir, I simply couldn't imagine why.' After a brief discussion, the formalities were completed and in a matter of minutes the meeting was over. In his diary, the King noted, 'He was full of fire & determination.'[1]

Churchill returned to the Admiralty as Prime Minister. The nation was in crisis. Less than three hundred miles away two million men were engaged in a furious battle. Events were moving at a stunning speed. Within weeks, Britain would be standing alone to face one of the most determined and ferocious enemies in its history. The burden on the new Prime Minister stepping up to lead the nation at this critical point was immense. Churchill must have felt doubts about what lay ahead. He confided to his detective in the car on the way back from the Palace: 'I hope it is not too late.' But he later wrote that he felt a profound sense of relief, that at last he had the authority to direct the entire operation of the war effort. In his Second World War history he wrote momentously, 'I felt as if I were walking with destiny, and that my past life had been but a preparation for this hour and for this trial.'[2]

At nine that evening Chamberlain broadcast to the nation, explaining that recent events made it clear that a national coalition government was needed. He told the British people that he had resigned and that Winston Churchill was their new Prime Minister. He asked everyone to give Churchill their full support. In Barrow-in-Furness, housewife Nella Last was keeping a diary for Mass Observation. In it she wrote that Churchill was a popular figure among the shipyard workers of the town and reflected that if she had to spend her 'whole life with a man, I'd choose Mr Chamberlain, but I think I would sooner have Mr Churchill if there was a storm and I was shipwrecked'.[3] The storm had arrived.

Churchill immediately started putting together his national government. And he set about restructuring the war effort to streamline the complex and cumbersome decision-making system that had been in existence up to this point. Later that same evening, he sent the King a letter outlining his top five appointments to the War Cabinet with Labour, Liberal and Conservative members in key positions. His government would be a true coalition, representing all political view-points across the nation. There was no vindictiveness towards Chamberlain, the man who had derided Churchill's views about the inevitability of war for years, who became Lord President of the Council. But this was not just an act of gen-erosity: Chamberlain was still leader of the Conservative Party and Churchill knew that he could not govern without his sup-port. Looking back at the end of a dramatic day, Churchill later wrote: 'I thought I knew a good deal about it all, and I was sure I would not fail. Therefore, although impatient for the morning, I slept soundly and had no need for cheering dreams. Facts are better than dreams.'[4]

It's difficult, knowing what we do today about events of the next few months and years, to realise that Churchill was by no means a universal choice as leader in May 1940. Officials in Whitehall were not at all heartened by his appointment. John Colville, one of Chamberlain's private secretaries at the time, remembers 'the mere thought of Churchill as Prime Minister sent a cold chill down the spines of the staff at 10 Downing Street ... His verbosity and restlessness made unnecessary work, prevented real planning and caused friction ... Our feel-ings ... were widely shared in the Cabinet offices, the Treasury and throughout Whitehall.'[5] This might be the sentiment of civil servants who feared change at a time of national crisis, but there was widespread suspicion of Churchill. He was thought to be impetuous, hot-headed and interfering. Even Halifax felt that he was led by his emotions rather than by reason. In British politics every Prime Minister has to have a substantial party base. But again, here Churchill was weak. Many Tories did not feel at all comfortable with him and had never forgiven him for deserting the party for the Liberals over thirty years earlier. He was seen as an opportunist and a chancer. Many felt like Lord Davidson that they simply 'don't trust Winston'. Old criticisms of him died hard. Alfred Lyttelton had said of him many decades before, 'He trims his sails to every passing wind.' Many Conservatives were also suspicious of his policies. He had supported Lloyd George's radical reforms of the Edwardian era, which had introduced unemployment benefits and state pensions. He had been a controversial Chancellor of the Exchequer in the 1920s. He had isolated himself over policy towards self-government in India. And, although his predictions about Hitler and Nazi aggression had been proved right, he had not won many friends in the Conservative Party, which had continued to support the policy of appeasement through the 1930s. Meanwhile, although the Labour Party now supported him as leader of a coalition government, this was more out of opposition to Chamberlain than active support for Churchill. And he was not a friend of the Left. He was still remembered for having threatened the miners at Tonypandy. Some newspapers, such as the *Daily Mirror* and the *Daily Mail*, were pro-Churchill. But the establishment paper, *The Times*, was unhesitatingly anti.

Without doubt, had he wanted to, Halifax could have become Prime Minister in May 1940. But it seems he saw the future as an impossible challenge, what might be described today as a 'no-win' situation. Churchill became Prime Minister partly by default, but also because his background, his love of military affairs and his sense of history made him (and others) feel that this was his moment, that his time had come. And he never lacked the confidence that he could govern and drive the country forwards to victory. In his first speech to Parliament as Prime Minister on 13 May, he repeated what he had said to his Cabinet colleagues earlier in the day, 'I have nothing to offer but blood, toil, tears and sweat.' Then he went on to give his first great speech as a wartime leader. As Hitler's panzers charged through Belgium, apparently unstoppable, Churchill told the House of Commons:

> We have before us an ordeal of the most grievous kind. We have before us many, many long months of struggle and of suffering. You ask, what is our policy? I will say: It is to wage war, by sea, land and air, with all our might and with all the strength that God can give us; to wage war against a monstrous tyranny, never surpassed in the dark, lamentable catalogue of human crime. That is our policy. You ask, what is our aim? I can answer in one word: It is victory, victory at all costs, victory in spite of all terror, victory, however long and hard the road may be; for without victory, there is no survival. Let that be realised. No survival for the British Empire, no survival for all that the British Empire has stood for . . . But I take up my task with buoyancy and with hope . . . and I say, 'Come then, let us go forward together with our united strength.'[6]

These were grand words and noble sentiments, but in the face of the rapid advance of Hitler's forces in Northern Europe they must have sounded hollow to those who heard them. How on earth could Churchill deliver?

Of the many tasks Churchill faced on becoming Prime Minister, first was the need to assemble his government. This was done while the war raged across the Channel. Some key members of what would become the War Lab were now put in place. At the centre of government, Churchill appointed himself Minister of Defence as well as Prime Minister. There was no precedent for this. It gave him unique authority to oversee all matters of military policy. The joint role put him in total control of Britain's war effort. There was virtually no aspect of war administration he could not influence. And this would be a vital feature of his leadership. There had been no such position as Minister of Defence in the First World War, and no ministry of this name during the 1930s. And, unlike from the 1960s onwards, no great department of state would report to him as Minister of Defence. The key adviser he appointed was General Sir Hastings Ismay, who would lead a small staff of a dozen officers and act like a staff officer, representing Churchill at Chiefs of Staff meetings and acting as his go-between with the military chiefs. Churchill called Ismay his 'eminence khaki' and told him that they must be very careful not to define their powers too precisely. He did not want to create a rulebook that hemmed in his authority. He wanted to range widely and without restraint across every aspect of the conduct of the war.[7] And this he did. Ismay became a faithful supporter and confidant of Churchill and he was one of the few who came into post in May 1940 and stayed with Churchill throughout the next five long and immensely challenging years. Their relationship was good, sometimes strained, but enduring. Churchill's affectionate nickname for Ismay was 'Pug'.

The War Cabinet was at the heart of the government. Churchill reduced it from nine to only five members, although later it increased in size. As we have seen, Chamberlain became Lord President of the Council. Clement Attlee, the leader of the

Labour Party, was Lord Privy Seal. Halifax remained Foreign Secretary. And Arthur Greenwood, the deputy Labour leader, became Minister without Portfolio. The ministers responsible for each of the services were not permanent members of the War Cabinet – another mark of the centralisation of military power and decision-making to Churchill himself.

The service ministers reflected the coalition nature of the new government. Sir Anthony Eden, the Conservative ex-Foreign Secretary who had resigned in 1938, was appointed Secretary of War. Sir Archibald Sinclair, leader of the Liberals as well as Churchill's good friend and his second-in-command in the trenches in the First World War, went to the Air Ministry. And Labour's A.V. Alexander replaced Churchill himself as First Lord of the Admiralty.

In less than a week, Churchill had appointed all thirty-four members of his government. The other key appointments here included Ernest Bevin, a trade union leader and for his day a real 'man of the people', as Minister of Labour. This was a brilliantly inspired appointment, and Bevin's total commitment to the war effort and to national unity helped keep many working people on side throughout the hardships that would follow. Lord Beaverbrook, the close friend of Churchill's from his 'court' at Chartwell, was appointed to the newly created post of Minister of Aircraft Production. The Canadian newspaper magnate was not a popular figure and many people were amazed at his appointment, but Churchill realised the vital need to increase the rate at which aircraft were being built in British factories, particularly the new fighter planes like the Hurricane and especially the Spitfire, which was suffering from huge delays in production. Churchill needed a human dynamo to create a flow of electricity to speed things up, and Beaverbrook provided the necessary spark. Sir John Anderson, an experienced administrator who had organised the evacuation of children at the beginning of the war, became Home Secretary. He gave his name to the corrugated-iron bomb shelters that almost everyone who had access to a garden would construct. Herbert Morrison, who had been the Labour leader of the London County Council and was a rising star within the party, was appointed Minister of Supply. Coincidentally, he gave his name to another type of bomb shelter.

Churchill also gathered around him a group of friends and advisers whose judgement he trusted and whose company he enjoyed. They had various jobs in what now became the court of King Winston, and they came nearest to a sort of central staff. Today, they would all become paid government consultants. Then, they remained on the fringes of government. But in essence Churchill created a private office in Downing Street that reported directly to him and served his interests and curiosity. At the centre of this would be his old friend Professor Frederick Lindemann (who later became Lord Cherwell), the rather pompous Oxford scientist universally known as 'the Prof'. He would meet with Churchill almost daily and advise him on a broad range of topics over the next few years. Another member of Churchill's inner team was his son-in-law, Duncan Sandys, who took on various roving missions. Brendan Bracken, another trusted friend from the old days, acted as a wide-ranging political adviser. Desmond Morton, the man who had supplied Churchill with valuable secret information during his wilderness years, became a sort of intelligence supremo. Sitting adjacent to the Cabinet Office, he had direct access to Churchill and acted as the Prime Minister's go-between with the various intelligence agencies. He was outgoing, with a strong sense of humour, and his raucous laughter echoed down the corridors of Downing Street. John Colville later described how these advisers arrived like 'Horsemen of the Apocalypse' in the government set-up.[8] Churchill's War Lab was beginning to take shape.

The military heads of the three services, known as the Chiefs of Staff, would meet daily in the morning. They constituted a sort of battle headquarters in London to assess and advise on the strategic direction of the war. Churchill would not attend these meetings as a matter of routine, but as Minister of Defence he could chair them if circumstances required it. Ismay, a member of the Chiefs of Staff Committee, would report daily to Churchill on the meetings and the issues that were discussed. Reporting to the Chiefs of Staff Committee were the Joint Planning Staff and the Joint Intelligence Committee. The latter group assembled and assessed the best intelligence about enemy actions and intentions. This was then distributed to Churchill, the War Cabinet and the Chiefs of Staff. This system was designed so that all the major decision-makers should have possession of all the key information.

The Chief of the Imperial General Staff (CIGS), a title inherited from the heyday of Empire, was another pivotal figure in the War Lab. When Churchill became Prime Minister, General Edmund Ironside was in the post. He was an impressive, dashing figure who in his youth had provided the model for Richard Hannay in John Buchan's *The Thirty-Nine Steps*. But he had fallen out with Churchill during the Norwegian debacle because he could not bear what he saw as the constant meddling of a politician who seemed to want to run a military campaign as though he were the field commander. A fortnight after Churchill took power, Ironside was replaced as CIGS by Sir John Dill, a tough Ulsterman greatly valued by Churchill for his abilities and strategic knowledge. But Dill seemed tired and lacked the vigour that was expected of him at this point of the war. Over time, Churchill would drive Dill to distraction with his constant attention to the sort of details the CIGS considered inappropriate for a Prime Minister to concern himself with. And Churchill would grow frustrated with Dill's slowness to respond, nicknaming him 'Dilly-Dally'. But this was in the future.

Under Chamberlain, the management of war policy had been confused and poorly thought through. Ironside commented in April 1940: 'Strategy is directed by odd people who collect odd bits of information. This is discussed quite casually by everyone.'[9] This was clearly not the way to run a war. Churchill, who had not only been at the heart of the management of war policy in the First World War but who had also seen how decision-making came about (or didn't come about) in the first eight months of the Second, brought in a new broom to sweep away Chamberlain's structure and make room for his own. Placing himself firmly in the coordinating chair, he established various groups who reported in with information and advice. The War Cabinet was responsible for the ultimate direction of war policy. The Chiefs of Staff reported to Churchill daily through Ismay. A new group known as the Defence Committee (Operations), consisting of the service ministers and the service chiefs, sent top-level strategic advice up the system. Another group, the Defence Committee (Supply), concerned itself with essential aspects of running and planning the war effort in a way that left the service chiefs free to concentrate on strategic thinking.

This might all sound like administrative game-playing at best or empire-building at worst. But these new structures, creating a new 'organogram' of power, were much more than this. One participant described the practical effects as 'revolutionary'.[10] It was essential that key information should flow in the most sensible way to those who needed to know what was going on and could then make sensible decisions in the light of this knowledge. It was essential to be able to focus first on the macro (or strategic) perspective on how to conduct the war. And then to see this through by attending to the micro (or tactical) detail of how to pursue it wisely. Finally, it was necessary to ensure that supply and logistics were focused on achieving and supporting the strategic war aims. At the centre of this new web of power was of course Churchill himself, in his joint role as Prime Minister and Minster of Defence. On him would fall the burden of understanding the big picture and deciding on myriad details that would make the war effort effective. Churchill now had to show how his years of military experience as a soldier and a deep understanding of military history would make him suitable as war leader for a nation in crisis.

Churchill committed himself to the tasks ahead with immense energy. An endless stream of instructions, requests, exhortations and diktats began to flow from the top, usually in the form of Churchill's increasingly familiar minutes. Rarely in history have so many orders come from the desk of one man. At no point in the Second World War was there anything comparable – not from Stalin after the invasion of the Soviet Union in June 1941, nor from Roosevelt after Pearl Harbor in December of that year. Churchill's first few months in office were more akin to President John F. Kennedy's first 'Hundred Days', and although there were grave crises in both, the nation's survival itself was not at stake when Kennedy took office. Over the next few weeks and months, Churchill was to enquire about and instruct on an enormously wide range of issues. What progress is being made with rockets, with sensitive fuses, with bomb sights and with Radio Detection-Finding? Can Turin and Milan be bombed from England? Can more trees be felled to reduce the reliance on imports and save shipping? Can regular troops be moved from India? Can a better reserve be built up in the Middle East? How are the coastal watches and coastal batteries being organised? How are harbour defences being built up? These minutes were often known by his staff as 'Churchill's prayers', because they usually began: 'Pray tell me . . .' or 'Pray explain why we cannot . . .'. To the Chiefs of Staff he would send directives for them to consider. His officials gave these their own names and references. Hence, a long and detailed directive beginning 'Renown awaits the Commander who first . . .' became known simply as 'Renown Awaits'. It was through these directives that Churchill tried to shape the conduct and strategy of the war.[11]

As with so much of Churchill's personal style of leadership, no detail was too small to escape his attention or interest. For instance, after Eden had suggested the creation of Local Defence Volunteer forces across the country – to utilise the skills and enthusiasm of ex-servicemen who were too old or otherwise unable to join the military but who wanted to 'do their bit' – Churchill wrote: 'I don't think much of the name "Local Defence Volunteers" for your very large new force. The word "Local" is uninspiring . . . I think "Home Guard" would be better. Don't hesitate to change on account of already having made armlets, etc.' And so, with the dash of a minute, Churchill created a name that became legendary in the collective British memory of the war.[12]

Churchill was a hard taskmaster and wanted things done his way. This was his prerogative as Prime Minister. What particularly frustrated a maverick like Churchill was the slowness of officialdom. Fighting a war with the intensity he now was, Churchill wanted action and he wanted it now – better still yesterday. He developed a variety of techniques to push things through and to attribute priorities. His dispatch box always had to have documents filed in a particular way, with the most urgent military matters at the top, and documents for reading at leisure (probably over a weekend) marked with an 'R' for 'Recreation' at the bottom. Officials had to act on items he had signed or authorised. And nothing typifies his desire to get things moving more than the red sticker he had specially made marked 'Action This Day'. When he attached this to a document or a minute the instructions or requests within were to be given top priority. Churchill wanted to hear back on it within the day.

Working for Churchill must have been extremely difficult. No doubt many of his minutes sidetracked exhausted officials from other duties. But Churchill also brought an immense, restless energy to the top of government. This had been badly lacking under Chamberlain, and almost certainly would have never happened under Halifax. As all management training makes clear today, change needs to start at the top. The chief executive has to be the model and to set the pace. Churchill instigated a brand of 'change management' (to use a phrase that would have meant nothing to the old man himself) that was dramatic, heartfelt and strikingly effective. Just when Britain needed it, the pace of government went up a gear. Lord Normanbrook, a senior civil servant in the Cabinet Office, wrote later:

> This stream of messages, covering so wide a range of subjects, was like the beam of a searchlight ceaselessly swinging round and penetrating into the remote recesses of the administration so that everyone, however humble his range or his function, felt that one day the beam might rest on him and light up what he was doing. In Whitehall the effect of this influence was immediate and dramatic. The machine responded at once to his leadership. It quickened the pace and improved the tone of administration. A new sense of purpose and urgency was created as it came to be realised that a firm hand guided by a strong will was on the wheel. Morale was high.[13]

Churchill's working day reflected this full-on approach, and it soon adopted a particular and rather unusual routine. Of course, every day was different. But even when travelling and working abroad Churchill would try to keep to some of his established routine. He would be woken every morning at about 8 a.m. Breakfast and the day's papers would be brought to him in bed on a tray. Along with these came the daily report from the Map Room. This was of vital importance to Churchill, who wanted to be kept up to date on the latest movements of armies and ships around the world. The report was often delivered in person by the naval officer in charge of the Map Room, Captain Richard Pim, who had been running it since Churchill's days at the Admiralty. Then, wearing his favourite dressing gown, which was green and gold with red dragons on it, he would sit in bed, propped up by pillows, and work on his boxes. He would read messages and communications, Cabinet papers, Foreign Office telegrams, military reports and so on. Throughout the morning, a female secretary or typist would be on hand to take down his dictation straight on to a specially made silent typewriter (the sound of punching the keys annoyed him). There was rarely time to take shorthand and then type it up later. It all had to be typed and signed immediately. The typists were led by Kathleen Hill, who knew his fancies and foibles inside out. The secretaries who joined his staff during the war at first found him a terrifying figure who would call out 'Gimme my box', 'Gimme Pug', which meant call for General Ismay, or 'Gimme Prof', which meant call for Professor Lindemann. On other occasions, he would just hold out his hand and say, 'Gimme', expecting the poor woman to know exactly what was meant, sometimes to pass a black pen, sometimes a red pen, a paper punch, which he called a 'Klop', some blotting paper, or the red 'Action This Day' label to stick on the front of a minute.[14]

Churchill would stay sitting up in bed, working and dictating, for as long as possible. Most mornings, the Chiefs of Staff would meet without the Prime Minister and Ismay would arrive to report back on their deliberations. Other officials or intimates might attend him in his bedroom. Several cigars would be smoked through the course of the morning, although most went out as Churchill's thoughts or dictation distracted him, and much fuss and effort would be devoted to relighting them. Often the War Cabinet would meet in the morning, daily in the early stages of the war and twice-weekly later. Half an hour before whatever meeting required his presence, Churchill would take a hot bath and would dress with the assistance of his valet, Frank Sawyers. Throughout the war Churchill kept up the Victorian habit of relying on a valet, and Sawyers was never far from his master, in London, at Chequers or abroad. Sawyers was short, plump, bald and, in the way of old-style servant relationships, utterly devoted to his boss. Churchill would always go out in public dressed immaculately in striped trousers, a black jacket with waistcoat, a spotted bow tie and a puffed handkerchief in his top pocket. However, if there were no meetings scheduled, he would often prefer to wear his siren suit, a one-piece boiler-type suit with a zip up the front, in Air Force blue. His staff called it his romper suit.

Lunch was usually served at 1.30 p.m., and provided an opportunity for Churchill to meet and talk with military personnel, politicians or his close set of advisers and friends. The afternoon was nearly always spent in meetings of one sort or another. Churchill had a private study next to the Cabinet Room in 10 Downing Street. Meetings could be held there or in the Annexe, a specially prepared set of rooms a few minutes' walk away at Storey's Gate. The Churchills had a small flat there as well. Below the Annexe, down a spiral staircase, were the Cabinet War Rooms, an underground complex supposed to be secure from bombing. This network of offices, communications, sleeping accommodation and a Cabinet Room were designed to provide all that was needed should central government have to carry on below ground. Churchill's Map Room was also located there.[15]

Every afternoon, as soon as possible after lunch, Churchill would take a nap for about an hour. His closest officials remarked on how quickly he could fall into a sound sleep, even during the most stressful times. This mid-afternoon rest did him immense good, and after it was over he would rise, take another hot bath if there were time, and like a giant awakened would be ready to start almost another full day's work, with the typists again standing by for dictation and officials hurrying in and out as required.

Dinner was always served around 8.30 p.m. This was another opportunity to meet and talk with senior officials or leading soldiers, sailors and airmen. It was always a big occasion. Reasonable amounts of wine would be served. The meal was four courses, beginning with soup. The soup course was invariably a restorative to Churchill. Whatever frame of mind he was in, no matter how much pressure he was under, his mood would lift as he ate the soup, and dinner usually became a lively, amusing and provocative affair. Most people who describe having dinner with Churchill talk of the countless witticisms and one-liners that he came up with during the meal. Strategy would be openly discussed, new ideas and potential solutions to challenges kicked around, and politics and military affairs freely debated. From about ten o'clock onwards, Churchill would then conduct more formal meetings or conferences, often with his CIGS or the other military chiefs. After these had ended, he would routinely dictate into the early hours – more minutes or directives to the Chiefs of Staff, or outlines for an upcoming speech or broadcast. He enjoyed these late hours and clearly some of his best ideas came to him then. General Sir Alan Brooke later said that Churchill was the sort of man who had ten ideas a day, only one of which was any good, but he never knew which one.[16]

The long hours were a strain on his staff. 'It's amazing how quickly you get used to going to bed at 2.30,' Elizabeth Layton, one of the secretaries, was told before she started to work for Churchill. His top military men, none of whom had enjoyed the benefit of a mid-afternoon siesta, often found the late-night sessions exhausting, but sometimes exhilarating too. Churchill would often use the tête-à-têtes as an occasion to make up after a demanding day or to make someone feel wanted who had been bullied or cajoled by his incessant demands. No matter how grumpy or stressed Churchill had been during the day, in the small hours he would always turn to his secretaries with a glowing smile and say, 'Good night and thank you,' making them feel appreciated. The working day could end at any time from about two in the morning onwards and sometimes as late as four. This schedule was kept up seven days a week. At Chequers there was often a film show after dinner, but otherwise the routine and the workload at the weekend remained the same. It was not an easy schedule to keep up with.[17]

Despite his authoritarian control over affairs, Churchill was no dictator. He dominated conversations, and his ubiquitous role at the centre of the political and military machinery of the war meant that his influence was immense But he listened to his professional advisers. He wanted them to argue their position forcefully and he relished the cut and thrust of debate. Often strong words were used and tempers frayed, but Churchill was well used to this from Parliament and throughout his life he rarely bore a grudge. So if his military chiefs stuck to their guns and opposed him, he would always back down. Not once during the war did he overrule his military advisers on a military question.[18]

At last, Britain's war effort was losing the complacency and hesitation that had characterised the Chamberlain era. At last, the country had a leader with the knowledge, the energy and the determination to get the machinery of war moving. But events now taking place in Belgium, Holland and France would soon show how limited Churchill's impact could be in this first phase of the war.

A major priority for Churchill as he threw himself into the business of leading the nation was to follow and to give every support to Britain's ally in the war waging across the Channel. He made five visits to France over the next six weeks, and sometimes these exposed him to considerable personal risk. It was characteristic of Churchill's style of leadership that he wanted to be in the thick of it. As Prime Minister, he would travel far more extensively than any of the other war leaders. Stalin left the Soviet Union just twice – to attend the Teheran and Potsdam summits. Roosevelt travelled abroad three times during the war, but in the main he expected Churchill to come to him, which was not particularly surprising bearing in mind his own disability and the fact that he was after all a head of state while Churchill was merely head of government. Hitler hardly ever travelled far from his favourite haunts in Bavaria, East Prussia and Berlin. Churchill strained every nerve and tried every trick to support the French in their life-and-death struggle with Germany. But his effectiveness here was severely limited by factors over which he had no control.

In the spring of 1940, French military thinking was still dominated by the experience of the First World War. The French Army was haunted by the memory of one and a half million deaths. It could think only in terms of defence, hence the vast expenditure on and commitment to the Maginot Line. Most of its senior commanders had obtained all their military knowledge between 1914 and 1918. There was little or no coordination between the army and the air force. The French Commander-in-Chief, General Maurice Gamelin, had no radio communication with his senior officers from his command headquarters at the Château de Vincennes. From there he conducted affairs in splendid isolation from day-to-day events, in an echo of Great War generals commanding their armies from comfortable châteaux miles behind the line. There was no clear delineation between the roles of Gamelin and his deputy, General Alphonse Georges, who held executive command over troops along the entire front. The whole French command structure was tangled and confused. At one critical point as the Germans swept into France, Gamelin began one of his orders with the apologetic words: 'Without wishing to intervene in the conduct of the battle in progress . . .' But what else should the Commander-in-Chief be doing?

Politically, too, France was weak and divided. Paul Reynaud had been Prime Minister for only seven weeks. And he had no time for Gamelin, whom he had tried to remove from command the day before the German onslaught overwhelmed them. The French had many skilled troops and some outstanding armoured units. But, as with so much in the French Army of 1940, the tank units were slow, poorly structured and ineffectively deployed on the battlefield.

The German Army, the Wehrmacht, on the other hand, was a thoroughly modern and effective fighting force. It had been almost entirely restructured during the 1930s, learning all the lessons of defeat in 1918. German military thinking incorporated the latest techniques for using fast-moving, armoured units in sharp hammer-blows against a narrow enemy front. Although the highest level of command was full of generals who doubted that France could be knocked out in a single, rapid blow, the middle-ranking officers who led men in battle were both highly motivated and trained to seize the initiative as and when they could. For instance, General Heinz Guderian was a great enthusiast for the armoured-warfare theories proposed by British strategists like Basil Liddell Hart and tank pioneers like Generals Fuller and Hobart (theories largely ignored by the British Army of 1940). Guderian commanded a panzer corps in the assault on Belgium and made it clear to all his senior officers that their overall objective was to force their way to the Channel coast in northern France as quickly as possible. They were to use their own initiative whenever necessary so long as it contributed towards this goal.

The British Army had sent a small expeditionary force to northern France, just as it had in 1914. The troops were well trained and reasonably well equipped. But as in the First World War, they were too few in number to make a substantial difference to the battle. Their commander, Viscount Gort, was a brave, courageous general who had won a Victoria Cross and a host of other commendations during the First World War. But although he had Churchill's confidence, he could not make up for years of peacetime neglect of the army. There was also confusion over how the British troops should fit into the French operation. Gort did his best to act as a loyal ally, but he was astonished and a little ashamed at how quickly French morale collapsed.

Despite the contrasting strengths and weaknesses of the Allied and Nazi units, the outcome of the battle that unfolded in May and June 1940 was by no means a certainty. The combined troops of the French, British, Belgian and Dutch armies slightly outnumbered the Wehrmacht. And the Allies even had more tanks than the Germans. But the German Air Force, the Luftwaffe, far outnumbered the combined Allied air forces, and no French fighter could match the Messerschmitt Me-109. The RAF Hurricanes and Spitfires were formidable flying machines, but as far as the French were concerned there were never enough of them. In addition, the Germans used their

Stuka dive-bombers brilliantly in close ground support. These aircraft had a siren fitted below the wings which emitted a screaming sound as they dived to drop their thousand-pound bomb, making them daunting terror weapons. Even the most experienced soldiers broke under bombardment from a wave of Stukas.

Using a strategy of fast-moving armoured units comprising massed phalanxes of panzers, with close air support for the ground advance, and choosing to fight over a narrow rather than a broad front, the German Army now rolled out its techniques for blitzkrieg or lightning war. This combination of surprise, speed, weight and numbers had been used very effectively in Poland. In France and Belgium, the Germans were up against tougher troops in much larger numbers, but the end result was the same. The Wehrmacht had been forged into a brilliant fighting machine with an iron sense of purpose and self-confidence. The Germans totally outperformed the Allies and enjoyed one of the most spectacular victories of the war.

From the beginning of their assault at dawn on 10 May, the initiative lay with the German troops. In a brilliant and daring action, about three hundred glider troops captured the giant, modern Belgian fortress at Eban Emael, reputed to be the strongest fort in the world. The well-defended position was overwhelmed in just a few hours. Simultaneously, a complete army group moved into Holland in the north, drew out the Dutch and Belgian armies and tempted the British forward, too. But this was part of the German master-plan to draw Allied forces away from the main strike, which fell in the centre of Belgium. Here, ten panzer divisions launched a lightning attack through the Ardennes forest, which the French had believed to be impenetrable and had left largely undefended. In a series of actions from 13 to 16 May along the banks of the river Meuse, the panzers crashed through French defences and established bridgeheads on the west side of the river.

After six days, the Dutch government gave in. The royal family escaped on a British destroyer and King George welcomed Queen Wilhelmina at Liverpool Street Station. Soon the Dutch government followed the Queen into exile in London. The breakneck speed of the German advance was beyond the comprehension of French generals who still thought in First World War terms of a few hundred yards lost or gained in a day. Their poor communications and divided command hampered effective resistance. On the eve of the sixth day of fighting, with the panzer breakout along the Meuse threatening to divide his entire army, Gamelin ordered a full withdrawal of all his troops from Belgium. Prime Minister Reynaud gave the order for the government to prepare to evacuate Paris and move to Tours. He rang Churchill in an 'excited mood' and said, 'We are defeated. We have lost the battle. The way to Paris lies open.' He asked Churchill to send all the troops and planes he could.[19]

On the following afternoon, Churchill flew to Paris. At 5.30 p.m. a historic meeting took place at the Quai d'Orsay. Reynaud, his Defence Minister Daladier and Gamelin met with the British Prime Minister, who was accompanied by Generals Ismay and Dill. Gamelin outlined the collapse of the front in a short speech to all those present. The meeting fell silent. In his best French, Churchill asked about the strategic reserve: '*Ou est la masse de manoeuvre?*' General Gamelin turned to him and with a shrug and a shake of the head replied: '*Aucune . . . Aucune*' – 'There is none.' Churchill wrote later: 'I was dumbfounded. What were we to think of the great French Army and its highest chiefs?'[20]

The French pressed Churchill to send more fighter squadrons. This had already been discussed by the War Cabinet. Air

Marshal Sir Hugh Dowding was in charge of RAF Fighter Command and had responsibility for the air defence of Britain. He argued against sending fighters to France because this would weaken the British air defensive system. Churchill felt that although it was a grave risk, something had to be done to 'bolster up the French'. He telegrammed London to say: 'It would not be good historically if their requests were denied and their ruin resulted.' The War Cabinet met at eleven o'clock that night to discuss this telegram and agreed to dispatch a total of ten fighter squadrons. Churchill immediately went to Reynaud's flat to tell him the news. After an interval, the French Prime Minister appeared from his bedroom in his dressing gown. Daladier was called to join them and he shook Churchill's hand in gratitude. Churchill got to bed at the British Embassy at about 2 a.m.

Over the next few days, the German panzers broke through and began their drive for the coast. The Allied position looked as though it were about to crumble. Gamelin was replaced by the sprightly seventy-two-year-old General Maxime Weygand, who tried to rally the troops but could do nothing to reverse the disasters that had already befallen the dispirited French Army. On 22 May, Churchill flew back to France to meet the French commanders at Vincennes. He was pleased to see that Weygand was reviving the French command, but by now the first German panzers had reached the Channel coast near Abbeville. The Allied armies were cut in two. The advanced panzer divisions moved north along the coast and after some bitter fighting captured first Boulogne, then Calais.

Ironside, the CIGS, was sent by the War Cabinet to visit Gort in the field and tell him to move his troops south-west. Gort carried out a small counter-attack against the advancing panzers near Arras which was successful. This forced even the elite panzers of the 7th Division, led by Erwin Rommel, to pause briefly and regroup. But the planned French support did not appear; and, fearing that his men would be cut off, Gort called off the counter-attack and, in defiance of his orders, began to retreat towards the coast.

At this point, General von Rundstedt, commander of the German army group in the centre of the battle, ordered his panzer units to pause. He was stunned by the speed of their advance, well over two hundred miles in little more than three days, and worried that they were now too exposed. In his diary, he noted that the enemy had been fighting 'with extraordinary tenacity', and he wanted to regroup and wait for the infantry to catch up. He was fearful of the very type of counter-attack that Weygand was in fact now planning. The German High Command debated whether to turn south and head for Paris or turn north to mop up the British and French armies first. At this point, Hitler arrived in person at von Rundstedt's headquarters. For the first time since the Battle of France had started he intervened directly and endorsed von Rundstedt's order. Maybe he thought it was more likely that the British would seek peace with Germany if their army had not been destroyed in the field. He almost certainly wanted to show his commanders that he was in control.[21] The panzers came to a halt, a few miles from the French port of Dunkirk.

On 27 May, an evacuation of British and French soldiers began around Dunkirk. The head of the Luftwaffe, Hermann Goering, told Hitler that his planes would finish off the Allied armies. And they nearly did so. Soldiers under constant harassment from the air cursed the RAF for not coming to their aid. But this was unfair. The RAF was attacking the German bomber formations as they assembled many miles away from the evacuation beaches. In a foretaste of what was to come later in the summer, the RAF pilots shot down large numbers of Goering's bombers but suffered substantial losses themselves. After a few days, the weather turned for the worse, the Luftwaffe could not fly, and the evacuation went up a gear. Boats of every shape and size came the twenty-odd miles from the Kent coast to assist the navy in the evacuation. Hundreds of these 'small ships' helped to get men off the beaches in what was now called the 'miracle of Dunkirk'. For several days and nights, the evacuation continued, with exhausted men clambering into fighting ships, trawlers, drifters, fishing boats, tugs, yachts and motor launches. The Admiralty initially estimated that they would be able to evacuate about 45,000 men. By 4 June, when the evacuation was finally called off, 338,226 men had been rescued, two-thirds of them British and one-third French, Belgian and Dutch.

Gort, the commander of British forces in France and Belgium and hero of the First World War, chose to stay with his men in the ever-shrinking defensive perimeter around the Dunkirk beaches, to face death or capture. However, Churchill thought his capture would provide the Germans with too great a trophy, so he ordered Gort to hand over to a deputy and evacuate. This he reluctantly did on 1 June, feeling bad about his escape. He believed that the criticism he later received for deserting his post was not fair as he had only been following Churchill's orders. But this was not the end of Gort's career and he would go on, two years later, to be Governor of Malta at a critical point in the war, when the survival of that beleaguered island was of vital importance.

In the last days of May, Churchill had faced another crisis. He had been Prime Minister for only two weeks, and his hold on the reins of power was by no means secure. Hitler thought Churchill would not last long and that the British would soon realise the folly of continuing to fight. Indeed, many in the British establishment were beginning to panic in the face of the disaster unfolding on the continent and the prospect of having to fight on alone. One Tory MP wrote in his diary: '"All is lost" sort of attitude in evidence in many quarters.'[22] And Halifax, very much a member of the establishment, believed that Britain should at least explore the possibility of negotiation with Hitler before facing the very real likelihood of total defeat. He made an approach to Mussolini, Hitler's ally, although at this point Italy was still not at war with Britain or France. In the War Cabinet, Halifax argued that Britain's long-term interests might be better secured by negotiating now before France fell, rather than later, under duress. The War Cabinet was divided. The two Labour members, Attlee and Greenwood, were opposed to any sort of negotiation with Hitler because they thought it would undermine the war effort if news of it ever got out. Chamberlain seems to have sat on the fence. Churchill, unsurprisingly, was instinctively opposed to any sort of parley with Hitler. 'Nations which went down fighting rose again, but those who surrender tamely were finished,' he argued.[23]

Matters came to a head on the afternoon of 28 May, when the War Cabinet discussed whether to open negotiations. Halifax was now in effect making a direct challenge to Churchill's leadership, not because he wanted to take over but because he thought the Prime Minister's thinking was wrong and a new course was needed. After an hour of passionate discussion, the War Cabinet was adjourned. Churchill had called a meeting of the full Cabinet at 5 p.m. In this he gave the twenty-five members of the Cabinet a frank account of the perilous situation in France. Hugh Dalton, the newly appointed Minister of Economic Warfare, wrote that Churchill 'was quite magnificent. The man, and the only man we have, for this hour.' He then recorded that Churchill said: 'I have thought carefully in these last days whether it was part of my duty to consider entering negotiations with That Man.' Churchill argued that Britain would not get any better terms by making peace with Hitler now than if the country went on and fought it out. Churchill continued: 'The Germans would demand our fleet – that would be called "disarmament" – our naval bases and much else. We should become a slave state.' He ended his speech by saying, 'We shall go on and fight it out, here or elsewhere, and if at last the long story [of British history] is to end, it were better it should end, not through surrender, but only when each one of us lies choking in his own blood upon the ground.' At this, a cheer went up around the table. Members of the Cabinet went over and congratulated Churchill, shook his hand and patted him on the back. Churchill was delighted by this spontaneous display of support from such a group of men, many of whom had long been his political adversaries. He later wrote: 'There is no doubt that had I at this juncture faltered at all in leading the nation, I should have been hurled out of office.' When the War Cabinet resumed its meeting at seven o'clock that evening, Churchill reported back on the strong support he had received. His resolve had been both personally and politically strengthened. There was to be no more talk of a parley with Hitler. Churchill had faced down Halifax. He had won. One historian has described this as a day that changed the course of world history, which would have been so different if Churchill had agreed to negotiate a deal with Hitler: 'Then and there he [Churchill] saved Britain, and Europe, and western civilisation.'[24]

On 31 May, in the midst of the Dunkirk evacuation, Churchill flew once again to Paris. He met with Reynaud and, for the first time since 1918, with Marshal Pétain, the legendary Great War hero who had been recalled as Deputy Prime Minister. Churchill repeated his line that Britain would fight on. In a conversation after the main meeting, he began to suspect that Pétain had now become a defeatist, and that he would agree to a separate peace treaty with Germany.

Churchill had not spent much time in the House of Commons since becoming Prime Minister. On 4 June, he reported to the

House what he described as the 'miracle of deliverance' at Dunkirk. But while celebrating the triumph of withdrawing so many men from the jaws of certain defeat and capture, he admitted: 'Wars are not won by evacuations.' Churchill hinted for the first time publicly in the speech that if France collapsed then Britain would fight on alone. In a passage that was partly intended to rally the British people to the struggle ahead, and partly intended to express Britain's resolve to overseas friends, especially in America, he concluded with some stirring phrases that have gone down in popular memory. He proclaimed:

Even though large tracts of Europe and many old and famous States have fallen or may fall into the grip of the Gestapo and all the odious apparatus of Nazi rule, we shall not flag or fail. We shall go on to the end. We shall fight in France, we shall fight in the seas and oceans, we shall fight with growing confidence and growing strength in the air; we shall defend our island whatever the cost may be. We shall fight on the beaches, we shall fight on the landing-grounds, we shall fight in the fields and in the streets, we shall fight in the hills; we shall never surrender.[25]

The speech was immensely well received by a packed House of Commons. One MP said it was worth 'a thousand guns'. In those days, Parliament was not broadcast, but the speech was very widely reported and had a great impact. Vita Sackville-West wrote to her husband, Harold Nicolson, after listening to a report of the speech on the radio: 'Even repeated by the announcer it sent shivers (not of fear) down my spine.'[26]

Belgium as well as Holland had now surrendered. The armies in the north had been defeated. Now Hitler's forces could turn south and move on Paris. On 5 June, the final phase of the Battle of France began. The British Army had evacuated from Dunkirk without most of its heavy weaponry, having abandoned more than 1400 artillery pieces, 38,000 vehicles and over 7000 tons of ammunition. There was precious little left to protect Britain should an invasion come. But Churchill knew that the military defeat of France would bring a political collapse. And the loss of an ally of this importance could be a fatal blow to Britain's own war effort. So he remained committed to the rapidly disintegrating French Army and sent two new and well-equipped divisions to north-west France.

Churchill requested another meeting with Reynaud to find out what the French were thinking. By now Paris had been abandoned and it was not easy to find a place to meet. On 11 June, Churchill and his small delegation flew to Briare on the Loire River for a meeting of the Supreme War Council. On arrival at the small landing strip, it was immediately apparent to Churchill how bad things had got. He tried to project a confident air. But the French were not responsive. A conference followed that evening in a nearby château that had been temporarily commandeered. It was woefully inadequate for this function and had only one telephone. General Weygand asked that every British fighter squadron should be sent to France. 'Here', he said, 'is the decisive point. Now is the decisive moment. It is therefore wrong to keep *any* squadrons back in England.' Churchill erupted. 'This is not the decisive point and this is not the decisive moment,' he declared forcefully. 'That moment will come when Hitler hurls his Luftwaffe against Great Britain. If we can keep command of the air, and if we can keep the seas open, as we certainly shall keep them open, we will win it all back for you.' In this atmosphere, no progress was made. Churchill heard after the meeting exactly how appalling the situation had become, with troops unable

The Young Winston

Churchill in his smart uniform in the 4th Hussars. But the cost of uniforms, horses, mess bills far exceeded the income.
(Getty Images)

ırchill in 1904, the year he the Conservatives and joined Liberals. As a young tician, Churchill was a nber of one of the great ırming governments of the ntieth century. (© Hulton-Deutsch ction/Corbis)

Churchill as prisoner of war, Pretoria, November 1899. He later wrote that he hat his period in captivity more than any other period in his whole life. (TopFoto)

Churchill and Lord Fisher in 1913. Churchill brought the ebullient Fisher back to the Admiralty in 1914 with disastrous consequences.

...rchill checking proofs in his study at Chartwell, February 1939. His years out of ...ce in the 1930s gave him plenty of time to develop his views on history and the ...cial destiny' of the British people. (Getty Images)

Churchill leaves Downing Street after a crisis War Cabinet on the day Hitler invaded Belgium and Holland, 10 May 1940. Later that same day he became Prime Minister. (Getty Images)

RAF Fighter Command Control Room, Bentley Priory. The command and control structure created by the RAF with input from scientists like Sir Henry Tizard on t eve of war worked brilliantly during the Battle of Britain. (Imperial War Museum, IWM)

...rchill and Captain Richard Pim in the Map Room at the Cabinet War Rooms.
...urchill eagerly followed troop and naval movements every day and Pim travelled
...h him setting up a temporary Map Room wherever he was. (IWM)

Churchill deep in conversation with Alex Henshaw, Spitfire test pilot. No doubt t
were discussing the strengths and weaknesses of the great British fighter aircraft. (I

Churchill visits Bristol, 12 April 1941, the day after a heavy bombing raid. His vis
to bomb-damaged cities were enormously popular. (IWM)

Churchill with his scientific guru Prof Lindemann (left with bowler hat), Air Chief Marshal Portal, Admiral Pound and General Ismay, all key players in his War Lab. (IWM)

scientists who contributed to new ideas during the war.

, Sir Solly Zuckerman who studied the impact of bombing and whose work was ɔrted by others. (Hamish Hamilton/Zuckerman family)

it, Alan Turing, the genius behind the 'Bombes' built at Bletchley Park to decode ɲan Enigma signals and one of the founders of the post-war computer industry.

Images)

Churchill poses with a Tommy gun sent in an arms shipment from America. He loved to get his hands on new weapons. (IWM)

to move along roads packed with refugees and everyone under constant machine-gun fire from German aircraft. He came away from the meeting convinced that a complete French military collapse was imminent. And he feared that Pétain would sign a peace treaty with Hitler. Only a meeting with a young French colonel, Charles de Gaulle, who had been appointed Under-Secretary for National Defence, cheered Churchill. De Gaulle favoured fighting a guerrilla war, and Reynaud seemed to like this approach. Churchill thought that maybe de Gaulle would take over from Reynaud if the latter stood down. But overall he left in a state of despair.

On the flight home, it was too cloudy for the Hurricane escort to accompany Churchill's plane. He chose to fly back anyway without it as there was much to do back in London. Over the French coast, the clouds cleared and Churchill looked down on Le Havre burning, the battle raging below. At this point, his aircraft dived steeply from eight thousand to about a hundred feet. German fighters had been spotted. The manoeuvre worked, and Churchill's plane flew on back to Britain, unnoticed and unharried.[27]

Two days later, the German Army entered Paris. Hitler's divisions then turned south and west, and within days had finished off the last French resistance. The military battle was over, but the political argument continued. Churchill made one final visit to France on 13 June. This time he flew to Tours to meet the French leaders. Such was the chaos on the ground that no one came out to meet the British Prime Minister. Churchill's delegation found a car and drove into the town along streets crowded with refugees and cars piled high with family possessions. Churchill couldn't even find somewhere for lunch. Eventually a café owner was persuaded to open up and serve the British leader a light meal. When Churchill finally met

Reynaud and the other French leaders it was obvious that final capitulation was near.

Over the following days, Churchill made it clear to the French leaders that he would not release them from the agreement made earlier in the year that neither country would seek a separate peace treaty. An extraordinary plan of a union between the two countries was suggested, with joint citizenship, so France could fight on. But nothing came of this. Any thought of rescuing France had now gone. Reynaud resigned on the 16th and was replaced by Pétain. Churchill hoped that the French government would move to North Africa and continue to fight from there, taking their fleet with them. He was particularly exercised by the fate of the French fleet, which he didn't want to fall into Nazi hands as this would give the German Navy a decisive advantage in the Mediterranean. He had obtained a promise from Admiral Darlan, the French naval commander, that he would never hand his fleet over to the Germans.

On taking power on 17 June, Pétain immediately opened negotiations with the Germans for an armistice. This was effectively the surrender of France. After a few days of delays, Hitler made it clear that the French must accept the terms on the table. On 22 June, the French generals signed the surrender at Compiègne. To rub in the humiliation, the Germans made the French sign the document in the same railway carriage in which the Germans had signed the Armistice in November 1918. Events had come full circle. The northern half of France would be occupied by German troops. The southern half would be run by Pétain from Vichy as a semi-independent but pro-German state.

A few days after the fall of Paris, Hitler – accompanied by Albert Speer, his favourite architect, a newsreel cameraman, and his bodyguard of SS troopers – was driven around the sights of the French capital. As he posed for the cameras in front of the Eiffel Tower, Hitler must have reflected on what a stunning victory his soldiers had won for him. For four whole years, from 1914 to 1918, the German Army had advanced only a few miles. Now, in just twelve weeks, since early April, his forces had conquered Denmark, Norway, Holland, Belgium, Luxembourg and France. In the previous ten months he had routed the Polish, Dutch, Belgian, French and British armies. Where would his triumphant war machine take him next?

Meanwhile, Winston Churchill, barely six weeks into his premiership, had to pick up the pieces after the utter catastrophe, for that's what it was, of France's surrender. But that had not been *his* battle. He had been able only to encourage and cajole from the sidelines. In the drama of the next conflict, the Battle of Britain, Churchill and his War Lab would play a leading role.

4

Spitfire Summer

Tuesday 18 June 1940 was the 125th anniversary of the Battle of Waterloo. At the time of the Napoleonic Wars, Britain had faced the possibility of an invasion from across the Channel. Now, with France defeated, the nation faced the possibility again. The guiding hand of history was never far from Churchill's shoulder. And on this day he felt it keenly. That afternoon, he addressed the House of Commons, reflecting on France's stunning defeat and looking ahead to Britain's prospects in fighting on alone. He said: 'What General Weygand called the Battle of France is over. I expect that the Battle of Britain is about to begin.' He wanted people at home and abroad to know that Britain would and could fight the battle on land, at sea and in the air. 'I look forward confidently to the exploits of our fighter pilots,' he told Parliament, 'who will have the glory of saving their native, their island home, and all they love, from the most deadly of all attacks.' He spoke of how all four dominion governments – Australia, New Zealand, Canada and South Africa – had guaranteed their support to Britain. But there was no doubt that with such a powerful foe only twenty-one miles across the Channel from southern England, the 'dread balance sheet' predicted a hard-fought battle ahead. Churchill argued: 'I see great reason for intense vigilance and exertion, but none whatsoever for panic or despair.'

He ended his address with a Shakespearean flourish, recalling Henry V's famous speech to his troops on the eve of the Battle of Agincourt. As ever, he spoke passionately of his belief in the special role carved out for Britain and its people. Churchill said of the upcoming Battle of Britain:

> Upon this battle depends the survival of Christian civilisation. Upon it depends our own British life and the long continuity of our institutions and our Empire. The whole fury and might of the enemy must very soon be turned on us. Hitler knows that he will have to break us in this island or lose the war. If we can stand up to him, all Europe may be free, and the life of the world may move forward into broad sunlit uplands; but if we fail, then the whole world, including the United States, and all that we have known and cared for, will sink into the abyss of a new dark age made more sinister, and perhaps more protracted, by the lights of a perverted science. Let us therefore brace ourselves to our duty and so bear ourselves that if the British Empire and its Commonwealth lasts for a thousand years, men will still say 'This was their finest hour.'[1]

Churchill was persuaded to broadcast this same speech to the nation on the BBC at nine o'clock that evening. This was one of his wartime speeches that would be heard not just in the House of Commons but by millions of people. The words of his flourishing finale are among the most famous Churchill ever uttered, and are almost as well known today as they were in the summer of 1940, having been repeated in countless television documentaries since. One vital part of Churchill's task over the next few months would be to rally public morale. Not only had he to lead Britain's war policy, but he must also call upon all the power of words and phrases that he could muster to encourage the nation to keep up the fight, despite what many saw as overwhelming odds against Britain's survival. The head of government had to display leadership, guidance, encouragement and the passionate inspiration to persuade the British people to fight on. This, we know, he did magnificently. Churchill really was walking with destiny now.

Ironically, to many who heard Churchill speak these famous words both in Parliament in the afternoon and then again on the radio in the evening, his radio performance came across as lacklustre. John Colville, his private secretary, thought he sounded tired and that he read the speech as though with a cigar in his mouth.[2] Harold Nicolson, Under-Secretary of State at the Ministry of Information, wrote to his wife:

How I wish Winston would not talk on the wireless unless he is feeling in good form. He hates the microphone and when we bullied him into speaking last night, he just sulked and read his House of Commons speech over again. Now, as delivered in the House of Commons, that speech was magnificent, especially the concluding sentences. But it sounded ghastly on the wireless. All the great vigour he put into it seemed to evaporate.[3]

Of course, Churchill's style of oratory long predated the advent of broadcasting. He had grown to political maturity accustomed to large-scale public speaking and to debating within the chamber of the House of Commons. He never seemed comfortable on the radio. This was probably because he was used to addressing an audience and relied upon the vibrancy of a 'live' public address. Speaking alone in a recording studio into a small microphone must have seemed a very artificial experience to him. From the time he became Prime Minister to the end of 1940, he made only seven speeches on the radio, and some of these were quite short. Many of his most famous speeches were made only in the House of Commons. They are familiar to so many people today because he recorded them on to gramophone discs for Decca Records after the war.[4]

It is interesting to speculate whether Churchill would ever have become a persuasive television performer. Although he lived on well into the TV era, he did not use the medium much. Some rushes of different takes have survived of him delivering a party political broadcast in 1950. He is not impressive although he seems more comfortable than he did on the radio – possibly because with a film crew present at least he had an audience of sorts.

Churchill had framed the fight to come in epic terms. And it proved to be one of the decisive battles of the Second World War. There was little Churchill could do to lead the Battle of Britain itself. That really had to be left to the RAF. The government's role was to ensure that, after years of neglect, the RAF now at this eleventh hour had enough fighting aircraft and had the correct command and control systems in place to take on the Luftwaffe. But Churchill himself had two additional tasks during the Battle of Britain. First, he had to secure and stir the determination of the British people to fight on. If the sort of defeatism that had spread among the upper classes in May 1940 before the rescue from Dunkirk had gained a widespread hold upon the nation, the political will to continue the battle might be undermined. That is why his speeches over the next few months would be so vital to the war effort. Second, he had to maximise the backing Britain received from its allies. More than anything else, this meant ensuring the support of the United States.

Churchill always favoured face-to-face discussions with friends or opponents. His five visits to France during the battle there were vital for his understanding of the French position and his reading of the differing views of the French leadership. It is no surprise then that he dedicated a large proportion of his time during the Second World War to fostering and building a direct and personal relationship with the US President, Franklin D. Roosevelt. The two men had met briefly at a dinner towards the end of the First World War, when Churchill had been Minister of Munitions and Roosevelt was Assistant Secretary of the Navy. At the time, Roosevelt was unimpressed and described Churchill as a 'stinker . . . lording it all over us'.[5] To his embarrassment, Churchill later forgot this early meeting. However, he sent Roosevelt signed copies of his Duke of Marlborough books, and Roosevelt's son visited him at Chartwell in 1933. When Churchill became First Lord of the Admiralty in September 1939, Roosevelt opened what would become a remarkable, historic correspondence. Roosevelt wrote to congratulate Churchill, saying: 'I shall at all times welcome it if you will keep me in touch personally with anything you want me to know about.'[6] This direct approach from the US President to a single government minister was highly unusual, to say the least. Roosevelt thought Churchill would soon become Britain's wartime leader and he wanted to get his hand in early.[7] Churchill asked the Prime Minister for permission to begin his own correspondence via telegram with the President. Chamberlain, who was keen to use any route to transmit the government's views to the White House, agreed. So Churchill began a long correspondence with Roosevelt characterised by his jokey signature on every telegram: initially 'Naval Person' and from the time he became Prime

Minister 'Former Naval Person', signifying the bond between them from the days when they were responsible for their navies.

Throughout the winter and early spring of 1939–40, Churchill telegrammed Roosevelt every few weeks to keep him up to date with British government thinking. Every message had Chamberlain's approval. In February, Roosevelt replied to one of Churchill's telegrams with the words: 'I wish much that I could talk things over with you in person – but I am grateful to you for keeping me in touch, as you do.'[8] He obviously appreciated this line of communication from a man he respected at the centre of the British government. And Churchill was well aware of their value, too. The US Ambassador in London at the time was Joseph Kennedy, the father of John, Robert and Edward. From a staunchly Irish-American clan, Kennedy was an Anglophobe who despised the British Empire and thought that British society was hopelessly antiquated. During the critical moments in 1940, he was convinced that Britain would not pull through, that its military would be defeated, and that Churchill, whom Kennedy thought epitomised everything that was old-fashioned and bad about Britain, would seek out a peace deal with Hitler. So Churchill's direct line to Roosevelt was a way to get a very different message directly to the heart of Washington.

When Churchill became Prime Minister in May, the tone of the correspondence changed. It became more personal and over time more friendly. But Churchill still wanted to get tough messages through to the White House. He wanted Roosevelt to realise the dire consequences of the current European events for US interests. On 15 May, Churchill sent his first message to Roosevelt as Prime Minister in continuation of what he described as 'our intimate, private correspondence'. He did not mince his words, telling the President:

If necessary, we shall continue the war alone, and we are not afraid of that. [This was in fact the first time the thought of continuing the war if France were defeated was raised.] But I trust you realise, Mr President, that the voice and force of the United States may count for nothing if they are withheld too long. You may have a completely subjugated Nazified Europe established with astonishing swiftness, and the weight may be more than we can bear.

The telegram went on to ask for the loan of forty or fifty destroyers, several hundred aircraft, anti-aircraft guns and ammunition, and a supply of steel.[9]

The American response was swift. Hundreds of aircraft, half a million rifles, and nearly one thousand 75mm guns were shipped up and sent across the Atlantic in less than a month.[10] The loan of destroyers was a more complex issue, and Roosevelt thought this would need approval from Congress, which he was unlikely to get. Churchill insisted in his next message: 'if American assistance is to play any part it must be available soon'.[11] Throughout the summer of 1940, Roosevelt did what he could to support the fragile British position. But he was constrained by several factors. As a neutral, under US law, he could go only so far in supplying arms to a belligerent nation without requesting the agreement of Congress. Here various US domestic factions came into play to balance out the widespread support felt for Britain. The German-American, Italian-American and even Irish-American groups were all opposed to offering aid to Britain. And Roosevelt faced a presidential election that autumn. To boost his chances he made several declarations guaranteeing that the United States would not get involved in the war raging in Europe. Churchill kept up the pressure on Roosevelt and spoke of 'the Common Cause' shared by the two English-speaking nations. He kept going back to request the urgent loan of destroyers, which he wanted to bolster Britain's defences against the submarine menace and against a possible invasion by sea. His messages included phrases like 'The need is extreme' and 'in the long history of the world this is a thing to do *now*'.[12] He was infuriated by the inability of many senior US officials to see the importance of this. Eventually, in August, Churchill's pleading paid off and a deal was struck whereby the United States agreed to loan Britain fifty antiquated destroyers in return for a lease on eight British naval bases in the Caribbean and the Atlantic. The Americans also insisted that if Britain were defeated, it would not surrender its fleet to the Germans but would send it abroad to defend other parts of the Empire. This deal, which later formed the basis of the Lend-Lease Agreement, clearly marked a move by the US towards an alliance with Britain, and it was a sign that the US would provide extensive military aid – almost everything short of joining the war.

The critical point is that through this correspondence, a direct line between Downing Street and the Oval Office, Churchill knew that he had the sympathy of the President and military support from America as far as it could go within the terms of US law. This 'special relationship' would grow and blossom as the war developed. There would be nearly two thousand telegrams, several hundred phone calls, and many person-to-person meetings and summits. But in the summer of 1940, that lay in the future. For now, Churchill's confidence, thanks to his secret correspondence, that he enjoyed Roosevelt's support gave him the courage and resolution to carry on the fight against Hitler.

One of the things that most agitated Churchill after France's defeat was the position of the powerful French fleet. As we have seen, Churchill had obtained a promise from Admiral Darlan the French naval commander that he would not hand the fleet over to the Germans. But Hitler had insisted on the surrender of the fleet in the terms of the armistice, and Pétain and Darlan, now Minister for the Marine in the new Vichy government, were determined to keep to the terms they had signed with the Nazis. The French Navy was scattered, and some of it was already in British hands. But a substantial battle fleet was now in Algeria, at the port of Mers el-Kebir. If this were used against Britain, it might turn the naval war almost overnight. The British Chiefs of Staff reviewed their options and offered the local French naval commander various choices: he could hand his warships over to the Royal Navy; sail to the West Indies and remove them from the war; or scuttle them. From Vichy, Darlan ordered his fleet commanders not to breech the terms of the armistice and to have no truck with the British demands. After several days of mounting crisis, an order was sent from London to Admiral Sir James Somerville, in command of Force H off Mers el-Kebir.

At 5.54 p.m. on 3 July, the heavy guns of the British battleships of Force H opened fire on the French warships in their Algerian harbour. The bombardment lasted for only about ten minutes. In that time the Royal Navy sank two French battleships and ran aground one of the newest French battle-cruisers. Elsewhere, British naval aircraft attacked French battleships, putting them out of action. In total, twelve hundred French sailors were killed. Churchill called it 'a hateful decision' to open fire on men who had been allies only weeks before, 'the most unnatural and painful in which I have ever been concerned'.[13] But no one in the War Cabinet or among the Chiefs of Staff had hesitated when it came to sending the order to open fire. The French fleet simply had to be put out of action to prevent the Nazis from using it against Britain. Around the world, and especially in Washington, governments saw the decision to destroy the fleet as a sign of the ruthlessness of the British war leadership to fight on with vigour and determination. It was a painful episode, but Churchill was convinced that it improved Britain's standing at a time of deep national crisis.

On the same day, the Soviet Ambassador to London, Ivan Maisky, paid Churchill a visit at Downing Street. Maisky describes Churchill as being 'full of life and energy . . . cheerful and fresh'. He asked the Prime Minister what was his general strategy, now that France had fallen. Churchill drew on his cigar and replied with a smile: 'My general strategy at present is to last out the next three months.'[14] Churchill knew that a German invasion could be attempted only during the summer months. Once autumn and winter set in, the opportunity would have passed. It was a modest target, to survive the next three months, but it was a realistic one. And it would not be easy.

Hitler's success in Northern Europe had not only astonished his enemies. It had surprised even his own generals. They were now left looking across the twenty-one miles of sea that separated northern France from the cliffs of Dover, wondering what to do next. There was no military plan in place for an invasion of Britain. But on 16 July, Hitler issued Führer Directive No. 16. In this he said: 'As England, in spite of her hopeless military situation, still shows no sign of willingness to come to terms, I have decided to prepare and if necessary to carry out, a landing operation against her.' He ordered his Armed Forces Supreme Headquarters to prepare an invasion plan. General Franz Halder, Chief of Staff, was put in charge. He saw Operation Sealion, as the projected invasion was called, as little more than a major river crossing on a broad front. Grand Admiral Erich Raeder had a different view. After the Norway campaign, he knew he could not match the firepower of the Royal Navy. He feared British warships would wreak havoc if they got in among his invasion fleet. Precious weeks were lost while the German High Command debated their options.

It was Hermann Goering – First World War fighter ace, Reichsmarschall, and probably the second most famous figure in the Nazi Party – who persuaded Hitler which course to follow. He said simply leave it to the Luftwaffe. His planes had already started a war of attrition against the RAF. He predicted that in four weeks he could force the British to surrender. Goering's argument helped to resolve the concerns of the German Navy. By destroying the RAF and winning air supremacy for Germany, the Luftwaffe would bring Britain to its knees. Maybe then an invasion would not even be necessary.

So, despite planning for an invasion, Hitler was confident he could force the British government to negotiate a peace deal. On 19 July, in a speech in Berlin, Hitler offered the British people a choice between peace with Germany or 'unending suffering and misery'. The mood in Britain was now far more defiant than it had been just two months before. The War Cabinet did not even discuss the matter. When Churchill was asked if he wanted to make a response, he wrote: 'I do not propose to say anything in reply to Herr Hitler's speech, not being on speaking terms with him.'[15]

The later myth created around the Battle of Britain was that the nation stood alone, hugely outnumbered by a superior and mighty foe. This ignores the fact that Britain was then at the head of a vast empire. Much of the world map was still coloured red. And pilots from around the Empire, especially from Canada, South Africa and New Zealand, rallied to the cause and fought bravely throughout the summer of 1940. In numerical terms, the RAF was outnumbered by roughly two-to-one: the Germans could call on about 1400 bombers, 300 dive-bombers, 800 single-engined Messerschmitt Me-109 fighters and about 240 twin-engined Messerschmitt Me-110 fighters, whereas RAF Fighter Command had only about 500 serviceable Hurricanes and Spitfires. But Lord Beaverbrook, as Minister of

Aircraft Production, was already making real increases in output by introducing round-the-clock shifts. And the factories in the Midlands and the South were soon producing about four hundred aircraft every month, enough not only to replace the losses but to grow the overall number of planes available. The problem would be the supply of trained pilots.

RAF Fighter Command had one vital advantage in the summer of 1940. Since Churchill had joined the secret Air Defence Research Committee in 1935, research into Radio Detection-Finding (later known by the American term 'radar') had developed considerably. During 1938 and 1939, British scientists based at Bawdsey on the Suffolk coast had designed and constructed a line of radar stations along the southern and eastern coasts of Britain called the 'Chain Home system'. This was an early warning system that enabled the RAF to spot and plot the course of German bombers and their fighter escorts as they crossed the Channel. Each radar station consisted of a set of giant towers that sent radio pulses out over the sea. At the base of the towers was a receiver hut where skilled operators, often members of the Women's Auxiliary Air Force (WAAF), would stare at cathode-ray tubes for hours on end. They measured the time it took for the radio waves to bounce back from approaching aircraft. By assessing the line of the approaching aircraft from two or more radar stations it was possible to predict with some accuracy the route of the raiders.

In the dogfights that followed, height proved a critical factor. If the RAF fighters could be at a higher altitude than the Luftwaffe bombers when they arrived over their targets, they would have the dual advantages of speed and surprise as they swept down from above, and so were more likely to inflict serious damage on the German aircraft. It took a fighter plane between thirteen and fifteen minutes from the order to scramble to get to its optimum height. But a German bomber could cross the English Channel in about five minutes. The key advantage provided by radar was that it gave the RAF the extra minutes it needed to get its fighters into the air and above the German bombers with accurate information as to where they were heading.

But radar was not the only vital ingredient in the RAF early warning system. The technology was still very basic. It worked well over the sea but not over the contours of land. So a second line of defence was formed by building a network of more than a thousand observation posts. From these, observers armed with little more than binoculars and aircraft recognition books identified and reported movements of enemy aircraft and telephoned the information to control rooms. At the peak of the Battle of Britain, more than fifty thousand members of the Observer Corps were in action reporting vital details of German aircraft movements.

The information provided by radar stations and the Observer Corps around the country was only as good as the intelligence interpreted from it. Air Marshal Sir Hugh Dowding had been Chief of RAF Fighter Command since July 1936. His encouragement of the development of radar and his conviction that all-metal, single-wing aircraft were the way of the future helped to shape RAF fighter defences by the time of war. But, with the input from some prominent scientists, Dowding also created a command and control system in the late 1930s that was able to analyse, interpret and focus the information from radar in a brilliantly effective way. The thousands of separate reports that came in from the radar stations and ground observers were fed to the Operations Room at RAF Fighter Command headquarters at Bentley Priory, near Stanmore in north London. Here the information was processed in filter rooms and then plotted on to a huge table map of southern and eastern England.

Highly trained young men and women wearing headsets would then move coloured markers around the table to represent enemy raiders and RAF interceptors.

From Bentley Priory, detailed information about enemy air raids was passed on to the four fighter Groups that each controlled a sector of the UK's fighter defence. Each Group had its own operational command centre mirroring the one at Bentley Priory. The Group Operation Rooms held lists of fighter squadrons and their states of readiness, from two minutes to twenty minutes, and a list of units currently in the air and in action. The decision to scramble the fighters would come from Group headquarters, as would requests for reserves during heavy raids. The fighters most often in the front line were those of 11 Group, led by a tough and determined New Zealander, Air Vice-Marshal Keith Park. His Group covered the whole of south-eastern England from its headquarters at Uxbridge in west London. This was the centre of the complex mass of communication links utilising hundreds of miles of telephone cables. The structure created under Dowding's supervision thankfully worked well during the Battle of Britain. The fate of the nation would hang on the split-second decisions made in these RAF command centres.

When all the information had been processed and the commands had been issued, it was, of course, down to the pilots and their aircraft to fight it out. RAF Fighter Command could pit two brilliant single-engined fighter aircraft against the Luftwaffe. Much has been written (and exaggerated) about the superiority of the Hawker Hurricane and the legendary Supermarine Spitfire over their German rivals. The Messerschmitt Me-109 was fast and agile, but its wings were weak and the pilots feared they would be pulled off in a fast dive or turn. This, naturally, slowed them down in combat from the maximum capable performance. The Hurricane and Spitfire were without doubt significantly more advanced than any previous British fighters. The Hurricane was a conventionally built aircraft, made of canvas stretched across a wooden frame. Its maximum speed was 330 m.p.h. – well below that of its German rival. But one of the advantages of the Hurricane was that it was easy to build and so could be produced in massive numbers. The Spitfire, by contrast, was made of stretched metal panels on an all-metal frame, which meant it was a much more complex machine to produce. Designed by R.J. Mitchell, its bird-like elliptical wings made it one of the great classics of aeronautics. The models used in the Battle of Britain could fly at 360 m.p.h., about the same speed as the Messerschmitt Me-109s, but the Spitfires were highly manoeuvrable, especially at altitude, and their pilots had better all-round vision out of the clear cockpit. Tens of thousands of words have been written arguing that the Spitfire was superior to the Hurricane, or vice versa. The truth is that the RAF needed both aircraft to fight the Battle of Britain. Often the Hurricanes would be directed at the slower-moving bombers and the Spitfires would be sent to attack the fast fighter escorts. So without the large numbers of the Hurricanes and the superb quality of the Spitfires, the outcome of the Battle of Britain would definitely have been very different.[16]

The RAF pilots were good, but they lacked the combat experience of their Luftwaffe rivals. And the German fighters were organised around the *Schwarm* – or finger-four – formation, which could easily break down into two leading planes each supported by a wingman. This gave the Luftwaffe tremendous flexibility in combat. Although the need for flexibility had been a lesson learned by both sides in First World War aerial combat, in Britain it had been lost somewhere in the inter-war years. Most RAF commanders still insisted on rigidly following the *Fighter Area Attack Manual*, which called for squadrons to fly in four flights of three aircraft each, in a tight V formation. Many pilots spent much of their time ensuring that they were flying in correct formation, rather than scanning the skies searching out enemy aircraft. Furthermore, RAF tactics were based upon the assumption that British fighters would be attacking bombers flying alone from bases in Germany. As soon as France and Belgium fell, the Luftwaffe transported its fighters to airbases only a few miles from the Channel coast, so they could escort the bombers over England. The RAF proved slow to adapt to the changed conditions of the actual combat they now faced. 'We did everything wrong that we could possibly do wrong,' said one fighter ace many years later. Rigidly adhering to outdated flying regulations cost the lives of many RAF pilots in the battle that summer.[17]

So, the RAF had some important advantages in intelligence, in command structure and in technology over the Luftwaffe. And most of the Luftwaffe effort in the war so far had been in ground support, attacking tactical targets set by the advancing army. This had proved fantastically effective in the invasions of Poland and France. But the Luftwaffe had not engaged in a bombing offensive before, let alone an offensive hundreds of miles from its bases across a sea. Nor did it have any four-engined bombers like those that would serve RAF Bomber Command so well later in the war. The Heinkel and Dornier bombers were good aircraft, but their bomb loads were small in comparison with the later British bombers. But the scene was now set for an intense aerial battle in which each side enjoyed some advantages over its enemy but suffered from disadvantages too.

The Battle of Britain was, by its nature, a defensive operation. But even at this stage of the war Churchill's restless mind constantly sought out opportunities for offensive action. Italy had declared war on 10 June, and with France now defeated,

Mussolini threatened British authority in the Mediterranean and Egypt. A huge Italian army of a quarter of a million men was assembling in Libya, near the Egyptian border. The commanding officer of British and imperial forces in the Middle East was General Archibald Wavell. He was in command of only some fifty thousand men in Egypt. So Churchill and the War Cabinet agreed during July to reinforce the Middle East garrison by sending shipments of light tanks to Egypt with a view to mounting a pre-emptive strike against the Italians. It was a brave move at a time when Britain itself was facing the threat of invasion. But it was typical of Churchill's belief in the need to seek out offensive measures. But the Italians were not yet ready to go on the attack in North Africa. Wavell was recalled to London for a series of meetings with Churchill. Wavell was an unusual senior officer, something of a poet and an academic, but socially timid, and he became tongue-tied in front of Churchill. Even worse, he did not stand up to the Prime Minister, who constantly requested information and wanted to debate every aspect of a military campaign. Churchill thought the worse of him for this, and their meetings were disastrous. He even considered replacing Wavell. But the situation at home was too serious and it was several months before the war in North Africa could get under way. It had to take a lower priority.

On 10 July, the first phase of the Battle of Britain began. The Luftwaffe's dive-bombers launched attacks on shipping in the Channel. They were led by the Junkers Ju-87, the Stuka. The siren that wailed as the plane went into its dive, which had caused such terror among troops and civilians across Poland and France, was now intended to have the same effect on Britain's mariners. But the attacks were fiercely defended by the young pilots of the RAF, whose fighters were faster and easily outperformed the dive-bombers. The Stukas began to suffer serious losses. On the first day of this phase of the battle, over twenty German aircraft were damaged with the loss of twenty-three aircrew. The Stukas soon began to be known by their German crews as 'flying coffins'.

Poor weather over the Channel caused something of a respite. But on 25 July visibility improved and the Luftwaffe mounted a further series of attacks on British shipping. These were intended to draw out more fighters, but Dowding was reluctant to respond as he wanted to maintain his strength for what he rightly saw as the tougher tests to come. Inspired by their war leader, the British people gritted their teeth in anticipation of the struggle ahead.

Meanwhile, in the Channel ports of France and Belgium, the Germans were busy assembling Rhine barges and other flat-bottom boats that could be used to land men and machines on the English coast. During July, RAF aerial reconnaissance flights brought back alarming evidence that huge numbers, up to about two thousand, of these barges were being assembled. At one point the photo-interpretation officer who was counting the barges threw down his equipment and said: 'We don't want these. They'd better give us rifles.'[18] They looked threatening at the time. But four years later the Allies would find that their landings in northern France were largely dictated by the availability of the right sort of specially built landing craft. The Germans were already learning how important landing craft were and so rapidly improvised whatever suitable vessels could be found for Operation Sealion.

There's no doubt that at this point the threat of invasion was putting Churchill under great strain. The line between cajoling and pushing his military chiefs, on the one hand, and bullying and threatening them, on the other, was always a fine one. At his best, Churchill knew how far he could push people without alienating them. But under pressure he could go too far. Such was the case at Chequers, the Prime Minister's weekend residence in Buckinghamshire, on 26 July, when Churchill's frustration with his military chiefs spilt over into direct rudeness. At dinner he questioned General Sir James Marshall-Cornwall about the readiness of his divisions that were stationed on the Welsh Marches. When he discovered that some of the information he had been given in a paper by the CIGS Sir John Dill was less than adequate, Churchill flew into a rage and threw the report at Dill, demanding that it be checked and returned to him the following day. After an awkward silence, Churchill turned to 'the Prof', Frederick Lindemann, who was a regular at the Chequers dinner table, and asked him what news he had to tell him. To the amazement of everyone at the table, Lindemann produced a Mills hand-grenade and proceeded to explain why it was an inefficient weapon. The Prof announced that he had designed a far more efficient alternative. Churchill was delighted, and with almost boyish glee he told Dill to scrap the Mills grenade immediately and introduce the Lindemann grenade. Dill, no doubt spluttering through his soup, announced that contracts had already been placed for millions of the Mills bombs in both Britain and America, and it was impossible to cancel them. Churchill must have known this was true, but he continued to berate Dill. The Prime Minister ended the evening after a further interrogation of the generals by muttering peevishly, 'You soldiers are all alike; you have no imagination.' The tirade seemed designed to humiliate the military men in front of Churchill's civilian cohorts. The military chiefs probably forgave him, understanding the pressure he was under, but this was certainly the war leader at his most infantile, on his worst behaviour and displaying an ill-judged outburst to men who were themselves under great strain. General Marshall-Cornwall later described the evening as 'The Mad Hatter's Dinner Party'.[19]

At the end of July, Hitler held a military conference at his retreat in the mountains above Berchtesgaden to review plans for the invasion of Britain. Admiral Raeder once again called for a postponement to May 1941. Hitler was not happy but agreed to push back Operation Sealion to mid-September. Everything hinged on Goering and the success of the Luftwaffe. So, in early August, Goering decided to change his tactics. The thirteenth of August was set for *Adlertag*, 'Eagle Day'. This marked the beginning of the next phase of the Battle of Britain. Now the focus would shift from attacking Channel shipping to an attempt to destroy the RAF either in the air or by bombing its air-fields. This was a gamble by Goering, but he was confident that he would destroy the RAF and leave the British begging to surrender.

In the twenty-four hours before Eagle Day, the Luftwaffe attacked several of the radar towers along the British coast. The towers stood some 360 feet tall and were easy targets to iden-tify. Two radar installations in Kent were attacked but survived. The station at Pevensey was hit hard and several operators were killed or wounded. At Rye in East Sussex and at Ventnor on the Isle of Wight there was severe damage. The Luftwaffe had identified the 'eyes' of the RAF defence system. But in a remarkable blunder by the Germans, the radar towers were not consistently targeted again. Within days, they were all back in full working order.

On Eagle Day itself, Goering sent a command to each unit: 'Within a short period you will wipe the British Air Force from the sky. Heil Hitler.' But the day began badly for the Luftwaffe. With thick cloud cover, Goering gave the order to recall the first assault wave. The fighters got the message and returned, but the bombers did not and carried on unescorted – to a mauling over southern England. Later in the day, however, as the skies cleared, a force of some three hundred planes headed off to

strike at the RAF airfields. By the end of the day, the Luftwaffe had lost 45 planes in action. The RAF had lost 13 fighters in the air and 47 aircraft on the ground – but only one of those was a fighter.

A major failing in the Luftwaffe was its inability to assess the damage it was causing the RAF accurately. Intelligence officers too willingly believed the daredevil claims of their pilots and repeatedly overestimated the number of 'kills'; consequently, they underestimated the number of planes the RAF could call upon. On the eve of Eagle Day, Luftwaffe intelligence officers estimated the RAF had 450 fighters left. In fact, the number was well above 600. And the Luftwaffe totally miscalculated the rate at which British factories were pouring out replacement aircraft. By late August, the Germans calculated that their enemy had barely 300 operational aircraft. In fact, the RAF had about 700 available fighters. Although Goering might have been delighted to hear the figures given by his intelligence officers, the pilots who flew daily over Britain grew to mistrust them, and this was appalling for morale.

As the battle continued to rage, with regular raids at dawn and dusk, Dowding's principal problem was not the numbers of aircraft but the loss of skilled pilots. A week after Eagle Day, four out of five squadron commanders in Fighter Command had been killed or wounded, or were resting after continuous combat. During August, Dowding reluctantly had to reduce the operational training period to two weeks. Before the war, it had been six months. So, at the height of the Battle of Britain, novice pilots with only a few flying hours under their belts were being thrown into the thick of the action.

The Hurricane and Spitfire pilots and their ground crews were on constant stand-by from half an hour before dawn, about 4.30 a.m., until around 9.00 p.m. The one feature nearly all of the pilots who survived the summer remembered was a feeling of

constant tiredness. No doubt the continuous strain of waiting for the order to scramble added further to this. Most pilots lounged around all day, playing cards or chess. Some were able to read a little, others would doze, others listened to gramophone records. When the order to scramble came they would race to their aircraft. Often the ground crew had already started the engine. Quickly kitted up with parachute, Mae West life-jacket, headgear and linked into the radio and oxygen supplies, the pilot would then throw the throttle forward and the aircraft rolled across the grass and into the air. Every second counted. On really intense days pilots would fly three, four or even five separate sorties. Between each one the hard-working ground crew had to service and refuel the aircraft, make any instant repairs and rearm the four guns in each wing, leaving the plane totally ready for the next scramble at a moment's notice.

All the dogfights took place in full view of the civilian population below. Factory workers, farmers, mothers at home and children at school would all strain their necks and look up at the vapour trails criss-crossing the blue skies above. When planes came crashing to the ground they were quickly surrounded by the Home Guard and any enemy pilots who survived were marched off to the local police or the military, and into captivity. Sometimes even RAF pilots were pursued by over-keen crowds. Squadron Leader James Nicolson was the only fighter pilot to win a VC in the Battle of Britain. But when he crash-landed his plane, badly burned on his hands and face, he was fired on by a trigger-happy member of the Home Guard. And, of course, for young boys nothing could beat the cachet of finding and keeping a piece of a downed aircraft. To many on the ground below, the British fighter pilots became instant heroes as they fought gladiatorial battles against heavy odds.

Throughout August, Churchill busied himself with preparations for the expected invasion. He inspected defensive positions along the beaches where it might take place; he issued instructions about the roles of the Home Guard, the police and the fire brigade; and he approved plans for the defence of central London in the event of a German assault by parachute commandos. And every day he received reports on the numbers of German planes shot down, of British aircraft and pilots lost, and of the big increase in output from Britain's aircraft factories. He visited 11 Group's Operations Room in Uxbridge on several occasions. On 16 August, he was particularly moved watching all the markers being moved forward on the big table map as each new wave of German aircraft approached England and the markers of each of the RAF fighter squadrons as they were scrambled to intercept them. When he left in his official car, he turned to General Ismay and said: 'Don't speak to me; I have never been so moved.' After about five minutes of silence, he turned again to Ismay and uttered the words, 'Never in the field of human conflict has so much been owed by so many to so few.' Ismay was touched by the phrase that would soon reach a far wider audience.[20]

In the second half of August, the air battles grew more and more desperate. On Sunday the 18th, which has since been called the 'hardest' day, wave after wave of German bombers came over to attack the RAF airfields along with the aircraft factories. A vast force of 108 bombers escorted by several hundred fighters went for the fighter base at Kenley. Squadrons from across 11 Group were scrambled, and as further waves of bombers approached reserves from 12 Group in East Anglia, led by Air Vice-Marshal Trafford Leigh-Mallory, were called in to help. At the end of the day, the tally recorded 69 Luftwaffe losses with another 31 aircraft badly damaged. The RAF had lost 63 fighters with another 62 damaged. However, each side claimed it had inflicted much more severe losses on its adversary. On the Luftwaffe side, these inflated figures were believed and the crews were told they were winning the battle. In Britain, the simple fact was that the RAF knew it could not go on losing this many planes. At this rate, the RAF would cease to exist in a few weeks.

On 20 August Churchill addressed the House of Commons, speaking for nearly an hour. He said that this war had not seen the 'prodigious slaughter' of the First World War, but was instead 'a conflict of strategy, of organisation, of technical apparatus, of science, mechanics and morale . . . [and] our science is definitely ahead of theirs'. Then he spoke of the RAF pilots who had become the heroes of the hour, 'whose brilliant actions we see with our own eyes day after day'. He said that everyone's 'gratitude . . . goes out to the British airmen who, undaunted by odds, unwearied in their constant challenge and mortal danger, are turning the tide of war by their prowess and by their devotion'. Even though the Battle of Britain was by no means won by this point, Churchill reworked the words he had said in the car to Ismay just a few days before, proclaiming: 'Never in the history of human conflict was so much owed by so many to so few.' Churchill ended by announcing that he had at last won US approval for the loan of the fifty destroyers in the 'destroyers for bases' deal. He said this would bring together the 'two great organisations of the English-speaking democracies, the British Empire and the United States' which he did not view 'with any misgivings'. He concluded by saying: 'I could not stop it if I wished; no one can stop it. Like the Mississippi, it just keeps rolling along. Let it roll. Let it roll on full flood, inexorable, irresistible, benignant, to broader lands and better days.' As he sat down the House rose to its feet, with members cheering. Then Churchill returned to Downing Street and his private secretary recorded that he sang 'Ol' Man River', out of tune, all the way back in the car.[21]

Churchill was carrying out one of his great tasks as war leader. He was rallying the nation and stirring the soul of almost everyone who heard or read the speech. And internationally, he was beginning to persuade people that Britain was not down and out, was not staring at defeat as France had done in the face of Nazi aggression, but had the determination to fight on. Also, he had provided a nickname that would stick to the RAF pilots on whom the nation's survival depended: 'the Few'. One friend wrote that his words would 'live as long as words are spoken and remembered'.[22] Over time, the reference to the Few became the enduring memory not only of Churchill's speech but of the months that became known as 'Spitfire Summer'. But that summer was by no means over yet.

On 26 August, there were three major assaults. The strains within Fighter Command were beginning to show, and at one point during the day 12 Group did not come to 11 Group's aid when all its squadrons had been scrambled. As a consequence, the airfield at Debden was left unprotected and suffered a heavy bombing raid. Leigh-Mallory, the commander of 12 Group, was beginning to take a different view from Park as to the best strategy for defending Britain. He came to believe that his fighters were most effective when they formed mass formations of three or more squadrons. On the other hand, Park thought it best to attack at squadron level, keeping other squadrons back in order to respond to later assaults and to prevent all his forces being drawn into action too early. The argument became known as the 'Big Wing' controversy and it began to split the unified ethos of Fighter Command.

In early September, the Battle of Britain entered its crucial phase. The Luftwaffe was now focusing its attacks on the RAF airfields in the south-east of England in a bid to break the fighter defence of London. On 3 September, the Luftwaffe and the RAF each lost sixteen aircraft. Two days later, the RAF lost twenty-two and the Luftwaffe twenty-one. True, if a British pilot baled out and survived, he could be patched up and back in action within days – in some famous cases pilots were back flying within hours of being shot down. Whereas Luftwaffe crews who survived being shot down were usually captured, taken prisoner and represented a total loss to the German war effort. But in a two-week period the RAF lost 103 pilots killed and 128 badly wounded, with 466 Spitfires and Hurricanes lost or seriously damaged. To replace them were 260 eager but inexperienced pilots straight out of training. The RAF simply could not go on enduring this level of losses. It looked as though the Germans might soon win the Battle of Britain.

Hitler had ordered the Luftwaffe not to bomb British civilian centres, but on 24 August a small number of Heinkel He-111s became separated from their squadron and dropped their bombs, in error, on the suburbs of London. Nine civilians were killed. Churchill ordered Bomber Command to retaliate, and over the next few nights about eighty Wellingtons bombed Berlin. They caused only a tiny amount of physical damage but Berliners were outraged. Goering had said that no enemy bombers would ever fly over the capital of the Reich. Hitler was furious and lifted his ban on bombing British cities. To a small gathering in Berlin, he announced that Britain's cities would be 'razed to the ground'. The crowd roared with hysterical approval.

Goering called a conference of his Luftwaffe commanders in The Hague. They were still puzzled as to how the RAF was managing to put up so many fighter aircraft. According to their intelligence estimates, Fighter Command had hardly any fighters left. But almost every time they arrived over a target the German crews found dogged British pilots waiting for them. The German pilots mocked their intelligence officers by reporting back that 'the last fifty Spitfires' had again been waiting to intercept them. Although the Luftwaffe could endure more losses than the RAF, the battle did not seem to be going well from their perspective. Goering demanded another change in tactics – the second in less than a month. With Hitler calling for reprisals against British cities, Goering now committed the blunder that ultimately lost the Battle of Britain for Germany.

At about 3.30 p.m. on Saturday 7 September, British radar picked up the biggest force yet of German raiders about to cross the Kent coast at Deal. This vast mass of bombers and fighters filled an airspace of about eight hundred square miles. At Bentley Priory, the plotting officers looked glum as further reports came in from observers across the South-East. Park scrambled several squadrons. But what happened next amazed everyone. The raiders flew on, over the airfields they had been bombing for days. They flew on across the green fields of Kent, and over the suburbs of south-east London. They flew on towards Goering's new target – the docks and factories of east London. Once the first wave had dropped incendiaries and created a huge inferno on the ground, the later waves came in one after another to bomb and destroy the network of warehouses and docklands below. The London docks were the heart of a vast trading empire. Enormous supplies of timber, paint, rubber, flour and dozens of other commodities were set ablaze. Firefighters struggled with fires that lit up the night sky. The bombers continued to arrive until the early hours of the following morning, and the 'all clear' was not sounded until 4.30 a.m.

Hundreds of acres of buildings burned to the ground. And in the densely packed streets of the East End, where most of the dockers lived, 448 civilians were killed and more than 1500 were injured. However, critically, the Luftwaffe had decided to give up attacking the RAF airfields as this didn't seem to be bringing victory. It was now going for civilian and industrial targets to try to break the morale of the people. This was the life-saver the RAF needed. Fighter Command simply could not have survived many more days of constant bombing of its airfields. Now it was the turn of the people of London.

During the course of this same Saturday, intelligence reports came in suggesting that the Germans were about to launch the invasion. Decrypted messages along with aerial photography seemed to show that barges in the French Channel ports were being readied for use. An emergency meeting of the Chiefs of Staff was called for 5.30 p.m. It was believed that the invasion might come on the following day. As the bombs started to fall on the docks and the East End, the Chiefs of Staff ordered all defence forces in the UK to 'stand by at immediate notice'. Just after eight o'clock that evening, General Headquarters, Home Forces, on their own initiative, sent out the code word 'Cromwell'. This was the sign that invasion was imminent. Across the country, the defence forces and the Home Guard went on to alert, and waited. But it was a false alarm. Hitler was not ready to invade.

Churchill visited several towns that had suffered from German bombing. He was very moved during a visit to Dover and Ramsgate in late August by the plight of those whose houses had been destroyed or badly damaged. He immediately said he would browbeat the Chancellor of the Exchequer into offering full compensation to the victims of Hitler's bombs. This policy was agreed by the War Cabinet in early September. The day after the bombing of the East End, Churchill visited the site of the heaviest devastation so far. Fires were still raging when he and his small entourage arrived. Whole rows of jerry-built houses had been reduced to piles of rubble. Tiny paper Union Jacks had been planted on some of these heaps of rubble. Today, one could imagine the survivors would turn on an authority figure and blame him for their lack of protection. But Churchill was literally mobbed. 'Good old Winnie!' people called out. 'We thought you'd come and see us. We can take it. Give it 'em back.' Churchill, who was always an emotional man, broke down in the face of this defiant response. General Ismay had the utmost difficulty escorting him through the crowd, and he heard one old woman say: 'You see, he really cares; he's crying.' Churchill remained in the Docklands until it began to get dark, refusing to leave despite pleas for him to get away. Then the air-raid sirens went off and the Luftwaffe's bombers returned. Churchill's car got caught in a street hemmed in by bomb damage, and a stick of incendiaries landed only a short distance away. When the party finally returned to Downing Street, Ismay was told off for taking such risks with the Prime Minister's life. He responded angrily by saying that anyone who thought they could control Churchill on jaunts like this was welcome to try on the next occasion.[23]

That Sunday night, 412 more civilians were killed in the bombing raids; and 370 on the following Monday. The Blitz on London had begun in earnest. On 11 September, the RAF lost thirty-one fighters. It was clear that the Battle of Britain was reaching a climax. Four days later, the Luftwaffe attacked in two large waves. Park's crews barely had time to refuel and rearm between the raids. But Leigh-Mallory's Big Wing came in from the north and caused serious havoc among the German bombers.

The Prime Minister chose this Sunday to visit Park's 11 Group headquarters at Uxbridge once again. Churchill's wartime memoir–history makes much of the visit. He describes sitting on the top level, looking down on the plotting table below, where twenty young men and women were moving the markers representing enemy formations. It was like a 'small theatre', where he and Clementine had seats in the 'Dress Circle'. He noticed the numbers of Park's squadrons written on the blackboards as 'Standing By', 'In Action' or 'Returning Home'.

Alongside were the numbers of Leigh-Mallory's squadrons as they came in to support. As the battle unfolded, more and more German formations moved across the big table-top map and Park 'in a calm, low monotone' ordered more squadrons to scramble. Everything Churchill witnessed was at the peak of efficiency in this 'elaborate instrument of war'. But there was no doubting the intensity of the drama unfolding in front of everyone. Late in the afternoon, Churchill went over to a tense-looking Park and asked: 'What other reserves have we?' Park came back with the curt but chilling reply: 'There are none.' Churchill looked grave. He later wrote: 'The odds were great; our margins small; the stakes infinite.' Five minutes passed. Then the markers were moved slowly back across the big table. The Germans were returning home. As Churchill emerged from his underground theatre the 'all clear' was sounding. When he got back to Chequers, he was told that 183 enemy planes had been shot down for the loss of just 40 British aircraft. (The actual figures later verified for that day were 56 German losses and 27 British.) Churchill later wrote that this day was the 'culminating date' of the Battle of Britain, which was 'one of the decisive battles of the war and, like the battle of Waterloo, it was on a Sunday'. The fifteenth of September has been commemorated as Battle of Britain Day ever since.[24]

At the time, neither Churchill nor Park knew that when the Luftwaffe crews landed the German pilots reported with astonishment the news of the Big Wing attack on them from the north. Believing the RAF had almost no fighters left, they could not understand where these squadrons of Spitfires kept coming from. Dispirited, they counted their losses. Losing 56 planes and their crews was a serious blow. This rate of attrition could not go on. Two days later, realising that he had failed to win mastery of the skies, Hitler issued a secret order postponing Operation Sealion. Within weeks, he had started to plan his invasion of Russia and the next dramatic extension of the war.

Daytime raids on airfields and cities continued sporadically into October. But from now the bombing of Britain moved into a new phase known generically as the Blitz. The Luftwaffe preferred night-time raids on the cities and industrial centres. London was blitzed, with only one night's respite, for seventy-six consecutive nights. The toll of cities across Britain being heavily bombed increased weekly – Portsmouth, Bristol, Plymouth, Birmingham and Liverpool all joined the list. The worst raid came on the night of 14 November, when Coventry was bombed. 554 civilians were killed and 1200 injured. There were so many corpses that they had to be lined up in rows for burial in mass graves. During the Blitz, the Second World War became the People's War. In total, about 43,000 civilians were killed, well over 150,000 were injured, and a quarter of a million were made homeless

But Churchill was right: 15 September had been the decisive day. And the Battle of Britain had been won. Not in the conventional sense, by destroying the enemy: the RAF had lost 1173 aircraft, with 510 pilots killed, while the Luftwaffe had lost 1733 aircraft, with over 3300 airmen killed, wounded or taken prisoner. But the Luftwaffe was still a major force, and would remain so for at least three more years. But it was a victory for Britain because Hitler had set out to destroy the RAF, to win mastery of the skies over England and then, possibly, to invade. And he had failed. As the invasion barges were quietly redeployed and sent back to their Rhineland owners, the RAF still ruled the skies over Britain. The British people had not been brought to their knees. And, in the longer spectrum of the war, Britain had survived as a base from where, when the Allies were ready, the invasion of Europe and the final defeat of Hitler's Third Reich could be launched.

Much has been written about the spirit that unified first Londoners and then the whole nation in the face of Hitler's Blitz. The traditional view that 'we was all one' and that divisions were put aside for the duration has been severely challenged by historians in recent decades.[25] There is no doubt that occasionally there was panic. At times local authorities failed miserably in their attempts to manage the chaos that befell their residents, and petty-officialdom left people frustrated, angry and vulnerable. At times people flooded out of the cities in fright, even when they were told not to. At times looting of bombed houses took place before their owners had returned from the air-raid shelters. People in Britain displayed all the traits that people everywhere exhibit during bombing. Fear becomes terror, which becomes anger, which becomes exhaustion, which extends into a burning desire for revenge. But there is also no doubt that Churchill had given the nation a fillip throughout this formidable summer. His visits to the sites of bomb attacks cheered the victims in a way that is difficult to imagine in today's more cynical age.

During the war years, British people made about twenty million visits to the cinema each week. It was a hugely popular medium for entertainment and before the main movie came the newsreel, twice-weekly compilations of news stories that were part of every cinema show. The newsreels were quite unlike today's television news. Reliant upon 35mm film that had to be processed, developed and edited, they were always a few days out of date. Nevertheless, some of the newsreels of this period capture the popular attitude towards Churchill very clearly. Unlike the heavily stage-managed performances seen in the newsreels of Hitler and Mussolini, Churchill was usually shown visiting bomb sites or touring factories. He always wore a hat which he would wave at the crowds or put on the end of his walking stick to wave in the air if the crowds around him could not see him clearly. He always had his characteristic cigar as a prop. And he would regularly hold up his fingers in the V-for-victory sign. He nearly always looked defiant and even when visibly moved by what he witnessed his bulldog spirit seemed to come across. These were not scenes directed by some clever news producer. This was not spin managed by the Ministry of Information or the Cabinet Office. It was just Churchill being himself. He would have made all of these visits even if the newsreel cameras had not been there to film him. And just as his spontaneous visits to victims of air raids proved popular to those who saw him in person, so the newsreel scenes projected to a much larger national audience the same message of encouragement and inspiration.

But it is for his words that Churchill is best remembered from the summer of 1940. Words had been vital to him since the beginning of his adult life. And from him came a torrent of words either performed as hundreds of speeches or dictated as dozens of books, thousands of articles, and innumerable memos, minutes and official state papers. The historian David Cannadine describes his extraordinary career as 'one sustained, brightly lit and scarcely interrupted monologue'.[26] For much of his life he had been respected for his oratory, but people had still been suspicious of him. Churchill could always find a brilliant phrase, but was he right in what he said? In the 1920s, Chamberlain had said his 'speeches are extraordinarily brilliant and men flock to hear them . . . The best show in London, they say. But so far as I can judge, they think of it as a show, and are not prepared at present to trust his character, still less his judgement.'[27] But during the summer of 1940 Churchill was perfectly attuned to the public mood. His black-and-white way of seeing things enabled him to present the struggle as a noble one between victory and defeat, freedom and tyranny, civilisation and barbarism. The vast majority of adult Britons listened to his broadcasts in 1940, nearly three out of four of the population.[28] Many people seem to have felt that Churchill was expressing their own feelings but in a way they could not. His speeches became weapons in the war against Hitler. When very little stood between the British people and the Luftwaffe, invasion and the great likelihood of defeat, Churchill's defiance and his sense of history gave Britons a feeling of pride that they were living through hours that were as vital as when the Spanish Armada had sailed or when Napoleon had threatened. His speeches hardened their resolve that Britain could take it – and hit back again. Humbly, Churchill later said that it fell to him to express the will of the nation but it was the people who had 'the lion heart. I had the luck to be called upon to give the roar.'[29] But this is to play down his role. A New Zealand editor wrote to the BBC, saying, 'A speech made by Mr Churchill is as good as a new battleship.'[30] The great American journalist Ed Murrow, who reported from London at the time, summed it up best when he observed that Churchill 'mobilized the English language and sent it into battle'.[31]

By September 1940, Churchill had become the unchallenged leader of the people of Britain. A Gallup Poll reported an extraordinarily high 88 per cent approval rating.[32] Doubts and scepticism about whether he was the right man for the job had been forgotten. All the fears of Conservatives that he could not be trusted, that he was unreliable and too much of a loose cannon, were put aside. When he had made his 'finest hour' speech in June, observers had noted that it was mostly the Labour benches that cheered him in the Commons. Now, the Conservatives were also behind him to a man. Never has the popularity of a prime minister risen so quickly and so dramatically as in the four historic months of the summer of 1940. It was an extraordinary turnaround. At the height of the battle, Churchill said to his dinner guests one evening that he was puzzled as to why he was so popular. Since he had come to power, 'everything had gone wrong, and he had nothing but disasters to announce' and his platform was only 'blood, sweat and tears'.[33] But this suited the mood of the people. Although no one knew for sure that the threat of invasion had been lifted as the Battle of Britain merged into the Blitz, Churchill had successfully led the nation through its darkest hour. But the task of going forward to victory would be long and arduous. Churchill had yet to prove that he had the right formula, and the right people around him, to meet this challenge.

5

The Wizard War

In the early hours of 5 November 1939, a parcel was left on the window ledge of the British Consulate in Oslo, in what was then still neutral Norway. Signed simply 'A German scientist who wishes you well', the parcel contained several typed pages which appeared to relate details of the latest German scientific research. This included information about radar equipment, new fuses for bombs and shells, the progress of the dive-bomber, the development of rocket technology, details of a large experimental establishment at Peenemünde on the Baltic, and a description of a radar aid to guide bombers at night, called 'Y-Geraet' (or 'Y-Apparatus'). When it was passed on to Scientific Intelligence in London, it was received with much scepticism and it was thought that the document was a plant to confuse or mislead British scientists. It was ordered that copies of the report should be destroyed. In fact, as the war unfolded, one after another of the details in the document known as the 'Oslo Report' came real. The Report revealed that the war would be fought between scientists as much as between soldiers, sailors and airmen. Churchill called this 'the Wizard War', and the scientists and innovators he called up in the service of Britain were essential members of his War Lab.

Probably ever since human beings first struck an animal with a stone, they have tried to improve the sharpness of the flint or the destructiveness of the stone. Ever since men first used metal weapons to strike at their adversaries, they have tried to improve the efficiency and power of their arms. And certainly ever since firearms were first introduced in the late Middle Ages, gunsmiths have tried to improve accuracy, the rate of fire and the general destructive capability of their weapons. Leonardo da Vinci is often remembered for the genius of his art, but he actually devoted more of his life to the improvement of military machines for his patrons and the invention of new devices for destroying the enemy. In other words, the application of science has never been far from the development of the technology of war.

But around the time of the Industrial Revolution, the military and the world of science, the soldier and the scientist, became separated. As the profession of arms became a full-time professional calling, it developed its own mores, customs and practices. Soldiers became convinced that they, and they alone, understood the business of war and needed to get on with it without interference from outsiders who lacked their professional expertise. During the nineteenth century, soldiering became an inherently conservative profession. Officers whose decisions could directly result in the death of their men, and generals whose strategies could end in massive loss of life or national humiliation, did not want to experiment with new methods and ideas that might lead to even greater losses on the battlefield. Around these attitudes grew up the rituals of officer life associated with the world of soldiering in many

Western countries – the customs of the regimental mess and the subtle but rigid social hierarchies of different regiments. Soldiering, at least as far as officers were concerned, generated a socially exclusive lifestyle based on tradition and the repetition of the same processes over and over again. In Britain, for example, it now seems astonishing how many admirals were reluctant to give up sail and embrace the transition to steamships. In the army, many generals continued to champion the value of cavalry units even as the world became dominated by the internal combustion engine. And with this conservative view on how to fight wars (it is often said that each new war is approached using the methods of the last), the unchallenged acceptance of command and authority became an inherent and vital feature of the military mind. While science was intended to challenge, to question and to change the world, the armies and navies of most developed nations chose to freeze their thinking, in well-established and proven systems. As Solly Zuckerman, an important player in this story, put it: 'Where it is the habit of the scientist to question, it is that of the soldier to obey.'[1]

This was the world that Churchill entered first at Sandhurst and then in the 4th Hussars, one of the elite cavalry regiments of the British Army. But as we have seen, Churchill was no model young cavalry subaltern. He read books to stretch his mind. Instead of fox-hunting during his long vacations, he travelled to distant military conflicts to get a taste of the action. Then he wrote about these experiences and even went so far as to question the decisions of his senior officers. Although Churchill entered the British Army at the peak of its Victorian mode of thinking, and although he enthusiastically took part in its last great cavalry charge, he did not possess the frame of mind required to progress to the top of the military system. His mind was too restless, and he was far too ambitious to settle for a career of slow and gradual promotion through the military hierarchy.

When he returned to the military world as First Lord of the Admiralty in 1911, Churchill was much more associated with radical thinking, so it was not surprising that his fertile mind found new ideas appealing. Hence his enthusiasm for the Royal Naval Air Service, his vigorous support for the transition from coal- to oil-fired turbines, and when war came his encouragement for a variety of new technologies – from Q-ships to the tank to the code-breaking carried out in Room 40. Churchill was deeply upset and offended when his idea for a mechanical device to cross the barbed wire of no man's land and penetrate the enemy's trenches (what became the tank) was rejected by the army as 'not likely to lead to success'. His anger is still there in the pages of *The World Crisis*, written some ten years later.[2] When it came to his spell as Minister of Munitions in the last fifteen months of the war, again he was eager to find new systems and new ways of operating that would increase output and efficiency. And in the post-war era he sought out more new technologies and new strategies to devise a role for the RAF to act as a form of imperial police force, and to establish new accords with old enemies, as in the Irish Treaty negotiations. Churchill was always up for a challenge, and nothing was sacred to him in the traditional world of military thinking. As a young man, he had been deeply opposed to stuffy, closed-minded, conservative military commanders. He had come across them in India, the Sudan, in the Boer War and at the Admiralty. And in many of his books he had written of the need for vigorous and inventive thinking. 'Nearly all the battles which are regarded as masterpieces of the military art . . . have been battles of manoeuvre in which very often the enemy has found himself defeated by some novel expedient or device, some queer, swift, unexpected thrust or stratagem.'[3] In a sense, this statement sums up his quest for new and radical solutions to military problems. By the 1940s, this inevitably meant some sort of marriage between the scientist and the soldier.

Churchill, of course, was the first to accept that he himself understood little about science and almost nothing about mathematics – the subject he had found so difficult to master at school, while his failures in maths exams had nearly prevented him from qualifying for the army. So it was that during the late 1920s Churchill developed a friendship and deep respect for Professor Frederick Lindemann, known always as simply 'the Prof'. Lindemann was in many ways the most unlikely member of Churchill's court at Chartwell. He was a vegetarian, and a non-smoking teetotaller! He always looked the same, dressing in a dark formal suit. He wore evening dress at dinner. And he always took a bowler hat and umbrella when going out, whatever the weather. He was an eccentric who seemed to enjoy annoying people. Whenever he crossed the road, he never stopped to look, he would just step off the pavement, waving his umbrella, and charge through the traffic (there was less then than today). In conversation, he liked to be blunt and provocative. When someone at Churchill's dinner table at Chartwell before the war asked him for a definition of morality, he replied: 'I define a moral action as one that brings advantage to my friends.' Clementine whispered to the person who had asked the question: 'Doesn't the Prof sometimes say dreadful things?'[4]

But Lindemann was a physicist of great standing and international renown. He had known Einstein before the First World War while carrying out research in Berlin. He had joined the Royal Aircraft Establishment at Farnborough in 1915 where he had carried out important work, including finding a way for pilots to pull out of a spin, which in those days was nearly always fatal. He is supposed to have learned how to fly in order to carry out tests to see if his mathematical calculations about this actually worked in practice. They did. In 1919, he went to Oxford as Professor of Experimental Philosophy. At that time, Oxford science was way behind that of Cambridge, and Lindemann gave a huge boost to the work of the Clarendon Laboratory, which had been severely neglected.

Churchill later described Lindemann's value as one who could explain to him 'in lucid, homely terms what the [scientific] issues were'. Lindemann's vast and wide-ranging scientific knowledge and his natural self-assurance enabled him to sum up almost any scientific question for Churchill, whether it be the potential power of the atom or (as we have seen) problems with the standard-issue Mills grenade. 'There are only twenty-four hours in the day,' Churchill wrote, 'of which at least seven must be spent in sleep and three in eating and relaxation. Anyone in my position would have been ruined if he had attempted to dive into depths which not even a lifetime of study could plumb. What I had to grasp were the practical results.'[5] And this was what Lindemann provided him with. His memos to Churchill were usually just two pages long, double spaced in large print. He always tried to condense even the most complex and demanding scientific ideas into these bite-sized chunks for his boss's consumption.

When Churchill returned to the Admiralty in 1939, he asked his friend to come with him, and Lindemann left Oxford to do so. When Churchill became Prime Minister, the Prof went on to be one of the key players in his War Lab. He was made head of the newly created Prime Minister's Statistical Branch, with a tiny team of some six or seven economists and a scientist. It acted like an independent think-tank for Churchill and had a roving commission to dig into any aspect of wartime government and administration. Lindemann met with Churchill almost daily, advising him on scientific matters, military issues, logistical problems and even the economy. Most weekends, he joined Churchill and his entourage at Chequers. And he sometimes accompanied Churchill when the Prime Minister travelled abroad. Lindemann sent Churchill about two thousand memos during the war, equivalent to roughly one per day. His biographer said his role as scientific adviser to Churchill gave him 'power greater than that exercised by any scientist in history'.[6] Inevitably, with such a difficult and combative man, this would prove controversial. And, equally inevitably, with his prickly and vain personality, often coming across as pompous and stiff, there would be major fallings-out between Lindemann and other key scientists.

But Churchill was worried that the Whitehall establishment would be slow to respond to new and dramatic developments in science, and that good advice would take too long to percolate up to him. So he wanted Lindemann at his side not only to explain in a way he could understand what the new science might be, but also to advise him on what else was needed in the wizard war. The Statistical Branch prepared albums of tables and charts to illustrate at a glance the strength of military units in various theatres, and to keep a running record of shipping losses in the Atlantic. Churchill was proud of these albums and used to show them off to the King and, later, to President Roosevelt.[7]

Back in the early 1930s, Prime Minister Stanley Baldwin had said in Parliament: 'the bomber will always get through'.[8] By this, he meant that there was no effective means of defence against enemy bombers. In the age of appeasement, it became government policy simply to accept the inevitability that Britain would be bombed in a future conflict. Churchill and Lindemann did not accept this defeatist attitude and Lindemann wrote to *The Times* on 8 August 1934:

Sir, In the debate in the House of Commons on Monday on the proposed expansion of our Air Forces, it seemed to be taken for granted on all sides that there is, and can be, no defence against bombing aeroplanes . . . That there is at present no means of preventing hostile bombers . . . I believe to be true; that no method can be devised to safeguard great centres of population from such a fate appears to me to be profoundly improbable . . . To adopt a defeatist attitude in the face of such a threat is inexcusable until it has definitely been shown that all the resources of science and invention have been exhausted.[9]

Lindemann's letter acted like a wake-up call. Something had to be done to develop defensive means against the bombing of Britain. This was where the wizards came in.

A committee was set up to investigate how scientific and technical advances could aid the detection of enemy aircraft. Sir Henry Tizard was asked to chair it. Tizard has been called one of Britain's greatest defence scientists.[10] He had begun as a chemist but had given up pure research and moved across to find ways of applying scientific advances to practical problems. Tizard was an excellent chairman and was known for asking clear and brilliant questions. At this point he was the rector of Imperial College, London, to which he had given a great boost – just as Lindemann had improved the standing of Oxford's Clarendon Laboratory. In many ways, Tizard's career closely paralleled that of Lindemann. Indeed, they had known each other in Berlin before the First World War and had become friends. But they had very different views on how to bring science into the mainstream. Tizard committed himself to public administration and worked tirelessly on several government committees. Lindemann attached himself to Churchill and saw political alignment as the way forward. When Lindemann pressed the Air Ministry to set up a committee to explore the science of air defence and discovered that Tizard was already running such a committee, he took this as a great personal affront by both Tizard and the ministry. Instead of working together, Lindemann fell out with Tizard. And once he held a grudge, the Prof was not one to forgive.

In this context, significant developments were made in Britain in Radio Detection-Finding, radar. When Churchill joined the Air Defence Research Committee in 1935 he first learned about the early development of radar from Tizard and others. Radar's origins lay in the bizarre quest to find a 'death ray' that would send enough energy along a beam to destroy an enemy aircraft. In 1935, Robert Watson-Watt, the superintendent of the National Physical Laboratory's Radio Research Station at Slough, was asked to investigate this. He very quickly proved that the amount of energy needed was so vast that the death ray would remain firmly in the realms of science fiction rather than science fact. But Watson-Watt was one of the outspoken mavericks of British science in the 1930s, with a strong sense of how science could be used to transform the future. He observed that radio waves will bounce off an aircraft and after tests using the BBC's short-wave radio transmitters at Daventry, he devised a system for measuring the position of a flying object. The Air Ministry quickly grasped the potential of this invention to give an early warning of the approach of enemy raiders, an advantage that in the age of 'the bomber will always get through' would prove vital.

Air Marshal Hugh Dowding was at this time in charge of RAF Research and Development, and he was impressed. He agreed to put up ten thousand pounds, a substantial sum, of research funding for the device to be tested. In simple surroundings first at Orfordness on the Suffolk coast and then at nearby Bawdsey, Watson-Watt and his small team of scientists developed one of the great inventions of the twentieth century. They began to find ways of measuring first the distance, then the height and finally the bearing of aircraft using radio transmitters and a cathode-ray tube. Despite the low level of defence spending, radar (or RDF) developed rapidly under Watson-Watt and both the army and the navy began to show an interest in his experiments as well. As we have seen, RAF Fighter Command when Dowding took it over developed a plan for the organisation of the air defence of England based on the construction of the Chain Home radar system. But the principal achievement of Dowding and his team of scientists was to integrate the scientific side with the operational, to filter and process the information gleaned from the new science into an effective battle plan. Tizard played a vital role in this development during a series of tests at Biggin Hill airfield in Kent, in the late 1930s. He calculated the angle at which the faster fighters needed to be directed in order to intercept the slower bombers. This became known as the 'Tizzy angle' and was used until the 1960s, when computers took over such calculations. The whole process marked a subtle but important shift. Pilots, who had traditionally operated under their own rules of patrol and observation, were now scrambled and directed to the enemy by their controllers, who acted according to strict scientific principles in reading, interpreting and predicting the Luftwaffe's flight path. This has been described as being 'of crucial importance in the new service–scientist relationship'.[11] During the Battle of Britain, radar literally meant the difference between victory and defeat. It was not the only element that helped bring victory to the RAF. But without radar, defeat would have been certain.

In the run-up to war, several senior scientists realised the important role science would play in the future conflict. Fearing that the government was not doing enough to prepare for war, they drew up a list of seven thousand scientists, some working in universities, others in industry. Each scientist's name and area of expertise were entered on to a card index known as the 'Central Register'. By this simple method, physicists, engineers, chemists, biologists, astronomers and botanists were all carefully listed. So, for instance, when the Merchant Navy needed a specialist in maritime refrigeration, the right person could be quickly found. Although many senior officers in the army and navy were still sceptical about how these scientists would fit into military work, the Air Ministry was more welcoming, as it had been with the integration of radar into an operational defence plan. The RAF was the youngest of the three services and needed science in obvious ways to improve its performance in the air. So it is not surprising that this new breed of scientist, known as the 'boffin', should have been welcomed first by the nation's aviators. 'Boffin' was the affectionate term that came into popular use during the war to describe a scientist known for his inventiveness, his persistence and his ability to come up with weird and wonderful solutions to problems. (They were nearly all men, as women received little encouragement in the sciences at this time.) Sometimes they joined the military, often they remained civilians, operating through a range of government advisory committees. There was a lot of potential for tension here. Senior military officers were usually drawn from the gentry or the upper middle classes and were of a conservative disposition. The boffins usually did not enjoy much social status, came from a variety of backgrounds, and were often radical in their approach. Nevertheless, the boffins would bring much to the military over the next few years, and without doubt they contributed significantly to the Allied victory.

One of the greatest triumphs of science in the war was the deciphering of German codes. In the 1930s, the German military had developed a form of top-secret communication using the Enigma machine. This was an electro-mechanical typing machine which was able to encode every letter of every message via a series of rotor blades. The scrambled message was then sent as a conventional radio signal. The Enigma machines for the various parts of the military were slightly different in their configurations, but the basic operating principle was the same. The operators would reset the rotor blades at the back of the machine every twenty-four hours, so that messages would be encoded according to a different formula each day. The German military were convinced that their Enigma codes were secure because, although it was theoretically possible for the enemy to decipher a message, it was reckoned that it would take so long that by the time it had been done the rotor blades would have been reset and a new code created. The Germans therefore put total faith in their Enigma codes, and the High Command communicated regularly with the Wehrmacht and the Luftwaffe, issuing orders and receiving field reports filled with precise details about locations, the strength of units, casualties, operational plans, and so on.[12]

Before the war, Polish Intelligence had captured an Enigma instruction booklet and had even got its hands on an Enigma machine, and so had been able to crack the German code system. In the summer of 1939, French Intelligence and the British Secret Intelligence Service started to get interested in this. Just before the outbreak of war, the Government Code and Cypher School moved its staff of about one hundred cryptographers to Bletchley Park, a country-house estate to the north of London. Additional teams of mathematicians were then recruited to work there, many from nearby Cambridge University. After the defeat of Poland and then France, Bletchley became the principal Allied centre for code-breaking. The amount of work that went on here soon outgrew the mansion house and stables, and dozens of brick huts were built across the grounds of the estate. Within a few years, seven thousand men and women were working at Bletchley, with even more at a series of outstations around the country, from Dorset to northern Scotland. They included radio operators, mathematicians, decryptologists, interpreters, and hundreds of clerical support staff working on the central index, many of whom came from the Women's Royal Naval Service.[13]

Of all the many extraordinarily brilliant personalities who worked at Bletchley, Alan Turing was one of the most exceptional. A top-level mathematician and mechanical engineer, he was a fellow of King's College, Cambridge, and had written a pioneering paper on computable numbers before the war. He was only in his late twenties when he arrived at Bletchley, with boyish looks but a totally dishevelled and eccentric air. His trousers were often held up with an old tie, he had stopped shaving regularly, his hair was scruffy and he spoke with a stutter. He was painfully shy and developed the habit of working continuously for days at a time before collapsing in exhaustion. His military masters never really understood him. But he ran Bletchley's famous Hut 8 where he helped design the first 'bombes', huge electrical machines six-foot-by-seven, consisting of thirty rotating drums that ran through thousands of letter possibilities at high speed to find the correct match of plain text with encrypted letters. Out of these later in the war came Colossus, the world's first operational computer, which could run through the tens of millions of computations that were necessary to decode some of the most complex messages. Initially it took days to decode a signal, but Colossus reduced this to hours and ultimately to minutes. It was a stunning breakthrough and Turing went on to help found the post-war computer industry. Hounded for being gay, he committed suicide in 1954 by biting on a poisoned apple.

Although exceptional, Turing was only one of many eccentric and remarkable characters working as code-breakers at Bletchley Park. Gordon Welchman, another pipe-smoking, studious Cambridge mathematician, was one of the first to recognise the scale of the task that faced code-breakers who had the potential to listen in to the German high commanders talking to each other on a daily or even an hourly basis. When more code-breakers were needed, he drove off to Cambridge in his Austin 7 and rounded up former colleagues and students to join his team. Peter Twinn, an Oxford mathematician, found that he was resented by the old school of cryptologists, who were all classicists and suspicious of what these bright young mathematicians could contribute. Stuart Milner-Barry was an international chess champion who was recruited at the start of the war. Josh Cooper was one of the strangest. He had the peculiar habit of putting his right hand behind his head and stroking his left shoulder when he was thinking. He was also known for every now and again missing his chair when he went to sit down and landing up on the floor. Mostly the newcomers were young, in their mid-twenties, but there was also a smattering of older men who had been members of the Admiralty's Room 40 in the First World War. Nigel de Grey was one of the most celebrated Great War code-breakers. Frank Birch, another Room 40 veteran, had combined life as an academic with a career on the pantomime stage. Some of the newcomers were women, like Diana Russell Clarke who worked in the Hut 6 Machine Room. She was renowned for driving her Bentley sports car at high speed through the local country lanes. Linguists Phoebe Senyard and Barbara Abernethy were also among the earliest recruits.

Today, the work of Bletchley Park (or Station X, as it was known) is famous. There have been novels, movies and TV series about the place. But between 1939 and 1945 it was the most highly secret operation in the entire war effort. Very few people, including most of the staff at Bletchley themselves, had any idea how crucial this code-breaking work was. The recruits were placed in a small group and got on with their own tasks, totally unaware of what was happening in any other group. Most of the new arrivals were selected because they were thought to be 100 per cent reliable, but on arriving at Bletchley many were often still met by a security officer who would draw his pistol. Everyone was told that he or she must never breathe a word of anything they did or knew about to anyone else. If they did, they were told, the officer would personally come and shoot them. The secrets of Bletchley Park lived on long after the war. It was only in the mid-1970s that stories began to emerge about the code-breaking that went on there and its importance to the Allied victory.

The information gleaned from breaking the German codes and listening in to the Enigma communications between field units and their headquarters was known generically as 'Ultra'. It began to come on line within weeks of Churchill becoming Prime Minister. The excitement of reading deciphered messages direct from the enemy appealed greatly to Churchill, just as it had in the First World War. He really enjoyed the magic and the mystery of it.[14] Instead of reading summaries of the messages, he asked to receive the information raw, as it had been decoded and translated. He did not like the idea of it being watered down or distorted to give him a rosier picture than was really the case. Every day, wherever he was, a special box in faded yellow leather was delivered to Churchill by a messenger from the Secret Intelligence Service (SIS). In this box were the latest decrypts, the decoded messages. Only Churchill held the key to this box, on his keyring. The boxes came to him from the director of SIS, the man known as 'C' (later the inspiration for 'M' in the James Bond stories written by Ian Fleming, who worked in

Naval Intelligence during the war). 'C' was Colonel Stewart Menzies, who ran SIS throughout the war and into the early 1950s. Desmond Morton coordinated the flow of Ultra from Menzies, but it all went directly to Churchill, who returned it after reading. To protect the source of this information, the code name 'Boniface' was used, suggesting to anyone who might by accident hear about it that it had been supplied by an agent, a spy operating somewhere inside Germany. Even Churchill's closest aides knew nothing about these decrypts. Only a tiny number of senior ministers and the Chiefs of Staff and their deputies, about thirty people in all, knew of the existence of this highly valuable top-secret intelligence. Over the next few years, the mass of information decoded from the Wehrmacht, the Luftwaffe, the Abwehr (German Military Intelligence) and even from the German police and railways revealed much about the enemy's military intentions. The German Navy used an even more sophisticated Enigma system with extra rotor blades, adding immensely to the challenge of the code-breakers. Only when these naval codes were finally broken in December 1942 did the Battle of the Atlantic begin to turn in Britain's favour. At the time, Churchill called the code-breakers 'the geese that laid the golden eggs and never cackled'.[15]

In September 1941, the Prime Minister made a personal visit to Bletchley Park to inspect the 'geese' for himself. Even he was surprised at the casual dress and eccentric behaviour he saw. He is supposed to have said to Menzies: 'I know I told you to leave no stone unturned to get staff but I didn't expect you to take me literally.'[16] He made a short and emotional speech to the code-breakers, telling them how important their work was. But because so few people in senior government positions were allowed to know about the work going on there, Bletchley Park was constantly turned down when it put in bids for much-needed extra staff and resources. By this time the volume of work coming through required a major expansion. So, a month after his visit, Turing, Welchman and two other leading code-breakers wrote directly to Churchill, telling him: 'We think you should know that this work is being held up, and in some cases not being done at all, principally because we cannot get sufficient staff to deal with it.' They went on to appeal above the heads of their bosses direct to the Prime Minister: 'For months we have done everything that we possibly can through the normal channels and we despair of any early improvement without your intervention.' They asked for additional typists, more clerks, and for the removal of various bottlenecks. When he received the letter, Churchill sent a minute to General Ismay, saying: 'Make sure they have everything they want as extreme priority and report to me that this has been done.' Then he stamped the minute with the red 'Action This Day' sticker. Within a month, the essential expansion at Bletchley Park had begun. The Ministry of Works started erecting new buildings and a recruitment programme for two thousand extra staff was launched. Once again, Churchill's personal intervention had made the key difference.[17]

Before the Battle of Britain had got fully under way and the genius of radar had proved its worth, the boffins again came to the aid of the military. A young research scientist who had worked for Lindemann at Oxford, Dr R.V. Jones, warned the Prof that the Germans had developed a sophisticated system of beams to guide their bombers to their targets. The beams could be used by day or night and in any weather conditions. Lindemann reported this warning to Churchill, who instantly recognised its importance. Without waiting for the slow-moving bureaucracy to assess the situation, Churchill called an urgent meeting on 21 June in the Cabinet Room. The new Minister for Air, Sir Archibald Sinclair, and the Minister for Aircraft Production, Lord Beaverbrook, were there along with

Tizard, Lindemann, Watson-Watt and several senior RAF figures. Jones was summoned to attend the meeting but when he got into work that morning and found the message calling him to the Cabinet Office he thought it was a practical joke. As a consequence he was about half an hour late. Soon after he arrived, Churchill asked him to outline the position. Jones was only twenty-eight years old, but undaunted by the top brass that now confronted him he launched into an explanation of how for some time he had been picking up reports that the Germans had developed a secret weapon, a new system of night bombing, on which they placed great hopes. It seemed to be linked to the code word *Knickebein*, which somewhat mysteriously translated as 'crooked leg'. A bomber had crash-landed earlier in the year and the phrase '*Knickebein* beacon' had been found in some documents. Captured Luftwaffe crew were interrogated and revealed the use of special new radio equipment. More shot-down aircraft were searched and further references to *Knickebein* were found, including one linking it to a location in Cleves, in north-western Germany. Meanwhile, aerial photography had revealed the existence of several strange towers that did not look like conventional radio beacons. After Luftwaffe prisoners of war were overheard saying, 'They'll never find where it is,' Jones had the idea that maybe this new device was contained within the existing system that enabled a pilot to land at night or in bad weather by tuning in to a beam. Sure enough, this equipment proved to be far more sensitive than was needed for landing purposes, and when an RAF aircraft tried it out, the plane picked up a whole series of signals linking it to a beam. It was then that Jones realised these could be used not for landing, but for guiding bombers to their targets.

Churchill and the distinguished gathering of senior officials listened to Jones as he told his story. Churchill later wrote 'For twenty minutes or more he spoke in quiet tones, unrolling his chain of circumstantial evidence, the like of which for its convincing fascination was never surpassed by the tales of Sherlock Holmes.'[18] Then there was a discussion around the table. Some of those present were incredulous. They argued that such a system was unnecessary and asked why the Luftwaffe pilots did not simply navigate by the stars, as RAF crews were trained to do. But Churchill, on the advice of Lindemann and against that of Tizard, who was sceptical about the existence of the beams, was ready to accept that the Germans had devised such a system. As the argument continued, Churchill grew angry and banged his fist on the table.[19] He ordered that countermeasures were to be investigated as a matter of priority. Jones went back to his desk in the Air Ministry to coordinate what became known as the 'Battle of the Beams'.

Conventional wisdom had it that short-wave radio beams did not have the accuracy to guide aircraft over the distances involved, that they would disperse like the beam of a searchlight with the curvature of the earth. But Jones persisted, and by flying with the captured German equipment, RAF pilots discovered a beam emanating from Cleves and directed on Derby in the East Midlands. This sent a cold chill down the spines of those involved. Derby was the location of the Rolls-Royce factory producing Merlin engines for Spitfires – vital for the Battle of Britain. This was probably the single most important target in Britain. Identification of this beam produced a near panic that the Germans could now bomb at night factories of such major importance to Britain's war effort. Scientists from the Air Ministry and the Telecommunications Research Establishment near Swanage in Dorset worked together at full speed. By the middle of August, all the *Knickebein* transmitting stations across northern France had been identified (the Cleves station had moved to Calais). Then the boffins found ways to jam the beams electronically, so the bombs would be dropped not on the intended targets but on open fields some fifteen or twenty miles away. The counter-measures were known by the code name 'Aspirin', as they helped clear the headache caused by *Knickebein*. By the time the Blitz began in earnest on 7 September with the big raid on the docks and East End of London, the first phase of the Battle of the Beams had been won.

Of course, the Germans soon realised that their beams had been identified and were being distorted. A new chapter in the scientific war unfolded when the Luftwaffe transferred to a new system called 'X-Geraet' (or 'X-Apparatus'). This was a more sophisticated device that used five very high-frequency, short-wavelength beams to guide the aircraft. When these beams intersected with cross-beams, a trained navigator could identify a target with great accuracy – it was estimated down to about one hundred yards. This system was used by only one formation, a special 'Pathfinder' group, Kampf Gruppe 100. The planes of KGr 100 would identify the target and drop incendiaries and the rest of that night's bombing force would then aim their explosives at the area of the flames.

On the evening of 5 November 1940, a Heinkel from KGr 100 crashed on the beach at West Bay, near Bridport in Dorset. As the sea lapped around the bomber a dispute ensued between the army, who turned up to salvage it, and the navy, who claimed that as it had landed in the sea the prize was theirs. As a consequence, the vital electronic equipment was initially lost and it took several days to find it. Even when it was finally recovered it proved difficult to piece together how it worked. It seemed the Germans transmitted eight beams, but only five of these were used in each raid. And they used two different types of signal, which the British called 'fine' and 'coarse'. But jamming or distorting the beams still proved impossible.

Using Ultra decrypts and a close study of how the beams were set up, by mid-November the boffins knew that a big series of raids was coming under the code name 'Moonlight Sonata'. But they were unable to predict the targets and still could not jam the beams. Sure enough, on the night of 14 November, the Luftwaffe mounted its biggest raid yet outside London when it bombed Coventry. The raid was one of the worst of the Blitz. In addition to the hundreds of civilian casualties, the cathedral and more than twenty factories were destroyed. A persistent myth still surounds this raid that Churchill knew the target was Coventry but failed to warn the city or order the jamming of the beams so as not to give away the fact that British boffins understood how the German system worked. It is clear from the evidence of those working long hours to understand and distort the beams that this was not the case. In fact, Churchill thought the raid was heading for London. He ordered his secretaries into underground shelters, telling them they were too young to die. Churchill himself could not sleep and spent much of the night on the Air Ministry roof, looking out for the expected bombers.[20]

By early 1941, a successful means had finally been found to block the X-Geraet system. The stronger counter-measures this time were known by the code name 'Bromide'. The Germans would turn on the beams in the evening before a raid and from this Jones and his team were eventually able to identify what that night's target would be. But the Germans, once again, soon developed yet another device, the Y-Geraet, or Y-Apparatus, an early version of which had been described in the Oslo Report. It used a highly sophisticated form of radar to guide an aircraft to its target. This system was identified and disrupted by the British boffins more quickly. In May 1941, it is thought that the twisting of these signals inadvertently led the Luftwaffe to bomb Dublin, in neutral Ireland, in error. The see-saw war of one side gaining an advantage, followed by the implementation of counter-measures to block this, continued until that May, when the Blitz on Britain was lifted as the majority of the Luftwaffe were sent east to a new target, the Soviet Union. Churchill estimated that the combination of British counter-measures and simple Luftwaffe inaccuracy meant that 80 per cent of German bombs missed their targets. This was, as he said, 'the equivalent of a considerable victory'.[21] Of course, this meant one in five bombs still hit home, and they caused dreadful losses throughout the winter and early spring of 1940–1. But without the boffins' work, the damage would have been much worse. The Battle of the Beams had proved to anyone who cared to doubt it that this would be a scientific war. But Churchill had already taken a major step to ensure that Britain would be on the winning side.

One of the unfortunate consequences of the big meeting held on 21 June, when Jones had first related to Churchill and the RAF bosses the story of the German *Knickebein* beams, was the resignation of Sir Henry Tizard. With Lindemann's close association to Churchill, their old rivalry re-emerged after he became Prime Minister and Tizard realised his position had become untenable. He also accepted that in not backing Jones in his suspicion that the Germans were using beams he had been wrong. He withdrew from his position at the apex of many government defence committees. But Churchill, unlike Lindemann, was not a man to hold a grudge. He recognised Tizard's ability and soon came up with a new mission for him.

During the summer of 1940, Churchill worked hard to persuade Roosevelt to increase the US commitment to the British war effort. We have seen that he was partially successful in this but at the end of July, Churchill personally took a dramatic and courageous decision that would have long-term consequences for Anglo-American cooperation during the war and for long after. With the threat of invasion and the possibility of defeat still real, Churchill decided to share Britain's scientific secrets with the Americans and the Canadians. Behind this extraordinary decision lay the idea that if Britain were defeated, then at least the New World could continue the fight using the latest technological advances. It was not an altruistic gesture. It was motivated by the desire to bring America further into the war. But for a nation at war to supply its top secrets to a non-belligerent country was an act of faith unique in world history. Churchill asked Tizard to chair the vital mission to the United States that would offer up those secrets.

Tizard was delighted with his new task. He hoped that he would succeed in bringing 'American scientists into the war before their Government' and that he could encourage the Americans to reciprocate by sharing some of their advances with Britain.[22] He gathered together a series of papers representing the most advanced thinking of British scientists on miniaturised radar which was being developed for air-to-air use, chemical warfare and on explosives. In addition, he boxed up and took with him actual examples of a variety of new devices. These included three power-driven gun turrets that were later used in bombers; proximity fuses that ignited when they came close to an aircraft, which the United States were to build in huge numbers; and a new predictor for the multiple-firing Bofors gun. But most important of all was a small black box containing the jewel in the crown of British science in the summer of 1940, the cavity magnetron.

The cavity magnetron had been developed by two scientists at Birmingham University, Professor John Randall and Dr Harry Boot, earlier in 1940. Radar, despite its great value, was limited by the inability to send out really short-wavelength radio signals. The cavity magnetron was a valve that overcame this problem by turning high voltages into short-wave signals of immense power. When combined with a receiving valve, the cavity magnetron revolutionised the power and range of a radar set almost overnight. Radar could now pick up and identify the movement of people, the positions of cliffs to assist in the radar navigation of naval vessels, and even the location of the conning tower of a submarine. And the way was opened for its use within aircraft and ships for blind navigation during fog or darkness. And radar's range was extended from forty or fifty to well over a hundred miles. The cavity magnetron was, literally, a war-winning device. When the box containing it was opened and it was shown off to a group of American scientists in a Washington hotel, they were almost blown away by what they saw. The official historian of the American scientific war later described this as nothing less than 'the most valuable cargo ever brought to our shores'.[23]

Churchill's decision to share Britain's secrets with America had long-term consequences of immense importance. A Scientific Office was opened in Washington to coordinate the further exchange of scientific ideas. Delegations of senior American officers and top scientists travelled to Britain to discuss ways of collaborating should the United States enter the war. America not only became a closer ally (Churchill's primary objective) but could now put its vast industrial muscle behind the development and manufacture of some of the latest scientific devices on a scale way beyond anything that was possible in Britain for the rest of the war.

In the summer of 1940, after France had fallen and with the Battle of Britain raging, it became obvious that heavy air raids would soon be made on Britain. But the state of the nation's anti-aircraft defences was poor. There were too few guns, and anyway the process of trying to hit a fast-moving target when it would take many seconds for the ack-ack shell to reach the right altitude, was still very hit and miss (mostly miss). Giant concave sound detectors were used to try to establish the height of enemy aircraft, but these were hopelessly inefficient. The officer in charge of Anti-Aircraft Command, General Frederick Pile, was an imaginative man keen to find any means to improve the accuracy of his gunners. After discussions with Tizard, it was decided to recruit a group of young scientists from the universities and industry from the Central Register drawn up before the war to tackle the problem. They were led by Professor Patrick Blackett, a leading physicist from Cambridge who had been an officer in the First World War and understood the army mentality. The team became known as 'Blackett's Circus'.

The Circus immediately got to work to try to bring scientific principles into the operation of the anti-aircraft batteries. Radar was used to try to predict the path, speed and altitude of enemy aircraft. But unlike the radar used by the RAF in the tall towers of the Chain Home sites, the portable radars used by the army alongside the ack-ack guns were never far off the ground and so were subject to massive interference from nearby buildings and even hills and valleys in the surrounding landscape. Experiments were carried out and it was discovered that placing wire netting around the radars provided a uniform reflecting surface which cut right back on interference. Within weeks, the army had requisitioned nearly all the available stocks of wire netting in the country and this was now laid out around the mobile radars at the batteries.

The second task was to link the guns' firing control with the radar signals to ensure that the batteries could fire at the position the enemy aircraft were going to arrive at in the number of seconds it took for the shells to reach the correct altitude. Masses of statistics were gathered as night after night the men of Blackett's Circus looked for ways to improve on the gun sighting mechanisms. Work was done in Richmond Park to calculate the optimum layout for a battery of guns and the best way to concentrate fire. Throughout the winter of 1940–1, as German bombers flew over almost nightly to blitz the cities of Britain, the men of Blackett's Circus observed the enemy raiders and worked out the best way to hit them.

This process of applying scientific, often mathematical, principles to observe, assess, review and ultimately to improve military operations was called Operational Research. It began to play an important part in the war effort and soon spread from the army to the navy and the RAF. All the services had their traditional ways of doing things, and the boffins of Operational Research were able to observe and assess these and sometimes find more efficient ways of achieving results. In 1941, Blackett summed this up by saying that Operational Research could encourage numerical or scientific thinking on operational matters in order 'to avoid running the war on gusts of emotion'.[24] This was at the heart of the wizard war: that scientific analysis could achieve better results than the time-honoured, traditional way so valued by soldiers, sailors and airmen.

Blackett himself went on to work for the navy and his Operational Research team helped in the deadly Battle of the Atlantic. It was found that aircraft painted white rather than the traditional black were more difficult to see from the sea. After the planes of Coastal Command were repainted, the number of U-boat sinkings increased. It was also discovered that something as simple as resetting depth charges to go off at twenty-five rather than a hundred feet resulted in many more kills. Indeed, losses went up so dramatically that captured U-boat crews said they thought the Royal Navy had developed a new weapon against them. At the height of the Battle of the Atlantic, Churchill became so concerned about the U-boat menace that he held fortnightly meetings at Downing Street which Blackett would attend in order to pass on the latest summaries and observations from his team (see Chapter 7).

The RAF had already embraced a form of Operational Research with the integration of radar technology into Fighter Command. The filter rooms which processed the inflow of information about the approach of enemy bombers and the command centres with their plotting tables and the movement of markers across maps that enabled orders to be sent to scramble the fighter squadrons had all been planned before the war. Soon Bomber Command established its own Operational Research unit, which again came up with a number of suggestions for improved operational efficiency. It was calculated that massed bomber attacks had more impact than a large number of scattered attacks. This thinking led to 'thousand-bomber' raids from May 1942. Scientists analysed how planes were shot down. Research found that most bombers returning from sorties had only one or two shell holes and were not structurally damaged. It was realised that most planes went down because of fires in their fuel tanks or the ignition of petrol vapour generated during a long flight. If an inert gas like nitrogen could be injected into the fuel tanks, then they would be less likely to burst into flames if hit by shrapnel from anti-aircraft fire. This discovery had long-term consequences, but only a limited improvement was possible during the war.[25]

Operational Research units were created in RAF commands overseas. One important unit was set up in Cairo to advise on issues relating to the war in North Africa and over the Mediterranean. But there was a shortage of scientists, particularly mathematicians, so many young men straight from university were put into uniform and rushed out to the Middle East.[26] From here, important work was done on improving Allied operations in the Mediterranean by assessing the strike rate of bombs versus torpedoes against enemy ships (torpedoes had a higher success rate), and discovering the best way to find and sink U-boats. Later, this group learned that orange life-vests and life-rafts were easier to spot in the sea than the traditional yellow ones. This apparently simple discovery would save the lives of hundreds of downed airmen long after the war was over.

The Operational Research teams were only ever advisers. They were often placed in command centres and worked along-side staff officers. Their research sometimes confirmed that the traditional ways of doing things were the best. But when they did come up with new recommendations it was still up to the generals, admirals and air chiefs to decide whether or not to implement them. The fact that the military commanders often did follow the scientists' advice is a sign of the changing balance between science and the military. The wizards were having a bigger impact than anyone could have imagined at the start of the war.

Another key player in Operational Research was Professor Solly Zuckerman. He had started his career as a zoologist and had done important research into the lives of apes and monkeys. When the war began, he was studying anatomy at Oxford. He and some colleagues wrote a short book, *Science at War*, in two weeks at the start of the conflict. Rushed out as a Penguin Special, this was almost a manifesto for the new science of Operational Research. Zuckerman went on to assess the effects of bomb blast on the human body and on buildings during the Blitz. He found that the body was far more able to withstand the blast than had previously been imagined and that most casualties were caused by indirect effects, such as the collapse of buildings. He began to calculate the number of casu-alties likely to be caused by the dropping of particular weights of bombs. Then he went to North Africa to survey bomb damage caused by air attacks on towns captured from the Germans and on military convoys crossing the desert. He used captured German documents as well as ground observations to make his assessments. Later, he looked at the impact of bombing on rail communications in Sicily and mainland Italy. His findings would play an important part in the debate about the bombing offensive which is dealt with in Chapter 8.[27]

Of course, all of this work went on without the direct involvement of Churchill. But his support for men of science, his enthusiasm for change and new thinking, and his desire for the military to keep up with the work of the wizards, created the climate in which this particular seed could grow into a forest. This all stemmed from his War Lab. However, Churchill's loyalty to the most prominent member of that group was both a hindrance as well as a help to the war effort.

In 1942, Churchill offered Lindemann a peerage and he became Lord Cherwell (the name by which he will be referred to from now on). Churchill also formalised his position in government by making him Postmaster General. But Churchill had become over-reliant upon Cherwell's scientific advice. It's unfortunate that Cherwell's abrasive personality meant he fell out with so many distinguished men. And of all those who Cherwell vehemently opposed, Sir Henry Tizard was without doubt the greatest loss to the war effort. Churchill was usually a good judge of character, and he should have insisted that Tizard remain in the positions he had occupied with real distinction since before the beginning of the war. However, the Prime Minister's friendship with Cherwell blinded him to Tizard's qualities and he allowed Tizard to take a back seat after 1940. Without doubt this was a great loss to the British war effort. Tizard graciously summed up the position of the new science when he asked a parliamentary committee in February 1942, 'What Prime Minister of England ever had a scientific adviser continually at his elbow?' And he went on to observe of wartime Britain: 'there is hardly a phase of the national life with which scientists are not associated. In fact a fighting friend of mine said that he could hardly walk in any direction in this war without tumbling over a scientist who had got in his way.'[28]

But by this time, Tizard was under-utilised by the War Lab. He held a variety of minor roles, but none of them compared with his earlier work on air defence or his mission to the United States in the summer of 1940. This had been one of the most important scientific journeys of the war. But there was yet another secret that Britain still had to share with America, one which would have even greater long-term consequences.

Before the First World War, Albert Einstein had reasoned that atoms, the basic unit of matter, were held together by forces that if released could produce huge amounts of energy. In the late 1930s, German scientists in Berlin had succeeded in splitting the atom. Then, in early 1940, two German émigrés working in Britain on ideas about nuclear fission and how to release the power of the atom, Rudolf Peierls and Otto Frisch, made an extraordinary claim. They calculated that the amount of uranium needed in a bomb to unleash the energy equivalent to about a thousand tons of high explosives could be measured not in tons, nor in hundreds of kilograms, but was as small as one pound, less than half a kilogram. Their findings were passed on to Tizard, who at that point was still chairing the Committee for the Scientific Study of Air Warfare. Tizard discussed the possibility of finding some form of military use for this remarkable equation with Professor George Thomson in his rooms at Oxford. Thomson led a group of scientists nicknamed the 'Balliol Beagles' – so called because they always seemed to be chasing after the latest scientific ideas. Tizard decided to form a committee under Professor Thomson to examine the possibility of producing an atomic bomb. For the first time anywhere in the world, a government committee now began to consider the possibility of producing nuclear weapons.

Soon after Thomson and his small team of experts began their deliberations, a strange message arrived from an exiled German physicist working in Sweden. It read: 'Met Niels and Margherita recently. Both well but unhappy about events. Please inform Cockcroft and Maud Ray Kent.' Niels was Niels Bohr, the distinguished Danish physicist who had worked on atomic science before the war. Cockcroft was Sir John Cockcroft, a brilliant Cambridge scientist and Nobel prize-winner who was already a member of Thomson's committee. But no one knew who Maud Ray Kent was. It was decided that the message was probably cryptic and could possibly be an anagram for 'Make Ur Day Nt' – a clue that the Germans were developing their own atomic bomb and that the British needed to speed up. Thomson's committee was renamed the Maud Committee and increased the pace of its work through the summer, autumn and winter of 1940–1.

In July 1941, the committee submitted its report, concluding that it was possible that an effective atomic bomb could be produced within two years. When Cherwell read the report, he was sceptical as the science was still unproven and the production of an atomic bomb would involve a massive reallocation of resources that were more profitably committed to other wartime technologies. However, he concluded to Churchill: 'I am quite clear that we must go forward. It would be unforgivable if we let the Germans develop a process ahead of us by means of which they could defeat us in war.'[29] Churchill agreed with the need to keep ahead of anything the Germans might be developing, so he set up a top-secret organisation under the code name 'Tube Alloys' to develop a nuclear bomb.

However, far more important than the creation of the British project was Churchill's agreement to forward the Maud Report to the Americans. The report was filed away in the United

States for several months until James B. Conant, the president of Harvard University and a senior scientific adviser to the US government, got to read it. Finally, in October 1941, he and other scientists persuaded President Roosevelt to commit the US government to developing and building an atomic bomb. Roosevelt offered to include the British in this effort but Churchill refused, believing that his scientists were ahead of their American counterparts (at this point, they were). However, once the United States came into the war after Pearl Harbor in December 1941, the Americans' work on their atom bomb went up a gear and rapidly pulled ahead of anything going on in Britain. In September 1942, General Leslie Groves was put in charge of the project, which now came under the supervision of the US Army. Three months later, the first nuclear reactor was built in Chicago. But the work involved in making a bomb proved far more complex than anything imagined by Thomson and his team in Britain. The Manhattan Project, as the US research came to be known, developed into one of the biggest scientific operations of all time, employing 120,000 people across 37 different research sites. Robert Oppenheimer led the scientific work and finally, four years after the Maud Report had been produced, in July 1945, an experimental bomb was successfully tested in Alamogordo, New Mexico. One of the scientists present at this test, code-named 'Trinity', wrote:

Suddenly there was an enormous flash of light, the brightest light that I have ever seen or that I think anyone has ever seen . . . as we looked toward the place where the bomb had been, there was an enormous ball of fire which grew and grew, and it rolled as it grew . . . A new thing had just been born; a new control; a new understanding of man, which man had acquired over nature.[30]

The war against Germany had already been won two months earlier. The war against Japan would be over within a month.

The atomic bomb had a strange lineage: from Germany to Britain, then through Tizard, Thomson and Cherwell to Churchill, and from him to the United States and into the full Manhattan Project. Only America had the vast resources needed for the development of a weapon that would transform world politics and the balance of power for the next fifty years. But Britain's War Lab had played a key role in starting the ball rolling. For good or ill, the partnership between scientists and soldiers had helped to produce the most destructive weapon known to mankind.

6

The Generals

Winston Churchill was a hard taskmaster, particularly for the military chiefs with whom he worked closely. He was demanding, demonstrative, convinced that he was always right, and kept them up half the night. He constantly felt that his generals, admirals and air marshals did not show enough aggressive instinct and that it was him against all of them. Overall, most of them admired him but felt they had the specific knowledge about the situation in the field that meant they were better judges than he was of what was possible and what was impossible. At best, Churchill viewed this as obstructive; at worst, plain defeatist. In one angry outburst in October 1941, he shouted at them: 'I sometimes think some of my generals don't want to fight the Germans!'[1] The Chiefs of Staff were all central players in the War Lab. But did Churchill cajole and bully them too much? Did he get the best out of them or did he push them too far? Building the right relationship with his military chiefs would be essential to winning the war. But it certainly would not be easy for Churchill, nor for his chiefs.

Churchill's military options were limited during the Battle of Britain and the Blitz. A stream of minutes still poured forth from his desk, demanding information, suggesting priorities, proposing objectives and calling for innovations. Many of them, as usual, required 'Action This Day'. But Britain was in a defensive mode and, as Churchill had told the Soviet Ambassador, his principal strategy was just to survive. Nevertheless, his instincts were all for taking the initiative and trying to throw the enemy on the back foot. In July 1940, when the Battle of Britain was about to begin, Churchill ordered the establishment of a top-secret special unit that would encourage sabotage and subversion behind enemy lines, in the hope of generating uprisings against Nazi occupation. This unit was called the Special Operations Executive (SOE) and Churchill famously instructed the minister he put in charge, Hugh Dalton, to 'set Europe ablaze'.

It was an ambitious, aggressive objective but there was little SOE could do to set fire to anything much in 1940. It had limited resources and was hemmed in by sceptical military bosses. But Dalton understood his mission. He said: 'Regular soldiers are not men to stir up revolution.' The idea was to drop small groups of well-trained saboteurs and assassins into occupied Europe. These would then act in tiny cells to hit at key targets and create a level of mayhem out of all proportion to their numbers. Churchill had long been keen on guerrilla tactics since he had observed them first hand as a young officer in Cuba and South Africa, where the Boers had used these tactics with great effect. With his lifelong enthusiasm for unorthodox methods of warfare, it is not surprising that he set up something like SOE so early in his premiership. He called it the 'Ministry for Ungentlemanly Warfare' and it was all very exciting cloak-and-dagger stuff.[2] But did it in reality do any good?

The people of occupied Europe were soon to feel the full force of the Nazi jackboot. Any uprising was met with ruthless and vicious reprisals. Dozens of innocent men and women would be killed for every action taken against the occupying forces. Thousands of others would be sent to concentration camps. Churchill wanted to provide a beacon to inspire and motivate uprisings while providing essential logistical support. The first parachute drops took place into occupied Poland in 1941. Later that year came operations in Norway and Sweden, but it was only in Yugoslavia that SOE could claim a significant impact. Even then, the eminent military historian John Keegan has claimed that SOE was an expensive and misguided failure, costing far more in the loss of innocent lives than it achieved in positive results.[3]

While Britain's back was very firmly against the wall, Churchill created two other new military forces with the intention of striking soon against Nazi-occupied Europe. The commandos (the term was first used by the Boers for their forces that struck behind enemy lines) were put under the command of Churchill's old hero from the First World War, Sir Roger Keyes. The first commando raids were combined operations with SOE against Norway to capture key pieces of Enigma technology in 1941. And, against much opposition, Churchill also insisted on the formation of a new paratroop regiment. The army chiefs argued that with the invasion scare at its height, skilled combat soldiers could not be spared for new units. But Churchill insisted. A call for volunteers went out and several hundred men came forward. Within a year, the core of the 1st Airborne Division had been trained up. Churchill kept up to date with developments in their training and watched a parachute test drop in person in July 1941. SOE, the commandos and the airborne units would all have notable successes later in the war.

With Cherwell's support Churchill also encouraged the development of a small experimental group to explore new forms of explosives. This was led by two maverick inventors, Major Millis Jefferis and Stuart Macrae, the ex-editor of *Armchair Science* magazine. Both men were brilliant and radical thinkers who over the next few years came up with a run of remarkable and slightly wacky devices, ranging from tiny booby traps to heavy guns, most of which had improbable names like the Kangaroo Bomb and the Beehive. They devised a magnetic naval limpet mine that was used in several commando raids, a sticky bomb that would attach to armour for five seconds before exploding, and a form of mortar that could fire a ring of bombs in a circular pattern against a U-boat, known as Hedgehog. By the end of the war, thirty-seven U-boats were confirmed as having been sunk with Hedgehog. Jefferis also invented a shoulder-fired anti-tank gun that eventually went into production as the PIAT gun and became the army's most effective infantry-operated anti-tank weapon. This was just the sort of unconventional, out-of-the-box thinking that Churchill loved to encourage in his War Lab.

Sometimes the work they did went wrong, and on at least one occasion there was an explosion that destroyed part of the unit's armoury at Whitchurch, near Aylesbury. Needless to say, the War Office and the Ministry of Supply were opposed to such unorthodox experiments and on several occasions tried to close down the whole operation. At one point, Churchill put the group under Ismay's authority and gave him instructions to keep an eye on it. Later, it came under Cherwell's direct control. It became known as 'Churchill's Toy Shop', and the Prime Minister loved visiting Whitchurch to see the latest inventions. On one occasion, Churchill was described as being 'like a small boy on holiday'.[4]

In the summer of 1940, the Mediterranean theatre, including

North Africa, was the only location where there was a remote possibility of taking the sort of aggressive action that Churchill longed for. And so campaigning here grew to obsessive proportions in Churchill's mind. There was a strategic debate about the Mediterranean. The First Sea Lord, Admiral Dudley Pound, proposed abandoning the eastern Med and the long-held British naval base in Alexandria to concentrate on Gibraltar. In July, Churchill vetoed this and decided to reinforce the garrison in Egypt against a likely attack by Italy. Even in this darkest hour, as the battered remnants of the British Army, hauled from the jaws of catastrophe at Dunkirk, desperately reassembled to prepare to defend the country from possible invasion, Churchill persuaded his Chiefs of Staff and the War Cabinet to send men and *matériel* to Egypt. About half of the best armour in the country, over 150 tanks, along with anti-tank weapons, anti-aircraft guns, field artillery, rifles and ammunition were loaded up. It was a courageous, possibly foolhardy, decision. It is probably a sign that Churchill never really believed that a German invasion was likely. The Ultra decrypts that he read often encouraged him in this view. But it was certainly going against the grain to deplete the national defences at such a critical time. Churchill later wrote that the decision 'was at once awful and right', but once he had convinced the other military and civilian chiefs, 'No one faltered.'[5] Churchill wanted to get the supplies to Egypt as quickly as possible and proposed sending them through the Mediterranean. Here he was overruled by the service chiefs, who argued that the route posed too great a risk to such a valuable cargo. After a fight, Churchill demurred and the convoy went by the long route around the Cape of Good Hope. It did not arrive in Egypt until the end of September.

As we have seen, the Commander-in-Chief in North Africa General Wavell came back to London in August 1940 to discuss strategy. Churchill was not impressed with him and his taciturn

manner and was tempted to replace him. But he had not done
so. Wavell returned to his command in Cairo, and he was there
to receive the reinforcements when they arrived in September.
Churchill then, once again, started to press for immediate
action. Wavell insisted on delaying until everything was ready.
In early November, reconnaissance aircraft photographed the
assembly of the Italian Mediterranean Fleet in the harbour at
Taranto. On the 11th, aircraft from the carrier HMS *Illustrious*
attacked the Italian fleet with torpedoes. Three battleships and
one cruiser were hit. The resounding success of this attack
helped shift the balance of naval power in the Mediterranean in
favour of the Royal Navy. This surprise attack upon the Italian
fleet in harbour was also the inspiration for the Japanese admirals a year later when planning their assault upon the American
Pacific Fleet at anchor in Pearl Harbor.

During the autumn of 1940, Mussolini invaded Greece and
an Italian army launched an attack on Egypt. The invasion
of Greece was stalled by the valiant defence of the Greek
Army. Then, on 9 December 1940, Churchill at last got his long-
awaited land offensive, by what he called the 'Army of the
Nile'. General Richard O'Connor led this modest affair, known
as 'Operation Compass', with only two Allied divisions. Nevertheless, the offensive was a stunning success. By the time it
came to a halt in February 1941, O'Connor had advanced five
hundred miles along the North African coast through Cyrenaica in Italian Libya as far west as Beda Fomm. The assault
had routed ten Italian divisions, and had captured 125,000
prisoners along with 400 tanks and 1200 guns. The newsreels contained footage of endless lines of Italian prisoners
as far as the eye could see. Not surprisingly, Churchill eagerly
embraced the good news, which was pretty well the first
British triumph of arms on land in the war so far. He wrote
to President Roosevelt, and to the Commonwealth prime

ministers, as he still needed the support of their armies in the
Middle East. But this was just the beginning of the see-saw
war in North Africa, which would be the principal theatre of
operations for the British Army for the next two years.

It will be remembered that Churchill had done much to
foster Roosevelt's support during the dark days of 1940. This
had led to America's supply of the second-hand destroyers
Churchill was so desperate for, along with tanks, artillery and
other weaponry, much of which had gone to buttress the army
in Egypt. However, before committing himself to more aid,
Roosevelt wanted to gauge the British war effort and particularly the determination of the British Prime Minister. In January
1941, he sent his close friend Harry Hopkins as his personal
emissary to Britain. Churchill really put himself out to charm
Hopkins and spent twelve evenings with him. His schedule
was carefully stage managed by Brendan Bracken. There was a
visit to Dover to review the defences and Hopkins peered
across the narrow Channel to occupied Europe; he toured
Britain and saw stout-hearted defenders everywhere, alongside
the damage caused by the Blitz; and he even travelled far north
to Scapa Flow to inspect the mighty fleet gathered there. He
also met the War Cabinet and the Chiefs of Staff.[6] Churchill did
not share with him the secret of Ultra. During his visit, further
intercepts came through, suggesting that the German invasion
had been called off. But Churchill kept these to himself and
instead talked up the threat of invasion, which he knew would
have the biggest impact upon the Americans.[7]

Hopkins was enraptured by Churchill and entirely won over.
At the end of his visit, he reported back to the President:

I have got a reasonably clear perception not only of the
physical defences of Britain, but of the opinions of the men
who are directing the forces of this nation. Your 'former

Navy person' is not only the Prime Minister, he is the directing force behind the strategy and conduct of the war in all its essentials . . . The spirit of this people and their determination to resist invasion is beyond praise. No matter how fierce the attack may be you can be sure they will resist it, and effectively.[8]

With the Blitz still on and with no end in sight, this was a fascinating verdict on Churchill's Britain in early 1941.

Roosevelt, reassured, pressed ahead with his support. The Lend-Lease Act passed through Congress. America could now build whatever was needed and lease it to Britain, who would pay up in full after the war was over. Before this, Britain must pay all the debts it could in gold and sell its commercial assets in the United States. It was a tough deal that totally drained the nation's reserves and in one sense left Britain bankrupt. But it marked a long-term commitment by the United States to Britain's war effort. It enabled Churchill to keep fighting the war. In a broadcast to America he used the famous phrase: 'Give us the tools and we will finish the job.' In the House of Commons he claimed that Lend-Lease was a 'monument of generous and far-seeing statesmanship'. And in a telegram to Roosevelt he wrote: 'Our blessings from the whole British Empire go out to you and the American nation for this very present help in time of trouble.' In private, however, he admitted that the sale of Britain's assets meant that 'we are not only to be skinned but flayed to the bone'![9]

The collapse of Mussolini's armies in both Greece and Libya now drew Hitler into the Mediterranean. In a sense this was a victory for Churchill's Mediterranean policy. At least he had found somewhere for offensive action to create an impact. But at the time, he once again felt that he was being let down by over-cautious thinking among his army chiefs. Having advanced far into Libya, O'Connor's offensive was called off because the intelligence coming through Ultra revealed that the Germans were preparing to intervene in Greece. At a meeting in mid-February, Churchill lost his temper with the CIGS, General John Dill, who told him troops could not be spared for Greece. Churchill could not fathom why, after orchestrating this great victory, with 300,000 men and all the supplies he had been sent, Wavell was unable to defend Greece and maintain the offensive campaign in North Africa at the same time. 'What you need out there is a Court Martial and a firing squad!' he shouted. Dill remained tight-lipped under the pressure of this Churchillian tantrum, but later he wished that he had replied: 'Whom do you want to shoot exactly?' But he didn't think of this until afterwards.[10]

The British intervention in Greece was a sorry affair. Churchill and the Chiefs of Staff ordered Wavell to halt the offensive in Libya and to dispatch troops to Greece. Reluctantly he did so. In April 1941, when the powerful German assault began, the British, Australian and New Zealand troops were both vastly outnumbered and outfought. They were forced back and on 17 April, Churchill sent agreement for their withdrawal in a sort of Greek Dunkirk. About 50,000 of the 62,000 men sent to Greece were evacuated by the Royal Navy, but they left behind most of their guns, tanks and transport. Crete was now reinforced and detailed plans were picked up in Ultra for a German airborne invasion of the island. However, the army and the intelligence people back in London, particularly Stewart Menzies, 'C', were desperate not to give away the fact that they had deciphered the German military messages. So the defence of Crete was not reorganised in a way that would have best prepared it for the German assault. General Bernard Freyburg, in command on Crete, was given full access to the Ultra decrypts and details of the planned airborne invasion, but effectively he was told not to act on them. 'The authorities in England

would prefer to lose Crete rather than risk jeopardising Ultra,'
Freyburg said later.[11] The New Zealand defenders fought
bravely, but in just a few days at the end of May they suffered
fifteen thousand men killed, captured or wounded, and Crete
was duly lost. For the German invaders, however, success came
at a high price. Seven thousand were killed during the assault,
and German airborne troops were never again used to assault
defended positions.

It is sometimes claimed that these actions in Southern Europe
at least delayed Hitler's assault on Russia, with the key consequence that his armies were unable to capture Moscow before
the onset of winter. It's unlikely in retrospect that they did have
this effect. More effective was an SOE-inspired anti-German
coup in Yugoslavia. This brought Hitler into the Balkans and
prompted his assault on Yugoslavia in order to secure his southern flank. It resulted in years of terror and repression in the
Balkans. And it was this action that delayed the start of his
assault upon the Soviet Union by a crucial five weeks.

Another consequence of Hitler's attempt to prop up his ally
Mussolini was the despatch to North Africa of General Erwin
Rommel, the man Hitler described as the most daring com-
mander in his army. Although initially Rommel had only
minimal forces at his disposal, these forerunners of the Afrika
Korps soon seized the initiative and rolled back the great
British advance across Libya. By the spring, Rommel and his
combined German and Italian troops had pushed the British
Army right back to the Egyptian border. To add to the humiliation, General O'Connor was captured as the British front
collapsed. This presented Churchill with yet another failure of
British arms. Only the port city of Tobruk managed to hold out
against Rommel's lightning advance, and was left behind as a
a besieged enclave.

Rommel sent messages to Berlin that his troops were exhausted and needed to rest. Two days later, the Ultra decrypts of these messages were in the faded yellow case on Churchill's desk. Once again, the Prime Minister chafed at the bit and demanded that Wavell launch a fresh assault. Another convoy of supplies, including more than two hundred new tanks, were sent to reinforce the Army of the Nile. This time, though, on Churchill's insistence, the convoy successfully took the quick route across the Mediterranean. Churchill signalled to Wavell: 'I have been working hard for you in the last few days . . . no Germans should remain in Cyrenaica by the end of June.'[12]

On 15 June, Wavell's new offensive, Operation Battleaxe, was launched. But Rommel had managed to decipher British Army messages sent from Middle East Command. Forewarned, he placed his front-line troops on full alert. They were waiting and ready for Battleaxe. After three days of fighting, Rommel cleverly outmanoeuvred the British and Wavell called off the failed offensive.

Churchill was furious. He felt like he was carrying the whole war effort on his shoulders. It seemed to him that he was facing cautious Chiefs of Staff, admirals who complained about exhausted ships, and generals in the field who lacked the will to fight. He now came to think he should take military command himself. On the other hand, for his generals the constant interference and sending of detailed memos with minute instructions about operational matters was severely wearing them down. Wavell complained to friends about the relentless 'barracking' from the Prime Minister. The reality was that Churchill did not have the right generals around him. So he did not appreciate their qualities and they were unable or unwilling to do his bidding. Churchill responded by dismissing Wavell immediately and swapping him with General Claude Auchinleck, who was commander-in-chief in India. Wavell was quickly packed off to Delhi, as Churchill put it, to sit 'under a pagoda tree'. Ismay, an old friend of Auchinleck, warned the new North African commander about Churchill's ways. His advice is fascinating. He told Auchinleck:

> The idea that he was rude, arrogant and self-seeking was entirely wrong . . . He was certainly frank in speech and writing but he expected others to be equally frank with him . . . He venerated tradition but ridiculed convention . . . His knowledge of military history was encyclopaedic and his grasp of the broad sweep of strategy unrivalled. At the same time he did not fully realise the extent to which mechanisation had complicated administrative arrangements . . . 'When I was a soldier' he would say, 'infantry used to walk and cavalry used to ride. But now the infantry require motor cars and even the tanks have to have horse boxes to take them into battle.'

Ismay also warned his friend that he would be bombarded by telegrams on every topic, 'many of which might seem irrelevant and superfluous'. But he was not to be irritated. Churchill was carrying the burden of fighting the whole war on every front, at land, at sea and in the air.[13] Auchinleck was stepping into the most difficult job in the British Army. Time would tell if Ismay's advice would bring him more success than his predecessor.

Within days of the failure of Operation Battleaxe, the whole shape of the war changed dramatically. At dawn on 22 June 1941, Hitler launched Operation Barbarossa, his invasion of the Soviet Union. For months intelligence reports had predicted the invasion, so Churchill had had plenty of time to think through his position. On the evening of Saturday 21 June, he told his dinner guests at Chequers, including the US Ambassador James Winant, that he was certain the Germans were about to attack Russia. He said he would instantly pledge Britain's support to

Stalin. Winant, who had discussed the matter with Roosevelt, agreed that this would also be the US position. John Colville, his private secretary, took a walk with Churchill in the garden after dinner and asked if supporting his old enemy would put him in a difficult position. Churchill replied that 'If Hitler invaded Hell he would at least make a favourable reference to the Devil.'[14]

In the early hours of the following morning, the news came through of the launch of Operation Barbarossa. That Sunday evening, knowing that he had US backing, Churchill announced the position of the British government on the BBC. It was an emotional broadcast, envisioning the noble defence by impoverished Russians of their beloved homeland against 'Hitler's blood-lust'. Churchill declared: 'Any man or state who fights on against Nazidom will have our aid.' He went on, 'The Russian danger is therefore our danger, and the danger of the United States, just as the cause of any Russian fighting for his hearth and home is the cause of free men and free peoples in every quarter of the globe.'[15] Despite a lifetime of personal hostility, and despite all that he had done to undermine the communist state in its early days, the Soviet Union was now Britain's ally – and that was official.

Ultra intelligence had for many months revealed that German troops were massing along the Soviet border, and Churchill had warned Stalin in a personal note of the possibility of invasion.[16] Stalin had received several other warnings of the imminent attack. But in one of the strangest blunders of the war, he ignored all of them and did nothing to prepare his vast land army or his air force. As a consequence, when Barbarossa was launched, the German military thrust forward with devastating speed. Three million men led the assault on the Soviet Union along a border of 450 miles, from the Baltic to the Black Sea. The Germans had a total of 120 divisions in three gigantic army groups supported by 3350 tanks. On the first morning, the Luftwaffe attacked the Soviet Air Force while it was still on the ground, destroying many aircraft before they were even able to get airborne. The Soviet Red Army was huge, but no match for the battle-hardened German infantry and panzer divisions. Hundreds of square miles were captured and occupied. One after another, major Soviet cities fell to the Nazi invaders – Minsk, Smolensk, Odessa. Six hundred thousand Russian soldiers were taken prisoner. Hitler spoke of his 'crusade' against communism. He called the Soviet state a 'rotten structure' that when kicked in would come 'crashing down'. It looked as though he would be proved right.

In London and Washington, the general feeling was that the Soviet Union would be overwhelmed within a few months. Barbarossa therefore injected a new intensity into the Anglo-Amereican relationship. Now it was time for a face-to-face meeting. On 4 August, amid tight security, Churchill along with his Chiefs of Staff boarded the newest battleship in the Royal Navy, HMS *Prince of Wales*, at Scapa Flow. Within minutes, the giant battleship slipped its moorings and was soon heading at full speed across the Atlantic. During the voyage, Churchill took his first break of the war. He loved life on board and found time for watching films (particularly historical movies like *Lady Hamilton)*, playing backgammon, and even reading a novel (*Captain Hornblower RN* by C.S. Forester). On the morning of 9 August, the battleship arrived at Placentia Bay off Newfoundland. It had been decided to meet on 'neutral' ground rather than in the United States. President Roosevelt arrived on the American heavy cruiser USS *Augusta* and Churchill, refreshed after the voyage, crossed to the American ship, where he was piped aboard. Within a few hours, observers were reporting that he and Roosevelt, who had been corresponding now for twenty-one months, were getting on famously.

The meeting at Placentia Bay provided a giant photo opportunity. On Sunday 10 August, Roosevelt visited the *Prince of Wales* for a church service held on deck. The prayers were carefully selected, as were the hymns, which included 'Onward Christian Soldiers'. The newsreel cameras rolled as the President and the Prime Minister sitting alongside each other led their men in the singing. 'You would have had to be pretty hard boiled not to be moved by it all – hundreds of men from both fleets all mingled together . . . It seemed a sort of marriage service between the two navies, already in spirit allies,' wrote John Martin, one of Churchill's secretaries, in his diary.[17] The meeting is famous for producing the Atlantic Charter, a joint Anglo-American declaration of principles respecting 'the rights of all peoples to choose the form of government under which they live'. It was a grand proclamation of the moral values of the democracies intended to act as a beacon to those under occupation. Its value was largely symbolic. But important business was also done, in great secrecy, at this momentous meeting.

Roosevelt promised to provide aid to the Soviet Union 'on a gigantic scale', and it was agreed to send an Anglo-American mission to Moscow to discuss the USSR's needs and to propose a summit meeting with Stalin. It was also decided to send a strong note to the Japanese, warning them against further encroachments in the Pacific. Critically, for Churchill, Roosevelt and his naval chiefs agreed to provide escorts for convoys across the Atlantic which, if attacked, would respond by firing on U-boats. And the United States would patrol the Atlantic to the west of Iceland. The two sets of Chiefs of Staff had useful meetings. It was clear there was a gulf between their thinking and that the Americans as yet had no plans in place should they become embroiled in the war. But useful personal contacts were made and the basis for future combined operations was laid.

For Churchill, most important of all was the personal time he spent with Roosevelt, building not just a working, professional relationship but a genuine mutual friendship that would be at the heart of the 'special relationship' for the next four years.

Churchill returned from Newfoundland to news of further German advances in the Soviet Union. The Wehrmacht now broke through into the giant, open prairie fields of the Ukraine. It seemed unstoppable. On 21 September, the Germans captured Kiev along with two-thirds of a million Soviet prisoners. Hitler called it the 'greatest battle in world history'. For Churchill, these were bleak times. He worried that if the Soviet Union were defeated, Hitler's triumphant armies would then turn once more on Britain. Again, he called for offensive action in North Africa, but Auchinleck his new commander told him the army would not be ready until November.

It was essential for Churchill to have the right men around him. Wavell had had to go. And so too would General Dill, whom Churchill thought off as being over-cautious, referring to him as 'Dilly-Dally'. It was a few months before the right moment came but later in the year he was replaced as Chief of the Imperial General Staff and sent off to Washington where he was to do an outstanding job. The man Churchill chose to replace Dill as CIGS, the army chief, was General Sir Alan Brooke (later Field Marshal Viscount Alanbrooke). Brooke was part of an Ulster Protestant family with a long tradition of service in the army. One of Churchill's close friends from his army days in India had been Victor Brooke, Alan's elder brother, who had been killed in 1914. And another brother, Ronald, had ridden with Churchill into Ladysmith to relieve the city during the Boer War. Alan Brooke himself had served with distinction in France in the spring of 1940 and had been put in command of the Home Forces in July 1940, when the possibility of invasion loomed. He had impressed Churchill with the way he had reinvigorated the defences of southern England around a more mobile strategy in order to respond with flexibility if an attack came. With frenetic energy he reorganised units that were still reeling from the loss of France. Churchill liked what he saw and the fact that Brooke had the self-confidence to stand up for himself and argue his case against anyone – including the Prime Minister. Churchill respected this and enjoyed the cut and thrust of debate. 'When I thump the table and push my face towards him what does he do? Thumps the table harder and glares back at me. I know these Brookes – stiff-necked Ulstermen and there's no one worse to deal with than that!' Churchill is reported to have said about Brooke to his deputy.[18] After a couple of late night sessions talking together, Churchill offered Brooke the top position.

So began one of the central partnerships of Churchill's War Lab. It endured for three and half years, to the end of the war. They would meet almost daily, and Brooke became Churchill's principal military adviser. To many outsiders it seemed that their relationship was difficult. They argued fiercely together and the atmosphere often seemed tense. Brooke, like his predecessor, was also infuriated by Churchill's micromanagement and by his meddling in minor tactical details, the stuff which Churchill of course loved. It always seemed that Churchill wanted to control every aspect of every battle plan. He interfered, it seemed to Brooke, without a full understanding of the situation in the field. Furthermore, Brooke was pushed to the brink of exhaustion by the hours Churchill kept. The Prime Minister would often call meetings late at night or even in the early hours of the morning and he always expected everyone to be at their best. But he would have enjoyed a leisurely morning, reading papers and dictating from his bed. The others would have worked a full, stressful day structured around a conventional time frame. Churchill never seemed to have consideration for the strain that others around him were also under.

But Brooke turned out to be the perfect foil to Churchill. He stood his ground against the Prime Minister's garrulous verbal assaults, and he never accepted a plan or endorsed a policy that he knew was wrong or would needlessly risk the lives of his men. Brooke could be as tough as nails. His nickname in the Cabinet Office was 'Colonel Shrapnel'. Churchill respected him for this. Although the Prime Minister would often cross-examine and criticise everything put before him, sometimes in an aggressive or bad-tempered way, Brooke knew that the very next day he might hear Churchill eagerly putting forward the same plan as though it were his own. And at heart, Brooke had great admiration for Churchill and for his leadership of Britain. Back in May 1941, before he became CIGS, he had the opportunity to observe Churchill at close quarters and had written: 'He is quite the most wonderful man I have ever met, and is a source of never ending interest studying and getting to realise that occasionally such human beings make their appearance on this earth. Human beings who stand out head and shoulders above all others.'[19] After the two had been at each other's throats in some gruelling encounter over the details of a battle plan Brooke would be heard to murmur, 'That man!' And then with a sigh to continue, 'But *what* would we do without him?'[20]

Over the years, both men were worn down by the strain of working together. Brooke often found Churchill petty, unfair and irrational, and his ideas wildly unrealistic. Totally against regulations, he kept a diary, which he wrote up late at night. For him, it provided relief from the stress of the day to scribble down his thoughts. Looking at the original diaries, it's easy to see how he wrote at speed, without much care for grammar or punctuation, almost in a stream of consciousness, to get his feelings off his chest. In one exhausted late-night entry from September 1944, after another bitter row, he recorded:

> We had another meeting with Winston at 12.00 noon. He was again in a most unpleasant mood. Produced the most ridiculous arguments that operations should be speeded up . . . He knows no details, has only got half the picture in his mind, talks absurdities and makes my blood boil to listen to his nonsense . . . Never have I admired and despised a man simultaneously to the same extent.[21]

But the fact is the tension in this love-hate relationship brought out the best in both men. Brooke was confident enough (just) to put up with Churchill's bullying. Churchill, for his part, respected Brooke as a supremely professional soldier, from a long line of soldiers, who always had the army's best interests at heart. And when faced with determined, well-argued opposition, Churchill never overruled Brooke. Churchill's undisciplined genius was tempered by Brooke's tough professionalism. It would be a war-winning partnership.

The very morning that Brooke began to work as CIGS, Auchinleck finally launched his offensive in the North African desert. Within days his men had advanced fifty miles, and on 29 November they relieved the siege of Tobruk. Churchill was delighted with their progress. Then intercepted Ultra messages enabled the RAF to locate and sink two vessels bringing vital fuel supplies across the Mediterranean to Rommel's forces. Churchill had just two ambitions in the closing months of 1941: to bring the United States into the war before the defeat of Stalin's Russia; and to win a victory in the Middle East. He telegraphed Auchinleck in Cairo: 'as long as you are closely locked with the enemy, the Russians cannot complain about no second front . . . the only thing that matters is to beat the life out of Rommel and Co.'[22]

Further Ultra decrypts reported that the German Army in Russia was running out of steam, and its commanders were concerned by lengthy supply lines and the ferocity of the Russian resistance. Churchill passed on details from several Ultra reports to Stalin, including an outline of the full German battle plan, which made it clear that the main German objective was not the oilfields of the Caucasus but Moscow itself. Without letting the Soviets know the source of the intelligence, Churchill forwarded message after message to Stalin. 'Has Joe [Stalin] seen this?' he would regularly ask Srewart Menzies.[23] The Soviets received high-grade information about German plans that they could not have obtained from any other source.

The first light snows fell in September, but the full force of winter swept across Russia in November. German troops had advanced to within thirty miles of Moscow. Advanced patrols could see the spires of the Kremlin through their binoculars.[24] But as the Soviet defence hardened, so the German forces came to a standstill. Then, on 5 December, Stalin did what the Germans had thought was impossible. Using fresh troops from eastern Asia, fully kitted out and trained for winter war, he launched a counter-attack. The German troops, unprepared for the freezing conditions, without winter clothing or suitable weapons, were thrown back. Moscow was saved. And for this winter at least, so was Stalin's Russia.

The weekend after the counter-attack, Churchill was at Chequers. Now his big worry was that Japan was showing signs of aggression towards British and Dutch territories as well as the independent Siam (now Thailand) in South-East Asia. Churchill got in touch with Roosevelt and they agreed to make it clear that an attack upon Siam would be regarded as an attack upon themselves. On Sunday 7 December, Churchill had just finished dinner with the US Ambassador and Averell Harriman, another American diplomat, when they turned on a small radio to hear the BBC's nine o'clock news. Churchill himself almost missed the piece that mentioned an attack by the Japanese on American shipping in Hawaii. The butler came in to confirm that he had heard the report also. Churchill immediately called the White House, and after a few minutes Roosevelt came on the line. 'It's quite true,' the President replied. 'They have attacked us at Pearl Harbor. We're all in the same boat now.'[25]

At this point, the full scale of the daring and unexpected Japanese attack on the US Navy's giant Pacific Fleet as it lay in harbour was unknown. Later, it became clear that four battleships and over two thousand American sailors had been lost that morning. Moreover, Japanese troops had launched simultaneous attacks upon British Malaya, the Dutch East Indies and Siam. The whole world was now at war. But Churchill instantly recognised this as the best news possible, America would at last be Britain's ally. He later wrote that he realised then

> We had won the war . . . Once again in our long Island history we should emerge, however mauled or mutilated, safe and victorious. We should not be wiped out. Our history would not come to an end. We might not even have to die as individuals. Hitler's fate was sealed. Mussolini's fate was sealed. And for the Japanese, they would be ground to powder.

With his staff buzzing around him, Churchill retired to bed, where he 'slept the sleep of the saved and thankful'.[26]

The following day, Britain declared war on Japan. And then Congress declared war. Roosevelt described 7 December 1941 as a 'date which will live in infamy'. Churchill immediately made plans to visit Washington, concerned that vital US supplies might now be cancelled in order to pursue the war with Japan. Then, on 11 December, Hitler chose to declare war on the United States. It was an extraordinary decision. Now it was imperative that the two leaders of Britain and the USA, at long last Allies in the war, should get together. On 13 December, Churchill set sail once again for the United States. It would be a long trip.

During the Atlantic crossing, HMS *Duke of York* was buffeted by heavy storms and made slow progress. En route Churchill received good news of further Soviet counter-attacks in the north at Leningrad and in the south along the Sea of Azov, and bad news of the Japanese attack upon Hong Kong. The long journey and forced inactivity on board gave Churchill and his Chiefs of Staff (the newly appointed Brooke as CIGS was not on this trip) plenty of time to reflect on the global conflict now raging. Churchill wrote three expansive papers on grand strategy. They show remarkable insight into the course the war would actually take. The first focused on the war in North Africa in 1942, arguing that it was essential for the United States and Britain to take control of the Mediterranean. The second was on the war in the Pacific against Japan and correctly foresaw that this would be a maritime struggle followed by a series of island invasions to recapture lost territory. The third addressed the strategic objectives for 1943 and rightly predicted that the conflict on the Eastern Front with the Soviet Union would become the central land conflict of Hitler's war. Although he correctly predicted several major events over the next few years, Churchill was a little optimistic with the timing of these events: he thought the Allied invasion of occupied Europe would occur in the summer of 1943, rather than June 1944.[27]

After ten days at sea, Churchill finally reached the United States and flew on to Washington, where Roosevelt met him and invited him to stay in the White House. They immediately began talks, while the British Chiefs of Staff met with their US counterparts, quickly establishing the basis of how they would work together from now on, a system of combined operations that lasted to the end of the war. They also agreed, after considerable pushing by the British, on the 'Germany First' principle: that is, American resources would be allocated to the defeat of Germany as the first priority in the global war. In retrospect, this was one of the most important strategic decisions of the war. It could so easily have gone the other way. The Americans were outraged at the unprovoked attack by Japan and were tempted to concentrate on the war in Asia with Europe as a secondary diversion. It was a tribute to Churchill and his team, as well as to the global view of the US leadership, that Germany First became the guiding beacon of the war effort.

Much future planning was debated and agreed during the Washington meetings, and once again Churchill enjoyed several hours each day of premium time with the President. They lunched together daily, usually with Harry Hopkins. Dinner was a more social occasion, with others also present. Churchill wrote that 'The President punctiliously made the preliminary cocktails himself, and I wheeled him in his chair from the drawing room to the lift as a mark of respect.'[28] (Churchill preferred whisky and soda to the President's cocktails. Roosevelt was amazed at but tolerant of the amount of alcohol Churchill consumed. However, Eleanor Roosevelt, the First Lady, regarded the Prime Minister as something of an alcoholic.) The bond of friendship between the two leaders grew stronger in the weeks that Churchill lived as Roosevelt's guest in the White House.

On 26 December, Churchill was invited to address both Houses of Congress. He had spent some time polishing his speech and it went down well. The newsreel cameras were there to record one of Churchill's finest, most assured performances. He began by saying, 'I cannot help reflecting that if my father had been American and my mother British, instead of the other way round, I might have got here on my own. In that case, this would not have been the first time you would have heard my voice.' The laughter at this quip turned into profound applause when, speaking of Japan's outrageous attack upon Pearl Harbor, he asked, 'What sort of people do they think we are?' He spoke about the 'long, hard war' ahead and came to a rousing conclusion: 'It is not given to us to peer into the mysteries of the future. Still, I avow my hope and faith, sure and inviolate, that in the days to come the British and American peoples will for their own safety and for the good of all walk together side by side in majesty, in justice and in peace.' These final words brought the cheering congressmen to their feet.[29]

A few hours later, back in the White House, Churchill went to bed but couldn't sleep. As it was a warm evening he tried to open the window. As he did so, he suddenly felt short of breath. He felt a dull pain over his heart which went down his left arm. He quickly recovered, but the following day he reported the incident with some concern to his doctor, Sir Charles Wilson, who was travelling with him. Wilson instantly recognised that Churchill had suffered a mild heart attack, what he called a 'coronary insufficiency'. While he examined Churchill with his stethoscope, Wilson thought hard about what to do. The textbook recovery period for this at the time was six weeks in bed. But Wilson knew that if he instructed Churchill to stop work at this critical juncture it would soon get out 'that the PM was an invalid' with heart problems. It could be the end of Churchill as an effective war leader. On the other hand, if he ignored it and Churchill had another, potentially fatal, seizure, 'the world would undoubtedly say that I had killed him through not insisting on rest'.

The doctor decided that as the attack had obviously been mild he would risk it. He told Churchill, 'There is nothing serious. You've been overdoing it.' When Churchill protested that there was no way he could take a rest now, Wilson replied, 'Your circulation was a bit sluggish . . . you musn't do more than you can help in the way of exertion for a little while.'[30] Despite his age (he was now sixty-seven), the immense strain he was under and the vast workload, Churchill kept going at full speed. Later in the war, he suffered further illnesses, but he was never incapacitated by another heart attack. Wilson had made the right call.

A couple of days later, Churchill visited Ottawa and addressed the Canadian Parliament. Again the speech was recorded on film, which captures the power of his oratory. He referred at one point to the French claim in June 1940 that, without France, Britain would have its neck wrung like a chicken in three weeks. 'Some chicken!' exclaimed Churchill. As the laughter died down he followed this up with 'Some neck!'

Churchill did take a short break for a few days in Florida, where he enjoyed swimming in the warm sea. Swimming was something that particularly appealed to the boyish side of Churchill. 'Winston basks half-submerged in the waters like a hippopotamus in a swamp,' recorded Wilson in his diary, no doubt relieved that at last a couple of days of relaxation had been squeezed into the schedule.[31] Then it was back to the White House, and agreement on a declaration that Roosevelt called the United Nations Pact. This was a follow-on from the Atlantic Charter signed the previous August, a further declaration of democratic principles. There were meetings of real substance about industrial output and a Combined Chiefs of Staff Committee was formed. Finally, it was decided to launch an invasion of French North Africa later in the year to help secure the Mediterranean. It was during this series of meetings that Sir John Dill started to forge an excellent relationship with General George Marshall, the US Army's sturdy and dependable Chief of Staff. When Churchill and the rest of the British team returned to Britain, Dill was left in Washington as head of the Joint Mission, a critical role in the Anglo-American relationship that he enthusiastically and ably fulfilled until his death in late 1944. By then, the man whom Churchill had nicknamed Dilly-Dally had finally proved his worth.

Churchill had been away for three weeks when it was decided business was done and it was time to go home. First he flew to Bermuda in a big Pan-American Boeing Clipper flying boat, and during the flight he took the controls for about twenty minutes. He had not outgrown his fascination with flying. With so many U-boats in the Atlantic and with the urgent need to get back to London, it was then decided that the best option was to continue the journey to Britain in the flying boat. It was an eighteen-hour flight, and towards the end the Clipper drifted slightly off course and dangerously near to the coast of occupied France. It veered north at the last minute and flew towards Plymouth at an angle that made it look like an approaching enemy bomber. Six Hurricanes were scrambled to intercept the Clipper, but fortunately the error was discovered in time and Churchill and his team landed safely.

The following few months saw disaster follow disaster for Britain. The Japanese made dramatic advances in the Far East in their version of the blitzkrieg. On 15 February 1942, the giant fortress at Singapore surrendered (see Chapter 7). It was a humiliating blow to British power and prestige in the East. Churchill described it as 'the greatest disaster to British arms which our history records'.[32] In North Africa, the gains of Auchinleck's offensive were reversed by Rommel. British troops began to retreat once more, although Tobruk again held out, offering some hope. Churchill worried that the British Army in the Far East and in North Africa did not seem to have the spirit to fight. Then the German Navy changed the configuration of their Enigma machine, which meant it was impossible to decipher their messages for most of the rest of the year. Shipping losses in the Atlantic rose alarmingly. And the convoys carrying supplies to Russia took a terrible battering from German aircraft and battle cruisers operating from northern Norway. As the strain grew, Churchill became very down. 'Papa is at a very low ebb . . . worn down by the continuous crushing pressure of events,' wrote his daughter, Mary, in her diary.[33]

With the worsening global situation, Churchill decided to call another conference with Roosevelt in mid-June. This time he flew across the Atlantic in the same flying boat he had used five months before. He spent a couple of days with Roosevelt in his house at Hyde Park, overlooking the Hudson River. On 20 June both men travelled to Washington in the presidential train. They were in a meeting in the White House the following morning when an aide came in and passed a pink slip of paper to the President. He read it, said nothing and passed it to Churchill. It read: 'Tobruk has surrendered with 25,000 men taken prisoner.' Churchill was thunderstruck by the news. He had placed so much weight on the North African campaign and now all of his hopes seemed to collapse. He despaired at the failure of the British Army to hold out even against inferior numbers of the enemy, at Singapore and now at Tobruk. He later wrote of this moment: 'This was one of the heaviest blows I can recall during the war . . . it had affected the reputation of the British armies . . . I did not attempt to hide from the President the shock I had received . . . Defeat is one thing, disgrace is another.' Roosevelt asked what he could do to help. Churchill replied that he needed more tanks. The President immediately summoned General Marshall to join them and within hours Marshall had come up with a plan to divert three hundred of the newest A4 Sherman tanks to North Africa. Marshall also agreed to send a hundred artillery pieces. These were soon on fast transports across the Atlantic. They would make a real difference to the North African campaign later in the year. It was a magnificent sign of Roosevelt's friendship for Churchill and of US support for Britain's fragile war effort.[34]

A few days later, Churchill returned home from Washington to face a vote of censure in the House of Commons. Constant news of defeats had created rumblings of discontent against his leadership, and this was the second parliamentary vote of no-confidence that year. The debate offered a sounding board for those who wanted to air their criticism, but this was not a time for a change of leader. Churchill won the vote by 475 votes to 25. On the same day, Rommel's troops reached a small railway station named El Alamein, only eighty miles from Cairo. Here they stopped, for now.

On the suggestion of the soldier son of a colleague who had just returned from Egypt, Churchill decided to visit the troops in the desert to assess for himself the state of the Army of the Nile. After another gruelling flight, this time in an unpressurised, unheated Liberator bomber (Churchill had his oxygen mask specially adapted so he could smoke a cigar while wearing it!), the Prime Minister landed in Cairo. Once again Charles Wilson accompanied him, and he recorded that Churchill arrived 'in great heart . . . A great feeling of elation stokes the marvellous machine, which seems quite impervious to fatigue.'[35]

Churchill soon picked up on the low morale in the 8th Army, and he and Brooke, who also accompanied him on this trip, realised that there must be something wrong with the command of the desert army. After a few days, Churchill decided to replace Auchinleck. He appointed General Harold Alexander as Commander-in-Chief. Alexander was a classic senior officer of the old school, an aristocrat and an ex-Guardsman, not too clever, but always willing. He had a distinguished war record from the Great War and had seemed to sail through life, effortlessly achieving whatever he set out to accomplish, always immaculately dressed and with film-star good looks. He had done well commanding an army corps guarding the evacuation at Dunkirk and was known as a safe pair of highly capable hands. Churchill admired him greatly and was sure he had the diplomatic skills necessary for senior command.

Brooke wanted to appoint General Bernard Montgomery as commander of the 8th Army. But Churchill had reservations about Montgomery and preferred General William Gott, a corps commander who was already in the desert. Brooke regarded Gott as too tired to take on this responsibility and thought Montgomery was more energetic and self-confident. Unusually for Brooke, he gave in to Churchill and agreed to appoint Gott. Then, a couple of days after his appointment, Gott was killed when his plane was shot down by German fighters outside Cairo. Churchill then agreed with Brooke's recommendation and decided on Montgomery to take command of the 8th Army. It proved to be an inspired choice.

Montgomery (better known as 'Monty'), who went on to become probably the best-known British general of the Second World War, had a complex personality. He was outwardly very assured, often abrasive towards those around him and keen on self-promotion – he always made himself available for photographers and film cameramen, no matter how busy and tense the situation was. But he was also something of a loner who did not fit in to the relaxed cycle of officer life in the British Army and seldom socialised in the conventional way. He had been a staff officer in the First World War and had learned the vital importance of thorough, detailed planning before combat. In the inter-war period, he was a training instructor for many

years and by 1939 he was a highly regarded, all-round professional soldier. He fought well in France in May–June 1940 and
impressed Churchill with his aggressive spirit when he was
then put in command of a division on the south coast waiting
for the anticipated German invasion. But Churchill also found
him an awkward man to work with. In many ways, Monty was
the opposite of the sort of general Churchill liked. He was
cautious, calculating and believed that no offensive action
should be taken until an army had built up an overwhelming
superiority of men, guns and equipment and could be sure of
supremacy in the air. He was lucky to arrive in Egypt just as
that was happening. With the new Sherman tanks and field
artillery arriving from America, as well as substantial reinforcements, Monty soon enjoyed a superiority of roughly two
to one over the Germans and Italians of Rommel's Afrika
Korps.

But Monty was more than just an excellent planner. He elec-
trified his headquarters and had an almost instant impact on
the morale of the men. He believed in constant training and the
need for physical toughness. He soon had the troops taking
daily exercises and endlessly preparing for battle. He also
believed a general should live among his men, and his constant
visits and pep-talks soon engendered a new fighting spirit. It
was Monty who would lead the next decisive phase of the
desert war. If he failed, and Rommel broke through to Cairo
and the Suez Canal, Hitler's plan was for the Afrika Korps to
link up with the southern flank of the army in Russia and to
capture the vast oilfields of the Caucasus and Persia. The stakes
could not have been higher.

Brooke felt 'that at last he [Churchill] is beginning to take my
advice', as the decision to appoint Alexander and Montgomery
to their key positions at this crucial moment had largely been
his.[36] As a result, Churchill at last had the right team in place.

He could work well with Brooke as his leading military adviser. And Alexander was the right strategic Commander-in-Chief for the Middle East, and did not interfere with Monty, who was left to make his own operational plans for battle.

The Ultra intelligence coming through about the state of the Afrika Korps was now really making a difference. Montgomery was forewarned about Rommel's next attack at El Alamein along the Alam Halfa Ridge at the end of August, so he reinforced his troops there. Rommel was unable to break through. By September, more Ultra decrypts helped the RAF to locate and sink about one-third of all the cargo that was sailing across the Mediterranean to reinforce the Afrika Korps, and almost half the Germans' fuel supplies. Increasingly, the intercepted messages reported how hard pressed the Afrika Korps were. Both sides continued to face each other in the desert, but the 8th Army was rapidly growing in men, equipment and, under Monty's inspired command, in self-confidence.

On the moonlit evening of 23 October 1942, after a huge artillery barrage, Monty launched his great offensive at El Alamein. His 8th Army consisted of British, Australian, New Zealand, Indian and South African troops. Monty feigned an attack in the south of his forty-mile front, which Rommel believed was the real thing. But his main thrust came in the north. For several days there was heavy fighting with neither side gaining a decisive advantage. But slowly the weight of armour as well as the persistence and determination of Monty and his men began to count. After twelve days, Montgomery wrote in his diary, 'The dam has burst,' and Rommel ordered his Afrika Korps to retreat. Harried constantly by the RAF, Rommel orchestrated a brilliant withdrawal along the coastal road, escaping to fight another day. Churchill was elated by the victory. The Battle of El Alamein proved to be a turning point in the war. In total, 8000 Germans and 22,000 Italians were taken prisoner, while 35,000 Afrika Korps and 13,000 Allied soldiers were killed or wounded. Montgomery had shown that the German Army was not invincible and that an Allied victory was a distant but real possibility.

In a speech in London, Churchill at last had some good news to announce. 'I have never promised anything but blood, tears, toil and sweat,' he said. 'Now however, we have a new experience. We have victory – a remarkable and definite victory . . . This is not the end. It is not even the beginning of the end. But it is, perhaps, the end of the beginning.'[37] On 8 November, Anglo-American troops landed in force along the French North African coast in Operation Torch. This was the first truly combined operation of the war and the result of the joint planning that had begun in Washington eleven months before. It was soon evident that the landings had been a success. Rommel was now in full retreat westwards from Egypt and troops from the Torch landings would begin to move east towards Tunisia. On 13 November, Monty's troops entered Tobruk, the loss of which had so upset Churchill five months earlier. On Sunday 15 November, Churchill ordered the church bells to be rung across Britain. Two years earlier, this would have been the signal that the German invasion had started. Now it was a sign of victory. At long last Churchill's generals had delivered him a victory that mattered.

7

The Admirals

With the whole French seaboard from Calais to Bordeaux under
Nazi control after the fall of France, the Germans lost no time
in building U-boat pens along the Atlantic coast. The U-boat
war now turned even deadlier. During the last six months of
1940, U-boats sank 471 ships in the Atlantic, a total of more than
two million tons of shipping. In the early months of 1941, the
losses continued to rise alarmingly. Churchill was very aware
of the need to keep the sea-lanes across the Atlantic open, not
only for the supplies of guns, tanks and ammunition that were
now coming out of America's factories under Lend-Lease, not
only for the reinforcements in troops and *matériel* from Canada
and the rest of the Empire, but for the foodstuffs, metal ores, oil,
chemicals and all the other imports that were essential for
Britain's survival. This was a struggle that Britain, as a trading
nation, could simply not afford to lose.

Looking back on the titanic struggle for the Atlantic,
Churchill wrote: 'The only thing that ever really frightened me
during the war was the U-boat peril. I was even more anxious

about this battle than I had been about the glorious air fight called the Battle of Britain.'[1] This was a conflict that could be followed only on charts, and with the accumulation of statistics on a weekly or monthly basis. The U-boats attacked in so-called 'wolf packs', assembling at night once a convoy had been spotted and then attacking in numbers, overwhelming the convoys' defences and sinking merchant ships almost at will. Added to the U-boat menace were the activities of surface raiders like the *Scharnhorst* and the *Gneisenau*, German battle cruisers that between them sank or captured twenty-two ships in early 1941. And the long-range Condor aircraft could also spot convoys and bomb them from the air. 'How willingly would I have exchanged a full-scale attempt at invasion for this shapeless, measureless peril, expressed in charts, curves and statistics!' wrote Churchill.[2] In February 1941, the command centre for the 'Western Approaches', as the Atlantic sea-lanes into Britain were called, was moved to Liverpool and Admiral Sir Percy Noble was put in command. The following month, after some particularly bad losses, Churchill met with Admiral Pound, the First Sea Lord, and told him that this struggle had to be given priority over everything else. Churchill gave a new name to this campaign: the 'Battle of the Atlantic'. As before, his use of words created a new battle-cry. By delineating the struggle for the Atlantic as a battle, just like the Battle of France or the Battle of Britain, Churchill concentrated minds, rallied government departments and focused the public's eye on a key matter of survival.[3]

A new committee dedicated to the Battle of the Atlantic was set up. For several months it met weekly, then fortnightly, to review all the information and to come up with new ideas and policies. It was chaired by Churchill himself and consisted of the rest of the War Cabinet, the naval and air Chiefs of Staff, other key ministers, and leading scientists such as Lord

Cherwell and Professor Blackett, who brought the skills of Operational Research to bear on the subject. Churchill wrote a directive listing thirteen points to get the new committee going. It was a magisterial document calling for an offensive against the U-boat menace – as ever, Churchill wanted to take the attack to the enemy. It helped to galvanise the minds of all the key players in this new battle. It was Churchill at his aggressive, motivational and coordinating best.[4]

At the beginning of the war, the only real weapon Britain had against the U-boat menace was Asdic, which the Admiralty had developed in the inter-war years. This was a system that sent out sound pulses that bounced back when they hit something, a bit like an underwater version of radar. At the Admiralty, Churchill had been keen on Asdic. But its range was limited and it was unreliable. It could be disrupted by water turbulence caused by the wakes of ships or by depth charges. However, by 1941, new measures against the U-boats had begun to appear. One of these was a radio direction finding system that picked up the enciphered messages of U-boats as they sent signals to their headquarters near L'Orient in France. These messages could not be deciphered, but that didn't matter as the objective was simply to locate where the signals were coming from. If two or more radio stations picked up the signals then they could 'fix' on the position of the U-boat. This could be done at long range and with impressive accuracy. The system, called 'High Frequency Direction Finding', or HF/DF, was nicknamed 'Huff Duff'. The wizards were beginning to influence the war at sea as well.

Other improvements in 1941 included readjusting the depth at which depth charges ignited, the use of new forms of radar and the deployment of fast-moving destroyers as convoy escorts. Hitler also inadvertently helped the Allies in the Battle of the Atlantic by ordering Admiral Karl Doenitz, the U-boat

Commander-in-Chief, to redeploy some of his vessels to the Mediterranean. But a decisive breakthrough came in May and June 1941, when the Royal Navy captured the German *U-110* submarine intact, along with two weather ships, and seized all of their Enigma code books. With them the code-breakers at Bletchley Park were at last able to break the German Navy's encrypted messages. By deciphering key signals to and from the 'wolf packs', it was possible to confirm their locations and their intentions. The convoys could then be routed away from the waiting U-boats. This dramatically reduced shipping losses, from an average of about a quarter of a million tons per month in the first six months of 1941 to roughly half of that, and by the end of the year even less. This was a victory for this phase of the Battle of the Atlantic. But it would not last long.

Another intense battle in the Atlantic attracted far more attention. After an intelligence tip-off from local agents, an RAF photographic reconnaissance Spitfire set out from Wick in the north of Scotland on 21 May 1941 and headed for the Norwegian fjords around Bergen. The pilots of these reconnaissance aircraft were true heroes. They flew without guns, sometimes for hours at a time, over enemy-occupied territory. Speed was their only weapon, and if fighters came after them it was only their ability to get away quickly at high altitude that saved them. On this afternoon, the pilot spotted a group of German warships, went down to have a look, then saw another two warships, one very large, about to sail. When the photographs were processed and examined, it transpired that the pilot had found the *Bismarck* and its support cruiser the *Prinz Eugen* about to head into the Atlantic. The *Bismarck* was the pride of Hitler's navy and its newest addition. It was the biggest German battleship ever built and boasted eight fifteen-inch guns. At 45,000 tons it was also heavier than the largest British battleship, but just as fast. If it got among the

Atlantic convoys it could cause mayhem. One of the most famous pursuits in naval history now began. The Admiralty ordered ships from Scapa Flow and from across the Atlantic to converge on the ice-bound stretch of water between Greenland and Iceland known as the Denmark Strait, where it was reckoned the *Bismarck* would attempt to pass into the ocean.

Churchill was at Chequers that weekend following the campaign that was raging on the island of Crete. At seven o'clock on the morning of Saturday 24 May, he was woken with dreadful news. In the first engagement with the *Bismarck*, HMS *Hood* had been sunk. *Hood* was the pride of the Royal Navy, one of its latest battleships. An inquiry found that a single shell from the *Bismarck* had penetrated the *Hood*'s ammunition store and the ship had exploded. Only three men from its crew of fifteen hundred survived. Another British battleship, HMS *Prince of Wales*, was also substantially damaged by the giant shells of the *Bismarck* and its bridge was put out of action. However, although it didn't realise it, the *Prince of Wales* had managed to hit the *Bismarck*, which had slowed it down.

The signal went out 'Sink the *Bismarck*' and all available warships in the Atlantic were ordered to join the pursuit. Battleships, cruisers, aircraft carriers and destroyers now raced to converge in the seas to the south of the Denmark Strait. On the evening of the 24th, Fleet Air Arm Swordfish aircraft flying from HMS *Victorious* spotted the *Bismarck*. The Swordfish was a biplane with canvas wings held together with bracing wire and was known by its crews as the 'Stringbag'. Although it looked like a leftover from another era, it was sturdy and reliable and carried a torpedo. One of these scored a direct hit under the bridge of the *Bismarck*. Then, at this critical moment, the pursuing cruisers lost radar contact with their prey. For a whole day, the *Bismarck* could not be found, despite a frantic search. In what direction was she now heading? On the 26th, a

Catalina flying boat from Lough Erne in Northern Ireland made a lucky identification. The *Bismarck* was heading for the port of Brest for repairs. It was about 700 miles out to sea. Soon, Swordfish from HMS *Ark Royal* found the battleship and more of their torpedoes hit home. Admiral Tovey, Commander-in-Chief of the Home Fleet, was aboard HMS *King George V*, which was now in hot pursuit along with HMS *Rodney*. But these two battleships were running low on fuel and it looked like they might have to give up the chase. Churchill ordered Admiral Pound to send a cable saying, '*Bismarck* must be sunk at all costs', even if one of the British battleships had to tow the other back afterwards.[5]

By now, the damage to the *Bismarck* had caused her rudder to jam and she could sail only hopelessly round and round in a circle. On the morning of the 27th, *King George V* and *Rodney* finally closed in for the kill. The *Bismarck*'s heavy guns were still firing and caused damage to the *Rodney*, but the German ship was a sitting duck and a combination of shells and torpedoes ultimately did for her. Admiral Lutjens, the German commander, sent a final signal: 'Ship unmanoeuvrable. We shall fight to the last shell. Long live the Fuehrer!' When the *Bismarck* went down, all but about 120 of its 2000-man crew, including Lutjens, went down with it. It was a victory for the Royal Navy, although with the loss of the *Hood*, a costly one. But it did deter the *Tirpitz*, another German heavy battleship, from ever putting to sea. Instead, it spent much of the war sheltering in the fjords of Norway.

Churchill had great experience of civilian command of the Royal Navy, going back thirty years to when he was appointed First Lord of the Admiralty in 1911. Back then, he had found the men who commanded the senior service very conservative and suspicious of change. Now, in the Second World War, armed with the confidence and conviction that he knew best, he was determined to have his say in operational matters. This led to considerable strain in his dealings with the admirals, just as it did with the generals when Churchill interfered in army affairs. But Admiral Pound knew Churchill well, having worked with him since September 1939 as First Lord of the Admiralty and then as Prime Minister on the Chiefs of Staff committee. He knew how to put up with him and they formed a good partnership. In December 1940, he told Admiral Cunningham, 'The PM is very difficult these days, not that he has not always been. One has however to take a broad view as one is dealing with a man who has proved to be a magnificent leader, and one just has to put up with his childishness as long as it isn't dangerous.' Later, Pound said to A.V. Alexander, Churchill's replacement as First Lord, 'At times you could kiss his [Churchill's] feet. At others you feel you could kill him.'[6]

Admiral Sir Andrew Browne Cunningham, universally known as 'ABC', commanded the Mediterranean Fleet until late 1943. He was the most successful British naval commander of the Second World War and has been called the greatest admiral since Nelson. He was behind the air attack on the Italian fleet at Taranto and masterminded the Battle of Matapan in March 1941, when he pursued his attack upon the Italian fleet at night and three Italian heavy cruisers were sunk for no British losses. He had a natural instinct to close with and destroy the enemy at every opportunity. Even when organising the evacuation of Greece and then Crete in April and May 1941, without air cover, he told his sailors that the 'Navy must not let the Army down'. But even he was subject to Churchill's detailed directives. Cunningham found these undermining, often believing that they cast doubt on his intention to take the fight to the enemy. Mostly he bit his lip and carried out his duties as best as he could. But after an argument over the blockading of Tripoli in April 1941, he admitted he was 'beginning to feel seriously annoyed' at being told how to do his job. He felt Churchill's instructions could have 'lost the whole fleet' if circumstances had turned out differently.[7]

But Churchill never maintained his criticism of anyone for long. Not only did he warmly congratulate Cunningham but he also offered him several promotions. Churchill was good at prioritising and at seeing the overview. He was brilliant at making things happen and refusing to take 'no' for an answer. And, of course, he had to balance all the competing demands for limited war supplies and to set overall priorities which were bound to annoy whichever party lost out. But he could go too far, and his micro-instructions turned potentially friendly military chiefs against him. At times, his interference even risked the lives of soldiers, sailors and airmen. His commanders were right to resist some of his demands and to argue back. A lid was kept on these arguments during the war, but some of the frustration came out in memoirs published after the war.[8]

We have seen how Hitler's invasion of the Soviet Union, the Japanese attack on Pearl Harbor and Germany's declaration of war on the United States truly created a world at war. The pressure on the Royal Navy, fighting in so many oceans, was now immense. Three days after Pearl Harbor, on the morning of 10 December, Churchill was still reading his boxes in bed when the phone rang. It was Admiral Pound. Churchill later wrote, 'His voice sounded odd. He gave a sort of cough and gulp and at first I could not hear him quite clearly.' The news he brought was shocking. HMS *Prince of Wales* and HMS *Repulse*, two battleships that had been sent to the Far East before the attack on Pearl Harbor in a bid to deter the Japanese, had been sunk by Japanese aircraft. Churchill was distraught. He had sailed on the *Prince of Wales* only a few months before to meet Roosevelt in Newfoundland. He knew many members of the crew well. 'In all the war I never received a more direct shock,' he wrote later. 'As I turned over and twisted in bed the full horror of the news sank in upon me.' Coming so soon after the disaster of Pearl Harbor, the sinking of the two ships meant there were now no Allied capital ships left in the Pacific. Churchill reflected: 'Over all this vast expanse of waters Japan was supreme, and we everywhere were weak and naked.'[9]

The sinking of the *Prince of Wales* and the *Repulse*, along with the pursuit of the *Bismarck*, proved how vital air power was at sea. The *Bismarck* had been found and critically injured by naval aircraft. The *Prince of Wales* and the *Repulse* had left their air cover behind and had been sunk by Japanese bombers. Then, the Battle of Midway in June 1942 was fought largely between aircraft flying from carriers. It would be one of the turning-point engagements of the Pacific naval war, with US naval aviators inflicting the loss of four aircraft carriers on the Japanese Imperial Navy. But still some in the Admiralty refused to recognise or accept the change that was taking place in naval warfare. The day of the heavy battleship operating as a floating steel platform for its giant guns was passing. The future, particularly in the Pacific, lay with aircraft carriers. And the United States soon began a huge aircraft-carrier building plan. By the end of the war in the Pacific, US shipyards had built twenty-four vast, 27,000-ton Essex-class carriers. They would slowly restore US naval supremacy across the 'vast expanse' of the Pacific Ocean.

But it would be some time before the disastrous defeats in the Far East could be avenged. More than any other incident, the humiliating loss of Singapore showed up British military weakness in Asia. Singapore is a small island at the tip of the five-hundred-mile-long Malayan peninsula. In the 1920s, it had been selected as the site for the construction of a huge naval base and a fortress with heavy guns as the centrepiece of British power in the region. Giant defences with heavy artillery pointing out to sea had been constructed to defend the city and the trading hub from seaborne attack. But Singapore's land defences were left almost non-existent, and it was from the land, down the Malayan peninsula, that the Japanese came. Without doubt, this was a disastrous lack of foresight and planning, a blunder of historic proportions. Arguments have raged for years over who was to blame. Certainly Churchill was partly responsible, as he was Chancellor of the Exchequer in the late 1920s and kept a tight rein on spending when the Singapore fortress was being built. And from 1939 he was first a senior member and then the leader of a government that failed to build up proper defences. But a war fought simultaneously with Germany, Italy and Japan had simply never been envisaged, and all planning since September 1939 had focused on Europe and North Africa. Despite his own culpability, though, Churchill was furious when he was told about the lack of defence against a land attack. He wrote that he was 'staggered', and in January 1942 he fumed to the Chiefs of Staff: 'What is the point of having an island for a fortress if it is not to be made into a citadel?' He continued that the provision of adequate land defence 'was an elementary peace-time provision which it is incredible did not exist in a fortress which has been twenty years building . . . How was it that not one of you pointed this out to me at any times when these matters have been under discussion?'[10]

Thousands of Allied land troops packed into Singapore after a demoralising and exhausting retreat down the length of Malaya. General Arthur Percival was in command. Churchill instructed him to stand and fight, and said that the unit in the forefront of the battle, 18th Division, 'has a chance to make its name in history . . . The honour of the British Empire and of the British Army is at stake.'[11] But the Japanese onslaught rolled relentlessly forward, and the dispirited defenders found they were in a hopeless situation. Water supplies were running out and the one million civilian inhabitants of the city were desperate. Ammunition and fuel reserves were also disastrously low. Churchill discussed the situation with Brooke and agreed that it was unrealistic to insist on holding out any longer. Through the regional commander, they gave Percival permission to cease resistance when he saw fit. On Sunday 15 February, Percival and his commanders marched out with white flags to signal the unconditional surrender of the fortress. Sixty-two thousand men went into captivity and began years of horror and torture in Japanese prisoner-of-war and work camps where half of them would die. Churchill wrote later that it was 'the worst disaster and largest capitulation in British history'.[12]

That evening Churchill announced the fall of Singapore on the BBC. It was an emotional speech in which Churchill sought to review the progress of the war by asking: 'Are we up or down?' He insisted that with both the United States and the Soviet Union as allies, victory was ultimately certain. But he admitted that the position for Britain was severe, and that the country faced hard struggles on every front. He ended with a typical rhetorical flourish by saying that under the shadow of a disastrous defeat, it was now one of those moments

> when the British race and nation can show their quality and their genius. This is one of those moments when it can draw from the heart of misfortune the vital impulses of victory . . . We must remember that we are no longer alone. We are in the midst of a great company . . . So far we have not failed. We shall not fail now. Let us move forward steadfastly together into the storm and through the storm.

Interestingly, the following day, Harold Nicolson wrote in his diary that Churchill's broadcast was not liked: 'The country is too nervous and irritable to be fobbed off with fine phrases.'[13] At this point of the war, it seems that the Churchillian magic was no longer working.

The global war was exacting its price. Neither the Royal Navy nor the British Army was capable of fighting effectively on so many fronts over such vast distances. Furthermore, Churchill never really empathised with the war in the Far East. He had never studied Japanese society and had very little understanding of Japan's military culture. He had a tendency, which he shared with his military chiefs, constantly to underestimate this new enemy's strength. Moreover, he had never visited Australia, and so never fully grasped the Australian fear that they were now at threat from the Japanese advance as it rolled mercilessly on across the region. He just couldn't see why the Australians felt the need to withdraw their troops from the Middle East.

For Churchill, the key front in the Far East was the defence of India, the jewel in the imperial crown, a place of course very close to his heart after his service there as a young cavalry officer and his championing of imperial interests in the country ever since. Defending India meant defending Burma, and so for Churchill this was the critical aspect of the war against Japan at this stage. In January 1942, he argued that Singapore should be abandoned in order to build up the defence of Rangoon, the Burmese capital. But to his regret, under pressure of other events he did not push for this. Burma fell to the Japanese in the spring. Sensing this moment of British weakness in Asia, a few months later the Congress Party in India launched a series of demonstrations and riots against British rule. With Germany advancing into southern Russia, potentially threatening the northwest frontier of India, and with Japan strident to the east, it looked to many that British rule in India might be entering its final days.

Back in the Atlantic, a fatal blow was struck when the German Navy changed the configuration of its Enigma machines. When the *Bismarck* had sailed, five supply ships had been dispatched to various points in the Atlantic so the mighty battleship could refuel at sea. Bletchley Park deciphered their codes, learned their locations, and passed on the information. Once the *Bismarck* had been sunk, four of the supply ships were tracked down and also sunk. The fifth was spotted by chance and sunk. Admiral Doenitz, the commander of the U-boat fleet, began to get suspicious that the British were decoding his Enigma signals. Then *U-570* was captured by a British destroyer south of Iceland, and it was feared that the Royal Navy might have seized the U-boat's Enigma machine and code books (in fact, this time, it had not). An investigation into possible code-breaking was carried out by Captain Stummel, an experienced naval signals officer with an almost comic-book Prussian appearance straight out of central casting with a glass eye and a limp. Stummel concluded that it was impossible to break Enigma, but Doenitz still wanted to tighten up the whole system. As a result, a fourth rotor blade was added to the Enigma machines, meaning that the code permutations were increased by a factor of twenty-six. The new system came into effect on 1 February 1942.[14]

Overnight, this resulted in a complete blackout at Bletchley Park of the German naval codes. The code-breakers called the new, seemingly impenetrable code 'Shark'. It created a major crisis in the Battle of the Atlantic. And it coincided with a glorious period for U-boats along the the eastern seaboard of the United States. Ignoring the lessons that had been so painfully learned by the British about the need for convoys, single ships continued to sail up and down the US coast and there was not even a blackout in the port towns. The U-boat crews enjoyed the easiest hunting of the war in what they called 'the happy time'. They sunk 31 American ships in January 1942, 69 in

February, and the numbers continued to rise over the next six months until sensible precautions and a system of integrated convoys were brought in.

From the summer of 1942, the number of ships lost crossing the Atlantic also grew to frightening levels. In the six months following the launch of the new Enigma system, U-boats sank about five hundred ships in Atlantic convoys, getting on for three million tons of shipping (in addition to all the ships lost along the eastern seaboard of the United States). At this rate many more ships were being sunk than could be built to replace them. And quite apart from the terrible loss of life, so many supplies were ending up at the bottom of the Atlantic that Britain risked running out of rations and the raw materials necessary to fight the war. By now, the Germans had also broken Britain's naval cipher and their code-breakers were picking up the routes of and instructions to the convoys as they set out from North America. The Admiralty stepped up the pressure on the code-breakers at Bletchley to crack the new Enigma. In Hut 8, where Alan Turing was based, they worked day and night. But they were operating almost blind and made little progress.

By November 1942, Churchill was once again facing a potentially catastrophic situation in the Atlantic. A second committee was formed, the Cabinet Anti-U-boat Warfare Committee. Like its successful 1941 predecessor, it was chaired by Churchill and consisted of senior ministers, the service chiefs and top scientists, including Robert Watson-Watt, Lord Cherwell and Professor Blackett. The presence of the scientists was key, and the committee increasingly brought scientific thinking to bear on the Battle of the Atlantic. A series of important developments soon followed. U-boats travelling on the surface had developed the technology to pick up traditional radar signals and therefore knew when they had been spotted by Allied aircraft. They could then dive below the surface and evade an air attack.

However, new, more sophisticated forms of short-wave radar (made possible by the development of the cavity magnetron at Birmingham) could not be detected by the U-boats. This dramatically increased the ability of patrolling aircraft to attack and sink U-boats, especially in the Bay of Biscay as they set out for or returned from their missions. A new searchlight known as the 'Leigh Lamp' was fitted to the aircraft so that they once they had tracked a U-boat using the new short-wave radar they could then attack at night. A new class of frigate was developed and dispatched in groups of four as independent flotillas to hunt down U-boats. Several escort carriers were built so that convoys could be accompanied by aircraft, and this extended the range at which U-boats could be hunted down. The boffins in Operational Research did their sums and noted that the U-boats were obviously limited by the number of torpedoes they could carry. So the loss rate was proportionately lower in a big convoy than in a small one. Accordingly, the convoys were enlarged. All of this helped. But some masterstroke was still needed to overcome Shark.

In fact, the lucky breakthrough had already occurred on 30 October, but it took some time for its impact to be realised. Early that morning, a Sunderland flying boat patrolling over the eastern Mediterranean picked up a radar contact with what it reported was possibly a submarine. A group of the latest class of Royal Navy destroyers was on patrol in the area and rushed to the coordinates supplied by the plane. The ships' Asdic underwater sonars picked up the presence of a U-boat and they began to launch depth charges. Throughout the afternoon and evening, the destroyers circled and dropped more explosives into the sea. The U-boat dropped to its maximum depth, below five hundred feet, but the charges continued to come. The stench of sweat, fear and diesel fumes inside the submarine grew worse and worse. At about 10 p.m she was struck despite her depth. The captain decided he had no alternative but to surface. When *U-559* came up, one of the circling destroyers, HMS *Petard*, opened fire and holed the conning tower. The U-boat crew abandoned ship and leapt into the sea. The *Petard*'s captain realised he might be able to capture the U-boat and tow it to port. So a boarding party was quickly sent across and clambered on to the U-boat. In this party was Lieutenant Anthony Fasson, who knew the importance of secret radio documents held on each U-boat. He descended into the U-boat, where the lights were still on. It was holed badly and taking in water. In the captain's cabin, Fasson broke open a cabinet, took a key and opened a drawer where he found books and papers. With the help of another member of the boarding party, Colin Grazier, Fasson brought up several piles of these documents to the conning tower. On their third trip back down to the captain's cabin, the U-boat suddenly started to sink. The officers on the conning tower managed to get off with most of the documents, but Fasson and Grazier were caught inside by the inrush of water and went down with the U-boat. They were both awarded posthumous George Crosses for their heroism.[15]

When the code books seized by Fasson and Grazier from *U-559* finally arrived at Bletchley Park, they provided the missing link. In the language of cryptology, the code-breakers were now able to find their cribs and kisses, and use their bombes. On the morning of 13 December, a cry went up from Hut 8: 'It's out!' They had cracked the four-rotor Enigma cipher. They could now read Shark. Within days, they had identified the positions of fifteen U-boats. Within weeks, the process of diverting convoys away from the waiting wolf packs could be resumed. By January and February 1943, shipping losses had dropped to half of what they had been before the breakthrough. It was the decisive moment in the Battle of the Atlantic. But the situation was to get a lot worse before it finally got better.

In the final months of 1942, the alliance of interests that had united Britain and the United States began to diverge. Admiral King, the head of the US Navy, and General Douglas MacArthur, the charismatic commander who had led the US garrison in the Philippines, both argued forcefully that more resources were needed for the war in the Pacific. This challenged the Germany First principle that Roosevelt had agreed with Churchill soon after Pearl Harbor. And General Marshall, the US Army Chief of Staff, who had gone along with the idea of Operation Torch and the landings in North Africa, now argued that an invasion of northern France in 1943 should be a higher priority than continuing the war in the Mediterranean. Roosevelt suggested to Churchill that they should meet with Stalin to review strategy for the year ahead. But Stalin announced that at this critical point in the Battle of Stalingrad, he could not leave Moscow. Churchill and Roosevelt decided to go ahead without him, and plans were drawn up for the two men to meet at Casablanca in Morocco. The summit was fittingly given the code name 'Symbol'.

On 12 January 1943, Churchill set off in a Liberator bomber for the nine-hour flight to Morocco. He travelled with his usual small entourage, his doctor, Sir Charles Wilson, John Martin from his private staff, his detective Tommy Thompson and his valet Frank Sawyers. It was, as ever, an uncomfortable flight, and at one point Churchill awoke to find a pipe overheating and feared that it would ignite petrol fumes in the cabin. But they arrived safely and the warm winter sun of Morocco brought welcome relief. 'Bright sunshine, oranges, eggs and razor-blades,' wrote Martin, all four items being in short supply in Britain at the time.[16] A small, discreet hotel had been taken over on the coast to the north of Casablanca. Churchill and Roosevelt had their own private villas, and the whole compound was sealed off and guarded by US Marines. Attending the conference were the British and American Chiefs of Staff, who met separately each day and then usually had two daily meetings together as the Combined Chiefs. The British had prepared their position and their arguments well. Churchill and his Chiefs of Staff had talked through all the key points and were now in agreement. The Americans were less well prepared and indeed had not even agreed on a unified position.

The conference formally opened on 13 January and the divisions between the military leaders immediately became evident. The Americans wanted to plan for an invasion of Northern Europe. The British wanted to concentrate on victory in the Mediterranean and considered an invasion of France in 1943 too great a risk. They argued for postponement until 1944, when more resources would be available and the U-boat threat should have been defeated. For several days, the two sides were locked in disagreement as to their strategy for the following year. General Brooke recorded in his diary the 'very heated' meetings with the Americans which seemed to be making 'no progress', and on the fifth day he wrote: 'A desperate day! We are further from obtaining agreement than we ever were!'[17] The British chiefs feared the Americans were already reallocating resources from Europe to the war in the Pacific. The Americans thought the British were obsessed with the Mediterranean for reasons of self-interest and traditional imperial concerns to retain the Suez Canal as a link to India.

While all of this was being thrashed out, Churchill and Roosevelt were getting on famously. The President seemed more relaxed than his Chief of Staff Marshall on the issue of the Mediterranean strategy. In return, Churchill responded to American fears that Britain would pull out of the war as soon as Germany was defeated by pledging to continue the fight against Japan. The warm friendship between the Prime Minister and the President blossomed in the winter sunshine.

And Churchill was in his element, with his military chiefs around him, seeing Roosevelt regularly, and being at the heart of a global war machine. Harold Macmillan, who joined the conference a few days after it had started, wrote: 'I have never seen him in better form. He ate and drank enormously all the time, settled huge problems, played bagatelle and bezique by the hour, and generally enjoyed himself.'[18]

On 18 January, the Combined Chiefs finally reached an agreement on strategy. Many of the Americans felt comfortable dealing with Field Marshal Sir John Dill who had been head of the British Mission in Washington for over a year and who was on excellent terms with Marshall. He played a central part in bringing both sides together. The Combined Chiefs presented their findings to Churchill and Roosevelt, who enthusiastically endorsed the new plans. Most of what the well-prepared British team had set out to achieve had been accepted. Defeat of Germany was still the first priority. Overcoming the U-boat threat and winning the Battle of the Atlantic was the leading objective. The Mediterranean strategy was endorsed, with agreement to invade Sicily once the Allies had finally expelled the Afrika Korps from North Africa. America agreed to support a British invasion of Burma later in the year. In Europe, Operation Bolero, the build-up of US troops in Britain, was to go ahead with maximum urgency. And the bombing offensive against Germany was to continue with new vigour. Later in the conference, Roosevelt added the condition that the Allies would accept only the 'unconditional surrender' of both Germany and Japan. This was agreed by Churchill on the spot and became the ultimate Allied war objective.

For the British planners, the summit was an enormous triumph. A joint strategy had been agreed by negotiation between the military chiefs, and the British had persuaded the Americans of the strengths of their case. It had not been handed down by edict from the US Commander-in-Chief and the British Prime Minister. In many ways, Casablanca represented the high water mark of British influence over the planning of the war. During 1943, the vast scale of the US war effort would over-take Britain and leave Churchill and the British chiefs as very much the junior partner in the alliance. But now, fittingly, Churchill and Roosevelt left Casablanca and travelled together to Marrakech, a city that Churchill had fallen in love with years before on holiday. The Prime Minister climbed to the roof of the villa that had been requisitioned for them to watch the beauti-ful sunset over the snow-capped Atlas mountains. He insisted that Roosevelt must see it too, and the disabled President was literally carried to the roof by two of his staff. Together they watched as the light magnificently changed colour in front of them. Churchill murmured that 'this was the most lovely spot in the whole world'. They concluded their business over dinner by drafting various communiqués, including a summary for Stalin of what had been agreed. And then they sang songs together.[19] The following morning, the President left for the United States and Churchill took a rare break. He painted the view of the mountains from the roof that he and Roosevelt had so admired the evening before. It was the only painting Churchill produced during the whole war.

Throughout 1942, U-boats had been launched at an average of eighteen vessels each month. By early 1943, Doenitz had about a hundred operating in the North Atlantic. There was a zone in the centre of the ocean that aircraft could not reach from either the United States or Britain. Inside this gap the U-boats continued their killing spree. Churchill came under consider-able pressure from the Admiralty to divert the big, four-engined RAF aircraft like the Liberator from Bomber Command to Coastal Command in order to fly sorties over the middle of the Atlantic to protect the convoys. But he and his advisers remained convinced that in the absence of a second front to satisfy Stalin, the bombing offensive was the principal method available to them to destroy the Nazi war machine. The Admiralty's request for the long-range aircraft was turned down. Instead, more bombing raids were made on the U-boat pens along the French coast. But the concrete roofs were so massive that despite literally thousands of bombing missions, not a single bomb ever penetrated to the U-boat docks below.

In March 1943, the sheer number of U-boats meant that shipping losses increased to over 600,000 tons, an appallingly high figure. Britain could not survive for long with this rate of loss. The Admiralty calculated that in the first twenty days of this month, communications between the Old World and the New nearly broke down completely. Stephen Roskill, the official naval historian, wrote: 'in the early spring of 1943 we had a very narrow escape from defeat in the Atlantic . . . had we suffered such a defeat, history would have judged that the main cause would have been the lack of two more squadrons of very long range aircraft for convoy escort duties'.[20] Churchill's adherence to the bombing offensive very nearly led to defeat in the Battle of the Atlantic.

The advances in science came to the rescue just in time. All of the developments that had been taking place at last began to kick in. With Bletchley Park now able to read the German naval signals again, with the new short-wave radar systems picking up more and more U-boats on the surface, and with the new escort groups in place, the hunters became the hunted. Aircraft patrolling the Bay of Biscay were spotting and sinking U-boats as they set off on or returned from their missions. In March and April, twenty-seven U-boats were sunk in the Atlantic, more than half by attack from the air. In May, forty were sunk, eighteen of them by air attack. In total, this amounted to over 50 per cent of the available U-boat fleet. No force could sustain this rate of loss. On 22 May, Doenitz called off the campaign and ordered the withdrawal of his U-boats from the North Atlantic. The convoy code-numbered SC130, which reached Liverpool on 23 May, was the last to be seriously menaced by U-boats.

The sea-lanes from North America to Britain had been cleared of the U-boat menace. It was as vital a turning point as Stalingrad or El Alamein. It was inconceivable that an invasion of Europe could have been mounted without mastery of the North Atlantic. And the great shipyards of North America were now working at full throttle, many producing what were known as 'Liberty Ships'. These were basic transport vessels that could be prefabricated in several parts. Henry Kaiser, the shipbuilding magnate, realised that speed of construction was of the essence, and that as the shipyards expanded much of the available labour was going to be unskilled. The genius of Kaiser's idea of prefabricating the ships was that many of the parts could be produced at inland factories, then transported by railway to shipyards on the coast for assembly. A giant ship's hull could be designed in a series of subsections, and new techniques like electric arc-welding were used to bond the plates together. This was faster than riveting and used less steel. More than 300,000 men and women were employed in the US shipyards up and down the east and west coasts. Many of them had never been near a shipyard in their lives before. Just as 'Rosie the Riveter' became the media darling of the aircraft manufacturing plants, so 'Wendy the Welder' became the generic name for women workers in the traditionally male-dominated world of heavy engineering and shipbuilding. The whole manufacturing process of the Liberty Ships was one of the most remarkable examples of mass production ever achieved. The speed at which these basic cargo ships could be assembled and launched got faster and faster. The first of the Liberty Ships took about 150 days from laying the keel to launch, itself impressively fast in shipbuilding terms. As techniques improved and systems became even more efficient, the time came down to fifty days. Then the American media got interested and a friendly rivalry was set up between the shipyards. Average production time fell to just ten days, and the fastest of all, the *Robert E. Parry*, was built at a yard in California in November 1942 in an incredible four days and fifteen hours. This speed of production was exceptional but in total 2700 Liberty Ships were manufactured during the war.

The U-boat threat was defeated by the application of scientific ideas at sea and by the revolutionary concept of mass-producing ships in America. As Professor Blackett put it: 'the anti-submarine campaign of 1943 was waged under closer scientific control than any other campaign in the history of the British Armed Forces'.[21] In July 1943, a key milestone was passed when the number of ships being built and launched exceeded the volume of shipping being lost. The War Lab had played its part and the Battle of the Atlantic had been won.

8

Bombing

On the night of 19 March 1940, a group of twenty Hampdens and thirty Whitleys of Bomber Command launched the first RAF bombing raid of the war on Germany. Their target was the German seaplane base of Hornum on the island of Sylt, a few miles west of the Danish border. From there, Luftwaffe seaplanes had been dropping mines in the North Sea. There was great excitement among the bomber crews, who had spent the first few months of the war doing nothing more than dropping propaganda leaflets over Germany. Such was the fascination with this first bombing raid that late that night in the House of Commons, Prime Minister Neville Chamberlain interrupted the session to announce that RAF bombers were obliterating the German airbase. Members cheered. The newspapers responded with a brace of headlines: 'Hangars And Oil Tanks Ablaze' and 'Night Sky Lit Up'. At last the RAF was dishing it out to the Nazis.

However, when the first aerial photographs of Hornum came back on the day after the raid they told a very different and rather surprising story. The photo interpreters could find no damage whatsoever to the hangars. The Heinkel seaplanes were still on their slipways and the oil tanks were all extant. The interpreters examined the photos over and over again. They considered the possibilities. Had the Luftwaffe managed a remarkable overnight feat of clearing up the destruction? Slowly, they came to an inescapable conclusion. Despite the enthusiastic post-flight debriefings of the crew, who told of blazing hangars and workshops below, the RAF bombers had entirely missed their targets. As a propaganda coup, the Germans invited neutral journalists to visit the base and see for themselves that no damage had been done. But this went unreported in Britain.

The RAF had learned its first depressing lesson about bombing at night. With the rudimentary navigation techniques then available, it was almost impossible to fly for seven or eight hours across a blacked-out and hostile Europe and hit the correct target. Navigation was mostly by sight, identifying landmarks below and charting a course from them. Obviously, cloud cover made this difficult. And bombers flew at high altitude to be above anti-aircraft defences and searchlights; dropping down low to identify a landmark brought obvious risks. Occasionally, crews flying above the clouds could use a sextant to read the stars as a guide to their location, but this took time and required flying on a consistent and level straight line for longer than most pilots felt comfortable doing. From the start of a flight, when an aircraft charted its course, the wind could blow it astray and evasive action like weaving could take it further off course. This was why the Germans had developed their network of *Knickebein* beams to guide bombers to their targets. But the RAF had nothing like this, so the consequences of its early bombing missions were mostly embarrassing.[1]

As soon as Churchill became Prime Minister and the war entered its critical phase, there was much to be done despite the difficulties. RAF bombers were assigned targets of rail junctions and airbases, and set off in their slow-moving aircraft to try to hit them. Mostly they failed. One RAF bomber in late May 1940 was sent to bomb a German airfield in Holland. It hit an electrical storm over the North Sea and became hopelessly lost. Eventually, totally confused, the crew identified what they thought was the Rhine estuary, found what they believed to be the target airfield, dropped their bombs on it, and returned home. When they found themselves over Liverpool, they realised something had gone dreadfully wrong. They had mistaken the Thames estuary for the Rhine and had bombed an RAF airfield by mistake. Bomber crews usually carried out their missions using 'ETA', dropping their bombs at the Estimated Time of Arrival over their target, but this meant they were often not just miles off their targets, but were sometimes tens or even hundreds of miles off course.[2]

Churchill, as ever, closely followed the progress of the bombing attacks on Germany and raised a host of questions and suggestions. Within five days of becoming Prime Minister he authorised a raid on the Ruhr industrial district. He asked what were the types of bombs in use and what improvements could be made to the aircraft? It will be remembered that he had orchestrated the first bombing attacks by primitive canvas and wire aircraft in the First World War, and he had been the minister in charge of the Royal Air Force after the end of that war. During the inter-war years, the RAF needed to find a role to secure its survival as a force that was independent of the army and navy. It did this by emphasising its ability to strike at the enemy. There were two elements to this: to undermine the ability or will of the enemy nation to fight by hitting their homeland (this was known as 'strategic bombing'); and to hit the enemy's armies, ammunition dumps, supply lines and operating ability in the field (known as 'tactical bombing'). This was the era when it was believed 'the bomber will always get through', as Stanley Baldwin had said, so maintaining a strong bomber force was intended to deter an enemy from making a first strike. Air Marshal Sir Hugh Trenchard, Chief of the Air Staff, preached this doctrine and largely defined the shape of the inter-war RAF, which had twice as many bombers as fighters. In the final years of peace, it was realised at the eleventh hour that the RAF's fighter capability had to be rapidly built up to defend Britain from enemy bombers. It was ironic that the first great success of the RAF in the war was not in the offensive bombing of German military targets, but in the purely defensive action of Sir Hugh Dowding's Fighter Command in fending off the attacks of Goering's Luftwaffe and preventing a German invasion in the summer and autumn of 1940. The first RAF heroes were not the bomber crews but the dashing fighter pilots who streaked across the sky in their Spitfires and Hurricanes.

Churchill instinctively recognised that the role of the bomber was to take the offensive action that he so dearly wanted to pursue. In early September 1940, while the Battle of the Britain was still raging above southern England, he wrote in a directive to ministers:

The Navy can lose us the war, but only the Air Force can win it . . . The Fighters are our salvation, but the Bombers alone provide the means of victory. We must therefore develop the power to carry an ever-increasing volume of explosives to Germany, so as to pulverise the entire industry and scientific structure on which the war effort and economic life of the enemy depend.[3]

But Churchill's ambitions for RAF Bomber Command would be totally impossible to achieve for some time to come.

For many months, photographic reconnaissance of sites that had been bombed continued to show that the damage caused was negligible. This was not what the chiefs of Bomber Command wanted to hear and they did not believe it could be true. They came up with a variety of reasons to disprove the photographic evidence. The photographs were of too small a scale to be able to spot the damage. The photo interpreters did not know what they were looking for. Some damage assessments came back with a note in the margin saying simply: 'I do not accept this report.' But the morale of the bomber crews who nightly put their lives at risk for what seemed no tangible gain slowly deteriorated. Some parts of Bomber Command did begin seriously to explore ways of improving navigational techniques. But overall, a growing sense of disappointment pervaded the missions. No one was particularly to blame for this. Years of financial cutbacks throughout the 1930s were once again showing through, just as they had in the army and navy. The RAF had poor aircraft. The Hampden could fly at only 155 m.p.h. The bombers could carry only small bomb loads that were largely ineffective even if, by some near miracle, they hit their target. And the crews lacked the navigational training to fly across hundreds of miles of occupied territory at night, often in freezing conditions and without properly pressurised cabins. It was hopeless to expect much from them, so although each night the BBC would broadcast that bombers were striking such-and-such armaments factory, the horrible reality was that it was mostly a waste of time. Frequently, from the dispersal of the bombs dropped, German Intelligence could not only fail to work out what the RAF's targets had been, but even which part of Germany they had been trying to hit.

Lord Cherwell, as we have seen, was never far from Churchill's side as his all-purpose scientific adviser. In late 1940, the Prof began to raise doubts in Churchill's mind about the accuracy of the RAF's bombing. The following year, Churchill instructed the Prof and a team from his statistical branch to carry out an investigation. David Butt of the War Cabinet secretariat analysed more than six hundred aerial photographs of post-bombing damage taken in June and July 1941. This analysis confirmed Cherwell's worst fears. When the moon was full, only 40 per cent of planes dropped their bombs within five miles of the target. In the absence of moonlight, a mere 7 per cent, only one out of every fifteen aircraft, got their bombs within five miles of the target. The Butt Report, as it was called, was immediately repudiated by the air marshals. Cherwell agreed that it was not a strictly accurate guide, but he argued that the figures 'are sufficiently striking to emphasise the supreme importance of improving our navigational methods'.[4] Churchill later wrote: 'The air photographs showed how little damage was being done. It also appeared that the crews knew this, and were discouraged by the poor results of so much hazard. Unless we could improve on this there did not seem much use in continuing night bombing.' He forwarded the report to the new Chief of the Air Staff, Air Chief Marshal Sir Charles Portal, with a covering note: 'This is a very serious paper, and seems to require your most urgent attention. I await your proposals for action.'[5] The future of the whole bombing campaign was in the balance.

In truth there was nothing much that Bomber Command could do at this point in time. The technology for improved navigational aids still lay in the future. The only realistic response was to abandon the concept of night-time precision bombing of specific factories or railway yards and to opt instead for the wholesale smashing of German cities on an indiscriminate basis, known as 'area bombing' or more colloquially as 'carpet bombing'. In September, Portal told the Prime Minister that if he were given a force of four thousand heavy bombers, he could bomb different cities each night and 'break Germany in six months'. This was dangerously close to the wild claims made by Goering in the summer and autumn of 1940 about what his Luftwaffe could do to Britain.

Churchill was in a dilemma. He had largely lost confidence in bombing as a key strategic offensive weapon against Germany. He wrote to Portal: 'It is very disputable whether bombing by itself will be a decisive factor in the present war. On the contrary, all that we have learnt since the war began shows that its effects, both physical and moral, are greatly exaggerated.'[6] After all, it was known that the Blitz had failed to destroy Britain's war economy and in the long run it had only increased the resolve of the British people to fight on. On the other hand, with the Soviet Union now in the war fighting for its survival, it was clear that one of the few ways in which Britain could help its new ally was by striking back through a bombing offensive to undermine the German war machine. The Chiefs of Staff, with Churchill's backing, had repeatedly stated that this was a major objective of the British war effort. Could it be abandoned now? And who would explain such a reversal of policy to Stalin?

The debate between Churchill and Portal continued. Then, on the night of 7 November 1941, four hundred aircraft were sent by Bomber Command to attack Berlin, the Ruhr and Cologne. Thirty-seven of the bombers, nearly one-tenth of the force, were shot down or failed to return. This was an unsustainable level of loss. Air Marshal Sir Richard Peirse, the commander of Bomber Command, was a guest at Chequers the following night. Churchill told Peirse how worried he was by the rate of casualties. He went further and said to Peirse that 'he did not think we had done any damage to the enemy lately'. Churchill insisted there must be a break in the bombing offensive in order for Bomber Command to 're-gather their strength for the spring'.[7] This matter was discussed by the War Cabinet and it was agreed that it was pointless to fritter away the bombing fleet in a series of small and largely ineffectual raids. It now became official policy to rest Bomber Command through the winter months. This was a vote of no-confidence in bombing as a strategy to win the war, as well as a vote of no-confidence in Peirse, who was soon removed from his command and sent to the Far East. Churchill needed a new, more dynamic figure to take over Bomber Command and realise the potential of the bombing campaign against Germany.

Arthur Harris was appointed as the new head of Bomber Command in February 1942. Harris shared many of Churchill's traits. He wanted to take the war to the enemy. He believed totally that you had to take offensive action to win wars. Harris was also a disciple of Trenchard and his belief in the power of bombing. He wanted to bomb German cities as powerfully and as destructively as the strength of his force would allow. This was how to win the war, he believed, hence his nickname, 'Bomber' Harris, although his crews knew him as the 'Butcher', usually abbreviated to 'Butch'. He was single-minded about this task – to the point of alienating other senior RAF figures who wanted him to take a more all-round view of the war. He opposed sending his valuable heavy bombers on long-range patrols to hunt down U-boats on the grounds that these were distractions to the main task. (He did let up slightly when it was pointed out to him that if Britain did not win the Battle of the Atlantic, there would be no petrol for his bombers.) Churchill liked his commitment and his realisation that tough things had to be done to win the war. Harris has been a controversial figure ever since, but he was a resolute commander who did not flinch when his own losses mounted horribly, or at the thought of the destruction his crews rained down on German cities. The nature of his character is revealed by a story of his pleasure in driving his two-seater Bentley fast on the roads into and out of London. One evening he was stopped by a traffic policeman who said reproachfully, 'You might have killed someone, sir.' Harris replied sombrely, 'Young man, I kill thousands of people every night.' He seemed to revel in the hard-man role he had cast for himself.[8]

Bomber Command headquarters, where Harris worked, was at High Wycombe in Buckinghamshire, not far from Chequers. In March 1942, Harris paid his first visit to the Prime Minister's country residence and spent an evening with Churchill. The two got on well, and Harris would have many more invites over the next two years, sometimes for an evening of chat, sometimes for a weekend as part of a larger company. This direct access to Churchill's ear was an important element in Harris's growing stature. And it generated much resentment, particularly among the admirals, who thought that Harris was advancing the cause of his command at their expense. But Churchill had confidence in Harris, and Harris took inspiration from their regular conversations. He later wrote: 'The worse the state of the war was, the greater was the support, enthusiasm, encouragement and constructive criticism from this extraordinary man . . . He did not mind your expressing views contrary to his own but he was difficult to argue with for the simple reason that he seldom seemed to listen long to sides of the question other than his own.'[9] Harris soon discovered, as others had done before, that the best way to get a new point across was to write a short two- or three-page note on a subject. The rapport Harris built up with Churchill was based on mutual respect rather than on real friendship, and it waned towards the end of the war. But like General Brooke as CIGS, Harris would stay in his post until final victory, and he was another core member of Churchill's War Lab.

In his first few months as head of Bomber Command, Harris orchestrated a few stunts to publicise and promote his new role. In April, a force of low-flying heavy bombers struck deep inside Germany at the U-boat engine production plant in Augsburg. For his daring and courage, the leader of the raid, Squadron Leader J.D. Nettleton, won the Victoria Cross. Then, after getting Churchill's agreement at a nocturnal session at Chequers, Harris launched the first 'thousand-bomber' raid of the war on the night of 30 May 1942 against the city of Cologne. This was lauded by the press and the newsreels, who were delighted that Britain was hitting back hard. Headlines talked of 'The Biggest Bombing Raid In History'. Both the Americans and the Russians were impressed. In fact, Harris had managed to rustle up the magic number of a thousand bombers only by deploying all his reserves, including every available training plane. Instructors as well as trainees flew on the raid. It was a huge risk but it paid off. Morale in Bomber Command shot up overnight. The damage to Cologne, though less than was claimed, was considerable. However, two later huge raids proved far less effective. A thousand bombers tried to hit the Krupp armaments factories at Essen in the Ruhr in June. But the target was more difficult to find and the bombs were widely dispersed. And nine hundred bombers targeted Bremen at the end of June, inflicting severe damage on the port but suffering substantial losses, too. Harris had put Bomber Command on the map, but raids on this scale could not be sustained and he had to settle for far more modest sorties for some time to come.

In early 1942, just as Harris was taking over at Bomber Command, there was an intensification of the debate about the bombing offensive. Cherwell once again took the initiative and instituted an investigation led by two scientists, Solly Zuckerman and J.D. Bernal. Zuckerman, as we have seen, had already carried out research into the impact of bombs on human beings and on their physical surroundings. Now, he and Bernal studied the German bombing of Birmingham and Hull with a view to finding some general principles for the impact of a bombing campaign upon urban centres. Cherwell kept in close touch with Zuckerman and Bernal, but before they had completed their research, he wrote a paper which he sent to Churchill on 30 March. In this he claimed that one ton of bombs dropped on a built-up area demolished between twenty and forty houses and turned '100–200 people out of house and home'. So if each of Britain's new heavy bombers were to drop about forty tons of bombs during its service life, then each would make between four thousand and eight thousand people homeless. He then calculated that if only half of the bombers in a force of ten thousand aircraft dropped their bombs on the biggest cities in the German Reich, 'about one third of the German population' would be made homeless. He concluded that the area bombing of German cities could therefore 'break the spirit of the people' and prompt a breakdown of communications and supply lines and the collapse of public services.[10] In other words, bombing could definitely help the Allies win the war against Germany.

Cherwell's paper is often said to be the prime document that persuaded Churchill to restart the bombing offensive. In fact, it provoked great controversy at the time and has continued to do so ever since. The debate about the impact of bombing opened up the old rivalry between Cherwell and Tizard, whose disagreement had first erupted nearly two years before, in the summer of 1940. Tizard criticised the mathematics by which Cherwell had made his calculations and challenged his assumption that there would ever be a force of ten thousand heavy bombers. He told Cherwell: 'I am afraid that I think the way you put the facts as they appear to you is extremely misleading and may lead to entirely wrong decisions being reached with a consequent disastrous effect on the war. I think, too, that you have got your facts wrong.' Professor Blackett, the doyen of Operational Research, also weighed into the debate. He said he thought Cherwell's estimate of what could be achieved was 'at least six hundred percent too high'.[11]

Cherwell wasn't the type to take a rebuke like this sitting down. He had Churchill's ear and he continued to press his case, claiming that his figures had merely been presented in a way that meant Churchill did not need to do the mathematical calculations himself. As we have seen, this was typical of the way Cherwell presented his papers to a Prime Minister who found mathematical explanations too complex to follow. In the end, of course, it was Churchill who had to take the final decision when it came to resolving the argument for competing claims to limited resources. And he took the side of Cherwell and Harris, against Tizard and Blackett. The official historians of the bombing offensive concluded that, because of his position when he submitted this note, 'Cherwell's intervention was of great importance. It did much to insure the concept of strategic bombing in its hour of crisis.'[12] The bombing offensive against Germany was on again. Area bombing was the new policy, and this time Bomber Command had a combative leader with great ambitions for his growing fleet of bombers.

There is no doubt that part of what lay behind Churchill's decision was his desire to show Stalin and the Soviet people that, while there was no second front in Europe, at least Britain was striking hard at the heart of the Nazi war machine. Accordingly, Churchill decided to make a personal visit to Stalin and to explain this face to face to the Soviet war leader. After his momentous visit to Cairo in August 1942 when he set the 8th Army on the path to victory (see Chapter 6), Churchill took an overnight flight in his uncomfortable Liberator bomber to Teheran. From there, he took another long, gruelling flight to

Moscow, skirting the fighting that was raging below. He was accompanied by Averill Harriman, representing the US President, and the British Chiefs of Staff. The Soviets had been pleading for a second front to be opened in France, so Churchill's principal mission was to explain why this could not be done, and to sell Operation Torch and the importance of the renewed bombing campaign to the Russian leader. It was, as Churchill confessed to Roosevelt, 'a somewhat raw job', but he wanted to express his personal support by taking the long, arduous route to Moscow in order to explain exactly what Stalin's allies were doing to help him in the gargantuan struggle playing out on the Eastern Front.

A few hours after his arrival in Moscow, on the evening of 12 August, Churchill had his first meeting with Stalin in the Kremlin. It lasted four hours. Stalin told Churchill about the immensity of the struggle the Red Army were engaged in along the Eastern Front. He said German troops were now beginning to press on the industrial city of Stalingrad on the river Volga. For his part, Churchill wanted to get all the bad news about not opening a second front over with first. As he listened, Stalin became glum and grew restless. He cheered up when he heard about the plans for the Torch landings in North Africa. When they went on to discuss the bombing offensive, Stalin said that he attached the greatest importance to this strategy and that he knew the air raids were having a tremendous effect upon morale in Germany. Churchill promised he would press on with the raids and would 'show no mercy' to the German people. Stalin smiled and said, 'May God prosper this undertaking.'[13] So far, so good.

The next meeting did not go well. It started at 11 p.m. in the Kremlin. Stalin accused Churchill and the British Army of being frightened of the Germans, and claimed that Britain and the United States had failed to deliver the supplies promised to

Russia, keeping the best for themselves. Then he accused Britain and the United States of reneging on firm promises to launch the second front in Europe. Churchill stood his ground and disagreed point by point. The dictator was not used to being contradicted. At one point, Churchill raised his voice and said in a passionate outburst that he had come a long way to establish good relations with Stalin and that victory must not be undermined by disagreements that could benefit only the enemy. Before this could be translated, Stalin responded by saying that he liked the tone of Churchill's speech. But it was clear that Stalin's position had hardened, and this did not look good for Anglo-Soviet relations.

The following night, Stalin hosted a dinner for his guests. A lavish banquet was served and several toasts were washed down with vodka. Churchill sat on Stalin's right, and although no serious business was done, the Soviet leader seemed in a far more friendly mood. The issue of Churchill's hostility to the birth of the Soviet Union came up and Churchill openly admitted this had been the case. Stalin smiled and Churchill asked, 'Have you forgiven me?' Stalin replied, 'All that is in the past and the past belongs to God.'[14] When Churchill left, exhausted, at 1.30 p.m. (Stalin's late-night hours even outdid his own), Stalin insisted on escorting him through endless corridors and staircases to the Kremlin's front door. The British Ambassador had to trot to keep up with the two leaders, and he later said that he had never known Stalin do this for any other guest.

During the next day, General Brooke, Air Marshal Arthur Tedder and General Wavell (who was there because he spoke fluent Russian) had detailed talks with their Soviet military counterparts. The discussions did not go well. When the British delegation asked for information, they were repeatedly told that the Soviet chiefs had 'no authority' to release such details. Instead, they kept repeating that they wanted a second front *now*. After the openness and informality of relations with their American allies, these talks were a very different affair. Brooke was particularly annoyed by the Russians and brought the series of meetings to an abrupt conclusion.

On the final evening, Churchill went once again to the Kremlin for a last hour with Stalin at 7 p.m. As Churchill got up to leave, Stalin became very chummy and invited him back to his private apartment for some drinks. There, in the Soviet leader's private dining room, his aged housekeeper began to assemble a meal. Stalin's pretty young daughter appeared and laid the table while her father uncorked an impressive array of bottles. With just Stalin, Molotov (the Soviet Foreign Minister) and Churchill present, each with his own translator, the two war leaders and one-time political foes talked on into the night. Occasionally they argued but always in a good-humoured way. No doubt the quality of the wine helped. Churchill talked about one of his pet projects, to invade northern Norway in order to create an easier passage for the Arctic convoys. They discussed the collectivisation of Soviet farming that Stalin had forced through in the pre-war years at the cost of millions of lives. At about 1 a.m., a huge suckling pig was brought in. Churchill finally left at about two-thirty. He felt that his mission to Moscow had been accomplished. He had built up a rapport with the Soviet leader.

As Churchill departed by air at dawn, only a couple of hours later, he was exhausted and, unusually for him, he had a split-ting headache. Over the next few days, he had time to reflect on his meetings in Moscow. He had been seriously offended by some of what Stalin had said, especially about Britain's cow-ardice in the face of the Nazis. And he was genuinely puzzled by the fluctuations in Stalin's mood. On the other hand, he appreciated that, with the Wehrmacht only fifty miles from Moscow and the huge struggle with Nazi Germany nearing its climax, the news he had brought had been a bitter blow to the Soviet leader. More than anything, Churchill now realised that the Anglo-American leadership must push their war machines and their men to the maximum in their campaigns in North Africa and in the bombing of Germany. The bombing offensive now took on a political role as well as being a military tool. Everything that could be done must be done to help their Soviet allies defeat the Nazi invaders.

So Churchill returned to Britain with renewed enthusiasm for the bombing offensive. Within weeks, he had agreed to increase Bomber Command from thirty-two to fifty operational squadrons. He gave support to Harris in his internal struggles within the RAF. But once again, conflicting priorities held back any dramatic developments and no further thousand-bomber raids took place that year. The war against the U-boats continued to raise questions about the deployment of long-range bombers over the Atlantic. And the war in North Africa dominated Churchill's and the nation's attention. Furthermore, the promised arrival of large numbers of US bombers failed to materialise during 1942. All the bombing raids on Germany that Churchill had eagerly boasted about to Stalin were carried out by the RAF with their meagre, but growing, resources.

Most importantly for the future of the bombing campaign, a series of significant developments took place in 1942. First, there were major advances in technology that enabled RAF bombers to find their targets with far greater accuracy. In an attack upon the Renault factory near Paris, in March 1942, a new navigational aid called 'Gee' was used for the first time. Gee had been developed by scientists at the Telecommunication Research Establishment (TRE) near Swanage in Dorset. Every Sunday, open meetings were held at TRE between operational flying officers and the scientists, and everyone, regardless of rank or status, was encouraged to speak their mind. They were known as the 'Sunday Soviets'. At one of these meetings in June 1940, a senior staff officer had deplored the inadequate results of the RAF's bombing missions. In response, one of the scientists came up with an old notion that had been partly developed before the war for sending out a set of pulses as a blind-landing aid. A group set to work to improve this system and eventually came up with Gee. A series of pulses was sent from three transmitting towers in southern Britain. As the signals from the first tower hit those from the other two, they created a lattice-type network extending for a few hundred miles across Northern Europe. A navigator on board his aircraft could then pick up these signals with a cathode-ray tube and read where he was on a chart that marked the grid of beams across Europe. Gee was accurate to within two miles. This was an enormous advance over navigating by identifying landmarks below or taking readings from the stars above. Gee was also better than the German *Knickebein* system and its follow-ups because the British grid covered the whole of Europe and the beams were not intended to guide aircraft to one particular spot. But the RAF was worried about one of its planes coming down over occupied Europe and the cathode-ray tube and accompanying charts falling into enemy hands. The Germans might then be able to figure out how the system worked and could even try to distort the pulses. So an elaborate deception was set up whereby it was leaked to the Germans through double agents working in Britain that the RAF now had a 'J' system (which sounded close to 'G'), based on the German *Knickebein* beams. A set of meaningless beams was duly transmitted and German Intelligence spent some time tracking them down and twisting them, while failing to identify the pulses that made up the new Gee system. Gee was successfully used for some years and remained in use after the war with the RAF and as an aid for shipping.

In addition to the development of this navigational aid, the RAF also needed a more precise blind-bombing guide, which would enable aircraft not just to bomb one part of a city, but to find and bomb a particular factory or military installation. Once again, it was the scientists at TRE who came up with the solution. It was called 'Oboe'. This system was based on two radar transmitters, one in Norfolk, known as 'Cat', and one in Kent, known as 'Mouse'. The two stations were linked and transmitted synchronised pulses. The pilot flew along the Cat beam across Europe towards the target. The operators of the Mouse beam could follow the aircraft and calculate its precise location. When it was over the target, they would transmit a signal to the plane's navigator, who would drop the bombs. Oboe had an accuracy of about a hundred yards, which was of a different order to anything that had gone before. When Oboe became operational in 1943, it was used by accurate Pathfinder aircraft, like the super-fast de Havilland Mosquito. These aircraft identified and hit the target with flares or incendiaries that the other bombers would then use as location finders.

Both Gee and Oboe were real achievements for the scientists, more strikes for Churchill's wizards. But they had their limitations. Gee had a range of about 450 miles from the British coast and Oboe about 250 miles. This was good enough to hit the Ruhr and many other prime targets, but not enough to penetrate the whole of occupied Europe. Something better was still needed.

Despite his call for improved navigational aids, Cherwell himself was not involved with the development of Gee and Oboe. He was however closely involved with the development of a new radar mapping system code-named 'H2S'. This was carried inside aircraft and at first utilised the revolutionary cavity magnetron, which enabled radars to work on a wavelength of 10cm, rather than 150cm as before. Aircraft that were

equipped with it could pick up buildings and the general landscape much more clearly. A rotating radar scanner was fitted in
a cupola below the belly of a heavy bomber and the navigator
read the landscape below on a circular screen. First trials took
place at the end of 1941. The team trying to develop this radar
mapping system encountered immense difficulties, including
the crash of the prototype bomber in which it was installed.
Many of the leaders of the research team were killed in that
accident. More delays followed when the RAF chiefs decided
that the cavity magnetron was so secret that it must not
fall into the hands of the enemy and therefore could not be
flown over occupied territory in case the plane crashed and it
was recovered by German scientists. So an alternative device,
the Klystron, was developed instead that was closer to known
existing German technology. The debate within the Air Staff
continued as to whether the concept of radar mapping could
ever work effectively, but Cherwell continued to support it and,
on his advice, so did Churchill. In June 1942, Churchill issued
one of his typical instructions to the Secretary for the Air, calling
for far greater effort in the manufacture of the new equipment
and the training of crews in its use. He insisted that 'nothing
should be allowed to stand in the way of this'.[15] The many
doubters would almost certainly have killed off the development of the ground-mapping radar system without Cherwell's
enthusiasm and Churchill's support. It finally came into operational use in 1943 and refinements continued to be made
throughout the war.

During 1942, another key development took place, the
arrival of the first of a new generation of heavy bombers.
Bomber Command had begun the war with their two-engined
Whitleys and Hampdens, later joined by the more robust
Wellington. But bombing on the scale that was now needed
required far larger aircraft that could carry much heavier bomb

loads. Britain's pre-war aircraft industry was lucky to have some visionary designers like Reginald Mitchell, who had designed the superlative Spitfire, and Roy Chadwick, who worked for the Avro company. Chadwick had already designed the two-engined Manchester bomber but decided it was too small to fit the bill, so he set to work on a four-engined giant that could carry more than three times the bomb load of the conventional bombers of the day up to a distance of two thousand miles. He used four Rolls-Royce Merlin engines, the same brilliant engine that was used in the Spitfire, to power his new beast, which was called the Lancaster. These new heavy bombers were designed to be mass produced and in early 1942 they began to come off the Avro production line, but still only in small numbers. It was not until the end of the year that the Lancaster and the other four-engined heavies, the Stirling and the Halifax, were available in significant numbers. The arrival of these heavies was similar in its impact to the arrival of jumbo jets to a later generation. Their vast scale seemed to dwarf almost everything that had flown before. Five thousand Lancasters would be built and the aircraft would come to symbolise the British bombing offensive against Germany, just as Boeing's B-17 'Flying Fortress' came to represent the American bombing campaign.

At the Casablanca Conference in January 1943, Roosevelt and Churchill fully endorsed the bombing strategy. Their directive to the British and American bomber commanders, which was approved by the Combined Chiefs of Staff, stated: 'Your primary objective will be the progressive destruction of the German military industrial and economic system, and the undermining of the morale of the German people to a point where their armed resistance is fatally weakened.'[16] A list of targets then followed, including submarine yards, aircraft factories, oil refineries, rubber and tyre plants, and factories for military transport. With American bombers now arriving in England in large numbers at last, and with all the improvements in technology and design, the bombing offensive would take off again during 1943. Churchill was keen to keep Stalin well informed of progress. He regularly sent him books of aerial photos of bomb-damage assessments. When congratulating the Soviet leader on his victory at Stalingrad, Churchill added, almost as a postscript: 'We last night dropped 142 tons of high explosives and 218 tons of incendiaries on Berlin.' Stalin replied: 'I wish the British Air Force further successes, most particularly in bombing Berlin.'[17]

The bombing offensive that now started in earnest against Germany was based on a strategy of RAF Bomber Command bombing by night, and the US Army Air Force (US AAF) bombing by day. The Americans had the Flying Fortress, which, with eight mounted heavy machine guns in four turrets and armour plating in the fuselage, was regarded as powerful enough to withstand attacks from enemy fighters. And the Americans had a bomb sight known as the 'Norden' that they regarded as supremely precise. 'You can drop a bomb in a pickle barrel from ten thousand feet' was the popular boast about the Norden. But it needed to be used in clear skies in daylight. The Americans rejected the policy of area bombing, which they thought was ineffective. Instead, they wanted to go for planned, precise attacks upon key elements of the German war economy that would cause maximum disruption. Churchill initially thought this was impossible to achieve, and along with Harris and his Chiefs of Staff wanted the Americans to join the night-time bombing campaign, adding their vast scale to the efforts of the RAF. But at Casablanca, Churchill met with General Ira Eaker, the commander of the USAAF in Britain. Eaker persuaded Churchill that by bombing around the clock, the combined RAF–USAAF operation would 'give the devils [i.e. the Germans] no rest'.[18] And so the strategy of twenty-four-hour bombing was endorsed, with the Americans going for precision bombing by day and the RAF opting for area bombing by night.

Harris could now at last take advantage of the advances in technology and make use of the growing supply of Lancasters. As Max Hastings has written, only in early 1943 did all the latest radio and radar equipment and the supply of heavy bombers enable Harris 'to bring the bomber offensive out of its cottage industry phase into the age of automated mass destruction'.[19] Most of the older, obsolete aircraft were pensioned off and his main force of about five hundred bombers was in a far better state to strike at the enemy than a year before. The spring offensive began on 5 March with an assault upon one of Harris's favourite targets, the giant Krupp armaments factory at Essen. Mosquitoes equipped with Oboe acted as Pathfinders to locate the target. The raid was a success, with a third of the force dropping its bombs within three miles of the aiming point, and 160 acres of Essen were flattened. But the Ruhr, Germany's industrial heartland, was well defended. As more raids on 'Happy Valley', as the bomber crews sarcastically called it, followed over the next three months, the number of bombers being shot down by radar-assisted German night fighters grew to alarming levels. Then, in July, Harris tried something new.

The scientists had come up with another simple innovation, the dropping of thousands of small metal foil strips which totally blinded the enemy radar. It was known as 'Window'. The technique had been worked out earlier, but Cherwell had pointed out that, as there was no known remedy for this, if the RAF tried out Window over Germany, the Luftwaffe was bound to use it when it next bombed Britain. Its use was delayed, and again it needed Churchill to intervene to settle the dispute. 'Let us open the window!' he ordered at the end of June, and on 24 July Window was used for the first time in a heavy raid on Hamburg. It was a total success. The night fighters completely failed to find the bombers and the mission was carried out with copybook precision. The US bombers followed up this initial attack with two days of daylight bombing on Hamburg. Then the RAF returned on the 27th and dropped incendiaries on the city. Fires were started that raged for days, strengthened by two further raids by Bomber Command over the next week. The devastation was extreme. The fires reached temperatures of a thousand degrees centigrade, and as the heat rose it sucked in more oxygen, creating whirlwinds or hurricanes of flame in a deadly, blazing inferno. Buildings disappeared in the firestorm. Bodies were incinerated. When the fires abated, it was estimated that 42,000 civilians had been killed, a million had fled into surrounding areas, and twenty-two square kilometres of the city had been razed to the ground. Forty thousand houses and more than five hundred factories had ceased to exist. The chief of the Hamburg fire brigade captured the terrible inferno on colour film which provides a permanent record of the terror of the fire raids.[20]

The Nazi leadership was truly shaken for the first time. Goebbels confided in his diary that the bombing of Hamburg was a 'catastrophe, the extent of which simply staggers the imagination'. Albert Speer, who had become Minister for War Production in February 1942, later said he told Hitler that if the Allies had mounted similar attacks against six cities in quick succession, German war production might have collapsed.[21] For Harris, of course, this was a triumphant success, but Bomber Command was wary about returning to the same location night after night, in case enemy fighters were waiting, and the terrible carnage of Hamburg was not replayed on other German cities until towards the very end of the war.

As the American fleet of heavy bombers grew in Britain, the debate about the objectives of the bombing campaign continued. After a discussion in Washington which Churchill, unusually for him, nodded through without challenge, the Combined Chiefs of Staff agreed to pursue Operation Pointblank. This summarised the objectives of the bombing and clearly shows that American influence dominated. A priority was given to targets relating to the German aircraft industry, with both factories and airbases to be attacked to eliminate the threat from the German fighters. Other industrial targets were also listed, and Pointblank referred to the need to try to destroy German morale. Harris seized on this last point to justify the continuation of area bombing, which he was convinced would win the war. On the other hand, the American commanders, Hap Arnold in Washington and General Carl Spaatz, head of the 8th Air Force in Britain, used Pointblank to justify precision attacks on industrial targets. From the start, the two bombing efforts increasingly went their separate ways.

Through the autumn and winter of 1943, Bomber Command turned its focus to what became known as the 'Battle of Berlin'. Twenty thousand sorties were flown against the German capital. Harris was supremely confident that this was the best way to defeat the Nazi war effort. But the city was out of range of Oboe so the crews relied upon H2S radar to identify their targets, a far more difficult tool to use effectively. Air defences grew in scale and expertise around the city. Huge towers were built to house powerful 88mm anti-aircraft guns. Losses mounted. Harris predicted to Churchill in November that 'We can wreck Berlin from end to end if the USAAF will come in on it. It will cost [us] between 400–500 aircraft. It will cost Germany the war.'[22] This was a rash claim that was used later against Harris. But by now Churchill did not interfere much in the development of air policy. He left it to Harris and his team to select targets and to pursue their aims. Harris became an increasingly rare visitor to Chequers. However, in March 1944, RAF losses from night-time bombing of Germany rose again to unacceptable levels of about 5 per cent of total aircraft. On one raid on Nuremberg it was as high as 9 per cent. With these levels, crews could not expect, statistically, to survive a single tour of duty. A pause was called in the bombing offensive. By now, fortunately for the crews, other priorities had arisen.

American confidence in the firepower of their Flying Fortress had proved not to be justified. Their daylight raids, flown unescorted over Germany, were subject to intense harassment from German fighters. Large numbers of B-17s were shot down and each aircraft down meant the loss of the ten members of its crew. Following their policy of hitting key targets, the US 8th Army Air Force based in Britain flew a series of raids in October 1943, culminating in an attack on the ball-bearing factory in Schweinfurt, deep in the heart of Germany. On the night of 14 October, 60 aircraft out of 291 on the raid were shot down. During that week, the Americans lost a total of 148 bombers. The US bombing offensive against Germany was postponed until long-range fighters were available to escort the bombers. This finally came about in the spring of 1944, when the P-51 Mustang was fitted with long-range fuel tanks, enabling it to fly all the way to Berlin and back. The sleek, silver Mustangs could defend the bombers from attack by enemy fighters, and on their return were told to seek out 'targets of opportunity', which usually meant swooping down to attack enemy air-craft on the ground. Only now did the Allies win daylight air supremacy over Germany. The story goes that when Goering looked up and saw enemy fighters over the skies of the German capital he pronounced: 'The jig is up,' meaning the war was lost.

The RAF had not entirely given up on daylight precision raids, although Harris was bitterly opposed to them as they distracted from the heavy area bombing that he favoured. Tension grew between the Ministry of Economic Warfare, which wanted to set targets whose destruction it believed would be critical to German's war economy, and Harris, who demanded the right to select his own targets. The ministry identified the dams that supplied the water and produced much of the electricity for the Ruhr as a key economic target. In early 1943, the inventor Barnes Wallis developed a way of spinning cylindrical, depth-charge-type bombs that could be dropped by low-flying Lancasters as 'bouncing bombs'. The idea was to bounce them over the German defences and destroy the dams. Harris was initially hostile, describing bouncing bombs as 'the maddest proposition as a weapon that we have yet come across'. He allowed one aircraft to be used for experimental purposes, but was not prepared to hand over any more of his precious Lancasters.[23]

However, on meeting Barnes Wallis in person, Harris was persuaded to give the idea a go. He agreed to create a special team, 617 Squadron, to train in the use of the bouncing bombs, and he suggested putting Wing Commander Guy Gibson in charge. Gibson was allowed to select his own elite crews from across Bomber Command. The attacks took place on 16 May 1943 and involved low-level precision flying across Holland and Germany by nineteen Lancasters. The heroics of the Dam Busters' raid, in which the bouncing bombs were dropped from only sixty feet, are now well known mainly from the triumphalist feature film that became a war classic in the 1950s.[24] The Mohne Dam was successfully breached and the Eder was damaged. However, the critical third dam at Sorpe was left intact and the power supply to the industries of the Ruhr was maintained. Despite this, Albert Speer later wrote that if the attack had been followed up, it could have ended the war that year.[25] The raid was immensely popular with the British press and public, and Guy Gibson was awarded a Victoria Cross for his heroism in leading the mission. However, as eight of his best crews had been lost in the raid, a 40 per cent loss rate, Harris concluded that such missions were not worth the cost. The ultimate lesson he took from this daring raid was of the need to maintain instead the policy of area bombing.

An aircraft more suited to low-level precision flying was the twin-engined Mosquito. With a top speed of nearly 400 m.p.h., it could out-fly just about anything in the pre-jet era. The frame of the Mosquito was built out of wood to get around the shortage of metal in wartime Britain. It was produced in large numbers but was in heavy demand for a variety of roles: as a night fighter, for photo reconnaissance, as a Pathfinder and as a light bomber. The Mosquito was used for several extraordinary operations. The most daring of these was a raid on the prison in the northern French town of Amiens on 18 February 1944. British Intelligence wanted to rescue a group of French Resistance leaders who were about to be executed by the Gestapo. A squadron of Mosquitoes was tasked with knocking down the walls of the prison, but in such a way as not to harm most of the prisoners, who would then be able to escape. The mission was called 'Operation Jericho'. Such accuracy would be difficult to attain even in today's era of GPS-guided missiles, but the Mosquito squadron achieved its objective with a superb display of flying. The planes approached fast and low, at about fifty feet, and hit the prison walls with pinpoint accuracy. Some prisoners were inevitably killed but over 250 French prisoners escaped in the resulting confusion.

Churchill loved to hear of missions like this. They were the RAF equivalent of commando raids. Soon he became involved in one debate which did not attract much attention at the time, but has since taken on major significance. In the summer of 1944, more and more shocking stories leaked out of occupied Europe about a terrible extermination camp in Poland where hundreds of thousands of Jews were being sent. Some of the thousands arriving each day were picked out by the SS guards as fit and able and were assigned to a brutal work camp, where most did not survive for long. The majority were sent straight to gas chambers, where they were killed. Their bodies were then burned in giant crematoria. The whole camp had been laid out with chilling efficiency to process and kill on an industrial scale – up to twelve thousand people each day. Its name was Auschwitz.

On 6 July 1944, the Jewish Agency sent two senior representatives to meet Anthony Eden, the Foreign Secretary, in London. They reported a sudden increase in the number of people being taken to Auschwitz as the Nazis geared up to exterminate the Jews of Hungary. They calculated that one and a half million Jews had already been killed. During the meeting, they made a formal request to bomb the camp. Eden passed this request on to Churchill, who had been a supporter of the Zionist cause since his visit to Palestine in 1921. He was shocked by the appalling estimates of the number of deaths. Churchill responded the following day by saying he agreed with the request to bomb the camp and wrote: 'Get anything you can out of the Air Force, and invoke me if necessary.'[26] Eden duly passed the request on to Sir Archibald Sinclair, the Minister for the Air.

There were several obvious difficulties with such a proposal. First, of course, the precise location of the camp had to be identified. Then a way of bombing it that minimised the risks to the inmates had to be found. The RAF considered the proposition and also considered bombing the railway lines leading to the camp. They concluded that although precision raids had been carried out in France, an attack on such a small target in distant Poland was virtually impossible. If it could be done at all, it could be achieved only by transferring much sought-after Mosquitoes from other essential duties. It was a critical point in the war. The Allies had still not broken out from the bridgehead they had established in Normandy. Flying bombs were being fired on London every day and the effort to locate and destroy their launch sites was a major priority. Neither Churchill nor Eden pressed the case and the request to bomb the camp was dropped as impractical. In an ironic twist, in July 1944, aerial reconnaissance photos were taken of the Monowitz chemical plant in Poland. Just outside this plant was the giant complex of Auschwitz–Birkenau. The camp was caught in perfect detail on the aerial photos. On one set, a train has just arrived and the SS are in the process of separating those who are disembarking. But the photo interpreters were not looking for an extermination camp and they never identified Auschwitz as such at the time. So the Allies did have a record of the exact location and layout of Auschwitz – even the gas chambers and ovens can clearly be seen.

In recent debates about the Holocaust, there has been much criticism of the Allies for their failure to bomb the extermination camps. The reality is that even if they had analysed the pictures correctly, a bombing raid against Auschwitz would still have been an immensely difficult mission to carry out. Although in retrospect it seems criminally negligent that the Allies did nothing to prevent the mass murder of the Holocaust from continuing, at the time there were simply too many other military priorities in the war effort.[27]

In early 1944, all Allied planning became dominated by the preparations for the D-Day landings in Normandy, Operation Overlord. A new debate began as to what role the Allied bombers should play in this huge operation. Harris and his

American counterpart, Spaatz, persisted in their view that bombing Germany was the main way in which the bombers could contribute towards the success of D-Day, by undermining German war production and civilian morale. But there was considerable scepticism among the army commanders about the claims of the bomber barons. There was no sign yet of the predicted collapse of the German war economy (as we shall see later, output was actually increasing) or breakdown of support for the war among the German people. General Eisenhower, who was appointed Supreme Commander of the Allied Forces for the invasion of France, insisted he must take direct command of the strategic bombing force. He wanted it to take on a new role.

Solly Zuckerman, the scientist who had studied the impact of German bombing on Birmingham and Hull, had gone on to analyse the impact of Allied bombing on enemy targets in North Africa, Sicily and southern Italy. This research had shown the devastating military consequences of bombing the railway networks. Zuckerman's work was enthusiastically taken up by Air Marshal Sir Arthur Tedder, head of the RAF in the Mediterranean, who was appointed Eisenhower's deputy. Zuckerman and Tedder drew up a plan for the bombing of railway marshalling yards across northern France and Belgium so that the Germans could not rush reserves to the area where the landings had taken place. This became known as the 'Transport Plan'. Eisenhower wanted to take command of the British and American bombers based in Britain as a tactical bombing force. Harris and Spaatz resisted this with all their energy. But Harris had few friends left in the Air Ministry, where officials had grown weary of his adversarial nature. He regarded any official who was not 100 per cent behind him as someone who was against him. It was reported that when he passed one particular civil servant in the Air Ministry he said: 'Good morning,

Abrahams, and what have you done to impede the war effort today?'[28] Neither was his cause helped by the inflated claims he repeatedly made for the success of his bombing campaign.

Churchill did not want to see the RAF fall under direct American command, and Cherwell was opposed to giving up the bombing offensive against Germany. It fell to Churchill himself eventually to come up with a compromise. Tedder was to have control of RAF's Bomber Command in the months before Overlord. This was acceptable to Eisenhower, and everyone was happy, except Harris. But Cherwell foresaw another problem. He calculated that bombing the French railways could kill up to forty thousand French civilians. Churchill took up this cause, worried that killing so many French men and women was not a good way to start a campaign to liberate their country. He wrote to Eisenhower in April that 'this might be held to be an act of very great severity' against Britain and America's 'friends'. The question was appealed to the President, who wrote back to Churchill: 'However regrettable the attendant loss of civilian lives is, I am not prepared to impose from this distance any restriction on military action by the responsible commanders that in their opinion might militate against the success of Overlord or cause additional loss of life to our Allied forces of invasion.' Roosevelt's response was, as Churchill later wrote, 'decisive'.[29] The Prime Minister raised no further objections. It was a sign of how far power and decision-making had shifted from the British to the Americans. Overlord was an American-led operation. The US commanders were calling the shots. And the President gave them his full support.

For several months, the heavy bombers targeted the railways of north-western Europe with great success. Coastal defences and other communication hubs were additional targets. Although as many as twelve thousand French and Belgian civilians were killed in the run-up to D-Day, this number was a lot less than had been feared. And the disruption caused inside France made it difficult for the German Army to bring up reserves in the wake of the invasion. The new tactical deployment of the bombing fleet made a major contribution to the success of this next vital chapter in the war.

Churchill's lack of interest in the bombing offensive in Germany from the summer of 1943 onwards is reflected in the lack of space he devotes to it in his war memoir–history.[30] This was partly down to his ambivalence about the role of bombing and partly down to the post-war debate about the wisdom and morality of the bombing campaign at the time when he was writing. But Churchill's influence was still to be felt over the final stages of the bombing offensive.

During 1944, the USAAF targeted German synthetic-oil production plants with stunning success and showed how effective the strategy called for in the Pointblank directive could be. The fuel supplies available to Hitler's army and air force were drastically reduced. The Allies now enjoyed total air superiority over Germany, with the surviving aircraft of the Luftwaffe largely grounded by their lack of fuel. Late in 1944, Bomber Command resumed its earlier policy of area bombing German cities by night. As the Red Army advanced westwards through Poland and approached the German border, there was a debate about how the bombers could be used in a way that would assist their progress. On 25 January 1945, a Joint Intelligence Committee report sent to Churchill and the Chiefs of Staff suggested using the heavy bombing force against targets south and east of Berlin. It was claimed this would disrupt troop reinforcements heading for the front, hamper the German administrative and military machine, and could even have 'a decisive effect on the length of the war'. Churchill discussed this with Archibald Sinclair and urged him to follow the recommendations and report back. Sinclair asked his staff to investigate the possibilities, explaining that Churchill was keen on 'blasting the Germans in their retreat from Breslau'.[31] This was reinforced when the Allied leaders met in early February at Yalta. Here the Soviet Chiefs of Staff made a formal request for British and American bombers to be used to paralyse German movements behind their retreating army.

The consequence of this was the combined bombing operation against the city of Dresden on the night of 13 February and over the following days. On the first night, a force of 900 RAF bombers dropped nearly 1500 tons of high explosive and over 1000 tons of incendiaries on the city. Hours later, US bombers followed this up with a massive daylight raid on the city. And that night the RAF returned. Once again, as in Hamburg, giant firestorms were ignited that destroyed vast areas of the city, leaving chaos and destruction in their wake. Dresden was an ancient city, a centre of art and culture, but much of its architecture was utterly destroyed in the flames. Days after the raid, photo interpreters were still unable to assess the damage because a pall of smoke hung across the city.

Dresden was packed with refugees fleeing the advancing Red Army, so it is impossible to know precisely how many people died. Estimates range from thirty thousand to about one hundred thousand. Whatever the true figure, the scale of destruction was immense and began to provoke revulsion. One news correspondent spoke of the 'deliberate terror bombing' of German cities. His report was censored in Britain but created a stir in the United States, where General Marshall made it clear that the raid was a consequence of a direct request from the Russians. Churchill had been involved in only the most generalised way by encouraging the implementation of an intelligence report to bomb eastern Germany. He had not mentioned Dresden specifically in conversations or in written minutes. But even he judged it was time to distance himself from the bombing campaign against Germany. In a memo on 28 March 1945, after he had been shown accounts of the raid, he wrote:

> It seems to me that the moment has come when the question of bombing of German cities simply for the sake of increasing the terror, though under other pretexts, should be reviewed ... The destruction of Dresden remains a serious query against the conduct of allied bombing ... I feel the need for more precise concentration upon military objectives, such as oil and communications behind the immediate battle zone, rather than on mere acts of terror and wanton destruction, however impressive.[32]

The wheel had come full circle. Churchill, who in 1940 had believed that the RAF could win the war, and who had backed his scientific and military advisers in their arguments in favour of area bombing, was now veering away from the terrible consequences of this policy, calling for more precise targeting of military objectives. The time to reassess had come.

So was the bombing offensive worthwhile? Questions about both the effectiveness of bombing Germany and the morality of killing civilians have raged since the last Lancaster returned from Dresden. In all, about 600,000 men, women and children were killed in the bombing of Germany, with about 20 per cent of homes in German cities damaged by aerial bombardment. But the morale of the population did not break until the very last months of the war, and this was caused more by the realisation that defeat was imminent, with the Red Army advancing relentlessly into Germany from the east and Allied troops advancing rapidly from the west. Moreover, although there is still much debate about this, the German war economy actually increased

...urchill and President Roosevelt at their first wartime meeting, August 1941, ...ging hymns together with their military chiefs. Churchill had specially selected ...hymns to emphasise unity between the two nations. (IWM)

General Sir Alan Brooke, Chief of the Imperial General Staff from 1941–5. A tough Ulsterman, he met with Churchill almost daily and had an often stormy, love-hat relationship with the PM. (IWM)

Air Marshal Sir Arthur 'Bomber' Harris looks at aerial photos on the wall. Photo-interpreters study aerial images in the foreground. Harris was totally committed to bombing as the way to end the war. (IWM)

...rchill surrounded by military chiefs in North Africa, June 1943. From left to ...t, General Sir Alan Brooke (with papers on his lap), Air Vice Marshal Sir Arthur ...der, Admiral Sir Andrew Cunningham, General Sir Harold Alexander, American ...erals George C. Marshall and Dwight D. Eisenhower (sitting) and General Sir ...nard Montgomery (standing). (Getty Images)

...rchill in his favourite ...ssing gown patterned ...h red dragons, Tunisia, ...istmas Day, 1943, with ...eral Eisenhower who ...just been appointed to ...mand Operation ...erlord. General ...xander behind them. ...rchill was recovering ...n a serious illness that at ...point threatened his life. ...)

Stalin proposes a toast to Churchill on his sixty-ninth birthday during the Teheran conference, 30 November 1943. Anthony Eden is on Churchill's right. The toasts went on throughout the evening. (IWM)

…rchill in Italy, August 1944, watching an artillery barrage on an enemy position.
…and the generals were within enemy artillery range. On his visits, Churchill liked
…et as near to the front as possible. (IWM)

Churchill arrives in Normandy six days after D-Day for a visit and is escorted off the beach by General Montgomery. Churchill had wanted to be present at D-Day itself. (IWM)

The British Mulberry harbour at Arromanches, June 1944. The huge caissons can clearly be seen along with miles of floating roadways. Churchill knew the building of two Mulberries would be a gigantic undertaking but persisted. Fittingly, this one became known as Port Winston. (Courtesy of the Medmenham Collection)

chilly day at the Yalta Conference, February 1945. Behind the Big Three stand
thony Eden, Foreign Secretary; Edward Stettinius, Secretary of State; and
acheslav Molotov, Soviet Foreign Secretary. Roosevelt is visibly ailing. He will not
e to see the victory. (Corbis)

Churchill the conquering hero. With trademark cigar in mouth, he leads Generals Brooke and Montgomery and a bevy of American starred generals on to the east bank of the Rhine, 25 March 1945. Later that day they came under fire and the PM had to be dragged away to safety. (IWM)

its output during the years of the bombing offensive. Armament production increased by about 80 per cent in 1942; by another 20 per cent in 1943; and by a further 40 per cent in the first six months of 1944. In other words it roughly trebled over the two and a half years. But part of this is explained by the fact that the German economy was geared to fighting a short, successful war in 1940 and 1941 and was by no means fully mobilised in those years. There was much spare capacity to call upon. The Nazi creed believed, for instance, that women should be mothers and wives, not industrial labourers, in the early years of war. Women were not deployed at first to anything like the same extent as they were in Britain and would later be in the United States. Also, by the end of the war, the German war machine was able to draw upon the forced labour of millions of slaves who were brought to the Reich from occupied territories and put to work, often in appalling conditions. Albert Speer claimed that the indiscriminate bombing of vast tracts of German cities was not the best strategy for the Allied bombers. He insisted that if the Allies had pressed on with their bombing of key targets like the ball-bearing factories, or had mounted a series of devastating raids like the fire raids on Hamburg, then the bombing offensive would have had far greater impact. On the other hand, specific elements of the bombing campaign had very clear and damaging results. The attacks on oil refineries and synthetic-oil production plants in 1944 led to serious fuel shortages which undermined the German Army's ability to fight in the final campaigns of the war. Moreover, the bombing kept about one million soldiers at home to man anti-aircraft defences, equivalent to about fifty divisions which otherwise could have swayed the war on the Eastern Front or in Normandy. Another one and a half million workers were tied up clearing rubble and in reconstruction simply to allow life to go on.

Ultimately, it is an ethical decision as to whether the bombing campaign against Germany was justified or was a war crime. Certainly, Churchill was an advocate of the campaign, albeit an uncertain and questioning one at times. Cherwell and 'Bomber' Harris were its chief protagonists. It's interesting to note that in the moral climate of the war the argument against bombing was made not on ethical but on practical grounds. Was it worth the massive effort in industrial output and in the lives of the RAF crews? After all, as was said over and over again during the war, it was the Germans who had started bombing cities, and the memories of Warsaw, Rotterdam, and the Blitz on London and Coventry were strong in everyone's minds. Harris told the newsreel cameras, 'They who sow the wind will reap the whirlwind,' and most Britons at the time felt he was right. Churchill was encouraged to 'give one back' to Hitler. And, in purely numerical terms, how does one compare the 600,000 German civilians who died as a consequence of Allied bombs with the two million Germans who died at the hands of advancing Soviet soldiers at the end of the war? Or with the six million Jews who were murdered during the Holocaust? Or with the US bombing offensive in Japan? Of course, that campaign culminated in the dropping of atomic bombs on Hiroshima and Nagasaki, which prompted the final Japanese surrender and the end of the war.

The arguments will rage on. Churchill, as the final decision-maker in the British war machine, must take his share of the responsibility for the adoption of the policy of area bombing and its consequences. He definitely listened too closely to Cherwell and did not pay enough heed to other advisers who argued a contrary point of view. But this was all about practicalities and effectiveness, not about the morality of bombing. At the end of the war, when he was perhaps reflecting more on the verdict of history than he had done earlier, Churchill distanced himself from the bombing campaign. Air Chief Marshal Harris was left out of the principal victory celebrations and no campaign medal was ever given to the crews of Bomber Command, despite the courage they had shown and the losses they had endured – 57,000 airmen killed during the war. Even the erection of a statue to Harris in London fifty years after the end of the war created intense controversy. The bombing offensive against Germany without doubt remains the most heavily criticised element of British strategy during the Second World War. Any evaluation of Churchill's reputation as a war leader will forever be bound up with it.

9

Overlord

After the successful summit with Roosevelt at Casablanca in January 1943 (from the British perspective at any rate), Churchill flew to Turkey, where he tried to persuade President Inonu to join the Allied war effort, without success. He then went on to inspect a victory parade of the 8th Army in Tripoli. After all the upsets of the war in North Africa, Churchill found this celebration very emotional and tears ran down his face. He then flew on to Algeria before returning to London after another long flight in the primitive Liberator bomber. When he got back to Paddington Station, thirteen ministers headed by Attlee, Eden and Bevin turned out to welcome him on the platform. He had been away for twenty-six days. Within a week of his return, he had been struck down with pneumonia. He was largely out of action for another month but, despite the illness, he continued to dictate minutes. General Brooke, who had been travelling with Churchill, was himself struck down with influenza for two weeks. Both men's illnesses are a sign of the strain they were under during these intense meetings abroad and the long, gruelling and sometimes dangerous travel involved.

By mid-March, Churchill was fighting fit again and back in control. But he still had to wait for the breakthrough in North Africa. Hitler had decided to reinforce his troops in Tunisia, and the battle to evict the German and Italian armies was progressing far more slowly than planned. Rommel was fighting a superb campaign of withdrawal. The raw American troops suffered a severe setback at the Kasserine Pass in February, and it took several weeks for their advance to pick up momentum again. Churchill once more tried to whip on his commanders and sent off a missive complaining about the 'many factors of safety' that were creeping into operational plans, which meant they were 'ceasing to be capable of making any form of aggressive war'.[1] As always, he called for his soldiers, sailors and airmen to take an aggressive line. In March, Montgomery broke through the German defences known as the 'Mareth Line'. And, finally, the following month, the American armies advancing eastwards met up with the 8th Army advancing westwards. The Axis forces were now surrounded and the Allied armies edged forward towards the city of Tunis, the site of Rommel's last stand in North Africa.

In early May, Churchill once again felt the need to cross the Atlantic with his Chiefs of Staff for another Washington conference. Planning for the invasion of Sicily, agreed at Casablanca, had fallen behind. Eisenhower sent a note to the Combined Chiefs of Staff saying that if there were more than two German divisions in Sicily, the landings might have to be postponed. Churchill erupted. He wrote to his Chiefs of Staff: 'If the presence of two German divisions is held to be decisive against any operation of an offensive or amphibious character open to the million men now in French North Africa, it is difficult to see how the war can be carried on.' He fumed against these 'pusillanimous and defeatist doctrines' and ended by asking 'what Stalin would think of this when he has 185 German divisions on his front'.[2]

Churchill was worried that there might be months during the summer when the Anglo-American armies would be fighting no Germans at all, while Stalin and the Red Army were engaged in a life-and-death struggle with the bulk of the Wehrmacht on the Eastern Front. Furthermore, it seemed to the British Chiefs of Staff that the Americans were directing more landing craft and supplies away from the European theatre and towards the Pacific. Churchill and his entourage, along with the Chiefs of Staff, sailed on the *Queen Mary*, the giant Cunard passenger ship that for several years pre-war had held the record as the fastest across the Atlantic but had now been requisitioned for war work. En route, Churchill and the Chiefs of Staff planned strategy. As they crossed the Atlantic, news came through of the final dramatic victory of the American and British armies in Tunisia. Rommel had got away but nine generals and about 240,000 men had been captured. Churchill ordered the church bells in England to be rung again, for the second time to mark a great victory.

Outwardly, the two weeks of meetings in Washington in May, code-named 'Trident', were a success. But yet again there were serious divisions not far below the surface of Anglo-American relations. Churchill convinced Roosevelt to mediate in the growing dispute between British scientists and their American counterparts, who were now keeping Britain out of the Manhattan Project, the giant scientific research programme to develop an atom bomb. Roosevelt agreed that the deal he had reached with Churchill was to make the results of this research jointly available, a success for the Prime Minister and for British science. The Combined Chiefs of Staff agreed to proceed with the invasion of Sicily now that there had been victory in North Africa, but there was a dispute as to where to go after that. The Americans favoured Sardinia. Churchill and Brooke argued that an invasion of the Italian mainland was the next logical step, with the objective of knocking Italy out of the war. Churchill said this would divert dozens of German divisions not only to fight in Italy but also to replace the Italian divisions currently operating in the Balkans. Here, SOE-encouraged uprisings were taking place and Tito and his Partisans were tying down about twenty enemy divisions. Churchill argued that this was the best support the Allies could give to Stalin during 1943. To his annoyance, the issue remained unresolved. 'I was deeply distressed at this,' he later remembered.[3] However, far and away the most important decision made at Trident was that serious planning should now begin for the invasion of Northern Europe.

As we have seen, the Americans had wanted to launch an invasion of Northern Europe as early as 1942, hoping to prevent a collapse of the Soviet Union and in the belief that victory in Europe could be achieved only by crushing the German armies in ground offensives. They regarded other campaigns as side-shows to this central and necessary assault. Churchill and Brooke, along with the rest of the British Chiefs of Staff, believed that such a complex operation as a cross-Channel invasion should be undertaken only when success was certain. And for success, the Allies first needed to defeat the U-boat menace in the Atlantic and then gain air supremacy over Northern Europe. In addition, the British argued that the army that waded ashore would have to be large enough to sustain the heavy counter-attacks that would be certain to follow. And it would take some time for sufficient supplies of troops and their vital equipment to be built up in southern England. So the British strategy, which had largely prevailed up to the spring of 1943, was to fight more limited campaigns in places where success was more certain, hence the battles in North Africa and the Mediterranean. The British remained sceptical about Operation Overlord, as the invasion plan became known, right up to the end. 'Why are we trying to do this?' Churchill cried out in a depressed moment to Brooke in February 1944.[4] Brooke himself remained fearful up to the eve of the invasion that if the landings failed, it would be the greatest disaster of the war. Nevertheless, at Trident, both Allies committed themselves to the invasion of Europe. A team led by British General Frederick Morgan and known as 'COSSAC' (Chief of Staff to the Supreme Allied Commander) was instructed to prepare outline plans for the invasion of Europe. And there was a date to work to, 1 May 1944, to be known as D-Day.

From Washington, Churchill flew with both the British and the US chiefs, Generals Brooke and Marshall, to Eisenhower's headquarters in Algiers. En route their Boeing Clipper was hit by lightning but not harmed. After the tense atmosphere in Washington, relations improved in the sunshine of Algiers. Marshall was happy to leave open the option of moving on to mainland Italy, depending upon progress in Sicily. Eisenhower impressed Churchill with his sense of authority and command of the situation. And Churchill wanted to ensure that the victorious army now poised in North Africa was kept busy with offensive action over the next year, until the invasion of Europe could be launched. Mostly, the generals agreed with him and he was delighted with the outcome of their meetings. He wrote later: 'I had never received so strong an impression of co-operation and control as during my visit.' After visiting the troops in Tunis and giving a speech to soldiers gathered in the dramatic setting of the ruins of an immense Roman amphitheatre in Carthage, Churchill set off for home. He later recalled: 'I have no more pleasant memories of the war than the eight days in Algiers and Tunis.'[5]

Churchill flew back via Gibraltar, where, because of the weather, he had to leave the luxurious Boeing Clipper and return in the far more basic Liberator. That same day, another plane was flying on a scheduled flight from Lisbon in neutral Portugal back to England. German agents at Lisbon airport noted a large man smoking a cigar boarding the flight and mistook him for Churchill. Luftwaffe fighters were scrambled and shot down the aircraft. All the passengers were killed. Churchill was not on board, but the leading actor Leslie Howard was. His death was a great loss to British cinema. Although Churchill was totally committed to these long-haul flights, each of them had its element of danger.

Back in London after another month away, there were jokes in the press about 'Prime Minister visits Britain'. But Churchill as ever threw himself into a full round of War Cabinet meetings, reports to Parliament and a packed schedule. The invasion of Sicily was launched on 10 July. There were some terrible mishaps at the start when airborne troops were dropped in entirely the wrong places, some of them even in the sea, but overall the landings were a success. Furthermore, many important lessons were learned of value to the later Overlord landings. The US Army advanced from the south of the island to Palermo while the British advanced up the east coast through Catania. General George S. Patton, the US commander, felt intense rivalry with General Montgomery and ended up racing him to Messina. Patton won. In just over five weeks, the whole island was in Allied hands.

Another summit with Roosevelt took place in mid-August in the Canadian city of Quebec, code-named 'Quadrant'. This time, unusually, Clementine accompanied her husband along with their daughter, Mary. At Quebec the same routine followed with the American and British Chiefs of Staff arguing over the details of military strategy while Roosevelt and

Churchill met to endorse the Allies' broad war aims. The Americans were still suspicious of British ambitions in the Mediterranean. And the British continued to press for an attack upon mainland Italy, where Mussolini had now fallen and been replaced by Pietro Badoglio as Chief Minister. But this time the American chiefs were determined not to be out-argued by the British. There was much discussion about policy in the Far East. As we have seen, the British interest here was principally to defend Burma in order to protect India from the Japanese. By contrast, the Americans wanted to use Burma to supply and reinforce the Chinese. In the British delegation was Brigadier Orde Wingate, fresh from leading his 'Chindits' in a long-range, three-month penetration raid behind Japanese lines. This was just the sort of high-risk operation that Churchill loved, and he possibly saw Wingate as a sort of Lawrence of Arabia figure. The Combined Chiefs of Staff agreed to support Wingate in future raids behind Japanese lines. They also agreed to appoint Lord Mountbatten as Supreme Commander in South-East Asia. But Roosevelt and Churchill never really saw eye to eye on the Pacific. Churchill's ambition was to win back all the colonies that had been lost in the Far East. The Americans had no desire to see the war strengthen the British Empire in a region they now regarded as their own.

With regard to Europe, Churchill agreed with Roosevelt that an American general, probably Marshall, should be appointed Supreme Commander for Overlord. Churchill had already offered the post to Brooke but now somewhat abruptly told him that it would be going to an American. He later wrote that Brooke bore his disappointment with 'soldierly dignity'.[6] But Churchill had failed to appreciate what a crushing blow this was to his closest military adviser and colleague. 'He offered no sympathy, no regrets at having had to change his mind, and dealt with the matter as if it were one of minor importance!'

Brooke later wrote. It took him several months to recover from the loss of a command that he had eagerly sought.[7] This was not Churchill at his best or his most considerate.

In the discussion about Overlord, Churchill again provoked American suspicions by suggesting that, if the German strength in Northern Europe proved too great, the Allies should have 'a second string to their bow'.[8] He proposed the invasion of northern Norway, an old hobby horse of his. It was not taken very seriously. More significantly, the Americans proposed an invasion of southern France, Operation Anvil, to coincide with Overlord. This was approved but would cause much tension later. In discussions about Overlord, the COSSAC plan was given preliminary approval. Three divisions of troops were to land not across the shortest stretch of the English Channel in the Pas de Calais, where German defences were at their strongest, but further west, in Normandy, where conditions were better and defences were weaker.

After Quadrant ended, Churchill took a brief holiday in the mountains. He quickly relaxed in his lakeside cabin, spending the days fishing and entertaining his guests at dinner by singing music-hall songs from his youth along with the latest from Noël Coward. On 1 September, he returned to Washington to rejoin Roosevelt, once again living in the White House as the President's guest. During the course of his stay, Italy formally surrendered. The first of Hitler's allies had been defeated. At the end of this visit, Roosevelt had to leave Washington and placed the White House at the Prime Minister's disposal. Here Churchill chaired a final meeting of the Combined Chiefs of Staff. He described this later as a great 'honour' – to preside over a meeting of the Allied chiefs in the Council Room of the White House. To him, it was 'an event in Anglo-American history.'[9]

In many ways, this moment was the peak of the special relationship between Churchill and Roosevelt. But the balance of that relationship was already changing. Churchill had kept Britain going through a critical period in 1940 and 1941. British soldiers and sailors had borne the brunt of the fighting in North Africa and the Mediterranean until the end of 1942. And British scientists had come up with fabulous technological advances to assist the war effort. But America was rapidly becoming predominant in the war in Europe, with ever more troops arriving in Britain to prepare for Overlord. Within months, there would be one million American GIs in Britain. American bombers were matching the efforts of the RAF in the bombing offensive against Germany. For the Pacific, the US Navy was launching ships on a prodigious scale and American marines and heavy bombers would soon play the dominant role in the war effort there. And as the 'arsenal of democracy', factories in the United States were producing tanks, weapons, planes and other vehicles on a previously unimaginable scale. Meanwhile, the Soviet Union had turned from being an ally facing imminent defeat into a superpower with the strongest army in the world. Like a gigantic steamroller, the Red Army was already driving westwards and engaging the lion's share of Hitler's ground forces.

Moreover, the autumn of 1943 saw the British war effort pushed to its extreme. There were now five million men and women in the armed services. Factories were going flat out. Resources were fully utilised. On 1 November, Churchill circulated a minute that noted: 'Our manpower is now fully mobilized for the war effort. We cannot add to the total; on the contrary it is already dwindling. All we can do is to make within that total such changes as the strategy of the war demands.' Britain was fully stretched and this would inevitably limit Churchill's ambition.[10]

Following the Italian surrender, Allied forces landed on the beaches in the Gulf of Salerno, south of Naples. Then Monty's

8th Army began a slow advance up the east coast of Italy. The Allies had missed the opportunity for a quick follow-up to the capture of Sicily and Hitler had reinforced his army in Italy. German troops moved into Rome, and the whole country was effectively occupied by the Wehrmacht. The six German divisions in Italy in the summer had become twenty-five by the autumn. And with the sudden withdrawal of the Italian Army from the Balkans and Greece, Hitler doubled the size of his garrison there, from twelve to twenty-four divisions. So the collapse in Italy had already achieved the first effect Churchill had wanted – to divert German divisions from the Eastern Front. Stalin sent a message to both Roosevelt and Churchill in September congratulating them and noting that 'the successful landing at Naples and the break between Italy and Germany will deal one more blow upon Hitlerite Germany and will considerably facilitate the actions of the Soviet armies at the Soviet-German front'.[11] On the other hand, the reinforcing of Italy by crack divisions from the East meant that the Allied advance up the 'soft underbelly of Europe', as Churchill called it, soon slowed to a crawl. This revived Marshall's fears that, far from offering up swift conquests, the Italian front would act as a drain on Allied resources and pin down troops that were needed for the bigger mission of Overlord. It had been agreed at Quebec that seven divisions would be withdrawn from Italy to aid in the build-up for Overlord in England in November, and that shipping, particularly landing craft, would be reassigned to the English Channel. But after requests from Eisenhower and an intervention from Churchill, the American chiefs reluctantly agreed to leave most of the landing craft in Italy.

Churchill still hankered after operations in the eastern Mediterranean and the Aegean to buttress Greece and to encourage Turkey to join the Allies. He was keen to seize Rhodes and the

Dodecanese islands along the Turkish coast. 'Improvise and dare,' he instructed General Maitland Wilson, the commander in the region.[12] Churchill argued his case in a long document sent to Roosevelt in October, and ended with a simple appeal: 'I beg you to consider this and not let it be brushed aside.' Roosevelt responded the very next day: 'I do not want to force on Eisenhower diversions which limit the prospects . . . of the Italian operations . . . It is my opinion that no diversion of forces or equipment should prejudice Overlord as planned. The American Chiefs of Staff agree.'[13] This unequivocal response made it quite clear who was in charge now.

Despite the put-down, Churchill was desperately anxious that plans for Overlord should not undermine the campaign in Italy, which he had championed for over a year. He felt that the Americans were being too rigid in their support for Overlord and that he was fighting with his hands tied behind his back. He went back to Roosevelt over and over again during that autumn with his concerns about the forthcoming invasion of France. 'My dear friend,' he concluded one of these messages, 'this is much the greatest thing we have ever attempted. And I am not satisfied that we have yet taken the measures necessary to give it the best chance of success.' Only a few days later in another message he said: 'I am more anxious about the campaign of 1944 than about any other with which I have been involved.'[14] Meanwhile, Stalin began to express his irritation with the slow progress of the Allied armies in Italy. He protested that, having fortified Italy, Hitler was now sending units back to the Eastern Front.

With these dilemmas and arguments in mind, at the end of November the Allied leaders, this time including Stalin, agreed to meet in Teheran for the first full summit of the war, the first of the 'Big Three' meetings. Churchill sailed from Plymouth on HMS *Renown* on 12 November. He would be away for two months and travelled with his usual team. First, there was the staff of his Map Room. Here, Captain Richard Pim constantly updated wall charts with pins and lines so Churchill could keep abreast of daily movements on every front and in every ocean. Pim packed up the Map Room and set it up wherever the Prime Minister was based. A complete signals unit travelled with him too, so Churchill could be kept in daily or even hourly contact with London, and through which he could send daily summaries to Deputy Prime Minister Attlee and other ministers. The vitally important Ultra reports were also sent to him by secret communication links to keep him updated. And, of course, there was the small group of secretaries who accompanied Churchill everywhere with their silent typewriters, ready and waiting at any hour of the day or night to type up minutes, briefing papers, speeches or any other message that the Prime Minister wanted to dictate. It is a sign of the success and stability of Churchill's regime that he could afford to travel and operate abroad for such long periods of time. Neither Hitler nor Stalin could have imagined being so far from his power base for so long.

The meeting in Teheran was preceded by another conference between Roosevelt and Churchill and their military chiefs in Cairo, code-named 'Sextant'. They wanted to get their position clear before presenting it to Stalin and his chiefs for the first time. But this meeting was unlike their previous conferences. Roosevelt set the agenda, literally. Much time was spent discussing the Far East and the Pacific. The presence of the Chinese Nationalist leader, Chiang Kai-shek, also meant the conference focused much more on the East. Plans were made for a big amphibious landing in the Bay of Bengal, to help provide supplies for China. This was to be called 'Operation Buccaneer'. Tensions between the British and American chiefs, never far below the surface, erupted in some violent exchanges.

In the afternoon session on 23 November, Admiral Ernest King and General Brooke argued particularly vehemently about the supply of landing craft. The American General Joseph Stilwell, who was present, wrote: 'Brooke got nasty and King got good and sore. King almost climbed over the table at Brooke. God he was mad! I wish he had socked him.'[15] Many unresolved and uncertain issues were taken on to Teheran. The prospects for a successful summit did not look good.

By the time the Big Three gathered in Teheran on 28 November, Churchill had gone down with a bug. He had left London two weeks earlier with a heavy cold and a sore throat. Now, after many late-night sessions in Cairo, he had, perhaps symbolically, lost his voice. His doctor, Charles Wilson, offered Churchill sprays to restore his vital weapon. Then, at the first dinner hosted by Roosevelt, the President had to withdraw with stomach ache. There were even rumours that he had been poisoned. But despite this inauspicious start, the summit proceeded reasonably well and after some tough talking, several significant decisions were reached. At the first plenary session, having been briefed about Overlord, Stalin surprised both Roosevelt and Churchill by eagerly picking up on the plans for Anvil, the invasion of southern France. No doubt the Soviet leader was already thinking of the post-war world, in which he had no desire to see Anglo-American forces in the Balkans. He wanted that part of South-East Europe in his own sphere of influence. By supporting Anvil, he probably believed he would divert Allied forces away from the Balkans. There was a discussion over the timing of Overlord. The Russians insisted on May 1944. The Americans and the British were now planning on June. Churchill still argued his standard line that he did not want to undermine the campaign in Italy, where there were twenty British or British-controlled divisions, simply to guarantee a 1 May date for Overlord.

Stalin kept up the pressure on the President and the Prime Minister. At the next plenary session, he asked who was going to command Overlord. Roosevelt responded that this had not yet been decided. Stalin retorted that the operation 'would come to nought' unless one man was placed in charge of both preparing and leading the invasion. And when Churchill spoke about the need to ensure that German forces in France were not strong enough to throw the Allies back into the sea, Stalin asked bluntly if 'the Prime Minister and the British staffs really believed in Overlord?' Churchill responded that, as long as conditions were right, British forces would hurl everything they had across the Channel at the Germans with 'every sinew of our strength'.[16] But Stalin kept pressing that the invasion must be launched in May. No delay was acceptable.

Roosevelt wanted to build up his own rapport with Stalin in Teheran, which inevitably meant distancing himself from Churchill. As the President put it, he could not appear to be 'ganging up with the British'. Churchill understood what was going on but sought to reassure Stalin during a personal meeting that he was entirely committed to Overlord, that he had no wish to intrude into the Balkans, and that his plans in Italy were limited.

Then, at the second dinner, hosted by Stalin, an unusual incident occurred. The discussion turned to the subject of punishing the Germans at the end of the war. Stalin suggested that there were fifty thousand leading Nazis who were really behind the whole German war effort, and when the war was won they should all be shot. Churchill was genuinely shocked and responded: 'The British Parliament and public will never tolerate mass executions.' Stalin persisted and Churchill said he would rather be taken out into the garden and shot there and then than sully his country's honour with such infamy. Roosevelt, trying to diffuse the brewing row with humour, suggested a compromise – only 49,000 need be shot. Then, to everyone's surprise, the President's son Elliott, who was attending the summit as a military attaché, rose to his feet. No doubt under the influence of the fine wine, he said the US Army would support Marshal Stalin's plan. Churchill, who was so used to being in command of the table talk, got up in disgust and walked out of the banquet and into an adjoining room. Only a minute had passed before he felt a hand on his shoulder. It was Stalin, grinning away, saying it had all been a joke and he had meant none of it. 'Stalin has a very captivating manner when he chooses to use it,' Churchill wrote later. The Prime Minister returned to the table and the rest of the dinner passed off pleasantly enough.[17]

Churchill was feeling the strain of losing the President's friendship and support and of being in the unfamiliar position of not getting his own way. Later that evening, Charles Wilson found him in a very depressed state, brooding on an apocalyptic vision of post-war Europe. The doctor took Churchill's pulse and told him it was high, probably because of the drink. 'It will soon fall,' mused Churchill. Then, returning to his gloom and despondency, he asked: 'Why do I plague my mind with these things? I never used to worry about anything. Stupendous issues are unfolding before our eyes, and we are only specks of dust, that have settled in the night on the map of the world.' He then turned to his doctor and asked abruptly: 'Do you think my strength will last out the war? I fancy sometimes that I am nearly spent.' Then he got into bed. The doctor waited a few minutes and asked if he wanted him to turn out the light. There was no answer. Churchill was already asleep.[18]

The following day, Stalin seemed more positive. He agreed to launch a major offensive on the Eastern Front to coincide with Overlord, in order to prevent German troops being diverted to the Western Front. He also announced that once

Germany had been defeated, the Soviet Union would join the other two Allies in their assault upon Japan. This transformed planning for the final stages of the war in the Far East. Roosevelt confirmed that Overlord would be launched in May 1944. The three leaders also discussed the value of deception tactics to confuse the enemy. Churchill agreed that 'truth should always be attended by a bodyguard of lies'.[19] And so Operation Fortitude was born, the secret deception plan for Overlord.

On this third evening, 30 November, it was Churchill's turn to host dinner. It was his sixty-ninth birthday. General Ismay remembered that the toasts and short speeches began as soon as everyone had sat down. In the Russian style, they then continued throughout the evening. Churchill spoke about the President's fine achievements and called the Russian leader 'Stalin the Great'. As the evening progressed, the toasts got merrier. At one point Churchill proposed a toast to the 'proletarian masses' and Stalin responded with a toast to the 'Conservative Party'! For Churchill, it was a memorable birthday: 'On my right sat the President of the United States, on my left the master of Russia. Together we controlled a large preponderance of the naval and three quarters of the air forces in the world, and could direct armies of nearly twenty millions of men, engaged in the most terrible of wars that had yet occurred in human history.' Later, he would describe the evening more amusingly: 'There I sat with the great Russian bear on one side of me, with paws outstretched, and on the other side the great American buffalo, and between the two sat the poor little English donkey who was the only one . . . who knew the right way home.'[20]

Back in Cairo after Teheran, Roosevelt took a momentous decision. He decided to appoint Eisenhower rather than Marshall as Supreme Commander for Overlord. The President explained this to Marshall by claiming that he would not be able to sleep at night if the general were to relinquish his role as Chief of Staff and be out of the country. If he were disappointed, Marshall did not show it. He said he would go along with whatever his commander-in-chief wanted. Roosevelt told Churchill of his decision during a short sightseeing visit to the Sphinx, a friendly and relaxed interlude after many days of tension. The two leaders gazed at the ancient statue for some minutes as the evening shadows fell, as if seeking guidance. But, as Churchill later put it, the Sphinx 'told us nothing and maintained her inscrutable smile'.[21]

Churchill was exhausted by the tensions of the previous weeks. General Smuts, the South African leader, told Brooke that he thought the Prime Minister was working too hard and that he was 'beginning to doubt whether he would stay the course'. Churchill himself admitted that he felt very tired and noted 'that I no longer dried myself after my bath, but lay on the bed wrapped in my towel till I dried naturally'.[22] He flew on to Eisenhower's headquarters at Carthage, outside Tunis, where he collapsed in exhaustion and went to bed.

At about four o'clock the following morning, 13 December, General Brooke was fast asleep when he was awoken by someone in his room mournfully calling out, 'Hulloo, Hulloo, Hulloo!' The most senior officer in the British Army leapt out of bed and turned on his torch to find the Prime Minister wandering around in his dressing gown with a brown bandage wrapped around his head. He was confused and thought this was his doctor's bedroom. When he finally found Charles Wilson, he was once again diagnosed with pneumonia. He was given a brand-new antibiotic sulphonamide called M&B that had been launched only recently on the market. But over the next few days Churchill's health rapidly deteriorated. Specialists were flown in from Cairo. On the night of the 15th, Churchill's heart began to fibrillate and his pulse became erratic. His doctor was seriously worried and thought this time he might not pull through. Churchill told his daughter Sarah, 'If I die, don't worry – the war is won.' John Martin, the Cabinet secretary who was accompanying him on this trip, alerted the War Cabinet in London. Grave announcements were issued to the press. At Carthage, Sarah read extracts from Jane Austen's *Pride and Prejudice* to her father. Clementine flew out from London to be with her husband. Then, suddenly, on the 17th, the antibiotics finally started to do their bit. From then on, Churchill recovered a little more each day. He started to dictate messages from his bed again and saw a constant stream of visitors until Clementine said all she could do was 'poke my nose around the corner of the door'. Churchill soon became irascible with his doctors, but they insisted he have at least a week's rest. So he spent a few more days in Carthage.

On Christmas Day, his first day out of bed, he had a conference with Eisenhower, Wilson, Alexander, Tedder and Cunningham to discuss plans for the landings at Anzio, south of Rome. Again the shortage of landing craft threatened the future of the whole operation. Churchill argued that the landings were essential to the Italian campaign, and the others agreed that they must go ahead, even if this led to a delay for Overlord. Two days later, Churchill and his entourage travelled on to the same villa in Marrakech where he and Roosevelt had watched the light over the mountains eleven months before. Churchill rested there for three weeks. He had suffered a serious, life-threatening illness and it had been an anxious time for everyone around him. But the old bulldog had pulled through.[23]

Throughout his illness, Churchill had been in contact with Roosevelt to agree the senior commanders for Overlord. Eisenhower was to take up his post as Supreme Commander as soon as he could leave his Italian command. Tedder was to be his deputy. And Montgomery was appointed Land Commander. Monty rushed back to London, leaving the 8th Army in Italy. On 2 January 1944, he attended a conference at St Paul's School (his old school in west London), which had been requisitioned by COSSAC, the group that had been quietly making plans for D-Day since the previous summer. After a briefing on the outline of the plans so far, Monty stood up and spoke. He tore the plans to shreds and said that the invasion was on too narrow a front with forces that were too small. He sent the COSSAC staff back to the drawing board to draw up a new and more ambitious plan. Later, Monty would claim that the redrawing of the invasion plans for Overlord was all his own doing. In fact, he and Eisenhower had already discussed the issue and agreed their line. And they knew that Churchill also thought more divisions were needed. The truth was that COSSAC had gone so far, but now that the Supreme Commander and his field commanders were in place, the whole operation could be scaled up. Serious planning for the invasion began at this point.

Eisenhower arrived in London in mid-January, and on the 21st he presided over the first meeting of his commanders and planners from the office that became known as Supreme Headquarters, Allied Expeditionary Force (SHAEF). From here the battle plan for the Overlord invasion soon expanded, as Eisenhower had the authority to convince Washington of the need for extra landing craft, air support, naval escorts, and the troops and *matériel* vital to launch a successful invasion across a hundred miles of the English Channel.

The invasion of Northern Europe was one of the most ambitious and risky operations of the Second World War. The scale of the challenge facing the planners was genuinely awesome. Each armoured division required forty ships to transport it. The Americans assembled in the South-West and the British troops concentrated in the South-East of England. Every unit required training camps, assembly areas and acres of space to gather their vehicles, armour and weaponry. A total of 137,000 wheeled and semi-tracked vehicles, 4000 full-tracked vehicles and 3500 artillery pieces were brought across the Atlantic in supply ships for the American armies alone. Jeeps from Detroit, K-rations from the farms of the Mid-West, shells, weapons, ammunition and medical supplies from across America were all delivered to the units assembling in England. Stretches of the Devon coast were evacuated of all their inhabitants so practice landings could take place using live ammunition. Ships and landing craft were lined up in all the major ports along the south coast of England. Hundreds of thousands of aerial photographs were taken up and down the French and Belgian coast and distributed so the troops could study the objectives that would face them. Divers crept ashore at night to collect samples of sand to calculate if it could support armoured vehicles, to measure the slope of the beaches and to assess the shore defences.

The final battle plan for D-Day was for three divisions of airborne troops to be dropped behind enemy lines to seize key targets on both flanks in the night before the invasion. During the morning of D-Day itself, four army corps would land on five Normandy beaches from the Cotentin peninsula in the west, on the right flank of the invasion, to the Orne River on the east. US, British and Canadian troops would charge ashore at dawn, and during the day about 170,000 men, 20,000 vehicles and thousands of tons of supplies would arrive to support them. Operational plans were drawn up and hundreds of pages of orders were circulated at corps level, then for divisions, brigades, regiments and companies. The five beaches were given code names, from west to east: Utah, Omaha, Gold, Juno and Sword. Each beach was divided into subsections and each unit assigned its targets from H-Hour, the moment when the first wave hit the beaches, onwards.

Churchill was too busy to engage with the day-to-day planning of the largest and most complex military operation of the war. But he still wrote minutes and issued his thoughts on matters like the waterproofing of vehicles, the onshore bombardment from naval ships and the number of transport aircraft available for the airborne assault. His influence was really felt when it came to his support for the Eisenhower–Montgomery plan to broaden the bridgehead and increase the number of men who would land ashore on D-Day. This would mean delaying the date of the invasion and reneging on the promise Roosevelt had made to Stalin at Teheran. The argument dragged on for a couple of months, until late March, when Washington finally agreed to the revised plan. Once that decision was made, and the idea of a May attack was abandoned, the next point when the moon and the tides would be right for a beach landing was from 5 to 7 June.

Churchill attended two presentations by Monty at St Paul's School, outlining the developing plans for Overlord. At the first on Good Friday, 7 April, Churchill was not well and he seems to have contributed little. The second, on 15 May, was a big show with dozens of senior officers from the British and American armies sitting in rows on benches, and the King, Churchill, Smuts, Brooke and the other Chiefs of Staff in VIP chairs at the front. Churchill was impressed by what he heard and said he was 'hardening' to the Overlord project.[24] Monty spent the last few weeks before the invasion on a whirlwind tour of southern England, inspecting the troops and visiting factories. His clipped, matter-of-fact style, captured in some of the newsreels, comes across as rather comical today. But it proved genuinely popular at the time. He addressed people in their own language, made them laugh and made them feel that they were really contributing to something important. And he seemed like a real soldier, rather than some aloof and remote château-general. The government was wary about Monty emerging as national figure, a popular warlord, but Churchill never did anything to prevent him from drumming up support.

As we saw in the last chapter, Churchill lost the struggle to keep RAF Bomber Command out of the planning for D-Day. Eisenhower brought all the British and American bombers in Britain under the command of SHAEF to enable strikes at tactical objectives along the beaches and at transport hubs inland. In order not to reveal that Normandy was the objective, this bombing had to be carried out along the whole French and Belgian coast.

Churchill's influence, however, was still considerable in important aspects of the Normandy invasion. A serious blot on his reputation for many years had been his involvement with the Dardanelles fiasco in 1915. Thousands of men had been landed along the coast at Gallipoli and it had been a near disaster. Obviously, Churchill did not want to be associated with the repetition of anything like this. And memories of the horrible slaughters resulting from First World War human-wave assaults against well-defended positions were strong in the minds of Churchill and the British generals, even if they were not for the American planners. As we know, from his early days, Churchill had been fascinated by new weapons and armoured vehicles of war, such as the tank which he had contributed to the development of in 1915. And in May 1940 he had asked Cherwell to review the production of tanks and called for the construction of an additional one thousand of them. One of the tank men who had given Churchill useful information during his 'wilderness years' about the parlous state of British armoured regiments was General Percy Hobart, then one of the most experienced commanders of armoured units in the army.

Churchill had been impressed with his fertile mind and his energy. But Hobart was a prickly figure and unpopular with his seniors in the army. In the summer of 1940, Churchill was appalled to discover that the Army High Command had pensioned off Hobart and he was serving his country only as a lance-corporal in the Home Guard. Churchill immediately called for his reinstatement as a major-general, and in a minute to his CIGS he wrote of Hobart's 'strong personality and original view'. He concluded in a way that perfectly summed up his view on these matters: 'We are now at war, fighting for our lives, and we cannot afford to confine Army appointments to persons who have excited no hostile comment in their career . . . This is a time to try men of force and vision and not to be exclusively confined to those who are judged thoroughly safe by conventional standards.' More prosaically, he was overheard saying to Dill: 'Remember it isn't only the good boys who help to win wars; it's the sneaks and stinkers as well.'[25]

Hobart was brought back into the army and given command of what became the 11th Armoured Division. He reorganised the structure of the unit to include a broad mix of heavy and light armour along with artillery, and can lay claim to having been the architect of the modern armoured division.[26] Churchill organised a series of four 'Tank Parliaments' at Downing Street in May and June 1941, another element in the War Lab. At these meetings, leading military figures and civilian experts met to exchange views about the future use of tanks, and of course to listen to Churchill's own thoughts on the subject. Hobart made an important contribution at these sessions. It is no surprise that the latest thirty-ton tank to roll off the production lines in 1941 was named the 'Churchill'. But the tank's namesake was distressed to discover that the mark-one Churchill had only a two-pound gun that was woefully inadequate for armoured warfare. It was unusual for anything with the name 'Churchill' to be known for its lack of bark. The gun was subsequently upgraded to a six-pounder.

In April 1943, Hobart was put in charge of the newly formed 79th Armoured Division, which became known as the 'Zoo' or 'Menagerie'. His task now was to devise a range of armoured devices to assist landing troops in getting through beach obstacles and in capturing the beachhead. The whole stretch of coast from Brittany to Norway had been heavily fortified. Concrete pill-boxes had been built with powerful heavy machine guns to provide arcs of fire across the beaches below. A huge array of steel obstacles had been set up along the beaches, and minefields had been laid in the sand dunes and at the head of each beach. In total, four million mines had been laid. The whole defensive line was called the 'Atlantic Wall'. In January 1944, in a strange twist of fate, Hitler appointed Field Marshal Rommel to take charge of it. Once again, Monty would be up against his old adversary from the desert war. With great vigour and energy, Rommel toured up and down the coast, reinforcing and building up the defences. It was Hobart's job to find the armoured machines that could penetrate the Atlantic Wall and support the infantry wading ashore.

Hobart turned his new division into a sort of think-tank for armoured warfare. Everyone was encouraged to come up with ideas. Floating tanks, known as 'Duplex Drives' (or DDs), had already been developed in the Mediterranean. They could be launched at sea with floating skirts around them so they could swim in with the landing craft carrying the infantry. Hundreds were built for D-Day. Hobart and his men devised minesweeping flail tanks with a giant rotor that spun a set of whirling chains on the ground to detonate mines ahead of the advancing tank. There were Bobbin tanks, which carried a metal track above the turret. Through an ingenious feeder mechanism, this could be laid in front of the advancing tank to cover ground where the sand was too soft to support tank tracks. Then there were tanks armed with flame throwers to flush out the enemy from well-defended bunkers. Tanks were adapted to lay bridges. And there were bulldozer tanks to remove obstacles. Hobart's inventiveness turned the British into pioneers of specialised armour, and the machines he devised became known as 'Hobart's Funnies'. Churchill was delighted with them. The Americans were more sceptical and used only the floating DD tanks on D-Day. Brooke wrote in his diary after a visit to Hobart to inspect the assault vehicles: 'Hobart has been doing wonders in his present job and I am delighted that we put him into it.'[27] Churchill's faith in Hobart had fully paid off.

Another aspect of the challenge of landing an army on beaches had exercised Churchill's mind for some time. A practice assault on an enemy-held harbour had been tried at Dieppe, in August 1942. It proved a disaster, with massive loss of life among the largely Canadian assault force. The lesson learned was that it was going to be very difficult to capture a heavily fortified port from the enemy. With thousands of tons of supplies needing to be brought ashore every day, the solution seemed to be for the Allies to build their own harbours along the invasion beaches. As early as May 1942, Churchill had sent a historic memo to Lord Mountbatten, who was then Chief of Combined Operations, about the problems of building a harbour on a shallow-water invasion beach. This included a handwritten comment that said the piers 'must float up and down with the tide. The anchor problems must be mastered. Let me have the best solutions worked out. Don't argue the matter. The difficulties will argue for themselves.'[28] This was typical of Churchill, and the last three sentences are still quoted in management training schools today as the attitude to adopt when facing a substantial challenge.

The War Office took on responsibility for pursuing this further, and Brigadier Bruce White was put in charge of the project. When Churchill sailed to the Quebec Conference on the *Queen Mary*, he debated the issue with his senior commanders. It had been decided to use blockships and giant concrete caissons to protect the harbours from the full force of the sea. Churchill did not understand how this would work, so an impromptu demonstration was staged in his bathroom. Several paper boats were launched and the water was splashed about. The paper boats sank. When a barrier was placed across the bath to represent a breakwater, no amount of splashing sank the little boats at the other end. General Ismay recalled:

> If a stranger had visited his bathroom, he might have seen a stocky figure in a dressing gown of many colours, sitting on a stool and surrounded by a number of what our American friends call 'Top Brass', while an admiral flapped his hands at one end of the bath . . . and a brigadier stretched a lilo across the middle . . . The stranger would have found it hard to believe that this was the British High Command studying the most stupendous and spectacular amphibious operation in the history of war.[29]

Churchill was now convinced it would work. The harbours were code-named 'Mulberry'. Two of the giant structures were to be built in Britain, one for the Americans off Omaha Beach and one for the British at Arromanches, off Gold Beach.

In a normal harbour, the quay remains fixed and the boats float up and down with the tide. In the Mulberry harbours, the piers had to float up and down with the ships. Giant pontoons were designed to be sunk on the seabed with four steel legs one hundred feet high. The floating pierheads would then be linked to the shore by a roadway strong enough to support thirty-ton tanks and other heavy vehicles. Major Alan Beckett, a distinguished engineer, came up with the design that combined both strength and flexibility using steel cables and heavy-duty ball-and-socket joints. A new form of anchor was also designed to secure all this to the seabed. And to protect it, huge concrete blockhouses, the caissons, each weighing six thousand tons, would be built in Britain and then floated across the Channel and sunk alongside a set of obsolete ships to form a harbour wall against the sea. The scale of the Mulberry project was gargantuan: 45,000 workers produced 147 caissons, 23 pierheads and 10 miles of floating roadway. This placed a near-impossible strain on British industry, which was already stretched to its limit.

In addition to the industrial challenge faced in the construction of the Mulberry harbours, there was endless bickering between the army, who had led the way on the project, and the navy, who regarded it as a matter for them. Churchill's constant requests for updates on the progress of his pet project no doubt prevented it from grinding to a complete halt. Despite endless delays, the many different parts were completed on time in ports and shipyards all around Britain. Like a giant jigsaw puzzle, the separate elements were then towed across the Channel and into position, and the two harbours were assembled a week after D-Day. It was an astonishing achievement on every level, and Churchill's enthusiasm and persistence had been vital to keep it going.

Throughout the whole planning for D-Day, the major fear was of a breach of secrecy – that somehow the plans would get out and the Germans would be waiting. Part of the attempt to prevent this was that huge operation of deception that had been born in the conversations with Stalin at Teheran. Through Operation Fortitude, the Allies tried to persuade the German

High Command that the real invasion would be launched along the shortest stretch of the Channel from England, on the Pas de Calais, and that the Normandy landings, when they came, were only a diversion. To this end, a false army known as '1st Army Group' was created in south-eastern England, complete with dummy tanks, trucks and fleets of dummy ships in the ports of Kent. A complete signals unit sent endless messages about training and assembly that could be picked up by the Germans. The 1st Army even had its own commander, the bullish General Patton, whom it was thought the Germans would believe was the most likely person to command the invasion forces. Patton made himself as visible as possible to add to the deception. Again, Churchill loved this sort of operation and gave it his full support.

Meanwhile, the advance in Italy, of which so much had been hoped by Churchill and others, had slowed to a snail's pace. The Germans had heavily fortified a defensive position known as the 'Gustav Line' across the central mountains, focused upon Monte Cassino, which dominated the road north to Rome. For four months, the Allies tried everything to destroy this citadel, including bombing the medieval Benedictine monastery that stood on its peak, destroying a library and antiquities that were over a thousand years old. But it was not until 18 May that Polish troops were able to capture the mountain that dominated the surrounding countryside. Finally, the troops advancing north met up with those who had landed at Anzio. They pressed onwards together, and on 4 June General Mark Clark led the Americans into Rome. It was splendid news which cheered Churchill and Roosevelt.

With the date for the invasion of France now fixed for 5 June, everything slowly came together. The men were trained and ready. They were in their final assembly camps near the embarkation points and received their final briefings. They were then issued with ammunition, seasickness pills and a leaflet about how to behave towards French civilians. From this point, no one was allowed to leave their base. Four thousand landing craft and hundreds of assault vehicles, along with dozens of escort ships, were ready. Thousands of light and heavy bombers were waiting to blitz the beach defences. The process of embarkation began. Anti-aircraft defences and fighter planes were on full alert, ready to attack any Luftwaffe bomber that dared to intervene. From Ipswich, along the whole south coast of Britain, and right round to Bristol, southern England had become an armed camp waiting for the order to go.

As we have seen, Churchill was eager to watch Overlord from HMS *Belfast*. But his senior commanders were horrified by the thought of the Prime Minister's being present near the landing beaches – not only for the danger it posed to him, but because of the fear that he might try to intervene at some critical juncture. In the end, to their relief, the King instructed Churchill to remain in England.

Then, at the last minute, the weather intervened. A storm blew up in the Atlantic and Eisenhower was advised that this might cause chaos for shipping and air support. At a late-night meeting on 3–4 June, he agreed to postpone D-Day for twenty-four hours. With 200,000 men in this state of readiness, it could be fatal to delay much longer. In the early hours of 5 June, Eisenhower gathered again with his commanders at his headquarters near Portsmouth. The predicted storm was raging and rain was lashing in horizontal streaks. The chief meteorologist, Group Captain Snagg, reported that he had spotted a slight break in the bad weather out in the Atlantic. He thought it would last for about thirty-six hours. Eisenhower had to make the biggest decision of his life. He turned to Montgomery and asked his opinion. He asked his deputy, Tedder, and the other senior commanders. The Supreme Commander listened carefully to their answers but knew that that only he had the authority to take the final decision. Eisenhower paused, then said, 'Let's go.' It was 4.15 a.m. on 5 June. The invasion was on.

Churchill, who had been sceptical of Overlord for so many months, had by now been won over and was optimistic. He invited the Chiefs of Staff to lunch and told them that the invasion was likely to be a success. Brooke, on the other hand, scribbled in his diary on the night before the invasion: 'I am very uneasy about the whole operation. At the best it will fall to very very far short of the expectation of the bulk of the people, namely all those who know nothing of its difficulties. At the worst it may well be the most ghastly disaster of the whole war. I wish to God it were safely over.'[30] Eisenhower chose that evening to visit the men of the 101st Airborne Division at Greenham Common airbase as they prepared to emplane for their drop behind enemy lines. His advisers had predicted they might suffer up to 80 per cent casualties, but he was cheered by their courage and enthusiasm. 'Now quit worrying, General,' one of them said, 'we'll take care of this thing for you.' Eisenhower had in his top tunic pocket a short, handwritten letter of resignation, accepting full responsibility for the failure of the invasion should everything go wrong.

At about 10 p.m. on the night of 5 June 1944, the aircraft carrying the airborne troops began to take off on their missions. They flew in a tight formation in a huge air armada across the Channel. In the west, the transport pilots encountered heavy anti-aircraft fire as they crossed the Cotentin Peninsula. In panic, many of the pilots pressed the green light, the signal to jump, and American paratroopers leapt out of the transport aircraft many miles from their intended drop zones. Some landed so far off course they could not even find where they were from their maps. In the east, some of the British glider troops, by contrast, landed within yards of their target, Pegasus Bridge. In minutes, they had seized control of Pegasus and another key bridge over the Orne. The first blood had been drawn and the 'Longest Day' had started.

The amphibious landings took place soon after dawn on 6 June. At the eastern end of Sword Beach the landing drill worked well. The DD tanks beached successfully and the flail tanks, known as 'Crabs', cleared the minefields as the men moved up and off the beach. The biggest problem came from traffic jams and bottlenecks as so many men and vehicles became entangled trying to get ashore. On Juno Beach, the Canadian landing went more slowly, but by late morning the bulldozer tanks were ashore and clearing obstacles, and the infantry advanced off the beach. After a few hours of fighting, the first coastal villages were liberated. At Gold Beach there was much heavier resistance and many of the tanks were taken out by the German anti-tank guns. But again the Crabs flailed through the minefields and the Bobbin tanks laid paths for vehicles and infantry to move forwards and capture the German strongholds. In total, the British and Canadians lost only 32 assault tanks out of 170. Hobart's 79th Armoured Division lost a total of 179 men killed or wounded. These numbers were way below the predicted casualty rates.

To the west on Omaha Beach, the story was entirely different. This was always going to be a tough landing, with two-hundred-foot cliffs at the head of the beach and well-prepared defenders inside thick concrete bunkers. A new German unit, the 352nd Division, had been assigned to this stretch of coast just a few days before the invasion. They were tougher and more determined than many of the other units in Normandy. At Omaha, the tanks were due to get to the beach at H-5, five minutes before the infantry arrived in their landing craft. But the sea was much rougher here in the aftermath of the storm. Many of the floating tanks were launched too far out and sank straight to the bottom. In one group, 29 out of 32 Sherman tanks sank on launching. And when the infantry waded ashore they were met with a furious enfilade of machine-gun and artillery fire. From their well-dug-in nests, the German machine gunners sprayed arcs of withering fire across the beach. Many men in the first wave never even got off the ramps of their landing craft. Others fell into the sea and drowned under the weight of all they were carrying. As landing craft were hit by mines or shells they blocked the beach for the next wave trying to get through behind them. The best the survivors could do was to take shelter behind the iron beach obstacles or under the sea wall. But moving off the beach under the intense fire seemed impossible. Casualties mounted to alarming levels. The first wave was almost entirely wiped out. Watching the massacre unfold from USS *Augusta* several miles out to sea, General Omar Bradley and his commanders tried to piece together what was going on and considered abandoning the landing. Naval destroyers came in as close to the beach as they dared, within about eight hundred yards, to fire directly into the German gun emplacements. Then, in the late morning, Brigadier Norman Cota, the energetic deputy commander of the 29th Division, showing great heroism, led a group of men up a gully and on to the cliffs above the beach. From here, they were slowly able to fan out and attack the German gun emplacements one by one. By early afternoon, the determination of the US infantry had won through. They had overpowered the German strongholds and cleared the beach exits. But by then there had been three thousand casualties on Omaha Beach.

On the westernmost beach, Utah, by contrast, things went extremely well. The current carried the landing craft more than a mile from their planned landing zone, but the beaches the American 4th Division hit were lightly defended and most of the armour got ashore without incident. Astonishingly, the casualties here during D-Day were lighter than on their last training exercise at Slapton Sands in Devon.

Overall, D-Day was a remarkable triumph. By the end of the day, 177,000 men and their equipment were ashore. Some units had penetrated five miles inland. The Allied air forces had flown 14,600 sorties. The Luftwaffe had barely put in an appearance all day. U-boats had got nowhere near the vast naval armada in the Channel. Hitler's supposedly impregnable Atlantic Wall had been breached. Not anticipating that the Allies would invade during the storm, Rommel had returned to Germany and so was not present when the landings took place. Other officers were away at an exercise in Rennes. Rommel rushed back later in the day, but only Hitler could order the deployment of the key panzer reserves. He believed that Normandy was just a side show, with the real landings to follow in the Pas de Calais. Operation Fortitude had been a success. So, in the first few critical hours, the panzer reserves waited but did not intervene.

Churchill followed events during the morning of 6 June in his Map Room. Later that day, he addressed a packed House of Commons. He paid fulsome tribute to the 'ingenious modifications of the British armour' and said:

> This vast operation is undoubtedly the most complicated and difficult that has ever taken place ... Nothing that equipment, science or forethought could do has been neglected and the whole process of opening up this great new front will be pursued with the utmost resolution both by the commanders and by the United States and British Governments whom they serve.[31]

He sent a message to Stalin, informing him of the initial success of the invasion. Stalin replied with wholehearted praise for the 'grandiose scale' on which the invasion had been carried out. As per the agreement at Teheran, on 10 June the Red Army's vast summer offensive began with an assault on the Leningrad front.

Churchill was still itching to get across to Normandy to see the bridgehead for himself. He asked Monty if he could pay a visit, saying: 'We do not wish in any way to be a burden to you or on your headquarters . . . We shall bring some sandwiches with us.'[32] On 12 June, Churchill crossed the Channel in a destroyer. Brooke, who accompanied him, noted: 'We continually passed convoys of landing craft, minesweepers, bits of floating breakwater being towed out, parts of the floating piers etc. And overhead, a continuous flow of planes going to and coming from France.' They were taken ashore in a DUKW, a floating truck, and were photographed and filmed as they disembarked on to the beach. Brooke was quite emotional at being back in France four years after he had left in the disastrous defeats of 1940. Monty met them and took the party to his headquarters about five miles inland, where he explained his dispositions and his plans. Then they had lunch in the grounds in a tent. Churchill asked how far away the enemy was. Monty told him about three miles and explained that there was not a continuous perimeter line. Churchill asked: 'What is there then to prevent an incursion of German armour breaking up our luncheon?' Monty replied that he didn't think they would come. Churchill and Brooke finished their tour by sailing up and down the invasion beaches and watching an LCT (Landing Craft Tank) disgorge its cargo of tanks and trucks on to the shore 'in a remarkably short time'. Finally, they witnessed a bombardment by two British battleships of positions about twelve miles inland. Churchill had never been on a Royal Navy ship firing in anger, so he asked the captain of his destroyer to fire off a salvo as well. This he did, and Churchill was quite disappointed when the enemy did not return their fire.[33]

Churchill and his team returned to Portsmouth that evening, having seen some of the giant pieces of the Mulberry harbours being assembled. When it was finally built, protected by the giant concrete caissons and sunken ships, with its floating pierheads and miles of roadway, the British harbour became known, fittingly, as 'Port Winston'. Although severely damaged in a storm, it continued to process literally millions of men, tens of thousands of tanks and other vehicles, and hundreds of thousands of tons of supplies for five months, until the Allies had advanced into Holland. The remnants of the giant concrete blocks can still be seen in the sea off the beach at Arromanches, the remains of one of the most extraordinary military engineering feats of the war.

The day after Churchill returned to London from his sightseeing trip to the invasion beaches, a mysterious new type of bomb exploded in a street in Bethnal Green, east London. Six people were killed and another nine injured. Hitler had been threatening to use secret terror weapons against Britain for some time. German science had advanced way ahead of what was happening in Britain. A campaign now began in which hundreds of flying bombs and then ballistic missiles were fired against London. Hitler was not defeated yet.

10

Victory and Defeat

On 15 May 1942, an aerial reconnaissance Spitfire was flying fast and high across the Baltic. Over the northern end of the forested island of Usedom, the pilot noticed a mass of new construction around what looked like an airfield. He turned his cameras on and took a series of photographs of the ground below. When they got back to the aerial photography interpretation centre located in a big country house at Medmenham in Buckinghamshire, the photo interpreters tried to work out what was going on. Medmenham was to aerial photography what Bletchley Park was to code-breaking. An unlikely group of academics, scientists, archaeologists and air force types had been assembled and were building up a detailed analysis of everything that was happening in occupied Europe. By constantly comparing new photos with previous ones, they were able to plot the building or extension of every new factory, every new stretch of road or railway, and every new gun emplacement across Europe. But the strange shapes in the photos taken along the Baltic coast, which included circular embankments, left the interpreters puzzled. It was decided to keep a close watch on developments in this place called Peenemünde.

Many months passed before reports started coming in to British Intelligence about long-range rockets being developed at Peenemünde. In the Oslo Report, the document that had been left on the window sill of the British Consulate in Oslo in November 1939, there had been references to the development of rocket technology. Now this suddenly seemed far more threatening and real. In April 1943, the Joint Intelligence Committee and the Chiefs of Staff thought that Churchill should be made aware of the intelligence reports. Churchill agreed to establish a group to investigate and assess the threat. Duncan Sandys, his son-in-law and an expert on weapons development, was put in charge of the investigation, code-named 'Operation Crossbow'.

Sandys and his team visited Medmenham and studied the aerial photographs, and went through the intelligence reports, some of which had come from the Polish Resistance. But none of it seemed to make much sense and there was an intense debate as to what the German scientists were up to. Then, in late June, a Mosquito photo reconnaissance aircraft made another pass across Peenemünde at high altitude. The day was clear and sunny and when the photographs were developed they revealed what seemed to be the answer to the mystery. The Mosquito had managed to photograph two rockets lying on their transporters alongside a tower structure. By measuring the shadows and knowing the exact time of day the photos had been taken, the interpreters were able to calculate that the rockets were thirty-eight feet long and that they were being assembled inside some sort of launch site.

On the evening of 29 June, Churchill chaired a high-level meeting of the Cabinet Defence Committee. Sandys and his team reported their fears that a form of long-range missile was being constructed. General Brooke, who was present, noted in his diary: 'Arrived at conclusion that definite threat exists.'[1] However, Lord Cherwell, who was also in attendance, was sceptical. He fiercely disputed that any sort of liquid fuel could have been developed as a propellant, and said that no rocket could be made to carry a sufficient payload to cause serious damage. On both these points he was proved entirely wrong. He argued that the Germans were probably developing some form of jet-propelled pilotless flying bomb. In this he was to be proved right. What the scientists in London did not know for sure was that the Germans were experimenting with the production of *two* new types of bomb at Peenemünde. The first, made by a team headed by the brilliant German rocket scientist Werner von Braun, was the A-4 ballistic missile, a rocket which could carry a one-ton payload over a distance of 90–130 miles at over 2000 m.p.h. Several of these missiles had already been successfully launched. Meanwhile, General Dornberger of the German Army, who was running the research station, was also developing a prototype cruise missile for the Luftwaffe, which was launched from a hundred-yard-long ramp.

For some time, the British research teams would be confused by the fact that the Germans were developing these two separate and distinct technologies simultaneously. There was considerable difference of opinion between the British scientists as to what was happening at Peenemünde, and as ever with Cherwell this soon became personal in his sharp criticism of Sandys. But at the key meeting on 29 June, Churchill sided with Sandys rather than Cherwell and authorised the heavy bombing of Peenemünde along with detailed surveillance of all of northern France within 130 miles of London to try to find launch sites for the secret weapons. The group agreed that London was the most likely target, and plans were laid in utmost secrecy for the mass evacuation of children and pregnant women in the event of the use of the terror weapons. It must have seemed that just as one threat to Britain's survival from the U-boats in the Atlantic had been defeated, another, potentially even more deadly threat had appeared.

In June, Hitler himself visited Peenemünde to inspect the progress of the experimental rocket research. He was delighted by what he saw. He believed that the use of these new weapons could turn the course of the war and he told his military chiefs that London would be flattened and Britain forced to capitulate. The date on which the attacks would begin was set for 20 October 1943. Hitler said that tens of thousands of the missiles would be used.

The debate on the scale of the threat continued in London with widespread divergence of views. The home security people believed the warheads could contain ten or even twenty tons of high explosive and were fearful of catastrophic damage to the capital. Cherwell continued to argue that nothing on this scale was technically possible. Churchill later wrote that listening to the opposing arguments, 'it might have seemed at times that the two protagonists were divided as to whether the attack by the self propelled weapons would be annihilating or comparatively unimportant'.[2]

On the night of 17 August, 571 heavy bombers hit Peenemünde. The bombing caused widespread destruction. More than seven hundred scientists and workers were killed, including Dornberger's deputy, who had designed the engine for the A-4 rocket. Forty of the bombers were shot down by enemy fighters. It was a high rate of loss, but the German research had been set back by several critical months. Furthermore, the Germans now decided to relocate this scientific work. Some of it was transferred to underground factories in the Harz Mountains. The work on the A-4 was relocated to an SS artillery range near Blizna in Poland. But it was the flying bombs, the prototype cruise missiles, that would be used first against Britain.

Assisted by reports coming in from the French Resistance, the scientists worked out what the launch sites for these new flying bombs looked like. Each site contained three buildings, the first about 260 feet long and 10 feet wide. It was here that the German engineers constructed the ramp from which the missile was fired. The other two buildings were smaller and always occupied the same relative positions to the long, thin building. In them the missiles were assembled, armed and fuelled. After scouring aerial photographs of the northern French coast, dozens of potential sites were identified by the photo interpreters at Medmenham. In each one, the ramp was being lined up to point exactly in the direction of London. A total of ninety-six of these sites were then bombed and destroyed. All of this further delayed the start of the flying bomb offensive. The first attack was made a week after D-Day, on 13 June 1944, nearly eight months after Hitler had said the missiles would be launched. Goebbels, the Nazi Propaganda Minister, named the missiles '*Vergeltungswaffe*' – literally 'retaliation' or 'vengeance weapons' for the invasion. The flying bomb became known in Britain as the 'V-1', with the 'V' standing for 'vengeance'. Eisenhower wrote later that if the Germans had got the V-1s operating six months earlier, as Hitler had planned, then they could have caused havoc with the preparations for D-Day. He even went as far as to say: '"Overlord" might have been written off.'[3]

As it was, Londoners now experienced a second Blitz. In the next five weeks about three thousand V-1s were fired at the capital. It was a terrible experience to be under these flying bombs. Londoners heard the buzz of their engines as they flew over, hence their popular names 'buzz bombs' and 'doodle-bugs'. Next the engine would cut out and everything fell silent for a few seconds. Then the bomb crashed to the ground, causing a huge explosion. The suspense was appalling. The flying bombs could come over at day or night and regardless of the weather. They were impersonal, indiscriminate killers and made people feel helpless as there was nothing they could do to defend themselves except run for the shelters if there were enough time.

At first it seemed as if there were little defence against the flying bombs once they had been launched. They were difficult to shoot down from the air because of their speed and small size. If an interceptor fighter aircraft got close enough to shoot at one, the fighter would probably be destroyed in the massive explosion that followed. The fastest RAF fighters, Spitfires and Tempests, stripped down to add a few extra miles per hour to their speed, were just about able to catch the jet-propelled flying bombs out over the Channel, and occasionally a brave pilot was able to get close enough to tip one with his wing, so as to deflect it off course and send it crashing into the sea. More effective was a new form of radar known as 'SCR-584' that was developed by scientists at the Radlab, a specialised unit at the Massachusetts Institute of Technology in America. This system could track a flying bomb and fire anti-aircraft shells automatically, bypassing manual operation of the guns. Churchill personally intervened to get this system shipped from America in significant numbers. Combining SCR-584 with new proximity fuses that ignited when the anti-aircraft shells were near to the bomb was the most effective way of striking at the V-1s. Another ingenious way of reducing their impact was by letting it be known that many of the bombs were overshooting London and landing to the north of the city. This piece of disinformation resulted in the Germans resetting the controls of the V-1s to crash to land earlier. This meant that hundreds of flying bombs landed harmlessly in the fields of Sussex or Kent and never reached London.

By the end of August, only one in seven of the flying bombs fired against London was getting through. Of the total 8500 bombs launched against London, a total of 2400 landed somewhere in the South-East. By September, the threat from the V-1s had virtually come to an end as the advancing armies had overrun most of the launch sites in northern France. However, 24,000 civilians were killed or seriously injured and 750,000 homes were damaged during the V-1 flying bomb offensive.

However, just as one threat faded, the second V-weapon began to land on London. These rocket missiles were propelled by the combustion of alcohol and liquid oxygen. Controlled by gyroscopes, they flew up to a height of about fifty miles before heading back to earth in a huge parabola. They had a range of about two hundred miles and the entire journey took just three or four minutes. Their one-ton warhead was about the same as that fitted to the V-1. After the plot on his life on 20 July 1944, Hitler put Himmler and the SS in charge of all his special weapons projects. The SS rushed through the readying of the rockets and the first one landed on Chiswick in west London on the evening of 8 September. There was absolutely no defence against this silent and deadly weapon, known as the 'V-2', other than to destroy the launch sites. As the Allied armies advanced through France and Belgium, most of the launch pads were moved to Holland, many near The Hague. The Germans thought the Allies would not want to bomb the Dutch capital. However, British and American bombers constantly harassed the known launch sites and the missile production centres. This reduced the number of missiles being produced from the intended number of nine hundred per month to roughly half of this. In total, over thirteen hundred V-2 rockets were fired on England and a slightly larger number were fired on Belgium, mostly on the giant port of Antwerp after the Allied armies had captured it. About five hundred reached London and over nine thousand civilians were killed or seriously injured. The V-2 threat was not finally lifted until the last launch sites were captured in March 1945.

The debate about the effectiveness of the V-weapons intensified after the war when Albert Speer, the German Minister of Munitions, said that they had been a massive waste of resources. Speer argued that if all the expertise and materials that had gone into flying bomb and rocket production had instead gone into the development of more fighter aircraft then the bombing offensive against Germany might have been defeated. In this sense, Hitler's obsession with his secret weapons that he thought could yet win the war was a stroke of luck for the Allies. But this new rocket missile technology was clearly a harbinger of things to come, and as the war came near to its end the Americans and Soviets raced to capture as much of the German rocket technology as possible. The United States launched Operation Paperclip, in which they rounded up many German scientists. Werner von Braun and his team preferred to surrender to the Americans rather than the Russians, and under Paperclip they were taken to White Sands in New Mexico, where a new US rocket research establishment was created. In the decades that followed, von Braun and his brilliant engineers played a key role in the American space programme. Twenty-seven years after the first ballistic missile had been launched from Peenemünde, *Apollo 11* astronauts walked on the moon.

With the war in its final phases, and with the Americans and Soviets taking on the major roles in defeating Hitler in Europe and the Japanese in the Pacific, Churchill's status clearly diminished. But there were still major disputes with his military commanders over how best to use the resources they had. The biggest disagreement arose over plans for the deployment of Britain's armed forces in the Far East. At the heart of the argument between Churchill and his Chiefs of Staff were two different approaches as to how best to defeat the Japanese. Churchill wanted to keep the core of the British effort in the Indian Ocean, directed at amphibious operations against Sumatra and further east towards Malaya and Singapore. The Chiefs of Staff wanted the limited British war effort in the Pacific to be lined up alongside the Americans. They produced powerful arguments to show that victory would come sooner if the ships of the Royal Navy, the aircraft of the RAF and the soldiers of the British Army were assembled in Australasia to fight along the left of the main American advance in the South-West Pacific and ultimately towards Japan. Churchill and the War Cabinet took a political view that British interests would be best served if British forces liberated the territories that had been lost in 1941 and 1942. This would help re-establish British power in the region as it had been before the war. The Chiefs of Staff took a more pragmatic view on how best to strike at the Japanese, recognising Britain's junior relationship in this American-dominated theatre. Churchill, as so often in his life, was more interested in maintaining British power and prestige in India than, in this case, advancing through lands he had barely heard of.

The dispute grew to a head in March 1944, three months before Overlord. In his diary, Brooke described several difficult and tense meetings with Churchill. After one such he wrote: 'Now that I know him well episodes such as Antwerp and the Dardanelles no longer puzzle me. But meanwhile I often doubt whether I am going mad or he is really sane.' Then, a few days later, he wrote of 'heated discussions' with Churchill and of a 'desperate meeting'. He was clearly at the end of his tether. Interestingly, later that day, Churchill invited Brooke to dinner. The CIGS thought he was going to be sacked for his outspoken opposition. Instead, Churchill was quite charming and clearly wanted to make up for some of the 'rough passages of the day'.

But the disagreement was a deep one and would not go away. After one Chiefs of Staff meeting, all the secretaries and minute-takers were asked to leave the room and the leaders of Britain's military machine discussed between themselves the possibility of a group resignation. Again Brooke wrote: 'I am shattered by the present condition of the PM. He has lost all balance and is in a very dangerous mood.'[4] General Ismay, the linchpin between Churchill and his War Cabinet, on the one hand, and his Chiefs of Staff, on the other, felt impelled to write to the Prime Minister that the division of opinion was so great there was talk of mass resignation. In Ismay's undoubtedly correct view, 'A breach of this kind, undesirable at any time, would be little short of cata-strophic at the present juncture' so close to D-Day.[5]

The argument seems an arcane one now, and it is difficult to imagine why the passions aroused should have been so intense. No doubt it was partly because of the general state of exhausted tension and stress felt by Churchill and his Chiefs of Staff. The campaign in Italy was going badly and the run-up to D-Day made this one of the most decisive moments in the war. And at the time, of course, no one could know that the war in the Pacific would end so soon after the end of the war in Europe. It was generally felt that the conflict against Japan would con-tinue at least into the summer of 1946 and that strategic decisions affecting that theatre were of vital significance. But it is difficult now to have much sympathy for either side in the dispute. Churchill, his Cabinet and the Foreign Office had all failed to spot the huge changes that had taken place in South-East Asia, where powerful anti-colonial movements had been unleashed by the Japanese successes. The prospect of restoring Britain's pre-war authority in the region was pure chimera. And the idea of landing troops in Sumatra now seems absurd. On the other hand, the soldier's job was to do whatever his polit-ical chiefs demanded, and Brooke's rigid hostility seems out of proportion and character. Even his supporters have not defended him in this quarrel.[6]

Churchill did as he often did at times of crisis and appealed to Roosevelt, who responded by telling him to concentrate on the Indian Ocean. After the Battles of Midway and the Coral Sea, the US Navy was already in command of much of the vastness of the Pacific, and later in the year it would win a decisive victory against the Imperial Japanese Navy at the Battle of Leyte Gulf in the Philippines. Churchill felt his case had been strengthened by the President's view and he wrote a paper outlining his position on future Pacific strategy that he asked the Chiefs of Staff to approve. Brooke wrote: 'We cannot accept it as it stands, and it would be better if we all three resigned rather than accept his solution.'[7] The crisis was defused only when the US Joint Chiefs of Staff announced there were no plans for a major amphibious operation in South-East Asia that year. Both Churchill's grand plan for Sumatra and the Chiefs of Staff's pro-American strategy were redundant. General William Slim would go on to win a considerable victory over Japanese land forces in Burma, so by the time the Pacific question next entered the frame it would be in completely different circumstances.

The crisis marks the lowest point in Churchill's relationship with Brooke and the Chiefs of Staff. Churchill was utterly exhausted by the unrelenting struggle of the war. After one meeting, Brooke wrote: 'He kept yawning and saying he felt desperately tired.' After another: 'PM aged, tired and failing to really grasp matters. It is a depressing sight to see him gradually deteriorating. I wonder how long he will last, not long enough to see the war through I fear.'[8]

But Churchill did recover his strength and his spirits, as he had done before. Only a month later, after dinner at Chequers, he took Brooke aside and told him how much he valued him. Brooke later reflected:

Considering the difficult times I had had recently with Winston I appreciated tremendously his kindness in passing on these remarks to me . . . He was an outstanding mixture, could drive you to complete desperation and to the brink of despair for weeks on end, and then would ask you to spend a couple of hours or so alone with him and would produce the most homely and attractive personality. All that unrelenting tension was temporarily relaxed . . . and you left him with the feeling that you would do anything within your power to help carry the stupendous burden he had shouldered.[9]

Churchill knew he could not push his military chiefs to resignation at this critical moment of the war. A brutal confrontation had been avoided and his charm had once again worked, for now.

The triumph of D-Day and the successful landing of men and *matériel* in Normandy were great boosts to Churchill and his Chiefs of Staff. One of the most complex and ambitious operations of the war had been a success and, despite a heavy storm in mid-June, Port Winston at Arromanches continued to operate as a floating harbour, receiving vast numbers of men and huge quantities of supplies. But the good news of the landings was soon followed by disappointing news as the Allies failed to extend their bridgehead in the way that had been hoped. Monty's troops took until the second week of July to capture the French city of Caen, only ten miles inland. Monty claimed his strategy was to draw the German armour to the east, around Caen, and so allow the Americans to break out in the west. After a slow start, the Germans sent heavy reinforcements to this front, including two crack SS panzer divisions from the Eastern Front, and tried repeatedly to split the bridgehead and throw the Allies back into the sea. Both sides refused to give an inch. The high, thick hedgerows that were common in Normandy made ideal conditions for defenders. By the end of June, one million soldiers were facing each other in bitter fighting. Monty tried to use his infantry to break through in an assault code-named 'Epsom' and then his armour in an attack code-named 'Goodwood'. But each attempt brought a tougher German defensive response. By mid-July, a total of eight panzer divisions, six of them elite SS units, were facing Monty's British and Canadian troops around Caen. It became clear to many that the German tanks, especially the massive sixty-ton Tiger, were far superior to the Allied armour. And the German artillery, particularly the much-feared 88mm gun, which was used as an anti-tank weapon, was superior to any artillery piece in the Allied arsenal.

In the circumstances, it might have been expected that Churchill would give vent to his frustrations at the slowness of the offensive, as he had done earlier in the war with Wavell and Auchinleck, by demanding action and pestering his field commanders with instructions and briefs. But Brooke managed to keep Churchill at arm's length from Monty, who was left to carry on with his operational planning unhindered by interventions from the Prime Minister. Churchill was also no doubt acutely aware of Monty's popularity with the public, which was at a different level to that of his previous generals. Unfortunately, no breakout came and it was Eisenhower who grew increasingly frustrated by Monty's lack of progress. The tension between the two commanders grew from this point and lasted right on to the battle of the memoirs and reputations in the post-war period.

When the breakout did finally take place in the last week of July, the American First Army commanded by General Bradley led the way in Operation Cobra. After a heavy air bombardment, the US VII Corps launched the assault near St Lô.

Monty's strategy of tying down the German armour in the east now paid off as there were still fourteen German divisions gathered around Caen, leaving only eleven weakened divisions facing fifteen American divisions in the west. Once the German line began to crumble, the American Sherman tanks were ordered in and their crews began to liberate town after town as they sped onwards. On 1 August, the US Army reorganised in Normandy and Bradley brought in General Patton to lead the newly created 3rd Army. Renowned for his aggressive spirit, Patton brought a new dynamism just when the breakout was gathering speed. A key bridge was captured intact at Pontauban, and Patton's men raced across it and fanned out into Brittany. Some of them advanced fifty miles in four days. Hitler ordered his commanders to give no ground, as he had done at Stalingrad, and replaced some of his senior generals. Rommel, who had done so much to hold up the Allied advance in Normandy, was severely wounded by an RAF attack upon his staff car. His career was over. Restrained by lack of fuel and ammunition, constantly harried from the air, and now prevented from making tactical withdrawals to reorganise in strength, the German troops still fought on. Especially tenacious were the fanatical SS panzer grenadiers whose ferocious support for their Fuehrer was only hardened after news got out of the unsuccessful bomb plot against his life. But no army, no matter how determined, could triumph against the overwhelming odds the Germans now faced. Every tank they lost was a permanent loss. For the Allies, every tank lost was replaced by two or three more within days.

Hitler, suspicious of all his army commanders after the plot against him, ordered General von Kluge, Rommel's replacement, to counter-attack. This he could do only reluctantly by moving his armour westwards. The counter-attack, inevitably, failed and now von Kluge's armour was deep inside an Allied encirclement as Patton's tanks raced eastwards towards the Loire and the Seine. The Canadians then broke through and advanced south while Patton turned north. The remnants of the German Army were surrounded. Some got away through the Falaise 'gap', but the bulk of Hitler's Army Group West was destroyed. Like the British Army at Dunkirk, the Germans had to abandon a lot of their heavy equipment. Ten thousand German soldiers had been killed and fifty thousand were taken prisoner. More than two thousand panzers had been lost. Twenty-seven divisions had ceased to exist. Von Kluge wrote a note to Hitler saying the war was as good as lost. Then, knowing he would be blamed for the defeat, he committed suicide. Four days after the collapse at Falaise, on 25 August, the German garrison in Paris surrendered. It was the culmination of a huge Allied victory.

Typically, Churchill seized every opportunity to visit the battlefront. He spent some time in Normandy in July and August, observing for himself the landscape of war, and eagerly followed the news of the breakout. He was concerned by the growing American hostility towards Monty. And there were still arguments over the planned landings in the south of France, now called 'Operation Dragoon'. Churchill did not want troops taken from the advance in northern Italy for a mission that he regarded as entirely unnecessary. Of 250,000 men in the 5th Army under General Alexander in Italy, roughly 100,000 would be taken away for Dragoon. Churchill knew that the advance through Italy and then the plan to cross the Alps and head towards Vienna would be slowed right down by diverting troops to the Côte d'Azur. This time his Chiefs of Staff agreed totally with him. Churchill appealed to Roosevelt to cancel the operation. The President again refused Churchill's plea and stood by his Joint Chiefs, who maintained their faith in the landings. On 5 August, Churchill spent more than six hours at

Eisenhower's headquarters in Portsmouth, trying to persuade him to cancel the operation. Eisenhower's aide-de-camp, Captain Harry Butcher, recalled that 'Ike said "No", continued saying "No" all afternoon, and ended saying "No" in every form of the English language at his command.'[10]

Six days later, Churchill flew to Italy to see the situation there for himself. He met with Marshal Tito, the leader of the Partisans in Yugoslavia, who had maintained an epic and brilliant struggle against the German occupying forces, supported by SOE. Churchill found Tito a curious but impressive figure and was pleased to hear that he was not committed to a communist future for Yugoslavia. Churchill then went on to witness the landings in southern France. He watched the shore bombardment from the British destroyer HMS *Kimberley*. For Churchill, the event was the great anticlimax he had predicted, and he noted that 'not a shot was fired either at the approaching flotillas or on the beaches'. His return was so uneventful that he even borrowed a novel from the ship's captain that he sat down and read. He wrote to Clementine that it was one of the best he had read in years.[11] Churchill travelled on to Naples, where he combined talks about the future of Italy with several swimming expeditions along the coast. The Mediterranean sunshine and the bathing refreshed his spirits. He returned to London rested and in good health.

Once again in the war, the victory in Normandy raised the question: what next? How should the Allies pursue their drive eastwards in what they hoped would be the final operation of the war? There were two views on this. Montgomery wanted to go for a single thrust of some forty divisions to strike forwards by the Ardennes, through the Ruhr and across the plains of northern Germany to Berlin. He wanted to lead this himself and so go down in history as the Allied general who won the war in Europe. Eisenhower, on the other hand, favoured a broader, two-pronged assault upon Germany, with Monty driving his forces to the north and a southern, American force heading below the Ardennes and crossing into Germany along the Saar River. This dispute between the two commanders, who were already not on the best of terms, grew in intensity over the weeks. Monty did not like being overruled. But Eisenhower was in command and the Americans were calling the shots. They would not accept that a British general could command US troops in such a key operation. Neither Churchill nor his Chiefs of Staff could do anything to prevent Eisenhower from getting his way.

In September, Monty launched his own highly imaginative thrust, code-named 'Operation Market Garden'. He intended to use a sequence of airborne drops to seize a series of key bridges across Holland right up to the Rhine. A relief column would then speed across country to link all the captured bridges and propel the Allies right into Germany itself. All the remaining V-2 launch sites would be captured and new ports would be opened up to the Allies to supply the advancing armies. It was an ambitious attempt to bring the war to a speedy end. Much of the plan was brilliantly executed. American paratroopers captured bridges at Eindhoven, Grave and Nijmegen. Unfortunately, alongside the last bridge to be seized by the British 1st Airborne at Arnhem, the Germans had located a rest camp for two SS panzer divisions that had been pulled out of the line. Photo reconnaissance had identified that these elite German units were in the vicinity, but the British commanders refused to adapt their plan. The British paratroopers, known as the 'Red Devils' and commanded by Colonel John Frost, conducted a heroic defence of the bridge. But the land troops failed to reach them and this led to the collapse of Monty's daring plan. The bridge at Arnhem is now remembered as the 'bridge too far'. With the failure here went all hope of a fast strike into Germany and the end of the war by Christmas.

In September, Churchill and his Chiefs of Staff travelled again to Quebec to meet Roosevelt and the Joint Chiefs for what proved to be the last Anglo-American summit of the war, code-named 'Octagon'. By this time, most of Churchill's attention was focused not so much on finishing the war, the result of which was by now a foregone conclusion, but on the post-war world and his fears of a dominant Russia. As the Red Army advanced west, beyond the borders of the Soviet Union, the question arose as to who should take over liberated territories. The first instance in which this became acute was in Poland. In the month before Octagon, the Polish Resistance rose up against the German occupation as the Red Army approached Warsaw. Their intention was to overthrow German rule and replace it with an independent Polish government based around the leadership in exile in London. The Germans responded by putting down the uprising with ferocious brutality. The Red Army now paused on the Vistula River, only a few miles from Warsaw, but Stalin ordered his soldiers not to intervene. He wanted his own communist supporters in the Polish Committee of National Liberation to take control, so he was happy to see the Poles who supported the London democrats massacred. Churchill and the Cabinet, along with public opinion in much of the West, were outraged by Stalin's refusal to help the Polish rebels. After all, Britain had gone to war in 1939 to defend Poland, and Churchill felt a particular responsibility for the country. He pleaded with Stalin to intervene. The Soviet leader said this was impossible – his troops needed time to regroup. There was nothing that British or American forces could do to aid the rebels as Warsaw was too far away to permit direct military intervention. All that could be done was for the Allied air forces to drop in supplies to assist the rebels. But no supply aircraft that could fly to Warsaw had the range to make it back, so they would have to land at a Soviet airfield to refuel

and return. Stalin absolutely prohibited this. Churchill was furious. The entire War Cabinet fumed and protested to Stalin. Still,
he did nothing. For sixty-three days, the Polish Resistance fighters held off the German onslaught armed only with rifles and
small arms. In the end 200,000 Poles were slaughtered by the
Nazis in an orgy of violence. Stalin had allowed the free Polish
Resistance movement to be destroyed so that he could hand
Poland over to his own stooges.

For Churchill, this rang alarm bells about the possibility of a
post-war Europe divided between East and West. At Quebec, it
was clear that Roosevelt was far less concerned about this. The
two leaders, along with the Combined Chiefs of Staff, discussed
and agreed the details for the next phase of the war. In Europe,
Eisenhower's plan for a two-pronged assault on Germany was
endorsed. In Italy, the Americans now raised no objections to an
advance across the Alps and into southern Europe. Churchill
talked about his plan to liberate Vienna. In the Far East,
Churchill wanted to assure the Americans of the British commitment to play its role in the defeat of Japan. He was again
thinking about the post-war era and wanted Britain to have
earned the right to restore its possessions that had been captured by Japan. He did not want these to be handed back by a
peace treaty; he wanted to win them back by force of arms.
However, the Americans were deeply suspicious of Britain's
imperial intentions in the Pacific. The US military chiefs wanted
to see Burma recaptured as this was vital to supplying China. But
Admiral King, who had never been much of a friend to Britain,
saw the naval war in the Pacific as an exclusively American
affair. In the end, the President overruled his own admiral and
agreed that the Royal Navy could contribute to the defeat of
Japan. But General Marshall pointed out that the United States
now had enough heavy bombers to carry out the bombing of
Japan. It seemed that once Germany had been defeated, the

RAF's role in the Far East would be limited to operations in Burma and the Indian Ocean. It was estimated that the war against Japan would continue for about eighteen months after the defeat of Germany.

At Octagon, Churchill's relationship with Roosevelt was much cooler than it had been earlier in the war. His friend and intermediary Harry Hopkins, who had done so much to help cement relations between Britain and the United States since 1941, had fallen out with the President and was not present in Quebec. Churchill spent a couple of days with Roosevelt at his home in Hyde Park after the summit, and then left for home.

Once the Octagon meetings had set the war strategy for the next six to twelve months, there was little in reality for Churchill to do as a warlord. It was up to the generals now to defeat Hitler in the West and to continue the advance towards Japan in the Pacific. But Churchill became even more concerned with the growing power of the Soviet Union as the Red Army looked set to liberate more of Eastern Europe. So, in October, he decided to pay another visit to 'Uncle Joe' in Moscow. Roosevelt was facing an election in November and could not travel, but he approved of the visit.

On 9 October, Churchill arrived in Moscow and late that evening he had his first meeting with Stalin. Anthony Eden, the Foreign Secretary, was with him. Molotov, the Soviet Foreign Minister, accompanied Stalin. Apart from the two translators, it was just these four men who met together late at night in the Kremlin. They talked about Poland and about Greece, and Churchill made it clear that he wanted to avoid civil wars in the countries of Europe over who should be in power after the war. The conversation was frank and was going well, so sensing this opening meeting was a good moment for business, Churchill suggested the two leaders try to settle their affairs in the Balkans. He said he had a 'naughty document'. Churchill proposed a simple breakdown of spheres of interest: Romania should be 90 per cent Soviet and 10 per cent British; Greece 90 per cent British-American and 10 per cent Soviet; Yugoslavia and Hungary both 50–50; and Bulgaria 75 per cent Soviet and 25 per cent British-American. While this was being translated, Churchill wrote it out on a piece of paper. There was a pause. Then Stalin reached for a blue pencil and put a big tick on the piece of paper. A long silence followed. Then Churchill said: 'Might it not be thought rather cynical if it seemed we had disposed of these issues, so fateful to millions of people in such an offhand manner? Let us burn the paper.' Stalin replied: 'No, you keep it.'[12]

Churchill was pleased with this exchange, although it led to much haggling between Eden and Molotov in the following days. Churchill was also delighted with the rapport he once again developed with Stalin in the face-to-face meetings that followed over the next ten days. There was agreement on nearly all the military issues. And there were discussions about the possibility of breaking up Germany after the war. Despite Stalin's joke a year before at Teheran about executing the top Nazis, the Soviet leader now firmly supported the idea of public trials of the Nazi leadership after the war was won. Only the issue of Poland continued to divide the two leaders. The pro-Western Polish politicians came to present their case to Churchill and Stalin in Moscow. Then the Soviet-backed team did the same. Churchill and Eden had no time for these pawns of Stalin. They thought, correctly, that the Polish communists were just repeating parrot-like a script that had been written for them by the Soviets. After one speech by the Polish communist leader, Churchill caught Stalin's look and saw 'an understanding twinkle in his expressive eyes, as much as to say, "What about that for our Soviet teaching!"'[13] Despite days of negotiations, the future frontiers and government of Poland were left unresolved.

Nevertheless, in the course of these meetings, Churchill and Stalin built up almost a friendship. More than anything else, they were united in their struggle to defeat Nazism. One evening they attended the Bolshoi Ballet, and when they appeared in the Royal Box together they received a long, rapturous reception from the audience. At several late-night sessions, many toasts were drunk to each other and to the joint interests of the British and Russian people. At one point, someone described the two leaders along with Roosevelt as the 'Holy Trinity'. Stalin responded by saying: 'If that is so, Churchill must be the Holy Ghost. He flies around so much.'[14] But despite the bonhomie, deep disagreements about the shape of the post-war world divided the two men. And however jovial Stalin might be in Churchill's presence, he would still ruthlessly pursue his own interests when it came to it.

Churchill continued to travel. He spent some time in Cairo on his return from Moscow. In November, he attended a parade down the Champs Elysées in Paris with Charles de Gaulle amid wildly cheering crowds. Meanwhile, the war was not going well. Churchill had refused to believe various intelligence reports that Germany would be defeated by the end of the year. He was right. In Italy, the advance came to a halt for the winter in the Apennine Mountains. In France, in mid-December, Hitler's armies launched one final surprise counter-attack in the Ardennes with ten panzer divisions in what came to be called the 'Battle of the Bulge' as German troops created a huge salient, or bulge, in the Allied line. The intention was to divide the British and American armies and strike at Antwerp. But the Germans never completely broke through. Their tanks were awesome weapons but, desperately short of fuel, the Germans could not afford to run them for long. This, along with a heroic stand by US soldiers at the major crossroads at Bastogne, defeated this last attempt by Hitler's armies to reverse the course of the war. But in the midst of a cold winter, further major campaigning had to be postponed to the spring.

Churchill felt a strong affinity for Greece, as British soldiers had fought and died there trying to defend the country in 1941. When the Germans withdrew their garrison in October 1944, a flying column of SAS troops entered the country and raced to Athens, where they were rapturously received as liberators. But the people of Greece were in a desperate state after four years of brutal German occupation. Many now went over to support ELAS, the communist nationalist movement, despite British attempts to install King George and a government led by Prime Minister George Papandreou. During December, the tensions erupted into civil war in Athens. Churchill ordered the British commander, General Ronald Scobie, to fire on the communists in order to maintain order. This sided Britain with the royalists in the civil war and looked like interference in a foreign state's internal politics. In the United States, it was seen as an attempt by Britain to sustain its power in the region and was widely denounced. Churchill once again felt he had to intervene in person. On the afternoon of 24 December, he decided to fly to Athens that night. At home, Clementine was preparing an eagerly anticipated family Christmas, beginning with a children's party that evening. Despite being so used to last-minute changes of plan, she was deeply upset by her husband's decision to leave. This was one of the few times in the whole war when she burst into 'floods of tears' and was 'laid low' by Winston's stubbornness.[15]

Churchill arrived in Athens on Christmas Day and had to be given an armed escort through the dangerously divided city, where British troops were still engaged in street fighting with the communists. It was decided that he would be safest on board HMS *Ajax* in Piraeus harbour. Here he met Archbishop Damaskinos, the Greek Orthodox Patriarch, a tall, impressive man who had once been a champion wrestler. To Churchill, Damaskinos seemed to have the authority to preside over matters. Churchill suggested calling a meeting of all rival groups on the following day, to be chaired by Damaskinos. The Patriarch agreed. The meeting was held in the Greek Foreign Ministry at 6 p.m. on Boxing Day. It was bitterly cold and there was no heating. A few hurricane lamps cast an eerie glow upon the scene. But all parties, including the communists, turned up for the roundtable talks. After opening the talks, Churchill and the British delegation then withdrew and left the tough negotiating to the Greeks themselves. A couple of days later, it was agreed that Churchill should ask the Greek King, who was in exile in London, to appoint the Archbishop as Regent. When he returned home, Churchill persuaded King George in an all-night session of the wisdom of this course of action. Damaskinos subsequently became Regent and the effective ruler of Greece. A truce was signed with the communists in January. Churchill was pleased that he had helped to save Greece from communist subjugation. He was convinced that, having defeated fascism in Europe, the next threat would be that of communism. In this he was way ahead of most Western leaders and was already anticipating the divisions of the Cold War. He saw Europe now made up of countries that would either fall under the 'heel' of communism or be saved for the West. He was convinced that he had done the right thing for Greece and would still try his best to rescue Poland.

In February 1945, the Big Three met once again, this time at the old Livadia summer palace of the tsars at Yalta in the Crimea. Roosevelt, who had been re-elected President at the end of 1944, was exhausted by the journey. In the group photos taken at Yalta he looks haggard and drawn. Churchill, too, was exhausted by the years and months of relentless pressure. In one sense, the meetings at Yalta were the high water mark of

Allied wartime collaboration. Stalin confirmed that he would join the war against Japan within three months of the defeat of Hitler. The Allied military leaders discussed what support they could give each other, and the Soviets formally requested bombing the cities behind the German lines in the East. This was one of the factors, as we have seen, that led to the destruction of Dresden by British and American heavy bombers. On the other hand, Yalta also represents the beginnings of the Cold War. Stalin was suspicious of Anglo-American plans for the United Nations Organisation that had been drawn up at Dumbarton Oaks in Washington. It was proposed there would be a consultative General Assembly, to which all nations could belong, and a Security Council. This Security Council would have the teeth that the failed League of Nations never had, with authority to order executive action on behalf of the UN, even to the extent of going to war on its behalf. Stalin thought the Soviet Union could easily be outvoted by Britain and America in such a body, and that the status the USSR had won by playing the major role in the defeat of Hitler was not reflected in the UN structure. It was agreed that various Soviet republics could also join the UN, and that each of the great powers would have a veto over Security Council resolutions.

There was still further dispute over the governance of Poland. Churchill again explained that this was a matter of 'honour' for Britain. Stalin explained that it was a matter of 'security' for him. Russia had been attacked twice in the last thirty years through the 'Polish corridor'. It must not be allowed to happen again. By this he clearly meant that he wanted control of the Polish government. And it was 'security' that underpinned Stalin's strategy for the whole of Eastern Europe. Churchill feared that Stalin wanted to create a buffer of satellite states. In the end, Roosevelt and Churchill largely gave in to Stalin's demands for a new border with Poland, which was now moved westwards. In compensation, Poland's border with Germany was shifted further west, into what had been German territory. Stalin agreed to free elections in Poland and he signed a Declaration on Liberated Europe that pledged support for reconstruction based on free elections. For now, the Western leaders took Stalin at his word.

It was agreed to divide Germany into four zones of military occupation: Soviet, American, British and, later, French. There was an argument over reparations. Stalin insisted on massive reparations, partly to compensate for the vast destruction caused by the German armies in the Soviet Union. Here, 32,000 factories were in ruin, 50,000 miles of railway track had been destroyed, 1710 towns had been devastated and about 100,000 collective farms had been burned to the ground. But Stalin also believed in reparations as a form of punishment and as a symbol of a victor's rights. The Western leaders thought that reparations had prevented Germany from recovering after the First World War. They took a more pragmatic view and wanted to restore Germany, not destroy it, after this war. Eventually, a compromise was agreed.

Yalta revealed major fissures in the Grand Alliance that had been held together by the common objective of defeating Hitler. Churchill was increasingly suspicious of Soviet post-war ambitions. Roosevelt, on the other hand, thought that collaboration with the Soviets was the only way of preventing post-war disputes. Churchill was pained by Roosevelt's attitude towards him at Yalta. In chummying-up to Stalin, the President seemed to be distancing himself from his old ally and friend.

After the summit, Churchill passed through Athens. This time, he was able to ride through the streets in an open-top car amid cheering crowds where only a few weeks before vicious street fighting had taken place. He went on to Alexandria in Egypt, where he had lunch with Roosevelt. Churchill noted how frail the President looked. After lunch Churchill said farewell to his friend. It was the last time he would see him.

In March, the Allied armies launched their final attack upon the Third Reich. The Rhine had been a barrier to the invasion of Germany since Roman times. Now it was the last major obstacle facing the Allies. Eisenhower was again in overall command. Monty and the 21st Army Group were to cross the Rhine in the north, between Cleves and Düsseldorf, and head across the German plain to Hamburg and the Baltic. Bradley and the 12th Army Group were to cross the river further south. It was a combined boat, air and land operation, the largest single offensive since D-Day. There were forty bridges across the Rhine. Nazi engineers planned to destroy all of them, but in a lucky break in early March, the US 9th Armored Division captured one bridge intact at Remagen. Tens of thousands of men and hundreds of tanks poured across it. Hitler was so furious when he heard of the failure to blow up the bridge that he sent out Gestapo squads to execute all those responsible. Later in the month, Patton launched an attack across the Rhine at Oppenheim. As in Sicily, Patton was determined to be ahead of Monty, and his men crossed the river one day before those of his British rival. Further north, Monty launched a massive artillery bombardment, followed by attacks with heavy bombers, against the German defenders who were dug in along the eastern bank of the river. On the night of 23 March, British commandos led the crossing at Wessel in armoured amphibious vehicles called 'Buffaloes'.

Churchill, always keen to be an observer at these big military shows, asked to join Monty at his headquarters for the crossing. Brooke, who accompanied him, was not happy. He wrote in his diary: 'All he will do is to endanger his life unnecessarily and to get in everybody's way and be a damned nuisance to everybody. However nothing on earth will stop him!'[16] They arrived at Monty's forward HQ on the evening of the attack, delighted to be on German soil. After dinner, Monty retired to bed and Churchill and Brooke went for a walk in the moonlight. A few miles away, a furious battle was taking place. The two men took this moment to look back over the struggles they had been through together. Churchill told his leading general how much he appreciated him. It was a moment of personal warmth on the fringes of the last great battle of the war involving British soldiers.

On the morning of 24 March, Churchill and Brooke were escorted to the top of a hill to watch the huge airborne landing behind German lines at Wessel. Called 'Operation Varsity', this was the biggest air drop since D-Day. The vast air armada, with over 1700 transport planes and 1300 gliders, took two hours to pass. Churchill was as thrilled to watch this huge military operation as he had been to observe the battle at Omdurman, when the British Army attacked at Khartoum, nearly fifty years before. The little boy in him who had enjoyed playing with his toy soldiers was still there. War was still a romantic and heroic escapade for Churchill, despite everything he had lived through. The following day, Churchill and Brooke even managed to cross the Rhine in a landing craft and stood for a few minutes on the eastern bank, examining the German defences. Back on the western bank, they scrambled about on the remains of the bridge at Wessel when they came under sniper fire. Then some shelling opened up near them. General Simpson, the local American commander, said he could no longer take responsibility for Churchill's presence and ordered him to leave the battlefield. Brooke remembered that 'The look on Winston's face was just like that of a small boy being called away from his sandcastles on the beach by his nurse! . . . Thank heaven he came away quietly, it was a sad wrench for him, he was enjoying himself immensely.'[17]

The Rhine crossing was a great military success. Within days, American and British troops, supported now by French soldiers, were striking hard into Germany. Eisenhower's northern and southern thrusts joined up, having encircled the Ruhr and its powerful defences. The German western front was collapsing.

Churchill's position in the spring of 1945 was difficult. He still had the personal prestige and status of a giant, the man who had led Britain from the abyss and was now one of the Big Three. But Britain was very much the junior partner in the alliance. The Soviet Union now had the largest army in history, and its enormous suffering in the war, estimated recently at about twenty-seven million dead, left Stalin with a legitimate claim to superpower status in the post-war world. Meanwhile, the United States was ending the war as the greatest industrial power in history. Its economy had more than doubled during the war. Its factories had become the 'arsenal of victory', producing the guns, ships, planes and tanks that had won the war. Nearly 50 per cent of all the world's goods were manufactured in America. There was no question that the United States would be a post-war superpower. Britain, however, was technically bankrupt. The only way it could have authority in world affairs after the war was as an ally of the United States. Churchill had to persuade Roosevelt that the new enemy was going to be the Soviet Union, and steps had to be taken to stand up to Stalin in what the Prime Minister saw as the inevitable East–West divide after the war. However, Roosevelt saw the future differently. He thought he could get along with Stalin and that the United Nations would be the agency of peace. In the end, Churchill's view was proved right. He had correctly foreseen the tensions of the imminent Cold War. Roosevelt's vision died with him.

Over the next month, Churchill continued to be agitated by the Soviet attitude to the end of the war in Europe and by the

lack of progress on Poland's future. It was clear to him that the
Soviets had no intention of implementing free elections there,
as had been agreed at Yalta. Churchill wanted to put pressure
on Stalin and tried to persuade Roosevelt to side with him. But
the President did not want to antagonise Stalin and suggested
a truce. There was a further dispute when the Soviets accused
the Western Allies of negotiating a separate peace treaty with
Germany. Roosevelt worked hard to resolve these issues. On 12
April, he sent a telegram to Churchill, saying: 'I would min-
imise the general Soviet problem as much as possible.'[18] A few
hours after sending this message, Roosevelt collapsed. He
never regained consciousness and died a few hours later. When
he heard the news, Churchill felt he had been struck a physical
blow. Although their views had diverged over recent months,
Roosevelt had been the great ally who had supported Britain's
war effort from the beginning. They had established an almost
daily correspondence. They had enjoyed nine separate meetings and had spent about 120 days in close personal contact.

But Churchill decided not to attend Roosevelt's funeral. This
was particularly surprising bearing in mind his enthusiasm for
getting on a plane and travelling almost anywhere. It was even
more remarkable bearing in mind the opportunity it offered to
meet with the new President and to try to influence his thinking. Churchill claimed he was under pressure to remain in
London during these last days of the war. But that had never
stopped him before. The only conclusion to be drawn is that he
felt seriously let down by the President over recent months.
Foreign Minister Eden attended the funeral on his behalf.

In accordance with the American constitution, the Vice-
President, Harry S Truman, immediately succeeded to the
presidency. 'I feel like I've been struck by a bolt of lightning,' he
told a colleague. Despite his ill health, Roosevelt had kept
Truman woefully in the dark about key strategic and political

developments in the war. Roosevelt had only two private meetings with his Vice-President in the five months since the election. Now, Truman had to go on a crash course in foreign and military affairs. Interestingly, he soon took up Churchill's view, believing that reconciliation with the Soviets was impossible because of their bully-boy tactics, and within months of taking office he became forcefully anti-Soviet.

In the meantime, for a variety of reasons, Eisenhower had decided not to try to capture the German capital. First, Berlin was well inside the Soviet zone of military occupation as agreed at Yalta, and it was more appropriate for the Red Army to capture the city that was only thirty-five miles from their front line. Second, he did not see Berlin as a major objective. He wanted to smash through to the centre of Germany, where he believed the Nazi government was planning to move. And finally, despite the German collapse, Eisenhower guessed that there would still be a ferocious battle for the capital of Hitler's Reich. So he approached Stalin directly and suggested Allied troops should halt on the river Elbe. Churchill was deeply opposed to this and wanted Western troops to seize the prize of Berlin. He thought this would leave the West in a stronger position in any post-war conflict. But Marshall and the American Joint Chiefs backed their field commander. No matter how much the Brits protested, they were going to finish off the war their way. And military rather than political priorities prevailed.[19]

It was Stalin who ordered the last assault on Hitler's capital. On 16 April, the final offensive began. Two and a half million men in the Red Army had assembled along the banks of the Oder and Neisse rivers. Facing them were 700,000 German troops. Many of them were poorly equipped. They included boys from the Hitler Youth and old men fighting to defend Hitler's capital from what they saw as the Bolshevik hordes. With them were the last Nazi die-hards. They all fought with a grim fanaticism. Stalin set off his two leading commanders, Marshals Zhukov and Koniev, in a race to battle their way into Berlin and win the accolade of taking the final German surrender.

On the morning of 20 April, the Allies launched their last 'thousand-bomber' raid against Berlin. When it was over, Hitler emerged from his bunker one last time to give medals to the defenders of the city. His hopes were placed in the fanatical determination of teenage boys. But the newsreel cameras caught the desperate twitch in his hands. The two huge Soviet armies advanced into the suburbs of Berlin, district by district, then street by street, then house by house. The fighting was as intense as Eisenhower had feared. The Soviet tanks that had led the Red Army fifteen hundred miles from Stalingrad to Berlin were no good in the urban environment and could be taken out at close range with primitive, easy-to-use weapons. German civilians hid in their cellars. SS execution squads roamed the city in search of deserters. Hundreds of thousands of German women were raped by Soviet soldiers as they advanced through the city. Hitler and his entourage in their bunker under the Reich Chancellery still believed there were armies waiting to rescue them. There were none. As the Red Army finally closed in on the centre of the city, Hitler at last accepted defeat. On the afternoon of 30 April, he shot himself. Churchill was having dinner when his private secretary, John Colville, brought him the news. According to German radio, Hitler had died 'fighting with his last breath against Bolshevism'. Churchill commented dryly: 'Well, I must say, I think he was perfectly right to die like that.'[20]

The fighting went on for a few days longer. The Red Flag was suspended from the top of the Reichstag, the symbol of Hitler's capital, in time for the great socialist parade of May Day. Three hundred thousand Russian soldiers lost their lives in the Battle of Berlin. A few days later, Hitler's generals tried to negotiate terms. They were told that only unconditional surrender of all German armies on every front was acceptable.

On 2 May, German forces in Italy surrendered. On 4 May, Montgomery, at his headquarters on Luneburg Heath, received the surrender of all German forces in north-western Germany, Denmark and Holland. That evening, Churchill called the Chiefs of Staff to the Cabinet Room in Downing Street and thanked them for all they had done. Then he shook their hands, one by one. Brooke noted he had tears in his eyes.[21] On 7 May, the German High Command finally signed a document of unconditional surrender. The guns at last fell silent. The war in Europe was over. Late that evening, Churchill called in Elizabeth Layton, one of his secretaries, to type up his dictation of the speech he would broadcast. 'Hullo, Miss Layton,' he said, 'well the war's over, you've played your part.'[22]

The following day, Tuesday 8 May, was proclaimed Victory in Europe or VE Day. Huge crowds gathered in London. At 3 p.m., Churchill broadcast the news of the surrender to the people of Britain and around the world. 'We may allow ourselves a brief period of rejoicing,' he said. 'But let us not forget for a moment the toil and efforts that lie ahead. Japan, with all her treachery and greed, remains unsubdued.' He ended the short broadcast with the words: 'We must now devote all our strength and resources to the completion of our task, both at home and abroad. Advance, Britannia! Long live the cause of freedom! God save the King.' On the words 'Advance, Britannia', Churchill's voice broke with emotion. That evening, he appeared on a balcony overlooking Whitehall, where vast crowds had assembled. The cheering was intense. 'God bless you all,' he said to the people below, 'this is your victory.' The crowd roared back: 'No – it's yours.'[23] Churchill also appeared with the King and Queen on the balcony of Buckingham Palace. The huge crowds once again cheered rapturously. It was almost five years to the day since Churchill had been appointed Prime Minister.

Churchill was still severely agitated by Soviet actions in the territories they had liberated, or captured, at the end of the war. On 12 May, he sent a message to President Truman using a phrase he would later make famous. He wrote: 'An iron curtain is drawn upon their [the Russian] front. We do not know what is going on behind.'[24] He feared that Stalin was imposing his own puppet governments in all the states of Eastern Europe. A conference was called for the victorious powers. They agreed to meet in Potsdam, outside devastated Berlin, in July.

Meanwhile, it was clear that the days were numbered for the coalition government Churchill had led for five years. The Labour Party took the view that, with Germany defeated, it was now time for a general election. After all, with all-party agreement, there had not been one for nearly ten years. Churchill himself argued that Japan should be defeated first, and nothing should detract from this major objective. However, everyone still expected that this would take another eighteen months. Attlee decided that the country could not wait that long and withdrew the Labour Party from the government. So, on 23 May, Churchill tendered his resignation to the King. He agreed to form a caretaker government until the election could be held on 5 July and all the votes from soldiers serving overseas counted. With the war in the Far East still raging, the campaigning began.

So great had been the burden of running Britain's war machine that Churchill had almost completely ignored domestic politics during his five years in office. He had been happy to leave the Home Front to Attlee, his deputy. And Churchill had not wanted to make promises about conditions after the war that he felt he could not deliver. He was very conscious that the promise to build 'Homes fit for Heroes' after the First World

War had backfired upon Lloyd George. So Churchill had completely failed to pick up on the sea change that had taken place in the thinking of the British people. He was revered as a war leader but in conventional politics he was seen as hopelessly old-fashioned. The country had made a major shift to the left. There was a strong feeling that, after all people had been through, there could be no return to the depression and misery of the 1930s. Men and women across Britain wanted full employment, better housing, national healthcare and social security. Many had thought long and hard about the future, even if Churchill had not. The Beveridge Report, which called for a welfare state to look after British citizens 'from the cradle to the grave', had sold 635,000 copies. Penguin Specials had debated every aspect of the future shape of Britain and had sold millions. Even inside the military, groups like the Army Bureau of Current Affairs (ABCA) had encouraged political debate about the post-war world and here, as elsewhere, a broad socialist perspective often prevailed. Churchill had been opposed to ABCA on the grounds that it would be bad for military discipline.[25] But now he looked old, tired and a leftover from an older Britain as he took up the mantle of leading the Conservative Party in the election campaign. Also, a remark in a party political broadcast that likened Labour Party tactics to those of the Gestapo in seeking to introduce a socialist state was very ill-judged and did him great harm.

Polling duly took place in early July, but because of the time it would take to collect and count the three million votes from army, navy and air force personnel around the world, the result would not be announced until the end of the month. Meanwhile, on the 15th, Churchill travelled to Potsdam for the end-of-war Big Three meeting. The next morning, he met President Truman for the first time and was impressed, even though Truman was still desperately new to the complexities of inter-power politics.

Accompanying the novice President was his Secretary of State, James Byrnes, who had been sworn in only three days before leaving for Europe. Before the formal sessions began, Churchill toured the ruins of Berlin. Outside the Chancellery building a small crowd of Berliners gathered. To Churchill's surprise, they cheered him. Already allegiances were changing.

When the conference began, Stalin again pledged his commitment to join the war against Japan. And agreement was swiftly reached on the military occupation of Germany in four separate zones. But there was still disagreement over the Polish borders and reparations. Then, on the 17th, extraordinary news arrived. The Americans had successfully carried out the first atomic bomb test in the New Mexico desert. Reports said the explosion was 'brighter than a thousand suns'. Truman and Churchill were told and immediately realised that this new weapon of war entirely transformed the struggle against Japan. US military planning was for an invasion of Japan some time between November 1945 and spring 1946. Nearly two million men would be involved. General Marshall feared that casualties would be extremely high. On Iwo Jima and Okinawa, Japanese soldiers had fought almost literally to the last bullet. And many had chosen suicide over surrender. Churchill was convinced that Truman would use the atom bomb and the war would be over in a matter of weeks. This meant that they no longer needed the Soviets to join in the war against Japan. The question was, how were they to explain this to Stalin?

Truman decided to tell the Soviet leader about the new bomb in person at the end of the session on 24 July. He walked across the room and casually informed Stalin that the United States now had a new weapon. Stalin knew all about the development of the atomic bomb through his spy network. He replied equally casually: 'Good, I hope the United States will use it.' Truman thought Stalin had not understood. But Uncle Joe realised immediately the significance of what he had been told. That evening, he instructed Molotov to speed up the development of the Soviet bomb.

The following day, Churchill flew back to London and the conference was put on hold while he awaited the results of the general election. Some party estimates suggested that the Conservatives would win with a majority of between fifty and eighty seats. On the morning of 26 July, Churchill followed the news of the results in his Map Room. One after another safe Conservative seat fell to Labour. By midday, it was becoming clear that the Labour Party had won a landslide victory. The decision of the British people was absolutely clear. Churchill was out.

Clementine was secretly relieved. After more than five years of relentless pressure, she wanted Winston to have a break rather than face the overwhelming challenges of managing the peace. Churchill, on the other hand, was utterly devastated by the news of his defeat. He could not understand how the very people he had led to victory, and who had cheered and mobbed him a few weeks before, had now rejected him. He was seventy years old. This might be the end of his political career. At lunch, Clementine told her husband that the result 'may well be a blessing in disguise'. Churchill replied: 'At the moment it seems quite effectively disguised.'[26] Churchill resigned that evening and Attlee, with a majority of 146, formed a Labour government. It would be one of the truly great reforming governments in British history.

On 6 August, an atom bomb was dropped on the Japanese city of Hiroshima. It exploded with the force of 13,000 tons of TNT. The heat it generated was so intense that it melted bricks and roof tiles, and incinerated human beings so completely that nothing remained of them except light outlines on scorched pavements. About a hundred thousand civilians died within hours. Thousands more died of radiation poisoning over the next few months and years. On 8 August, Stalin declared war on Japan and the Red Army entered Manchuria and then Korea, at that time a part of Japan. On 9 August, with minimal strategic need, a second atom bomb was dropped on the city of Nagasaki. The following day, the Japanese Emperor announced his intention to surrender. Terms were agreed shortly after and the Japanese surrender was formally signed a few weeks later on board the battleship USS *Missouri* in Tokyo harbour. The Second World War was over. The atomic age had begun. On that same day, Churchill at last took off on a holiday.

11

Churchill's War

Winston Churchill remains one of the most fascinating figures of the twentieth century. Aware of how history judges individuals, he was determined to be one of the first to write his own account of the war years. He said he would be happy for the judgement of events to be left to history – but that he would be one of the historians.[1] The massive six-volume memoir–history of the Second World War that he published from 1948 to 1954 presented his own interpretation of events very clearly and lucidly. Backing up his narrative, he provided a mass of documents he had special clearance from the Cabinet to publish.[2] Up to his death, most of the memoirs and accounts that were published painted a positive picture of his leadership, with the exception of Arthur Bryant's working of General Brooke's diaries. These first appeared in Bryant's two books *The Turn of the Tide 1939–43* and *Triumph in the West 1943–46* in the late 1950s. Churchill was extremely hurt and offended by the publication of these diary entries frequently written in anger and despair while events were still unfolding, often late at night, and without the mediation and reflection of time. According to John Colville, Churchill deliberately and ostentatiously turned his back on Brooke, by then Viscount Alanbrooke, after the publication of Bryant's books. Colville said he knew of no other person who received similar treatment from Churchill.[3] But after Churchill's death, the pendulum began to swing and several historians took a more robust and often hostile view of the great man.[4] More recently, the pendulum has swung back again. In 2002, Churchill was voted 'Greatest Briton' in a BBC television series.

One of the key questions when it comes to evaluating his leadership of Britain during the Second World War is: what difference did he make? Churchill later said that all he did was 'to let the Lion roar', that the British people were the lion-hearted nation and it was his good luck to lead them.[5] But in this, rarely for once, he underplays his own role. In May and June 1940, when France was disastrously overrun in a matter of weeks, when Britain faced the possibility of invasion and attack from the air, and when the sea-lanes that kept the nation functioning might have been cut, the situation seemed truly hopeless. At that time, what was the real view of the British people? We will never know for sure, but Churchill had only a fragile hold on Downing Street. Most members of the Conservative Party, by far the largest number of MPs in the Commons, were far from convinced that he was the right man to lead the nation in its hour of peril. Moreover, there is plenty of evidence to suggest that if another leader, perhaps Lord Halifax, had told the British people at that moment that the only sensible option was to make peace with Germany, then Britons might well have eagerly gone along with him. And as several commentators have said, the ensuing history of Europe would have taken a very different course. As it was, Churchill, with his strong sense of history and an equally strong sense of destiny, would have 'no parley' with the Nazis. His speeches and his courage at this moment without question had an immense impact on the course of events. First to the War Cabinet, then to the full Cabinet, then to Parliament, and then to the people at large, Churchill provided a direction and a leadership that filled them with pride and the resolution to fight on against an evil regime. This was not just a question of clever oratory, of fine eloquence, it was a question of saying what needed to be said. Hitler had to be stopped, and the only way this was possible was by defeating him in war. Had Churchill dropped dead of a heart attack a few months later, as he could well have done, his contribution to world history would still have been immense. But as it was he went on saying what needed to be said to keep the British people determined to fight on against what looked like impossible odds, until first the Soviet Union and then the United States joined the struggle. From May 1940 until November 1942, he kept the war effort going before the contribution of those new allies really made a difference to the balance of the war. He stayed put in London when it was wise to do so. He visited bomb-damaged cities when he needed to. And he visited the Allies and the military front in a seemingly endless round of travels in order to understand better what was going on and to inspire and motivate those he met.

In the latter part of the war, as Britain's contribution to the defeat of fascism in Europe and militarism in Japan was far exceeded by those of the United States and the Soviet Union, inevitably Churchill's ability to make a difference lessened. But through his Chiefs of Staff he convinced the Americans to postpone D-Day until 1944, a postponement which few historians today regard as anything other than essential for final victory. And Churchill was the first leader to identify the Soviet Union as the next antagonist of the West although he failed to convince Roosevelt of this. But in the years to come Americans would see him almost as a prophet for this vision.

As a military man, he certainly had courage, and luck. He understood how armies and navies worked and he was able to get things done. He had closely observed and reflected on the process of government during war, and when he came to lead he knew exactly how he wanted to structure things. He knew the strengths and weaknesses of experts and advisers. He did not want to be given an over-rosy interpretation of events; nor did he want to hide disasters from the public when they happened, as they did in plenty. But even when conveying bad news he had the ability to exude confidence.[6] The biggest criticism against him on this point is that he listened too unquestioningly to Lord Cherwell, his principal scientific aide. Cherwell was to be proved wrong on many key matters – from the effectiveness of bombing as a way to destroy the German war economy to the ability of the Germans to produce rocket missiles. Even though he was over-reliant on this single individual at the expense of other great wartime scientists, Churchill valued science and technology highly, at least as far as they could improve military actions, at a time when there was much suspicion of scientists. And he liked fresh, unconventional, even unorthodox thinking. He could inspire people. His words inspired a generation living through the war. No matter how old-fashioned or out of place he seemed in 1940, he said what people wanted to hear in those extreme circumstances. He made people feel important and that their lives were linked to a long and great history. He had the ability to push individuals, sometimes beyond what they thought they were capable of.

This account has been full of quotes from men and women who felt lit up in his presence. R.V. Jones, the young scientist who first met the Prime Minister when he arrived late for the crucial Downing Street meeting that ushered in the Battle of the Beams in June 1940, had several meetings with Churchill through the war. Thirty years later, reflecting on being with Churchill, he wrote: 'I had the feeling of being recharged by contact with a source of living power. Here was strength, resolution, humour, readiness to listen, to ask the searching question and when convinced, to act.'[7] Even accounting for the impression an elder statesman would naturally make on a younger man, this describes a rare quality in leadership. Churchill had led a team of scientists and military chiefs, he had cut through red tape, encouraged innovation and fresh thinking. The War Lab he developed around him helped Britain survive and did much to contribute to victory.

The other side of this is that he cajoled and sometimes bullied his military chiefs beyond what was fair and reasonable, although not usually beyond endurance. He usually knew when to stop, and when a kind word was needed. When pushing one of his secretaries, Elizabeth Layton, at a critical moment late at night he paused, realising her exhaustion, and said: 'We must go on like the gun horses until we drop.'[8] Of course she was then willing to go that extra mile for him and with him. He probably came nearest to a full-scale falling out with General Brooke, particularly when exhaustion had reduced both men to a fragile state in the spring of 1944, and they argued intensely about future strategy. But even here, Churchill did not push Brooke into resignation, although he and the Chiefs of Staff came near to it. And, as Brooke's diary recorded, Churchill was keen to make up and express his appreciation for his CIGS when he felt he had gone too far.

As we have seen throughout this book, Churchill's intervention was critical at many key moments. From getting extra resources for the much-needed expansion of the code-breaking centre at Bletchley Park to focusing both government and military thinking on solving the U-boat threat; from giving the go-ahead to constructing the floating Mulberry harbours to pausing the bombing offensive until navigation techniques could be improved. These are just a few of his many key interventions. And of course, more than anything else, Churchill realised the importance of the 'special relationship' with the United States. This awareness began well before he came to office but it became a life-saver during the Spitfire Summer of 1940. Despite his differences with President Roosevelt, differences that have often been overlooked in the rosy glow of victory, Churchill worked immensely hard in building not just a strong personal relationship but a system of collaboration between two military operations that not only survived the war but became a key alliance of the post-war world.

When it came to shaping military strategy, Churchill's record is more chequered. He has been criticised a lot for his 'dispersionist' strategy, always looking for a flank to attack, for his obsession with dispersing his forces to surprise the enemy by attacking where they least expect it. This, in essence, was what the Dardanelles campaign was all about. And, in part, it was what was behind his Mediterranean strategy. But sometimes it worked brilliantly. In 1941, there was nowhere else realistically to attack Axis forces than in North Africa. By dragging Hitler into this theatre of war, and later into Italy to defend his Italian ally, and by diverting his forces from elsewhere, Churchill's strategy worked. He had a canny ability to sense where the enemy was weak and to attack there. But Nigel Knight, among others, believes that, as an overall strategy, this is fundamentally flawed and wars are won by concentrating forces against the enemy, not by dispersing them. Knight claims that Churchill might have extended the war by as much as a year by pursuing this strategy.[9] Of course, this can never be proven. Churchill's unrealised pet project, to attack Norway, probably helped to keep a dozen German divisions in that country when they could have turned the tide of battle elsewhere. On the other hand, his plan to invade Sumatra in 1944 seems ridiculous today.

There is also the controversy of the bombing offensive and accusations have even been made that by ordering the area bombing of German towns and cities Churchill was effectively a war criminal. But it is profoundly *un*-historical to apply the moral criteria of one age to individuals living in a different era. Today, when war deaths are reported in the mass media and in Parliament name by name, it is difficult to imagine a context in which thousands or even tens of thousands of people lost their lives in a single day. So it would be historically wrong to condemn Churchill for being the political leader of a nation that left a trail of such devastating loss of life across German cities. At the time, in the aftermath of Hitler's Blitz on British cities, there was no moral condemnation of the bombing of Germany, just a debate as to whether the ends (the partial destruction of the German war economy) justified the means (the vast allocation of resources within the US and British war economies and the huge loss of life among the bomber crews). Later, this became a political and a moral issue. Political in that no campaign medal was ever given to the men of Bomber Command. Moral in that it has been said that the killing of civilians in war is *always* wrong. But it still goes on today despite our moral revulsion. And the moral debate about Churchill continues.

Did Churchill have doubts? Certainly he did. He would not have been human otherwise. On the day he became Prime Minister, driving back to the Admiralty, his personal detective offered his congratulations and Churchill responded grimly

that he hoped it was not too late. Returning from his penulti-
mate meeting with the French leaders in June 1940, he turned
to General Ismay and said: 'We fight alone.' When Ismay tried
to cheer him up by saying he was glad of it, and that 'We'll win
the Battle of Britain,' Churchill turned to him, gave him a look
and said: 'You and I will be dead in three months' time.'[10] On
many occasions over the following years he was brought low
by depression, his 'black dog'. In the First World War, he had
admitted to 'terrible and reasonless depressions'.[11] In the
Second, he was worried by recurring fears that, for instance, the
British soldier no longer had the warrior spirit to fight with the
determination that would bring victory. He was also terribly
upset on hearing news of losses, particularly at sea. Despite the
strength of his oratory and the courage he displayed, he wore
his emotions on his sleeve for most of the war. There are dozens
of accounts of tears falling down his cheeks at emotional
moments, not something it is easy to imagine with more recent
leaders.

The telephone calls Churchill frequently had with Roosevelt
over the first ever 'hot-line', which was set up between the
Cabinet War Rooms and the Oval Office, had to be listened to
by a censor because they were sent by radio and although
scrambled they could be intercepted by the Germans (as indeed
they were). Ruth Ive, then in her early twenties, was one
of those who listened in to these phone calls and she was
instructed to interrupt the two leaders if certain security pro-
tocols were breached. She could always tell when Churchill was
in a depressed frame of mind. She was always alarmed by hearing him in this depressed state, wondering at times if he were
capable of carrying on.[12] Many others who worked with him
closely had the same worries.

So Churchill was only human after all, which should be no
surprise. He needed the right people around him to bring out

the best in him, and for him to bring out the best in them. And they in turn passed on his passion and his inspiration to others. That was what his War Lab was all about. So, yes, he really did make a difference. At a time of a national, European and world crisis, when leadership mattered, Britain for once had the right man in the right place doing the right job.

Notes

Introduction

1. This account is based on Winston Churchill *My Early Life* pp. 12–20.
2. This account is based on Winston Churchill *My Early Life* pp. 179–93.
3. This account is taken from John Wheeler-Bennett *King George VI* pp. 601–5 and from Winston Churchill *Second World War Vol. V* pp. 546–51. The King's letter to Churchill is quoted in both.
4. Ronald Clark *The Rise of the Boffins* p. 162, and see p. 177–8 of this book.
5. R.V. Jones 'Churchill and Science' in Robert Blake and Wm. Roger Louis (eds) *Churchill* p. 437.
6. Piers Brendon *Winston Churchill: A Brief Life* pp. 148–50.
7. Winston Churchill *The Second World War Vol. I* pp. 526–7.

Chapter 1 – Preparation: The Army and the Navy

1. See David Cannadine *The Decline and Fall of the British Aristocracy* pp. 113 and 397–8.
2. Churchill always claimed he was born premature. He could have been conceived before his parents were married in April 1874. We will never know which is true.
3. Winston Churchill *My Early Life* pp. 4–5.
4. Winston Churchill *My Early Life* pp. 15–16.
5. Winston Churchill *My Early Life* p. 76.
6. Randolph Churchill *Winston S. Churchill Vol I. Youth: 1874–1900 Companion Volume II 1896–1900* p. 930.

7. Randolph Churchill *Winston S. Churchill Vol. I: Youth 1874–1900* p. 418.

8. This book does not attempt to be any sort of political biography of Churchill, nor to provide a critique of his political views. Of recent biographies, the best political account comes in Roy Jenkins *Churchill.*

9. Randolph Churchill *Winston S. Churchill Vol. I: Youth* p. 463.

10. Winston Churchill *My Early Life* p. 248.

11. Winston Churchill *My Early Life* p. 256.

12. Winston Churchill *My Early Life* p. 277.

13. The whole story of his capture and escape is told in detail in Celia Sandys *Churchill Wanted Dead or Alive.* Sandys, his granddaughter, corrects some of the myths Churchill himself created about this episode.

14. Randolph Churchill *Winston S. Churchill Vol. I: Youth 1874–1900* p. 524.

15. Martin Gilbert *Churchill: A Life* p. 85.

16. Winston Churchill *My Early Life* p. 298.

17. Randolph Churchill *Winston S. Churchill Vol. II: Young Statesman* p. 71.

18. Randolph Churchill *Winston S. Churchill Vol. II: Young Statesman* p. 228.

19. Clementine had a Higher School Certificate (roughly equivalent to A Levels today) in French, German and Biology from Berkhamsted High School. Her headmistress wanted her to go on to university but her mother decided when she was eighteen that she had had enough education and that it was time to enter society and find a husband. She had had two engagements, both broken off by her, before she met Churchill. See Mary Soames *Clementine Churchill* pp. 22–34.

20. A selection of these letters, which beautifully captures the ups and downs of their relationship, features in *Speaking for Themselves: The Personal Letters of Winston and Clementine Churchill*, edited by their daughter Mary Soames.

21. Winston Churchill *The World Crisis Vol. I* p. 49 (this and all subsequent volume and page references are from the 1939 edition of *The World Crisis*).

22. A variation of this appears in Winston Churchill *The World Crisis Vol. I* p. 24: 'The Admiralty had demanded six ships; the economists offered four; and we finally compromised on eight.'

23. Winston Churchill *The World Crisis Vol. I* pp. 51–70, quoted in Stephen Roskill *Churchill and the Admirals* p. 30.
24. Randolph Churchill *Winston S. Churchill Vol. II: Young Statesman* p. 703.
25. Randolph Churchill *Winston S. Churchill Vol. II: Young Statesman* p. 686.
26. Winston Churchill *The World Crisis Vol. I* pp. 155–7.
27. Randolph Churchill *Winston S. Churchill Vol. II: Young Statesman* p. 710.
28. Martin Gilbert *Winston S. Churchill Vol. III* p. 31.

Chapter 2 – Preparation: The War and the Wilderness

1. David Kahn *Seizing the Enigma* pp. 15ff. and David Stafford *Churchill and Secret Service* pp. 70ff.
2. Winston Churchill *World Crisis Vol. II* p. 562.
3. Winston Churchill *World Crisis Vol. I* p. 414.
4. Nicholas Rankin *Churchill's Wizards* pp. 13–14.
5. Letter from the Master General of the Ordnance, 26 February 1915, quoted in Winston Churchill *The World Crisis Vol. II* p.512.
6. Martin Gilbert *Winston S. Churchill Vol. III: 1914–16* p. 537; see also Winston Churchill *The World Crisis Vol. II* pp. 508–16.
7. Winston Churchill *The World Crisis Vol. II* p. 466.
8. Martin Gilbert *Winston S. Churchill Vol. III: 1914–16* p. 465.
9. Martin Gilbert *Winston S. Churchill Vol. III: 1914–16* pp. 579–80 and 574.
10. Martin Gilbert *Winston S. Churchill Vol. III: 1914–16* pp. 610, 686, 705 and 745.
11. Martin Gilbert *Winston S. Churchill Vol. III: 1914–16* pp. 609 and 748.
12. Gary Sheffield and John Bourne (eds) *Douglas Haig: War Diaries and Letters* pp. 315 and 371.
13. Winston Churchill *The World Crisis Vol. IV* p. 543.
14. The book is part history and part autobiography of Churchill's own contribution to events from the time he was appointed First Lord of the Admiralty in 1911. His political opponent Bonar Law cruelly but amusingly described the book as 'an autobiography disguised as an history of the universe'.
15. This line was remembered by Lady Violet Bonham Carter; see Martin Gilbert *Winston S. Churchill Vol. IV: 1916–1922* p. 278.

16. Martin Gilbert *Winston S. Churchill Vol. IV: 1916–1922* p. 332.
17. Winston Churchill *Thoughts and Adventures* p. 213.
18. Paul Addison *Churchill on the Home Front*, p. 243.
19. Piers Brendon *Winston Churchill: A Brief Life* p. 100.
20. Chartwell is today owned by the National Trust and is open to visitors; see http://www.nationaltrust.org.uk/main/w-chartwell.htm.
21. Piers Brendon *Winston Churchill: A Brief Life* p. 118.
22. Maurice Ashley *Churchill as Historian* p. 18.
23. See J.H. Plumb 'The Historian' in A.J.P. Taylor et al. *Churchill: Four Faces and the Man* p. 119–29. Plumb rightly draws a distinction between Churchill's histories of events with which he was not personally involved and his histories of the two world wars, which, as has already been noted, are much more autobiographical and so have great value as guides to Churchill's thinking at the times they describe.
24. Geoffrey Best *Churchill: A Study in Greatness* pp. 146–7 and David Stafford *Churchill and Secret Service* p. 180.
25. Hansard *Parliamentary Debates* House of Commons, 21 February 1938.
26. Martin Gilbert *Winston S. Churchill Vol. V: 1922–39* p. 917.
27. Hansard *Parliamentary Debates* House of Commons, 5 October 1938.
28. Martin Gilbert *Winston S. Churchill Vol. V: 1922–39* p. 1106.
29. For instance, the broadcast features in the Ministry of Information documentary *The First Days* produced by Alberto Cavalcanti, directed by Humphrey Jennings, Harry Watt, Pat Jackson and others.
30. Martin Gilbert *Winston S. Churchill Vol. VI: Finest Hour* p. 4.
31. Winston Churchill *The Second World War Vol. I* p. 320. Some scholars have suggested that this could have been a message of warning rather than of welcome, for example Geoffrey Best *Churchill and War* p. 107. Other scholars have doubted that the message was ever sent. Whether apocryphal or not, it is entirely believable.
32. Sir Alan Brooke quoted in Nicholas Rankin *Churchill's Wizards* p. 237.
33. Martin Gilbert *Winston S. Churchill Vol. VI: Finest Hour* pp. 156–7.
34. Martin Gilbert *Winston S. Churchill Vol. VI: Finest Hour* p. 62. The story of the sinking of HMS *Royal Oak* and the dreadful loss of life soon became known. However, the Admiralty did not reveal the number of boy sailors who went down with the ship. It did, though, change the policy with regard to boy sailors, who were henceforth no longer allowed to serve on ships that were on active duty.

35. Peter Calvocoressi and Guy Wint *Total War* p. 100.

36. John Keegan (ed.) *Churchill's Generals* p. 27.

37. For instance, from Bob Boothby and from Harold Macmillan; see Martin Gilbert *Winston S. Churchill Vol. VI: Finest Hour* pp. 302ff. and Harold Macmillan *The Blast of War 1939–45* p. 74.

38. From the diary of Henry 'Chips' Channon, quoted in Martin Gilbert *Winston S. Churchill Vol. VI: Finest Hour* p. 294.

39. Hansard *Parliamentary Debates* House of Commons, 8 May 1940.

40. Winston Churchill *The Second World War Vol. I* pp. 523–4.

41. From John Colville's interview for *The World at War* Thames Television documentary series, 1973, producer Jeremy Isaacs. See also John Colville *The Fringes of Power – Downing Street Diaries 1939–45* p. 123.

42. Churchill wrongly dates the meeting as being on 10 May, whereas all other accounts place it on the 9th. Also, Churchill forgets that David Margesson, the Tory Chief Whip, was present. Halifax's diary is quoted in Robert Blake 'How Churchill Became Prime Minister' in Robert Blake and Wm. Roger Louis (eds) *Churchill* pp. 265–7. Other accounts have led Andrew Roberts to give another version of these critical few hours in *Hitler and Churchill: Secrets of Leadership* pp. 94–100. Roberts, who is also Halifax's biographer, recounts several discussions between Chamberlain and Halifax, in which the Prime Minister proposed Halifax as his successor and in which Halifax literally felt pain in the pit of his stomach. Roberts also quotes the recently published diaries of the American ambassador, Joseph Kennedy, who discussed the meeting with Chamberlain later. In both Blake's and Roberts's accounts, Chamberlain is more active in trying to prevent Churchill from becoming Prime Minister, and Churchill is more determined to grasp the position.

43. Martin Gilbert *Winston S. Churchill Vol. VI: Finest Hour* p. 305.

Chapter 3 – Action This Day

1. The King's diary is quoted in John Wheeler-Bennett *King George VI: His Life and Reign* p. 444. Churchill's account is in Winston Churchill *The Second World War Vol. I* p. 525.

2. Winston Churchill *The Second World War Vol. I* pp. 525–7.

3. Richard Broad and Suzie Fleming (eds) *Nella Last's War* p. 55.

4. Winston Churchill *The Second World War Vol. I* p. 527.

5. John Colville in Lord Normanbrook (and others) *Action This Day: Working with Churchill* p. 48.
6. Hansard *Parliamentary Debates* House of Commons, 13 May 1940.
7. Hastings Ismay *Memoirs* p. 158.
8. John Colville *The Churchillians* pp. 205–6.
9. John Keegan (ed.) *Churchill's Generals* p. 27.
10. Hastings Ismay *Memoirs* p. 159.
11. John Colville *The Churchillians* p. 146.
12. Ronald Lewin *Churchill as Warlord* pp. 41–2.
13. Lord Normanbrook *Action This Day* p. 22.
14. Elizabeth Nel [née Layton] *Mr Churchill's Secretary* pp. 29–30.
15. The Cabinet War Rooms, restored as they were left at the end of the war, can be visited today as a part of the Imperial War Museum. See: http://cwr.iwm.org.uk/server/show/nav.221
16. John Keegan (ed.) *Churchill's Generals* p. 7.
17. Many of those who worked closely with Churchill describe the tough, demanding hours he worked, for instance John Colville *The Fringes of Power passim* and *The Churchillians* pp. 64ff.; Field Marshal Lord Alanbrooke *War Diaries passim*; and Elizabeth Nel (née Layton) *Mr Churchill's Secretary* pp. 27ff.
18. Hastings Ismay *Memoirs* pp. 164–5 and John Colville *The Churchillians* p. 146.
19. Martin Gilbert *Winston S. Churchill Vol. VI: Finest Hour* pp. 339–40 and Winston Churchill *The Second World War Vol. II* p. 38–9
20. Winston Churchill *The Second World War Vol. II* p. 42.
21. There has been much debate about Hitler's intervention confirming von Rundstedt's halt order; see, for instance, Andrew Roberts *Hitler and Churchill: Secrets of Leadership* pp. 105–7 and *The Storm of War* pp. 60–4. Roberts does not accept the argument that Hitler allowed the British Expeditionary Forces to escape in order to get better terms in negotiations with Britain.
22. John Lukacs *Five Days in London May 1940* p. 19.
23. Minutes of the War Cabinet, ref: CAB 65/13, WM 145.
24. In *The Second World War* Churchill does not relate the events of the Halifax challenge to his leadership, perhaps not wanting to cast a shadow over Halifax's reputation, perhaps because he felt awkward about having been nearly deflected at this critical point. He does recount the support he received at the full Cabinet meeting on the

afternoon of 28 May 1940 in *Vol. II* pp. 87–8. The account of the meeting in Hugh Dalton's diaries and his memoirs is quoted in John
Lukacs *Five Days in London May 1940* pp. 4–5 and 183–4. And in the
same book Lukacs talks of the momentousness of this day on p. 2.

25. Hansard *Parliamentary Debates* House of Commons, 4 June 1940.
26. Martin Gilbert *Winston S. Churchill Vol. VI: Finest Hour* p. 469. It has
    been claimed by David Irving in *Churchill's War Vol. I* p. 313 that the
    BBC transmitted a version of this speech that evening that was not
    read by Churchill but by an actor, Norman Shelley, well known at the
    time for playing Larry the Lamb in the BBC's *Children's Hour*. In fact,
    extracts of the speech on the BBC Home Service News that evening
    were read by the newsreader, as the Vita Sackville-West comment
    makes clear. It is possible that Shelley recorded a version of the
    speech for transmission overseas, but this was not heard in the UK.
    See D.J. Wenden 'Churchill, Radio, and Cinema' in Robert Blake and
    Wm. Roger Louis (eds) *Churchill* pp. 236–7.
27. Winston Churchill *The Second World War Vol. II* pp. 136–42 relates the
    whole story of this trip to France and Churchill's return.

Chapter 4 – Spitfire Summer

1. Hansard *Parliamentary Debates* House of Commons, 18 June 1940.
2. John Colville *The Fringes of Power* p. 165. Listening to the speech held
   in the BBC Archives today, he does not come across as tired, nor sound
   like he is smoking a cigar. But by this point Colville was working with
   Churchill virtually all day, every day, so his impression is interesting.
   One of Colville's dinner companions, who listened to the speech on the
   radio with him, thought that Churchill sounded like 'a bishop'!
3. Martin Gilbert *Winston S. Churchill Vol. VI: Finest Hour* p. 571.
4. D.J. Wenden 'Churchill, Radio, and Cinema' in Robert Blake and
   Wm. Roger Louis (eds) *Churchill* p. 238. They were recorded by
   Churchill in 1949 and were released by Decca as a set of LPs. Some
   of the versions of Churchill's wartime speeches that are available
   today are these later recordings.
5. Warren Kimball *Forged in War* p. 15 and David Stafford *Roosevelt and
   Churchill* p. xvi.
6. Martin Gilbert *Winston S. Churchill Vol. VI: Finest Hour* p. 52.
7. Warren Kimball *Forged in War* pp. 3ff.

364 Churchill's War Lab

8. Martin Gilbert *Winston S. Churchill Vol. VI: Finest Hour* p. 146.
9. Martin Gilbert *Winston S. Churchill Vol. VI: Finest Hour* pp. 345–6.
10. Ronald Lewin *Churchill as Warlord* p. 37.
11. Martin Gilbert *Winston S. Churchill Vol. VI: Finest Hour* p. 356.
12. Martin Gilbert *Winston S. Churchill Vol. VI: Finest Hour* pp. 427 and 689.
13. Winston Churchill *The Second World War Vol. II* p. 206.
14. Ivan Maisky *Memoirs of a Soviet Ambassador: The War 1939–43* pp. 99–100.
15. John Colville *The Fringes of Power* p. 200.
16. For the Spitfire story, see Taylor Downing and Andrew Johnston *Battle Stations* pp. 11–35 and Leo McKinstry *Spitfire: Portrait of a Legend*.
17. Quote from Bob Doe, the third-highest-scoring ace in the Battle of Britain, in *Battle Stations – Spitfire Squadron*, producer Taylor Downing, director Andrew Johnston, Flashback Television, 2000; and quoted in Taylor Downing and Andrew Johnston *Battle Stations* p. 44. See also Bob Doe *Fighter Pilot*.
18. Constance Babington Smith *Evidence in Camera* p. 62.
19. The evening is recounted in James Marshall-Cornwall *Rumours of War* pp. 166–71. See also Martin Gilbert *Winston S. Churchill Vol. VI: Finest Hour* pp. 682–5.
20. Hastings Ismay *Memoirs* pp. 179–80.
21. The speech is from Hansard *Parliamentary Debates* House of Commons, 20 August 1940; see John Colville *The Fringes of Power* p. 227 for the anecdote about the car journey.
22. Violet Bonham Carter in Martin Gilbert *Winston S. Churchill Vol. VI* p. 742.
23. Hastings Ismay *Memoirs* pp. 183–4.
24. Winston Churchill *The Second World War Vol. II* pp. 293–7.
25. For instance, in Angus Calder *The People's War: Britain 1939–45* and in the spate of books it ushered in. And more recently in Juliet Gardiner *Wartime Britain 1939–45* pp. 530ff.
26. David Cannadine (ed.) *Winston Churchill: Blood, Toil, Tears and Sweat; The Great Speeches* p. xiv.
27. Quoted in David Cannadine (ed.) *Winston Churchill: Blood, Toil, Tears and Sweat; The Great Speeches* p. xxxiii.
28. Asa Briggs *The War of Words* pp. 187 and 297.
29. From a speech given at Westminster Hall, London, 30 November 1954 on the occasion of a parliamentary tribute to his eightieth birthday – he was the first prime minister since Gladstone to be in power at the age of eighty.

30. Asa Briggs *The War of Words* p. 10.

31. E. Bliss (ed.) *In Search of Light: The Broadcasts of Edward R. Murrow* p. 237.

32. David Reynolds '1940: The Worst and Finest Hour' in Robert Blake and Wm. Roger Louis (eds) *Churchill* p. 254.

33. John Colville *The Fringes of Power* p. 217.

Chapter 5 – The Wizard War

1. Sir Solly (later Lord) Zuckerman *Scientists and War* p. 9.

2. See Winston Churchill *The World Crisis Vol. II* pp. 508–26.

3. Winston Churchill *The World Crisis Vol. II* p. 464.

4. Thomas Wilson *Churchill and the Prof* p. 12.

5. Winston Churchill *The Second World War Vol. II* p. 338.

6. Lord Birkenhead *The Prof in Two Worlds* p. 159.

7. Thomas Wilson *Churchill and the Prof* pp. 29–30.

8. Hansard *Parliamentary Debates* House of Commons, 10 November 1932.

9. Thomas Wilson *Churchill and the Prof* p. 33.

10. Ronald Clark *The Rise of the Boffins* p. 161; see also Ronald Clark *Tizard passim*.

11. Ronald Clark *The Rise of the Boffins* p. 51; see also Ronald Clark *Tizard* pp. 149–63.

12. David Kahn *Seizing the Enigma* pp. 68ff.

13. See F.H. Hinsley and Alan Stripp (eds) *Code Breakers: The Inside Story of Bletchley Park passim* and Michael Smith *Station X* pp. 16ff.

14. Ronald Lewin *Ultra Goes to War* p. 183.

15. Martin Gilbert *Winston S. Churchill Vol. VI: Finest Hour* pp. 611–13, and Ronald Lewin *Churchill as Warlord* p. 75 and *Ultra Goes to War* p. 64.

16. Michael Smith *Station X* p. 78.

17. Martin Gilbert *Winston S. Churchill Vol. VI: Finest Hour* pp. 1185–6 and Michael Smith *Station X* pp. 79–81.

18. Winston Churchill *The Second World War Vol. II* p. 340. The meeting is also recounted in R.V. Jones *Most Secret War* pp. 100–5.

19. R.V. Jones *Most Secret War* pp. 101–2 and Martin Gilbert *Winston S. Churchill Vol. VI: Finest Hour* pp. 380–2.

20. R.V. Jones *Most Secret War* pp. 149–51, and John Colville *The Fringes of Power* pp. 294–5 and *The Churchillians* pp. 62–3.

21. Winston Churchill *The Second World War Vol. II* p. 343. There are several accounts of the Battle of the Beams, including Ronald Clark

The Rise of the Boffins pp. 98–125, Brian Johnson *The Secret War* pp. 11–61 and R.V. Jones *Most Secret War* pp. 92–188.

22. Ronald Clark *The Rise of the Boffins* p. 136; see also Ronald Clark *Tizard* pp. 248-252.

23. The official historian was James Phinney Baxter, quoted in Robert Buderi *The Invention that Changed the World* pp. 27 and 36–7 and Ronald Clark *Tizard* p. 268.

24. Ronald Clark *The Rise of the Boffins* p. 215.

25. *The Origins and Development of Operational Research in the Royal Air Force* HMSO Air Ministry Publication 3368, 1962.

26. For instance, the author's father, Peter Downing, was recruited into the RAF on graduation from King's College, London, with a mathematics degree, made a Pilot Officer, given radar operator's wings and sent immediately by Imperial Airways flying boat to Cairo, a sign of the urgent need for Operational Research mathematicians in the Middle East.

27. See Sir (later Lord) Solly Zuckerman's memoirs, *From Apes to Warlords*. Zuckerman later became Chief Scientific Adviser to the Ministry of Defence (1960–4) and then Chief Scientific Adviser to the British Government (1964–71). Despite his senior position he was an outspoken critic of the policy of nuclear deterrence.

28. Ronald Clark *The Rise of the Boffins* p. 162.

29. Tom Shachtman *Laboratory Warriors* p. 157.

30. Jeremy Isaacs and Taylor Downing *Cold War* p. 18.

Chapter 6 – The Generals

1. Ronald Lewin *Churchill as Warlord* p. 84.

2. Martin Gilbert *Winston S. Churchill Vol. VI: Finest Hour* p. 667.

3. John Keegan *Churchill* pp. 127–8 and 'Churchill's Strategy' in Robert Blake and Wm. Roger Louis (eds) *Churchill* pp. 333–4.

4. Patrick Delaforce *Churchill's Secret Weapons* p. 45 and Martin Gilbert *Winston S. Churchill Vol. VI: Finest Hour* pp. 746–7.

5. Winston Churchill *The Second World War Vol. II* p. 379.

6. Martin Gilbert *Winston S. Churchill Vol. VI: Finest Hour* pp. 981–1000.

7. David Stafford *Churchill and Secret Service* pp. 231–3.

8. Robert E. Sherwood *The White House Papers of Harry L. Hopkins Vol. I* pp. 256–7.

9. Winston Churchill *The Second World War Vol. III* p. 111, and Martin Gilbert *Winston S. Churchill Vol. VI: Finest Hour* pp. 1031–3 and *Churchill: A Life* p. 254.

10. Ronald Lewin *Churchill as Warlord* p. 57.

11. David Stafford *Churchill and Secret Service* pp. 250–4.

12. Ronald Lewin *Churchill as Warlord* p. 73 and Winston Churchill *The Second World War Vol. III* p. 223.

13. John Keegan (ed.) *Churchill's Generals* p. 80 and Hastings Ismay *Memoirs* pp. 269–71.

14. John Colville *Fringes of Power* p. 404. Colville and Churchill also discussed Wavell's dismissal in this after-dinner conversation in the garden. Colville told Churchill that Wavell would probably write his memoirs after the war and put his own side of the story of his dispute with the Prime Minister. Churchill replied that he would write his version as well 'and would bet he sold more copies'! This amusing aside proves that Churchill was thinking about writing his own account of the war as early as 1941.

15. Winston Churchill *The Second World War Vol. III* pp. 331–3.

16. Winston Churchill *The Second World War Vol. III* pp. 320–3. In this account, written in the late 1940s, Churchill was careful not to reveal the Ultra secret. He used phrases like 'Intelligence reports from one of our most trusted sources' and spoke of 'reliable agents' in the neutral countries. The story of breaking the Enigma codes was not made public until the 1970s. See also David Stafford *Churchill and Secret Service* pp. 258–9.

17. Sir John Martin *Downing Street: The War Years* p. 58.

18. David Fraser *Alanbrooke* p. 202.

19. Alex Danchev and Daniel Todman (eds) *Field Marshal Lord Alanbrooke's War Diaries* pp. 160–1.

20. John Keegan (ed.) *Churchill's Generals* p. 90.

21. Alex Danchev and Daniel Todman (eds) *Field Marshal Lord Alanbrooke's War Diaries* p. 590. In their 'Introduction' to the *War Diaries*, Danchev and Todman explore the circumstances of the writing of the diaries: pp. xiff. The original diaries are held at the Liddell Hart Centre for Military Archives at King's College, London.

22. Martin Gilbert *Winston S. Churchill Vol. VI: Finest Hour* p. 1251.

23. David Stafford *Churchill and Secret Service* p. 261.

24. Eyewitness interview with Colonel Manteuffel in Thames TV's *The World at War* episode 'Barbarossa', producer Jeremy Isaacs, director Peter Batty. See also Richard Holmes *The World at War* p. 191.

25. Winston Churchill *The Second World War Vol. III* p. 538.

26. Winston Churchill *The Second World War Vol. III* pp. 539–40.

27. These three papers are reproduced in Winston Churchill *The Second World War Vol. III* pp. 572–86.

28. Winston Churchill *The Second World War Vol. III* p. 588.

29. The speech is quoted in full in David Cannadine (ed.) *Winston Churchill: Blood, Toil, Tears and Sweat; The Great Speeches* pp. 226–33.

30. Lord Moran *Churchill at War 1940–45* pp. 17–18.

31. Lord Moran *Churchill at War 1940–45* p. 22.

32. Martin Gilbert *Winston S. Churchill Vol. VII: Road to Victory* p. 78.

33. Martin Gilbert *Winston S. Churchill Vol. VII: Road to Victory* p. 67.

34. Winston Churchill *The Second World War Vol. IV* pp. 343–4. General Brooke comments in his diary on the generosity of the US offer of Sherman tanks, which had already been allocated to a US armoured division: see Alex Danchev and Daniel Todman (eds) *Field Marshal Lord Alanbrooke's War Diaries* p. 269.

35. Lord Moran *Churchill at War 1940–45* pp. 57–8.

36. Alex Danchev and Daniel Todman (eds) *Field Marshal Lord Alanbrooke's War Diaries* p. 293. Churchill had initially offered Auchinleck's role to Brooke himself, who had been sorely tempted by 'the finest command I could hope for'. But he felt he lacked experience in desert warfare and was 'able to render better services to my country' by remaining as CIGS. See *Field Marshal Lord Alanbrooke's War Diaries* pp. 293–7.

37. Martin Gilbert *Winston S. Churchill Vol. VII: Road to Victory* p. 254.

Chapter 7 – The Admirals

1. Winston Churchill *The Second World War Vol. II* p. 529.

2. Winston Churchill *The Second World War Vol. III* p. 101.

3. Winston Churchill *The Second World War Vol. III* p. 106 and Ronald Lewin *Churchill as Warlord* p. 61.

4. Churchill liked to include documents that showed him in a good light in his post-war history and this directive is reproduced in full in Winston Churchill *The Second World War Vol. III* pp. 107–8.

5. Stephen Roskill, the official historian of the naval war, is highly critical

of this instruction, which he calls one of the most extraordinary signals of the war. See Stephen Roskill *Churchill and the Admirals* p. 125.

6. Stephen Roskill *Churchill and the Admirals* pp. 178 and 125.

7. Stephen Roskill *Churchill and the Admirals* pp. 183ff. and Richard Ollard 'Churchill and the Navy' in Robert Blake and Wm. Roger Louis (eds) *Churchill* pp. 392–3.

8. The most obvious example of this was in Alan Brooke's war diaries. These first came out when released to Arthur Bryant for his two books *The Turn of the Tide 1939–43* and *Triumph in the West 1943–46* in 1957 and 1959. By contrast, Andrew Cunningham in *Admiral A.B. Cunningham: A Sailor's Odyssey*, Arthur Harris in *Bomber Offensive* and Montgomery in his memoirs were all quite bland about their disagreements with the Prime Minister.

9. Winston Churchill *The Second World War Vol. III* p. 551.

10. Winston Churchill *The Second World War Vol. IV* pp. 43–4.

11. Winston Churchill *The Second World War Vol. IV* pp. 87–8.

12. Winston Churchill *The Second World War Vol. IV* p. 81.

13. Martin Gilbert *Winston S. Churchill Vol. VII: Road to Victory* pp. 57–9.

14. David Kahn *Seizing the Enigma* pp. 195–213.

15. This incident was transformed in the movie *U-571*, written and directed by Jonathan Mostow, 2000. In one of the worst Hollywood distortions of history, *U-571* shows a group of *American* submariners deceiving a U-boat into surrendering so they can capture the vital Enigma machine and code books. The derring-do of the U-boats, their captains and their crews has generated lots of films, from *The Enemy Below* (1957) to *Das Boot* (1981).

16. Sir John Martin *Downing Street: The War Years* p. 97.

17. Alex Danchev and Daniel Todman (eds) *Field Marshal Lord Alanbrooke's War Diaries* p. 361.

18. Harold Macmillan *War Diaries: Politics and War in the Mediterranean, January 1943 to May 1945* p. 9.

19. Lord Moran *Churchill at War* p. 99.

20. Ronald Lewin *Churchill as Warlord* p. 186.

21. P.M.S. Blackett *Studies of War* p. 238.

Chapter 8 – Bombing

1. Constance Babbington Smith *Evidence in Camera* pp. 71–6 and Max Hastings *Bomber Command* pp. 80–3.

2. Max Hastings *Bomber Command* pp. 82–8.
3. Winston Churchill *The Second World War Vol. II* pp. 405–6.
4. Sir Charles Webster and Noble Frankland *The Strategic Air Offensive against Germany Vol. I* p. 179.
5. Winston Churchill *Second World War Vol. IV* p. 250.
6. Sir Charles Webster and Noble Frankland *The Strategic Air Offensive against Germany Vol. I* p. 182.
7. Sir Charles Webster and Noble Frankland *The Strategic Air Offensive against Germany Vol. I* p. 186 and Winston Churchill *The Second World War Vol. III* p. 748.
8. Max Hastings *Bomber Command* p. 135.
9. Sir Arthur Harris *Bomber Offensive* pp. 151–5 and Henry Probert *Bomber Harris* pp. 133–4.
10. Cherwell's minute is quoted at length in Thomas Wilson *Churchill and the Prof* p. 74.
11. Ronald Lewin *Churchill as Warlord* p. 101.
12. Sir Charles Webster and Noble Frankland *The Strategic Air Offensive against Germany Vol. I* p. 336.
13. Winston Churchill *The Second World War Vol. IV* p. 433.
14. Winston Churchill *The Second World War Vol. IV* p. 443.
15. Winston Churchill *The Second World War Vol. IV* p. 253.
16. Sir Charles Webster and Noble Frankland *The Strategic Air Offensive against Germany Vol. II* pp. 12–13.
17. Martin Gilbert *Winston S. Churchill Vol. VII: Road to Victory* pp. 295 and 302.
18. Martin Gilbert *Winston S. Churchill Vol. VII: Road to Victory* p. 303.
19. Max Hastings *Bomber Command* p. 189.
20. This film is held at the Landesmedienzentrum in Hamburg. Clips of the film are regularly shown in television documentaries.
21. The Goebbels quote is from his diary entry of 29 July 1943; Albert Speer *Inside the Reich* pp. 283–4.
22. Max Hastings *Bomber Command* p. 257.
23. Henry Probert *Bomber Harris* p. 221.
24. *The Dam Busters*, producer Robert Clark, director Michael Anderson, starring Michael Redgrave as Barnes Wallis and Richard Todd as Guy Gibson, Associated British Picture Coproration, 1954. The film is based on a book by Paul Brickhill.
25. Albert Speer *Inside the Reich* pp. 280–1.

26. Martin Gilbert *Auschwitz and the Allies* p. 270.
27. Martin Gilbert *Auschwitz and the Allies* p. 285. For the recent debate about whether the Allies should have bombed Auschwitz, see William D. Rubinstein *The Myth of Rescue: Why the Democracies Could Not Have Saved More Jews from the Nazis* and Michael J. Neufeld and Michael Berenbaum (eds) *The Bombing of Auschwitz: Should the Allies Have Attempted It?* For the aerial photographs themselves and a summary of these issues, see the TV documentary *Auschwitz: The Forgotten Evidence*, producer Taylor Downing, director Lucy Carter, Flashback Television, 2005.
28. Max Hastings *Bomber Command* p. 244.
29. Winston Churchill *The Second World War Vol. IV* pp. 466 and 468.
30. See David Reynolds *In Command of History* pp. 320–4 and 396–8.
31. Martin Gilbert *Winston S. Churchill Vol. VII: Road to Victory* pp. 1160–1.
32. Martin Gilbert *Winston S. Churchill Vol. VII: Road to Victory* p. 1257.

Chapter 9 – Overlord

1. Ronald Lewin *Churchill as Warlord* p. 190
2. Martin Gilbert *Winston S. Churchill Vol. VII: Road to Victory* pp. 379–80.
3. Winston Churchill *The Second World War Vol. IV* p. 724.
4. Max Hastings *Overlord* p. 23. See also Alex Danchev and Daniel Todman (eds) *Field Marshal Lord Alanbrooke's War Diaries* p. 527.
5. Winston Churchill *The Second World War Vol. IV* pp. 729 and 741.
6. Winston Churchill *The Second World War Vol. V* p. 76.
7. Alex Danchev and Daniel Todman (eds) *Field Marshal Lord Alanbrooke's War Diaries* pp. 441–2.
8. Martin Gilbert *Winston S. Churchill Vol. VII: Road to Victory* p. 480 and see also p. 445.
9. Winston Churchill *The Second World War Vol. V* p. 123.
10. Ronald Lewin *Churchill as Warlord* p. 219.
11. Winston Churchill *The Second World War Vol. V* p. 128.
12. Martin Gilbert *Winston S. Churchill Vol. VII: Road to Victory* p. 497.
13. Martin Gilbert *Winston S. Churchill Vol. VII: Road to Victory* pp. 522 and 524 and Ronald Lewin *Churchill as Warlord* p. 222.
14. Martin Gilbert *Winston S. Churchill Vol. VII: Road to Victory* pp. 539 and 543.
15. Quoted from the Stilwell Papers in Ronald Lewin *Churchill as Warlord*

p. 228. See also Alex Danchev and Daniel Todman (eds) *Field Marshal Lord Alanbrooke's War Diaries* p. 478. Brooke had wanted the conference to be over before it had begun, knowing how unpleasant it would be 'the most unpleasant we have had yet, and that is saying a good deal'. *Field Marshal Lord Alanbrooke's War Diaries* p. 475.

16. Martin Gilbert *Winston S. Churchill Vol. VII: Road to Victory* pp. 578–9.
17. Winston Churchill *The Second World War Vol. V* pp. 329–30.
18. Lord Moran *Churchill at War* p. 171.
19. Martin Gilbert *Winston S. Churchill Vol. VII: Road to Victory* p. 586 and Winston Churchill *The Second World War Vol. V* p. 338.
20. Winston Churchill *The Second World War Vol. V* p. 339 and Ronald Lewin *Churchill as Warlord* p. 231.
21. Winston Churchill *The Second World War Vol. V* p. 371.
22. Martin Gilbert *Winston S. Churchill Vol. VII: Road to Victory* p. 602 and Winston Churchill *The Second World War Vol. V* p. 372.
23. Winston Churchill *The Second World War Vol. V* pp. 372–87, Martin Gilbert *Winston S. Churchill Vol. VII: Road to Victory* pp. 604–28, Lord Moran *Churchill at War* pp. 181–91, Alex Danchev and Daniel Todman (eds) *Field Marshal Lord Alanbrooke's War Diaries* pp. 497–8, and Sir John Martin *Downing Street: The War Years* pp. 124–33.
24. Martin Gilbert *Winston S. Churchill Vol. VII: Road to Victory* p. 771.
25. Winston Churchill *The Second World War Vol. II* p. 602 and John Colville *The Fringes of Power* p. 275.
26. Patrick Delaforce *Churchill's Secret Weapons* pp. 27–8.
27. Alex Danchev and Daniel Todman (eds) *Field Marshal Lord Alanbrooke's War Diaries* pp. 516–17.
28. The minute is reproduced as a facsimile with Churchill's handwritten notes in Winston Churchill *The Second World War Vol. V* opposite p. 78; see also J. Evans, E. Palmer and R. Walter (eds) *A Harbour Goes to War* pp. 5ff.
29. Hastings Ismay *Memoirs* p. 309.
30. Alex Danchev and Daniel Todman (eds) *Field Marshal Lord Alanbrooke's War Diaries* p. 554.
31. Hansard *Parliamentary Debates* House of Commons, 6 June 1944.
32. Martin Gilbert *Winston S. Churchill Vol. VII: Road to Victory* p. 802.
33. Winston Churchill *The Second World War Vol. VI* pp. 10–12 and Alex Danchev and Daniel Todman (eds) *Field Marshal Lord Alanbrooke's War Diaries* pp. 556–8.

Chapter 10 – Victory and Defeat

1. Alex Danchev and Daniel Todman (eds) *Field Marshal Lord Alanbrooke's War Diaries* p. 424.
2. Winston Churchill *The Second World War Vol. V* p. 206.
3. Dwight D. Eisenhower *Crusade in Europe* p. 260.
4. Alex Danchev and Daniel Todman (eds) *Field Marshal Lord Alanbrooke's War Diaries* pp. 521, 525 and 528.
5. Ronald Lewin *Churchill as Warlord* p. 238.
6. John Keegan (ed.) *Churchill's Generals* p. 99.
7. Alex Danchev and Daniel Todman (eds) *Field Marshal Lord Alanbrooke's War Diaries* p. 533.
8. Alex Danchev and Daniel Todman (eds) *Field Marshal Lord Alanbrooke's War Diaries* pp. 535 and 537.
9. Alex Danchev and Daniel Todman (eds) *Field Marshal Lord Alanbrooke's War Diaries* p. 544.
10. Captain Harry C. Butcher *Three Years with Eisenhower* p. 545; see also Ronald Lewin *Churchill as Warlord* p. 251 and Martin Gilbert *Winston S. Churchill Vol. VII: Road to Victory* p. 877.
11. Winston Churchill *The Second World War Vol. VI* p. 85 and Martin Gilbert *Winston S. Churchill Vol. VII: Road to Victory* p. 899.
12. Winston Churchill *The Second World War Vol. VI* p. 198. Churchill tells this story in the last volume of his memoir–history, published in 1954, after Stalin's death. Martin Gilbert notes that some of the official record of this discussion was later removed as it might 'seem most inappropriate for a record of this importance': see Martin Gilbert *Winston S. Churchill Vol. VII: Road to Victory* p. 992. The original piece of paper clearly showing Stalin's blue tick is reproduced in Jeremy Isaacs and Taylor Downing *Cold War* p. 12.
13. Winston Churchill *The Second World War Vol. VI* p. 205.
14. Martin Gilbert *Winston S. Churchill Vol. VII: Road to Victory* p. 1017.
15. Mary Soames *Clementine Churchill* p. 364.
16. Alex Danchev and Daniel Todman (eds) *Field Marshal Lord Alanbrooke's War Diaries* p. 673.
17. Alex Danchev and Daniel Todman (eds) *Field Marshal Lord Alanbrooke's War Diaries* pp. 676–7.
18. Martin Gilbert *Winston S. Churchill Vol. VII: Road to Victory* p. 1289.
19. Stephen Ambrose *Eisenhower and Berlin 1945: The Decision to Halt at the Elbe* pp. 53–65.

20. John Colville *The Fringes of Power* pp. 595–6.
21. Alex Danchev and Daniel Todman (eds) *Field Marshal Lord Alanbrooke's War Diaries* p. 687.
22. Elizabeth Nel (née Layton) *Mr Churchill's Secretary* p. 176.
23. Martin Gilbert *Winston S. Churchill Vol. VII: Road to Victory* p. 1347.
24. Winston Churchill *The Second World War Vol. VI* pp. 498–9.
25. Paul Addison *The Road to 1945* pp. 150–1.
26. Winston Churchill *The Second World War Vol. VI* p. 583.

Chapter 11 – Churchill's War

1. John Colville *The Fringes of Power* p. 509.
2. David Reynolds *In Command of History* pp. 28ff.
3. John Colville *The Churchillians* p. 143.
4. Robert Rhodes James *Churchill: A Study in Failure* is an early example, from 1970; Clive Ponting *Churchill* (1994) and Nigel Knight *Churchill: The Greatest Briton Unmasked* (2008) are later examples of this more hostile take on Churchill.
5. Speech given at Westminster Hall, London, 30 November 1954, on his eightieth birthday, quoted in David Cannadine (ed.) *Winston Churchill: Blood, Toil, Tears and Sweat; The Great Speeches* pp. 334–7.
6. Asa Briggs *The War of Words* pp. 9–10.
7. R.V. Jones *Most Secret War* p. 107.
8. Elizabeth Nel (née Layton) *Mr Churchill's Secretary* p. 58 and in interview with Flashback Television in 2006.
9. Nigel Knight *Churchill: The Greatest Briton Unmasked passim*. One of the great British military strategists, Basil Liddell Hart, also criticised Churchill's strategic vision in A.J.P. Taylor *et al. Churchill: Four Faces and the Man* pp. 155–202.
10. David Reynolds '1940: The Worst and Finest Hour' in Robert Blake and Wm. Roger Louis (eds) *Churchill* p. 249.
11. Martin Gilbert *Winston S. Churchill Vol. III: 1914–1916* p. 693.
12. Ruth Ive *The Woman Who Censored Churchill* p. 75 and in an interview for *Churchill and the President*, producer Taylor Downing, director Patrick King, Flashback Television, 1999.

Bibliography

Books by Winston Churchill

The World Crisis 1911–1918 First published in 5 vols, Odhams, London
 1923–31; republished in 2 vols, Odhams, London, 1939
My Early Life Thornton Butterworth, London, 1930; republished
 Eland, London, 2000
Thoughts and Adventures Thornton Butterworth, London, 1932
Great Contemporaries Thornton Butterworth, London, 1937
Marlborough: His Life and Times 4 vols, Harrap & Co, London, 1933–8
The Second World War 6 vols, Cassell, London, 1948–54

Official biography

Randolph Churchill *Winston S. Churchill Vol. I: Youth 1874–1900*
 Heinemann, London, 1966
Randolph Churchill *Winston S. Churchill Vol. II: Young Statesman
 1901–1914* Heinemann, London, 1967
Martin Gilbert *Winston S. Churchill Vol. III: 1914–1916* Heinemann,
 London, 1971
Martin Gilbert *Winston S. Churchill Vol. IV: 1916–1922* Heinemann,
 London, 1975
Martin Gilbert *Winston S. Churchill Vol. V: 1922–1939* Heinemann,
 London, 1976

Martin Gilbert *Winston S. Churchill Vol. VI: Finest Hour 1939–1941*
Heinemann, London, 1983

Martin Gilbert *Winston S. Churchill Vol. VII: Road to Victory 1941–1945*
Heinemann, London, 1986

Complementing these biographies are several volumes of documents
edited by Martin Gilbert called *Companion* volumes, the most relevant
of which for this study are:

*The Churchill War Papers Vol. I: At the Admiralty September 1939 to May
1940* Heinemann, London, 1993

*The Churchill War Papers Vol. II: Never Surrender May 1940 to December
1940* Heinemann, London, 1994

The Churchill War Papers Vol. III: The Ever Widening War 1941 Heinemann, London, 2000

**Wartime memoirs and accounts by those who worked with or knew
Churchill:**

Field Marshal Lord Alanbrooke *War Diaries 1939–1945* ed. by Alex
Danchev and Daniel Todman, Weidenfeld and Nicolson,
London, 2001

Maurice Ashley *Churchill as Historian* Charles Scribner's Sons, New
York, 1968

P.M.S. Blackett *Studies of War* Oliver & Boyd, Edinburgh, 1962

Violet Bonham Carter *Winston Churchill as I Knew Him* Eyre and
Spottiswoode, London, 1965

Joan Bright Astley *The Inner Circle: A View of War at the Top* First published Hutchinson, London, 1971; republished The Memoir
Club, Stanhope, 2007

Harry C. Butcher *My Three Years with Eisenhower* Simon & Schuster,
New York, 1946

John Colville *The Churchillians* Weidenfeld and Nicolson, London,
1981

John Colville *The Fringes of Power – Downing Street Diaries 1939–45*
Hodder and Stoughton, London, 1985

Andrew Cunningham *Admiral A.B. Cunningham: A Sailor's Odyssey* Hutchinson, London, 1951

Dwight D. Eisenhower *Crusade in Europe* Doubleday, New York, 1948

Sir Arthur Harris *Bomber Offensive* First published Collins, London, 1947; republished Greenhill, London, 1990

Hastings Ismay *The Memoirs of Lords Ismay* Heinemann, London, 1960

Ruth Ive *The Woman Who Censored Churchill* The History Press, Stroud, 2008

R.V. Jones *Most Secret War* Hamish Hamilton, London, 1978

Harold Macmillan *The Blast of War 1939–45*, Macmillan, London, 1977

Harold Macmillan *War Diaries: Politics and War in the Mediterranean, January 1943 to May 1945* Macmillan, London, 1984

Ivan Maisky *Memoirs of a Soviet Ambassador: The War 1939–43* trans. by Andrew Rothstein, Hutchinson, London, 1967

James Marshall-Cornwall *Rumours of War* Martin Secker & Warburg, London, 1984

Sir John Martin *Downing Street: The War Years* Bloomsbury, London, 1991

Field Marshal Viscount Montgomery of Alamein *Normandy to the Baltic* Hutchinson, London, 1947

Joanna Moody *From Churchill's War Rooms: Letters of a Secretary 1943–45* Tempus, Stroud, 2007

Lord Moran *Churchill at War 1940–45* First published Constable, London, 1966; republished Robinson, London, 2002

Elizabeth Nel (née Layton) *Mr Churchill's Secretary* First published Hodder and Stoughton, London, 1958; republished as *Winston Churchill by His Personal Secretary* iUniverse, New York, 2007

Lord Normanbrook (and others) *Action This Day: Working with Churchill* Macmillan, London, 1968

Mary Soames *Clementine Churchill* Cassell, London, 1979

Mary Soames (ed.) *Speaking for Themselves: The Personal Letters of Winston and Clementine Churchill* Doubleday, London, 1998

Robert E. Sherwood *The White House Papers of Harry L. Hopkins* Eyre & Spottiswoode, London, 1948

Albert Speer *Inside the Reich* Weidenfeld and Nicolson, London, 1970

Solly Zuckerman *From Apes to Warlords* Hamish Hamilton, London, 1978

Secondary accounts

Paul Addison *The Road to 1945: British Politics and the Second World War* Jonathan Cape, London, 1975

Paul Addison *Churchill on the Home Front* Jonathan Cape, London, 1992

Stephen Ambrose *Eisenhower and Berlin 1945: The Decision to Halt at the Elbe* Norton & Co, New York, 1967

Stephen Ambrose *D-Day* Simon & Schuster, New York, 1994

Constance Babington Smith *Evidence in Camera: The Story of Photographic Intelligence in the Second World War* First published Chatto & Windus, London, 1957; republished Sutton, Stroud, 2004

Joseph Balkoski *Beyond the Beachhead: The 29th Infantry Division in Normandy* Stackpole Books, Mechanicsburg, 1989

Correlli Barnett *The Audit of War* Macmillan, London, 1986

Geoffrey Best *Churchill: A Study in Greatness* Penguin, London, 2002

Geoffrey Best *Churchill and War* Hambledon, London, 2005

Lord Birkenhead *The Prof in Two Worlds: The Official Life of Professor F.A. Lindemann Viscount Cherwell* Collins, London, 1961

Robert Blake and Wm. Roger Louis (eds) *Churchill* Oxford University Press, 1993

Piers Brendon *Winston Churchill: A Brief Life* Pimlico, London, 2001

Asa Briggs *The History of Broadcasting in the United Kingdom Vol. III: The War of Words* 2nd revised edition, Oxford University Press, Oxford, 1995

Richard Broad and Suzie Fleming (eds) *Nella Last's War: A Mother's Diary 1939–45* Falling Wall Press, Bristol, 1981

William F. Buckingham *Arnhem 1944* Tempus, Stroud, 2002

Robert Buderi *The Invention that Changed the World: How a Small Group of Radar Pioneers Won the Second World War* Simon & Schuster, New York, 1996

Angus Calder *The People's War: Britain 1939–45* Jonathan Cape, London, 1969

Peter Calvocoressi and Guy Wint *Total War* Penguin, London, 1972

David Cannadine *The Decline and Fall of the British Aristocracy* Yale University Press, London, 1990

David Cannadine (ed.) *Winston Churchill: Blood, Toil, Tears and Sweat; The Great Speeches* Penguin Classics, London, 2007

Ronald W. Clark *The Rise of the Boffins* Phoenix House, London, 1962

Ronald W. Clark *Tizard* Methuen, London, 1965

John Costello *The Pacific War 1941–1945* HarperCollins, New York, 1982

Len Deighton and Max Hastings *Battle of Britain* Jonathan Cape, London, 1980

Patrick Delaforce *Churchill's Secret Weapons: The Story of Hobart's Funnies* Pen & Sword, Barnsley, 2006

Bob Doe *Fighter Pilot* CCB Associates, Selsdon, 1999

Taylor Downing and Andrew Johnston *Battle Stations: Decisive Weapons of the Second World War* Pen & Sword, Barnsley, 2000

J. Evans, E. Palmer and R. Walter (eds) *A Harbour Goes to War: The Story of Mulberry and the Men Who Made It Happen* Brook House Publishing, Wigtownshire, 2000

David Fraser *Alanbrooke* HarperCollins, London, 1982

Juliet Gardiner *Wartime Britain 1939–45* Headline Books, London, 2004

Martin Gilbert *Churchill: A Life* Heinemann, London, 1991

Martin Gilbert *Auschwitz and the Allies* Pimlico, London, 2001

Ian Grant *Cameramen at War* Patrick Stephens, Cambridge, 1980

Max Hastings *Bomber Command* Penguin, London, 1999

Max Hastings *Overlord* Pan Macmillan, London, 1999

Richard Havers *Here is the News: The BBC and the Second World War* Sutton Publishing, Stroud, 2007

F.H. Hinsley and Alan Stripp (eds) *Code Breakers: The Inside Story of Bletchley Park* Oxford University Press, Oxford, 1993

Richard Holmes *In the Footsteps of Churchill* BBC Books, London, 2006

Richard Holmes *The World at War: The Landmark Oral History* Ebury, London, 2007

Alistair Horne with David Montgomery *The Lonely Leader: Monty 1944–1945* Macmillan, London, 1994

Jeremy Isaacs and Taylor Downing *Cold War* Transworld, London, 1998 and republished by Little, Brown, London, 2008

Brian Johnson *The Secret War* BBC Books, London, 1978

David Kahn *Seizing the Enigma* Arrow, London, 1996

John Keegan *Six Armies in Normandy: From D-Day to the Liberation of Paris* Jonathan Cape, London, 1982

John Keegan *Churchill* Weidenfeld & Nicolson, London, 2002

John Keegan (ed.) *Churchill's Generals* Abacus, London, 1999

Warren Kimball *Forged in War: Roosevelt, Churchill and the Second World War* William Morrow and Company, New York, 1997

Nigel Knight *Churchill: The Greatest Briton Unmasked* David & Charles, Newton Abbot, 2008

Ronald Lewin *Churchill as Warlord* Batsford, London, 1973

Ronald Lewin *Ultra Goes to War: The Secret Story* Hutchinson, London, 1978

Adrian R. Lewis *Omaha Beach: A Flawed Victory* Tempus, Stroud, 2004

John Lukacs *Five Days in London May 1940* Yale University Press, London, 1999

Leo McKinstry *Spitfire: Portrait of a Legend* John Murray, London, 2007

Michael J. Neufeld and Michael Berenbaum (eds) *The Bombing of Auschwitz: Should the Allies Have Attempted It?* University Press of Kansas, Lawrence, 2003

Richard Overy *Russia's War* Allen Lane, London, 1998

Richard Overy *The Battle of Britain* Penguin, London, 2000

Clive Ponting *Churchill* Sinclair-Stevenson, London, 1994

Henry Probert *Bomber Harris: His Life and Times* Greenhill, London, 2003

Nicholas Rankin *Churchill's Wizards: The British Genius for Deception 1914–1945* Faber and Faber, London, 2008

David Reynolds *In Command of History: Churchill Fighting and Writing the Second World War* Allen Lane, London, 2004

Robert Rhodes-James *Churchill: A Study in Failure 1900–39* Weidenfeld and Nicolson, London, 1970

Andrew Roberts *Hitler and Churchill: Secrets of Leadership* Phoenix, London, 2003

Andrew Roberts *Masters and Commanders: How Roosevelt, Churchill, Marshall and Alanbrooke Won the War in the West* Allen Lane, London, 2008

Andrew Roberts *The Storm of War: A New History of the Second World War* Allen Lane, London, 2009

Stephen Roskill *Churchill and the Admirals* First published William Collins, London, 1977; republished as a Pen & Sword Military Classic, Barnsley, 2004

William D. Rubinstein *The Myth of Rescue: Why the Democracies Could Not Have Saved More Jews from the Nazis* Routledge, London, 1997

Celia Sandys *Churchill Wanted Dead or Alive* HarperCollins, London, 1999

L.A. Sawyer and W.H. Mitchell *The Liberty Ships* Lloyds of London, London, 1985

Tom Shachtman *Laboratory Warriors: How Allied Science and Technology Tipped the Balance in World War Two* HarperCollins, New York, 2003

Gary Sheffield and John Bourne (eds) *Douglas Haig: War Diaries and Letters* Phoenix, London, 2006

Michael Smith *Station X: The Codebreakers of Bletchley Park* Channel Four Books, London, 1998

David Stafford *Roosevelt and Churchill: Men of Secrets* Little, Brown, London, 1999

David Stafford *Churchill and Secret Service* Abacus, London, 2000

A.J.P. Taylor *English History 1914–1945* Oxford University Press, Oxford, 1965

A.J.P. Taylor, R.R. James, J.H. Plumb, B.L. Hart and A. Storr *Churchill: Four Faces and the Man* Allen Lane, London, 1969

Sir Charles Webster and Noble Frankland *The Strategic Air Offensive against Germany 1939–1945* 4 vols, HMSO, London, 1961

John Wheeler-Bennett *King George VI: His Life and Reign* Macmillan, London, 1958

Thomas Wilson *Churchill and the Prof* Cassell, London, 1995

Solly Zuckerman *Scientists and War: The Impact of Science on Military and Civil Affairs* Hamish Hamilton, London, 1966

Acknowledgements

I have been lucky enough to have produced many documentaries at Flashback Television relating to several of the subject areas covered in this book. And I have been privileged to interview some of the individuals who feature in the book or who knew those who feature. So the ideas here have been mulling over in my mind for many years after discussions and debate with a large number of people whom I would like to thank. First of all, there is my business and creative partner David Edgar, who deserves special thanks for coming up with the title. Then there are many other fellow travellers with whom I have had the pleasure of working on television documentaries in this area. They include Andrew Johnston, Patrick King, Colin Barratt, Chris Warren, David Caldwell-Evans, Steve Baker, Paul Nelson, Jobim Sampson, James Barker, Lucy Carter and Dunja Noack. I need to thank all of them. Also, working with Sir Jeremy Isaacs has always been pleasurable and rewarding. I have benefited from discussions with several professional historians, including Professors David Cannadine, Richard Overy, Richard Holmes and Gary Sheffield. Phil Reed, director of the Imperial War Museum's Cabinet War Rooms and Churchill Museum, has always been wonderfully helpful and open.

I should like to thank Tim Whiting, Iain Hunt and Philip Parr at Little, Brown for their continuing support and encouragement, and Linda Silverman for the photo research; and the staff of the London Library for their efficient support. Extracts from the writings of Winston Churchill are reproduced with permission of Curtis Brown Ltd, London, on behalf of The Estate of Winston Churchill, copyright © Winston S. Churchill. Finally, my thanks, as always, go to Anne for her patience and her support.

Index

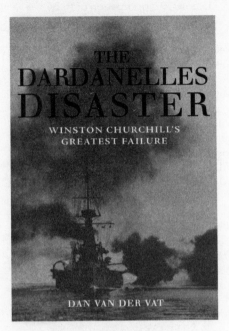
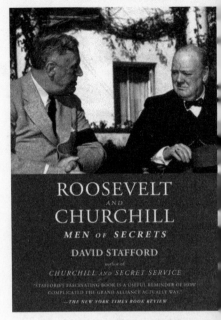

"Why do engineers prefer this FE/EIT study guide?"

Reader remarks from the GLP in-basket....

"After looking at several other books, I am convinced your *Fundamentals of Engineering* is the best review around. It is very well organized, thorough, and concise. An outstanding book."

—Paul Griesmer, Cleveland, Ohio

"I tell everyone I know about the *Fundamentals of Engineering* review by Potter. You can recommend this book to anyone. The problems on the actual exam were just like the problems in your book—it is absolutely great!"

—Krzysztof Kopec, New York

"In your FE book you cut to the chase and don't embellish it... Yours is the only review that doesn't scare the pants off people. It's exactly what I want for teaching my review course."

—John Thorington

"A student told me that the problems on the actual FE exam were like the problems in your book —verbatim. It's the best review I've ever seen. When we started using your review, our students' pass rates went up 20%! We'll continue to use your book because we take professional licensing seriously."

—Dr. Gary Rogers, Virginia Military Institute

"Your FE study guide is very thorough, well-organized and easy to use. It was instrumental in helping me brush up on engineering material I had not seen for 5 years. I passed the FE the first time!"

—Brian Campbell, Project Engineer, Trailmaster Corp, Ft. Worth, TX

"Thank you for the book! I passed the test because of it. Stuff I hadn't studied for more than 15 years came back to me clearly. The two practice exams are what helped me the most."

—Juan Alfaro, College Park, MD

"Three years out of school and all I needed to pass the FE exam, on the first try, was your review book! I have recommended it to everyone I know. I look forward to using your PE reference."

—David Robins, Syracuse, NY

"Your book is great! Very easy to use. Although I only had time to skim through it, it helped me review the very basics I needed to know (i.e., Chemistry, Econ). I passed without a problem! Thanks! I'm keeping it as a handy reference."

—Julie Volby, Civil Engineering Student, Univ of Minnesota

"Your review material is perfect for the non-traditional night student. It refreshes and restores many years of part-time study, without being overly exhaustive."

—Jerome Bobak, Designer Mechanical Engineer, Grand Island, NY

"This book provided all of the necessary information for passing the FE exam. I was able to review for and *pass* the exam in only 3 weeks!"

—Joseph Rozza, Recent Graduate, Orlando, FL

Important Information

FE examination date: _____ time: _____

Location: _____

_____

Examination Board Address: _____

_____

_____

Phone: _____

Application was requested on this date: _____

Application was received on this date: _____

Application was accepted on this date: _____

This book belongs to: _____

_____

_____

_____

Phone: _____

...from the Professors who know it best...

FUNDAMENTALS OF ENGINEERING
REVIEW

•For the Morning & General Afternoon Tests•

Authors:

J. Dilworth, PhD	Ethics
D. Farnum, PhD	Chemistry
F. Hatfield, PhD, PE	Civil Engineering
G. Mase, PhD	Engineering Mechanics
K. Mukherjee, PhD	Materials Science
M. Potter, PhD, PE	Mechanical Engineering
J. Soper, PhD	Electrical Engineering
B. Weinberg, PhD, PE	Computer Science

Our authors are award-winning professors. All are from Michigan State University, with the exception of Dr. Soper of Michigan Technological University, and Dr. Dilworth of Western Michigan University.

GREAT LAKES PRESS

Okemos, MI / Wildwood, MO
Customer Service: (636) 273-6016
Fax: (636) 273-6086
Website: www.glpbooks.com
Email: custserv@glpbooks.com

International Standard Book Number 1-881018-44-X

Cover and page design by Ross W. Orr.

All comments and inquiries should be addressed to:
    Great Lakes Press
    PO Box 550
    Wildwood, MO 63040-0550
    Phone (636) 273-6016
    Fax (636) 273-6086
    custserv@glpbooks.com
    www.glpbooks.com

Library of Congress Card Number: 2001086473

Printed in the USA by Sheridan Books, Inc. of Ann Arbor, Michigan.

10 9 8 7 6 5 4

Table of Contents

Preface   **1**

"STEP ONE: Study these strategies for passing the FE/EIT Exam"

PART I
Passing the FE/EIT
Exam   **3**

"STEP TWO: Take the FE/EIT Diagnostic Exam"

PART II
FE/EIT Diagnostic
Exam   **15**

"STEP THREE: Study the *Fundamentals of Engineering Review*"

Chapter 3
MATERIALS SCIENCE
        167

Chapter 4
CHEMISTRY   **211**

Chapter 5
ENGINEERING
ECONOMICS   **247**

Chapter 6
ELECTRICAL THEORY
289

Chapter 7
THERMODYNAMICS
337

"STEP FOUR: Take the FE/EIT Practice Exam—You're Ready!"

Preface

This FE review takes about half the time to work through compared with other available reviews. It is as thick as it is due to its spacious page layout which is designed for pleasant reviewing. Our eight professors used a streamlined approach to create the most effective review possible for the FE exam.

This review is targeted closely to the test with no extraneous material. For those who wish to save time, as well as to avoid the kind of mental clutter that lowers test scores, this review is best for *any* user, no matter if they just graduated or have been working in the field for years. There is never a need to prepare for an exam like this with over-detailed study. It is a competence test and it covers only the basics. Unfortunately, those who have been out of school awhile are often most worried about the test and take on too much study material. More than anyone, they need to stick to familiarizing themselves only with the subject areas covered by an easy majority of test questions. Over-study or diffuse reviewing brings on much more risk of failure than the exam itself! Focus to pass!

An Efficient Review is Key for *Any* Test-taker!

All test-takers must take the general morning exam but then they have a choice of six discipline-specific (DS) exams for the afternoon session: chemical, civil, electrical, industrial, mechanical, and general. Every test-taker should at least consider taking the general exam for the afternoon session. Pass/fail rates seem to be about the same by and large, though scores on the discipline tests were slightly higher—but overall general test preparation should be simpler. Each person must prepare for the morning general exam, so the simplest approach would be to continue reviewing those same topics for the afternoon session. *If you opt for the general afternoon test, check with your state board to make sure that your pass will be recognized in your state for your specialty.*

On the other hand, some test-takers reported that they switched from the general to a DS test upon evaluating each of them at the exam site—it appeared

Strategy Options

to them that the DS test was easier. Even so, to properly prepare for the numerous subjects of an afternoon area exam in addition to the 12 subjects of the morning exam might be a significant challenge.

Lecturing professors—who we asked to help create this book—are clearly the people who know how to teach the material best, as the FE is an exam that has a strictly academic basis. The result of their efforts is a succinct, authoritative review for the Fundamentals of Engineering (FE) Examination—formerly known as the Engineer-In-Training (EIT) Examination.

This volume reviews the most important terms, concepts and major equations in each of the twelve major subject areas covered by the FE exam. *The goal of this review is to enable the reader to pass the FE exam.* Therefore, minor topics that make up an insignificant portion of the exam have been intentionally omitted for the sake of efficiency. By far the vast majority of question topics are covered.

Free! Interactive CD with Study-Director™

With the purchase of this book, an interactive CD with two full-length exams with solutions and our powerful Study-Director™ software is available to you FREE. To obtain your free copy, simply tear out the business reply card at the back of this book and pop it in any mailbox to return it postpaid to: GLP, PO Box 550, Wildwood, MO 63040. You should receive your CD within 2-3 weeks.

Study-Director™ •calculates your score at the end of a test, •indicates pass/fail, •determines areas of strength or weakness, •directs you to sections in the book which might require further study, •prints out your report...and more!

Sample Problems Like the FE Questions

All our practice problems are designed to be as exam-like as possible. We have included theory questions as well as numerical problems, now with four-part multiple-choice answers—just like the exam. In the more extensive chapters, selected problems are starred (*) so that choosing to work only those problems gives you the option of a quicker review. (We have not starred any problems in the mathematics chapter; you should make sure that you have a solid math capability by working *all* of those problems.) It may seem that some of our questions are simplistic. This, too, is intentional. By and large, most of the exam questions will be quite simple, with only one principle involved. After reviewing this material and working the practice problems, you should be ready to pass the FE exam.

Mix Practice Tests with Study for Best Results

To give you further confidence, we have included two full 8-hour practice exams that provide an excellent indicator of whether you are completely ready for the examination. You may never have taken an eight-hour exam before; it is very demanding intellectually, physically and emotionally. Actual simulations of the exam will prepare you for the total experience. The first exam, called a Diagnostic Examination, is intended to be taken when you begin your review—it will reveal your weak areas. The review material comes next, and finally the second exam to determine if you're completely ready.

Keep in mind that the objective of your preparation is to pass the Fundamentals of Engineering Examination—your first step toward becoming a licensed engineer. The point is *not* to develop an exhaustive proficiency in all subject areas included on the exam.

Use your time most wisely by reviewing in detail the subject areas that you are most familiar with. Get a good night's sleep before the exam, and we here at Great Lakes Press wish you well!

—Dr. Merle C. Potter, editor

Passing the FE/EIT Exam

Part I

A Brief Outline Of This Review

This book presents an efficient review of the general subject areas covered by the FE/EIT morning session and by the General Test in the afternoon. Considering the reality of preparing for 12 topics to satisfy the demands of the General morning test that everyone takes, many test-takers prefer to take the General test in the afternoon session, as well. This review is ideal for both sessions.

GLP has prepared separate reviews for those who will take one of the Discipline tests in the afternoon. Topics include: civil, mechanical, electrical, industrial and chemical. Call 1-800-837-0201 for information and ordering.

This book contains:

- A full 8-hour Diagnostic Exam with solutions. (Simulates the morning test and afternoon General test)

- Short, succinct reviews of the theoretical aspects of the morning and General Test subject areas

- Equation Summary Sheets which allow optimum use of the NCEES Reference Handbook

- Example Problems with detailed solutions illustrating important concepts

- Practice Problems like those that will be on the FE/EIT morning test and afternoon General test

- Solutions to all Practice Problems

- A full 8-hour Practice Exam with solutions—a final readiness check. (Simulates the morning test and afternoon General test)

- A coupon to obtain a free CD with 6 practice exams (2 General and 4 Disciplines) and a reference key for all problems—plus the Study-Director score analyzer.

Why We Created This FE Review

In 1983, we at Great Lakes Press developed this reference with the cooperation of a team of colleagues in response to our experience in coordinating FE/EIT review courses. The kind of well-planned material that an engineer naturally desires to use did not exist at the time. The options were either to pick and choose from a large, encyclopedia-like book that covers almost every topic in engineering, or to use material that didn't even attempt to cover the topics tested on the exam. It was either feast or famine. And both options were often rather expensive! So we recruited popular lecturers from the university campus and prepared this study guide. Its overwhelming acceptance has encouraged us to keep it continuously in tune with the changing tenor of the FE/EIT exam. (And there have been many drastic changes over the years! We stay ahead of them for you, while others take years to catch up.)

We believe in reasonable testing. The FE exam is not intended to torture anyone. But that's not always how it's presented. We've proved that with proper, targeted prep any competent engineer can readily pass, whether they're fresh out of school or have been in the field for years. We find that fails are *very often* due to over-ambitious study of too much material and a resulting lack of focus.

On a daily basis we act as advocate for the test-taker in our involvement with engineering departments, associations, review courses and registration governing bodies. We are dedicated to making the entire licensing and registration process as reasonable as possible. Our combination of a pre-study diagnostic exam plus concise, focused exam-topic reviews, followed by a final readiness-check practice test, makes for ideal preparation.

How To Become A Professional Engineer

To become registered as an engineer, a state may require that you:
1. Graduate from an ABET-accredited engineering program
2. Pass the *Fundamentals of Engineering* exam
3. Pass the *Principles and Practice of Engineering* (PE) exam after several years of engineering experience

Requirements vary from state to state, so you should obtain local guidelines and follow them carefully.

Why Get an Engineering License?

Registration is necessary if an engineer works as a consultant, and is highly recommended in certain industries—especially when one is, or hopes to be, in a management position.

How The FE Exam Is Scored

In the morning session, each of the 120 problems is worth **one-half** point. Thus a maximum score of 60 is possible.

The afternoon session is *different* from the morning in that each problem is worth **one** point. With half the number of questions, the maximum possible score in the afternoon session is also 60.

The two-session total is 120 points, with both sessions having equal weight. A predetermined passing percentage is not established, nor is the exam graded on a curve. From recent history, a score of 60 (50% correct) would probably be a passing score.

Examination Format

The FE is composed of a four-hour general-subject morning session, followed by a one-hour break, then a four-hour discipline-specific afternoon session. The sessions have a total of 180 4-part multiple-choice questions covering the subject areas listed in the tables on the following page.

Morning Session

Subject Area	*Approximate Number*
Chemistry	11
Computers	6
Dynamics	10
Economics	5
Electrical Circuits	12
Ethics	5
Fluids	8
Materials Science	8
Mathematics	24
Mechanics of Materials (Solids)	8
Statics	12
Thermodynamics	11

Total Questions: 120

Afternoon Session

Subject Area .... (for the General Test only!)	*Number*
Chemistry	4
Computers	3
Dynamics	4
Economics	3
Electrical	6
Ethics	3
Fluids	5
Material Science	3
Mathematics	12
Mechanics of Materials (Solids)	5
Statics	6
Thermodynamics	6

Total Questions: 60

Subject Lists of the Discipline-Specific Afternoon Tests

General • See subjects above

Civil • Construction, Environmental, Hydraulics, Hydrology, Numerical Methods, Legal, Soils, Foundations, Structural, Design, Surveying, Water Treatment, Waste Water

Mechanical • Controls, Computers, Systems, Energy Conversion, Power Plants, Turbomachines, Fluids, Heat Transfer, Materials, Instrumentation, Design, HVAC, Solids, Thermodynamics

Electrical • Analog, Communication, Numerical Methods, Computer Hardware, Software, Controls, Systems, Digital, Electromagnetics, Instrumentation, Networks, Power, Signal Processing, Solid State

Chemical • Reactions, Thermodynamics, Numerical Methods, Heat Transfer, Mass Transfer, Energy, Pollution, Controls, Design, Economics, Equipment, Safety, and Transport Phenomena

Industrial • Design, Economics, Statistics, Facilities, Cost Analysis, Computer Modeling, Ergonomics, Management, Systems, Manufacturing, Material Handling, Optimization, Production, Productivity, Queuing, Simulation, Quality Control, Quality Management, Performance

Why a Discipline Test Might Not Be Your Best Choice

To prepare for any of the above Discipline-Specific (DS) Tests, it is necessary to review up to 15 to 20 textbooks, some of which were not studied as an undergraduate. Since all questions must be answered in the afternoon exam, it is not possible to select only some of the subjects listed—all subjects are included in a particular DS test. Consequently, some FE/EIT test-takers may prefer to elect the General Test for the afternoon session. If your state is one of the very few that will not accept the General Test for the afternoon session, you could simply take the test in a neighboring state that does—reciprocity has been recognized in the past and undoubtedly will be recognized in the future. If, however, you decide to take one of the DS p.m. tests, we also publish the *FE/EIT Discipline Reviews* —call 1-800-837-0201 to inquire or order.

Recommended Materials for FE/EIT Preparation

1. *Fundamentals of Engineering—General Review*; GLP (this book)
2. *FE/EIT Discipline Reviews: Civil, Mechanical, Electrical, IE, ChemE*, 5th ed.; GLP
3. *FE/EIT Quick Prep*—for General topics; GLP
4. HP 48GX Programmable Calculator
5. *Jump Start the HP 48G/GX*; GLP
6. NCEES FE/EIT Sample Exam
7. NCEES Reference Handbook

Available from GLP by calling 1-800-837-0201 or visiting www.glpbooks.com.

A Video Course is an Ideal Supplement!

Can't find a suitable review course? Want intensive study at home? GLP now offers 12-hour video courses for the FE exam, General and Discipline, produced by ASCE and ASME. (FYI, We also offer 24-hour courses for the CE and ME PE exams.) Tapes are available for sale or rent. Call 1-800-837-0201 for details.

How to Handle the NCEES Handbook

A copy of the NCEES FE Handbook may be mailed to you sometime after you register. Your first impression of this Handbook may leave you overwhelmed! It has a tremendous amount of equations, figures, and information that may, at first glance, seem unfamiliar to you. Indeed, afternoon DS test info is mixed in with morning General info. In our review we have used the NCEES Handbook to compile summaries of the more important equations from the most significant General subject areas. We have attempted to adapt our nomenclature to that of the NCEES Handbook. If you do not receive a Handbook, call us to purchase one.

We strongly urge you to have the official NCEES Reference Handbook by your side the entire time you study and to use a highlighter to identify the equations you most often use. Initially, you can use our Equation Summary Sheets and your own best judgment to highlight the key equations.

Familiarize yourself with the location of these equations so you can quickly locate them during the actual exam in the new handbook that will be given to you at the test site. If you do not prepare this way, you might become lost in the handbook during the exam.

Strategies for Study

The following strategies will help you to use this book:

1. Focus your review on the eight subjects that have the most exam questions: Chemistry, Dynamics, Electrical, Fluids, Math, Solids, Statics, and Thermo.

2. *Quickly* review the remaining four major subject areas: Computers, Economics, Ethics, and Materials Science.

3. Spend the majority of your time reviewing material with which you are *most* familiar.

4. You may receive a copy of the NCEES Handbook when you register for the exam; you can order a copy from GLP by calling 1-800-837-0201. You will not be allowed to bring this Handbook (or any other material except for a calculator— see page 9) with you into the exam. However, a clean copy of this same Handbook will be given to you upon entering the exam site. The new Handbook is particularly confusing. It includes about 85 pages that cover the General subjects (a.m. and p.m.) and 40 pages that cover the Discipline-Specific subjects. The trouble is that the a.m. and p.m. subjects are intermixed! Thus, you'll find Heat Transfer (for the ME DS Test) covered early in the pamphlet, hidden in with most of the General topics. If you elect to take the General Test, boldly mark the pages that cover the general subjects. In our book, we have provided most of the same equations that you will find in the NCEES Handbook for the major a.m. and General p.m. test subjects. Then search through the Handbook and highlight those important equations. This will allow you to familiarize yourself with the location of the equations you need most, and you will be able to quickly locate those equations in the Handbook during the exam. You will find this particularly helpful since the Handbook is filled with plenty of extraneous material. If you do not train yourself in this way, you may well find it difficult to quickly locate the appropriate equations during the exam.

Outline of A Good Study Program For Quick Progress

For a senior in an engineering college who has a busy schedule, we suggest 8 weeks as an ideal study period. During those 8 weeks, you must be willing to perform a fairly concentrated study. You should set aside blocks of 3 hours at least 2 days a week. In any case, we recommend that you study no less than 4 weeks for the FE exam. For those of you who have been away from this material for a while, base the length of your study period on the number of years you have been away from school and your own memory capability.

Perform an initial review during the first half of your selected study period (for engineering seniors, 4 weeks). But if you are trying to get through your review quickly, only the Practice Problems that have been starred (*) should be worked and studied.

Halfway through your review, set aside 9 hours to take the Practice Exam. Start at 8 a.m., take a one-hour break from 12 to 1 p.m., and finish at 5 p.m. If this is not possible for you, set aside two 4-hour blocks of time within 2 days of each other, one to take the Morning Session and the second to take the Afternoon Session of the Practice Exam. It is best if you simulate the true FE Exam experience and attempt a continuous 8-hour exam session. In any case, try to take the Practice Exam during the morning or afternoon, and avoid taking it late at night.

Upon scoring your Practice Exam, you should be able to select no more than 5 key areas out of the 12 subject areas that need the most additional review. If you are weak in more than five areas, you need substantially more study. Be sure not to select subject areas that are tested lightly as your key areas of concentration. For the next half of your study period (engineering seniors: 4 weeks) you may be able to reduce your study to 2 hours at least 2 days a week. Or, you may realize that you need to study an additional day a week or increase your study session to 4 hours. By this time you should have a definite plan of how much time you will commit to each key subject area and distribute your study time evenly throughout the 4 week period—an even, consistent study schedule builds skills best and minimizes stress and fatigue.

Two days prior to exam day, review all subject areas briefly, using your high-lighted Handbook of equations and tables. Be sure you can quickly find the equations you will use most often in the *unmarked* Handbook you will be given on exam day.

The day before the exam, relax and go to bed early. Do *not* cram or perform any panic studying. By then, you will be as prepared as you can be for the exam.

The morning of your test, get up early and have a light, healthy breakfast (and maybe some coffee!). Arrive at the exam site at least 20 minutes early. You need to allow time for parking and getting settled—be sure to bring some change to pay for parking! During the one-hour lunch break, it is best to plan to meet with a friend who can help you relax and get refreshed for the Afternoon Session. If there are no restaurants nearby, bring a bag lunch and eat outside on the lawn somewhere. Get some fresh air. Do *not* spend the entire hour reviewing. Try not to talk to other test-takers about how it is going for them. This can easily induce either insecurity or false confidence. If you understand engineering principles and have prepared well, after the dust of test day clears you'll find you've passed!

Pacing Yourself During the FE Exam

The problems in the morning session are, for the most part, unrelated. Consequently, *two minutes* (on the average) can be spent on each problem. This makes fast recall *essential*, as time does not allow you to contemplate various methods of solution. But each problem is only worth one-half point—so do not fall into the trap of spending too much time on any one problem from the morning session.

In the afternoon session, you can spend an average of 4 minutes per individual question. (Many questions in the afternoon are multi-part.)

Process of Elimination

Sometimes the best way to find the right answer is to look for the wrong ones and cross them out. On questions which are difficult for you, wrong answers are often much easier to find than right ones!

Answers are seldom given with more than three significant figures, and may be given with two significant figures. The choice *closest* to your own solution should be selected.

There is no penalty for *guessing*. Use the *process of elimination* when guessing at an answer. If only one answer is negative and three answers are positive, eliminate the one odd answer from your guess. Also, when in doubt, work backwards and eliminate those answers that you believe are untrue, and then guess. By using a combination of methods, you greatly improve your odds of answering correctly.

Should I Guess?

Leave the last ten minutes of each session for making educated guesses. **Do not leave any answers blank** on your answer key. A guess *cannot* hurt you, it can only help you. Your score is based on the number of questions you answer correctly. An incorrect answer does not harm your score.

Place a question mark beside choices you are uncertain of, but seem correct. If time prevents you from re-working that problem, you will have at least identified your best guess.

Difficult Problems

If at first glance you know that a certain problem will require much time and is exceptionally difficult for you, make your best guess, then *skip right over it*. Be sure to mark the problem in a unique manner (we suggest that you circle the

INTRO

problem number) so that if time permits you may come back to it. (Note: it is not possible to return to the Morning Session problems in the Afternoon Session.)

When you are working through a problem and decide to move on due to some difficulty, be sure to write down in your test booklet your notes and conclusions up to that point in case you have time to return to it. Then make your best guess and circle the problem number to return to if you have time.

If you feel you know how to work a difficult problem and could answer it with more time, identify it by circling the entire problem, not just the problem number—this identifies it as a 'most likely' candidate for your set-aside ten minutes of 'guess time'.

Once you determine your answer, *always write the letter corresponding to the correct answer in the margin of the test booklet* beside the question. At the end of the page, you can then transfer all the answers from that page to the answer key at once. This will save you considerable time and help you maintain concentration as well!

Cross out choices that you have eliminated in your test booklet on the problems you will return to. Otherwise, you will have to reread them as you make your last-ditch deliberations.

Time-Saving Tips for Test Day!

Feel free to write all over the writing space provided for you in your test booklet. Do not hesitate to work out a problem, no matter how simple it may be. Doing as much work as you can on paper will ease your mind and leave it less 'cluttered'—and it will help you if you need to return to a problem. You may think you're saving time, but your exam performance is *not* improved when you work problems in your head. (Note: Room for working out problems is provided in the test booklet.)

Write Out Your Work

You must take a silent calculator (it may be preprogrammed) into the exam. A calculator is essential when solving many problems. In fact, with the exception of a couple of states, the premier engineering calculator, the HP 48GX from Hewlett-Packard, is allowed into the exam (check with your state board!). This calculator is a hand computer which has hundreds of basic equations and constants pre-programmed. This really helps! We at GLP offer this calculator for sale at a substantial discount. It accepts custom-programmed cards. We now offer cards expressly designed for the FE and PE exams, with hundreds of actual NCEES Handbook equations built-in—these are legal at most test-sites. Call for information! We offer an engineering-oriented manual, *Jump Start the HP 48G/GX*, to guide you through the steps to using this calculator effectively for the FE Exam. (The manufacturer's manual is difficult to use for even basic operations.) Call us at 1-800-837-0201 for ordering or information, or browse our website at www.glpbooks.com.

Bring a Calculator —Ideally, an HP 48GX

Some questions from the Solids chapter can be worked using either English units or SI units in the morning session only. The afternoon session will use only SI units. We recommend that all test takers prepare using only SI units. Since you must use SI units in the afternoon session, it's reason enough to prepare using SI units. The afternoon Civil test may use both sets of units in some of the subjects areas (e.g., Soils). A table of conversion factors is presented in Appendix B of this book.

English vs. SI Units

State Boards of Registration Information

All State Boards of Registration administer the National Council of Engineering Examiners and Surveyors (NCEES) uniform examination. The dates of the exams cover a span of three days in mid-April and three days in late October. The specific dates are selected by each State Board. To be accepted to take the FE exam, an applicant must apply well in advance. For information regarding the specific requirements in your state, contact your State Board's office. If contact information has changed from what we have listed here, your correct State Board information can be obtained from the Executive Director of NCEES, P. O. Box 1686, Clemson, SC 29633-1686, phone (803) 654-6824, or www.NCEES.org. Any comments relating to the exam or the Reference Handbook should be addressed to NCEES .

The answers to the following questions are answered alongside each listing:

1. *Do you provide an NCEES Handbook for all registrants?*
2. *Do you allow CE's, ME's, EE's, IE's, ChemE's to take the afternoon General Exam?*
3. *Are advanced calculators, such as the HP48GX, allowed?*

The three columns at left are headed:
- NCEES Handbook at signup?
- Can all take Gen'l Exam?
- Advanced calculators allowed?

Handbook	Gen'l	Calc	Listing
Y	Y	Y	**ALABAMA:** State Board of Licensure for Professional Engineers, P. O. Box 304451, Montgomery 36130-4451. Executive Secretary, Telephone: (334) 242-5568, engineer@dsmd.dsmd.state.al.us.
Y	Y	Y	**ALASKA:** State Board of Registration for Engineers, Pouch D, Juneau 99811. Licensing Examiner, Telephone: (907) 465-2540, marcia_pappas@dced.state.ak.us, www.commerce.state.ak.us/occ/pael/htm.
N	N	Y	**ARIZONA:** State Board of Technical Registration, 1990 W. Camelback Rd., Suite 406, Phoenix 85015. Executive Director, Telephone: (602) 255-4053, btrlvd@yahoo.com, www.btr.state.az.us.
Y	Y	'Y'	**ARKANSAS:** State Board of Registration for Professional Engineers and Land Surveyors, P. O. Box 3750, Little Rock 72203. Secretary-Treasurer, Telephone: (501) 682-2824, joe.clements@mail.state.ar.us. www.state.ar.us/pels. (No pre-programmed calculator cards allowed.)
Y	Y	Y	**CALIFORNIA:** Board for Professional Engineers and Land Surveyors, 2535 Capitol Oaks Dr #300, Sacramento 95833. Executive Secretary, Telephone: (916) 263-2222, www.dca.ca.gov/pels.
'Y'	Y	Y	**COLORADO:** State Board of Registration for Professional Engineers, 1560 Broadway, Suite 1370, Denver 80202. Program Administrator, Telephone: (303) 894-7788, www.dora.state.co.us/engineers. (Handbooks avail. while they last.)
N	Y	Y	**CONNECTICUT:** State Board of Registration for Professional Engineers, The State Office Building, Rm 110, 165 Capitol Ave, Hartford 06106. Administrator, Telephone: (860) 713-6145.

	NCEES Book?	Gen'l Exam?	Calculators?
DELAWARE: Association of Professional Engineers, 56 W. Main St, Suite 208, Christina 19702. Executive Secretary, Telephone: (302) 368-6708, peggy@dape.org, www.dape.org.	Y	Y	Y
DISTRICT OF COLUMBIA: Board of Registration for Professional Engineers, 941 N. Capitol St., OPLA Rm 2200 Washington 20002. Executive Secretary, Telephone: (202) 442-4320.	Y	Y	Y
FLORIDA: Board of Professional Engineers, 1208 Hays St., Tallahassee 32301-0755. Executive Director, Telephone: (850) 521-0500, board@fbpe.org, www.fbpe.org.	N	Y	Y
GEORGIA: State Board of Registration for Professional Engineers, 237 Coliseum Dr., Macon, 31217-3858. Executive Director, Telephone: (912) 207-1450, pels@sos.state.ga.us, www.sos.state.ga.us/ebd–pels.	Y	Y	Y
GUAM: Territorial Board of Registration for Professional Engineers, Architects and Land Surveyors, Department of Public Works, Government of Guam, P. O. Box 2950, Agana 96911. Chairman, Telephone: (671) 646-3115/3138.	?	?	?
HAWAII: State Board of Registration for Professional Engineers, P. O. Box 3469, Honolulu 96801. Executive Secretary, Telephone: (808) 586-2702.	N	N	Y
IDAHO: Board of Professional Engineers, 600 S. Orchard, Suite A, Boise 83705-1242. Executive Secretary, Telephone: (208) 334-3860, dcurtis@ipels.state.id.us, www.state.id.us/ipels.	Y	Y	Y
ILLINOIS: State Board of Professional Engineers, 320 West Washington, 3rd Fl, Springfield 62786. Unit Manager, Telephone: (217) 785-0820, question@dpr084.1.state.il.us, www.state.il.us.	N	Y	N
INDIANA: State Board of Registration for Professional Engineers, 302 W. Washington St., E034, Indianapolis 46204. Executive Director, Telephone: (317) 232-3902, www.ai.org/pla.	Y	Y	'Y'
IOWA: Engineering Examining Board, 1918 S.E. Hulsizer, Ankeny 50021. Executive Secretary, Tel: (515) 281-5602, jolene.schmitt@comm7,state.ia.us, www.state.ia.us/proflic.	N	Y	Y
KANSAS: State Board of Technical Professions, 900 Jackson, Suite 507, Topeka 66612. Executive Secretary, Telephone: (785) 296-3053, www.ink.org/public/ksbtp.	Y	N	Y
KENTUCKY: State Board of Licensure for Professional Engineers, 160 Democrat Dr., Frankfort 40601. Executive Director, Telephone: (502) 573-2680, larry.perkins@mail.state.ky.us, www.kyboels.	Y	Y	Y

NCEES Book?	Gen'l Exam?	Calculators?	
Y	Y	Y	**LOUISIANA:** State Board of Registration for Professional Engineers, 10500 Coursey Blvd Suite 107, Baton Rouge. Executive Secretary, Telephone: (225) 295-8522, www.lapels.com.
Y	Y	Y	**MAINE:** State Board of Registration for Professional Engineers, 92 State House, Station, Augusta 04333-0092. Secretary, Telephone: (207) 287-3236, pengineers@ctel.net, www.professionalsmaineusa,com.
N	Y	Y	**MARYLAND:** Board for Professional Engineers, 500 N. Calvert St, Rm 308, Baltimore 21202-3651. Executive Secretary, Telephone: (410) 230-6322, dmatricciani@dllr.state.md.us, www.dllr.state.md.us.
N	Y	Y	**MASSACHUSETTS:** State Board of Registration of Professional Engineers, 239 Canseway St, Boston 02114. Secretary, Telephone: (617) 727-3074, marie.e.deveau@state.ma.us, www.state.ma.us/reg.
'Y'	Y	Y	**MICHIGAN:** Board of Professional Engineers, P. O. Box 30018, Lansing 48909. Administrative Secretary, Telephone: (517) 241-9253, jack.sharpe@cis.state.mi.us. (NCEES Handbook provided upon signup if requested.)
Y	N	N	**MINNESOTA:** State Board of Registration for Engineers, 85 E. 7th Pl, Suite 160, St. Paul 55101. Executive Secretary, Telephone: (651) 296-2388, sheri.lindemann@state.mn.us, www.aelslagid.state.mn.us.
Y	Y	Y	**MISSISSIPPI:** State Board of Registration for Professional Engineers, P. O. Box 3, Jackson 39205. Executive Director, Telephone: (601) 359-6160, information@pepls.state.ms.us, www.peplsstate.ms.us.
N	Y	Y	**MISSOURI:** Board of Professional Engineers, P. O. Box 184, Jefferson City 65102. Executive Director, Telephone: (573) 751-0047, moapels@mail.state.mo.us, www.ecodev.state.mo.us/pr/apels.
N	Y	Y	**MONTANA:** State Board of Professional Engineers and Land Surveyors, Department of Commerce, 111 N. Jackson, P. O. Box 200513, Helena 59620-0513. Administrative Secretary, Telephone: (406) 444-1667, compolpel@state.my.us, www.com.state.mt.us/license/POL/pol_boards.
Y	N	Y	**NEBRASKA:** State Board of Professional Engineers, 301 Centennial Mall South, 6th Fl, Lincoln 68508. Executive Director, Telephone: (402) 471-2021, execdir@nol.org, www.nol.org/home/NBOP.
Y	Y	Y	**NEVADA:** State Board of Professional Engineers, 1755 East Plum Lane, Ste. 135, Reno 89502. Executive Secretary, Telephone: (775) 688-1231, nevengsur@natinfo.net, www.state.nv.us/BOE.

	NCEES Book?	Gen'l Exam?	Calculators?
NEW HAMPSHIRE: State Board of Professional Engineers, 57 Regional Drive, Concord 03301. Executive Secretary, Telephone: (603) 271-2219, llavertu@nhsa.state.nh.us, www.state.nh.us/jtboard/home.	Y	Y	Y
NEW JERSEY: State Board of Professional Engineers and Land Surveyors, P. O. Box 45015, Newark 07101. Executive Secretary-Director, Telephone: (973) 504-6460.	Y	Y	Y
NEW MEXICO: State Board for Professional Engineers, 1010 Marquez Pl., Santa Fe 87501. Secretary, Telephone: (505) 827-7561, amanda.lopez@state.nm.us, www.state.nm.us/pepsboard.	Y	Y	N
NEW YORK: State Board for Engineering, Cultural Education Center, Rm 3019, Albany 12230. Executive Secretary, Telephone: (518) 474-3846, enginbd@mail.nysed.gov, www.nysed.gov/prof/pe.	N	Y	Y
NORTH CAROLINA: State Board of Professional Engineers, 310 W Millbrook Rd, Raleigh 27609. Executive Secretary, Telephone (919) 841-4000, ncboard@ncbels.org, www.ncbels.org.	Y	Y	Y
NORTH DAKOTA: State Board of Registration for Professional Engineers, P. O. Box 1357, Bismarck 58502. Executive Secretary, Telephone: (701) 258-0786.	Y	Y	'N'
OHIO: State Board of Registration for Professional Engineers, 77 S. High St., 16th Fl., Columbus 43266-0314. Executive Secretary, Telephone: (614) 466-3650, mjacob@mail.peps.state.oh.us, www.peps.state.oh.us.	Y	Y	Y
OKLAHOMA: State Board of Registration for Professional Engineers, 201 N.E. 27th Street, Rm 120, Oklahoma City, 73105-2788. Executive Secretary, Telephone: (405) 521-2874, www.okpels.org.	Y	Y	Y
OREGON: State Board of Engineering Examiners, Department of Commerce, 728 Hawthorne Ave NE, Salem 97301. Executive Secretary, Telephone: (503) 362-2666, grahame@osbeels.org, www.osbeels.org.	Y	Y	Y
PENNSYLVANIA: State Registration Board for Professional Engineers, P. O. Box 2649, Harrisburg 17105-2649. Administrative Assistant, Telephone: (717) 783-7049, engineer@pados.dos.state.pa.us, www.dos.state.pa.us/bpoa/engbd.	N	Y	Y
PUERTO RICO: Board of Examiners of Engineers, P. O. Box 9023271, San Juan 00907-3271. Director, Examining Boards, Telephone: (728) 722-4816.	?	?	?
RHODE ISLAND: Board of Registration for Professional Engineers, 1 Capitol Hill, 3rd Fl, Providence 02908, Administrative Assistant, Telephone: (401) 222-2565.	N	N	Y

NCEES Book?	Gen'l Exam?	Calculators?	
Y	Y	Y	SOUTH CAROLINA: State Board of Registration for Professional Engineers, P. O. Box 11597, Columbia 29211-1597. Agency Director, Tele-phone: (803) 896-4422, engls@mail.llr.state.sc.us, www.llr.state.sc.us.
N	Y	Y	SOUTH DAKOTA: Board of Technical Professions, 2040 West Main St, Suite 304, Rapid City 57702-2447. Executive Secretary, Telephone: (605) 394-2510, snwhillpe@aol.com, www.state.sd.us/dcr/engineer.
N	Y	Y	TENNESSEE: State Board of Engineering Examiners, 500 James Robertson Pkwy, 3rd Fl,, Nashville 37243. Administrator, Telephone: (615) 741-3221, bbowling@mail.state.tn.us, www.state.tn.us/commerce/ae.
N	Y	Y	TEXAS: Board of Professional Engineers, P. O. Drawer 18329, Austin 78760-8329. Executive Director, Telephone: (512) 440-7723, peboard@mail.capnet.state.tx.us, www.main.org/peboard.
N	Y	Y	UTAH: Division of Occupational and Professional Licensing, P. O. Box 146741, Salt Lake City 84114-6741. Director, Telephone: (801) 530-6511, brcmrc.brdopl.dfairhur@email.state.ut.us.
Y	Y	Y	VERMONT: State Board of Registration for Professional Engineering, 26 Terrace St, Drawer 09, Montpelier 05609-1106. Executive Secretary, Telephone: (802) 828-2875, cpreston@sec.state.vt.us, www.sec.state.vt.us.
N	Y	Y	VIRGINIA: State Board of Professional Engineers, 3600 W Broad St, Richmond 23230. Assistant Director, Telephone: (804) 367-8512, apelsla@dpor.state.va.us, www.va.us/dpor.
N	Y	Y	VIRGIN ISLANDS: Board for Architects, Engineers and Land Surveyors, Bldg 1, Sub-Base, Rm 205, St. Thomas 00802. Secretary, Telephone: (340) 773-2226.
Y	Y	Y	WASHINGTON: State Board of Registration for Professional Engineers and Land Surveyors, P. O. Box 9649, Olympia 985047-9649 Executive Secretary, Telephone: (360) 753-6966, engineers@dol.wa.gov, www.wa.gov/dol/bpd/engfront.
N	Y	Y	WEST VIRGINIA: State Board of Registration for Professional Engineers, 608 Union Building, Charleston 25301-2703. Executive Director, Telephone: (304) 558-3554.
Y	Y	Y	WISCONSIN: State Examining Board of Professional Engineers, P. O. Box 8935, Madison 53708-8935. Administrator, Telephone: (608) 266-5511, dorl@mail.state.wi.us, www.badger.state.wi.us/agencies/drl.
Y	Y	Y	WYOMING: State Board of Examining Engineers, 2424 pioneer Ave, Suite 400, Cheyenne 82001. Secretary-Accountant, Telephone: (307) 777-6155, cturk@wyoming.com, www.wrds.uwyo.edu/wrds/borpe/borpe.

FE/EIT Diagnostic Examination

Part II

This diagnostic exam is designed to indicate your areas of relative strength to help you prioritize your subsequent study. The morning session covers the same subjects for all test-takers. The afternoon sessions of both tests in this volume cover only the General DS subject area. To prepare for tests in other major DS areas, refer to our *FE/EIT Discipline Review* volume.

We at GLP have developed a CD that you may obtain at no charge by mailing in the reply card found at the back of this Review. It contains the same two exams that are found in this book presented in a lively, easy-to-use format which closely simulates the real testing experience. The CD will also provide you with a detailed score analysis of each exam via our Study-Director™ feature. Solutions with text references are also provided on the CD. If you are interested in the General Morning Session only, you can take and analyze that session only. The CD for our *"FE/EIT Discipline Review"* can be used for any afternoon Discipline test (except ChemE). So, if you plan on using the CD to take the exam, do not preview this Diagnostic Examination!

New! Interactive CD Exams with Study-Director™

Until you sit to take it, do not look or even glance at the material in this exam. To properly take this exam, spend at most four hours on each section. You may use only the Reference Handbook supplied by NCEES. One may be sent to you after you register for the exam or you may order a copy by calling Great Lakes Press at 1-800-837-0201. If you are studying without the NCEES Handbook, use the Equation Summaries provided at the end of this manual.

Taking the Diagnostic Exam

Battery-operated, silent, programmable calculators are allowed in nearly every state (see page 9 for info about the best FE exam calculator). Indicate your answers on the separate answer sheet. Be sure and answer all questions. Guess at those you do not have time to work through! Scratch paper is not allowed during the actual examination; large margins both here and on the test provide sufficient work space.

To score yourself, add your correct responses from the afternoon part to one-half of your correct responses from the morning part (a maximum score of 120). If you score less than 60 (50%) you may have difficulty with the actual examination. If your score is substantially greater than 60, you should be ready to pass!

The problems in the actual exam will be organized differently than in this sample exam.

FUNDAMENTALS OF ENGINEERING EXAM

Morning Session—Diagnostic Exam

(Simulated answer form with topical breakout and scoring grid.)

BE SURE EACH MARK IS DARK AND COMPLETELY FILLS THE INTENDED SPACE AS ILLUSTRATED HERE: ●.

MATH	MATERIALS	ECONOMICS	THERMODYNAMICS	DYNAMICS	FLUID MECHANICS
1 Ⓐ Ⓑ Ⓒ Ⓓ	31 Ⓐ Ⓑ Ⓒ Ⓓ	50 Ⓐ Ⓑ Ⓒ Ⓓ	67 Ⓐ Ⓑ Ⓒ Ⓓ	90 Ⓐ Ⓑ Ⓒ Ⓓ	108 Ⓐ Ⓑ Ⓒ Ⓓ
2 Ⓐ Ⓑ Ⓒ Ⓓ	32 Ⓐ Ⓑ Ⓒ Ⓓ	51 Ⓐ Ⓑ Ⓒ Ⓓ	68 Ⓐ Ⓑ Ⓒ Ⓓ	91 Ⓐ Ⓑ Ⓒ Ⓓ	109 Ⓐ Ⓑ Ⓒ Ⓓ
3 Ⓐ Ⓑ Ⓒ Ⓓ	33 Ⓐ Ⓑ Ⓒ Ⓓ	52 Ⓐ Ⓑ Ⓒ Ⓓ	69 Ⓐ Ⓑ Ⓒ Ⓓ	92 Ⓐ Ⓑ Ⓒ Ⓓ	110 Ⓐ Ⓑ Ⓒ Ⓓ
4 Ⓐ Ⓑ Ⓒ Ⓓ	34 Ⓐ Ⓑ Ⓒ Ⓓ	53 Ⓐ Ⓑ Ⓒ Ⓓ	70 Ⓐ Ⓑ Ⓒ Ⓓ	93 Ⓐ Ⓑ Ⓒ Ⓓ	111 Ⓐ Ⓑ Ⓒ Ⓓ
5 Ⓐ Ⓑ Ⓒ Ⓓ	35 Ⓐ Ⓑ Ⓒ Ⓓ	54 Ⓐ Ⓑ Ⓒ Ⓓ	71 Ⓐ Ⓑ Ⓒ Ⓓ	94 Ⓐ Ⓑ Ⓒ Ⓓ	112 Ⓐ Ⓑ Ⓒ Ⓓ
6 Ⓐ Ⓑ Ⓒ Ⓓ	36 Ⓐ Ⓑ Ⓒ Ⓓ		72 Ⓐ Ⓑ Ⓒ Ⓓ	95 Ⓐ Ⓑ Ⓒ Ⓓ	113 Ⓐ Ⓑ Ⓒ Ⓓ
7 Ⓐ Ⓑ Ⓒ Ⓓ	37 Ⓐ Ⓑ Ⓒ Ⓓ	Score: _____	73 Ⓐ Ⓑ Ⓒ Ⓓ	96 Ⓐ Ⓑ Ⓒ Ⓓ	114 Ⓐ Ⓑ Ⓒ Ⓓ
8 Ⓐ Ⓑ Ⓒ Ⓓ	38 Ⓐ Ⓑ Ⓒ Ⓓ		74 Ⓐ Ⓑ Ⓒ Ⓓ	97 Ⓐ Ⓑ Ⓒ Ⓓ	115 Ⓐ Ⓑ Ⓒ Ⓓ
9 Ⓐ Ⓑ Ⓒ Ⓓ		**ELECTRICAL**	75 Ⓐ Ⓑ Ⓒ Ⓓ	98 Ⓐ Ⓑ Ⓒ Ⓓ	
10 Ⓐ Ⓑ Ⓒ Ⓓ	Score: _____		76 Ⓐ Ⓑ Ⓒ Ⓓ	99 Ⓐ Ⓑ Ⓒ Ⓓ	Score: _____
11 Ⓐ Ⓑ Ⓒ Ⓓ		55 Ⓐ Ⓑ Ⓒ Ⓓ	77 Ⓐ Ⓑ Ⓒ Ⓓ		
12 Ⓐ Ⓑ Ⓒ Ⓓ	**CHEMISTRY**	56 Ⓐ Ⓑ Ⓒ Ⓓ		Score: _____	**ETHICS**
13 Ⓐ Ⓑ Ⓒ Ⓓ		57 Ⓐ Ⓑ Ⓒ Ⓓ	Score: _____		
14 Ⓐ Ⓑ Ⓒ Ⓓ	39 Ⓐ Ⓑ Ⓒ Ⓓ	58 Ⓐ Ⓑ Ⓒ Ⓓ		**MECHANICS**	116 Ⓐ Ⓑ Ⓒ Ⓓ
15 Ⓐ Ⓑ Ⓒ Ⓓ	40 Ⓐ Ⓑ Ⓒ Ⓓ	59 Ⓐ Ⓑ Ⓒ Ⓓ	**STATICS**		117 Ⓐ Ⓑ Ⓒ Ⓓ
16 Ⓐ Ⓑ Ⓒ Ⓓ	41 Ⓐ Ⓑ Ⓒ Ⓓ	60 Ⓐ Ⓑ Ⓒ Ⓓ		100 Ⓐ Ⓑ Ⓒ Ⓓ	118 Ⓐ Ⓑ Ⓒ Ⓓ
17 Ⓐ Ⓑ Ⓒ Ⓓ	42 Ⓐ Ⓑ Ⓒ Ⓓ	61 Ⓐ Ⓑ Ⓒ Ⓓ	78 Ⓐ Ⓑ Ⓒ Ⓓ	101 Ⓐ Ⓑ Ⓒ Ⓓ	119 Ⓐ Ⓑ Ⓒ Ⓓ
18 Ⓐ Ⓑ Ⓒ Ⓓ	43 Ⓐ Ⓑ Ⓒ Ⓓ	62 Ⓐ Ⓑ Ⓒ Ⓓ	79 Ⓐ Ⓑ Ⓒ Ⓓ	102 Ⓐ Ⓑ Ⓒ Ⓓ	120 Ⓐ Ⓑ Ⓒ Ⓓ
19 Ⓐ Ⓑ Ⓒ Ⓓ	44 Ⓐ Ⓑ Ⓒ Ⓓ	63 Ⓐ Ⓑ Ⓒ Ⓓ	80 Ⓐ Ⓑ Ⓒ Ⓓ	103 Ⓐ Ⓑ Ⓒ Ⓓ	
20 Ⓐ Ⓑ Ⓒ Ⓓ	45 Ⓐ Ⓑ Ⓒ Ⓓ	64 Ⓐ Ⓑ Ⓒ Ⓓ	81 Ⓐ Ⓑ Ⓒ Ⓓ	104 Ⓐ Ⓑ Ⓒ Ⓓ	Score: _____
21 Ⓐ Ⓑ Ⓒ Ⓓ	46 Ⓐ Ⓑ Ⓒ Ⓓ	65 Ⓐ Ⓑ Ⓒ Ⓓ	82 Ⓐ Ⓑ Ⓒ Ⓓ	105 Ⓐ Ⓑ Ⓒ Ⓓ	
22 Ⓐ Ⓑ Ⓒ Ⓓ	47 Ⓐ Ⓑ Ⓒ Ⓓ	66 Ⓐ Ⓑ Ⓒ Ⓓ	83 Ⓐ Ⓑ Ⓒ Ⓓ	106 Ⓐ Ⓑ Ⓒ Ⓓ	
23 Ⓐ Ⓑ Ⓒ Ⓓ	48 Ⓐ Ⓑ Ⓒ Ⓓ		84 Ⓐ Ⓑ Ⓒ Ⓓ	107 Ⓐ Ⓑ Ⓒ Ⓓ	
24 Ⓐ Ⓑ Ⓒ Ⓓ	49 Ⓐ Ⓑ Ⓒ Ⓓ	Score: _____	85 Ⓐ Ⓑ Ⓒ Ⓓ		
			86 Ⓐ Ⓑ Ⓒ Ⓓ	Score: _____	
Score: _____	Score: _____		87 Ⓐ Ⓑ Ⓒ Ⓓ		
			88 Ⓐ Ⓑ Ⓒ Ⓓ		
COMPUTERS			89 Ⓐ Ⓑ Ⓒ Ⓓ		
25 Ⓐ Ⓑ Ⓒ Ⓓ			Score: _____		
26 Ⓐ Ⓑ Ⓒ Ⓓ					
27 Ⓐ Ⓑ Ⓒ Ⓓ					
28 Ⓐ Ⓑ Ⓒ Ⓓ					
29 Ⓐ Ⓑ Ⓒ Ⓓ					
30 Ⓐ Ⓑ Ⓒ Ⓓ					
Score: _____					

cut here!

Morning Session—Diagnostic Exam

4 hours maximum

Each of the 120 problems is followed by four answers.
Select the response that is best and circle the corresponding letter on the answer sheet.

Workspace Below

1. Determine the equation of a straight line that passes through the point (6, –3) if it is perpendicular to the line $y = 2x - 3$.
    (A) $y = -\frac{1}{2}x$
    (B) $y = \frac{1}{2}x - 6$
    (C) $y = -\frac{1}{2}x - 6$
    (D) $y = 2x - 15$

2. The equation $x^2 - 4xy + y^2 + 4x - 6y + 12 = 0$ represents:
    (A) a circle
    (B) an ellipse
    (C) a parabola
    (D) a hyperbola

3. The expression $\frac{\cos\theta}{\sin\theta} + \frac{\sin\theta}{\cos\theta}$ can be written as:
    (A) $\frac{1}{\sin 2\theta}$
    (B) $\frac{\sin 2\theta}{2}$
    (C) $\frac{2}{\cos 2\theta}$
    (D) $\frac{2}{\sin 2\theta}$

4. $(1 - 2i)^{-1}$ can be written as:
    (A) $\frac{1}{5} + \frac{2}{5}i$
    (B) $\frac{1}{5} - \frac{2}{5}i$
    (C) $-\frac{1}{3} - \frac{2}{3}i$
    (D) $-\frac{1}{3} + \frac{2}{3}i$

Workspace Below

5. Find the adjoint of $\begin{bmatrix} 2 & 3 \\ -1 & 0 \end{bmatrix}$.

    (A) $\begin{bmatrix} \frac{1}{2} & \frac{1}{3} \\ -1 & 0 \end{bmatrix}$

    (B) $\begin{bmatrix} 2 & 3 \\ -1 & 0 \end{bmatrix}$

    (C) $\begin{bmatrix} 0 & -3 \\ 1 & 2 \end{bmatrix}$

    (D) $\begin{bmatrix} 0 & 1 \\ -3 & 2 \end{bmatrix}$

6. Determine y if $\begin{array}{rrrr} x & -y & +z & = 2 \\ x & & -z & = 0 \\ x & +y & & = -3 \end{array}$.

    (A) $-\dfrac{2}{3}$

    (B) -8

    (C) $-\dfrac{4}{3}$

    (D) $-\dfrac{8}{3}$

7. Find the eigenvalues associated with the matrix $\begin{bmatrix} 1 & 1 \\ 2 & 0 \end{bmatrix}$.

    (A) $0, 1$

    (B) $-2, 1$

    (C) $0, -1$

    (D) $2, -1$

8. What is the particular solution to the differential equation $\dot{y} + 4y = 3e^{-t}$?

    (A) $3e^{-t}$

    (B) e^{-4t}

    (C) $c_1 e^{-4t}$

    (D) e^{-t}

9. A spring-mass system is modeled by the differential equation $\ddot{y} + 4\dot{y} + 4y = 8\sin 2t$. What is the amplitude of the steady-state solution?

    (A) 1

    (B) 2

    (C) 4

    (D) 6

10. The parabola $x = 2y^2$ is rotated about the y-axis. What is the volume between $y = 0$ and $y = 2$?

    (A) $\dfrac{512\pi}{5}$

    (B) $\dfrac{128\pi}{5}$

    (C) 8π

    (D) 32π

11. If a vector field is conservative which of the following is zero?

    (A) curl

    (B) cross product

    (C) divergence

    (D) dot product

12. The cross product of $\mathbf{A} = 4\mathbf{i} + 2\mathbf{j}$ with $\mathbf{B}$ is zero. The dot product $\mathbf{A} \cdot \mathbf{B} = 30$. Find $\mathbf{B}$.

    (A) $-6\mathbf{i} - 3\mathbf{j}$

    (B) $6\mathbf{i} - 3\mathbf{j}$

    (C) $6\mathbf{i} + 3\mathbf{j}$

    (D) $-6\mathbf{i} + 3\mathbf{j}$

13. What is the component of $\mathbf{A}$ in the direction of $\mathbf{B}$ if $\mathbf{A} = \mathbf{i} - 4\mathbf{j}$ and $\mathbf{B} = 2\mathbf{i} - 4\mathbf{j} - 4\mathbf{k}$?

    (A) -3

    (B) -2

    (C) 1

    (D) 3

14. About how many times out of 12,000 attempts would a person roll all the same numbers using 5 dice?

    (A) 50

    (B) 9

    (C) 4

    (D) 2

15. Find the y-coordinate of the centroid of the area bounded by $x = 2y^2$, the x-axis, and the line $x = 2$.

    (A) $2/5$

    (B) $1/4$

    (C) $3/8$

    (D) $1/2$

Workspace Below

16. The differential equation $y'' + 3x^2 y' + \sin x = 0$ is:
    (A) linear, homogeneous, constant coefficient
    (B) nonlinear, homogeneous, constant coefficient
    (C) linear, nonhomogeneous, variable coefficient
    (D) nonlinear, nonhomogeneous, variable coefficient

17. Select the Taylor series representation of $\cos 2x$.

    (A) $2x - \dfrac{4x^3}{3} + \dfrac{4x^5}{15} + \cdots$

    (B) $1 + 2x^2 + \dfrac{2x^4}{3} + \cdots$

    (C) $1 - \dfrac{x^2}{2} + \dfrac{x^4}{24} + \cdots$

    (D) $1 - 2x^2 + \dfrac{2x^4}{3} + \cdots$

18. A chain saw makes a 10-inch straight cut in the side of a 24-inch diameter tree. Calculate the angle made by the two radii connecting the ends of the cut. The cut is perpendicular to the tree's axis.
    (A) 131°
    (B) 49.2°
    (C) 45.2°
    (D) 24.6°

19. Find the y-intercept of the line tangent to the parabola $x = 2y^2$ at the point (2, 1).
    (A) −7
    (B) 7
    (C) 3/2
    (D) 1/2

20. Find $\sqrt{i}$.
    (A) $\sqrt{2}i$
    (B) $\sqrt{2}(-1+i)$
    (C) $(-1+i)/\sqrt{2}$
    (D) $(1+i)/\sqrt{2}$

21. Express the product $(1+2i)(5+3i)$ in polar form.
    (A) $17.03\,e^{1.494i}$
    (B) $13.04\,e^{-1.494i}$
    (C) $13.04\,e^{1.648i}$
    (D) $17.03\,e^{-1.494i}$

Questions 22–23:

22. What is $\lim\limits_{x \to 0} \dfrac{f^2}{g^2}$ if $f(x) = \sin 2x$ and $g(x) = x$?

    (A) 0

    (B) 2

    (C) 4

    (D) -2

23. What is $\int\limits_0^\pi f(x)g(x)dx$?

    (A) $\pi/2$

    (B) $-\pi/2$

    (C) 0

    (D) $-\pi$

24. What function $f(t)$ has a Laplace transform $\dfrac{s+3}{s^2 + 4s + 8}$?

    (A) $\left(\cos 2t + \frac{1}{2}\sin 2t\right)e^{-2t}$

    (B) $(\cos 2t + \sin 2t)e^{-2t}$

    (C) $e^{-2t}\cos 2t$

    (D) $(\cos 4t + \sin 4t)e^{-2t}$

25. Express the base 4 number 101.1 as a base 10 number.

    (A) 17.25

    (B) 68.25

    (C) 21.25

    (D) 20.25

26. A 64K × 16-bit read/write memory ensemble is to be made using 4K × 8-bit RAM cells. How many cells are required?

    (A) 16

    (B) 256

    (C) 32

    (D) 8

27. Encode the base-10 number 21.75 into an unsigned binary form with a minimum number of bits.

    (A) 1101011

    (B) 10100.011

    (C) 10101.011

    (D) 10101.11

Workspace Below

28. The hexadecimal string C31 has an equivalent BCD (binary coded decimal) encoding of what?

    (A) 1231

    (B) 3121

    (C) 1100 0011 0001

    (D) Cannot be encoded.

29. Consider the following program segment:

    ```
    #include <iostream.h>
    main ( )
    {
        int amount = 55;
        cout << dec << amount << ' '
             << oct << amount << ' '
             << hex <<  amount:
    }
    ```

    This program segment prints out which of the following?

    (A) 55 55 55

    (B) 55 67 37

    (C) amount = 55

    (D) dec 55 oct 55 hex 55

30. An A/D (analog-to-digital) converter has a range of –5 V to +5 V and an 8-bit output. An output of 0110 1100 corresponds approximately to what input voltage?

    (A) –0.78 volts

    (B) 4.22 volts

    (C) 0.8 volts

    (D) –4.0 volts

31. A solid is a good electrical conductor if

    (A) the electronic band-gap is > 10 eV

    (B) the electronic band-gap is < 5 eV

    (C) the conduction band is full

    (D) the conduction band is half full

32. An *n*-type semiconductor is a covalent solid in which

    (A) the energy gap is very small

    (B) an impurity level just above the valence band is added by the impurity atoms

    (C) an impurity level just below the conduction band is added by the impurity atoms

    (D) the solid is of ultra high purity

33. In a covalently bonded solid, the bonding is produced by
    (A) sharing of electrons between adjacent atoms
    (B) the coulombic attraction between oppositely charged atoms
    (C) the minimization of kinetic energy of free electrons
    (D) the delocalization of electrons associated with individual atoms

34. Which of the following statements about atomic packing in a crystal lattice are true?
    (A) Highest packing fraction is only possible in a FCC crystal.
    (B) Packing fraction for a BCC lattice is higher than that for a HCP lattice.
    (C) Packing fraction for a HCP lattice is the same as for a FCC lattice.
    (D) Packing fraction of a BCC lattice is 0.74.

35. The intercepts of a crystallographic plane with the three crystallographic axes, x, y, z, are expressed as fractions of the unit cell dimension along a given direction. Thus, the intercepts of (120) plane are:
    (A) $1, \frac{1}{2}, \infty$
    (B) $2, 1, 0$
    (C) $0, 2, 1$
    (D) $1, \frac{1}{2}, 0$

36. If the hardening of an alloy is induced by diffusion controlled precipitation of second phase particles, then the rate of hardening is
    (A) exponentially dependent on time
    (B) independent of time
    (C) independent of temperature
    (D) exponentially dependent on temperature

37. All of the following statements about metallic corrosion are true except:
    (A) Corrosion requires simultaneous oxidation and reduction reactions.
    (B) Iron does not rust if it is kept immersed in water which does not have any dissolved oxygen or air.
    (C) Iron corrodes substantially when in contact with zinc, in an aqueous environment.
    (D) Magnesium, which is more anodic than aluminum, is protected by aluminum in a corrosive environment.

Workspace Below

38. The following statements about toughness of a material are true except:
    (A) Charpy impact test is a measure of toughness.
    (B) High hardness is an indication of high toughness.
    (C) In a tough material extensive necking occurs before tensile failure.
    (D) The area under the tensile stress-strain curve up to fracture is large.

39. The nucleus of a neutral atom contains 42 protons and 54 neutrons. The element is
    (A) calcium
    (B) manganese
    (C) gold
    (D) molybdenum

40. How many protons, neutrons, and electrons are in an ion of the rhodium isotope $^{103}Rh^{3+}$?

	Protons	Neutrons	Electrons
(A)	45	103	45
(B)	45	58	45
(C)	45	58	42
(D)	45	55	45

41. Which compound does not contain a covalent bond?
    (A) HBr
    (B) $NaNO_3$
    (C) KCl
    (D) CH_4

42. Which ion does not have the same electron configuration as a noble gas?
    (A) O^{2-}
    (B) Pb^{2+}
    (C) Mg^{2+}
    (D) Br^-

43. In the presence of an iron catalyst, hydrogen gas can be produced from carbon monoxide gas and steam according to the equation:

$$CO(g) + H_2O(g) = CO_2(g) + H_2(g)$$

At a certain temperature, analysis showed the presence of 0.80 mol of CO, 0.25 mol of water vapor, 0.50 mol of H_2, and 2.4 mol of carbon dioxide in a liter of the equilibrium mixture. What is the value of the equilibrium constant at that temperature?

(A) 12.0

(B) 6.0

(C) 4.8

(D) 1.5

44. How many valence electrons does an element, such as arsenic, from Group 5A have?

(A) 3

(B) 4

(C) 5

(D) 6

45. What is the ground-state electron configuration of a barium ion, Ba^{2+}?

(A) $[Rn]$

(B) $[Xe]\, 6s^2$

(C) $[Xe]$

(D) $[Ar]$

46. What is the percentage by mass of carbon in the hydrocarbon propane, C_3H_8?

(A) 18

(B) 36

(C) 44

(D) 82

47. When a nonmetallic element in Group 6A reacts to form an ionic compound, the element usually gains an ionic charge of

(A) –2

(B) –1

(C) 0

(D) +1

Workspace Below

48. Nitric acid will oxidize sulfur to sulfur dioxide. What is the mole ratio of sulfur to nitric acid in the balanced redox equation?

    (A)   1:2

    (B)   1:3

    (C)   2:3

    (D)   3:4

49. Which of the following factors does not influence the rate of a chemical reaction?

    (A)   The nature of the reactants

    (B)   The amount of a solid reactant present

    (C)   The reactant concentrations or state of subdivision

    (D)   The temperature

50. At the end of each of twelve months Terry deposited $100 in a savings account that pays 6% annual interest compounded monthly. Compute the balance in Terry's account immediately after the twelfth payment.

    (A) $1200

    (B) $1206

    (C) $1234

    (D) $1272

51. How many years are required for an amount of money to triple if it is invested at a 4% interest rate?

    (A)   3

    (B)   7

    (C)   13

    (D)   28

52. Twenty-one equal end-of-year deposits are made into a savings account that pays 4% interest. Compute the amount of each deposit that will permit withdrawals of $10,000 at the ends of the eighteenth through twenty-first years, leaving the account empty.

    (A) $1328

    (B) $1667

    (C) $1905

    (D) $2123

53. Profits generated by Excelsys Inc. were $10,000 for the first year and increased by $1000 each year. If the profits for five years of operation were invested at an 8% rate of return, how much money had accumulated at the end of the fifth year?

   (A) $47,300

   (B) $55,000

   (C) $60,000

   (D) $69,500

54. Development costs of a new product are estimated to be $70,000 per year for three years. Annual profits from the sale of the new product, estimated to be $80,000, will begin in the fourth year and continue for ten years. Using a rate of return of 20%, compute the present value of the venture.

   (A) $14,300

   (B) $46,600

   (C) $187,900

   (D) $309,200

55. The equivalent resistance between terminals *a–b* in ohms is:

   (A) 3

   (B) 5

   (C) 8

   (D) 10

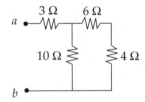

56. The Thevinen Equivalent voltage between terminals *a–b* is, in volts:

   (A) 3

   (B) 4

   (C) 6

   (D) 9

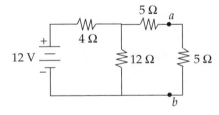

Workspace Below

57. The power delivered by the 12-volt battery, above, in watts, is:

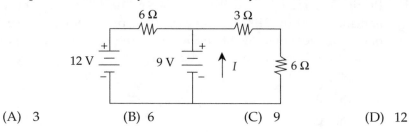

(A) 3   (B) 6   (C) 9   (D) 12

58. The *rms* current through the 45-ohm resistor in the circuit shown is:

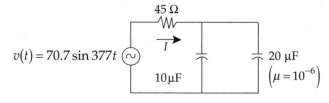

$v(t) = 70.7 \sin 377t$

(A) 0.15 A   (B) 0.25 A   (C) 0.40 A   (D) 0.50 A

59. The rms voltage across the 40-ohm resistor is, in volts:

(A) 20
(B) 30
(C) 40
(D) 50

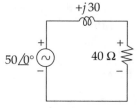

60. The power delivered to the 40-ohm resistor in Problem 59 is:
(A) 20 W
(B) 30 W
(C) 40 W
(D) 50 W

61. The instantaneous current through the inductor at $t = 0.001$ sec in amperes is:
(A) 0.175
(B) 0.260
(C) 0.355
(D) 0.495

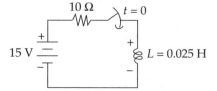

Workspace Below

62. The instantaneous voltage across the inductor at $t = 0.001$ sec
    in the circuit of Problem 61 is, in volts:

    (A) 6.75

    (B) 8.25

    (C) 9.15

    (D) 10.05

63. The current in the 100-ohm resistor is:

    (A) 1.5 A

    (B) 3.0 A

    (C) 4.5 A

    (D) 6.0 A

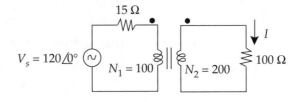

64. Two parallel conductors carry 50 amperes each in the same direc-
    tion. The conductors are 5 cm apart. What is the magnetic force on
    a 1 meter length of one conductor in newtons?

    (A) 0.01

    (B) 0.02

    (C) 0.03

    (D) 0.04

65. Two parallel flat plates are separated by 2 cm. A voltage of 500 V is
    applied to the parallel plates. What is the maximum electric field
    force experienced by an electron passing between the plates?

    (A) 4×10^{-15} N

    (B) 20×10^{-15} N

    (C) 30×10^{-15} N

    (D) 40×10^{-15} N

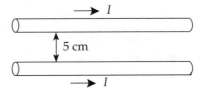

66. A copper conductor 10 m long and 3 mm in diameter has a
    resistance of 0.024 ohms at room temperature (20°C). What is
    the temperature in degrees Celsius of this conductor if it has a
    resistance of 0.036 ohms? ($\alpha_c = 0.0039$.)

    (A) 87

    (B) 118

    (C) 128

    (D) 148

Workspace Below

67. Select the best response for an isolated system.
   (A) The entropy of system remains constant.
   (B) The heat transfer equals the work done.
   (C) The heat transfer equals the internal energy change.
   (D) The heat transfer is zero.

68. When one system interacts with another system which of the following is possible?
   (A) Internal energy can be transferred from one system to the other.
   (B) Entropy can be transferred from one system to the other.
   (C) One system can induce a force on the other system.
   (D) Temperature can be transferred from one system to the other.

69. The pressure-temperature diagram for water is shown. The names for points A and B and line ℓ are, respectively:
   (A) triple, critical, fusion
   (B) critical, triple, sublimation
   (C) triple, critical, sublimation
   (D) critical, triple, fusion

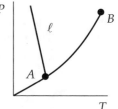

70. A tank contains 0.02 m³ of liquid and 1.98 m³ of vapor. If the density of the liquid is 960 kg/m³ and that of the vapor is 0.5 kg/m³, what is the quality of the mixture?
   (A) 5.2%
   (B) 4.9%
   (C) 2.04%
   (D) 1.01%

71. Two kilograms of air are contained in a cylinder. If 80 kJ of heat are added to the air, estimate the temperature rise if the pressure is held constant. $c_p = 1.0$, $c_v = 0.716$ kJ/kg·K, $k = 1.4$.
   (A) 56°C
   (B) 40°C
   (C) 33°C
   (D) 28°C

72. Clothes are hung out to dry in very cold weather. The water in the clothes freezes, but a day later when the clothes are brought inside they are dry. By what process did the drying occur?

    (A) vaporization

    (B) condensation

    (C) evaporation

    (D) sublimation

73. Air is compressed in an ideal, adiabatic compressor from 100 kPa and 20°C to 800 kPa. What is the temperature at the compressor exit? $k = 1.4$.

    (A) 1440°C

    (B) 368°C

    (C) 258°C

    (D) 167°C

74. Vapor refrigerant enters and liquid refrigerant leaves the coils on the back of a refrigerator. These coils are the:

    (A) evaporator

    (B) intercooler

    (C) reheater

    (D) condenser

75. Steam at high temperature and pressure passes through a half open globe valve. Select the property that remains constant through the valve.

    (A) enthalpy

    (B) temperature

    (C) pressure

    (D) entropy

76. Air undergoes a three-process cycle of a constant pressure process (1)-(2), an isothermal process (2)-(3), and a constant volume process (3)-(1). Select the correct response for the piston-cylinder arrangement.

    (A) $W_{1-2} = 0$

    (B) $Q_{3-1} = 0$

    (C) $Q_{2-3} = 0$

    (D) $W_{3-1} = 0$

Workspace Below

77. A 2.5-cm-thick substance has a thermal resistance of 2.0 hr·m·°C/kJ. Estimate the heat transferred in 15 minutes through a 3 m by 8 m wall if the inside and outside temperatures are –10°C and 25°C, respectively.

 (A) 6300 kJ

 (B) 5400 kJ

 (C) 4800 kJ

 (D) 4200 kJ

78. Determine the magnitude of the resultant of the following three forces:

$$\mathbf{F}_1 = 100\mathbf{i} - 200\mathbf{k} \qquad \text{acting at } (0,\ 0,\ 0)$$
$$\mathbf{F}_2 = 50\mathbf{j} + 50\mathbf{k} \qquad \text{acting at } (3,\ 1,\ 2)$$
$$\mathbf{F}_3 = -200\mathbf{i} + 100\mathbf{j} \qquad \text{acting at } (0,\ 2,\ 0)$$

 (A) 457

 (B) 365

 (C) 283

 (D) 234

79. Find the tension in cable *AB*.

 (A) 706 N

 (B) 530 N

 (C) 264 N

 (D) 72 N

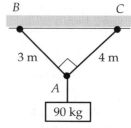

80. The *z*-component of the moment of the force $\mathbf{F} = 20\mathbf{i} - 30\mathbf{j} + 40\mathbf{k}$ acting at $(1, 2, 3)$ about the point $(0, 2, 0)$ is

 (A) 89

 (B) 80

 (C) 60

 (D) 30

81. If two forces hold a rigid body in equilibrium, they must

 (A) form a couple

 (B) be non-concurrent

 (C) be collinear

 (D) act at a right angle

82. A force and a moment are needed at the wall to hold the rigid link in equilibrium. What is the moment?
    - (A) 20 N·m
    - (B) 40 N·m
    - (C) 140 N·m
    - (D) 240 N·m

83. Find the force in member *AB*.
    - (A) 0
    - (B) 200 N
    - (C) 400 N
    - (D) 600 N

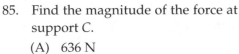

84. What force will cause the 20 kg block to move?
    - (A) 103 N
    - (B) 121 N
    - (C) 134 N
    - (D) 149 N

85. Find the magnitude of the force at support *C*.
    - (A) 636 N
    - (B) 537 N
    - (C) 387 N
    - (D) 300 N

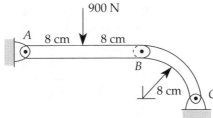

86. A 4-m-long chain lies in a straight line on a table. How much of the chain can hang over an end of the table without the entire chain slipping off? $\mu = 0.4$.
    - (A) 1.02 m
    - (B) 1.14 m
    - (C) 1.92 m
    - (D) 2.67 m

87. A wire connects the middle of the two links. What is the tension in the wire?
    - (A) 540 N
    - (B) 405 N
    - (C) 270 N
    - (D) 195 N

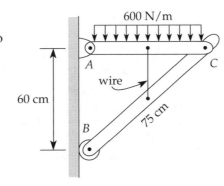

Workspace Below

88. A plane area has its centroid C at (2 cm, 4 cm). If its area is 100 cm^2 and $I_y = 2000$ cm^4, what is $(I_y)_C$?

    (A) 1600 cm^4

    (B) 1200 cm^4

    (C) 1000 cm^4

    (D) 800 cm^4

89. The U-beam is composed of two 2 cm by 10 cm plates and a 2 cm by 4 cm plate. What is the y-coordinate of the centroid?

    (A) 4.83 cm

    (B) 4.69 cm

    (C) 4.52 cm

    (D) 4.33 cm

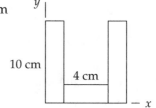

90. An object experiences rectilinear acceleration $a(t) = 10 - 2t$. How far does it travel in 6 seconds if its initial velocity is 10 m/s?

    (A) 182 m

    (B) 168 m

    (C) 142 m

    (D) 126 m

91. A wheel is rotating at 4000 rpm. If it experiences a deceleration of 20 rad/s^2, through how many revolutions will it rotate before it stops?

    (A) 4400

    (B) 3200

    (C) 2100

    (D) 700

92. An 80-cm-diameter wheel is accelerating at 10 m/s^2 without slipping on a flat surface. What is the magnitude of the acceleration of the very top of the wheel when the velocity of the wheel is 4 m/s?

    (A) 20 m/s^2

    (B) 25 m/s^2

    (C) 40 m/s^2

    (D) 45 m/s^2

93. If $\omega = 10$ rad/s, find the velocity of slider A.

    (A) 0.5 m/s

    (B) 0.577 m/s

    (C) 0.6 m/s

    (D) 0.866 m/s

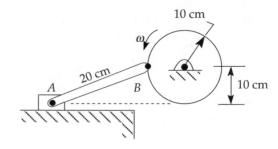

Workspace Below

94. If the angular acceleration of the driver wheel in Problem 93 is zero, find the acceleration of slider A.

(A) 12.6 m/s^2

(B) 15.1 m/s^2

(C) 17.7 m/s^2

(D) 20.3 m/s^2

95. Find the tension in the string connecting the two masses. The pulley is massless and frictionless.

(A) 240 N

(B) 560 N

(C) 1260 N

(D) 2050 N

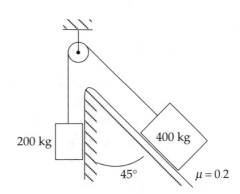

96. The force $F(t)$ acts on the mass shown. What is its velocity after 20 s if it starts from rest?

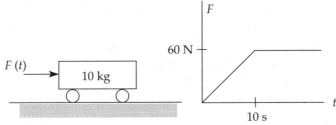

(A) 60 m/s

(B) 70 m/s

(C) 80 m/s

(D) 90 m/s

97. The spring is stretched until the force it exerts on the cylinder is 400 N. It is attached to a rope wrapped around the stationary cylinder. What is the cylinder's speed when the spring force is zero? (No slipping occurs.)

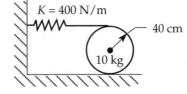

(A) 5.16 m/s

(B) 5.98 m/s

(C) 6.32 m/s

(D) 7.48 m/s

Workspace Below

98. A constant thrust of 20 000 N launches on a 1500-kg rocket vertically upward. If the drag force F_D is related to the velocity, as shown, find the velocity of the rocket after 20 seconds.

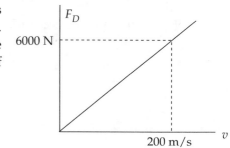

(A) 38 m/s

(B) 42 m/s

(C) 58 m/s

(D) 70 m/s

99. The two identical balls collide as shown. What is v_2' if the coefficient of restitution is 0.8?

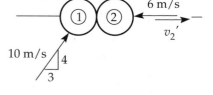

(A) 5.4 m/s

(B) 5.2 m/s

(C) 5.0 m/s

(D) 4.8 m/s

100. A solid steel cylinder of radius r and a hollow brass cylinder of outer radius $3r/2$ support the load. If both cylinders are of the same length, what percentage of the load is carried by the steel cylinder? ($E_{steel} = 2E_{brass}$.)

(A) 72.5%

(B) 61.5%

(C) 55.5%

(D) 42.5%

101. Steel is used to reinforce concrete because

(A) its density is correctly related to the density of concrete.

(B) it is relatively inexpensive compared to other metals.

(C) its coefficient of thermal expansion is the same as that of concrete.

(D) its Poisson's ratio is the same as that of concrete.

102. Calculate the maximum shearing stress at a point where
$\tau_{xy} = 10$ MPa, $\sigma_x = 40$ MPa, and $\sigma_y = 50$ MPa.

  (A) 46.1 MPa

  (B) 36.5 MPa

  (C) 23.2 MPa

  (D) 11.2 MPa

103. A simply-supported beam of length L has a uniform load w over the entire length. What is the ratio of the maximum normal stress to the maximum vertical shearing stress if the cross section is a square $b \times b$?

  (A) L/b

  (B) $2L/b$

  (C) $3L/b$

  (D) $4L/b$

104. The bending moment diagram of a simply-supported beam with a uniform load over the entire length has the shape of a

  (A) rectangle

  (B) triangle

  (C) parabola

  (D) circle

105. A hollow shaft with an inner radius of 2 cm and an outer radius of 3 cm transmits a torque of 300 N·m. What is the maximum shearing stress?

  (A) 17.6 MPa

  (B) 14.2 MPa

  (C) 12.6 MPa

  (D) 8.81 MPa

106. Find the maximum tensile stress if the rectangular cross-section is 2 cm × 6 cm (6 cm is vertical).

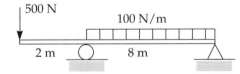

  (A) 92.3 MPa

  (B) 83.3 MPa

  (C) 72.5 MPa

  (D) 64.8 MPa

Workspace Below

107. A 4-cm-diameter cantilever steel beam is 6 m long. A uniform load of 100 N/m is applied over 4 m, beginning from the wall. The remaining 2 m is unloaded. What is the deflection of the free end? ($E_{steel} = 210 \times 10^6$ kPa.)

(A) 20.2 cm

(B) 16.4 cm

(C) 14.7 cm

(D) 12.1 cm

108. The viscosity of a gas increases with increased temperature because

(A) internal stickiness of the gas decreases.

(B) internal molecular activity decreases.

(C) internal stickiness of the gas increases.

(D) molecular activity increases.

109. Find the difference in pressure between the water and oil if $H = 25$ cm. See above sketch.

(A) 42.3 kPa

(B) 37.2 kPa

(C) 34.8 kPa

(D) 30.6 kPa

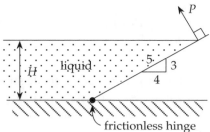

110. Find an expression for the force P needed to hold the gate of width w in the position shown.

(A) $\frac{5}{18} \gamma w H^2$

(B) $\frac{1}{6} \gamma w H^2$

(C) $\frac{2}{9} \gamma w H^2$

(D) $\frac{1}{2} \gamma w H^2$

111. Water flows in a pipe of diameter D with a velocity V. It enters at the center of two parallel disks of radius R separated by a distance t. The water flows radially outward between the disks. The velocity with which the water leaves the disks is

(A) $\dfrac{D^2 V}{4R^2}$

(B) $\dfrac{D^2 V}{8Rt}$

(C) $\dfrac{DtV}{8R^2}$

(D) $\dfrac{DtV}{4R^2}$

112. Bernoulli's equation cannot be used to approximate the pressure drop for which of the following?

(A) across an orifice through which water flows

(B) across a nozzle through which water flows

(C) from the free stream to the stagnation point on an airfoil of a small aircraft

(D) across a Venturi meter

113. The pressure drop over 15 m of 2-cm-diameter galvanized iron pipe is measured to be 60 kPa. If the pipe is horizontal, estimate the flow rate of water. ($v = 10^{-6}\ \mathrm{m^2/s}$)

(A) 6.82 L/s

(B) 2.18 L/s

(C) 0.682 L/s

(D) 0.218 L/s

114. The pressure drop across a valve, through which 0.04 m³/s of water flows, is measured to be 100 kPa. Estimate the loss coefficient if the nominal diameter of the valve is 8 cm.

(A) 0.32

(B) 0.79

(C) 3.2

(D) 8.7

115. What is the energy requirement of an 85% efficient pump that transports 0.04 m³/s of water if it increases the pressure from 200 kPa to 1200 kPa?

(A) 4.8 kW

(B) 14.2 kW

(C) 34.0 kW

(D) 47.1 kW

Workspace Below

116.   A person's behavior is ethical when one

(A)   does what is best for oneself

(B)   has good intentions, no matter how things turn out

(C)   does what is most tempting

(D)   does what is best for everyone

117.   Engineers need a code of ethics because

(A)   it keeps the government off their backs

(B)   it provides a clear definition of what the public has a right to expect from responsible engineers

(C)   it will make engineers look good in court, when they can prove they followed the code

(D)   it raises the image of the profession and hence gets engineers more pay

118.   Engineers should act ethically because

(A)   if they don't, they risk getting demoted or fired

(B)   that's the way responsible engineers behave

(C)   the boss wants you to

(D)   it feels good

119.   The first and foremost obligation of registered professional engineers is to

(A)   the public welfare

(B)   their own career advancement

(C)   their employer

(D)   the government

120.   Registered professional engineers should undertake services for clients only when

(A)   they really need the fees

(B)   their own bid is the lowest one

(C)   they are fully technically competent to carry out the services

(D)   carrying out the services wouldn't involve excessive time or effort

STOP!
•The Afternoon Session is Next•

If you finish before 4 hours have elapsed, you may return to any of the problems in the morning session. **Do not look** at the afternoon session problems. Take a 1-hour break and then continue with the afternoon session.

FUNDAMENTALS OF ENGINEERING EXAM

Afternoon Session—Diagnostic Exam

(Simulated answer form with topical breakout and scoring grid.)

BE SURE EACH MARK IS DARK AND COMPLETELY FILLS THE INTENDED SPACE AS ILLUSTRATED HERE:●.

MATH	MATERIALS	STATICS	MECHANICS	THERMO/FLUIDS	ETHICS
1 Ⓐ Ⓑ Ⓒ Ⓓ	16 Ⓐ Ⓑ Ⓒ Ⓓ	23 Ⓐ Ⓑ Ⓒ Ⓓ	33 Ⓐ Ⓑ Ⓒ Ⓓ	44 Ⓐ Ⓑ Ⓒ Ⓓ	58 Ⓐ Ⓑ Ⓒ Ⓓ
2 Ⓐ Ⓑ Ⓒ Ⓓ	17 Ⓐ Ⓑ Ⓒ Ⓓ	24 Ⓐ Ⓑ Ⓒ Ⓓ	34 Ⓐ Ⓑ Ⓒ Ⓓ	45 Ⓐ Ⓑ Ⓒ Ⓓ	59 Ⓐ Ⓑ Ⓒ Ⓓ
3 Ⓐ Ⓑ Ⓒ Ⓓ	18 Ⓐ Ⓑ Ⓒ Ⓓ	25 Ⓐ Ⓑ Ⓒ Ⓓ	35 Ⓐ Ⓑ Ⓒ Ⓓ	46 Ⓐ Ⓑ Ⓒ Ⓓ	60 Ⓐ Ⓑ Ⓒ Ⓓ
4 Ⓐ Ⓑ Ⓒ Ⓓ		26 Ⓐ Ⓑ Ⓒ Ⓓ	36 Ⓐ Ⓑ Ⓒ Ⓓ	47 Ⓐ Ⓑ Ⓒ Ⓓ	
5 Ⓐ Ⓑ Ⓒ Ⓓ	Score: _____	27 Ⓐ Ⓑ Ⓒ Ⓓ	37 Ⓐ Ⓑ Ⓒ Ⓓ	48 Ⓐ Ⓑ Ⓒ Ⓓ	Score: _____
6 Ⓐ Ⓑ Ⓒ Ⓓ		28 Ⓐ Ⓑ Ⓒ Ⓓ		49 Ⓐ Ⓑ Ⓒ Ⓓ	
7 Ⓐ Ⓑ Ⓒ Ⓓ	**CHEMISTRY**		Score: _____	50 Ⓐ Ⓑ Ⓒ Ⓓ	
8 Ⓐ Ⓑ Ⓒ Ⓓ		Score: _____		51 Ⓐ Ⓑ Ⓒ Ⓓ	
9 Ⓐ Ⓑ Ⓒ Ⓓ	19 Ⓐ Ⓑ Ⓒ Ⓓ		**ELECTRICAL**	52 Ⓐ Ⓑ Ⓒ Ⓓ	
10 Ⓐ Ⓑ Ⓒ Ⓓ	20 Ⓐ Ⓑ Ⓒ Ⓓ	**DYNAMICS**		53 Ⓐ Ⓑ Ⓒ Ⓓ	
11 Ⓐ Ⓑ Ⓒ Ⓓ	21 Ⓐ Ⓑ Ⓒ Ⓓ		38 Ⓐ Ⓑ Ⓒ Ⓓ	54 Ⓐ Ⓑ Ⓒ Ⓓ	
12 Ⓐ Ⓑ Ⓒ Ⓓ	22 Ⓐ Ⓑ Ⓒ Ⓓ	29 Ⓐ Ⓑ Ⓒ Ⓓ	39 Ⓐ Ⓑ Ⓒ Ⓓ		
		30 Ⓐ Ⓑ Ⓒ Ⓓ	40 Ⓐ Ⓑ Ⓒ Ⓓ	Score: _____	
Score: _____	Score: _____	31 Ⓐ Ⓑ Ⓒ Ⓓ	41 Ⓐ Ⓑ Ⓒ Ⓓ		
		32 Ⓐ Ⓑ Ⓒ Ⓓ	42 Ⓐ Ⓑ Ⓒ Ⓓ	**ECONOMICS**	
			43 Ⓐ Ⓑ Ⓒ Ⓓ		
COMPUTERS		Score: _____		55 Ⓐ Ⓑ Ⓒ Ⓓ	
			Score: _____	56 Ⓐ Ⓑ Ⓒ Ⓓ	
13 Ⓐ Ⓑ Ⓒ Ⓓ				57 Ⓐ Ⓑ Ⓒ Ⓓ	
14 Ⓐ Ⓑ Ⓒ Ⓓ					
15 Ⓐ Ⓑ Ⓒ Ⓓ				Score: _____	
Score: _____					

cut here!

Afternoon Session Diagnostic—General DS

4 hours maximum

Each of the 60 problems is followed by four answers. Select the response that is best and circle the corresponding letter on the answer sheet.

Workspace Below

Questions 1–2:

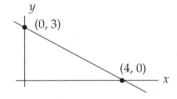

1. What is the equation of the line passing through the two points shown?

   (A) $y = -\frac{4}{3}x + 3$

   (B) $4y - 3x = 12$

   (C) $3y - 4x = 12$

   (D) $4y + 3x = 12$

2. Which integral would be used to provide the second moment about the x-axis of the area formed by the straight line, the x-axis, and the y-axis?

   (A) $\int_0^3 y^2 x \, dy$

   (B) $\int_0^4 x^2 y \, dx$

   (C) $\int_0^3 y x^2 \, dy$

   (D) $\int_0^4 y^2 x \, dy$

Workspace Below

Questions 3–6:

Given the three matrices:

$$A = \begin{bmatrix} 2 & 1 & -2 \\ 0 & 1 & 0 \\ 1 & 2 & 0 \end{bmatrix}, \qquad B = \begin{bmatrix} 1 & -2 & 0 \end{bmatrix}, \qquad C = \begin{bmatrix} 3 \\ -1 \\ 0 \end{bmatrix}$$

3. Find $|A|$.

   (A) 0

   (B) 1

   (C) 2

   (D) -2

4. Find **BC**.

   (A) 0

   (B) $\begin{bmatrix} 3 & -6 & 0 \\ -1 & 2 & 0 \\ 0 & 0 & 0 \end{bmatrix}$

   (C) $\begin{bmatrix} 3 \\ 2 \\ 0 \end{bmatrix}$

   (D) $[5]$

5. Which of the following is an eigenvalue of **A**?

   (A) -1

   (B) 0

   (C) 1

   (D) 2

6. If $Ax = C$, what is x_1?

   (A) 0

   (B) 1

   (C) 2

   (D) -2

Questions 7–8:

Given the vectors $\quad \mathbf{A} = 3\mathbf{i} + 2\mathbf{j} - \mathbf{k}$

$\mathbf{B} = x\mathbf{i} - 3yz\mathbf{j} + y\mathbf{k}$

$\mathbf{C} = xy\mathbf{i} - y^2\mathbf{j} - yz\mathbf{k}$

7. Find $\mathbf{A} \times \mathbf{B} \cdot \mathbf{C}$ at $(1, 2, 0)$.

   (A) $4\mathbf{i} - 7\mathbf{j} - 2\mathbf{k}$

   (B) 28

   (C) $8\mathbf{i} + 28\mathbf{j}$

   (D) 36

8. Find $\nabla \cdot \mathbf{C}$ at $(1, 2, 0)$ if $\nabla = \dfrac{\partial}{\partial x}\mathbf{i} + \dfrac{\partial}{\partial y}\mathbf{j} + \dfrac{\partial}{\partial z}\mathbf{k}$

   (A) $2\mathbf{i} - 4\mathbf{j} - 2\mathbf{k}$

   (B) -2

   (C) $\mathbf{i} - 2\mathbf{j}$

   (D) -4

Questions 9–12:

A certain phenomenon is modeled with the following differential equation:

$$\frac{d^2x}{dt^2} + C\frac{dx}{dt} + 4x = f(t)$$

with initial conditions $x(0) = 0$ and $x'(0) = 10$.

9. If $C = 0$, the homogenous solution is

   (A) $c_1 e^{2t} + c_2 e^{-2t}$

   (B) $c_1 e^{2it} + c_2 e^{-2it}$

   (C) $c_1 \cos 4t + c_2 \sin 4t$

   (D) $c_1 e^{2t} + c_2 t e^{2t}$

10. If $C = 0$ and $f(t) = 8e^{2t}$, the particular solution is

    (A) e^{2t}

    (B) Ate^{2t}

    (C) $At^2 e^{2t}$

    (D) e^{2it}

11. If $C = 5$ and $f(t) = 20\sin 2t$, the solution of the initial-value problem is

    (A) $e^{-t} - e^{-4t} + 20\sin 2t$

    (B) $6\sin t - 4\cos 4t + 4\cos 2t$

    (C) $4\cos t - 6\sin 4t - 4\cos 2t$

    (D) $6e^{-t} - 4e^{-4t} - 2\cos 2t$

Workspace Below

12. If $C = 0$ and $f(t) = 4\cos \omega t$, select the value for ω that would make $x(t)$ unbounded as $t \to \infty$.

(A) 0

(B) 1

(C) 2

(D) 3

13. Given the base 10 number 27.625, which of the following representations is correct?

(A) 11002.101 base 2, 19.5 base 16

(B) 121.22 base 4, 16.6 base 16

(C) 33.5 base 8, 1B.A base 16

(D) 11001.101 base 2, 123.22 base 4

14. In a standard spreadsheet format, cells D3, E3 and F3 contain the values 1, 4, and 10, respectively. Cell G3 contains the formula @AVG(D3..F3). This formula is copied into cells H3 and I3. The value in cell I3 is then most nearly:

(A) 5.0

(B) 6.3

(C) 3.3

(D) 7.1

15. A multiplexer is a Boolean logical device that has k selection inputs that determine which of the 2^k data inputs will be connected to the single output. Consider a 4 data input (I0, I1, I2, I3) multiplexer. If the 2 selection inputs are S1, S0 then:

S1 S0	output
0 0	I 0
0 1	I 1
1 0	I 2
1 1	I 3

(A) output $= \overline{S1}\,\overline{S0}\,\text{I0} + \overline{S1}\,S0\,\text{I1} + S1\,\overline{S0}\,\text{I2} + S1\,S0\,\text{I3}$

(B) output $= \overline{S0}\,\overline{S1}\,\text{I0} + \overline{S0}\,S1\,\text{I1} + S0\,\overline{S1}\,\text{I2} + S0\,S1\,\text{I3}$

(C) output $= \left(\overline{S1}+\overline{S0}\right)\text{I0} + \left(\overline{S1}+S0\right)\text{I1} + \left(S1+\overline{S0}\right)\text{I2} + \left(S1+S0\right)\text{I3}$

(D) output $= \left(\overline{S0}+\overline{S1}\right)\text{I0} + \left(\overline{S0}+S1\right)\text{I1} + \left(S0+\overline{S1}\right)\text{I2} + \left(S0+S1\right)\text{I3}$

16. Yield point phenomenon in mild steel occurs due to

(A) large grain size

(B) poor tempering

(C) presence of too much martensite

(D) interaction of carbon with dislocations

17. In this phase diagram, the following are true except:

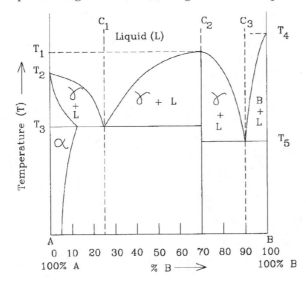

(A) an eutectic reaction occurs at a temperature T_3

(B) an eutectic reaction occurs at a temperature T_5

(C) an eutectic reaction occurs at a composition C_1

(D) an eutectic reaction occurs at a composition C_2

18. In the phase diagram for the problem above, the following are true except:

(A) an intermetallic phase γ forms at composition C_2

(B) an eutectic reaction occurs at a composition of 25% A and 75% B and at a temperature T_3

(C) pure solid B melts at a temperature T_4

(D) an eutectic reaction occurs at a composition of 90% B and 10% A and at a temperature T_5

19. What is the electron configuration of gallium?

(A) $1s^2\, 2s^2\, 2p^6\, 3s^2\, 3p^6\, 4s^2\, 3d^{10}\, 4p^1$

(B) $1s^2\, 2s^2\, 2p^6\, 3s^2\, 3p^6\, 3d^6\, 3p^7$

(C) $1s^2\, 2s^2\, 2p^6\, 3s^2\, 2p^6\, 4s^2\, 4p^6\, 4d^5$

(D) $1s^2\, 2s^2\, 2p^6\, 3s^2\, 3p^6\, 4s^2\, 3d^8\, 4p^1$

20. In the exothermic reaction

$$C(s) + O_2(g) + 2HCl = COCl_2(g) + H_2O(g)$$

at equilibrium, how is it possible to increase the amount of heat evolved?

(A) increase the pressure

(B) add water

(C) add a catalyst

(D) increase the volume

21. Which of the following equilibrium constant expressions is associated with the equation: $BaO(s) + CO_2(g) = Ba\,CO_3(s)$?
    (A) $K_p = 1/p(CO_2)$
    (B) $K_p = p(BaCO_3)/[p(BaO) \times p(CO_2)]$
    (C) $K_p = 1/[p(BaO) \times p(CO_2)]$
    (D) $K_p = 1/p(BaCO_3)$

22. In the following reaction, determine the change, if any, that occurs in the oxidation number of the underlined element, and whether the element is oxidized, reduced, or unchanged:

$$3Mg + \underline{N}_2 \rightarrow Mg_3\underline{N}_2$$

    (A) from 0 to +3; oxidized

    (B) from 0 to –3; oxidized

    (C) from +3 to +5; oxidized

    (D) from 0 to –3; reduced

Questions 23–25:

Each link has a circular cross section of radius 8 mm and is made of steel.
$E_{steel} = 210 \times 10^6$ kPa, $\alpha = 11.7 \times 10^{-6}\ ^\circ C^{-1}$

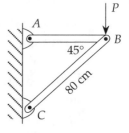

23. Find the force in member AB if $P = 400$ N.
    (A) 0
    (B) 283 N
    (C) 400 N
    (D) 476 N

24. What force P is required to just buckle link BC?
    (A) 9430 N
    (B) 7370 N
    (C) 5980 N
    (D) 4720 N

25. If the temperature of link BC were increased 40°C while that of link AB were held constant, how far would point B move vertically up? (Omit force P.)
    (A) 0.187 mm
    (B) 0.265 mm
    (C) 0.529 mm
    (D) 0.765 mm

Questions 26–28:

All members are the same length.

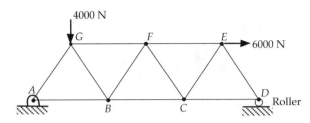

26. Calculate the magnitude of the reaction at *A*.
    (A) 1600 N
    (B) 2800 N
    (C) 4000 N
    (D) 6200 N

27. Calculate the force in link *CD*.
    (A) 2399 N ten
    (B) 2770 N comp
    (C) 2770 N ten
    (D) 1380 N ten

28. If the cross-section of link *CD* is as shown, find $I_{N.A.}$.
    (A) 576 cm^4
    (B) 864 cm^4
    (C) 1150 cm^4
    (D) 1460 cm^4

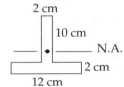

Workspace Below

Questions 29–32:

The 50 kg solid cylinder rolls without slipping. It is initially at rest.

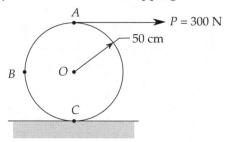

29. Find the speed of point B when the speed of A is 20 m/s.
    (A) 20 m/s
    (B) 14.14 m/s
    (C) 12.12 m/s
    (D) 10 m/s

30. Find the acceleration of point O.
    (A) 20 m/s²
    (B) 16 m/s²
    (C) 12 m/s²
    (D) 8 m/s²

31. Find the friction force.
    (A) 100 N right
    (B) 100 N left
    (C) 50 N right
    (D) 50 N left

32. If P acts over a distance of 2 m, what is the velocity of point O?
    (A) 4 m/s
    (B) 6 m/s
    (C) 8 m/s
    (D) 10 m/s

Questions 33–35:

$$I_{N.A.} = 1.848 \times 10^{-6} \text{ m}^4$$
$$E = 210 \times 10^9 \text{ Pa}$$

33. The maximum tensile stress in the beam is
    (A) 112 MPa
    (B) 91.2 MPa
    (C) 76.5 MPa
    (D) 49.1 MPa

34. The maximum vertical shearing stress in the beam is
    (A) 1240 kPa
    (B) 1060 kPa
    (C) 840 kPa
    (D) 720 kPa

35. Estimate the deflection of the free end.
    (A) 51.2 mm
    (B) 63.6 mm
    (C) 77.9 mm
    (D) 86.4 mm

Workspace Below

Questions 36–37:

The stress state at a point in a beam is as shown.

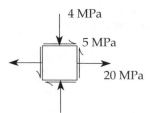

36. What is the maximum tensile stress at the point?
    (A) 5 MPa
    (B) 13 MPa
    (C) 21 MPa
    (D) 26 MPa

37. The element can be rotated through an angle ϕ such that there is no normal stress on the face with the 4 MPa stress shown. Find ϕ.
    (A) 8°
    (B) 13°
    (C) 16°
    (D) 19°

38. What value of R_X in the circuit shown will make $I_G = 0$?
    (A) 10
    (B) 20
    (C) 30
    (D) 40

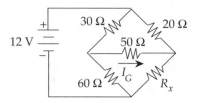

39. The magnitude and phase of the current in the circuit is
    (A) 1.72 ∠45° A
    (B) 3.54 ∠45° A
    (C) 4.62 ∠–45° A
    (D) 5.00 ∠0° A

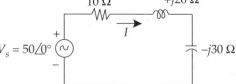

40. The power delivered to the load $R_L = 100\ \Omega$ is
    (A) 15.6 W
    (B) 28.1 W
    (C) 32.4 W
    (D) 39.1 W

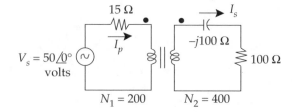

41. The current in a circuit is digital as shown in the scope trace. The *rms* value of this current is

    (A) 0 A

    (B) 8.71 A

    (C) 16.33 A

    (D) 20.0 A

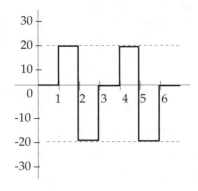

42. Compute the reactive power in volt amperes delivered by the source in the circuit shown.

    (A) 741

    (B) 892

    (C) 1287

    (D) 1623

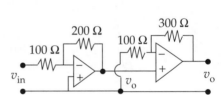

43. The gain (v_{out}/v_{in}) of the op-amp circuit shown is

    (A) +2

    (B) −4

    (C) +6

    (D) −8

Workspace Below

Questions 44–49:

This cycle occurs in a piston-cylinder arrangement. Assume air to be an ideal gas with constant specific heats.

$$T_{high} = 1200°C$$

$$T_{low} = 20°C$$

$$P_{low} = 100 \text{ kPa}$$

$$\text{compression ratio} = 8$$

$$R_{air} = 0.287 \frac{kJ}{kg \cdot K}$$

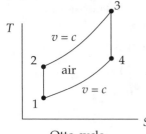

Otto cycle

44. Find the added heat.
    - (A) 440 kJ/kg
    - (B) 575 kJ/kg
    - (C) 620 kJ/kg
    - (D) 800 kJ/kg

45. Find the net work per cycle.
    - (A) 325 kJ/kg
    - (B) 400 kJ/kg
    - (C) 425 kJ/kg
    - (D) 450 kJ/kg

46. The efficiency of the Otto cycle is
    - (A) 42%
    - (B) 46%
    - (C) 56%
    - (D) 68%

47. The efficiency of a Carnot cycle operating between the same limits as this Otto cycle is
    - (A) 42%
    - (B) 46%
    - (C) 56%
    - (D) 80%

48. The work needed to compress the air from BDC to TDC is approximated by which expression?
    - (A) $RT_2 \ln v_1/v_2$
    - (B) $c_p(T_2 - T_1)$
    - (C) $P_2(v_1 - v_2)$
    - (D) $c_v(T_2 - T_1)$

49. The Otto cycle is used to simulate the operation of
    - (A) a gasoline engine
    - (B) a diesel engine
    - (C) a gas turbine
    - (D) a jet engine

Questions 50–54:

pipe diameter = 1.2 m
pipe length = 800 m
water viscosity = 10^{-3} N·s/m^2
flow rate = 0.8 m^3/s
z_1 = 40 m
z_2 = 10 m
z_3 = 0

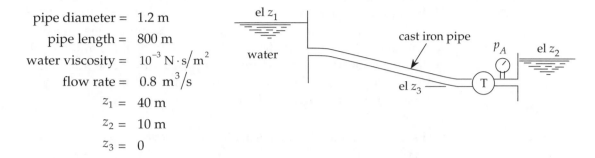

50. Estimate the pressure p_A just upstream of the pipe exit.
    (A) 102 kPa
    (B) 98 kPa
    (C) 82 kPa
    (D) 76 kPa

51. Estimate the pressure in the pipe at the turbine inlet. (The turbine is located near the pipe exit.)
    (A) 356 kPa
    (B) 365 kPa
    (C) 372 kPa
    (D) 389 kPa

52. If the turbine is 89% efficient, what is the power output?
    (A) 161 kW
    (B) 186 kW
    (C) 207 kW
    (D) 236 kW

53. The turbine has a set of nozzles that direct high speed water into the turbine blades. What is the maximum velocity that the water can have exiting the nozzles?
    (A) 31.3 m/s
    (B) 27.9 m/s
    (C) 23.2 m/s
    (D) 20.1 m/s

54. If a model study were used to study the proposed designs of the blades on the turbine, which of the following parameters would be used in the study?
    (A) Reynolds number
    (B) Froude number
    (C) Weber number
    (D) Cauchy number

EXAM 1

Workspace Below

Questions 55–57:

Flood damage to businesses and homes in Riverbend City averages five million dollars annually. A levee system costing fifty million dollars would prevent all flood damage. The annual maintenance and interest costs for the levee system would be three million dollars. Riverbend City could finance construction by selling bonds with a 20-year term that would pay 5% interest on par value. The market rate for similar bonds is 6%.

55. Estimate the rate of return provided by the levee system.
   (A) 4%
   (B) 5%
   (C) 6%
   (D) 10%

56. Compute the benefit/cost ratio for the levee system using 6% interest rate.
   (A) 0.10
   (B) 0.50
   (C) 0.67
   (D) 1.00

57. Estimate the market price for a bond with $5000 par value.
   (A) $2867
   (B) $4426
   (C) $5000
   (D) $5574

58. You are the engineer of record on a building project which is behind schedule and urgently needed by the clients. Your boss wants you to certify some roofing construction as properly completed even though you know some questionable installation techniques were used. What should you do?
   (A) Certify it, and demand a raise from your boss as your price for doing so.
   (B) Refuse to certify it.
   (C) Tell the clients about the problem, saying that you'll certify it if they want you to.
   (D) Certify it, but keep a close watch on the project in future in case any problems develop.

59. You are the engineer responsible for monitoring and fixing any pollution problems associated with a production site. Your routine tests turn up levels of pollution which are somewhat higher than legally allowed (but not very much higher). What is your best course of action?

    (A) Tell your bosses, and let them decide whether or not to fix it.

    (B) Ignore the problem, since it isn't a significant one.

    (C) Fix the problem, no matter what it costs, and even if your bosses tell you to ignore it.

    (D) Fix the problem only if it can be done relatively cheaply.

60. You are an engineer and a manager at an aerospace company with an important government contract supplying parts for a space shuttle. As an engineer, you know that a projected launch would face unknown risks, because the equipment for which you are responsible would be operating outside its tested range of behaviors. However, since you are also a manager you know how important it is to your company that the launch be carried out promptly. What should you do?

    (A) Allow your judgment as a manager to override your judgment as an engineer, and so permit the launching.

    (B) Allow your judgment as an engineer to override your judgment as a manager, and so do not permit the launching.

    (C) Toss a coin to decide, since one's engineering and managerial roles are equally important, so neither should take precedence over the other.

    (D) Go along with whatever is the majority decision of the company's managers and engineers.

STOP!

•You are finished with the Diagnostic Exam!•

If you finish before 4 hours have elapsed, you may return to any of the problems in the afternoon session. You may not return to the morning session.

FUNDAMENTALS OF ENGINEERING EXAM

ANSWER KEY—Morning—Diagnostic Exam

(Answer key with topical breakout and scoring grid.)

BE SURE EACH MARK IS DARK AND COMPLETELY FILLS THE INTENDED SPACE AS ILLUSTRATED HERE: ●.

MATH

1 ●ⒷⒸⒹ
2 ⒶⒷⒸ●
3 ⒶⒷⒸ●
4 ●ⒷⒸⒹ
5 ⒶⒷ●Ⓓ
6 ⒶⒷⒸ●
7 ⒶⒷⒸ●
8 ⒶⒷⒸ●
9 ●ⒷⒸⒹ
10 Ⓐ●ⒸⒹ
11 ●ⒷⒸⒹ
12 ⒶⒷ●Ⓓ
13 ⒶⒷⒸ●
14 Ⓐ●ⒸⒹ
15 ⒶⒷ●Ⓓ
16 ⒶⒷ●Ⓓ
17 ⒶⒷⒸ●
18 Ⓐ●ⒸⒹ
19 ⒶⒷⒸ●
20 ⒶⒷⒸ●
21 ⒶⒷ●Ⓓ
22 ⒶⒷ●Ⓓ
23 Ⓐ●ⒸⒹ
24 ●ⒷⒸⒹ

Score: _____

COMPUTERS

25 ●ⒷⒸⒹ
26 ⒶⒷ●Ⓓ
27 ⒶⒷⒸ●
28 ⒶⒷⒸ●
29 Ⓐ●ⒸⒹ
30 ●ⒷⒸⒹ

Score: _____

MATERIALS

31 ⒶⒷⒸ●
32 ●ⒷⒸⒹ
33 ●ⒷⒸⒹ
34 ⒶⒷ●Ⓓ
35 ●ⒷⒸⒹ
36 ⒶⒷⒸ●
37 ⒶⒷ●Ⓓ
38 Ⓐ●ⒸⒹ

Score: _____

CHEMISTRY

39 ⒶⒷⒸ●
40 ⒶⒷ●Ⓓ
41 ⒶⒷ●Ⓓ
42 Ⓐ●ⒸⒹ
43 Ⓐ●ⒸⒹ
44 ⒶⒷ●Ⓓ
45 ⒶⒷ●Ⓓ
46 ⒶⒷⒸ●
47 ●ⒷⒸⒹ
48 ⒶⒷⒸ●
49 Ⓐ●ⒸⒹ

Score: _____

ECONOMICS

50 ⒶⒷ●Ⓓ
51 ⒶⒷⒸ●
52 ●ⒷⒸⒹ
53 ⒶⒷⒸ●
54 Ⓐ●ⒸⒹ

Score: _____

ELECTRICAL

55 ⒶⒷ●Ⓓ
56 ⒶⒷⒸ●
57 Ⓐ●ⒸⒹ
58 ⒶⒷⒸ●
59 ⒶⒷ●Ⓓ
60 ⒶⒷ●Ⓓ
61 ⒶⒷⒸ●
62 ⒶⒷⒸ●
63 ●ⒷⒸⒹ
64 ●ⒷⒸⒹ
65 ●ⒷⒸⒹ
66 ⒶⒷⒸ●

Score: _____

THERMODYNAMICS

67 ⒶⒷⒸ●
68 ⒶⒷ●Ⓓ
69 ●ⒷⒸⒹ
70 Ⓐ●ⒸⒹ
71 Ⓐ●ⒸⒹ
72 ⒶⒷⒸ●
73 ⒶⒷ●Ⓓ
74 ⒶⒷⒸ●
75 ●ⒷⒸⒹ
76 ⒶⒷⒸ●
77 ⒶⒷⒸ●

Score: _____

STATICS

78 ⒶⒷⒸ●
79 ●ⒷⒸⒹ
80 ⒶⒷⒸ●
81 ⒶⒷ●Ⓓ
82 Ⓐ●ⒸⒹ
83 ⒶⒷⒸ●
84 ⒶⒷ●Ⓓ
85 ●ⒷⒸⒹ
86 Ⓐ●ⒸⒹ
87 ⒶⒷ●Ⓓ
88 ●ⒷⒸⒹ
89 ⒶⒷⒸ●

Score: _____

DYNAMICS

90 Ⓐ●ⒸⒹ
91 ⒶⒷⒸ●
92 ⒶⒷⒸ●
93 Ⓐ●ⒸⒹ
94 ⒶⒷ●Ⓓ
95 ⒶⒷⒸ●
96 ⒶⒷⒸ●
97 ●ⒷⒸⒹ
98 ⒶⒷ●Ⓓ
99 ⒶⒷⒸ●

Score: _____

MECHANICS

100 Ⓐ●ⒸⒹ
101 ⒶⒷ●Ⓓ
102 ⒶⒷⒸ●
103 ●ⒷⒸⒹ
104 ⒶⒷ●Ⓓ
105 ⒶⒷⒸ●
106 Ⓐ●ⒸⒹ
107 ●ⒷⒸⒹ

Score: _____

FLUID MECHANICS

108 ⒶⒷⒸ●
109 ⒶⒷ●Ⓓ
110 ●ⒷⒸⒹ
111 Ⓐ●ⒸⒹ
112 ●ⒷⒸⒹ
113 ⒶⒷⒸ●
114 ⒶⒷ●Ⓓ
115 ⒶⒷⒸ●

Score: _____

ETHICS

116 ⒶⒷⒸ●
117 Ⓐ●ⒸⒹ
118 Ⓐ●ⒸⒹ
119 ●ⒷⒸⒹ
120 ⒶⒷ●Ⓓ

Score: _____

Diagnostic Exam Solutions—Morning

1. **A**   The slope of the line $y = 2x - 3$ is 2. Its negative reciprocal is $-\frac{1}{2}$.

   Hence, $y = -\frac{1}{2}x + b$ is the line. Substitute in:

   $-3 = -\frac{1}{2}(6) + b.$ $\therefore b = 0$ and $y = -\frac{1}{2}x.$

2. **D**   Refer to the general form $Ax^2 + 2Bxy + Cy^2 + \cdots = 0.$

   $B^2 - AC = (-2)^2 - (1)(1) = 3.$ Since $B^2 - AC > 0$, this is a hyperbola.

3. **D** $\dfrac{\cos\theta}{\sin\theta} + \dfrac{\sin\theta}{\cos\theta} = \dfrac{\cos^2\theta + \sin^2\theta}{\cos\theta\sin\theta} = \dfrac{1}{\cos\theta\sin\theta} = \dfrac{2}{2\cos\theta\sin\theta} = \dfrac{2}{\sin 2\theta}.$

4. **A** $(1 - 2i)^{-1} = \dfrac{1}{1 - 2i} = \dfrac{1}{1 - 2i}\dfrac{1 + 2i}{1 + 2i} = \dfrac{1 + 2i}{1 + 4} = \dfrac{1}{5} + \dfrac{2}{5}i.$

5. **C** $\text{adj}\begin{bmatrix} 2 & 3 \\ -1 & 0 \end{bmatrix} = \begin{bmatrix} 2 & 3 \\ -1 & 0 \end{bmatrix}^{+} = \begin{bmatrix} 0 & 1 \\ -3 & 2 \end{bmatrix}^{T} = \begin{bmatrix} 0 & -3 \\ 1 & 2 \end{bmatrix}.$

   Note: The elements in the transpose are the cofactors of the elements of

   $\begin{bmatrix} 2 & 3 \\ -1 & 0 \end{bmatrix}.$

6. **D** $y = \dfrac{\begin{vmatrix} 1 & 2 & 1 \\ 1 & 0 & -1 \\ 1 & -3 & 0 \end{vmatrix}}{\begin{vmatrix} 1 & -1 & 1 \\ 1 & 0 & -1 \\ 1 & 1 & 0 \end{vmatrix}} = \dfrac{-8}{3} = -\dfrac{8}{3}$

7. **D** $\begin{vmatrix} 1 - \lambda & 1 \\ 2 & -\lambda \end{vmatrix} = (1 - \lambda)(-\lambda) - 2 = \lambda^2 - \lambda - 2 = 0.$ $(\lambda - 2)(\lambda + 1) = 0.$ $\therefore \lambda = 2, \ -1.$

8. **D**   Let $y_p = Ae^{-t}.$ Substitute in:

   $-Ae^{-t} + 4Ae^{-t} = 3e^{-t}.$ $\therefore -A + 4A = 3.$ $\therefore 3A = 3.$ $A = 1.$ $\therefore y_p(t) = e^{-t}.$

9. **A**   Damping makes $y_h \to 0$ as $t \to \infty.$ $\therefore y_{\text{steady-state}} = y_p.$ Let

   $y_p = A\sin 2t + B\cos 2t.$ Substitute in:

   $-4A\sin 2t - 4B\cos 2t + 8A\cos 2t - 8B\sin 2t + 4A\sin 2t + 4B\cos 2t = 8\sin 2t.$

   $\therefore 8A = 0$ and $-8B = 8.$ $\therefore A = 0$ and $B = -1.$ $\therefore$ Amplitude $= 1.$

10. **B** $V = \int_0^2 \pi x^2\, dy = \int_0^2 \pi 4y^4\, dy = 4\pi\left(\dfrac{2^5}{5}\right) = \dfrac{128\pi}{5}.$

11. **A**   The curl of a vector field is zero if it is conservative.

12.   **C** $\mathbf{A} \times \mathbf{B} = (4\mathbf{i} + 2\mathbf{j}) \times (B_x\mathbf{i} + B_y\mathbf{j}) = 0.$ $\therefore 4B_y - 2B_x = 0.$

$\mathbf{A} \cdot \mathbf{B} = (4\mathbf{i} + 2\mathbf{j}) \cdot (B_x\mathbf{i} + B_y\mathbf{j}) = 30.$ $\therefore 4B_x + 2B_y = 30.$

$B_y = 3.\ B_x = 6.$

$\therefore \mathbf{B} = 6\mathbf{i} + 3\mathbf{j}.$

13.   **D** $\mathbf{A} \cdot \mathbf{i}_B = \mathbf{A} \cdot \mathbf{B} / |\mathbf{B}|$

$= (\mathbf{i} - 4\mathbf{j}) \cdot \dfrac{2\mathbf{i} - 4\mathbf{j} - 4\mathbf{k}}{\left(2^2 + 4^2 + 4^2\right)^{1/2}}$

$= (2 + 16)/6 = 3$

14.   **B**   The first dice has a probability of 1 of rolling a number. The second dice has a probability of $1/6$ of rolling the same number:

$$P = 1 \times \frac{1}{6} \times \frac{1}{6} \times \frac{1}{6} \times \frac{1}{6} \times 12,000 = 9.26\ .$$

15.   **C** $\bar{y} = \dfrac{\int y\, dA}{\int dA} = \dfrac{\displaystyle\int_0^1 y\left(2 - 2y^2\right) dy}{\displaystyle\int_0^1 \left(2 - 2y^2\right) dy} = \dfrac{1 - \dfrac{2}{4}}{2 - \dfrac{2}{3}} = \dfrac{1/2}{4/3} = \dfrac{3}{8}.$

16.   **C**   The term $\sin x$ makes it nonhomogeneous. (If it were $\sin y$ it would be nonlinear.) It has a variable coefficient, x^2. It is linear since the dependent variable y (or its derivatives) appear to the first power.

17.   **D** $\cos 2x = 1 - \dfrac{(2x)^2}{2!} + \dfrac{(2x)^4}{4!} - \cdots = 1 - 2x^2 + \dfrac{2}{3}x^4 - \cdots.$

Note: Since $\cos 0 = 1$, the series must begin with 1. This is a Taylor series with $a = 0$:

$\cos 2x = \cos(0) + \dfrac{-2\sin(2 \cdot 0)}{1!}x + \dfrac{-4\cos(2 \cdot 0)}{2!}x^2 + \cdots = 1 + 0 - \dfrac{4}{2}x^2 + \cdots.$

18.   **B**   Sketch the circle: $\sin\dfrac{\theta}{2} = \dfrac{5}{12}.$ $\therefore \dfrac{\theta}{2} = 24.62°$ and $\theta = 49.2°.$

19.   **D**   At the point $(2, 1)$ the slope of $x = 2y^2$ is found by differentiating:

$1 = 2(2y)\dfrac{dy}{dx}.$ $\therefore \dfrac{dy}{dx} = \dfrac{1}{4}.$ Hence the line is $y = \dfrac{1}{4}x + b.$ If it passes through $(2, 1)$, then $1 = \dfrac{1}{4}(2) + b.$ $\therefore b = \dfrac{1}{2}.$

20.   **D** $i = e^{\pi i/2}.$ $i^{1/2} = e^{(\pi i/2)/2} = e^{\pi i/4} = \cos\dfrac{\pi}{4} + i\sin\dfrac{\pi}{4} = \dfrac{1}{\sqrt{2}} + i\dfrac{1}{\sqrt{2}} = (1 + i)\ \sqrt{2}.$

21. **C** $(1+2i)(5+3i) = 5 - 6 + 10i + 3i = -1 + 13i = re^{i\theta}$. $r = \sqrt{13^2 + 1^2} = 13.04$.

     $\theta = \tan^{-1}\dfrac{13}{-1} = -85.6°$. $\therefore \theta = 180 - 85.6 = 94.4° = 1.648$ rad.

     Note: $0 < \theta \le 180°$, so it is in the second quadrant.

22. **C** $\lim\limits_{x\to 0}\dfrac{\sin^2 2x}{x^2} = \lim\limits_{x\to 0}\dfrac{2\sin 2x(2\cos 2x)}{2x} = \lim\limits_{x\to 0}\dfrac{2\sin 2x\cos 2x}{x}$

$$= \lim_{x\to 0}\frac{2\left[2\cos^2 2x - 2\sin^2 2x\right]}{1} = 4.$$

     Note: We had to differentiate twice.

23. **B** $\displaystyle\int_0^\pi x\sin 2x\,dx \begin{pmatrix} u = x; & dv = \sin 2x\,dx \\[4pt] du = dx; & v = -\dfrac{1}{2}\cos 2x \end{pmatrix} = -\dfrac{x}{2}\cos 2x\Big|_0^\pi + \dfrac{1}{2}\int_0^\pi \cos 2x\,dx$

$$= -\frac{\pi}{2}(1) + \frac{1}{4}\sin 2x\Big|_0^\pi = -\frac{\pi}{2}.$$

24. **A** $\dfrac{s+3}{s^2+4s+8} = \dfrac{(s+2)+1}{(s+2)^2+4} = \dfrac{s+2}{(s+2)^2+4} + \dfrac{1}{(s+2)^2+4}$.

     $\therefore f(t) = e^{-2t}\cos 2t + \dfrac{1}{2}e^{-2t}\sin 2t$.

25. **A** $(101.1)_4 = 1\times 4^2 + 0\times 4^1 + 1\times 4^0 + 1\times 4^{-1} = 16 + 0 + 1 + 0.25 = 17.25$.

26. **C** $\dfrac{64\text{K}}{4\text{K}} \times \dfrac{16}{8} = 32$ cells

27. **D** $20_{10} = 1\times 2^4 + 0\times 2^3 + 1\times 2^2 + 0\times 2^1 + 1\times 2^0 = 10101_2$

     $.75 = 1\times 2^{-1} + 1\times 2^{-2} = .11$

     Answer $= 10101.11$

28. **D**   Cannot be encoded since C is out of the BCD digit range.

29. **B**   It prints 55 in decimal, octal and hex (55, 67, 37) with spaces (' ') in between.

30. **A**   8-bit $2^8 = 256$ levels

     voltage range = 10 volts

     $\therefore 10/256 = .0391$ volts/step

     $01101100 = 108$ steps

     $.0391$ volts/step $\times$ 108 steps $= 4.2228$ V

     $-5 + 4.2228 = -0.7772$ volts

31. **D**   The half-filled conduction band has the available energy levels for Fermi electrons to move up by acquiring extra kinetic energy when an electrical potential is applied.

32. **A**   The energy gap between the impurity level and the bottom of the conduction band is small, and thus electrons from the impurity level can

be thermally activated to the conduction band. This is called *n*-type because the charge carriers are negative (electrons).

33. **A**   Covalent bonding is produced by electron sharing between atoms as in the case of diamond (carbon) or *Si*.

34. **C**   Packing factor of a BCC lattice is less than that for a FCC lattice since the packing factors for BCC and FCC lattice are 0.68 and 0.74, respectively. Packing factor for FCC and HCP are equal, and it is 0.74. Note that (111) plane of a FCC lattice is the most densely packed plane, whereas (001) type planes are the most densely packed in HCP.

35. **A**   The three Miller indices are reciprocals of the intercepts. Note that the plane (120) is parallel to the z-axis, i.e., its intercept with this axis is at ∞.

36. **D**   Diffusional processes are thermally activated and the rate increases exponentially with increasing temperature.

37. **C**   Iron is actually protected by zinc. *Zn*, being more anodic in Galvanic series than iron, is preferentially corroded while iron is protected. Zinc in this case acts as the sacrificial electrode.

38. **B**   High hardness does not mean high toughness. To the contrary, brittle materials (low toughness) often have high hardness.

39. **D**   The number of protons (42) defines the element. From the Periodic Table it must be Molybdenum (*Mo*), number 42.

40. **C**   The symbol (*Rh*) identifies the atom as number 45 in the Periodic Table. It must, therefore have 45 protons. The atomic mass (103) tells you it must have $103 - 45 = 58$ neutrons. In order to have a charge of +3 it must have $45 - 3 = 42$ electrons.

41. **C**   Covalent bonds occur between atoms of similar electronegativity. Hydrogen always forms covalent bonds. Ionic bonds form between atoms of very different electronegativity. Only *KCl* has no possibility of covalent bonding. $NaNO_3$ contains Na^+ ions and NO_3^- ions, but the N-O bond is covalent.

42. **B**   Find the column or Group for each element in the Periodic Table, then move one column to the right for each negative charge, or one column to the left for each positive charge. If you end up in Group O, the Noble Gases, then the ion has the same electron configuration as a Noble Gas. For example: O^{2-}; Oxygen is in Group 6A. Two columns to the right (because there are 2 negative charges) brings you to Group O, the Noble Gases. Therefore O^{2-} does have a Noble Gas electron configuration. Pb^{2+}; Lead (82) is in Group 4A. Two columns left brings you to Group 2B, which is not the Noble Gases. Therefore the correct answer is Pb^{2+}.

43. **B**   The equilibrium constant (in moles/L) is $[CO_2][H_2]/[CO][H_2O] = [2.4][0.50]/[0.80][0.25] = 6$

44. **C** *As* (element number 33) has 33 electrons. The first three shells accommodate $2 + 8 + 18 = 28$ electrons. *As* therefore has $33 - 28 = 5$ valence electrons.

45. **C** From the Periodic Table, neutral Barium (number 56) has 56 electrons. Ba^{2+} has 56-2 = 54 electrons, the same as *Xe* (number 54).

46. **D** The mass of Carbon in a mole of propane equals 3 (the number of atoms of carbon per molecule) times 12 (the atomic weight of carbon) = 36 g. The mass of propane in a mole = $36 + 8 = 44$ g (the molecular weight of propane = 44). The %C = 100(36)/44 = 82%.

47. **A** Elements in Group 6A are two electrons short of a Noble Gas configuration. Therefore they will gain a charge of –2.

48. **D** First you must find the change in oxidation numbers for *S* and *N*. Sulfur changes from 0 to +4, a change of +4. Nitrogen changes from +5 to +2, a change of –3. Therefore 4 equivalents of nitric acid must react with three equivalents of sulfur to balance the change in oxidation numbers. The S/HNO_3 ratio = 3/4.

49. **B** There are few reaction variables that do not influence the reaction rate. The amount of a solid reactant present is one of them. A change in the total amount of material present without changing concentrations is another (i.e., the rate of conversion of one liter of NO_2 to N_2O_4 at STP is the same as the rate of conversion of 2 liters at STP).

50. **C** $F = 100(F/A)_{12}^{0.5} = 1234$.

51. **D** $3P = P(F/P)_n^4$. $(F/P)_n^4 = (1.04)^n = 3$. $\therefore n = 28$.

52. **A** $0 = x(F/A)_{21}^4 - 10,000(F/A)_4^4$. $\therefore x = 1328$.

53. **D** $F = 10,000(F/A)_5^8 + 1000(F/A)_5^8(A/G)_5^8 = 69,500$.

54. **B** $P = -70,000(P/A)_3^{20} + 80,000(P/A)_{10}^{20}(P/F)_3^{20} = 46,600$.

55. **C**

56. **D** With terminal *a–b* open, there is no current in the 5 Ω resistor, therefore no voltage drop in the 5 Ω resistor.

$$V_{ab} = \frac{12\Omega}{(12\Omega + 4\Omega)} \times 12 \text{ volts} = 9 \text{ volts} = V_{\text{Thevinen}}.$$

57. **B**

Write KVL $= \sum V_{drop} = 0$

Loop 1 : $\quad -12 + 6I_1 + 9 = 0$

Loop 2 : $\quad -9 + 9(I_1 + I) = 0$

Solve Loop 1: $I_1 = \dfrac{12 - 9}{6} = 0.5$.   Solve Loop 2: $I_1 + I = 1, \quad I = 1 - 0.5 = 0.5$ A.

$$\therefore \text{Power} = VI = 12 \times 0.5 = 6 \text{ W}.$$

58. **D**   Combine the parallel capacitors:

$v(t) = 70.7 \sin 377t$

$V_{rms} = \dfrac{V_{max}}{\sqrt{2}} = \dfrac{70.7}{1.414} = 50$

$X_C = \dfrac{1}{\omega C} = \dfrac{1}{377 \times 30 \times 10^{-6}} = 88.42$

$I = \dfrac{50\angle 0°}{45 - j88.42} = 0.504\angle 63°$ amp

59. **C** $I = \dfrac{50\angle 0°}{40 + j30} = \dfrac{50\angle 0°}{50\angle 36.9°} = 1\angle -36.9°, \quad V_{40} = IR = 40$ V.

60. **C** $P = |I|^2 R = (1)^2 \, 40 = 40$ W.

61. **D** $I(t) = I_\infty + (I_0 - I_\infty)e^{-\frac{t}{T}}, \quad I_0 = 0, \quad I_\infty = \dfrac{15 \text{ V}}{10 \text{ }\Omega} = 1.5$ A,

$T = \dfrac{L}{R} = \dfrac{0.025}{10} = 0.0025$.

$I(t) = 1.5 + (0 - 1.5)e^{-\frac{t}{0.0025}}, \quad I(0.001) = 1.5e^{-0.4} = 0.495$ A.

62. **D** $V_L = L\dfrac{dI}{dt} = 0.025\dfrac{d}{dt}\left[1.5 - 1.5e^{-\frac{t}{0.0025}}\right] = 0.025\left[0 + \dfrac{1.5}{0.0025}e^{-\frac{t}{0.0025}}\right]$

$= 15e^{-\frac{0.001}{0.0025}} = 15e^{-0.4} = 10.05$ V

63. **A**   Reflect the 100 Ω resistance to the primary side:

$Z_P = \left(\dfrac{N_1}{N_2}\right)^2 Z_S = \left(\dfrac{100}{200}\right)^2 100 = 25 \ \Omega$

$I_P = \dfrac{120\angle 0°}{40} = 3\angle 0°$ A

$I_S = \left(\dfrac{N_1}{N_2}\right)I_P = \left(\dfrac{100}{200}\right)3 = 1.5$ A

64. **A** $\mathbf{F} = \mathbf{I}L \times \mathbf{B}, \quad B = \dfrac{\mu I}{2\pi r}$ where r is the distance between the wires.

$B = \dfrac{4\pi \times 10^{-7} \times 50}{2\pi \times 0.05} = \dfrac{10^{-5}}{0.05} = 20 \times 10^{-5}$.

$\therefore F = 50 \times 1 \times 20 \times 10^{-5} = 10^{-2}$ N.

65. **A**   The field between the plates is $E = \dfrac{V}{d} = \dfrac{500}{0.02} = 25\,000$ V/m.

The force on the electron: $F = qE = 1.6 \times 10^{-19} \times 25\,000 = 4 \times 10^{-15}$ N.

66. **D** $R = R_0\big[1 + \alpha(T - T_0)\big], \quad 0.036 = 0.024\big[1 + 0.0039(T - 20)\big]$.
Solve for T: $T = 148$ °C.

67. **D**   An isolated system is defined as a system that does not interact with its surroundings, i.e., $Q = W = 0$. Even though $Q = W$, $Q = 0$ is the best response.

68. **C**   Work can occur by one system inducing a force on the other.

69. **A**

70. **B** $x = \dfrac{m_g}{m_g + m_f} = \dfrac{1.98 \times 0.5}{1.98 \times 0.5 + 0.02 \times 960} = 0.049$ or 4.9%.

71. **B** $Q = m\Delta h = mc_p\Delta T. \qquad 80 = 2 \times 1.00\Delta T. \qquad \therefore \Delta T = 40$°C.

72. **D**   Ice changes directly to vapor by the process called sublimation.

73. **C** $T_2 = T_1\left(\dfrac{P_2}{P_1}\right)^{\frac{k-1}{k}} = 293\left(\dfrac{800}{100}\right)^{\frac{0.4}{1.4}} = 531$ K or 258° C.

74. **D**   The refrigerant enters as a vapor and leaves as a liquid: a condenser.

75. **A**   The energy equation: $q - w_s = \Delta h$ gives $\Delta h = 0$ with $q = w_s = 0$. Note: w_s is the shaft work. It differs from the total work w by the flow work Pv. For steam $h = h(T, P)$ so $\Delta T \neq 0$, in general.

76. **D** $W = \int P dV = 0$ if $dV = 0$. Note: $W_{2-3} = Q_{2-3} = mRT \ln V_2/V_1$.

77. **D** $Q = -kA\dfrac{\Delta T}{L}\Delta t = -\dfrac{1}{2} \times (3 \times 8)\dfrac{35}{0.025} \times \dfrac{15}{60} = -4200$ kJ.

Note: Make sure the units all check out: $\dfrac{\text{kJ} \cdot \text{m}^2 \cdot {}^\circ\text{C} \cdot \text{hr}}{\text{hr} \cdot \text{m} \cdot {}^\circ\text{C} \cdot \text{m}} = \text{kJ}$.

78. **D** $\mathbf{F}_1 + \mathbf{F}_2 + \mathbf{F}_3 = 100\mathbf{i} - 200\mathbf{k} + 50\mathbf{j} + 50\mathbf{k} - 200\mathbf{i} + 100\mathbf{j} = -100\mathbf{i} + 150\mathbf{j} - 150\mathbf{k}$.
$F = \sqrt{100^2 + 150^2 + 150^2} = 234$.

79. **A**   Sum forces along AB: $90 \times 9.8\cos\theta = F_{AB}$.

$\cos\theta = \dfrac{4}{5}$ so that $F_{AB} = 706$ N. Note: Exaggerate the angle in your sketch so you know that θ is the small angle, i.e., $\cos\theta = 4/5$, and not $3/5$.

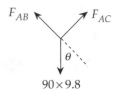

80. **D** $\mathbf{M} = \mathbf{r} \times \mathbf{F} = \big[(0-1)\mathbf{i} + (2-2)\mathbf{j} + (0-3)\mathbf{k}\big] \times (20\mathbf{i} - 30\mathbf{j} + 40\mathbf{k})$
$= (-\mathbf{i} - 3\mathbf{k}) \times (20\mathbf{i} - 30\mathbf{j} + 40\mathbf{k})$.
The z-component is $-\mathbf{i} \times (-30\mathbf{j}) = 30\mathbf{k}$.

81. **C**

82. **B** $M_{wall} = 600 \times 0.4 - 400 \times 0.5 = 240 - 200 = 40$ N·m.

83. **D** $\sum M_A$: $4 \times C_y = 2 \times 800 + 2 \times 400$. $\therefore C_y = 600$ N. $F_{CD} = 0$ from point D.

$\therefore (F_{EC})_y = 600$ N. $(F_{EC})_x = 600$ N $= F_{BC} = F_{AB}$.

84. **C**   <u>If the block slides:</u>

Friction force $= \mu N = \mu W \cos 30° = 0.3 \times (20 \times 9.8) \times 0.866 = 50.9$ N.

$\therefore F = W \sin 30° + 50.9 = 20 \times 9.8 \times 0.5 + 50.9 = 149$ N.

<u>If the block tips:</u>

$F \times \ell = Wg \cos 30° \times \dfrac{\ell}{2} + Wg \sin 30° \times \dfrac{\ell}{2}$. $\therefore F = 20 \times 9.8 \left(\dfrac{0.866}{2} + \dfrac{0.5}{2} \right) = 134$ N.

85. **A**   Since link BC is a two-force member, $\mathbf{F}_{BC}$ must be directed from B to C.

$\therefore C_x = C_y$ $\sum M_A$: $900 \times 8 = C_y \times 24 - C_x \times 8$. $\therefore C_y = 450$ N.

$\therefore F_C = \sqrt{450^2 + 450^2} = 636$ N.

86. **B**   Length $= 4$. Length over $= \ell$. Friction force $= (4 - \ell)mg\mu$.

Weight of part hanging over $= mg\ell$.

$\therefore mg\ell = (4 - \ell)mg\mu$,   or $\ell = (4 - \ell) \times 0.4$. $\therefore \ell = 1.14$ m.

Note: We let m be the mass per unit length of chain.

87. **C** $L_{AC} = \sqrt{75^2 - 60^2} = 45$ cm $\sum M_A$: $B_x \times 60 = (600 \times 0.45) \times \dfrac{45}{2}$. $\therefore B_x = 101$ N.

$\sum M_C$ on link BC: $101 \times 60 = F_{wire} \times \dfrac{45}{2}$. $\therefore F_{wire} = 270$ N.

88. **A** $I_y = (I_y)_C + Ad^2$. $2000 = (I_y)_C + 100 \times 2^2$. $\therefore (I_y)_C = 1600$ cm^4.

89. **D** $y_c = \dfrac{y_{c1}A_1 + y_{c2}A_2 + y_{c3}A_3}{A_1 + A_2 + A_3} = \dfrac{5 \times 20 + 1 \times 8 + 5 \times 20}{20 + 8 + 20} = 4.33$ cm.

90. **B** $a = \dfrac{dv}{dt} = 10 - 2t$. $\therefore \int_{10}^{v} dv = \int_{0}^{t} (10 - 2t)dt$. $v - 10 = 10t - t^2$.

$\therefore v = \dfrac{ds}{dt} = 10t - t^2 + 10$. $\therefore \int_{0}^{s} ds = \int_{0}^{6} (10t - t^2 + 10)dt$.

$s = 5 \times 6^2 - \dfrac{6^3}{3} + 10 \times 6 = 168$ m. $\left(\text{Make sure } v \neq 0 \text{ for } 0 < t < 6.\right)$

91. **D** $\alpha = \dfrac{d\omega}{dt}$. $\omega = \dfrac{d\theta}{dt}$ or $dt = \dfrac{d\theta}{\omega}$. $\therefore \alpha = \omega \dfrac{d\omega}{d\theta}$. $\int_{0}^{\theta} \alpha d\theta = \int_{\omega_0}^{0} \omega d\omega$.

$\therefore \alpha\theta = -\dfrac{\omega_0^2}{2}$. $-20\theta = -\dfrac{1}{2} \left(\dfrac{4000 \times 2\pi}{60} \right)^2$. $\therefore \theta = 4386.5$ rad or 698 rev.

92. D $\quad \mathbf{a}_T = \mathbf{a}_O + \mathbf{a}_{T/O} = 10\mathbf{i} + 0.4 \times 25\mathbf{i} - 0.4 \times 10^2 \mathbf{j} = 20\mathbf{i} - 40\mathbf{j}.$

$a = \sqrt{20^2 + 40^2} = 44.7 \text{ m/s}^2.$

We used $\alpha = \dfrac{a_O}{r} = \dfrac{10}{0.4} = 25 \text{ rad/s}^2$ and $\omega = \dfrac{v}{r} = \dfrac{4}{0.4} = 10 \text{ rad/s}.$

93. B $\quad \mathbf{v}_A = \mathbf{v}_B + \mathbf{v}_{A/B}.$ $\quad v_B = r\omega = 0.1 \times 10 = 1 \text{ m/s}.$

$\therefore v_A = v_B \times \dfrac{10}{\sqrt{300}} = 0.577 \text{ m/s}.$

Note: The velocity triangle is similar to the triangle with legs 10 and $\sqrt{300}$.

94. C $\quad \mathbf{a}_A = \mathbf{a}_B + \mathbf{a}_{A/B}.$ From the velocity diagram of Number 93,

$v_{A/B} = 0.2\omega_{AB} = 1 \times \dfrac{20}{\sqrt{300}}.$ $\quad \therefore \omega_{AB} = 5.77 \text{ rad/s}.$

$r\omega^2 = 0.1 \times 10^2 = 10 \text{ rad/s}^2$ and $.2\omega_{AB}^2 = 6.66.$

Finally, recognizing that a_A is horizontal,

$a_A = 10 + 6.66 / \cos 30° = 17.7 \text{ m/s}^2.$

95. D $\quad$ Assume the 200 kg mass rises: $T - 200 \times 9.8 = 200a.$ $\quad \therefore T = 200a + 1960.$
The friction force is $0.2(400 \times 9.8 \times 0.707) = 554.3 \text{ N}.$ Then summing forces on the 400-kg mass:

$400 \times 9.8 \times 0.707 - 554.3 - T = 400a.$

Substituting T from above:

$2217 - 200a - 1960 = 400a. \quad \therefore a = 0.429 \text{ m/s}^2$ and $T = 2046 \text{ N}.$

96. D $\quad$ Impulse-momentum:

$Fdt = mdv.$ $\quad \displaystyle\int_0^{10} 6t\,dt = \int_0^{v_1} 10\,dv.$ $\quad 300 = 10v_1.$ $\quad \therefore v_1 = 30 \text{ m/s}.$

$\displaystyle\int_{10}^{20} 60\,dt = \int_{30}^{v_2} 10\,dv.$ $\quad 60(20 - 10) = 10(v_2 - 30).$ $\quad \therefore v_2 = 90 \text{ m/s}.$

97. A $\quad$ Work-energy:

$\dfrac{1}{2}Kx^2 = \dfrac{1}{2}mv^2 + \dfrac{1}{2}I\omega^2.$ $\quad \dfrac{1}{2} \times 400 \times \left(\dfrac{400}{400}\right)^2 = \dfrac{1}{2} \times 10v^2 + \dfrac{1}{2}\left(\dfrac{1}{2}10 \times 0.4^2\right)\dfrac{v^2}{0.4^2}.$

$\therefore v = 5.16 \text{ m/s}.$

We used $\omega = v/r$ and $I = \frac{1}{2}mr^2$ for a cylinder.

98. C $\quad F_D = 30v.$ Sum forces:

$20\,000 - 1500 \times 9.8 - 30v = 1500\dfrac{dv}{dt}.$ $\quad 5300 - 30v = 1500\dfrac{dv}{dt},$ or

$\dfrac{-30dv}{5300 - 30dv} = \dfrac{-dt}{50}.$ $\quad \therefore \displaystyle\int_0^v \dfrac{-30dv}{5300 - 30v} = -\int_0^{20} \dfrac{dt}{50}.$ $\quad \ln\dfrac{5300 - 30v}{5300} = -\dfrac{20}{50}.$

$\therefore v = 58.2 \text{ m/s}.$

99. **D** Along the centerline connecting the two balls:

$$e = \frac{v_2' - v_1'}{6 - (-6)} = 0.8. \quad \therefore v_2' - v_1' = 9.6.$$

Also, for the normal direction,

$$m_1 \times 6 - m_2 \times 6 = m_1 v_1' + m_2 v_2'. \quad \text{Since } m_1 = m_2, \; v_1' = -v_2'$$
$$\therefore v_2' = 4.8 \text{ m/s}.$$

100. **B** $\delta_B = \delta_S$ or $\dfrac{P_B L_B}{A_B E_B} = \dfrac{P_S L_S}{A_S E_S}.$ $\quad \therefore P_S = P_B \dfrac{A_S}{A_B} \dfrac{E_S}{E_B} = P_B \dfrac{\pi r^2}{\frac{9}{4}\pi r^2 - \pi r^2} \dfrac{2E_B}{E_B} = \dfrac{8}{5} P_B.$

$$P = P_S + P_B = P_S + \frac{5}{8} P_S. \quad \therefore P_S = \frac{8}{13} P \quad \text{or} \quad P_S = 0.615P \quad \text{or} \quad 61.5\% \text{ of } P.$$

101. **C**

102. **D** The center of Mohr's circle is at 45.

$$\therefore \tau_{\max} = \text{radius} = \sqrt{5^2 + 10^2} = 11.2 \text{ MPa}.$$

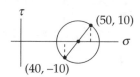

103. **A** $V_{\max} = wL/2.$ $M_{\max} = wL^2/8.$ $\sigma_{\max} = \dfrac{My}{I} = \dfrac{\left(wL^2/8\right)\left(b/2\right)}{b^4/12} = \dfrac{3wL^2}{4b^3}.$

$$\tau_{\max} = \frac{VQ}{Ib} = \frac{\left(wL/2\right)\left(b^3/8\right)}{\left(b^4/12\right)b} = \frac{3wL}{4b^2}. \quad \sigma_{\max}/\tau_{\max} = \frac{3wL^2}{4b^3} \times \frac{4b^2}{3wL} = \frac{L}{b}.$$

Note: $Q = b \times \dfrac{b}{2} \times \dfrac{b}{4} = b^3/8.$

104. **C** The vertical shear diagram is triangular.

105. **D** $\tau = \dfrac{Tr}{J} = \dfrac{300 \times 0.03}{\pi\left(.03^4 - .02^4\right)/2} = 8.81 \times 10^6 \text{ Pa or } 8.81 \text{ MPa}.$

106. **B** The force on the left support is found from $800 \times 4 + 500 \times 10 = 8P.$
$\therefore P = 1025 \text{ N}.$ The force on the right support is 275 N. The greatest moment is at the left support: $M_{\max} = 500 \times 2 = 1000 \text{ N} \cdot \text{m}.$
$$\therefore \sigma_{\max} = My/I = 1000 \times 0.03 / \left(0.02 \times 0.06^3/12\right) = 83.3 \times 10^6 \text{ Pa}.$$

107. **A** $\delta = \dfrac{wL^4}{8EI} + \phi_{\max} \times \ell =$

$$\frac{100 \times 4^4}{8 \times 210 \times 10^9 \times \pi\left(0.02^4\right)/4} + \frac{100 \times 4^3}{6 \times 210 \times 10^9 \times \pi\left(0.02^4\right)/4} \times 2 = 0.202 \text{ m}.$$

108. **D**

109. **C** $p_w + \gamma H = p_o + 0.8\gamma(2H) + 13.6\gamma H.$
$$p_w - p_o = 14.2\gamma H = 14.2 \times 9800 \times 0.25 = 34\,790 \text{ Pa}.$$

110. **A** $F = \gamma h_c A = \gamma \dfrac{H}{2}\left(\dfrac{5}{3}Hw\right) = \dfrac{5}{6}\gamma H^2 w.$ This force acts $1/3$ up from hinge.

$$\therefore P = F/3 = \dfrac{1}{2}\left(\dfrac{5}{6}\gamma H^2 w\right) = \dfrac{5}{18}\gamma H^2 w$$

111. **B** $\dfrac{\pi D^2}{4}\times V = 2\pi Rt \times V_2.$ $\therefore V_2 = \dfrac{D^2 V}{8Rt}.$

112. **A** All choices except A involve flows in which the losses are negligible.

113. **C** $\dfrac{e}{D} = \dfrac{0.15}{20} = 0.0075.$ $\therefore f = 0.034$ (assume fully rough).

$$\Delta p = f\dfrac{L}{D}\dfrac{V^2}{2g}\gamma.\quad 60\,000 = 0.034\dfrac{15}{0.02}\dfrac{V^2}{2\times 9.8}\times 9800.\quad \therefore V = 2.17\ \text{m/s}.$$

$$Q = AV = \pi \times .01^2 \times 2.17 = 6.82\times 10^{-4}\ \text{m}^3/\text{s}\ \text{ or }\ 0.682\ \text{L/s}.$$

114. **C** $h_f = \dfrac{\Delta p}{\gamma} = C\dfrac{V^2}{2g}.$ $V = \dfrac{Q}{A} = \dfrac{0.04}{\pi \times .04^2} = 7.96\ \text{m/s}.$

$$\therefore C = \dfrac{100\,000 \times 2 \times 9.8}{9800 \times 7.96^2} = 3.16.$$

115. **D** Use Eq. 11.4.12: $\dot{W}_p = Q\gamma h = 0.04 \times 9800 \times \dfrac{1200 - 200}{9800} = 40\ \text{kW}.$

$$\therefore \left(\dot{W}_p\right)_{\text{req'd}} = \dfrac{40}{0.85} = 47.1\ \text{kW}.$$

Note: If pressure is in kPa, $\dot{W}$ will be in kW.

116. **D**

117. **B**

118. **B**

119. **A**

120. **C**

FUNDAMENTALS OF ENGINEERING EXAM—General

ANSWER KEY—Afternoon—Diagnostic Exam

(Answers with topical breakout and scoring grid.)

BE SURE EACH MARK IS DARK AND COMPLETELY FILLS THE INTENDED SPACE AS ILLUSTRATED HERE: ●.

MATH

1 ●BCD
2 ABC●
3 ABC●
4 ●BCD
5 AB●D
6 ABC●
7 ABC●
8 ABC●
9 ●BCD
10 A●CD
11 ●BCD
12 AB●D

Score: _____

COMPUTERS

13 AB●D
14 ABC●
15 ●BCD

Score: _____

MATERIALS

16 ABC●
17 ABC●
18 ABC●

Score: _____

CHEMISTRY

19 ●BCD
20 ●BCD
21 ●BCD
22 ABC●

Score: _____

STATICS

23 AB●D
24 A●CD
25 AB●D
26 ABC●
27 ABC●
28 ●BCD

Score: _____

DYNAMICS

29 A●CD
30 ABC●
31 ●BCD
32 ●BCD

Score: _____

MECHANICS

33 ABC●
34 A●CD
35 ABC●
36 AB●D
37 ●BCD

Score: _____

ELECTRICAL

38 ABC●
39 A●CD
40 A●CD
41 AB●D
42 ABC●
43 ABC●

Score: _____

THERMO/FLUIDS

44 A●CD
45 ●BCD
46 AB●D
47 ABC●
48 ABC●
49 ●BCD
50 A●CD
51 ABC●
52 AB●D
53 ●BCD
54 ●BCD

Score: _____

ECONOMICS

55 ●BCD
56 AB●D
57 A●CD

Score: _____

ETHICS

58 A●CD
59 AB●D
60 A●CD

Score: _____

Diagnostic Exam Solutions—Afternoon

1. **D** The slope is $m = \frac{-3}{4}$. $\therefore y = -\frac{3}{4}x + 3$, or $4y + 3x = 12$.

2. **A** Using a horizontal strip: $I = \int_A y^2 \, dA = \int_0^3 y^2 x \, dy$.

3. **C** $|\mathbf{A}| = \begin{vmatrix} 2 & 1 & -2 \\ 0 & 1 & 0 \\ 1 & 2 & 0 \end{vmatrix} = 2.$ $\begin{matrix} 2 & 1 & -2 & 2 & 1 \\ 0 & 1 & 0 & 0 & 1 \\ 1 & 2 & 0 & 1 & 2 \end{matrix}$ $= 0 + 0 + 0 - (-2) - 0 - 0 = 2$.

4. **D** $\begin{bmatrix} 1 & -2 & 0 \end{bmatrix} \begin{bmatrix} 3 \\ -1 \\ 0 \end{bmatrix} = [3 + 2 + 0] = [5]$.

5. **C** $\begin{vmatrix} 2-\lambda & 1 & -2 \\ 0 & 1-\lambda & 0 \\ 1 & 2 & -\lambda \end{vmatrix} = (1-\lambda)[(2-\lambda)(-\lambda) + 2] = (1-\lambda)(\lambda^2 - 2\lambda + 2) = 0.$

   $\therefore \lambda = 1$ is one of the eigenvalues.

6. **C** $\begin{bmatrix} 2 & 1 & -2 \\ 0 & 1 & 0 \\ 1 & 2 & 0 \end{bmatrix} \begin{bmatrix} x_1 \\ x_2 \\ x_3 \end{bmatrix} = \begin{bmatrix} 3 \\ -1 \\ 0 \end{bmatrix}.$ $x_1 = \dfrac{\begin{vmatrix} 3 & 1 & -2 \\ -1 & 1 & 0 \\ 0 & 2 & 0 \end{vmatrix}}{\begin{vmatrix} 2 & 1 & -2 \\ 0 & 1 & 0 \\ 1 & 2 & 0 \end{vmatrix}} = \dfrac{4}{2} = 2.$

7. **D** At $(1, 2, 0)$ we find $(3\mathbf{i} + 2\mathbf{j} - \mathbf{k}) \times (\mathbf{i} + 2\mathbf{k}) = -6\mathbf{j} - 2\mathbf{k} + 4\mathbf{i} - \mathbf{j} = 4\mathbf{i} - 7\mathbf{j} - 2\mathbf{k}$.
   Then, $(4\mathbf{i} - 7\mathbf{j} - 2\mathbf{k}) \cdot (2\mathbf{i} - 4\mathbf{j}) = 8 + 28 = 36$.

8. **D** $\nabla \cdot \mathbf{C} = \left(\dfrac{\partial}{\partial x} \mathbf{i} + \dfrac{\partial}{\partial y} \mathbf{j} + \dfrac{\partial}{\partial z} \mathbf{k} \right) \cdot \mathbf{C}$
   $= y - 2y - y = -2y = -4$

9. **B** $x'' + 4x = 0$ is the homogeneous equation. $r^2 + 4 = 0$. $r = \pm 2i$.
   $\therefore x(t) = C_1 e^{2it} + C_2 e^{-2it} = A \cos 2t + B \sin 2t$. Either form is acceptable.

10. **A** Assume $x_p(t) = Ae^{2t}$. $x_p' = 2Ae^{2t}$ and $x_p'' = 4Ae^{2t}$.
    Then $4Ae^{2t} + 4Ae^{2t} = 8e^{2t}$. $\therefore 8A = 8$. $\therefore A = 1$ and $x_p(t) = e^{2t}$.

11. **D** $x'' + 5x' + 4x = 0.$ $r^2 + 5r + 4 = 0.$ $(r+4)(r+1) = 0.$ $r = -4, \ -1.$

$\therefore x_h(t) = C_1 e^{-4t} + C_2 e^{-t}.$

Assume $x_p(t) = A \sin 2t + B \cos 2t.$ Then

$-4A \sin 2t - 4B \cos 2t + 10A \cos 2t - 10B \sin 2t + 4A \sin 2t + 4B \cos 2t = 20 \sin 2t.$

$\therefore A = 0$ and $-10B = 20$ or $B = -2.$

$\therefore x_p(t) = C_1 e^{-4t} + C_2 e^{-t} - 2 \cos 2t.$ $\left. \begin{array}{l} x(0) = 0 = C_1 + C_2 - 2. \\ x'(0) = 10 = -4C_1 - C_2 \end{array} \right\} \therefore C_1 = -4$ and $C_2 = 6.$

12. **C**   This is resonance: the input frequency ω equals the natural frequency of 2 rad/s. (See Problem 9 for the natural frequency.)

13. **C**

14. **D**   The value in cell G3 will be AVG (1, 4, 10) = 5. The value in cell H3 will be AVG (4, 10, 5) = 6.3333... The value in cell I3 will be AVG (10, 5, 6.3333...) + 7.1111...

15. **A**

16. **D**   Carbon atoms form a locking of dislocations (called Cottrell atmosphere) thereby a higher stress is necessary to initiate dislocation motion. Once the dislocations are freed, they can move under a lower applied stress, and thus the stress drops giving rise to an yield point.

17. **D**   An eutectic point is where two solids coexist with one liquid. Composition C_2 is not such a composition.

18. **B**

19. **A**   Gallium, element number 31 in the Periodic Table, has 31 electrons. Answer (D) has only 29 electrons. Answer (B) has $3f$ electrons. There are no f orbitals in the 3 shell. Answer (C) has empty $3d$ orbitals. Only (A) remains and is correct.

20. **A**   In this reaction the pressure decreases as products on the right are formed since there are 3 molecules of gaseous reactants on the left (O_2 + 2HCl) and only 2 on the right. therefore increasing the pressure should drive the reaction to the right in order to decrease the pressure (Le Chatelier Principle)and will increase the amount of heat evolved.

21. **A**   Since solids do not enter into the equilibrium constant only p(CO_2) is important.

22. **D**   An atom bonded only to itself has oxidation number = 0. In Mg_3N_2, Mg has oxidation no. 2^+ (an alkaline earth). $\therefore$ to make a net 0, N must have 3^-. Any reduction in oxidation no. (0 to –3) reduces the element.

23. **C** $\sum M_C = 0.$ $\therefore 400 \times 80 \cos 45° = F_{AB} \times 80 \sin 45°.$ $\therefore F_{AB} = 400$ N.

24. **B** Link BC is pinned at both ends.

$$\therefore P_{cr} = \frac{\pi^2 EI}{L^2} = \frac{\pi^2 \times 210 \times 10^9 \times \pi \times .008^4/4}{.8^2} = 10\,420 \text{ N.}$$

The force in link BC is $\sqrt{2}P$. $\therefore P = 10\,420/\sqrt{2} = 7366$ N.

25. **C** $\delta_{BC} = \alpha L(T_2 - T_1) = 11.7 \times 10^{-6} \times 800 \times 40 = 0.374$ mm.

$\therefore \overline{BB}' = \sqrt{2} \times .374 = .529$ mm.

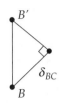

26. **D** $0.866\,L \times 6000 - 4000 \times 2.5L + 3LA_y = 0$. $\therefore A_y = 1601$ N.

$A_x = 6000$ N. $\therefore A = \sqrt{A_x^2 + A_y^2} = 6210$ N.

27. **D** $D_y + A_y = 4000$. $\therefore D_y = 4000 - 1601 = 2399$ N.

$F_{DE} \times 0.866 = 2399$. $\therefore F_{DE} = 2770$ N. $F_{CD} = 0.5\,F_{DE} = 1385$ N.

28. **A** $\bar{y} = \dfrac{24(6) + 20 \times 1}{2 \times 12 + 10 \times 2} = 3.727$ cm

$$I_{\text{N.A.}} = I_{\text{base}} - Ad^2$$
$$= 2 \times 12^3/3 + 10 \times 2^3/3 - 44 \times 3.727^2 = 576 \text{ cm}^4$$

29. **B** Point C is the instant center for velocity. $\therefore \omega = \dfrac{v}{r} = \dfrac{20}{1.00} = 20$ rad/s.

The speed of point B is $v_B = r_{BC}\omega = 0.5\sqrt{2} \times 20 = 14.14$ m/s.

30. **D** There is a friction force acting at C in the x-direction.

$$\sum F_x = ma_O \qquad \sum M_O = I\alpha$$
$$P - F = ma_O \qquad Pr + Fr = \frac{1}{2}mr^2\alpha$$

Combine the two equations, letting $r\alpha = a_O$, and

$$2P = \frac{3}{2}ma_O. \therefore a_O = \frac{4P}{3m} = \frac{4 \times 300}{3 \times 50} = 8 \text{ m/s}^2.$$

31. **A** $F = P - ma_O = 300 - 50 \times 8 = 300 - 400 = -100$ N. $\therefore F$ acts to the right.

32. **A** Work-energy since force and distance are specified:

Work $= 300 \times 2 = 600$ N·m.

$$\text{Energy} = \frac{1}{2}mv_0^2 + \frac{1}{2}I\omega^2 = \frac{1}{2}50v_0^2 + \frac{1}{2}\left(\frac{1}{2}50 \times .5^2\right)\frac{v_0^2}{.5^2} = \frac{3}{4} \times 50v_0^2.$$

$$\therefore 600 = \frac{3}{4} \times 50v_0^2. \therefore v_0 = 4 \text{ m/s.}$$

Note: The friction force does no work since point C moves vertically.

33. **D** $\sigma_{max} = \dfrac{My}{I} = \dfrac{3300 \times .0275}{1.848 \times 10^{-6}} = 49.1 \times 10^6$ Pa.

34. **B** $\tau_{max} = \dfrac{VQ}{Ib} = \dfrac{1000 \times .01 \times (.09 - .0275)^2 / 2}{1.848 \times 10^{-6} \times .01} = 1.057 \times 10^6$ Pa.

35. **D** $\delta = \delta_P + \delta_w + \ell\theta_w = \dfrac{P(2\ell)^3}{3EI} + \dfrac{w_0\ell^4}{8EI} + \ell\dfrac{w_0\ell^3}{6EI}$

$= \left(\dfrac{400 \times 6^3}{3} + \dfrac{200 \times 3^4}{8} + \dfrac{200 \times 3^4}{6} \right) \Big/ 210 \times 10^9 \times 1.848 \times 10^{-6} = 0.0864$ m.

36. **C** $2\ell = 20 - (-4) = 24.$ $\therefore \ell = 12.$

$\therefore r = \sqrt{12^2 + 5^2} = 13.$

$\therefore \sigma_{max} = 20 - \ell + r = 20 - 12 + 13 = 21$ MPa.

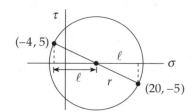

37. **A** $\sin 2\alpha = \dfrac{5}{13}.$ $\therefore 2\alpha = 22.62°$

$\sin(2\alpha + 2\phi) = \dfrac{12 - 4}{13}.$ $\therefore 2\alpha + 2\phi = 37.98°.$

$\therefore \phi = 7.7°.$

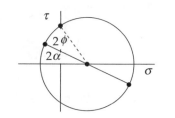

38. **D**   If $I_G = 0$ then the current in the $30\,\Omega$ resistor equals the current in the $60\,\Omega$ resistor, likewise in R_X and the $20\,\Omega$ resistor. Therefore

$\left. \begin{array}{c} I_1 30 = I_2 20 \\ I_1 60 = I_2 R_X \end{array} \right\} \Rightarrow R_X = \dfrac{60}{30} \times 20 = 40\ \Omega.$

39. **B** $V_S - I(10) - I(j20) - I(-j30) = 0.$

$I = \dfrac{V_S}{10 + j20 - j30} = \dfrac{50\angle 0°}{10 - j10} = 2.5 + j2.5 = 3.54\angle 45°$ A.

40. **B**   First reflect the $100\ \Omega$ resistor to the transformer primary and find I_P.

$Z_P = \left(\dfrac{N_1}{N_2} \right)^2 Z_S = \left(\dfrac{1}{2} \right)^2 (100 - j100) = 25 - j25$

$I_P = \dfrac{50\angle 0°}{40 - j25} = 1.06\angle 32°$ A

$I_S = \left(\dfrac{N_1}{N_2} \right) I_P = \left(\dfrac{1}{2} \right) 1.06 = 0.53$ A

$P = I^2 R = (0.53)^2 100 = 28.1$ W.

41. **C** $I_{rms} = \sqrt{\dfrac{1}{T} \int_0^T i^2(t)dt}$, find $\int_0^T i^2(t)dt$ graphically.

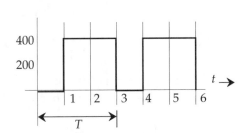

$$\int_0^T i^2 dt = 400 \times 2 = 800 \ \text{amp}^2 \cdot \text{sec}$$

$$I_{rms} = \sqrt{\frac{1}{3} \times 800} = 16.33 \ \text{A}$$

42. **D**   Find the source current I_S. Reactive power $Q = V_S I_S \sin\theta$. The total impedance seen at the source is:

$$Z_S = +j4 + \frac{(-j10)(25+j25)}{(-j10)+(25+j25)} = 8.30\angle -69.25° \ \text{ohm}$$

$$I_S = \frac{120\angle 0°}{8.30\angle -69.25°} = 14.46\angle 69.25°$$

$$Q = (120)(14.46)\sin 69.25 = 1623 \ \text{VARS}.$$

43. **D**   The gain of stage 1: $\dfrac{v_{01}}{v_{in}} = -\dfrac{R_F}{R_i} = -\dfrac{200}{100} = -2$

The gain of stage 2: $\dfrac{v_0}{v_{01}} = \left(1 + \dfrac{R_F}{R_i}\right) = 1 + \dfrac{300}{100} = 4$

The overall gain: $\dfrac{v_0}{v_{in}} = \dfrac{v_{01}}{v_{in}} \times \dfrac{v_0}{v_{01}} = (-2)(4) = -8.$

44. **B** $q_{in} = q_{2-3} = u_3 - u_2 + \cancel{w_{2-3}}^{\,0} = c_v(T_3 - T_2)$

$\qquad\quad = 0.718(1473 - 673) = 574 \ \text{kJ/kg}.$

We used $T_2 = T_1\left(\dfrac{v_1}{v_2}\right)^{k-1} = 293 \times 8^{1.4-1} = 673 \ \text{K}.$

45. **A** $w_{net} = q_{net} = q_{in} - q_{out}. \qquad q_{out} = -q_{4-1} = c_v(T_4 - T_1).$

$\qquad\quad = 574 - 0.718(641 - 293) = 324 \ \text{kJ/kg}.$

We used $T_4 = T_3\left(\dfrac{v_4}{v_3}\right)^{k-1} = 1473\left(\dfrac{1}{8}\right)^{0.4} = 641 \ \text{K}.$

Note: q_{in} was taken from Problem 44. Also, $w_{net} = q_{net}$ is the 1st law for a cycle.

46. **C** $\eta = \dfrac{w_{net}}{q_{add}} = \dfrac{324}{574} = 0.564.$

47. **D** $\eta_{Carnot} = 1 - \dfrac{T_L}{T_H} = 1 - \dfrac{293}{1473} = 0.801.$

48. **D** $-w_{1-2} = (u_2 - u_1) = c_v(T_2 - T_1)$. Note: q_{1-2} is zero since it's an isentropic process. We use Δu since it's a piston-cylinder, i.e., a system (not a control volume).

49. **A**

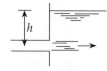

50. **B** $p_A = \gamma h = 9800 \times 10 = 98\,000$ Pa.

Note: The pressure inside the exiting stream is the same as that outside the stream. So the pressure is simply due to the static head.

51. **D** $V = \dfrac{Q}{A} = \dfrac{0.8}{\pi \times 0.6^2} = 0.707$ m/s. $\dfrac{e}{D} = \dfrac{0.25}{1200} = 0.00021$.

$\text{Re} = \dfrac{0.707 \times 1.2}{10^{-6}} = 8.5 \times 10^5$. $\therefore f = 0.015$.

Energy:

$40 = \dfrac{p_i}{9800} + \dfrac{0.707^2}{2 \times 9.8} + \left(0.5 + 0.015 \times \dfrac{800}{1.2}\right)\dfrac{0.707^2}{2 \times 9.8}$. $\therefore p_i = 389\,000$ Pa.

52. **C** $h_T = \dfrac{\Delta p}{\gamma} = \dfrac{389\,000 - 98\,000}{9800} = 29.7$ m.

$\therefore \dot{W}_T = Q\gamma h_T \eta = 0.8 \times 9800 \times 29.7 \times 0.89 = 2.07 \times 10^5$ W

53. **A** $p_{\min} = -100$ kPa. $\dfrac{0.707^2}{2 \times 9.8} + \dfrac{389\,000}{9800} = \dfrac{V_{\max}^2}{2 \times 9.8} + \dfrac{-100\,000}{9800}$.

$\therefore V_{\max} = 31.3$ m/s.

Note: The lowest possible pressure at the nozzle exit is absolute zero (vapor pressure is quite close to absolute zero).

54. **A**   Flow around blades is an internal flow that involves viscous and inertia forces: Reynolds number.

55. **A** $0 = (5 - 3) \times 10^6 (P/A)_\infty^i - 50 \times 10^6$. $(P/A)_\infty^i = 1/i = 25$. $\therefore i = 4\%$.

56. **C** $B/C = \left[(5 - 3) \times 10^6\right]\Big/\left[50 \times 10^6 (A/P)_\infty^6\right] = 0.67$.

57. **B** $A = 0.05 \times 5000 = \$250$. $P = 250(P/A)_{20}^6 + 5000(P/F)_{20}^6 = \$4426$.

58. **B**

59. **C**

60. **B**

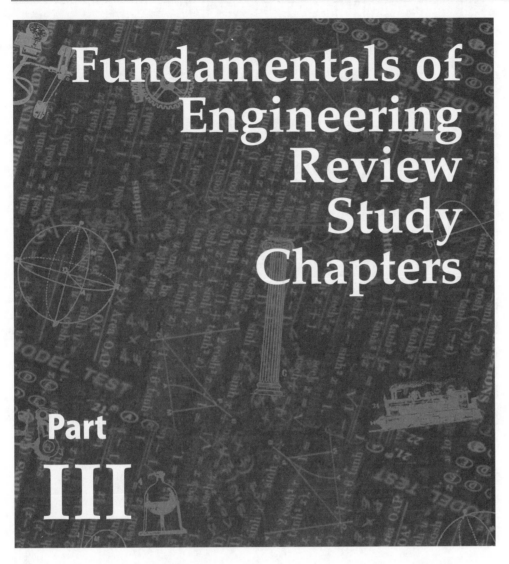

Fundamentals of Engineering Review Study Chapters

Part III

If you seek to reduce the amount of time required for your review, ideally you will have by now completed the Diagnostic Exam and identified your weakest subjects. You may then concentrate your review on your weaker areas.

However, if you are reviewing all the material, the chapters are organized so that you may begin with the Math chapter and continue in sequence through the book. Note that we present Statics, then Dynamics, then Solid Mechanics, then Fluid Mechanics—the same order in which the courses are offered in most engineering programs. The remaining subjects can be reviewed in any order.

You'll find that the chapters with numerous Practice Problems will have some of the problems starred with asterisks. If you are trying to save time, then work only the starred problems, which cover only the most essential information.

The problem solutions following each chapter outline only the most crucial steps. The examples in each chapter provide more detailed analyses of the most essential problem-solving methods. By both studying the examples and working the Practice Problems, you should be well prepared for the FE/EIT examination.

Use the NCEES Handbook as you work through the Practice Problems of the review chapters. It is essential that you become familiar with that Handbook so you will quickly know which equations to use when taking the test.

Mathematics

by Merle C. Potter

Chapter 1

Strategic Study Note

If you're planning a short review and you're outlining the NCEES Handbook, omit reviewing the following Handbook subjects since they will not likely be tested in the FE/EIT exam:

- Progressions and Series
- Probability and Statistics (except mean, median, and mode values)
- Curvature
- Fourier Series
- Fourier Transforms
- Difference Equations
- Numerical Methods

Introduction

The engineer uses mathematics as a tool to help solve the problems encountered in the analysis and design of physical systems. We will review those parts of mathematics that are used fairly often by the engineer and which may appear on the exam. The topics include: algebra, trigonometry, analytic geometry, linear algebra (matrices), calculus, differential equations, and probability and statistics. The review here is intended to be brief and not exhaustive. The majority of the questions on the exam will be based on the material included in this chapter. There may be a few questions, however, that will require information not covered here; to cover all possible points would not be in the spirit of an efficient review.

1.1 Algebra

It is assumed that the reader is familiar with most of the rules and laws of algebra as applied to both real and complex numbers. We will review some of the more important of these and illustrate several with examples. The three basic rules are:

commutative law:	$a + b = b + a$	$ab = ba$	**(1.1.1)**
distributive law:	$a(b + c) = ab + ac$		**(1.1.2)**
associative law:	$a + (b + c) = (a + b) + c$	$a(bc) = (ab)c$	**(1.1.3)**

Exponents

Laws of exponents are used in many manipulations. For positive x and y we use

$$x^{-a} = \frac{1}{x^a}$$

$$x^a x^b = x^{a+b}$$

$$(xy)^a = x^a y^a \qquad \textbf{(1.1.4)}$$

$$x^{ab} = \left(x^a\right)^b$$

Logarithms

Logarithms are actually exponents. For example if $b^x = y$ then $x = \log_b y$; that is, the exponent x is equal to the logarithm of y to the base b. Most engineering applications involve common logs which have a base of 10, written as $\log y$, or natural logs which have a base of e ($e = 2.7183 \cdots$), written as $\ln y$. If any other base is used it will be so designated, such as $\log_5 y$.

Remember, logarithms of numbers less than one are negative, the logarithm of one is zero, and logarithms of numbers greater than one are positive. The following identities are often useful when manipulating logarithms:

$$\ln x^a = a \ln x$$
$$\ln(xy) = \ln x + \ln y$$
$$\ln(x/y) = \ln x - \ln y$$
$$\ln x = 2.303 \log x$$
$$\log_b b = 1 \qquad \textbf{(1.1.5)}$$
$$\ln 1 = 0$$
$$\ln e^a = a$$
$$\log_a y = x \quad \text{implies } a^x = y$$

The Quadratic Formula and the Binomial Theorem

We often encounter the quadratic equation $ax^2 + bx + c = 0$ when solving engineering problems. The *quadratic formula* provides its solution; it is

$$x = \frac{-b \pm \sqrt{b^2 - 4ac}}{2a} \qquad \textbf{(1.1.6)}$$

If $b^2 < 4ac$, the two roots are complex numbers. Cubic and higher order equations are most often solved by trial and error.

The *binomial theorem* is used to expand an algebraic expression of the form $(a + x)^n$. It is

$$(a + x)^n = a^n + na^{n-1}x + \frac{n(n-1)}{2!}a^{n-2}x^2 + \cdots \qquad \textbf{(1.1.7)}$$

If n is a positive integer, the expansion contains $(n + 1)$ terms. If it is a negative integer or a fraction, an infinite series expansion results.

A rational fraction $P(x) / Q(x)$, where $P(x)$ and $Q(x)$ are polynomials, can be resolved into partial fractions for the following cases.

Partial Fractions

Case 1: $Q(x)$ factors into n different linear terms,

$$Q(x) = (x - a_1)(x - a_2)...(x - a_n)$$

Then

$$\frac{P(x)}{Q(x)} = \sum_{i=1}^{n} \frac{A_i}{x - a_i} \qquad \text{(1.1.8)}$$

Case 2: $Q(x)$ factors into n identical terms,

$$Q(x) = (x - a)^n$$

Then

$$\frac{P(x)}{Q(x)} = \sum_{i=1}^{n} \frac{A_i}{(x - a)^i} \qquad \text{(1.1.9)}$$

Case 3: $Q(x)$ factors into n different quadratic terms,

$$Q(x) = \left(x^2 + a_1 x + b_1\right)\left(x^2 + a_2 x + b_2\right)...\left(x^2 + a_n x + b_n\right)$$

Then

$$\frac{P(x)}{Q(x)} = \sum_{i=1}^{n} \frac{A_i\, x + B_i}{x^2 + a_i\, x + b_i} \qquad \text{(1.1.10)}$$

Case 4: $Q(x)$ factors into n identical quadratic terms,

$$Q(x) = \left(x^2 + ax + b\right)^n$$

Then

$$\frac{P(x)}{Q(x)} = \sum_{i=1}^{n} \frac{A_i\, x + B_i}{\left(x^2 + a\, x + b\right)^i} \qquad \text{(1.1.11)}$$

Case 5: $Q(x)$ factors into a combination of the above. The partial fractions are the obvious ones from the appropriate expansions above.

Example 1.1

The temperature at a point in a body is given by $T(t) = 100e^{-0.02t}$. At what value of t does $T = 20$?

Solution. The equation takes the form

$$20 = 100e^{-0.02t}$$

$$0.2 = e^{-0.02t}$$

Take the natural logarithm of both sides and obtain

$$\ln 0.2 = \ln e^{-0.02t}$$

Using a calculator, we find

$$-1.6094 = -0.02t$$

$$\therefore t = 80.47$$

Example 1.2

Solve for V if $3V^2 + 6V = 10$.

Solution. Use the quadratic formula, Eq. 1.1.6. In standard form, the equation is

$$3V^2 + 6V - 10 = 0$$

The solution is then

$$V = \frac{-6 \pm \sqrt{36 - 4 \times 3 \times (-10)}}{2 \times 3} = \frac{-6 \pm 12.49}{6}$$
$$= 1.082 \quad \text{or} \quad -3.082$$

Note: Some problems may not permit a negative answer, so $V = 1.082$ would be the selection.

Example 1.3

Resolve $\dfrac{3x - 1}{x^2 + x - 6}$ into partial fractions.

Solution. The denominator is factored into

$$x^2 + x - 6 = (x + 3)(x - 2)$$

Using Case 1 there results

$$\frac{3x - 1}{x^2 + x - 6} = \frac{A_1}{x + 3} + \frac{A_2}{x - 2}$$

This can be written as

$$\frac{3x - 1}{x^2 + x - 6} = \frac{A_1(x - 2) + A_2(x + 3)}{(x + 3)(x - 2)}$$

$$= \frac{(A_1 + A_2)x - 2A_1 + 3A_2}{(x + 3)(x - 2)}$$

The numerators on both sides must be equal. Equating the coefficients of the various powers of x provides us with two equations:

$$A_1 + A_2 = 3$$
$$-2A_1 + 3A_2 = -1$$

These are solved quite easily to give $A_2 = 1$, $A_1 = 2$. Finally,

$$\frac{3x - 1}{x^2 + x - 6} = \frac{2}{x + 3} + \frac{1}{x - 2}$$

1.2 Trigonometry

The primary functions in trigonometry involve the ratios between the sides of a right triangle. Referring to the right triangle in Fig. 1.1, the functions are defined by

$$\sin \theta = \frac{y}{r}, \qquad \cos \theta = \frac{x}{r}, \qquad \tan \theta = \frac{y}{x} \tag{1.2.1}$$

In addition, there are three other functions that find occasional use, namely,

$$\cot \theta = \frac{x}{y}, \qquad \sec \theta = \frac{r}{x}, \qquad \csc \theta = \frac{r}{y} \tag{1.2.2}$$

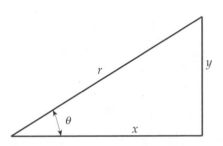

$$r^2 = x^2 + y^2$$

Figure 1.1 A right triangle.

The angle θ is usually given in radians for mathematical equations.

The trig functions $\sin \theta$ and $\cos \theta$ are periodic functions with a period of 2π. Fig. 1.2 shows a plot of the three primary functions.

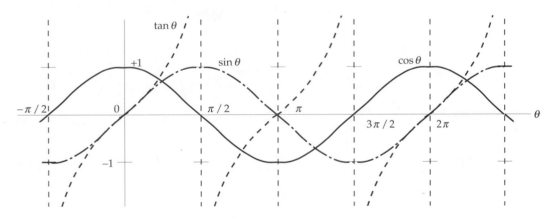

Figure 1.2 The trig functions.

In the above relationships, the angle θ is usually given in radians for mathematical equations. It is possible, however, to express the angle in degrees; if that is done it may be necessary to relate degrees to radians. This can be done by remembering that there are 2π radians in $360°$. Hence, we multiply radians by $(180/\pi)$ to obtain degrees, or multiply degrees by $(\pi/180)$ to obtain radians. A calculator may use either degrees or radians for an input angle.

Most problems involving trigonometry can be solved using a few fundamental identities. They are

$$\sin^2\theta + \cos^2\theta = 1 \tag{1.2.3}$$

$$\sin 2\theta = 2\sin\theta\cos\theta \tag{1.2.4}$$

$$\cos 2\theta = \cos^2\theta - \sin^2\theta \tag{1.2.5}$$

$$\sin(\alpha \pm \beta) = \sin\alpha\cos\beta \pm \sin\beta\cos\alpha \tag{1.2.6}$$

$$\cos(\alpha \pm \beta) = \cos\alpha\cos\beta \mp \sin\alpha\sin\beta \tag{1.2.7}$$

A general triangle may be encountered such as that shown in Fig. 1.3. For this triangle we may use the following equations:

$$\text{law of sines: } \frac{\sin\alpha}{a} = \frac{\sin\beta}{b} = \frac{\sin\gamma}{c} \tag{1.2.8}$$

$$\text{law of cosines: } c^2 = a^2 + b^2 - 2ab\cos\gamma \tag{1.2.9}$$

Note that if $\gamma = 90°$, the law of cosines becomes the *Pythagorean Theorem*

$$c^2 = a^2 + b^2 \tag{1.2.10}$$

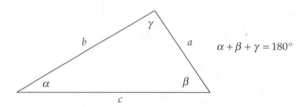

$$\alpha + \beta + \gamma = 180°$$

Figure 1.3 A general triangle.

The hyperbolic trig functions also find occasional use. They are defined by

$$\sinh x = \frac{e^x - e^{-x}}{2}, \quad \cosh x = \frac{e^x + e^{-x}}{2}, \quad \tanh x = \frac{\sinh x}{\cosh x} \tag{1.2.11}$$

Useful identities follow:

$$\cosh^2 x - \sinh^2 x = 1 \tag{1.2.12}$$

$$\sinh(x \pm y) = \sinh x \cosh y \pm \cosh x \sinh y \tag{1.2.13}$$

$$\cosh(x \pm y) = \cosh x \cosh y \pm \sinh x \sinh y \tag{1.2.14}$$

The values of the primary trig functions of certain angles are listed in Table 1.1.

TABLE 1.1 Functions of Certain Angles

	0	30°	45°	60°	90°	135°	180°	270°	360°
$\sin\theta$	0	$1/2$	$\sqrt{2}/2$	$\sqrt{3}/2$	1	$\sqrt{2}/2$	0	-1	0
$\cos\theta$	1	$\sqrt{3}/2$	$\sqrt{2}/2$	$1/2$	0	$-\sqrt{2}/2$	-1	0	1
$\tan\theta$	0	$1/\sqrt{3}$	1	$\sqrt{3}$	∞	-1	0	$-\infty$	0

Example 1.4

Express $\cos^2 \theta$ as a function of $\cos 2\theta$.

Solution. Substitute Eq. 1.2.3 into Eq. 1.2.5 and obtain

$$\cos 2\theta = \cos^2 \theta - \left(1 - \cos^2 \theta\right)$$

$$= 2\cos^2 \theta - 1$$

There results

$$\cos^2 \theta = \frac{1}{2}\left(1 + \cos 2\theta\right)$$

Example 1.5

If $\sin \theta = x$, what is $\tan \theta$?

Solution. Think of $x = x/1$. Thus, the hypotenuse of an imaginary triangle is of length unity and the side opposite θ is of length x. The adjacent side is of length $\sqrt{1 - x^2}$. Hence,

$$\tan \theta = \frac{x}{\sqrt{1 - x^2}}$$

Example 1.6

An airplane leaves Lansing flying due southwest at 300 km/hr, and a second leaves Lansing at the same time flying due west at 500 km/hr. How far apart are the airplanes after 2 hours?

Solution. After 2 hours, the respective distances from Lansing are 600 km and 1000 km. A sketch is quite helpful. The distance d that the two airplanes are apart is found using the law of cosines:

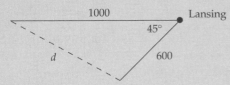

$$d^2 = 1000^2 + 600^2 - 2 \times 1000 \times 600 \cos 45^\circ$$

$$= 511470$$

$$\therefore d = 715.2 \text{ km}$$

1.3 Geometry

A regular polygon with n sides has a vertex angle (the central angle subtended by one side) of $2\pi/n$. The included angle between two successive sides is given by $\pi(n-2)/n$. Some common geometric shapes are displayed in Fig. 1.4.

The equation of a straight line can be written in the general form

$$Ax + By + C = 0 \qquad \text{(1.3.1)}$$

There are three particular forms that this equation can take. They are:

$$\text{Point} - \text{slope:} \qquad y - y_1 = m(x - x_1) \qquad \text{(1.3.2)}$$

$$\text{Slope} - \text{intercept:} \quad y = mx + b \qquad \text{(1.3.3)}$$

$$\text{Two} - \text{intercept:} \quad \frac{x}{a} + \frac{y}{b} = 1 \qquad \text{(1.3.4)}$$

In the above equations m is the slope, (x_1, y_1) a point on the line, "a" the x-intercept, and "b" the y-intercept (see Fig. 1.5). The perpendicular distance d from the point (x_3, y_3) to the line $Ax + By + C = 0$ is given by (see Fig. 1.5)

$$d = \frac{\left| Ax_3 + By_3 + C \right|}{\sqrt{A^2 + B^2}} \qquad \text{(1.3.5)}$$

The equation of a plane surface is given as

$$Ax + By + Cz + D = 0 \qquad \text{(1.3.6)}$$

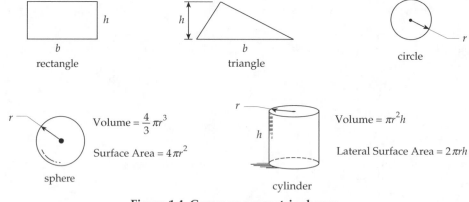

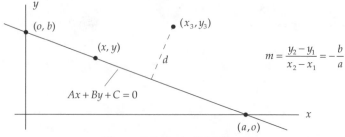

Figure 1.4 Common geometric shapes.

Figure 1.5 A straight line.

The general equation of second degree

$$Ax^2 + 2Bxy + Cy^2 + 2Dx + 2Ey + F = 0 \qquad \textbf{(1.3.7)}$$

represents a set of geometric shapes called *conic sections*. They are classified as follows:

Ellipse: $B^2 - AC < 0$ (circle: $B = 0$, $A = C$)

Parabola: $B^2 - AC = 0$ **(1.3.8)**

Hyperbola: $B^2 - AC > 0$

If $A = B = C = 0$, the equation represents a line in the xy-plane, not a parabola. Let's consider each in detail.

Circle: The circle is a special case of an ellipse with $A = C$. Its general form can be expressed as

$$(x-a)^2 + (y-b)^2 = r^2 \qquad \textbf{(1.3.9)}$$

where its center is at (a, b) and r is the radius.

Ellipse: The sum of the distances from the two foci, F, to any point on an ellipse is a constant. For an ellipse centered at the origin

$$\frac{x^2}{a^2} + \frac{y^2}{b^2} = 1 \qquad \textbf{(1.3.10)}$$

where a and b are the semi-major and semi-minor axes. The foci are at $(\pm c, 0)$ where $c^2 = a^2 - b^2$. See Fig. 1.6a.

Parabola: The locus of points on a parabola are equidistant from the focus and a line (the directrix). If the vertex is at the origin and the parabola opens to the right, it is written as

$$y^2 = 2px \qquad \textbf{(1.3.11)}$$

where the focus is at $(p/2, 0)$ and the directrix is at $x = -p/2$. See Fig. 1.6b. For a parabola opening to the left, simply change the sign of p. For a parabola opening upward or downward, interchange x and y.

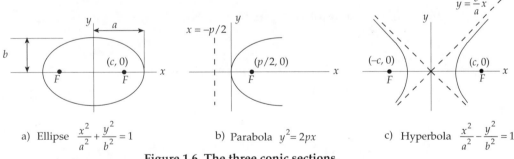

a) Ellipse $\dfrac{x^2}{a^2} + \dfrac{y^2}{b^2} = 1$ b) Parabola $y^2 = 2px$ c) Hyperbola $\dfrac{x^2}{a^2} - \dfrac{y^2}{b^2} = 1$

Figure 1.6 The three conic sections.

Hyperbola: The difference of the distances from the foci to any point on a hyperbola is a constant. For a hyperbola centered at the origin opening left and right, the equation can be written as

$$\frac{x^2}{a^2} - \frac{y^2}{b^2} = 1 \qquad \textbf{(1.3.12)}$$

The lines to which the hyperbola is asymptotic are asymptotes:

$$y = \pm \frac{b}{a} x \qquad \textbf{(1.3.13)}$$

If the asymptotes are perpendicular, a rectangular hyperbola results. If the asymptotes are the x and y axes, the equation can be written as

$$xy = \pm k^2 \tag{1.3.14}$$

Finally, in our review of geometry, we will present three other coordinate systems often used in engineering analysis. They are the polar (r, θ) coordinate system, the cylindrical (r, θ, z) coordinate system, and the spherical (r, θ, ϕ) coordinate system. The polar coordinate system is restricted to a plane:

$$x = r\cos\theta, \quad y = r\sin\theta \tag{1.3.15}$$

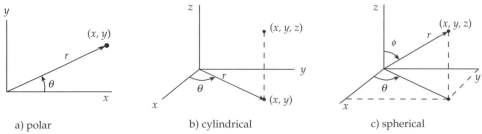

a) polar   b) cylindrical   c) spherical

Figure 1.7 The polar, cylindrical and spherical coordinate systems.

For the cylindrical coordinate system

$$x = r\cos\theta, \quad y = r\sin\theta, \quad z = z \tag{1.3.16}$$

And, for the spherical coordinate system

$$x = r\sin\phi\cos\theta,$$
$$y = r\sin\phi\sin\theta,$$
$$z = r\cos\phi \tag{1.3.17}$$

Example 1.7

What conic section is represented by $2x^2 - 4xy + 5x = 10$?

Solution. Comparing this with the general form Eq. 1.3.7, we see that

$$A = 2, \qquad B = -2, \qquad C = 0$$

Thus, $B^2 - AC = 4$, which is greater than zero. Hence, the conic section is a hyperbola.

Example 1.8

Calculate the radius of the circle given by $x^2 + y^2 - 4x + 6y = 12$.

Solution. Write the equation in standard form (see Eq. 1.3.9):

$$(x - 2)^2 + (y + 3)^2 = 25$$

The radius is $r = \sqrt{25} = 5$.

Note: the terms $-4x$ and $6y$ demanded that we write $(x - 2)^2$ and $(y + 3)^2$.

Example 1.9

Write the general form of the equation of a parabola, vertex at (2, 4), opening upward, with directrix at $y = 2$.

Solution. The equation of the parabola (see Eq. 1.3.11) can be written as

$$(x - x_1)^2 = 2p(y - y_1)$$

where we have interchanged x and y so that the parabola opens upward. For this example, $x_1 = 2$, $y_1 = 4$ and $p = 4$ ($p/2$ is the distance from the vertex to the directrix). Hence, the equation is

$$(x - 2)^2 = 2(4)(y - 4)$$

or, in general form,

$$x^2 - 4x - 8y + 36 = 0$$

1.4 Complex Numbers

A complex number consists of a real part x and an imaginary part y, written as $x + iy$, where $i = \sqrt{-1}$. (In electrical engineering, however, it is common to let $j = \sqrt{-1}$ since i represents current.) In real number theory, the square root of a negative number does not exist; in complex number theory, we would write $\sqrt{-4} = \sqrt{4(-1)} = 2i$. The complex number may be plotted using the real x-axis and the imaginary y-axis, as shown in Fig. 1.8.

> 🔑 A complex number consists of a real part x and an imaginary part y, written as $x + iy$, where $i = \sqrt{-1}$.

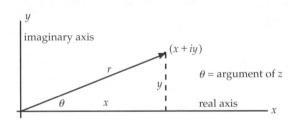

Figure 1.8 The complex number.

It is often useful to express a complex number in polar form as (both $re^{i\theta}$ and $r\angle\theta$ are polar forms)

$$x + iy = re^{i\theta} \quad \text{or} \quad r\angle\theta \tag{1.4.1}$$

where we use *Euler's equation*

$$e^{i\theta} = \cos\theta + i\sin\theta \tag{1.4.2}$$

to verify the relations

$$x = r\cos\theta, \quad y = r\sin\theta \tag{1.4.3}$$

Note that $e^{i\theta} = e^{i(\theta + 2n\pi)}$ where n is an integer. This simply adds 360° (2π radians) to θ and hence in Fig. 1.8 $re^{i\theta}$ and $re^{i(\theta + 2n\pi)}$ represent the identical point.

Multiplication and division are accomplished with either form:

$$(a+ib)(c+id) = ac - bd + i(ad+bc)$$

$$= r_1 e^{i\theta_1} r_2 e^{i\theta_2} = r_1 r_2 e^{i(\theta_1+\theta_2)} \qquad (1.4.4)$$

$$= r_1 r_2 \angle \theta_1 + \theta_2$$

$$\frac{a+ib}{c+id} = \frac{a+ib}{c+id} \frac{c-id}{c-id} = \frac{(a+ib)(c-id)}{c^2+d^2}$$

$$= \frac{r_1}{r_2} e^{i(\theta_1-\theta_2)} = \frac{r_1}{r_2} \angle \theta_1 - \theta_2 \qquad (1.4.5)$$

It is usually easier to find powers and roots of complex numbers using the polar form:

$$(x+iy)^k = r^k e^{ik\theta}, \quad (x+iy)^{1/k} = r^{1/k} e^{i\theta/k} \qquad (1.4.6)$$

When finding roots, more than one root results by using $e^{i\theta}$ and $e^{i(\theta+2n\pi)}$. An example illustrates. Remember, in mathematical equations we usually express θ in radians; however, when displaying the angle as $\angle\theta$ it is expressed in degrees.

Using Euler's equation we can show that

$$\sin\theta = \frac{e^{i\theta} - e^{-i\theta}}{2i}, \qquad \cos\theta = \frac{e^{i\theta} + e^{-i\theta}}{2} \qquad (1.4.7)$$

Example 1.10

Divide $(3 + 4i)$ by $(4 + 3i)$.

Solution. We perform the division as follows:

$$\frac{3+4i}{4+3i} = \frac{3+4i}{4+3i} \cdot \frac{4-3i}{4-3i} = \frac{12+16i-9i+12}{16+9} = \frac{24+7i}{25} = 0.96 + 0.28i$$

Note that we multiplied the numerator and the denominator by the *complex conjugate* of the denominator. A complex conjugate is formed simply by changing the sign of the imaginary part.

Example 1.11

Find $(3+4i)^6$.

Solution. This can be done multiplying six times or using the polar form. Polar form is

$$r = \sqrt{3^2 + 4^2} = 5, \quad \theta = \tan^{-1} 4/3 = 0.9273 \text{ rad}$$

We normally express θ in radians. The complex number, in polar form, is

$$3+4i = 5 e^{0.9273i}$$

Thus,

$$(3+4i)^6 = 5^6 e^{6(0.9273)i} = 5^6 e^{5.564i}$$

Converting back to rectangular form we have

$$5^6 e^{5.564i} = 15\,625(\cos 5.564 + i\sin 5.564)$$

$$= 11\,755 - 10\,293\,i$$

Alternatively, we recognize that this could be expressed in polar form as $15\,625\underline{/318.8°}$ or $15\,625\underline{/-41.2°}$, where a positive angle is measured counterclockwise.

Example 1.12

Find the three roots of 1.

Solution. We express the complex number in polar form as

$$1 = 1e^{0i}$$

Since the trig functions are periodic, we know that

$$\sin\theta = \sin(\theta + 2\pi) = \sin(\theta + 4\pi)$$
$$\cos\theta = \cos(\theta + 2\pi) = \cos(\theta + 4\pi)$$

Thus, in addition to the first form, we have

$$1 = e^{2\pi i} = e^{4\pi i}$$

Taking the one-third root of each form, we find the three roots to be

$$1^{1/3} = 1e^{0i/3} = 1$$
$$1^{1/3} = 1e^{2\pi i/3}$$
$$= \cos 2\pi/3 + i\sin 2\pi/3 = -0.5 + 0.866i \quad \text{or} \quad 1\underline{/120°}$$
$$1^{1/3} = 1e^{4\pi i/3}$$
$$= \cos 4\pi/3 + i\sin 4\pi/3 = -0.5 - 0.866i \quad \text{or} \quad 1\underline{/240°}$$

If we added 6π to the angle we would be repeating the first root, so obviously this is not done.

An $m \times n$ matrix multiplied by an $n \times s$ matrix produces an $m \times s$ matrix.

1.5 Linear Algebra

The primary objective in linear algebra is to find the solution to a set of n linear algebraic equations for n unknowns. To do this we must learn how to manipulate a matrix, a rectangular array of quantities arranged into rows and columns.

An $m \times n$ matrix has m rows (the horizontal lines) and n columns (the vertical lines). An $m \times n$ matrix multiplied by an $n \times s$ matrix produces an $m \times s$ matrix. When multiplying two matrices the columns of the first matrix must equal the rows of the second. Their product is a third matrix:

$$\left[c_{ij}\right] = \sum_{k=1}^{n}\left[a_{ik}\right]\left[b_{kj}\right] \tag{1.5.1}$$

We are primarily interested in square matrices since we usually have the same number of equations as unknowns, such as

$$a_{11}x_1 + a_{12}x_2 + a_{13}x_3 + a_{14}x_4 = r_1$$

$$a_{21}x_1 + a_{22}x_2 + a_{23}x_3 + a_{24}x_4 = r_2$$

$$a_{31}x_1 + a_{32}x_2 + a_{33}x_3 + a_{34}x_4 = r_3 \qquad \text{(1.5.2)}$$

$$a_{41}x_1 + a_{42}x_2 + a_{43}x_3 + a_{44}x_4 = r_4$$

In matrix form this can be written as

$$\left[a_{ij}\right]\left[x_j\right] = \left[r_i\right] \quad \text{or} \quad \mathbf{A}\mathbf{x} = \mathbf{r} \qquad \text{(1.5.3)}$$

where $\left[x_j\right]$ and $\left[r_i\right]$ are column matrices. (A column matrix is often referred to as a *vector*.) The coefficient matrix $\left[a_{ij}\right]$ and the column matrix $\left[r_i\right]$ are assumed to be known quantities. The solution $\left[x_j\right]$ is expressed as

> The cofactor is defined to be $(-1)^{i+j}$ times the *minor*, the determinant obtained by deleting the ith row and the jth column.

$$\left[x_j\right] = \left[a_{ij}\right]^{-1}\left[r_i\right] \quad \text{or} \quad \mathbf{x} = \mathbf{A}^{-1}\mathbf{r} \qquad \text{(1.5.4)}$$

where $\left[a_{ij}\right]^{-1}$ is the *inverse* matrix of $\left[a_{ij}\right]$. It is defined as

$$\left[a_{ij}\right]^{-1} = \frac{\left[a_{ij}\right]^+}{\left|a_{ij}\right|} \quad \text{or} \quad \mathbf{A}^{-1} = \frac{\mathbf{A}^+}{|\mathbf{A}|} \qquad \text{(1.5.5)}$$

where $\left[a_{ij}\right]^+$ is the *adjoint* matrix and $\left|a_{ij}\right|$ is the *determinant* of $\left[a_{ij}\right]$. Let us review how the determinant and the adjoint are evaluated.

In general, the determinant may be found using the *cofactor* A_{ij} of the element a_{ij}. The cofactor is defined to be $(-1)^{i+j}$ times the *minor*, the determinant obtained by deleting the ith row and the jth column. The determinant is then

$$\left|a_{ij}\right| = \sum_{j=1}^{n} a_{ij}\,A_{ij} \qquad \text{(1.5.6)}$$

where i is any value from 1 to n. Recall that the third-order determinant can be evaluated by writing the first two columns after the determinant and then summing the products of the elements of the diagonals, using negative signs with the diagonals sloping upward.

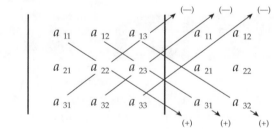

The elements of the adjoint $[a_{ij}]^+$ are the cofactors A_{ij} of the elements a_{ij}; for the matrix $[a_{ij}]$ of Eq. 1.5.2 we have

$$\left[a_{ij}\right]^+ = \begin{bmatrix} A_{11} & A_{21} & A_{31} & A_{41} \\ A_{12} & A_{22} & A_{32} & A_{42} \\ A_{13} & A_{23} & A_{33} & A_{43} \\ A_{14} & A_{24} & A_{34} & A_{44} \end{bmatrix} \qquad \text{(1.5.7)}$$

Note that A_{ij} takes the position of a_{ji}.

Finally, the solution $[x_j]$ of Eq. 1.5.4 results if we multiply the square matrix $[a_{ij}]^{-1}$ by the column matrix $[r_i]$. In general, we multiply the elements in each left-hand matrix row by the elements in each right-hand matrix column, add the products, and place the sum at the location where the row and column intersect. The following examples will illustrate.

Before we work some examples though, we should point out that the above matrix presentation can also be presented as *Cramer's rule*, which states that the solution element x_n can be expressed as

$$x_n = \frac{|b_{ij}|}{|a_{ij}|} \qquad (1.5.8)$$

where $|b_{ij}|$ is formed by replacing the nth column of $|a_{ij}|$ with the elements of the column matrix $[r_i]$.

Notes: If the system of equations is homogeneous, i.e., $r_i = 0$, a solution may exist if $|a_{ij}| = 0$. If the determinant of a matrix is zero, that matrix is *singular* and its inverse does not exist.

In the solution of a system of first-order differential equations, we encounter the matrix equation

$$(\mathbf{A} - \lambda \mathbf{I})\mathbf{x} = 0 \qquad (1.5.9)$$

The scalar λ is the *eigenvalue* and the vector $\mathbf{x}$ is the *eigenvector* associated with the eigenvalue. The matrix $\mathbf{I}$ is called the *unit matrix*, which for a 2×2 matrix is $\begin{bmatrix} 1 & 0 \\ 0 & 1 \end{bmatrix}$. If $\mathbf{A}$ is 2×2, λ has two distinct values, and if $\mathbf{A}$ is 3×3 it has three distinct values. Since $r_i = 0$ in Eq. 1.5.9, the scalar equation

$$|\mathbf{A} - \lambda \mathbf{I}| = 0 \qquad (1.5.10)$$

provides the equation that yields the eigenvalues. Then Eq. 1.5.9 is solved with each eigenvalue to give the eigenvectors. We often say that λ represents the eigenvalues of the matrix $\mathbf{A}$.

> If the determinant of a matrix is zero, that matrix is *singular* and its inverse does not exist.

Example 1.13

Calculate the determinants of $\begin{bmatrix} 2 & -3 \\ 1 & 4 \end{bmatrix}$ and $\begin{bmatrix} 1 & 0 & -2 \\ -1 & 2 & 0 \\ 1 & 2 & 1 \end{bmatrix}$.

Solution. For the first matrix we have

$$\begin{vmatrix} 2 & -3 \\ 1 & 4 \end{vmatrix} = 2 \times 4 - 1(-3) = 11$$

The second matrix is set up as follows:

$$= 2 + 0 + 4 + 4 - 0 - 0 = 10$$

Example 1.14

Multiply the two matrices $\begin{bmatrix} 1 & 1 \\ -1 & -1 \end{bmatrix}$ and $\begin{bmatrix} 1 & 1 \\ -1 & -1 \end{bmatrix}$.

Solution. Multiply the two matrices using Eq. 1.5.1. If we desire c_{12}, we use the first row of the first matrix and the second column of the second matrix so that

$$c_{12} = a_{11}b_{12} + a_{12}b_{22} = 1(1) + 1(-1) = 0$$

Doing this for all elements we find

$$\begin{bmatrix} 1 & 1 \\ -1 & -1 \end{bmatrix} \begin{bmatrix} 1 & 1 \\ -1 & -1 \end{bmatrix} = \begin{bmatrix} 0 & 0 \\ 0 & 0 \end{bmatrix}$$

Note: Even though a matrix has no zero elements, its square may be zero. Matrix multiplication is not like other forms of multiplication.

Example 1.15

Find the adjoint of the matrix

$$[a_{ij}] = \begin{bmatrix} 1 & 0 & -2 \\ -1 & 2 & 0 \\ 1 & 2 & 1 \end{bmatrix}$$

Solution. The cofactor of each element of $[a_{ij}]$ must be determined. The cofactor is found by multiplying $(-1)^{i+j}$ times the determinant formed by deleting the ith row and the jth column. They are found to be

$$A_{11} = 2, \qquad A_{12} = 1, \qquad A_{13} = -4$$

$$A_{21} = -4, \qquad A_{22} = 3, \qquad A_{23} = -2$$

$$A_{31} = 4, \qquad A_{32} = 2, \qquad A_{33} = 2$$

The adjoint is then

$$[a_{ij}]^+ = [A_{ji}] = \begin{bmatrix} 2 & -4 & 4 \\ 1 & 3 & 2 \\ -4 & -2 & 2 \end{bmatrix}$$

Note: The matrix $[A_{ji}]$ is called the *transpose* of $[A_{ij}]$, i.e., $[A_{ji}] = [A_{ij}]^T$.

Example 1.16

Find the inverse of the matrix $[a_{ij}] = \begin{bmatrix} 1 & 0 & -2 \\ -1 & 2 & 0 \\ 1 & 2 & 1 \end{bmatrix}$

Solution. The inverse is defined to be the adjoint matrix divided by the determinant $|a_{ij}|$. Hence, the inverse is (see Examples 1.13 and 1.15)

$$[a_{ij}]^{-1} = \frac{1}{10}\begin{bmatrix} 2 & -4 & 4 \\ 1 & 3 & 2 \\ -4 & -2 & 2 \end{bmatrix} = \begin{bmatrix} 0.2 & -0.4 & 0.4 \\ 0.1 & 0.3 & 0.2 \\ -0.4 & -0.2 & 0.2 \end{bmatrix}$$

Example 1.17

Find the solution to

$$\begin{aligned} x_1 \quad\quad - 2x_3 &= 2 \\ -x_1 + 2x_2 \quad\quad &= 0 \\ x_1 + 2x_2 + x_3 &= -4 \end{aligned}$$

Solution. The solution matrix is (see Example 1.13 and 1.15 or use $[a_{ij}]^{-1}$ from Example 1.16)

$$[x_j] = [a_{ij}]^{-1}[r_i] = \frac{[a_{ij}]^+}{|a_{ij}|}[r_i]$$

$$= \frac{1}{10}\begin{bmatrix} 2 & -4 & 4 \\ 1 & 3 & 2 \\ -4 & -2 & 2 \end{bmatrix}\begin{bmatrix} 2 \\ 0 \\ -4 \end{bmatrix}$$

First, let's multiply the two matrices; they are multiplied row by column as follows:

$$2\cdot2 + (-4)\cdot0 + 4\cdot(-4) = -12$$

$$1\cdot2 + 3\cdot0 + 2\cdot(-4) = -6$$

$$-4\cdot2 - 2\cdot0 + 2\cdot(-4) = -16$$

The solution vector is then

$$[x_i] = \frac{1}{10}\begin{bmatrix} -12 \\ -6 \\ -16 \end{bmatrix} = \begin{bmatrix} -1.2 \\ -0.6 \\ -1.6 \end{bmatrix}$$

In component form, the solution is

$$x_1 = -1.2, \quad\quad x_2 = -0.6, \quad\quad x_3 = -1.6$$

Example 1.18

Use Cramer's rule and solve

$$
\begin{aligned}
x_1 \qquad\;\; - 2x_3 &= 2 \\
-x_1 + 2x_2 \qquad &= 0 \\
x_1 + 2x_2 + x_3 &= -4
\end{aligned}
$$

Solution. The solution is found (see Example 1.14) by evaluating the ratios as follows:

$$
x_1 = \dfrac{\begin{vmatrix} 2 & 0 & -2 \\ 0 & 2 & 0 \\ -4 & 2 & 1 \end{vmatrix}}{D} = \dfrac{-12}{10} = -1.2
\qquad
x_2 = \dfrac{\begin{vmatrix} 1 & 2 & -2 \\ -1 & 0 & 0 \\ 1 & -4 & 1 \end{vmatrix}}{D} = \dfrac{-6}{10} = -0.6
$$

$$
x_3 = \dfrac{\begin{vmatrix} 1 & 0 & 2 \\ -1 & 2 & 0 \\ 1 & 2 & -4 \end{vmatrix}}{D} = \dfrac{-16}{10} = -1.6
$$

where

$$
D = \begin{vmatrix} 1 & 0 & -2 \\ -1 & 2 & 0 \\ 1 & 2 & 1 \end{vmatrix} = 10
$$

Note that the numerator is the determinant formed by replacing the ith column with right-hand side elements r_i when solving for x_i.

Example 1.19

Find the eigenvalues of $\mathbf{A} = \begin{bmatrix} 4 & 0 & 2 \\ 0 & 8 & 0 \\ 3 & 0 & 5 \end{bmatrix}$ and one of its eigenvectors.

Solution. To find the eigenvalues of the matrix, we form the equation

$$
|\mathbf{A} - \lambda\mathbf{I}| = 0 \qquad \text{or} \qquad \begin{vmatrix} 4-\lambda & 0 & 2 \\ 0 & 8-\lambda & 0 \\ 3 & 0 & 5-\lambda \end{vmatrix} = 0
$$

Expanding the determinant using cofactors we have

$$
(8-\lambda)\begin{vmatrix} 4-\lambda & 2 \\ 3 & 5-\lambda \end{vmatrix} = (8-\lambda)\left[(4-\lambda)(5-\lambda)-6\right] = (8-\lambda)\left[\lambda^2 - 9\lambda + 14\right] = 0
$$

or

$$
(8-\lambda)(\lambda-7)(\lambda-2) = 0
$$

The eigenvalues are then $\lambda = 8, 7, 2$.

To find an eigenvector (calculation of eigenvectors will not likely be on the exam), use $l = 2$. Then Eq. 1.5.9 is

$$(\mathbf{A} - 2\mathbf{I})\mathbf{x} = \mathbf{0} \quad \text{or} \quad \begin{bmatrix} 2 & 0 & 2 \\ 0 & 6 & 0 \\ 3 & 0 & 3 \end{bmatrix} \begin{bmatrix} x_1 \\ x_2 \\ x_3 \end{bmatrix} = \begin{bmatrix} 0 \\ 0 \\ 0 \end{bmatrix}$$

Write out the three equations:

$$2x_1 + 2x_3 = 0$$
$$6x_2 = 0$$
$$3x_1 + 3x_3 = 0$$

The only solution is

$$x_2 = 0$$
$$x_1 = -x_3$$

An eigenvector is then

$$\mathbf{x} = \begin{bmatrix} 1 \\ 0 \\ -1 \end{bmatrix}$$

Note that eigenvectors are not unique. We simply select $x_1 = 1$ so that $x_3 = -1$. We could have selected $x_1 = -1$ so that $x_3 = 1$, an equally valid result. Or we could select x_1, x_2, and x_3 so that a unit vector results.

1·MATH

1.6 Calculus

Differentiation

The slope of a curve $y = f(x)$ is the ratio of the change in y to the change in x as the change in x becomes infinitesimally small. This is the first derivative, written as

$$\frac{dy}{dx} = \lim_{\Delta x \to 0} \frac{\Delta y}{\Delta x} \tag{1.6.1}$$

This may be written using abbreviated notation as

$$\frac{dy}{dx} = Dy = y' = \dot{y} \tag{1.6.2}$$

The second derivative is written as

$$\frac{d^2 y}{dx^2} = D^2 y = y'' = \ddot{y} \tag{1.6.3}$$

and is defined by

$$\frac{d^2 y}{dx^2} = \lim_{\Delta x \to 0} \frac{\Delta y'}{\Delta x} \tag{1.6.4}$$

Some derivative formulas, where f and g are functions of x, and k is constant, are given below.

$$\frac{dk}{dx} = 0$$

$$\frac{d(k x^n)}{dx} = k n x^{n-1}$$

$$\frac{d}{dx}(f + g) = f' + g'$$

$$\frac{df^n}{dx} = n f^{n-1} f'$$

$$\frac{d}{dx}(fg) = fg' + gf' \tag{1.6.5}$$

$$\frac{d}{dx}(\ln x) = \frac{1}{x}$$

$$\frac{d}{dx}\left(e^{kx}\right) = ke^{kx}$$

$$\frac{d}{dx}(\sin x) = \cos x$$

$$\frac{d}{dx}(\cos x) = -\sin x$$

If a function f depends on more than one variable, partial derivatives are used. If $z = f(x, y)$, then $\partial z / \partial x$ is the derivative of z with respect to x holding y constant. It would represent the slope of a line tangent to the surface in a plane of constant y.

Derivatives are used to locate points of inflection, maxima, and minima. Note the following:

$$f'(x) = 0 \text{ at a maximum or a minimum.}$$

$$f''(x) = 0 \text{ at an inflection point.}$$

$$f''(x) > 0 \text{ at a minimum.}$$

$$f''(x) < 0 \text{ at a maximum.}$$

An inflection point always exists between a maximum and a minimum.

Maxima and Minima

Differentiation is also useful in establishing the limit of $f(x)/g(x)$ as $x \to a$ if $f(a)$ and $g(a)$ are both zero or $\pm\infty$. *L'Hospital's rule* is used in such cases and is as follows:

$$\lim_{x \to a} \frac{f(x)}{g(x)} = \lim_{x \to a} \frac{f'(x)}{g'(x)} = \lim_{x \to a} \frac{f''(x)}{g''(x)} \qquad (1.6.6)$$

L'Hospital's Rule

Derivatives are used to expand a continuous function as a power series around $x = a$. Taylor's series is as follows:

$$f(x) = f(a) + (x-a)f'(a) + (x-a)^2 f''(a)/2! + \cdots \qquad (1.6.7)$$

Taylor's Series

This series is often used to express a function as a polynomial near a point $x = a$ providing the series can be truncated after a few terms. Using Taylor's series we can show that (expanding about $a = 0$):

$$\sin x = x - x^3/3! + x^5/5! - \cdots$$

$$\cos x = 1 - x^2/2! + x^4/4! - \cdots$$

$$\ln(1+x) = x - x^2/2 + x^3/3 - \cdots \qquad (1.6.8)$$

$$\frac{1}{1-x} = 1 + x + x^2 + \cdots$$

$$e^x = 1 + x + x^2/2! + x^3/3! + \cdots$$

When expanding with $a = 0$, the Taylor series may be called a *Maclaurin series*.

The inverse of differentiation is the process called integration. If a curve is given by $y = f(x)$, then the area under the curve from $x = a$ to $x = b$ is given by

$$A = \int_a^b y\,dx \qquad (1.6.9)$$

Integration

The length of the curve between the two points is expressed as

$$L = \int_a^b \left(1 + y'^2\right)^{1/2} dx \qquad (1.6.10)$$

If the integral has limits, it is a *definite integral*.

Volumes of various objects are also found by an appropriate integration.

If the integral has limits, it is a *definite integral*; if it does not have limits, it is an *indefinite integral* and a constant is always added. Some common indefinite integrals follow:

$$\int dx = x + C$$

$$\int cy\,dx = c\int y\,dx$$

$$\int x^n dx = \frac{x^{n+1}}{n+1} + C \quad n \ne -1$$

$$\int x^{-1} dx = \ln x + C$$

$$\int e^{ax} dx = \frac{1}{a} e^{ax} + C$$

$$\int \sin x\,dx = -\cos x + C$$

$$\int \cos x\,dx = \sin x + C$$

$$\int \cos^2 x\,dx = \frac{x}{2} + \frac{1}{4}\sin 2x + C$$

$$\int u\,dv = uv - \int v\,du$$

(1.6.11)

This last integral is often referred to as "integration by parts." If the integrand (the coefficients of the differential) is not one of the above, then in the last integral, $\int v\,du$ may in fact be integrable. An example will illustrate.

Example 1.20

Find the slope of $y = x^2 + \sin x$ at $x = 0.5$.

Solution. The derivative is the slope:

$$y'(x) = 2x + \cos x$$

At $x = 0.5$ the slope is

$$y'(0.5) = 2 \cdot 0.5 + \cos 0.5 = 1.878$$

Example 1.21

Find $\frac{d}{dx}(\tan x)$.

Solution. Writing $\tan x = \sin x / \cos x = f(x) \cdot g(x)$ we find

$$\frac{d}{dx}(\tan x) = \frac{1}{\cos x}\frac{d}{dx}(\sin x) + \sin x \frac{d}{dx}(\cos x)^{-1}$$

$$= \frac{\cos x}{\cos x} + \frac{\sin^2 x}{\cos^2 x} = 1 + \tan^2 x$$

$$= \frac{\cos^2 x + \sin^2 x}{\cos^2 x} = \frac{1}{\cos^2 x} = \sec^2 x$$

Either expression is acceptable.

1·MATH

Example 1.22

Locate the maximum and minimum points of the function $y(x) = x^3 - 12x - 9$ and evaluate y at those points.

Solution. The derivative is

$$y'(x) = 3x^2 - 12$$

The points at which $y'(x) = 0$ are at

$$x = 2, -2$$

At these two points the extrema are:

$$y_{min} = (2)^3 - 12 \cdot 2 - 9 = -25$$

$$y_{max} = (-2)^3 - 12(-2) - 9 = 7$$

Let us check the second derivative. At the two points we have:

$$y''(2) = 6 \cdot 2 = 12$$

$$y''(-2) = 6 \cdot (-2) = -12$$

Obviously, the point $x = 2$ is a minimum since its second derivative is positive there.

Example 1.23

Find the limit as $x \to 0$ of $\sin x / x$.

Solution. If we let $x = 0$ we are faced with the ratio of 0/0, an indeterminate quantity. Hence, we use L'Hospital's rule and differentiate both numerator and denominator to obtain

$$\lim_{x \to 0} \frac{\sin x}{x} = \lim_{x \to 0} \frac{\cos x}{1}$$

Now, we let $x = 0$ and find

$$\lim_{x \to 0} \frac{\sin x}{x} = \frac{1}{1} = 1$$

Example 1.24

Verify that $\sin x = x - x^3/3! + x^5/5! - \cdots$.

Solution. We expand in a Taylor's series about $x = 0$:

$$f(x) = f(0) + x f'(0) + x^2 f''(0) / 2! + \cdots$$

Letting $f(x) = \sin x$ so that $f' = \cos x$, $f'' = -\sin x$, etc., there results

$$\sin x = 0 + x(1) + x^2(0/2!) + x^3(-1)/3! + \cdots$$

$$= x - x^3/3! + x^5/5! - \cdots$$

Example 1.25

Find the area of the shaded area in the figure.

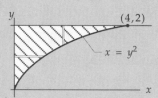

Solution. We can find this area by using either a horizontal strip or a vertical strip. We will use both. First, for a horizontal strip:

$$A = \int_0^2 x\,dy$$

$$= \int_0^2 y^2\,dy = \frac{y^3}{3}\Big|_0^2 = 8/3$$

Using a vertical strip we have

$$A = \int_0^4 (2-y)\,dx$$

$$= \int_0^4 \left(2 - x^{1/2}\right)dx = \left[2x - \frac{2}{3}x^{3/2}\right]_0^4 = 8 - \frac{2}{3}8 = 8/3$$

Either technique is acceptable. The first appears to be the simpler one.

Example 1.26

Find the volume enclosed by rotating the shaded area of Example 1.25 about the y-axis.

Solution. If we rotate the horizontal strip about the y-axis we will obtain a disc with volume

$$dV = \pi x^2 dy$$

This can be integrated to give the volume, which is

$$V = \int_0^2 \pi x^2 dy$$

$$= \pi \int_0^2 y^4 dy = \frac{\pi y^5}{5}\Big|_0^2 = \frac{32\pi}{5}$$

Now, let us rotate the vertical strip about the y-axis to form a cylinder with volume

$$dV = 2\pi x(2-y)dx$$

This can be integrated to yield

$$V = \int_0^4 2\pi x (2 - y)\,dx$$

$$= \int_0^4 2\pi x \left(2 - x^{1/2}\right)dx = 2\pi \left[x^2 - \frac{2x^{5/2}}{5} \right]_0^4 = \frac{32\pi}{5}$$

Again, the horizontal strip is simpler.

Example 1.27

Show that $\int x e^x\,dx = (x-1)e^x + C$.

Solution. Let's attempt the last integral of (1.6.11). Define the following:

$$u = x, \quad dv = e^x\,dx$$

Then,

$$du = dx, \quad v = \int e^x\,dx = e^x$$

and we find that

$$\int x e^x\,dx = x\,e^x - \int e^x\,dx$$

$$= x\,e^x - e^x + C = (x-1)e^x + C$$

1.7 Differential Equations

A differential equation is *linear* if no term contains the dependent variable or any of its derivatives to a power other than one (terms that do not contain the dependent variable are not considered in the test of linearity). For example,

$$y'' + 2xy' - y\sin x = 3x^2 \tag{1.7.1}$$

is a linear differential equation. The dependent variable is y and the independent variable is x. If a term contained y'^2, or $y^{1/2}$ or $\sin y$ the equation would be non-linear. We use either primes or dots to denote a derivative, i.e., $\dot{y} = y' = dy/dx$.

A differential equation is *homogeneous* if all of its terms contain the dependent variable. Eq. 1.7.1 is *nonhomogeneous* because of the term $3x^2$.

The *order* of a differential equation is established by its highest order derivative. Eq. 1.7.1 is a second order differential equation.

The general solution of a differential equation involves a number of arbitrary constants equal to the order of the equation. If conditions are specified, the arbitrary constants may be calculated.

A first order differential equation is *separable* if it can be expressed as

$$M(x)\,dx + N(y)\,dy = 0 \tag{1.7.2}$$

The solution follows by integrating each of the terms. This equation is, in general, nonlinear.

Terms that do not contain the dependent variable are not considered in the test of linearity.

First Order

If a first order differential equation is not separable, we will consider only those that are linear with a constant coefficient, written as

$$y' + ay = f(x) \tag{1.7.3}$$

For the homogeneous equation, $f(x) = 0$, it has the solution

$$y(x) = Ce^{-ax} \tag{1.7.4}$$

The constant C would be determined from an imposed condition

$$y(0) = C \tag{1.7.5}$$

Second Order

The general form of a second order, linear, homogeneous differential equation with constant coefficients is

$$y'' + 2ay' + by = 0 \tag{1.7.6}$$

To find a solution we assume $y = e^{rx}$ and solve the *characteristic equation*

$$r^2 + 2ar + b = 0 \tag{1.7.7}$$

Let r_1 and r_2 be its roots. If $r_1 \neq r_2$ and both are real, the general solution is

$$y(x) = C_1 e^{r_1 x} + C_2 e^{r_2 x} \tag{1.7.8}$$

If $r_1 = r_2$, the general solution is

$$y(x) = C_1 e^{r_1 x} + C_2 x e^{r_2 x} \tag{1.7.9}$$

Finally, if $r_1 = \alpha + i\beta$ and $r_2 = \alpha - i\beta$, the general solution is

$$y(x) = (c_1 \sin \beta x + c_2 \cos \beta x) e^{\alpha x} \tag{1.7.10}$$

where $\beta = \sqrt{b - a^2}$ and $\alpha = -a$.

Linear, Nonhomogeneous, with Constant Coefficients

If Eq. 1.7.6 were nonhomogeneous, it would be written as

$$y'' + 2ay' + by = f(x) \tag{1.7.11}$$

The general solution is found by finding the solution $y_h(x)$ to the homogeneous equation (simply let the right-hand side be zero and solve the equation as in Section 1.7.2) and adding to it a particular solution $y_p(x)$ found by using Table 1.2. This is expressed as

$$y(x) = y_h(x) + y_p(x) \tag{1.7.12}$$

TABLE 1.2 Particular Solutions

$f(x)$	$y_p(x)$	provisions
A	C	
$Ax + B$	$Cx + D$	
$e^{\alpha x}$	$Ce^{\alpha x}$	if r_1 or $r_2 \neq \alpha$
	$Cxe^{\alpha x}$	if r_1 or $r_2 = \alpha$
$B \sin \alpha x$	$C \sin \alpha x + D \cos \alpha x$	if $r_{1,2} \neq \pm \alpha i$
	$Cx \sin \alpha x + Dx \cos \alpha x$	if $r_{1,2} = \pm \alpha i$
$B \cos \alpha x$	(same as above)	

Example 1.28

Find the general solution to $2xy' + y = 2$.

Solution. Write the differential equation as

$$2x\frac{dy}{dx} = 2 - y$$

This is separable and written as

$$\frac{2dy}{(2-y)} = \frac{dx}{x}$$

This is rewritten as

$$\frac{2dy}{2-y} = \frac{dx}{x}$$

Integrating provides a solution:

$$-2\ln(2-y) = \ln x - \ln C$$

where the constant of integration is $-\ln C$. Rewrite this as

$$\ln C(2-y)^{-2} = \ln x$$

Finally, one form of the solution is

$$\frac{C}{(2-y)^2} = x \quad \text{or} \quad y(x) = 2 - \sqrt{\frac{C}{x}}$$

Example 1.29

Find the solution to

$$y' + 2y = 4x, \quad y(0) = 2$$

Solution. We will use the method outlined in Section 1.7.2. The characteristic equation of the homogeneous equation is

$$r + 2 = 0. \quad \therefore r = -2$$

The homogeneous solution is then

$$y_h(x) = Ce^{-2x}$$

The particular solution is assumed to be of the form

$$y_p(x) = Ax + B$$

Substituting this into the original differential equation gives

$$A + 2(Ax + B) = 4x. \quad \therefore A = 2, \quad B = -1$$

The solution is then

$$y(x) = y_h(x) + y_p(x)$$

$$= Ce^{-2x} + 2x - 1$$

Using the given condition

$$y(0) = 2 = C - 1. \quad \therefore C = 3$$

Finally,

$$y(x) = 3e^{-2x} + 2x - 1$$

Example 1.30 (Refer to page 17 in the NCEES Handbook, 3rd ed.)

The motion of a simple spring-mass system is represented by

$$M\ddot{y} + C\dot{y} + Ky = F(t)$$

where the mass M, the damping coefficient C, the spring constant K, and the forcing function $F(t)$ have the appropriate units. Find the general solution if $M = 2$, $C = 0$, $K = 50$, and $F(t) = 0$.

Solution. The differential equation simplifies to $2\ddot{y} + 50y = 0$.

The characteristic equation is then

$$2r^2 + 50 = 0$$

$$\therefore r_1 = 5i, \quad r_2 = -5i$$

The solution is then (see Eq. 1.7.10)

$$y(t) = C_1 \sin 5t + C_2 \cos 5t$$

This situation with zero damping represents simple *harmonic motion*.

Note that we have used dots to represent the time derivative $dy/dt = \dot{y}$. Also, note that the coefficient of t in the undamped system is the *natural frequency* $\omega_n = \sqrt{K/M}$; the frequency in hertz is $f = \omega_n/2\pi$; and the *period* is $\tau = f^{-1} = 2\pi/\omega_n$. For this problem $\omega_n = 5$ rad/s, $f = 5/2\pi$ Hz, and $\tau = 2\pi/5$ seconds.

Example 1.31

In the equation of Ex. 1.30, let $M = 2$, $C = 12$, $K = 50$, and $F(t) = 60 \sin 5t$. Find the general solution.

Solution. The differential equation is

$$2\ddot{y} + 12\dot{y} + 50y = 60 \sin 5t$$

The characteristic equation of the homogeneous differential equation is found by letting $y = e^{rx}$:

$$2r^2 + 12r + 50 = 0$$

$$\therefore r_1 = -3 + 4i, \quad r_2 = -3 - 4i$$

The homogeneous solution is (see Eq. 1.7.10)

$$y_h(t) = e^{-3t}\left(C_1 \sin 4t + C_2 \cos 4t\right)$$

The particular solution is found by assuming that

$$y_p(t) = A \sin 5t + B \cos 5t$$

Substitute this into the original differential equation:

$$2\left[-25A \sin 5t - 25B \cos 5t\right] + 12\left[5A \cos 5t - 5B \sin 5t\right] + 50\left[A \sin 5t + B \cos 5t\right]$$
$$= 60 \sin 5t$$

Equating coefficients of sin terms and then cos terms:

$$-50A - 60B + 50A = 60. \quad \therefore B = -1$$

$$-50B + 60A + 50B = 0. \quad \therefore A = 0$$

The two solutions are superposed as in Eq. 1.7.12 to give

$$y(t) = \left(C_1 \sin 4t + C_2 \cos 4t\right) e^{-3t} - \cos 5t$$

Laplace Transforms

The solution of nonhomogeneous, constant coefficient, linear differential equations can be obtained quite easily using Laplace transforms. The initial conditions <u>must</u> be given and with them we obtain the solution directly; we do not superpose homogeneous and particular solutions.

The *Laplace transform F(s)* of *f(t)* is defined as

$$F(s) = \int_0^\infty f(t)e^{-st}\,dt \qquad \textbf{(1.7.13)}$$

We also use the notation

$$\mathcal{L}(f) = F(s) \qquad \textbf{(1.7.14)}$$

where $\mathcal{L}(f)$ is the Laplace transform of *f(t)*.

By applying Eq. 1.7.13 to a variety of functions, including derivatives, we can obtain the Laplace transforms presented in Table 1.3.

TABLE 1.3 Laplace Transforms

$f(t)$	$F(s)$	$f(t)$	$F(s)$
(t), Impulse at $t = 0$	1	$\sin \beta t$	$\beta/(s^2 + \beta^2)$
$u(t)$, Step at $t = 0$	$1/s$	$\cos \beta t$	$s/(s^2 + \beta^2)$
$t\,u(t)$, Ramp at $t = 0$	$1/s^2$		
$e^{-\alpha t}$	$1/(s+\alpha)$	df/dt	$sF(s) - f(0)$
$te^{-\alpha t}$	$1/(s+\alpha)^2$	d^2f/dt^2	$s^2F(s) - sf(0) - f'(0)$
$e^{-\alpha t}\sin \beta t$	$\beta/\left[(s+\alpha)^2 + \beta^2\right]$	$d^n f(t)/dt^n$	$s^nF(s) - \sum_{m=0}^{n-1} s^{n-m-1}\dfrac{d^m f(0)}{dt^m}$
$e^{-\alpha t}\cos \beta t$	$(s+\alpha)/\left[(s+\alpha)^2 + \beta^2\right]$	$\int_0^t f(\tau)d\tau$	$(1/s)F(s)$
$t \sin \beta t$	$2bs/\left(s^2 + \beta^2\right)^2$	$\int_0^t f(t-\tau)h(\tau)d\tau$	$F(s)H(s)$
$t \cos \beta t$	$\left(s^2 - \beta^2\right)/\left(s^2 + \beta^2\right)^2$	$\lim_{t\to\infty} f(t)$	$\lim_{s\to 0} sF(s)$
		$\lim_{t\to 0} f(t)$	$\lim_{s\to\infty} sF(s)$

We can now use Table 1.3 to solve ordinary differential equations. We can write:

$$\mathcal{L}\{y'(t)\} = sY(s) - y(0)$$
$$\mathcal{L}\{y''(t)\} = s^2Y(s) - sy(0) - y'(0)$$

(1.7.15)

If we take the Laplace transform of Eq. 1.7.11, replacing the independent variable x with t, we find the *subsidiary* equation:

$$s^2Y(s) + 2asY(s) + bY(s) - sy(0) - y'(0) - 2ay(0) = F(s)$$

(1.7.16)

This can be rearranged as

$$Y(s) = \frac{sy(0) + y'(0) + y(0)}{s^2 + 2as + b} + \frac{F(s)}{s^2 + 2as + b}$$

(1.7.17)

The solution $y(t)$ is then the inverse Laplace transform

$$y(t) = \mathcal{L}^{-1}\{Y(s)\}$$

(1.7.18)

To find the inverse Laplace transform we find the inverse functions of the fractions on the right-hand side of Eq. 1.7.17. Section 1.1.4 on partial fractions will aid in this process.

Example 1.32

Solve the differential equation $2y'' + 12y' + 50y = 60\sin 5t$ if $y(0) = 0$ and $y'(0) = 10$.

Solution. We will find the solution using Laplace transforms. The Laplace transform of our differential equation is (first divide by 2 so that the coefficient of y'' is 1)

$$s^2Y(s) + 6sY(s) + 25Y(s) - s\,y(0)^{\,0} - 10 - 6y(0)^{\,0} = \frac{30(5)}{s^2 + 5^2}$$

where we have used $\alpha = 0$ and $\beta = 5$ in the Laplace transform of $e^{-\alpha t}\sin\beta t$. Next, we see, with some algebra, that

$$Y(s) = \frac{10}{s^2 + 6s + 25} + \frac{150}{(s^2 + 25)(s^2 + 6s + 25)}$$

$$= \frac{10}{s^2 + 6s + 25} + \frac{-s}{s^2 + 25} + \frac{s + 6}{s^2 + 6s + 25}$$

$$= \frac{13}{(s+3)^2 + 16} - \frac{s}{s^2 + 25} + \frac{s + 3}{(s+3)^2 + 16}$$

The inverse Laplace transform is found using Table 1.3 to be:

$$y(t) = \frac{13}{4}e^{-3t}\sin 4t - \cos 5t + e^{-3t}\cos 4t$$

$$= \left(\frac{13}{4}\sin 4t + \cos 4t\right)e^{-3t} - \cos 5t$$

Compare this solution to that of Example 1.31. Also, check and make sure that those initial conditions are satisfied.

1.8 Vectors

There are two vector multiplications. The first, the *scalar product*, or *dot product*, is the scalar defined by

$$\mathbf{A} \cdot \mathbf{B} = AB\cos\theta \tag{1.8.1}$$

where θ is the angle between the two vectors, as shown in Fig. 1.9, and A and B are the magnitudes of the two vectors. In a rectangular coordinate system the dot product becomes

$$\begin{aligned}
\mathbf{A} \cdot \mathbf{B} &= \left(A_x\mathbf{i} + A_y\mathbf{j} + A_z\mathbf{k}\right) \cdot \left(B_x\mathbf{i} + B_y\mathbf{j} + B_z\mathbf{k}\right) \\
&= A_xB_x + A_yB_y + A_zB_z
\end{aligned} \tag{1.8.2}$$

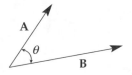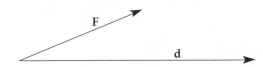

Figure 1.9 Vectors.

The scalar quantity *work* can be defined using the dot product:

$$w = \mathbf{F} \cdot \mathbf{d} \tag{1.8.3}$$

where $\mathbf{d}$ is the directed distance moved by the force.

The second, the *vector product*, or *cross product*, of the two vectors $\mathbf{A}$ and $\mathbf{B}$ is a vector defined by

$$\mathbf{C} = \mathbf{A} \times \mathbf{B} \tag{1.8.4}$$

where the magnitude of $\mathbf{C}$ is given by

$$C = AB\sin\theta \tag{1.8.5}$$

The vector $\mathbf{C}$ acts in a direction perpendicular to the plane of $\mathbf{A}$ and $\mathbf{B}$ so that the three vectors form a right-handed set of vectors. (If the fingers curl $\mathbf{A}$ into $\mathbf{B}$, the thumb points in the direction of $\mathbf{C}$.) In a rectangular coordinate system the cross product is

$$\mathbf{A} \times \mathbf{B} = \begin{vmatrix} \mathbf{i} & \mathbf{j} & \mathbf{k} \\ A_x & A_y & A_z \\ B_x & B_y & B_z \end{vmatrix} = \left(A_yB_z - A_zB_y\right)\mathbf{i} + \left(A_zB_x - A_xB_z\right)\mathbf{j} + \left(A_xB_y - A_yB_x\right)\mathbf{k} \tag{1.8.6}$$

The magnitude of $\mathbf{C}$ is the area of the parallelogram with sides $\mathbf{A}$ and $\mathbf{B}$.

The volume of the parallelepiped with sides $\mathbf{A}$, $\mathbf{B}$, and $\mathbf{C}$ is the scalar triple product given by

$$\mathbf{A} \times \mathbf{B} \cdot \mathbf{C} = \begin{vmatrix} A_x & A_y & A_z \\ B_x & B_y & B_z \\ C_x & C_y & C_z \end{vmatrix} \tag{1.8.7}$$

Using the above definition we can produce the following identities:

$$\mathbf{i} \cdot \mathbf{i} = \mathbf{j} \cdot \mathbf{j} = \mathbf{k} \cdot \mathbf{k} = 1$$
$$\mathbf{i} \times \mathbf{i} = \mathbf{j} \times \mathbf{j} = \mathbf{k} \times \mathbf{k} = 0$$
$$\mathbf{A} \cdot \mathbf{B} = 0 \quad \text{if} \quad \mathbf{A} \perp \mathbf{B}$$
$$\mathbf{A} \cdot \mathbf{B} = AB \quad \text{if} \quad \mathbf{A} \| \mathbf{B}$$

$$\mathbf{i} \cdot \mathbf{j} = \mathbf{j} \cdot \mathbf{k} = \mathbf{k} \cdot \mathbf{i} = 0$$
$$\mathbf{i} \times \mathbf{j} = \mathbf{k}, \quad \mathbf{j} \times \mathbf{k} = \mathbf{i}, \quad \mathbf{k} \times \mathbf{i} = \mathbf{j}$$
$$\mathbf{A} \times \mathbf{B} = 0 \quad \text{if} \quad \mathbf{A} \| \mathbf{B}$$

(1.8.8)

Example 1.33

Find the projection of **A** on **B** if $\mathbf{A} = 12\mathbf{i} + 6\mathbf{k}$ and $\mathbf{B} = -4\mathbf{j} + 3\mathbf{k}$.

Solution. Find the unit vector $\mathbf{i}_B$ in the direction of **B**:

$$\mathbf{i}_B = \frac{\mathbf{B}}{B} = \frac{-4\mathbf{j} + 3\mathbf{k}}{\sqrt{4^2 + 3^2}} = \frac{1}{5}\left(-4\mathbf{j} + 3\mathbf{k}\right)$$

The projection of **A** on **B** is then

$$\mathbf{A} \cdot \mathbf{i}_B = (12\mathbf{i} + 6\mathbf{k}) \cdot \frac{1}{5}\left(-4\mathbf{j} + 3\mathbf{k}\right)$$
$$= 18/5$$

Example 1.34

Find the area of a parallelogram with two sides identified by vectors from the origin to the points (3, 4) and (8, 0).

Solution. The two vectors are represented by

$$\mathbf{A} = 3\mathbf{i} + 4\mathbf{j}, \qquad \mathbf{B} = 8\mathbf{i}$$

The area of the parallelogram is then

$$|\mathbf{A} \times \mathbf{B}| = |(3\mathbf{i} + 4\mathbf{j}) \times 8\mathbf{i}| = 32$$

since $\mathbf{i} \times \mathbf{i} = 0$ and $\mathbf{j} \times \mathbf{i} = -\mathbf{k}$.

Example 1.35

Find a unit vector perpendicular to the plane that contains both $\mathbf{A} = \mathbf{i} - 2\mathbf{j}$ and $\mathbf{B} = \mathbf{i} - \mathbf{k}$.

Solution. The vector $\mathbf{C} = \mathbf{A} \times \mathbf{B}$ is perpendicular to the plane of **A** and **B**. Using Eq. 1.8.6,

$$\mathbf{C} = \left[-2(-1) - 0 \times 2\right]\mathbf{i} + \left[0 \times 1 - 1(-1)\right]\mathbf{j} + \left[1 \times 0 - (-2) \times 1\right]\mathbf{k}$$
$$= 2\mathbf{i} + \mathbf{j} + 2\mathbf{k}$$

A unit vector in the direction of **C** is the desired unit vector:

$$\mathbf{i}_c = \frac{2\mathbf{i} + \mathbf{j} + 2\mathbf{k}}{\sqrt{2^2 + 1^2 + 2^2}} = \frac{1}{3}\left(2\mathbf{i} + \mathbf{j} + 2\mathbf{k}\right)$$

We define a vector differential operator $\mathbf{V}$, referred to as *del*, to be

$$\mathbf{V} = \frac{\partial}{\partial x}\mathbf{i} + \frac{\partial}{\partial y}\mathbf{j} + \frac{\partial}{\partial z}\mathbf{k} \qquad (1.8.9)$$

The Gradient

(This section may not be tested.)

The *gradient* of a scalar function ϕ is

$$\mathbf{V}\phi = \frac{\partial\phi}{\partial x}\mathbf{i} + \frac{\partial\phi}{\partial y}\mathbf{j} + \frac{\partial\phi}{\partial z}\mathbf{k} \qquad (1.8.10)$$

It is a vector quantity that points in the direction of the maximum rate of change of ϕ; hence, it is normal to a constant ϕ surface.

The *divergence* of a vector function $\mathbf{u}$ is the scalar quantity

$$\mathbf{V}\cdot\mathbf{u} = \frac{\partial u_x}{\partial x} + \frac{\partial u_y}{\partial y} + \frac{\partial u_z}{\partial z} \qquad (1.8.11)$$

The *curl* of a vector function $\mathbf{u}$ is the vector quantity

$$\mathbf{V}\times\mathbf{u} = \left(\frac{\partial u_z}{\partial y} - \frac{\partial u_y}{\partial z}\right)\mathbf{i} + \left(\frac{\partial u_x}{\partial z} - \frac{\partial u_z}{\partial x}\right)\mathbf{j} + \left(\frac{\partial u_y}{\partial x} - \frac{\partial u_x}{\partial y}\right)\mathbf{k} \qquad (1.8.12)$$

The *Laplacian* of a scalar function is, using $\mathbf{V}\cdot\mathbf{V} = \mathbf{V}^2$,

$$\mathbf{V}^2\phi = \frac{\partial^2\phi}{\partial x^2} + \frac{\partial^2\phi}{\partial y^2} + \frac{\partial^2\phi}{\partial z^2} \qquad (1.8.13)$$

and *Laplace's equation* is

$$\mathbf{V}^2\phi = 0 \qquad (1.8.14)$$

A vector function $\mathbf{u}$ is a *conservative* (or *irrotational*) vector function if it is given by the gradient of a scalar function ϕ, i.e.,

$$\mathbf{u} = \mathbf{V}\phi \qquad (1.8.15)$$

The curl of a conservative vector function is always zero. A vector field is *solenoidal* if its divergence is zero.

Example 1.36

Find a unit vector in the direction of the maximum rate of change of $\phi = x^2 - 2yz + xy$ at the point $(2, -1, -1)$.

Solution. The gradient of ϕ is

$$\mathbf{V}\phi = \frac{\partial\phi}{\partial x}\mathbf{i} + \frac{\partial\phi}{\partial y}\mathbf{j} + \frac{\partial\phi}{\partial z}\mathbf{k}$$

$$= (2x + y)\mathbf{i} + (-2z + x)\mathbf{j} + (-2y)\mathbf{k} = 3\mathbf{i} + 4\mathbf{j} + 2\mathbf{k}$$

A unit vector in the direction of $\mathbf{V}\phi$ is

$$\mathbf{i_n} = \frac{\mathbf{V}\phi}{|\mathbf{V}\phi|} = \frac{3\mathbf{i} + 4\mathbf{j} + 2\mathbf{k}}{\sqrt{3^2 + 4^2 + 2^2}} = \frac{1}{\sqrt{29}}(3\mathbf{i} + 4\mathbf{j} + 2\mathbf{k})$$

Example 1.37

Given a vector function $\mathbf{u} = x^2\mathbf{i} + 2yz\mathbf{j} + y^2\mathbf{k}$, find a) the divergence, b) the curl, and c) its associated scalar function.

Solution.　a) The divergence is the scalar function

$$\nabla \cdot \mathbf{u} = \frac{\partial u_x}{\partial x} + \frac{\partial u_y}{\partial y} + \frac{\partial u_z}{\partial z}$$

$$= 2x + 2z + 0 = 2(x + z)$$

b)　The curl is the vector function

$$\nabla \times \mathbf{u} = \left(\frac{\partial u_z}{\partial y} - \frac{\partial u_y}{\partial z}\right)\mathbf{i} + \left(\frac{\partial u_x}{\partial z} - \frac{\partial u_z}{\partial x}\right)\mathbf{j} + \left(\frac{\partial u_y}{\partial x} - \frac{\partial u_x}{\partial y}\right)\mathbf{k}$$

$$= (2y - 2y)\mathbf{i} + (0 - 0)\mathbf{j} + (0 - 0)\mathbf{k} = 0$$

c) We know that an associated scalar function exists since the curl is everywhere zero. It is found by equating the scalar components of Eq. 1.8.15:

$$u_x = \frac{\partial \phi}{\partial x} \Rightarrow x^2 = \frac{\partial \phi}{\partial x}. \quad \therefore \phi = \frac{x^3}{3} + f(y, z)$$

$$u_y = 2yz = \frac{\partial \phi}{\partial y} = \frac{\partial}{\partial y}\left[\frac{x^3}{3} + f(y, z)\right] = \frac{\partial f}{\partial y}$$

$$\therefore \frac{\partial f}{\partial y} = 2yz \quad \text{and} \quad f(y, z) = y^2 z + g(z)$$

$$u_z = y^2 = \frac{\partial \phi}{\partial z} = \frac{\partial}{\partial z}\left[\frac{x^3}{3} + y^2 z + g(z)\right] = y^2 + \frac{dg}{dz}$$

$$\therefore \frac{dg}{dz} = 0 \quad \text{so that} \quad g(z) = c$$

Finally,

$$\phi = \frac{x^3}{3} + y^2 z + c$$

1.9 Probability and Statistics

Events are independent if the probability of occurrence of one event does not influence the probability of occurrence of other events. The number of permutations (a particular sequence) of n things taken r at a time is

$$P(n,r) \;=\; \frac{n!}{(n-r)!} \tag{1.9.1}$$

If the starting point is unknown, as in a ring, the *ring permutation* is

$$P(n,r) \;=\; \frac{(n-1)!}{(n-r)!} \tag{1.9.2}$$

The number of *combinations* (no order-conscious arrangement) of n things taken r at a time is given by

$$C(n,r) \;=\; \frac{n!}{r!(n-r)!} \tag{1.9.3}$$

For independent events of two sample groups A and B the following rules are necessary:

1. The probability of A or B occurring equals the sum of the probability of occurrence of A and the probability of occurrence of B; that is,
$$P(A \text{ or } B) = P(A) + P(B) \tag{1.9.4}$$

2. The probability of both A and B occurring is given by the product
$$P(A \text{ and } B) = P(A)P(B) \tag{1.9.5}$$

3. The probability of A not occurring is given as
$$P(\text{not } A) = 1 - P(A) \tag{1.9.6}$$

4. The probability of either A or B occurring is given by
$$P(A \text{ or } B) = P(A) + P(B) - P(A)P(B) \tag{1.9.7}$$

The probability of an event occurring is in the range of 0 to 1. An impossible event has a probability of 0 and an event that is certain to occur has a probability of 1.

The data gathered during an experiment can be analyzed using quantities defined by the following:

1. The arithmetic mean $\bar{x}$ is the average of the observations; that is,
$$\bar{x} = \frac{x_1 + x_2 + x_3 + \cdots + x_n}{n}$$

2. The median is the middle observation when all the data is ordered by magnitude; half the values are below the median. The median for an even number of data is the average of the two middle values.

3. The mode is the observed value that occurs most frequently.

4. The standard deviation σ of the sample is a measure of variability. It is defined as

$$\sigma = \left[\frac{(x_1 - \bar{x})^2 + (x_2 - \bar{x})^2 + \cdots + (x_n - \bar{x})^2}{n-1} \right]^{1/2} \tag{1.9.8}$$

$$= \left[\frac{x_1^2 + x_2^2 + \cdots + x_n^2 - n\bar{x}^2}{n-1} \right]^{1/2} \tag{1.9.9}$$

For large observations (over 50), it is customary to simply use n, rather that $(n-1)$, in the denominators of the above. In fact, if n is used in the above equations, σ is often referred to as the *standard deviation of the population*.

5. The *variance* is defined to be σ^2.

Example 1.38

How many different ways can seven people be arranged in a lineup? In a circle?

Solution. This is the number of permutations of seven things taken seven at a time. The answer is

$$P(7,7) = \frac{n!}{(n-r)!}$$

$$= \frac{7!}{(7-7)!} = 5040$$

In a circle we use the ring permutation:

$$P(7,7) = \frac{(n-1)!}{(n-r)!}$$

$$= \frac{(7-1)!}{(7-7)!} = 720$$

Note that $0! = 1$.

Example 1.39

How many different collections of eight people can fit into a six-passenger vehicle? (Only six will fit at a time.)

Solution. The answer does not depend on the seating arrangement. If it did, it would be a permutation. Hence, we use the combination relationship and find

$$C(8,6) = \frac{n!}{(n-r)!\,r!}$$

$$= \frac{8!}{(8-6)!\,6!} = 28$$

Example 1.40

A carnival booth offers $10 if you pick a red ball and then a white ball (the first ball is re-inserted) from a bin containing 60 red balls, 15 white balls, and 25 blue balls. If $1 is charged for an attempt, will the operator make money?

Solution. The probability of drawing a red ball on the first try is 0.6. If it is then re-inserted, the probability of drawing a white ball is 0.15. The probability of accomplishing both is then given by

$$P(\text{red and white}) = P(\text{red})\,P(\text{white})$$
$$= 0.6 \times 0.15 = 0.09$$

or 9 chances out of 100 attempts. Hence, the entrepreneur will pay out $90 for every $100 taken in and will thus make money.

Example 1.41

If the operator of the bin of balls in Example 1.40 offers a $1.00 prize to contestants who pick either a red ball or a white ball from the bin on the first attempt, and charges $0.75 per attempt, will the operator make money?

Solution. The probability of selecting either a red ball or a white ball on the first attempt is

$$P(\text{red and white}) = P(\text{red}) + P(\text{white})$$
$$= 0.6 + 0.15 = 0.75$$

Consequently, 75 out of 100 gamblers will win and the operator must pay out $75 for every $75 taken in. The operator would not make any money.

Example 1.42

If the operator of Example 1.41 had two identical bins and offered a $1.00 prize for successfully withdrawing a red ball from the first bin or a white ball from the second bin, will the operator make money if he charges $0.75 per attempt?

Solution. The probability of selecting a red ball from the first bin (sample group A_i) or a white ball from the second bin (sample group B_i) is

$$P(\text{red or white}) = P(\text{red}) + P(\text{white}) - P(\text{red})\,P(\text{white})$$
$$= 0.6 + 0.15 - 0.6 \times 0.15 = 0.66$$

For this situation the owner must pay $66 to every 100 gamblers who pay $75 to participate. The profit is $9.

Example 1.43

The temperature at a given location in the south at 2 p.m. each August 10 for 25 consecutive years was measured, in degrees Celsius, to be 33, 38, 34, 26, 32, 31, 28, 39, 29, 36, 32, 29, 31, 24, 35, 34, 32, 30, 31, 32, 26, 40, 27, 33, 39. Calculate the arithmetic mean, the median, the mode and the sample standard deviation.

Solution. Using the appropriate equations, we calculate the arithmetic mean:

$$\overline{T} = \frac{T_1 + T_2 + \cdots + T_{25}}{25}$$

$$= \frac{33 + 38 + 34 + \cdots + 39}{25} = \frac{801}{25} = 32.04°\mathrm{C}$$

The median is found by first arranging the values in order. We have 24, 26, 26, 27, 28, 29, 29, 30, 31, 31, 31, 32, 32, 32, 32, 33, 33, 34, 34, 35, 36, 38, 39, 39, 40. Counting 12 values in from either end, the median is found to be 32°C.

The mode is the observation that occurs most often; it is 32°C.

The sample standard deviation is found to be

$$\sigma = \left[\frac{T_1^2 + T_2^2 + \cdots + T_{25}^2 - n\overline{T}^2}{n-1} \right]^{1/2}$$

$$= \left[\frac{33^2 + 38^2 + \cdots + 39^2 - 25 \times 32.04^2}{25-1} \right]^{1/2} = \sqrt{\frac{26,099 - 25,664}{24}} = 4.26$$

Practice Problems

1.1   A growth curve is given by $A = 10\,e^{2t}$. At what value of t is $A = 100$?

Algebra

   a) 5.261   b) 3.070   c) 1.151   d) 0.726

1.2   If $\ln x = 3.2$, what is x?

   a) 18.65   b) 24.53   c) 31.83   d) 64.58

1.3   If $\log_5 x = -1.8$, find x.

   a) 0.00483   b) 0.0169   c) 0.0552   d) 0.0783

1.4   One root of the equation $3x^2 - 2x - 2 = 0$ is

   a) 1.215   b) 1.064   c) 0.937   d) 0.826

1.5 $\sqrt{4 + x}$ can be written as the series

   a) $2 - x/4 + x^2/64 + \cdots$ c) $2 - x^2/4 - x^4/64 + \cdots$

   b) $2 + x/8 - x^2/128 + \cdots$ d) $2 + x/4 - x^2/64 + \cdots$

1.6   Resolve $\dfrac{2}{x\left(x^2 - 3x + 2\right)}$ into partial fractions.

   a) $\dfrac{1}{x} + \dfrac{1}{x-2} - \dfrac{2}{x-1}$ c) $\dfrac{2}{x} - \dfrac{1}{x-2} - \dfrac{2}{x-1}$

   b) $\dfrac{1}{x} - \dfrac{2}{x-2} + \dfrac{1}{x-1}$ d) $-\dfrac{1}{x} + \dfrac{2}{x-2} + \dfrac{1}{x-1}$

1.7   Express $\dfrac{4}{x^2\left(x^2 - 4x + 4\right)}$ as the sum of fractions.

   a) $\dfrac{1}{x} - \dfrac{1}{x-2} + \dfrac{1}{(x-2)^2}$

   b) $\dfrac{1}{x} + \dfrac{1}{x^2} - \dfrac{1}{x-2} + \dfrac{1}{(x-2)^2}$

   c) $\dfrac{1}{x^2} + \dfrac{1}{(x-2)^2}$

   d) $\dfrac{1}{x} + \dfrac{1}{x^2} + \dfrac{1}{x-2} + \dfrac{1}{(x-2)^2}$

1.8   A germ population has a growth curve of $Ae^{0.4t}$. At what value of t does its original value double?

   a) 9.682   b) 7.733   c) 4.672   d) 1.733

Trigonometry

1.9   If $\sin\theta = 0.7$, what is $\tan\theta$?

a) 0.98   b) 0.94   c) 0.88   d) 0.85

1.10   If the short leg of a right triangle is 5 units long and the long leg is 7 units long, find the angle opposite the short leg, in degrees.

a) 26.3   b) 28.9   c) 31.2   d) 35.5

1.11   The expression $\tan\theta\sec\theta\,(1-\sin^2\theta)/\cos\theta$ simplifies to

a) $\sin\theta$ b) $\cos\theta$ c) $\tan\theta$ d) $\sec\theta$

1.12   A triangle has sides of length 2, 3 and 4. What angle, in radians, is opposite the side of length 3?

a) 0.55   b) 0.61   c) 0.76   d) 0.81

1.13   The length of a lake is to be determined. A distance of 850 m is measured from one end to a point x on the shore. A distance of 732 m is measured from x to the other end. If an angle of 154° is measured between the two lines connecting x, what is the length of the lake?

a) 1542   b) 1421   c) 1368   d) 1261

1.14   Express $2\sin^2\theta$ as a function of $\cos 2\theta$.

a) $\cos 2\theta - 1$ b) $\cos 2\theta + 1$ c) $\cos 2\theta + 2$ d) $1 - \cos 2\theta$

Geometry

1.15   The included angle between two successive sides of a regular eight-sided polygon is

a) 150°   b) 135°   c) 120°   d) 75°

1.16   A large 15-m-dia cylindrical tank that sits on the ground is to be painted. If one liter of paint covers 10 m², how many liters are required if it is 10 m high? (Include the top.)

a) 65   b) 53   c) 47   d) 38

1.17   The equation of a line that has a slope of –2 and intercepts the x-axis at $x = 2$ is

a) $y + 2x = 4$ c) $y + 2x = -4$

b) $y - 2x = 4$ d) $2y + x = 2$

1.18   The equation of a line that intercepts the x-axis at $x = 4$ and the y-axis at $y = -6$ is

a) $2x - 3y = 12$ c) $2x + 3y = 12$

b) $3x - 2y = 12$ d) $3x + 2y = 12$

1.19   The shortest distance from the line $3x - 4y = 3$ to the point $(6, 8)$ is

a) 4.8   b) 4.2   c) 3.8   d) 3.4

1.20   The equation $x^2 + 4xy + 4y^2 + 2x = 10$ represents which conic section?

a) circle   b) ellipse   c) parabola   d) hyperbola

1.21   The x- and y-axes are the asymptotes of a hyperbola that passes through the point $(2, 2)$. Its equation is

a) $x^2 - y^2 = 0$ b) $xy = 4$ c) $y^2 - x^2 = 0$ d) $x^2 + y^2 = 4$

1.22   A 100-m-long track is to be built 50 m wide. If it is to be elliptical, what equation could describe it if the 100-m length is along the x-axis?

a) $50x^2 + 100y^2 = 1000$ c) $4x^2 + y^2 = 2500$

b) $2x^2 + y^2 = 250$ d) $x^2 + 2y^2 = 250$

1.23   The cylindrical coordinates $(5, 30°, 12)$ are expressed in spherical coordinates as

a) $(13, 30°, 67.4°)$ c) $(15, 52.6°, 22.6°)$

b) $(13, 30°, 22.6°)$ d) $(15, 52.6°, -22.6°)$

1.24   The equation of a 4-m-radius sphere using cylindrical coordinates is

a) $x^2 + y^2 + z^2 = 16$ c) $r^2 + z^2 = 16$

b) $r^2 = 16$ d) $x^2 + y^2 = 16$

Complex Numbers

1.25   Divide $3 - i$ by $1 + i$.

a) $1 - 2i$ b) $1 + 2i$ c) $2 - i$ d) $2 + i$

1.26   Find $(1 + i)^6$.

a) $1 + i$ b) $1 - i$ c) $8i$ d) $-8i$

1.27   Find the root of $(1+i)^{1/5}$ with the smallest argument.

a) $0.168 + 1.06i$ c) $1.06 - 0.168i$

b) $1.06 + 0.168i$ d) $0.168 - 1.06i$

1.28   Express $(3+2i)\,e^{2it} + (3-2i)\,e^{-2it}$ in terms of trigonometric functions.

a) $3\cos 2t - 4\sin 2t$ c) $6\cos 2t - 4\sin 2t$

b) $3\cos 2t - 2\sin 2t$ d) $3\sin 2t + 2\sin 2t$

Linear Algebra

1.29 Subtract $5e^{0.2i}$ from $6e^{2.3i}$. Express the answer in polar form.

a) $9.56\angle{-21.4°}$ c) $3.59\angle{255.5°}$

b) $9.56\angle{158.6°}$ d) $3.59\angle{201.4°}$

1.30 Find the value of the determinant $\begin{vmatrix} 3 & 2 & 1 \\ 0 & -1 & -1 \\ 2 & 0 & 2 \end{vmatrix}$.

a) 8   b) 4   c) –8   d) –4

1.31 Evaluate the determinant $\begin{vmatrix} 1 & 0 & 1 & 1 \\ 2 & -1 & 0 & 1 \\ 0 & 0 & 2 & 0 \\ 3 & 2 & 1 & 1 \end{vmatrix}$.

a) 8   b) 4   c) 0   d) –4

1.32 The cofactor A_{21} of the determinant of Prob. 1.30 is

a) –5   b) –4   c) 3   d) 4

1.33 The cofactor A_{34} of the determinant of Prob. 1.31 is

a) 4   b) 6   c) –6   d) –4

1.34 Find the adjoint matrix of $\begin{vmatrix} 1 & -4 \\ 0 & 2 \end{vmatrix}$.

a) $\begin{bmatrix} 4 & 2 \\ 0 & 1 \end{bmatrix}$ b) $\begin{bmatrix} 1 & 0 \\ 4 & 2 \end{bmatrix}$ c) $\begin{bmatrix} 2 & 4 \\ 1 & 0 \end{bmatrix}$ d) $\begin{bmatrix} 2 & 4 \\ 0 & 1 \end{bmatrix}$

1.35 The inverse matrix of $\begin{bmatrix} 2 & 3 \\ 1 & 1 \end{bmatrix}$ is

a) $\begin{bmatrix} -1 & 3 \\ 1 & -2 \end{bmatrix}$ b) $\begin{bmatrix} 1 & -1 \\ -3 & 2 \end{bmatrix}$ c) $\begin{bmatrix} -1 & 1 \\ -3 & 2 \end{bmatrix}$ d) $\begin{bmatrix} -2 & 3 \\ 1 & -1 \end{bmatrix}$

1.36 Calculate $\begin{bmatrix} 2 & -1 \\ 3 & 2 \end{bmatrix}\begin{bmatrix} 2 \\ 1 \end{bmatrix}$.

a) $\begin{bmatrix} 8 \\ 3 \end{bmatrix}$ b) $\begin{bmatrix} 3 \\ 8 \end{bmatrix}$ c) $\begin{bmatrix} -3 \\ -8 \end{bmatrix}$ d) $[3,8]$

1.37 Determine $\begin{bmatrix} 1 & 2 \\ 2 & 1 \end{bmatrix}\begin{bmatrix} -1 & 0 \\ 1 & 2 \end{bmatrix}$.

a) $\begin{bmatrix} 1 & 4 \\ -1 & 2 \end{bmatrix}$ b) $\begin{bmatrix} 1 & -1 \\ 4 & 2 \end{bmatrix}$ c) $\begin{bmatrix} 1 \\ -1 \end{bmatrix}$ d) $\begin{bmatrix} 4 \\ 2 \end{bmatrix}$

1.38 Solve for $[x_i]$.

$$3x_1 + 2x_2 \qquad = -2$$
$$x_1 - x_2 + x_3 = 0$$
$$4x_1 \qquad + 2x_3 = 4$$

a) $\begin{bmatrix} 2 \\ 4 \\ -6 \end{bmatrix}$ 　　b) $\begin{bmatrix} -2 \\ 4 \\ 12 \end{bmatrix}$ 　　c) $\begin{bmatrix} 2 \\ 8 \\ 4 \end{bmatrix}$ 　　d) $\begin{bmatrix} -6 \\ 8 \\ 14 \end{bmatrix}$

1.39 Find the eigenvalues of $\begin{bmatrix} 1 & 2 \\ 3 & 2 \end{bmatrix}$

a) 4, –1 　　b) 4, 1 　　c) 1, –4 　　d) 3, 2

1.40 Find an eigenvector of $\begin{bmatrix} 1 & 2 \\ 3 & 2 \end{bmatrix}$

a) $\begin{bmatrix} 4 \\ -1 \end{bmatrix}$ 　　b) $\begin{bmatrix} 2 \\ 3 \end{bmatrix}$ 　　c) $\begin{bmatrix} 1 \\ 4 \end{bmatrix}$ 　　d) $\begin{bmatrix} -3 \\ 2 \end{bmatrix}$

Calculus

1.41 The slope of the curve $y = 2x^3 - 3x$ at $x = 1$ is

a) 3 　　b) 5 　　c) 6 　　d) 8

1.42 If $y = \ln x + e^x \sin x$, find dy/dx at $x = 1$.

a) 1.23 　　b) 3.68 　　c) 4.76 　　d) 6.12

1.43 At what value of x does a maximum of $y = x^3 - 3x$ occur?

a) 2 　　b) 1 　　c) 0 　　d) –1

1.44 Where does an inflection point occur for $y = x^3 - 3x$?

a) 2 　　b) 1 　　c) 0 　　d) –1

1.45 Evaluate $\displaystyle\lim_{x \to \infty} \frac{2x^2 - x}{x^2 + x}$.

a) 2 　　b) 1 　　c) 0 　　d) –1

1.46 If a quantity η and its derivatives η' and η'' are known at a point, its approximate value at a small distance h is

a) $\eta + h^2 \eta'' / 2$ 　　　　c) $\eta + h\eta' + h^2 \eta'' / 2$

b) $\eta + h\eta / 2 + h^2 \eta''$ 　　d) $\eta + h\eta' + h^2 \eta''$

1.47 Find an approximation to $e^x \sin x$ for small x.

a) $x - x^2 + x^3$ 　　　　c) $x - x^2/2 + x^3/6$

b) $x + x^2 + x^3/3$ 　　d) $x + x^2 - x^3/6$

1.48 Find the area between the y-axis and $y = x^2$ from $y = 4$ to $y = 9$.

a) 29/3 　　b) 32/3 　　c) 34/3 　　d) 38/3

1.49 The area contained between $4x = y^2$ and $4y = x^2$ is

a) 10/3   b) 11/3   c) 13/3   d) 16/3

1.50 Rotate the shaded area of Example 1.25 about the x-axis. What volume is formed?

a) 4π b) 6π c) 8π d) 10π

1.51 Evaluate $\int_0^2 \left(e^x + \sin x \right) dx$.

a) 7.81   b) 6.21   c) 5.92   d) 5.61

1.52 Evaluate $2\int_0^1 e^x \sin x \, dx$.

a) 1.82   b) 1.94   c) 2.05   d) 2.16

1.53 Derive an expression $\int x \cos x \, dx$.

a) $x \cos x - \sin x + C$ c) $x \sin x - \cos x + C$
b) $x \sin x + \cos x + C$ d) $x \cos x + \sin x + C$

Differential Equations

1.54 The differential equation $y'' + x^2 y' + y + 2 = 0$ is

a) linear and homogeneous.   c) nonlinear and homogeneous.
b) linear and nonhomogeneous.   d) nonlinear and nonhomogeneous.

1.55 Given: $y' + 2xy = 0,$ $y(0) = 2$. Find : $y(2)$.

a) 0.0366   b) 0.127   c) 0.936   d) 2.36

1.56 Given: $y' + 2x = 0,$ $y(0) = 1$. Find: $y(10)$.

a) –100   b) –99   c) –91   d) –86

1.57 A spring-mass system is represented by $2\ddot{y} + \dot{y} + 50y = 0$. What frequency, in hertz, is contained in the solution?

a) 0.79   b) 1.56   c) 2.18   d) 3.76

1.58 Find the solution to $\ddot{y} + 16y = 0$.

a) $C_1 \cos 4t + C_2 \sin 4t$ c) $C_1 e^{4t} + C_2 t e^{4t}$
b) $C_1 e^{4t} + C_2 e^{-4t}$ d) $C_1 \cos 4t + C_2 t \cos 4t$

1.59   Find the solution to $\ddot{y} + 8\dot{y} + 16y = 0$.

   a) $C_1 \cos 4t + C_2 \sin 4t$ c) $C_1 e^{-4t} + C_2 t e^{-4t}$

   b) $C_1 t \cos 4t + C_2 \cos 4t$ d) $C_1 e^{4t} + C_2 t e^{4t}$

1.60   Solve the equation $\ddot{y} - 5\dot{y} + 6y = 4e^t$.

   a) $C_1 e^{2t} + C_2 e^{3t}$ c) $C_1 e^{2t} + C_2 t e^{3t} + 2e^t$

   b) $C_1 e^{-2t} + C_2 e^{-3t} + 2e^t$ d) $C_1 e^{2t} + C_2 e^{3t} + 2e^t$

1.61   Solve $\ddot{y} + 16y = 8 \sin 4t$.

   a) $C_1 \sin 4t + C_2 \cos 4t - t \cos 4t$ c) $C_1 \sin 4t + C_2 \cos 4t - \cos 4t$

   b) $C_1 \sin 4t + C_2 \cos 4t + t \cos 4t$ d) $C_1 \sin 4t + C_2 \cos 4t + \cos 4t$

1.62   Solve $\ddot{y} + 5\dot{y} + 6y = 0$ if $y(0) = 2$ and $\dot{y}(0) = 0$. Use Laplace transforms.

   a) $2e^{-3t} - 3e^{-2t}$ c) $4e^{-3t} - 6e^{-2t}$

   b) $2e^{3t} - 3e^{2t}$ d) $-4e^{-3t} + 6e^{-2t}$

1.63   Solve $\ddot{y} + y = 120te^{-t}$ if $y(0) = 0$ and $\dot{y}(0) = 12$.

   a) $8te^{-t} + \sin 4t$ c) $6te^{-t} + 6\sin t$

   b) $4te^t + 2\sin 4t$ d) $60\left(e^{-t} + te^{-t}\right) + 12\sin t - 60\cos t$

Vector Analysis

1.64   Given: $\mathbf{A} = 3\mathbf{i} - 6\mathbf{j} + 2\mathbf{k}$, $\mathbf{B} = 10\mathbf{i} + 4\mathbf{j} - 6\mathbf{k}$. Find: $\mathbf{A} \cdot \mathbf{B}$.

   a) $-6\mathbf{i}$ b) 6   c) -6 d) $30\mathbf{i} - 24\mathbf{j} - 12\mathbf{k}$

1.65   Given: $\mathbf{A} = 2\mathbf{i} - 5\mathbf{k}$, $\mathbf{B} = \mathbf{j}$. Find: $\mathbf{A} \times \mathbf{B}$.

   a) 0   b) $5\mathbf{i} + 2\mathbf{k}$ c) -3 d) $-3\mathbf{k}$

1.66   Find the projection of **A** in the direction of **B** if $\mathbf{A} = 14\mathbf{i} - 7\mathbf{j}$ and $\mathbf{B} = 6\mathbf{i} + 3\mathbf{j} - 2\mathbf{k}$.

   a) 9   b) $12\mathbf{i} - 3\mathbf{j}$ c) 0   d) 15

1.67   The equation of a plane perpendicular to and passing through the end of the vector $\mathbf{A} = 2\mathbf{i} - 4\mathbf{j} + 6\mathbf{k}$ is given by $2x - 4y + 6z = k$ where k is

   a) 56   b) 24   c) 0   d) -8

1.68   Estimate the area of the parallelogram with sides $\mathbf{A} = 2\mathbf{i} + 3\mathbf{j}$ and $\mathbf{B} = 4\mathbf{i} - 6\mathbf{j} + 5\mathbf{k}$.

a) 32   b) 30   c) 26   d) 20

1.69   Find a unit vector normal to the surface $x^2 + 3y^2 - 3z = 4$ at the point (1,1,0).

a) $\dfrac{\mathbf{i} + \mathbf{j}}{\sqrt{2}}$ b) $\dfrac{2\mathbf{i} - 3\mathbf{j}}{\sqrt{13}}$ c) $\dfrac{\mathbf{i} + 3\mathbf{j} - 3\mathbf{k}}{\sqrt{19}}$ d) $\dfrac{2\mathbf{i} + 6\mathbf{j} - 3\mathbf{k}}{7}$

1.70   The divergence of $\mathbf{u} = x^2\mathbf{i} + y^2\mathbf{j} + z^2\mathbf{k}$ at the point (1,1,1) is

a) $2\mathbf{i} + 2\mathbf{j} + 2\mathbf{k}$ b) $\mathbf{i} + \mathbf{j} + \mathbf{k}$ c) 3   d) 6

1.71   The curl of $\mathbf{u} = x^2\mathbf{i} + y^2\mathbf{j} + z^2\mathbf{k}$ at the point (1,1,1) is

a) $2\mathbf{i} + 2\mathbf{j} + 2\mathbf{k}$ b) $\mathbf{i} + \mathbf{j} + \mathbf{k}$ c) 3   d) 0

1.72   The vector function $\mathbf{u} = yz\mathbf{i} + xz\mathbf{j} + xy\mathbf{k}$ is

a) conservative and solenoidal   c) solenoidal only
b) conservative only   d) neither conservative nor solenoidal

Probability and Statistics

1.73   You reach into a jelly bean bag and grab one bean. If the bag contains 30 red, 25 orange, 15 pink, 10 green, and 5 black beans, the probability that you will get a black bean or a red bean is nearest to

a) 0.6   b) 0.5   c) 0.4   d) 0.3

1.74   Two jelly bean bags are identical to that of Prob. 1.73. One bean is to be selected from each bag. The probability of selecting a black bean from the first bag and a red bean from the second bag is nearest to

a) 1/100   b) 2/100   c) 3/100   d) 4/100

1.75   From the original bag of Prob. 1.73, the probability of selecting 5 beans, the first three of which are red and the next two of which are orange, is nearest to

a) 3/1000   b) 4/1000   c) 5/1000   d) 6/1000

1.76   Two bags each contain 2 black balls, 1 white ball, and 1 red ball. One ball is to be selected from each bag. What is the probability of selecting the white ball from the first bag or the red ball from the second bag?

a) 1/2   b) 7/16   c) 1/4   d) 3/8

1.77   A professor gives the following scores to her students. What is the mode?

frequency	1	3	6	11	13	10	2
score	35	45	55	65	75	85	95

a) 65   b) 75   c) 85   d) 11

1.78   For the data of Prob. 1.77, what is the arithmetic mean?

   a) 68.5   b) 68.9   c) 69.3   d) 70.2

1.79   Calculate the sample standard deviation for the data of Prob. 1.77.

   a) 9.27   b) 10.11   c) 11.56   d) 13.78

Questions 1.80–1.82
   A complex number is given by $z = 0.3 - 0.4i$.

**Afternoon Session
Practice Problems**

1.80   The magnitude of the complex number is

   a) 0.3   b) 0.4   c) 0.5   d) 0.7

1.81   The reciprocal of the complex number is

   a) $1.2 + 1.6i$ b) $1.6 + 1.2i$ c) $1.2 - 1.6i$ d) $1.6 - 1.2i$

1.82   The square root of the complex number is nearest

   a) $0.71 - 0.94i$ b) $0.53 - 0.71i$ c) $0.53 + 0.71i$ d) $0.63 - 0.32i$

Questions 1.83–1.84
   Cottages A, B and C are located on the shore of a lake. The straight-line distance from A to B is 120 meters and the straight-line distance from B to C is 80 meters. The angle between these two lines is 115°.

1.83   Calculate the distance from A to C.

   a) 129 m   b) 158 m   c) 172 m   d) 193 m

1.84   What is the angle between the line connecting B and C and the line connecting A and C?

   a) 72.1°   b) 68.4°   c) 51.2°   d) 43.6°

Questions 1.85–1.89
   The equations $\begin{array}{l} x - y = 3 \\ 2x + y = -6 \end{array}$ can be written in matrix form as $\mathbf{Ax} = \mathbf{r}$.

1.85   The matrix $\mathbf{r}$ is

   a) a square matrix
   b) a row matrix
   c) a column matrix
   d) a one by two matrix

1.86   The adjoint of **A** is

a) $\begin{bmatrix} 1 & 1 \\ -2 & 1 \end{bmatrix}$ b) $\begin{bmatrix} 1 & 2 \\ -1 & 1 \end{bmatrix}$ c) $\begin{bmatrix} 1 & -2 \\ 1 & 1 \end{bmatrix}$ d) $\begin{bmatrix} 1 & -1 \\ 2 & 1 \end{bmatrix}$

1.87   The solution vector is

a) $\begin{bmatrix} -4 \\ -1 \end{bmatrix}$ b) $\begin{bmatrix} -1, & -4 \end{bmatrix}$ c) $\begin{bmatrix} -1 \\ -4 \end{bmatrix}$ d) $\begin{bmatrix} -4, & -1 \end{bmatrix}$

1.88   The inverse of **A** is

a) $\frac{1}{3}\begin{bmatrix} 1 & 1 \\ -2 & 1 \end{bmatrix}$ b) $\frac{1}{3}\begin{bmatrix} 1 & 2 \\ -1 & 1 \end{bmatrix}$ c) $\frac{1}{3}\begin{bmatrix} 1 & -2 \\ 1 & 1 \end{bmatrix}$ d) $\frac{1}{3}\begin{bmatrix} 1 & -1 \\ 2 & 1 \end{bmatrix}$

1.89   The product $\mathbf{r}\mathbf{x}^T$ is

a) $\begin{bmatrix} -12 & -3 \\ 24 & 6 \end{bmatrix}$ b) $\begin{bmatrix} -12, & 6 \end{bmatrix}$ c) $\begin{bmatrix} -12 \\ 6 \end{bmatrix}$ d) -6

Questions 1.90–1.93

Given $f(x) = e^x \sin x$ and $g(x) = e^x - 1$.

1.90   Find $\lim\limits_{x \to 0} \dfrac{f(x)}{g(x)}$.

a) -1 b) 0 c) 1 d) ∞

1.91   Expand $f(x)$ in a Taylor series about $x = 0$. The first three terms are

a) $1 + x + x^2$

b) $x + x^2 + \frac{1}{3}x^3$

c) $x + \frac{1}{2}x^2 - \frac{1}{3}x^3$

d) $x - \frac{2}{3}x^3 + \frac{3}{5}x^5$

1.92   Find $\int_{-1}^{1} g(x)\,dx$.

a) $e - e^{-1} - 2$

b) $(e-1)(e+1)/e$

c) $e^2 - 1$

d) $e(e-1)(e+1)$

1.93   The first inflection point of $f(x)$ for $x > 0$ is found at

a) $\pi/4$ b) $\pi/2$ c) π d) $3\pi/2$

Questions 1.94–1.96

Given $f(x) = x^3$ and $g(x) = x$.

1.94 The area in the first quadrant bounded by $f(x)$ and $g(x)$ is

    a) $1/2$ b) $3/8$ c) $1/4$ d) $1/8$

1.95 The volume between $y = 0$ and $y = 1$ generated by rotating $f(x)$ about the y-axis (let $f = y$) is

    a) $\pi/5$ b) $2\pi/5$ c) $3\pi/5$ d) $4\pi/5$

1.96 The centroid of the area bounded by $f(x)$, $x = 1$ and the x-axis is found at what value of y?

    a) $4/7$ b) $3/7$ c) $2/7$ d) $1/7$

Questions 1.97–1.100

A differential equation is given by $y'' + 2y' + y = 2\sin x$.

1.97 The differential equation is

    a) linear   b) non-linear   c) first order   d) homogeneous

1.98 The homogeneous equation provides a solution which is

    a) underdamped
    b) overdamped
    c) undamped
    d) critically damped

1.99 The particular solution is

    a) $\sin x$ b) $-\sin x$ c) $\cos x$ d) $-\cos x$

1.100 The solution of the homogeneous equation is

    a) $C_1 + C_2 e^{-x}$

    b) $(C_1 + C_2 x)e^{-x}$

    c) $C_1 e^x + C_2 e^{-x}$

    d) $Ce^{-x/2}$

Questions 1.101–1.105

A differential equation is given by $y'' + 4y = f(t)$ with $y(0) = 0$ and $y'(0) = 0$.

1.101 If $f(t) = 0$, the solution represents a motion that is

a) underdamped

b) overdamped

c) undamped

d) critically damped

1.102 The solution of the homogeneous equation can be written as

a) $(C_1 \sin 2t + C_2 \cos 2t)e^{2t}$

b) $C_1 \sin 4t + C_2 \cos 4t$

c) $C_1 \sin(2t + C_2)$

d) $C_1 \cos(4t + C_2)$

1.103 The natural frequency of the system represented by this differential equation is

a) 4 rad/s   b) 4 Hz   c) 2 rad/s   d) 2 Hz

1.104 The function $f(t)$ that would not lead to resonance is

a) $2 \sin 2t$ b) $3 \cos 2t$ c) e^{2it} d) e^{2t}

1.105 If $f(t) = 6 \sin t$, the solution of the differential equation satisfying the initial conditions is

a) $2 \sin t - \sin 2t$ c) $\cos t - \cos 2t$

b) $\cos t - \sin 2t$ d) $2 \sin t - \cos 2t$

Questions 1.106–1.109

Given vectors $\mathbf{A} = 6\mathbf{i} - 8\mathbf{j}$, $\mathbf{B} = \mathbf{i} - 3\mathbf{j} + \mathbf{k}$ and $\mathbf{C} = 2\mathbf{i}$.

1.106 Find the component of $\mathbf{B}$ in the direction of $\mathbf{A}$.

a) 3   b) 26   c) –26   d) 30

1.107 The angle between $\mathbf{A}$ and $\mathbf{B}$ is nearest

a) 40°   b) 35°   c) 30°   d) 25°

1.108 If $\mathbf{C}$ is the gradient of a scalar function, that function could be

a) $2x + 10$ b) $8x$ c) $2y$ d) $5y$

1.109 The vector product $\mathbf{A} \times \mathbf{C} \cdot \mathbf{B}$ is

a) –16   b) 0   c) 8   d) 16

Solutions to Practice Problems

1.1 **c)** $100 = 10e^{2t}$. $\therefore \ln e^{2t} = \ln 10$. $\therefore 2t = 2.303$ $\therefore t = 1.151$

1.2 **b)** $\ln x = 3.2$. $\therefore e^{3.2} = x$. $\therefore x = 24.53$

1.3 **c)** $\log_5 x = -1.8$. $\therefore 5^{-1.8} = x$. $\therefore x = 0.0552$

1.4 **a)** $x = \dfrac{-(-2) \pm \sqrt{2^2 - 4(3)(-2)}}{3 \cdot 2} = 1.215$

1.5 **d)** $(4+x)^{\frac{1}{2}} = 4^{1/2} + \dfrac{1}{2} 4^{-1/2} x + \dfrac{\frac{1}{2}\left(1 - \frac{1}{2}\right)}{2} 4^{-3/2} x^2 + \cdots = 2 + x/4 - x^2/64 + \cdots$

1.6 **a)** $\dfrac{2}{x\left(x^2 - 3x + 2\right)} = \dfrac{A_1}{x} + \dfrac{A_2}{x-2} + \dfrac{A_3}{x-1} = \dfrac{A_1\left(x^2 - 3x + 2\right) + A_2\left(x^2 - x\right) + A_3\left(x^2 - 2x\right)}{x\left(x^2 - 3x + 2\right)}$

$$\left.\begin{array}{r} A_1 + A_2 + A_3 = 0 \\ -3A_1 - A_2 - 2A_3 = 0 \\ 2A_1 = 2 \end{array}\right\} \quad \left.\begin{array}{r} A_1 = 1 \\ A_2 + A_3 = -1 \\ -A_2 - 2A_3 = 3 \end{array}\right\} \quad \begin{array}{l} A_3 = -2 \\ A_2 = 1 \end{array}$$

1.7 **b)** $\dfrac{4}{x^2\left(x^2 - 4x + 4\right)} = \dfrac{A_1}{x} + \dfrac{A_2}{x^2} + \dfrac{A_3}{x-2} + \dfrac{A_4}{(x-2)^2}$

$$= \dfrac{A_1\left(x^3 - 4x^2 + 4x\right) + A_2\left(x^2 - 4x + 4\right) + A_3\left(x^3 - 2x^2\right) + A_4 x^2}{x^2(x-2)^2}$$

$$\left.\begin{array}{r} A_1 + A_3 = 0 \\ -4A_1 + A_2 - 2A_3 + A_4 = 0 \\ 4A_1 - 4A_2 = 0 \\ 4A_2 = 4 \end{array}\right\} \quad \begin{array}{l} A_2 = 1 \\ A_1 = 1 \\ A_3 = -1 \\ A_4 = 1 \end{array}$$

1.8 **d)** at $t = 0$, population $= A$. $\therefore 2A = Ae^{0.4t}$. $\ln 2 = 0.4t$. $\therefore t = 1.733$

1.9 **a)** $\sin \theta = 0.7$ $\therefore \theta = 44.43°$. $\tan 44.43° = 0.980$

1.10 **d)** $\tan \theta = 5/7$. $\therefore \theta = 35.54°$

1.11 **c)** $\tan \theta \sec \theta \left(1 - \sin^2 \theta\right)\Big/ \cos \theta = \tan \theta \dfrac{1}{\cos \theta} \cos^2 \theta \dfrac{1}{\cos \theta} = \tan \theta$

1.12 **d)** $3^2 = 4^2 + 2^2 - 2 \cdot 2 \cdot 4 \cos \theta$. $\therefore \cos \theta = 0.6875$. $\theta = 46.6°$. $\therefore \text{rad} = 0.813$

1.13 **a)** $L^2 = 850^2 + 732^2 - 2 \cdot 850 \cdot 732 \cos 154°$. $\therefore L = 1542$ m

1.14 **d)** $\cos 2\theta = \cos^2 \theta - \sin^2 \theta = 1 - \sin^2 \theta - \sin^2 \theta = 1 - 2\sin^2 \theta$. $\therefore 2\sin^2 \theta = 1 - \cos 2\theta$

1.15 b) $\theta = \pi(n-2)/n = \pi(8-2)/8$ radians. $\frac{6\pi}{8} \times \frac{180}{\pi} = 135°$

1.16 a) Area $= \text{Area}_{top} + \text{Area}_{sides} = \pi R^2 + \pi DL$

$$= \pi \times 7.5^2 + \pi \times 15 \times 10 = 648 \text{ m}^2. \quad 648 \div 10 \approx 65$$

1.17 a) $y = mx + b. \quad y = -2x + b. \quad 0 = -2(2) + b. \quad \therefore b = 4. \quad \therefore y = -2x + 4$

1.18 b) $y = mx + b. \quad 0 = 4m + b. \quad -6 = b. \quad \therefore m = 3/2. \quad \therefore y = 3x/2 - 6 \quad$ or $\quad 2y = 3x - 12$

1.19 d) $3x - 4y - 3 = 0. \quad A = 3, B = -4. \quad d = \frac{|3 \times 6 - 4 \times 8 - 3|}{\sqrt{3^2 + (-4)^2}} = 3.4$

1.20 c) $B^2 - AC = 2^2 - 1 \times 4 = 0. \quad \therefore$ parabola

1.21 b) $xy = \pm k^2 = 4$

1.22 c) $\frac{x^2}{25^2} + \frac{y^2}{50^2} = 1. \quad \therefore 4x^2 + y^2 = 2500$

1.23 b) $x = r\cos\theta = 5 \times 0.866 = 4.33. \quad y = r\sin\theta = 5 \times 0.5 = 2.5$
Spherical coordinates:

$$r = \sqrt{4.33^2 + 2.5^2 + 12^2} = 13. \quad \phi = \cos^{-1}\frac{z}{r} = \cos^{-1}\frac{12}{13} = 22.6°.$$

$$\theta = \tan^{-1}\frac{y}{x} = \tan^{-1}\frac{2.5}{4.33}. \quad \therefore \theta = 30°.$$

1.24 c) a) is rectangular coordinates. **b)** is spherical coordinates.

1.25 a) $\frac{3-i}{1+i} = \frac{3-i}{1+i}\frac{1-i}{1-i} = \frac{3-1-4i}{1-(-1)} = \frac{1}{2}(2-4i) = 1-2i$

1.26 d) $1+i = re^{i\theta}. \quad r = \sqrt{1^2 + 1^2} = \sqrt{2}. \quad \theta = \tan^{-1}\frac{1}{1} = \pi/4 \text{ rad.} \quad \therefore 1+i = \sqrt{2}e^{i\pi/4}.$

$$\therefore (1+i)^6 = \left(\sqrt{2}\right)^6 e^{i\pi 3/2} = 8\left(\cos\frac{3\pi}{2} + i\sin\frac{3\pi}{2}\right) = -8i. \text{ Note: angles are in radians.}$$

1.27 b) $1+i = \sqrt{2}e^{i\pi/4}. \quad \therefore (1+i)^{1/5} = 1.414^{1/5}e^{i\pi/20} = 1.072\left(\cos\frac{\pi}{20} + i\sin\frac{\pi}{20}\right)$

$$= 1.06 + 0.168i$$

1.28 c) $(3+2i)(\cos 2t + i\sin 2t) + (3-2i)(\cos 2t - i\sin 2t) = 6\cos 2t + 4i(i\sin 2t)$

$$= 6\cos 2t - 4\sin 2t$$

1.29 b) $6(\cos 2.3 + i\sin 2.3) - 5(\cos 0.2 + i\sin 0.2) = 6(-0.666 + 0.746i) - 5(0.98 + 0.199i)$

$$= -8.90 + 3.48i$$

$$= 9.56 \angle 158.6°$$

1.30 c) $\begin{vmatrix} 3 & 2 & 1 \\ 0 & -1 & -1 \\ 2 & 0 & 2 \end{vmatrix} = -6 - 4 + 2 = -8$

1.31 **a)** $\begin{vmatrix} 1 & 0 & 1 & 1 \\ 2 & -1 & 0 & 1 \\ 0 & 0 & 2 & 0 \\ 3 & 2 & 1 & 1 \end{vmatrix} = 2 \begin{vmatrix} 1 & 0 & 1 \\ 2 & -1 & 1 \\ 3 & 2 & 1 \end{vmatrix} = 2(-1 + 4 + 3 - 2) = 8$

Note : Expand using the third row.

1.32 **b)** $(-1)^3 \begin{vmatrix} 2 & 1 \\ 0 & 2 \end{vmatrix} = -4$

1.33 **c)** $(-1)^7 \begin{vmatrix} 1 & 0 & 1 \\ 2 & -1 & 0 \\ 3 & 2 & 1 \end{vmatrix} = -(-1 + 4 + 3) = -6$

1.34 **d)** $\left[a_{ij} \right]^+ = \begin{bmatrix} A_{11} & A_{21} \\ A_{12} & A_{22} \end{bmatrix} = \begin{bmatrix} 2 & 4 \\ 0 & 1 \end{bmatrix}$

1.35 **a)** $\left[a_{ij} \right]^{-1} = \dfrac{\left[a_{ij} \right]^+}{\left| a_{ij} \right|} = \dfrac{\begin{bmatrix} 1 & -3 \\ -1 & 2 \end{bmatrix}}{-1} = \begin{bmatrix} -1 & 3 \\ 1 & -2 \end{bmatrix}$

1.36 **b)** $\begin{bmatrix} 2 & -1 \\ 3 & 2 \end{bmatrix} \begin{bmatrix} 2 \\ 1 \end{bmatrix} = \begin{bmatrix} 4 - 1 \\ 6 + 2 \end{bmatrix} = \begin{bmatrix} 3 \\ 8 \end{bmatrix}$

1.37 **a)** $\begin{bmatrix} 1 & 2 \\ 2 & 1 \end{bmatrix} \begin{bmatrix} -1 & 0 \\ 1 & 2 \end{bmatrix} = \begin{bmatrix} 1 & 4 \\ -1 & 2 \end{bmatrix}$

1.38 **d)** $\left[a_{ij} \right] = \begin{bmatrix} 3 & 2 & 0 \\ 1 & -1 & 1 \\ 4 & 0 & 2 \end{bmatrix}.$ $\left[a_{ij} \right]^+ = \begin{bmatrix} -2 & -4 & 2 \\ 2 & 6 & -3 \\ 4 & 8 & -5 \end{bmatrix}.$ $\left| a_{ij} \right| = -2.$

$\therefore \left[a_{ij} \right]^{-1} = \dfrac{\left[a_{ij} \right]^+}{\left| a_{ij} \right|} = \begin{bmatrix} 1 & 2 & -1 \\ -1 & -3 & 3/2 \\ -2 & -4 & 5/2 \end{bmatrix}.$ $\left[x_j \right] = \left[a_{ij} \right]^{-1} \left[r_i \right] = \left[a_{ij} \right]^{-1} \begin{bmatrix} -2 \\ 0 \\ 4 \end{bmatrix} = \begin{bmatrix} -6 \\ 8 \\ 14 \end{bmatrix}$

1.39 **a)** $\begin{vmatrix} 1 - \lambda & 2 \\ 3 & 2 - \lambda \end{vmatrix} = \lambda^2 - 3\lambda + 2 - 6 = \lambda^2 - 3\lambda - 4 = 0.$

$(\lambda - 4)(\lambda + 1) = 0. \quad \therefore \ \lambda = 4, -1$

1.40 **b)** Use $\lambda = 4.$ $\begin{bmatrix} -3 & 2 \\ 3 & -2 \end{bmatrix} \begin{bmatrix} x_1 \\ x_2 \end{bmatrix} = 0.$

$\begin{aligned} -3x_1 + 2x_2 &= 0. \\ 3x_1 - 2x_2 &= 0. \end{aligned} \quad \therefore \ \mathbf{x} = \begin{bmatrix} 2 \\ 3 \end{bmatrix}$

Any multiple is also an eigenvector, e.g., $\mathbf{x} = \begin{bmatrix} 1 \\ 3/2 \end{bmatrix}$ or $\mathbf{x} = \begin{bmatrix} 2/\sqrt{13} \\ 3/\sqrt{13} \end{bmatrix}$

1.41 **a)** $\dfrac{dy}{dx} = 6x^2 - 3 = 6(1)^2 - 3 = 3$

1.42 **c)** $\dfrac{dy}{dx} = \dfrac{1}{x} + e^x \cos x + e^x \sin x = 1 + e \cos 1 + e \sin 1 = 4.76.$ ($\cos 1 = \cos 57.3°$)

1.43 **d)** $\dfrac{dy}{dx} = 3x^2 - 3 = 0.$ $\therefore x^2 = 1.$ $\therefore x = \pm 1.$ $\dfrac{d^2 y}{dx^2} = 6x.$ $\therefore x = -1$ is a maximum.

1.44 **c)** $y' = 3x^2 - 3.$ $y'' = 6x.$ $\therefore x = 0$ is inflection.

1.45 **a)** $\lim\limits_{x \to \infty} \dfrac{2x^2 - x}{x^2 + x} = \lim\limits_{x \to \infty} \dfrac{4x - 1}{2x + 1} = \lim\limits_{x \to \infty} \dfrac{4}{2} = 2$

1.46 **c)** $\eta(x + h) = \eta + h\eta' + \dfrac{h^2}{2}\eta''$

1.47 **b)** $e^x \sin x = \left(1 + x + \dfrac{x^2}{2}\right)\left(x - \dfrac{x^3}{6}\right) = x + x^2 + \dfrac{x^3}{2} - \dfrac{x^3}{6} = x + x^2 + x^3/3$

1.48 **d)** Area $= \int\limits_{4}^{9} x\,dy = \int\limits_{4}^{9} y^{1/2}\,dy = \dfrac{2}{3}(27 - 8) = 12\,\dfrac{2}{3}$

1.49 **d)** Area $= \int\limits_{0}^{4}(x_2 - x_1)\,dy = \int\limits_{0}^{4}\left(2y^{1/2} - \dfrac{y^2}{4}\right)dy$

$= 2 \times \dfrac{2}{3} \times 8 - \dfrac{1}{12} \times 64 = 16/3$

1.50 **c)** $V = \int\limits_{0}^{2} 2\pi y\, x\,dy = 2\pi \int\limits_{0}^{2} y^3\,dy = 2\pi \times \dfrac{2^4}{4} = 8\pi$

1.51 **a)** $\int\limits_{0}^{2}\left(e^x + \sin x\right)dx = e^x - \cos x\Big|_0^2 = e^2 - 1 - \cos 2 + 1 = 7.81$

1.52 **a)** $\int\limits_{0}^{1} e^x \sin x\,dx = e^x \sin x\Big|_0^1 - \int\limits_{0}^{1} e^x \cos x\,dx$ $\begin{array}{ll} u = \sin x & dv = e^x dx \\ du = \cos x\,dx & v = e^x \end{array}$

$\underbrace{}_{\text{1st integral}}$

$\begin{array}{ll} u = \cos x & dv = e^x dx \\ v = e^x & du = -\sin x\,dx \end{array}$

$\underbrace{}_{\text{2nd integral}}$

$\therefore \int\limits_{0}^{1} e^x \sin x\,dx = e \sin 1 - \left[e^x \cos x\Big|_0^1 + \int\limits_{0}^{1} e^x \sin x\,dx \right]$

$\therefore 2\int\limits_{0}^{1} e^x \sin x\,dx = e \sin 1 - e \cos 1 + 1 \times 1 = 1.819.$ $\therefore \int\limits_{0}^{1} e^x \sin x\,dx = 0.909$

1.53 **b)** $\int x \cos x \, dx = x \sin x - \int \sin x \, dx = x \sin x + \cos x + C$

$$\begin{array}{cc} u = x & dv = \cos x \, dx \\ du = dx & v = \sin x \end{array}$$

$$\underbrace{}_{\text{1st integral}}$$

1.54 **b)** linear and nonhomogeneous. The term (+2) makes it nonhomogeneous. $x^2 y'$ is linear.

1.55 **a)** $\dfrac{dy}{dx} = -2xy.$ $\dfrac{dy}{y} = -2x \, dx.$ $\therefore \ln y = -x^2 + C.$ $\ln 2 = 0 + C.$ $\therefore C = \ln 2.$

$y(2) = \exp\left(-2^2 + \ln 2\right) = 0.0366$

1.56 **b)** $\dfrac{dy}{dx} = -2x.$ $dy = -2x \, dx.$ $\therefore y = -x^2 + C.$ $1 = 0 + C.$ $\therefore C = 1.$

$y(10) = -10^2 + 1 = -99$

1.57 **a)** $2m^2 + m + 50 = 0.$ $\therefore m = \dfrac{-1 \pm \sqrt{1 - 400}}{4} = -\dfrac{1}{4} \pm 4.99i.$

$\therefore y(t) = e^{-t/4}\left(A \cos 4.99t + B \sin 4.99t\right).$

$\therefore \omega = 4.99 \text{ rad/s}.$ $\therefore f = \dfrac{\omega}{2\pi} = \dfrac{4.99}{2\pi} = 0.794 \text{ hertz}$

1.58 **a)** $m^2 + 16 = 0.$ $\therefore m = \pm 4i.$ $\therefore y(t) = C_1 \cos 4t + C_2 \sin 4t$

1.59 **c)** $m^2 + 8m + 16 = 0.$ $(m + 4)^2 = 0.$ $m = -4, -4.$ $\therefore y(t) = C_1 e^{-4t} + C_2 t e^{-4t}$

1.60 **d)** $m^2 - 5m + 6 = 0.$ $m = \dfrac{5 \pm \sqrt{25 - 24}}{2} = 3, 2.$ $\therefore y_h = C_1 e^{3t} + C_2 e^{2t}.$

Assume $y_p = Ae^t.$ Then $Ae^t - 5Ae^t + 6Ae^t = 4e^t.$ $\therefore A = 2.$

1.61 **a)** homogeneous: $m^2 + 16 = 0.$ $\therefore m = \pm 4i.$ $\therefore y_h(t) = C_1 \sin 4t + C_2 \cos 4t$

particular: $y_p = At \cos 4t.$ (This is resonance.) $\dot{y}_p = A \cos 4t - 4At \sin 4t$

$\therefore -4A \sin 4t - 4A \sin 4t - 16At \cos 4t + 16At \cos 4t = 8 \sin 4t$

$\therefore -8A = 8.$ $A = -1.$ $\therefore y = y_h + y_p = C_1 \sin 4t + C_2 \cos 4t - t \cos 4t$

1.62 **d)** $s^2 Y - 2s + 5sY - 10 + 6Y = 0.$ $Y = \dfrac{2s + 10}{s^2 + 5s + 6} = \dfrac{-4}{s + 3} + \dfrac{6}{s + 2}.$

$\therefore y(t) = -4e^{-3t} + 6e^{-2t}$

1.63 **d)** $s^2 Y - 12 + Y = \dfrac{120}{(s + 1)^2}.$ $Y = \dfrac{12}{s^2 + 1} + \dfrac{120}{(s + 1)^2(s^2 + 1)}$

$$= \dfrac{12}{s^2 + 1} + \dfrac{60}{s + 1} + \dfrac{60}{(s + 1)^2} - \dfrac{60s}{s^2 + 1}$$

$\therefore y(t) = 12 \sin t - 60 \cos t + 60\left(e^{-t} + te^{-t}\right)$

1.64 **c)** $\mathbf{A} \cdot \mathbf{B} = 3 \cdot 10 + (-6) \cdot 4 + 2(-6) = -6$

1.65 **b)** $\mathbf{A} \times \mathbf{B} = (2\mathbf{i} - 5\mathbf{k}) \times \mathbf{j} = 2\mathbf{i} \times \mathbf{j} - 5\mathbf{k} \times \mathbf{j} = 2\mathbf{k} - 5(-\mathbf{i}) = 5\mathbf{i} + 2\mathbf{k}$

1.66 **a)** $\mathbf{i_B} = (6\mathbf{i} + 3\mathbf{j} - 2\mathbf{k}) / \sqrt{6^2 + 3^2 + 2^2} = \frac{1}{7}(6\mathbf{i} + 3\mathbf{j} - 2\mathbf{k})$

$\mathbf{A} \cdot \mathbf{i_B} = [14 \cdot 6 - 7(3)]/7 = 12 - 3 = 9$

1.67 **a)** $[(x\mathbf{i} + y\mathbf{j} + z\mathbf{k}) - (2\mathbf{i} - 4\mathbf{j} + 6\mathbf{k})] \cdot (2\mathbf{i} - 4\mathbf{j} + 6\mathbf{k}) = 0.$

$2(x - 2) - 4(y + 4) + 6(z - 6) = 0. \quad \therefore 2x - 4y + 6z = 56$

1.68 **b)** $|\mathbf{A} \times \mathbf{B}| = |15\mathbf{i} - 10\mathbf{j} - 24\mathbf{k}| = \sqrt{901} \cong 30$

1.69 **d)** $\nabla\phi = 2x\mathbf{i} + 6y\mathbf{j} - 3\mathbf{k} = 2\mathbf{i} + 6\mathbf{j} - 3\mathbf{k}. \quad |\nabla\phi| = 7. \quad \therefore \mathbf{i_n} = \nabla\phi/|\nabla\phi| = (2\mathbf{i} + 6\mathbf{j} - 3\mathbf{k})/7$

1.70 **d)** $\nabla \cdot u = 2x + 2y + 2z = 2 + 2 + 2 = 6$

1.71 **d)** $\nabla \times \mathbf{u} = (0 - 0)\mathbf{i} + (0 - 0)\mathbf{j} + (0 - 0)\mathbf{k} = 0$

1.72 **a)** $\nabla \cdot \mathbf{u} = 0 + 0 + 0 = 0. \quad \therefore$ solenoidal. $\nabla \times \mathbf{u} = (x - x)\mathbf{i} + (y - y)\mathbf{j} + (z - z)\mathbf{k} = 0.$

$\therefore$ conservative and solenoidal.

1.73 **c)** $P(A_1 \text{ or } A_2) = P(A_1) + P(A_2) = \frac{5}{85} + \frac{30}{85} = 0.41$

1.74 **b)** $P(A_1 \text{ and } B_1) = P(A_1)P(B_1) = \frac{5}{85} \times \frac{30}{85} = 0.0208 \text{ or } 2/96.3$

1.75 **b)** $P = \frac{30}{85} \times \frac{29}{84} \times \frac{28}{83} \times \frac{25}{82} \times \frac{24}{81} = 0.0037 \text{ or } 4/1077$

1.76 **b)** $P(A \text{ or } B) = P(A) + P(B) - P(A)P(B) = \frac{1}{4} + \frac{1}{4} - \frac{1}{4} \times \frac{1}{4} = 7/16$

1.77 **b)** The mode is the observation that occurs most frequently. It is 75.

1.78 **d)** $\bar{x} = \dfrac{35 + 3 \times 45 + 6 \times 55 + 11 \times 65 + 13 \times 75 + 10 \times 85 + 2 \times 95}{1 + 3 + 6 + 11 + 13 + 10 + 2} = \dfrac{3230}{46} = 70.217$

1.79 **d)** $\sigma = \sqrt{\dfrac{35^2 + 3 \times 45^2 + 6 \times 55^2 + 11 \times 65^2 + 13 \times 75^2 + 10 \times 85^2 + 2 \times 95^2 - 46 \times 70.217^2}{45}} = 13.78$

1.80 **c)** $\sqrt{0.3^2 + 0.4^2} = 0.5$

1.81 **a)** $\dfrac{0.3 + 0.4i}{(0.3 - 0.4i)(0.3 + 0.4i)} = \dfrac{1}{0.9 + 0.16}(0.3 + 0.4i) = 4(0.3 + 0.4i) = 1.2 + 1.6i$

1.82 **d)** $0.3 - 0.4i = 0.5e^{-0.927i}$ where $\theta = \tan^{-1}\dfrac{-0.4}{0.3} = 0.927$

$\therefore \sqrt{0.3 - 0.4i} = \sqrt{0.5}e^{-0.927i/2} = 0.707\left(\cos\dfrac{-0.927}{2} + i\sin\dfrac{-0.927}{2}\right)$

$= 0.632 - 0.316i$

1.83 **c)** $z^2 = x^2 + y^2 - 2xy\cos\alpha = 120^2 + 80^2 - 2 \times 120 \times 80\cos 115° = 28\,910$ m. $\therefore\ z = 170$ m.

1.84 **d)** $\dfrac{120}{\sin\alpha} = \dfrac{157.7}{\sin 115°}.$ $\therefore \sin\alpha = 0.6896.$ $\therefore \alpha = 43.6°$

1.85 **c)**

1.86 **a)** $\mathbf{A} = \begin{bmatrix} 1 & -1 \\ 2 & 1 \end{bmatrix}.$ $\therefore \operatorname{adj}\mathbf{A} = \begin{bmatrix} 1 & 1 \\ -2 & 1 \end{bmatrix}.$ Remember, the cofactor of the −1 element is
−2 and it is placed in the position of the 2 element.

1.87 **c)** By inspection: $x = -1$ and $y = -4$. The solution vector is $\begin{bmatrix} x \\ y \end{bmatrix} = \begin{bmatrix} -1 \\ -4 \end{bmatrix}$

1.88 **a)** $\mathbf{A}^{-1} = \dfrac{\operatorname{adj}\mathbf{A}}{\det\mathbf{A}} = \dfrac{\begin{bmatrix} 1 & 1 \\ -2 & 1 \end{bmatrix}}{1+2} = \dfrac{1}{3}\begin{bmatrix} 1 & 1 \\ -2 & 1 \end{bmatrix}$

1.89 **a)** $\mathbf{r}\,\mathbf{x}^T = \begin{bmatrix} 3 \\ -6 \end{bmatrix}[-4,-1] = \begin{bmatrix} -12 & -3 \\ 24 & 6 \end{bmatrix}$

1.90 **c)** $\dfrac{f(0)}{g(0)} = \dfrac{0}{0} = \text{undefined.}$ $\dfrac{f'(0)}{g'(0)} = \dfrac{1-0}{1} = 1$

1.91 **b)** $e^x = 1 + x + \dfrac{1}{2}x^2 + \cdots,$ $\sin x = x - \dfrac{1}{6}x^3 + \cdots$

$\therefore e^x \sin x = (1 + x + \dfrac{1}{2}x^2 + \cdots)(x - \dfrac{1}{6}x^3 + \cdots) = x + x^2 + \dfrac{1}{3}x^3 + \cdots$

1.92 **a)** $\displaystyle\int_{-1}^{1}(e^x - 1)dx = \left[e^x - x\right]_{-1}^{1} = e - 1 - e^{-1} - 1 = e - e^{-1} - 2$

1.93 **b)** $f'(x) = e^x \cos x + e^x \sin x.$ $f''(x) = 2e^x \cos x.$

$2e^x \cos x = 0.$ $\therefore \cos x = 0.$ $\therefore x = \pi/2$

1.94 **c)** Let $f = y.$ area $= \displaystyle\int_{0}^{1} x\,dy - \dfrac{1}{2}(1 \times 1) = \int_{0}^{1} x(3x^2 dx) - \dfrac{1}{2}$

$= 3\displaystyle\int_{0}^{1} x^3 dx - \dfrac{1}{2} = \dfrac{3}{4} - \dfrac{1}{2} = \dfrac{1}{4}$

1.95 **c)** Let $f = y.$ volume $= \displaystyle\int_{0}^{1} \pi x^2 dy = \pi\int_{0}^{1} x^2(3x^2 dx) = 3\pi\dfrac{1}{5}$

1.96 **c)** $y_c = \dfrac{\int_{0}^{1}\frac{1}{2}y(y\,dx)}{\int_{0}^{1} y\,dx} = \dfrac{\frac{1}{2}\int_{0}^{1} x^6 dx}{\int_{0}^{1} x^3 dx} = \dfrac{1}{2}\dfrac{1/7}{1/4} = \dfrac{2}{7}.$ Note: we used $(y/2)dA$ in the
numerator since we selected a vertical strip. With a horizontal strip we would
use $y\,dA$ but it would be somewhat more difficult to use since $dA = (1 - x)dy.$

1.97 **a)** It's linear, second order, non-homogeneous with constant coefficients.

1.98 **d)** $r^2 + 2r + 1 = 0$. $\therefore r = -1, -1$. $\therefore y(x) = (C_1 + C_2 x)e^{-x}$

1.99 **d)** $y_p(x) = A \sin x + B \cos x$. Substitute into the diff eq and find

$$-A \sin x - B \cos x + 2A \cos x - 2B \sin x + A \sin x + B \cos x = 2 \sin x$$

$$\therefore\ 2A = 0,\ \ -2B = 2.\ \ \therefore A = 0,\ \ B = -1.\ \ \therefore y_p(x) = -\cos x$$

1.100 **b)** The characteristic equation is $r^2 + 2r + 1 = 0$ or $(r + 1)(r + 1) = 0$.

$$\therefore r = -1, -1.\ \ \therefore y_h(x) = (C_1 + C_2 x)e^{-x}$$

1.101 **c)** There is no y'-term.

1.102 **b)** The characteristic equation is $r^2 + 4 = 0$. $\therefore r = \pm 2i$.

$\therefore y(t) = C_1 \sin 2t + C_2 \cos 2t$ which can be written as $A \sin(2t + B)$

since this is $A(\sin 2t \cos B + \cos 2t \sin B) = A \cos B \sin 2t + A \sin B \cos 2t$.

Let $A \cos B = C_1$ and $A \sin B = C_2$. The two solutions are equivalent.

1.103 **c)** The natural frequency is $\sqrt{k/m} = \sqrt{4/1} = 2$ rad/s. Note: k is the coefficient of y and m is the coefficient of y''.

1.104 **d)** If the frequency of the forcing function $f(t)$ is the same as the natural frequency, resonance will result. Only (d) has no forcing frequency of 2 rad/s. Note: $e^{2it} = \cos 2t + i \sin 2t$.

1.105 **a)** Let $y_p(t) = A \sin t + B \cos t$. Substitute into the diff eq:

$$-A \sin t - B \cos t + 4A \sin t + 4B \cos t = 6 \sin t.\ \ \therefore B = 0,\ \ A = 2.$$

The solution is then $y(t) = C_1 \sin 2t + C_2 \cos 2t + 2 \sin t$. This must satisfy the initial conditions :

$$\left.\begin{array}{l} y(0) = C_2 = 0 \\ y'(0) = 2C_1 + 2 = 0 \end{array}\right\}\ \ \therefore C_2 = 0,\ \ C_1 = -1\ \text{and}\ y(t) = 2 \sin t - \sin 2t$$

1.106 **a)** $\mathbf{i}_A = \dfrac{\mathbf{A}}{A} = \dfrac{6\mathbf{i} - 8\mathbf{j}}{10}$. $\mathbf{B} \cdot \mathbf{i}_A = (\mathbf{i} - 3\mathbf{j} + \mathbf{k}) \cdot \dfrac{6\mathbf{i} - 8\mathbf{j}}{10} = 0.6 + 2.4 = 3$

1.107 **d)** $\mathbf{A} \cdot \mathbf{B} = AB \cos\theta$. $(6\mathbf{i} - 8\mathbf{j}) \cdot (\mathbf{i} - 3\mathbf{j} + \mathbf{k}) = 10 \times \sqrt{11} \cos\theta$.

$$\therefore \cos\theta = \frac{6 + 24}{10 \times \sqrt{11}} = 0.9045.\ \ \therefore \theta = 25.2°$$

1.108 **a)** $2 = \dfrac{\partial\phi}{\partial x}$. $\therefore \phi = 2x + C$.   Let $C = 10$.

1.109 **d)** $\mathbf{A} \times \mathbf{C} = 16\mathbf{k}$. $16\mathbf{k} \cdot (\mathbf{i} - 3\mathbf{j} + \mathbf{k}) = 16$.

Digital Computing

by Bernhard Weinberg

Chapter 2

Digital computing crosses the boundaries of Mathematics and Engineering. For the most part, it is a tool to be used for the more important tasks at hand. The topics covered here are relevant to the FE/EIT exam; the subject of computing is not covered in any comprehensive manner. The basics of number systems, spreadsheet usage, and the elementary notions of programming are considered. Some comments are also related to Operating Systems.

2.1 Number Systems

A number may be represented as a polynomial in powers of its *base* or *radix*. Most digital computers represent numbers internally in base 2 (*binary*) rather than base 10 (*decimal*). For clarification, consider the following example.

> **Example 2.1**
>
> Evaluate the base 2 number 1101.01 to the base 10 equivalent value.
>
> **Solution.** The base conversion proceeds as follows:
>
> $$1101.01_2 = 1 \times 2^3 + 1 \times 2^2 + 0 \times 2^1 + 1 \times 2^0 + 0 \times 2^{-1} + 1 \times 2^{-2} = 13.25_{10}$$

Of necessity, all numbers in a digital computer are of finite length and, hence, numerical precision must always be a consideration. It is convenient when handling long binary numbers to group the digits (*bits*) into groups of three or four. If grouped in threes, the numerical value for each group is between 0 and 7; if grouped in fours, the range is from 0 to 15. Thus, by grouping bits, a binary number may be conveniently represented either as a base 8 (*octal*) or base 16 (*hexadecimal*) number. In the case of hexadecimal, a convenient notation for digits larger than 9 is to use the letters A through F for the digits equivalent to 10 through 15. Thus, the integer 28_{10} is 34_8 or $1C_{16}$. The integer $3AC_{16}$ is 1110101100_2 or 940_{10}.

Assume the integer to be converted is I_0; the problem is to solve the equation

$$I_0 = d_n r^n + \ldots + d_2 r^2 + d_1 r + d_0 \qquad (2.1.1)$$

for the values of d_i which are the digits of the base r equivalent. Recall that if two integers are divided, the result is another integer plus a fractional remainder. We begin with

$$\frac{I_0}{r} = \underbrace{d_n r^{n-1} + \ldots + d_2 r + d_1}_{I_1} + \underbrace{\frac{d_0}{r}}_{F_1} \qquad (2.1.2)$$

The fractional remainder is the low order digit. The next lower order digit may be obtained by dividing the above integral part by r:

$$\frac{I_1}{r} = \underbrace{d_n r^{n-2} + \ldots + d_3 r + d_2}_{I_2} + \underbrace{\frac{d_1}{r}}_{F_2} \qquad (2.1.3)$$

The process may be repeated to obtain the base r digits from right to left while the integer part I_i is not zero. The base r digits are expressed in their decimal equivalents.

Example 2.2

Convert the base 10 integer 45 to the base 16 equivalent value.

Solution. Refer to Eq. 2.1.2 and we have

$$\frac{45}{16} = 2, \quad \text{remainder} = 13; \quad \frac{2}{16} = 0, \quad \text{remainder} = 2$$

Consequently, there results

$$45_{10} = 2D_{16}$$

Negative binary integers may be represented using either 1's complement or 2's complement notation. The 1's complement negation of a binary integer requires that each bit of the number be "flipped" independently; that is, a 0 becomes a 1 and a 1 becomes a 0. The left-most bit of a number indicates it's a sign, a 0 indicates positive and a 1 indicates negative. This implies that the decimal integer 27 be represented by at least 6 bits as 011011. If interpreted as a signed number, the pattern 11011 is equivalent to –4 and not 27. The 1's complement representation of 0 is either 0...0 or 1...1. Because of the dual representation of 0, arithmetic with 1's complement numbers may require corrective measures.

The easiest way to obtain the 2's complement of a number is to add 1 to the 1's complement of the number. The 2's complement of N is equivalent to 0–N. A useful hexadecimal trick is to scan the number from right to left. The right-most zeros are copied. The right-most non-zero digit is subtracted from 16. The remaining left digits are subtracted from 15.

All arithmetic operations with complement numbers must be done with a sufficient number of bits to include the value and sign. If 1's complement is used, all carries (borrows) out of the left-most sign bit must be brought around and added (subtracted) into the right-most bit position. The sign bit carry (borrow) is ignored with 2's complement arithmetic, as the following example illustrates.

Example 2.3

Add −5 to 7 using 6-bit 1's and 2's complement representation.

Solution. We use the above described steps:

	1's complement		2's complement	
7	000111		000111	
−5	111010		111011	
2	1 000001	end-around	1 000010	ignore carry
	1	carry	000010	
	000010			

When negative numbers are represented in complement form, the sign bit is treated as an ordinary numerical bit. The end-around carry (borrow) in 1's complement signals the need for the result correction because of the dual representation of zero. Numerical overflow during addition is signaled by two numbers of the same sign yielding a sum of the opposite sign. Numerical overflow during subtraction may occur only with oppositely signed numbers. It occurs when the sign of the difference is the opposite sign of the subtrahend (second number).

A collection of 8 bits, without regard to any numerical implications, is called a *byte*. An *ASCII* text character requires one byte. A half byte, or 4 bits, is called a *nibble*. When dealing with large binary numbers, the value $1024 = 2^{10}$ is abbreviated K. The value $1,048,576 = 2^{20}$ is abbreviated by M. Thus, a computer memory that has $16M$ bytes actually has 16,777,216 bytes.

Real numbers are represented by a signed exponent and signed mantissa similar to scientific notations. Most commonly, a *single precision* real number uses 32-bit representation and a *double precision* real number uses a 64-bit representation.

2.2 Spreadsheets

The *spreadsheet* is essentially a rectangular grid wherein each cell can contain numerical or textual data. The data within cells may be operated on to produce new data. One of the more desirable features of a spreadsheet is that the data presentation possibilities range from a straight data listing using any of a variety of equations to the production of graphs and pie charts. This section will concentrate only on numerical computation features.

Each cell in a spreadsheet is referenced by a column-row coordinate system. Columns are indicated by one or more letters, whereas rows are indicated by one or more digits. Computations are done by placing a formula in an indicated cell. The formula is essentially an arithmetic expression specifying the operand cell coordinate. Cell coordinates may be either absolute or relative. An absolute coordinate always refers to the specified cell. Absolute coordinates are usually specified by placing a special character, such as a $, in front of both the column and row specifier. A relative coordinate is specified without any special character indication. The following example illustrates relative coordinates and shows how they differ from absolute coordinates.

> 🔑 Columns are indicated by one or more letters, whereas rows are indicated by one or more digits.

Example 2.4

Add the contents of cell B4 with cells A3 and E7 placing the two sums into cells D5 and H9, respectively.

Solution. Enter the formula = A3 + $B$4 into D5. Assuming that cells A3 and B4, have numbers in them, the sum will appear in cell D5. If the formula entered in D5 is copied into cell H9, the sum of cells E7 (providing it has a number in it) and B4 will appear in cell H9.

The appearance of the D5 sum is straight forward; the H9 sum is the result of absolute and relative coordinates. When a formula is copied from one cell to another, and a relative coordinate is specified, the cell used has the same relative position to the target as the original cell did to the original target. In other words, A3 is 3 columns to the left and 2 rows above the target D5. Note that E7 is 3 columns to the left and 2 rows above the target H9. If the cell B4 were not specified as absolute, cell G8 would be used for the second operand.

The copy operation is usually labeled as "copy/cut and paste" and works on single cells or a range of cells.

An absolute coordinate specification can be absolute in both the column and row, or in either the column or the row. The specification $Q12 implies that the column is absolute while the row is relative. In addition to having the usual arithmetic operators, a spreadsheet also has a number of functions including trigonometric and statistical functions. Particularly in the statistical functions, it is useful to specify a range of cells to be operated on rather than name each cell individually. Thus, to add a column of numbers, the formula with a range "= sum(R10:R35)" is more convenient than writing "= sum(R10, R11, ..., R34, R35)".

Example 2.5

Calculate the range of a cannonball assuming air resistance proportional to v^2. Assume a muzzle velocity of $V = 200$ m/s, a firing angle of $30°$, and a normalized air resistance drag of $0.25mgv^2/V^2$.

Solution. The differential equations that describe the flight of the cannonball are

$$m\frac{dv_y}{dt} = -mg - 0.25mg\frac{|v_y|v_y}{V^2}$$

$$m\frac{dv_x}{dt} = -0.25mg\frac{v_x^2}{V^2}$$

$$\frac{ds_y}{dt} = v_y$$

$$\frac{ds_x}{dt} = v_x$$

For no air resistance, the drag is zero and a closed-form solution yields the "time of flight" and the "horizontal range" as

$$t = \frac{2V\sin\theta}{g} \qquad R = \frac{2V^2\sin\theta\cos\theta}{g}$$

For this example the closed-form solutions give $t = 20.39$ seconds and $R = 3531$ meters using $g = 9.81$ m/s^2.

If 100 steps for the numerical integration are chosen, the ideal time of flight yields a Δt value of 0.204 seconds. The initial horizontal and vertical velocities are $V\cos\theta$ and $V\sin\theta$, respectively. The initial horizontal and vertical distances are both 0. The spreadsheet solution begins with the following steps where the cell numbers are arbitrarily selected. Some spreadsheets may require the angle in radians rather than degrees.

Cell	Entry	Comment
A1	200.0	Muzzle velocity
B1	30.0	Angle
C1	0.25	Relative drag
D1	9.81	Gravity
E1	0.2039	Δt for integration
F1	=C1*D1/(A1*A1)	Drag factor
A5	=A1*sin(B1)	Initial Y velocity
B5	0.0	Initial Y position
C5	=A1*cos(B1)	Initial X velocity
D5	0.0	Initial X position

Now the actual numerical integration can begin. When finished, cells, A5: A105, B5: B105, C5: C105 and D5: D105 will contain, respectively, the y velocity, y position, x velocity, and x position at the end of each time increment. The following steps will perform the integration.

Cell	Entry	Comment
A6	=A5-($D$1+$F$1*A5*abs(A5))*$E$1	*y* velocity
A7:A105	copy A6 formula	integration
B6	=B5+A6*$E$1	*y* position
B7:B105	copy B6 formula	integration
C6	=C5-$F$1*C5*C5*$E$1	*x* velocity
C7:C105	copy C6 formula	integration
D6	=D5+C6*$E$1	*x* position
D7:D105	copy D6 formula	integration

The last several rows of the spreadsheet reveal the answer sought.

	A	B	C	D
100	-90.55	45.88	143.60	3047.4
101	-92.44	27.03	143.34	3076.754
102	-94.34	7.796	148.09	3105.8
103	-96.23	-11.8	142.83	3135.0
104	-98.11	-31.8	142.58	3164.0
105	99.99	-52.2	142.32	3193.0

The maximum range is the *x* position (Column D) where the cannon ball has zero altitude (Column B). Thus from row 102 and row 103, the range is about 3120 meters, some 400 meters short because of air resistance.

A side benefit of using a spreadsheet to make a calculation is that if a parameter is changed, a recalculation of all dependent values is done automatically. Suppose, in the above example, that the firing angle is changed from 30 to 40 degrees. Then the entire calculation would be redone without any further intervention.

2.3 Programming

Although the Spreadsheet is a powerful computational tool, there is a class of problems which require complex decision making in their solution. For such problems, a programming solution may be the best way to obtain the desired results.

A program can be written using only three instruction flow constructs:

* **Sequence**   A linear sequence of constructs.

* **Selection**   The choosing of a particular construct from several possible constructs according to some condition.

* **Repetition**   The repeated execution of a construct as long as some condition is satisfied.

These constructs can be illustrated either by *pseudo code* or *flow charts*. Pseudo code is programming language like notation that can range from a plain-word description of the computation to the program itself. Flow charts are graphical representations of the computation. There are two types of flow charts, structured and unstructured. The structured form is composed of nested rectangular boxes which have a single entry at the top and a single exit at the bottom. The unstructured form consists of boxes connected by lines. It is possible, but certainly not recommended, that these unstructured flow charts be drawn with multiple entries and exits, hence they are referred to as *spaghetti* because of the resulting jumble of connections.

Sequence is just a series of statements, executed serially. Fig.2.1 shows the three forms for sequence. The execution order of Stmt 1 and Stmt 2 is not important and is implied from both statements being within the same block of the flow charts. Order-critical execution such as Stmt 1-2 coming before Stmt 3 is implied with a separate box.

Selection is analogous to **IF ELSE**, **IF**, or **CASE** statements. Fig.2.2 illustrates the **IF ELSE** construction. The Spaghetti flow chart allows the two alternatives to have individual exits. This should be avoided, especially in a language that permits the **GOTO** statement.

> Flow charts are graphical representations of the computation.

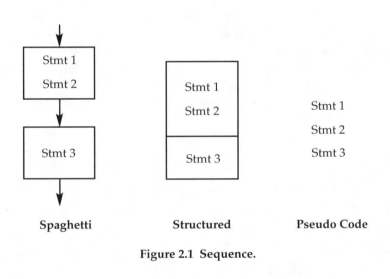

Spaghetti   **Structured**   **Pseudo Code**

Figure 2.1 Sequence.

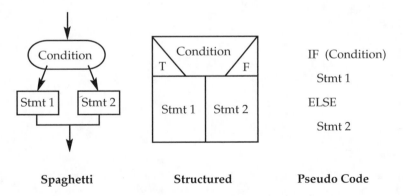

Spaghetti   **Structured**   **Pseudo Code**

Figure 2.2 Selection.

Repetition is known as *looping*. Most programming languages support one or more of the looping statements such as **WHILE**, **FOR**, and **REPEAT**. The **WHILE** and **FOR**, as shown in Fig. 2.3, are *top tested* loops. The condition is evaluated before the body of the loop is executed, and consequently the body is executed zero or more times. The **REPEAT** is a *bottom tested* loop wherein the body is executed before the condition is evaluated. Therefore, the body may be executed one or more times. The **REPEAT** is not illustrated—some variants terminate when the condition is true, others when the condition is false.

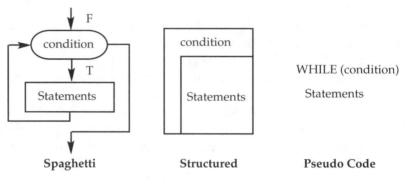

| Spaghetti | Structured | Pseudo Code |

Figure 2.3   Repetition.

Programs are constructed by using these three generic structures as building blocks. It should be relatively easy to write a program in your favorite language once the computational steps are expressed either by flow chart or pseudo code. If the computation involves any degree of complexity, a flow chart or pseudo code prepared before actual programming goes a long way in insuring that the computation will be correct.

Example 2.6

Design the logic of a program to evaluate roman numerals.

Solution. The first step is to convert each roman character into its numerical equivalent. The following table gives the equivalent values:

Roman Character	I	V	X	L	C	D	M
Numerical Value	1	5	10	50	100	500	1000

A pseudo code solution to the character conversion is:

```
IF( char = 'I' )
    value = 1
ELSE
  IF( char = 'V' )
     value = 5
  ELSE
    IF( char = 'X' )
       value = 10
    ELSE
      IF( char = 'L' )
         value = 50
```

```
ELSE
    IF( char = 'C' )
        value = 1
    ELSE
        IF( char = 'D' )
            value = 500
        ELSE
            IF( char = 'M' )
                value = 1000
            ELSE
                value = 0
```

An illegal roman character is arbitrarily assigned a value of 0.

The roman numeral evaluation algorithm is to read the digits left to right. If a digit is greater or equal to its right neighbor, the value of that digit is added to the current numeral value. If a digit is less than its right neighbor, the value of that digit is subtracted from the current numeral value. Of course the value of the next digit to the right cannot be known unless that digit is read. Consequently, the comparisons are made between the previous digit and the current digit. The algorithm is stated as a structured flow chart in Fig. 2.4. Note the nesting of the constructs and the invocation of the character conversion module defined earlier.

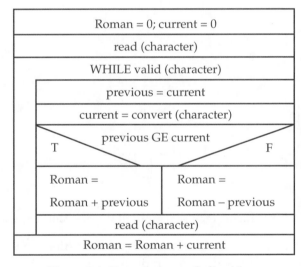

Figure 2.4   Roman numeral algorithm.

2.4 Combinational Logic

Boolean algebra deals with logical values, such as false or true, zero or one. The basic operations are "negation" or "NOT," usually indicated by an overscore; "union" or "OR," usually indicated by a plus sign; and "intersection" or "AND," usually indicated by a multiplication sign, a dot, or implied. These basic operations are supplemented by the "NAND" (Not AND), "NOR" (Not OR), and "XOR" (exclusive OR). These operations are defined in Fig. 2.5 with the standard schematic symbols shown. Other schematic symbols are also in common usage. All the operations may be extended to functions of more than two variables.

A given "black box" may not be classified as to its logical function without a knowledge of how its inputs and output(s) are mapped according to the Boolean values of "0" and "1." Consider a black box whose output is at 0 volts if one, two, or three of its three inputs are at 0 volts, and the output is at 5 volts only if all three inputs are at 5 volts. If 0 and 5 volts are equivalent to the Boolean 0 and 1, respectively, then this black box is a three-input AND gate. If, however, 0 and 5 volts are equivalent to the Boolean 1 and 0, respectively, then this black box is a three-input OR gate.

🔑 The Karnaugh map simplifies functions with respect to NOT, OR, and AND operations.

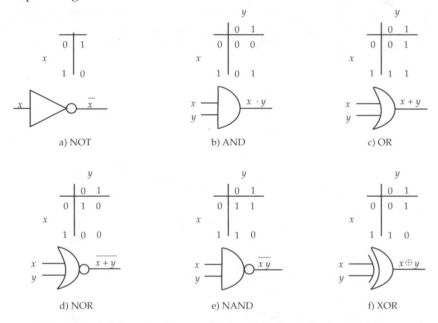

Figure 2.5 Schematic representations of the basic logic operations.

The Karnaugh map is a tool for simplifying the functions of two, three, or four variables. But beyond four variables it rapidly loses its usefulness because of geometric considerations. The map simplifies functions with respect to NOT, OR, and AND operations. Because of input-output loading limitations (fan-in, fan-out) on the electrical circuitry of the gates, the most economical implementation of a Boolean function is not necessarily the simplest. This is particularly true if NAND, NOR, or XOR gates are to be used.

The Karnaugh map displays all 2^N combinations of N variables labeled such that vertically or horizontally adjacent squares differ by only one variable change. The left and right cells are considered adjacent and the top and bottom cells are adjacent. After plotting the function as a '1' for those variable combinations where it is true and a '0' (sometimes omitted) where it is false, simplification may begin. Simplification consists of trying to surround the 1's of the function with the largest possible "circles" consisting of 1, 2, 4, 8, or 16 cells. The minimum number of "circles" are selected such that all the 1's of the function are covered. The larger a "circle" is, the fewer the variables required to describe it. The fewest number of "circles" means the fewest number of terms in the simplification.

There are times when it is known that certain combinations of the variables cannot exist from the physical consideration of the problem. The combinations are called *don't care* functions and may be used in simplifications. They are plotted on the Karnaugh map using an "X" rather than a "1." The name "don't care" arises because the use of an "X" is optional; they may be used as needed to make the largest possible circles and they do not have to be covered. Fig. 2.6 illustrates.

A function may also be simplified algebraically by the method of *prime implicants*. The details of this method will not be shown here, but it follows directly from the map method. The first step is to obtain the prime implicants. They are simply all the possible circles. The second step is to then obtain the minimal covering: select a minimum set of the largest prime implicants (the ones with the fewest variables) in order to cover the original function. Again, "don't care" functions may be used.

> The minimum number of "circles" are selected such that all the 1's of the function are covered.

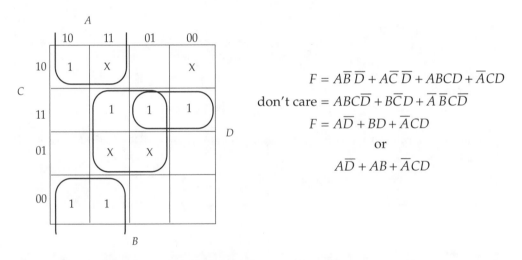

$$F = A\overline{B}\,\overline{D} + A\overline{C}\,\overline{D} + ABCD + \overline{A}CD$$

$$\text{don't care} = ABC\overline{D} + B\overline{C}D + \overline{A}\,\overline{B}C\overline{D}$$

$$F = A\overline{D} + BD + \overline{A}CD$$

$$\text{or}$$

$$A\overline{D} + AB + \overline{A}CD$$

Figure 2.6 A Karnaugh map.

There are two canonical forms for representing Boolean functions. The first is a *sum of products* or *minterm*. The second is a *product of sums* or *maxterm*. Each minterm or maxterm contains all N variables of the function. The function itself may contain a maximum of 2^N min or max terms. Each square on a Karnaugh map represents a minterm.

A function may be negated using a Karnaugh map. The function is plotted as before but the 0's are covered instead. An example is shown below.

Example 2.7

Negate the function $A + \overline{B}C$ using a Karnaugh map.

Solution.

$$A$$

	10	11	01	00
C 1	1	1		1
0	1	1		

$$B$$

$$F = A + \overline{B}C$$

$$\overline{F} = \overline{A}B + \overline{A}\,\overline{C}$$

A function may be negated algebraically with *DeMorgan's Law*. All variables are complemented, with AND and OR interchanged. The trick is to properly parenthesize the expression so the priority of AND over OR is explicit rather than implicit in all cases and then doing the interchanging and complementing. Some parentheses may be removed afterwards.

The dual of a function is obtained by interchanging the AND and OR operators. It is similar to negation but the variables are not complemented. Again, the proper parenthesization should be done beforehand.

> The state table describes the output(s) and the next state as functions of the input and present state.

Example 2.8

Negate the function $F = A + \overline{B}\,C$ with DeMorgan's Law.

Solution. We may write

$$F = A + \overline{B}\,C = A + \left(\overline{B} * C\right)$$

Upon complementing the variables and interchanging the AND-OR operators, the function becomes

$$\overline{F} = \overline{A} * \left(B + \overline{C}\right) = \overline{A}B + \overline{A}\,\overline{C}$$

2.5 Sequential Logic

The output in a combinational or memoryless logic circuit is a function of the current input only. If the output is a function of both the current input and past inputs (or outputs), then the circuit is sequential or has memory in it.

The behavior of a sequential circuit is described by a *state table*. The state table describes the output(s) and the next state as functions of the input and present state. The *state* represents the memory. There may exist equivalent *machines* exhibiting identical behavior requiring a lesser number of states. If the outputs of a sequential circuit or machine are a function only of the state, the circuit is classified as a *Moore machine*. In another type called a *Mealy machine*, the outputs are a function of the state and the input. A state is represented by a state variable configuration. N state variables can implement up to 2^N states.

Sequential machines are either synchronous or asynchronous. *Synchronous* machines are defined only at discrete times controlled by an external clock. Their state variables must be implemented with flip-flops in order to hold the state variable values between clock pulses. The *asynchronous* machine is defined for all time and therefore does not need explicit memory for the state variables.

The asynchronous machine, although simpler in concept than a synchronous one, has two implementation restrictions necessary to ensure correct operation due to inherent circuit delays:

1. No more than one input variable may change at a time.
2. State variables must be assigned in such a way that no more than one state variable changes for any possible state changes.

Because of finite signal propagation times, it cannot be assumed that two variables which are supposed to change simultaneously will indeed do so or will always pass through the same intermediate configuration. The actual state transition may depend upon which path wins the "race." For example, the variable change $00 \rightarrow 11$ may actually be $00 \rightarrow 01 \rightarrow 11$ or $00 \rightarrow 10 \rightarrow 11$. Asynchronous machines will not be discussed further. There are no restrictions on the number of variable changes for synchronous machines. Either machine may have "don't care" entries.

Four types of flip-flops are in common usage. If X is the current flip-flop output, these four may be defined in either state table or equation form as shown in Fig. 2.7. The flip-flops also have a "clear" input, which when asserted, forces the output to 0. The general form of the state variable equation is

$$X_{next} = AX + B\overline{X}$$

(2.5.1)

where X is the state variable and A, B are not functions of X. For a given state variable application, the flip-flop input(s) must be found. This may be done by equating the desired flip-flop equation (Fig 2.7) to the state variable equation

> There are no restrictions on the number of variable changes for synchronous machines.

D	X_{next}
0	0
1	1

$X_{next} = D$

D Flip-Flop

T	X_{next}
0	X
1	$\overline{X}$

$X_{next} = \overline{T}X + T\overline{X}$

T Flip-Flop

J K	X_{next}
0 0	X
0 1	0
1 0	1
1 1	$\overline{X}$

$X_{next} = \overline{K}X + J\overline{X}$

J-K Flip-Flop

S R	X_{next}
0 0	X
0 1	0
1 0	1
1 1	undefined

$X_{next} = S + \overline{R}X$,   where $SR = 0$

S-R Flip-Flop

Figure 2.7 The four common flip-flops.

(Eq. 2.5.1) and finding solutions for the input(s). The general solution for each type are:

$$D = AX + B\overline{X} \qquad\qquad \text{D Flip-Flop} \qquad \textbf{(2.5.2)}$$

$$T = \overline{A}X + B\overline{X} \qquad\qquad \text{T Flip-Flop} \qquad \textbf{(2.5.3)}$$

$$J = B \qquad\qquad K = \overline{A} \qquad\qquad \text{J-K Flip-Flop} \qquad \textbf{(2.5.4)}$$

$$S = B\overline{X}, = B \qquad R = \overline{A}X, = \overline{A} \text{ if } \overline{A}B = 0 \qquad \text{S-R Flip-Flop} \qquad \textbf{(2.5.5)}$$

The next example illustrates the above.

Example 2.9

A synchronous Mealy machine with one input, one output, and six states as described below is to be realized. *A* is the initial state.

Present State	Input		Present State	Input	
	0	1	PQR	$\bar{I}$	I
A	C/0	C/0	000	001/0	001/0
B	A/0	A/0	100	000/0	000/0
C	D/0	E/0	001	110/0	111/0
D	B/0	F/0	110	100/0	010/0
E	F/0	F/0	111	010/0	010/0
F	A/0	A/1	010	000/0	000/1
			011	xxx/x	xxx/x
			101	xxx/x	xxx/x

next state/output

Solution. This is a minimal state machine requiring at least three state variables. Although state variable assignment is arbitrary, the following rules of thumb seem to yield reduced cost logic:

1. Give adjacent assignments to a state and the state that follows it.

2. If two present states have the same next states, the present states should have adjacent assignments.

3. Use a minimum number of state variables.

These rules of thumb may be contradictory and compromises may have to be made in the assign-ment. Consider, for example, the following assignments:

$A = 000, B = 100, C = 001, D = 110, E = 111, F = 010$ a nd "don't care" = 101,011

Note that with these assignments, the initial state may be forced by clearing the state variable flip-flops. By naming the state variables $P, Q,$ and R, and the input variable I, the state and output equations become

$$P_{next} = P\left(Q\bar{R}\bar{I}\right) + \bar{P}(R)$$

$$Q_{next} = Q(R + PI) + \bar{Q}(R)$$

$$R_{next} = R\left(\bar{P}\,I\right) + \bar{R}\left(\bar{P}\,\bar{Q}\right)$$

$$\text{output} = \bar{P}\,Q\bar{R}\,I$$

Note that the form of each state equation is the same as that of Eq. 2.5.1.

Arbitrarily, let the P and Q state variables be implemented with J-K flip-flops and the R state variable be implemented by a T flip-flop. The flip-flop inputs become

$$J_P = R*\text{clock},$$
$$J_Q = R*\text{clock},$$
$$T_R = \left(PR + \bar{I}R + \bar{P}\,\bar{R}\,\bar{Q}\right) * \text{clock}$$

$$K_P = \left(\bar{Q} + R + I\right)*\text{clock}$$

$$K_Q = \bar{R}\left(\bar{P} + \bar{I}\right)*\text{clock}$$

Some flip-flops have a clock input built in and therefore do not require the explicit AND of the clock with all inputs. The resulting machine is shown as follows:

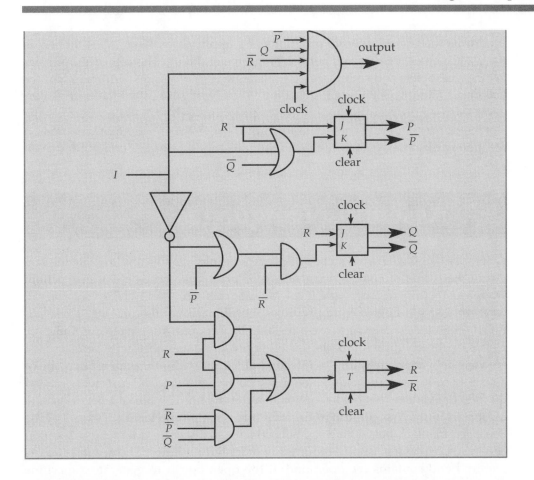

2.6 Operating Systems

Simply stated, an *operating system* is a program for interfacing between the user and the hardware. Its purpose is to provide an environment in which a user may execute programs conveniently and efficiently. The operating system may serve any number of users concurrently and independently.

A *batch* operating system never interacts with the user once the job is submitted. A *time-sharing* or *interactive* system allows the user to interact with the execution of the job. Interaction is accomplished by sharing the processor time and other resources by allocating each user a *time slice* in succession. An operating system that allows multiple jobs for a user to proceed concurrently is called *multi-tasking*. Multi-tasking is also accomplished by time-slicing. A measure of *goodness* is the average response time to a user directive. A *real time* operating system is one that services an external plant that has strict time constraints on response, such as process control. Most operating systems are *multi-programmed*, wherein several user jobs reside within the computer system at any one time.

A more precise definition of an operating system is a collection of code transparently activated by user application software to provide common tasks such as file storage and character input-output. It is an interface between user application software, not user programs and hardware. The typical application software that comes with an operating system includes a shell, a text editor, language processors, library and file system. The *shell* is the user interface to the operating system.

It permits the user to execute programs and applications. The *text editor* allows the user to enter, modify and correct programs and data. The *language processors* are the assemblers and compilers for translating user programs written in "source language" into the machine's instructions. The *library*, also called the *loader-linker*, allows a user program to access utility programs. The *file system* permits the storage of user programs and data for future use. Files are commonly stored on magnetic disks or magnetic tape.

2.7 Assembly Languages

Assembly languages are a means of programming symbolically in machine language. Each line of code writing normally produces one machine instruction. Opposed to this are the high level languages such as FORTRAN or Pascal, wherein a single line of code produces many machine instructions. These so-called "high-level" languages are translated by a process known as compiling.

It is extremely difficult to discuss assembly languages abstractly because they are very dependent upon the architecture of the individual machine. Each line of assembly code has four fields, some of which are optional. The first field is called the *label* or *location*. This field is optional and if the line contains a label, it usually must start in the first column of the line. If the line has no label, column 1 of the line is left blank. Labels define symbols which usually represent memory location addresses. They are usually required to start with a letter. The second field is required and contains the operation. If the operation is to generate a machine instruction, then the field contains the *op-code*. If the operation is a directive to the assembler, then this field contains a *pseudo-op*. Pseudo-ops are also used to generate data items. The third field is called the *operand* or *address*. It generally contains symbolic register names or memory locations for op-codes. For data generation pseudo-ops, this field contains the data; there are some operations which do not use this field. The last field is for comments. Fields are separated by one or more blanks or are assumed to start at certain columns in the case of fields following optional or non-required fields. Most assemblers treat an entire line as a comment if it starts with a special symbol such as an asterisk or a "C" in column 1.

Assembly languages have a feature that does not appear in most high-level languages—the *macro* definition. The macro allows the programmer to name and define parameterized sequences of code that may be referred to later in the program. This facility differs from a subroutine or procedure in that the body of the macro is inserted or assembled into the program at each place the macro name is invoked. If an assembler permits the use of macros, it probably permits *conditional assembly*. Conditional assembly allows the testing of parameter attributes and the subsequent conditional generation or assembly of the code, depending upon the test outcome. Strictly speaking, a conditional assembly facility is independent of the macro facility of an assembler. It is, however, of very limited utility outside the macro context.

High-level languages are either compiled into native code for direct execution on the machine or into a pseudo-code for an interpretive execution. The advantage of an interpreter is that the programmer is allowed a much greater degree of interaction with the executing program than if it were allowed to execute directly on the machine itself. The chief disadvantage of an interpreter is that execution time is much slower than direct execution. Slow-down factors of 5 to 20 are common. FORTRAN is most often compiled into native code, while BASIC is mostly interpreted. Pascal seems to be available both ways.

FORTRAN (FORmula TRANslator) was the first commercial high-level language and is the language still used most often by scientists and engineers. It is primarily a numerical computation language and one of the few which directly permits complex number arithmetic. It is easy to use and has a large library. BASIC (Beginner's All-purpose Symbolic Instruction Code) is a variant of FORTRAN. It does not require a differentiation between real and integer variables; nor are any variable declarations required. BASIC is a very easy language to use. Pascal (named after the French mathematician Blaise Pascal) is a "modern" language. It requires that all variables be declared before their use and imposes a rigid structure upon the form of the program code and logic. The use of the "GOTO" is permitted but strongly discouraged by the availability of looping and control constructs. A program written in Pascal requires more preliminary design work before coding than would the same program written in either FORTRAN or BASIC. The net practical effect is that once the compiler-detectable errors are corrected, Pascal programs tend to be more execution-time error-free than either FORTRAN or BASIC programs. Current opinion among software engineers is that FORTRAN and BASIC are suitable for one-off programs, but not for commercial quality, error-free, large programs.

FORTRAN (FORmula TRANslator) was the first commercial high-level language and is the language still used most often by scientists and engineers.

2-COMPUTERS

Practice Problems

Number Systems

2.1 – 2.3: Convert the following numbers to their base 10 equivalents.

2.1   101101.11 (base 2)

    a) 42.25

    b) 45.75

    c) 48.68

    d) 52.3

2.2   24.6 (base 8)

    a) 12.3

    b) 14.75

    c) 20.6

    d) 20.75

2.3   3FC.A (base 16)

    a) 986.5

    b) 995.625

    c) 1010.25

    d) 1020.625

2.4–2.6: Convert the following numbers to 8-digit binary using 1's complement.

2.4   21 (base 10)

    a) 00010001

    b) 00010101

    c) 10010101

    d) 11101110

2.5   −29 (base 10)

    a) 00101001

    b) 00011101

    c) 11100010

    d) 11100000

2.6   −40 (base 10)

    a) 11000000

    b) 00101000

    c) 11011000

    d) 11010111

2.7   Convert the base 5 number 123.4_5 to its base 10 equivalent.

   a) 26.6_{10}

   b) 38.8_{10}

   c) 45.8_{10}

   d) 123.4_{10}

2.8   Convert the base 16 number $2ED.89_{16}$ to its base 8 equivalent.

   a) 764.33_8

   b) 1174.22_8

   c) 1355.422_8

   d) 3217.44_8

2.9   Convert the base 10 integer 432_{10} to its base 16 equivalent.

   a) $1B0_{16}$

   b) $1FC_{16}$

   c) $2A3_{16}$

   d) 1420_{16}

2.10   What is the base 10 equivalent of the 32 bit, signed integer expressed in base 16, 2's complement notation as $FFFFFFE2_{16}$?

   a) -29_{10}

   b) -30_{10}

   c) -31_{10}

   d) -226_{10}

2.11   What is the 16-bit sum of the following 16-bit numbers expressed in hexadecimal: $24CA + E173$?

   a) $1063D_{16}$

   b) 10703_{16}

   c) 0503_{16}

   d) 1053_{16}

2.12–2.14: Convert the following numbers to 8-digit binary using 2's complement.

2.12 21_{10}

   a)   0001001

   b)   00010101

   c)   10101010

   d)   11101110

2.13 -29_{10}

   a)   11100010

   b)   11100011

   c)   11100100

   d)   00101000

2.14 -40_{10}

   a)   11011000

   b)   11010111

   c)   00100111

   d)   00101000

2.15   How many bytes does a 48K computer memory contain?

   a)   47,256

   b)   48,000

   c)   48,512

   d)   49,152

2.16   How would you modify the range calculation of the Example 2.5 cannon-ball if the air resistance is linear rather than quadratic in v^2? Assume all other factors are the same. Indicate only the spreadsheet changes.

a)

Cell	Entry	Comment
F1	$= C1 * D1/A1$	Drag factor
A6	$= A5 - (D1 + F1 * A5) * E1$	Y velocity
C6	$= C5 - F1 * C5 * E1$	X velocity

b)

Cell	Entry	Comment
F1	$= C1 * D1/A1$	Drag factor
A6	$= A5 - (D1 + \$F\$1 * A5) * \$E\$1$	Y velocity
C6	$= C5 - F1 * C5 * \$E\$1$	X velocity

c)

Cell	Entry	Comment
F1	$= C1 * D1/A1$	Drag factor
A6	$= A5 - (\$D\$1 + F1 * A5) * \$E\$1$	Y velocity
C6	$= C5 - \$F\$1 * C5 * E1$	X velocity

d)

Cell	Entry	Comment
F1	$= C1 * D1/A1$	Drag factor
A6	$= A5 - (\$D\$1 + \$F\$1 * A5) * \$E\$1$	Y velocity
C6	$= C5 - \$F\$1 * C5 * \$E\$1$	X velocity

2.17   An instructor has exam grades entered on a spreadsheet and needs a way to get the total points to be normalized between 0 and 1. Assume that the student names occupy columns *A* and *B*. There are three exam scores for each student in columns *C*, *D*, and *E*. The 35 students in the class occupy rows 6 through 40. Row 5 contains the maximum points obtainable for each exam. The first exam is to contribute 20, the second 30, and the third 50 of the total points. Give a spreadsheet solution.

a)

Cell	Entry
G5	= C5 * 0.2/C5 + D5 * 0.3/D5 + E5 * 0.5/E5
G6 : G40	Copy the G5 formula

b)

Cell	Entry
G5	= C5 * 0.2/$C$5 + D5 * 0.3/$D$5 + E5 * 0.5/$E$5
G6 : G40	Copy the G5 formula

c)

Cell	Entry
G5	= C5 * 0.2 + D5 * 0.3 + E5 * 0.5
G6 : G40	Copy the G5 formula

d)

Cell	Entry
G5	= C5/$C$5 + D5/$D$5 + E5/$E$5
G6 : G40	Copy the G5 formula

2.18   Suppose your favorite programming language does not support **repeat** statements but does support **while**, **if**, and **if-else** statements. The repeat is to terminate when the condition is true. How would you get around this with what is available?

```
              repeat
                  stmt;    ⟹
              until (cond);
```

a)
```
  if (cond)
      while (not cond)
          stmt;
```
b)
```
  if (cond)
      stmt;
  else
      while (cond)
          stmt;
```
c)
```
  stmt;
  if (not cond)
      stmt;
```
d)
```
  stmt;
  while (not cond)
    stmt;
```

2.19   Suppose your favorite programming language does not support **if else** statements but does support **if** statements. How would you get around this with what is available?

$$\begin{array}{l} \textbf{if}\ (\text{cond}) \\ \quad \text{Stmt1;} \quad \Rightarrow \\ \textbf{else} \\ \quad \text{Stmt2;} \end{array}$$

a)
```
  if (cond)
    Stmt1;
  if (not cond)
    Stmt2;
```

b)
```
  if (not cond)
    Stmt1;
  if (cond)
    Stmt2;
```

c)
```
  if (cond)
    Stmt1;
  Stmt2;
```

d)
```
  Stmt1;
  if (not cond)
    Stmt2;
```

2.20   Complete a pseudo-code program to calculate the trajectory of the Example 2.5 cannonball. The program is to input the muzzle velocity, firing angle, and drag factor. The output of the program is a listing of the horizontal and vertical velocities and positions over approximately 100 intervals. The program outline is:

```
G := 9.81;
read( muzzle, angle, F );
vel_x := muzzle*cos(angle);
vel_y := muzzle*sin(angle);
pos_x := 0;
pos_y := 0;
drag := F*G/(muzzle*muzzle);
delta_t := vel_y/(G*50);
for( i := 1 to 100 )
   integrate( );
   print( vel_x, pos_x, vel_y, pos_y );
endfor;
```

Give the pseudo-code that replaces the "integrate( )" statement.

a)
```
 vel_x := vel_x + drag*vel_x*vel_x*delta_t;
pos_x := pos_x + vel_x*delta_t;
vel_y := vel_y + (G + drag*vel_y*abs(vel_y))*delta_t;
pos_y := pos_y + vel_y*delta_t;
```

b)
```
 vel_x := vel_x – drag*vel_x*vel_x*delta_t;
pos_x := pos_x + vel_x*delta_t;
vel_y := vel_y – (G + drag*vel_y*abs(vel_y))*delta_t;
pos_y := pos_y + vel_y*delta_t;
```

c)
```
 vel_x := vel_x – drag*vel_x*vel_x*delta_t;
pos_x := pos_x – vel_x*delta_t;
vel_y := vel_y – (G + drag*vel_y*abs(vel_y))*delta_t;
pos_y := pos_y – vel_y*delta_t;
```

d)
```
 vel_x := –drag*vel_x*vel_x*delta_t;
pos_x := vel_x*delta_t;
vel_y := –(G + drag*vel_y*abs(vel_y))*delta_t;
pos_y := vel_y*delta_t;
```

Simplify the following Boolean functions.

2.21 $AB + A\bar{B}C + \bar{A}C$

a) $AB + BC$ b) $AC + B$ c) $AB + C$ d) A

2.22 $F = \bar{B}\bar{C} + \bar{A}C + A\bar{B}C$,   don't care $= ABC + \bar{A}B\bar{C}$

a) AC b) $A + C$ c) $AB + \bar{C}$ d) $\bar{B} + C$

2.23 $F = \bar{A}BC + \bar{A}BD$,   don't care $= (AB + \bar{A}\,\bar{B})(C + D)$

a) $BC + BD$ b) $BC + \bar{A}D$ c) $\bar{A}C + AD$ d) $\bar{A}C + BD$

Give the simplified complement of the following functions.

2.24 $\bar{C}D + BD$

a) $B + CD$ b) $\bar{C}D + BD$ c) $\bar{D} + \bar{B}C$ d) $\bar{B} + CD$

2.25 $A\bar{B}C + A\bar{B}\,\bar{D} + BD$

a) $\bar{A}\bar{B} + B\bar{D} + \bar{B}\,\bar{C}D$

b) $AB + \bar{B}\,\bar{D} + \bar{C}D$

c) $A\bar{B}C + D$

d) $AD + BC$

Sequential Logic

Given the transition table of the synchronous Mealy machine and the state variable assignment, answer Problem 2.26–2.28.

| | | MN, input | | | |
PQ	state	00	01	11	10
00	a	a/0	a/0	b/0	b/0
01	b	c/0	d/0	c/1	c/1
11	c	a/0	a/0	a/1	–/–
10	d	c/0	a/0	a/0	c/0

2.26   What is the output equation?

a) MQ b) $N\bar{P} + Q$ c) $M\bar{Q}$ d) $\bar{P}\bar{N} + PN$

2.27   If the P state variable is implemented with a J-K flip-flop, what is the "J" equation?

a) Q b) P c) $Q + N$ d) $\bar{Q} + N$

2.28   If the Q state variable is implemented with a S-R flip-flop, what is the "R" equation?

a) $\bar{P}N + \bar{P}M$ b) $(\bar{P}N + \bar{P}M)Q$ c) $(P + \bar{M}N)Q$ d) Q

Operating Systems

2.29   An operating system that allows the user to correct input data has:

a) language processing

b) multiprogramming

c) text editing

d) file storage

Solutions to Practice Problems

2.1   **b)** $101101.11_2 = 32 + 8 + 4 + 1 + 1/2 + 1/4 = 45.75$

2.2   **d)** $24.6_8 = 2 \times 8 + 4 + 6/8 = 20.75$

2.3   **d)** $3FC.A_{16} = 3 \times 256 + 15 \times 16 + 12 + 10/16 = 1020.625$

2.4   **b)** $21_{10} = 16 + 4 + 1 = 00010101_2$

2.5   **c)** $29_{10} = 16 + 8 + 4 + 1 = 00011101_2$
             $-29_{10} = 11100010_2$ 1's comp.

2.6   **d)** $40_{10} = 32 + 8 = 00101000_2$
             $-40_{10} = 11010111_2$ 1's comp.

2.7   **b)** $1 \times 5^2 + 2 \times 5^1 + 3 \times 5^0 + 4 \times 5^{-1} = 38.8_{10}$

2.8   **c)** $2ED.89_{16} = 0010\ 1110\ 1101.1000\ 1001_2$

                $= 001\ 011\ 101\ 101.100\ 010\ 010_2 = 1355.422_8$

2.9   **a)** $432 \div 16 = 27$, remainder $= 0$

             $27 \div 16 = 1$, remainder $= 11 = B_{16}$

             $1 \div 16 = 0$, remainder $= 1$. Thus, $432_{10} = 1B0_{16}$

2.10 **b)**   This is a negative number because the left-most bit $= 1$.
             Complementing to the positive version, $0000001E_{16} = 30_{10}$. Thus,
             $FFFFFFE2_{16} = -30_{10}$.

2.11 **a)**

2.12 **b)** $21_{10} = 16 + 4 + 1 = 00010101_2$

2.13 **b)** $-29_{10} = 11100010_2$ 1's comp.
                   $= 11100011_2$ 2's comp.

2.14 **a)** $-40_{10} = 11010111_2$ 1's comp.
                   $= 11011000_2$ 2's comp.

2.15 **d)** $48 \times 1024 = 49\ 152$

2.16 **d)**   The range is approximately 2980 meters.

2.17 **b)**   Each of the three exams will have to be multiplied by a scale factor
             which will add to 1.0 for anyone who received the maximum points on
             all exams.

2.18 **d)**

2.19 **a)**

2.20 **b)**

2.21 c)

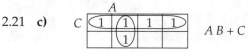

$AB + C$

2.22 d)

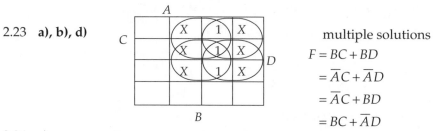

$F = \overline{B} + C$

2.23 a), b), d)

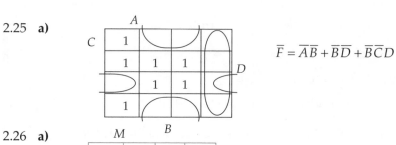

multiple solutions

$F = BC + BD$

$= \overline{A}C + \overline{A}D$

$= \overline{A}C + BD$

$= BC + \overline{A}D$

2.24 c)

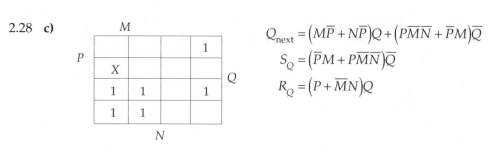

$\overline{F} = \overline{D} + \overline{B}C$

2.25 a)

C				
	1		
	1	1	1
		1	1
	1		

$\overline{F} = \overline{A}\,\overline{B} + \overline{B}\,\overline{D} + \overline{B}\,\overline{C}D$

2.26 a)

P | M | | |
---|---|---|---|---
 | X | 1 | |
 | 1 | 1 | |
 | | | |

OUTPUT $= MQ$

2.27 a)

P | M | | |
---|---|---|---|---
 | 1 | | | 1
 | X | | |
 | 1 | 1 | 1 | 1
 | | | |

$P_{\text{next}} = \overline{Q}\,\overline{N}P + Q\overline{P}$

$J_P = Q \ ; \ K_P = Q + N$

2.28 c)

P | M | | |
---|---|---|---|---
 | | | | 1
 | X | | |
 | 1 | 1 | | 1
 | 1 | 1 | |

$Q_{\text{next}} = \left(M\overline{P} + N\overline{P}\right)Q + \left(P\overline{M}\,\overline{N} + \overline{P}M\right)\overline{Q}$

$S_Q = \left(\overline{P}M + P\overline{M}\,\overline{N}\right)\overline{Q}$

$R_Q = \left(P + \overline{M}N\right)Q$

2.29 c)

Materials Science

by Kalinath Mukherjee

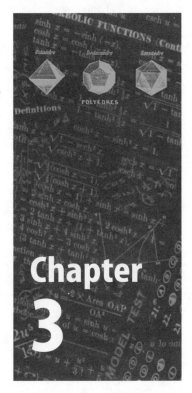

Chapter 3

Materials science is a very broad field of study covering the structures and properties of metallic materials, ceramics, polymers and composites. Hence, it is necessary to discuss the electronic, magnetic, optical, mechanical and chemical properties of various materials in the materials science discipline.

A review of past Fundamentals of Engineering exams indicates that there are two major areas emphasized in materials science. These are related to the fundamentals of 1) strength, deformation and plasticity of crystalline solids, and 2) phase equilibria in metallic systems. Typically, the latter is troublesome to engineers who do not have a metallurgy-materials science background. In this review, therefore, these two subject areas are thoroughly treated. (For a more complete understanding of the topic, we recommend that you simply refer to appropriate texts.)

We include a discussion of various solid types, and the nature of atomic bonding, which gives rise to different classes of materials. We discuss fundamentals of crystallography, since a majority of engineering solids are crystalline. Thus, it is important to know how to define crystal planes and directions which play an important role in mechanical deformation, as we will see. Some discussion on atomic mobility (diffusion) in solids is included, since this mobility is very closely related to phase changes, hardening through heat-treatment, etc. A brief discussion of electrical and electrochemical properties is also presented. Please note that corrosion of metallic materials, which can be understood in terms of electrochemical behavior of a solid, is a very important consideration in some branches of engineering. Finally, it may be worth considering that the majority of FE exam materials questions usually hinge on the subjects of our first two articles, with the final eight "capsule" reviews representing the remainder.

A majority of engineering solids are crystalline.

• Atomic mobility is very closely related to phase changes.

• The majority of FE exam materials questions usually hinge on the subjects of our first two articles.

3.1 Mechanical Properties of Metals and Alloys

There are several standard experimental techniques used to determine how a material responds to an applied state of stress. The specific responses and the corresponding tests may be summarized as follows:

- Capacity to withstand static load → Tension or compression test
- Resistance to permanent deformation → Hardness test
- Toughness of a material under shock loading → Impact test
- The useful life of a material under cyclic loading → Fatigue test
- Elevated temperature behavior → Creep and stress rupture tests

In tension testing, there are two distinct stages of deformation:

1) Elastic deformation (reversible)

2) Plastic deformation (irreversible)

The elastic range is characterized by *Hooke's law*, which is the linear equation

$$\sigma = E\varepsilon \tag{3.1.1}$$

where σ and ε are the stress and strain, respectively, and E (the slope of the line) is the *Young's modulus* of the material, also called the *modulus of elasticity*. Beyond the elastic range, the material undergoes *plastic deformation*. In this range, the stress-strain relation is nonlinear. It is important to note that, unlike elastic deformation, the volume of the material remains constant during plastic deformation (we will see later why this is so). The stress at which this nonlinearity begins is called the *yield stress* σ_y.

Very frequently it is difficult to obtain a reliable value of σ_y from experimental data because the linear to nonlinear transition of the stress-strain diagram is rather gradual. To avoid this difficulty, an *off-set yield stress* $\sigma_{0.2}$ is defined at a specified percentage of plastic strain (usually 0.2% plastic strain).

🔑 The volume of the material remains constant during plastic deformation, unlike elastic deformation.

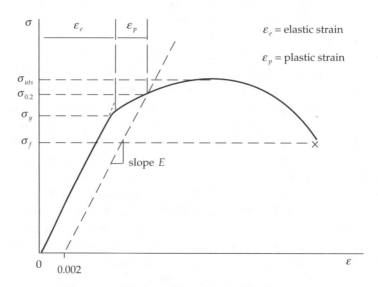

Figure 3.1 Engineering stress-strain diagram.

The engineering stress-strain curve (Fig. 3.1) shows a maximum value of stress called the *ultimate tensile strength* σ_{uts}. Beyond this value, the engineering stress decreases and the sample fails in tension at a *fracture stress* σ_f, which is (usually) less than σ_{uts}. The diagram in Fig. 3.1 shows various features of the engineering stress-strain diagram.

The reason $\sigma_f < \sigma_{uts}$ is that the engineering stress is obtained by dividing the load by the original cross-sectional area of the sample. At stresses $\geq \sigma_{uts}$ the sample starts to neck locally, tri-axial stresses develop and eventually the sample breaks. Since the cross-sectional area is less at the necking, the load bearing capacity decreases. This load divided by the original area is less than the "true" stress beyond this point.

> The engineering stress is obtained by dividing the load by the original cross-sectional area of the sample.

The extent of necking depends on the *ductility* of the material. If the material is very *brittle*, that is, has little or no ductility, there will be very little necking strain, and in that case $\sigma_f \equiv \sigma_{uts}$. Often it is possible to make a qualitative assessment of ductility from the nature of the tensile fracture. Fig. 3.2 shows three types of necking which might be observed.

a) Very ductile

b) Ductile; cup and cone

c) Very brittle

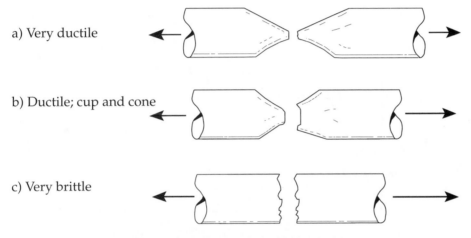

Figure 3.2 Examples of tensile failure.

Plastic deformation at ordinary temperature introduces some additional strength to many metals and alloys. This is called *work-hardening* or *strain-hardening*. The nature of this hardening can be understood by studying Fig. 3.3. If the material is loaded in the plastic range to strain ε_1 and then unloaded, the "apparent" yield stress σ_{y2} on reloading is greater than σ_{y1}. Such a "hardness" is imparted on cold-forged tools, for example. It must be noted that although the yield strength has apparently increased, the material loses some amount of its plastic flow property. The "extra strength" is removed if the material is annealed at an elevated temperature.

> Plastic deformation introduces additional strength to many metals and alloys.

In steel and other ferrous alloys, the stress strain curve might look like the one shown in Fig. 3.4 (depending on carbon and other alloy content). The quantities σ_u and σ_l are called *upper* and *lower yield points*. This peculiarity of yielding occurs due to the interaction of carbon atoms with atomic scale defects called *dislocations*.

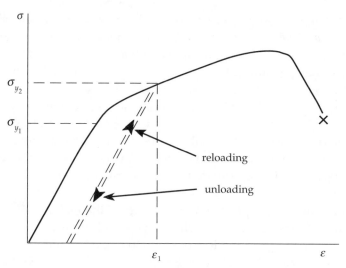

Figure 3.3 Tensile loading-unloading curve.

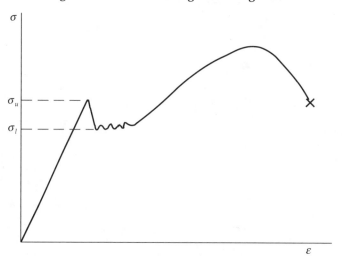

Figure 3.4 Stress-strain diagram of mild steel.

Nature of Plastic Flow

🔑 Slip takes place on those crystal planes which have the densest atomic packing.

In crystalline materials (all metals and alloys are crystalline) plastic flow or plastic deformation involves the *sliding* of atomic planes, analogous to shearing a deck of cards, as shown in Fig. 3.5. The sliding of atomic planes is called *slip deformation*. Under an applied stress, slip takes place on those crystal planes which have the densest atomic packing. Furthermore, slip directions are restricted to the crystallographic directions along which the atoms are most closely packed.

The combination of a close-packed plane and a close-packed direction is called a *slip system*. Depending on the crystal structure, some metals and alloys will have more slip systems than others. The higher the number of planes and directions along which slip can take place, the easier it is to produce plastic deformation without brittle fracture.

Slip occurs when the resolved component of shear stress τ_R, given by the expression on the slip plane along the slip direction,

$$\tau_R = \frac{P}{A}\cos\phi\cos\lambda \qquad (3.1.2)$$

exceeds a critical value called *critical resolved shear stress* $(\tau_R)_{crit}$ (see Fig. 3.6). This critical value is a property of the material.

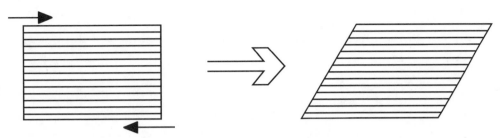

Figure 3.5 Shearing of a deck of cards. (Note shape change, but no volume change.)

The experimental value of $(\tau_R)_{crit}$ is found to be at least five times smaller than the theoretically calculated value based on the force necessary to slide closely packed planes of atoms. The apparent anomaly here was resolved when dislocations were discovered. Slip becomes easier if dislocations are present. Let us consider an analogy. A long narrow rug on a hallway is to be moved x meters to the right, as shown in Fig. 3.7a. This could be done by pulling, as shown. It must be noted that considerable friction must be overcome to do this. Alternately, a bulge could be made as shown in Fig. 3.7b and then this bulge could be "walked" to the right. When the bulge exits on the right, the rug has moved x meters to the right. Considerably less effort is required in the second procedure.

Analogous to the bulge, there is an extra half-plane of atoms in an *edge dislocation* as shown in Fig. 3.8. The row of atoms at the end of the half-plane is situated between two equilibrium sites. Thus, it takes less force to move this plane.

When the extra half-plane emerges on the surface, we have one elementary slip step. The row of atoms at the end of the half-plane can be viewed as a line called a *dislocation line*. When a dislocation line moves, plastic deformation occurs.

Slip becomes easier if dislocations are present.

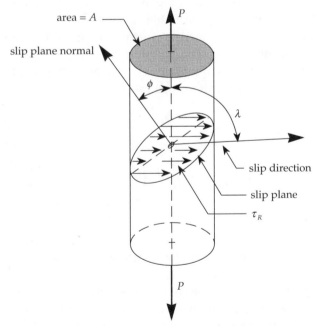

Figure 3.6 Resolved shear stress on the slip plane.

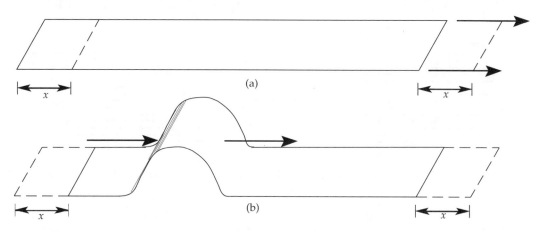

Figure 3.7 Analogy of a dislocation motion.

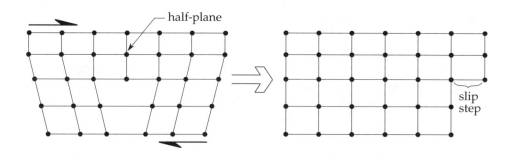

Figure 3.8 An edge dislocation.

It has been established that existing dislocation lines in a material can multiply under an applied stress, as shown in Fig. 3.9. This mechanism is called a *Frank-Reed source* and is experimentally verifiable.

Since dislocation motion ≡ plastic deformation, strength can be increased if dislocation motion is blocked. Indeed, the strengthening of alloys can be traced to the interaction of dislocations with dispersed phases, with grain boundaries, and with stress fields of other dislocations (e.g., strain hardening).

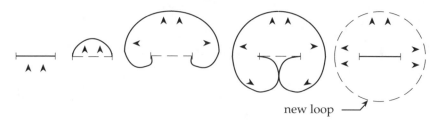

Figure 3.9 Frank-Reed dislocation source.

Compressive Strength

A material's response to a compressive stress is similar to that for a tensile stress, except for the fact that there is no necking involved in pure compression. Compression test data is especially useful for those materials which are quite brittle in tension but have significant compressive load bearing capacities (concrete, cast iron, etc.).

Hardness of Materials

A hardness test is an empirical method which determines the resistance of a material to the penetration of an indenter. Hardness measurement can be useful for obtaining a qualitative estimate of service wear, strength and toughness. Furthermore, for steel, an empirical correlation exists between hardness and tensile strength. The most commonly used hardness tests are:

1) Brinell
2) Rockwell
3) Vickers
4) Microhardness (Vickers or Knoop indenters)

Rockwell hardness has scales, A through V (depending on load and type of indenter). Scales A, B, C, and D are commonly used for various steels. Table 3.1 shows a few hardness values along with the tensile strength of steel for comparison.

> Hardness measurement can be useful for obtaining a qualitative estimate of service wear, strength and toughness.

TABLE 3.1 Hardness and Strength of Steel[*]

Brinell	Rockwell			Vickers	Tensile Strength MPa (1000 psi)
	C	**D**	**A**		
601	57.3	68.7	79.8	640	2120 (308)
495	51.0	63.8	76.3	528	1740 (253)
401	43.1	57.8	72.0	425	1380 (201)
302	32.1	49.3	66.3	319	1030 (150)
229	20.5	40.5	60.8	241	760 (111)

[*] A more complete table can be found in "The Testing and Inspection of Engineering Materials": H. F. Danis, G. E. Trowell and C. T. Wiskocil, McGraw Hill Book Co., NY.

Fatigue Test

Life in cyclic loading is important in many applications. Fatigue life is determined from experimental data relating number of cycles (N) to failure with cyclic stress amplitude (S). A schematic S vs. N curve is shown in Fig. 3.10. Note that for steel there is a critical value of stress S_{crit} below which fatigue life is virtually infinity. This limit is called the *endurance limit*. Notice that no such endurance limit exists for *Al* (or many other nonferrous metals and alloys). Fatigue fractures are progressive, beginning as minute cracks that grow under the action of the fluctuating stress. Fatigue strength is defined as the maximum cyclic stress amplitude for a specified number of cycles until failure.

Fatigue is a surface-active failure. Fatigue cracks start at the surface; surface defects such as notches can initiate a crack. A rough surface may reduce fatigue strength by as much as 25%. Cold rolling or shot peening (which introduces surface compressive stress) can increase fatigue strength by as much as 25%. *Corrosion-fatigue* is an important cause of service failure if a corrosive environment and cyclic stresses co-exist. For example, it has been shown that the endurance limit of a steel (tested in air) is altogether eliminated when the sample is tested in pure water. Fatigue life or fatigue strength can be improved by:

1) A highly polished surface
2) Surface hardening (carburizing, nitriding, etc.)
3) Surface compressive stresses (shot peening, cold rolling, etc.)

> Fatigue life is determined from experimental data relating number of cycles (N) to failure with cyclic stress amplitude.
> • Cold rolling or shot peening (which introduces surface compressive stress) can increase fatigue strength by as much as 25%.

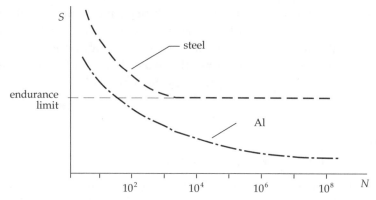

Figure 3.10 *S-N* **diagram (schematic) of aluminum and steel.**

Toughness and Impact Testing

The *impact value* is a simple evaluation of the notch toughness of the material. And *toughness* is a measure of energy absorbed by the material before fracture. Two types of machines, the Charpy and the Izod, are commonly used to test these qualities, both of which use swinging-pendulum loading with notched-bar samples. In tension, the area under the stress-strain curve is the energy/unit volume to fracture (see Fig. 3.11). The area under the stress-strain diagram of material *A* is less than that of material *B*. The area has the dimension of stress (force/unit area), which, if multiplied and divided by length, results in energy/volume. Hence, material *B* is tougher than material *A*.

🔑 Temperature has a pronounced effect on the energy absorption and fracture behavior of steel in a notch condition.

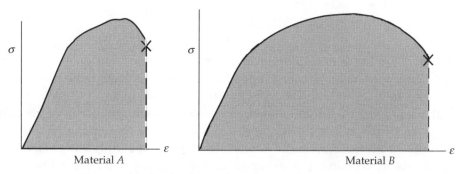

Figure 3.11 Comparison of toughness of two materials.

The presence of a notch introduces tri-axial stresses. Many materials become more brittle under such a state of stress than under uni-axial tension or compression. Temperature has a pronounced effect on the energy absorption and fracture behavior of steel in a notch condition. The sharpness of the transition from tough to brittle fracture depends on the material and also on the notch geometry.

Frequently, Charpy values will change from 35 or 40 to as low as 7 N·m over a temperature interval of 4 to 10°C. Fig. 3.12 shows the qualitative nature of ductile-brittle transition (also the behavior of *Ni*, which does not have a ductile-brittle transition). Service failures testify to the increased hazards of subnormal temperature, and so determination of transition temperature has come to be an important criterion for materials selection. It must be noted that in a large rigid structure, the transition temperature would be considerably higher than that for a standard Charpy sample.

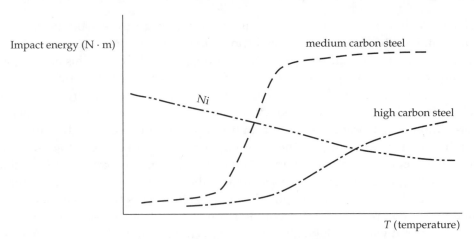

Figure 3.12 Impact energy vs. temperature.

The progressive deformation of a material at constant stress is called *creep*. Below about 40% of the absolute melting temperature, creep strain is negligible for most structural metals and alloys. An idealized shape of a creep curve is shown in Fig. 3.13. Andrade's empirical formula for the creep curve is given by

$$\varepsilon = \varepsilon_0 \left(1 + \beta t^{1/3}\right)e^{kt} \qquad (3.1.3)$$

where ε is the strain in time t, ε_0 is the initial elastic strain, and β and k are material constants.

The stress-rupture test is basically similar to a creep test except that the test is always carried out to failure. Elongation, time to failure, applied load, and temperature are all reported for the purpose of design data.

One particular mode of failure of polycrystalline metals and alloys at elevated temperatures is *grain boundary sliding*. The influence of grain size on creep resistance is not clear-cut. There is some evidence, however, to indicate that creep rate is lower in large-grain materials. Because grain boundaries are the nucleation sites for high-temperature fracture, the control (or elimination) of grain boundaries will suppress fracture and increase rupture life. It must be noted that the environment plays an important role in high-temperature mechanical properties. The nature of oxides, for example, can influence creep and stress-rupture.

Creep at High Temperature; Stress Rupture

🔑 The progressive deformation of a material at constant stress is called *creep*.

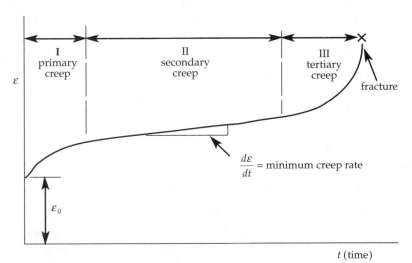

Figure 3.13 A typical creep curve showing three stages of creep.

Sound Velocity in Solids and Damping Capacity

Under a rapid cyclic loading of a solid in the elastic range, the elastic stress-strain curve shows a hysteresis. The area inside a hysteresis loop is a measure of energy dissipation per cycle of rapid elastic loading and unloading. This energy loss is said to be due to "internal friction" of the solid. Internal friction is closely related to elastic aftereffect associated with adiabatic temperature rise in the solid. Internal boundaries and defects also contribute to internal friction. Energy dissipation of a vibrating solid through internal friction damps the vibration amplitude. Thus, the higher the internal friction of a solid, the higher is its "damping capacity". In many applications, high damping capacity is a desirable property. High damping capacity also retards the sound propagation through the solid. Note that sound propagation through a solid occurs through elastic wave (alternating compression and decompression cycles) propagation. Thus, the velocity of sound wave through an elastic solid is related to the density of the solid and its compressibility.

Metallurgical Variables in Material Response to Stresses

Microstructural conditions, heat treatment, processing variables, and service conditions can all influence mechanical properties of metals and alloys.

Microstructural conditions

• Grain size effect: At ordinary temperatures, fine grain is better for strength. At high temperatures, perhaps a larger grain size is desirable.

• Single-phase vs. multiphase alloys: Many times a second phase might have a profound effect on the mechanical properties; for example, the retained austenite may be a problem in fatigue. Deformation behavior of phases may be different, and a simple averaging of properties might not be appropriate.

• Porosity and inclusions: Poor mechanical properties result from high porosity and inclusions.

• Directionality of microstructure: Rolling direction vs. transverse direction will have different mechanical properties. These also introduce anisotropy of properties.

Effects of heat treatment

• Annealing: Softening, ductile behavior (depending on alloy).

• Quenching of steel: Martensite formation, strong but brittle. In high carbon steel, quench-cracks may form.

• Tempering of martensite: Hardness decreases but toughness increases. Strength is sacrificed to avoid brittle failure.

• Age hardening: Depending on alloy composition, fine scale ($\approx 10^{-7} M$) precipitation may be formed which interacts with dislocations. Increased strength is thus obtained.

• Case hardening: A hard surface and soft core combination is obtained by carburizing and nitriding. Fatigue strength can be increased by this method. A better wear-resistant surface can be produced.

Effects of some processing variables

• Welding: The heat-affected zone with large grain size will have poorer mechanical properties. Local chemical composition changes can occur, including a loss of carbon in steel. Large parts can have quench cracking due to rapid quenching effects.

- Flame cutting: Drastic changes of microstructure occur near the flame-cut surface and these changes affect the mechanical properties.
- Machining, grinding: Cold work results in strain hardening. Excessive cold work may produce surface cracks.

Effects of service conditions

- Extreme low temperature: Ductile-brittle transition occurs in steel.
- Extreme high temperature: Causes corrosion and oxidation of surface. Surface cracks may form. Results in problems with corrosion fatigue, creep and rupture.
- Impact loading: Notch sensitivity, surface scratches or corrosion pits can initiate brittle fracture.
- Corrosive environment: Stress-corrosion, pitting corrosion, and corrosion fatigue result.

These are but a few examples of the service and material variables which can influence the mechanical response of a material. Often, deterioration of material properties over time leads to a service failure. But the most important function of an appropriate materials input in engineering design is to prevent unexpected catastrophic failure.

> The most important function of an appropriate materials input in engineering design is to prevent unexpected catastrophic failure.

3.2 Equilibrium Phase Diagrams

For most practical purposes, alloy compositions are listed in weight percentage (wt. %). For example, 70-30 brass means 70 wt. % Cu and 30 wt. % Zn. In this discussion, we will consider a binary alloy (two chemical elements) of elements A and B (e.g., $A = Cu$, $B = Zn$). Sometimes, however, it is convenient to express an alloy composition in atomic percentage (at. %). Weight percent composition can be converted to atomic percent by using the following formulas:

$$\text{at.\% } A = \frac{W_A}{W_A + (M_A / M_B)W_B} \times 100 \tag{3.2.1}$$

$$\text{at.\% } B = \frac{W_B}{W_B + (M_B / M_A)W_A} \times 100 \tag{3.2.2}$$

where W_A and W_B are the weight percents in the alloy of elements A and B, respectively, and M_A and M_B are the respective atomic weights. Similarly, at. % can be converted to wt. % by using the following formulas:

$$\text{wt.\% } A = \frac{P_A M_A}{P_A M_A + P_B M_B} \times 100 \tag{3.2.3}$$

$$\text{wt.\% } B = \frac{P_B M_B}{P_A M_A + P_B M_B} \times 100 \tag{3.2.4}$$

where P_A and P_B are atomic percents of A and B, respectively.

There are various methods for determining equilibrium phase diagrams: X-ray diffraction, optical microscopy, and calorimetric and thermal analyses. We will consider thermal analysis here (i.e., the cooling curve method) since it is very instructive.

The equilibrium phase diagrams show the existence or coexistence of phases at any given temperature and alloy composition. The term *equilibrium* implies that the alloy is cooled at such a slow rate that thermodynamic equilibrium is

> Equilibrium phase diagrams show the existence or coexistence of phases at any given temperature and alloy composition.

attained at each temperature. A *phase* is a volume of material bounded by a distinct boundary within which the chemical composition is uniform. A phase has a fixed crystal structure and thermo-physical properties at a given temperature. The equilibrium between phases is determined by Gibb's phase rule

$$P + F = C + 2 \qquad \textbf{(3.2.5)}$$

where P = number of phases, C = number of chemical elements in the alloy and F = the degrees of freedom, i.e., the number of independent variables. Eq. 3.2.5 is the generalized phase rule where both pressure and temperature are independent external variables. If the pressure is kept constant, as is the usual case (usually 1 atmosphere), then we have the *condensed phase rule* given by

$$P + F = C + 1 \qquad \textbf{(3.2.6)}$$

> A phase has a fixed crystal structure and thermo-physical properties at a given temperature.

We will use Eq. 3.2.6 in our discussion. As an example, consider a binary alloy in which $C = 2$. In this case, if the number of phases P in equilibrium is 3, then Eq. 3.2.6 predicts that $F = 0$, i.e., no degree of freedom. Thus, in such a case, the composition of the phases and the temperature at which the three phases coexist are fixed: no degree of freedom.

Consider the cooling of pure molten metal in a furnace which has the cooling curve depicted in Fig. 3.14a. If we now place a thermocouple in the molten metal and plot the temperature of the metal as it cools, we will obtain the curve shown in Fig. 3.14b. The horizontal shelf $\overline{ab}$ is the *thermal arrest* at a temperature T_m. In this case T_m is the freezing (or melting) point of the metal where liquid and solid coexist. Until all of the molten metal is solidified, the temperature does not change. An analogy is the equilibrium between ice and water: until the ice cubes melt, the temperature of a glass of water remains at $0°C$.

If we now add a small amount of an alloying element in a pure metal and repeat the cooling curve experiment, we will obtain the curve shown in Fig. 3.15. Comparing Fig. 3.15 with Fig. 3.14b we note that, unlike a single arrest temperature, we have a change in slope at point a. Actually, freezing begins at point a and is completed at point b. Thus, within the range of temperatures T_1 and T_2, we have a mixture of solid and liquid.

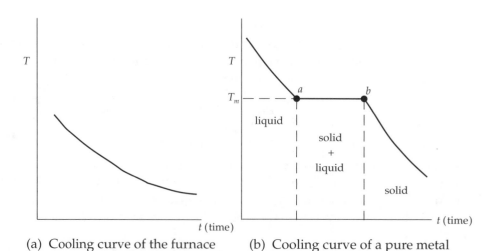

(a) Cooling curve of the furnace   (b) Cooling curve of a pure metal

Figure 3.14 The cooling of a pure metal in a furnace.

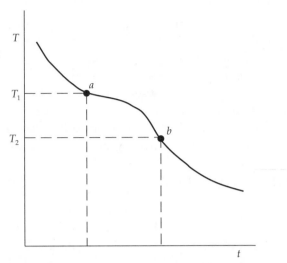

Figure 3.15 Cooling curve of liquid dilute alloy.

If the alloying element has a higher melting point (or freezing point) than the host pure metal, then at temperature T_1 this element starts to freeze and the remaining liquid has less of the alloying element in solution. Thus, the new liquid has a lower freezing temperature. This process continues until an almost pure host element freezes at temperature T_2.

Consider now a series of alloys of nickel (*Ni*) and copper (*Cu*); we note that the melting point of *Ni* is higher than that of *Cu* and addition of *Cu* to *Ni* lowers the freezing point (analogous to the lowering of the freezing point of water when salt is added). Several such cooling curves are shown in Fig. 3.16. In all these curves, point *a* corresponds to the beginning of freezing and point *b* the end of freezing. We now plot these temperatures of beginning and end of freezing in a diagram with temperature and alloy composition as coordinates. Such a diagram is shown in Fig. 3.17.

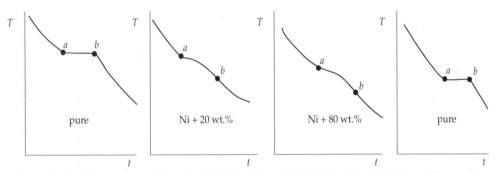

Figure 3.16 Schematic cooling for *Ni*, *Ni* + 20 wt. % *Cu*, *Ni* + 80 wt. % *Cu*, and pure *Cu*.

Figure 3.17 is indeed an *equilibrium phase diagram* of the *Ni-Cu* alloy system. The upper curve defines the temperature above which the alloy is liquid and is called the *liquidus*; the lower curve defines the temperature below which the alloy is solid and is called the *solidus*. The area bounded by the liquidus and the solidus is the region of two phases: solid + liquid.

Let us now analyze the cooling of an alloy of composition C as shown in Fig. 3.18. At temperature T_1—which is above the liquidus—the alloy of composition C is entirely liquid. At temperature T_2 an extremely minute quantity of solid forms and at T_3 we are in the two-phase $S + L$ region. At T_3 we have a mixture of solid and liquid, and the composition of the solid is given by the intersection of the temperature-horizontal with the solidus curve. The composition of the liquid phase is given by the intersection of the temperature-horizontal with the liquidus line. The compositions can be obtained by drawing vertical lines through these intersection points—that is, C_L and C_S in the figure are the compositions of the liquid and solid phases, respectively.

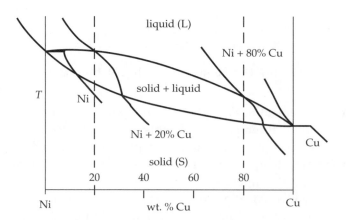

Figure 3.17 Arrest temperatures vs. composition.

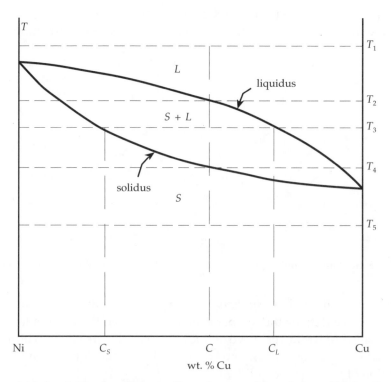

Figure 3.18 Analysis of cooling an alloy of composition C; S = solid, L = liquid.

The next situation we should work through is this: If two phases are present, what are the proportions of these phases? For example, at T_3 in Fig. 3.18 what are the weight percentages of the solid and the liquid phases? These percentages are given by the well-known *Lever rule*. The principle of the Lever rule is based on balancing two weights on a weightless beam across a fulcrum as shown in Fig. 3.19. The alloy composition is the fulcrum, and weights of phases (S and L) are suspended to balance the beam. The beam will balance if the moments of the weights are equal, i.e.,

$$W_S \times \overline{CC_S} = W_L \times \overline{CC_L} \tag{3.2.7}$$

It is easy to see from the above that

$$\text{wt. } \% \, S = \frac{C_L - C}{C_L - C_S} \times 100 \tag{3.2.8}$$

$$\text{wt. } \% \, L = \frac{C - C_S}{C_L - C_S} \times 100 \tag{3.2.9}$$

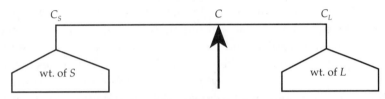

Figure 3.19 Principle of the Lever rule.

The *Ni-Cu* equilibrium diagram is a very simple case where *Ni* and *Cu* remain in solution in the solid phase. Such an alloy is called a *solid-solution* alloy. Some elements, however, do not like to remain in solution in the solid state. In some others, the two elements might form a compound at a fixed (or nearly fixed) composition. In others, other phases might form. Thus, in such cases the shapes of the equilibrium diagram are quite different. For example, if the two elements do not mix at all in the solid state, we obtain a phase diagram as shown in Fig. 3.20. This is a *eutectic* diagram.

In this diagram (Fig. 3.20), the elements A and B do not remain in solution below the *eutectic temperature* T_e. If we choose an alloy of composition C_e (as shown in the figure) at T_e, there is a three-phase equilibrium for this composition at point E. Point E is known as the *eutectic point*. At a temperature infinitesimally below T_e, solidification starts. Since A and B do not mix in the solid state, the solidification process must separate out pure A and B. In the previous diagram we assumed that the melting point of A is higher than that for pure B, and thus, a speck of pure A solidifies first. This makes the remaining liquid richer in B and a speck of pure B solidifies. In such a way alternate layers of plates of pure A and B solidify to give rise to a *eutectic microstructure*.

In some cases there might be a limited solid solubility of the two elements. For such a case we obtain a diagram as shown in Fig. 3.21. Below T_e we have two solid phases which we have designated as α and β. Although there are some standard notations—α, β, γ, depending on the crystal structure of the phases—it is important to note that α is, in this case, a solid solution which primarily consists of element A with some small amount of B dissolved in it. Similarly, β is primarily B with some small amount of A in it.

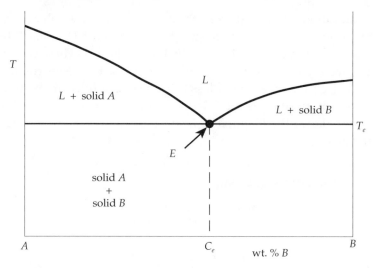

Figure 3.20 A eutectic diagram.

Consider the freezing of an alloy of composition C as shown in Fig. 3.21. At temperature T_1 the alloy is in the single-phase liquid region. At temperature T_2 the alloy is in the two-phase liquid + α region. Note that the intersection point between the composition-vertical and temperature-horizontal lies in the two-phase region. This region is defined by the liquidus line which delineates the boundary of the liquid, and the solidus line which defines the boundary of the solid α-phase. Thus, the region consists of solid α and the liquid alloy. At T_2 the temperature horizontal intersects the solidus and the liquidus. If we drop perpendiculars from these points to the composition axis, we obtain C_1 as the composition of solid α in equilibrium with a liquid of composition C_2 at that temperature. Applying the Lever rule at temperature T_2:

$$\text{wt. \% solid} = \frac{C_2 - C}{C_2 - C_1} \times 100 \qquad \textbf{(3.2.10)}$$

$$\text{wt. \% liquid} = \frac{C - C_1}{C_2 - C_1} \times 100 \qquad \textbf{(3.2.11)}$$

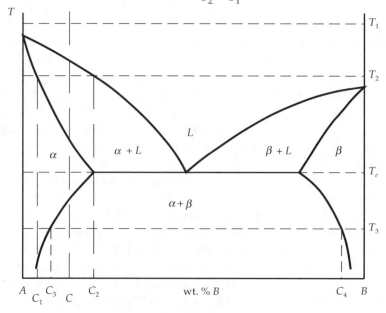

Figure 3.21 Eutectic diagram with limited solid solubility.

Similarly, at temperature T_3 the temperature horizontal intersects lines which separate α and β. Thus, at T_3 the two equilibrium phases, for the alloy composition C, are solid α of composition C_3 and solid β of composition C_4, respectively. The proportions of the phases are

$$\text{wt. } \% \ \alpha = \frac{C_4 - C}{C_4 - C_3} \times 100 \tag{3.2.12}$$

$$\text{wt. } \% \ \beta = \frac{C - C_3}{C_4 - C_3} \times 100 \tag{3.2.13}$$

Some elements might form a compound-like mixture at a fixed composition such as 75 atomic % A + 25 atomic % B, or 50 atomic % A + 50 atomic % B. These may be correspondingly designated as A_3B (75%: 25%), or AB (50%: 50%), as if they have a molecular formula like H_2O. When such compounds form, they behave more like pure metal and melt at a fixed single temperature. Formation of a compound splits the phase diagram.

It is easier to depict compound-forming alloys if we plot the phase diagram in at. % composition. Figures 3.22a and b schematically show two cases where the compound formation can be viewed as a separation of the phase diagram into two regions of eutectic type diagrams. Consider alloys of composition C_1 and A + 50% B in Fig. 3.22b. At temperature T_1 alloy C_1 is liquid, at T_2 it is in two-phase L + (AB) regions (note that (AB) is a compound), and at T_3 it is in two-phase α + (AB) regions. Note the intersection points of the temperature-horizontals with the various phase boundaries. For the alloy with A + 50 at. % B, T_1 is the region of liquid phase, but at both T_2 and T_3 the alloy is in a single-phase AB compound.

The eutectic diagram, as discussed earlier, can be viewed as if a chemical reaction occurs at the eutectic point; i.e., in melting a eutectic solid, two solids react to form a liquid of fixed composition. Thus, a eutectic phase separation is sometimes referred to as a *eutectic reaction*.

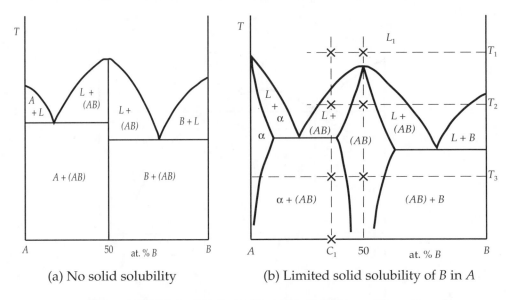

(a) No solid solubility   (b) Limited solid solubility of B in A

Figure 3.22 Schematic phase diagrams showing an AB compound.

Other reactions in various binary alloys are similar to the eutectic reaction. For example, a *peritectic reaction* is one in which a liquid L_I reacts with a solid S_I to form a second solid phase S_{II}. Fig. 3.23 shows a schematic diagram with a peritectic reaction. The point P is the peritectic point, and T_p and C_p are the peritectic temperature and composition, respectively. At T_p liquid of composition C_{L_I} reacts with solid α of composition C_α to form a new solid β; for example,

$$L_I + \alpha \rightarrow \beta \qquad\qquad (3.2.14)$$

A peritectic reaction is one in which a liquid L_I reacts with a solid S_I to form a second solid phase.

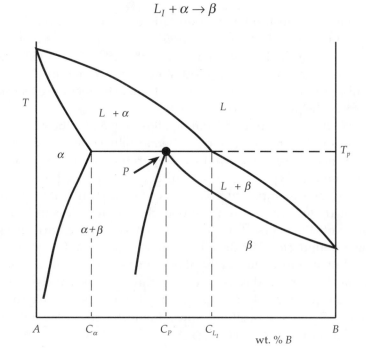

Figure 3.23 Schematic diagram showing a peritectic reaction.

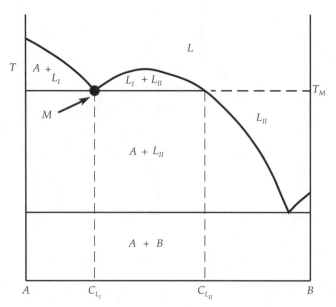

Figure 3.24 Schematic presentation of a monotectic reaction.

Another type of reaction, known as the *monotectic* reaction, is shown in Fig. 3.24. In this diagram M is the monotectic point. At the monotectic temperature T_M, liquid of composition C_{L_I} reacts with pure A to form another liquid of composition $C_{L_{II}}$. Note that the diagram shows a region where two immissible liquids, L_I and L_{II}, coexist.

Thus, the monotectic reaction in the above diagram could be written as:

$$\text{Solid } A + \text{ liquid } L_I \to L_{II} \qquad \textbf{(3.2.15)}$$

Analogous to the eutectic and peritectic reactions during the freezing of an alloy, we find two other reactions in the solid state diffusion-controlled phase separation. These are called *eutectoid* and *peritectoid* reactions. For a eutectoid reaction, we can write

$$\text{Solid}_I \to \text{Solid}_{II} + \text{Solid}_{III} \qquad \textbf{(3.2.16)}$$

$$\text{e.g., } \quad \gamma \to \alpha + \beta$$

and for a peritectoid reaction, we have

$$\text{Solid}_I + \text{Solid}_{II} \to \text{Solid}_{III} \qquad \textbf{(3.2.17)}$$

$$\text{e.g., } \quad \alpha + \gamma \to \beta$$

An important practical example showing a eutectoid reaction is the iron-carbon diagram. Figures 3.25a and b show some of the important features of the iron-carbon diagram. This diagram is very useful in the determination of heat-treatment procedure for steels.

The eutectoid reaction in the *Fe-C* system produces an alternate plate-like microstructure known as *pearlite*. The alternate plates consist of *ferrite* and *cementite*. Ferrite, denoted by α, is almost pure iron with a small amount of carbon ($\leq 0.02\%$). Cementite, also known as *carbide*, has a composition $Fe + 6.7$ wt. % C, and in atomic % has a formula Fe_3C. The phase, designated as γ in this diagram, is known as *austenite*. Since the eutectoid reaction at $\approx 723°C$ is controlled by solid state diffusion, this reaction can be suppressed by a rapid quenching of γ. In that case, austenite (γ) can transform to a metastable phase known as *martensite*. Martensite is the phase responsible for the dramatic increase of hardness of steels upon quenching. A steel with $< 0.8\%$ C is called a *hypoeutectoid* steel, and one with $> 0.8\%$ is called a *hypereutectoid* steel.

Martensite is the phase responsible for the dramatic increase of hardness of steels upon quenching.

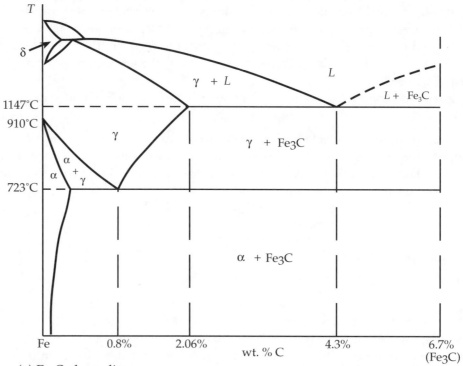

(a) Fe-C phase diagram.

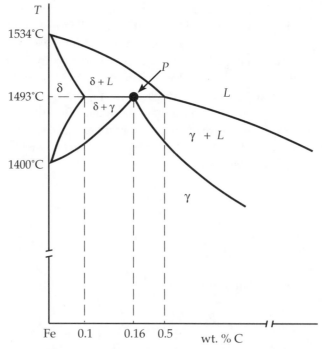

(b) A magnified view of the δ-Fe region. Point *P* is a peritectic point.

Figure 3.25 The iron-carbon diagram.

3.3 Atomic Bonding and Solid Types

A pure chemical element (or a mixture of elements) can exist in three different forms: (a) gaseous state, (b) liquid state, and (c) solid state. In the gas phase, atoms or molecules are randomly distributed in a given volume, and they are relatively far apart. They are free to move within the volume of the container that confines the gas. In the liquid form, however, the atoms or molecules are situated at distances comparable to atomic dimensions. A liquid, we know, cannot hold its own shape, but takes the shape of the container. A solid, on the other hand, can maintain its own shape and it has rigidity and strength to withstand a contact pressure. For our present purpose we focus our attention on solids only.

A solid material could be amorphous, crystalline or a mixture of both. In the amorphous form, the atoms or molecules are randomly distributed without any periodicity of arrangement. Glass, for example, is such an amorphous solid. Sometimes we can consider an amorphous solid as a "super cooled liquid." That is, the distribution of the atoms or molecules is similar to that in a liquid, but they are "frozen" in 3-dimensional space by super-cooling below its freezing point. In a crystalline solid the atoms or molecules are organized in a distinct 3-dimensional pattern. Like a pattern in a wallpaper, which repeats a basic "motif" or pattern to fill a large 2-dimensional space, in a crystalline solid space is filled by the repetition of a 3-dimensional "motif" called a "unit cell" of the solid. Crystallography is a subject which deals with the symbolic presentation and analysis of the unit cell of a crystalline solid. Before we discuss crystallography, it will be instructive to review the nature and type of interatomic forces which hold the atoms or molecules in a solid. Basically there are three types of primary bonds between atoms and molecules in an engineering solid. These are: (1) Ionic bonds, (2) Covalent bonds, and (3) Metallic bonds. These bond types are primarily dependent on the electronic structure of the atoms. First, we very briefly review the electronic structure of atoms.

> In the amorphous form, the atoms or molecules are randomly distributed without any periodicity of arrangement.

3.4 Electronic Structure of Atoms

Energy of electrons, orbiting around the nucleus of an atom, is quantized. The main quantized energy levels are designated by the primary quantum number n, where $n = 1, 2, 3$, etc. The energy level associated with the quantum number n is called the nth electronic shell. The number of electrons in a shell is given by $2n^2$. Thus the first shell ($n = 1$) has 2 electrons, the second shell ($n = 2$) has 8 electrons, etc.

A second quantum number l determines the energy sub-levels or sub-shells within a main energy level. The value of the second quantum number can be 0, 1, 2, ...(n–1). A notation of s, p, d, f is used for $l = 0, 1, 2, 3$, respectively. Thus, when $n = 1$, l can only be 0 (i.e., n–1), and the first energy level has no sub-level, and the shell is symbolically denoted by 1(s) (1 for $n = 1$, and s for l being equal to zero). For $n = 2$, l has a value of 0 and 1 (that is, s and p) and symbolically the two sub-shells are denoted as 2(s) and 2(p), respectively.

> The number of electrons in a shell is given by $2n^2$.

The Pauli exclusion principle states that no more than two electrons of opposite spin can occupy a "quantum state."

• The total number of electrons in an atom is equal to the number of protons in the atom.

• The filled outermost (s) and (p) shells are associated with the inertness or the very high stability of the atom.

Within an energy level, there could be several "quantum states" arising from a third quantum number, called the magnetic quantum number. We will use m for this quantum number. This quantum number can have values ranging from $-l$ to $+l$, including 0. Unlike n and l, different values of m, although it is a different quantum state, do not give rise to different values of electronic energy. Different quantum states which have the same energy are called degenerate states. Note that for $l = 2$ for example, m has values of $-2, -1, 0, +1, +2$, i.e., there are 5 degenerate quantum states in the 3rd shell ($n = 3$, since $l = n–1$).

A fourth quantum number is the spin quantum number s, which has values of $+1/2$ or $-1/2$. Each quantum state can accommodate two electrons of opposite spins ($+1/2$ or $-1/2$ are conventions of electronic spin up or down, respectively). The Pauli exclusion principle states that no more than two electrons of opposite spin can occupy a "quantum state." Note that the Pauli exclusion principle applies to quantum states and not to energy levels. Thus, for the above example, $n = 3$ gives $l = 0, 1, 2$, i.e., s, p, and d, respectively. For $l = 0$, that is s state, $m = 0$, and 2 electrons (spin up and spin down) occupy this shell. This is denoted by $3(s)^2$. Note that the first number is for n, and s within the parentheses stands for the s-state ($l = 0$), and the superscript 2 stands for the two electrons as discussed above. In the same example, for $n = 3$, and $l = 1$ that is p-state, m has values of -1, 0, $+1$; i.e., three quantum states, and each of these states holds two electrons, i.e., a total of 6 electrons. This is denoted by $3(p)^6$. Again, 3 for $n = 3$, p stands for $l = 1$, the superscript 6 is for the six electrons as discussed above. For $n = 3$, and $l = 2$, $m = -2, -1, 0, +1, +2$, i.e., 5 quantum states. Each of these five quantum states holds two electrons. Thus a total of 10 electrons. This configuration is denoted by $3(d)^{10}$. The $n = 3$ electron shell then consists of 2 electrons in the $3(s)$ state, another 6 electrons in the $3(p)$ state and an additional 10 electrons in $3(d)$ state. Thus a total of 18 electrons in the energy level associated with the primary quantum number $n = 3$, and it satisfies the requirement that the total number of electrons is given by $2(3)^2$. In symbolic form, the above mentioned sequence could be written as $3(s)^2 3(p)^6 3(d)^{10}$. It is easy to see that for $n = 1$, we have only $1(s)^2$, for $n = 2$, we have the sequence $2(s)^2 2(p)^6$.

In some elements, the $4(s)$ state might be filled before the $3(d)$ state has all ten electrons. This is the case in transition elements such as *Fe*, *Ni*, etc. For example, in the above example, if all of the quantum states of an atom up to $3(d)$ were sequentially filled, there will be a total of 28 electrons in the atom. This is because the total number of electrons in an atom is equal to the number of protons in the atom (which defines the atomic number Z). *Ni*, a transition element, has the atomic number 28. In nickel, the sequence of filled quantum states is given by $1(s)^2 2(s)^2 2(p)^6 3(s)^2\ 3(p)^6 3(d)^8 4(s)^2$. It is then clear that the $3(d)$ state of *Ni* is only partially filled.

If we examine the inert gases, *He*, *Ne*, *Ar*, etc., we find that in *He* the filled electronic shell is $1(s)^2$ (the atomic number of *He* is 2 and thus a total of 2 electrons), in *Ne*, the filled shells are sequentially given by $1(s)^2 2(s)^2 2(p)^6$; i.e., 10 electrons, which corresponds to the atomic number of *Ne*. Similarly for *Ar*, the sequence is $1(s)^2 2(s)^2 2(p)^6 3(s)^2 3(p)^6$, 18 electrons in total, which corresponds to the atomic number of *Ar*. In *He*, there is of course no p-shell, but its s-shell is filled. In *Ne*, the outermost states are filled; i.e., $2(s)^2 2(p)^6$; in *Ar* the outermost states $3(s)^2 3(p)^6$ are also filled. Similarly in *Kr*, and in *Xe*, the outermost states are given by $4(s)^2 4(p)^6$ and $5(s)^2 5(p)^6$, respectively. Thus, the filled outermost (s) and (p) shells are associated with the inertness or the very high stability of the atom. The electrons which are situated in the outermost *s* and *p* states are called *valence* electrons. In *He*, the outermost *s* shell is filled since it has two electrons. Likewise, in *Ne*, there are 8 electrons in the $2(s)2(p)$ states, and in *Ar* there are 8 electrons in the $3(s)3(p)$ states, and so on. These above mentioned elements have a full count (i.e., 8 electrons except in *He*) of valence electrons, and we also note that these are chemically inert elements. If we examine the periodic table, we notice that the "metallic elements" have partially filled valence states.

3.5 Ionic Bonding

An electropositive element such as Na and an electronegative element such as *Cl* can form a strong bond by transferring an electron from *Na* to *Cl*. This electron transfer process creates a positively charged Na^+ ion and a negatively charged Cl^- ion. The coulombic force then creates an attraction between these two charges when the pair of ions are not too far from each other. As this attractive force pulls the ions together, and they come in proximity to each other, a short-range repulsive force then operates due to a repulsion between the negative charge of the electron cloud of the ions. There exists a mutual separation distance at which the attractive and repulsive forces exactly balance each other. At this separation, the potential energy of the system is minimum. The coulomb attractive force is inversely proportion to r^2, where r is the separation distance between the ions. The repulsive force, on the other hand, is inversely proportional to r^n, where $n > 2$ ($\approx$ 6 to about 13). We note that the first derivative of potential energy with respect to separation distance is the force. As a convention, we choose the potential energy resulting from the attractive force as negative, and the potential energy resulting from the repulsive force as positive. In Fig. 3.26, we see that the equilibrium position is obtained by the algebraic summation of the attractive and the repulsive potentials.

The coulomb attractive force is inversely proportion to r^2. The repulsive force, on the other hand, is inversely proportional to r^n, where $n > 2$.

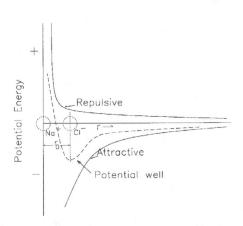

Figure 3.26 Equilibrium positions of atoms as determined by the potential energy minimum. The equilibrium separation distance is r_0.

The resulting potential energy curve has a minimum corresponding to the equilibrium separation. The potential energy minimum, commonly referred to as the "potential well," is a preferred site for an atom in a solid. Even in other types of bonding, potential energy minima associated with equilibrium atomic separation (as shown in Fig. 3.26) exist. What has been said for a pair of ions can be extended to a group of such ions. The arrangement in such a case is an alternate pairing of + and − ions in the three dimensional space. The situation in a two-dimensional plane of a ionic crystal is shown in Fig. 3.27. The ions in this plane are highly organized, and the separation distance a is the "interatomic distance" (please note that in the potential energy diagram for a pair of ions, we called this distance r_o).

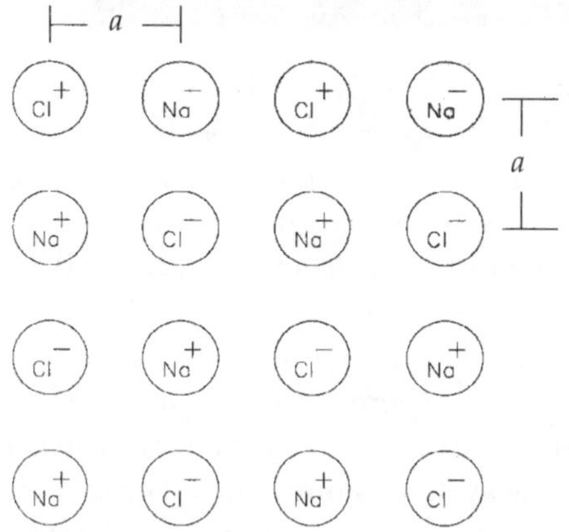

Figure 3.27 A two-dimensional diagram showing a plane of atoms of an ionic solid.

3.6 Covalent Bonding

> We define a bond between two similarly charged ions as covalent bonding.

We saw that in ionic bonding one atom gives up an electron, and another atom gains this electron, thus the donor atom becomes a positively charged ion and the other atom becomes a negatively charged ion. Then the coulombic attraction between these two ions is the force that binds a pair of atoms. Thus, the genesis of an ionic bond is the opposite polarity of the ions. We could define a bond between two similarly charged ions as a homopolar bonding. In homopolar or covalent bonding, instead of giving up or receiving electrons, the atoms *share* electrons. The bond strength is then derived from this electron sharing. To understand this mechanism, please refer to Section 3.4. Consider two hydrogen atoms adjacent to each other. Hydrogen (atomic number 1) has one electron only, and this electron resides in the s-state, i.e., the state is symbolically represented by $1(s)^1$. The "inert" element He (atomic number 2) has two electrons, and its state is represented by $1(s)^2$. Thus, two hydrogen atoms, in close proximity to each other, can share or "pool their two electrons" in a "common orbit" to mimic $1(s)^2$ orbital of the He atom. This bonding in hydrogen is a strong covalent bonding commonly referred to as a hydrogen bond. It is as if the two electrons spend part of the time in the $1(s)$ orbital of each atom. In a similar fashion, in other covalently bonded materials, valence electrons are shared by adjacent atoms in a solid to produce stability, i.e., bonding. The stability is related to the full outermost shell of the type $2(s)^2 2(p)^6$, $3(s)^2 3(p)^6$, etc. The number of nearest neighbors with which an atom can share its electrons, in a homopolar bond, is given by $8 − N$, where N

is the number of valence electrons in the atom. Now consider carbon (atomic number 6) which has an electron configuration given by $1(s)^2 2(s)^2 2(p)^2$. That is, the number of valence electrons in carbon is 4, 2 in $2(s)$ and 2 in $2(p)$. Hence carbon can make $8 - 4 = 4$ bond pairs. Such is the case in diamond, one of the hardest materials, where 4 very strong covalent bonds are made between 4 nearest carbon atoms in the crystalline solid. Similarly, technologically a very important element *Si* (extensively used for semiconductors), has 4 valence electrons $3(s)^2 3(p)^2$, and this element crystallizes via a very strong covalent bonding.

3.7 Metallic Bonding

It has been stated earlier that in metallic elements, the number of valence electrons is one or two. The valence electrons are, furthermore, "free" to move around the entire solid piece of metal. The valence electrons are no longer "localized" to individual atoms as in the case of ionic and covalent bonds. Instead, these electrons contribute to a common "sea" of electrons, in which the ions are immersed in a three-dimensional periodic pattern. The bonding in the solids then is due to an attraction between the positively charged ions and the negatively charged sea of electrons. The motion of these free electrons through the periodic lattice, however, is governed by quantum mechanical laws. The subject of metallic bonding is much more complicated than that described here. The interested student is advised to read any textbook in solid state physics.

3.8 Electrical Properties

Insulators

In a solid in which the bonding between the atoms is either ionic or covalent in nature, valence electrons are localized near the atoms. In ionic solids an electron is actually transferred to the adjacent atom, and in a covalent solid an electron is shared by two adjacent atoms. In either case the electron orbits are tightly bound to the atoms. Thus in these types of solids electrons cannot freely move around to produce a current flow when an electrical potential gradient (voltage) is established. These solids are called *insulators*. Insulators have very high electrical resistivity on the order of 10^{16} ohm·cm, compared with a good metallic conductor, which has a resistivity on the order of 10^{-6} ohm·cm.

In ionic solids, a current flow can occur if the ions (which carry a positive or a negative charge) can migrate through the solid as charge carriers instead of the electrons. Such an ion mobility, however, requires solid state diffusion. As discussed before, the rate of solid state diffusion increases exponentially with increasing temperature. Thus, the electrical conductivity of ionic solids increases with temperature (i.e., resistivity decreases).

Conductors

In metallic solids, valence electrons are not bound to individual atoms. Instead, these electrons form what may be called a "free electron gas." This electron gas obeys quantum statistical laws rather than the classical statistical mechanics laws which apply to molecular gases. In a crystalline metallic solid, individual atoms are placed in a periodic manner within a "sea" of free electrons. Since the free electrons are not strongly bound to individual atoms, they can easily move through the solid metal, where a very small electrical potential gradient (voltage) is established. Because of the high mobility of the free electrons, the electrical resistivity of a good metallic conductor like *Cu* is about 1.7×10^{-6} ohm·cm. Electrical resistance, R, of a conductor of length l cm, a cross-sectional area a cm² (normal to the direction of current flow) and resistivity ρ, is given by Ohm's law:

$$R = \rho l / a \qquad \qquad \text{(3.8.1)}$$

In a metallic conductor, the moving electrons periodically collide with oscillating atoms in the lattice. The average distance traveled by an electron between two successive collisions is called the "mean free path" of an electron. A higher value of the mean free path gives a higher value of conductivity (i.e., lower resistivity). As temperature increases, the amplitude of thermal oscillation of lattice atoms increases, and the mean free path decreases. Thus, in metallic solids resistivity (thus resistance) increases with increasing temperature. Note that this behavior is opposite of that for an ionic conductor as discussed before.

Energy Band

Free atoms have discrete quantum states or levels as has been discussed before. For example, *Na* (a metallic element of atomic number 11) has 11 electrons in energy levels described by: $1(s)^2 2(s)^2 2(p)^6 3(s)^1$. When sodium atoms are brought close together to form a solid, the electronic energy levels of individual atoms overlap. As the atoms come closer together, the energy levels split, and each discrete energy level becomes an energy band with quasi-continuous energy sublevels within each band. If we consider a solid *Na* block, containing N atoms of *Na* (for example $N \approx 10^{23}$ for one gram-atom of *Na*), then $1(s)$ and $2(s)$ bands each contain $2N$ electrons, and $2(p)$ band contains $6N$ electrons (each N atom contributing 6 electrons to this band). The outermost band $3(s)$ can accommodate $2N$ electrons; however, each Na atom can only contribute 1 electron to this band. Thus the $3(s)$ band is *only half full*. Figure 3.28 shows a schematic picture of energy levels and energy bands of a single Na atom and a crystalline solid block of *Na* containing N atoms.

Within each energy band, the Pauli exclusion principle holds, and no more than 2 electrons of opposite spin can stay in each of the states within an energy band as described above. Each band has a quasi-continuous set of energy levels. Electrons fill the bands from the lowest to the highest energy levels. This is a simple manifestation of energy minimization principle. When additional energy is supplied to an electron either by supplying thermal energy or by setting up an electrical potential, the kinetic energy of an electron must increase. Quantum mechanically, then, this electron must move up to a higher energy level. Since all of the energy levels from the ground level up are filled, and since the Pauli exclusion principle applies, the only electrons which can take up the extra energy and move up to a higher empty level are those near the top of a band.

The probability of finding an electron in a particular energy state E is given by the Fermi-Dirac distribution function $P(E)$,

$$P(E) = \frac{1}{[e(E - E_f) / kT] - 1} \qquad \qquad \text{(3.8.2)}$$

where E_f is called the Fermi energy, k is Boltzmann's constant and T is the Kelvin temperature. At $T = 0$, $P(E) = 1$ for $E < E_f$, and $P(E) = 0$ for $E > E_f$. At $T > 0$ K, $P(E)$

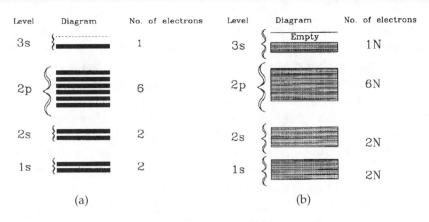

Figure 3.28 (a) Schematic energy level diagram of a single *Na* atom, and (b) the energy bands of a solid *Na* containing *N* atoms.

$= 1/2$ for $E = E_f$. Figures 3.29a and b show the variation of $P(E)$ as a function of energy E at $T = 0$, and at $T > 0$ K, respectively. We note from the above discussion that at temperatures $T > 0$ K, a small fraction of the energy levels below the Fermi energy are empty, and a small fraction of the number of energy levels above the Fermi level are occupied.

At $T = 0$ K, the Fermi level E_f coincides with the middle line of the half-filled $3(s)$ band in *Na*. When an electric field is applied at a temperature greater than absolute zero, the electrons very near the Fermi energy can acquire incremental kinetic energy, and thus must move up to a higher empty level. Note that the energy bands are separated by forbidden energy gaps. If a solid is such that the topmost band is completely full, which is followed by an energy gap and a completely empty band above that, then the conductivity of this solid depends on the magnitude of the energy gap E_g. At a temperature T, if E_g is less than kT (note that kT has the dimension of energy), then conductivity rises when electrons are raised to the upper empty band. The upper empty band is called the "conduction band," and the filled band immediately below it is called the "valence band". In a good insulator, E_g is very large, on the order of 10 electron volts (eV).

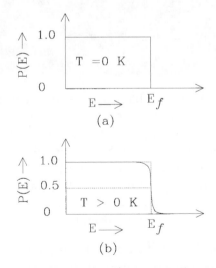

Figure 3.29 *P(E)* v. *E* plots; (a) showing that at $T = 0$ K the probability of finding an electron up to Fermi level is 1; (b) at $T > 0$ K, there is a finite probability of finding some electrons above the Fermi level.

Semiconductors

In a material in which the value of E_g is relatively small (on the order of 1 eV), conduction can occur at higher temperatures through electrons which are raised from the full valence band to the empty conduction band across the band gap, via thermal activation. The thermally activated electrons, which are placed in the conduction band, can now move under the influence of an electrical potential. At $T = 0$ K, the conduction band is empty, and has no current flows when an electrical potential is applied. Such a material is called an "intrinsic semiconductor." Si and Ge are two very common intrinsic semiconductors used in technology today.

Adding impurities, called "doping," to a semiconductor can significantly modify the electrical properties. If an impurity atom is such that it adds an electronic energy level within the E_g and near the bottom of the conduction band, then the electrons from this impurity level can be thermally activated to the empty conduction band, and thus provide a current flow when a voltage is applied. The impurity in this case is called a "donor," since it donates electrons to the conduction band. The energy gap between the donor level and the bottom of the conduction band is typically 0.05 eV. The donor level provides negatively charged electrons for conduction in such a doped material. The semiconductor doped in this fashion is called an "n-type" semiconductor. If, however, an added impurity is such that it creates an electron-deficient level near the top of the valence band, and this level is separated by an energy gap on the order of 0.05 eV, then electrons can be thermally activated to this donor band, and once again conduction could occur. This impurity level is called "acceptor," since it accepts electrons. When electrons from the filled valence band are promoted to the acceptor level, "holes" are left in the previously filled valence band. Conduction occurs as if by the migration of "holes" in such a semiconductor. Compared with the n-type semiconductors where the charge carrier is negative (electrons), these hole conduction type semiconductors are called p-type (positive carriers) semiconductors. Materials in which semiconducting behavior is ushered in by doping of impurities are called "extrinsic semiconductors."

3.9 Crystalline State and Crystallography

The glassy or the amorphous state has no long-range periodicity of atomic positions. As opposed to an amorphous solid, a crystalline solid is composed of atoms (henceforth "atoms" will be interchangeably used for ions, molecules or atoms) which are arranged in regular periodic patterns. These solid materials where the atoms are arranged in a regular periodic and repetitive manner, following certain geometric and mathematical laws, are called crystalline solids. Many of the engineering solids are crystalline in nature. By long-range periodicity we mean periodicity over thousands of atoms in any given direction.

Unit Cell and Lattice Parameters

The fundamental building block of a crystalline solid, in an atomic scale, is called an unit cell or a lattice. A three-dimensional stacking of such unit cells produces a macroscopic crystalline solid. An unit cell or a lattice can be defined by three vectors x, y, and z as shown in Fig. 3.30.

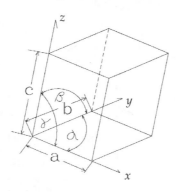

Figure 3.30 Unit cell of a crystal lattice. The dimensions *a*, *b*, *c* and the angles α, β, and γ are the lattice parameters.

In Fig. 3.30, *a*, *b*, and *c* define the dimensions of the three sides of the parallelepiped. The three mutually inclined (non-orthogonal) vectors *x*, *y*, and *z* are chosen to represent a general case. If we now put eight atoms at the eight corners of the parallelepiped shown in Fig. 3.30, then we have what we may call a unit cell. Note that the size and shape of this unit cell are determined by the three angles, and the three lengths of the three adjacent sides. A special case is when $a = b = c$, and $\alpha = \beta = \gamma = 90°$. In that case the shape is a cube, and the unit cell, as shown in Fig. 3.31, is called a simple cubic lattice. The quantities *a*, *b*, *c*, α, β, and γ are called lattice parameters. For an orthogonal axis system, such as the cubic crystal, only one lattice parameter, *a*, is sufficient to define the unit cell size and shape.

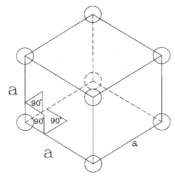

Figure 3.31 A simple cubic unit cell or a simple cubic lattice.

Seven Crystal Systems

Only seven distinct shapes of unit cells can be generated by various combinations of values of *a*, *b*, *c*, α, β, and γ. These are called the seven crystal systems. Note that these crystal unit cells are defined by putting one atom in each corner of the cell. These seven systems are shown in Fig. 3.32.

Note that in the case of a hexagonal crystal, only one-third of the volume shown in Fig. 3.32 is taken as the unit cell. This volume is a rectangular parallelepiped with two sides equal (shown as *a* in Fig. 3.32), and the third side is *c*. The included angle between the two axes, defined as α, is 120°. The various relationships between the dimensions and the angles for the seven crystal systems are shown in Table 3.2.

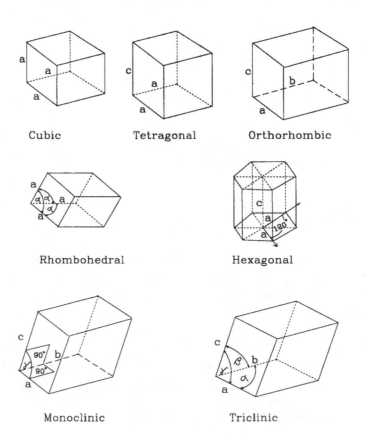

Figure 3.32 Seven crystal systems.

TABLE 3.2 Properties of the Seven Crystal Systems

Crystal system	Dimensions of a, b, and c	Angles between the three axes
Cubic	$a = b = c$	$\alpha = \beta = \gamma = 90°$
Tetragonal	$a = b \neq c$	$\alpha = \beta = \gamma = 90°$
Orthorhombic	$a \neq b \neq c$	$\alpha = \beta = \gamma = 90°$
Rhombohedral	$a = b = c$	$\alpha = \beta = \gamma \neq 90°$
Hexagonal	$a = b \neq c$	$\alpha = 120°, \beta = \gamma = 90°$
Monoclinic	$a \neq b \neq c$	$\alpha = \beta = 90° \neq \gamma$
Triclinic	$a \neq b \neq c$	$\alpha \neq \beta \neq \gamma \neq 90°$

Bravais Lattice and Atom Positions

If we place an atom (remember that we are using "atom" as a generic term for atoms, molecules or ions) at the eight corners of each of the seven cells shown in Fig. 3.32, we obtain seven unit cells. Please note again that for the hexagonal cell, we take one-third of the volume shown in Fig. 3.32. This volume is defined by two axes which have an included angle of 120°, and the third axis is perpendicular to the plane containing the other two axes. With these seven types of elementary unit cells, we can fill up a three-dimensional space by stacking them together, much like stacking bricks to form a massive structure. If we examine such a large mass, we see that the adjacent atoms along any direction are obtained by "translations" of vectors along the three defining vectors (called basis vectors) of the unit cell. This is shown in Fig. 3.33. This space-filling also produces an identical surrounding for each atom (i.e., number and distance of nearest neighbors to each atom).

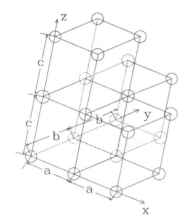

Figure 3.33   Unit translation of atoms along *x*-, *y*-, and *z*-directions for 3-dimensional space filling.

The above mentioned seven unit cells are not the only possibilities where each atom has an identical surrounding. In fact, altogether fourteen unit cells can be constructed from the above mentioned seven cells where each atom has an identical surrounding. These fourteen are called the *Bravais lattices*. Because of the brevity of this treatment, we will consider only the cubic and the hexagonal systems, which include a large number of engineering solids.

A simple cubic lattice is very easy to visualize. It consists of an elementary cube, in which the eight corners of the cube are occupied by eight atoms. This unit cell is already shown in Fig. 3.31.

Simple Cubic Lattice

A body-centered unit cell is shown in Fig. 3.34. Aside from the eight corners, there is another atom situated in the interior of the cube. At the center of the body, defined by the point of intersections of the body diagonals as shown, thus the name body-centered cubic (BCC) is used. Many metals and alloys crystallize in this form (notably iron and steel).

Body Centered Cubic Lattice (BCC)

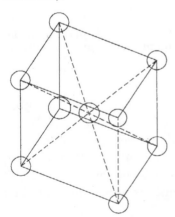

Figure 3.34 Body-centered cubic lattice (BCC).

Face Centered Cubic Lattice (FCC)

A face centered unit cell (FCC) is shown in Fig. 3.35a. Here, six additional atoms are located at the center of each face of the cube. Hence the name face centered cubic (FCC) is used. The six atom positions are obtained by drawing diagonal lines from the opposite corners of each face as shown in Fig. 3.35b.

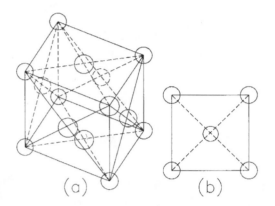

Figure 3.35 a) A face centered cubic lattice. b) The location of the face center atom is at the intersection of the face diagonals.

Note that an FCC lattice is a "close-packed" lattice. By this it is meant that, if the atoms are assumed to be like ball bearings of equal size, then this structure provides the maximum packing density. In Fig. 3.36a is shown a plane of atoms in which the atoms are most closely packed. The arrangement of atoms in this plane is shown in Fig. 3.36b. We will return to this subject later.

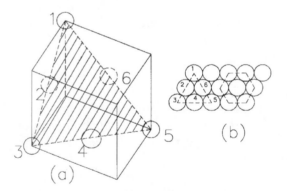

Figure 3.36 a) shows a "close packed" plane of the FCC lattice (not all atoms of the cell are shown, and b) shows the arrangement of atoms in this plane.

Hexagonal Close Packed lattice (HCP)

A hexagonal unit cell is shown in Fig. 3.37a. This lattice is <u>not</u> a close packed cell. Fig. 3.37b is a hexagonal close packed cell (HCP). Note in 3.37b, that there are three additional atoms inside the hexagonal frame, aside from the external corner atoms (not shown in b for clarity). The close packed plane is the bottom plane (called the basal plane) and it is shown in Fig. 3.37c. The second layer of atoms (i.e., the interior three atoms) are shown by dotted circles in this figure. Please compare figures 3.36b and 3.37c.

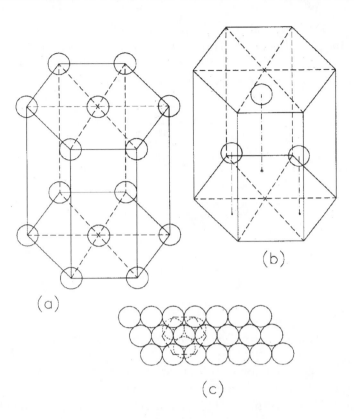

Figure 3.37 Hexagonal lattice: a) simple hexagonal, b) hexagonal close packed HCP, and c) atomic packing on the basal plane.

Miller indices is a system of notations used for denoting planes and directions in crystals. Letters h, k, and l are used as the indices, and these indices are usually written as (hkl) without commas between them. Miller indices are all integers, and they do not contain a common factor. For example (111), (121), etc., are permissible but indices (222), (242) are not used, since taking the common factor out (222) is reduced to (111), and (242) is reduced to (121).

If a, b, and c are the three dimensions of a unit cell, then a plane with Miller indices (hkl) intersects the three coordinate axes x, y, and z as shown in Fig. 3.38a. The intercepts are a/h, b/k, and c/l, respectively. If a plane intersects the three axes of the crystal at distances equal to the three dimensions a, b, and c of the unit cell, then the miller indices of the plane is (111). For example the cross-hatched plane shown in Fig. 3.38a, intersects the x, y, and z axes at distances equal to the dimension of the side of the cube, and thus this plane is (111). Note, therefore, that the (111) plane of an FCC crystal is the close packed plane. To determine the Miller indices of a plane we take the intercepts of the plane in terms of the fractions of the lattice dimensions along the three directions. As an example consider an unit cell of dimensions a, b, and c, and a plane which intersects the x-axis at a distance of a, the y-axis at $b/2$ and the z-axis at $c/2$. Thus the $b/2$ and $c/2$ intercepts are 1, 1/2, 1/2. We now take reciprocal of these intercepts, i.e., 1, 2, 2, and write it in the form (122), which is the Miller indices of the plane. Note that this gives the intercepts $a/1$, $b/2$, and $c/2$ as discussed earlier. A plane which intersects the three axes at $a/2$, $b/2$, and $c/2$, has intercepts 1/2, 1/2, 1/2, reciprocals of which are 2, 2, 2. We eliminate the common factor and write (111) as the Miller indices of that plane. Note that what it means is that the (222) plane

Miller Indices of Planes and Directions

To determine the Miller indices of a plane we take the intercepts of the plane in terms of the fractions of the lattice dimensions along the three directions.

is parallel to (111) plane. Note that if a plane is parallel to an axis, the intercept is infinity (the reciprocal is zero). Thus, for example, we recognize that the (110) plane is parallel to the z-axis. A plane which intersects the x-axis at unit distance is parallel to the y- and z-axes and has Miller indices (100), etc.

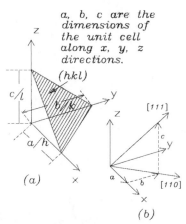

Figure 3.38 Miller indices of planes and directions: a) planes, b) directions.

Miller indices of a direction are obtained by the vector sum of the component vectors along the three axes of the unit cell. Usually Miller indices of a direction are written as [hkl]. for example, [110] is a direction on the x-y plane obtained by adding one lattice vector along the x-direction and one lattice vector along the y-direction as shown in Fig. 3.38b. Also shown is the [111] direction.

Primitive Cell

A unit cell which only has corner atoms (ions, molecules) is called a primitive cell. Thus, a simple cubic lattice is a primitive cell. Similarly, a hexagonal lattice (note that one-third of the hexagon, as discussed earlier, is the unit cell) only has corner atoms, and thus it is a primitive lattice. However, BCC, FCC, and HCP are not primitive cells.

Number of Atoms per Unit Cell

Consider a simple cubic lattice. There are eight atoms at the eight corners of a single cell. However, when we pack unit cells to fill up a three-dimensional space, each corner atom is shared by eight other adjacent cells. Thus on the average, only one eighth of a corner atom belongs to one unit cell. Hence, $1/8 \times 8 = 1$ atom per unit cell. In FCC, each atom at the center of each of the six faces is shared by two adjacent cells during stacking of such cubes. Thus, on the average $1/2$ of each face atom belongs to one cell. Thus, in FCC, six faces have each half an atom, and each corner has $1/8$ of an atom. Therefore, the total number of atoms per unit cell in FCC is $(1/8 \times 8 + 1/2 \times 6) = 4$ atoms. In BCC, the body center atom is not shared by any other cells, and thus BCC has 2 atoms per unit cell.

Interplaner Spacing d_{hkl}

In many problems in materials science, the distance between parallel planes in a given lattice is an important parameter. Interplaner distance d_{hkl} is the perpendicular distance between equivalent planes as shown in Fig. 3.39. The planes shown are of the type are (100), (110) and (111). Note that (100) planes are parallel to the y- and z-axes, with an intercept on the x-axis equal to the unit cell dimension in that direction. Similarly, (110) is parallel to the z-axis with unit intercepts along the x- and y-axes. For the (111) plane the intercepts along the x, y

and z directions are equal to the unit cell dimensions along those directions. Distance between crystallographic planes of a unit cell is expressed in Angstrom units. One Angstrom is equal to 10^{-8} cm, and it is written as Å.

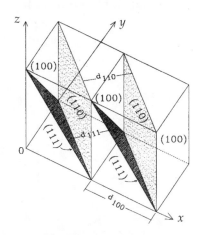

Figure 3.39 Interplaner distance d_{hkl}.

FCC and HCP are two of the close packed lattices. If we try to arrange a number of dimes or nickels in such a way as to have a most efficient coverage of a two-dimensional space, we obtain a configuration similar to the arrangement of atoms on the (111) planes of a FCC lattice or the basal plane of a HCP lattice (see Figs. 3.36b and 3.37c). In examining the close packed arrangement of the coins, we find that there are empty spaces around them. Similarly in close packing of hard spheres, we have empty spaces surrounding the spheres. Thus, the volume bounded by the unit cell consists of the volume occupied by the atoms plus the empty space. We could define an atomic packing factor (APF) as the ratio of the volume of atoms to the volume of the cell.

Close Packing of Atoms, and Packing Factor

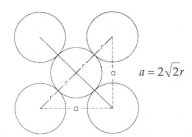

Figure 3.40 Atomic packing on a face plane of a FCC lattice.

Figure 3.40 shows the arrangement of atoms on one of the faces of a FCC unit cell. We note that the face diagonal is equal to four atomic radii, $4r$. The dimension of the side of the square faces is a. Thus from the geometry, we have,

$$a = 2\sqrt{2}r \tag{3.9.1}$$

In an FCC unit cell there are 4 atoms per cell, as before. The volume of four atoms is given by

$$\text{volume occupied by atoms} = 4 \times (4/3)\,\pi\, r^3 \tag{3.9.2}$$

From Eq. 3.9.1, we can write

$$\text{volume of the unit cell} = a^3 = (2\sqrt{2})^3 r^3 \tag{3.9.3}$$

Thus, for FCC, the atomic packing factor is given by

$$APF = [\,4 \times (4/3)\,\pi\,r^3\,]/[\,(2\sqrt{2})^3 r^3\,] = 0.74 \qquad (3.9.4)$$

In a BCC cell, the atoms touch along the body diagonal as shown in Fig. 3.41a. The geometry of the body diagonal and its relationship with the unit cell dimension *a* is shown in Fig. 3.41b.

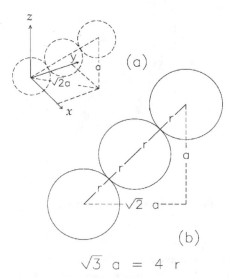

Figure 3.41 Atomic packing along a body diagonal of a BCC cell.

From Fig. 3.41b, we see that

$$\sqrt{3}\ a = 4r \qquad (3.9.5)$$

In a BCC unit cell there are 2 atoms per unit cell. The volume occupied by the atoms in the cell is given by

$$\text{volume occupied by atoms} = 2 \times (4/3)\,\pi\,r^3 \qquad (3.9.6)$$

From Eq. 3.9.5 we can write

$$\text{volume of the unit cell} = a^3 = (4/\sqrt{3})^3 r^3 \qquad (3.9.7)$$

Thus, for BCC, the atomic packing factor is given by

$$APF = \frac{2(4/3)\pi r^3}{(4/\sqrt{3})^3 r^3} = 0.68 \qquad (3.9.8)$$

We note that the packing efficiency in FCC is higher than in BCC. As the name implies, FCC is a close packed structure, whereas BCC is not a close packed structure.

X-Ray Crystallography

X-ray diffraction is a powerful tool for crystal structure determination. For example, if we determine the spacing of the planes which define the faces of a unit cell, we can determine the size and shape of the unit cell. The well known Bragg's law of X-ray diffraction is given by

$$2d_{hkl}\,\sin\theta = n\,\gamma \qquad (3.9.9)$$

where d_{hkl} is the spacing of a set of planes for which an X-ray diffraction maximum is obtained when the angle of incidence of the X-ray beam, measured from the surface of the plane, is θ. γ is the wave length of the incident X-ray, and *n* is an integer called the order of reflection, and it can have values of 1, 2, 3, ... $n = 1$ is the first order reflection, $n = 2$ is the second order reflection, etc.

3.10 Atomic Mobility, Solid State Diffusion, and Atomic Scale Defects

In the solid state, migration of atoms from one location to another (one lattice site to another) occurs very slowly at ordinary temperatures. However, this atomic migration (called diffusion), at elevated temperatures can cause many important changes, such as recrystallization, precipitation of phases, and decomposition of phases. Diffusion also plays a role in high-temperature creep, and creep rupture failure of metals and alloys.

In a crystalline solid, each atomic site is a "potential well" corresponding to the potential energy minima as illustrated in Fig. 3.42. Adjacent atoms in a crystalline solid are situated at the bottom of a periodic well. Separating any two such wells is a potential energy hill. Thus diffusion requires that an atom has sufficient energy to climb the hill.

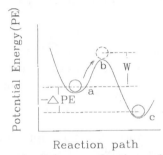

Figure 3.42 Potential wells, potential energy barrier and atomic migration in a solid.

The concept of a potential energy barrier in atomic migration is illustrated in Fig. 3.42. In the solid state, atoms are constantly oscillating about the lattice sites. As the temperature increases, the amplitude of oscillation of the atoms increases. In the figure, the potential well on the right is deeper (i.e., a site with lower potential energy) than the one on the left. A net release of potential energy equal to ΔPE occurs if the atom from site a can move over to site c. However, separating sites a and b is the hill of height W. As the temperature increases, the thermal oscillation of the atom increases, and it attempts to surmount the hill. The rate or the kinetics of the atomic migration, in such a case, is then determined by the number of attempts the atom makes per unit time to approach the top of the hill, and the probability that this atom has the additional energy W. The number of attempts an atom makes is related to its vibration frequency (number of cycles per second). The rate of such a thermally activated process is given by

$$\text{rate} = fe^{-W/kT} \tag{3.10.1}$$

where f is the oscillation frequency of the atom, W is the activation barrier, called the activation energy, k is Boltzmann's constant, and T is Kelvin temperature. Note that the rate of any such process increases exponentially with temperature. Note also that an atom can move to another lattice site only if that site is empty. Indeed, such empty sites called vacancies exist in crystalline solids. Thus, the presence of vacancies is essential to solid state diffusion. Vacancies are also known as point defects.

3.11 Metallic Corrosion

🔑 Oxidation of a metal (anodic) takes place when the metal gives up its valence electrons.

Metallic corrosion is intuitively identified with rusting and perforation of automobile bodies. Billions of dollars are wasted every year due to corrosion damage of engineering structures such as bridges, highways (steel reinforcement bars), storage tanks, automobiles, and machinery. The basic phenomenon of corrosion can be recognized as "rusting." The fundamental mechanism of rusting is oxidation-reduction reactions. It is recognized that oxidation reactions go hand in hand with reduction reactions. In corrosion, this oxidation-reduction process is electrochemical in nature.

Oxidation is associated with anodic reaction, as in an anode of a battery. Reduction reaction, on the other hand, is associated with a cathodic reaction. Oxidation of a metal (anodic) takes place when the metal gives up its valence electrons. Reduction, a cathodic reaction, on the other hand occurs through a reaction which accepts the electrons liberated by the anodic reaction. For example, oxidation of two iron atoms could be expressed as follows:

$$2\ Fe \rightarrow 2\ Fe^{+2} + 4e \qquad \qquad \textbf{(3.11.1)}$$

where each divalent *Fe* atom gives up two of its valence electrons to become an Fe^{+2} ion. There must be a corresponding reduction reaction to accept these four liberated electrons. Such a reduction reaction occurs in oxygenated water as

$$O_2 + 2H_2O + 4e \rightarrow 4(OH)^- \qquad \qquad \textbf{(3.11.2)}$$

That is, oxygen and two molecules of water combine with four electrons to produce four negatively charged $(OH)^-$ ions. It can be seen that the two Fe^{+2} ions (total positive charge of +4), can be neutralized through the reaction with four $(OH)^-$ ions (total charge –4). This is the basis of oxidation or rusting of iron. Please note that iron will not rust in water which does not have dissolved air or oxygen.

Another form of corrosion is often encountered in improperly designed engineering structures which combine different metals and alloys. This type of corrosion is called "galvanic corrosion," When two dissimilar metals (or alloys) are immersed in a saline solution or in a weak acid solution, and there exists an electrical contact between them, one of the two metals corrodes away and an electrical current flows between them. (This is how batteries operate; the metal that corrodes acts as the anode.) Which of the two metals corrodes depends on their relative positions on the "galvanic series." An *emf* or a galvanic series can be constructed starting from the most corrosion resistance (noble metal or cathodic metal) to the least corrosion (anodic, or base metal) metals and alloys. A partial list of such a galvanic series is shown:

Noble   **Anodic** $\rightarrow\rightarrow\rightarrow$ **Base**
Pt, Au, ...Ag,......Ni, ...Cu, ...Sn, Pb, ..., Fe, ...Al, ...Zn, Mg
$\leftarrow\leftarrow\leftarrow$ **Cathodic**

It is essential for a design engineer to consult a table of galvanic series before selecting dissimilar metallic materials to be incorporated in a design.

Practice Problems

3.1   Deformation is irreversible if

    a)   Hooke's law holds.

    b)   the deformation rate is slow.

    c)   applied stress is greater than the yield stress.

    d)   there is no work hardening.

3.2   Off-set yield stress is defined as

    a)   stress at which yielding starts.

    b)   stress required for inhomogenous deformation.

    c)   stress corresponding to a specific plastic strain.

    d)   stress at the proportional limit.

3.3   Ultimate tensile strength is

    a)   the theoretical strength of metal.

    b)   the stress to initiate plastic flow.

    c)   the fracture stress.

    d)   the maximum engineering stress.

3.4   All of the following statements about fracture are correct, except:

    a)   extent of necking depends on ductility

    b)   ductile fracture produces a cup and cone fracture surface

    c)   in a ductile fracture the reduction in area is zero

    d)   a low carbon steel can be more brittle at low temperatures

3.5   All of the following statements about yield-point phenomenon are true, except:

    a)   dislocation motion is responsible for yield point

    b)   presence of carbon in iron is responsible for yield point in steels

    c)   upper and lower yield points are found in many aluminum alloys

    d)   yield point indicates inhomogenous deformation

3.6   Plastic deformation is caused by

    a)   stored elastic energy.   c)   low value of modulus.

    b)   dislocation motion.   d)   complex elastic stresses.

3.7   All of the following statements regarding slip deformation are correct, except:

    a)   a volume change is associated with slip

    b)   slip occurs along close-packed directions

    c)   some crystals have more slip systems than others

    d)   dislocation motion is necessary for slip

3.8   All of the following statements regarding metal fatigue are correct, except:

    a)   surface roughness decreases fatigue life
    b)   thermal cycling of a metal can produce fatigue failure
    c)   carburizing treatment can improve fatigue life
    d)   a fatigue endurance limit is observed in pure aluminum

3.9   A solid-solution alloy is

    a)   produced by melting two metals together which do not mix in the solid state.
    b)   an alloy of two solid phases.
    c)   homogeneous and single phase at ordinary temperatures.
    d)   quickly attacked by an acid.

3.10   All of the following statements regarding a eutectic alloy are correct, except:

    a)   eutectic temperature is invariant
    b)   an alloy of eutectic composition solidifies within a range of temperatures
    c)   two elements must be partially insoluble in the solid state to form a eutectic
    d)   eutectic microstructure is easily detectable under a microscope

3.11   A peritectic reaction is defined as

    a)   two solids reacting to form a liquid.
    b)   two liquids reacting to form a solid.
    c)   a liquid and a solid reacting to form another solid.
    d)   two solids reacting to form a third solid.

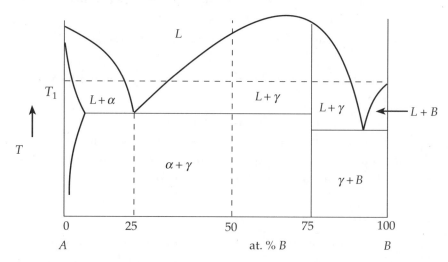

3.12   In the above diagram, which of the following compound or compounds are present?

    a) AB b) AB_2 c) A_3B_2 d) AB_3

3.13 For an alloy of A + 50 at. % B as shown in the diagram for Problem 3.12, which phases are present at the temperature T_1?

   a) single phase liquid (L)   c) liquid + α
   b) liquid + γ d) $\alpha + \gamma$

3.14 For the iron-carbon diagram shown in Fig. 3.25, all of the following are true, except:

   a) a eutectoid reaction at 1147°C
   b) a peritectic reaction at 1493°C
   c) maximum carbon content of austenite is 2.06%
   d) γ to δ transformation temperature is 1400°C

3.15 A binary alloy of composition 50 wt. % A and 50 wt. % B has two equilibrium phases, α and β, at a temperature T_1. The composition of α-phase is 75 wt. % A and 25 wt. % B. The composition of β-phase is 25 wt. % A and 75 wt. % B. The proportions of α- and β-phases are

   a) 25 wt. % α, 75 wt. % β.
   b) 75 wt. % α, 25 wt. % β.
   c) 50 wt. % α, 50 wt. % β.
   d) 80 wt. % α, 20 wt. % β.

3.16 The most efficient packing of atoms is found in which of the following crystalline lattices:

   I)   simple cubic
   II)   face centered cubic
   III) body centered tetragonal
   IV)   rhombohedral
   V)   hexagonal close packed

   a) I only   c) III only
   b) II only   d) II and V only

3.17 Doped-semiconducting materials have which of the following properties:

   I)   an energy gap on the order of 10 eV between the valence band and the conduction band
   II) an energy gap on the order of 0.05 eV between the valence band and the conduction band
   III) electrical conductivity increases with increasing temperature

   a) I only
   b) II only
   c) III only
   d) II and III only

3.18   A solid is an intrinsic semiconductor if

a)   there are no electrons in the conduction band, and the band-gap is large

b)   the conduction band is half full with electrons

c)   the conduction band is empty and the band-gap is about ≈ 1 eV or less at ordinary temperature

d)   the impurity atoms provide extra electrons

3.19   Miller indices of a plane which intersects the three crystal axes at distances equal to $a/2$, $b/3$ and $c/1$ are given by:

a)   (1/2 ↖ 1)

b)   (312)

c)   (2,3,1)

d)   (231)

3.20   In a crystalline solid, the rate of a process which is diffusion controlled

I)   is a linear function of temperature

II)   varies exponentially with temperature

III) is controlled by an activation barrier

a)   I only

b)   II only

c)   III only

d)   II and III only

3.21   A given monovalent metallic crystal has 2×10^{10} atoms. Which of the following statements are true for this crystal?

a)   There are 2×10^{10} electrons in the valence band.

b)   There are 2×10^{10} empty states in the valence band.

c)   There are 4×10^{10} available quantum states in the valence band.

d)   There are 2×10^{10} unoccupied quantum states in the valence band.

3.22   In a cubic lattice, which of the following directions are perpendicular to the (111) plane?

a)   [110]

b)   [111]

c)   [100]

d)   [010]

Solutions to Practice Problems

3.1   **c)**   If applied stress is greater than yield stress, a permanent deformation occurs and the strain is irreversible.

3.2   **c)**   Off-set yield stress is defined as the stress corresponding to a specified plastic strain, usually 0.2%.

3.3   **d)**   When stress is calculated by using the original cross-sectional area, the stress is called the engineering stress. When necking occurs, cross-section decreases and the engineering stress decreases. It reaches a maximum value before the onset of necking.

3.4   **c)**   The higher the ductility, the smaller the cross-section at fracture, i.e., the greater is the reduction in area. Reduction in area is zero for very brittle material.

3.5   **c)**   Yield point phenomenon is peculiar to carbon steels. Nonferrous alloys, such as aluminum alloys, do not show a yield point.

3.6   **b)**   In a crystalline solid, slip is the primary mode of plastic deformation. Dislocation motion is necessary for slip.

3.7   **a)**   Slip produces a change in shape without producing a change in volume, like shearing a deck of cards.

3.8   **d)**   In pure aluminum, as the amplitude of alternating stress decreases, the fatigue life monotonically increases. There is no threshold stress and thus there is no endurance limit.

3.9   **c)**   The two elements in a binary alloy must be soluble in a solid state to produce a solid solution alloy.

3.10 **b)**   The eutectic temperature is invariant, i.e., the solidification of the eutectic composition occurs at the single temperature rather than over a range of temperature.

3.11 **c)**   A liquid phase of a fixed composition reacts with a solid phase of another fixed composition to produce a new solid phase at the peritectic temperature.

3.12 **d)** AB_3 is the only intermetallic compound in this diagram. It consists of 75 at. % B and 25 at. % A.

3.13 **b)**   The horizontal line corresponding to T_1 intersects the vertical, $A + 50$ at. % B within the $L + \gamma$ region.

3.14 **a)**   According to Fig. 3.25a, 1147°C is the temperature the liquid solidified into γ (solid) and Fe_3C (solid). Thus, this is the eutectic temperature.

3.15 **c)** The composition of alloy is A + 50 wt. % B. Composition of α is A + 25% B and that of β is A + 75% B. Thus, the lever rule can be applied as follows:

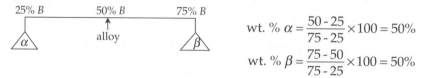

$$\text{wt. } \% \ \alpha = \frac{50 - 25}{75 - 25} \times 100 = 50\%$$

$$\text{wt. } \% \ \beta = \frac{75 - 50}{75 - 25} \times 100 = 50\%$$

3.16 **d)** They both have the same packing density.

3.17 **d)**

3.18 **c)** In such a material, electrons from the valence band can be thermally activated across the band-gap to the conduction band, and once thus promoted the electrons have mobility under an applied voltage.

3.19 **d)**

3.20 **d)**

3.21 **d)** If there are N atoms then each atom contributes 2 s-states in s-band. Thus there are $2N$ available states in the s-band. However, if the atom is a monovalent metal then only N electrons are available. That is, half of the states in the s-band are unoccupied.

3.22 **b)** In a cubic crystal, Miller indices of a direction perpendicular to a plane are the same as that of the plane. Note that [111] is the body diagonal of a cubic lattice. If you draw the (111) plane, you will note that one of the body diagonals is perpendicular to this plane.

Chemistry

by Donald G. Farnum

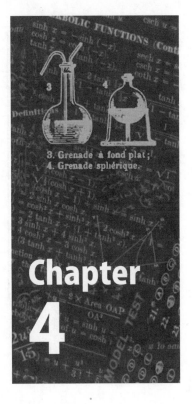

Chemistry attempts to describe and predict the macroscopic behavior of matter in terms of the properties of the submicroscopic *atoms* and *molecules* of which it consists. Although the physical properties of matter are of some interest to chemists because of what they reveal about the nature of atoms and molecules, the chemical properties or *chemical reactions* of matter are far more important. Thus, an understanding of the definition, structure, and properties of atoms and molecules, the definition of a chemical reaction, and the effect of variables on a chemical reaction are fundamental to understanding chemistry.

Each element is composed of only one kind of atom, and is represented by a *chemical symbol.*

4.1 Atoms

An *atom* is the smallest subdivision or particle of an element that enters into the chemical reactions of that element. An *element* is a pure substance that cannot be decomposed into other pure substances. Each element is composed of only one kind of atom, and is represented by a *chemical symbol.* Thus, gold is an element represented by the symbol *Au*, and is composed entirely of atoms of gold. No chemical or physical process can separate a sample of gold into any other pure substance.

The chemical and physical properties of the elements follow a pattern that is revealed in the *periodic table of the elements* (Table 4.1). In the table, the elements are ordered according to their atomic weights. Note: ordering according to atomic weights—an experimental observation—results in ordering according to *atomic numbers*, an inferred quantity often denoted by Z. The significance of this

The Periodic Table of Elements

4•CHEMISTRY

TABLE 4.1. The Periodic Chart of the Elements

IA	IIA	IIIB	IVB	VB	VIB	VIIB	VIIIB			IB	IIB	IIIA	IVA	VA	VIA	VIIA	0
1 H 1.0080																	2 He 4.003
3 Li 6.940	4 Be 9.013											5 B 10.82	6 C 12.011	7 N 14.008	8 O 16.000	9 F 19.00	10 Ne 20.183
11 Na 22.991	12 Mg 24.32											13 Al 26.98	14 Si 28.09	15 P 30.975	16 S 32.066	17 Cl 35.457	18 Ar 39.944
19 K 39.100	20 Ca 40.08	21 Sc 44.96	22 Ti 47.90	23 V 50.95	24 Cr 52.01	25 Mn 54.94	26 Fe 55.85	27 Co 58.94	28 Ni 58.71	29 Cu 63.54	30 Zn 65.38	31 Ga 69.72	32 Ge 72.60	33 As 74.91	34 Se 78.96	35 Br 79.916	36 Kr 83.80
37 Rb 85.48	38 Sr 87.63	39 Y 88.92	40 Zr 91.22	41 Nb 92.91	42 Mo 95.95	43 Tc (99)	44 Ru 101.1	45 Rh 102.91	46 Pd 106.4	47 Ag 107.880	48 Cd 112.41	49 In 114.82	50 Sn 118.70	51 Sb 121.87	52 Te 127.61	53 I 126.91	54 Xe 131.30
55 Cs 132.91	56 Ba 137.36	57 *La 138.92	72 Hf 178.50	73 Ta 180.95	74 W 183.86	75 Re 186.22	76 Os 190.2	77 Ir 192.2	78 Pt 195.09	79 Au 197.0	80 Hg 200.61	81 Tl 204.39	82 Pb 207.21	83 Bi 209.00	84 Po (210)	85 At (210)	86 Rn (222)
87 Fr (223)	88 Ra (226)	89 †Ac (227)	104 Ku (261)	105 Ha (260)													

← VIII B

* **Lanthanides**

58 Ce 140.13	59 Pr 140.92	60 Nd 144.27	61 Pm (147)	62 Sm 50.35	63 Eu 152.0	64 Gd 157.26	65 Tb 158.93	66 Dy 162.51	67 Ho 164.94	68 Er 167.27	69 Tm 168.94	70 Yb 173.04	71 Lu 174.99

+ **Actinides**

90 Th (232)	91 Pa (231)	92 U 238.07	93 Np (237)	94 Pu (242)	95 Am (243)	96 Cm (247)	97 Bk (249)	98 Cf (251)	99 Es (254)	100 Fm (253)	101 Md (256)	102 No (253)	103 Lw (257)

fact will be discussed when atomic structure is discussed. The *atomic weight* of an element is the weight of an atom of that element in atomic mass units. One *atomic mass unit (amu)* is one-twelfth the mass of one normal *C* atom, very close to that of one *H* atom. Thus, the approximate atomic weight of an element is the weight of one atom (or 10, or 6×10^{23} atoms) of that atomic element relative to the weight of one atom (or 10, or 6×10^{23} atoms) of hydrogen. When ordered in the periodic table according to their atomic weights, the elements fall into families of related physical and chemical properties. A thorough understanding of the periodic table enables one to infer the properties of an unknown element with some reliability from its determined position in the table. Perhaps more important, it is not necessary to memorize the properties of all 106 known elements to have a reasonable grasp of them. It is sufficient to know the properties of a few representative elements and understand the trends within the table. Thus, if you know that the element sodium (*Na*), is a soft, malleable solid with a metallic luster, and that it can be cut with a knife, conducts heat and electricity, and reacts vigorously with water with bubbling, you can expect that cesium (*Cs*)—in the same column or group—will show the same properties, more or less. The principles discussed here and in Section 4.3 on Chemical Reactions, when combined with practice and experience, will allow the skillful use of the periodic table.

There is a greater change in the properties of the elements across the table (the rows or *periods*) than there is down the table (the columns, *families*, or *groups*). Note: Hydrogen, the simplest element, is an exception. It exhibits some of the properties of both groups I A and VII A as well as some unique ones. Thus lithium (*Li*, group I A) is much more like francium (*Fr*, group I A) than it is like fluorine (*F*, group VII A). As a result, the elements can be divided into two general classes, the metals and non-metals, by a more or less vertical line. The *metals* are conducting and have low *electron affinities* (tendency to accept an electron). Therefore, they tend to give up electrons easily to form positive ions, and are reducing agents. The *non-metals* are non-conducting and have high electron affinities. They, therefore, tend to accept electrons to form negative ions, and are oxidizing agents. Metallic properties tend to increase for the elements of higher atomic number. As a result, polonium (*Po*, element number 84) is more metallic than tellurium (*Te*, element number 52), and, even though these elements are in the same family (group VI A), polonium is classified as a metal and tellurium as a non-metal. The increase in metallic properties as the atomic number increases thus accounts for the diagonal division separating the metals from the non-metals. The *transition metals* (elements number 21-29, 39-47, 57-79, 89-106) are classified together since their properties are very similar. The changes across the table are dramatically attenuated for the transition metals and they represent a gradual transition from the group II A metals to the group II B metals.

The common names of some of the groups, or families, of elements in the periodic table are as follows:

Group I A: *alkali metals*

Group II A: *alkaline earth metals*

Group VII A: *halogens*

Group 0: *noble gases*

Elements 57-71: *lanthanides* or *rare earths*

Elements 89-106: *actinides*

Groups I B-VII B, VIII: *transition metals*

The periodic table enables one to infer the properties of an unknown element with some reliability from its determined position in the table.

General Trends in the Periodic Table

The elements can be divided into two general classes, the metals and non-metals.

Atomic Structure and the Properties of the Elements

The periodicity in the properties of the elements can be understood in terms of the structures of their atoms. An atom consists of an extremely dense *nucleus* of *protons* (particles with a unit positive charge and a mass very close to 1 *amu*) and *neutrons* (neutral particles of essentially the same mass as the proton), and a very diffuse surrounding electron cloud containing enough *electrons* (entities with a unit negative charge and a comparatively negligible mass—about 5.5×10^{-4} *amu*) to exactly balance the nuclear charge. Thus, for any atom, the total number of protons equals the total number of electrons. The chemistry of an element is essentially determined by the electron cloud in the atoms of that element. The periodicity of the properties of the elements is thus a reflection of the periodicity of the structure of the electron clouds in atoms. It should now be apparent that the atomic number, which corresponds to the number of protons in the atomic nucleus (hence the number of electrons in the electron cloud), is actually the parameter which determines the position of an element in the periodic table, rather than the atomic weight (which is the sum of the masses of the protons, neutrons, and electrons in the atom).

For any atom, the total number of protons equals the total number of electrons.

• An orbital can be defined by three *quantum numbers*.

Electron Orbitals

The theory of wave mechanics applied to atomic structure tells us that electrons (which appear to have properties of both waves and particles) occupy regions in space of specific shape and size called *orbitals*. Note: The older term, *orbit*, derives from a planetary theory of the atom which did not take into account the wave nature of electrons. An orbital can be defined by three *quantum numbers*: $n = 1, 2, 3, \cdots$, which defines the size of the orbital *shell*; $\ell = 0, 1, 2, \cdots, n-1$, which defines the shape of the orbital *subshell*; and $m = 0, \pm1, \pm2, \cdots, \pm\ell$, which defines the orientation of the orbital subshell in space. The larger the *principal quantum number*, n, the larger the orbital, and the further the average negative charge of the electron from the positive nucleus, hence the higher the energy.

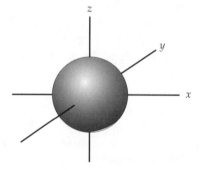

Figure 4.1 Boundary surface representation of an electron in the $n = 1$ state of the hydrogen atom. (Volume encloses 90% of the electron density. Nucleus is at the origin.)

For a principal quantum number $n = 4$, there are different orbital shapes corresponding to the *subsidiary quantum numbers* $\ell = 0, 1, 2, 3$. These shapes are often identified by letter symbols instead of number symbols. An *s* orbital has $\ell = 0$ and is spherical in shape (Fig. 4.1). A *p* orbital has $\ell = 1$ and is dumbbell shaped (Fig. 4.2). A *d* orbital has $\ell = 2$ and is still more complex in shape. An *f* orbital has $\ell = 3$, and so on. There is only one orientation in space for a spherical shape, and therefore only one value (0) for *m*, the *magnetic orbital quantum number*, for an *s* orbital. However, the dumbbell-shaped *p* orbital has three perpendicular orientations in space (see Fig. 4.2), and has three values for *m*, ($m = +1, 0, -1$). That is, for a given principal quantum number *n* there is only one *s* orbital, but there are three *p* orbitals. For the *d* orbital, there are five values for *m*, ($m = +2, +1, 0, -1, -2$), hence five different *d* orbitals. The quantum numbers for the thirty atomic orbitals of the first four shells are presented in Table 4.2.

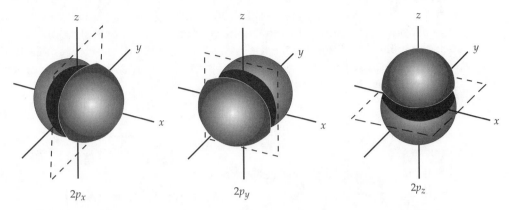

Figure 4.2 Boundary surface diagrams for the 2*p* orbitals.

TABLE 4.2 The Orbitals of the First Four Shells

Shell *n*	Subshell *ℓ*	Orbital *m*	Subshell Notation	Orbitals per Subshell
1	0	0	1*s*	1
2	0	0	2*s*	1
	1	+1, 0, −1	2*p*	3
3	0	0	3*s*	1
	1	+1, 0, −1	3*p*	3
	2	+2, +1, 0, −1, −2	3*d*	5
4	0	0	4*s*	1
	1	+1, 0, −1	4*p*	3
	2	+2, +1, 0, −1, −2	4*d*	5
	3	+3, +2, +1, 0, −1, −2, −3	4*f*	7

Electron Configurations of the Elements

The state of an electron in an atom is completely described by the three quantum numbers defining the electron orbital, and a fourth quantum number m_s, the magnetic spin number, derived from the magnetic field of the spinning electron. The value of m_s can only be $\pm 1/2$. Therefore, a given orbital can represent two, and only two, electrons with opposite spin. No two electrons can have all four quantum numbers identical. From this *Pauli exclusion principle* and the fact that electrons will assume the lowest values possible for the quantum numbers *n* and *ℓ*, the electron configuration for the atoms of the first 18 elements can be described. The higher ones are more complex.

Example 4.1

What is the electron configuration for an aluminum atom?

Solution. From the periodic table we see that aluminum, *Al*, is element No. 13, and therefore has 13 electrons in its atom. From Table 4.2 we can simply fill in up to two electrons in each subshell orbital until we reach 13. Therefore, aluminum has 2 electrons in the 1*s* orbital, 2 electrons in the 2*s* orbital (= 4), 2 electrons in each of the three 2*p* orbitals (total = 10), 2 electrons in the 3*s* orbital, and 1 in the 3*p* orbital (total = 13). This, in shorthand notation, is as follows: 1*s* (2), 2*s* (2), 2*p* (6), 3*s* (2), 3*p* (1).

Example 4.2

What is the electron configuration of a phosphorus atom?

Solution. Phosphorus, *P*, is element 15. Therefore we must arrange 15 electrons as follows: 1*s* (2), 2*s* (2), 2*p* (6), 3*s* (2), 3*p* (3).

In Example 4.2 there is an ambiguity about the state of the 3*p* electrons. We don't know whether to put two of them in one 3*p* orbital or put each of the three in a different 3*p* orbital. This ambiguity is removed by *Hund's rule of maximum multiplicity* which states that, whenever possible, the electrons in a subshell will have the same value for the magnetic spin quantum number, m_s. For phosphorus, this is possible for the 3*p* subshell electrons if each electron is in a different orbital with $m_s = +1/2$ (or $-1/2$). Since the spins of electrons with opposite signs for m_s are said to be paired, an alternate way of stating Hund's rule is that the electrons are distributed among the orbitals of a subshell in a way that gives the maximum number of unpaired electrons with parallel spins. We might, therefore, write the electron configuration of a phosphorus atom in more detail as follows: 1*s* (2), 2*s* (2), 2*p* (6), 3*s* (2), $3p_x$ (1), $3p_y$ (1), $3p_z$ (1). The maximum numbers of electrons that can occupy each subshell for the first four shells are given in Table 4.3.

> Hund's rule states that the electrons are distributed among the orbitals of a subshell in a way that gives the maximum number of unpaired electrons with parallel spins.

TABLE 4.3 **Maximum Number of Electrons for the Subshells of the First Four Shells**

Subshell Notation	Orbitals per Subshell	Electrons per Subshell	Electrons per Shell ($2n^2$)
1*s*	1	2	2
2*s*	1	2	8
2*p*	3	6	
3*s*	1	2	18
3*p*	3	6	
3*d*	5	10	
4*s*	1	2	32
4*p*	3	6	
4*d*	5	10	
4*f*	7	14	

The periodicity of the properties of the elements revealed in the periodic table can now be seen to have its origins in the periodicity of the electronic configurations of the atoms. The chemical properties of an atom are determined by the electrons with the largest value of n, that is, the outer shell or *valence electrons*. Thus, the properties of lithium are determined by its lone $2s$ electron, those of sodium by its lone $3s$ electron, those of potassium by its lone $4s$ electron, and those of francium by its lone $7s$ electron. All the atoms of the elements of Group 0, the noble gases, have *closed-shell configuration*, that is, all the orbitals of the highest principal quantum number are full of electrons. The closed-shell configuration represents a particularly stable state. Any further electrons would have to occupy higher principal quantum number (and therefore higher energy, less stable) orbital states. All the atoms of the halogens (Group VII A) are one electron short of closed-shell configurations, and hence can accept an electron very readily.

> *Closed-shell configuration* means that all the orbitals of the highest principal quantum number are full of electrons.

Example 4.3

Determine the electron configuration of the valence electrons of an atom of *N*, and compare it with that for *As*.

Solution. *N* has 7 electrons. The electron configuration is $1s$ (2), $2s$ (2), $2p_x$ (1), $2p_y$ (1), $2p_z$ (1). The valence electrons are those with $n = 2$: $2s$ (2), $2p_x$ (1), $2p_y$ (1), $2p_z$ (1). *As* has 33 electrons. The first three shells ($n = 1, 2, 3,$) are completely filled to account for $2 + 8 + 18 = 28$ electrons (see Table 4.3). That leaves 5 electrons for the fourth shell, $n = 4$. Therefore, the configuration of the valence electrons of *As* is $4s$ (2), $4p_x$ (1), $4p_y$ (1), $4p_z$ (1). Note the similarity to *N* in the filled s orbital and three singly occupied p orbitals.

The similarities in the properties of the elements in each group or family in the periodic table are simply a manifestation of the similarities in the electronic configurations of the valence electrons of the corresponding atoms. Some of those properties will now be examined for the more common families of elements.

The Properties of the Families of Elements

Group I A—The Alkali Metals

The alkali metal atoms of Group I A all have one s electron beyond a closed-shell configuration. They therefore tend to lose an electron very readily to the environment to give a positively charged species—a *cation*, with a closed-shell configuration—as shown in the following simple chemical equation for sodium:

$$Na \rightarrow Na^+ + 1e^-$$

One sodium atom yields one sodium cation plus one electron.

They are thus said to have a low electron affinity, or desire to accept electrons, and a low *ionization energy*—that is, it doesn't take much energy to make them lose an electron to form a cation. Note: This does not mean that the converse reaction, $Na + 1e^- \rightarrow Na^-$, is impossible, but only that it is extraordinarily difficult. This atomic property of the alkali metals is reflected in their metallic luster and their conductivity (electrons are readily available to form a *conducting band*). It is also reflected in their chemical reactivity as *reducing agents*. Reducing agents give up electrons easily to other substances and are themselves oxidized in the process. A simple example is the chemical reaction of a sodium atom and a chlorine atom:

$$Na + Cl \rightarrow Na^+ Cl^-$$

One sodium atom plus one chlorine atom yields one sodium cation plus one chloride anion.

In the above example, an electron is transferred from sodium to chlorine, and the sodium atom is oxidized and the chlorine atom is reduced. The sodium atom acts as a reducing agent and the chlorine atom acts as an oxidizing agent.

Since the higher atomic number elements in a family have larger electron clouds which screen the nuclear positive charge, electron affinity decreases as the atomic number increases within a family. Thus, potassium (atomic No. 19) is a more powerful reducing agent than lithium (atomic No. 3).

Reducing agents give up electrons easily and are oxidized in the process.

Example 4.4

Complete the following chemical reaction:

$$Rb + F \rightarrow ?$$

Solution. Since rubidium, *Rb*, is in the same family as sodium, it is a reducing agent. Since fluorine, *F*, is in the same family as chlorine, it is an oxidizing agent. Hence, an electron will transfer from rubidium to fluorine:

$$Rb + F \rightarrow Rb^+ + F^-$$

Group II A—The Alkaline Earth Metals

The lightest of the Group II A elements, beryllium (*Be*, atomic No. 4), has the electronic configuration 1s (2), 2s (2). The *s* electrons in the second shell are easily lost to give Be^{+2} with a closed-shell configuration in the first shell. The alkaline earth metals are thus typically reducing agents that give up two electrons. They are said to be *divalent*.

The alkaline earths are less powerful reducing agents than the alkali metals since the higher nuclear charge tends to hold the valence electrons more tightly. In fact, electron affinity increases across the periodic table and decreases down the periodic table, i.e., reducing power decreases across the periodic table and increases down the table.

The alkaline earth metals have a metallic luster and are harder than the alkali metals. They are good conductors of electricity.

Reducing power decreases across the periodic table and increases down the table.

Example 4.5

Complete the following chemical reaction:

$$Ca + 2Br \rightarrow ?$$

Solution. Calcium (*Ca*, atomic No. 20) has the following electron configuration: 1s (2), 2s (2), 2p (6), 3s (2), 3p (6), 4s (2). It is an alkaline earth with two valence electrons in the fourth shell. It is, therefore, a reducing agent with a tendency to give up two electrons. Bromine, like chlorine, can accept one electron to give a closed-shell anion. Therefore, two bromine atoms can accept one electron each from one calcium atom:

$$Ca + 2Br \rightarrow Ca^{+2} + 2Br^-$$

Example 4.6

Assign the ionization energies in the column on the right to the elements in the column on the left:

Element	Ionization Energy (kJ/mol)
Cs	738
Mg	503
Ca	590
Ba	376

Solution. Magnesium (*Mg*, No. 12), calcium (*Ca*, No. 20), and barium (*Ba*, No. 56) are all alkaline earths. The first ionization energy, the energy required to remove the first valence electron, should decrease with increasing atomic number. Cesium (*Cs*, No. 55) is an alkali metal and should have a lower ionization energy than the next alkaline earth, barium. Cesium, therefore, has the lowest ionization energy of the four, and the correct answer is:

Cs	376
Mg	738
Ca	590
Ba	503

Group VII A—The Halogens

The halogen atoms of Group VII A are all one electron short of a closed-shell configuration. Because they have high nuclear charges which hold their valence electrons very tightly, it is no surprise that they have high electron affinities. They therefore tend to accept electrons readily to give closed-shell configuration anions, and are oxidizing agents. Chlorine (*Cl*, No. 17) is typical with electron configuration $1s$ (2), $2s$ (2), $2p$ (6), $3s$ (2), $3p$ (5):

$$Cl + 1e \rightarrow Cl^-$$

Reactions of halogen atoms as oxidizing agents with metals acting as reducing agents have already been illustrated above. An example is

$$I + K \rightarrow I^- + K^+$$

As you might expect, the oxidizing power of the halogens is greatest for fluorine (*F*, No. 9) and decreases down the table, the inverse of the reducing power of the metals. The halogens tend to be colored. Thus, chlorine is a green gas, bromine is a red volatile liquid, and iodine is a deep purple, volatile solid.

Halogen atoms tend to accept electrons readily and are oxidizing agents.

4·CHEMISTRY

Example 4.7

Which of the following chemical reactions has the greatest tendency to take place?

$$Cl + K \rightarrow Cl^- + K^+$$

$$Br + K \rightarrow Br^- + K^+$$

$$Cl + Li \rightarrow Cl^- + Li^+$$

$$Br + Li \rightarrow Br^- + Li^+$$

Solution. Since oxidizing power decreases down the table, chlorine, *Cl*, is a more powerful oxidizing agent than bromine, *Br*. Since reducing power increases down the table, potassium, *K*, is a more powerful reducing agent than lithium, *Li*. The reaction with the greatest tendency to take place is the one between the best oxidizing and best reducing agents, i.e.,

$$Cl + K \rightarrow Cl^- + K^+$$

Group 0 —The Noble Gases

The noble gases are the only non-metallic elements that exist as single atoms in the elemental state.

The noble gases of Group 0 all have closed-shell configurations. They therefore have both low electron affinities and high ionization potentials. An added electron would have to go into the next orbital shell of much higher energy, and removal of an electron would have to take place from the closed shell. Because of these properties, the noble gases enter into chemical reactions with extreme reluctance. Some of the properties of the noble gases are given in Table 4.4.

TABLE 4.4 Some Properties of the Noble Gases

Gas	Melting Point (°C)	Boiling Point (°C)	Ionization Energy (kJ/mol)	Abundance in Atmosphere (Volume %)
He	—	−268.9	2.37×10^3	5×10^{-4}
Ne	−248.6	−245.9	2.08×10^3	2×10^{-3}
Ar	−189.3	−185.8	1.52×10^3	0.93
Kr	−157	−152.9	1.35×10^3	1×10^{-4}
Xe	−112	−107.1	1.17×10^3	8×10^{-4}
Rn	−71	−61.8	1.04×10^3	trace

The noble gases are the only non-metallic elements that exist as single atoms in the elemental state. All the others exist as clusters of atoms bonded together as molecules. Thus, the low melting points and boiling points of the noble gases reflect the stability of the atoms. However, in order to understand the chemical and physical properties of the rest of the elements, it is necessary to understand the molecule and the nature of chemical bonds between atoms.

4.2 Molecular Structure

A *molecule* is the smallest subdivision or particle of a chemical compound that enters into the chemical reactions of that compound. A *chemical compound* is a substance containing more than one element combined in definite proportions. The molecules of a chemical compound are all identical clusters of atoms held together by chemical bonds. Thus, the chemical compound water consists of molecules containing two hydrogen atoms and one oxygen atom joined together by chemical bonds, symbolized by the structure shown in Fig. 4.3.

Molecules are clusters of atoms held together by chemical bonds.

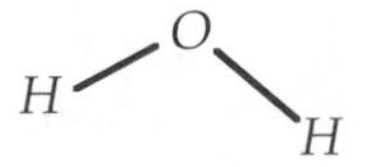

Figure 4.3 The structure of water.

The term *structure* can be used in chemistry on a number of levels, expressed by symbols of different complexity. At the simplest level, the structure of water is defined by its *molecular formula*, H_2O. A molecular formula defines the number of atoms of each element in the molecule of a compound. Thus, water has two hydrogen atoms and one oxygen atom in each molecule. At the next level, the structure of water is further defined by *HOH*, which defines the order in which the atoms are attached to one another. Thus, the two hydrogen atoms are attached to the one oxygen atom. At the next level, the shape of the molecule might be defined as either linear (*H—O—H*), or bent (   ). The water molecule is bent. The shape might then be more precisely defined in terms of the actual bond angles and bond lengths involved. The structure of water (see Fig. 4.4): bond angle 104.5°, *O—H* bond length = 0.96 Å = 0.096 nm = 96 pm. Molecular distances are often given in Angstrom units (Å): one Å = 10^{-8} centimeters (cm) = 0.1 nanometers (nm) = 100 picometers (pm).

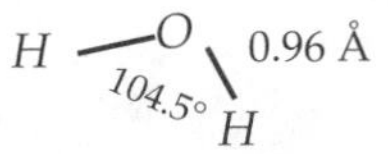

$$H \overset{}{\underset{104.5°}{\diagup}} \overset{O}{\diagdown}{}_{0.96 \text{ Å}} \; H$$

Figure 4.4 The detailed structure of water.

For more complex molecules, a structure might include a description of the three-dimensional shape of the molecule. For example, the molecule of methane (the main component of marsh gas and natural gas) has the molecular formula CH_4. The *H—C—H* bond angles are all exactly 109°28′, and the *C—H* bond lengths are all 1.09 Å. A qualitative representation of the methane structure might look like that of Fig. 4.5. Thus the carbon atom and the two hydrogens attached to it with solid lines are implied to be in the plane of the paper. The wedged bond (*C ◀H*) is intended to project above the paper, while the dashed bond (*C- -H*) is intended to project below the paper.

Figure 4.5 The structure of methane.

Perhaps the most complete, though not always the most useful, definition of the structure of a molecule would be a mathematical description of the geometry and motions of the atoms and the states of all the electrons in it. Molecular structures thus require different approaches for each level of complexity.

Determination of the Molecular Formula

If all molecules of a pure compound contain the same elements in the same ratios, then the compound will always contain the same elements combined in the same proportions by mass. This is the *law of definite proportions*. Therefore, if we know the mass ratio of oxygen to hydrogen in water and know the atomic masses of oxygen and hydrogen, we can determine the ratio of oxygen atoms to hydrogen atoms in the water molecule, that is, the *empirical formula*. If we know the mass of a molecule of water, the *molecular mass,* then we can determine the actual number of oxygen and hydrogen atoms in a water molecule, the *molecular formula*.

The empirical formula can also be determined in some instances by application of *Avogadro's law*, which states: equal volumes of all gases at the same temperature and pressure contain equal numbers of molecules.

Avogadro's law: equal volumes of all gases at the same temperature and pressure contain equal numbers of molecules.

Example 4.8

Water can be broken down into elemental hydrogen and oxygen by electrolysis. Every 100 g of water gives 88.8 g of oxygen and 11.2 g of hydrogen. What is the empirical formula of water?

Solution. The atomic mass of oxygen is 16.0, while that of hydrogen is 1.008. The ratio of hydrogen atoms to oxygen atoms is therefore

$$\frac{11.2 / 1.008}{88.8 / 16.0} = 2.00$$

The empirical formula of water is therefore H_2O.

Example 4.9

Electrolysis of 18 g of water gives 22.4 L of hydrogen gas and 11.2 L of oxygen gas at 22°C and 1 atmosphere pressure. What is the empirical formula of water?

Solution. Since the ratio of the volumes of hydrogen to oxygen is 2:1, Avogadro's law tells us that the ratio of the number of molecules of hydrogen to the number of molecules of oxygen is also 2:1. If hydrogen and oxygen molecules each contain the same number of atoms, then the empirical formula of water is H_2O.

There are several ways of determining the molecular mass of a pure compound. At the present time, an instrument called a *mass spectrometer* is most often used. However, if the compound is a gas at known temperature and pressure, then the volume of a given mass of the gas can be used to determine the molecular mass. For this purpose, the *mole* is a useful and important concept. The *molar mass* of an element is an amount in grams numerically equal to the atomic mass. Thus, 1.000 moles of sodium atoms contains 22.9 grams of sodium. A mole of a pure molecular compound is that amount of the compound numerically equal in grams to the molecular mass of the compound. Thus, 1.000 moles of water contains $2(1.008)+16.00 = 18.02$ grams of water. A mole of an ionic compound is that amount of the compound numerically equal in grams to the *formula mass*.

Since the weight ratio of a mole of sodium atoms to a mole of hydrogen atoms is the same as the ratio of the atomic masses of the elements $(23.0:1.0)$, a mole of sodium contains the same number of atoms of sodium as a mole of hydrogen atoms contains atoms of hydrogen. Similarly, a mole of water contains the same number of water molecules as a mole of methane contains methane molecules. In fact, the number of atoms in a mole of any element and the number of molecules in a mole of any compound is a constant. The constant is called Avogadro's number and has been experimentally determined to be 6.02205×10^{23}. The amount of any substance that contains Avogadro's number of elementary units is called a mole (abbreviated mol).

With the exception of the noble gases, which are monatomic, all elements which are gases at ordinary temperatures and pressures are diatomic, that is, they contain two atoms per molecule (e.g., N_2, O_2, Cl_2). Note that one mole of any gas will occupy 22.4 L at 0°C and 1 atm—the same as one mole of helium (Avogadro's law). This temperature and pressure is called *Standard Temperature and Pressure*, or STP. Hence, 1 mol of any gas at STP contains 22.4 L.

> A mole of a pure molecular compound is that amount of the compound numerically equal in grams to the molecular mass of the compound.
> • The amount of any substance that contains Avogadro's number of elementary units is called a mole (abbreviated mol).
> • All elements which are gases at ordinary temperatures and pressures are diatomic, that is, they contain two atoms per molecule.

4-CHEMISTRY

Example 4.10

A sample of helium gas weighing 4.00 g occupies 22.4 L. The same volume of hydrogen gas weighs 2.02 g. What is the molecular formula of hydrogen gas?

Solution. Since the atomic mass of helium is 4.00, the sample of helium is 1.00 mole. Since the atomic mass of hydrogen is 1.008, the sample of hydrogen is 2.00 moles of hydrogen atoms and must contain twice as many atoms as the helium sample. Since both occupy the same volume, both must contain the same number of molecules (Avogadro's law). Therefore, a molecule of hydrogen contains twice as many atoms as a molecule of helium. If we assume that a molecule of helium contains only one atom (reasonable, since helium is an unreactive noble gas), then a molecule of hydrogen contains two atoms and has the molecular formula H_2.

Example 4.11

A sample of steam weighing 27.0 g occupies the same volume as a sample of hydrogen weighing 3.02 g at 110°C and 1 atm. What is the molecular formula for water?

Solution. Since the two samples occupy the same volume under the same conditions, they have the same number of molecules. Therefore, the ratio of their masses, $27.0 : 3.02$, is equal to the ratio of their molecular masses. If the molecular mass of hydrogen (H_2) is 2.02, the molecular mass of water is 18.0. Thus, the molecular formula for water is H_2O (see Ex. 4.9).

Example 4.12

A sample of ethane is burned in air to give carbon dioxide (molecular formula CO_2) and water. The ratio of the volume of water vapor to that of carbon dioxide at 110° and 1 atm is 3:2. If 1 L of ethane gas at STP gives 2 L of CO_2 gas at STP, how many carbon and hydrogen atoms are there in a molecule of ethane?

Solution. The burning of ethane can be represented symbolically by the following expression:

$$\text{ethane } (g) \ + \ O_2(g) \rightarrow CO_2(g) + H_2O(l)$$

Note: The letters in parentheses simply indicate whether the substance is a gas (*g*), liquid (*l*), or solid (*s*) at STP.

Since equal volumes of CO_2 gas and H_2O gas at the same temperature and pressure will contain equal numbers of molecules, there are twice as many hydrogen atoms per unit volume in the water as there are carbon atoms per unit volume in the carbon dioxide. Since burning ethane gives 3 volumes of water vapor to 2 volumes of carbon dioxide, the ratio of hydrogen atoms to carbon atoms in ethane is $(3 \times 2) : (2 \times 1) = 3 : 1$.

Since 1 L of ethane gives 2 L of carbon dioxide, each molecule of ethane must give two molecules of carbon dioxide. Therefore, there must be two carbon atoms in each molecule of ethane. A molecule of ethane, therefore, contains 2 carbon atoms and 6 hydrogen atoms. Note that we do not yet know the molecular formula of ethane completely, since it may contain other atoms as well (e.g., oxygen).

We can now convert the symbolic expression for the burning or combustion of ethane in Example 4.12 into a *balanced chemical equation*. A balanced chemical equation is a symbolic representation of a chemical change in which the number of each kind of atoms on the left side of the equation, the reactants, is equal to the number of each kind of atoms on the right side of the equation, the products:

$$C_2H_6 + \frac{7}{2}O_2 \rightarrow 2CO_2 + 3H_2O$$

Example 4.13

The density of ethane gas at STP is 1.34 g/L. What is the molecular weight and molecular formula for ethane?

Solution. The molar mass is (22.4 L × 1.34 g/L) = 30 g. The molecular formula is therefore C_2H_6. Any additional atoms in the molecule would increase the molar mass.

The determination of the structure of a complex substance of known molecular formula is often a very difficult research task, requiring years of effort, including the analysis of chemical reactions and the use of sophisticated instruments. Perhaps the most powerful technique is *x-ray crystallography*, in which an x-ray picture is taken of the arrangement of the atoms in the regularly spaced molecules of a crystalline substance; pictures taken from several angles allow an accurate three-dimensional structure of the molecule to be constructed. For simpler molecules, a knowledge of *chemical bonding* principles can at least limit the number of possible structures for a given molecular formula.

Determination of Chemical Structure

Example 4.14

Given that a carbon atom can bond with no more than four other atoms, and hydrogen with only one, what is the order of connection of atoms in ethane, C_2H_6?

Solution. There is only one logically possible arrangement:

$$
\begin{array}{ccc}
H & & H \\
| & & | \\
H-C- & C & -H \\
| & & | \\
H & & H
\end{array}
$$

There are two limiting types of chemical bonds which hold atoms together—the *ionic bond* and the *covalent bond*. *Metal bonding*, a third and very different type of bonding, is found in the metals where the atoms are bonded together as cations in a "sea" of conducting valence electrons.

The ionic bond, such as that found in sodium chloride, Na^+Cl^-, occurs whenever there is a complete transfer of one or more electrons from one atom to another to give oppositely charged ions. A crystal of sodium chloride, or table salt, might be regarded as a single enormous molecule in which all of the positive sodium ions and neighboring negative chloride ions are bonded together by ionic bonds in the crystal lattice. Ionic bonds are formed between atoms of very different electron affinities, and the electron transfer usually brings both atoms to their closed-shell configurations.

The covalent bond, present in the hydrogen molecule (H_2), water (H_2O), methane (CH_4), and ethane (C_2H_6), occurs whenever one or more electrons are shared between two atoms. The force holding the atoms together is then the electrostatic attraction between the shared electrons and the positively charged nuclei. The hydrogen molecule might be regarded as two positively charged protons suspended at equilibrium distance in a diffuse elliptical cloud of two electrons. The covalent bond is formed between atoms of similar electron affinities, the shared electrons generally being sufficiently numerous to bring both atoms to their noble gas configurations. Thus, the two shared electrons in the hydrogen molecule can be considered to fill the $1s$ shell of each hydrogen atom. Although most bonds can be easily classified as ionic or covalent, in practice there is a spectrum of bond types from pure covalent through highly polar covalent to ionic bonds.

Chemical Bonds

The ionic bond occurs whenever there is a transfer of one or more electrons from one atom to another.

• The covalent bond occurs whenever one or more electrons are shared between two atoms.

Example 4.15

Arrange the following chemical bonds in order of increasing ionic character: *CCl*, *LiCl*, *LiI*, *CC*, *KCl*, *CAl*, *CMg*.

Solution. The most covalent bond is, the *C-C* bond, between identical atoms. The most ionic is the *K⁺Cl⁻* bond between the atom of lowest electron affinity, *K*, and the one of highest electron affinity, *Cl*. *Li⁺Cl⁻* will be less ionic (*Li* has a higher electron affinity than *K*), *Li⁺I⁻* still less (*I* has a lower electron affinity than *Cl*), then *CMg*, *CCl*, and *CAl* (reflecting the relative differences in electron affinities). Note that the partial electron transfer is from *C* to *Cl*, leaving carbon partially positive for *CCl*, while it is from metal to carbon for *CMg* and *CAl*, leaving carbon partially negative. The correct order of *increasing* ionic character is then: *CC < CAl < CCl < CMg < LiI < LiCl < KCl*.

The number of electrons "transferred" in an ionic bond, and the number of covalent bonds formed to a given atom, is limited by the number of electrons in the valence shell. A convenient, though somewhat arbitrary, way of keeping track of the number of electrons transferred is the *oxidation number*, or oxidation state, or *valence*. (Valence is an older term whose meaning has become confused and is, therefore, rarely used now.) The oxidation number may be defined as the total number of electrons transferred or partially transferred to or from an atom in the bonds it forms with other atoms in the compound. If the electrons are transferred *from* the atoms, its oxidation number is positive. If they are transferred *to* the atoms, its oxidation number is negative. For example, in potassium chloride, one electron is transferred from potassium to chlorine. The oxidation number of potassium is therefore 1+, while that of chlorine is 1−. It is obvious that the oxidation numbers of monatomic ions in ionic compounds are equivalent to the charges on the ions. The oxidation number of the atoms in a covalently bonded molecule or ion can be determined by assuming that the electrons are transferred to the atom with the higher electron affinity. For example, in the covalent molecule *H-Cl* we assume that one electron is transferred from hydrogen to chlorine. The oxidation number of hydrogen is therefore 1+ and that of chlorine 1−. For a neutral molecule, the sum of the oxidation numbers of all the atoms must, of course, be zero. For a charged molecule ion or complex ion, the sum of the oxidation numbers of all the atoms must equal the charge on the ion. A covalent bond between two atoms of the same element results in no electron transfer and no change in oxidation number.

The concept of oxidation number is a powerful tool for the analysis of a type of chemical reaction called an *oxidation-reduction* reaction or *Redox reaction*.

Example 4.16

Assign oxidation numbers to all of the atoms in each of the following compounds: $NaBr$, $BaCl_2$, CaO, NH_3, CCl_4, OF_2, O_2, C_2H_6, CO, CO_2, Na_2SO_4, $K_2Cr_2O_7$.

Solution:

Compound	Atom	Oxidation Number	Explanation
$NaBr$	Na	1+	One electron is transferred from *Na* to *Br*.
	Br	1–	Oxidation number = charge.
$BaCl_2$	Ba	2+	Two electrons transferred from *Ba*,
	Cl	1–	One to each *Cl*.
CaO	Ca	2+	Two electrons transferred from the
	O	2–	alkaline earth, *Ca*, to oxygen.
NH_3	H	1+	*H* is 1+. Therefore, *N* must be 3– for a net = 0
	N	3–	
CCl_4	Cl	1–	One electron considered transferred to each
	C	4+	*Cl* (higher electron affinity (*e.a.*)).
OF_2	F	1–	*F* has the highest *e.a.* of all. It is 1– except
	O	2+	in F_2.
O_2	O	0	Same element. No *e* transfer.
C_2H_6	H	1+	*H* is always 1+ with non-metals. *C* must be 3–
	C	3–	for net = 0.
CO	O	2–	*O* generally 2–. *C* must be 2+.
	C	2+	
CO_2	O	2–	*C* must be 4+ for net = 0.
	C	4+	
Na_2SO_4	Na	1+	*Na* must be 1+. The anion must be SO_4^{-2}.
	O	2–	If *O* is 2–, then *S* must be 6+.
	S	6+	
$K_2Cr_2O_7$	K	1+	The complex dichromate ion must be $Cr_2O_7^{-2}$.
	O	2–	If *O* is 2–, the two *Cr* atoms must total 12+.
	Cr	6+	Assuming they are in the same oxidation state, they are each 6+.

4.3 Chemical Reactions

A *chemical reaction* occurs whenever a chemical compound is formed from the elements or from another chemical compound. Thus, a chemical reaction involves the transformation of the arrangement of atoms in the molecules of the starting materials, or *reactants*, into the arrangement of atoms in the molecules of the *products*. The two main types of variables that affect the course of a reaction are the quantities of reactants and the conditions (e.g., temperature and either pressure for reactions of gases, or concentration for reactions in solution). The two main characteristics of the reaction which affect its course are the *rate* and the *equilibrium*.

Balancing Chemical Equations

In order to understand the effect of the quantities of reactants on the course of a chemical reaction, it is necessary to have a *balanced chemical equation* for the reaction. In a chemical equation, the structures or condensed structures of the reactants and products are written on the left and right, respectively, with an arrow between the two. In a balanced chemical reaction, the numbers of molecules of reactants and products are adjusted in such a way that both the total number of atoms and the total charge of each element on the left is equal to that of the same element on the right. Thus, reaction of magnesium with bromine to give magnesium bromide is symbolized: $Mg + Br_2 \rightarrow MgBr_2$. Reaction of potassium with chlorine to give potassium chloride is symbolized: $2K + Cl_2 \rightarrow 2KCl$. Note that the smallest integers possible are used. We would not write $2Mg + 2Br_2 \rightarrow 2MgBr_2$. However, one might sometimes write $K + \frac{1}{2}Cl_2 \rightarrow KCl$. For the reaction of sodium with water to give sodium hydroxide and hydrogen gas, we might write either $2Na + 2H_2O \rightarrow 2NaOH + H_2$, or $Na + H_2O \rightarrow \frac{1}{2}H_2 + NaOH$.

Slightly more complex reactions can often be balanced by trial and error. For example, rust formation is illustrated by the (unbalanced) equation:

$$Fe + H_2O \rightarrow Fe_2O_3 + H_2$$

In order to balance this equation, we might first locate the molecule that has the largest number of atoms of the elements—the most complex molecule. In this case, it is Fe_2O_3. For a balanced equation we must therefore have at least two atoms of iron in the reactants and three molecules of water:

$$2Fe + 3H_2O \rightarrow Fe_2O_3 + 3H_2$$

Example 4.17

Balance the chemical equation for the complete combustion (with oxygen) of ethane (C_2H_6) to carbon dioxide and water.

Solution. Since ethane has two carbon atoms and six hydrogen atoms, we know that each molecule of ethane must give two molecules of CO_2 and three of H_2O:

$$C_2H_6 + \frac{7}{2}O_2 \rightarrow 2CO_2 + 3H_2O$$

or

$$2C_2H_6 + 7O_2 \rightarrow 4CO_2 + 6H_2O$$

The balanced chemical equation of Ex. 4.17 tells us a number of useful facts. It tells us that two molecules of ethane require seven molecules of oxygen for complete combustion to give four molecules of carbon dioxide and six molecules of water. It tells us that 2 L of ethane requires 7 L of oxygen for complete combustion; less would give incomplete combustion. It tells us that 60 g of ethane (2 mol) will give 108 g of water (6 mol) upon complete combustion.

More complex chemical equations can often be balanced by the use of oxidation numbers. For example, consider the unbalanced reaction:

$$\overset{5+}{H\,N}O_3 + H_2\overset{2-}{S} \rightarrow \overset{2+}{N}O + \overset{0}{S} + H_2O$$

The oxidation numbers of N and S in reactants and products have been identified. N undergoes a change of −3 (5+ to 2+) from reactants to products. Sulfur undergoes a change of +2 (2− to 0). The total change in oxidation number for the reaction must be zero. Therefore, all we need to do is find the common denominator for 2 and 3, namely 6. Hence we can write

$$2HNO_3 + 3H_2S \rightarrow 2NO + 3S + H_2O$$

The remainder of the equation can be balanced by inspection. Thus, there are eight hydrogen atoms on the left, requiring four water molecules on the right. The balanced equation is then

$$2HNO_3 + 3H_2S \rightarrow 2NO + 3S + 4H_2O$$

Example 4.18

Balance the following equation:

$$I_2 + H_2O + ClO_3^- \rightarrow IO_3^- + Cl^- + H^+$$

Solution. First identify the oxidation numbers:

$$H_2O + \overset{0}{I_2} + \overset{5+}{Cl}O_3^- \rightarrow \overset{5+}{I}O_3^- + \overset{1-}{Cl}^- + H^+$$

The change for I_2 is +10 (there are 2 I atoms in I_2). The change for Cl is −6. The common denominator is 30:

$$H_2O + 3I_2 + 5ClO_3^- \rightarrow 6IO_3^- + 5Cl^- + H^+$$

The remainder is balanced by inspection. There are 18 oxygen atoms on the right, requiring 3 from the H_2O on the left, and $6H^+$ on the right:

$$3H_2O + 3I_2 + 5ClO_3^- \rightarrow 6IO_3^- + 5Cl^- + 6H^+$$

Note that the charge also balances.

Chemical Equilibrium

🔑 An arrow pointing in both directions implies that the reaction can proceed in either direction.

If a sample of the colorless gas N_2O_4 is placed in a container at 25°C and 1 atm pressure, it will slowly turn orange because of the formation of the orange gas NO_2. The balanced chemical reaction can be written as

$$N_2O_4 \leftrightarrow 2\,NO_2$$

Note the arrow pointing in both directions. This implies that the reaction can proceed in either direction. In fact, if a pure sample of the orange gas NO_2 is placed in a container at 25°C and 1 atm, the color will become lighter as N_2O_4 is formed. Whether we start from N_2O_4 or NO_2, the reaction mixture will eventually stabilize at the same color, the same final concentration of N_2O_4 being formed per second from NO_2 as there is dissociating to give NO_2.

The Equilibrium Constant

The position of equilibrium for a given reaction can be defined by the equilibrium constant K, a constant for the reaction which is dependent only upon the temperature. The form of the equilibrium constant depends on the *stoichiometry* of the reaction as shown for each of the following reaction types:

Reaction Type	Form of K
$A \leftrightarrow B$	$[B]/[A]$
$A + B \leftrightarrow C$	$[C]/[A][B]$
$A + B \leftrightarrow C + D$	$[C][D]/[A][B]$
$A \leftrightarrow 2\,B$	$[B]^2/[A]$
$A + 2\,B \leftrightarrow C + D$	$[C][D]/[A][B]^2$

The numerator in the expression for the equilibrium constant can be obtained by writing the product of the concentrations of each of the substances on the right-hand side of the equation (the products) raised to the power of the number of molecules of that substance in the equation. The denominator is obtained by the same operation for the substances on the left-hand side of the equation (the reactants).

Example 4.19

Write the expression for the equilibrium constant for each of the following chemical reactions (each equation is balanced):

1. $N_2O_4(g) \leftrightarrow 2NO_2(g)$
2. $H_2(g) + I_2(g) \leftrightarrow 2HI(g)$
3. $2CO(g) + O_2(g) \leftrightarrow 2CO_2(g)$
4. $N_2(g) + 3H_2(g) \leftrightarrow 2NH_3(g)$

Solution.

1. $K = [NO_2]^2/[N_2O_4]$
2. $K = [HI]^2/[H_2][I_2]$
3. $K = [CO_2]^2/[CO]^2[O_2]$
4. $K = [NH_3]^2/[N_2][H_2]^3$

Example 4.20

At 1 atm and 25 °C, the concentrations of the components of an equilibrium mixture of NO_2 and N_2O_4 are $[N_2O_4] = 4.27 \times 10^{-2}$ mol/L, $[NO_2] = 1.41 \times 10^{-2}$ mol/L. What is the equilibrium constant for the reaction at 25°C (expressed as $N_2O_4 \leftrightarrow 2\,NO_2$)?

Solution. The equilibrium constant is calculated as follows:

$$K_{25°} = [NO_2]^2 / [N_2O_4]$$

$$= \left(1.41 \times 10^{-2}\right)^2 (\text{mol} / \text{L})^2 / 4.27 \times 10^{-2} (\text{mol} / \text{L})$$

$$= 4.66 \times 10^{-3} \text{mol} / \text{L}$$

The chemical reactions in Ex. 4.19 have all reactants and products in the gas phase. For reactions in which one or more of the components are pure solids or liquids, the derivation of the equilibrium constant expression is modified. Since the concentration of pure liquids and solids remains constant, it is not necessary to include them in the expression for the equilibrium constant; their values are absorbed in the constant K. For example, consider the following reaction:

$$CaCO_3 \leftrightarrow CaO + CO_2$$

Since $CaCO_3$ and CaO are pure solids, their concentrations do not appear in the equilibrium constant expression, which is

$$K = [CO_2]$$

That is to say, the concentration of CO_2 over a mixture of $CaCO_3$ and CaO at a given temperature is always the same. It does not depend on the quantities of $CaCO_3$ and CaO present. Similarly, for the reaction of HNO_3 in dilute aqueous solution, the H_2O concentration does not appear in the expression for the equilibrium constant:

$$HNO_3 + H_2O \leftrightarrow H_3O^+ + NO_3^-$$

$$K = [H_3O^+][NO_3^-] / [HNO_3]$$

Since water is the solvent, it is present in large excess and its essentially constant concentration is included in the value of K.

4·CHEMISTRY

Example 4.21

Write the expression for the equilibrium constant for the following reaction:

$$C(s) + CO_2(g) \leftrightarrow CO(g)$$

Solution. First we must balance the equation:

$$C(s) + CO_2(g) \leftrightarrow 2\,CO(g)$$

Then the equilibrium constant may be written as

$$K = [CO]^2 / [CO_2]$$

Note that solid carbon does not appear in the expression.

Since the partial pressure of a gas is a measure of its concentration, equilibrium constants for reactions involving gases may be written in terms of partial pressures. An equilibrium constant expressed this way is designated K_p. For example, the equilibrium constant expressed in partial pressures for the first reaction of Example 4.19-1 is

$$K_P = \left(p_{NO_2}\right)^2 / \left(p_{N_2O_4}\right)$$

K_p and K are related by the following expression:

$$K_p = K(RT)^{\Delta n}$$

where Δn is the change in the number of moles of gases between reactants and products. For the reaction under consideration,

$$N_2O_4(g) \leftrightarrow 2\,NO_2(g)$$

One mole of reactants gives two moles of products, $\Delta n = +1$. The equilibrium constant is then given by

$$K_p = K(RT)^{+1} = KRT$$

For a reaction with no change in the number of moles of gases, i.e., $\Delta n = 0$, $K_p = K$.

Example 4.22

K_p is 167.5 atm at 1000°C for the following reaction:

$$C(s) + CO_2(g) \leftrightarrow 2\,CO(g)$$

What is the partial pressure of $CO(g)$ in equilibrium when the partial pressure of $CO_2(g)$ is 1.0 atm, and when it is 0.1 atm?

Solution. The equilibrium constant is

$$K_P = \left(p_{CO}\right)^2 / \left(p_{CO_2}\right) = 167.5 \text{ atm}$$

There then follows

$$\left(p_{CO}\right)^2 / 1 \text{ atm} = 167.5 \text{ atm}$$

When $p_{CO_2} = 1.0$ atm, the partial pressure of carbon monoxide is

$$p_{CO} = 12.9 \text{ atm}$$

Likewise, for 0.1 atm

$$\left(p_{CO}\right)^2 / 0.1 \text{ atm} = 167.5 \text{ atm}$$

$$\therefore p_{CO} = 41.0 \text{ atm}$$

Factors Affecting Chemical Equilibrium

The value of the equilibrium constant is characteristic of the particular reaction at a particular temperature. It depends on the relative stability of reactants and products. If the products are very much more stable than the reactants, then K will be much greater than 1 and the reaction will tend to proceed to complete formation of products, with the generation of a large amount of heat. Such a reaction is said to be *exothermic* as indicated by the following:

$$A + B \leftrightarrow C + D + \text{Heat}$$

In an exothermic reaction, $K \gg 1$.

If the reactants are very much more stable than the products, then K will be much less than 1 and the reaction will tend to favor reactants and will generally proceed with the absorption of heat. Such a reaction, said to be *endothermic*, is indicated by the following:

$$A + B \leftrightarrow C + D - \text{Heat}$$

In an endothermic reaction, $K \ll 1$.

Although external conditions do not generally affect the equilibrium constant significantly, they can affect the relative concentrations of reactants and products dramatically. In Ex. 4.22, for instance, the ratio p_{CO} / p_{CO_2} is 12.9 when p_{CO_2} is 1.0 atm, but changes to 4.1 when p_{CO_2} is 0.10 atm. Note that reducing the pressure on the system increases the relative amount of CO. Concentration changes can have the same effect for certain reactions.

> If the products are very much more stable than the reactants the reaction is *exothermic*.
> • If the reactants are very much more stable than the products the reaction is *endothermic*.

4·CHEMISTRY

Example 4.23

Calculate the ratio of the concentration of N_2O_4 to NO_2 at equilibrium at 25°C if the concentration of NO_2 is 1 mol/L (see Ex. 4.20). Compare it to the ratio in Ex. 4.20.

Solution. The equilibrium constant is calculated to be

$$K = [NO_2]^2 / [N_2O_4] = 4.66 \times 10^{-3} \text{ mol} / \text{L}$$

Hence, there results

$$\frac{1 \text{ mol}^2 / L^2}{[N_2O_4]} = 4.66 \times 10^{-3} \text{ mol} / \text{L}$$

This leads to

$$[N_2O_4] = 2.15 \times 10^2 \text{ mol} / \text{L}$$

or

$$[N_2O_4]/[NO_2] = 2.15 \times 10^2$$

From Ex. 4.20

$$[N_2O_4]/[NO_2] = 4.27 \times 10^{-2} / 1.41 \times 10^{-2}$$
$$= 3.03$$

Note that at the higher concentration of NO_2, the ratio $[N_2O_4]/[NO_2]$ is higher.

Observations of the effects of concentration, pressure, and temperature on the equilibrium composition of chemical reactions led to the formulation of *LeChatelier's Principle*: A system at equilibrium responds to stress to establish a new equilibrium composition that reduces the stress. For instance, in CO-CO_2 equilibrium, an increase in pressure results in the formation of less CO, which reduces the pressure (since there are 2 equivalents of CO formed from each equivalent of CO_2). In the N_2O_4-NO_2 system, an increase in the concentration of NO_2 results in the formation of more N_2O_4, thus decreasing the concentration of NO_2. The extension of LeChatelier's Principle to cover temperature effects suggests that increasing the temperature of an exothermic reaction should cause the equilibrium to shift to the left (more reactants) so that less heat is evolved. Increasing the temperature of an endothermic reaction should cause the equilibrium to shift to the right (more products) so that more heat is absorbed. These predictions are generally true. However, note the important difference that the effect of temperature actually changes the value of the equilibrium constant, while the effect of pressure and concentration changes the composition without changing the value of K.

Example 4.24

For each of the following reactions, give the effect of the indicated stress on the stated quantity.

1. $2SO_2(g) + O_2(g) \leftrightarrow 2SO_3(g) + \text{Heat}$

What is the effect on p_{SO_3} / p_{SO_2} of

        a. Increased total pressure?
        b. Decreased temperature?

2. $CO_2(g) + H_2(g) \leftrightarrow CO(g) + H_2O(g) - \text{Heat}$

What is the effect on p_{CO} / p_{CO_2} of

        a. Increased total pressure?
        b. Decreased temperature?

3. $2Pb_3O_4(s) \leftrightarrow 6PbO(s) + O_2(g) - \text{Heat}$

What is the effect on p_{O_2} of

        a. Increased T?
        b. Increased total pressure?
        c. Added Pb_3O_4?

What is the effect on the ratio of the total quantity of O_2 to that of Pb_3O_4 of

        d. Increased T?
        e. Increased total pressure?
        f. Added Pb_3O_4?

Solutions.

1a. p_{SO_3} / p_{SO_2} will increase. Since there are three equivalents of gases on the left and two on the right, the system will respond to an increase in total pressure by shifting to the right, thereby reducing the number of molecules and the pressure.

1b p_{SO_3} / p_{SO_2} will increase. The reaction is exothermic. Therefore, decreasing the temperature will cause a shift to the right to liberate more heat.

2a. p_{CO} / p_{CO_2} will not change. Since there is no difference in the number of gaseous molecules on the two sides of the equation, pressure changes will not change the composition.

2b. p_{CO} / p_{CO_2} will decrease. The reaction is endothermic. A decrease in temperature will result in a shift to the left to liberate more heat (i.e., the reverse reaction is exothermic).

3a. p_{O_2} will increase. The reaction is endothermic. An increase in T will cause a shift to the right with the absorption of more heat.

3b. p_{O_2} will decrease. Since O_2 is the only gas present, an increase in total pressure will reduce the concentration of O_2 in the gas phase in order to reduce the pressure.

3c. p_{O_2} will not change. The concentration of solids remains constant.

3d. O_2/Pb_3O_4 will increase. Although the *concentration* of Pb_3O_4 is constant, more of it will be converted to PbO and O_2 at higher temperatures for this endothermic reaction.

3e. O_2/Pb_3O_4 will decrease. At higher total pressure O_2 and PbO will combine to form more Pb_3O_4, thus reducing the pressure.

3f. O_2/Pb_3O_4 will decrease. The added Pb_3O_4 will not affect the total quantity of O_2 present.

Reaction Rate

The fact that a chemical reaction is exothermic and has a large, favorable equilibrium constant does not ensure that products will be formed. For instance, the reaction of the hydrocarbons (compounds containing only carbon and hydrogen, e.g., ethane, C_2H_6) in gasoline with the oxygen in air to give carbon dioxide and water is an exothermic reaction with a large, favorable equilibrium constant. Yet gasoline can stand in air for years without transforming into carbon dioxide and water. However, let someone strike a match or spark, and the favorable equilibrium constant and exothermicity is immediately and dramatically revealed. The problem is, of course, in the reaction rate. Unless there is an available chemical path (a mechanism) to get from reactants to products, the rate of conversion of reactants to products will be too slow to be observed.

The effect of variables on reaction rate can be understood in terms of the following expression derived from the collision theory of reaction rates. For the reaction

$$A + B \rightarrow \text{products}$$

the reaction rate is

$$\text{Rate} = Af(t) \times [A][B]$$

The first part that contributes to the reaction rate, $Af(t)$, represents a temperature dependent constant characteristic of the reaction; the second part, $[A][B]$, represents the effect of the concentration variable. Thus, increasing the temperature of the reaction increases the rate by affecting the rate constant, while increasing the pressure of a gas phase reaction, or the concentration of reactants in a solution reaction, increases the rate by increasing the total collision frequency. For the combustion of gasoline, the match provides the high temperature necessary to obtain an initial high rate of reaction; the heat necessary to maintain a high rate of reaction is provided by the exothermicity of the reaction itself.

> Unless there is an available chemical mechanism to get from reactants to products, the rate of conversion of reactants to products will be too slow to be observed.

Electrochemical Reactions

Figures 4.6a and 4.6b illustrate schematically two types of *electrochemical cells*. In Fig. 4.6a, a favorable chemical oxidation-reduction (redox) reaction is used to provide a voltage in a *voltaic cell* or battery. In Fig. 4.6b, a voltage is used to drive an unfavorable redox reaction in an *electrolysis cell*. Both illustrations can be used to give a simplified description of the essential events occurring in a rechargeable ni-cad battery. The reaction which provides the voltage in a ni-cad battery is

$$Cd(s) + Ni^{2+}(aq) \rightarrow Cd^{2+}(aq) + Ni(s)$$

During discharge of the battery, cadmium metal gives up electrons to the electrode in the left-hand compartment (the *anode*) and is oxidized. The resulting cadmium ions enter the solution. The electrons released flow to the electrode in the *cathode* compartment where they are taken up by the nickel ions which are *reduced* to form metallic nickel. In order to maintain charge balance in the solution the negatively charged *anions* flow through the ion permeable barrier to the anode, while the positively charged *cations* flow to the cathode. During the discharge cycle, chemical change produces electrical work. The electrode in the anode compartment is the negative pole of the battery, while that in the cathode compartment is the positive pole. Electrons flow externally through the wire from the anode to the cathode. Note that internally oxidation takes place at the anode and anions flow towards it, while reduction takes place at the cathode and cations flow toward it.

> Oxidation takes place at the anode and anions flow towards it, while reduction takes place at the cathode and cations flow toward it.

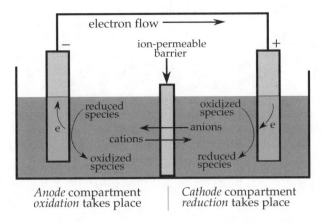

Anode compartment
oxidation takes place

Cathode compartment
reduction takes place

(a) A voltaic cell or battery

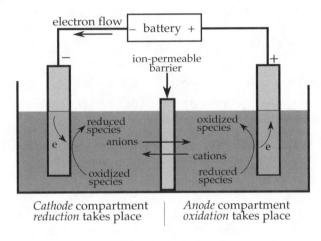

Cathode compartment
reduction takes place

Anode compartment
oxidation takes place

(b) An electrolysis cell

Figure 4.6   Electrochemical cells.

During the recharging cycle (see Fig. 4.6b) the process is reversed. A positive potential applied to a battery to the right-hand compartment results in the removal of electrons from the nickel metal, which is oxidized to nickel ions. In order to maintain charge balance in the solution, anions flow into this compartment, which is now, therefore, an anode. Electrons are "pumped" into the left-hand compartment where they reduce the cadmium ions to cadmium metal. In order to maintain charge balance, cations flow into this compartment, which is now, therefore, the cathode. During the recharging cycle, electrical work produces chemical change. The electrode in the anode compartment is positive, while that in the cathode compartment is negative. Electrons flow externally through the wire and the battery from the anode to the cathode. Note the recurrence of the definition: *Oxidation takes place at the anode and anions flow toward it; reduction takes place at the cathode and cations flow toward it.*

During the recharging cycle the electrode in the anode compartment is positive.

4-CHEMISTRY

Example 4.25

The following reaction is used to construct a voltaic cell.

$$Ni(s) + 2Ag^+ \rightarrow Ni^{2+}(aq) + 2Ag(s)$$

Write the two half reactions for the process. Which is an oxidation? Which is a reduction? Which occurs at the anode? Which occurs at the cathode? What is the direction of electron flow in an external wire connecting the two electrodes? If the salt that carries the charge (the electrolyte) is KNO_3, what is the direction of flow of the nitrate ions in the cell?

Solution. One half reaction:

$$Ni \rightarrow Ni^{2+} + 2 \text{ electrons } (e^-)$$

This is an oxidation (electrons are removed). Oxidation takes place at the anode.

The other half reaction:

$$Ag^+ + e^- \rightarrow Ag$$

This is a reduction (electrons are added). Reduction takes place at the cathode.

Electrons flow externally from the nickel to the silver electrode (electrons always flow externally from the anode to the cathode).

The nitrate ions flow toward the anode (anions always flow toward the anode to maintain charge balance in the solution).

The quantity of chemical change that takes place in an electrolysis cell in a given period of time can be determined from the quantity of charge passed and the charge carried by a mole of electrons. The quantity of charge is measured in coulombs,

$$C = \text{current (amps)} \times \text{time (seconds)}$$

The charge carried by one mole of electrons is the Faraday constant = 96,485.31 C/mole.

Example 4.26

A current of 2.0 amps is passed through an electrolysis cell containing copper ions for 10.0 min. What is the mass of copper deposited at the cathode?

Solution. The reduction half reaction is

$$Cu^{2+} + 2e^- \rightarrow Cu$$

Therefore, two moles of electrons are required to deposit one mole of copper metal. A current of 2.0 amps for 600 seconds yields a charge of $2 \times 600 = 1.2 \times 10^3$ C. The number of moles of electrons is

$1.2 \times 10^3 / 9.65 \times 10^4$ (the Faraday constant) $= 1.24 \times 10^{-2}$ moles

The mass of copper deposited is

$$63.54 \text{ (the atomic mass)} \times 1.24 \times 10^{-2} / 2 = 0.394 \text{ g or } 394 \text{ mg}$$

Practice Problems

4.1   Which statement is incorrect?

a)   Solutions may be homogeneous or heterogeneous.

b)   Matter may be homogeneous or heterogeneous.

c)   Both elements and compounds are composed of atoms.

d)   All substances contain atoms.

4.2   Which of the following statements is not correct?

a)   An element may be separated into atoms.

b)   An element may be a gas, a liquid, or a solid.

c)   A compound can be separated into its elements by chemical means.

d)   An element is always heterogeneous.

4.3   In relation to the proton, the electron is

a)   about the same mass and of opposite charge.

b)   about the same mass and of the same charge.

c)   about the same mass and with no charge.

d)   much lighter and of opposite charge.

4.4   A negative ion of a certain element can be formed by

a)   subtraction of a proton from an atom of that element.

b)   subtraction of an electron from an atom of that element.

c)   subtraction of a neutron from an atom of that element.

d)   addition of an electron to an atom of that element.

4.5   Metallic conduction involves

a)   migration of cations toward a positively charged electrode.

b)   migration of cations toward a negatively charged electrode.

c)   migration of anions toward a positively charged electrode.

d)   passage of electrons from one atom of a metal to another.

4.6   Which of the following statements is correct?

a)   Within a group of elements in the periodic table, the largest atom has the highest ionization potential.

b)   Within a period of elements in the periodic table, the noble gas has the highest ionization potential.

c)   When all valence p orbitals of an atom are half filled, the ionization potential of that atom is lower than the ionization potential of an atom with only two electrons in the valence p orbitals.

d)   It is easier to form a 2+ ion than a 1+ ion.

4.7   Which one of the following elements has the largest atomic radius?

a) lithium   b) sodium   c) beryllium   d) magnesium

4.8   In the series of elements *B, Al, Ga, In,* which of the following is true?

a)   Metallic character increases from *B* to *In*.
b)   Electronegativity increases from *B* to *In*.
c)   Ionization energy increases from *B* to *In*.
d)   Nonmetallic character increases from *B* to *In*.

4.9   Which of the following lists contains only nonmetals?

a)   beryllium (*Be*), hydrogen (*H*), osmium (*Os*)
b)   germanium (*Ge*), palladium (*Pd*), silicon (*Si*)
c)   carbon (*C*), sulfur (*S*), fluorine (*F*)
d)   calcium (*Ca*), chlorine (*Cl*), boron (*B*)

4.10   In an element

a)   the atomic number is equal to the number of neutrons in the atom.
b)   the number of protons always equals the number of neutrons in the atom.
c)   the mass number is equal to the number of electrons in the atom.
d)   the atomic number is equal to the number of protons in the atom.

4.11   What is the ground state electron configuration of aluminum (*Al, Z* = 13)?

a) $1s^2\,2s^2\,2p^5\,3s^2\,3p^1$
b) $1s^2\,2s^2\,2p^6\,3s^2\,3p^1$
c) $1s^2\,2s^2\,2p^6\,3s^2\,4s^1$
d) $1s^2\,2s^2\,2p^6\,3s^2\,3p^2$

4.12   Which of the following electron configurations is *inconsistent* with Hund's rule (the principle of maximum multiplicity)?

a) $[Kr]\,5s^2\,4d^{10}\,5p_x^2\,5p_y^1\,5p_z^0$
b) $[Kr]\,5s^2\,4d^{10}\,5p_x^1\,5p_y^0\,5p_z^0$
c) $[Kr]\,5s^2\,4d^{10}\,5p_x^1\,5p_y^1\,5p_z^1$
d) $[Kr]\,5s^2\,4d^{10}\,5p_x^2\,5p_y^1\,5p_z^1$

4.13   Which of these electron configurations is found in periodic Group VI?

a) $\cdots ns^2\,np^6$ b) $\cdots np^6$ c) $\cdots ns^6$ d) $\cdots ns^2\,np^4$

4.14   From a consideration of electron configurations, which of the following elements would you expect to be most similar in chemical properties to strontium (*Sr, Z* = 38)?

a) *Rb*   b) *V*   c) *Sc*   d) *Ba*

4.15   The principal quantum number designates the

   a)   shape of an orbital.
   b)   main energy level in which an electron is found.
   c)   sublevel of energy in which an electron is found.
   d)   number of electrons allowed in a main energy level.

4.16   In any atom, what is the total number of electrons which can have a principal quantum number of 5 and a secondary quantum number (ℓ) of zero?

   a) 2   b) 4   c) 5   d) 6

4.17   For a neutral atom of an element in its ground state, 35 electrons occupy the energy levels up to and including the $n = 4$ energy level. If all electrons in the valence (outermost) p-orbitals are removed by ionization, how many electrons remain in the resulting ion?

   a) 18   b) 20   c) 28   d) 30

4.18   How many electrons does a phosphorus atom have in its set of valence shell p orbitals?

   a) 0   b) 1   c) 2   d) 3

4.19   An atom of an unknown element Q has a mass number of 31 and the nucleus contains 15 protons. The element is:

   a)   gallium, Ga
   b)   sulfur, S
   c)   phosphorus, P
   d)   palladium, Pd

4.20   An ion of an unknown element has an atomic number of 15 and contains 18 electrons. The ion is:

   a) P^{3-} b) Ar c) O^{2-} d) Si^{3-}

Molecules

4.21   Consider the following statements about ionic and covalent bonds. Which statement is true?

   a)   In a covalent molecule, each atom is bonded to only two other atoms.
   b)   An ionic bond is an electrostatic interaction localized between two definite ions of identical electrical charge.
   c)   A covalent bond occurs when electrons are completely transferred from one atom to another.
   d)   When a covalent bond forms between two atoms with different electronegativities, the bond is always polar.

4.22   Which one of the following compounds is classified as an alkane?

   a) ethylene   b) benzene   c) propane   d) acetylene

4.23   Which one of the following bonds is most covalent?

a) *MgCl*   b) *AlP*   c) *NaCl*   d) *MgS*

4.24   The sum of the oxidation states of all the atoms in a neutral molecule

a)   must be a small positive number.
b)   must be a small negative number.
c)   must be zero.
d)   can be either positive or negative, but not zero.

4.25   The oxidation state of an element bonded only to itself

a)   must be a small positive number.
b)   must be a small negative number.
c)   can be either positive or negative, but not zero.
d)   must be zero.

4.26   The oxidation state of sulfur (S) in the ion SO_3^{2-} is

a) 1+   b) 2+   c) 3+   d) 4+

4.27   A mole

a)   is a unit of measurement applicable only to molecules.
b)   equals the number of atoms in one gram of carbon-12.
c)   equals the number of molecules in 20 liters of air.
d)   is Avogadro's number of anything.

4.28   Which statement is incorrect?

a)   Avogadro's number equals the number of molecules in one mole of nitrogen molecules.
b)   Avogadro's number equals the number of atoms in one mole of nitrogen atoms.
c)   Avogadro's number equals the number of atoms in one mole of nitrogen molecules.
d)   Avogadro's number equals 6.02×10^{23}.

4.29   An empty aluminum Coke can weighs 50 grams. How many moles of aluminum does one Coke can contain? (Atomic weight of *Al* = 27)

a) 1,350   b) 1.85   c) 1.0×10^{25} d) 3.0×10^{25}

4.30   A 27 gram sample of oxygen difluoride, OF_2, contains how many molecules? (Atomic weights: $O = 16$, $F = 19$; Avogadro's number: 6.0×10^{23})

a) 3.0×10^{23}
b) $2 \times 6.0 \times 10^{23}$
c) $6.0 \times 10^{23} / 4$
d) $3.0 \times 10^{23} \times 54$

4.31   How many grams are there in 0.01 mole of Na_2SO_4?

   a) 7.1 g   b) 14.2 g   c) 9.6 g   d) 1.42 g

4.32   What is the volume at standard temperature and pressure of 16 grams of gaseous sulfur dioxide, SO_2?

   a) 22.4 liters   b) 11.2 liters   c) 5.6 liters   d) 16.8 liters

4.33   What is the percentage by weight of aluminum, Al, in alumina, Al_2O_3? (Atomic weights: $Al = 27$, $O = 16$)

   a) 63   b) 37   c) 23   d) 53

4.34   A certain compound consists only of sulfur (S) and chlorine (Cl). It contains 47.5 percent by weight of sulfur and has a molecular weight of 135. What is its molecular formula? (Atomic weights: $S = 32$, $Cl = 35.5$)

   a) SCl_2 b) SCl c) S_2Cl_2 d) S_2Cl

4.35   An unknown organic compound was analyzed and found to contain 34.6 percent carbon, 3.8 percent hydrogen, and 61.5 percent oxygen. Which one of the following compounds could the unknown be?

   a)   methanol, CH_3OH

   b)   oxalic acid, CO_2H—CO_2H

   c)   acetic acid, CH_3—CO_2H

   d)   malonic acid, CO_2H—CH_2—CO_2H

4.36   What is the expression for the equilibrium constant for the following system?

Reactions

$$2\ NOCl\ (g) \leftrightarrow 2NO\ (g) + Cl_2\ (g)$$

   a) $K = [NO]^2[Cl_2]^2/[NOCl]^2$

   b) $K = 2[NO][Cl_2]/2[NOCl]$

   c) $K = [NO]^2[Cl_2]/[NOCl]^2$

   d) $K = [NO]^2[Cl_2]^2/[NOCl]^2$

4.37   For the reaction of solid BaO with carbon dioxide according to the equation $BaO(s) + CO_2(g) \leftrightarrow BaCO_3(s)$, the equilibrium constant may be represented as:

   a) $[BaCO_3]/[BaO]$

   b) $1/[CO_2]$

   c) $[BaO][CO_2]/[BaCO_3]$

   d) $[CO_2]$

4.38   Assume excess oxygen reacts with methane to form 14 grams of carbon monoxide according to the equation $2CH_4 + 3O_2 \leftrightarrow 2CO + 4H_2O$. How many moles of methane will be consumed?

a)   2.0 moles methane

b)   one-third mole methane

c)   0.25 moles methane

d)   0.5 moles methane

4.39   What coefficient is required for NO_2 in order to balance the equation

$$2Pb(NO_3)_2 \rightarrow 2PbO + NO_2 + O_2$$

a) 0.5   b) 1   c) 1.5   d) 4

4.40   What coefficient is required for H_2O in order to balance the equation

$$Be_3N_2 + H_2O \rightarrow 3Be(OH)_2 + 2NH_3$$

a) 1   b) 2   c) 3   d) 6

4.41   According to the equation $2Al + 6HCl \rightarrow 2AlCl_3 + 3H_2$,

a)   production of 1 mole of H_2 requires 3 moles of HCl.

b)   production of 1 mole of $AlCl_3$ requires 3 moles of HCl.

c)   production of 2 moles of H_2 requires 2 moles of HCl.

d)   production of 2 moles of H_2 requires 5 moles of HCl.

4.42   When crystals of sodium sulfate are dissolved in water, the resulting solution feels warmer. The solubility of Na_2SO_4 could be increased by

a)   increasing the temperature.

b)   increasing the pressure.

c)   decreasing the temperature.

d)   adding more solute to the solution.

4.43   In which one of the following reactions would an increase in the volume of the container cause an increase in the amount of products at equilibrium? (All substances are gases unless marked otherwise.)

a) $2NO + 5H_2 \leftrightarrow 2NH_3 + 2H_2O$

b) $CH_3CHO + \text{heat} \leftrightarrow CH_4 + CO$

c) $SO_2 \leftrightarrow S(s) + O_2$

d) $SO_3 + HF \leftrightarrow HSO_3(l)$

4.44   Electrolysis of a $NiCl_2$ solution produces nickel metal

a)   at the positive polarity anode.

b)   at the negative polarity anode.

c)   at the positive polarity cathode.

d)   at the negative polarity cathode.

Solutions to Practice Problems

4.1 **a)** A solution is defined as homogeneous.

4.2 **d)** An element is a pure substance and is homogeneous.

4.3 **d)** By definition.

4.4 **d)** By definition.

4.5 **d)** Conduction is a flow of electrons.

4.6 **b)** The noble gases have closed shell, stable electronic configurations.

4.7 **b)** Atomic radius increases down the periodic table, and decreases across (left to right).

4.8 **a)** Metallic character increases down the table.

4.9 **c)** See the periodic table.

4.10 **d)** By definition.

4.11 **b)** The 13 electrons must be in the lowest energy orbitals available. Thus, at each quantum level (n = 1, 2, 3) the s-orbitals, then the p-orbitals must be filled in order.

4.12 **a)** The $5p_x^2$ configuration has two paired electrons which could be un-paired, i.e., $5p_x'$, $5p_y'$, $5p_2'$.

4.13 **d)** Group VI is two electrons short of a closed shell configuration, there-fore must have 2 electrons in a valence s-orbital, and 4 in the p-orbitals.

4.14 **d)** Ba, Z = 56, has a valence electron configuration $6s^2$. Sr, Z = 38, has $5s^2$.

4.15 **b)** By definition.

4.16 **a)** If ℓ = 0, the orbital is an s-orbital. There can be only one s-orbital for a given principal quantum number. Therefore there can be only two electrons.

4.17 **d)** There are 28 electrons in the n = 1, 2, 3 energy levels (see Table 4.3). The configuration for the n = 4 level is, therefore $4s^2$, $4p^5$. If the 5 p-elec-trons are removed that leaves 30 electrons.

4.18 **d)** Phosphorus, Z = 15 (Table 4.1), has electronic configuration $1s^2, 2s^2, 1p^6, 3s^2, 3p^3$ (see Table 4.3).

4.19 **c)** See Table 4.1 for atomic number 15.

4.20 **a)** The element must be P(Z = 15). The 18 electrons are 3 in excess of the nuclear charge.

4.21 **d)** Electrons are polarized toward the more electronegative atom.

4.22 **c)** Alkane names always end in "ane."

4.23 **b)** Al and P are the closest in the periodic table.

4.24 **c)** By definition.

4.25 d) No net electron transfer.

4.26 d) O is 2^-. Three oxygens is 6^-. The net charge is 2^-. $\therefore$ s must be 4^+, i.e., $4 - 6 = -2$.

4.27 d) By definition.

4.28 c) Molecular nitrogen is N_2. There are therefore 2 moles of N atoms in a mole of nitrogen molecules, and twice Avogadro's number of atoms.

4.29 b) $50/27 = 1.85$ mol.

4.30 a) Molecular wt. of
$$OF_2 = 16 + (2 \times 19) = 54. \quad 27g = 0.5 \text{ mol.} \quad 0.5 \times 6 \times 10^{23} = 3 \times 10^{23}.$$

4.31 d) Mol wt. $Na_2SO_4 = (2 \times 23) + 32 + (4 \times 16) = 142. \quad 0.01 \times 142 = 1.42\,g$.

4.32 c) Mol wt. $SO_2 = 32 + 2 \times 16 = 64. \quad 16g$ of $SO_2 = 16 \div 64 = \frac{1}{4}$ mol.

One mol $= 22.4$ L at STP. $\therefore$ $1/4$ mol $= \frac{1}{4} \times 22.4 = 5.6$ L at STP.

4.33 d) Mol wt. $Al_2O_3 = 2 \times 27 + 3 \times 16 = 102$. wt % $Al = (54/102) \times 100 = 53\%$.

4.34 c) Compound contains $.475 \times 135 = 64.1g$ S per mol.

$\therefore$ there are $64.1/32 = 2.0$ mol S per mol compound.

The remaining mol wt, $135 - 64 = 71$ is Cl (Atomic wt $= 35.5$).

There are $\therefore$ 2 mol per mol compound. $\therefore$ formula S_2Cl_2.

4.35 d) Atomic ratio of $C/H = \dfrac{34.6}{12} \div \dfrac{3.8}{1} = 0.75$, i.e., $3 : 4$ or C_3H_4. Malonic acid

is $C_3H_4O_4$. To confirm, the atomic ratio of $O/H = \dfrac{61.5}{16} \div 3.8 = 1.0$.

4.36 c) See Example 4.18.

4.37 b) Solids do not enter into the K_{eq}.

4.38 d) Mol wt $CO = 28$. $14g$ $CO = 14/28 = .5$ mol. Each mol of CH_4 gives 1 mol CO. $\therefore \frac{1}{2}$ mol $CH_4 \to \frac{1}{2}$ mol CO.

4.39 d) $2\,Pb(NO_3)_2$ gives $4\,N$ atoms, requiring $4\,NO_2$.

4.40 d) There are 12 H atoms on the right requiring $6\,H_2O$ on the left (note that oxygen balances).

4.41 b) The balanced equation shows that 6 moles of HCL gives 2 moles of $AlCl_3$ or 3 moles gives 1 mole.

4.42 c) LeChatelier principle.

4.43 b) LeChatelier principle.

4.44 d) The half reaction that produces solid nickel is
$$Ni_{2+} + 2e- \to Ni(s)$$

This is a reduction and must therefore take place at the cathode. In an electrolytic cell, electrons are pumped into the cathode, making it negative.

Engineering Economics

by Frank Hatfield

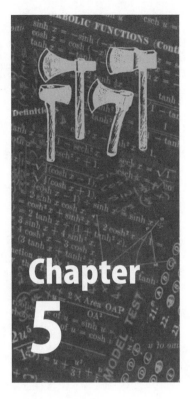

Chapter 5

Engineering designs are intended to produce good results. In general, the good results are accompanied by undesirable effects including the costs of manufacturing or construction. Selecting the best design requires the engineer to anticipate and compare the good and bad outcomes. If outcomes are evaluated in dollars, and if "good" is defined as positive monetary value, then design decisions may be guided by the techniques known as *engineering economy*. Decisions based solely on engineering economy may be guaranteed to result in maximum goodness only if all outcomes are anticipated and can be monetized (measured in dollars).

5.1 Value and Interest

"Value" is not synonymous with "amount." The value of an amount of money depends on when the amount is received or spent. For example, the promise that you will be given a dollar one year from now is of less value to you than a dollar received today. The difference between the anticipated amount and its current value is called *interest* and is frequently expressed as a time rate. If an interest rate of 10% per year is used, the expectation of receiving $1.00 one year hence has a value now of about $0.91. In engineering economy, interest usually is stated in percent per year. If no time unit is given, "per year" is assumed.

> The difference between the anticipated amount and its current value is called *interest*.

Example 5.1

What amount must be paid in two years to settle a current debt of $1,000 if the interest rate is 6%?

Solution. Value after one year $= 1000 + 1000 \times 0.06$

$$= 1000(1 + 0.06)$$

$$= \$1060$$

Value after two years $= 1060 + 1060 \times 0.06$

$$= 1000(1 + 0.06)^2$$

$$= \$1124$$

Hence, $1,124 must be paid in two years to settle the debt.

5.2 Cash Flow Diagrams

In a cash flow diagram income is up and expenditures are down.

• The error introduced by neglecting interest for partial years is usually insignificant compared to uncertainties in the estimates of future amounts.

As an aid to analysis and communication, an engineering economy problem may be represented graphically by a horizontal time axis and vertical vectors representing dollar amounts. The cash flow diagram for Example 5.1 is sketched in Fig. 5.1. Income is up and expenditures are down. It is important to pick a point of view and stick with it. For example, the vectors in Fig. 5.1 would have been reversed if the point of view of the lender had been adopted. It is a good idea to draw a cash flow diagram for every engineering economy problem that involves amounts occurring at different times.

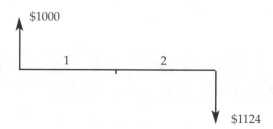

Figure 5.1 Cash flow diagram for Example 5.1.

In engineering economy, amounts are almost always assumed to occur at the ends of years. Consider, for example, the value today of the future operating expenses of a truck. The costs probably will be paid in varied amounts scattered throughout each year of operation, but for computational ease the expenses in each year are represented by their sum (computed without consideration of interest) occurring at the end of the year. The error introduced by neglecting interest for partial years is usually insignificant compared to uncertainties in the estimates of future amounts.

5.3 Cash Flow Patterns

Engineering economy problems involve the following four patterns of cash flow, both separately and in combination:

P-pattern: A single amount P occurring at the beginning of n years. P frequently represents "present" amounts.

F-pattern: A single amount F occurring at the end of n years. F frequently represents "future" amounts.

A-pattern: Equal amounts A occurring at the ends of each of n years. The A-pattern frequently is used to represent "annual" amounts.

G-pattern: End-of-year amounts increasing by an equal annual gradient G. Note that the first amount occurs at the end of the second year. G is the abbreviation of "gradient."

The four cash flow patterns are illustrated in Fig. 5.2.

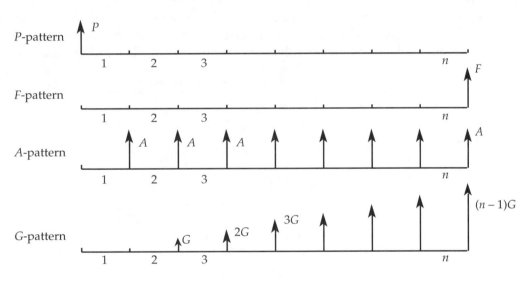

Figure 5.2 Four cash flow patterns.

5.4 Equivalence of Cash Flow Patterns

The letters in the parentheses together with the sub- and super-scripts constitute a single symbol.

Two cash flow patterns are said to be equivalent if they have the same value. Most of the computational effort in engineering economy problems is directed at finding a cash flow pattern that is equivalent to a combination of other patterns. Example 5.1 can be thought of as finding the amount in an F-pattern that is equivalent to $1,000 in a P-pattern. The two amounts are proportional, and the factor of proportionality is a function of interest rate i and number of periods n. There is a different factor of proportionality for each possible pair of the cash flow patterns defined in Section 5.3. To minimize the possibility of selecting the wrong factor, mnemonic symbols are assigned to the factors. For Example 5.1, the proportionality factor is written $(F/P)_n^i$ and solution is achieved by evaluating

$$F = (F/P)_n^i \, P \tag{5.4.1}$$

To analysts familiar with the canceling operation of algebra, it is apparent that the correct factor has been chosen. However, the letters in the parentheses together with the sub- and super-scripts constitute a single symbol; therefore, the canceling operation is not actually performed. Table 5.1 lists symbols and formulas for commonly used factors. Table 5.2, located at the end of this chapter, presents a convenient way to find numerical values of interest factors. Those values are tabulated for selected interest rates i and number of interest periods n; linear interpolation for intermediate values of i and n is acceptable for most situations.

TABLE 5.1 Formulas for Interest Factors

Symbol	To Find	Given	Formula
$(F/P)_n^i$	F	P	$(1+i)^n$
$(P/F)_n^i$	P	F	$\dfrac{1}{(1+i)^n}$
$(A/P)_n^i$	A	P	$\dfrac{i(1+i)^n}{(1+i)^n - 1}$
$(P/A)_n^i$	P	A	$\dfrac{(1+i)^n - 1}{i(1+i)^n}$
$(A/F)_n^i$	A	F	$\dfrac{i}{(1+i)^n - 1}$
$(F/A)_n^i$	F	A	$\dfrac{(1+i)^n - 1}{i}$
$(A/G)_n^i$	A	G	$\dfrac{1}{i} - \dfrac{n}{(1+i)^n - 1}$
$(F/G)_n^i$	F	G	$\dfrac{1}{i}\left[\dfrac{(1+i)^n - 1}{i} - n \right]$
$(P/G)_n^i$	P	G	$\dfrac{1}{i}\left[\dfrac{(1+i)^n - 1}{i(1+i)^n} - \dfrac{n}{(1+i)^n} \right]$

Example 5.2

Derive the formula for $\left(F/P\right)_n^i$:

Solution. For $n = 1$,

$$F = (1+i)P$$

that is,

$$\left(F/P\right)_1^i = (1+i)^1$$

For any n,

$$F = (1+i)\left(F/P\right)_{n-1}^i P$$

that is,

$$\left(F/P\right)_n^i = (1+i)\left(F/P\right)_{n-1}^i$$

By induction,

$$\left(F/P\right)_n^i = (1+i)^n$$

Example 5.3

A new widget twister, with a life of six years, would save $2,000 in production costs each year. Using a 12% interest rate, determine the highest price that could be justified for the machine. Although the savings occur continuously throughout each year, follow the usual practice of lumping all amounts at the ends of years.

Solution. First, sketch the cash flow diagram.

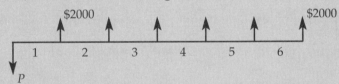

The cash flow diagram indicates that an amount in a P-pattern must be found that is equivalent to $2,000 in an A-pattern. The corresponding equation is

$$P = \left(P/A\right)_n^i A$$

$$= \left(P/A\right)_6^{12\%} 2000$$

Table 5.2 is used to evaluate the interest factor for $i = 12\%$ and $n = 6$:

$$P = 4.1114 \times 2000$$

$$= \$8223$$

Example 5.4

How soon does money double if it is invested at 8% interest?

Solution. Obviously, this is stated as

$$F = 2P.$$

Therefore,

$$\left(F/P\right)_n^{8\%} = 2$$

In the 8% interest table, the tabulated value for (F/P) that is closest to 2 corresponds to $n = 9$ years.

Example 5.5

Find the value in 1987 of a bond described as "Acme 8% of 2000" if the rate of return set by the market for similar bonds is 10%.

Solution. The bond description means that the Acme company has an outstanding debt that it will repay in the year 2000. Until then, the company will pay out interest on that debt at the 8% rate. Unless otherwise stated, the principal amount of a single bond is $1,000. If it is assumed that the debt is due December 31, 2000, interest is paid every December 31, and the bond is purchased January 1, 1987, then the cash flow diagram, with unknown purchase price P, is:

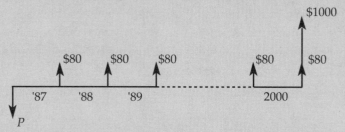

The corresponding equation is

$$P = \left(P/A\right)_{14}^{10\%} 80 + \left(P/F\right)_{14}^{10\%} 1000$$

$$= 7.3667 \times 80 + 0.2633 \times 1000$$

$$= \$853$$

That is, to earn 10% the investor must buy the 8% bond for $853, a "discount" of $147. Conversely, if the market interest rate is less than the nominal rate of the bond, the buyer will pay a "premium" over $1,000.

The solution is approximate because bonds usually pay interest semiannually, and $80 at the end of the year is not equivalent to $40 at the end of each half year. But the error is small and is neglected.

Example 5.6

You are buying a new appliance. From past experience you estimate future repair costs as:

First Year	$ 5
Second Year	15
Third Year	25
Fourth Year	35

The dealer offers to sell you a four-year warranty for $60. You require at least a 6% interest rate on your investments. Should you invest in the warranty?

Solution. Sketch the cash flow diagram.

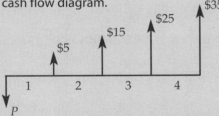

The known cash flows can be represented by superposition of a $5 *A*-pattern and a $10 *G*-pattern. Verify that statement by drawing the two patterns. Now it is clear why the standard *G*-pattern is defined to have the first cash flow at the end of the second year. Next, the equivalent amount *P* is computed:

$$P = \left(P/A\right)_4^{6\%} A + \left(P/G\right)_4^{6\%} G$$
$$= 3.4651 \times 5 + 4.9455 \times 10$$
$$= \$67$$

Since the warranty can be purchased for less then $67, the investment will earn a rate of return greater than the required 6%. Therefore, you should purchase the warranty.

If the required interest rate had been 12%, the decision would be reversed. This demonstrates the effect of a required interest rate on decision-making. Increasing the required rate reduces the number of acceptable investments.

Example 5.7

Compute the annual equivalent maintenance costs over a 5-year life of a laser printer that is warranted for two years and has estimated maintenance costs of $100 annually. Use $i = 10\%$.

Solution. The cash flow diagram appears as:

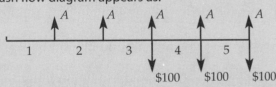

There are several ways to find the 5-year *A*-pattern equivalent to the given cash flow. One of the more efficient methods is to convert the given 3-year *A*-pattern to an *F*-pattern, and then find the 5-year *A*-pattern that is equivalent to that *F*-pattern. That is,

$$A = \left(A/F\right)_5^{10\%} \left(F/A\right)_3^{10\%} 100$$
$$= \$54$$

5.5 Unusual Cash Flows and Interest Periods

Occasionally an engineering economy problem will deviate from the year-end cash flow and annual compounding norm. The examples in this section demonstrate how to handle these situations.

Example 5.8

PAYMENTS AT BEGINNINGS OF YEARS

Using a 10% interest rate, find the future equivalent of:

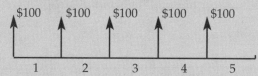

Solution. Shift each payment forward one year. Therefore,

$$A = \left(F/P\right)_1^{10\%} 100 = \$110$$

This converts the series to the equivalent A-pattern:

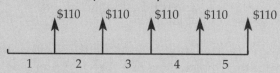

and the future equivalent is found to be

$$F = \left(F/A\right)_5^{10\%} 110 = \$672$$

Alternative Solution. Convert to a six-year series:

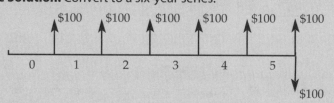

The future equivalent is

$$F = \left(F/A\right)_6^{10\%} 100 - 100 = \$672$$

Example 5.9

SEVERAL INTEREST AND PAYMENT PERIODS PER YEAR

Compute the present value of eighteen monthly payments of $100 each, where interest is 1/2% per month.

Solution. The present value is computed as

$$P = \left(P/A\right)_{18}^{1/2\%} 100 = \$1717$$

Example 5.10

ANNUAL PAYMENTS WITH INTEREST COMPOUNDED m TIMES PER YEAR

Compute the effective annual interest rate equivalent to 5% nominal annual interest compounded daily. (There are 365 days in a year.)

Solution. The legal definition of nominal annual interest is

$$i_n = mi$$

where i is the interest rate per compounding period. For the example,

$$i = i_n/m$$
$$= 0.05/365 = 0.000137 \quad \text{or} \quad 0.0137\% \text{ per day}$$

Because of compounding, the effective annual rate is greater than the nominal rate. By equating (F/P)-factors for one year and m periods, the effective annual rate i_e may be computed as follows:

$$\left(1 + i_e\right)^1 = \left(1 + i\right)^m$$

$$i_e = \left(1 + i\right)^m - 1$$

$$= \left(1.000137\right)^{365} - 1 = 0.05127 \text{ or } 5.127\%$$

Example 5.11

CONTINUOUS COMPOUNDING

Compute the effective annual interest rate i_e equivalent to 5% nominal annual interest compounded continuously.

Solution. As m approaches infinity, the value for i_e is found as follows:

$$i_e = e^i - 1$$

$$= e^{0.05} - 1$$

$$= 0.051271 \text{ or } 5.1271\%$$

Example 5.12

ANNUAL COMPOUNDING WITH m PAYMENTS PER YEAR

Compute the year-end amount equivalent to twelve end-of-month payments of $10 each. Annual interest rate is 6%.

Solution. The usual simplification in engineering economy is to assume that all payments occur at the end of the year, giving an answer of $120. This approximation may not be acceptable for a precise analysis of a financial agreement. In such cases, the agreement's policy on interest for partial periods must be investigated.

Example 5.13

ANNUAL COMPOUNDING WITH PAYMENT EVERY *m* YEARS

With interest at 10% compute the present equivalent of

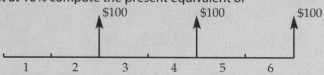

Solution. First convert each payment to an *A*-pattern for the *m* preceding years. That is,

$$A = \left(A/F\right)_2^{10\%} 100$$

$$= \$47.62$$

Then, convert the *A*-pattern to a *P*-pattern:

$$P = \left(P/A\right)_6^{10\%} 47.62$$

$$= \$207$$

5.6 Evaluating Alternatives

The techniques of engineering economy assume the objective of maximizing net value. For a business, "value" means after-tax cash flow. For a not-for-profit organization, such as a government agency, value may include non-cash benefits, such as clean air, improved public health, or recreation to which dollar amounts have been assigned.

This section concerns strategies for selecting alternatives in such a way that net value is maximized. The logic of these methods will be clear if the following distinctions are made between two different types of interest rates, and between two different types of relationships among alternatives.

Types of Interest Rates

•*Rate of Return (ROR)*: The estimated interest rate produced by an investment. It may be computed by finding the interest rate in such a way that the estimated income and non-cash benefits (positive value), and the estimated expenditures and non-cash costs (negative value), sum to a net equivalent value of zero.

•*Minimum Attractive Rate of Return (MARR)*: The lowest rate of return that the organization will accept. In engineering economy problems, it is usually a given quantity and may be called, somewhat imprecisely, "interest," "interest rate," "cost of money," or "interest on capital."

Types of Alternative Sets

•*Mutually Exclusive Alternatives*: Exactly one alternative must be selected. Examples: "Shall Main Street be paved with concrete or with asphalt?" "In which room will we put the piano?" If a set of alternatives is mutually exclusive, it is important to determine whether the set includes the null (do nothing) alternative. Serious consequences can arise from failure to recognize the null alternative.

•*Independent Alternatives*: It is possible (but not necessarily economical) to select any number of the available alternatives. Examples: "Which streets should be paved this year?" "Which rooms shall we carpet?"

The estimated income and benefits (positive) and expenditures and costs (negative) associated with an alternative are converted to the equivalent A-pattern using an interest rate equal to *MARR*. The A-value is the *annual net equivalent value* (*ANEV*) of the alternative. If the alternatives are mutually exclusive, the one with the largest *ANEV* is selected. If the alternatives are independent, all that have positive *ANEV* are selected.

Annual Equivalent Cost Comparisons

Example 5.14

A new cap press is needed. Select the better of the two available models described below. *MARR* is 10%.

Model	Price	Annual Maintenance	Salvage Value	Life
Reliable	11,000	1,000	1,000	10 years
Quicky	4,000	1,500	0	5 years

Solution. The *ANEV* is calculated for each model:

Reliable: $\quad ANEV = -(A/P)_{10}^{10\%}11000 - 1000 + (A/F)_{10}^{10\%}1000$

$$= -\$2730$$

Quicky: $\quad ANEV = -(A/P)_{5}^{10\%}4000 - 1500$

$$= -\$2560$$

Negative *ANEV* indicates a rate of return less than *MARR*. However, these alternatives are mutually exclusive and the null is not available. The problem is one of finding the less costly way to perform a necessary function. Therefore, *Quicky* is selected. If *MARR* had been much lower, *Reliable* would have been selected. By setting the *MARR* relatively high, the organization is indicating that funds are not available to invest now in order to achieve savings in the future.

The estimated income and benefits (positive) and expenditures and costs (negative) associated with an alternative are converted to the equivalent *P*-pattern using an interest rate equal to *MARR*. The *P*-value is the *present net equivalent value* (*PNEV*) of the alternative. If the alternatives are mutually exclusive, the one with the largest *PNEV* is selected. *PNEV* is also called "life cycle cost," "present worth," "capital cost," and "venture worth." If the alternatives are independent, all that have positive *PNEV* are selected.

The present equivalent cost method requires that alternatives be evaluated over the same span of time. If their lives are not equal, the lowest common multiple of the lives is used for the time span, with each alternative repeated to fill the span. A variation, called the *capitalized cost method*, computes the *PNEV* for repeated replacement of the alternatives for an infinite time span. The capitalized cost *P* of an infinite series of equal amounts *A* is given by

Present Equivalent Cost Comparisons

$$P = A(P/A)_{\infty}^{i} = A/i \qquad (5.6.1)$$

Example 5.15

Repeat Example 5.14 using the present equivalent cost method.

Solution. The *PNEV* is calculated for each model:

$$\text{Reliable: } PNEV = -11000 - (P/A)_{10}^{10\%}1000 + (P/F)_{10}^{10\%}1000$$

$$= -\$16,760$$

$$\text{Quicky: } PNEV = -4000 - (P/F)_{5}^{10\%}4000 - (P/A)_{10}^{10\%}1500$$

$$= -\$15,700$$

Note that *Quicky* was replaced in order to fill the ten-year time span. As in Example 5.14, *Quicky* is selected. The two methods will always give the same decision if used correctly. Observe that for both alternatives

$$PNEV = (P/A)_{10}^{10\%} ANEV$$

Incremental Approach

For a set of mutually exclusive alternatives, only the differences in amounts need to be considered. Compute either the *ANEV* or the *PNEV* and base the decision on the sign of that value.

Example 5.16

Repeat Example 5.14 using an incremental present net equivalent value approach.

Solution. *Reliable* costs $7,000 more than *Quicky* but saves $500 each year in maintenance expenses and eliminates the need for a $4,000 replacement after five years. In addition, *Reliable* has a $1,000 salvage value whereas *Quicky* has none.

Reliable – Quicky:

$$PNEV = -7000 + (P/A)_{10}^{10\%}500 + (P/F)_{5}^{10\%}4000 + (P/F)_{10}^{10\%}1000$$

$$= -\$1060$$

The negative result dictates selection of *Quicky*. That is, the additional initial cost required to purchase *Reliable* is not justified.

Rate of Return Comparisons

The expression for *ANEV* or *PNEV* is formulated and then solved for the interest rate that will give a zero *ANEV* or *PNEV*. This interest rate is the rate of return (*ROR*) of the alternative. To apply the rate-of-return method to mutually exclusive alternatives requires incremental comparison of each possible pair of alternatives; increments of investment are accepted if their rates of return exceed *MARR*. For independent alternatives, all those with *ROR* exceeding *MARR* are accepted. The rate-of-return method permits conclusions to be stated as functions of *MARR*, which is useful if *MARR* has not been determined precisely.

Example 5.17

A magazine subscription costs $50 for one year or $80 for two years. If you want to receive the magazine for at least two years, which alternative is better?

Solution. The two-year subscription requires an additional initial investment of $30 and eliminates the payment of $50 one year later. The rate of return formulation is:

$$PNEV = 0$$

$$-30 + 50(P/F)_1^i = 0$$

The solution for *i* is as follows:

$$-30 + 50\frac{1}{(1+i)} = 0$$

$$i = 0.67 \text{ or } 67\%$$

Therefore, if your *MARR* is less than 67%, subscribe for two years.

Example 5.18

Repeat Example 5.14 using the rate-of-return method.

Solution. Use the incremental expression derived in Example 5.16, but set *PNEV* equal to zero and use the interest rate as the unknown:

$$-7000 + (P/A)_{10}^i\,500 + (P/F)_5^i\,4000 + (P/F)_{10}^i\,1000 = 0$$

By trial and error, the interest rate is found to be 6.6%. Therefore, *Reliable* is preferred if, and only if, *MARR* is less than 6.6%.

The benefit/cost ratio is determined from the formula:

Benefit/Cost Comparisons

$$\frac{B}{C} = \frac{\text{Uniform net annual benefits}}{\text{Annual equivalent of initial cost}} \qquad (5.6.2)$$

where *MARR* is used in computing the *A*-value in the denominator. As with the rate-of-return method, mutually exclusive alternatives must be compared incrementally, the incremental investment being accepted if the benefit/cost ratio exceeds unity. For independent alternatives, all those with benefit/cost ratios exceeding unity are accepted.

Note that the only pertinent fact about a benefit/cost ratio is whether it exceeds unity. This is illustrated by the observation that a project with a ratio of 1.1 may provide greater net benefit than a project with a ratio of 10 if the investment in the former project is much larger than the investment in the latter. It is incorrect to rank mutually exclusive alternatives by their benefit/cost ratios as determined by comparing each alternative to the null (do nothing) alternative.

The benefit/cost ratio method will give the same decision as the rate-of-return method, present equivalent cost method, and annual equivalent cost method if the following conditions are met:

1. Each alternative is comprised of an initial cost and uniform annual benefit.
2. The form of the benefit/cost ratio given above is used without deviation.

5-ECON

> **Example 5.19**
>
> A road resurfacing project costs $200,000, lasts five years, and saves $100,000 annually in patching costs. *MARR* is 10%. Should the road be resurfaced?
>
> **Solution.** The benefit/cost ratio is
>
> $$\frac{B}{C} = \frac{100,000}{(A/P)_5^{10\%} \, 200,000} = 1.9$$
>
> Since the ratio exceeds unity, the resurfacing is justified.

A Note on *MARR*

In engineering economy examination problems, *MARR* is a given quantity. However, the following discussion of the determination of *MARR* will help clarify the logic underlying the various comparison methods.

In general, an organization will be able to identify numerous opportunities to spend money now that will result in future returns. For each of these independent investment opportunities, an expected rate-of-return can be estimated. Similarly, the organization will be able to find numerous sources of funds for investment. Associated with each source of funds is an interest rate. If the source is a loan, the associated interest rate is simply that charged by the lender. Funds generated by operations of the organization, or provided by its owners (if the organization is a business), or extracted from taxpayers (if the organization is a government agency) can be thought of as being borrowed from the owners or taxpayers. Therefore, such funds can be assigned a fictitious interest rate, which should not be less than the maximum rate-of-return provided by other opportunities in which the owners or taxpayers might invest.

Value will be maximized if the rates of return of all the selected investments exceed the highest interest rate charged for the money borrowed, and if every opportunity has been taken to invest at a rate-of-return exceeding that for which money can be borrowed. That rate is the Minimum Attractive Rate-of-return. No investments should be made that pay rates of return less than *MARR*, and no loans should be taken that charge interest rates exceeding *MARR*. Furthermore, the organization should exploit all opportunities to borrow money at interest rates less than *MARR* and invest it at rates of return exceeding *MARR*.

To estimate *MARR* precisely would require the ability to foresee the future, or at least to predict all future investment and borrowing opportunities and their associated rates. A symptom of *MARR* being set too low is insufficient funds for all the investments that appear to be acceptable. Conversely, if *MARR* has been set too high, some investments will be rejected that would have been profitable.

Replacement Problems

How frequently should a particular machine be replaced? This type of problem can be approached by varying the life *n*. For each value of *n*, the annual costs and salvage value are estimated, and then the *ANEV* is computed. The value of *n* resulting in the smallest annual equivalent cost is the optimum, or economic, life of the machine. This approach is complicated by technological improvements in replacement machinery, which may make it advantageous to replace a machine before the end of its economic life. In practice, technological advances are difficult to anticipate.

Another form of the replacement problem asks if an existing asset should be replaced by a new (and possibly different) one. Again, the annual equivalent cost method is recommended. The *ANEV* of the replacement is computed, using its economic life for *n*. However, the annual cost of the existing asset is simply the estimated expense for one more year of operation. This strategy is based on the assumption that the annual costs of the existing asset increase monotonically as it ages.

Engineering economy, and decision-making in general, deals with alternatives. But there is only one past, and it affects all future alternatives equally. Therefore, past costs and income associated with an existing asset should not be included in computations that address the question of replacing the asset. Only the estimated cash flows of the future are relevant.

Always Ignore the Past

The mistake of counting past costs is common in everyday affairs. For example, a student may say, "I paid $90 for this textbook, so I will not sell it for $20." A more rational approach would be to compare the highest offered price to the value of retaining the text.

Example 5.20

Yesterday a machine was bought for $10,000. Estimated life is ten years, with no salvage value at the end of its useful life. Current book value is $10,000. Today a vastly improved model was announced. It costs $15,000, has a ten-year life and no salvage value, but reduces operating costs by $4,000 annually. The current resale value of the older machine has dropped to $1,000 due to this stunning technological advance. Should the old model be replaced with a new model at this time?

Solution. The purchase price of the old machine, its book value, and the loss on the sale of the old machine are irrelevant to the analysis. The incremental cost of the new machine is $14,000 and the incremental income is $4,000 annually. A rate-of-return comparison is formulated as follows:

$$-14,000 + (P/A)_{10}^{i} \, 4000 = 0$$

Solving for rate-of-return gives *i* = 26%, indicating that the older machine should be replaced immediately if *MARR* is less than 26%.

A break-even point is the value of an independent variable where two alternatives are equally attractive. For values of the independent variable above the break-even point, one of the alternatives is preferred; for values of the independent variable below the break-even point, the other alternative is preferred. Break-even analysis is particularly useful for dealing with an independent variable that is subject to change or uncertainty, since the conclusion of the analysis can be stated as a function of the variable. The rate-of-return method, as applied to mutually exclusive alternatives, is an example of break-even analysis. The independent variable is *MARR*.

Break-Even Analysis

Example 5.21

An item can be manufactured by hand for $5. Alternatively, the item can be produced by a machine at a fixed annual equivalent cost of $4,000 plus a variable cost of $1 per item. Assume that the cost of laying off and hiring workers is zero. For each of the two manufacturing processes, answer the following questions:

a) For what production rate is one method more economical than the other?
b) If the item is sold for $6, how many must be sold to make a profit?
c) How low must the price fall, in the short term, before production is discontinued?

Solution.

a) Let P be production rate in units per year. Production costs for the two processes are equated:

$$\text{Cost by machine} = \text{Cost manually}$$

$$4000 + 1P = 5P$$

$$\therefore P = 1000$$

If annual production is expected to be less than 1,000 units, the manual process is more economical. For production rates exceeding 1,000 units per year, the machine process is preferred.

b) Setting profit equal to zero is expressed as:

$$\text{gross income} - \text{cost} = 0$$

$$\text{Manual production:} \quad 6P - 5P = 0$$

$$\therefore P = 0$$

$$\text{Machine production:} \quad 6P - (4000 + 1P) = 0$$

$$\therefore P = 800$$

With price maintained at $6, the mechanized operation will be unprofitable if production rate is less than 800 units per year, but the manual operation is profitable at all production rates.

c) Manual production becomes unprofitable if the price drops below $5, and production will cease at that level. For the machine, the $4,000 cost continues whether or not the machine is running. Incremental income is generated so long as the price stays above the variable (per item) cost. Therefore, production will continue at any price over $1, even though a net loss may be sustained. Of course, if it appears that the price and production rate will not soon increase sufficiently to provide a profit, then the operation will be terminated.

5.7 Income Tax and Depreciation

Business pays to the federal government a tax that is a proportion of taxable income. Taxable income is gross revenue less operating costs (wages, cost of materials, etc.), interest payments on debts, and depreciation. Depreciation is different from the other deductions in that it is not a cash flow.

Depreciation is an accounting technique for charging the initial cost of an asset against two or more years of production. For example, if you buy a $50,000 truck for use in your construction business, deducting its total cost from income during the year of purchase gives an unrealistically low picture of income for that year, and an unrealistically high estimate of income for the succeeding years during which you use the truck. A more level income history would result if you deducted $10,000 per year for five years. In fact, the Internal Revenue Service (IRS) requires that most capital assets used in business be depreciated over a number of years rather than being deducted as expenses during the year of purchase.

An asset is depreciable if it is used to produce income, has a determinable life greater than one year, and decays, wears out, becomes obsolete, or gets used up. Examples include tools, production machinery, computers, office equipment, buildings, patents, contracts, franchises, and livestock raised for wool, eggs, milk or breeding. Non-depreciable assets include personal residence, land, natural resources, annual crops, livestock raised for sale or slaughter, and items intended primarily for resale, such as stored grain and the merchandise in a department store.

Since depreciation is not a cash flow, it will not directly enter an engineering economy analysis. However, depreciation must be considered when estimating future income taxes, which are cash flows.

The IRS requires that the Modified Accelerated Cost Recovery System (MACRS) be applied to most tangible property placed in service after 1986. In general, MACRS is based on computing depreciation using a declining-balance method or the straight-line method treating the property as being placed in service and retired from service at midpoints of tax years, and setting salvage value equal to zero. Older methods, such as the Accelerated Cost Recovery System (ACRS) or the straight-line method with a non-zero salvage value, may still show up in engineering economy problems, and therefore are included in this discussion. The following notation will be used in defining methods for computing depreciation:

B — the installed first cost, or basis
n — recovery period in years
D_x — depreciation in year x at age n
V_x — undepreciated balance at the end of year x, also book value
V_n — estimated salvage at age n

In computing depreciation there is no attempt to equate book value with resale value, productive worth, or any other real figure. A business is not obliged to keep an asset for exactly n years, nor to sell it for exactly its book value or estimated salvage value. These, then, are the depreciation methods:

1. *Declining Balance*: Depreciation is taken as a proportion of book value:

$$D_x = V_{x-1}C/n \qquad \textbf{(5.7.1)}$$

    where n is the recovery period. For values of C equaling 1.25, 1.5 and 2 the method is called, respectively: 125% declining balance, 150% declining balance, and double declining balance.

2. *Straight Line Depreciation*: Depreciation is the same for every full year and is calculated as

$$D_x = (B - V_n)/n \tag{5.7.2}$$

3. *Accelerated Cost Recovery System (ACRS)*: An asset is classed as having a recovery period n of 3, 5, 10, or 15 years using IRS guidelines. For each class, a set of annual rates R_x is specified by the IRS. With 3-year property, for example, $R_1 = 0.25$, $R_2 = 0.38$, $R_3 = 0.37$. Depreciation is calculated as follows:

$$D_x = R_x B \tag{5.7.3}$$

By definition, the salvage value using *ACRS* is zero.

Example 5.22

The purchase price of an over-the-road tractor unit is $100,000, its recovery period is three years, and it can be sold for an estimated $20,000 at that time. Compute the depreciation schedules using each of the methods described.

Solution.

Double Declining Balance (MACRS)

Year	Depreciation	Book Value
		$100,000
1	$0.5 \times (\$100,000 \times 2/3) = \$33,333$	$ 66,667
2	$\$66,667 \times 2/3 = \$44,444$	$ 22,222
3	$\$22,222 \times 2/3 = \$14,815$	$ 7,407
4	$7407	$ 0

*The book value must be zero after three years of service, so the formula was not used for the last year.

Straight Line (MACRS)

Year	Depreciation	Book Value
		$100,000
1	$\$100,000/3 \times 0.5 = \$16,667$	$ 83,333
2	$\$100,000/3 = \$33,333$	$ 50,000
3	$\$100,000/3 = \$33,333$	$ 16,667
4	$\$100,000/3 \times 0.5 = \$16,667$	$ 0

Straight Line (General)

Year	Depreciation	Book Value
		$100,000
1	$(100,000 - 20,000)/3 = \$26,667$	$ 73,333
2	$26,667	$ 46,667
3	$26,667	$ 20,000

Accelerated Cost Recovery System (ACRS]

Year	Depreciation	Book Value
		$100,000
1	$0.25 \times \$100,000 = \$25,000$	$ 75,000
2	$0.38 \times \$100,000 = \$38,000$	$ 37,000
3	$0.37 \times \$100,000 = \$37,000$	$ 0

Note: The factor 0.5 in the MACRS results from the requirement to use the midpoint of a tax year.

5.8 Inflation

The "buying power" of money changes with time. A decline in "buying power" is experienced due to a general increase in prices, called "inflation."

Inflation, if it is anticipated, can be exploited by fixing costs and allowing income to increase. A manufacturing business can fix its costs by entering long-term contracts for materials and wages, by purchasing materials long before they are needed, or by stockpiling its product for later sale. Income is allowed to respond to inflation by avoiding long-term contracts for the product. Borrowing becomes more attractive if inflation is expected, since the debt will be paid with the less valuable cash of the future.

MARR may be adjusted for anticipated uniform inflation using the formula

$$d = i + f + if \tag{5.8.1}$$

where d is inflation-adjusted *MARR*, i is unadjusted *MARR*, and f is the rate of inflation. This formula facilitates the solution of some types of engineering economy problems.

Example 5.23

A machine having a five-year life can replace a worker who is compensated $20,000 per year with 5% annual "cost of living" increases. Operating and maintenance costs for the machine are negligible. *MARR* is 10%. Find the maximum price that can be justified for the machine if:

   a)   general price inflation is 5%

   b)   general price inflation is zero

Solution.

a) Although the worker gets a larger amount of money each year, her raises are exactly matched by increased prices, including those of her employer's product. "Buying power" of her annual compensation remains equal to the current value of $20,000. Hence, the maximum justifiable price for the machine is

$$P = (P/A)_5^{10\%} \, 20,000 = \$75,816$$

b) The maximum justifiable price of the machine is equal to the present equivalent value of the annual amounts of compensation:

$$(P/F)_1^{10\%}(1.05) \; 20,000 = \$19,090$$

$$(P/F)_2^{10\%}(1.05)^2 \, 20,000 = \$18,224$$

$$(P/F)_3^{10\%}(1.05)^3 \, 20,000 = \$17,394$$

$$(P/F)_4^{10\%}(1.05)^4 \, 20,000 = \$16,604$$

$$(P/F)_5^{10\%}(1.05)^5 \, 20,000 = \underline{\$15,850}$$

$$\text{therefore,} \qquad P = \$86,162$$

Example 5.24

Recompute the value, in terms of 1987 "buying power," of the "Acme 8% of 2000" bond discussed in Example 5.5, but assume 6% annual inflation.

Solution. The cash flow for each year must be divided by an inflation factor, as well as multiplied by an interest factor, and then the factored cash flows are added:

$$\left(P/F\right)_1^{10\%} \quad 80/(1.06) = \$ \quad 69$$

$$\left(P/F\right)_2^{10\%} \quad 80/(1.06)^2 = \$ \quad 59$$

$$\left(P/F\right)_3^{10\%} \quad 80/(1.06)^3 = \$ \quad 50$$

$$\vdots$$

$$\left(P/F\right)_{13}^{10\%} \quad 80/(1.06)^{13} = \$ \quad 11$$

$$\left(P/F\right)_{14}^{10\%} \quad 80/(1.06)^{14} = \$ \quad 9$$

$$\left(P/F\right)_{14}^{10\%} \quad 1000/(1.06)^{14} = \underline{\$\ 116}$$

$$\text{therefore,} \qquad P = \$\ 541$$

Note that investors can account for anticipated inflation simply by using increased values of *MARR*. A *MARR* of 16.6% gives the same conclusions as a *MARR* of 10% with 6% inflation.

Alternative Solution. Using inflation-adjusted *MARR* we have

$$d = i + f + if$$
$$= .10 + .06 + .10 \times .06$$
$$= .166 \quad \text{or} \quad 16.6\%$$

The value of the bond is

$$P = \left(P/A\right)_{14}^{16.6\%} 80 + \left(P/F\right)_{14}^{16.6\%} 1000$$
$$= 5.3225 \times 80 + .1165 \times 1000$$
$$= \$542$$

Formulas from Part 5.4 (a table in the NCEES Handbook) were used to evaluate the interest factors.

Practice Problems

(If you attempt only a few, select those with an asterisk.)

5.1 Which of the following would be most difficult to monetize?

a) maintenance cost   b) selling price   c) fuel cost   d) prestige

Value and Interest

*5.2 If $1,000 is deposited in a savings account that pays 6% annual interest and all the interest is left in the account, what is the account balance after three years?

a) $840   b) $1,000   c) $1,180   d) $1,191

*5.3 Your perfectly reliable friend, Merle, asks for a loan and promises to pay back $150 two years from now. If the minimum interest rate you will accept is 8%, what is the maximum amount you will loan him?

a) $119   b) $126   c) $129   d) $139

5.4 $12,000 is borrowed now at 12% interest. The first payment is $4000 and is made 3 years from now. The balance of the debt immediately after the payment is

a) $4000   b) $8000   c) $12,000   d) $12,860

5.5 An alumnus establishes a perpetual endowment fund to help Saint Louis University. What amount must be invested now to produce income of $100,000 one year from now and at one-year intervals forever? Interest rate is 8%.

a) $8000   b) $100,000   c) $1,250,000   d) $10,000,000

Equivalence of Cash Flow Patterns

*5.6 The annual amount of a series of payments to be made at the end of each of the next twelve years is $500. What is the present worth of the payments at 8% interest compounded annually?

a) $500   b) $3,768   c) $6,000   d) $6,480

*5.7 Consider a prospective investment in a project having a first cost of $300,000, operating and maintenance costs of $35,000 per year, and an estimated net disposal value of $50,000 at the end of thirty years. Assume an interest rate of 8%.

What is the present equivalent cost of the investment if the planning horizon is thirty years?

a) $670,000   b) $689,000   c) $720,000   d) $791,000

If the project replacement will have the same first cost, life, salvage value, and operating and maintenance costs as the original, what is the capitalized cost of perpetual service?

a) $670,000   b) $689,000   c) $720,000   d) $765,000

*5.8   Maintenance expenditures for a structure with a twenty-year life will come as periodic outlays of $1,000 at the end of the fifth year, $2,000 at the end of the tenth year, and $3,500 at the end of the fifteenth year. With interest at 10%, what is the equivalent uniform annual cost of maintenance for the twenty-year period?

    a) $200   b) $262   c) $300   d) $325

5.9   An alumnus has given Michigan State University ten million dollars to build and operate a laboratory. Annual operating cost is estimated to be one hundred thousand dollars. The endowment will earn 6% interest. Assume an infinite life for the laboratory and determine how much money may be used for its construction.

    a) 5.00×10^6 b) 8.33×10^6 c) 8.72×10^6 d) 9.90×10^6

5.10   An investment pays $6000 at the end of the first year, $4000 at the end of the second year, and $2000 at the end of the third year. Compute the present value of the investment if a 10% rate-of-return is required.

    a) $8333   b) $9667   c) $10,300   d) $12,000

5.11   An amount F is accumulated by investing a single amount P for n compounding periods with interest rate of i. Select the formula that relates P to F.

    a) $P = F(1+i)^{-n}$ b) $P = F(1+i)^{n}$ c) $P = F(1+n)^{-i}$ d) $P = F(1+ni)^{-1}$

5.12   At the end of each of the next ten years, a payment of $200 is due. At an interest rate of 6%, what is the present worth of the payments?

    a) $27   b) $200   c) $1472   d) $2000

5.13   The purchase price of an instrument is $12,000 and its estimated maintenance costs are $500 for the first year, $1500 for the second and $2500 for the third year. After three years of use the instrument is replaced; it has no salvage value. Compute the present equivalent cost of the instrument using 10% interest.

    a) $14,070   b) $15,570   c) $15,730   d) $16,500

5.14   If an amount invested five years ago has doubled, what is the annual interest rate?

    a) 15%   b) 12%   c) 10%   d) 6%

5.15   After a factory has been built near a stream, it is learned that the stream occasionally overflows its banks. A hydrologic study indicates that the probability of flooding is about 1 in 8 in any one year. A flood would cause about $20,000 in damage to the factory. A levee can be constructed to prevent flood damage. Its cost will be $54,000 and its useful life is thirty years. Money can be borrowed at 8% interest. If the annual equivalent cost of the levee is less than the annual expectation of flood damage, the levee should be built. The annual expectation of flood damage is $(1/8) \times 20{,}000 = \$2{,}500$. Compute the annual equivalent cost of the levee.

    a) $1,261   b) $1,800   c) $4,320   d) $4,800

5.16 If $10,000 is borrowed now at 6% interest, how much will remain to be paid after a $3,000 payment is made four years from now?

    a) $7,000   b) $9,400   c) $9,625   d) $9,725

*5.17 A piece of machinery costs $20,000 and has an estimated life of eight years and a scrap value of $2,000. What uniform annual amount must be set aside at the end of each of the eight years for replacement if the interest rate is 4%?

    a) $1,953   b) $2,174   c) $2,250   d) $2,492

*5.18 The maintenance costs associated with a machine are $2,000 per year for the first ten years, and $1,000 per year thereafter. The machine has an infinite life. If interest is 10%, what is the present worth of the annual disbursements?

    a) $16,145   b) $19,678   c) $21,300   d) $92,136

*5.19 A manufacturing firm entered into a ten-year contract for raw materials which required a payment of $100,000 initially and $20,000 per year beginning at the end of the fifth year. The company made unexpected profits and asked that it be allowed to make a lump sum payment at the end of the third year to pay off the remainder of the contract. What lump sum is necessary if the interest rate is 8%?

    a) $85,600   b) $92,700   c) $122,300   d) $196,700

Unusual Cash Flows and Interest Payments

5.20 A bank currently charges 10% interest compounded annually on business loans. If the bank were to change to continuous compounding, what would be the effective annual interest rate?

    a) 10%   b) 10.517%   c) 12.5%   d) 12.649%

*5.21 Terry bought a CD-ROM drive for $50 down and $30 per month for 24 months. The same drive could have been purchased for $675 cash. What nominal annual interest rate is Terry paying?

    a) 7.6%   b) 13.9%   c) 14.8%   d) 15.2%

5.22 How large a contribution is required to endow perpetually a research laboratory which requires $500,000 for original construction, $200,000 per year for operating expenses, and $100,000 every three years for new and replacement equipment? Interest is 4%.

    a) $700,000   b) $6,300,000   c) $7,900,000   d) $10,000,000

5.23 A set of speakers may be purchased now for $400 or by making a down payment of $35 and additional payments of $45 at the end of each of the next ten months. Compute the nominal annual interest rate for the time payment plan.

a) 11.2%   b) 21.2%   c) 23.3%   d) 48.0%

5.24 Same as preceding question, except find the effective annual interest rate.

a) 60.1%   b) 48%   c) 23.3%   d) 21.2%

5.25 A $1000 debt is to be repaid in four weekly payments of $300 each, beginning one week after the debt is incurred. Compute the nominal annual interest rate.

a) 8%   b) 20%   c) 240%   d) 400%

Annual Equivalent Cost Comparisons

*5.26 One of the two production units described below must be purchased. The minimum attractive rate-of-return is 12%. Compare the two units on the basis of equivalent annual cost.

	Unit A	Unit B
Initial Cost	$16,000	$30,000
Life	8 years	15 years
Salvage value	$ 2,000	$ 5,000
Annual operating cost	$ 2,000	$ 1,000

a) A—$5,058; B—$5,270

b) A—$4,916; B—$4,872

c) A—$3,750; B—$2,667

d) A—$1,010; B—$1,010

5.27 Tanks to hold a corrosive chemical are now being made of material A, and have a life of eight years and a first cost of $30,000. When these tanks are four years old, they must be relined at a cost of $10,000. If the tanks could be made of material B, their life would be twenty years and no relining would be necessary. If the minimum rate-of-return is 10%, what must be the first cost of a tank made of material B to make it economically equivalent to the present tanks?

a) $38,764   b) $42,631   c) $51,879   d) $58,760

Present Equivalent Cost Comparisons

5.28 Compute the life cycle cost of a reciprocating compressor with first cost of $120,000, annual maintenance cost of $9,000, salvage value of $25,000 and life of six years. The minimum attractive rate-of-return is 10%.

a) $120,000   b) $145,000   c) $149,000   d) $153,280

5.29 A punch press costs $100,000 initially, requires $10,000 per year in maintenance expenses, and has no salvage value after its useful life of ten years. With interest of 10%, the capitalized cost of the press is:

a) $262,700   b) $200,000   c) $197,300   d) $100,000

5.30　A utility is considering two alternatives for serving a new customer. Both plans provide twenty years of service, but plan *A* requires one large initial investment, while plan *B* requires additional investment at the end of ten years. Neglect salvage value, assume interest at 8%, and determine the present cost of both plans.

	Plan A	Plan B
Initial investment	$50,000	$30,000
Investment at end of 10 years	none	$30,000
Annual property tax and maintenance, years 1–10	$ 800	$ 500
Annual property tax and maintenance, years 11–20	$ 800	$ 900

a)　*A*—$48,780; *B*—$49,250

b)　*A*—$50,000; *B*—$30,000

c)　*A*—$50,000; *B*—$60,000

d)　*A*—$57,900; *B*—$50,000

*5.31　The heat loss of a bare stream pipe costs $206 per year. Insulation *A* will reduce heat loss by 93% and can be installed for $116; insulation *B* will reduce heat loss by 89% and can be installed for $60. The insulations require no additional expenses and will have no salvage value at the end of the pipe's estimated life of eight years. Determine the present net equivalent value of the two insulations if the interest rate is 10%.

a)　A—$116; B—$90

b)　A—$906; B—$918

c)　A—$1,022; B—$978

d)　A—$1,417; *B*—$1,406

Incremental Approach

5.32　A desalinator is needed for six years. Cost estimates for two are:

	The Life of Brine	The Salty Tower
Price	$95,000	$120,000
Annual maintenance	3,000	9,000
Salvage value	12,000	25,000
Life in years	3	6

With interest at 10%, what is the annual cost advantage of the Salty Tower?

a) 0　　　　b) $4,260　　　　c) $5,670　　　　d) $5,834

5.33　A motor costs $20,000 and has an estimated life of six years. By the addition of certain auxiliary equipment, an annual savings of $300 in operating costs can be obtained, and the estimated life of the motor extended to nine years. Salvage value in either case is $5,000. Interest on capital is 8%. Compute the maximum expenditure justifiable for the auxiliary equipment.

a) $1,149　　　　b) $1,800　　　　c) $2,700　　　　d) $7,140

*5.34 An existing electrical power line needs to have its capacity increased, and this can be done in either of two ways. The first method is to add a second conductor to each phase wire, using the same poles, insulators and fittings, at a construction cost of $15,000. The second method for increasing capacity is to build a second line parallel to the existing line, using new poles, insulators and fittings, at a construction cost of $23,000. At some time in the future, the line will require another increase in capacity, with the first alternative now requiring a second line at a cost of $32,500, and the second alternative requiring added conductors at a cost of $23,000. If interest rate is 6%, how many years between the initial expenditure and the future expenditure will make the two methods economically equal?

    a) 1   b) 3   c) 5   d) 10

Replacement Problems

5.35 One year ago machine *A* was purchased at a cost of $2,000, to be useful for five years. However, the machine failed to perform properly and costs $200 per month for repairs, adjustments and shut-downs. A new machine *B* designed to perform the same functions is quoted at $3,500, with the cost of repairs and adjustments estimated to be only $50 per month. The expected life of machine *B* is five years. Except for repairs and adjustments, the operating costs of the two machines are substantially equal. Salvage values are insignificant. Using 8% interest rate, compute the incremental annual net equivalent value of machine *B*.

    a) – $877   b) $923   c) $1,267   d) $1,800

Break-Even Analysis

5.36 Bear Air, an airline serving the Arctic, serves in-flight snacks on some routes. Preparing these snacks costs Bear Air $5000 per month plus $1.50 per snack. Alternatively, prepared snacks may be purchased from a supplier for $4.00 per snack. What is the maximum number of snacks per month for which purchasing from the supplier is justified economically?

    a) 769   b) 1250   c) 2000   d) 3333

*5.37 Bear Air has been contracting its overhaul work to Aleutian Aeromotive for $40,000 per plane per year. Bear estimates that by building a $500,000 maintenance facility with a life of 15 years and a salvage value of $100,000, they could handle their own overhauls at a variable cost of only $30,000 per plane per year. The maintenance facility could be financed with a secured loan at 8% interest. What is the minimum number of planes Bear must operate in order to make the maintenance facility economically feasible?

    a) 5   b) 6   c) 10   d) 40

5.38 It costs Bear Air $1,200 to run a scheduled flight, empty or full, from Coldfoot to Frostbite. Moreover, each passenger generates a cost of $40. The regular ticket costs $90. The plane holds 65 people, but it is running only about 20 per flight. The sales director has suggested selling introductory tickets for $50 to people who have never flown Bear Air.

What is the minimum number of introductory tickets that must be sold in order for a flight to produce a profit?

    a) 5   b) 10   c) 15   d) 20

5.39   What would be the total profit on the flight from Coldfoot to Frostbite of Problem 5.38 if all 65 passengers claimed introductory tickets?

a) – $800   b) – $550   c) 0   d) $400

5.40   Two electric motors are being considered for an application in which there is uncertainty concerning the hours of usage. Motor A costs $4,500 and has an efficiency of 90%. Motor B costs $3,000 and has an efficiency of 89%. Each motor has a ten-year life and no salvage value. Electric service costs $18.70 per year per kW of demand and $0.10 per kWh of energy. The output of the motors is to be 75 kW, and interest rate is 8%. At how many hours usage per year would the two motors be equally economical? If the usage is less than this amount, which motor is preferable?

a) 1800, A b) 1800, B c) 2200, A d) 2200, B

Income Tax and Depreciation

5.41   A drill press is purchased for $10,000 and has an estimated life of twelve years. The salvage value at the end of twelve years is estimated to be $1,300. Using general straight-line depreciation, compute the book value of the drill press at the end of eight years.

a) $1,300   b) $3,333   c) $3,475   d) $4,200

5.42   Excelsys Inc. purchased a desktop computer for $4500. Using the general straight line method, compute the depreciation for the first year if the recovery period is three years and the salvage value is $1500.

a) $500   b) $750   c) $1000   d) $1500

5.43   A grading contractor owns earth-moving equipment that costs $300,000 and is classed as 7-year property. After seven years of use, its salvage value will be $50,000. Using the general straight line method, compute the first two depreciation deductions and the book value at the end of four years.

a) $35,714; $35,714; $157,143

b) $85,714; $85,714; $0

c) $21,429; $42,857; $150,000

d) $42,857; $73,469; $93,711

5.44   Rework Prob. 5.43 using the MACRS straight line method to compute the first two depreciation deductions and the book value at the end of the fourth tax year.

a) $35,714; $35,714; $157,143

b) $85,714; $85,714; $0

c) $21,429; $42,857; $150,000

d) $42,857; $73,469; $93,711

5.45 Rework Prob. 5.43 using the general double-declining balance method to compute the first two depreciation deductions and the book value at the end of the four years.

   a) $85,714; $61,224; $78,092

   b) $85,714; $85,714; $0

   c) $21,429; $42,857; $150,000

   d) $42,857; $73,469; $93,711

5.46 Rework Prob. 5.43 using the MACRS double-declining balance method to compute the first two depreciation deductions and the book value at the end of the fourth tax year.

   a) $35,714; $35,714; $157,143

   b) $85,714; $85,714; $0

   c) $21,429; $42,857; $150,000

   d) $42,857; $73,469; $93,711

General

Questions 5.47–5.50

The market for laser ignition units is estimated to be 1000 per month if the selling price is $400 per unit. The monthly cost of production is

$$C = 35,000 + 0.5S^2$$

where S is the number of units produced each month. Assume that monthly sales and production rates are equal.

5.47 Compute the monthly profit if production is 1000 units per month.

   a) –$135,000   b) $112   c) $135   d) $35,800

5.48 Compute the profitable range of production rates.

   a) 100–400 units/mo   c) 265–400 units/mo

   b) 100–700 units/mo   d) 265–700 units/mo

5.49 Compute the maximum possible monthly profit.

   a) $45,000   b) $35,800   c) $135   d) –$135,000

5.50 Compute the maximum possible profit per unit.

   a) –$135,000   b) $112   c) $135   d) $35,800

Questions 5.51-5.52

A new bus route was added last week, but the average number of passengers on that bus has been only 20; the capacity is 60. The fare is $0.50 and the cost of operating the bus is $0.05 per passenger plus $25 per trip. The marketing director suggests offering a $0.25 fare to people who have never before taken the bus.

5.51 Assume that the director's suggestion is implemented, and that 15 additional passengers per trip are gained. The total profit per trip will be

a) –$26.75   b) –$13   c) –$3.75   d) $10

5.52 Assume that the director's suggestion is implemented, and that 15 additional passengers per trip are gained, but that all passengers claim the $0.25 fare. The total profit per trip will be

a) –$25   b) –$23   c) –$18   d) $7

Questions 5.53-5.57

A corporation evaluates all capital investments using a 20% annual rate-of-return before taxes. The corporation must purchase a new tangent scanner. The following estimates pertain to the two models available:

	Scanx	**Holo-Scan**
First cost	$90,000	$170,000
Life (years)	5	5
Salvage value	$15,000	$ 50,000
Annual cost	$44,000	$ 70,000
Generated income (annual)	$100,000	$160,000

5.53 Using general straight line depreciation, compute the book value of the Scanx at the end of two years.

a) $15,000   b) $30,000   c) $45,000   d) $60,000

5.54 Suppose the Scanx is depreciated by the general double declining balance method. At the end of which year will book value be reduced to salvage value?

a) 1   b) 2   c) 3   d) 4

5.55 If income is disregarded, an annual cost comparison indicates that the preferred model is

a) Scanx by about $22,000/yr.   c) Scanx by about $48,000/yr.

b) Scanx by about $26,000/yr.   d) Holo-Scan by about $2700/yr.

5-ECON

5.56   The present worth of costs and income for the two models indicates that Holo-Scan is worth about how much more than Scanx?

a) $80,000   b) $65,000   c) $45,000   d) $36,000

5.57   The scanner is served by high-voltage electric lines. Total cost of the lines is $F + tI + L/t$ where t is the thickness of insulation on the lines, F is a fixed cost independent of insulation, tI is the cost of insulation, and L/t is the cost of leakage through the insulation. The thickness of the insulation that will give the lowest cost is

a) $\sqrt{L/I}$ b) $F + L/I$ c) $\sqrt{I/L}$ d) $\left[(I+F)/L\right]^{2}$

Afternoon Session Practice Problems

Questions 5.58 – 5.60

A bond that pays no periodic interest is called a zero-coupon bond. A $10,000 zero-coupon bond was purchased today for $4000. It matures in ten years.

5.58   Compute the rate of return.

a) 0 %

b) 9.6%

c) 25%

d) 250%

5.59   If the buyer's minimum attractive rate of return is 8%, the net present worth of the bond is most nearly

a) $600

b) $4000

c) $6000

d) $10000

5.60   If the expected annual rate of inflation is 4% and the buyer's unadjusted minimum attractive rate of return is 8%, what is the inflation-adjusted net present worth of the bond?

a) –$870

b) $600

c) $2760

d) $4050

Questions 5.61 – 5.63

Each member of a three-person field crew is paid $20 per hour. The same work could be done by a Hydro-Swift that costs $100,000 and is operated by one person who would be paid $30 per hour. Assume that the life of the Hydro-Swift is five years and that there are 1500 hours of field work per year. Minimum attractive rate of return in 20%.

5.61 The present net equivalent value of the Hydro-Swift is most nearly

    a) $35,000

    b) $100,000

    c) $125,000

    d) $135,000

5.62 Compute the benefit-cost ratio of the Hydro-Swift.

    a) cannot be determined since there is no annual cost

    b) 0.7

    c) 1.3

    d) 2.25

5.63 Compute the minimum number of hours of field work per year that would justify purchase of the Hydro-Swift.

    a) 670

    b) 1100

    c) 1300

    d) 1500

Questions 5.64 – 5.66

Natasha, Nathan and Nadim are planning to start the 3N Corporation, a communications service business. They expect 3N to have net operating losses of $120,000 per year for the first two years, followed by net operating profits of $240,000 per year for the next eight years. The minimum attractive rate of return is 20%.

5.64 The net present worth of the expected cash flow is most nearly

    a) $500,000

    b) $800,000

    c) $1,000,000

    d) $1,800,000

5.65   Assume that the losses will be covered by borrowing $10,000 at the end of each of the first 24 months at a monthly interest rate of 2%. If the debt is repaid as rapidly as possible, during what year will the balance of the debt reach zero?

  a) 2

  b) 3

  c) 4

  d) never

5.66   Assume that the losses will be covered by a single loan taken at the beginning of the first year, to be repaid in ten equal annual payments starting at the end of the first year. If the lender charges 12% interest, how much must be borrowed?

  a) $203,000

  b) $240,000

  c) $290,000

  d) $301,000

Questions 5.67 – 5.69

   A new BioVue instrument costs $50,000. Operating, maintenance and repair costs are $10,000 for the first year, $25,000 for the second year, $40,000 for the third year, and $55,000 for the fourth year. Minimum attractive rate of return is 10%.

5.67 Compute the annual net equivalent cost if the BioVue is kept for four years

  a) $10,000

  b) $12,500

  c) $45,000

  d) $46,500

5.68 How frequently should the BioVue be replaced?

  a) every year

  b) every two years

  c) every three years

  d) every four years

5.69 Assume that company policy is to replace a BioVue when it is three years old. How much should the company be willing to pay for a one-year old BioVue?

  a) 0

  b) $20,800

  c) $33,300

  d) $35,000

Solutions to Practice Problems

5.1 **d)** Prestige.

5.2 **d)** $1000 \times 1.06^3 = \$1191$.

5.3 **c)** $150 / 1.08^2 = \$129$.

5.4 **d)** $F = 12,000 (F/P)_3^{12} - 4000 = \$12,860$.

5.5 **c)** $P = 100,000 (P/A)_\infty^8 = \$1,250,000$.

5.6 **b)** $500 (P/A)_{12}^8 = 500 \times 7.536 = \$3768$.

5.7 **b), d)** $A: \ 300,000 + 35,000 (P/A)_{30}^8 - 50,000 (P/F)_{30}^8 = \$689,000$
$\qquad B: \ 689,000 (A/P)_{30}^8 (P/A)_\infty^8 = \$765,000$.

5.8 **b)** $\left[1000 (P/F)_5^{10} + 2000 (P/F)_{10}^{10} + 3500 (P/F)_{15}^{10} \right] (A/P)_{20}^{10} = \$262$.

5.9 **b)** $10 \times 10^6 = X + 0.1 \times 10^6 (P/A)_\infty^6$. $\quad \therefore X = 8.33 \times 10^6$.

5.10 **c)** $P = 6000 (P/A)_3^{10} - 2000 (P/G)_3^{10} = 10,300$.

5.11 **a)** By inspection.

5.12 **c)** $P = 200 (P/A)_{10}^6 = \$1472$.

5.13 **b)** $P = 12,000 + 500 (P/A)_3^{10} + 1000 (P/G)_3^{10} = \$15,570$.

5.14 **a)** $2P = (F/P)_5^i P. \quad (F/P)_5^i = (1+i)^5 = 2. \quad \therefore i = 15\%$.

5.15 **d)** $54,000 (A/P)_{30}^8 = \$4800$.

5.16 **c)** $10,000 (F/P)_4^6 - 3000 = \$9625$.

5.17 **a)** $18,000 (A/F)_8^4 = \$1953$.

5.18 **a)** $1000 (P/A)_\infty^{10} + 1000 (P/A)_{10}^{10} = \$16,145$. Note: for the first 10 years, this accounts for \$2000/yr.

5.19 **a)** $20,000 (P/A)_6^8 (P/F)_1^8 = \$85,600$.

5.20 **b)** $e^{0.1} - 1 = 0.10517$ or 10.517%.

5.21 **b)** $675 = 50 + 30 (P/A)_{24}^i$. $\therefore (P/A)_{24}^i = 20.833$.
        $\therefore$ by trial and error $i = 0.0116$. $\therefore 12i = 0.139$ or 13.9%.

5.22 **b)** $500,000 + \left[200,000 + 100,000 (A/F)_3^4\right](P/A)_\infty^4 = \$6,300,000$.

5.23 **d)** $400 = 35 + 45 (P/A)_{10}^i$. $(P/A)_{10}^i = 8.11$. $i = 4\%$. $i_n = 12i$. $\therefore i_n = 48\%$.

5.24 **a)**   From preceding solution $i = 4\%$.
        $i_e = (1 + 0.04)^{12} - 1 = 0.601$. $\therefore i_e = 60.1\%$.

5.25 **d)** $1000 = 300 (P/A)_4^i$. $(P/A)_4^i = 3.33$. $i = 7.7\%$. $\therefore i_n = 52 \times 7.7 = 400\%$.

5.26 **a)** $A: -16,000 (A/P)_8^{12} - 2000 + 2000 (A/F)_8^{12} = -\$5058$.
        $B: -30,000 (A/P)_{15}^{12} - 1000 + 5000 (A/F)_{15}^{12} = -\$5270$

5.27 **d)** $P(A/P)_{20}^{10} = \left[30,000 + 10,000 (P/F)_4^{10}\right](A/P)_8^{10}$. $\therefore P = \$58,760$.

5.28 **b)** $120,000 + 9000 (P/A)_6^{10} - 25,000 (P/F)_6^{10} = \$145,000$.

5.29 **a)** $\left[100,000 (A/P)_{10}^{10} + 10,000\right](P/A)_\infty^{10} = \$262,700$.

5.30 **d)** $A: 50,000 + 800 (P/A)_{20}^8 = \$57,900$
        $B: 30,000 + 500 (P/A)_{20}^8 + \left[30,000 + 400 (P/A)_{10}^8\right](P/F)_{10}^8 = \$50,000$.

5.31 **b)** $A: -116 + 0.93 \times 206 (P/A)_8^{10} = \$906$
        $B: -60 + 0.89 \times 206 (P/A)_8^{10} = \$918$

5.32 **b)** $A: \left[-25,000 + 83,000 (P/F)_3^{10}\right](A/P)_6^{10} - 6000 + 13,000 (A/F)_6^{10} = \$4260$.

5.33 **d)** $(20,000 + P)(A/P)_9^8 - 300 - 5000 (A/F)_9^8 = 20,000 (A/P)_6^8 - 5000 (A/F)_6^8$.
        $\therefore P = \$7140$.

5.34 **b)** $(23,000 - 15,000) + (23,000 - 32,500)(P/F)_N^6 = 0$. $(1.06)^{-N} = 0.84$.
        $\therefore N = 3$ yrs.

5.35 **b)** $-3500(A/P)_5^8 + 12(200-50) = \$923$.

5.36 **c)** $5000 + 1.50n = 4.00n$. $\therefore n = 2000$.

5.37 **b)** $40,000x = 500,000(A/P)_{15}^8 - 100,000(A/F)_{15}^8 + 30,000x$.
$\therefore x = 5.47$.   Use $x = 6$.

5.38 **d)** $1200 + 40(20+x) = 90(20) + 50x$. $\therefore x = 20$

5.39 **b)** $65(50) - 65(40) - 1200 = -550$

5.40 **d)** $4500(A/P)_{10}^8 + (18.7+.1x)75/.9 = 3000(A/P)_{10}^8 + (18.7+.1x)75/.89$.
$\therefore x = 2200$ hr., B

5.41 **d)** $10,000 - (10,000 - 1300)8/12 = 4200$

5.42 **c)** $D = (4500 - 1500)/3 = 1000$

5.43 **a)** $(300,000 - 50,000)/7 = 35,714$
$300,000 - 4(35,714) = 157,143$

5.44 **c)** $(300,000/7)0.5 = 21,419$
$300,000/7 = 42,857$
$300,000 - 3.5(42,857) = 150,000$

5.45 **a)** $300,000 \times 2/7 = 85,714$
$(300,000 - 85,714)2/7 = 61,224$
$300,000 - 85,714 - 61,224 - 43,732 - 31,237 = 78,092$

5.46 **d)** $(300,000 \times 2/7)0.5 = 42,857$
$(300,000 - 42,857)2/7 = 73,469$
$300,000 - 42,857 - 73,469 - 52,478 - 37,484 = 93,711$

5.47 **a)** $P = 400S - (35000 + 0.5S^2)$. $S = 1000$ gives $P = -\$135,000$

5.48 **b)** $P = 0$. $S = \left(-400 \pm \sqrt{400^2 - 4 \times 0.5 \times 35000}\right)/(-2 \times 0.5)$.
$\therefore S = 400 \pm 300$ units/mo

5.49 **a)** $dP/dS = 400 - 2 \times 0.5S = 0$. $S = 400$. $P = \$45,000$ per month.

5.50 **c)** $U = P/S = 400 - (35000S^{-1} + 0.5S)$. $dU/dS = 35,000S^{-2} - 0.5 = 0$.
$S = 265$. $U = \$135/$unit.

5.51 **b)** $P = 20 \times (0.50 - 0.05) + 15(0.25 - 0.05) - 25 = -\$13$.

5.52 **c)** $P = (20+15) \times (0.25 - 0.05) - 25 = -\$18$.

5.53 **d)** $D = \dfrac{(90,000 - 15,000)}{5} = 15,000; \quad V_2 = 90,000 - 2 \times 15,000 = \$60,000$

5.54 **d)** $D_1 = \dfrac{90,000 \times 2}{5} = 36,000. \quad V_1 = 90,000 - 36,000 = 54,000$

$D_2 = \dfrac{54,000 \times 2}{5} = 21,600. \quad V_2 = 54,000 - 21,600 = 32,400$

$D_3 = \dfrac{32,400 \times 2}{5} = 12,960. \quad V_3 = 32,400 - 12,960 = 19,440$

$D_4 = \dfrac{19,440 \times 2}{5} = 7,776. \quad V_4 = 19,440 - 7,776 = 11,664 < 15,000$

5.55 **c)** $\text{ANEV} = -(170,000 - 90,000)(A/P)_5^{20} - (70,000 - 44,000)$

$+ (50,000 - 15,000)(A/F)_5^{20} = -\$48,000$

5.56 **d)** $\text{PNEV} = (160,000 - 100,000)(P/A)_5^{20} - (170,000 - 90,000)$

$-(70,000 - 44,000)(P/A)_5^{20} + (50,000 - 15,000)(P/F)_5^{20} = \$36,000.$

5.57 **a)** $dC/dt = I - \left(L/t^2\right) = 0; \quad t = \sqrt{L/I}\,.$

5.58 **b)** $(1 + i)^{10} \times 4,000 = 10,000. \quad 1 + i = 2.5^{0.1}. \quad \therefore i = 0.096$

5.59 **a)** $P = 10,000(1 + 0.08)^{-10} - 4000 = \$632$

5.60 **a)** $d = 0.08 + 0.04 + 0.08 \times 0.04 = 0.1232$

$\therefore P = 10,000(1 + 0.1232)^{-10} - 4000 = -\$871$

5.61 **a)** $P = (P/A)_5^{20} \times (3 \times 20 - 30) \times 1500 - 100,000 = \$34,600$

5.62 **c)**   c) $\dfrac{B}{C} = \dfrac{(3 \times 20 - 30) \times 1500}{(A/P)_5^{20} \times 100,000} = 1.3$

5.63 **b)** $100,000 = (P/A)_5^{20} \times (3 \times 20 - 30) \times N. \quad \therefore N = 1115$

5.64 **a)** $P = (P/F)_2^{20}(P/A)_8^{20} \times 240,000 - (P/A)_2^{20} \times 120,000 = \$456,000$

5.65 **c)** $(F/A)_{24}^2 \times 10,000 = \$304,200$

$304,200 = (P/A)_n^2 \times 20,000. \quad \therefore (P/A)_n^2 = \dfrac{304,200}{20,000} = 15.2$

By inspection of the tables $n = 18$ months (approx) so debt will be paid off during the fourth year.

5.66　**c)**　$A = (A/P)_{10}^{12} \times P$

$P = (P/A)_{2}^{12} \times (120,000 + A)$
Substitute the first equation into the second and solve: $P = \$289{,}400$.

5.67　**d)**　The $ANEC$ = Annual Net Equivalent Cost. It is

$ANEC_4 = (A/P)_4^{10} \times 50000 + 10,000 + (A/G)_4^{10} \times 15,000 = \$46,500$

5.68　**c)**　$ANEC_n$ is least if $n = 3$ years.　$\therefore\ ANEC_3 = \$44,154$

5.69　**b)**　$ANEC_3 = 44,154 = (A/P)_2^{10} \times P + 25,000 + (A/G)_2^{10} \times 15,000$
Solve for $P = \$20,800$

Interest Tables

TABLE 5.2 .c.Compound Interest Factors

$i = \frac{1}{2}\%$

n	(P/F)	(P/A)	(P/G)	(F/P)	(F/A)	(A/P)	(A/F)	(A/G)	n
1	.9950	0.995	0.000	1.005	1.000	1.0050	1.0000	0.000	1
2	.9901	1.895	0.990	1.010	2.005	0.5038	0.4988	0.499	2
3	.9851	2.970	2.960	1.015	3.015	0.3367	0.3317	0.997	3
4	.9802	3.950	5.901	1.020	4.030	0.2531	0.2481	1.494	4
5	.9754	4.926	9.803	1.025	5.050	0.2030	0.1980	1.990	5
6	.9705	5.896	14.655	1.030	6.076	0.1696	0.1646	2.485	6
7	.9657	6.862	20.449	1.036	7.106	0.1457	0.1407	2.980	7
8	.9609	7.823	27.176	1.041	8.141	0.1278	0.1228	3.474	8
9	.9561	8.779	34.824	1.046	9.182	0.1139	0.1089	3.967	9
10	.9513	9.730	43.386	1.051	10.228	0.1028	0.0978	4.459	10
11	.9466	10.677	52.853	1.056	11.279	0.0937	0.0887	4.950	11
12	.9419	11.619	63.214	1.062	12.336	0.0861	0.0811	5.441	12
13	.9372	12.556	74.460	1.067	13.397	0.0796	0.0746	5.930	13
14	.9326	13.489	86.583	1.072	14.464	0.0741	0.0691	6.419	14
15	.9279	14.417	99.574	1.078	15.537	0.0694	0.0644	6.907	15
16	.9233	15.340	113.424	1.083	16.614	0.0652	0.0602	7.394	16
17	.9187	16.259	128.123	1.088	17.697	0.0615	0.0565	7.880	17
18	.9141	17.173	143.663	1.094	18.786	0.0582	0.0532	8.366	18
19	.9096	18.082	160.036	1.099	19.880	0.0553	0.0503	8.850	19
20	.9051	18.987	177.232	1.105	20.979	0.0527	0.0477	9.334	20
21	.9006	19.888	195.243	1.110	22.084	0.0503	0.0453	9.817	21
22	.8961	20.784	214.061	1.116	23.194	0.0481	0.0431	10.299	22
23	.8916	21.676	233.677	1.122	24.310	0.0461	0.0411	10.781	23
24	.8872	22.563	254.082	1.127	25.432	0.0443	0.0393	11.261	24
25	.8828	23.446	275.269	1.133	26.559	0.0427	0.0377	ll.N1	25
26	.8784	24.342	297.228	1.138	27.692	0.0411	0.0361	12.220	26
28	.8697	26.068	343.433	1.150	29.975	0.0384	0.0334	13.175	28
30	.8610	27.794	392.632	1.161	32.280	0.0360	0.0310	14.126	30
∞	0	200.000	40000.0	∞	∞	.0050	0	200.00	∞

$i = 2.00\%$

n	(P/F)	(P/A)	(P/G)	(F/P)	(F/A)	(A/P)	(A/F)	(A/G)	n
I	.9804	0.9804	0.0000	1.0200	1.0000	1.0200	1.0000	0.0000	1
2	.9612	1.9416	0.9612	1.0404	2.0200	0.5150	0.4950	0.4950	2
3	.9423	2.8839	2.8458	1.0612	3.0604	0.3468	0.3268	0.9868	3
4	.9238	3.8077	5.6173	1.0824	4.1216	0.2626,	0.2426	1.4752	4
5	.9057	4.7135	9.2403	1.1041	5.2040	0.2122	0.1922	1.9604	5
6	.8880	5.6014	13.6801	1.1262	6.3081	0.1785	0.1585	2.4423	6
7	.8706	6.4720	18.905	1.1487	7.4343	0.1545	0.1345	2.9208	7
8	.8535	7.3255	24.8779	1.1717	8.5830	0.1365	0.1165	3.3961	8
9	.8368	8.1622	31.5720	1.1951	9.7546	0.1225	0.1025	3.8681	9
10	.8203	8.9826	38.9551	1.2190	10.9497	0.1113	0.0913	4.3367	10
11	.8043	9.7868	46.9977	1.2434	12.1687	0.1022	0.0822	4.8021	11
12	.7885	10.5753	55.6712	1.2682	13.4121	0.0946	0.0746	5.2642	12
13	.7730	11.3484	64.9475	1.2936	14.6803	0.0881	0.0681	5.7231	13
14	.7579	12.1062	74.7999	1.3195	15.9739	0.0826	0.0626	6.1786	14
15	.7430	12.8493	85.2021	1.3459	17.2934	0.0778	0.0578	6.6309	15
16	.7284	13.5777	96.1288	1.3728	18.6393	0.0737	0.0537	7.0799	16
17	.7142	14.2919	107.5554	1.4002	20.0121	0.0700	0.0500	7.5256	17
18	.7002	14.9920	119.4581	1.4282	21.4123	0.0667	0.0467	7.9681	18
19	.6864	15.6785	131.8139	1.4568	22.8406	0.0638	0.0438	8.4073	19
20	.6730	16.3514	144.6003	1.4859	24.2974	0.0612	0.0412	8.8433	20
21	.6598	17.0112	157.7959	1.5157	25.7833	0.0588	0.0388	9.2760	21
22	.6468	17.6580	171.3795	1.5460	27.2990	0.0566	0.0366	9.7055	22
23	.6342	18.2922	185.3309	1.5769	28.8450	0.0547	0.0347	10.1317	23
24	.6217	18.9139	199.6305	1.6084	30.4219	0.0529	0.0329	10.5547	24
25	.6095	19.5235	214.2592	1.6406	32.0303	0.0512	0.0312	10.9745	25
26	.5976	20.1210	229.1987	1.6734	33.6709	0.0497	0.0297	11.3910	26
28	.5744	21.2813	259.9392	1.7410	37.0512	0.0470	0.0270	12.2145	28
30	.5521	22.3965	291.7164	1.8114	40.5681	0.0446	0.0246	13.0251	30
∞	.0000	50.0000	2500.0000	∞	∞	0.0200	0.0000	50.0000	∞

TABLE 5.2 Compound Interest Factors (continued)

$i = 4.00\%$

n	(P/F)	(P/A)	(P/G)	(F/P)	(F/A)	(A/P)	(A/F)	(A/G)	n
1	.9615	0.9615	-0.0000	1.0400	1.0000	1.0400	1.0000	-0.0000	1
2	.9246	1.8861	0.9246	1.0816	2.0400	0.5302	0.4902	0.4902	2
3	.8890	2.7751	2.7025	1.1249	3.1216	0.3603	0.3203	0.9739	3
4	.8548	3.6299	5.2670	1.1699	4.2465	0.2755	0.2355	1.4510	4
5	.8219	4.4518	8.5547	1.2167	5.4163	0.2246	0.1846	1.9216	5
6	.7903	5.2421	12.5062	1.2653	6.6330	0.1908	0.1508	2.3857	6
7	.7599	6.0021	17.0657	1.3159	7.8983	0.1666	0.1266	2.8433	7
8	.7307	6.7327	22.1806	1.3686	9.2142	0.1485	0.1085	3.2944	8
9	.7026	7.4353	27.8013	1.4233	10.5828	0.1345	0.0945	3.7391	9
10	.6756	8.1109	33.8814	1.4802	12.0061	0.1233	0.08333	4.1773	10
11	.6496	8.7605	40.3772	1.5395	13.4864	0.1141	0.0741	4.6090	11
12	.6246	9.3851	47.2477	1.6010	15.0258	0.1066	0.0666	5.0343	12
13	.6006	9.9856	54.4546	1.6651	16.6268	0.1001	0.0601	5.4533	13
14	.5775	10.5631	61.9618	1.7317	18.2919	0.0947	0.0547	5.8659	14
15	.5553	11.1184	69.7355	1.8009	20.0236	0.0899	0.0499	6.2721	15
16	.5339	11.6523	77.7441	1.8730	21.8245	0.0858	0.0458	6.6720	16
17	.5134	12.1657	85.9581	1.9479	23.6975	0.0822	0.0422	7.0656	17
18	.4936	12.6593	94.3498	2.0258	25.6454	0.0790	0.0390	7.4530	18
19	.4746	13.1339	102.8933	2.1068	27.6712	0.0761	0.0361	7.8342	19
20	.4564	13.5903	111.5647	2.1911	29.7781	0.0736	0.0336	8.2091	20
21	.4388	14.0292	120.3414	2.2788	31.9692	0.0713	0.0313	8.5779	21
22	.4220	14.4511	129.2024	2.3699	34.2480	0.0692	0.0292	8.9407	22
23	.4057	14.8568	138.1284	2.4647	36.6179	0.0673	0.0273	9.2973	23
24	.3901	15.2470	147.1012	2.5633	39.0826	0.0656	0.0256	9.6479	24
25	.3751	15.6221	156.1040	2.6658	41.6459	0.0640	0.0240	9.9925	25
26	.3607	15.9828	165.1212	2.7725	44.3117	0.0626	0.0226	10.3312	26
28	.3335	16.6631	183.1424	2.9987	49.9676	0.0600	0.0200	10.9909	28
30	.3083	17.2920	201.0618	3.2434	56.0849	0.0578	0.0178	11.6274	30
∞	.0000	25.000	625.0000	∞	∞	0.0400	0.0000	25.0000	∞

$i = 6.00\%$

n	(P/F)	(P/A)	(P/G)	(F/P)	(F/A)	(A/P)	(A/F)	(A/G)	n
1	.9434	0.9434	–0.0000	1.0600	1.0000	1.0600	1.0000	-0.0000	1
2	.8900	1.8334	0.8900	1.1236	2.0600	0.5454	0.4854	0.4854	2
3	.8396	2.6730	2.5692	1.1910	3.1836	0.3741	0.3141	0.9612	3
4	.7921	3.4651	4.9455	1.2625	4.3746	0.2886	0.2286	1.4272	4
5	.7473	4.2124	7.9345	1.3382	5.6371	0.2374	0.1774	1.8836	5
6	.7050	4.9173	11.4594	1.4185	6.9753	0.2034	0.1434	2.3304	6
7	.6651	5.5824	15.4497	1.5036	8.3938	0.1791	0.1191	2.7676	7
8	.6274	6.2098	19.8416	1.5938	9.8975	0.1610	0.1010	3.1952	8
9	.5919	6.8017	24.5768	1.6895	11.4913	0.1470	0.0870	3.6133	9
10	.5584	7.3601	29.6023	1.7908	13.1808	0.1359	0.0759	4.0220	10
11	.5268	7.8869	34.8702	1.8983	14.9716	0.1268	0.0668	4.4213	11
12	.4970	8.3838	40.3369	2.0122	16.8699	0.1193	0.0593	4.8113	12
13	.4688	8.8527	45.9629	2.1329	18.8821	0.1130	0.0530	5.1920	13
14	.4423	9.2950	51.7128	2.2609	21.0151	0.1076	0.0476	5.5635	14
15	.4173	9.7122	57.5546	2.3966	23.2760	0.1030	0.0430	5.9260	15
16	.3936	10.1059	63.4592	2.5404	25.6725	0.0990	0.0390	6.2794	16
17	.3714	10.4773	69.4011	2.6928	28.2129	0.0954	0.0354	6.6240	17
18	.3503	10.8276	75.3569	2.8543	30.9057	0.0924	0.0324	6.9597	18
19	.3305	11.1581	81.3062	3.0256	33.7600	0.0896	0.0296	7.2867	19
20	.3118	11.4699	87.2304	3.2071	36.7856	0.0872	0.0272	7.6051	20
21	.2942	11.7641	93.1136	3.3996	39.9927	0.0850	0.0250	7.9151	21
22	.2775	12.0416	98.9412	3.6035	43.3923	0.0830	0.0230	8.2166	22
23	.2618	12.3034	104.7007	3.8197	46.9958	0.0813	0.0213	8.5099	23
24	.2470	12.5504	110.3812	4.0489	50.8156	0.0797	0.0197	1.87951	24
25	.2330	12.7834	115.9732	4.2919	54.8645	0.0782	0.0182	9.0722	25
26	.2198	13.0032	121.4684	4.5494	59.1564	0.0769	0.0169	9.3414	26
28	.1956	13.4062	132.1420	5.1117	68.5281	0.0746	0.0146	9.8568	28
30	.1741	13.7648	142.3588	5.7435	79.0582	0.0726	0.0126	10.3422	30
∞	.0000	16.6667	277.7778	∞	∞	0.0600	0.0000	16.667	∞

5·ECON

TABLE 5.2 Compound Interest Factors (continued)

$i = 8.00\%$

n	(P/F)	(P/A)	(P/G)	(F/P)	(F/A)	(A/P)	(A/F)	(A/G)	n
1	.9259	0.9259	−0.0000	1.0800	1.0000	1.0800	1.0000	−0.0000	1
2	.8573	1.7833	0.8573	1.1664	2.0800	0.5608	0.4808	0.4808	2
3	.7938	2.5771	2.4450	1.2597	3.2464	0.3880	0.3080	0.9487	3
4	.7350	3.3121	4.6501	1.3605	4.5061	0.3019	0.2219	1.4040	4
5	.6806	3.9927	7.3724	1.4693	5.8666	0.2505	0.1705	1.8465	5
6	.6302	4.6229	10.5233	1.5869	7.3359	0.2163	0.1363	2.2763	6
7	.5835	5.2064	14.0242	1.7138	8.9228	0.1921	0.1121	2.6937	7
8	.5403	5.7466	17.8061	1.8509	10.6366	0.1740	0.0940	3.0985	8
9	.5002	6.2469	21.8081	1.9990	12.4876	0.1601	0.0801	3.4910	9
10	.4632	6.7101	25.9768	2.1589	14.4866	0.1490	0.0690	3.8713	10
11	.4289	7.1390	30.2657	2.3316	16.6455	0.1401	0.0601	4.2395	11
12	.3971	7.5361	34.6339	2.5182	18.9771	0.1327	0.0527	4.5957	12
13	.3677	7.9038	39.0463	2.7196	21.4953	0.1265	0.0465	4.9402	13
14	.3405	8.2442	43.4723	2.9372	24.2149	0.1213	0.0413	5.2731	14
15	.3152	8.5595	47.8857	3.1722	27.1521	0.1168	0.0368	5.5945	15
16	.2919	8.8514	52.2640	3.4259	30.3243	0.1130	0.0330	5.9046	16
17	.2703	9.1216	56.5883	3.7000	33.7502	0.1096	0.0296	6.2037	17
18	.2502	9.3719	60.8426	3.9960	37.4502	0.1067	0.0267	6.4920	18
19	.2317	9.6036	65.0134	4.3157	41.4463	0.1041	0.0241	6.7697	19
20	.2145	9.8181	69.0898	4.6610	45.7620	0.1019	0.0219	7.0369	20
21	.1987	10.0168	73.0629	5.0338	50.4229	0.0998	0.0198	7.2940	21
22	.1839	10.2007	76.9257	5.4365	55.4568	0.0980	0.0180	7.5412	22
23	.1703	10.3711	80.6726	5.8715	60.8933	0.0964	0.0164	7.7786	23
24	.1577	10.5288	84.2997	6.3412	66.7648	0.0950	0.0150	8.0066	24
25	.1460	10.6748	87.8041	6.8485	73.1059	0.0937	0.0137	8.2254	25
26	.1352	10.8100	91.1842	7.3964	79.9544	0.0925	0.0125	8.4352	26
28	.1159	11.0511	97.5687	8.6271	95.3388	0.0905	0.0105	8.8289	28
30	.0994	11.2578	103.4558	10.0627	113.2832	0.0888	0.0088	9.1897	30
∞	.0000	12.500	156.2500	∞	∞	0.0800	0.0000	12.5000	∞

$i = 10.00\%$

n	(P/F)	(P/A)	(P/G)	(F/P)	(F/A)	(A/P)	(A/F)	(A/G)	n
1	.9091	0.9091	−0.0000	1.1000	1.0000	1.1000	1.0000	−0.0000	1
2	.8264	1.7355	0.8264	1.2100	2.1000	0.5762	0.4762	0.4762	2
3	.7513	2.4869	2.3291	1.3310	3.3100	0.4021	0.3021	0.9366	3
4	.6830	3.1699	4.3781	1.4641	4.6410	0.3155	0.2155	1.3812	4
5	.6209	3.7908	6.8618	1.6105	6.1051	0.2638	0.1638	1.8101	5
6	.5645	4.3553	9.6842	1.7716	7.7156	0.2296	0.1296	2.2236	6
7	.5132	4.8684	12.7631	1.9487	9.4872	0.2054	0.1054	2.6216	7
8	.4665	5.3349	16.0287	2.1436	11.4359	0.1874	0.0874	3.0045	8
9	.4241	5.7590	19.4215	2.3579	13.5795	0.1736	0.0736	3.3724	9
10	.3855	6.1446	22.8913	2.5937	15.9374	0.1627	0.0627	3.7255	10
11	.3505	6.4951	26.3963	2.8531	18.5312	0.1540	0.0540	4.0641	11
I2	.3186	6.8137	29.9012	3.1384	21.3843	0.1468	0.0468	4.3884	12
13	.2897	7.1034	33.3772	3.4523	24.5227	0.1408	0.0408	4.6988	13
14	.2633	7.3667	36.8005	3.7975	27.9750	0.1357	0.0357	4.9955	14
15	.2394	7.6061	40.1520	4.1772	31.7725	0.1315	0.0315	5.2789	15
16	.2176	7.8237	43.4164	4.5950	35.9497	0.1278	0.0278	5.5493	16
17	.1978	8.0216	46.5819	5.0545	40.5447	0.1247	0.0247	5.8071	17
18	.1799	8.2014	49.6395	5.5599	45.5992	0.1219	0.0219	6.0526	18
19	.1635	8.3649	52.5827	6.1159	51.1591	0.1195	0.0195	6.2861	19
20	.1486	8.5136	55.4069	6.7275	57.2750	0.1175	0.0175	6.5081	20
21	.1351	8.6487	58.1095	7.4002	64.0025	0.1156	0.0156	6.7189	21
22	.1228	8.7715	60.6893	8.1403	71.4027	0.1140	0.0140	6.9189	22
23	.1117	8.8832	63.1462	8.9543	79.5430	0.1126	0.0126	7.1085	23
24	.1015	8.9847	65.4813	9.8497	88.4973	0.1113	0.0113	7.2881	24
25	.0923	9.0770	67.6964	10.8347	98.3471	0.1102	0.0102	7.4580	25
26	.0839	9.1609	69.7940	11.9182	109.1818	0.1092	0.0092	7.6186	26
28	.0693	9.3066	73.6495	14.4210	134.2099	0.1075	0.0075	7.9137	28
30	.0573	9.4269	77.0766	17.4494	164.4940	0.1061	0.0061	8.1762	30
∞	.0000	10.0000	100.0000	∞	∞	0.1000	0.0000	10.0000	∞

TABLE 5.2 Compound Interest Factors (continued)

$i= 12.00\%$

n	(P/F)	(P/A)	(P/G)	(F/P)	(F/A)	(A/P)	(A/F)	(A/G)	n
1	.8929	0.8929	-0.0000	1.1200	1.0000	1.1200	1.0000	-0.0000	1
2	.7972	1.6901	0.7972	1.2544	2.1200	0.5917	0.4717	0.4717	2
3	.7118	2.4018	2.2208	1.4049	3.3744	0.4163	0.2963	0.9246	3
4	.6355	3.073	4.1273	1.5735	4.7793	0.3292	0.2092	1.3589	4
5	.5674	3.6048	6.3970	1.7623	6.3528	0.2774	0.1574	1.7746	5
6	.5066	4.1114	8.9302	1.9738	8.1152	0.2432	0.1232	2.1720	6
7	.4523	4.5638	11.6443	2.2107	10.0890	0.2191	0.0991	2.5515	7
8	.4039	4.9676	14.4714	2.4760	12.2997	0.2013	0.0813	2.9131	8
9	.3606	5.3282	17.3563	2.7731	14.7757	0.1877	0.0677	3.2574	9
10	.3220	5.6502	20.2541	3.1058	17.5487	0.1770	0.0570	3.5847	10
11	.2875	5.9377	23.1288	3.4785	20.6546	0.1684	0.0484	3.8953	11
12	.2567	6.1944	25.9523	3.8960	24.1331	0.1614	0.0414	4.1897	12
13	.2292	6.4235	28.7024	4.3635	28.0291	0.1557	0.0357	4.4683	13
14	.2046	6.6282	31.3624	4.8871	32.3926	0.1509	0.0309	4.7317	14
15	.1827	6.8109	33.9202	5.4736	37.2797	0.1468	0.0268	4.9803	15
16	.1631	6.9740	36.3670	6.1304	42.7533	0.1434	0.0234	5.2147	16
17	.1456	7.1196	38.6973	6.8660	48.8837	0.1405	0.0205	5.4353	17
18	.1300	7.2497	40.9080	7.6900	55.7497	0.1379	0.0179	5.6427	18
19	.1161	7.3658	42.9979	8.6128	63.4397	0.1358	0.0158	5.8375	19
20	.1037	7.4694	44.9676	9.6463	72.0524	0.1339	0.0139	6.0202	20
21	.0926	7.5620	46.8188	10.8038	81.6987	0.1322	0.0122	6.1913	21
22	.0826	7.6446	48.5543	12.1003	92.5026	0.1308	0.0108	6.3514	22
23	.0738	7.7184	50.1776	13.5523	104.6029	0.1296	0.0096	6.5010	23
24	.0659	7.7843	51.6929	15.1786	118.1552	0.1285	0.0085	6.6406	24
25	.0588	7.8431	53.1046	17.0001	133.3339	0.1275	0.0075	6.7708	25
26	.0525	7.8957	54.4177	19.0401	150.3339	0.1267	0.0067	6.8921	26
28	.0419	7.9844	56.7674	23.8839	190.6989	0.1252	0.0052	7.1098	28
30	.0334	8.0552	58.7821	29.9599	241.3327	0.1241	0.0041	7.2974	30
∞	.0000	8.333	69.4444	∞	∞	0.1200	0.0000	8.3333	∞

$i = 20.00\%$

n	(P/F)	(P/A)	(P/G)	(F/P)	(F/A)	(A/P)	(A/F)	(A/G)	n
1	.8333	0.8333	-0.0000	1.2000	1.0000	1.2000	1.0000	-0.0000	1
2	.6944	1.5278	0.6944	1.4400	2.2000	0.6545	0.4545	0.4545	2
3	.5787	2.1065	1.8519	1.7280	3.6400	0.4747	0.2747	0.8791	3
4	.4823	2.5887	3.2986	2.0736	5.3680	0.3863	0.1863	1.2742	4
5	.4019	2.9906	4.9061	2.4883	7.4416	0.3344	0.1344	1.6405	5
6	.3349	3.3255	6.5806	2.9860	9.9299	0.3007	0.1007	1.9788	6
7	.2791	3.6046	8.2551	3.5832	12.9159	0.2774	0.0774	2.2902	7
8	.2326	3.8372	9.8831	4.2998	16.4991	0.2606	0.0606	2.5756	8
9	.1938	4.0310	11.4335	5.1598	20.7989	0.2481	0.0481	2.8364	9
10	.1615	4.1925	12.8871	6.1917	25.9587	0.2385	0.0385	3.0739	10
11	.1346	4.3271	14.2330	7.4301	32.1504	0.2311	0.0311	3.2893	11
12	.1122	4.4392	15.4667	8.9161	39.5805	0.2253	0.0253	3.4841	12
13	.0935	4.5327	16.5883	10.6993	48.4966	0.2206	0.0206	3.6597	13
14	.0779	4.6106	17.6008	12.8392	59.1959	0.2169	0.0169	3.8175	14
15	.0649	4.6755	18.5095	15.4070	72.0351	0.2139	0.0139	3.9588	15
16	.0541	4.7296	19.3208	18.4884	87.4421	0.2114	0.0114	4.0851	16
17	.0451	4.7746	20.0419	22.1861	105.9306	0.2094	0.0094	4.1976	17
18	.0376	4.8122	20.6805	26.6233	128.1167	0.2078	0.0078	4.Z975	18
19	.0313	4.8435	21.2439	31.9480	154.7400	0.2065	0.0065	4.3861	19
20	.0261	4.8696	21.7395	38.3376	186.6880	0.2054	0.0054	4.4643	20
21	.0217	4.8913	22.1742	46.0051	225.0256	0.2044	0.0044	4.5334	21
22	.0181	4.9094	22.5546	55.2061	271.0307	0.2037	0.0037	4.5941	22
23	.0151	4.9245	22.8867	66.2474	326.2369	0.2031	0.0031	4.6475	23
24	.0126	4.9371	23.1760	79.4968	392.4842	0.2025	0.0025	4.6943	24
25	.0105	4.9476	23.4276	95.3962	471.9811	0.2021	0.0021	4.7352	25
26	.0087	4.9563	23.6460	114.4755	567.3773	0.2018	0.0018	4.7709	26
28	.0061	4.9697	23.9991	164.8447	819.2233	0.2012	0.0012	4.8291	28
30	.0042	4.9789	24.2628	237.3763	1181.8816	0.2008	0.0008	4.8731	30
∞	.0000	5.0000	25.0000	∞	∞	0.2000	0.0000	5.5000	∞

Electrical Theory

by Jon A. Soper

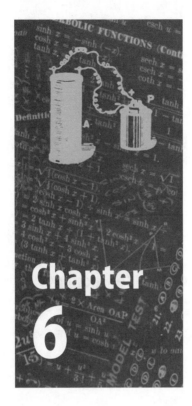

A review of basic concepts in Electrical Engineering of interest to all engineers is presented in this chapter. The subjects include circuits, electromagnetics, the fundamentals of operational electronics, and electric power distribution and machinery. Each section begins with a brief statement of the concepts to be covered and a listing of pertinent formulas with units.

6.1 Circuits

Electric circuits are an interconnection of electrical components for the purpose of either generating and distributing electrical power; converting electrical power to some other useful form such as light, heat, or mechanical torque; or processing information contained in an electrical form (i.e., electrical signals). Most electrical circuits contain a source (or sources) of electrical power, passive components which store or dissipate energy, and possibly active components which change the electrical form of the energy or information being processed by the circuit.

Circuits may be classified as *Direct Current* (DC) circuits when the currents and voltages do not vary with time and as *Alternating Current* (AC) circuits when the currents and voltage vary sinusoidally with time. Both DC and AC circuits are said to be operating in the *steady state* when their current/voltage time variation is purely constant or purely sinusoidal with time. A *transient circuit* condition occurs when a switch is thrown that turns a source either on or off. This review will cover the DC steady-state and DC transient circuit conditions and the AC steady-state circuit condition. The primary quantities of interest in making circuit calculations are presented in Table 6.1.

Circuits are said to be operating in the *steady state* when their current/voltage time variation is purely constant or purely sinusoidal with time.

TABLE 6.1 Quantities Used in Electric Circuits

Quantity	Symbol	Unit	Defining Equation	Definition
Charge	Q	coulomb	$Q = \int I dt$	
Current	I	ampere	$I = \dfrac{dQ}{dt}$	Time rate of flow of charge past a point in the circuit.
Voltage	V	volt	$V = \dfrac{dW}{dQ}$	Energy per unit charge either gained or lost through a circuit element.
Energy	W	joule	$W = \int V dQ = \int P dt$	
Power	P	watt	$P = \dfrac{dW}{dt} = IV$	Power is the time rate of energy flow.

Circuit Components

The circuits reviewed in this section will contain one or more sources interconnected with passive components. These passive circuit components include resistors, inductors and capacitors. They are described as follows:

a) *Resistors* are energy absorbing components and have a resistance value R measured in ohms:

$$I = \frac{V}{R} \quad \text{or} \quad V = IR \tag{6.1.1}$$

$$\text{AMPERES} = \frac{\text{VOLTS}}{\text{OHMS}}$$

b) *Inductors* are energy storage components and have an inductance value L measured in henries:

$$I = \frac{1}{L}\int V dt \quad \text{or} \quad V = L\frac{dI}{dt} \tag{6.1.2}$$

$$\text{AMPERES} = \frac{\text{VOLT} \cdot \text{SECONDS}}{\text{HENRIES}}$$

c) *Capacitors* are energy storage components and have a capacitance value C measured in farads:

$$I = C\frac{dV}{dt} \quad \text{or} \quad V = \frac{1}{C}\int I dt \tag{6.1.3}$$

$$\text{AMPERES} = \frac{\text{FARAD} \cdot \text{VOLTS}}{\text{SECONDS}}$$

Sources of Electrical Energy

Sources in electric circuits can be independent of current and/or voltage values elsewhere in the circuit, or they can be dependent upon them. In this section only independent sources will be considered. Figure 6.1 shows both ideal and linear models for current and voltage sources.

6·ELECTRICAL

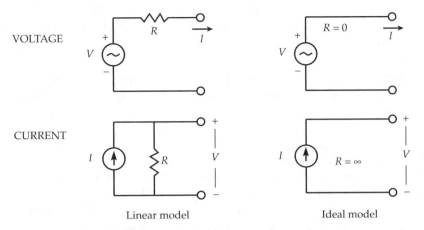

Figure 6.1 Ideal and linear models of current and voltage sources.

Two laws of conservation govern the behavior of all electrical circuits:

Kirchhoff's Laws

a) *Kirchhoff's Voltage Law* (KVL), for the conservation of energy, states that the sum of voltage rises or drops around any closed path in an electrical circuit must be zero:

$$\sum V_{DROPS} = 0 \quad \sum V_{RISES} = 0 \quad \text{(around close path)} \qquad \textbf{(6.1.4)}$$

b) *Kirchhoff's Current Law* (KCL), for the conservation of charge, states that the flow of charges either into (positive) or out of (negative) any node in a circuit must add to zero:

$$\sum I_{IN} = 0 \quad \sum I_{OUT} = 0 \quad \text{(at node)} \qquad \textbf{(6.1.5)}$$

Ohm's Law

Ohm's Law is a statement of the relationship between the voltage across an electrical component and the current through the component. For DC circuits, where the components are resistors, Ohm's law is

$$V = IR \quad \text{or} \quad I = V/R \qquad \textbf{(6.1.6)}$$

For AC circuits, with resistors, capacitors and inductors, Ohm's law, stated in terms of the component impedance Z (see Table 6.3), is

$$V = IZ \quad \text{or} \quad I = V/Z \qquad \textbf{(6.1.7)}$$

Reference Voltage Polarity and Current Direction

where all variables can be complex. Circuit analysis requires defining first a reference current direction with an arrow placed next to the circuit component. For each of the components a reference current direction is arbitrarily defined. Once the current reference direction is defined, the voltage reference polarity marks can be placed on each component. The polarity marks on passive components are always placed so that the current flows from the plus (+) mark to the minus (–) mark, the passive sign convention.

  Current values can be either positive or negative. A positive current value shows that the current does in fact flow in the reference direction. A negative current value shows that the current flows opposite to the reference direction. Voltage values can be either positive or negative. A positive voltage value indicates a loss of energy or reduction in voltage when moving through the circuit from the plus polarity mark to the minus polarity mark. A negative voltage value

6-ELECTRICAL

indicates a gain of energy when moving through the circuit from the plus polarity mark to the minus polarity mark.

It is proper electrical terminology to talk about voltage drops and voltage rises. A voltage drop is experienced when moving through the circuit from the plus (+) polarity mark to the minus (–) polarity mark. A voltage rise is experienced when moving through the circuit from the minus (–) polarity mark to the plus (+) polarity mark.

Circuit Equations

When writing circuit equations, the current is assumed to have a positive value in the reference direction and the voltage is assumed to have a positive value as indicated by the polarity marks. To write the KVL circuit equation one must move around a closed path in the circuit and sum all the voltage rises or all the voltage drops. For example, for the circuit in Fig. 6.2 begin at point a and move to b, then c, then d, and back to a. For $\sum V_{RISES} = 0$ obtain

$$V_s - IR_1 - IR_2 - IR_3 = 0 \tag{6.1.8}$$

For $\sum V_{DROPS} = 0$ obtain

$$-V_s + IR_1 + IR_2 + IR_3 = 0 \tag{6.1.9}$$

Either of these equations can now be solved for the one unknown current:

$$I = \frac{V_s}{R_1 + R_2 + R_3} = \frac{V_s}{R_{eq}} \tag{6.1.10}$$

where R_{eq} is the equivalent resistance for the circuit.

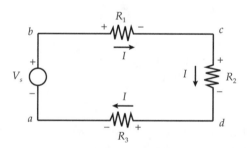

Figure 6.2 A simple circuit.

Circuit Equations Using Branch Currents

The circuit in Fig. 6.3 has meshes around which two voltage equations (KVL) can be written. There are, however, three branches in the circuit. An unknown current with a reference direction is assumed in each branch. The polarity marks are indicated for each resistor so the KVL can be written. Write two KVL equations, one around each mesh. Using $\sum V_{DROPS} = 0$ obtain:

$$-V_s + I_1 R_1 + I_3 R_2 + I_1 R_3 = 0$$
$$-I_3 R_2 + I_2 R_4 + I_2 R_5 + I_2 R_6 = 0 \tag{6.1.11}$$

Write one KCL equation at circuit node a. This additional equation is necessary since there are three unknown currents:

$$I_1 - I_2 - I_3 = 0 \tag{6.1.12}$$

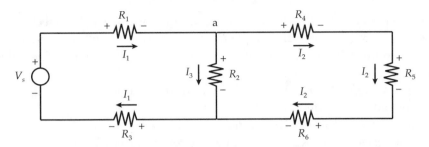

Figure 6.3 A circuit with two meshes and three branches.

These three equations can be solved for I_1, I_2 and I_3. The current I_1 is

$$I_1 = \frac{\begin{vmatrix} V_s & 0 & R_2 \\ 0 & R_4 + R_5 + R_6 & -R_2 \\ 0 & -1 & -1 \end{vmatrix}}{\begin{vmatrix} R_1 + R_3 & 0 & R_2 \\ 0 & R_4 + R_5 + R_6 & -R_2 \\ 1 & -1 & -1 \end{vmatrix}} \tag{6.1.13}$$

A simplification in writing the circuit equations for Fig. 6.3 occurs if mesh currents are used. Note that

$$I_3 = I_1 - I_2 \tag{6.1.14}$$

Redefine the reference currents in the network of Fig. 6.3 as shown in Fig. 6.4. Now there are only two unknown currents to solve for instead of the three in Fig. 6.3. The current through R_1 and R_3 is I_1. The current through R_4, R_5 and R_6 is I_2. The current through R_2 is $I_1 - I_2$ which is consistent with the KCL equation written for the network of Fig. 6.3. Write two KVL equations, one around each mesh:

$$-V_s + I_1(R_1 + R_2 + R_3) - I_2 R_2 = 0$$

$$-I_1 R_2 + I_2(R_2 + R_4 + R_5 + R_6) = 0 \tag{6.1.15}$$

These two equations can be solved for I_1 and I_2. The current I_1 is equivalent to that of Eq. 6.1.13:

$$I_1 = \frac{\begin{vmatrix} V_s & -R_2 \\ 0 & R_2 + R_4 + R_5 + R_6 \end{vmatrix}}{\begin{vmatrix} R_1 + R_2 + R_3 & -R_2 \\ -R_2 & R_2 + R_4 + R_5 + R_6 \end{vmatrix}} \tag{6.1.16}$$

Circuit Equations Using Mesh Currents

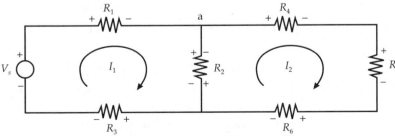

Figure 6.4 A circuit with two meshes.

Thévenin Equivalent Circuit

It is often convenient to model a complex circuit which has many electrical components by a single source and single resistor (or impedance) in series. This simplified circuit is called a *Thévenin Equivalent*, as shown in Fig. 6.5. The values of V_{eq} and R_{eq} are found as follows:

- The voltage drop is V_{oc} from a to b in the complex circuit with R_{LOAD} removed. It is evident that V_{oc} is also the open circuit (R_{LOAD} removed) voltage across a–b in the Thévenin equivalent.
- The resistance is R_{eq} looking in at the terminals (a-b) with R_{LOAD} removed and all voltage sources shorted out and all current sources opened (or removed). Any technique for finding equivalent resistance may then be used. A second way to find R_{eq}, once V_{oc} is known, is to short circuit the terminals (a-b) and solve for the current I_{sc} through the short circuit without removing any sources in the complex circuit. Then

$$R_{eq} = \frac{V_{oc}}{I_{sc}} \qquad \text{(6.1.17)}$$

Example 6.3 illustrates the above.

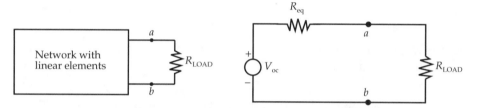

Figure 6.5 A complex circuit and its Thévenin equivalent.

Norton Equivalent Circuit

Any network of R's, L's and C's, voltage sources and current sources can be replaced at any two terminals with a *Norton Equivalent Current Source*. The easiest way to find the Norton Equivalent is to convert from the Thévenin Equivalent as shown in Fig. 6.6. If we replace R_L in the Thévenin Equivalent by a short circuit, the current through a-b will be

$$I_{sc} = \frac{V_{oc}}{R_{eq}} \qquad \text{(6.1.18)}$$

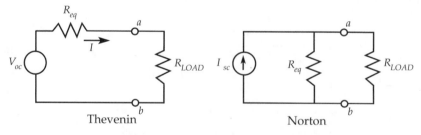

Figure 6.6 The Norton Equivalent Circuit.

To find R_{eq} we short out the voltage source and open circuit the current source, then evaluate the resistance looking in at terminal a-b. It is apparent that the value of R_{eq} is the same for both networks, i.e.,

$$\text{Thévenin } R_{eq} = \text{Norton } R_{eq}$$

We have just observed that it is possible to simplify a circuit using source equivalents. It is also possible to simplify a circuit by combining components of the same kind that are grouped together in the circuit. The formulas for combining several R's to a single R, several L's to a single L and several C's to a single C are found using Kirchhoff's laws (see Eq.6.1.10). Consider two inductors in series as shown in Fig. 6.7. We see that $L_{eq} = L_1 + L_2$. Combinations of circuit components are summarized in Table 6.2.

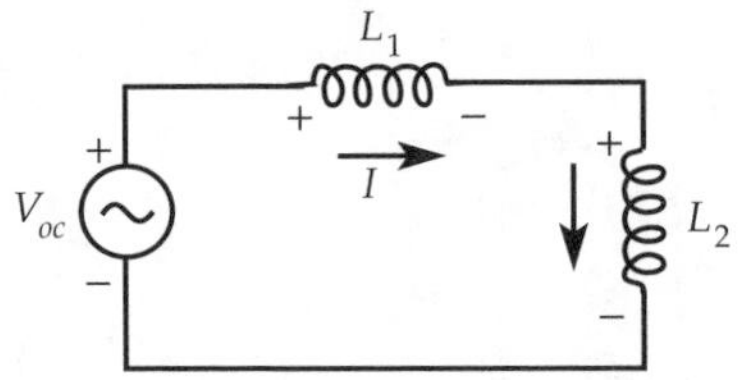

Circuit Simplification

$$V - L_1 \frac{dI}{dt} - L_2 \frac{dI}{dt} = 0$$

$$V - (L_1 + L_2) \frac{dI}{dt} = 0$$

$$V - L_{eq} \frac{dI}{dt} = 0$$

Figure 6.7 Circuit Simplification.

TABLE 6.2 Circuit Components in Series and Parallel

Component	Series	Parallel
R	$R_{eq} = R_1 + R_2 + \cdots + R_N$	$\frac{1}{R_{eq}} = \frac{1}{R_1} + \frac{1}{R_2} + \cdots + \frac{1}{R_N}$
L	$L_{eq} = L_1 + L_2 + \cdots + L_N$	$\frac{1}{L_{eq}} = \frac{1}{L_1} + \frac{1}{L_2} + \cdots + \frac{1}{L_N}$
C	$\frac{1}{C_{eq}} = \frac{1}{C_1} + \frac{1}{C_2} + \cdots + \frac{1}{C_N}$	$C_{eq} = C_1 + C_2 + \cdots + C_N$

In a DC circuit the only crucial components are resistors. Another component, the inductor, appears as a zero resistance connection (or short circuit) and a third component, a capacitor, appears as an infinite resistance, or open circuit. The three circuit components are summarized in Table 6.3.

DC Circuits

TABLE 6.3 DC Circuit Components

Component		Impedance	Current	Power	Energy Stored
Resistor	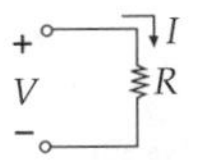	R	$I = V/R$	$P = I^2 R = V^2 / R$	None stored
Inductor	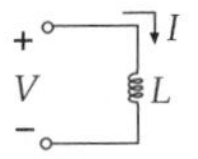	Zero (Short Circuit)	Unconstrained	None dissipated	$W_L = \frac{1}{2} L I^2$
Capacitor	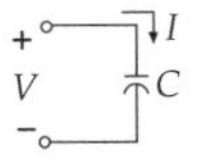	Infinite (Open Circuit)	Zero	None dissipated	$W_C = \frac{1}{2} C V^2$

Example 6.1

Compute the current in the $10\,\Omega$ resistor.

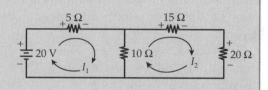

Solution. Assume loop currents I_1 and I_2. Write KVL around both meshes:

$$\sum V_{DROPS} = 0$$

Mesh 1: $-20 + 5I_1 + 10I_1 - 10I_2 = 0$

Mesh 2: $-10I_1 + 10I_2 + 15I_2 + 20I_2 = 0$

These are arranged as

$$15I_1 - 10I_2 = 20$$
$$-10I_1 + 45I_2 = 0$$

The solution is

$$I_1 = 1.57 \text{ A}, \qquad I_2 = 0.35 \text{ A}$$

The current in the $10\,\Omega$ resistor is

$$I = I_1 - I_2$$
$$= 1.57 - 0.35 = 1.22 \text{ A}$$

Example 6.2

Compute the power delivered to the $6\,\Omega$ resistor.

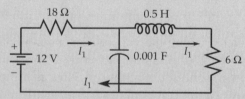

Solution. Only one current path exists since no DC current flows through a capacitor; the voltage drop across the inductor is zero. Write KVL:

$$\sum V_{DROPS} = 0$$

$$-12 + 18I_1 + 6I_1 = 0$$

$$I_1 = 0.5 \text{ A}$$

The power is then

$$P = I^2 R$$
$$= 0.5^2 \times 6 = 1.5 \text{ W}$$

Example 6.3

Calculate the Thévenin equivalent circuit between points *a* and *b* for the circuit shown.

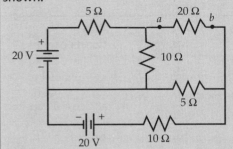

Solution. V_{eq} is the voltage across *a-b* with the 20 Ω resistor out of the circuit. R_{eq} is the resistance across *a-b* with the 20 Ω resistor removed and the 20 V sources replaced by short circuits.

The voltage V_{eq} is formed as follows:

$$I_1 = \frac{20}{15} = \frac{4}{3} \text{ A}$$

$$I_2 = \frac{20}{15} = \frac{4}{3} \text{ A}$$

$$-V_{ab} + 10I_1 - 5I_2 = 0$$

$$\therefore V_{ab} = 10 \times \frac{4}{3} - 5 \times \frac{4}{3} = 6.67$$

$$\therefore V_{eq} = 6.67 \text{ V}$$

To find R_{eq} the voltage sources are replaced by short circuits:

$$R_{eq} = \frac{1}{\frac{1}{5} + \frac{1}{10}} + \frac{1}{\frac{1}{10} + \frac{1}{5}} = 6.67 \, \Omega$$

Single phase AC circuits operate with sinusoidal signal sources and are assumed to be operating steady state, that is, all transients have long since died out. Sinusoidal currents and voltages can be represented either as trigonometric expressions or as complex numbers where the explicit time dependence has been dropped. Consider the following two notations representing a sinusoidal voltage:

Trigonometric	Complex
$V(t) = V_m \cos(\omega t + \phi)$	$V = \dfrac{V_m}{\sqrt{2}} e^{j\phi} = V_{rms} e^{j\phi}$

$$\text{(6.1.19)}$$

where V_m is the maximum voltage and $j = \sqrt{-1}$. The magnitude of the complex voltage is called the *rms value* and is given by $V_m / \sqrt{2}$ where V_m is the maximum of the sinusoidal voltage. The conversion from trigonometric to complex notation is given by the expression:

$$V(t) = \text{Re}\left[V_m e^{j\phi} e^{j\omega t}\right] = \text{Re}\left[\sqrt{2} V_{rms} e^{j\phi} e^{j\omega t}\right]$$

$$\text{(6.1.20)}$$

where "Re" means "the real part of." Once sinusoidal currents and voltages are expressed in complex notation, the solution of AC circuits becomes nearly identical to the solution of DC circuits. The difference is that inductors and capacitors

AC Circuits —Single Phase

The magnitude of the complex voltage is called the *rms value* and is given by $V_m / \sqrt{2}$ where V_m is the maximum of the sinusoidal voltage.

6·ELECTRICAL

can no longer be considered short or open circuit components; in addition, the algebra is done using complex numbers.

TABLE 6.4 AC Circuit Components

Component	Impedance (ohms)	Admittance (siemens)	Current (amperes)	Power (watts or vars)
Resistor	R	$G = \dfrac{1}{R}$	$I = \dfrac{V}{R}$	$P = I^2 R = \dfrac{V^2}{R}$ active/dissipated
Inductor	$jX_L = j\omega L$	$-jB_L = \dfrac{-j}{X_L}$	$I = \dfrac{-jV_L}{\omega L}$	$Q_L = I^2 X_L = \dfrac{V_L^2}{X_L}$ reactive/stored
Capacitor	$-jX_C = \dfrac{-j}{\omega C}$	$jB_C = \dfrac{j}{X_C}$	$I = jV_C \omega C$	$Q_C = I^2 X_C = \dfrac{V_C^2}{X_C}$ reactive/stored
R, L, C	Z	Y	$I = V/Z$	—

Table 6.4 presents the definitions and relationships between current, voltage, and power for the passive circuit components R, L, and C when used in an AC circuit. All currents and voltages in Table 6.4 and in the rest of this article are rms values.

For a series connection of components, the impedances sum to give a total impedance for the combination. There results:

Series R–L: $Z = R + jX_L = \sqrt{R^2 + X_L^2}\ \angle{\theta_L} = |Z|\ \angle{\theta_L} \quad \theta_L = \tan^{-1} x_L/R$

(6.1.21)

Series R–C: $Z = R - jX_C = \sqrt{R^2 + X_C^2}\ \angle{\theta_C} = |Z|\ \angle{\theta_C} \quad \theta_C = -\tan^{-1} x_C/R$

For a parallel connection of components, the admittances sum to give a total admittance as follows:

Parallel R–L: $Y = G - jB_L = \sqrt{G^2 + B_L^2}\ \angle{\theta_L} = |Y|\ \angle{\theta_L}$

(6.1.22)

Parallel R–C: $Y = G + jB_C = \sqrt{G^2 + B_C^2}\ \angle{\theta_C} = |Y|\ \angle{\theta_C}$

The relationship between Z and Y is always $Z = 1/Y$.

Each circuit parameter in an AC circuit can be represented by a complex number, where a subscript "r" denotes the real part, a subscript "x" denotes the imaginary part, and an asterisk denotes the complex conjugate:

$$\text{Current:} \quad I = I_r + jI_x = |I|\ \angle{\theta}$$

$$\text{Voltage:} \quad V = V_r + jV_x = |V|\ \angle{\theta}$$

(6.1.23)

$$\text{Complex Power:} \quad S = VI^* = P + jQ$$

where

$$P = \text{real dissipated power (watts)}$$

$$= \text{Re}\left[VI^*\right] = |V||I|\cos\theta \qquad\qquad \textbf{(6.1.24)}$$

$$Q = \text{reactive stored power (vars)}$$

$$= \text{Im}\left[VI^*\right] = |V||I|\sin\theta \qquad\qquad \textbf{(6.1.25)}$$

and θ in these power equations is as displayed in Fig. 6.8. The quantity $\cos\theta$ is often referred to as the *power factor, pf*. These complex quantities can be visualized using the phasor diagrams and triangles shown in Fig. 6.8.

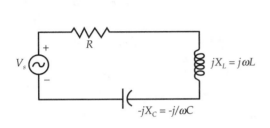

a) A simple AC circuit

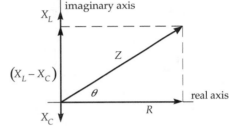

b) Impedance triangle

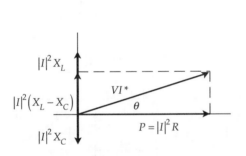

c) The power triangle

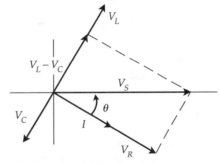

d) Current and voltage phasors

Figure 6.8 Diagrams for the simple AC circuit.

Resonance in an AC circuit occurs at that frequency at which the applied voltage and the input current are in phase, as shown in Fig. 6.9.

Resonance requires that the AC circuit have both capacitive and inductive components, i.e., energy storage components. At resonance, the energy stored in the inductor is equal to the energy stored in the capacitor, and the circuit timing is such that this energy oscillates back and forth between the inductive and capacitive components. If the circuit did not have any resistance (loss of energy) the oscillations would continue forever.

Resonance

Resonance requires that the AC circuit have both capacitive and inductive components.

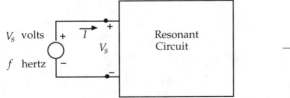

Figure 6.9 Resonance in an AC circuit.

Table 6.5 shows the simple series resonant and parallel resonant circuits along with the input impedance for each circuit. Since the input impedance must be real in order to have the input voltage and current in phase, the reactive part of the input impedance must be zero. This leads to the formulas for the resonant frequencies as shown. See Table 6.4 for the formulas to calculate I, V, and P for each component in a resonant circuit.

TABLE 6.5 Resonant Circuits

Circuit	Resonant Frequency	Impedance/Admittance
Series	$f = \dfrac{1}{2\pi\sqrt{LC}}$	$Z_{IN} = R + j\left(\omega L - \dfrac{1}{\omega C}\right)$ But $\omega L = \dfrac{1}{\omega C}$ $\therefore\ Z_{IN} = R$
Parallel	$f = \dfrac{1}{2\pi\sqrt{LC}}$	$Y_{IN} = \dfrac{1}{R} + j\left(\omega C - \dfrac{1}{\omega L}\right)$ But $\omega C = \dfrac{1}{\omega L}$ $\therefore\ Y_{IN} = \dfrac{1}{R}$

Example 6.4

Compute the power delivered to the 25 Ω resistor.

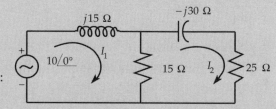

Solution. Use the KVL as follows:

$$\sum V_{DROPS} = 0$$

$$-10 + j15I_1 + 15I_1 - 15I_2 = 0$$

$$-15I_1 + 15I_2 - j30I_2 + 25I_2 = 0$$

These are written as

$$(15 + j15)I_1 - 15I_2 = 10$$

$$-15I_1 + (40 - j30)I_2 = 0$$

A simultaneous solution yields

$$I_2 = 0.179\underline{/10.3°}\,\text{A}$$

The power delivered is then

$$P = |I_2|^2 R = 0.179^2 \times 25 = 0.800\ \text{W}$$

Example 6.5

Compute the value of X_C so that I is in phase with V_S.

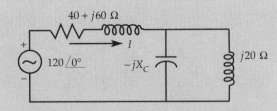

Solution. The impedance of the parallel load is

$$Z_{load} = \frac{-jX_C(j20)}{-jX_C + j20} = \frac{20X_C}{j(20 - X_C)}$$

To make I in phase with V_S, the total impedance seen by the generator must have a zero imaginary part:

$$j60 + \frac{-j20X_C}{20 - X_C} = 0$$
$$\therefore X_C = 15\,\Omega$$

Example 6.6

Compute the current I if the load dissipates 240 W of real power and −140 vars of reactive power.

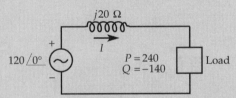

Solution. The complex power consumed by the series combination of the 20 Ω inductor and the load is VI^*. The inductor power is $Q_L = |I|^2 X_L$. The unknown load power is $S = 240 - j140$. Therefore,

$$VI^* = S + jQ_L$$

$$(120\underline{/0°})(I_r - jI_x) = j|I|^2 X_L + (240 - j140)$$

This equation can be visualized with the power triangle shown below. Rearranging the equation gives:

$$120(I_r - jI_x) = 240 + j\left[20(I_r^2 + I_x^2) - 140\right]$$

Equate real and imaginary parts:

$$\therefore 120I_r = 240 \quad \text{and} \quad -120I_x = 20(I_r^2 + I_x^2) - 140$$

The solution is, $I_r = 2$, $I_x = 0.464$, -6.464.

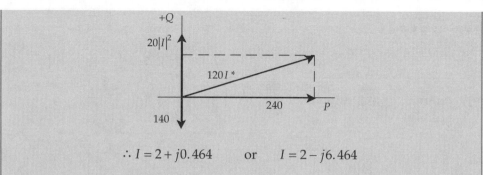

$$\therefore I = 2 + j0.464 \qquad \text{or} \qquad I = 2 - j6.464$$

Additional information would be needed to narrow the selection to one of the above answers.

The advantage of three-phase circuits is that the instantaneous power flow is uniform, and not pulsating as it is in a single-phase circuit.

Example 6.7

Compute the resonant frequency and the current through the inductor and capacitor at resonance for the circuit shown.

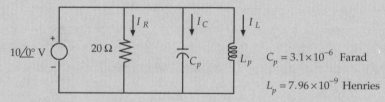

Solution. From Table 6.5 the resonant frequency is

$$f = \frac{1}{2\pi\sqrt{LC}} = \frac{1}{2\pi\sqrt{7.96 \times 10^{-9} \times 3.1 \times 10^{-6}}} = 1.013 \times 10^{6} \text{ Hz}$$

The angular frequency is $\omega = 2\pi f$. From Table 6.4 the desired currents are

$$I_C = jV\omega C = j10\left(6.36 \times 10^{6}\right) \times \left(3.1 \times 10^{-6}\right) = j197 \quad \text{or} \quad 197\underline{/90^\circ} \text{ A}$$

$$I_L = -\frac{jV}{\omega L} = -\frac{j10}{\left(6.36 \times 10^{6}\right) \times \left(7.96 \times 10^{-9}\right)} = -j197 \quad \text{or} \quad 197\underline{/-90^\circ} \text{ A}$$

AC Circuits —Three Phase

Three-phase circuits are composed of three single-phase circuits where the source voltages for each phase are 120° apart. The load impedances for three-phase circuits can be connected in either a wye (Y) connection or a delta (Δ) connection as shown in Fig. 6.10. Phasor diagrams for a typical set of source voltages are given in Fig. 6.11. One may further specify the source voltage to be either line-to-line or line-to-neutral. Figure 6.11 shows both the line-to-neutral voltages which can be used for a wye-connected load, and the line-to-line voltages which can be used for either a delta- or a wye-connected load. The advantage of three-phase circuits is that the instantaneous power flow is uniform, and not pulsating as it is in a single-phase circuit.

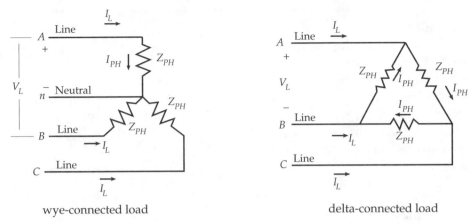

wye-connected load   delta-connected load

Figure 6.10 Load impedances.

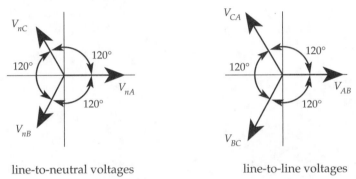

line-to-neutral voltages   line-to-line voltages

Figure 6.11 Phasor diagrams.

🔑 Where all three-phase impedances are equal, the circuits are balanced.

Kirchhoff's circuit laws apply to three-phase circuits just as they apply to all other circuits; however, it is typically not necessary to write complex sets of circuit equations to solve the simple balanced circuits being considered here. Just remember that where all three-phase impedances are equal, the circuits are balanced. The expressions used in solving balanced circuits are tabulated in Table 6.6.

TABLE 6.6 AC Circuit Expressions (Three-Phase)

Load	Current	Voltage	Power
wye load	$I_L = I_{PH} = \dfrac{V_{PH}}{Z_{PH}}$	$V_L = \sqrt{3}\,V_{PH}$	$P = 3P_{PH} = 3|V_{PH}||I_{PH}|\cos\theta$
			$= \sqrt{3}|V_L||I_L|\cos\theta$
			$Q = 3Q_{PH} = 3|V_{PH}||I_{PH}|\sin\theta$
			$= \sqrt{3}|V_L||I_L|\sin\theta$
delta load	$I_L = \sqrt{3}I_{PH}$	$V_L = V_{PH} = I_{PH}Z_{PH}$	same as above

Example 6.8

A balanced delta-connected load is driven from a 208-volt line to a line system as shown. Calculate the line current I_A.

Solution. Sketch the phasor diagram to assist in the calculations. The currents are calculated as follows:

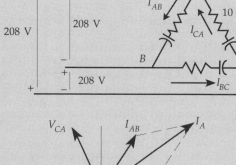

$$I_{AB} = \frac{V_{AB}}{10 - j20} = \frac{208 \underline{/0^\circ}}{10 - j20} = 9.30 \underline{/63.4}$$

$$\therefore I_{CA} = 9.30 \underline{/183.4^\circ}$$

Kirchhoff's Current Law allows us find the line current as

$$I_A = I_{AB} - I_{CA}$$

$$= 9.30 \underline{/63.4^\circ} - 9.30 \underline{/183.4^\circ}$$

$$= 4.17 + j8.32 - (-9.28 - j0.55) = 13.45 + j8.87 = 16.11 \underline{/33.41^\circ} \text{ A}$$

We could have found the line current magnitude as follows:

$$I_{PH} = \frac{V_{PH}}{Z_{PH}} = \frac{208}{\sqrt{10^2 + 20^2}} = 9.30 \text{ A}$$

$$\therefore I_L = \sqrt{3} I_{PH} = \sqrt{3} \times 9.30 = 16.11 \text{ A}$$

Example 6.9

A balanced Y-connected load is attached to a 3 ϕ four-wire line with a 120 V line to neutral voltages as shown. Sketch a phasor diagram showing all line and phase currents and voltages. Assume V_{nA} to be at zero phase angle.

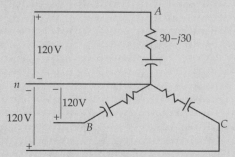

Solution. The phase voltages are expressed as

$$V_{nA} = 120 \underline{/0^\circ} \quad V_{nB} = 120 \underline{/-120^\circ} \quad V_{nC} = 120 \underline{/120^\circ}$$

The line voltages are then,

$$V_{AB} = V_{An} + V_{nB} = 208 \underline{/-150°}$$

$$V_{BC} = V_{Bn} + V_{nC} = 208 \underline{/90°}$$

$$V_{CA} = V_{Cn} + V_{nA} = 208 \underline{/-30°}$$

The line currents and phase currents are equal so that

$$I_A = \frac{V_{nA}}{Z_{PH}} = \frac{120 \underline{/0°}}{30 - j30} = 2.83 \underline{/45°}$$

$$I_B = 2.83 \underline{/-75°} \quad I_C = 2.83 \underline{/165}$$

The phasor diagram is sketched.

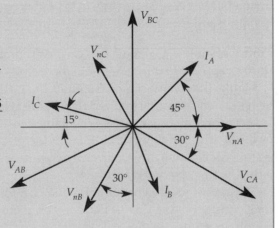

Example 6.10

A balanced Y-connected load is connected to a three-phase source as shown. Determine the power delivered to the load.

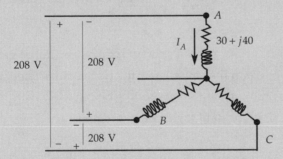

Solution. First calculate the phase voltage V_{PH}:

$$V_{PH} = \frac{V_L}{\sqrt{3}} = V_{nA} = \frac{208 \underline{/150°}}{\sqrt{3}} = 120 \underline{/150°} \text{ V}$$

Note: If V_{AB} is assumed to be at 0°, then V_{nA} is at −150° (see Example 6.9). The phase current is

$$I_{PH} = \frac{V_{PH}}{Z_{PH}} = \frac{120 \underline{/150°}}{50 \underline{/53.1°}} = 2.4 \underline{/96.9°} \text{ A}$$

The power dissipated in phase *A* is,

$$P_{PH} = |V_{PH}||I_{PH}|\cos\theta$$

$$= 120 \times 2.40 \times \cos 53.1° = 172.9 \text{ W}$$

$$P_{\text{total}} = 3 \times 172.9 = 519 \text{ W}$$

This could also have been computed as

$$P_{\text{total}} = \sqrt{3}|V_L||I_L|\cos\theta$$

$$= \sqrt{3} \times 208 \times 2.40 \cos 53.1° = 519 \text{ W}$$

DC Transients

🔑 If only a single inductor or a single capacitor is contained in a circuit, the current will either grow or decay exponentially.

Transients in a DC circuit can exist any time a sudden change is made in the sources applied to the circuit or in the circuit configuration.

Unlike the steady state solution of DC circuits, transient solutions require the inclusion of capacitive and inductive effects as functions of time. If only a single inductor or a single capacitor is contained in a circuit, the current will either grow or decay exponentially. If both an inductor and a capacitor are included in the circuit, oscillations can occur. Only circuits with a single capacitor and/or single inductor are considered here.

For exponentially changing functions, a time constant (T) can be defined. The time constant is the time it takes to complete 63.2% of the change that will ultimately be made (see Fig. 6.12). This is a practical number since in a time corresponding to four or five time constants most transients have disappeared from a circuit.

Several general expressions can be written for the voltage and current in a DC transient circuit. Two of these are

$$I(t) = I_\infty + (I_0 - I_\infty)e^{-t/T}$$

$$V(t) = V_\infty + (V_0 - V_\infty)e^{-t/T}$$

(6.1.26)

where

I_0 and V_0	are at the instant of a sudden change, i.e., initial values
I_∞ and V_∞	will exist in the circuit after the transient has died away (let $t = \infty$)
$T = L/R$	the time constant for series R–L circuit
$T = RC$	the time constant for series R–C circuit

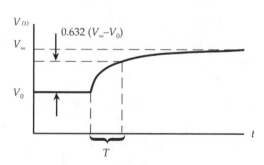

Figure 6.12 A DC transient.

Example 6.11

The switch is closed at $t = 0$. Determine the current in the circuit at $t = 2T$, two time constants after the switch is closed.

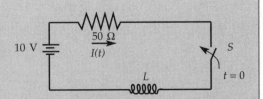

Solution. The general expression for the transient current in a series _R-L_ or _R-C_ circuit is

$$I(t) = I_\infty + (I_0 - I_\infty)e^{-t/T}$$

For the case being considered

$$I_0 = 0, \quad I_\infty = \frac{V}{R} = \frac{10}{50} = 0.2$$

Thus

$$I(2T) = 0.2 - 0.2e^{-2} = 0.173 \text{ A}$$

6.2 Static Electric Fields

Electric fields exist any time an electric charge is present in the region. The presence of an electric field causes many things to happen. It produces forces on stationary charges, forces on charges moving in conductors and, therefore, forces on the conductors themselves. The forces on the charges in a conductor also cause the motion of those charges to produce current. Forces on the charges in an atom can cause the atom to come apart, creating a material breakdown. In addition to their usefulness in calculating forces, electric field quantities can be used to calculate stored energy and capacitance for any shape of electrodes on which the original charge may exist, as well as the potential difference between those electrodes. Here we will examine only the most basic concepts of electric field theory and attempt to do so with minimal use of mathematics.

The presence of an electric field produces forces on the conductors

The two most basic field quantities are _electric field intensity_ **E** (newtons/coulomb or volts/meter) and _electric flux density_ **D** (coulombs/meter²). These are defined as follows:

$$\mathbf{E} = \mathbf{F}/Q \tag{6.2.1}$$
$$E = dV/dL$$

For the derivative definition, **E** is in the direction of the maximum rate of change. The electric flux density is a vector quantity whose magnitude is the maximum value of the derivative

$$D = dQ/dA \tag{6.2.2}$$

and **D** is perpendicular to the surface dA.

The two basic field quantities are related to each other by

$$E = D/\varepsilon \tag{6.2.3}$$

where $\varepsilon = \varepsilon_0 \varepsilon_r$, $\varepsilon_0 = 8.85 \times 10^{-12}$ F/m (the permittivity of free space). The *relative permittivity* ε_r depends on the material and will be specified in a particular problem. The field quantities for some simple geometries are especially useful. They follow:

Point of charge Q (C): $\qquad\qquad D = \dfrac{Q}{4\pi r^2} \qquad E = \dfrac{Q}{4\pi\varepsilon r^2}$ **(6.2.4)**

with vectors **D** and **E** directed radially away from the point charge.

Uniform line of charge ρ_L (C/m): $D = \dfrac{\rho_L}{2\pi r} \qquad E = \dfrac{\rho_L}{2\pi\varepsilon r}$ **(6.2.5)**

with vectors **D** and **E** normal to the line of charge.

Uniform sheet of charge $\rho_s \left(\text{C}/\text{m}^2 \right)$: $D = \dfrac{\rho_s}{2} \qquad E = \dfrac{\rho_s}{2\varepsilon}$ **(6.2.6)**

with vectors **D** and **E** directed normally away from the plane.

If D and E are not known they must be calculated (from the known voltages or charges) using Eqs. 6.2.1 and 6.2.2. Once D and E are known they can be used to calculate the following quantities:

Voltage: $\qquad\qquad\qquad\qquad V = \int \mathbf{E} \cdot d\mathbf{L}$ **(6.2.7)**

Charge: $\qquad\qquad\qquad\qquad Q = \oiint \mathbf{D} \cdot d\mathbf{S}$ **(6.2.8)**

Stored electrical energy: $\qquad W_E = \dfrac{1}{2}\iiint \mathbf{D} \cdot \mathbf{E}\, dv = \dfrac{1}{2}CV^2$ **(6.2.9)**

Capacitance: $\qquad\qquad\quad C = Q/V = 2W_E \big/ V^2$ **(6.2.10)**

Current: $\qquad\qquad\qquad\quad I = \iint \sigma \mathbf{E} \cdot d\mathbf{S}$ **(6.2.11)**

Force on a charge Q: $\qquad\quad \mathbf{F} = Q\mathbf{E}$ **(6.2.12)**

The following examples illustrate the use of several of the above relationships.

The *relative permittivity* ε_r depends on the material.

Example 6.12

A point charge of $Q = 5 \times 10^{-9}$ coulombs is located in rectangular coordinates at (1, 3, 5) and a line charge $\rho_L = 1.5 \times 10^{-9}$ coulomb/m is located parallel to the *x*-axis at $y = 3$ and $z = 0$. Find the point where the net electric field is zero.

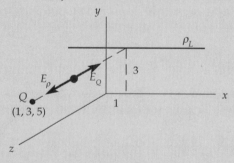

Solution. The field intensity from the line charge is

$$E_L = \frac{\rho_L}{2\pi\varepsilon_0 r}$$

The field intensity from the point charge is

$$E_Q = \frac{Q}{4\pi\varepsilon_0 r^2}$$

Since the E fields from the sources are in opposite directions, we simply equate the above two expressions, letting $r = z$ in the expression for E_L:

$$\frac{1.5 \times 10^{-9}}{2\pi z \varepsilon_0} = \frac{5 \times 10^{-9}}{4\pi\varepsilon_0 (5-z)^2}$$

The quadratic $3z^2 - 35z + 75 = 0$ results. The appropriate root is $z = 2.829$ m.

Example 6.13

Concentric coaxial cylinders 50 cm long are separated by air with permittivity ε_0. If the radius of the inner conductor is 0.2 cm and the inner radius of the outer conductor is 1.0 cm, compute the capacitance per meter between the cylinders.

Solution. Assume a charge ρ_L on the inner conductor, $-\rho_L$ on the outer conductor, and compute the potential difference V. Combining Eqs. 6.2.5 and 6.2.7 we have the voltage on the outer conductor:

$$V = \int_{0.2}^{1.0} \mathbf{E} \cdot d\mathbf{L} = \int_{0.2}^{1.0} \frac{\rho_L}{2\pi r \varepsilon_0} dr$$

$$= \frac{\rho_L}{2\pi\varepsilon_0} \ln \frac{1.0}{0.2}$$

To find the capacitance per meter between the cylinders we use Eq. 6.2.10, replace Q with ρ_L, and obtain

$$C = \frac{\rho_L}{V} = \frac{2\pi\varepsilon_0}{\ln 5}$$

$$= \frac{2\pi \times 8.85 \times 10^{-12}}{\ln 5} = 34.55 \times 10^{-12} \text{ F/m}$$

Example 6.14

The voltage distribution between two coaxial cylinders is given by

$$V = 50 \ln \frac{2.5}{r} \text{ volts}$$

where r varies from 0.5 cm to 2.5 cm. At what radius r between the cylinders does the largest magnitude of the E field exist?

Solution. The E field is given by

$$E = \frac{dV}{dr}$$

$$= 50 \frac{1}{2.5/r} \left(-\frac{2.5}{r^2} \right) = -\frac{50}{r}$$

By observation the largest magnitude of the E field occurs at the minimum value of r, i.e., $r = 0.5$ cm.

6.3 Static Magnetic Fields

Magnetic Fields

Magnetic fields exist any time there is a moving charge or electric current in the region. Just as electric fields interact with charges, magnetic fields interact with moving charges or currents. A current-carrying conductor in a magnetic field will have a force exerted on it due to its presence in that magnetic field. In addition to their usefulness in calculating forces, magnetic field quantities can be used to calculate energy stored in a magnetic field and inductance for any configuration of current-carrying conductors.

The two most basic magnetic field quantities are *magnetic field intensity* **H** (amperes/meter) and *magnetic flux density* **B** (webers/meter^2 or tesla). Magnetic field intensity is defined by

$$H = dI/dL \tag{6.3.1}$$

> 🔑 A current-carrying conductor in a magnetic field will have a force exerted on it due to its presence in that magnetic field.
>
> • The relationship between *B* and *H* depends on the material in which the field exists through a material parameter called the *permeability*.

where **H** is in the direction of the maximum rate of change. Magnetic flux density is defined by

$$B = F/IL \tag{6.3.2}$$

where **B** is perpendicular to both **F** and *I***L**. **F** is the force on the current element *I***L** residing in a field with flux density **B**. The relationship between B and H depends on the material in which the field exists through a material parameter called the *permeability*, μ. The relationship is

$$H = B/\mu \tag{6.3.3}$$

where $\mu = \mu_0 \mu_r$, $\mu_0 = 4\pi \times 10^{-7}$ H/m (the permeability of free space). The *relative permeability* μ_r depends on the material and will be specified in a particular problem.

The expression for the magnetic field produced by a straight conductor carrying a current I is especially useful. It is

$$B = \frac{\mu I}{4\pi r}\left(\sin\theta_1 + \sin\theta_2\right) \tag{6.3.4}$$

where **B** is in a direction perpendicular to a plane containing the point and the straight wire, and where r is the perpendicular distance shown (see fig. 6.13). A general expression, called *Ampere's Rule*, for computing the field B given a known current distribution is

$$\mathbf{B} = \frac{\mu}{4\pi}\int \frac{I d\mathbf{L} \times \mathbf{a}_R}{R^2} \tag{6.3.5}$$

The parameters for Eq. 6.3.5 are defined in Fig. 6.14; $\mathbf{a}_R$ is a unit vector. Once B is known, the energy W_H stored in the magnetic field of an inductor can be found using

$$W_H = \frac{1}{2}\int \mathbf{B}\cdot\mathbf{H}\,d\mathcal{V}$$
$$= \frac{1}{2}LI^2 \tag{6.3.6}$$

where I is the current producing the field **B**. Knowing **B**, the total force on a current-carrying conductor in the field can be computed using

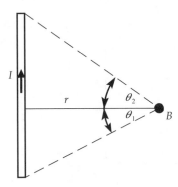

Figure 6.13 Magnetic field due to a straight conductor.

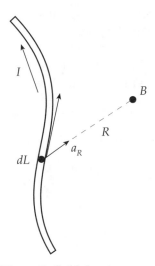

Figure 6.14 Magnetic field due to a curved conductor.

$$\mathbf{F} = I\mathbf{L} \times \mathbf{B} \qquad\qquad \textbf{(6.3.7)}$$

where $\mathbf{L}$ is the length vector of the conductor.

The total *magnetic flux* ψ_m passing through an area can be found once the flux density $\mathbf{B}$ is known:

$$\psi_m = \iint_{area} \mathbf{B} \cdot d\mathbf{A} \qquad\qquad \textbf{(6.3.8)}$$

If $\mathbf{B}$ is constant this reduces to

$$\psi_m = B\,A \qquad\qquad \textbf{(6.3.9)}$$

where A is the area being considered.

Magnetic Circuits

A magnetic circuit is formed when a magnetic field is confined inside a closed circuit of magnetic material. If one recognizes the analogies, the solution of a magnetic circuit is similar to the solution of an electric circuit. Figure 6.15 shows a simple magnetic circuit along with an analogous electric circuit. The equation similar to Kirchhoff's voltage law is

$$NI = HL \qquad\qquad \textbf{(6.3.10)}$$

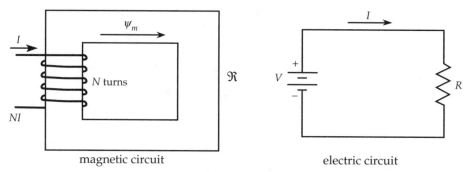

Figure 6.15 A magnetic circuit with its analogous electric circuit.

The magnetic flux in the magnetic circuit is similar to the current *I* in the electric circuit.

• The primary difference between the electric circuit and the magnetic circuit is that *R* is linear whereas $\Re$ is nonlinear.

NI is the *mmf* due to the current (*I*) in the coil and is similar to the *emf* of the battery in the electric circuit. *HL* is the magnetic potential drop in the magnetic circuit and is similar to the *IR* voltage drop in the electric circuit. The magnetic flux ψ_m, measured in webers, in the magnetic circuit is similar to the current *I* in the electric circuit and is related to the constant flux density *B* by

$$\psi_m = BA \tag{6.3.11}$$

where *A* is the cross sectional area. Using Eqs. 6.3.3 and 6.3.8 this can be put in the form

$$\psi_m = \frac{\mu NIA}{L} = \frac{NI}{\Re} \tag{6.3.12}$$

where we have used

$$\Re = \frac{L}{\mu A} \tag{6.3.13}$$

The quantity $\Re$ is called the *reluctance* of the magnetic circuit and is similar to the resistance of the electric circuit. The primary difference between the electric circuit and the magnetic circuit is that *R* is linear whereas $\Re$ is nonlinear. This means that the solution of a magnetic circuit is best done graphically. An electric current analogy can only be used when $\Re$ is assumed to be linear over the range of flux through which the circuit operates.

Induced Voltages

Time varying magnetic fields will induce voltages in a conductor (see Fig. 6.16) according to Faraday's law:

$$V(t) = N\frac{d\psi_m(t)}{dt} \qquad \text{volts} = \frac{\text{webers}}{\text{seconds}} \tag{6.3.14}$$

where $\psi_m(t)$ is the total magnetic flux "linking" the conductor, and *N* is the number of turns on the coil.

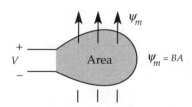

Figure 6.16 Induced voltage due to a magnetic field.

Transformers

A transformer is a magnetic circuit that has two coils or windings wound on it. A typical transformer is shown in Fig. 6.17. The rate of change of magnetic flux is the same in both coils:

$$V_1(t) = N_1 \frac{d\psi_m}{dt} \qquad V_2(t) = N_2 \frac{d\psi_m}{dt} \qquad \text{(6.3.15)}$$

resulting in

$$\frac{V_1}{N_1} = \frac{V_2}{N_2} \qquad \text{(6.3.16)}$$

This leads to the expression for the voltage ratio of the transformer:

$$\frac{V_1}{V_2} = \frac{N_1}{N_2} = a \qquad \text{(6.3.17)}$$

where a is the transformer turns ratio. A current ratio can be found knowing that the coil ampere-turns of the input coil are opposed by equal ampere-turns in the output coil:

$$N_1 I_1 = N_2 I_2 \qquad \text{or} \qquad \frac{I_1}{I_2} = \frac{N_2}{N_1} \qquad \text{(6.3.18)}$$

This leads to the impedance transformation ratio of the transformer:

$$\frac{V_1}{I_1} = \frac{\dfrac{N_1}{N_2} V_2}{\dfrac{N_2}{N_1} I_2} \qquad \text{or} \qquad \frac{Z_1}{Z_2} = \left(\frac{N_1}{N_2}\right)^2 \qquad \text{(6.3.19)}$$

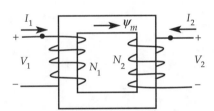

Figure 6.17 A transformer.

Example 6.15

Compute the value of the magnetic flux density at the point (1, –1) in the figure shown.

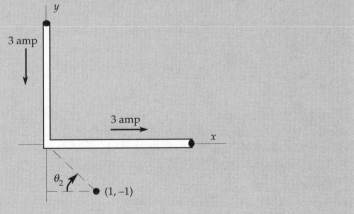

Solution. The field from a straight wire is given by

$$\mathbf{B} = \frac{\mu I}{4\pi r}\left(\sin\theta_1 + \sin\theta_2\right)\mathbf{a_R}$$

For the length along the y-axis,

$$\mathbf{B} = \frac{3\mu}{4\pi \times 1}\left(\sin 90° - \sin 45°\right)\mathbf{z}$$

$$= \frac{3\mu}{4\pi}\left(1 - \frac{1}{\sqrt{2}}\right)\mathbf{z}$$

For the length along the *x*-axis,

$$\mathbf{B} = \frac{3\mu}{4\pi \times 1}\left(\sin 90° + \sin 45°\right)(-\mathbf{z})$$

$$= -\frac{3\mu}{4\pi}\left(1 + \frac{1}{\sqrt{2}}\right)\mathbf{z}$$

Adding:

$$\mathbf{B}_{total} = -\frac{3\mu}{2\pi\sqrt{2}}\mathbf{z} \quad \text{webers}/\text{m}^2$$

Example 6.16

Two parallel conductors each carry 50 amperes, but in opposite directions. If the conductors are one meter apart, compute the force in newtons per meter on either conductor.

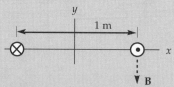

Solution. First, it is necessary to compute the field *B* that one conductor produces at the location of the other conductor; it is, using μ_0 for air,

$$B = \frac{\mu_0 I}{2\pi r}$$

$$= \frac{4\pi \times 10^{-7} \times 50}{2\pi \times 1} = 10^{-5} \quad \text{Wb/m}$$

If the wires are aligned parallel to the *z*-axis as shown, then $\mathbf{B} = -10^{-5}\mathbf{y}$ where $\mathbf{y}$ is a unit vector in the *y*-direction. This is the field at the right conductor due to the current in the left conductor. Then, using Eq. 6.3.7 there results

$$\mathbf{F} = I L \times \mathbf{B}$$

$$50(1)\mathbf{z} \times \left(-10^{-5}\mathbf{y}\right) = 50 \times 10^{-5}\mathbf{x} \quad \text{N}$$

Note that the conductors repel one another.

Example 6.17

A magnetization curve for the cast steel of an inductor core is shown. The magnetic flux in the steel is $\psi_m = 8 \times 10^{-5}$ Wb. Find the current I.

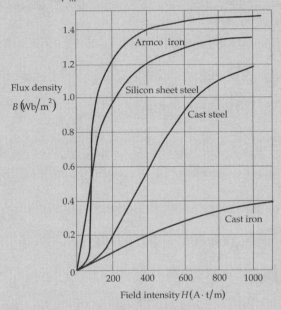

Flux density $B \, (\text{Wb}/\text{m}^2)$

Field intensity $H \, (\text{A} \cdot \text{t/m})$

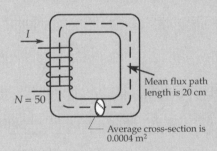

I

$N = 50$

Mean flux path length is 20 cm

Average cross-section is 0.0004 m²

Solution. The flux density B is

$$B = \frac{\psi_m}{A}$$

$$= \frac{8 \times 10^{-5}}{0.0004} = 0.2 \text{ tesla}$$

Using the appropriate curve we find H to be

$$H = 200 \ \text{A} \cdot \text{turns/m}$$

Using Equation 6.3.10, the current is found to be

$$I = \frac{HL}{N}$$

$$= \frac{200 \times 0.2}{50} = 0.8 \text{ A}$$

Example 6.18

A rectangular coil of wire with 100 turns is placed next to a long straight conductor carrying a 60 hertz sinusoidal current with an *rms* value of 25 amperes. What is the *rms* voltage induced in the coil?

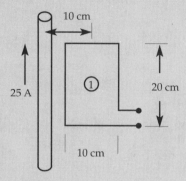

$$B = \frac{\mu I}{2\pi r} = \frac{\mu}{2\pi \times 0.1}\sqrt{2} \times 25\sin(2\pi 60t) \quad \text{webers} / \text{m}^2$$

$$\psi_m = BA = \frac{\mu}{2\pi \times 0.1}\sqrt{2} \times 25 \times 0.1 \times 0.2\sin(2\pi 60t)$$

$$V = N\frac{d\psi_m}{dt} = 100\frac{\mu}{2\pi}\sqrt{2} \times 5(2\pi 60)\cos(2\pi 60t)$$

$$= \sqrt{2}\mu\, 30\,000\cos(2\pi 60t) \text{ volts}$$

$$\therefore \quad V_{rms} = 30\,000\mu$$

Since we know that $\mu = 4\pi \times 10^{-7}$ we have

$$V_{rms} = 12\pi \times 10^{-3} \text{ volts} = 37.7 \text{ millivolts}$$

Example 6.19

A transformer with a turns ratio of 100 has a 50-ohm resistor connected across the output. What is the resistance observed at the input?

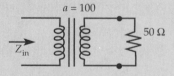

$$a = \frac{N_1}{N_2} = 100$$

We then have

$$Z_1 = \left(\frac{N_1}{N_2}\right)^2 Z_2$$

$$= 100^2 \times 50 = 50 \times 10^4 = 500 \text{ k}\Omega$$

6.4 Electronics

Electronics is the study of circuits which are used to process electrical signals (voltages or currents) which contain information. It involves the use of both passive circuit components—which have been previously discussed—as well as active and/or nonlinear circuit components, which have not yet been discussed in the review.

This review of electronics will include simple diodes and operational amplifiers. Diodes are non-linear devices which are used to build circuits which can be used to integrate and differentiate signals, sum signals together, and filter portions of signals out, as well as amplify signals.

The forward and reverse characteristics of an actual diode are shown in Fig. 6.18 along with the characteristics of an ideal diode. An ideal diode has zero current flow in the reverse direction and zero voltage drop across the diode when current is flowing in the forward direction. The analysis of diode circuits is greatly simplified when ideal diodes are assumed. Table 6.7 gives the characteristics of some simple diode circuits, assuming that they are ideal.

Diodes

An ideal diode has zero current flow in the reverse direction and zero voltage drop across the diode when current is flowing in the forward direction.
• *Gain* is defined as the ratio of the output voltage to the input voltage.

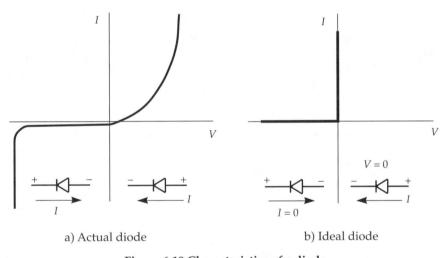

a) Actual diode   b) Ideal diode

Figure 6.18 Characteristics of a diode.

The symbolic representation of an operational amplifier is shown in Fig. 6.19. The OP-AMP, as it is often called, has two inputs. One is marked with a "+" sign and is called the non-inverting input, which means that the output is of the same polarity as the input. If the input is positive with respect to ground, then the output is also positive. The other input is marked with a "–" and is called the inverting input, which means that the output is opposite in polarity to the input with respect to ground.

The most important feature of the OP-AMP is the extremely high gain A that it possesses. *Gain* is defined as the ratio of the output voltage to the input voltage. With an extremely high gain it only requires a very, very small input signal to realize a finite output signal. The input current is, in fact, so small that it may safely

Operational Amplifiers

6•ELECTRICAL

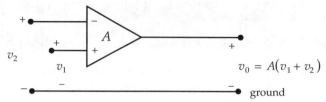

Figure 6.19 An operational amplifier.

be assumed to be zero. In the analysis of OP-AMP circuits the input current to either of the input ports is assumed to be zero and the two inputs are assumed to be at the same voltage. Normally, the non-inverting input is tied to ground, so the inverting input is assumed to be at ground potential also.

TABLE 6.7 Some Simple Diode Circuits

	Input v_{in}	Circuit	Output v_O
half-wave rectifier			$V_{DC} = V_m/\pi$
bridge rectifier			$V_{DC} = 2V_m/\pi$
peak clipping			

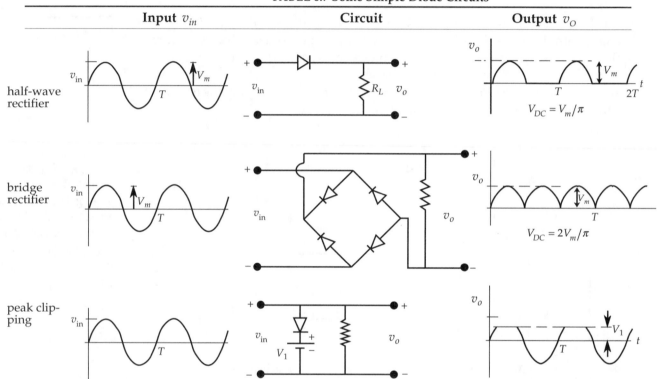

The typical circuit for an OP-AMP is shown in Fig. 6.20. It has an input impedance Z_i connected in series with the inverting input and a feedback impedance Z_f connected from the output back to the inverting input. The ratio of the output voltage to the input voltage for this circuit configuration is also given in the figure.

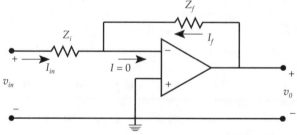

$$I_{in} + I_f = 0$$

$$\frac{v_{in}}{Z_i} + \frac{v_o}{Z_f} = 0$$

$$\therefore \quad \frac{v_o}{v_{in}} = -\frac{Z_f}{Z_i}$$

Figure 6.20 A typical OP-AMP circuit.

TABLE 6.8 Operational Amplifier Functions

Name	Circuit	Output
Amplifier		For arbitrary time functions $$v_o(t) = -\frac{R_f}{R_i} v_i(t)$$ For periodic functions $$V_o = -\frac{R_f}{R_i} V_i$$
Summer		$$v_o = -\frac{R_f}{R_1} v_{i1} - \frac{R_f}{R_2} v_{i2}$$ $$V_o = -\frac{R_f}{R_1} V_{i1} - \frac{R_f}{R_2} V_{i2}$$
Integrator		$$v_o = -\frac{1}{R_i C} \int v_i dt$$ $$V_o = \frac{j}{\omega R_i C} V_i$$
Differentiator		$$v_o = -\frac{L}{R_i} \frac{dv_i}{dt}$$ $$V_o = -j\frac{\omega L}{R_i} V_i$$
Low Pass Filter		For sinusoidal functions $$V_o = -\frac{R_f}{R_i\left(1 + j\omega R_f C\right)} V_i$$

The impedances Z_i and Z_f can be varied, as indicated in Table 6.8, to cause the OP-AMP to perform many different functions. In this table, the lower case v's represent arbitrary functions of time and the upper case V's represent *rms* values of sinusoidal voltages.

Example 6.20

A half-wave rectifier circuit uses an ideal diode. If the desired DC load voltage is 9 V, what is the *rms* value of the source?

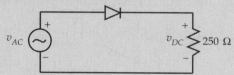

Solution. The time-dependent voltages v_{AC} and v_{DC} appear as sketched below.

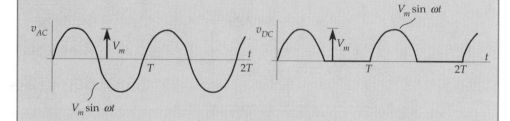

The average, or DC value, of the rectified voltage is given by the integral

$$V_{DC} = \frac{1}{T}\int_0^T v_{DC}(t)\,dt = \frac{V_m}{\pi}$$

$$\therefore V_m = \pi V_{DC} = 9\pi \ \text{volts}$$

The required *rms* value of the source is therefore

$$V_{rms} = \frac{V_m}{\sqrt{2}} = \frac{9\pi}{\sqrt{2}} = 19.99 \ \text{volts}$$

Example 6.21

Determine the gain of the OP-AMP circuit shown.

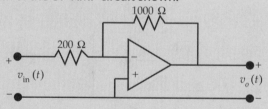

Solution. The gain expression for an OP-AMP circuit is
$$A = -Z_f/Z_i = -R_f/R_i$$

so the OP-AMP gain is
$$A = -1000/200 = -5$$

Example 6.22

A square wave with extrema ± 1 is input to the OP-AMP circuit shown. Sketch $v_0(t)$.

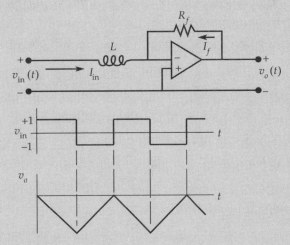

Solution. The KCL allows us to write

$$I_{in} + I_f = 0$$

But we know that

$$I_{in} = \frac{1}{L} \int v_{in} dt \qquad I_f = \frac{v_0}{R_f}$$

Hence,

$$\frac{1}{L} \int v_{in} dt + \frac{v_0}{R_f} = 0$$

or

$$v_0(t) = -\frac{R_f}{L} \int v_{in} dt$$

The circuit shown is an integrator, so the output voltage is proportional to the integral of the input voltage.

Practice Problems

(If you attempt only a few, select those with a star.)

DC Circuits

*6.1 For the circuit below, with voltages' polarities as shown, KVL in equation form is

a) $v_1 + v_2 + v_3 - v_4 + v_5 = 0$

b) $-v_1 + v_2 + v_3 - v_4 + v_5 = 0$

c) $v_1 + v_2 - v_3 - v_4 + v_5 = 0$

d) $-v_1 - v_2 - v_3 + v_4 + v_5 = 0$

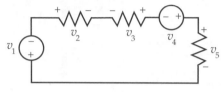

6.2 Find I_1 in amps.

a) 12

b) 15

c) 18

d) 21

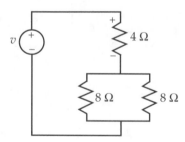

*6.3 Find the magnitude and sign of the power, in watts, absorbed by the circuit element in the box.

a) –20

b) –8

c) 8

d) 12

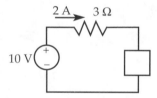

*6.4 For the circuit shown, the voltage across the 4 ohm resistor is, with $v = 1$ V

a) 1/4

b) 1/2

c) 2/3

d) 2

6.5 The total conductance, in mhos, in the circuit shown below is

a) 1/5

b) 1/2

c) 2

d) 5

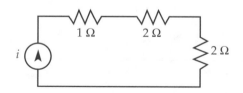

6.6   The voltage across the 5 ohm
        resistor in the circuit shown is
        a) 1.0
        b) 2.5
        c) 3.0
        d) 5.83

6.7   The power delivered to the
        5 ohm resistor is
        a) 1.5
        b) 2.15
        c) 2.85
        d) 3.2

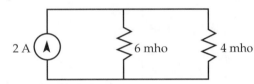

6.8   The power, in watts, absorbed by the 6 mho conductance in the circuit below is
        a) −0.24
        b) 0.2
        c) 0.24
        d) 0.48

*6.9   The equivalent resistance, in ohms, between points *a* and *b* in the circuit below is
        a) 3
        b) 5
        c) 7
        d) 8

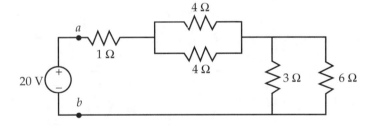

6.10   The voltage V_2 is
        a) 6.4
        b) 4.0
        c) 2.0
        d) 5.6

6.11   Find I_1 in amperes.
        a) 4.0
        b) 2.0
        c) 4.11
        d) 2.11

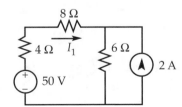

AC Circuits
—Single Phase

*6.12 $(2 + j2)(3 - j4)$ is most nearly

    a) $6.0\underline{/-21.8°}$ b) $14.1\underline{/-21.8°}$ c) $14.1\underline{/-8.1°}$ d) $28.0\underline{/-8.1°}$

*6.13 The following sinusoid is displayed on an oscilloscope. The RMS voltage and the radian frequency are most nearly

    a) 1, 8.33

    b) 0.7071, 52.36

    c) 1.4142, 52.36

    d) 2, 8.33

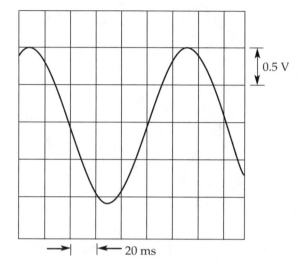

6.14 Find I_2 in amperes.

    a) $0.29 + j0.68$

    b) $-0.12 + j0.69$

    c) $-0.82 - j0.37$

    d) $1 - j2$

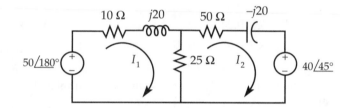

*6.15 Calculate the magnitude of the node voltage V_{AB}.

    a) 85.1

    b) 77.2

    c) 68.8

    d) 92.2

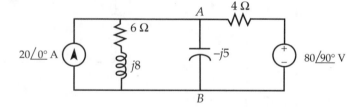

6.16 The DC (average) current through the $+j\,40$ ohm inductor is

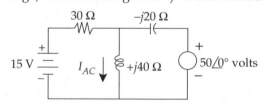

    a) 0.3 A   b) 0.5 A   c) 0.8 A   d) 1.2 A

6.17 The rms current through the $+j\,40$ ohm inductor of Problem 6.16 is

    a) 0.5 A   b) 0.93 A   c) 1.58 A   d) 3.04 A

6.18   The current through the capacitor is

   a) 0.21 A
   b) 0.57 A
   c) 1.0 A
   d) 4.85 A

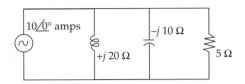

6.19   The voltage across the 5-ohm resistor of Problem 6.18 is

   a) 0.50 V
   b) 1.61 V
   c) 2.06 V
   d) 48.5 V

6.20   The peak value of $V(t)$ in the circuit shown is approximately

   a) 2.0
   b) 3.68
   c) 25.9
   d) 50.0

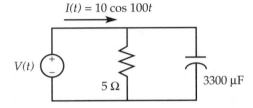

*6.21 The power factor of the circuit shown is most nearly

   a) 0.5
   b) 0.6
   c) 0.7
   d) 0.8

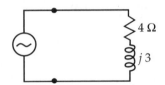

6.22   What value of ω will make the *rms* of $|I_S|$ a minimum in the circuit shown?

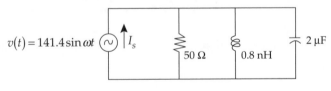

   a) 2×10^6 b) 8×10^6 c) 25×10^6 d) 50×10^6

6.23   What is the *rms* magnitude of the minimum source current in the circuit of Problem 6.22?

   a) 1.0   b) 1.5   c) 2.0   d) 2.5

6.24   For the circuit shown, the value of capacitance C that will give a power factor of 1.0 is most nearly

   a) 0.0173
   b) 0.0519
   c) 0.0938
   d) 0.0393

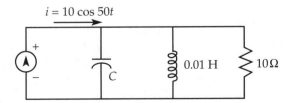

6.25 For maximum power dissipation in the load of the circuit shown, R (in ohms) and L (in milli-henries) should be chosen as

a) 26, 50

b) 20, 100

c) 20, 50

d) 25, 100

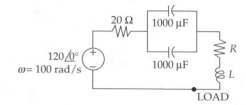

AC Circuits —Three Phase

*6.26 Calculate the total average power, in watts, dissipated in the balanced three phase load.

a) 2507

b) 5276

c) 3456

d) 978

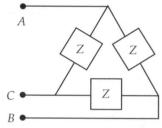

$Z = 10 + j5$

$V_{AC} = 120$ V

6.27 The value of the line current I_{aA} in the balanced Y-connected system shown is most nearly

a) $20.6 \underline{/30°}$

b) $35.3 \underline{/-45°}$

c) $35.3 \underline{/45°}$

d) $15.1 \underline{/-30°}$

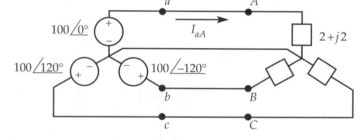

*6.28 For a balanced Y-connected system identify the incorrect statement.

a) $V_{PH} = V_L / \sqrt{3}$

b) $I_L = I_{PH}$

c) $P_{total} = 3 P_{PH}$

d) All phase impedances are equal.

6.29 A 100 µF capacitor has $I_C(t)$. The capacitor voltage $V_c(t)$ at $t = 2.5$ seconds $\left(V(0) = 1.0 \text{ V} \right)$ is most nearly

a) –24

b) –25

c) 25

d) 26

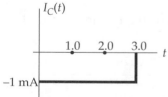

6.30   The voltage across a 10 μF capacitor is $50t^2$ V. The time, in seconds, it will take to store 200 J of energy is most nearly

a) 0.15   b) 0.21   c) 1.38   d) 11.25

*6.31   The value of the voltage across C at $t = 30 \times 10^{-6}$ s, if the switch is closed at $t = 0$, is

a) 3.51
b) 4.51
c) 5.46
d) 6.32

S   50 Ω

10 V   C 10^{-6} F

6.32   How long, in microseconds, does it take for the current to reach half its final value, if the switch is closed at $t = 0$?

a) 3.1
b) 4.7
c) 5.2
d) 7.3

S   20 Ω

10 V   150 μH

*6.33   The electric flux passing out through a closed surface is equal to

a) the line integral of the current around the surface.
b) zero.
c) the flux density at the surface.
d) the total charge enclosed by the surface.

Electric Fields

*6.34   The direction of the force acting on a moving charge placed in a magnetic field is

a) perpendicular to the magnetic field.
b) opposite to the direction of motion of the charge.
c) along the direction of the magnetic field.
d) along the direction of motion of the charge.

6.35   Two infinitely long lines of charge are parallel to the z-axis and located as shown. The force on an electron at $(1, 0, 0)$ will be in the direction

a) +x
b) −x
c) +y
d) −y

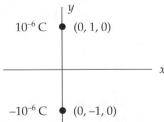

10^{-6} C • (0, 1, 0)

-10^{-6} C • (0, −1, 0)

6.36   A point charge of 2×10^{-7} C is located at the origin of coordinates. A spherical shell with center at the origin and radius of 20 cm has a surface charge density 1×10^{-7} C/m^2. The electric flux density at $r = 50$ cm, in C/m^2, is

a) 3.18×10^{-8} b) 7.96×10^{-8} c) 9.55×10^{-8} d) 11.14×10^{-8}

*6.37 A uniform line charge of $\rho_L = 30$ nC/m lies along the z-axis. The flux density D at (3, –4, 5) is:

a) 1.91×10^{-10} c) 11.94×10^{-10}

b) 9.55×10^{-10} d) 15.92×10^{-10}

6.38 An electric field in rectangular coordinates is given by $\mathbf{E} = 4y\mathbf{x} + 4x\mathbf{y}$ V/m. The voltage drop from (1, 1, 1) to (5, 1, 1) is

a) +12   b) –12   c) +16   d) –16

6.39 Static electric field distributions refer to cases where

a) all time derivatives of field quantities are zero.
b) the time derivatives of the displacement current are not zero.
c) the electric fields vary with time.
d) the electric scalar potential is two-dimensional.

*6.40 A point charge of 50×10^{-9} C is placed 10 cm above a perfectly conducting infinitely large flat ground plane. What is the voltage 5 cm above the ground with respect to zero volts on the ground?

a) 3000   b) 4000   c) 5000   d) 6000

Magnetic Fields

*6.41 Two long, straight conductors located at (0, 3, z) and (0, –3, z) each carry 5 amperes in the same direction (distances are in meters). The magnitude of magnetic field intensity at (4, 0, 0) is

a) $1/\pi$ b) $2/5\pi$ c) $3/5\pi$ d) $4/5\pi$

6.42 A solenoid has 1000 turns and carries a current of 5 amperes. If $L = 50$ cm and $r_c = 2.5$ cm, what is the magnetic field intensity on the solenoid axis at the center of the solenoid?

a) 10^4 b) 2×10^5 c) 5×10^4 d) 10^5

*6.43 The inductor shown has an inductance of 4 mH. In order to increase the inductance to 40 mH,

a) increase the current by 10.
b) increase the mean flux path length by 10.
c) increase the number of turns to 10 N.
d) increase the cross sectional area of the iron by 10.

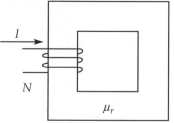

6.44 An iron ring with a mean diameter of 20 cm is wound with a coil of 200 turns. The permeability of the iron is $4\pi \times 10^{-4}$ H/m. A current of 0.05 A is passed through the coil. The magnetic flux density in the iron, in W/m^2, is

a) 0.02   b) $0.01\pi^2$ c) $100/\pi$ d) π

*6.45 An iron core is shown. The relative permeability of the iron is 4000. The reluctance, in H^{-1}, of the magnetic circuit shown is

a) $1/(\pi \times 10^{-8})$

b) $1/(4\pi \times 10^{-5})$

c) $1/(4\pi \times 10^{-8})$

d) $1/(16\pi \times 10^{-8})$

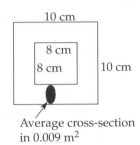

10 cm

8 cm

8 cm

10 cm

10 cm

Average cross-section
in 0.009 m²

Diodes

*6.46 If the desired DC load voltage is 9 volts, what is the rms value of the source?

a) 4.1

b) 12.7

c) 20.0

d) 28.3

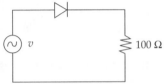

v

100 Ω

6.47 If the source voltage in the circuit of Prob. 6.46 is $v = 100 \sin 377t$, the peak reverse voltage applied to the diode would be

a) 2.5   b) 100   c) 141.4   d) 31.8

6.48 If $R_L = 600\ \Omega$, what must be the rms value of the sinusoidal voltage v if $I = 150$ mA?

a) 60

b) 80

c) 100

d) 120

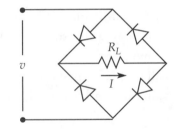

v

R_L

I

Operational Amplifiers

*6.49 Calculate R, in kΩ, so that

$v_o/v_{in} = -200$.

a) 50 kΩ

b) 100

c) 200

d) 300

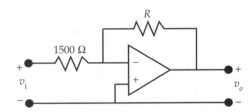

R

1500 Ω

v_i

v_o

6.50   The gain of the following
        OP-AMP circuit is

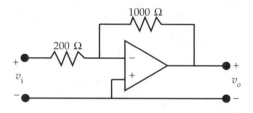

   a) –0.2
   b) –1.2
   c) –4
   d) –5

6.51   Given the voltages into the following OP-AMP network, the output voltage is

   a) –2
   b) –4
   c) –7
   d) –10

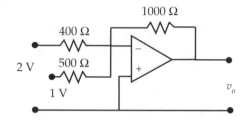

*6.52   The OP-AMP circuit below performs the function of

   a) amplification
   b) integration
   c) differentiation
   d) summing

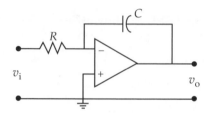

6.53   An OP-AMP integrator is used
        to integrate the square wave
        shown. What must be the
        value of R to make the peak
        value of the triangular wave
        equal 150 volts?
   a) 10 000 ohms
   b) 16 667 ohms
   c) 25 000 ohms
   d) 33 333 ohms

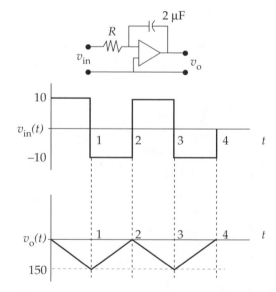

Solutions to Practice Problems

6.1 c)   Beginning at lower left, sum the voltage drops around the closed path:

$$v_1 + v_2 - v_3 - v_4 + v_5 = 0$$

6.2 a)   An equivalent circuit is:
Use current divider:

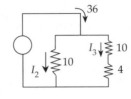

$$I_2 = \frac{14}{24} \times 36 = 21 \text{ A}$$

$$I_1 = \frac{20}{25} I_3 = \frac{20}{25}(36 - 21) = 12 \text{ A}$$

6.3 c) $P_{source} = VI = 10 \times 2 = 20 \text{ W}$

$P_{resistor} = I^2 R = 2^2 \times 3 = 12 \text{ W}.$

$\therefore P_{box} = 20 - 12 = 8 \text{ W}$

6.4 b)   A simplified circuit is shown.
$v - 4I - 4I = 0. \quad \therefore I = v/8.$

$v_4 = IR = \frac{v}{8} \times 4 = v/2.$

$\therefore$ Voltage across 4Ω resistor if $v = 1V$ is $1/2 V$.

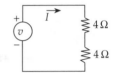

6.5 a)   Total Resistance $= 1 + 2 + 2 = 5 \Omega$
Conductance $= 1/R = 1/5$ siemens

6.6 b) $9 = 18I. \quad \therefore I = 1/2. \quad \therefore V = IR = \frac{1}{2}(5) = 2.5V.$

6.7 d)   First find the voltage across the 5Ω resistor. $V_{ab} = \frac{4}{12} \times 12 = 4$ volts

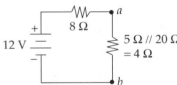

$$P_5 = \frac{V_{ab}^2}{R} = \frac{4^2}{5} = 3.2 \text{ W}.$$

6.8 c)   An equivalent circuit is shown.
Voltage across 10 mho :
$V = I/G = 2/10 = 0.2$ Volts
Current in 6 mho $= I = VG = 0.2 \times 6 = 1.2 \text{ A}$
$P = I^2/G = 1.2^2/6 = 0.24 \text{ W}.$

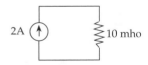

6.9 b)   An equivalent circuit is shown.
$R_{eq} = 1 + 2 + 2 = 5 \Omega$

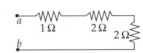

6.10 d)   At pt. 1 sum currents:

$$2 - \frac{V_1}{4} - \frac{V_1 - V_2}{2} = 0$$

At pt. 2 sum currents:

$$1 - \frac{V_2}{4} - \frac{V_2 - V_1}{2} = 0$$

The above equations are: $\left.\begin{array}{c} 3V_1 - 2V_2 = 8 \\ -2V_1 + 3V_2 = 4 \end{array}\right\}$ $\therefore V_2 = 5.6$

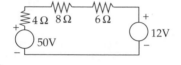

6.11 d)   Convert the 2 A current source with parallel resistor to a voltage source with series resistor. Summing voltages:

$$50 - 4I - 8I - 6I - 12 = 0. \quad \therefore I = 38/18 = 2.11 \text{ A}.$$

6.12 c) $(2 + j2)(3 - j4) = \left(2.82 \angle 45°\right)\left(5 \angle -53.13°\right) = 14.1 \angle -8.13°$.

6.13 b)   From graph $V_{max} = 1.0$ V. $\therefore V_{rms} = \dfrac{V_{max}}{\sqrt{2}} = 0.707$ V.

The period $T = 120$ ms. $\therefore f = \dfrac{1}{T} = \dfrac{1}{120 \times 10^{-3}} = 8.33$ Hz

$\therefore$ radian frequency $= \omega = 2\pi f = 52.36$ rad/s.

6.14 c)   Write the mesh current equations:

$$50 \angle 180° - (10 + j20) I_1 - 25I_1 + 25I_2 = 0$$

$$25I_1 - 25I_2 - (50 - j20) I_2 - 40 \angle 45° = 0$$

$$(35 + j20) I_1 - 25I_2 = 50 \angle 180°$$

$$-25I_1 + (75 - j20) I_2 = -40 \angle 45°$$

$$\therefore I_2 = \frac{2285 \angle 233°}{2530 \angle 18.4°} = 0.90 \angle 214.6° = -.82 - j.37$$

6.15 a)   Convert voltage source to current source:
Write KCL at A:

$$20 \angle 0° - \frac{V_A}{6 + j8} - \frac{V_A}{-j5} - \frac{V_A}{4} + 20 \angle 90° = 0.$$

$$\therefore V_A = \frac{20 \angle 0° + 20 \angle 90°}{\left(\dfrac{1}{6 + j8} - \dfrac{1}{j5} + \dfrac{1}{4}\right)} = \frac{20 + j20}{(.06 - j.08 + j.2 + .25)} = \frac{20 + j20}{.31 + j.12}$$

$$= \frac{28.28 \angle 45°}{0.33 \angle 21.16°} = 85.1 \angle 23.84°$$

6.16 b)   Sketch the DC circuit, inductor = short, capacitor = open:

$$I_{DC} = \frac{15}{30} = 0.5 \text{ amp}$$

6.17 d)   The rms current through the inductor is composed of I_{DC} and I_{AC}:

$I_{rms} = \sqrt{I_{DC}^2 + I_{AC}^2}$, $I_{DC} = 0.5$ A, from Problem 6.16. Sketch the AC circuit (the battery is a short):

$$I_{AC} = \frac{36 + j48}{-j20 + \dfrac{(30)(+j40)}{30 + j40}} = \frac{36 + j48}{19.2 - j5.6} = 3 \underline{/69.4^\circ}$$

$$I_{rms} = \sqrt{(0.5)^2 + (3)^2} = 3.04 \text{ A}$$

6.18 d)   Find the voltage across the parallel combination $V = Iz_{eq}$ where

$$I = 10\underline{/0^\circ}, \quad \frac{1}{z_{eq}} = \frac{1}{z_1} + \frac{1}{z_2} + \frac{1}{z_3} = \frac{1}{j20} + \frac{1}{-j10} + \frac{1}{5} = 0.2 + j0.05,$$

$$z_{eq} = 4.71 - j1.18$$

$$V = (10\underline{/0^\circ})(4.71 - j1.18) = 47.1 - j11.8 = 48.5 \underline{/-14.04^\circ} \text{ V}$$

$$I_c = \frac{V}{z_c} = \frac{48.5\underline{/-14.04^\circ}}{-j10} = 4.85\underline{/76^\circ} \text{ A}$$

6.19 d)   From Problem 6.18, $V = 48.5\angle -14^\circ$ volts

6.20 c)   Convert to phasors:

The current $i = 10 \cos 100\, t$ becomes

$$I = \frac{10}{\sqrt{2}}\underline{/0^\circ} \text{ A}, \quad \omega = 100 \frac{\text{rad}}{\text{sec}}$$

$$-j\frac{1}{\omega c} = -j\frac{1}{100 \times 3300 \times 10^{-6}} = -j3.03$$

Find parallel equivalent impedance:

$$Z = \frac{-j3.03 \times 5}{5 - j3.03} = \frac{15.15\ \underline{-90^\circ}}{5.85\ \underline{-31.2^\circ}} = 2.59\ \underline{-58.8^\circ}$$

$$V = IZ = \left(\frac{10}{\sqrt{2}}\underline{/0^\circ}\right)(2.59\ \underline{-58.8^\circ}) = 18.32\ \underline{-58.8^\circ}$$

$$v(t) = 25.9 \cos(100t - 58.8^\circ)$$

6.21 d) $Z = 4 + j3 = 5\underline{/36.9^\circ} \quad \therefore \theta = 36.9^\circ. \quad pf = \cos\theta = \cos 36.9^\circ = 0.8$

6-ELECTRICAL

6.22 c)   Recall $I_S = V_S Y_T$ where Y_T is the total parallel admittance of the circuit:

$$Y_T = \frac{1}{Z_T} = \frac{1}{Z_R} + \frac{1}{Z_L} + \frac{1}{Z_C} = \frac{1}{50} + \frac{1}{j\omega L} + \frac{1}{\frac{1}{j\omega C}} = 0.02 - j\frac{1}{\omega L} + j\omega C$$

If Y_T is minimum, the $I_S = V_S Y_T$ is minimum. For Y_T minimum, set

$$-j\frac{1}{\omega L} + j\omega C = 0 \Rightarrow \omega^2 = \frac{1}{LC} \quad \therefore \text{Resonance.}$$

$$\omega = \frac{1}{\sqrt{8 \times 10^{-10} \times 2 \times 10^{-6}}} = 0.25 \times 10^8 = 25 \times 10^6 \text{ rad/s.}$$

6.23 c)   rms $V_S = \dfrac{V_{max}}{\sqrt{2}} = \dfrac{141.4}{\sqrt{2}} = 100.$ I_S min $= 100 \times 0.02 = 2$ A.

6.24 d)   For $pf = 1$: $Y = G + j(\omega C - 1/\omega L) = G + j0$ or $\omega C = \dfrac{1}{\omega L}$.

$$\therefore \ C = \frac{1}{\omega^2 L} = \frac{1}{50^2 \times .01} = 0.04$$

6.25 c)   For max. power dissipation choose $z_L = \tilde{z}_{gen}$.

$$Z_{gen} = 20 - j\frac{1}{100 \times 2000 \times 10^{-6}} = 20 - j5.$$

$$\therefore Z_L = 20 + j5. \quad \therefore R = 20 \text{ and } \omega L = 5.$$

$$\therefore \ L = \frac{5}{100} = .05$$

6.26 c) $\theta_{ph} = \tan^{-1}\dfrac{5}{10} = 26.6°.$ $V_{ph} = 120.$ $I_{ph} = \dfrac{120}{|10 + j5|} = 10.73.$

$$\therefore \ P_L = 3V_{ph}I_{ph}\cos\theta_{ph} = 3 \times 120 \times 10.73 \cos 26.6° = 3456.$$

6.27 b) $I_L = I_{ph} = \dfrac{V_{ph}}{Z_{ph}} = \dfrac{100\angle 0°}{2 + j2} = \dfrac{100\angle 0°}{2.83\angle 45°} = 35.36\angle{-45°}$

6.28 a) (a) should be $V_L = \sqrt{3}\ V_{ph}$

6.29 a) $v = \dfrac{1}{C}\int idt + v_o = \dfrac{1}{100 \times 10^{-6}}\left(-10^{-3} \times 2.5\right) + 1.0 = -24$

6.30 d) $w_C(t) = \dfrac{1}{2}Cv^2 = \dfrac{1}{2}\left(10 \times 10^{-6}\right)\left(50t^2\right)^2 = 200.$ $\therefore \ t^4 = 16000.$ $\therefore t = 11.25\,s$

6.31 b) $T = RC = 50 \times 10^{-6}$ sec.

$$v_C(t) = V_\infty + \left(V_o - V_\infty\right)e^{-t/T} = 10 + (0 - 10)e^{-\frac{30\times 10^{-6}}{50\times 10^{-6}}} = 10 - 10e^{-.6} = 4.51.$$

6.32 c) $I_\infty = 10/20 = 0.5$ A. $T = L/R = 150 \times 10^{-6}/20 = 7.5 \times 10^{-6}$

$$i(t) = I_\infty + \left(I_o - I_\infty\right)e^{-t/T}$$

$$\therefore \ \frac{0.5}{2} = 0.5 + (0 - 0.5)e^{-t/7.5\times 10^{-6}}$$

$$\therefore \ t = 5.20 \times 10^{-6} \text{ sec.}$$

6.33 d)   This is Gauss' Law.

6.34 a) $\mathbf{F} = q\mathbf{V} \times \mathbf{B}$.   ∴ $\mathbf{F} \perp \mathbf{B}$

6.35 c)   The x-components of $\mathbf{F}_- + \mathbf{F}_+$ cancel and
∴ $\mathbf{F}_{\text{total}}$ is in y-direction.

6.36 b)   For the surface charge: $D_s = \rho_s \dfrac{4\pi R^2}{4\pi r_s^2}$.

For the point charge: $D_q = \dfrac{q}{4\pi r_s^2}$.

∴ The total is $D_t = \dfrac{10^{-7} \times 0.2^2}{0.5^2} + \dfrac{2 \times 10^{-7}}{4\pi \times 0.5^2} = 7.96 \times 10^{-8} \ \text{C/m}^2$

6.37 b)   From the z-axis to $(3, -4, 5)$ the distance is
$$r = \sqrt{3^2 + 4^2} = 5$$
$$|D| = \frac{\rho_\ell}{2\pi r} = \frac{30 \times 10^{-9}}{2\pi \times 5} = 9.55 \times 10^{-10} \ \text{C/m}^2$$

6.38 c) $V = \int_a^b \mathbf{E} \cdot d\mathbf{L} = \int_a^b E_x dx + E_y dy^{\,0} + E_z dz^{\,0}$
$= \int_1^5 E_x dx = \int_1^5 4y\,dx = \int_1^5 4 \times 1\,dx = 4 \times 4 = 16 \ \text{volts}$

6.39 a)   "Static" implies no time variation in any quantity.

6.40 d)   Use image theory and place a second charge at $(0, -10 \ \text{cm})$. The second charge must be negative.

∴ $V = V_+ + V_- = \dfrac{q}{4\pi\varepsilon r_+} + \dfrac{-q}{4\pi\varepsilon r_-} = \dfrac{q}{4\pi\varepsilon}\left(\dfrac{1}{r_+} - \dfrac{1}{r_-}\right)$

$= \left(50 \times 10^{-9}\right)\left(9 \times 10^9\right)\left(\dfrac{1}{.05} - \dfrac{1}{.15}\right) = 6000 \ \text{volts}$.

We used $\dfrac{1}{4\pi\varepsilon} = 9 \times 10^9$.

6.41 d)   Each H is $\perp$ plane containing wire and point.
$\theta = \tan^{-1}\dfrac{3}{4} = 36.9°$, $H = \dfrac{I}{2\pi r} = \dfrac{5}{2\pi 5} = \dfrac{1}{2\pi}$
∴ $H_t = 2H\cos\theta = 2 \times \dfrac{1}{2\pi} \times 0.8 = 4/5\pi$

6.42 a) $H_{\text{center}} = \dfrac{NI}{\ell} = \dfrac{1000 \times 5}{0.5} = 10^4 \ \text{A/m}$.

6.43 d) $L = \dfrac{N}{I}\Psi = \dfrac{N}{I}\left(\dfrac{NI}{\Re}\right) = N^2/\Re = N^2 \Big/ \left(\dfrac{\ell}{\mu A}\right) = N^2 \mu A / \ell$.

To increase L from 4 to 40 increase A by a factor of 10.

6.44 **a)** $B = \dfrac{\Psi}{A} = \dfrac{1}{A}\dfrac{NI}{\Re} = \dfrac{1}{A}NI\left(\dfrac{\mu A}{\ell}\right) = \dfrac{NI\mu}{\ell}$

$$= \dfrac{200 \times 0.05 \times 4\pi \times 10^{-4}}{\pi \times 0.2} = 0.02 \text{ Wb/m}^2.$$

6.45 **b)** $\Re = \dfrac{\ell}{\mu A} = \dfrac{\ell}{\mu_o \mu_r A} = \dfrac{4 \times 0.09}{4\pi \times 10^{-7} \times 4000 \times 0.009} = \dfrac{1}{4\pi \times 10^{-5}} \text{ H}^{-1}$

6.46 **c)** $V_{DC} = V_{max}/\pi$

$9 = V_{max}/\pi.$

$\therefore V_{max} = 9\pi.$

$V_{rms} = V_{max}/\sqrt{2} = 9\pi/\sqrt{2} = 20$

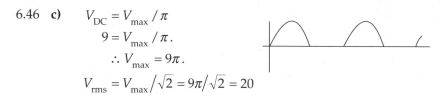

6.47 **b)** The peak reverse voltage occurs when the diode is reverse biased and does not conduct. $\therefore PRV = V_{max} = 100$ volts.

6.48 **c)** For a bridge rectifier

$$V_{DC} = 2V_{max}/\pi.$$

$$V_{DC} = I_L R_L = 0.150 \times 600 = 90.$$

$$\therefore V_{max} = \dfrac{\pi}{2} \times 90 = 45\pi. \quad \therefore V_{rms} = \dfrac{45\pi}{\sqrt{2}} = 100 \text{ volts}.$$

6.49 **d)** The gain of an OP-AMP is

$$\dfrac{v_o}{v_{in}} = -\dfrac{R_f}{R_i} = -\dfrac{R_2}{1500} = -200. \quad \therefore R_2 = 300\,000 \ \Omega$$

$$\text{or } 300 \text{ k}\Omega$$

6.50 **d)** $A = -\dfrac{R_f}{R_i} = -\dfrac{1000}{200} = -5$

6.51 **c)** $v_o = -\dfrac{R_f}{R_1}v_1 - \dfrac{R_f}{R_2}v_2$

$$= -\dfrac{1000}{400} \times 2 - \dfrac{1000}{500} \times 1$$

$$= -5 - 2 = -7 \text{ volts}$$

6.52 **b)** The OP-AMP circuit with capacitor feedback performs integration.

6.53 **d)** For the integrator $v_0 = \dfrac{1}{RC}\int v_i dt$. Note from the plot of v_i that $\int v_i dt = 10 \times 1 = 10$.

$$\therefore v_0 = 150 = \dfrac{1}{RC}(10), \quad R = \dfrac{10}{150C} = \dfrac{10}{150 \times 2 \times 10^{-6}} = \dfrac{10^7}{300} = 33\,333 \ \Omega.$$

Thermodynamics

by Merle C. Potter

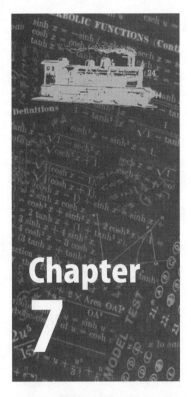

Chapter

7

Strategic Study Note

If you're planning a short review and you're outlining the NCEES Handbook, omit reviewing the following Handbook subjects since they will not likely be tested in the FE/EIT exam:

- Ideal Gas Mixtures
- Phase Relations
- Vapor–Liquid Mixtures

Overview, Definitions and Laws

Thermodynamics involves the storage, transformation and transfer of energy. It is stored as internal energy, kinetic energy and potential energy; it is transformed between these various forms; and it is transferred as work or heat transfer.

The *macroscopic* approach is used in this presentation, that is, we assume matter occupies all points in a region of interest. This is acceptable providing the density is sufficiently large, which it is in most engineering situations.

Both a *system*, a fixed quantity of matter, and a *control volume*, a volume into which and/or from which a substance flows, can be used in thermodynamics. (A control volume may also be referred to as an *open system*.) A system and its surroundings make up the *universe*. Some useful definitions follow:

phase — matter that has the same composition throughout; it is homogeneous

mixture — a quantity of matter that has more than one phase

property — a quantity which serves to describe a system

simple system — a system composed of a single phase, free of magnetic, electrical, and surface effects. Only two properties are needed to fix a simple system

state — the condition of a system described by giving values to its properties at the given instant

intensive property	—	a property that does not depend on the mass
extensive property	—	a property that depends on the mass
specific property	—	an extensive property divided by the mass
thermodynamic equilibrium	—	when the properties do not vary from point to point in a system and there is no tendency for additional change
process	—	the path of successive states through which a system passes
quasi-equilibrium	—	if, in passing from one state to the next, the deviation from equilibrium is infinitesimal. It is also called a quasistatic process
reversible process	—	a process which, when reversed, leaves no change in either the system or surroundings
isothermal	—	temperature is constant
isobaric	—	pressure is constant
isometric	—	volume is constant
isentropic	—	entropy is constant
adiabatic	—	no heat transfer

Experimental observations are organized into mathematical statements or *laws*. Some of those used in thermodynamics follow:

zeroith law of thermodynamics	—	If two bodies are equal in temperature to a third, they are equal in temperature to each other.
first law of thermodynamics	—	During a given process, the net heat transfer minus the net work output equals the change in energy.
second law of thermodynamics	—	A device cannot operate in a cycle and produce work output while exchanging heat with a single constant temperature reservoir.
Boyle's law	—	The volume varies inversely with pressure for an ideal gas.
Charles' law	—	The volume varies directly with temperature for an ideal gas.
Avogadro's law	—	Equal volumes of different ideal gases with the same temperature and pressure contain an equal number of molecules.

We will present thermodynamics using SI units only. Because there will be no choice of English units, we are omitting all problems with English units. We will, however, maintain some English units in the text and in the tables. The afternoon civil engineering area exam will have some English units; all other afternoon subject exams will use SI units.

7.1 Density, Pressure, and Temperature

The density ρ is the mass divided by the volume,

$$\rho = \frac{m}{V} \qquad \text{(7.1.1)}$$

The specific volume is the reciprocal of the density,

$$v = \frac{1}{\rho} = \frac{V}{m} \qquad \text{(7.1.2)}$$

The pressure P is the normal force divided by the area upon which it acts. In thermodynamics, it is important to use *absolute pressure*, defined by

$$P_{abs} = P_{gauge} + P_{atmospheric} \qquad \text{(7.1.3)}$$

where the atmospheric pressure is taken as 100 kPa (14.7 psi), unless otherwise stated. If the gauge pressure is negative, it is a *vacuum*.

The temperature scale is established by choosing a specified number of divisions, called degrees, between the ice point and the steam point, each at 101 kPa absolute. In the Celsius scale, the ice point is set at 0°C and the steam point at 100°C. **In thermodynamics, pressures are always assumed to be given as absolute pressures.** Expressions for the absolute temperature in kelvins and degrees Rankine are, respectively,

$$T = T_{celsius} + 273; \quad T = T_{fahrenheit} + 460 \qquad \text{(7.1.4)}$$

The temperature, pressure and specific volume for an ideal (perfect) gas are related by the *ideal gas law*

$$Pv = RT, \quad P = \rho RT, \quad \text{or } PV = mRT \qquad R = \overline{R}/M \qquad \text{(7.1.5)}$$

where the *universal gas constant* $\overline{R} = 8.314$ kJ/kmol·K $\left(1545 \text{ ft-lbf/lbmol-°R}\right)$, M is the molar mass, and R is the gas constant; for air it is 0.287 kJ/kg·K (53.3 ft-lbf / lbm-°R). (Note: the NCEES Handbook does not list R_{air}. It is a good idea to memorize R_{air} since it is used so often.) Below moderate pressure this equation can be used if the temperature exceeds twice the critical temperature, the temperature above which the liquid and vapor phases do not coexist (or above which vaporization does not occur). Thus, if the temperature of the steam is greater than 800°C (1500°F), Equation 7.1.5 can be used with $R = 0.462$ kJ/kg·K (85.7 ft-lbf / lbm-°R) if the pressure is not excessive; for high pressure ($P > 10$ MPa) the temperature should be higher than 1000°C if Equation 7.1.5 is to be used.

If the temperature is less than twice the critical temperature, tables relating the three variables P, v and T must usually be used. For water such tables are called the "steam tables" and are presented in Table 7.3.1. Data is presented in Table 7.3.1 and 7.3.2 that is used to relate P, v and T when water exists in the liquid phase, as a liquid/vapor mixture, or in the saturated vapor phase. These situations are best described referring to a T-v diagram, shown in Figure 7.1. Suppose we start with a constant pressure container (a cylinder with a floating piston) containing water

🔑 The temperature scale is established by choosing a specified number of divisions, called degrees, between the ice point and the steam point.

• If the temperature is less than twice the critical temperature, tables relating the three variables P, v and T must usually be used.

7-THERMO

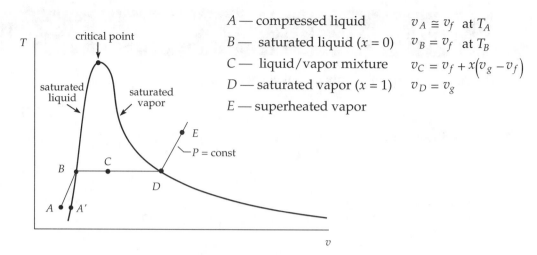

Figure 7.1 A *T-v* diagram.

at room temperature; it would undergo the following changes if heat is trans-ferred to the volume:

- The temperature would rise above T_A in the *compressed liquid* and $v_A \cong v_{A'}$.
- At state *B saturated liquid* phase results and vaporization (boiling) begins; $v_B = v_f$. A subscript *f* will always denote a saturated liquid.
- At state *C* the liquid phase and the vapor phase are in equilibrium; a *liquid/vapor mixture* occurs and

$$v = v_f + x\left(v_g - v_f\right) \quad \text{or} \quad v = xv_g + \left(1 - x\right)v_f \qquad \textbf{(7.1.6)}$$

where *x* is the *quality*. Sometimes we let $v_{fg} = v_g - v_f$.

- At state *D* a *saturated vapor* exists and vaporization is complete; a subscript *g* will always denote a saturated vapor: $v_D = v_g$.
- At state *E* the vapor is *superheated* and *v* is found in Table 7.3.3.

Equation 7.1.6 above results from the definition of *quality*, the ratio of the vapor mass to the total mass:

$$x = \frac{m_{vapor}}{m_{total}} = \frac{m_g}{m_g + m_f} \qquad \textbf{(7.1.7)}$$

Note that the entries in the tables at the end of this chapter are in absolute pressure.

An alternative to the tabulated properties is the *P-h* diagram which includes the properties *P*, *h*, *T*, *v* and *s*. If internal energy is required we use the relation $u = h - Pv$ (see Eq. 7.2.10). We will illustrate its use in Article 7.3.

The NCEES Reference Handbook contains a much shorter version of the steam tables; it is important that you become familiar with the tables.

🔑 An alternative to the tabulated properties is the *P-h* diagram which includes the properties *P*, *h*, *T*, *v* and *s*.

7·THERMO

Example 7.1

What mass of air is contained in a room 20 m × 40 m × 3 m at standard conditions?

Solution. Standard conditions are $T = 25°C$ and $P = 100$ kPa. Using $M = 28.97$,

$$\rho = \frac{P}{RT}$$

$$= \frac{100}{0.287 \times 298} = 1.17 \text{ kg/m}^3, \quad \text{where} \quad R = \frac{8.314}{28.97} = 0.287$$

$$\therefore m = \rho V$$

$$= 1.17 \times 20 \times 40 \times 3 = 2810 \text{ kg}$$

Example 7.2

What mass of water contained in 2m^3 at 2000 kPa and 200°C?

Solution. The specific volume of compressed water is insensitive to pressure, so we use v_f at 200°C. It is, using Table 7.3.1,

$$v_f = 0.001156 \text{ m}^3/\text{kg}$$

The mass is then

$$m = V/v$$

$$= 2/0.001156 = 1730 \text{ kg}$$

Note: Liquid water has mass density of about 1000 kg/m^3 or $v = 0.001 \text{ m}^3/\text{kg}$. This is good if the temperature is relatively low, say below 100°C.

Example 7.3

The volume occupied by 20 kg of a water-vapor mixture at 200°C is 2m^3. Calculate the quality.

Solution. The specific volume is
$$v = V/m$$
$$= 2/20 = 0.1 \text{ m}^3/\text{kg}$$

Using Equation 7.1.6, and Table 7.3.1, we have

$$x = \frac{v - v_f}{v_g - v_f}$$

$$= \frac{0.1 - 0.001156}{0.1274 - 0.001156} = 0.783 \text{ or } 78.3\%$$

Example 7.4

Find the volume occupied by 20 kg of steam at 4 MPa and 400°C.

Solution. The specific volume is found in Table 7.3.3 to be

$$v = 0.07341 \text{ m}^3/\text{kg}$$

The volume is then

$$V = mv$$

$$= 20 \times 0.07341 = 1.468 \text{ m}^3$$

7·THERMO

7.2 The First Law of Thermodynamics for a System

The first law of thermodynamics, referred to as the "first law" or the "energy equation," is expressed for a cycle as

$$Q_{net} = W_{net} \tag{7.2.1}$$

and for a process as

$$Q - W = \Delta E \tag{7.2.2}$$

where Q is the heat transfer, W is the work, and E represents the energy (kinetic, potential, and internal) of the system*. In thermodynamics attention is focused on internal energy with kinetic and potential energy changes neglected (unless otherwise stated) so that we have

$$Q - W = \Delta U \quad \text{or} \quad q - w = \Delta u \tag{7.2.3}$$

where the specific internal energy is

$$q = \frac{Q}{m}, \quad w = \frac{W}{m}, \quad u = \frac{U}{m} \tag{7.2.4}$$

> 🔑 In thermodynamics attention is focused on internal energy with kinetic and potential energy changes usually neglected.

Heat transfer may occur during any of the three following modes :

•**Conduction**—heat transfer due to molecular activity. For steady-state heat transfer through a constant wall area *Fourier's law* states[†]

$$\dot{Q} = kA\Delta T/L = A\Delta T/R \tag{7.2.5}$$

where k is the *conductivity* (dependent on the material), R is the *resistance factor*, and the length, L, is normal to the heat flow.

•**Convection**—heat transfer due to fluid motion. The mathematical expression used is

$$\dot{Q} = hA\Delta T = A\Delta T/R \tag{7.2.6}$$

where h is the *convective heat transfer coefficient* (dependent on the surface geometry, the fluid velocity, the fluid viscosity and density, and the temperature difference). The *Nusselt number* ($Nu = hL/k$) is the dimensionless convective heat transfer coefficient.

•**Radiation**—heat transfer due to the transmission of waves. The heat transfer from body 1 is

$$\dot{Q} = \sigma \varepsilon A\left(T_1^{\,4} - T_2^{\,4}\right)F_{1-2} \tag{7.2.7}$$

in which the *Stefan-Boltzmann constant* is $\sigma = 5.67 \times 10^{-11}\,\text{kJ/s}\cdot\text{m}^2\cdot\text{K}^4$ ($1.714 \times 10^{-9}\,\text{Btu/hr-ft}^2\text{-}^\circ\text{R}^4$), ε is the *emissivity* ($\varepsilon = 1$ for a black body), and F_{1-2} is the *shape factor* ($F_{1-2} = 1$ if body 2 encloses body 1).

---

*In this book, heat transferred to the system is positive and work done by the system is positive. It is also conventional to define work done on the system as positive so that $Q + W = \Delta U$.

[†]A dot signifies a rate, so that $\dot{Q}$ has units of J/s (Btu/sec).

For a two layer composite wall with an inner and outer convection layer we use the resistance factors and obtain

$$\dot{Q} = A\Delta T / (R_i + R_1 + R_2 + R_o) = UA\Delta T \qquad \text{(7.2.8)}$$

where U is the *overall heat transfer coefficient*. It is not to be confused with internal energy of Eq. 7.2.3.

In thermodynamics, the heat transfer is usually specified or calculated using Equation 7.2.3; it is usually not calculated with the previous four equations. The equations in the one-dimensional form above and in two dimensions are the focus of attention in a course in Heat Transfer. Thermal properties are presented in Tables 7.5 and 7.6.

Work can be accomplished mechanically by moving a boundary, resulting in a quasi-equilibrium work mode

$$W = \int P dV \qquad \text{(7.2.9)}$$

It can also be accomplished in non-quasi-equilibrium modes such as with a paddle wheel or by electrical resistance. But then Equation 7.2.9 cannot be used.

We introduce *enthalpy* for convenience, and define it to be

$$H = U + PV \qquad \text{(7.2.10)}$$
$$h = u + Pv$$

For substances such as steam, the specific internal energy and specific enthalpy are either found in the steam tables or from a *P-h* diagram. For a compressed liquid, u and h are insensitive to pressure and are found in the Table 7.3.1 with the "*f*" subscripts under the specified temperature. For the liquid/vapor mixture we use

$$u = u_f + x(u_g - u_f) \qquad \text{(7.2.11)}$$
$$h = h_f + x h_{fg}$$

where $h_{fg} = h_g - h_f$.

For ideal gases we assume constant specific heats and use

$$\Delta u = c_v \Delta T \qquad \text{(7.2.12)}$$
$$\Delta h = c_p \Delta T \qquad \text{(7.2.13)}$$

where c_v is the *constant volume specific heat*, and c_p is the *constant pressure specific heat*. From the differential forms of the above we can find

$$c_p = c_v + R \qquad \text{(7.2.14)}$$

We also define the *ratio of specific heats k* to be

$$k = c_p / c_v \qquad \text{(7.2.15)}$$

For air $c_v = 0.716$ kJ/kg·K (0.171 Btu/lbm - °R), $c_p = 1.00$ kJ/kg·K (0.24 Btu/lbm - °R), $k = 1.4$. For most solids and liquids we can find the heat transfer using

$$Q = m c_p \Delta T \qquad \text{(7.2.16)}$$

For water $c_p = 4.18$ kJ/kg·°K (1.00 Btu/lbm - °R), and for ice $c_p \cong 2.1$ kJ/kg·°K (0.40 Btu/lbm - °R).

When a substance changes phase, *latent heat* is involved. The energy necessary to melt a unit mass of a solid is the *heat of fusion*; the energy necessary to vaporize a unit mass of liquid is the *heat of vaporization*, equal to $(h_g - h_f)$; the energy nec-

Work is accomplished mechanically by moving a boundary, or with a paddle wheel or by electrical resistance.

7·THERMO

essary to vaporize a unit mass of solid is the *heat of sublimation.* For ice, the heat of fusion is approximately 320 kJ/kg (140 Btu/lbm) and the heat of sublimation is about 2040 kJ/kg (877 Btu/lbm); the heat of vaporization varies from 2050 kJ/kg at 0°C (1075 Btu/lbm at 32°F) to zero at the critical point.

For specific processes, we consider the preceding paragraphs and summarize as follows:

Constant Temperature (Isothermal)

$$1\text{st law}: \quad Q - W = m\Delta u \qquad \text{or} \qquad q - w = \Delta u \tag{7.2.17}$$

$$\text{ideal gas}: \quad Q = W = mRT \ln \frac{v_2}{v_1} = mRT \ln \frac{P_1}{P_2} \tag{7.2.18}$$

$$P_2 = P_1 v_1 / v_2 \tag{7.2.19}$$

Constant Pressure (Isobaric)

$$1\text{st law}: \qquad Q = m\Delta h \qquad \text{or} \quad q = \Delta h \tag{7.2.20}$$

$$W = mP\Delta v \tag{7.2.21}$$

$$\text{ideal gas}: \qquad Q = mc_p \Delta T \tag{7.2.22}$$

$$T_2 = T_1 v_2 / v_1 \tag{7.2.23}$$

Constant Volume (Isometric)

🔑 A *polytropic process* results if *k* is replaced with *n*.

$$1\text{st law}: \qquad Q = m\Delta u \qquad \text{or} \quad q = \Delta u \tag{7.2.24}$$

$$W = 0 \tag{7.2.25}$$

$$\text{ideal gas}: \qquad Q = mc_v \Delta T \tag{7.2.26}$$

$$T_2 = T_1 P_2 / P_1 \tag{7.2.27}$$

Adiabatic Process (Isentropic)

$$1\text{st law}: \qquad -W = m\Delta u \qquad \text{or} \qquad -w = \Delta u \tag{7.2.28}$$

$$Q = 0 \tag{7.2.29}$$

$$\text{ideal gas}: \quad -W = mc_v \Delta T \tag{7.2.30}$$

$$T_2 = T_1 (v_1 / v_2)^{k-1} = T_1 (P_2 / P_1)^{(k-1)/k} \tag{7.2.31}$$

$$P_2 = P_1 (v_1 / v_2)^k \tag{7.2.32}$$

A *polytropic process* results if *k* in Equations 7.2.31 and 7.2.32 is replaced with *n*. Then *n* must be specified. Note that the adiabatic, quasi-equilibrium process is often referred to as an *isentropic process.*

Example 7.5

How much heat must be added to 2 kg of steam contained in a rigid volume, if the initial pressure of 2 MPa is increased to 5 MPa? $T_1 = 300°C$.

Solution. The first law with $\Delta KE = \Delta PE = 0$ is

$$Q - W = \Delta U$$

For a rigid container $W = 0$ so that
$$Q = m(u_2 - u_1)$$

From the steam Table 7.3.3, we find $u_1 = 2772.6$ kJ/kg and $v_1 = 0.1255$ m^3/kg. We can locate state 2 because the container is rigid, so that

$$v_2 = v_1 \cong 0.126 \ \text{m}^3/\text{kg}$$

The temperature T_2 that has $P_2 = 5$ MPa and $v_2 = 0.126$ m^3/kg is 1100°C. At that state $u_2 = 4246$ kJ/kg. Thus,

$$Q = m(u_2 - u_1)$$
$$= 2(4246 - 2773) = 2946 \ \text{kJ}$$

Example 7.6

Calculate the heat transfer necessary to raise the temperature of 2 kg of saturated water vapor to 600°C if the pressure is maintained constant at 2000 kPa.

Solution. The first law, for a constant pressure process, is

$$Q = m(h_2 - h_1)$$

Using Tables 7.3.2 and 7.3.3, we find $h_1 = 2799.5$ and $h_2 = 3690.1$ kJ/kg. Hence, we have

$$Q = 2(3690.1 - 2799.5) = 1781 \ \text{kJ}$$

Example 7.7

How much heat is needed to completely vaporize 100 kg of ice at $T_1 = -10°C$ if the pressure is held constant at 200 kPa?

Solution. The heat transfer is related to the enthalpy by

$$Q = m\Delta h$$
$$= m(c_p \Delta T_{ice} + \text{heat of fusion} + c_p \Delta T_{water} + \text{heat of vaporization})$$

Using the values given in Article 7.2, Table 7.2, and Table 7.3.2,

$$Q = 100(2.1 \times 10 + 320 + 4.18 \times 120.2 + 2201.9)$$
$$= 304 \ 500 \ \text{kJ or} \ 304.5 \ \text{MJ}$$

Example 7.8

Estimate the heat transfer necessary to increase the pressure of 50% quality steam from 200 kPa to 800 kPa if the volume is kept constant.

Solution. The first law, with $W = 0$ for a constant volume process, is

$$q = u_2 - u_1$$

To find state 2 we must use $v_1 = v_2$. At state 1 we have

$$v_1 = v_f + x(v_g - v_f)$$
$$= 0.00106 + 0.5(0.8857 - 0.00106) = 0.4434 \ \text{m}^3/\text{kg}$$

$$u_1 = u_f + x(u_g - u_f)$$
$$= 504.5 + 0.5(2529.5 - 504.5) = 1517 \ \text{kJ/kg}$$

At state 2, $P_2 = 0.8$ MPa and $v_2 = 0.4434$ m³/kg (note: state 2 is superheat) so that at this superheated state $u_2 = 3126$ kJ/kg. Hence,

$$q = 3126 - 1517 = 1609 \ \text{kJ/kg}$$

Note that we have used q rather than Q since mass was not specified.

Example 7.9

Calculate the work done by a piston if the 2 m³ volume of air is tripled while the temperature is maintained at 40°C. The initial pressure is 400 kPa.

Solution. The mass is needed in order to use Equation 7.2.18 to find the work; it is, using $R = \overline{R}/M = 8.314/28.97 = 0.287 \, \text{kJ/kg} \cdot \text{K}$,

$$m = \frac{PV}{RT}$$
$$= \frac{400 \times 2}{0.287 \times 313} = 8.91 \ \text{kg}, \qquad R = \frac{8.314}{28.97} = 0.287$$

The work is then found to be

$$W = mRT \ln v_2/v_1$$
$$= 8.91 \times 0.287 \times 313 \ln 3 = 879 \ \text{kJ}$$

Note: The temperature is expressed as $40 + 273 = 313$ K.

Example 7.10

How much work is necessary to compress air in an insulated cylinder from 0.2 m³ to 0.01 m³? Use $T_1 = 20°C$ and $P_1 = 100$ kPa.

Solution. For an adiabatic process $Q = 0$ so that the first law is

$$-W = m(u_2 - u_1)$$
$$= mc_v(T_2 - T_1)$$

To find the mass m we use the ideal gas equation with

$$R = \overline{R}/M = 8.314/28.97 = 0.287 \text{ kJ/kg} \cdot \text{K} :$$

$$m = \frac{PV}{RT}$$

$$= \frac{100 \times 0.2}{0.287 \times 293} = 0.2378 \text{ kg}$$

The temperature T_2 is found to be

$$T_2 = T_1(v_1/v_2)^{k-1}$$

$$= 293(0.2/0.01)^{0.4} = 971.1 \text{ K}$$

The work is then

$$W = 0.2378 \times 0.716(971.1 - 293) = 115.5 \text{ kJ}$$

Example 7.11

A 10-cm-thick wall made of pine wood is 3 m high and 10 m long. Calculate the heat transfer rate if the temperature is 25°C on the inside and –20°C on the outside. Neglect convection.

Solution. The heat transfer occurs due to conduction. Using k from Table 7.5, Eq. 7.2.5 provides

$$\dot{Q} = kA\Delta T/L$$

$$= 0.15 \times (3 \times 10) \times [25 - (-20)]/0.1 = 2025 \text{ J/s}$$

Example 7.12

The surface of the glass in a 1.2 m $\times$ 0.8 m skylight is maintained at 20°C. If the air temperature is –20°C, estimate the rate of heat loss from the window. Use $h = 12$ J/s·m^2·°C.

Solution. The convective heat transfer coefficient depends on several parameters so, as usual, it is specified. Using Equation 7.2.6 the rate of heat loss is

$$\dot{Q} = hA\Delta T$$

$$= 12 \times (1.2 \times 0.8) \times [20 - (-20)] = 461 \text{ J/s}$$

Example 7.13

A 2-cm-diameter heating oven is maintained at 1000°C and the oven walls are at 500°C. If the emissivity of the element is 0.85, estimate the rate of heat loss from the 2-m-long element.

Solution. The heat loss will be primarily due to radiation. Neglecting any convection loss, using $F_{1-2} = 1$ since the oven encloses the element, and Eq. 7.2.7 provides us with

7·THERMO

$$\dot{Q} = \sigma \varepsilon A (T_1^{\,4} - T_2^{\,4})$$

$$= 5.67 \times 10^{-11} \times 0.85 \times (\pi \times 0.02 \times 2)(1273^4 - 773^4) = 13.7 \text{ kJ/s}$$

Note that absolute temperature must be used. Also, the area A is the surface area of the cylinder, i.e., $\pi D L$.

Example 7.14

Estimate the rate of heat loss from a 3 m × 10 m wall if it is composed of 2.5 cm of pine wood, 8 cm of wool insulation, and 1.5 cm of plaster. The room is at 22°C. and the outside air is at –20°C. Also, calculate the overall heat transfer coefficient.

Solution. The resistance coefficient is L/k for a material layer and $1/h$ for an air layer. Using Equation 7.2.8, and values from Table 7.5, we have

$$\dot{Q} = A\Delta T \big/ \big(R_i + R_1 + R_2 + R_3 + R_o \big)$$

$$= A\Delta T \bigg/ \bigg(\frac{1}{h_i} + \frac{L_1}{k_1} + \frac{L_2}{k_2} + \frac{L_3}{k_3} + \frac{1}{h_o} \bigg)$$

$$= \frac{(3 \times 10)[22 - (-20)]}{\dfrac{1}{12} + \dfrac{0.025}{0.15} + \dfrac{0.08}{0.038} + \dfrac{0.015}{0.81} + \dfrac{1}{12}} = 513 \text{ J/s}$$

The overall heat transfer coefficient is found as follows:

$$\dot{Q} = UA\Delta T = U \times 30 \times 42 = 513.$$

$$\therefore U = 0.407 \text{ J/s} \cdot \text{m}^2 \cdot {}^{\circ}\text{C}$$

7.3 The First Law of Thermo-dynamics for a Control Volume

The dot signifies a rate so that $\dot{Q}$ and $\dot{W}_S$ have the units of kJ/s.

The continuity equation, which accounts for the conservation of mass, may be used in certain situations involving control volumes. It is stated as

$$\dot{m} = \rho_1 A_1 V_1 = \rho_2 A_2 V_2 \tag{7.3.1}$$

where, in control volume formulations, V is the velocity; $\dot{m}$ is called the *mass flux*. In the above continuity equation, we assume *steady flow*, that is, the variables are independent of time. For such steady state flow situations, the first law takes the form:

$$\frac{\dot{Q} - \dot{W}_S}{\dot{m}} = \frac{V_2^{\,2} - V_1^{\,2}}{2} + h_2 - h_1 + g(z_2 - z_1) \tag{7.3.2}$$

where the dot signifies a rate so that $\dot{Q}$ and $\dot{W}_S$ have the units of kJ/s. In most devices the potential energy is negligible. Also, the kinetic energy change can often be ignored (but if sufficient information is given, it should be included) so that the first law is most often used in the simplified form

$$\dot{Q} - \dot{W}_S = \dot{m}(h_2 - h_1) \quad \text{or} \quad q - w_S = h_2 - h_1 \tag{7.3.3}$$

Particular devices are of special interest. The energy equation for a *valve* or a *throttle plate* is simply

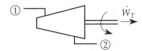

$$h_2 = h_1 \qquad \textbf{(7.3.4)}$$

providing kinetic energy can be neglected.

For a *turbine* expanding a gas, the heat transfer is negligible so that

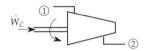

$$\dot{W}_T = \dot{m}(h_1 - h_2) \qquad \text{or} \qquad w_T = h_1 - h_2 \qquad \textbf{(7.3.5)}$$

The work input to a *gas compressor* with negligible heat transfer is

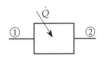

$$\dot{W}_C = \dot{m}(h_2 - h_1) \qquad \text{or} \qquad w_C = h_2 - h_1 \qquad \textbf{(7.3.6)}$$

A *boiler* and a *condenser* are simply heat transfer devices. The first law then simplifies to

$$\dot{Q} = \dot{m}(h_2 - h_1) \qquad \text{or} \qquad q = h_2 - h_1 \qquad \textbf{(7.3.7)}$$

For a *nozzle* or a *diffuser* there is no work or heat transfer; we must include, however, the kinetic energy change, resulting in

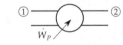

$$0 = \frac{V_2^{\,2} - V_1^{\,2}}{2} + h_2 - h_1 \qquad \textbf{(7.3.8)}$$

For a *pump* or a *hydroturbine* we take a slightly different approach. We return to Equation 7.3.2 and write it using $v = 1/\rho$, and with Equation 7.2.10, as

$$\frac{\dot{Q} - \dot{W}_S}{\dot{m}} = \frac{V_2^{\,2} - V_1^{\,2}}{2} + u_2 - u_1 + \frac{P_2 - P_1}{\rho} + g(z_2 - z_1) \qquad \textbf{(7.3.9)}$$

For an ideal situation we do not transfer heat and assume constant temperature so that $u_2 = u_1$. Neglecting kinetic and potential energy changes we find that

$$-\dot{W}_S = \dot{m}\,\frac{P_2 - P_1}{\rho} \qquad \textbf{(7.3.10)}$$

Efficiency is based on an isentropic process

This would provide the minimum pump power requirement or the maximum turbine power output. The inclusion of an efficiency would increase the pump power requirement or decrease the turbine output.

A gas turbine or compressor efficiency is based on an isentropic process ($s_2 = s_1$) as the ideal process. For a gas turbine or a compressor we have

$$\eta_T = \frac{\dot{W}_a}{\dot{W}_s} = \frac{w_a}{w_s} \qquad\qquad \eta_C = \frac{\dot{W}_s}{\dot{W}_a} = \frac{w_s}{w_a} \qquad \textbf{(7.3.11)}$$

where $\dot{W}_a$ is the actual power and $\dot{W}_s$ is the power assuming an isentropic process.

7·THERMO

Example 7.15

Refrigerant-134a expands through a valve from a state of saturated liquid at 800 kPa to a pressure of 100 kPa. What is the final quality?

Solution. The first law states that

$$h_1 = h_2$$

Using Fig. 7.9 (at the end of the chapter) for Refrigerant-134a we find, using $h_1 = h_f$,

$$h_1 = 240 \text{ kJ/kg}$$

There follows at $P_2 = 100$ kPa, using $h_2 = 240$,

$$x = 0.35 \quad \text{or} \quad 35\%$$

Example 7.16

Steam expands through a turbine from 6 MPa and 600°C to 2 kPa with $x_2 = 1.0$. Find the work output.

Solution. The first law gives

$$w_T = h_1 - h_2$$
$$= 3658.4 - 2533.5 = 1125 \text{ kJ/kg}$$

where h_2 is h_g at $P_2 = 0.002$ MPa, as given in Table 7.3.2.

Example 7.17

What is the turbine efficiency in Example 7.16?

Solution. The turbine efficiency is based on an isentropic process. Let state 2' be at 2 kPa with

$$s_{2'} = s_1 = 7.1677 \text{ kJ/kg} \cdot \text{K}$$

At 0.002 MPa we find, from Table 7.3.2

$$s_{2'} = s_f + x_{2'} s_{fg}$$
$$7.1677 = 0.2606 + x_{2'}(8.4639)$$
$$\therefore x_{2'} = 0.816$$

At this ideal state we find

$$h_{2'} = h_f + x_{2'} h_{fg}$$
$$= 73.5 + 0.816 \times 2460 = 2080 \text{ kJ/kg}$$

Finally, we use w_T as the answer in Example 7.16 and obtain

$$\eta_T = \frac{w_T}{w_S} = \frac{w_T}{h_1 - h_2}$$
$$= \frac{1125}{3658.4 - 2080} = 0.713 \text{ or } 71.3\%$$

Example 7.18

What is the minimum power requirement of a pump that is to increase the pressure from 2 kPa to 6 MPa for a mass flux of 10 kg/s of water?

Solution. With a liquid we let $h_2 - h_1 = u_2 - u_1 + (P_2 - P_1)v$ since $v = $ const. We let $u_2 - u_1 = 0$ so that the first law simplifies to

$$\dot{W}_P = \dot{m}\frac{P_2 - P_1}{\rho}$$

$$= 10\frac{6000 - 2}{1000} = 59.98 \text{ kW}$$

Note how small this is relative to the power output of the turbine of example 7.16 operating between the same pressures. Because this is less than 1% of the turbine output, the pump work may usually be neglected in the analysis of a cycle involving a steam turbine and a pump.

Example 7.19

A nozzle accelerates air from 100 m/s, 400°C and 400 kPa to a receiver where $P = 20$ kPa. Assuming an isentropic process, find V_2.

Solution. The energy equation takes the form

$$0 = \frac{V_2^2 - V_1^2}{2} + h_2 - h_1$$

Assuming air to be an ideal gas with constant c_p we have

$$c_p(T_1 - T_2) = \frac{V_2^2 - V_1^2}{2}$$

We can find T_2 from Equation 7.2.31 to be

$$T_2 = T_1(P_2 / P_1)^{k-1/k}$$

$$= 673(20 / 400)^{0.4/1.4} = 286 \text{ K}$$

The exiting velocity is found as follows:

$$1000(673 - 286) = \frac{V_2^2 - 100^2}{2}$$

$$\therefore V_2 = 885 \text{ m/s}$$

Note: c_p must be used as 1000 J / kg · K so that the units are consistent.

7.4 The Second Law of Thermodynamics

The two scientific statements of the second law of thermodynamics can be shown to be equivalent. They are stated and shown schematically in Figure 7.2.

Clausius Statement—A device which operates in a cycle cannot transfer heat from a cooler body to a hotter body without a work input.

Kelvin-Planck Statement—A device which operates in a cycle cannot produce work while exchanging heat with a single constant temperature reservoir.

Figure 7.3 shows an engine (it produces work) and a refrigerator (it transfers heat from a body at low temperature) that satisfy the second law. The devices of Figure 7.2 do not violate the first law—energy is conserved—however, they represent impossibilities, violations of the second law.

> Losses, friction, unrestrained expansion, and most important, heat transfer across a finite temperature difference all lead to irreversibilities.

To write a mathematical statement of the second law, we use entropy, defined by $dS = \delta Q/T$. The net entropy change during any process is given by

$$\Delta S_{universe} = \Delta S_{system} + \Delta S_{surroundings} \geq 0 \tag{7.4.1}$$

The equal sign applies to a reversible process, the greater-than sign applies to an irreversible (or real) process. Losses, friction, unrestrained expansion, and most important, heat transfer across a finite temperature difference all lead to irreversibilities. This latter irreversibility results in the relatively low efficiencies of power plants and auto engines. Entropy changes can be found using tables, or for an ideal gas with constant specific heats we can use

$$\Delta s = c_p \ln \frac{T_2}{T_1} - R \ln \frac{P_2}{P_1} \tag{7.4.2}$$

For constant temperature processes, such as heat transfer to a reservoir, we use

$$\Delta S = \frac{Q}{T} \tag{7.4.3}$$

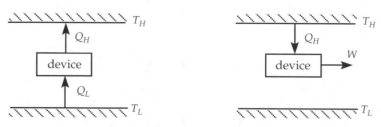

Figure 7.2 Violations of the second law.

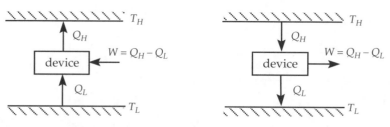

Figure 7.3 Devices that satisfy the second law.

For a solid or a liquid we use

$$\Delta S = mc \ln \frac{T_2}{T_1} \qquad \textbf{(7.4.4)}$$

where $c = c_p$ found in Table 7.2.

In general, for a reversible process, we have, from the definition of entropy,

$$Q = \int T dS \qquad \textbf{(7.4.5)}$$

which is analogous to $W = \int P dV$ for such a process.

A Carnot engine or refrigerator is a fictitious device that operates with reversible processes. It provides us with the maximum possible efficiency of an engine in terms of temperatures:

$$\eta = \frac{W_{out}}{Q_{in}}, \qquad \eta_{\max} = 1 - \frac{T_L}{T_H} \qquad \textbf{(7.4.6)}$$

> A Carnot engine or refrigerator is a fictitious device that operates with reversible processes.

It provides the maximum possible *coefficient of performance*, COP, of a refrigerator,

$$\text{COP} = \frac{Q_L}{W_{in}}, \qquad \text{COP}_{\max} = \frac{1}{T_H / T_L - 1} \qquad \textbf{(7.4.7)}$$

or, the upper limit for the COP of a heat pump,

$$\text{COP} = \frac{Q_H}{W_{in}}, \qquad \text{COP}_{\max} = \frac{1}{1 - T_L / T_H} \qquad \textbf{(7.4.8)}$$

T_H is the temperature of the high temperature reservoir and T_L is the temperature of the low temperature reservoir.

The vapor power cycle is the basic cycle for most power plants; it is sketched in Figure 7.4a. The vapor refrigeration cycle is shown in Figure 7.4b.

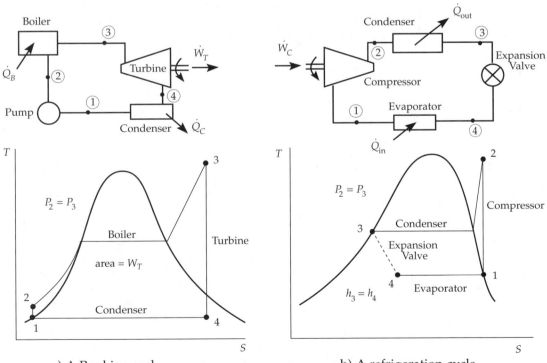

a) A Rankine cycle.   b) A refrigeration cycle.

Figure 7.4 Vapor cycles.

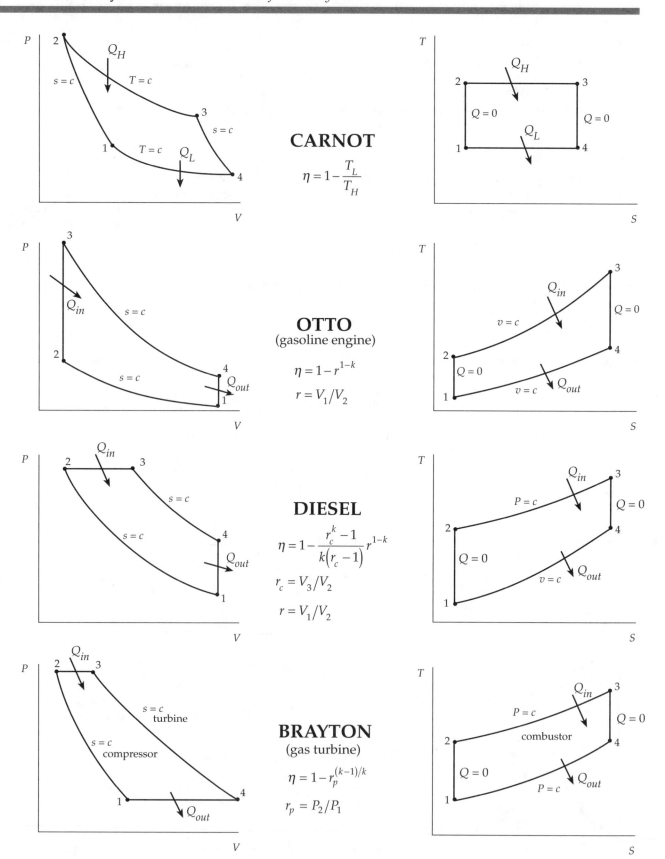

Figure 7.5 Common thermodynamic gas cycles.

The Carnot cycle is sketched in Figure 7.5 along with some other common gas cycles. The efficiency of each of the other cycles is less than that of the Carnot cycle, primarily due to the transfer of heat across a finite temperature difference.

Note that all of the above cycles are ideal cycles; the entropy is assumed constant in two processes in each cycle (except for the refrigeration cycle). Actual processes deviate from these ideal processes, resulting in lower cycle efficiencies than predicted by the above.

To determine an expression for the maximum work output of a steady flow device, use the first law, neglecting kinetic and potential energy changes, in the form:

$$\dot{Q} - \dot{W}_s = \dot{m}(h_2 - h_1) \tag{7.4.9}$$

If we assume that heat is transferred to the surroundings at atmospheric temperature T_o we can relate

$$\dot{m}(s_2 - s_1) = \dot{Q}/T_o \tag{7.4.10}$$

Substituting into the Equation 7.4.9 we have

$$\dot{W}_{max} = \dot{m}(h_1 - T_o s_1) - \dot{m}(h_2 - T_o s_2)$$
$$= \dot{m}(\phi_1 - \phi_2) \tag{7.4.11}$$

where ϕ is the *availability*. Hence, the maximum work output is the change in the availability.

Example 7.20

Ten kilograms of ice at 0°C are melted in 100 kg of water initially at 25°C. Calculate the final temperature and the entropy change. Assume no heat transfer to the surroundings.

Solution. The first law is applied to the ice-water system:

$$Q_{gain} = Q_{lost}$$
$$10 \times 320 + 10(T - 0) \times 4.18 = 100(25 - T) \times 4.18$$
$$\therefore T = 15.8°C$$

The entropy change is found as follows:

$$\text{ice}: \quad \Delta S = \frac{Q}{T_1} + mc \ln \frac{T_2}{T_1}$$
$$= \frac{10 \times 320}{273} + 10 \times 4.18 \ln \frac{288.8}{273} = 14.073 \text{ kJ/K}$$
$$\text{water}: \quad \Delta S = mc \ln \frac{T_2}{T_1}$$
$$= 100 \times 4.18 \ln \frac{288.8}{298} = -13.107 \text{ kJ/K}$$

The net entropy change is

$$\Delta S_{net} = 14.073 - 13.107 = 0.966 \text{ kJ/K}$$

This is positive, as required by the second law.

Example 7.21

An inventor claims to have invented an engine, using a 160°C geothermal heat source, which operates with an efficiency of 30%. If it exhausts to the 20°C atmosphere, is the invention possible?

Solution. The maximum possible efficiency, as limited by the second law, is given by

$$\eta_{max} = 1 - \frac{T_L}{T_H}$$

$$= 1 - \frac{293}{433} = 0.323 \ \text{ or } \ 32.3\%$$

The proposal is a possibility. However, the proposed efficiency is quite close to the maximum efficiency. It would be extremely difficult to obtain the 30% because of the losses due to heat transfer across a finite temperature difference and friction.

Example 7.22

A heat pump delivers 20 000 kJ /hr of heat with a 1.39 kW input. Calculate the COP.

Solution. Using the definition of the COP we find

$$\text{COP} = \frac{\dot{Q}_H}{\dot{W}_{in}}$$

$$= \frac{20\ 000\ /\ 3600}{1.39} = 4.00$$

Note, the factor 3600 converts hours into seconds.

Example 7.23

Compare the efficiency of an Otto cycle operating on an 8 to 1 compression ratio ($r = 8$) with a Diesel cycle that has a 20 to 1 compression ratio and a cut-off ratio of 2 to 1 ($r_c = 2$). Use air.

Solution. The efficiency of an Otto cycle (see Figure 7.5) is

$$\eta = 1 - r^{1-k}$$

$$= 1 - 8^{-0.4} = 0.565 \ \text{ or } \ 56.5\%$$

where air is assumed to be the working fluid.

The efficiency of the Diesel cycle is

$$\eta = 1 - \frac{r_c^{\ k} - 1}{k(r_c - 1)} r^{1-k}$$

$$= 1 - \frac{2^{1.4} - 1}{1.4(2 - 1)} 20^{-0.4} = 0.647 \ \text{ or } \ 64.7\%$$

The efficiency of the Diesel cycle is higher than that of the Otto cycle because it operates at a higher compression ratio. If the Otto cycle could operate at $r = 20$, its efficiency would be greater than that of the Diesel.

Example 7.24

If a power plant operates on a simple Rankine cycle using water between 600°C, 6 MPa and a low pressure of 10 kPa, calculate η_{max}.

Solution. Referring to Figure 7.4a, we define the efficiency to be

$$\eta_{max} = \frac{\dot{W}_T}{\dot{Q}_B}$$

The pump work is neglected (see Example 7.18). To find $\dot{W}_T$ we must find h_4. This is accomplished using $P_3 = 6$ MPa and $T_3 = 600\,°C$, as follows:

$$s_4 = s_3 = 7.168 \ \text{kJ/kg·K}$$

$$\text{At } P = 10 \text{ kPa}: \quad 7.168 = 0.6491 + x_4(7.5019)$$

$$\therefore \ x_4 = 0.869$$

$$\therefore \ h_4 = 191.8 + 0.869 \times 2392.8 = 2271 \ \text{kJ/kg}$$

The turbine output is then (assuming $\dot{m} = 1$ kg / s since it is not given; alternatively we could let $w_T = h_3 - h_4$)

$$\dot{W}_T = \dot{m}(h_3 - h_4)$$
$$= 1 \times (3658.4 - 2271) = 1387 \ \text{kW}$$

The energy input occurs in the boiler. It is

$$\dot{Q}_B = \dot{m}(h_3 - h_2)$$
$$= 1 \times (3658.4 - 191.8) = 3467 \ \text{kW}$$

Note: Be careful finding h_2. We ignore the energy of the pump since it is always quite small; then $h_2 \cong h_1 = h_f$ at 10 kPa.

Finally, the efficiency of this idealized cycle is

$$\eta_{max} = \frac{1387}{3467} = 0.400 \ \text{ or } \ 40.0\%$$

Example 7.25

A refrigeration system, using Refrigerant-134a, operates between –20°C and 40°C. What is the maximum possible COP?

Solution. The refrigeration effect takes place in the evaporator. Hence, referring to Figure 7.4b, the COP is defined as

$$\text{COP} = \frac{\dot{Q}_{in}}{\dot{W}_C}$$

To find $\dot{W}_C$ we must locate state 2. This is done by following the constant entropy line $(s_1 = s_2 \cong 1.74)$ in Fig. 7.9 at the end of this chapter. Locating states 1 and 2 we find

$$h_1 \cong 385 \ \text{kJ/kg}$$
$$h_2 \cong 425 \ \text{kJ/kg}$$

The compressor work is, assuming $\dot{m} = 1$ kg / s,

$$\dot{W}_C = \dot{m}(h_2 - h_1)$$
$$= 1 \times (425 - 385) = 40 \text{ kW}$$

To find $\dot{Q}_{in}$ we recognize that $h_4 = h_3 = 255$ kJ/kg, using Fig. 7.4b. Thus we find,

$$\dot{Q}_{in} = \dot{m}(h_1 - h_4)$$
$$= 1 \times (385 - 255) = 130 \text{ kW}$$

The maximum COP for this idealized cycle is

$$\text{COP} = \frac{130}{40} = 3.25$$

Example 7.26

The maximum pressure in an Otto cycle is 8 MPa. Air is compressed from 85 kPa and 22°C with a compression ratio of 8. What is the required heat addition? Assume constant specific heats.

Solution. Referring to the diagrams of the Otto cycle

$$P_1 = 85 \text{ kPa} \quad, \quad T_1 = 22°C. \qquad \therefore v_1 = \frac{RT_1}{P_1} = \frac{0.287 \times 295}{85} = 0.9961 \text{ m}^3/\text{kg}$$

Since the compression ratio is a volume ratio we have

$$v_3 = v_2 = v_1/8 = 0.9961/8 = 0.1245 \text{ m}^3/\text{kg}$$

We know that $P_3 = 8$ MPa . Thus

$$T_3 = \frac{P_3 v_3}{R} = \frac{8000 \times 0.1245}{0.287} = 3471 \text{ K}$$

The isentropic process from 1 to 2 allows us to find T_2:

$$T_2 = T_1 \left(\frac{v_1}{v_2} \right)^{k-1} = 295 \times 8^{0.4} = 677.7 \text{ K}$$

Finally, since the process from 2 to 3 is at constant volume with a system,

$$q_{2-3} = c_v(T_3 - T_2) = 0.717(3471 - 677.7) = 2003 \text{ kJ/kg}$$

Example 7.27

Steam at 200°C and 200 kPa is available to produce work by expanding it to the atmosphere at 20°C and 100 kPa. What is $\dot{W}_{max}$ if $\dot{m} = 2$ kg / s?

Solution. We will use the equation

$$\dot{W}_{max} = \dot{m}(\phi_1 - \phi_2)$$

The availabilities are found to be (using Table 7.3)

$$\phi_1 = h_1 - T_o s_1$$
$$= 2870.5 - 293 \times 7.5066 = 671 \text{ kJ/kg}$$
$$\phi_2 = h_2 - T_o s_2$$
$$= 83.9 - 293 \times 0.2965 = -3.0 \text{ kJ/kg}$$

Note: State 2 is at 20°C and 100 kPa. This is the liquid state so we use $h_2 = h_f$ and $s_2 = s_f$ at 20°C (see Table 7.3.1), and simply ignore the pressure. Finally,

$$\dot{W}_{max} = 2[671 - (-3.0)] = 1348 \text{ kW}$$

7.5 Psychrometrics

Air is primarily a mixture of nitrogen, oxygen, argon and water vapor. When water vapor is absent, it is *dry air*. In most problems water vapor does not influence calculations, e.g., the problems considered earlier in this chapter. It must, however, be accounted for in problems involving combustion and air conditioning. Here we will present the primary quantities when considering *atmospheric air*, air that contains water vapor. We will make our calculations using the *psychrometric chart*, found in Fig. 7.8 at the end of this chapter or the NCEES Handbook.

The atmospheric pressure P is the sum of the partial pressure P_a of dry air and the partial pressure P_v of the water vapor:

$$P = P_a + P_v \qquad (7.5.1)$$

Relative humidity ϕ is

$$\phi = \frac{m_v}{m_g} \qquad (7.5.2)$$

$$= \frac{P_v}{P_g}$$

where P_g is the saturation pressure at temperature of the air (found in Table 7.3.1) and m_g is the maximum mass of water vapor that the air can hold at air temperature, usually called the *dry-bulb temperature T_{db}*. We have assumed that the water vapor contained in atmospheric air acts as an ideal gas.

The *specific humidity* (or *humidity ratio*) ω is

$$\omega = \frac{m_v}{m_a} \qquad (7.5.3)$$

$$= 0.622 \frac{P_v}{P_a}$$

The enthalpy of the atmospheric air is

$$h = h_a + \omega h_v \qquad (7.5.4)$$

The *dew-point temperature T_{dp}* is the temperature at which condensation begins. The *wet-bulb temperature T_{wb}* is the temperature that a thermometer would read if a saturated wick were attached to its bulb and whirled around through the air. On the T-s diagram shown here, $T_1 = T_2 = T_{db}$, $T_3 = T_{dp}$, and T_{wb} would be between T_2 and T_3.

The quantities T_{db}, T_{dp}, T_{wb}, ω, ϕ, and h can be read directly from the psychrometric chart so that the above equations are not needed in most air conditioning problems. Consider a state A, on the psychrometric chart shown, located by specifying the dry-bulb temperature T_{db} and the relative humidity ϕ. We would read T_{wb} at 1, T_{dp} at 2, h at 3, and ω at 4. A detailed psychrometric chart is in Fig. 7.8 or the NCEES Handbook.

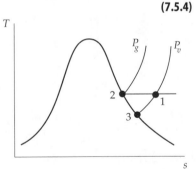

Figure 7.6 Water vapor.

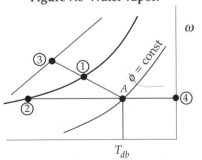

Figure 7.7 Psychrometric chart.

Water vapor must be accounted for in problems involving air conditioning.

• The *wet-bulb temperature* T_{wb} is the temperature that a thermometer would read if a saturated wick were attached to its bulb and whirled around through the air.

7·THERMO

Example 7.28

A thermometer with a wet cloth attached to its bulb reads 20°C when air is blown around it. If the atmospheric air is 33°C, what is the relative humidity and dew-point temperature? How much water could be condensed out of a 100-m³ volume?

Solution. From the psychrometric chart we read

$$\phi = 30\% \quad \text{and} \quad T_{dp} = 13.2°C. \quad \text{Also,} \quad \omega = 0.0093 \text{ kg water/kg air}$$

The amount of water that could be condensed out is

$$\omega \, \rho_{air} V_{air} = 0.0093 \times \frac{100}{0.287 \times 306} \times 100 = 1.06 \text{ kg} \quad \text{or} \quad 1.06 \text{ Liters}$$

Example 7.29

It is desired to condition 35°C, 80% humidity air to 24°C and 50% humidity. If 100 m³/min of air is to be conditioned, how much energy is required in the cooling process, and how much in the heating process?

Solution. To decrease the moisture content in the air we first cool the air from 1 to 2 at constant ω and then remove water by cooling it further to 3 (along the 100% humidity line). In this process

$$\dot{Q}_{cool} = \dot{m}\Delta h = \frac{100}{60}\rho_a \big(h_1 - h_3\big) + h_f\big(\omega_1 - \omega_3\big)$$

$$= \frac{100}{60}\frac{1}{0.913}(105 - 37) = 124 \text{ kJ/s}.$$

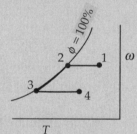

Heating takes place from 3 to 4 at constant ω:

$$\dot{Q}_{heat} = \dot{m}\big(h_4 - h_3\big) = \frac{100}{60}\frac{1}{0.823}(48 - 37) = 18.3 \text{ kJ/s}$$

We obtained $v = 1/\rho$ and the above properties from the psychrometric chart found in Fig. 7.8 or the NCEES Handbook.

Practice Problems

(If you choose to work only a few problems, select those with an asterisk.)

General

*7.1   Which of the following would be considered a system rather than a control volume?
a) a pump   b) a tire   c) a pressure cooker   d) a turbine

*7.2   Which of the following is an extensive property?
a) Temperature   b) Velocity   c) Pressure   d) Mass

7.3   An automobile heats up while sitting in a parking lot on a sunny day. The process can be assumed to be:
a) isothermal   b) isobaric   c) isometric   d) isentropic

*7.4   If a quasi-equilibrium process exists, we have assumed
a) the pressure at any instant to be everywhere constant.
b) an isothermal process.
c) the heat transfer to be small.
d) the boundary motion to be infinitesimally small.

*7.5   A scientific law is a statement that
a) we postulate to be true.
b) is generally observed to be true.
c) is a summary of experimental observation.
d) is agreed upon by the scientific community.

7.6   Which of the following is not an extensive property?
a) Momentum   b) Kinetic energy   c) Enthalpy   d) Density

7.7   In a quasiequilibrium process involving a system
a) the pressure remains constant.
b) the pressure varies with temperature.
c) the pressure is constant at an instant at each point in the system.
d) the pressure force results in a positive work input.

7.8   Which of the following is not an acceptable SI unit?
a) Distance measured in centimeters.
b) Temperature measured in kelvins.
c) Density measured in grams per cubic centimeter.
d) Volume measured in cubic centimeters.

7.9   A long metal rod can be used as a very stiff spring. The deformation of a rod is given by $\delta = PL/AE$, as defined in Mechanics of Materials. What is the "spring constant" of the metal rod?

    a) AE/L b) $1/AE$ c) L/AE d) AE

Density, Pressure and Temperature

*7.10   The density of air at vacuum of 40 kPa and –40°C is, in kg/m^3,

    a) 0.598   b) 0.638   c) 0.897   d) 0.753

7.11   The specific volume of water is 0.5 m^3/kg at a pressure of 200 kPa. Find the quality.

    a) 0.623   b) 0.564   c) 0.478   d) 0.423

7.12   The specific volume of steam at 4 MPa and 1200°C, in m^3/kg, is

    a) 0.20   b) 0.19   c) 0.18   d) 0.17

7.13   Water with quality $x = 50\%$ is contained in a rigid vessel. If more heat is added

    a) x increases.

    b) x decreases.

    c) x remains relatively constant.

    d) x may increase or decrease.

7.14   There are 20 kg of steam contained in 2 m^3 at 4 MPa. What is the temperature in °C?

    a) 600   b) 610   c) 620   d) 630

7.15   The pressure in a cylinder containing water is 200 kPa and the temperature is 115°C. What state is it in?

    a) compressed liquid

    b) saturated liquid

    c) liquid/vapor mixture

    d) saturated vapor

*7.16   A cold tire has a volume of 0.03 m^3 at –10°C and 180 kPa gage. If the pressure and temperature increase to 210 kPa gage and 30°C, find the final volume in m^3.

    a) 0.0304   b) 0.0308   c) 0.0312   d) 0.0316

The First Law for a System

*7.17   A 300-watt light bulb provides energy in a 10-m-dia spherical space. If the outside temperature is 20°C, find the inside steady-state temperature, in °C, if $R = 1.5\ hr \cdot m^2 \cdot °C/kJ$ for the wall.

    a) 40.5   b) 35.5   c) 32.6   d) 25.2

7.18   A 10 kg mass, which is attached to a pulley and a paddle wheel submerged in water, drops 3 m. Find the subsequent heat transfer, in joules, needed to return the temperature of the water to its original value.

    a) –294   b) –195   c) –126   d) –30

*7.19 Select a correct statement of the first law.

 a) Heat transfer equals the work done for a process.

 b) Net heat transfer equals the net work for a cycle.

 c) Net heat transfer equals net work plus internal energy change for a cycle.

 d) Heat transfer minus work equals change in enthalpy.

7.20 Which of the following first law statements is wrong?

 a) The internal energy change equals the work of a system for an adiabatic process.

 b) The net heat transfer equals the work output for an engine operating on a cycle.

 c) The heat transfer equals the quasi equilibrium work of a system for a constant volume process in which the internal energy remains constant.

 d) For an adiabatic process the heat transfer equals the enthalpy change.

*7.21 Which of the following statements about work for a quasi equilibrium process is wrong?

 a) Work is the area under a curve on the P-T diagram.

 b) The differential of work is inexact.

 c) Work is energy crossing a boundary.

 d) Work is a path function.

7.22 Select the correct statement for an incompressible substance.

 a) The enthalpy depends on temperature only.

 b) The specific heat is always constant.

 c) The specific volume depends on the pressure.

 d) The internal energy depends on temperature only.

*7.23 A cycle undergoes the following processes. All units are kJ. Find E_{after} for the process $1 \rightarrow 2$.

	Q	W	ΔE	E_{before}	E_{after}
$1 \rightarrow 2$	20		5		10
$2 \rightarrow 3$			−5	5	
$3 \rightarrow 1$	30				30

 a) 10 b) 15 c) 20 d) 25

7.24 For the cycle of Problem 7.23 find W_{3-1}.

 a) 50 b) 60 c) 70 d) 80

7.25 A 2000 kg automobile traveling at 25 m/s strikes a plunger in 10 000 cm^3 of water, bringing the auto to a stop. What is the maximum temperature rise, in °C, in the water?

 a) 5 b) 10 c) 15 d) 20

7.26 Ten kilograms of –10°C ice is added to 100 kg of 20°C water. What is the eventual temperature, in °C, of the water? Assume an insulated container.
a) 9.2   b) 10.8   c) 11.4   d) 12.6

*7.27 Of the following first law statements, choose the one that is wrong:
a) The net heat transfer equals the net work for a cycle.
b) The heat transfer cannot exceed the work done.
c) The heat transfer equals the work plus the energy change.
d) The heat transfer equals the energy change if no work is done.

7.28 Select the incorrect statement. $(Q - W = \Delta U)$
a) Work and heat transfer represent energy crossing a boundary.
b) The differentials of work and heat transfer are exact.
c) Work and heat transfer are path integrals.
d) Net work and net heat transfer are equal for a cycle.

Isothermal Process

*7.29 Determine the work, in kJ, necessary to compress 2 kg of air from 100 kPa to 4000 kPa if the temperature is held constant 300°C.
a) –1210   b) –1105   c) –932   d) –812

*7.30 Steam is compressed from 100 kPa to 4000 kPa holding the temperature constant at 300°C. What is the internal energy change, in kJ, for $m = 2$ kg?
a) –180   b) –170   c) –160   d) –150

7.31 How much heat transfer, in kJ, is needed to convert 2 kg of saturated liquid water to saturated vapor if the temperature is held constant at 200°C?
a) 2380   b) 2980   c) 3880   d) 4160

Constant Pressure Process

7.32 There are 200 people in a 2000 m^2 room, lighted with 30 W/m^2. Estimate the maximum temperature increase, in °C, if the ventilation system fails for 20 min. Each person generates 400 kJ/h. The room is 3 m high.
a) 5.6   b) 6.8   c) 8.6   d) 13.4

*7.33 Estimate the average c_p value, in kJ/kg·K, of a gas if 522 kJ of heat are necessary to raise the temperature from 300 K to 800 K holding the pressure constant.
a) 1.000   b) 1.026   c) 1.038   d) 1.044

*7.34 How much heat, in kJ, must be transferred to 10 kg of air to increase the temperature from 10°C to 230°C if the pressure is maintained constant?
a) 2200   b) 2090   c) 1890   d) 1620

7.35 Ten kilograms of water, initially at 10°C, is heated until $T = 300$°C. Estimate the heat transfer, in MJ, if the pressure is held constant at 200 kPa.
a) 29.2   b) 29.7   c) 30.3   d) 30.9

7•THERMO

7.36   Calculate the work done, in MJ, in Problem 7.35.
    a) 2.63   b) 4.72   c) 8.96   d) 11.4

7.37   How much heat, in kJ, must be added to a rigid volume, containing 2 kg of water/vapor mixture with $x = 0.5$, to increase the temperature from 200°C to 500°C?
    a) 2730   b) 2620   c) 2510   d) 2390

Constant Volume Process

*7.38   A tire is pressurized to 100 kPa gauge in Michigan where $T = 0$°C. In Arizona the tire is at 70°C. Assuming a rigid tire, estimate the pressure in kPa gauge.
    a) 120   b) 130   c) 140   d) 150

7.39   A sealed, rigid, 10 m^3 air tank is heated by the sun from 20°C to 80°C. How much energy, in kJ, is transferred to the tank? Assume $P_1 = 100$ kPa.
    a) 720   b) 680   c) 510   d) 400

7.40   Ten kilograms of water is heated in a rigid container from 10°C to 200°C. What is the final quality if $Q = 9000$ kJ?
    a) 0.258   b) 0.162   c) 0.093   d) 0.052

Isentropic Process

*7.41   Air expands in an insulated cylinder from 200°C and 400 kPa to 20 kPa. Find T_2 in °C.
    a) –24   b) –28   c) –51   d) –72

*7.42   During an isentropic expansion of air, the volume triples. If the initial temperature is 200°C, find T_2 in °C.
    a) 32   b) 28   c) 16   d) 8

7.43   Superheated steam expands isentropically from 600°C and 6 MPa to 10 kPa. Find the final quality.
    a) 0.79   b) 0.83   c) 0.87   d) 0.91

7.44   Superheated steam expands isentropically from 600°C and 6 MPa to 400 kPa. Find T_2 in °C.
    a) 220   b) 200   c) 190   d) 160

7.45   Find the work, in kJ/kg, needed to compress air isentropically from 20°C and 100 kPa to 6 MPa.
    a) –523   b) –466   c) –423   d) –392

*7.46   During an isentropic process, which one of the following is true?
    a) The temperature increases as the pressure decreases.
    b) The temperature increases as the volume increases.
    c) The heat transfer equals the enthalpy change.
    d) The heat transfer is zero.

7-THERMO

*7.47 Which of the following entropy relationships is wrong?

    a) water: $\Delta s = c_p \ln T_2 / T_1$ b) air, $V = $ const : $\Delta s = c_v \ln T_2 / T_1$

    c) copper: $\Delta s = c_p \ln T_2 / T_1$ d) reservoir: $\Delta s = c_p \ln T_2 / T_1$

7.48 An isentropic process

    a) is adiabatic if it is reversible.

    b) is reversible but may not be adiabatic.

    c) is never irreversible.

    d) occurs at constant pressure but not constant temperature.

Polytropic Process

*7.49 Find T_2, in °C, if the pressure triples and $T_1 = 10$°C. Let $n = 1.2$.

    a) 179   b) 113   c) 67   d) 52

The First Law for a Control Volume

7.50 Steam enters a turbine in a 20-cm-dia pipe at 600°C and 6 MPa. It exits from a 5-cm-dia pipe at 20 kPa with $x = 1$. What is the velocity ratio V_{out}/V_{in}?

    a) 1880   b) 1640   c) 1210   d) 820

*7.51 Water enters a boiler at 60°C and 4 MPa. How much energy, in kJ/kg, must be added to obtain 600°C at the exit if the pressure remains constant?

    a) 2340   b) 2630   c) 3420   d) 3680

7.52 A condenser is cooled by heating water from 20°C to 30°C. If the condenser inlets 10 kg/s of saturated water vapor at 20 kPa and exits saturated liquid, what is the mass flux, in kg/s, of the cooling water?

    a) 640   b) 560   c) 500   d) 410

7.53 Steam at 400°C and 4 MPa expands isentropically through a turbine to 10 kPa. Estimate the maximum work output in kJ/kg.

    a) 1030   b) 1050   c) 1070   d) 1090

*7.54 What is the energy requirement, in kW, for a pump that is 75% efficient if it increases the pressure of 10 kg/s of water from 10 kPa to 6 MPa?

    a) 60   b) 70   c) 80   d) 90

7.55 A river 60 m wide and 2 m deep flows at 2 m/s. A hydro plant develops a pressure of 300 kPa gage just before the turbine. What maximum power, in MW, is possible?

    a) 72   b) 64   c) 56   d) 48

*7.56 A nozzle expands air isentropically from 400°C and 2 MPa to the atmosphere at 80 kPa. If the inlet velocity is small, what exit velocity, in m/s, can be expected?

    a) 500   b) 600   c) 900   d) 1200

7.57 If the efficiency of a turbine that expands steam at 400°C and 6 MPa to 20 kPa is 87%, find the work output in kJ/kg.

a) 723   b) 891   c) 933   d) 996

7.58 Select the assumption that we make when deriving the continuity equation $\dot{m}_1 = \dot{m}_2$.

a) constant density   b) steady flow
c) uniform flow   d) constant velocity

7.59 The term $\dot{m}\Delta h$ in the control volume equation $\dot{Q} - \dot{W}_S = \dot{m}\Delta h$

a) accounts for the change in energy in the control volume.
b) represents the change in energy between the outlet and the inlet.
c) is often neglected in control-volume applications.
d) includes the work due to the pressure forces.

The Second Law

*7.60 An inventor proposes to take 10 kg/s of geothermal water at 120°C and generate 4180 kW of energy by exhausting very near to the ambient temperature of 20°C. This proposal should not be supported because

a) it violates the first law.
b) it violates the second law.
c) it would be too expensive.
d) friction must be accounted for.

*7.61 The net entropy change in the universe during any real process

a) is equal to zero.
b) is positive.
c) is negative.
d) must be calculated to determine its sense.

*7.62 A Carnot engine

a) provides a fictitious model which is of little use.
b) can be experimentally modeled.
c) supplies us with the lower limit for engine efficiency.
d) operates between two constant temperature reservoirs.

7.63 Ninety kilograms of ice at 0°C is completely melted. Find the entropy change, in kJ/K, if $T_2 = 0$°C.

a) 0   b) 45   c) 85   d) 105

7.64 Forty kilograms of ice at 0°C is mixed with 100 kg of water at 20°C. What is the entropy change, in kJ/K?

a) 2.36   b) 2.15   c) 1.04   d) 0.96

*7.65 An inventor proposes to have developed a small power plant that operates at 70% efficiency. It operates between temperature extremes of 600°C and 50°C. Your analysis shows that the maximum possible efficiency is

a) 56   b) 63   c) 67   d) 72

*7.66 Select the process that is most nearly reversible in today's processes.

a) Compressing gas in a cylinder

b) Transferring heat in a heat exchanger

c) Combustion in a cylinder while the piston is stationary

d) Electrical resistance heating in a rigid container

7.67 Select an acceptable paraphrase of the Kelvin-Planck statement of the second law.

a) No process can produce more work than the heat that it accepts.

b) No engine can produce more work than the heat that it intakes.

c) An engine cannot produce work without accepting heat.

d) An engine has to reject heat.

7.68 Which one of the following second law statements is wrong?

a) Heat must always be rejected from a heat engine.

b) The entropy of an isolated process must remain constant or increase.

c) The entropy of a hot copper block decreases as it cools.

d) If ice is melted in water in an insulated container, the net entropy decreases.

Power Cycles

*7.69 A Carnot cycle operates on air such that $P_4 = 160$ kPa and $v_4 = 0.5$ m^3/kg (see Fig. 7.5). If 30 kJ/kg of heat is added at $T_H = 200$°C, find the work produced in kJ/kg.

a) 20.3   b) 18.2   c) 12.3   d) 6.2

7.70 An Otto cycle operates with volumes of 40 cm^3 and 400 cm^3 at top dead center (TDC) and bottom dead center (BDC), respectively. If the power output is 100 kW, what is the heat input in kJ/s? Assume $k = 1.4$.

a) 166   b) 145   c) 110   d) 93

7.71 The volumes of states 1, 2, and 3 in Fig. 7.5 of the Diesel cycle are 450 cm^3, 25 cm^3 and 45 cm^3, respectively. If the power produced is 120 kW, what is the required heat input in kJ/s? Assume that $k = 1.4$.

a) 187   b) 172   c) 157   d) 146

7.72 A simple Rankine cycle operates between superheated steam at 600°C and 6 MPa entering the turbine, and 10 kPa entering the pump. What is the maximum possible efficiency, as a percent?

a) 30   b) 35   c) 40   d) 45

7.73   The water vapor that expands from 600°C and 6 MPa in a turbine of a Rankine cycle is intercepted at 200 kPa and reheated at constant pressure to 600°C in the boiler, after which it is re-injected in the turbine and expanded to 10 kPa. (This is the *reheat cycle*.) Calculate the maximum possible efficiency, as a percent?

    a) 32   b) 37   c) 41   d) 45

7.74   The primary effect of reheating, as illustrated in Problem 7.61 (compare with the result in Problem 7.60), is to

    a) increase the efficiency.

    b) decrease or eliminate moisture condensation in the turbine.

    c) decrease the heat requirement.

    d) eliminate unnecessary piping.

*7.75 Which of the following will not increase the efficiency of a Rankine cycle?

    a) Increase boiler exit temperature

    b) Increase turbine exit pressure

    c) Increase pump exit pressure

    d) Decrease condenser exit pressure

7.76   The area under the *T-s* diagrams for the power cycles represents:

    a) the net work output   b) the heat input

    c) the total enthalpy change   d) the heat output

7.77   The efficiency of an Otto cycle depends on only one parameter. It is (refer to the Otto cycle):

    a) T_2 / T_1 b) T_3 / T_2 c) T_4 / T_1 d) T_4 / T_2

Refrigeration Cycles

7.78   A refrigeration cycle operates with Refrigerant-134a between 100 kPa and 1000 kPa. What is the maximum possible COP?

    a) 1.5   b) 2   c) 2.5   d) 3

7.79   The quality of the refrigerant immediately after the expansion valve of the cycle of Problem 7.78 is

    a) 0.58   b) 0.54   c) 0.42   d) 0.38

Availability

7.80   Determine the maximum possible power output, in kW, if 10 kg/s of air is expanded in a turbine from 100°C and 6 MPa to the surroundings at 20°C and 80 kPa.

    a) 3720   b) 2610   c) 2030   d) 1890

7.81   The change in thermodynamic availability is equal to

    a) the quantity $T \Delta S$.
    b) the change in enthalpy.
    c) the actual work output.
    d) the maximum possible work output.

Heat Transfer
(See Article 7.2)

*7.82 Heat transfer decreases with increased
a) conductivity   b) *R*-factor   c) emissivity   d) *U*-factor

*7.83 Heat transfer due to convection can be determined if we know the temperature difference, fluid properties, the geometry, and the
a) Reynolds No.   b) Nusselt No.   c) Prandtl No.   d) Froude No.

*7.84 Frozen soil at –15°C and water at 10°C are separated by a 50 cm-thick concrete wall. Estimate the rate of heat transfer, in J/s, if the wall is 2 m × 8 m.
a) 180   b) 140   c) 100   d) 50

7.85 The rate of heat loss, due to 150 °C air blowing over a 4-cm-dia cylinder, is measured to be 1500 kJ over a 10 minute time period. If the cylinder is 1.0-m-long and is maintained at 40°C, estimate the convection heat transfer coefficient in $J/s \cdot m^{2 \cdot °}C$.
a) 180   b) 140   c) 100   d) 50

7.86 A filament with a surface area of 0.8 cm^2 is positioned in a spherical space whose surface is at 80°C. Estimate the temperature of the filament , in °C, if 100 W of power is dissipated. Assume a black body filament.
a) 3000   b) 2600   c) 2300   d) 1900

7.87 Calculate the overall *R*-factor, in $m^{2 \cdot °}C \cdot s / J$, for a wall composed of 2.5 cm of polystyrene, 8 cm of wool insulation, and 2 cm of pine wood. Assume $h = 10 \ J/s \cdot m^{2 \cdot °}C$.
a) 3.2   b) 3.0   c) 2.8   d) 2.6

Psychrometrics

7.88 How much liquid water, in liters, is contained in a $3m \times 10m \times 20m$ room if $T = 25°C$ and the humidity is 60%?
a) 5.1   b) 6.6   c) 8.2   d) 9.8

7.89 A "swamp" cooler operates by blowing relatively dry air past a network of wet wicks. What maximum exiting temperature can be realized if the air is at 35°C with a humidity of 20%?
a) 28°C   b) 25°C   c) 22°C   d) 19°C

7.90 Outside air at 40°C and 20% relative humidity is cooled to 25°C without removing moisture. What is the final humidity? (Use the chart.)
a) 59%   b) 51%   c) 46%   d) 37%

Questions 7.91–7.95

A fictitious power cycle operates on 0.04 kg of air using the following three processes with a piston-cylinder arrangement:

$1 \rightarrow 2$: Constant pressure, $P_1 = 2000$ kPa, $T_1 = 20°C$

$2 \rightarrow 3$: Constant volume, $T_2 = 800°C$

$3 \rightarrow 1$: Constant temperature

7.91   At state 1 the volume of the air is nearest

    a) 1370 cm^3 b) 1680 cm^3 c) 1970 cm^3 d) 2360 cm^3

7.92   The volume at state 3 is nearest

    a) 3790 cm^3 b) 4180 cm^3 c) 5230 cm^3 d) 6160 cm^3

7.93   The heat required for a piston to move from state 1 to state 2 is nearest

    a) 56 kJ   b) 45 kJ   c) 31 kJ   d) 22 kJ

7.94   The work input needed to move a piston from state 3 to state 1 is nearest

    a) 2.6 kJ   b) 4.4 kJ   c) 16.7 kJ   d) 22 kJ

7.95   The heat that must be rejected as the piston moves from state 2 to state 3 is

    a) 56 kJ   b) 45 kJ   c) 31 kJ   d) 22 kJ

Questions 7.96–7.98

A nozzle accelerates air from 10 m/s and 20°C to 300 m/s and 100 kPa. The inlet diameter and pressure are 20 cm and 200 kPa, respectively.

7.96   The mass flow rate is nearest

    a) 0.36 kg/s   b) 0.47 kg/s   c) 0.52 kg/s   d) 0.75 kg/s

7.97   The exit temperature is nearest

    a) 0°C   b) –25°C   c) –38°C   d) –52°C

7.98   The efficiency of the nozzle is nearest

    a) 93%   b) 91%   c) 88%   d) 85%

7-THERMO

Questions 7.99–7.101

Two kilograms of steam at 6 MPa and 600°C enters an insulated turbine each second and exits the turbine at 10 kPa with a quality of 1.0.

7.99 If the exit diameter is 120 cm, the exit velocity is nearest

a) 26 m/s   b) 21 m/s   c) 16 m/s   d) 12 m/s

7.100 The power output of the turbine is nearest

a) 1.07 MW   b) 1.86 MW   c) 2.15 MW   d) 2.56 MW

7.101 The efficiency of the turbine is nearest

a) 77%   b) 82%   c) 86%   d) 91%

Questions 7.102–7.104

A Carnot cycle operates between temperatures of 20°C and 400°C. It rejects 100 kJ of heat each cycle.

7.102 What is the efficiency of the cycle?

a) 43.5%   b) 56.5%   c) 72.5%   d) 95.1%

7.103 How much heat must be added each cycle?

a) 57 kJ   b) 159 kJ   c) 192 kJ   d) 230 kJ

7.104 The entropy change during the heat addition process is nearest

a) 0.341 kJ/K   b) 0.961 kJ/K   c) 1.26 kJ/K   d) 5.03 kJ/K

Questions 7.105–7.108

An Otto cycle intakes air at 20°C and 100 kPa. The high temperature is 1000°C and the compression ratio is 8. Assume constant specific heats.

7.105 The efficiency of the cycle is nearest

a) 0.62   b) 0.59   c) 0.56   d) 0.47

7.106 Calculate the heat added.

a) 600 kJ/kg   b) 520 kJ/kg   c) 430 kJ/kg   d) 380 kJ/kg

7.107 The work done during the expansion process is nearest

a) 600 kJ/kg   b) 520 kJ/kg   c) 430 kJ/kg   d) 380 kJ/kg

7.108 If the mass of air in a cylinder is 0.002 kg, the clearance volume is nearest

a) 210 cm^3 b) 180 cm^3 c) 120 cm^3 d) 90 cm^3

<u>Questions 7.109–7.114</u>

Assume an adiabatic turbine and no pressure drop in the water as it flows through the boiler, superheater, and condenser in the Rankine cycle shown. Neglect kinetic and potential energy changes. Use the steam tables for the needed properties.

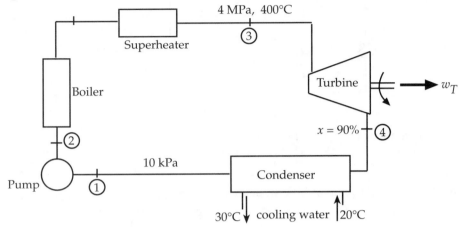

7.109 The energy requirement of the pump is nearest

    a) 4 kJ/kg   b) 40 kJ/kg   c) 400 kJ/kg   d) 4000 kJ/kg

7.110 The work output of the turbine is nearest

    a) 660 kJ/kg   b) 710 kJ/kg   c) 870 kJ/kg   d) 1200 kJ/kg

7.111 The cycle efficiency is nearest

    a) 41%   b) 37%   c) 33%   d) 29%

7.112 If the turbine output is 2 MW, the mass flow rate of water in the cycle is nearest

    a) 1.6 kg/s   b) 2.3 kg/s   c) 2.8 kg/s   d) 3.6 kg/s

7.113 The efficiency of the turbine is nearest

    a) 81%   b) 84%   c) 87%   d) 90%

7.114 The ratio of the mass flow rate of cooling water to the mass flow rate of steam in the condenser is nearest

    a) 9.2   b) 16.7   c) 32.3   d) 51.5

Questions 7.115–7.119

The ideal refrigeration cycle shown operates with Refrigerant HFC-134a between 100 kPa and 1 MPa. It provides five tons of cooling. Refer to Fig. 7.9 for data.

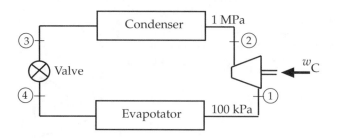

7.115   The quality of state 4 is nearest

    a) 0.43   b) 0.39   c) 0.35   d) 0.31

7.116   The mass flow rate of HFC-134a is nearest

    a) 19 kg/min   b) 15 kg/min   c) 12 kg/min   d) 8.5 kg/min

7.117   The work required by the compressor is nearest

    a) 40 kJ/kg   b) 50 kJ/kg   c) 60 kJ/kg   d) 60 kJ/kg

7.118   The COP for this cycle is nearest

    a) 1.4   b) 2.0   c) 2.5   d) 3.2

7.119   If a Carnot refrigeration cycle operated between the limits of this cycle, its COP would be nearest

    a) 3.4   b) 3.8   c) 4.5   d) 5.2

Questions 7.120–7.123

Two hundred cubic meters per minute of outside air at 80% relative humidity, 10°C and 100 kPa are heated to 20°C. Moisture is added so that the conditioned air is at 60% relative humidity.

7.120   If no moisture is added to the air, the relative humidity of the conditioned air would be nearest

    a) 37%   b) 43%   c) 49%   d) 58%

7.121   The dew point of the conditioned air is nearest

    a) 6.4°C   b) 8.2°C   c) 11.3°C   d) 15.2°C

7.122   The mass of water that must be added per hour is nearest

    a) 28 kg   b) 34 kg   c) 41 kg   d) 56 kg

7.123   The heat required is nearest

    a) 260 MJ/hr   b) 220 MJ/hr   c) 180 MJ/hr   d) 100 MJ/hr

Solutions to Practice Problems

7.1 b)   A tire. All other devices have fluid entering and/or leaving.

7.2 d)   Mass. All other quantities do not depend on the mass.

7.3 b)   Isobaric. The pressure will remain constant due to the inlets and outlets for air.

7.4 a)   All properties are uniform throughout the volume.

7.5 c)   A scientific law results from experimental observations.

7.6 d)   Density does not depend on the mass, i.e., when the mass is increased the density does not increase simultaneously.

7.7 c)   All properties are uniform throughout the volume.

7.8 c)   Distance, area, or volume may be measured in cm, cm^2, or cm^3, respectively, but grams are not acceptable in SI and cm cannot be used in combination with other units.

7.9 a) $F = Kx.$ $P = \dfrac{AE}{L}\delta.$ $\therefore K = \dfrac{AE}{L}.$

7.10 c) $\rho = 1/v = P/RT = (-40 + 100)/.287 \times (-40 + 273) = 0.897 \ \text{kg/m}^3.$
   $R = 8.314/28.97 = .287.$

7.11 b) $v = v_f + x\left(v_g - v_f\right)$ $P = 0.2 \ \text{MPa}$
   $0.5 = .001 + x(.8857 - .001)$ TABLE 7.3.2
   $\therefore x = 0.564$

7.12 d)   If the state is beyond Table 7.3.3 use the equation of state with
   $R = \dfrac{8.314}{18} = 0.462.$
   $$v = \dfrac{RT}{P} = \dfrac{0.462 \times 1473}{4000} = 0.17 \ \text{m}^3/\text{kg}.$$
   Use $T = 1200 + 273 = 1473 \ \text{K}, \quad P = 4000 \ \text{kPa}$

7.13 a)   In a rigid vessel, the volume remains constant. If we move straight up on the T-v diagram, x increases. (Temperature increases as heat is added.) Note: it is important to know that the diagram is skewed quite markedly to the left.

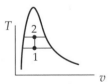

7.14 b) $v = \dfrac{V}{m} = \dfrac{2}{20} = 0.1, \quad P = 4 \ \text{MPa}.$
   From Table 7.3.3 interpolation gives
   $$T = \dfrac{0.1 - 0.09885}{0.1109 - 0.09885} \times 100 + 600 = 610° \ \text{C}.$$

7.15 a)   Using Table 7.3.2 we see that $115°C < 120.2°C$. $\therefore$ compressed.

7.16 **c)** $m = \dfrac{P_1 V_1}{RT_1} = \dfrac{280 \times .03}{.287 \times 263} = 0.1113$ kg, where $R = \dfrac{8.314}{28.97} = 0.287$.

$\therefore V_2 = \dfrac{mRT_2}{P_2} = \dfrac{.1113 \times .287 \times 303}{310} = 0.0312 \ \text{m}^3$

7.17 **d)** $\dot{Q} = \dfrac{1}{R} A \Delta T \qquad A = 4\pi r^2$

$\dfrac{300}{1000} = \dfrac{1}{1.5} 4\pi \times 5^2 (T - 20)\dfrac{1}{3600}. \quad \therefore \ T = 25.2°\text{C}.$

The 1000 converts J/s to kJ/s.

The 3600 converts hr to seconds.

7.18 **a)** $W = F \times d = (10 \times 9.8) \times 3 = 294$ N·m input. $\therefore$ W $= -294$ N·m.

$\therefore Q = W = -294\,\text{J}. \ \left(\text{Heat output is negative.}\right)$

7.19 **b)**   For a cycle, the change in internal energy is zero.

7.20 **d)**   For an adiabatic process the heat transfer is zero.

7.21 **a)**   Work is the area under the *P-V* diagram.

7.22 **d)**   If it's incompressible, the volume does not change.

7.23 **d)** $Q - W = E_a - E_b.$

$20 - 5 = E_a - 10. \quad \therefore \ E_a = 25 \text{ kJ}.$

7.24 **a)**   For $2 \to 3 \quad Q - (-5) = 5. \quad \therefore Q_{2-3} = 0$

$\therefore Q_{\text{net}} = 20 + 0 + 30 = 50$

$Q_{\text{net}} = W_{\text{net}} = 5 - 5 + W_{3-1} = 50.$

$\therefore W_{3-1} = 50 \ \text{kJ}.$

7.25 **c)** $Q = mc\Delta T. \quad$ Here $Q = \dfrac{1}{2}mV^2, \quad m = V\!\rho$

$\dfrac{1}{2} \times 2000 \times 25^2 = 10\ 000 \times 10^{-6} \times 1000 \times 4180 \ \Delta T$

$\therefore \ \Delta T = 14.95°\text{C}$

7.26 **b)** $(mc\Delta T)_{\text{ice}} + (mc\Delta T)_{\substack{\text{melted} \\ \text{ice}}} + mh_{\text{fusion}} = (mc\Delta T)_{\text{water}}$

$10 \times 2.1 \times 10 + 10 \times 4.18(T - 0) + 10 \times 320 = 100 \times 4.18(20 - T). \quad \therefore T = 10.77°\text{C}.$

7.27 **b)**   The heat transfer exceeds the work done if $\Delta E > 0$.

7.28 **b)** δW and δQ are inexact differentials. That's why we don't write dW and dQ.

7.29 **a)** $W = mRT \ln P_1/P_2$

$\quad = 2 \times .287 \times 573 \ln 100/4000 = -1213 \text{ kJ}$

7.30 **b)** $\Delta U = m\left(u_2 - u_1\right) \qquad \text{Table 7.3.3}$

$\quad = 2(2725.3 - 2810.4) = -170.2 \text{ kJ}$

7.31 **c)** $Q = m\Delta h = mh_{fg} = 2 \times 1940.8 = 3881.6 \text{ kJ}$

7.32 **d)**   Assume $P = \text{const}$ since doors would be opened. Cracks abound.

$$Q = mc_p\Delta T$$

$$\frac{400 \times 200}{3600} + \frac{30 \times 2000}{1000} = \frac{6000 \times 1.23 \times 1.00\Delta T}{20 \times 60} . \qquad \therefore \Delta T = 13.37°\text{ C}$$

7.33 d) $Q = m\Delta h = mc_p\Delta T$

$522 = 1 \times c_p \times (800 - 300). \quad \therefore c_p = 1.044\dfrac{\text{kJ}}{\text{kg} \cdot \text{K}}$

7.34 a) $Q = m\Delta h = mc_p\Delta T = 10 \times 1.00 \times (230 - 10) = 2200 \text{ kJ}$

7.35 c) $Q = m\Delta h = 10[3072 - 42] = 30\,300 \text{ kJ}$

7.36 a) $W = P\Delta V = mP\Delta v = 10(1.316 - .001) \times 200 = 2630 \text{ kJ}$

7.37 a) $Q = m\Delta u \qquad u_1 = 851 + .5(2595 - 851) = 1723 \text{ kJ/kg}.$

$T_2 = 500°\text{C}$

$v_2 = .0642 \qquad v_1 = .001 + .5(.1274 - .001) = .0642 \text{ m}^3/\text{kg}.$

Use Table 7.3.3 :

$u_2 = \dfrac{.0642 - .0566}{.0686 - .0566}(3091 - 3082) + 3082 = 3088$

$\therefore Q = 2(3088 - 1723) = 2730 \text{ kJ}$

7.38 d) $\dfrac{P_1}{T_1} = \dfrac{P_2}{T_2} . \qquad (p_2 + 100)273 = (100 + 100)343$

$\therefore P_2 = 151 \text{ kPa gage}$

7.39 c) $Q = m\Delta u = mc_v\Delta T \qquad m = \dfrac{PV}{RT} = \dfrac{100 \times 10}{.287 \times 293} = 11.89 \text{ kg}$

$= 11.89 \times .716 \times 60 = 511 \text{ kJ}$

7.40 d) $Q = m\Delta u. \quad 9000 = 10(u_2 - 42) \qquad \therefore u_2 = 942 \text{ kJ/kg}$

$942 = 851 + x_2(2595 - 851) \qquad \therefore x_2 = .0522$

7.41 d) $T_2 = T_1\left(\dfrac{P_2}{P_1}\right)^{k-1/k} = 473\left(\dfrac{20}{400}\right)^{0.4/1.4} = 201\text{K or } -72°\text{C}$

7.42 a) $T_2 = T_1\left(\dfrac{v_1}{v_2}\right)^{k-1} = 473\left(\dfrac{1}{3}\right)^{0.4} = 305\text{K or } 31.8°\text{C}$

7.43 c) $s_2 = s_1 = 7.1685 \quad$ from Table 7.3.2, $\; 7.1685 = .649 + 7.502x_2 . \quad \therefore \; x_2 = .869$

7.44 b) $s_2 = s_1 = 7.1685 \quad$ from Table 7.3.3. This is slightly less than $s = 7.171$
at $T = 200°\text{C}$ and $P = 0.4\,\text{MPa}. \quad \therefore T_2 = 199°\text{C}.$

7.45 b) $T_2 = T_1\left(\dfrac{P_2}{P_1}\right)^{k-1/k} = 293\left(\dfrac{6000}{100}\right)^{.4/1.4} = 944 \text{ K}.$

$W = -m\Delta u = -mc_v\Delta T \qquad (\text{let } m = 1)$

$= -.716(944 - 293) = -466 \text{ kJ/kg}.$

7.46 d)   The heat transfer must be zero.

7.47 d)   A reservoir is at constant temperature so $\Delta s = Q/T$.

7.48 a)   Isentropic means the entropy is constant. A paddle wheel in a volume with heat leaving the volume could maintain the entropy.

7.49 c) $T_2 = T_1\left(\dfrac{P_1}{P_2}\right)^{n-1/n} = 283 \times 3^{.2/1.2} = 340$ K   or $66.9°$C

7.50 a) $\rho_1 = \dfrac{1}{v_1} = \dfrac{1}{.06525} = 15.33$ Table 7.3.3

$\rho_2 = \dfrac{1}{v_2} = \dfrac{1}{7.649} = 0.1307$ Table 7.3.2

$\rho_1 A_1 V_1 = \rho_2 A_2 V_2$. $15.33\pi \times \dfrac{.2^2}{4} V_1 = .1307\pi \times \dfrac{.05^2}{4} V_2$. $\therefore \dfrac{V_2}{V_1} = 1877$

7.51 c) $Q = h_2 - h_1$. $h_1 = 251$ from Table 7.3.1.
  $= 3674 - 251 = 3423$ kJ/kg

7.52 b) $\dot{Q} = \dot{m}_w c\Delta T = \dot{m}_s \Delta h$.   Table 7.3.2, $h_{fg} = 2358$ kJ/kg.

$\dot{m} \times 4.18(30 - 20) = 10 \times 2358$. $\therefore \dot{m} = 564$ kg / s

7.53 c) $s_2 = s_1 = 6.7698 = .649 + 7.502 x_2$. $\therefore x_2 = .816$.

$\therefore h_2 = 192 + .816 \times 2393 = 2144$. $W = h_1 - h_2 = 3213.5 - 2144 = 1069$ kJ/kg

7.54 c) $\dot{W}_P = \dot{m}\dfrac{\Delta P}{\rho\eta} = 10\dfrac{6000 - 10}{1000 \times .75} = 79.9$ kW

7.55 a) $\dot{W}_T = \dot{m}\dfrac{\Delta P}{\rho} = 60 \times 2 \times 2 \times 1000\dfrac{300}{1000} = 72\,000$ kW

7.56 c) $T_2 = T_1\left(\dfrac{P_2}{P_1}\right)^{k-1/k} = 673\left(\dfrac{80}{2000}\right)^{.4/1.4} = 268$ K.

$V_2^2/2 = h_1 - h_2 = c_p(T_1 - T_2) = 1000(673 - 268)$. $\therefore V_2 = 900$ m/s.

7.57 b) $h_1 = 3177$ $s_{2'} = s_1 = 6.5415 = .832 + x_{2'}7.0774$. $\therefore x_{2'} = .807$.

$\therefore h_{2'} = 251 + .807 \times 2358 = 2153$. $w = 0.87 \times (3177 - 2153) = 891$ kJ/kg.

7.58 b)   For an unsteady flow an additional term must be added.

7.59 d)   The work term $\dot{W}_S$ is called the shaft work (or power) because the work due to the pressure force has been added to the internal energy term to provide the enthalpy term.

7.60 b) $\eta_{max} = 1 - \dfrac{T_L}{T_H} = 1 - \dfrac{293}{393} = 0.254$

$\eta = \dfrac{4180}{10 \times 4.18(120 - 20)} = 1.00$. $\therefore$ impossible

7.61 b) $\Delta s_{net} > 0$ for all processes.

7.62 d)   Operates between constant temperature reservoirs.

7.63 d) $\Delta S > Q/T = 90 \times 320/273 = 105.5$ kJ/K

7.64　**c)**　$40(320 + 4.18T_2) = 100 \times 4.18(20 - T_2)$.　$\therefore T_2 = -7.6°C$.

Impossible.　$\therefore T_2 = 0°C$.　$320\,m = 100 \times 4.18 \times 20$.　$\therefore m = 26.1$ kg.

$\Delta s = 26.1 \times 320 / 273 + 100 \times 4.18 \ln 273 / 293 = 1.04$

7.65　**b)**　$\eta_{max} = 1 - \dfrac{T_L}{T_H} = 1 - 323 / 873 = 0.63$

7.66　**a)**　All other terms are highly irreversible. Heat transfer across a large temperature difference is very irreversible. It's a process that is most difficult to make reversible, the primary reason why the efficiency of engines are so much lower than their respective Carnot efficiencies.

7.67　**d)**　Heat must be rejected by all engines operating on a cycle. Of course, all engines with which we are familiar operate on a cycle.

7.68　**d)**　If the container is insulated, it is isolated from its surroundings. The net entropy must increase.

7.69　**c)**　$T_4 = P_4 v_4 / R = 160 \times .5 / .287 = 279$ K.

$w = q\eta = 30(1 - 279 / 473) = 12.3$ kJ/kg

7.70　**a)**　$\eta = 1 - (400/40)^{-.4} = 0.602$.　$\therefore \dot{Q} = \dot{W} / \eta = 100 / .602 = 166$ kW.

7.71　**a)**　$r_C = 45 / 25 = 1.8$.　$r = 450 / 25 = 18$.

$\dot{Q} = \dot{W} / \eta = 120 / \left[1 - \dfrac{1.8^{1.4} - 1}{1.4(1.8 - 1)} 18^{-.4} \right] = 187$ kJ/s.

7.72　**c)**　$s_4 = s_3 = 7.1677 = .649 + 7.502x_4$.　$\therefore x_4 = .869$.

$h_4 = 192 + .869 \times 2393 = 2272$.　$h_3 = 3658$,　$h_1 = 192$.

$\eta = \dfrac{w}{q} = (3658 - 2272)/(3658 - 192) = 0.40$

7.73　**c)**　$s_4 = s_3 = 7.168$.　$\therefore$ ④ superheat　$\therefore h_4 = 2722$.　$h_3 = 3658$.

After reheat $h_5 = 3704$.　$s_6 = s_5 = 8.778$.

$\therefore h_6 = \dfrac{8.777 - 8.448}{8.9038 - 8.448}(2879.5 - 2688) + 2783 = 2826$.

$\eta = \dfrac{w_{3-4} + w_{5-6}}{q_{2-3} + q_{4-5}} = \dfrac{3658 - 2722 + 3704 - 2826}{3658 - 192 + 3704 - 2722} = 0.408$

7.74　**b)**　Decrease moisture content in the turbine.

7.75　**b)**　All other conditions increase the efficiency.

7.76　**a)**　The net work output is equal to the net heat required during a cycle. The area under the *T-s* diagram is the net heat transfer which is equal to the net work output.

7.77　**a)**　$\dfrac{T_2}{T_1} = \left(\dfrac{v_1}{v_2} \right)^{k-1} = r^{k-1}$. The efficiency depends on *r* and hence (a).

7.78 c) $s_2 = s_1 = 1.75$.   Refer to Fig. 7.4a : $h_1 = 380$, $h_2 = 430$, $h_3 = 255 = h_4$.

$$COP = \frac{q_{4-1}}{w_{1-2}} = \frac{380 - 255}{430 - 380} = 2.5.$$

7.79 c) $h_4 = h_3 = 255 = h_f + x_4\left(h_g - h_f\right)$

$$= 165 + x_4(380 - 165). \quad \therefore x_4 = 0.42 .$$

7.80 a) $\dot{W}_{max} = \dot{m}\left(h_1 - T_o s_1\right) - \dot{m}\left(h_2 - T_o s_2\right)$

$$= \dot{m}\left[\left(h_1 - h_2\right) + T_o\left(s_2 - s_1\right)\right] = \dot{m}\left[c_p\Delta T + T_o\left(c_p \ln \frac{T_2}{T_1} - R\ln \frac{P_2}{P_1}\right)\right]$$

$$= 10\left[1.00(100 - 20) + 293\left(1.00\ln \frac{293}{373} - .287\ln \frac{80}{6000}\right)\right] = 3723 \text{ kW}$$

7.81 d) $\phi_2 - \phi_1 = w_{max}$.

7.82 b)

7.83 b)

7.84 c) $\dot{Q} = .13 \times 2 \times 8 \times \dfrac{25}{.5} = 104 \text{ J/s}$

7.85 a) $\dfrac{1\,500\,000}{10 \times 60} = h \times \pi \times .04 \times (150 - 40). \quad \therefore h = 181 \text{ J/s} \cdot \text{m}^2 \cdot {}^\circ\text{C}$

7.86 d) $100 = 5.67 \times 10^{-8} \times \left(.8 \times 10^{-4}\right)\left(T^4 - 353^4\right).$

$$\therefore T = 2167 \text{ K} \quad \text{or} \quad 1894^\circ \text{ C}$$

7.87 b) $R = \dfrac{1}{h} + \dfrac{L_1}{k_1} + \dfrac{L_2}{k_2} + \dfrac{L_3}{k_3} + \dfrac{1}{h}$

$$= \frac{1}{10} + \frac{.025}{.04} + \frac{.08}{.038} + \frac{.02}{.15} + \frac{1}{10} = 3.06 \ \frac{\text{s} \cdot \text{m}^2 \cdot {}^\circ\text{C}}{\text{J}}$$

7.88 c) $\omega = 0.0118. \quad \therefore m_v = \omega m_a = \omega V/v$

$$= .0118 \times 600/.861$$

$$= 8.2 \text{ kg} \quad \text{or} \quad 8.2 \text{ L}$$

7.89 d)   The enthalpy remains constant since $\dot{W} = \dot{Q} = 0$. States 1 and 2 lie on a constant enthalpy line on the psychrometric chart with $\phi_2 = 100\%$. From Fig. 7.8 $T_2 = 19^\circ\text{C}$.

7.90 c)   A horizontal line is followed on the psychrometric chart.

7.91 b)   Sketch the cycle on a T - v diagram:

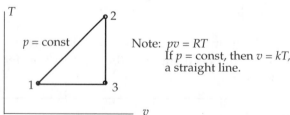

$$PV = mRT. \quad \therefore 2000V = 0.04 \times 0.287 \times 293. \quad \therefore V = 0.00168 \text{ m}^3$$

7.92 d) For a constant pressure process, $\dfrac{T_1}{V_1} = \dfrac{T_2}{V_2}$.

$$\therefore V_3 = V_2 = V_1 \frac{T_2}{T_1} = 1680 \frac{1073}{293} = 6160 \text{ cm}^3$$

7.93 c) For this constant pressure process

$$Q = m\Delta h = mc_p\Delta T$$

$$= 0.04 \text{ kg} \times 1.00 \frac{\text{kJ}}{\text{kg} \cdot \text{K}} \times (1073 - 293) = 31.2 \text{ kJ}$$

7.94 b) For this constant temperature process

$$W = mRT \ln\frac{V_2}{V_1} = mRT \ln\frac{T_2}{T_1}$$

$$= 0.04 \text{ kg} \times 0.287 \frac{\text{kJ}}{\text{kg} \cdot \text{K}} \times 293 \text{ K} \times \ln\frac{1073}{293} = 4.37 \text{ kJ}$$

7.95 d) For the constant volume process the work is zero. Thus

$$Q = \Delta U = mc_v\Delta T$$

$$= 0.04 \times 0.717(800 - 20) = 22.4 \text{ kJ}$$

7.96 d) The mass flow rate is, using v from Table 7.3.2 with $P = 0.01$ MPa,

$$v = \frac{RT}{P} = \frac{0.287 \times 293}{200} = 0.42 \text{ m}^3/\text{kg}$$

$$\dot{m} = \frac{1}{v}AV = \frac{1}{0.42} \times \pi \times 0.1^2 \times 10 = 0.75 \text{ kg}/\text{s}$$

7.97 b) The energy equation with $Q = W = 0$ provides

$$0 = \Delta h + \frac{V_2^2 - V_1^2}{2} = c_p(T_2 - T_1) + \frac{V_2^2 - V_1^2}{2}$$

$$= 1.0(T_2 - 20) + \frac{300^2 - 10^2}{2 \times 1000}. \quad \therefore T_2 = -25°\text{C}$$

7.98 d) The efficiency is based on an isentropic flow so that

$$T_2 = T_1\left(\frac{P_2}{P_1}\right)^{\frac{k-1}{k}} = 293\left(\frac{100}{200}\right)^{\frac{0.4}{1.4}} = 240.4 \text{ K}$$

$$\eta = \frac{\Delta KE_{\text{actual}}}{\Delta KE_{\text{max}}} = \frac{\left(300^2 - 10^2\right)/2 \times 1000}{1.0(293 - 240.4)} = 0.855$$

7.99 a) The velocity is found from the equation for mass flow rate:

$$\dot{m} = \rho AV = \frac{1}{v}AV$$

$$2 = \frac{1}{14.67} \frac{\pi \times 1.2^2}{4} V_2. \quad \therefore V_2 = 25.9 \text{ m}/\text{s}$$

The specific volume $v = v_g$ was found in Table 7.3.2 with $P = 0.01$ MPa.

7.100 c) The 1st law for a control volume is used:

$$\dot{W}_T = -\dot{m}\Delta h = \dot{m}(h_1 - h_2)$$

$$= 2(3658.4 - 2584.6) = 2148 \text{ kW}$$

7-THERMO

The enthalpy h_1 is from Table 7.3.3 and $h_2 = h_g$ is from Table 7.3.2.

7.101 **a)** First, let's find h_2 assuming an isentropic process:

$$s_1 = s_2 = 7.1677 = 0.6491 + x_{2s}(7.5019). \quad \therefore x_{2s} = 0.8689$$

$$\therefore h_{2s} = h_{2f} + x_{2s} \times h_{2fg} = 191.8 + 0.689 \times 2392.8 = 2271$$

Finally,

$$\eta = \frac{h_1 - h_2}{h_1 - h_{2s}} = \frac{3658.4 - 2584}{3658.4 - 2271} = 0.774$$

7.102 **b)** $\eta = 1 - \dfrac{T_L}{T_H} = 1 - \dfrac{293}{673} = 0.5646$

7.103 **d)** The cycle efficiency can also be expressed as

$$\eta = \frac{W}{Q_H} = \frac{Q_H - Q_L}{Q_H} = 1 - \frac{Q_L}{Q_H}. \quad \therefore 0.5646 = 1 - \frac{100}{Q_H}. \quad \therefore Q_H = 229.7 \text{ kJ}$$

7.104 **a)** Since the temperature is constant, the entropy change is

$$\Delta S = \frac{Q_H}{T_H} = \frac{Q_L}{T_L} = \frac{100}{293} = 0.341 \text{ kJ/K}$$

7.105 **c)** The efficiency for an Otto cycle is

$$\eta = 1 - r^{1-k} = 1 - 8^{1-1.4} = 0.5647$$

7.106 **c)** Refer to the Otto cycle diagrams:

$$T_2 = T_1 \left(\frac{v_1}{v_2} \right)^{k-1} = 293 \times 8^{0.4} = 673 \text{ K}$$

$$q_{2\text{-}3} = c_v(T_2 - T_1) = 0.717(1273 - 673) = 430.2 \text{ kJ/kg}$$

7.107 **b)** Refer to the Otto cycle diagrams:

$$T_4 = T_3 \left(\frac{v_3}{v_4} \right)^{k-1} = 1273 \times \left(\frac{1}{8} \right)^{0.4} = 554 \text{ K}$$

$$w_{3\text{-}4} = -\Delta u = -c_v(T_4 - T_3) = 0.717(1273 - 554) = 516 \text{ kJ/kg}$$

7.108 **a)** First, let's find the pressure at state 2:

$$P_2 = P_1 \left(\frac{v_1}{v_2} \right)^k = 100 \times 8^{1.4} = 1838 \text{ kPa}$$

$$\therefore V_2 = \frac{mRT}{P_2} = \frac{0.002 \times 0.287 \times 673}{1838} = 2.1 \times 10^{-4} \text{ m}^3 \text{ or } 210 \text{ cm}^3$$

7.109 **a)** For a liquid we assume $v = 1/\rho = \text{const}$ and neglect Δu:

$$w_P = \Delta h = \Delta u + \Delta(Pv) = 0 + \frac{\Delta P}{\rho}$$

$$= \frac{4000 - 10}{1000} = 3.99 \text{ kJ/kg}$$

7.110 **c)** Use data from Tables 7.3.3 and 7.3.2 with the 1st law:

$$h_3 = 3213.6 \text{ kJ/kg}$$

$$h_4 = h_f + x \times h_{fg} = 191.8 + 0.9 \times 2392.8 = 2345 \text{ kJ/kg}$$

$$w_T = h_3 - h_4 = 3213.6 - 2345 = 869 \text{ kJ/kg}$$

7.111 **d)** We can neglect the small pump energy requirement so that $h_1 = h_2 = 192$ kJ/kg:

$$q_{in} = h_3 - h_2 = 3214 - 192 = 3022 \text{ kJ/kg}$$

$$\eta = \frac{w_T}{q_{in}} = \frac{869}{3022} = 0.288 \text{ or } 28.8\%$$

7.112 **b)** From $W = mw$ we write $\dot{W} = \dot{m}w$. Hence

$$\dot{W}_T = \dot{m}w_T. \quad \therefore 2000 = \dot{m} \times 869. \quad \therefore \dot{m} = 2.3 \text{ kg/s}$$

7.113 **a)** The efficiency is based on an isentropic process:

$$s_3 = s_4 = 6.769 = 0.649 + x_4 \times 7.5019. \quad \therefore x_4 = 0.816$$

$$\therefore h_{4s} = 191.8 + 0.816 \times 2392.8 = 2144 \text{ kJ / kg}$$

$$\therefore \eta = \frac{h_3 - h_4}{h_3 - h_{4s}} = \frac{3213.6 - 2345}{3213.6 - 2144} = 0.812 \text{ or } 81.2\%$$

7.114 **d)** The heat that leaves the condenser enters the cooling water:

$$\dot{m}_s \Delta h_s = \dot{m}_w \Delta h_w \quad \text{or} \quad \dot{m}_s(h_4 - h_1) = \dot{m}_w(c_p)_w \Delta T_w$$

$$\therefore \frac{\dot{m}_w}{\dot{m}_s} = \frac{2345 - 192}{4.18 \times (30 - 20)} = 51.5$$

7.115 **a)** For a valve the 1st law with $Q = 0$ and $W = 0$ provides

$$h_3 = h_4 = 258 = 165 + x_4(382 - 165). \quad \therefore x_4 = 0.429$$

7.116 **d)** Cooling takes place in the evaporator where $W = 0$:

$$\dot{Q}_E = \dot{m}(h_1 - h_4)$$

$$5 \times 3.52 = \dot{m}(382 - 258). \quad \therefore \dot{m} = 0.142 \text{ kg/s}$$

7.117 **b)** We assume that $Q = 0$ for the isentropic compressor:

$$w_C = h_2 - h_1$$

$$\left. \begin{array}{l} s_2 = s_1 = 1.75 \\ P_2 = 1 \text{ MPa} \end{array} \right\} \quad \therefore h_2 = 431 \text{ kJ/kg}$$

$$\therefore w_C = 431 - 382 = 49 \text{ kJ/kg}$$

7.118 **c)** The COP is output divided by input:

$$\text{COP} = \frac{q_{4\text{-}1}}{w_{1\text{-}2}} = \frac{382 - 258}{431 - 382} = 2.53$$

7.119 **d)** We use the maximum and minimum temperatures:

$$T_L = -27°C = 246 \text{ K}, \quad T_H = 50°C = 323 \text{ K}$$

$$\therefore \text{COP}_{Carnot} = \text{COP}_{max} = \frac{T_L}{T_H - T_L} = \frac{246}{323 - 246} = 3.19$$

7·THERMO

7.120 **b)** Refer to the psychrometric chart assuming ω = const:

$$\omega_1 = \omega_2. \quad \therefore \phi = 43\%$$

7.121 **d)** At 20°C and 60% relative humidity we read from the psychrometric chart with constant humidity ratio that $T_{dp} = 15.2°C$.

7.122 **c)** First let's find the mass flow rate of air (read v_a from the chart):

$$\dot{m}_a = 200\rho = 200\frac{1}{v_a} = 200\frac{m^3}{min}\frac{1}{0.81\ m^3/kg} = 247\ kg/min$$

$$\therefore \dot{m}_v = \dot{m}_a(\omega_2 - \omega_1) = 247(0.0088 - 0.006) = 0.69\ kg/min\ \text{ or }\ 41\ kg/hr$$

7.123 **a)** The 1st law provides

$$\dot{Q} = \dot{m}(h_2 - h_1) = 247(43 - 25) = 4400\ kJ/min\ \text{ or }\ 260\ MJ/hr$$

Tables for Thermodynamics

TABLE 7.1 Properties of Ideal Gases — Metric Units

Gas	Chemical Formula	Molar Mass	$R\ \dfrac{kJ}{kg \cdot K}$	$c_p\ \dfrac{kJ}{kg \cdot K}$	$c_v\ \dfrac{kJ}{kg \cdot K}$	k
Air	—	28.97	0.287 00	1.0035	0.7165	1.400
Argon	Ar	39.948	0.208 13	0.5203	0.3122	1.667
Butane	C_4H_{10}	58.124	0.143 04	1.7164	1.5734	1.091
Carbon Dioxide	CO_2	44.01	0.188 92	0.8418	0.6529	1.289
Carbon Monoxide	CO	28.01	0.296 83	1.0413	0.7445	1.400
Ethane	C_2H_6	30.07	0.276 50	1.7662	1.4897	1.186
Ethylene	C_2H_4	28.054	0.296 37	1.5482	1.2518	1.237
Helium	He	4.003	2.077 03	5.1926	3.1156	1.667
Hydrogen	H_2	2.016	4.124 18	14.2091	10.0849	1.409
Methane	CH_4	16.04	0.518 35	2.2537	1.7354	1.299
Neon	Ne	20.183	0.411 95	1.0299	0.6179	1.667
Nitrogen	N_2	28.013	0.296 80	1.0416	0.7448	1.400
Octane	C_8H_{18}	114.23	0.072 79	1.7113	1.6385	1.044
Oxygen	O_2	31.999	0.259 83	0.9216	0.6618	1.393
Propane	C_3H_8	44.097	0.188 55	1.6794	1.4909	1.126
Steam	H_2O	18.015	0.461 52	1.8723	1.4108	1.327

TABLE 7.2 Specific Heats of Liquids and Solids — Metric Units

c_p kJ/(kg·°C)

A. LIQUIDS

Substance	State	c_p	Substance	State	c_p
Water	1 atm, 25°C	4.177	Glycerin	1 atm, 10°C	2.32
Ammonia	sat., −20°C	4.52	Bismuth	1 atm, 425°C	0.144
	sat., 50°C	5.10	Mercury	1 atm, 10°C	0.138
Refrigerant 12	sat., −20°C	0.908	Sodium	1 atm, 95°C	1.38
	sat., 50°C	1.02	Propane	1 atm, 0°C	2.41
Benzene	1 atm, 15°C	1.80	Ethyl Alcohol	1 atm, 25°C	2.43

B. SOLIDS

Substance	T, °C	c_p	Substance	T, °C	c_p
Ice	−11	2.033	Lead	−100	0.118
	−2.2	2.10		0	0.124
Aluminum	−100	0.699		100	0.134
	0	0.870	Copper	−100	0.328
	100	0.941		0	0.381
Iron	20	0.448		100	0.393
Silver	20	0.233			

TABLE 7.3 Thermodynamic Properties of Water (Steam Tables) — Metric Units

7.3.1 Saturated H₂O — Temperature Table

T, °C	P, MPa	Volume, m³/kg		Energy, kJ/kg		Enthalpy, kJ/kg			Entropy, kJ/(kg·K)		
		v_f	v_g	u_f	u_g	h_f	h_{fg}	h_g	s_f	s_{fg}	s_g
0.010	0.0006113	0.001000	206.1	0.0	2375.3	0.0	2501.3	2501.3	0.0000	9.1571	9.1571
5	0.0008721	0.001000	147.1	21.0	2382.2	21.0	2489.5	2510.5	0.0761	8.9505	9.0266
10	0.001228	0.001000	106.4	42.0	2389.2	42.0	2477.7	2519.7	0.1510	8.7506	8.9016
20	0.002338	0.001002	57.79	83.9	2402.9	83.9	2454.2	2538.1	0.2965	8.3715	8.6680
30	0.004246	0.001004	32.90	125.8	2416.6	125.8	2430.4	2556.2	0.4367	8.0174	8.4541
40	0.007383	0.001008	19.52	167.5	2430.1	167.5	2406.8	2574.3	0.5723	7.6855	8.2578
50	0.01235	0.001012	12.03	209.3	2443.5	209.3	2382.8	2592.1	0.7036	7.3735	8.0771
60	0.01994	0.001017	7.671	251.1	2456.6	251.1	2358.5	2609.6	0.8310	7.0794	7.9104
70	0.03119	0.001023	5.042	292.9	2469.5	293.0	2333.8	2626.8	0.9549	6.8012	7.7561
80	0.04739	0.001029	3.407	334.8	2482.2	334.9	2308.8	2643.7	1.0754	6.5376	7.6130
90	0.07013	0.001036	2.361	376.8	2494.5	376.9	2283.2	2660.1	1.1927	6.2872	7.4799
100	0.1013	0.001044	1.673	418.9	2506.5	419.0	2257.0	2676.0	1.3071	6.0486	7.3557
120	0.1985	0.001060	0.8919	503.5	2529.2	503.7	2202.6	2706.3	1.5280	5.6024	7.1304
140	0.3613	0.001080	0.5089	588.7	2550.0	589.1	2144.8	2733.9	1.7395	5.1912	6.9307
160	0.6178	0.001102	0.3071	674.9	2568.4	675.5	2082.6	2758.1	1.9431	4.8079	6.7510
180	1.002	0.001127	0.1941	762.1	2583.7	763.2	2015.0	2778.2	2.1400	4.4466	6.5866
200	1.554	0.001156	0.1274	850.6	2595.3	852.4	1940.8	2793.2	2.3313	4.1018	6.4331
220	2.318	0.001190	0.08620	940.9	2602.4	943.6	1858.5	2802.1	2.5183	3.7686	6.2869
240	3.344	0.001229	0.5977	1033.2	2604.0	1037.3	1766.5	2803.8	2.7021	3.4425	6.1446
260	4.688	0.001276	0.04221	1128.4	2599.0	1134.4	1662.5	2796.9	2.8844	3.1184	6.0028
280	6.411	0.001332	0.03017	1227.4	2586.1	1236.0	1543.6	2779.6	3.0674	2.7905	5.8579
300	8.580	0.001404	0.02168	1332.0	2563.0	1344.0	1405.0	2749.0	3.2540	2.4513	5.7053
320	11.27	0.001499	0.01549	1444.6	2525.5	1461.4	1238.7	2700.1	3.4487	2.0883	5.5370
340	14.59	0.001638	0.01080	1570.3	2464.6	1594.2	1027.9	2622.1	3.6601	1.6765	5.3366
360	18.65	0.001892	0.006947	1725.2	2351.6	1760.5	720.7	2481.2	3.9154	1.1382	5.0536
374.136	22.088	0.003155	0.003155	2029.6	2029.6	2099.3	0.0	2099.3	4.4305	0.0000	4.4305

7.3.2 Saturated H₂O — Pressure Table

P, MPa	T, °C	Volume, m³/kg		Energy, kJ/kg		Enthalpy, kJ/kg			Entropy, kJ/(kg·K)		
		v_f	v_g	u_f	u_g	h_f	h_{fg}	h_g	s_f	s_{fg}	s_g
0.001	7.0	0.001000	129.2	29.3	2385.0	29.3	2484.9	2514.2	0.1059	8.8706	8.9765
0.002	17.5	0.001001	67.00	73.5	2399.5	73.5	2460.0	2533.5	0.2606	8.4639	8.7245
0.01	45.8	0.001010	14.67	191.8	2437.9	191.8	2392.8	2584.6	0.6491	7.5019	8.1510
0.02	60.1	0.001017	7.649	251.4	2456.7	251.4	2358.3	2609.7	0.8319	7.0774	7.9093
0.04	75.9	0.001026	3.993	317.5	2477.0	317.6	2319 1	2636.7	1.0260	6.6449	7.6709
0.06	85.9	0.001033	2.732	359.8	2489.6	359.8	2293.7	2653.5	1.1455	6.3873	7.5328
0.08	93.5	0.001039	2.087	391.6	2498.8	391.6	2274.1	2665.7	1.2331	6.2023	7.4354
0.1	99.6	0.001043	1.694	417.3	2506.1	417.4	2258.1	2675.5	1.3029	6.0573	7.3602
0.12	104.8	0.001047	1.428	439.2	2512.1	439.3	2244.2	2683.5	1.3611	5.9378	7.2989
0.16	113.3	0.001054	1.091	475.2	2521.8	475.3	2221.2	2696.5	1.4553	5.7472	7.2025
0.2	120.2	0.001061	0.8857	504.5	2529.5	504.7	2201.9	2706.6	1.5305	5.5975	7.1280
0.4	143.6	0.001084	0.4625	604.3	2553.6	604.7	2133.8	2738.5	1.7770	5.1197	6.8967
0.6	158.9	0.001101	0.3157	669.9	2567.4	670.6	2086.2	2756.8	1.9316	4.8293	6.7609
0.8	170.4	0.001115	0.2404	720.2	2576.8	721.1	2048.0	2769.1	2.0466	4.6170	6.6636
1	179.9	0.001127	0.1944	761.7	2583.6	762.8	2015.3	2778.1	2.1391	4.4482	6.5873
1.2	188.0	0.001139	0.1633	797.3	2588.8	798.6	1986.2	2784.8	2.2170	4.3072	6.5242
1.6	201.4	0.001159	0.1238	856.9	2596.0	858.8	1935.2	2794.0	2.3446	4.0780	6.4226
2	212.4	0.001177	0.09963	906.4	2600.3	908.8	1890.7	2799.5	2.4478	3.8939	6.3417
4	250.4	0.001252	0.04978	1082.3	2602.3	1087.3	1714.1	2801.4	2.7970	3.2739	6.0709
6	275.6	0.001319	0.03244	1205.4	2589.7	1213.3	1571.0	2784.3	3.0273	2.8627	5.8900
8	295.1	0.001384	0.02352	1305.6	2569.8	1316.6	1441.4	2758.0	3.2075	2.5365	5.7440
12	324.8	0.001527	0.01426	1472.9	2513.7	1491.3	1193.6	2684.9	3.4970	1.9963	5.4933
16	347.4	0.001711	0.009307	1622.7	2431.8	1650.0	930.7	2580.7	3.7468	1.4996	5.2464
20	365.8	0.002036	0.005836	1785.6	2293.2	1826.3	583.7	2410.0	4.0146	0.9135	4.9281
22.088	374.136	0.003155	0.003155	2029.6	2029.6	2099.3	0.0	2099.3	4.4305	0.0000	4.4305

7.3.3 Superheated Steam

°C	v	u	h	s	v	u	h	s	v	u	h	s
		P = .010 MPa				P = .050 MPa				P = .10 MPa		
100	17.196	2515.5	2687.5	8.4479	3.418	2511.6	2682.5	7.6947	1.6958	2506.7	2676.2	7.3614
200	21.825	2661.3	2879.5	8.9038	4.356	2659.9	2877.7	8.1580	2.172	2658.1	2875.3	7.8343
300	26.445	2812.1	3076.5	9.2813	5.284	2811.3	3075.5	8.5373	2.639	2810.4	3074.3	8.2158
400	31.063	2968.9	3279.6	9.6077	6.209	2968.5	3278.9	8.8642	3.103	2967.9	3278.2	8.5435
500	35.679	3132.3	3489.1	9.8978	7.134	3132.0	3488.7	9.1546	3.565	3131.6	3488.1	8.8342
600	40.295	3302.5	3705.4	10.1608	8.057	3302.2	3705.1	9.4178	4.028	3301.9	3704.7	9.0976
700	44.911	3479.6	3928.7	10.4028	8.981	3479.4	3928.5	9.6599	4.490	3479.2	3928.2	9.3398
800	49.526	3663.8	4159.0	10.6281	9.904	3663.6	4158.9	9.8852	4.952	3663.5	4158.6	9.5652
900	54.141	3855.0	4396.4	10.8396	10.828	3854.9	4396.3	10.0967	5.414	3854.8	4396.1	9.7767
1000	58.757	4053.0	4640.6	11.0393	11.751	4052.9	4640.5	10.2964	5.875	4052.8	4640.3	9.9764

°C	v	u	h	s	v	u	h	s	v	u	h	s
		P = .20 MPa				P = .40 MPa				P = .60 MPa		
200	1.080	2654.4	2870.5	7.5066	.5342	2646.8	2860.5	7.1706	.3520	2638.9	2850.1	6.9665
300	1.316	2808.6	3071.8	7.8926	.6548	2804.8	3066.8	7.5662	.4344	2801.0	3061.6	7.3724
400	1.549	2966.7	3276.6	8.2218	.7726	2964.4	3273.4	7.8985	.5137	2962.1	3270.3	7.7079
500	1.781	3130.8	3487.1	8.5133	.8893	3129.2	3484.9	8.1913	.5920	3127.6	3482.8	8.0021
600	2.013	3301.4	3704.0	8.7770	1.0055	3300.2	3702.4	8.4558	.6697	3299.1	3700.9	8.2674
700	2.244	3478.8	3927.6	9.0194	1.1215	3477.9	3926.5	8.6987	.7472	3477.0	3925.3	8.5107
800	2.475	3663.1	4158.2	9.2449	1.2372	3662.4	4157.3	8.9244	.8245	3661.8	4156.5	8.7367
900	2.706	3854.5	4395.8	9.4566	1.3529	3853.9	4395.1	9.1362	.9017	3853.4	4394.4	8.9486
1000	2.937	4052.5	4640.0	9.6563	1.4685	4052.0	4639.4	9.3360	.9788	4051.5	4638.8	9.1485
1100	3.168	4257.0	4890.7	9.8458	1.5840	4256.5	4890.2	9.5256	1.0559	4256.1	4889.6	9.3381

°C	v	u	h	s	v	u	h	s	v	u	h	s
		P = .80 MPa				P = 1.00 MPa				P = 2.00 MPa		
200	.2608	2630.6	2839.3	6.8158	.2060	2621.9	2827.9	6.6940				
300	.3241	2797.2	3056.5	7.2328	.2579	2793.2	3051.2	7.1229	.1255	2772.6	3023.5	6.7664
400	.3843	2959.7	3267.1	7.5716	.3066	2957.3	3263.9	7.4651	.1512	2945.2	3247.6	7.1271
500	.4433	3126.0	3480.6	7.8673	.3541	3124.4	3478.5	7.7622	.1757	3116.2	3467.6	7.4317
600	.5018	3297.9	3699.4	8.1333	.4011	3296.8	3697.9	8.0290	.1996	3290.9	3690.1	7.7024
700	.5601	3476.2	3924.2	8.3770	.4478	3475.3	3923.1	8.2731	.2232	3470.9	3917.4	7.9487
800	.6181	3661.1	4155.6	8.6033	.4943	3660.4	4154.7	8.4996	.2467	3657.0	4150.3	8.1765
900	.6761	3852.8	4393.7	8.8153	.5407	3852.2	4392.9	8.7118	.2700	3849.3	4389.4	8.3895
1000	.7340	4051.0	4638.2	9.0153	.5871	4050.5	4637.6	8.9119	.2933	4048.0	4634.6	8.5901
1100	.7919	4255.6	4889.1	9.2050	.6335	4255.1	4888.6	9.1017	.3166	4252.7	4885.9	8.7800

°C	v	u	h	s	v	u	h	s	v	u	h	s
		P = 3.0 MPa				P = 4.0 MPa				P = 5.0 MPa		
300	.08114	2750.1	2993.5	6.5390	.05884	2725.3	2960.7	6.3615	.04532	2698.0	2924.5	6.2084
400	.09936	2932.8	3230.9	6.9212	.07341	2919.9	3213.6	6.7690	.05781	2906.6	3195.7	6.6459
500	.11619	3108.0	3456.5	7.2338	.08643	3099.5	3445.3	7.0901	.06857	3091.0	3433.8	6.9759
600	.13243	3285.0	3682.3	7.5085	.09885	3279.1	3674.4	7.3688	.07869	3273.0	3666.5	7.2589
700	.14838	3466.5	3911.7	7.7571	.11095	3462.1	3905.9	7.6198	.08849	3457.6	3900.1	7.5122
800	.16414	3653.5	4145.9	7.9862	.12287	3650.0	4141.5	7.8502	.09811	3646.6	4137.1	7.7440
900	.17980	3846.5	4385.9	8.1999	.13469	3843.6	4382.3	8.0647	.10762	3840.7	4378.8	7.9593
1000	.19541	4045.4	4631.6	8.4009	.14645	4042.9	4628.7	8.2662	.11707	4040.4	4625.7	8.1612
1100	.21098	4250.3	4883.3	8.5912	.15817	4248.0	4880.6	8.4567	.12648	4245.6	4878.0	8.3520
1200	.22652	4460.9	5140.5	8.7720	.16987	4458.6	5138.1	8.6376	.13587	4456.3	5135.7	8.5331

°C	v	u	h	s	v	u	h	s	v	u	h	s
		P = 6.0 MPa				P = 8.0 MPa				P = 10.0 MPa		
300	.03616	2667.2	2884.2	6.0674	.02426	2590.9	2785.0	5.7906				
400	.04739	2892.9	3177.2	6.5408	.03432	2863.8	3138.3	6.3634	.02641	2832.4	3096.5	6.2120
500	.05665	3082.2	3422.2	6.8803	.04175	3064.3	3398.3	6.7240	.03279	3045.8	3373.7	6.5966
600	.06525	3266.9	3658.4	7.1677	.04845	3254.4	3642.0	7.0206	.03837	3241.7	3625.3	6.9029
700	.07352	3453.1	3894.2	7.4234	.05481	3443.9	3882.4	7.2812	.04358	3434.7	3870.5	7.1687
800	.08160	3643.1	4132.7	7.6566	.06097	3636.0	4123.8	7.5173	.04859	3628.9	4114.8	7.4077
900	.08958	3837.8	4375.3	7.8727	.06702	3832.1	4368.3	7.7351	.05349	3826.3	4361.2	7.6272
1000	.09749	4037.8	4622.7	8.0751	.07301	4032.8	4616.9	7.9384	.05832	4027.8	4611.0	7.8315
1100	.10536	4243.3	4875.4	8.2661	.07896	4238.6	4870.3	8.1300	.06312	4234.0	4865.1	8.0237
1200	.11321	4454.0	5133.3	8.4474	.08489	4449.5	5128.5	8.3115	.06789	4444.9	5123.8	8.2055

°C	v	u	h	s	v	u	h	s	v	u	h	s
		P = 15.0 MPa				P = 20.0 MPa				P = 40.0 MPa		
400	.01564	2740.7	2975.5	5.8811	.00994	2619.3	2818.1	5.5540	.001908	1854.6	1930.9	4.1135
500	.02080	2996.6	3308.6	6.3443	.01477	2942.9	3238.2	6.1401	.005622	2678.4	2903.3	5.4700
600	.02491	3208.6	3582.3	6.6776	.01818	3174.0	3537.6	6.5048	.008094	3022.6	3346.4	6.0114
700	.02861	3410.9	3840.1	6.9572	.02113	3386.4	3809.0	6.7993	.009941	3283.6	3681.2	6.3750
800	.03210	3610.9	4092.4	7.2040	.()2385	3592.7	4069.7	7.0544	.011523	3517.8	3978.7	6.6662
900	.03546	3811.9	4343.8	7.4279	.02645	3797.5	4326.4	7.2830	.012962	3739.4	4257.9	6.9150
1000	.03875	4015.4	4596.6	7.6348	.02897	4003.1	4582.5	7.4925	.041324	3954.6	4527.6	7.1356
1100	.04200	4222.6	4852.6	7.8283	.03145	4211.3	4840.2	7.6874	.015642	4167.4	4793.1	7.3364
1200	.04523	4433.8	5112.3	8.0108	.03391	4422.8	5101.0	7.8707	.016940	4380.1	5057.7	7.5224

Figure 7.8 Psychrometric Chart — Metric Units

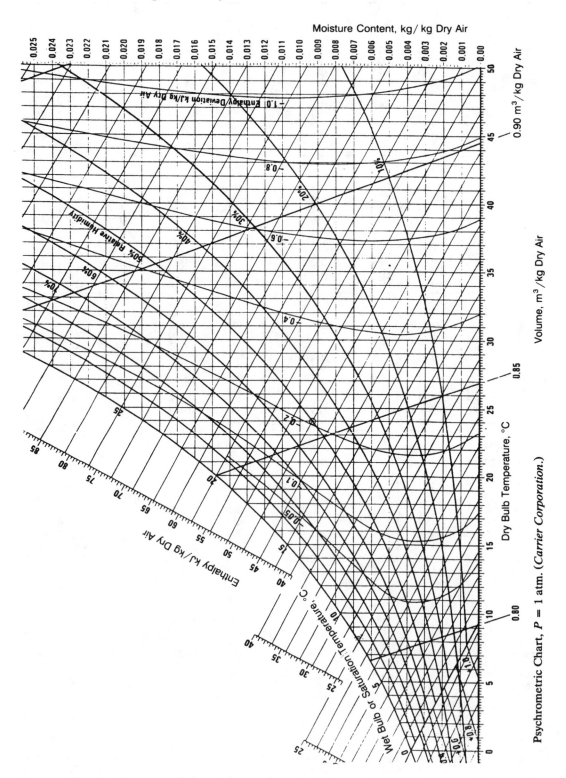

Psychrometric Chart, $P = 1$ atm. *(Carrier Corporation.)*

Figure 7.9 *P-h* Diagram for Refrigerant 134a —Metric Units

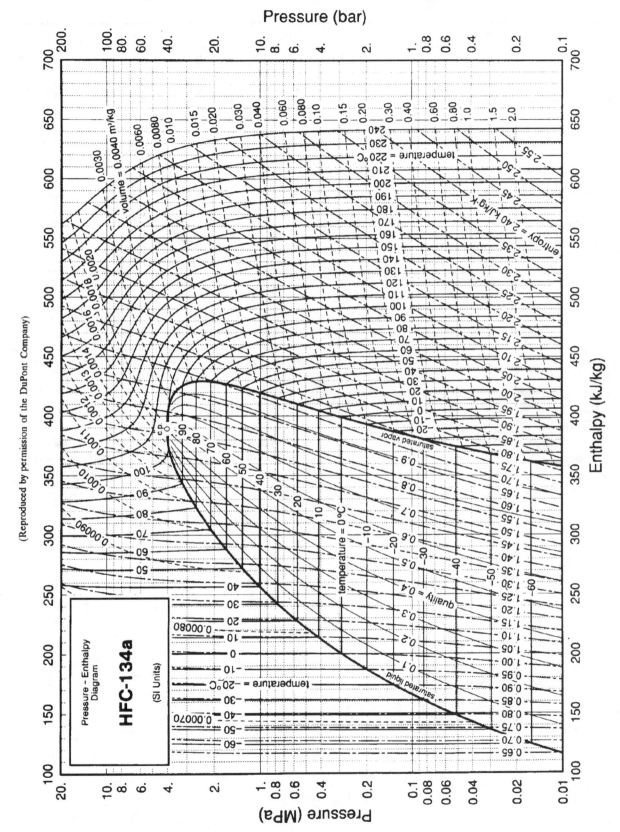

7•THERMO

TABLE 7.5 Thermal Properties of Various Materials at 20°C or 68°F.

Material	Density – ρ		Specific Heat – c_p		Conductivity – k	
	kg/m³	lb/ft³	J/kg·K	BTU/lbm-°R	J/s·m·°C	BTU/hr-ft-°F
Aluminum	2700	167	896	0.214	237	136
Bronze	8670	541	343	0.0819	26	15
Concrete	500	30	840	0.2	0.13	0.075
Copper	8930	557	383	0.0915	400	230
Glass	2800	175	800	0.2	0.81	0.47
Ice	910	57	1830	0.44	2.2	1.3
Plaster	1800	112			0.81	0.47
Polystyrene	1210	75			.04	.023
Steel (1% C)	7800	487	473	0.113	43	25
Wood (pine)	420	26	2700	0.64	0.15	0.087
Wool (insulation)	200	12			0.038	0.022

TABLE 7.6 Typical Convective Coefficients h.

Fluid	J/s · m² · °C	BTU/hr-ft²-°F
Air, free convection	6 to 30	1 to 5
Air, forced convection	30 to 300	5 to 50
Superheated steam, forced convection	30 to 300	5 to 50
Water, forced convection	300 to 12 000	50 to 2000
Water, boiling	3000 to 60 000	500 to 20,000
Steam, condensing	6000 to 120 000	1000 to 20,000

TABLE 7.1E Properties of Ideal Gases—English Units

Gas	Chemical Formula	Molecular Weight	$R \dfrac{ft-lb}{lbm \cdot °R}$	$c_p \dfrac{BTU}{lbm \cdot °R}$	$c_v \dfrac{BTU}{lbm \cdot °R}$	k
Air	$\cdots$	28.97	53.34	0.240	0.171	1.400
Argon	Ar	39.94	38.68	0.1253	0.0756	1.667
Butane	C_4H_{10}	58.124	26.58	0.415	0.381	1.09
Carbon Dioxide	CO_2	44.01	35.10	0.203	0.158	1.285
Carbon Monoxide	CO	28.01	55.16	0.249	0.178	1.399
Ethane	C_2H_6	30.07	51.38	0.427	0.361	1.183
Ethylene	C_2H_4	28.054	55.07	0.411	0.340	1.208
Helium	He	4.003	386.0	1.25	0.753	1.667
Hydrogen	H_2	2.016	766.4	3.43	2.44	1.404
Methane	CH_4	16.04	96.35	0.532	0.403	1.32
Neon	Ne	20.183	76.55	0.246	0.1477	1.667
Nitrogen	N_2	28.016	55.15	0.248	0.177	1.400
Octane	C_8H_{18}	114.22	13.53	0.409	0.392	1.044
Oxygen	O_2	32.000	48.28	0.219	0.157	1.395
Propane	C_3H_8,	44.097	35.04	0.407	0.362	1.124
Steam	H_2O	18.016	85.76	0.445	0.335	1.329

TABLE 7.2E Specific Heats of Liquids and Solids—English Units
c_p BTU/(lbm-°F)

A. LIQUIDS

Substance	State	c_p	Substance	State	c_p
Water	1 atm, 77°F	1.00	Glycerin	1 atm, 50°F	0.555
Ammonia	sat., –4°F	1.08	Bismuth	1 atm, 800°F	0.0344
	sat., 120°F	1.22	Mercury	1 atm, 50°F	0.0330
Refrigerant-12	sat.,–4°F	0.217	Sodium	1 atm, 200°F	0.330
	sat., 120°F	0.244	Propane	1 atm, 32°F	0.577
Benzene	1 atm, 60°F	0.431	Ethyl Alcohol	1 atm, 77°F	0.581

B. SOLIDS

Substance	T, °F	c_p	Substance	T, °F	c_p
Ice	–76	0.392	Silver	–4	0.0557
	12	0.486	Lead	–150	0.0282
	28	0.402		30	0.0297
Aluminum	–150	0.167		210	0.0321
	30	0.208	Copper	–150	0.0785
	210	0.225		30	0.0911
Iron	–4	0.107		210	0.0940

TABLE 7.3E Thermodynamic Properties of Water (Steam Tables)—English Units

7.3.1E Saturated H₂0—Temperature Table

T, °F	P, psia	Volume, ft³/lbm		Energy, BTU/lbm		Enthalpy, BTU/lbm			Entropy, BTU/lbm-°R		
		v_f	v_g	u_f	u_g	h_f	h_{fg}	h_g	s_f	s_{fg}	s_g
32.018	0.08866	0.016022	3302	0.00	1021.2	0.01	1075.4	1075.4	0.00000	2.1869	2.1869
40	0.12166	0.016020	2445	8.02	1023.9	8.02	1070.9	1078.9	0.01617	2.1430	2.1592
60	0.2563	0.016035	1206.9	28.08	1030.4	28.08	1059.6	1087.7	0.05555	2.0388	2.0943
80	0.5073	0.016073	632.8	48.08	1037.0	48.09	1048.3	1096.4	0.09332	1.9423	2.0356
100	0.9503	0.016130	350.0	68.04	1043.5	68.05	1037.0	1105.0	0.12963	1.8526	1.9822
120	1.6945	0.016205	203.0	87.99	1049.9	88.00	1025.5	1113.5	0.16465	1.7690	1.9336
140	2.892	0.016293	122.88	107.95	1056.2	107.96	1014.0	1121.9	0.19851	1.6907	1.8892
160	4.745	0.016395	77.23	127.94	1062.3	127.96	1002.2	1130.1	0.23130	1.6171	1.8484
180	7.515	0.016509	50.20	147.97	1068.3	147.99	990.2	1138.2	0.26311	1.5478	1.8109
200	11.529	0.016634	33.63	168.04	1074.2	168.07	977.9	1145.9	0.29400	1.4822	1.7762
212	14.698	0.016716	26.80	180.11	1077.6	180.16	970.3	1150.5	0.31213	1.4446	1.7567
220	17.188	0.016772	23.15	188.17	1079.8	188.22	965.3	1153.5	0.32406	1.4201	1.7441
240	24.97	0.016922	16.327	208.36	1085.3	208.44	952.3	1160.7	0.35335	1.3609	1.7143
260	35.42	0.017084	11.768	228.64	1090.5	228.76	938.8	1167.6	0.38193	1.3044	1.6864
280	49.18	0.017259	8.650	249.02	1095.4	249.18	924.9	1174.1	0.40986	1.2504	1.6602
300	66.98	0.017448	6.472	269.52	1100.0	269.73	910.4	1180.2	0.43720	1.1984	1.6356
340	117.93	0.017872	3.792	310.91	1108.0	311.30	879.5	1190.8	0.49031	1.0997	1.5901
380	195.60	0.018363	2.339	352.95	1114.3	353.62	845.4	1199.0	0.54163	1.0067	1.5483
420	308.5	0.018936	1.5024	395.81	1118.3	396.89	807.2	1204.1	0.59152	0.9175	1.5091
460	466.3	0.019614	0.9961	439.7	1119.6	441.4	764.1	1205.5	0.6404	0.8308	1.4712
500	680.0	0.02043	0.6761	485.1	1117.4	487.7	714.8	1202.5	0.6888	0.7448	1.4335
540	961.5	0.02145	0.4658	532.6	1111.0	536.4	657.5	1193.8	0.7374	0.6576	1.3950
580	1324.3	0.02278	0.3225	583.1	1098.9	588.6	589.3	1178.0	0.7872	0.5668	1.3540
620	1784.4	0.02465	0.2209	638.3	1078.5	646.4	505.0	1151.4	0.8398	0.4677	1.3075
660	2362	0.02767	0.14459	702.3	1042.3	714.4	391.1	1105.5	0.8990	0.3493	1.2483
700	3090	0.03666	0.07438	801.7	947.7	822.7	167.5	990.2	0.9902	0.1444	1.1346
705.44	3204	0.05053	0.05053	872.6	872.6	902.5	0	902.5	1.0580	0	1.0580

7.3.2E Saturated H₂0—Pressure Table

P, psia	T, °F	Volume, ft³/lbm		Energy, BTU/lbm		Enthalpy, BTU/lbm			Entropy, BTU/lbm-°R		
		v_f	v_g	u_f	u_g	h_f	h_{fg}	h_g	s_f	s_{fg}	s_g
1.0	101.70	0.016136	333.6	69.74	1044.0	69.74	1036.0	1105.8	0.13266	1.8453	1.9779
2.0	126.04	0.016230	173.75	94.02	1051.8	94.02	1022.1	1116.1	0.17499	1.7448	1.9198
4.0	152.93	0.016358	90.64	120.88	1060.2	120.89	1006.4	1127.3	0.21983	1.6426	1.8624
6.0	170.03	0.016451	61.98	137.98	1065.4	138.00	996.2	1134.2	0.24736	1.5819	1.8292
10	193.19	0.016590	38.42	161.20	1072.2	161.23	982.1	1143.3	0.28358	1.5041	1.7877
14.696	211.99	0.016715	26.80	180.10	1077.6	180.15	970.4	1150.5	0.31212	1.4446	1.7567
20	227.96	0.016830	20.09	196.19	1082.0	196.26	960.1	1156.4	0.33580	1.3962	1.7320
30	250.34	0.017004	13.748	218.84	1088.0	218.93	945.4	1164.3	0.36821	1.3314	1.6996
40	267.26	0.017146	10.501	236.03	1092.3	236.16	933.8	1170.0	0.39214	1.2845	1.6767
50	281.03	0.017269	8.518	250.08	1095.6	250.24	924.2	1174.4	0.41129	1.2476	1.6589
60	292.73	0.017378	7.177	262.06	1098.3	262.25	915.8	1178.0	0.42733	1.2170	1.6444
70	302.96	0.017478	6.209	272.56	1100.6	272.79	908.3	1181.0	0.44120	1.1909	1.6321
80	312.07	0.017570	5.474	281.95	1102.6	282.21	901.4	1183.6	0.45344	1.1679	1.6214
90	320.31	0.017655	4.898	290.46	1104.3	290.76	895.1	1185.9	0.46442	1.1475	1.6119
100	327.86	0.017736	4.434	298.28	1105.8	298.61	889.2	1187.8	0.47439	1.1290	1.6034
120	341.30	0.017886	3.730	312.27	1108.3	312.67	878.5	1191.1	0.49201	1.0966	1.5886
140	353.08	0.018024	3.221	324.58	1110.3	325.05	868.7	1193.8	0.50727	1.0688	1.5761
160	363.60	0.018152	2.836	335.63	1112.0	336.16	859.8	1196.0	0.52078	1.0443	1.5651
180	373.13	0.018273	2.533	345.68	1113.4	346.29	851.5	1197.8	0.53292	1.0223	1.5553
200	381.86	0.018387	2.289	354.9	1114.6	355.6	843.7	1199.3	0.5440	1.0025	1.5464
300	417.43	0.018896	1.5442	393.0	1118.2	394.1	809.8	1203.9	0.5883	0.9232	1.5115
400	444.70	0.019340	1.1620	422.8	1119.5	424.2	781.2	1205.5	0.6218	0.8638	1.4856
500	467.13	0.019748	0.9283	447.7	1119.4	449.5	755.8	1205.3	0.6490	0.8154	1.4645
600	486.33	0.02013	0.7702	469.4	1118.6	471.7	732.4	1204.1	0.6723	0.7742	1.4464
800	518.36	0.02087	0.5691	506.6	1115.0	509.7	689.6	1199.3	0.7110	0.7050	1.4160
1000	544.75	0.02159	0.4459	538.4	ll 09.9	542.4	650.0	1192.4	0.7432	0.6471	1.3903
1400	587.25	0.02307	0.3016	592.7	l 096.0	598.6	575.5	1174.1	0.7964	0.5497	1.3461
2000	636.00	0.02565	0.18813	662.4	1066.6	671.9	464.4	1136.3	0.8623	0.4238	1.2861
3000	695.52	0.03431	0.08404	783.4	968.8	802.5	213.0	1015.5	0.9732	0.1843	1.1575
3203.6	705.44	0.05053	0.05053	872.6	872.6	902.5	0	902.5	1.0580	0	1.0580

7.3.3E Superheated Vapor

°F	v	u	h	s	v	u	h	s	v	u	h	s
		1 psia					10 psia				14.7 psia		
200	392.5	1077.5	1150.1	2.0508	38.85	1074.7	1146.6	1.7927	...	...	...	...
300	452.3	1112.1	1195.8	2.1153	45.00	1110.6	1193.9	1.8595	30.53	1109.7	1192.8	1.8160
400	511.9	1147.0	1241.8	2.1720	51.03	1146.1	1240.5	1.9171	34.67	1145.6	1239.9	1.8741
500	571.5	1182.8	1288.5	2.2235	57.04	1182.2	1287.7	1.9690	38.77	1181.8	1287.3	1.9263
600	631.1	1219.3	1336.1	2.2706	63.03	1218.9	1335.5	2.0164	42.86	1218.6	1335.2	1.9737
700	690.7	1256.7	1384.5	2.3142	69.01	1256.3	1384.0	2.0601	46.93	1256.1	1383.8	2.0175
800	750.3	1294.9	1433.7	2.3550	74.98	1294.6	1433.3	2.1009	51.00	1294.4	1433.1	2.0584
1000	869.5	1373.9	1534.8	2.4294	86.91	1373.8	1534.6	2.1755	59.13	1373.7	1534.5	2.1330
1200	988.6	1456.7	1639.6	2.4967	98.84	1456.5	1639.4	2.2428	67.25	1456.5	1639.3	2.2003
1400	1107.7	1543.1	1748.1	2.5584	110.76	1543.0	1748.0	2.3045	75.36	1543.0	1747.9	2.2621
		20 psia					60 psia				100 psia		
300	22.36	1108.8	1191.6	1.7808	7.259	1101.0	1181.6	1.6492	...	...	...	...
400	25.43	1145.1	1239.2	1.8395	8.353	1140.8	1233.5	1.7134	4.934	1136.2	1227.5	1.6517
500	28.46	1181.5	1286.8	1.8919	9.399	1178.6	1283.0	1.7678	5.587	1175.7	1279.1	1.7085
600	31.47	1218.4	1334.8	1.9395	10.425	1216.3	1332.1	1.8165	6.216	1214.2	1329.3	1.7582
700	34.47	1255.9	1383.5	1.9834	11.440	1254.4	1381.4	1.8609	6.834	1252.8	1379.2	1.8033
800	37.46	1294.3	1432.9	2.0243	12.448	1293.0	1431.2	1.9022	7.445	1291.8	1429.6	1.8449
1000	43.44	1373.5	1534.3	2.0989	14.454	1372.7	1533.2	1.9773	8.647	1371.9	1532.1	1.9204
1200	49.41	1456.4	1639.2	2.1663	16.452	1455.8	1638.5	2.0448	9.861	1455.2	1637.7	1.9882
1400	55.37	1542.9	1747.9	2.2281	18.445	1542.5	1747.3	2.1067	11.060	1542.0	1746.7	2.0502
1600	61.33	1633.2	1860.1	2.2854	20.44	1632.8	1859.7	2.1641	12.257	1632.4	1859.3	2.1076
		120 psia					160 psia				200 psia		
400	4.079	1133.8	1224.4	1.6288	3.007	1128.8	1217.8	1.5911	2.361	1123.5	1210.8	1.5600
500	4.633	1174.2	1277.1	1.6868	3.440	1171.2	1273.0	1.6518	2.724	1168.0	1268.8	1.6239
600	5.164	1213.2	1327.8	1.7371	3.848	1211.1	1325.0	1.7034	3.058	1208.9	1322.1	1.6767
700	5.682	1252.0	1378.2	1.7825	4.243	1250.4	1376.0	1.7494	3.379	1248.8	1373.8	1.7234
800	6.195	1291.2	1428.7	1.8243	4.631	1289.9	1427.0	1.7916	3.693	1288.6	1425.3	1.7660
1000	7.208	1371.5	1531.5	1.9000	5.397	1370.6	1530.4	1.8677	4.310	1369.8	1529.3	1.8425
1200	8.213	1454.9	1637.3	1.9679	6.154	1454.3	1636.5	1.9358	4.918	1453.7	1635.7	1.9109
1400	9.214	1541.8	1746.4	2.0300	6.906	1541.4	1745.9	1.9980	5.521	1540.9	1745.3	1.9732
1600	10.212	1632.3	1859.0	2.0875	7.656	1631.9	1858.6	2.0556	6.123	1631.6	1858.2	2.0308
1800	11.209	1726.2	1975.1	2.1413	8.405	1725.9	1974.8	2.1094	6.722	1725.6	1974.4	2.0847
		250 psia					300 psia				400 psia		
500	2.150	1163.8	1263.3	1.5948	1.7662	1159.5	1257.5	1.5701	1.2843	1150.1	1245.2	1.5282
600	2.426	1206.1	1318.3	1.6494	2.004	1203.2	1314.5	1.6266	1.4760	1197.3	1306.6	1.5892
700	2.688	1246.7	1371.1	1.6970	2.227	1244.6	1368.3	1.6751	1.6503	1240.4	1362.5	1.6397
800	2.943	1287.0	1423.2	1.7401	2.442	1285.4	1421.0	1.7187	1.8163	1282.1	1416.6	1.6844
900	3.193	1327.6	1475.3	1.7799	2.653	1326.3	1473.6	1.7589	1.9776	1323.7	1470.1	1.7252
1000	3.440	1368.7	1527.9	1.8172	2.860	1367.7	1526.5	1.7964	2.136	1365.5	1523.6	1.7632
1200	3.929	1453.0	1634.8	1.8858	3.270	1452.2	1633.8	1.8653	2.446	1450.7	1631.8	1.8327
1400	4.414	1540.4	1744.6	1.9483	3.675	1539.8	1743.8	1.9279	2.752	1538.7	1742.4	1.8956
1600	4.896	1631.1	1857.6	2.0060	4.078	1630.7	1857.0	1.9857	3.055	1629.8	1855.9	1.9535
1800	5.376	1725.2	1974.0	2.0599	4.479	1724.9	1973.5	2.0396	3.357	1724.1	1972.6	2.0076
		600 psia					800 psia				1000 psia		
500	0.7947	1128.0	1216.2	1.4592	...	...	...	...	...	...	...	...
600	0.9456	1184.5	1289.5	1.5320	0.6776	1170.1	1270.4	1.4861	0.5140	1153.7	1248.8	1.4450
700	1.0727	1231.5	1350.6	1.5872	0.7829	1222.1	1338.0	1.5471	0.6080	1212.0	1324.6	1.5135
800	1.1900	1275.4	1407.6	1.6343	0.8764	1268.5	1398.2	1.5969	0.6878	1261.2	1388.5	1.5664
900	1.3021	1318.4	1462.9	1.6766	0.9640	1312.9	1455.6	1.6408	0.7610	1307.3	1448.1	1.6120
1000	1.4108	1361.2	1517.8	1.7155	1.0482	1356.7	1511.9	1.6807	0.8305	1352.2	1505.9	1.6530
1200	1.6222	1447.7	1627.8	1.7861	1.2102	1444.6	1623.8	1.7526	0.9630	1441.5	1619.7	1.7261
1400	1.8289	1536.5	1739.5	1.8497	1.3674	1534.2	1736.6	1.8167	1.0905	1531.9	1733.7	1.7909
1600	2.033	1628.0	1853.7	1.9080	1.5218	1626.2	1851.5	1.8754	1.2152	1624.4	1849.3	1.8499
1800	2.236	1722.6	1970.8	1.9622	1.6749	1721.0	1969.0	1.9298	1.3384	1719.5	1967.2	1.9046
		2000 psia					3000 psia				4000 psia		
700	0.2487	1147.7	1239.8	1.3782	0.09771	1003.9	1058.1	1.1944	0.02867	742.1	763.4	0.9345
800	0.3071	1220.1	1333.8	1.4562	0.17572	1167.6	1265.2	1.3675	0.10522	1095.0	1172.9	1.2740
900	0.3534	1276.8	1407.6	1.5126	0.2160	1241.8	1361.7	1.4414	0.14622	1201.5	1309.7	1.3789
1000	0.3945	1328.1	1474.1	1.5598	0.2485	1301.7	1439.6	1.4967	0.17520	1272.9	1402.6	1.4449
1200	0.4685	1425.2	1598.6	1.6398	0.3036	1408.0	1576.6	1.5848	0.2213	1390.1	1553.9	1.5423
1400	0.5368	1520.2	1718.8	1.7082	0.3524	1508.1	1703.7	1.6571	0.2603	1495.7	1688.4	1.6188
1600	0.6020	1615.4	1838.2	1.7692	0.3978	1606.3	1827.1	1.7201	0.2959	1597.1	1816.1	1.6841
1800	0.6656	1712.0	1958.3	1.8249	0.4416	1704.5	1949.6	1.7769	0.3296	1697.1	1941.1	1.7420
2000	0.7284	1810.6	2080.2	1.8765	0.4844	1803.9	2072.8	1.8291	0.3625	1797.3	2065.6	1.7948

7-THERMO

Statics

by George E. Mase

Chapter 8

Statics is concerned primarily with the equilibrium of bodies subjected to force systems. Also, traditionally in engineering statics we consider centroids, center of gravity and moments of inertia.

8.1 Forces, Moments and Resultants

A force is the manifestation of the action of one body upon another. Forces arise from the direct action of two bodies in contact with one another, or from the "action at a distance" of one body upon another as occurs with gravitational and magnetic forces. We classify forces as either *body forces*, which act (and are distributed) throughout the volume of the body, or as *surface forces*, which act over a surface portion (either external or internal) of the body. If the surface over which the force system acts is very small, we usually assume localization at a specific point in the surface and speak of a *concentrated force* at that point.

Mathematically, forces are represented by *vectors*. Geometrically, a vector is a directed line segment having a head and a tail, i.e., an arrow. The length of the arrow corresponds to the magnitude of the force, its orientation defines the line of action, and the direction of the arrow (tail to head) gives the sense of the force.

Systems of concentrated forces are listed as *concurrent* when all of the forces act, or could act, at a single point; otherwise they are termed *non-concurrent* systems. Parallel force systems are in this second group. Also, force systems are often described as two-dimensional (acting in a single plane), or three-dimensional (spatial systems).

In addition to the "push or pull" effect on the point at which it acts, a force creates a *moment* about other points of the body. Conceptually, a moment may be

> If the surface over which the force system acts is very small, we usually assume localization at a specific point in the surface and speak of a *concentrated force* at that point.

thought of as a torque. Mathematically, the moment of the force **F** with respect to point A when the force acts at point B is defined by the vector cross product

$$\mathbf{M}_A = \mathbf{r}_{B/A} \times \mathbf{F} \tag{8.1.1}$$

where $\mathbf{r}_{B/A}$ is the position vector of B relative to A as shown by Fig. 8.1. Actually, it is easily shown that

$$\mathbf{M}_A = \mathbf{r}_{Q/A} \times \mathbf{F} = \mathbf{r}_{B/A} \times \mathbf{F} \tag{8.1.2}$$

where Q is any point on the line of action of **F**, as shown in Fig. 8.1.

A moment must always be designated with respect to a specific point, and is represented by a vector perpendicular to the plane of **r** and **F**. Moment vectors are sometimes denoted by double-headed arrows to distinguish them from force vectors. The component of the moment vector in the direction of any axis (line) passing through A is said to be the moment of the force about that axis. If the direction of the axis is defined by the unit vector $\boldsymbol{\lambda}$, the moment component, a scalar along that axis, is given by

$$M_\lambda = \mathbf{r} \times \mathbf{F} \cdot \boldsymbol{\lambda} \tag{8.1.3}$$

The *resultant* of a system of forces is the equivalent force and moment of the total system at any point.

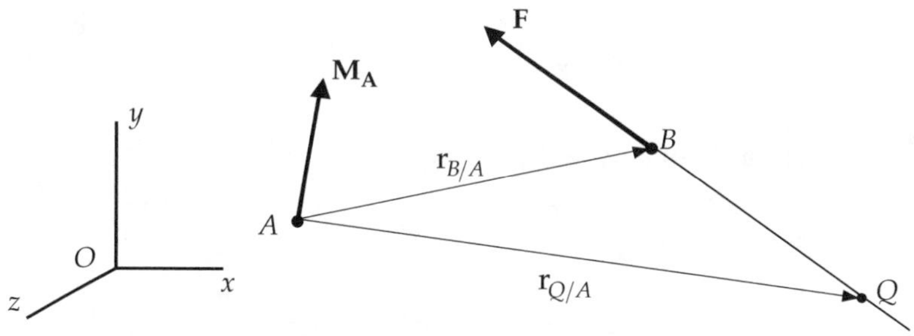

Figure 8.1 Moment of F about A.

The "turning effect" about the hinge axis of a door due to the application of a force to the doorknob is an example. If $\boldsymbol{\lambda} = \mathbf{k}$ in Eq. 8.1.3, the moment component is labeled M_z, the scalar moment about the z-axis, and we find that

$$M_z = xF_y - yF_x \tag{8.1.4}$$

where x and y are the components of $\mathbf{r}_{B/A}$ of Fig. 8.1. Similarly, for $\boldsymbol{\lambda} = \mathbf{j}$ and $\boldsymbol{\lambda} = \mathbf{i}$, respectively,

$$M_y = zF_x - xF_z \tag{8.1.5}$$

$$M_x = yF_z - zF_y \tag{8.1.6}$$

Furthermore, it may be shown from Eq. 8.1.4 that the scalar moment about any point A in the plane of **r** and **F** is given by

$$M_A = F \times d \tag{8.1.7}$$

where d is the perpendicular distance from A to the line of action of **F**.

The *resultant* of a system of forces is the equivalent force and moment of the total system at any point. Thus, the resultant of a concurrent force system is a single force acting at the point of concurrency, and is the vector sum of the individual forces. In contrast, the resultant of a non-concurrent system depends upon the point at which it is determined, and in general consists of a resultant force and resultant moment. Actually, the resultant force (the vector sum of the individual forces) is the same at all points, but the resultant moment will vary (in magnitude and direction) from point to point.

The resultant of a pair of equal but oppositely directed parallel forces, known as a *couple*, is simply a moment having a magnitude $F \times d$ where F is the magnitude of the forces and d the perpendicular distance between their lines of action. Figure 8.2 illustrates equivalent couples and the curly symbol often used.

A pair of equal but oppositely directed parallel forces is known as a *couple*.

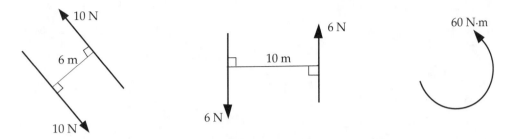

Figure 8.2 Equivalent couples.

Example 8.1

Determine the resultant force for the (a) plane, and (b) space concurrent systems shown.

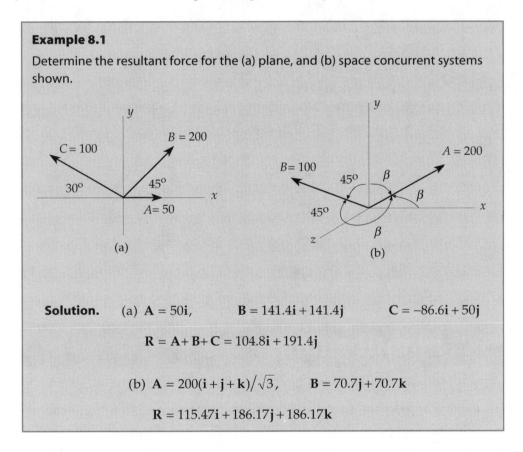

Solution.   (a) $\mathbf{A} = 50\mathbf{i},$ $\mathbf{B} = 141.4\mathbf{i} + 141.4\mathbf{j}$ $\mathbf{C} = -86.6\mathbf{i} + 50\mathbf{j}$

$$\mathbf{R} = \mathbf{A} + \mathbf{B} + \mathbf{C} = 104.8\mathbf{i} + 191.4\mathbf{j}$$

(b) $\mathbf{A} = 200(\mathbf{i} + \mathbf{j} + \mathbf{k})/\sqrt{3},$ $\mathbf{B} = 70.7\mathbf{j} + 70.7\mathbf{k}$

$$\mathbf{R} = 115.47\mathbf{i} + 186.17\mathbf{j} + 186.17\mathbf{k}$$

Example 8.2

Determine the moment of force **F**

    (a) with respect to the origin. (b) with respect to point Q. (c) about the axis OQ.

    (d) about the x-axis.   (e) about the y-axis.

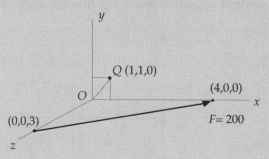

Solution. $\mathbf{F} = 0.8(200)\mathbf{i} - 0.6(200)\mathbf{k} = 160\mathbf{i} - 120\mathbf{k}$.

(a) $\mathbf{M}_O = 4\mathbf{i} \times (160\mathbf{i} - 120\mathbf{k}) = 3\mathbf{k} \times (160\mathbf{i} - 120\mathbf{k}) = 480\mathbf{j}$

(b) $\mathbf{M}_O = (3\mathbf{i} - \mathbf{j}) \times (160\mathbf{i} - 120\mathbf{k}) = (-\mathbf{i} - \mathbf{j} + 3\mathbf{k}) \times (160\mathbf{i} - 120\mathbf{k}) = 120\mathbf{i} + 360\mathbf{j} + 160\mathbf{k}$

(c) $M_{OQ} = (120\mathbf{i} + 360\mathbf{j} + 160\mathbf{k}) \cdot (\mathbf{i} + \mathbf{j})/\sqrt{2}$

       $= (120 + 360)/\sqrt{2} = 480/\sqrt{2} = 339.5$

(d) $M_x = 0$ (force **F** intersects the x - axis)

(e) $M_y = Fd = 200(3 \cos\beta) = 200(2.4) = 480$

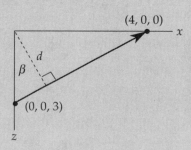

8.2 Equilibrium

If the system of forces acting on a body is one whose resultant is absolutely zero (vector sum of all forces is zero, and the resultant moment of the forces about every point is zero) the body is in *equilibrium*. Mathematically, equilibrium requires the equations

$$\sum \mathbf{F} = 0, \qquad \sum \mathbf{M}_A = 0 \qquad\qquad (8.2.1)$$

to be simultaneously satisfied, with A arbitrary. These two vector equations are equivalent to the six scalar equations:

$$\sum F_x = 0 \qquad \sum M_x = 0$$

$$\sum F_y = 0 \qquad \sum M_y = 0 \qquad \textbf{(8.2.2)}$$

$$\sum F_z = 0 \qquad \sum M_z = 0$$

which must hold at every point A for any orientation of the xyz-axes. The moment components in Eq. 8.2.2 are the coordinate axes components of $\mathbf{M}_A$. If the forces are concurrent and their vector sum is zero, the sum of moments about every point will be satisfied automatically.

If all the forces act in a single plane, say the xy-plane, one of the above force equations, and two of the moment equations are satisfied identically, so that equilibrium requires only

$$\sum F_x = 0, \qquad \sum F_y = 0, \qquad \sum M_z = 0 \qquad \textbf{(8.2.3)}$$

In this case we can solve for only three unknowns instead of six as when Eqs. 8.2.2 are required.

The solution for unknown forces and moments in equilibrium problems rests firmly upon the construction of a good *free body diagram*, abbreviated FBD, from which the detailed equations 8.2.2 or 8.2.3 may be obtained. A free body diagram is a neat sketch of the body (or of any appropriate portion of it) showing all forces and moments acting on the body, together with all important linear and angular dimensions.

> A free body diagram is a neat sketch of the body showing all forces and moments acting on the body.

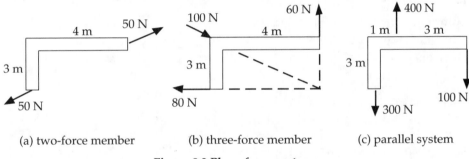

| (a) two-force member | (b) three-force member | (c) parallel system |

Figure 8.3 Plane force systems.

A body in equilibrium under the action of two forces only is called a *two-force member*, and the two forces must be equal in magnitude and oppositely directed along the line joining their points of application. If a body is in equilibrium under the action of three forces (a *three-force member*) those forces must be coplanar, and concurrent (unless they form a parallel system). Examples are shown in Fig. 8.3.

A knowledge of the possible reaction forces and moments at various supports is essential in preparing a correct free body diagram. Several of the basic reactions are illustrated in Fig. 8.4 showing a block of concrete subjected to a horizontal pull P, Fig. 8.4a, and a cantilever beam carrying both a distributed and concentrated load, Fig. 8.4b. The correct FBDs are on the right.

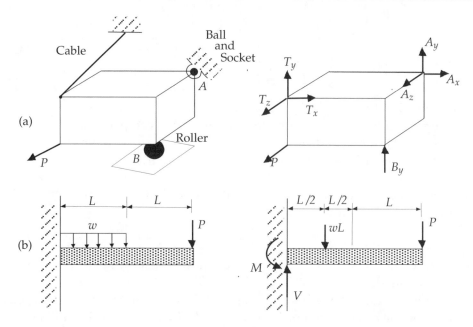

Figure 8.4 Free body diagrams.

Example 8.3

Determine the tension in the two cables supporting the 700 N block.

Solution. Construct the FBD of junction A of the cables. Sum forces in x and y directions:

$$\sum F_x = -0.707T_{AB} + 0.8T_{AC} = 0$$
$$\sum F_y = 0.707T_{AB} + 0.6T_{AC} - 700 = 0$$

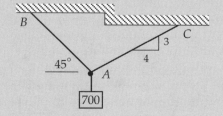

Solve, simultaneously, and find

$$T_{AC} = 700/1.4 = 500 \text{ N}$$
$$T_{AB} = 0.8(500)/0.707 = 565.8 \text{ N}$$

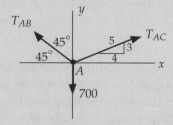

Alternative solution. Draw the force polygon (vector sum of forces) which must close for equilibrium. Determine angles, and use law of sines:

$$\frac{700}{\sin 81.87°} = \frac{T_{AB}}{\sin 53.1°} = \frac{T_{AC}}{\sin 45°}$$

$$T_{AC} = \frac{700(0.707)}{(0.99)} = 500 \text{ N}$$

$$T_{AB} = \frac{700(0.8)}{(0.99)} = 565.8 \text{ N}$$

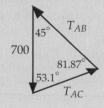

Example 8.4

A 12-m bar weighing 140 N is hinged to a vertical wall at *A*, and supported by the cable *BC*. Determine the tension in the cable together with the horizontal and vertical components of the force reaction at *A*.

Solution. Construct the FBD showing force components at *A* and *B*. Write the equilibrium equations and solve:

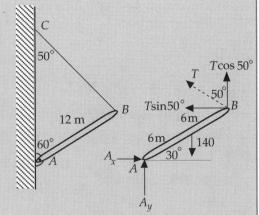

$$\sum M_A = 6T \sin 50° + 6\sqrt{3}T \cos 50° - 140(6)\sqrt{3}/2 = 0$$

$$\therefore T = 64.5 \text{ N}$$

$$\sum F_x = A_x - T \sin 50° = A_x - 64.5(0.766) = 0$$

$$\therefore A_x = 49.4 \text{ N}$$

$$\sum F_y = A_y + T \cos 50° - 140 = A_y + 64.5(0.643) - 140 = 0$$

$$\therefore A_y = 98.5 \text{ N}$$

8.3 Trusses and Frames

> 🔑 All members are assumed to be two-force members and are therefore in simple (axial) tension or compression.

Simple pin-connected trusses and plane frames provide us with elementary examples of structures that may be solved by the equilibrium concepts of statics.

The classic truss problem resembles the one-lane country bridge, as shown schematically in Fig. 8.5a. All members are assumed to be two-force members and are therefore in simple (axial) tension or compression. All loads are assumed to act at the joints (labeled *A*, *B*, *C*, etc.) where the members are pinned together. External reactions such as A_x, A_y and E_y may be determined as a non-concurrent force problem from a FBD of the entire truss. Following that, the internal forces in the members themselves may be determined from a FBD of each joint in turn

(a)

(b)

Figure 8.5 Simple truss.

(method of joints) starting, for example, with joint E of the truss as shown in Fig. 8.5b. Thus, we solve a sequence of concurrent force problems at successive joints having only two unknowns. As noted by Fig. 8.5b we may assume the unknown internal forces such as F_{ED}, F_{EF}, etc., to be tension. A negative result indicates compression.

Example 8.5

Using the right sub-truss of Fig 8.6, determine the forces in members CD, CF and FG.

Solution. Summing moments about pin F of the FBD of the right sub-truss,

$$\sum M_F = F_{DC}(\sqrt{3}L/2) + 10P(L) - 6P(L/2) = 0$$
$$\therefore F_{DC} = -8.085P \text{ (comp)}$$

Summing vertical forces on the sub-truss,

$$\sum F_y = 10P - 3P - 6P + 0.866F_{FC} = 0$$
$$\therefore F_{FC} = -1.156P \text{ (comp)}$$

Summing horizontal forces,

$$\sum F_x = -F_{FG} + 8.085P + 1.156P/2 = 0$$
$$\therefore F_{FG} = 8.663P \text{ (tens)}$$

Note: These results agree with those determined by the method of joints in Example 8.6.

Example 8.6

Determine the forces in the members of the pin-connected truss loaded as shown below. All members have length L.

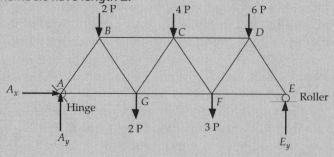

Solution. Summing moments about pin A we solve for the reaction at roller E (counterclockwise moments are positive):

$$\sum M_A = 3LE_y - 2PL - 3P(2L) - 2P(L/2) - 4P(3L/2) - 6P(5L/2) = 0$$
$$\therefore E_y = 10P$$

Also,

$$\sum M_E = -3LA_y + 3P(L) + 2P(2L) + 6P(L/2) + 4P(3L/2) + 2P(5L/2) = 0$$

$$\therefore A_y = 7P$$

Summing Horizontal forces,

$$\sum F_x = A_x = 0$$

Consider joint E (see FBD at right),

$$\sum F_y = T_{ED} \sin 60° + 10P = 0$$

$$\therefore T_{ED} = -11.55P \text{ (comp)}$$

$$\sum F_x = -T_{EF} - T_{ED} \cos 60° = 0$$

$$\therefore T_{EF} = 5.775P \text{ (tens)}$$

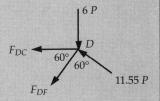

Consider next joint D (see FBD at right),

$$\sum F_y = -6P - 0.866F_{DF} + 0.866(11.55P) = 0$$

$$\therefore F_{DF} = 4.62P \text{ (tens)}$$

$$\sum F_x = -F_{DC} - 0.5(11.55P) - 0.5(4.62P) = 0$$

$$\therefore F_{DC} = -8.085P \text{ (comp)}$$

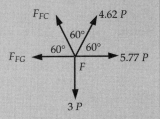

Consider next joint F (see FBD at right),

$$\sum F_y = -3P + 0.866(4.62P) + 0.866F_{FC} = 0$$

$$\therefore F_{FC} = -1.156P \text{ (comp)}$$

$$\sum F_x = -F_{FG} - 0.5(-1.156P) + 0.5(4.62P) + 5.775P = 0$$

$$\therefore F_{FG} = 8.663P \text{ (tens)}$$

Note: This example should be completed by considering joint C next, then joint G, and so on.

If the internal forces in only a few selected members are required, the *method of sections* may be used. For example, to obtain only the forces in members CD, CF and GF of the above truss, we "section" it into two portions by cutting across those members as shown in Fig. 8.6. Each portion becomes a sub-truss, and the internal forces of the sectioned members become external reactions of the two sub-trusses. Both force $\left(\sum F = 0 \right)$ and moment $\left(\sum M_A = 0 \right)$ equations are useful in this method.

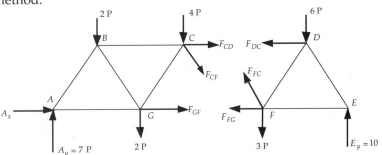

Figure 8.6 Sectioned truss.

A plane frame is a structure that consists of both two-force and three-force members, or even four-force members, etc. Loads may act at any location on the frame. The problem is to determine the components of the reactions at all pins of the frame. This usually requires not only a FBD of the entire frame, but also a FBD of each member. We illustrate by the following example.

Example 8.7

For the frame shown, determine the horizontal and vertical components of the reactions at all pins.

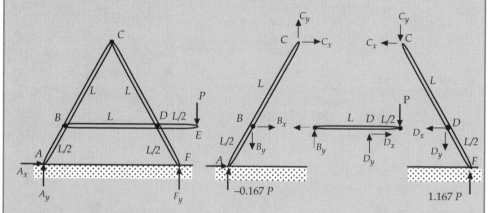

Solution. From a FBD of entire frame,

$$\sum F_x = A_x = 0 \qquad\qquad \therefore A_x = 0$$

$$\sum M_A = (1.5L)F_y - (1.75L)P = 0 \qquad\qquad \therefore F_y = 1.167P$$

$$\sum F_y = A_y + 1.167P - P = 0 \qquad\qquad \therefore A_y = -0.167P$$

From a FBD of member *BDE*,

$$\sum M_D = -(L)B_y - (L/2)P = 0 \qquad \therefore B_y = -0.5P$$

$$\sum F_y = -0.5P + D_y - P = 0 \qquad \therefore D_y = 1.5P$$

Transfer the vertical components at *B* and *D* of members *BDE* to members *ABC* and *CDF* by changing directions (action and reaction principle). From a FBD of member *ABC*,

$$\sum F_y = -0.167P + 0.5P + C_y = 0 \qquad\qquad \therefore C_y = -0.333P$$

$$\sum M_B = -(\sqrt{3}L/2)C_x - (L/2)0.333P + (L/4)0.167P = 0 \qquad\qquad \therefore C_x = -0.144P$$

$$\sum F_x = B_x - 0.144P = 0 \qquad\qquad \therefore B_x = 0.144P$$

Transfer horizontal components B_x and C_x to members *BDE* and *CDF*. From a FBD of member *BDE*,

$$\sum F_x = -0.144P + D_x = 0 \qquad \therefore D_x = 0.144P$$

From a FBD of member *CDF*,

$$\sum F_y = 0.333P + D_y + 1.167P = 0 \qquad \therefore D_y = -1.5P$$

Completed FBDs of all members are shown on the next page.

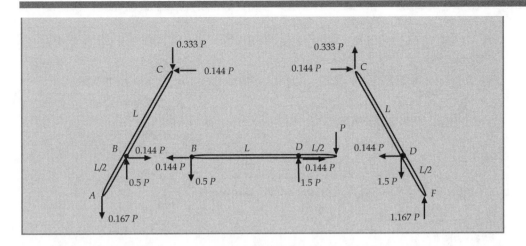

8.4 Friction

Consider a block of weight W at rest on a dry, rough, horizontal plane, Fig. 8.7a. Let a horizontal force P act to the right on the block, Fig. 8.7b. A *friction force F* is developed at the surface of contact between the block and plane, and maintains equilibrium ($F = P$) as long as $P < \mu_s N = \mu_s W$, where μ_s is the *static coefficient of friction*. If P is increased until $P = P^* = \mu_s N = \mu_s W$ (Fig. 8.7c), the equilibrium state is on the verge of collapse, and motion to the right is impending. In summary, dry *Coulomb friction* described here is governed by

$$F \leq \mu_s N \qquad \textbf{(8.4.1)}$$

If relative motion between the block and the plane occurs (Fig. 8.7d), the friction force is given by

$$F = \mu_k N \qquad \textbf{(8.4.2)}$$

where μ_k is the *kinetic coefficient of friction*, slightly less in value than μ_s, with both coefficients having a range $0 \leq \mu \leq 1$.

At impending motion, the equality holds in Eq. 8.4.1 and the resultant R of F and N makes an angle ϕ with the normal N, called the *friction angle*. From Fig. 8.8a it is clear that

$$\phi = \tan^{-1} \mu_s \qquad \textbf{(8.4.3)}$$

Also, it may be readily shown that a block will remain at rest (in equilibrium) on a rough inclined plane, Fig. 8.8b, as long as $\beta < \phi$ for the surfaces of contact.

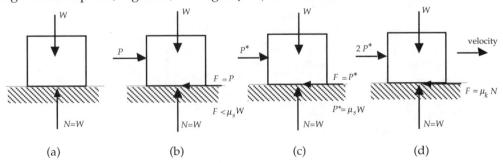

Figure 8.7 Friction forces.

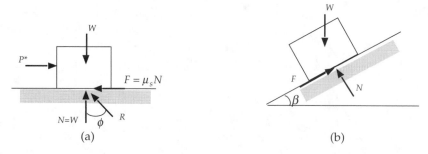

Figure 8.8 Friction angle.

Example 8.8

Determine the horizontal force P required to cause impending motion of the 50 kg block, (a) up the plane, (b) down the plane, if $\mu_s = 0.6$ between the block and plane.

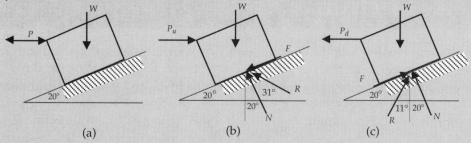

Solution. Note that, $\phi = \tan^{-1}(0.6) = 31°$ so that the block would remain in place if undisturbed.

(a) At impending motion up the plane, Fig. b, the resultant R of the friction force F and normal force N makes an angle of $51°$ to the right of the vertical and from the FBD of the block,

$$\sum F_x = P_u - R\sin 51° = 0$$

$$\sum F_y = R\cos 51° - 50 \times 9.81 = 0$$

Solving these equations,

$$R = 779 \text{ N}, \qquad P_u = 606 \text{ N}$$

(b) At impending motion down the plane, R makes an angle of $11°$ to the left of the vertical, Fig. c, so that now

$$\sum F_x = -P_d + R\sin 11° = 0$$

$$\sum F_y = R\cos 11° - 50 \times 9.81 = 0$$

Therefore

$$R = 499 \text{ N}, \qquad P_d = 95.2 \text{ N}$$

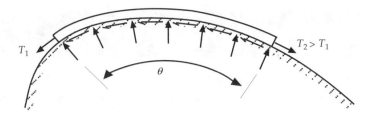

Figure 8.9 A belt with friction.

If a belt, or rope, is pressed firmly against some portion of a rough stationary curved surface, and pulled in one direction or the other, the tension in the belt will increase in the direction of pull due to the frictional resistance between the belt and surface, as shown in Fig. 8.9. It may be shown that

$$T_2 = T_1 e^{\mu_s \theta} \qquad T_2 > T_1 \qquad\qquad (8.4.4)$$

where θ is the angle of contact, in radians, and μ_s is the static coefficient of friction.

Tension in a belt will increase in the direction of pull due to the frictional resistance.

Example 8.9

A 100 kg block rests on a 30° rough inclined plane ($\mu_s = 0.4$) and is attached by a rope to a mass m in the arrangement shown. If the static coefficient of friction between the rope and the circular support is 0.25, determine the maximum m that can be supported without slipping.

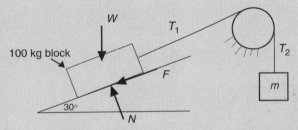

Solution. Summing forces perpendicular to the plane we determine

$$N = 981 \cos 30° = 849.5 \text{ N}$$

Thus,

$$F = 0.4(849.5) = 339.8 \text{ N}$$

at impending motion, and by summing forces along the plane

$$T_1 = 339.8 + 981 \sin 30° = 830.3 \text{ N}$$

For the circular support we have,

$$T_2 = T_1 e^{(0.25)(120 \times \pi/180)} = 830.3(1.69) = 1403 \text{ N}$$

and

$$m = 1403/9.81 = 143 \text{ kg}$$

8.5 Properties of Plane Areas

Associated with every plane area A (in the xy-plane, for example) there is a point C, known as the *centroid*, whose coordinates $\bar{x}$ and $\bar{y}$ are defined by the integrals

$$\bar{x} = \frac{\int_A x \, dA}{\int_A dA} \qquad \bar{y} = \frac{\int_A y \, dA}{\int_A dA} \qquad (8.5.1)$$

where dA is differential element of area having coordinates x and y as shown in Fig. 8.10a.

Although the integrals in Eq. 8.5.1 may be evaluated by a double integration using $dA = dx\,dy$, in practice it is often advantageous to calculate centroidal coordinates by a single integration using either a horizontal or vertical strip for dA (Fig. 8.10b and Fig. 8.10c) for which Eq. 8.5.1 may be expressed in the form where

$$\bar{x} = \frac{\int_A x_e \, dA}{\int_A dA} \qquad \bar{y} = \frac{\int_A y_e \, dA}{\int_A dA} \qquad (8.5.2)$$

x_e and y_e are the coordinates of the centroids of the strip elements as shown.

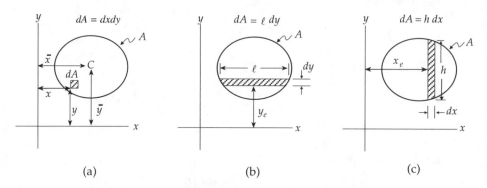

(a)   (b)   (c)

Figure 8.10 Plane area centroid.

The *plane moments of inertia* I_x and I_y of A with respect to the x and y axes, respectively, are defined by

$$I_x = \int_A y^2 \, dA, \qquad I_y = \int_A x^2 \, dA \qquad (8.5.3)$$

where in integrating for I_x we use the horizontal strip for dA, and for I_y the vertical strip. The *polar moment of inertia* with respect to the origin O is defined by

$$J_O = \int_A r^2 \, dA = \int_A (x^2 + y^2) \, dA = I_x + I_y \qquad (8.5.4)$$

All moments of inertia may be expressed in terms of their respective *radii of gyration*. Thus,

$$I_x = r_x^2 A, \qquad I_y = r_y^2 A, \qquad J_O = r_O^2 A \qquad (8.5.5)$$

The *product of inertia* of A is defined with respect to a pair of perpendicular axes. For the coordinate axes we have

$$I_{xy} = \int_A xy \, dA \qquad (8.5.6)$$

which normally must be evaluated by a double integration over A. If either one (or both) of the reference axes is an axis of symmetry, the product of inertia is zero relative to that pair of axes.

The *transfer theorem* establishes a relationship between the moment of inertia about an arbitrary axis and the moment of inertia about a parallel axis passing through the centroid C. Thus

$$I_P = I_C + Ad^2, \qquad J_P = J_C + Ad^2 \tag{8.5.7}$$

where the subscript C indicates the centroidal moment of inertia, subscript P indicates the moment of inertia about the parallel axis, A is the area, and d the distance separating the two axes. Similarly, for products of inertia,

$$I_{x_P y_P} = I_{x_C y_C} + A x_1 y_1 \tag{8.5.8}$$

where x_1 and y_1 are the distances between axes x and x_C, and y and y_C, respectively.

Example 8.10

For the shaded area shown by the sketch, determine $\bar{x}$, $\bar{y}$, I_x, I_y, J_O, I_{xy}, $(I_x)_C$, $(I_y)_C$, J_C and $I_{x_C y_C}$. Units are mm.

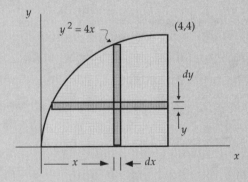

Solution. First we calculate A using the vertical strip, $dA = y\,dx = 2\sqrt{x}\,dx$:

$$A = \int_0^4 2\sqrt{x}\,dx = 32/3 \text{ mm}^2$$

Thus, from Eq. 8.5.1, with $dA = 2\sqrt{x}\,dx$,

$$\bar{x} = \frac{3}{32}\int_0^4 x(2\sqrt{x})\,dx = 2.4 \text{ mm}$$

and, using the horizontal strip $dA = (4 - y^2/4)\,dy$,

$$\bar{y} = \frac{3}{32}\int_0^4 y(4 - y^2/4)\,dy = 1.5 \text{ mm}$$

From Eq. 8.5.3, with $dA = (4 - y^2/4)\,dy$,

$$I_x = \int_0^4 y^2(4 - y^2/4)\,dy = 34.13 \text{ mm}^4$$

and, using $dA = 2\sqrt{x}\,dx$,

$$I_y = \int\limits_0^4 x^2 (2\sqrt{x})dx = 73.14 \text{ mm}^4$$

From Eq. 8.5.4

$$J_O = I_x + I_y = 34.13 + 73.14 = 107.27 \text{ mm}^4$$

From Eq. 8.5.6, with $dA = dxdy$,

$$I_{xy} = \int\limits_0^4 \int\limits_0^{2\sqrt{x}} xy\, dydx = \int\limits_0^4 \left[\frac{xy^2}{2}\right]_0^{2\sqrt{x}} dx = \int\limits_0^4 2x^2 dx = 42.67 \text{ mm}^4$$

From Eq. 8.5.7,

$$(I_x)_C = I_x - Ad^2 = 34.13 - 10.67(1.5)^2 = 10.13 \text{ mm}^4$$

$$(I_y)_C = I_y - Ad^2 = 73.14 - 10.67(2.4)^2 = 11.68 \text{ mm}^4$$

$$J_C = J_O - Ad^2 = 107.27 - 10.67\left[(1.5)^2 + (2.4)^2\right] = 21.80 \text{ mm}^4$$

Note that moments of inertia are always minimum about a centroidal axis. Finally, from Eq. 8.5.8,

$$I_{x_C y_C} = I_{xy} - A(-1.5)(-2.4) = 42.67 - 38.40 = 4.27 \text{ mm}^4$$

Example 8.11

Determine I_x and J_O for the circular sector shown below.

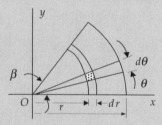

Solution. Using polar coordinates with $dA = rdrd\theta$ and $y = r\sin\theta$ in Eq. 8.5.3:

$$I_x = \int\limits_0^\beta \int\limits_0^a (r\sin\theta)^2 rdrd\theta = \frac{a^4}{4}\left[\frac{\beta}{2} - \frac{\sin 2\beta}{4}\right]$$

When $\beta = \pi/2$,

$$I_x = \pi a^4/16$$

From Eq. 8.5.4,

$$J_O = \int\limits_0^\beta \int\limits_0^a r^3 drd\theta = \frac{a^4 \beta}{4}$$

When $\beta = \pi/2$,

$$J_O = \pi a^4/8$$

TABLE 8.1. Properties of Areas

Shape	Dimensions	Centroid	Inertia
Rectangle		$\bar{x} = b/2$ $\bar{y} = h/2$	$I_C = bh^3/12$ $I_x = bh^3/3$ $I_y = hb^3/3$
Triangle		$\bar{y} = h/3$	$I_C = bh^3/36$ $I_x = bh^3/12$
Circle		$\bar{x} = 0$ $\bar{y} = 0$	$I_x = \pi r^4/4$ $J = \pi d^4/32$
Quarter Circle		$\bar{y} = 4r/3\pi$	$I_x = \pi r^4/16$
Half Circle		$\bar{y} = 4r/3\pi$	$I_x = \pi r^4/8$

The properties of common areas may be determined by integration. A brief list is given in Table 8.1.

Using data from Table 8.1, we may calculate centroids and moments of inertia of *composite areas* made up of combinations of two or more (including cutouts) of the common areas. Thus,

$$\bar{x} = \frac{\sum_{i=1}^{N} x_i A_i}{\sum_{i=1}^{N} A_i}, \qquad \bar{y} = \frac{\sum_{i=1}^{N} y_i A_i}{\sum_{i=1}^{N} A_i} \qquad \text{(8.5.9)}$$

where N is the number of areas, and x_i is the centroidal distance for area A_i. Likewise, for moments of inertia

$$I = \sum_{i=1}^{N} I_i = I_1 + I_2 + \ldots + I_N \qquad \text{(8.5.10)}$$

An example illustrates.

Example 8.12

Determine the centroidal coordinates, and I_x and I_y for the composite area shown.

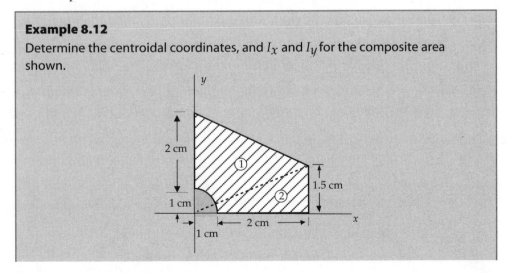

Solution. Decompose the composite into two triangular areas 1 and 2, and the negative quarter circular area 3:

$$A = A_1 + A_2 + A_3 = 4.5 + 2.25 - \pi/4 = 5.97 \text{ cm}^2$$
$$A\bar{x} = x_1 A_1 + x_2 A_2 + x_3 A_3$$
$$= (1)(4.5) + (2)(2.25) + (4/3\pi)(-\pi/4) = 8.67$$
$$\therefore \bar{x} = 8.67/5.97 = 1.45 \text{ cm}$$
$$A\bar{y} = y_1 A_1 + y_2 A_2 + y_3 A_3$$
$$= (1.5)(4.5) + (0.5)(2.25) + (4/3\pi)(-\pi/4) = 7.54$$
$$\therefore \bar{y} = 7.54/5.97 = 1.26 \text{ cm}$$
$$I_x = I_{1x} + I_{2x} + I_{3x}$$
$$= \left\{ 2\left[3(1.5)^3/36 \right] + (4.5)(1.5)^2 \right\} + 3(1.5)^3/12 - \pi/16 = 11.33 \text{ cm}^4$$

where we have used the parallel-axis theorem to obtain I_{1x}. Finally,

$$I_y = I_{1y} + I_{2y} + I_{3y}$$
$$= 3(3)^3/12 + 1.5(3)^3/4 - \pi/16 = 16.68 \text{ cm}^4$$

8.6 Properties of Masses and Volumes

The coordinates of the *center of gravity* G of an arbitrary mass m occupying a volume V of space are defined by

$$x_G = \frac{\int_V x\rho \, dV}{\int_V \rho \, dV}, \qquad y_G = \frac{\int_V y\rho \, dV}{\int_V \rho \, dV}, \qquad z_G = \frac{\int_V z\rho \, dV}{\int_V \rho \, dV} \qquad \textbf{(8.6.1)}$$

where ρ is the mass density, dV is the differential element of volume, and x, y and z are the coordinates of dV, as shown in Fig. 8.11.

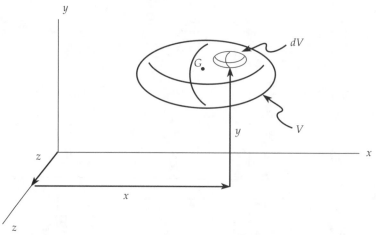

Figure 8.11 Center of gravity of an arbitrary mass.

The density may be a function of the space variables, $\rho = \rho(x,y,z)$. If the density is constant throughout the volume, the integrals in Eq. 8.6.1 reduce to

$$x_C = \frac{\int_V x\,dV}{V}, \qquad y_C = \frac{\int_V y\,dV}{V}, \qquad z_C = \frac{\int_V z\,dV}{V} \qquad (8.6.2)$$

which defines the coordinates of the centroid C of volume V. If ρ is constant, G and C coincide for a given body. As with areas, if an axis of symmetry exists for the volume, C is on that axis. The coordinates of G and C are readily calculated for geometries having an axis of revolution.

Example 8.13

Let the area of Example 8.10 be rotated about the x-axis to form a solid (volume) of revolution. Determine (a) G for the solid if $\rho = \rho_o x$ where ρ_o is a constant, (b) C for the volume.

Solution. Since there is symmetry about the x-axis, and since ρ is at most a function of x we have

$$y_G = z_G = y_C = z_C = 0$$

(a) Let the element of mass be a thin disk for which $\rho\,dV = \rho_o x \pi y^2 dx$. Therefore,

$$x_G = \frac{\int_0^4 \rho_o \pi x^2 (4x)\,dx}{\int_0^4 \rho_o \pi x (4x)\,dx} = \frac{4 \times 4^4 / 4}{4 \times 4^3 / 3} = 3.00 \text{ mm}$$

(b) For the same element with $\rho = \rho_o$

$$x_C = \frac{\int_0^4 \rho_o \pi x (4x)\,dx}{\int_0^4 \rho_o \pi (4x)\,dx} = \frac{4 \times 4^3 / 3}{4 \times 4^2 / 2} = 2.67 \text{ mm}$$

Because the topic of mass moments of inertia properly belongs in the subject of dynamics, and is not a factor in statics, we present only a brief comment or two here for comparison with area moments of inertia. The *mass moment of inertia* of the three-dimensional body in Fig. 8.11 about any axis is defined by the integral

$$I = \int_V r^2 \rho\,dV = \int_V r^2 dm \qquad (8.6.3)$$

where r is the perpendicular distance of the mass element dm from the axis. With respect to the coordinate axes, Eq. 8.6.3 may be specialized to yield

$$I_x = \int_V (y^2 + z^2)\,dm \qquad (8.6.4)$$

$$I_y = \int_V (z^2 + x^2)\,dm \qquad (8.6.5)$$

$$I_z = \int_V (x^2 + y^2)\,dm \qquad (8.6.6)$$

8·STATICS

There is also a parallel-axis theorem for mass moments of inertia, namely,

$$I_P = I_G + md^2 \qquad \textbf{(8.6.7)}$$

with d being the distance between the center of gravity axis and the parallel axis of interest. Several mass moments of inertia are presented in Table 8.2.

TABLE 8.2 Mass Moments of Inertia

Shape	Dimensions	Moment of Inertia
Slender rod		$I_y = mL^2/12$ $I_{y'} = mL^2/3$
Circular cylinder		$I_x = mr^2/2$ $I_y = m(L^2 + 3r^2)/12$
Disk		$I_x = mr^2/2$ $I_y = mr^2/4$
Rectangular parallelepiped		$I_x = m(a^2 + b^2)/12$ $I_y = m(L^2 + b^2)/12$ $I_z = m(L^2 + a^2)/12$ $I_{y'} = m(4L^2 + b^2)/12$
Sphere		$I_x = 2mr^2/5$

Practice Problems

(If you choose to work only a few problems, select those with a star.)

*8.1 Find the component of the vector $\mathbf{A} = 15\mathbf{i} - 9\mathbf{j} + 15\mathbf{k}$ in the direction of $\mathbf{B} = \mathbf{i} - 2\mathbf{j} - 2\mathbf{k}$.

a) 1   b) 3   c) 5   d) 7

8.2 Find the magnitude of the resultant of $\mathbf{A} = 2\mathbf{i} + 5\mathbf{j}$, $\mathbf{B} = 6\mathbf{i} - 7\mathbf{k}$, and $\mathbf{C} = 2\mathbf{i} - 6\mathbf{j} + 10\mathbf{k}$.

a) 8.2   b) 9.3   c) 10.5   d) 11.7

*8.3 Determine the moment about the y-axis of the force $\mathbf{F} = 200\mathbf{i} + 400\mathbf{j}$ acting at (4, –6, 4).

a) 0   b) 200   c) 400   d) 800

8.4 What total moment do the two forces $\mathbf{F_1} = 50\mathbf{i} - 40\mathbf{k}$ and $\mathbf{F_2} = 60\mathbf{j} + 80\mathbf{k}$ acting at (2, 0, –4) and (–4, 2, 0), respectively, produce about the x-axis?

a) 0   b) 80   c) 160   d) 240

*8.5 The force system shown may be referred to as being

a) non-concurrent, non-coplanar

b) coplanar

c) parallel

d) two-dimensional

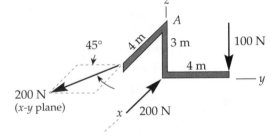

8.6 If equilibrium exists due to a rigid support at A in the figure of Prob. 8.5, what reactive force must exist at A?

a) $-59\mathbf{i} - 141\mathbf{j} + 10\mathbf{k}$ c) $341\mathbf{i} - 141\mathbf{j} - 100\mathbf{k}$

b) $59\mathbf{i} + 141\mathbf{j} + 100\mathbf{k}$ d) $341\mathbf{i} + 141\mathbf{j} - 100\mathbf{k}$

*8.7 If equilibrium exists on the object in Prob. 8.5, what reactive moment must exist at the rigid support A?

a) $600\mathbf{i} + 400\mathbf{j} + 564\mathbf{k}$ c) $400\mathbf{i} - 600\mathbf{j} + 564\mathbf{k}$

b) $400\mathbf{i} + 564\mathbf{k}$ d) $400\mathbf{i} - 600\mathbf{j}$

*8.8 If three nonparallel forces hold a rigid body in equilibrium, they must

a) be equal in magnitude.

b) be concurrent.

c) be non-concurrent.

d) form an equilateral triangle.

*8.9 A truss member

a) is a two-force body.
b) is a three-force body.
c) resists forces in compression only.
d) may resist three concurrent forces.

*8.10 Find the magnitude of the re-
action at support *B*.

a) 400
b) 500
c) 600
d) 700

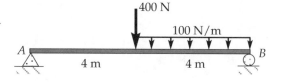

8.11 What moment *M* exists at support *A*?

a) 5600
b) 5000
c) 4400
d) 4000

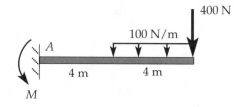

8.12 Calculate the reactive force at support *A*.

a) 250
b) 350
c) 450
d) 550

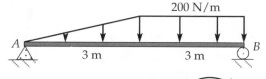

8.13 Find the support moment at *A*.

a) 66
b) 77
c) 88
d) 99

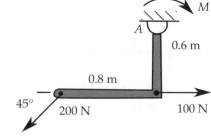

*8.14 To ensure equilibrium, what couple must be applied to this member?

a) 283 cw
b) 283 ccw
c) 400 cw
d) 400 ccw

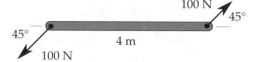

*8.15 Calculate the magnitude of the equilibrating force at *A* for the three-force
body shown.

a) 217
b) 287
c) 343
d) 385

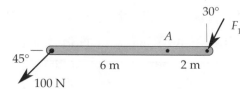

8.16   Find the magnitude of the equilibrating force at point *A*.

a) 187   c) 114

b) 142   d) 84

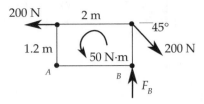

8.17   Find F_{DE} if all angles are equal.

a) 189   c) 163

b) 176   d) 142

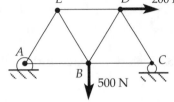

Trusses and Frames

---

*8.18   Find F_{DE}.

a) 0   c) 2000

b) 1000   d) 2500

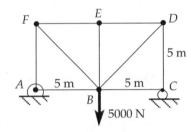

8.19   What is the force in member *DE*?

a) 1532   c) 1895

b) 1768   d) 1946

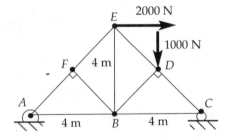

---

*8.20   Calculate F_{FB} in the truss of Problem 8.19.

a) 0   b) 932   c) 1561   d) 1732

8.21   Find the force in member *IC*.

a) 0

b) 1000

c) 1250

d) 1500

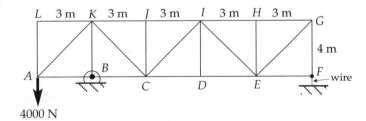

4000 N

8.22   What force exists in member *BC* in the truss of Prob. 8.21?

a) 0   b) 1000   c) 2000   d) 3000

8.23 Find the force in member *FC*.

a) 5320   c) 2560

b) 3420   d) 0

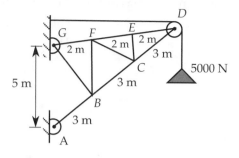

8.24 Determine the force in member *BC* in the truss of Prob. 8.23.

a) 3560   b) 4230   c) 5820   d) 6430

*8.25 Find the magnitude of the reactive force at support *A*.

a) 1400   c) 1200

b) 1300   d) 1100

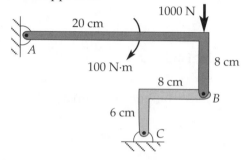

8.26 Determine the distributed force intensity *w*, in N/m, for equilibrium to exist.

a) 2000   c) 6000

b) 4000   d) 8000

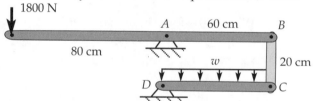

*8.27 Find the magnitude of the reactive force at support *A*.

a) 2580   c) 2790

b) 2670   d) 2880

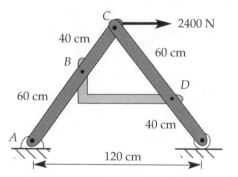

8.28 Calculate the magnitude of the force in member *BD* of Prob. 8.27.

a) 2590   b) 2670   c) 2790   d) 2880

Friction

*8.29 What force, in newtons, will cause impending motion up the plane?

   a) 731   c) 973

   b) 821   d) 1245

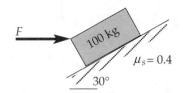

*8.30 What is the maximum force F, in newtons, that can be applied without causing motion to impend?

   a) 184   c) 316

   b) 294   d) 346

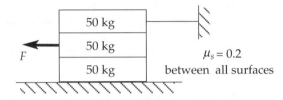

*8.31 Only the rear wheels provide braking. At what angle θ will the car slide if $\mu_s = 0.6$?

   a) 10   c) 16

   b) 12   d) 20

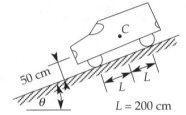

8.32 Find the minimum h value at which tipping will occur.

   a) 8 cm   c) 12 cm

   b) 10 cm   d) 14 cm

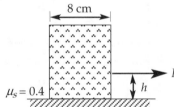

*8.33 What force F, in newtons, will cause impending motion?

   a) 240   c) 280

   b) 260   d) 320

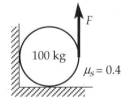

8.34 The angle θ at which the ladder is about to slip is

   a) 50   c) 42

   b) 46   d) 38

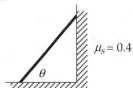

*8.35 A boy and his dad put a rope around a tree and stand side by side. What force by the boy can resist a force of 800 N by his dad? Use $\mu_s = 0.5$.

    a) 166 N   b) 192 N   c) 231 N   d) 246 N

8.36 What moment, in N·m, will cause impending motion?

    a) 88

    b) 99

    c) 110

    d) 121

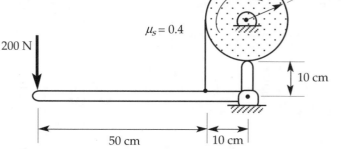

8.37 A 12-m-long rope is draped over a horizontal cylinder of 1.2-m-diameter so that both ends hang free. What is the length of the longer end at impending motion? Use $\mu_s = 0.5$.

    a) 6.98 m   b) 7.65 m   c) 7.92 m   d) 8.37 m

Centroids and Moments of Inertia

*8.38 Find the x-coordinate of the centroid of the area bounded by the x-axis, the line $x = 3$, and the parabola $y = x^2$.

    a) 2.0   b) 2.15   c) 2.20   d) 2.25

8.39 What is the y-coordinate of the centroid of the area of Prob. 8.38?

    a) 2.70   b) 2.65   c) 2.60   d) 2.55

8.40 Calculate the x-coordinate of the centroid of the area enclosed by the parabolas $y = x^2$ and $x = y^2$.

    a) 0.43   b) 0.44   c) 0.45   d) 0.46

8.41 Find the y-component of the centroid of the area shown.

    a) 3.35   c) 3.45

    b) 3.40   d) 3.50

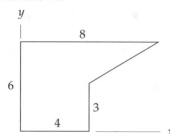

*8.42 Calculate the y-component of the centroid of the area shown.

    a) 3.52   c) 3.60

    b) 3.56   d) 3.68

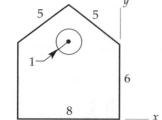

8.43 Find the *x*-component of the center of gravity of the three objects.

a) 2.33

b) 2.42

c) 2.84

d) 3.22

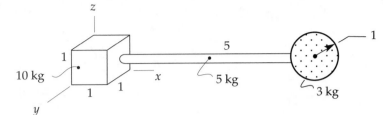

*8.44 Calculate the moment of inertia about the *x*-axis of the area of Prob. 8.38.

a) 94

b) 104

c) 112

d) 124

8.45 What is I_x for the area of Prob. 8.42?

a) 736

b) 842

c) 936

d) 1056

*8.46 Find I_y for the symmetrical area shown.

a) 4267

b) 4036

c) 3827

d) 3652

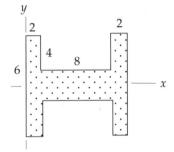

8.47 Determine the mass moment of inertia of a cube with edges of length *b*, about an axis passing through an edge.

a) $2mb^2/3$

b) $mb^2/6$

c) $3mb^2/2$

d) $mb^2/2$

*8.48 Find the mass moment of inertia about the *x*-axis if the mass of the rods per unit length is 1.0 kg/m.

a) 224

b) 268

c) 336

d) 432

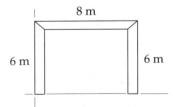

Afternoon Session
Practice Problems

Questions 8.49 – 8.51 relate to the truss shown. All angles are equal.

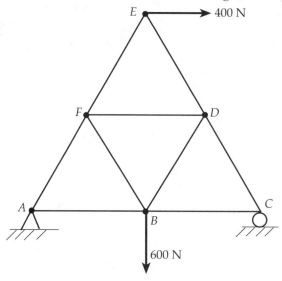

8.49   The magnitude of the reaction at A is

a)   403 N

b)   527

c)   672 N

d)   748 N

8.50   The force in link BC is

a)   169 N

b)   373 N

c)   532 N

d)   746 N

8.51   The force in link EF is

a)   100 N

b)   200 N

c)   300 N

d)   400 N

Questions 8.52 – 8.54 relate to the frame shown. Each link is 80 cm long and the wire is in the middle of the link.

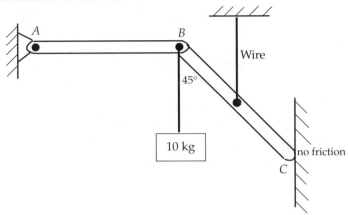

8.52   The force in the wire is

   a) 137 N   b) 98 N   c) 49 N   d) 10 N

8.53   The magnitude of the force at *A* is

   a) 137 N   b) 98 N   c) 49 N   d) 10 N

8.54   If the wire were cut, the force at *C* would

   a) increase

   b) stay the same

   c) decrease

   d) can't say, need more information

Questions 8.55 – 8.56 relate to the figure shown. Motion is impending and $\mu_A = 0.3$, $\mu_B = 0.5$ and $\mu_C = 0$.

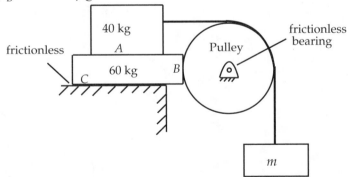

8.55   The tension in the rope where it attaches to the 40-kg mass is nearest

   a) 90 N   b) 120 N   c) 150 N   d) 180 N

8.56   The mass *m* for impending motion is nearest

   a) 18 kg   b) 22 kg   c) 28 kg   d) 40 kg

Questions 8.57 – 8.59 relates to the following figure.

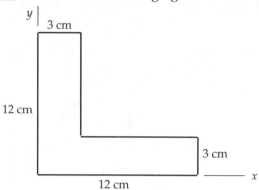

8.57   Find I_x.

a) 2372 cm^4 b) 2185 cm^4 c) 1809 cm^4 d 1567 cm^4

8.58   Find the y-coordinate of the centroid.

a) 3.21 cm   b) 4.07 cm   c) 5.12 cm   d) 6.32 cm

8.59   Find the second moment of the area about the centroidal axis, i.e., I_{x_c}.

a) 475 cm^4 b) 525 cm^4 c) 685 cm^4 d) 765 cm^4

Solutions to Practice Problems

8.1 **a)** $\quad \mathbf{i}_B = \dfrac{\mathbf{i} - 2\mathbf{j} - 2\mathbf{k}}{\sqrt{1+4+4}} = \dfrac{1}{3}\left(\mathbf{i} - 2\mathbf{j} - 2\mathbf{k}\right)$

$\quad \mathbf{A} \cdot \mathbf{i}_B = \left(15\mathbf{i} - 9\mathbf{j} + 15\mathbf{k}\right) \cdot \dfrac{1}{3}\left(\mathbf{i} - 2\mathbf{j} - 2\mathbf{k}\right) = 5 + 6 - 10 = 1$

8.2 **c)** $\quad \mathbf{A} + \mathbf{B} + \mathbf{C} = \left(2\mathbf{i} + 5\mathbf{j}\right) + \left(6\mathbf{i} - 7\mathbf{k}\right) + \left(2\mathbf{i} - 6\mathbf{j} + 10\mathbf{k}\right) = 10\mathbf{i} - \mathbf{j} + 3\mathbf{k}$

$\quad \text{magnitude} = \sqrt{10^2 + 1^2 + 3^2} = 10.49$

8.3 **d)** $\quad \mathbf{M} = \mathbf{r} \times \mathbf{F} = \left(4\mathbf{i} - 6\mathbf{j} + 4\mathbf{k}\right) \times \left(200\mathbf{i} + 400\mathbf{j}\right). \quad M_y = 4 \times 200 = 800 \quad \text{since } \mathbf{k} \times \mathbf{i} = \mathbf{j}$

8.4 **c)** $\quad \mathbf{M} = \mathbf{r}_1 \times \mathbf{F}_1 + \mathbf{r}_2 \times \mathbf{F}_2 = \left(2\mathbf{i} - 4\mathbf{k}\right) \times \left(50\mathbf{i} - 40\mathbf{k}\right) + \left(-4\mathbf{i} + 2\mathbf{j}\right) \times \left(60\mathbf{j} + 80\mathbf{k}\right)$

$\quad M_x = 2 \times 80 = 160 \quad \text{since } \mathbf{j} \times \mathbf{k} = \mathbf{i}$

8.5 **a)** $\quad$ Concurrent $\Rightarrow$ all pass through a point.

$\qquad$ Coplanar $\Rightarrow$ all in the same plane.

$\qquad$ The forces are three-dimensional.

8.6 **b)** $\quad \sum \mathbf{F} = 0. \quad \therefore \mathbf{R} + 141\mathbf{i} - 141\mathbf{j} - 200\mathbf{i} - 100\mathbf{k} = 0$

$\quad \therefore \mathbf{R} = 59\mathbf{i} + 141\mathbf{j} + 100\mathbf{k}$

8.7 **c)** $\quad \sum \mathbf{M} = 0. \quad \therefore \mathbf{M}_A + \left(4\mathbf{j} - 3\mathbf{k}\right) \times \left(-100\mathbf{k}\right) - 3\mathbf{k} \times \left(-200\mathbf{i}\right) + 4\mathbf{i} \times \left(141\mathbf{i} - 141\mathbf{j}\right) = 0$

$\quad \therefore \mathbf{M}_A = 400\mathbf{i} - 600\mathbf{j} + 564\mathbf{k}$

8.8 **b)** $\quad$ They must be concurrent, otherwise a resultant moment would occur.

8.9 **a)** $\quad$ It is a two-force body.

8.10 **b)** $\quad \sum M_A = 0. \quad F_B \times 8 = 400 \times 4 + 400 \times 6. \quad \therefore F_B = 500 \text{ N}$

8.11 **a)** $\quad M_A = 400 \times 8 + 400 \times 6 = 5600 \text{ N} \cdot \text{m}$

8.12 **b)** $\quad \sum M_B = 0. \quad 6F_A = 4 \times 300 + 600 \times 3/2. \quad \therefore F_A = 350 \text{ N}$

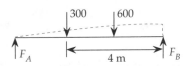

8.13 **c)** $\quad M_A = 0.6 \times 100 - 141 \times 0.6 + 141 \times 0.8 = 88.2$

8.14 **a)** $\quad M = 100 \sin 45° \times 4 = 282.8 \text{ cw}$

8.15 **c)** $\sum M_A = 0.$ $\therefore 6 \times 70.7 = 2 \times 0.866 F_1.$ $\therefore F_1 = 245$

$\sum F_x = 0.$ $\therefore -70.7 - 245 \times 0.5 + F_{Ax} = 0.$ $\therefore F_{Ax} = 193$

$\sum F_y = 0.$ $\therefore -70.7 - 245 \times 0.866 + F_{Ay} = 0.$ $\therefore F_{Ay} = 283$

$\therefore F_A = \sqrt{F_{Ax}^2 + F_{Ay}^2} = \sqrt{193^2 + 283^2} = 343$

8.16 **d)** $\sum M_A = 0.$ $\therefore 2F_B + 1.2 \times 200 - 141.4 \times 2 - 141.4 \times 1.2 + 50 = 0.$ $\therefore F_B = 81.2$

$\sum F_x = 0.$ $\therefore F_{Ax} - 200 + 141.4 = 0.$ $\therefore F_{Ax} = 58.6$

$\sum F_y = 0.$ $\therefore F_{Ay} + 81.2 - 141.4 = 0.$ $\therefore F_{Ay} = 60.2$

$\therefore F_A = \sqrt{F_{Ax}^2 + F_{Ay}^2} = \sqrt{58.6^2 + 60.2^2} = 84.0$

8.17 **a)** $\sum M_A = 0.$ $\therefore 500\ell + 200 \times 0.866\ell - F_C \times 2\ell = 0.$ $\therefore F_C = 337$

$0.866 F_{DC} = 337.$ $\therefore F_{DC} = 389$

$0.866 \times 389 = 0.866 F_{BD}.$ $\therefore F_{BD} = 389$

$-F_{DE} + 200 - 389 \times 0.5 - 389 \times 0.5 = 0.$ $\therefore F_{DE} = -189$

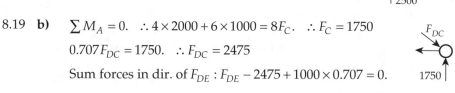

8.18 **d)** $\sum M_A = 0.$ $\therefore 5 \times 5000 = 10 \times F_C.$ $\therefore F_C = 2500$ $\therefore F_{DC} = 2500$

$0.707 F_{BD} = 2500.$ $\therefore F_{BD} = 3536$

$0.707 \times 3536 = F_{DE}.$ $\therefore F_{DE} = 2500$

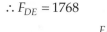

8.19 **b)** $\sum M_A = 0.$ $\therefore 4 \times 2000 + 6 \times 1000 = 8 F_C.$ $\therefore F_C = 1750$

$0.707 F_{DC} = 1750.$ $\therefore F_{DC} = 2475$

Sum forces in dir. of F_{DE} : $F_{DE} - 2475 + 1000 \times 0.707 = 0.$

$\therefore F_{DE} = 1768$

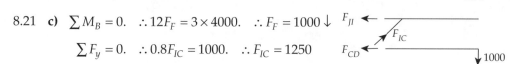

8.20 **a)**   Sum forces in dir. of F_{FB} at $F.$ $F_{FB} = 0.$

8.21 **c)** $\sum M_B = 0.$ $\therefore 12 F_F = 3 \times 4000.$ $\therefore F_F = 1000 \downarrow$

$\sum F_y = 0.$ $\therefore 0.8 F_{IC} = 1000.$ $\therefore F_{IC} = 1250$

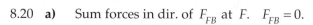

8.22 **d)**   Cut vertically through link $KA.$ Then $F_{KA} = 5000.$
Obviously, $F_{AL} = 0.$ $\therefore F_{AB} = 3000.$ $\therefore F_{BC} = 3000$

8.23 **d)**   At E we see that $F_{EC} = 0.$ $\therefore$ At $C,$ $F_{FC} = 0$

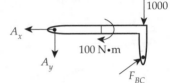

8.24 c) $9^2 = 6^2 + 5^2 - 2 \times 5 \times 6 \cos\theta.$ $\therefore \theta = 109.5°$

$6^2 = 9^2 + 5^2 - 2 \times 9 \times 5 \cos\alpha.$ $\therefore \alpha = 38.9°$

From pts E, C, F, B we see that $F_{EC} = F_{FC} = F_{FB} = F_{GB} = 0.$

Also, $F_A = F_{BC}.$ $\sum M_G = 0.$

$\therefore 5 \times F_A \sin 38.9° + 5000 \times 6 \sin 70.5° = 5000 \times 6 \cos 70.5°.$

$\therefore F_A = -5817$ N

8.25 b)   Recognize that link BC is a two-force member. $\sum M_A = 0.$

$\therefore 0.2 \times 1000 + 100 = 0.08 \times F_{BC} \times 0.8 + 0.2 \times F_{BC} \times 0.6$

$\therefore F_{BC} = 1630.$ $A_x = 1630 \times 0.8 = 1304.$ $A_y = 1630 \times 0.6 - 1000 = -22$

$\therefore F_A = \sqrt{1304^2 + 22^2} = 1304$ N

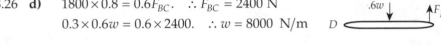

8.26 d) $1800 \times 0.8 = 0.6 F_{BC}.$ $\therefore F_{BC} = 2400$ N

$0.3 \times 0.6w = 0.6 \times 2400.$ $\therefore w = 8000$ N/m

8.27 d) $\sum M_A = 0.$ $\therefore 1.2 F_E = 0.8 \times 2400.$ $\therefore F_E = 1600$

$\therefore A_x = 2400.$ $A_y = 1600$

$\therefore F_A = \sqrt{2400^2 + 1600^2} = 2884$ N

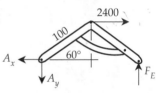

8.28 a)   Link BD is a two-force member. $\therefore$ the force acts from D to B. Hence, the angles are found.

$120^2 = 100^2 + 100^2 - 2 \times 100 \times 100 \cos\beta.$ $\therefore \beta = 73.7°$

$\overline{BD}^2 = 60^2 + 40^2 - 2 \times 60 \times 40 \cos 73.7°.$ $\therefore BD = 62.1$

$\dfrac{62.1}{\sin 73.7°} = \dfrac{40}{\sin\phi}.$ $\therefore \phi = 38.2°.$ $\alpha = (180 - 73.7)/2 = 53.2°$

$\sum M_C = 0.$ $1600 \times 100 \cos 53.2° = 60 \times F_{BD} \sin 38.2°.$ $\therefore F_{BD} = 2587$

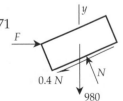

8.29 d) $\sum F_y = 0.$ $N \times 0.866 - 980 - 0.4N \times 0.5 = 0.$ $\therefore N = 1471$

$\sum F_x = 0.$ $F = 1471 \times 0.5 + 0.4 \times 1471 \times 0.866 = 1245$ N

8.30 b) $N_1 = 490.$ $N_2 = 980.$ $\therefore F = 0.2(490 + 980) = 294$

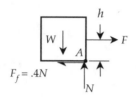

8.31 c) $\sum M_{\text{front wheel}} = 0.$ $\therefore 400 N_2 - W \cos\theta \times 200 + W \sin\theta \times 50 = 0$

$\sum F_x = 0.$ $\therefore 0.6 N_2 = W \sin\theta.$

$\therefore 400 (W \sin\theta)/0.6 + 50 W \sin\theta = 200 W \cos\theta$

$\therefore \dfrac{\sin\theta}{\cos\theta} = \dfrac{200}{716.7} = \tan\theta.$ $\therefore \theta = 15.6°$

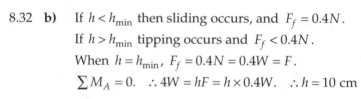

8.32 b)   If $h < h_{\min}$ then sliding occurs, and $F_f = 0.4N$.
If $h > h_{\min}$ tipping occurs and $F_f < 0.4N$.
When $h = h_{\min}$, $F_f = 0.4N = 0.4W = F$.
$\sum M_A = 0.$ $\therefore 4W = hF = h \times 0.4W.$ $\therefore h = 10$ cm

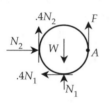

8.33 d) $\sum F_x = 0.$ $\therefore N_2 = 0.4 N_1.$ Also, $W = 980$

$\sum M_A = 0.$ $\therefore W \cdot r = (N_1 + 0.4 N_1 + 2 \times 0.4 N_2)r.$

$\therefore N_1 = 0.5814W = 570$

$\sum F_y = 0.$ $\therefore F = 980 - 570 - 0.16 \times 570 = 319$

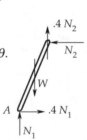

8.34 b) $\sum F_x = 0.$ $\therefore N_2 = 0.4 N_1.$ $\sum F_y = 0.$ $\therefore N_1 + 0.4 N_2 = W.$

$\therefore N_2 = 0.345W$

$\sum M_A = 0.$ $\therefore \dfrac{L}{2} \times W \cos\theta = N_2 \times L \sin\theta + 0.4 N_2 \times L \cos\theta.$

This gives $\tan\theta = 1.049.$ $\therefore \theta = 46.4°$

8.35 a) $F_B = F_D e^{-\mu\theta} = 800 e^{-0.5\pi} = 166\,\text{N}$

8.36 a) $\sum M_A = 0.$ $\therefore 200 \times 0.6 = 0.1 \times T_1 + 0.1 \times T_2.$

$T_1 = T_2 e^{0.4 \times 3\pi/2} = 6.59 T_2.$ Thus, $T_2 = 158$ and $T_1 = 1042.$

$\sum M_{\text{center}} = 0.$ $\therefore M = 0.1 \times (1042 - 158) = 88.4\ \text{N}\cdot\text{m}$

8.37 d)   Let h = long end. m = mass/unit length. Then,
$(12 - 1.88 - h)mg e^{0.5\pi} = hmg.$ $\therefore h = 8.38$ m

8.38 **d)** $\bar{x} = \dfrac{\int_0^3 xy\,dx}{\int_0^3 y\,dx} = \dfrac{\int_0^3 x^3\,dx}{\int_0^3 x^2\,dx} = \dfrac{3^4/4}{3^3/3} = 2.25$

8.39 **a)** $\bar{y} = \dfrac{\int_0^3 \frac{y}{2}\,y\,dx}{\int_0^3 y\,dx} = \dfrac{\frac{1}{2}\int_0^3 x^4\,dx}{\int_0^3 x^2\,dx} = \dfrac{3^5/10}{3^3/3} = 2.7$

8.40 **c)** $\bar{x} = \dfrac{\int_0^1 \left(\sqrt{x} - x^2\right)x\,dx}{\int_0^1 \left(\sqrt{x} - x^2\right)dx} = \dfrac{\frac{1}{5/2} - \frac{1}{4}}{\frac{1}{3/2} - \frac{1}{3}} = 0.45$

8.41 **b)** $\bar{y} = \dfrac{24 \times 3 + 6 \times 5}{6 \times 4 + 4 \times 3/2} = 3.4$

8.42 **d)** $\bar{y} = \dfrac{48 \times 3 + 12 \times 7 - \pi \times 6}{8 \times 6 + 3 \times 4 - \pi} = 3.68$

8.43 **b)** $\bar{x} = \dfrac{10 \times \frac{1}{2} + 5 \times 3.5 + 3 \times 7}{10 + 5 + 3} = 2.42$

8.44 **b)** $I_x = \int_0^3 y^3\,dx/3 = \int_0^3 x^6\,dx/3 = 3^7/21 = 104.1.$

With a horizontal strip: $I_x = \int_0^9 y^2(3 - x)\,dy = \int_0^9 y^2\left(3 - \sqrt{y}\right)dy = 9^3 - \dfrac{9^{7/2}}{7/2} = 104.1$

8.45 **d)** $I_x = 8 \times 6^3/3 + \left(8 \times 3^3/36 + 12 \times 7^2\right) - \left(\pi \times 1^4/4 + \pi \times 6^2\right) = 1056$

8.46 **a)** $I_y = 12 \times 12^3/3 - \left(8 \times 8^3/12 + 64 \times 6^2\right) = 4267.$ Or, alternatively:

$I_y = 8 \times 2^3/3 + 4 \times 12^3/3 + 8 \times 2^3/12 + 16 \times 11^2 = 4267$

8.47 **a)** $I_{\text{edge}} = I_{\text{c.g.}} + Md^2 = \dfrac{1}{12}M\left(b^2 + b^2\right) + M\dfrac{b^2}{2} = \dfrac{2}{3}Mb^2$

8.48 **d)** $I_x = \dfrac{1}{3}(6m) \times 6^2 \times 2 + 8m \times 6^2 = 432$ with $m = 1$

8.49 **a)**   All lengths must also be equal. Sum moments about C:

$\Sigma M_C = 0.$ $400 \times 0.866 \times 2L - 600L = 2L \times F_{Ay}.$ $\therefore F_{Ay} = 46.4\text{ N} \downarrow$

$\Sigma F_x = 0.$ $\therefore F_{Ax} = 400\text{ N}.$ $\therefore F_A = \sqrt{46.4^2 + 400^2} = 403\text{ N}$

8-STATICS

8.50 b)   Find the force acting at C:

$$\Sigma M_A = 0. \quad 2L \times F_C = 2L \times 0.866 \times 400 + 600L.$$

$$\therefore F_C = 646.4 \text{ N.} \quad \text{Sketch the force situation at } C.$$

$$0.866 \times F_{CD} = 646.4. \quad \therefore F_{CD} = 746.4.$$

$$F_{BC} = F_{CD} \sin 60° = 746.4 \times 0.5 = 373.2 \text{ N}$$

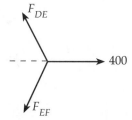

8.51 d)   Consider the force situation at E:

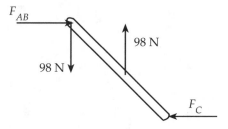

$$\Sigma F_x = 0.$$

$$\therefore F_{EF} \cos 60° = \frac{1}{2} \times 400.$$

$$\therefore F_{EF} = 400 \text{ N}$$

8.52 b)   Link AB is a two-force member so that the force in link AB is in the x-direction only. A free-body diagram of link BC *provides the solution:*

Since there are only two vertical

forces acting on the link, they

must be equal :

$$\therefore F_{wire} = 10 \times 9.8 = 98 \text{ N}$$

8.53 c)   The force in the two-force member is found from moments on the free-body of Problem 8.52:

$$98 \times 40 \sin 45° = F_{AB} \times 80 \sin 45°. \quad \therefore F_{AB} = 49 \text{ N}$$

8.54 c)   The force would reduce to zero since the two links would be free to simply fall and assume a vertical position.

8.55 b)   Draw a free-body diagram of the upper block:

$$N_A = W = 40 \times 9.8 = 392 \text{ N}$$

$$\mu_A N_A = 0.3 \times 392 = 117.6 \text{ N} = T_1$$

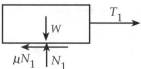

8.56 a)   From a free-body of the lower block we see that $N_B = 117.6$ N. Draw a free-body diagram of the pulley:

$$\therefore N_B = 117.6. \quad \mu_B N_B = 0.5 \times 117.6 = 58.8$$

$$\Sigma M_{pulley} = 0. \quad \therefore m \times 9.8 = T_1 + \mu_B N_B$$

$$\therefore m = (117.6 + 58.8)/9.8 = 18 \text{ kg}$$

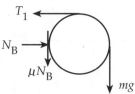

8.57　**c)**　Use two rectangles, one 3 cm by 12 cm and the other 3 cm by 9 cm:

$$I_x = \left(\frac{bh^3}{3}\right)_1 + \left(\frac{bh^3}{3}\right)_2 = \frac{3 \times 12^3}{3} + \frac{9 \times 3^3}{3} = 1809 \text{ cm}^4$$

8.58　**b)**　Use the two rectangles of Problem 8.57:

$$y_c = \frac{y_{c_1} A_1 + y_{c_2} A_2}{A_1 + A_2} = \frac{6 \times 36 + 1.5 \times 27}{36 + 27} = 4.07 \text{ cm}$$

8.59　**d)**　Use the parallel-axis-transfer theorem:

$$I_{x_c} = I_x - a y_c^2 = 1809 - 63 \times 4.07^2 = 765 \text{ cm}^4$$

Dynamics

by Merle C. Potter

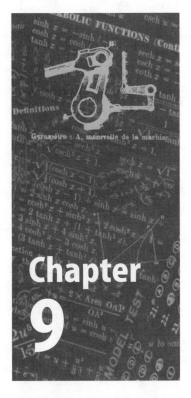

Chapter 9

Dynamics is separated into two major divisions: *kinematics*, which is a study of motion without reference to the forces causing the motion, and *kinetics*, which relates the forces on bodies to their resulting motions. Newton's laws of motion are necessary in relating forces to motions; they are:

Overview

1st law: A particle remains at rest or continues to move in a straight line with a constant velocity if no unbalanced force acts on it.

2nd law: The acceleration of a particle is proportional to the force acting on it and inversely proportional to the particle mass; the direction of acceleration is the same as the force direction.

3rd law: The forces of action and reaction between contacting bodies are equal in magnitude, opposite in direction, and colinear.

Law of gravitation: The force of attraction between two bodies is proportional to the product of their masses and inversely proportional to the square of the distance between their centers.

9.1 Kinematics

In kinematics we will consider three different kinds of particle motion: rectilinear motion, angular motion, and curvilinear motion. These will be followed by a review of motion of rigid bodies.

In rectilinear motion of a particle in which the particle moves in a straight line, the acceleration a, the velocity v, and the displacement s are related by

Rectilinear Motion

$$a = \frac{dv}{dt}, \qquad v = \frac{ds}{dt}, \qquad a = \frac{d^2s}{dt^2} = v\frac{dv}{ds} \tag{9.1.1}$$

If the acceleration is a known function of time, the above can be integrated to give $v(t)$ and $s(t)$. For the important case of constant acceleration, integration yields

$$v = v_o + at$$

$$s = v_o t + at^2/2 \tag{9.1.2}$$

$$v^2 = v_o^2 + 2as$$

where at $t = 0$, $v = v_o$ and $s_o = 0$.

Angular Motion

Angular displacement is the angle θ that a line makes with a fixed axis, usually the positive x-axis. Counterclockwise motion is assumed to be positive, as shown in Fig. 9.1. The angular acceleration α, the angular velocity ω, and θ are related by

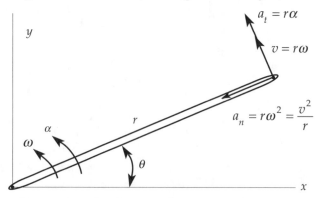

Figure 9.1 Angular motion.

$$\alpha = \frac{d\omega}{dt}, \qquad \omega = \frac{d\theta}{dt}, \qquad \alpha = \omega\frac{d\omega}{d\theta} = \frac{d^2\theta}{dt^2} \tag{9.1.3}$$

If α is a constant, integration of these equations gives

$$\omega = \omega_o + \alpha t$$

$$\theta = \omega_o t + \alpha t^2/2 \tag{9.1.4}$$

$$\omega^2 = \omega_o^2 + 2\alpha\theta$$

where we have assumed that $\omega = \omega_o$ and $\theta_o = 0$ at $t = 0$.

Curvilinear Motion

When a particle moves on a plane curve as shown in Fig. 9.2, the motion may be described in terms of coordinates along the normal n and the tangent t to the curve at the instantaneous position of the particle.

The acceleration is the vector sum of the normal acceleration a_n and the tangential acceleration a_t. These components are given as

$$a_n = \frac{v^2}{r}, \qquad a_t = \frac{dv}{dt} \tag{9.1.5}$$

where r is the radius of curvature and v is the magnitude of the velocity. The velocity is always tangential to the curve, so no subscript is necessary to identify the velocity.

It should be noted that a rigid body traveling without rotation can be treated as particle motion.

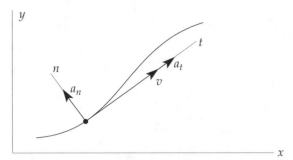

Figure 9.2 Motion on a plane curve.

Example 9.1

The velocity of a particle undergoing rectilinear motion is $v(t) = 3t^2 + 10t$ m/s. Find the acceleration and the displacement at $t = 10$ s, if $s_o = 0$ at $t = 0$.

Solution. The acceleration is found to be

$$a = \frac{dv}{dt}$$

$$= 6t + 10 = 6 \times 10 + 10 = 70 \text{ m/s}^2$$

The displacement is found by integration

$$s = \int_0^{10} v \, dt$$

$$= \int_0^{10} (3t^2 + 10t)dt = t^3 + 5t^2 \Big|_0^{10} = 1500 \text{ m}$$

Example 9.2

An automobile skids to a stop 60 m after its brakes are applied while traveling 25 m/s. What is its acceleration?

Solution. We use the relationship

$$v^2 = v_o{}^2 + 2as$$

Letting $v = 0$, we find,

$$a = -\frac{v_o{}^2}{2s}$$

$$= -\frac{25^2}{2 \times 60} = -5.21 \text{ m/s}^2$$

Example 9.3

A wheel, rotating at 100 rad/s ccw (counterclockwise), is subjected to an angular acceleration of 20 rad/s^2 cw. Find the total number of revolutions (cw plus ccw) through which the wheel rotates in 8 seconds.

Solution. The time at which the angular velocity is zero is found as follows:

$$\cancel{\omega}^{\,0} = \omega_o + \alpha t$$

$$\therefore t = -\frac{\omega_o}{\alpha} = -\frac{100}{-20} = 5 \text{ s}.$$

After three additional seconds the angular velocity is determined by

$$\omega = \cancel{\omega_o}^{\,0} + \alpha t$$

$$= -20 \times 3 = -60 \text{ rad / s}.$$

The angular displacement from 0 to 5 s is

$$\theta = \omega_o t + \alpha t^2 / 2$$

$$= 100 \times 5 - 20 \times 5^2 / 2 = 250 \text{ rad}$$

During the next 3 s, the angular displacement is

$$\theta = \alpha t^2 / 2$$

$$= -20 \times 3^2 / 2 = -90 \text{ rad}$$

The total number of revolutions rotated is

$$\theta = (250 + 90) / 2\pi = 54.1 \text{ rev}$$

Example 9.4

Consider idealized projectile motion (no air drag) in which $a_x = 0$ and $a_y = -g$. Find expressions for the range R and the maximum height H in terms of v_o and θ.

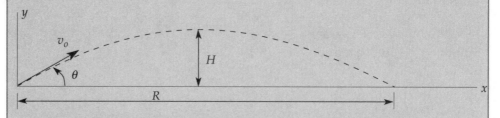

Solution. Using Eq. 9.1.2 for constant acceleration we have the point $(R, 0)$:

$$\cancel{y}^{\,0} = (v_o \sin \theta)t - g t^2 / 2.$$

$$\therefore t = 2v_o \sin \theta / g.$$

From the x-component equation:

$$x = (v_o \cos \theta)t + \cancel{a_x t^2}^{\,0} / 2.$$

$$\therefore R = (v_o \cos \theta) 2v_o \sin \theta / g = v_o^2 \sin 2\theta / g.$$

Obviously, the maximum height occurs when the time is one-half that which yields the range R. Hence,

$$H = (v_o \sin \theta)\frac{v_o \sin \theta}{g} - \frac{g}{2}(\frac{v_o \sin \theta}{g})^2$$

$$= \frac{v_o^2}{2g} \sin^2 \theta$$

Note: The maximum R for a given v_o occurs when $\sin 2\theta = 1$, which means $\theta = 45°$ for R_{max}.

Example 9.5

It is desired that the normal acceleration of a satellite be 9.6 m/s^2 at an elevation of 200 km. What should be the velocity for a circular orbit? The radius of the earth is 6400 km.

Solution. The normal acceleration, which points toward the center of the Earth, is

$$a_n = \frac{v^2}{r}$$

$$\therefore v = \sqrt{a_n r}$$

$$= \sqrt{9.6 \times (6400 + 200) \times 1000} = 7960 \text{ m/s}$$

The normal acceleration is essentially the value of gravity near the Earth's surface. Gravity varies only slightly if the elevation is small with respect to the Earth's radius.

The motion of a rigid body can be described using the relative velocity and relative acceleration equations

$$\mathbf{v}_A = \mathbf{v}_B + \mathbf{v}_{A/B}$$
$$\mathbf{a}_A = \mathbf{a}_B + \mathbf{a}_{A/B} \qquad \text{(9.1.6)}$$

where the velocity $\mathbf{v}_{A/B}$ is the velocity of point A with respect to point B and the acceleration $\mathbf{a}_{A/B}$ is the acceleration of point A with respect to point B. If points A and B are on the same rigid body then point A must move perpendicular to the line AB and

$$v_{A/B} = r\omega \qquad \text{(9.1.7)}$$

$$\left(a_{A/B}\right)_n = r\omega^2$$

$$\left(a_{A/B}\right)_t = r\alpha$$

where ω is the angular velocity, α is the angular acceleration of the body, and r is the length of $\overline{AB}$. If point A is located on a body which moves with a constant velocity v relative to a coincident point B which is located on a second body rotating with an angular velocity ω (see Fig. 9.3), the acceleration of A with respect to

Rigid Body Motion

If points A and B are on the same rigid body then point A must move perpendicular to the line AB.

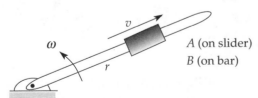

A (on slider)
B (on bar)

Figure 9.3 Coriolis acceleration.

9•DYNAMICS

B is called the *Coriolis acceleration*, given by

$$\mathbf{a}_{A/B} = 2\boldsymbol{\omega} \times \mathbf{v} \qquad\qquad (9.1.8)$$

We note that the Coriolis acceleration acts normal to both vectors $\boldsymbol{\omega}$ (use the right-hand rule) and $\mathbf{v}$. Thus it acts normal to the arm.

A final note regarding the instant center of zero velocity (a point which is often off the body, that has zero velocity): if such a point *B* can be located, then the magnitude of the velocity of point *A* is simply $r\omega$.

> 🔑 The instant center of zero velocity is a point which is often off the body that has zero velocity.

Example 9.6

Find the magnitude of the velocity and acceleration of point *A*.

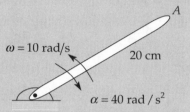

Solution. The velocity is found to be

$$v_A = r\omega$$
$$= 0.2 \times 10 = 2 \text{ m/s}$$

The acceleration components are

$$a_n = r\omega^2 = 0.2 \times 10^2 = 20 \text{ m/s}^2$$
$$a_t = r\alpha = 0.2 \times 40 = 8 \text{ m/s}^2$$

Thus,

$$a = \sqrt{a_n^2 + a_t^2} = \sqrt{20^2 + 8^2} = 21.5 \text{ m/s}^2$$

Example 9.7

Find the velocity of *C* and ω_{BC}.

Solution. The velocity of *B* is normal to $\overline{AB}$ and is equal to

$$v_B = r\omega$$
$$= 0.4 \times 100 = 40 \text{ m/s}$$

To find v_C we use the relative motion equation

$$\mathbf{v}_C = \mathbf{v}_B + \mathbf{v}_{C/B}$$

The velocity of C must be horizontal and $\mathbf{v}_{C/B}$ must be normal to $\overline{BC}$. This can be displayed in a velocity polygon as follows:

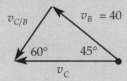

From the velocity polygon we use some simple trigonometry and find v_C to be to the left with magnitude

$$v_C = 44.6 \ \text{m/s}$$

The angular velocity of $\overline{BC}$ is found to be

$$\omega_{BC} = v_{C/B}/r_{BC}$$
$$= 32.7/0.5656 = 57.8 \ \text{rad/s} \quad \text{cw}$$

Example 9.8

Find the acceleration of C in Example 9.7, assuming $\alpha_{AB} = 0$.

Solution. The acceleration of B is

$$(a_B)_n = r\omega^2$$
$$= 0.4 \times 100^2 = 4000 \ \text{m/s}^2$$

The relative acceleration equation

$$\mathbf{a}_C = \mathbf{a}_B + \mathbf{a}_{C/B}$$

can be displayed in an acceleration polygon, realizing that $\mathbf{a}_C$ must be horizontal, and $\mathbf{a}_{C/B}$ has both normal and tangential components. We find $(a_{C/B})_n$ to be

$$\left(a_{C/B}\right)_n = r_{BC}\omega_{BC}^2$$
$$= 0.5656 \times 57.8^2 = 1890 \ \text{m/s}^2$$

The acceleration polygon is shown. From the polygon we can find a_C to be to the left with magnitude

$$a_C = 3380 \ \text{m/s}^2$$

Example 9.9

The wheel is rolling with no slip. Find v_A and a_A.

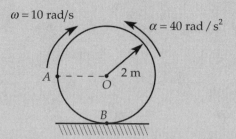

Solution. At this instant the wheel rotates about B. Hence, we can find v_A by using

$$v_A = r_{AB}\omega$$

$$= \frac{2}{\sin 45°} \times 10 = 28.3 \text{ m/s}$$

To find the acceleration we relate A to the center O and use

$$\mathbf{a}_A = \mathbf{a}_O + \mathbf{a}_{A/O}$$

The acceleration polygon follows using

$$a_O = r\alpha = 2 \times 40 = 80 \text{ m/s}^2$$

$$(a_{A/O})_t = r\alpha = 2 \times 40 = 80 \text{ m/s}^2$$

$$(a_{A/O})_n = r\omega^2 = 2 \times 10^2 = 200 \text{ m/s}^2$$

From the polygon we find a_A to be $a_A = 144 \text{ m/s}^2$.

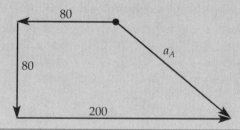

Example 9.10

Calculate a_A where A is on the slider.

Solution. The relative acceleration equation is

$$\mathbf{a}_A = \mathbf{a}_B + \mathbf{a}_{A/B}$$

where point B is on the arm, coincident with point A. We know that

$$(a_B)_n = r\omega^2 = 0.4 \times 10^2 = 40 \ \text{m/s}^2$$

$$(a_B)_t = r\alpha = 0.4 \times 40 = 16 \ \text{m/s}^2$$

$$(a_{A/B})_t = 60 \ \text{m/s}^2$$

$$(a_{A/B})_C = 2\omega v = 2 \times 10 \times 5 = 100 \ \text{m/s}^2$$

The acceleration polygon appears as follows:

The acceleration a_A is found to be $a_A = 86.4 \ \text{m/s}^2$.

9.2 Kinetics

To relate the force acting on a body to the motion of that body we use Newton's laws of motion. Newton's 2nd law is used in the form

$$\sum \mathbf{F} = m\mathbf{a} \tag{9.2.1}$$

where the mass of the body is assumed to be constant and $\mathbf{a}$ is the acceleration of the center of mass (center of gravity) if the body is rotating. We also require

$$\sum M = I\alpha \tag{9.2.2}$$

where the moments must be summed about an axis passing through the center of mass. The mass moment of inertia I is often found by using the radius of gyration k and the relation $I = mk^2$.

The gravitational attractive force between one body and another is given by

$$F = K\frac{m_1 m_2}{r^2} \tag{9.2.3}$$

where $K = 6.67 \times 10^{-11} \ \text{N} \cdot \text{m}^2/\text{kg}^2$.

Note: Since metric units are used in the above relations, mass must be measured in kilograms. The weight is related to the mass by

$$W = mg \tag{9.2.4}$$

where we will use $g = 9.8 \ \text{m/s}^2$, unless otherwise stated.

Example 9.11

Find the tension in the rope and the distance the 600 kg mass moves in 3 seconds. The mass starts from rest and the mass of the pulleys is negligible.

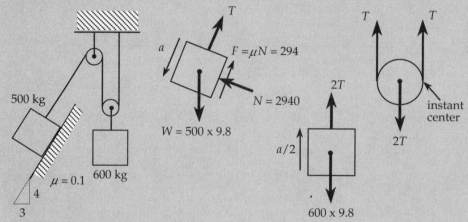

Solution. Applying Newton's 2nd law to the 500 kg mass gives

$$\sum F = ma$$
$$0.8 \times 500 \times 9.8 - 294 - T = 500\, a$$

By studying the lower pulley we observe the 600 kg mass to be accelerating at $a/2$. Hence, we have

$$\sum F = ma$$
$$2T - 600 \times 9.8 = 600 \times a/2$$

Solving the above equations simultaneously results in

$$a = 1.055 \ \text{m}\!\left/\!\text{s}^2\right., \qquad T = 3100 \ \text{N}$$

The distance the 600 kg mass moves is

$$s = \frac{1}{2}\frac{a}{2}t^2$$
$$= \frac{1}{2} \times \frac{1.055}{2} \times 3^2 = 2.37 \ \text{m}$$

Example 9.12

Find the tension in the string if at the position shown, $v = 4$ m/s. Calculate the angular acceleration.

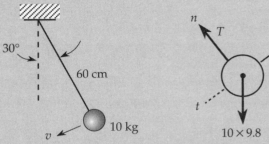

Solution. Sum forces in the normal direction and obtain

$$\sum F_n = ma_n = mv^2/r$$

$$T - 10 \times 9.8 \cos 30° = 10 \times 4^2/0.6$$

$$\therefore\ T = 352\ \text{N}$$

Sum forces in the tangential direction and find

$$\sum F_t = ma_t = mr\alpha$$

$$10 \times 9.8 \sin 30° = 10 \times 0.6\alpha$$

$$\therefore\ \alpha = 8.17\ \text{rad/s}^2$$

Example 9.13

Find the angular acceleration of the 60 kg cylindrical pulley, and the tension in the rope.

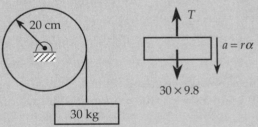

Solution. Summing forces on the 30 kg mass gives

$$\sum F = ma$$

$$-T + 30 \times 9.8 = 30 \times 0.2\alpha$$

Summing moments about the center of the pulley yields

$$\sum M = I\alpha$$

$$T \times 0.2 = \frac{1}{2} \times 60 \times 0.2^2\alpha$$

where $I = mr^2/2$ for a cylinder (see Table 8.2). A simultaneous solution results in

$$\alpha = 24.5\ \text{rad/s}^2, \qquad T = 147\ \text{N}$$

9.3 Work and Energy

Work is defined to be the dot product between a force and the distance it moves, that is,

$$W = \int \mathbf{F} \cdot d\mathbf{s} \qquad \qquad (9.3.1)$$

or, if the force is constant,

$$W = \mathbf{F} \cdot \Delta \mathbf{s} \qquad \qquad (9.3.2)$$

For a rotating body the work is

$$W = M \Delta \theta \qquad \qquad (9.3.3)$$

The *work-energy equation*, which results from integrating Newton's 2nd law, Eqs. 9.2.1 and 9.2.2, states that the net work done on a body (or several connected bodies) equals the change in energy of the body (or several bodies). This is expressed as

$$W_{net} = \Delta E \qquad \qquad (9.3.4)$$

where E represents the kinetic energy, given by

$$E = \frac{1}{2} m v^2 \qquad \qquad (9.3.5)$$

for a translating body, and

$$E = \frac{1}{2} I \omega^2 \qquad \qquad (9.3.6)$$

for a rotating body. For a translating and rotating body, refer v and I to the mass center. Potential energy can be realized by allowing the body forces to do work; or they can be incorporated in the ΔE-term by using the potential energy as

$$E_p = mgh \qquad \qquad (9.3.7)$$

where h is the distance above a selected datum.

By applying Eq. 9.3.1 to a spring, the work necessary to compress that spring a distance x is

$$W = \frac{1}{2} K x^2 \qquad \qquad (9.3.8)$$

The quantity $Kx^2/2$ can be considered the potential energy stored in the spring.

The net work done on a body equals the change in energy of the body.

Example 9.14
Neglecting friction, find v of the slider when it hits B if it starts from rest at A.

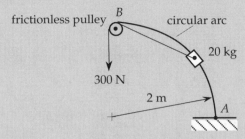

Solution. The distance the force F moves is

$$s = \frac{2}{\sin 45^\circ} = 2.828 \text{ m.}$$

The work-energy equation is written as

$$W_{net} = \frac{1}{2}mv^2$$

$$300 \times 2.828 - (20 \times 9.8) \times 2 = \frac{1}{2} \times 20v^2$$

$$\therefore v = 6.76 \text{ m/s}$$

Note that the body force does negative work since the motion is up and the body force acts down.

Example 9.15
Neglect friction and estimate the angular velocity of the cylinder after the mass falls 2 m from rest.

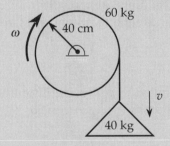

Solution. The work-energy equation provides

$$W_{net} = \frac{1}{2}mv^2 + \frac{1}{2}I\omega^2$$

$$(40 \times 9.8) \times 2 = \frac{1}{2} \times 40 \times (0.4\omega)^2 + \frac{1}{2}(\frac{1}{2} \times 60 \times 0.4^2)\omega^2$$

$$\therefore \omega = 11.83 \text{ rad/s}$$

Example 9.16

What is the velocity of the 40 kg mass after it falls 20 cm from rest? The spring is initially stretched 10 cm.

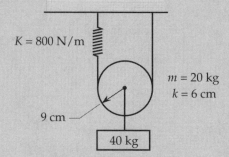

$K = 800$ N/m

$m = 20$ kg
$k = 6$ cm

9 cm

40 kg

Solution. The spring will stretch an additional 40 cm. Thus, the work-energy equation results in

$$W_{net} = \frac{1}{2}mv^2 + \frac{1}{2}I\omega^2$$

$$(20+40) \times 9.8 \times 0.2 - \frac{1}{2}800\left(0.5^2 - 0.1^2\right) = \frac{1}{2}(20+40)v^2 + \frac{1}{2}\left(20 \times 0.06^2\right)\left(\frac{v}{0.09}\right)^2$$

$$\therefore v = 0.792 \text{ m/s}$$

9.4 Impulse and Momentum

The impulse-momentum equations also result from integrating Newton's 2nd law. *Impulse* is defined for linear and rotating bodies, respectively, as

$$i_\ell = \int F dt$$
$$i_r = \int M dt$$

(9.4.1)

Momentum is velocity multiplied by mass. The impulse-momentum equations for a constant force and moment take the form (see Eqs. 9.2.1 and 9.2.2)

$$F\Delta t = m\Delta v$$
$$M\Delta t = I\Delta\omega$$

(9.4.2)

Objects impacting each other with no external forces acting experience a conservation of momentum. The *coefficient of restitution e* is used in such problems. It is defined as

$$e = \frac{\text{relative separation velocity}}{\text{relative approach velocity}}$$

(9.4.3)

If $e = 1$, the collision is *elastic* with no energy loss. If $e = 0$, the collision is *plastic* with maximum energy loss.

Example 9.17

Neglecting friction, estimate the angular velocity of the cylinder after 2 seconds if the motion starts from rest.

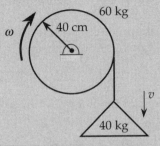

Solution. The impulse-momentum equation is used as follows:

$$M\Delta t = I\Delta\omega + m\Delta v \times r$$

$$0.4 \times (40 \times 9.8) \times 2 = \frac{1}{2} \times 60 \times 0.4^2\omega + 40 \times 0.4\omega \times 0.4$$

$$\therefore \omega = 28.0 \text{ rad/s}$$

Example 9.18

Find v' and θ if the coefficient of restitution is 0.8.

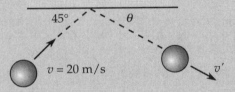

Solution. The coefficient of restitution is based on the normal components of velocity. Thus,

$$e = \frac{v' \sin\theta}{v \sin 45°}$$

$$\therefore v' \sin\theta = 0.8 \times 20 \times 0.707 = 11.31$$

The tangential velocity component remains unchanged so that

$$v' \cos\theta = 20 \cos 45° = 14.14$$

Simultaneous solution of the above results in

$$v' = 18.11 \text{ m/s}, \qquad \theta = 38.65°$$

Practice Problems

(If you choose to work only a few problems, select those with a star.)

Rectilinear Motion

*9.1   An object is moving with an initial velocity of 20 m/s. If it is decelerating at 5 m/s^2 how far does it travel, in meters, before it stops?

a) 10   b) 20   c) 30   d) 40

9.2   If the particle starts from rest, what is its velocity, in m/s, at $t = 4$ s?

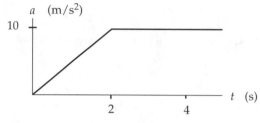

a) 10   b) 20   c) 30   d) 40

*9.3   A projectile is shot straight up with $v_o = 40$ m/s. After how many seconds will it return if drag is neglected?

a) 4   b) 6   c) 8   d) 10

*9.4   An automobile is traveling at 25 m/s. It takes 0.3 s to apply the brakes after which the deceleration is 6.0 m/s^2. How far does the automobile travel, in meters, before it stops?

a) 40   b) 45   c) 50   d) 60

Angular Motion

9.5   A wheel accelerates from rest with $\alpha = 6$ rad/s^2. How many revolutions are experienced in 4 s?

a) 7.64   b) 9.82   c) 12.36   d) 25.6

*9.6   A 2-m-long shaft rotates about one end at 20 rad/s. It begins to accelerate with $\alpha = 10$ rad/s^2. After how long, in seconds, will the velocity of the free end reach 100 m/s?

a) 3   b) 4   c) 5   d) 6

Curvilinear Motion

*9.7   A roller-coaster reaches a velocity of 20 m/s at a location where the radius of curvature is 40 m. Calculate the acceleration, in m/s^2.

a) 8   b) 9   c) 10   d) 12

9.8   A bucket full of water is to be rotated in the vertical plane. What minimum angular velocity, in rad/s, is necessary to keep the water inside if the rotating arm is 120 cm?

a) 2.86   b) 3.15   c) 3.86   d) 4.26

9.9   An automobile is accelerating at 5 m/s^2 on a straight road on a hill where the radius of curvature of the hill is 200 m. What is the magnitude of the total acceleration when the car's speed is 30 m/s?

a) 5   b) 5.46   c) 6.04   d) 6.73

9.10   A particle experiences the displacement shown. What is its velocity at $t = 1$ s?

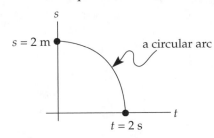

a) –0.58 m/s   b) – 0.76 m/s   c) –0.92 m/s   d) –1.0 m/s

9.11   Neglecting the change of gravity with elevation, estimate the speed a satellite must have to orbit the earth at an elevation of 100 km. Earth's radius = 6400 km.

a) 4000   b) 6000   c) 8000   d) 10 000

Projectile Motion

9.12   Find an expression for the maximum range of a projectile with initial velocity v_0 at angle θ with the horizontal.

a) $\dfrac{v_0^2}{g}\sin 2\theta$ b) $\dfrac{v_0^2}{2g}\sin^2\theta$ c) $\dfrac{v_0^2}{2g}\sin\theta$ d) $\dfrac{v_0^2}{g}\cos\theta$

*9.13   Find the maximum height, in meters.

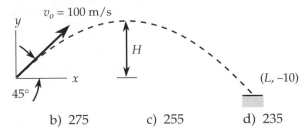

a) 295   b) 275   c) 255   d) 235

9.14   Calculate the time, in seconds, it takes the projectile of Problem 9.13 to reach the low point.

a) 14.6   b) 12.2   c) 11.0   d) 10.2

9.15   What is the distance L, in meters, in Problem 9.13?

a) 530   b) 730   c) 930   d) 1030

*9.16   The acceleration of the center O is given by

a) $r\omega^2$ c) 0

b) v^2/r d) ω^2/r

Rigid Body Motion

9.17   The spool rolls without slipping. Find v_o in m/s.

a) 30   c) 20

b) 25   d) 10

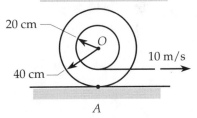

*9.18 The acceleration a_A, in m/s^2, in Problem 9.17 is
    a) 1000   b) 800   c) 600   d) 400

*9.19 If the acceleration of B is $60i - 20j$ m/s^2,
find $\mathbf{a}_A$ in m/s^2.
    a) $220i + 60j$
    b) $100i + 20j$
    c) $-100i + 20j$
    d) $-100i - 20j$

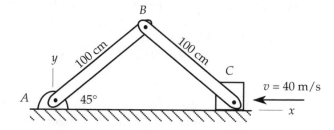

*9.20 Find ω_{AB} in rad/s.
    a) 56.6 ccw
    b) 56.6 cw
    c) 34.1 ccw
    d) 28.3 ccw

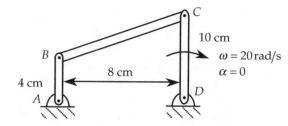

*9.21 What is ω_{BC}, in rad/s, for the linkage of Problem 9.20?
    a) 28.3 cw   b) 56.6 cw   c) 34.1 ccw   d) 28.3 ccw

9.22 Determine α_{AB}, in rad/s^2, if $a_C = 0$, in Problem 9.20.
    a) 800 cw   b) 800 ccw   c) 1160 cw   d) 3200 cw

9.23 What is $\mathbf{a}_B$, in m/s^2, if $a_C = 0$, in Problem 9.20?
    a) $1130\,\mathbf{i}$ b) $-1130\,\mathbf{i}$ c) $1130\,\mathbf{j}$ d) $-1130\,\mathbf{j}$

9.24 Find ω_{BC} in rad/s.
    a) 20 ccw
    b) 0
    c) 10 ccw
    d) 10 cw

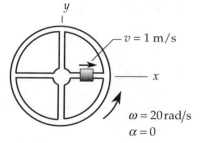

9.25 Find α_{BC}, in rad/s^2 in Problem 9.24.
    a) 750 cw   b) 750 ccw   c) 400 cw   d) 1000 cw

*9.26 What is the acceleration, in m/s^2, of the
bead if it is 10 cm from the center?
    a) $20\,i + 40\,j$
    b) $-40\,i - 20\,j$
    c) $-40\,i + 40\,j$
    d) $20\,i - 40\,j$

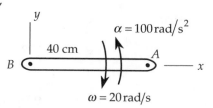

9.27 A boy moves toward the center of a merry-go-round at 4 m/s. If the merry-go-round rotates at 5 rev/min., calculate the acceleration component of the boy normal to the radius.

   a) 6.7   b) 6.1   c) 5.8   d) 4.2

*9.28 What is a_A in m/s^2 ?

   a) 2.09
   b) 1.85
   c) 1.63
   d) 1.47

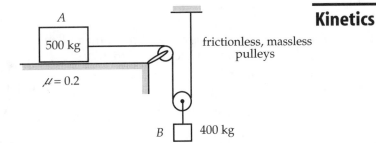

Kinetics

frictionless, massless pulleys

*9.29 How far, in meters, will the weight move in 10 s, if released from rest?

   a) 350   c) 250

   b) 300   d) 200

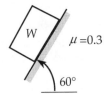

*9.30 At what angle, in degrees, should a road be slanted to prevent an automobile traveling at 25 m/s from tending to slip? The radius of curvature is 200 m.

   a) 22   b) 20   c) 18   d) 16

9.31 A satellite orbits the Earth 200 km above the surface. What speed, in m/s, is necessary for a circular orbit? The radius of the Earth is 6400 km and $g = 9.2\ m/s^2$.

   a) 7800   b) 7200   c) 6600   d) 6000

9.32 Determine the mass of the Earth, in kg, if the radius of the Earth is 6400 km.

   a) 6×10^{22} b) 6×10^{23} c) 6×10^{24} d) 6×10^{25}

9.33 The coefficient of sliding friction between rubber and asphalt is about 0.6. What minimum distance, in meters, can an automobile slide on a horizontal surface if it is traveling at 25 m/s?

   a) 38   b) 43   c) 48   d) 53

*9.34 The center of mass is 30 cm in front of the rear wheel of a motorcycle and 80 cm above the roadway. What maximum acceleration, in m/s^2, is possible?

   a) 4.5   b) 4.3   c) 3.7   d) 3.2

9.35 Find the ratio of the tension in the wire before and immediately after the string is cut.

   a) $2/\sqrt{3}$ c) 2/3

   b) 4/3   d) 3/4

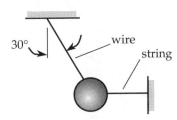

*9.36 Find the force, in kN, on the
front wheels if $a = 2$ m/s^2.
The center of mass is at G.

a) 58.2

b) 47.3

c) 41.6

d) 36.8

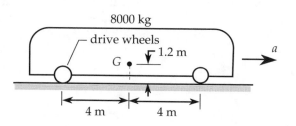

9.37 The radius of gyration of the pulley
is 10 cm. Calculate α in rad/s^2.

a) 8.52

b) 7.26

c) 6.58

d) 3.11

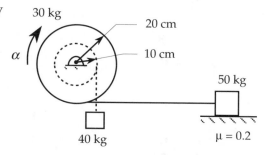

9.38 What is the force at O immediately after the
string is cut?

a) $\dfrac{mg}{2}$ c) $\dfrac{mg}{4}$

b) $\dfrac{mg}{3}$ d) $\dfrac{mg}{5}$

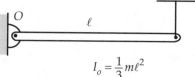

$I_o = \dfrac{1}{3}m\ell^2$

Work Energy

9.39 Find the velocity, in m/s, after the mass moves 10 m if it starts from rest.

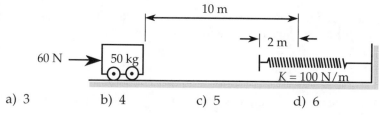

a) 3   b) 4   c) 5   d) 6

*9.40 If the force acts through 4 m, what is the an-
gular velocity, in rad/s, of the solid cylinder? Assume no slip and the cylinder starts
from rest.

a) 18   c) 14

b) 16   d) 12

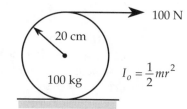

*9.41 The spring is initially free. Calcu-
late the velocity, in m/s, of the 2
kg mass after it falls 40 cm. It
starts from rest.

a) 4.62

b) 3.84

c) 2.96

d) 2.42

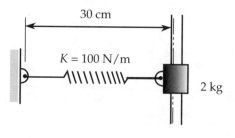

9.42 Find the velocity, in m/s, of the end of the 10 kg bar as it passes *A*. The free spring length is 30 cm. The moment of inertia of a bar about its mass center is $m\ell^2/12$.

a) 5.2

b) 4.6

c) 3.5

d) 1.2

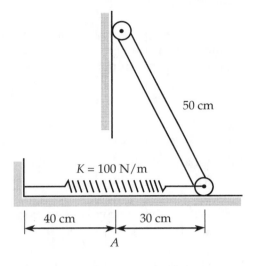

*9.43 If the force in Problem 9.40 acts for 4 seconds, find the angular velocity, in rad/s, assuming no slip. The cylinder starts from rest.

a) 2.4   b) 5.2   c) 8.6   d) 26.7

Impulse-Momentum

*9.44 Find the velocity, in m/s, of a 100 kg mass at $t = 2$ s. The coefficient of friction is 0.2.

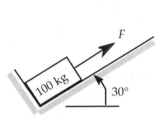

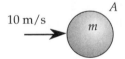

a) 0.245   b) 0.345   c) 0.456   d) 0.567

*9.45 If the coefficient of restitution is 0.8, find v'_B in m/s.

a) 16

b) 13

c) 11

d) 7

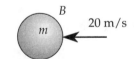

*9.46 Calculate the energy lost, in joules, in the collision of Problem 9.45 if $m = 2$ kg.

a) 200   b) 180   c) 160   d) 140

Afternoon Session
Practice Problems

Questions 9.47–9.49

The force $F(t)$ acts on a 2-kg mass that moves in a straight line on a frictionless plane. It starts from rest at $x = 0$ at $t = 0$.

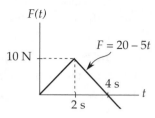

9.47 What is the displacement x after 2 seconds?

a) 5   b) 5/3   c) 3   d) 10/3

9.48 What is the velocity after 4 seconds?

a) 10   b) 9   c) 8   d) 7

9.49 How long does it take for the mass to reach its maximum displacement from $x = 0$?

a) 2 s   b) 4 s   c) 6.83 s   d) 7.24 s

Questions 9.50–9.53

A projectile is fired over a 10-m-high barrier, as shown.

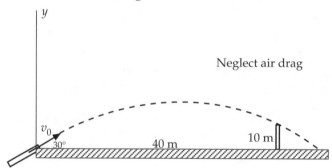

9.50 The velocity needed for the projectile to just clear the barrier is nearest

   a) 10 m/s
   b) 20 m/s
   c) 30 m/s
   d) 40 m/s

9.51 The time it takes for the projectile to just clear the barrier is nearest

   a) 2.92 sec
   b) 2.01 sec
   c) 1.82 sec
   d) 1.63 sec

9.52   If $v_0 = 40$ m/s, what's the maximum horizontal distance the projectile travels?

a) 100 m

b) 120 m

c) 140 m

d) 160 m

9.53   If the 2-kg projectile requires 80 cm to reach its velocity of 40 m/s, what average force is required?

a) 2000 N

b) 1600 N

c) 800 N

d) 200 N

Questions 9.54–9.57

A 10-kg mass is suspended form a spring as shown.

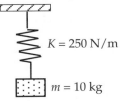

$K = 250$ N/m

$m = 10$ kg

9.54   The spring hangs freely. The mass is attached and allowed to slowly drop until it comes to rest in equilibrium. It will drop a distance of nearly

a) 30 cm

b) 40 cm

c) 50 cm

d) 60 cm

9.55   If the mass is released from rest 10 cm from its equilibrium position and allowed to vibrate freely, its frequency of oscillation will be nearest

a) 5 Hz

b) 5 rad/s

c) 31.4 Hz

d) 31.4 rad/s

9.56   The maximum velocity attained by the mass of Problem 9.55 is nearest

a) 2.0 m/s

b) 1.5 m/s

c) 1.0 m/s

d) 0.5 m/s

9.57   The time required for the mass of Problem 9.55 to complete one cycle is nearest

a) 1.26 sec

b) 1.02 sec

c) 0.91 sec

d) 0.79 sec

Questions 9.58–9.61

A piston-crank setup is shown.

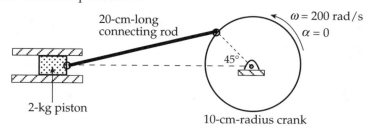

20-cm-long connecting rod

$\omega = 200$ rad/s

$\alpha = 0$

45°

2-kg piston

10-cm-radius crank

9.58   How far is the instantaneous center of rotation from the piston?

a) 25 cm

b) 30 cm

c) 35 cm

d) 40 cm

9.59   The velocity of the piston is nearest

a) 10 m/s

b) 15 m/s

c) 20 m/s

d) 25 m/s

9.60   The acceleration of the piston is nearest

a) 2000 m/s^2

b) 1500 m/s^2

c) 1000 m/s^2

d) 500 m/s^2

9.61   The force exerted on the piston by the connecting rod is nearest

a) 500 N

b) 1000 N

c) 1500 N

d) 2000 N

Solutions to Practice Problems

9.1 **d)** $v^2 = v_o^2 + 2as.$ $0 = 20^2 - 2 \times 5s$ $\therefore$ $s = 40$ m

9.2 **c)** $a = 5t$ $t \le 2$ $v = \int a\,dt = \int_0^2 5t\,dt + \int_2^4 10\,dt = 5\dfrac{2^2}{2} + 10(4-2) = 30$ m/s

9.3 **c)** $v = v_o + at.$ $0 = 40 - 9.8t$ $\therefore$ $t = 4.08$ s. $\therefore$ $t_{total} = 2t = 8.16$ s

9.4 **d)** $\Delta s = v\Delta t = 25 \times 0.3 = 7.5$ m

$v^2 = v_o^2 + 2as.$ $0 = 25^2 - 2 \times 6s$ $\therefore$ $s = 52.1$ m

$\therefore$ $s_{total} = 7.5 + 52.1 = 59.6$ m

9.5 **a)** $\theta = \alpha t^2 / 2 = 6 \times 4^2 / 2 = 48$ rad. $48/2\pi = 7.64$ rev.

9.6 **a)** $\omega = \omega_o + \alpha t = 20 + 10t.$ $\omega = v/L = 100/2 = 50.$

$\therefore$ $20 + 10t = 50.$ $\therefore$ $t = 3$ s.

9.7 **c)** $a = \dfrac{v^2}{r} = \dfrac{20^2}{40} = 10$ m/s^2

9.8 **a)** $\dfrac{v^2}{r} = g.$ $\dfrac{v^2}{1.20} = 9.8.$ $\therefore$ $v = 3.43$ m/s.

$v = r\omega$ $\therefore$ $\omega = 3.43/1.2 = 2.86$ rad/s

9.9 **d)** $a_t = 5.$ $a_n = \dfrac{v^2}{R} = \dfrac{30^2}{200} = 4.5.$ $a = \sqrt{a_t^2 + a_n^2} = \sqrt{5^2 + 4.5^2} = 6.73$ m/s^2.

9.10 **a)**   The equation of the circle is

$s^2 + t^2 = 4.$ $2s\dfrac{ds}{dt} + 2t = 0.$ $\therefore \dfrac{ds}{dt} = -\dfrac{2t}{2s} = -\dfrac{t}{s} = -\dfrac{1}{\sqrt{4-1}} = -0.577$ m/s.

9.11 **c)** $g = \dfrac{V^2}{R}.$ $9.8 = \dfrac{V^2}{6\,400\,000}.$ $\therefore V = 7920$ m/s.

9.12 **a)**   Because of symmetry, the time is twice that to reach the maximum height.

Let $v_y = 0$: $gt = v_0 \sin\theta.$ $\therefore t = 2\left(\dfrac{v_0}{g}\sin\theta\right).$

$\therefore x_{max} = v_0\left(\dfrac{2v_0}{g}\sin\theta\right)\cos\theta = \dfrac{v_0^2}{g}\sin 2\theta.$

9.13 **c)** $H = v_0^2 \sin^2\theta / 2g = 100^2 \times .707^2 / 2 \times 9.8 = 255$ m

9.14 **a)** $y = v_o t\sin\theta - gt^2 / 2.$ $-10 = 100t \times .707 - 9.8t^2 / 2.$ $\therefore t = 14.6$ s

9.15 **d)** $x = v_o t\cos\theta = 100 \times 14.6 \times 0.707 = 1032$ m

9.16 c) The acceleration of the point of contact is v^2/r or $r\omega^2$. The acceleration of the center is 0.

9.17 c) Motion is about the point of contact. Thus,
$\omega = 10/0.2 = 50$ rad/s. $v = r\omega = 0.4 \times 50 = 20$ m/s.

9.18 a) $a = v^2/r = 20^2/0.4 = 1000$ m/s^2

9.19 c) $\mathbf{a}_A = \mathbf{a}_B + \mathbf{a}_{A/B}$
$$= 60\mathbf{i} - 20\mathbf{j} - .4 \times 20^2\mathbf{i} + .4 \times 100\mathbf{j} = -100\mathbf{i} + 20\mathbf{j}$$

9.20 d) $v_B = 40\cos 45° = 28.3 = r\omega_{AB} = 1.0\omega_{AB}$
$\therefore\ \omega_{AB} = 28.3$ ccw.

9.21 a) $v_{C/B} = 40\sin 45° = 28.3 = r_{BC}\omega_{BC} = 1.0\omega_{BC}$. $\therefore\ \omega_{BC} = 28.3$ cw

9.22 a) $\mathbf{a}_C = \mathbf{a}_B + \mathbf{a}_{C/B}$
$r_{AB}\omega_{AB}^2 = 1.0 \times 28.3^2 = 800$
$r_{BC}\omega_{BC}^2 = 1.0 \times 28.3^2 = 800$
Then, $r_{AB}\alpha_{AB} = 800$. $\therefore\ \alpha_{AB} = 800$ cw

9.23 d) $\mathbf{a}_B = \mathbf{a}_A + \mathbf{a}_{B/A}$
$r\omega^2 = 1.0 \times 28.3^2 = 800$
$r\alpha = 1.0 \times 800 = 800$
$\therefore\ \mathbf{a}_B = -1130\mathbf{j}$

9.24 b) $\mathbf{v}_B = \mathbf{v}_C + \mathbf{v}_{B/C}$. $v_{B/C} = r\omega_{BC} \perp \overline{BC}$. But, $\mathbf{v}_B$ and $\mathbf{v}_C$ are both horizontal. Thus, $\mathbf{v}_{B/C} = 0$ and $\omega_{BC} = 0$.

9.25 b) $v_B = v_C = 20 \times 0.1 = 0.04\,\omega_{AB}$.
$\therefore\ \omega_{AB} = 50$. $r_{CD}\omega_{CD}^2 = .1 \times 20^2 = 40$
$r_{AB}\omega_{AB}^2 = .04 \times 50^2 = 100$.
$\therefore\ r_{BC}\alpha_{BC} = \dfrac{60}{0.8} = 75$.
But, $r_{BC} = 0.1$. $\therefore\ \alpha_{BC} = 750$ ccw.

9.26 c) $\mathbf{a} = -r\omega^2\mathbf{i} + 2\omega v\mathbf{j} = -0.1 \times 20^2\mathbf{i} + 2 \times 20 \times 1.0\mathbf{j} = -40\mathbf{i} + 40\mathbf{j}$

9.27 d) $a_{\text{Coriolis}} = 2v\omega = 2 \times 4 \times \dfrac{5 \times 2\pi}{60} = 4.19$ m/s^2.

9.28 c) $a_A = 2a_B$ (from small pulley above B)

$$400 \times 9.8 - 2T = 400\frac{a_A}{2} \qquad \text{(body } B\text{)}$$

$$T - 0.2 \times 500 \times 9.8 = 500\, a_A \quad \text{(body } A\text{)}, \qquad \therefore\ a_A = 1.63 \text{ m/s}^2$$

9.29 a) $W\cos 30° - W\mu \sin 30° = \dfrac{W}{g}a.$

$$\therefore\ a = 9.8(0.866 - 0.3 \times 0.5) = 7.02 \text{ m/s}^2. \quad \therefore\ s = at^2/2 = 7.02 \times 10^2/2 = 351 \text{ m}$$

9.30 c) $W\sin\theta = \dfrac{W}{g}\dfrac{v^2}{r}\cos\theta \qquad \tan\theta = \dfrac{25^2}{200 \times 9.8}. \quad \therefore\ \theta = 17.7°$

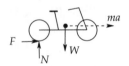

9.31 a) $W = \dfrac{W}{g}\dfrac{v^2}{r}. \quad \therefore\ v = \sqrt{9.2 \times 6\ 600\ 000} = 7790 \text{ m/s}$

9.32 c) $F = k\dfrac{m_1 m_2}{r^2}. \qquad W = k\dfrac{m_e W/g}{r^2}.$ (Let W be your weight!)

$$\therefore\ m_e = r^2 g/k = 6\ 400\ 000^2 \times 9.8/6.67 \times 10^{-11} = 6 \times 10^{24} \text{ kg}$$

9.33 d) $v^2 = v_0^2 + 2as. \quad -0.6W = \dfrac{W}{g}a. \quad \therefore\ a = -.06g. \quad 0 = 25^2 - 2 \times .6 \times 9.8s.$

$$\therefore\ s = 53.2 \text{ m}$$

9.34 c) $\Sigma M = 0$

For maximum accel. the force on the front wheel $= 0$.

Thus, $30W = 80\,ma. \quad \therefore\ a = \dfrac{30 \times 9.8}{80} = 3.68 \text{ m/s}^2$

9.35 b) Before : $\Sigma F_y = 0. \quad T\cos 30° = W. \quad \therefore\ T = \dfrac{W}{0.866}$

After : $F = 0, \quad \Sigma F_n = ma_n. \quad n \perp t. \quad \therefore\ T = W\cos\ = 0.866\ W.$

ratio $= \dfrac{\text{before}}{\text{after}} = \dfrac{1}{0.866 \times 0.866} = 1.33$

9.36 d) Take moments about the back wheels.

$$4W - 8N_2 = 1.2\frac{W}{g} \times 2. \quad \therefore\ N_2 = 0.469W = .469 \times 8000 \times 9.8 = 36\ 800 \text{ N}$$

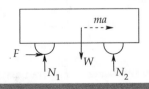

9.37 d)   Acceleration of block $= 0.2\alpha$. Thus, $T = 50 \times 0.2\alpha + 50 \times 9.8 \times 0.2$.

$\Sigma M = I\alpha$.   Use $I = mk^2$. $(40 \times 9.8 - 40\alpha) \times 0.1 - (10\alpha + 98) \times 0.2 = 30 \times 0.1^2 \alpha$.

$\therefore \alpha = 3.11 \text{ rad/s}^2$

9.38 c) $\Sigma M_o = I_o \alpha$. $mg \times \dfrac{\ell}{2} = \dfrac{1}{3} m\ell^2 \alpha$. $\therefore \alpha = \dfrac{3g}{2\ell}$.

$\Sigma F_y = m\vec{a}$ $(\vec{a}$ is acc. of mass center$)$.

$mg - F_o = m\dfrac{\ell}{2}\alpha = m\dfrac{3}{4}g$. $\therefore F_o = \dfrac{mg}{4}$.

9.39 b) $W_{net} = \Delta E = \dfrac{1}{2}mv^2$. $60 \times 10 - \dfrac{1}{2} \times 100 \times 2^2 = \dfrac{1}{2} 50v^2$. $\therefore v = 4$ m/s

9.40 d) $W_{net} = \Delta KE = \dfrac{1}{2}mv^2 + \dfrac{1}{2}I\omega^2$. $v = r\omega$.

$\therefore 100 \times 4 = \dfrac{1}{2} \times 100(0.2\omega)^2 + \dfrac{1}{2}\left(\dfrac{1}{2} \times 100 \times .2^2\right)\omega^2$. $\therefore \omega = 11.55$ rad/s

9.41 d) $W_{net} = \Delta KE = \dfrac{1}{2}mv^2$. $\Delta x = 50 - 30 = 20$.

$\therefore 2 \times 9.8 \times 0.4 - \dfrac{1}{2} \times 100 \times .2^2 = \dfrac{1}{2} \times 2v^2$. $\therefore v = 2.42$ m/s

9.42 d) $W_{net} = \Delta KE = \dfrac{1}{2}mv^2 + \dfrac{1}{2}I\omega^2$.

$\dfrac{1}{2}100\left(.4^2 - .1^2\right) - 10 \times 9.8(.25 - .20) = \dfrac{1}{2}10\left(\dfrac{v}{2}\right)^2 + \dfrac{1}{2}\left(10 \times .5^2 / 12\right)\left(\dfrac{v}{.5}\right)^2$

where $\overline{v} = v/2$ and $\omega = v/.5$. The above gives $v = 1.25$ m/s.

9.43 b) $\Sigma M_C \Delta t = I_C \omega$ where C is the point of contact. $I_C = I_o + mr^2 = \dfrac{3}{2}mr^2$.

$100 \times 0.4 \times 4 = \dfrac{3}{2} \times 100 \times .2^2 \omega$. $\therefore \omega = 26.7$ rad/s.

9.44 a)   Integrate Eq. 9.2.1 as follows: $\int F dt = m\Delta v$. $F = 400t$.

$F_f = \mu N = 0.2 \times 100 \times 0.866 \times 9.8 = 170$

$400t = 100 \times 0.5 \times 9.8 + 170$. $\therefore t = 1.65$ s   when motion initiates.

$\displaystyle\int_{1.65}^{2.0} 400t\,dt - (170 + 50 \times 9.8) \times 0.35 = 100v$. $\therefore v = 0.245$ m/s

9.45 d) $10\,m - 20\,m = v'_A m + v'_B m$. $\therefore v'_A + v'_B = -10$

$0.8 = \dfrac{v'_B - v'_A}{20 + 10}$. $\therefore v'_B - v'_A = 24$.   Simultaneous solutions yields $v'_B = 7$ m/s,

$v'_A = -17$ m/s.

9.46 c) $\Delta KE = \dfrac{1}{2}mv_A^2 + \dfrac{1}{2}mv_B^2 - \dfrac{1}{2}mv'^2_A - \dfrac{1}{2}mv'^2_B = \dfrac{2}{2}\left(10^2 + 20^2\right) - \dfrac{2}{2}\left(7^2 + 17^2\right) = 162$ J.

9.47 **d)** $F = 5t$ for $t < 2$ s. $\therefore 5t = 2\dfrac{dv}{dt}$ or $\displaystyle\int_0^t 5t\,dt = \int_0^v 2\,dv$. $\therefore v = \dfrac{5}{4}t^2$.

$v = \dfrac{dx}{dt} = \dfrac{5}{4}t^2$. $\therefore \displaystyle\int_0^x dx = \dfrac{5}{4}\int_0^2 t^2\,dt$ and $x = \dfrac{5}{4}\times\dfrac{2^3}{3} = \dfrac{10}{3}$ m.

9.48 **a)** $v = \dfrac{5}{4}t^2 = \dfrac{5\times 2^2}{4} = 5$ m/s after 2 seconds. For $t > 2$, $20 - 5t = 2\dfrac{dv}{dt}$.

$\therefore \displaystyle\int_2^4 (20 - 5t)\,dt = 2\int_5^v dv.$ $20\times(4-2) - \dfrac{5}{2}(16-4) = 2(v-5)$. $\therefore v = 10$ m/s.

9.49 **c)** From Problem 9.48,

$\displaystyle\int_2^t (20 - 5t)\,dt = 2\int_5^v dv$ or $20(t-2) - \dfrac{5}{2}\left(t^2 - 4\right) = 2(v-5)$.

The mass reaches its maximum displacement when $v = 0$. Set $v = 0$ and solve for t:

$20t - 40 - \dfrac{5}{2}t^2 + 10 = -10$. $\therefore t^2 - 8t + 8 = 0$. $\therefore t = \dfrac{8 \pm \sqrt{64 - 32}}{2} = 6.83$ s.

9.50 **c)** $x = v_o t \cos\theta$. $\therefore 40 = v_o t \times \cos 30°$

$y = v_o t \sin\theta - \dfrac{g}{2}t^2$. $\therefore 10 = v_o t \sin 30° - \dfrac{9.8}{2}t^2$

Solve the two equations:

$-13.09 = -4.9t^2$. $\therefore t = 1.634$ sec and $v_o = 28.3$ m/s

9.51 **d)** See the solution for t in Problem 9.50.

9.52 **c)** $y = v_o t \sin\theta - \dfrac{g}{2}t^2$. $\therefore 0 = 40t \times \sin 30° - \dfrac{9.8}{2}t^2$. $\therefore t = 4.082$ sec

$x = v_o t \cos\theta = 40 \times 4.082 \times \cos 30° = 141$ m

9.53 **a)** Work-energy: Work $= \Delta KE$. $\therefore F \times 0.8 = \dfrac{1}{2}\times 2\times 40^2$. $\therefore F = 2000$ N

9.54 **b)** $W = K \times d$. $10 \times 9.8 = 250 \times \delta_{st}$. $\therefore \delta_{st} = 0.392$ m

9.55 **b)** $m\ddot{x} + kx = 0$. $10\ddot{x} + 250x = 0$ or $\ddot{x} + 25x = 0$

$\therefore \omega_n = \sqrt{25} = 5$ rad/s

9.56 **d)** $x = C_1 \cos 5t + C_2 \sin 5t$

$\dot{x} = -5C_1 \sin 5t + 5C_2 \cos 5t$

$\left.\begin{array}{l} 0.1 = C_1 \\ 0 = 5C_2 \cos 5t \end{array}\right\}$ $\therefore C_1 = 0.1$, $C_2 = 0$ and $x(t) = 0.1\cos 5t$

Finally, $\dot{x} = 0.5\sin 5t$ so that $\dot{x}_{max} = 0.5$ m/s

9.57 **a)** $\tau = \dfrac{2\pi}{\omega_n} = \dfrac{2\pi}{5} = 1.26$ sec

9.58   **a)** First, sketch the triangles that locate the instant center:

We seek the quantity y. It is found from the triangles as follows:

The lower leg has length, using the law of cosines

$$20^2 = c^2 + 10^2 - 2 \times c \times 10 \cos 45°$$

$$\therefore c = 25.78 \text{ cm } = y$$

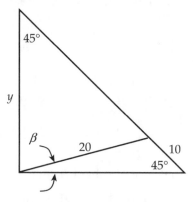

9.59   **c)** Sketch the velocity polygon:

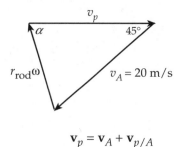

$$\mathbf{v}_p = \mathbf{v}_A + \mathbf{v}_{p/A}$$

Point A is where the rod connects to the crank. The angle β is found from the figure of Prob. 58:

$$10^2 = 25.78^2 + 20^2 - 2 \times 25.78 \times 20 \cos \beta$$

$$\therefore \beta = 20.72° \text{ and } \alpha = 69.28° \text{ so that the}$$

remaining angle is 65.72°. The law of sines:

$$\frac{v_p}{\sin 65.72°} = \frac{20}{\sin 69.28°}. \quad \therefore v_p = 19.49 \text{ m/s}$$

9.60   **d)** Sketch the acceleration polygon:

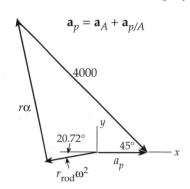

$$\mathbf{a}_p = \mathbf{a}_A + \mathbf{a}_{p/A}$$

From the velocity polygon we find:

$$0.2\omega \times \sin 69.28° = 14.14$$

$$\therefore \omega = 75.59 \text{ rad/s.} \quad \therefore r_{rod}\omega^2 = 1143 \text{ rad/s}^2$$

From the acceleration polygon:

$$1143 \times \sin 20.72° + 4000 \times \sin 45° = r\alpha \sin 69.28°$$

$$\therefore r\alpha = 3456 \text{ rad/s}^2.$$

$$\therefore a_p = 4000 \cos 45° - 1143 \cos 20.72° - 3456 \cos 69.28°$$

$$= 536 \text{ m/s}^2$$

9.61   **b)** Use Newton's second law:

$$F = ma = 2 \times 536 = 1072 \text{ N}$$

Mechanics of Materials

by George E. Mase

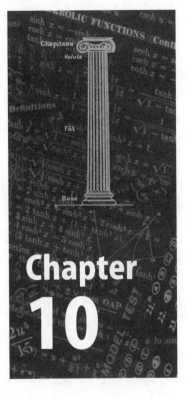

Chapter 10

Strategic Study Note

If you're planning a short review and you're outlining the NCEE Handbook, omit reviewing the following Handbook subjects, since they are not expected to be tested in the FE/EIT exam:

•Static Loading Failure Theories   •Elastic Strain Energy

Introduction

The mechanics of materials is one of a number of names given to the study of deformable solids subjected to applied forces and moments. The foundations of this subject reside in three basic topics:

1. internal equilibrium (stress concepts)
2. geometry of deformation (strain concepts)
3. mechanical and thermal properties (by which stress and strain are related)

Additionally, we assume homogeneity (properties are independent of position) and isotropy (absence of directional properties) in the materials considered.

🗝 We assume homogeneity and isotropy in the materials considered.

10.1 Stress and Strain, Elastic Behavior

Consider a prismatic bar of length L and a cross sectional area A situated along the x-axis as shown in Fig. 10.1a. Let the bar be subjected to a constant axial force P applied at the centroids of the end faces so as to stretch the bar by an amount δ, Fig. 10.1b.

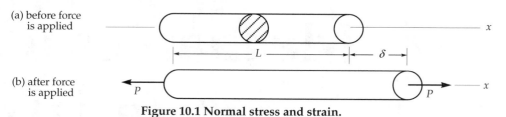

(a) before force
is applied

(b) after force
is applied

Figure 10.1 Normal stress and strain.

We define the *longitudinal*, or *normal strain* ε_x by the ratio

$$\varepsilon_x = \delta/L \qquad \text{(10.1.1)}$$

Strain is dimensionless, having the units of m/m, or in/in, etc. Normal strains are positive if due to elongation, negative if the result is shortening. The stress

$$\sigma_x = P/A \qquad \text{(10.1.2)}$$

A positive longitudinal strain is accompanied by a negative lateral strain.

• Stress is always accompanied by strain, but strain may occur without stress.

is the *normal*, or *axial stress* in the bar. Stress has units of $\mathrm{N/m^2}$, $\mathrm{lbs/in^2}$ (psi) or $\mathrm{kips/in^2}$ (ksi). One newton per square meter is called a *pascal*, abbreviated Pa. Note that the stress and strain defined here are averages, constant over the length of the bar, and uniform over its cross section. By contrast, for a tapered bar hanging from the ceiling under its own weight, the stress and strain would vary along the bar. Also, it is natural that a positive longitudinal strain will be accompanied by a negative lateral strain. Indeed, this ratio

$$\nu = -\frac{\text{lateral strain}}{\text{longitudinal strain}} \qquad \text{(10.1.3a)}$$

is called *Poisson's ratio*, an important property of a given material. Thus, for the bar in Fig. 10.1,

$$\varepsilon_y = \varepsilon_z = -\nu\varepsilon_x \qquad \text{(10.1.3b)}$$

If the bar in Fig. 10.1 is made of a *linear elastic* material, its axial stress and strain are related by the formula, often called *Hooke's law*,

$$\sigma_x = E\varepsilon_x \qquad \text{(10.1.4)}$$

where E is a material constant called *Young's modulus*, or the *modulus of elasticity*. The units of E are the same as those of stress. By inserting Eqs. 10.1.1 and 10.1.2 into Eq. 10.1.4 and solving for δ we obtain the useful formula

$$\delta = \frac{PL}{AE} \qquad \text{(10.1.5)}$$

Stress is always accompanied by strain, but strain may occur without stress. In particular, a temperature change in an unconstrained bar will cause it to expand (or shrink) inducing a thermal deformation

$$\delta_t = \alpha L(T - T_o) \qquad \text{(10.1.6)}$$

where α is the *coefficient of thermal expansion*, and $(T - T_o)$ the temperature change. Typical units of α are meters per meter per degree Celsius ($°\mathrm{C}^{-1}$). Important properties of several materials are listed in Table 10.1.

Next consider a material cube subjected to a pair of equilibrating couples acting in the plane of the faces of the cube as shown pictorially in Fig. 10.2a, and schematically in Fig. 10.2b. For a cube whose faces have an area A we define the *shear stress* in a plane parallel to those on which the forces act as

$$\tau_{xy} = F/A \qquad \text{(10.1.7)}$$

TABLE 10.1 Average Material Properties

	Modulus of Elasticity E		Shear Modulus G		Poisson's Ratio ν	Density ρ		Coefficient of Thermal Expansion α	
	$\times 10^6$ kPa	$\times 10^6$ psi	$\times 10^6$ kPa	$\times 10^6$ psi		kg/m³	lb/ft³	$\times 10^{-6}$ °C^{-1}	$\times 10^{-6}$ °F^{-1}
steel	210	30	83	12	0.28	7850	490	11.7	6.5
aluminum	70	10	27	3.9	0.33	2770	173	23.0	12.8
magnesium	45	6.5	17	2.4	0.35	1790	112	26.1	14.5
cast iron	140	20	55	8	0.27	7080	442	10.1	5.6
titanium	106	15.4	40	6	0.34	4520	282	8.8	4.9
brass	100	15	40	6	0.33	8410	525	21.2	11.8
concrete	20	3	—	—	—	2400	150	11.2	6.2

Note: Material properties may not be known exactly, so various tables may list values differing by quite a bit, sometimes as much as 40%. For that reason, answers to more than four significant digits are avoided.

If the material of the cube is linearly elastic, the top will be displaced relative to the bottom as shown in Fig. 10.2c. The angle γ_{xy} measures the *shear strain* of the cube, and since for elastic behavior this angle is very small, we define the shear strain as

> There are only two independent material properties in an isotropic, elastic solid.

$$\gamma_{xy} \approx \tan \gamma_{xy} = \Delta x / h \qquad \textbf{(10.1.8)}$$

Also, for elastic behavior,

$$\tau_{xy} = G\gamma_{xy} \qquad \textbf{(10.1.9)}$$

where G is the *shear modulus*, or *modulus of rigidity*, having the units of Pa or psi. It is related to E and ν by

$$G = \frac{E}{2(1+\nu)} \qquad \textbf{(10.1.10)}$$

There are only two independent material properties in an isotropic, elastic solid. These properties may depend on position as in a heat-treated steel.

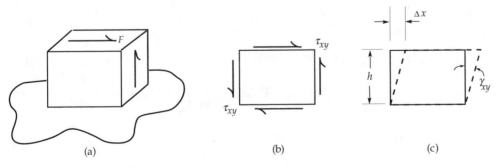

Figure 10.2 Shear stress and strain.

Example 10.1

A 2 cm × 2 cm square aluminum bar *AB* supported by 1.25 cm diameter steel cable *BC* carries a 7000 N load in the arrangement shown. Determine the stresses in the steel and in the aluminum. Also, calculate the elongation of the cable and the shortening of the bar.

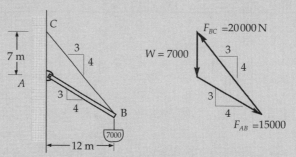

Solution.   As shown by the force polygon for the equilibrium, $F_{AB} = -15\,000$ N and $F_{BC} = 20\,000$ N. Thus there results

$$\sigma_{al} = \frac{P}{A} = -\frac{15\,000}{0.02 \times 0.02} = -37.5 \times 10^6 \text{ Pa} \quad \text{or} \quad -37.5 \text{ MPa}$$

$$\sigma_{st} = \frac{P}{A} = \frac{20\,000}{\pi(0.0125)^2/4} = 163 \times 10^6 \text{ Pa} \quad \text{or} \quad 163 \text{ MPa}$$

From Table 10.1 and Eq. 10.1.5,

$$\delta_{al} = \frac{PL}{AE} = \frac{-15\,000(15)}{0.02 \times 0.02 \times 70 \times 10^9} = -0.00804 \text{ m} \quad \text{or} \quad -8.04 \text{ mm}$$

$$\delta_{st} = \frac{PL}{AE} = -\frac{20\,000(20)}{(\pi \times 0.0125^2/4) \times 210 \times 10^9} = 0.0155 \text{ m} \quad \text{or} \quad 15.5 \text{ mm}$$

Example 10.2

A 5-cm-dia, 80-cm-long steel bar is restrained from moving. If its temperature is increased 100°C, what compressive stress is induced?

Solution. The strain can be calculated using the deformation of Eq. 10.1.6:

$$\varepsilon = \frac{\delta_t}{L} = \alpha(T - T_o)$$

$$= 11.7 \times 10^{-6} \times 100 = 11.7 \times 10^{-4}$$

Hence, the induced stress is

$$\sigma = \varepsilon E = 11.7 \times 10^{-4} \times 210 \times 10^6 = 246\,000 \text{ kPa}$$

Example 10.3

The steel block ($G = 83 \times 10^6$ kPa) is welded securely to a horizontal platen and subjected to 1000 kN horizontal force as shown. Determine the shear stress in a typical horizontal plane of the block, and the horizontal displacement of the top edge *AB*.

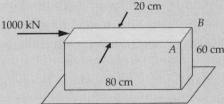

Solution. From Eq. 10.1.7

$$\tau = \frac{F}{A} = \frac{1000}{(0.8)(0.2)} = 6250 \text{ kPa}$$

From Eq. 10.1.9

$$\gamma_{xy} = \frac{\tau_{xy}}{G} = \frac{6250}{83 \times 10^6} = 7.53 \times 10^{-5} \text{ rad}$$

From Eq. 10.1.8 the horizontal displacement is

$$\Delta x = h\gamma_{xy} = 600(7.53 \times 10^{-5}) = 0.0452 \text{ mm}$$

10.2 Torsion

A straight member subjected to a twisting couple is said to be in *torsion*.

A straight member of constant circular cross section subjected to a twisting couple at each end is said to be in *torsion*, and such a member is called a *shaft*. For an elastic shaft of length L and radius a subjected to a *torque* T (pair of equilibrium couples), as shown in Fig. 10.3a, the angular displacement of one end relative to the other is given by the angle ϕ (in radians) as

$$\phi = \frac{TL}{JG} \tag{10.2.1}$$

where $J = \pi a^4/2$ is the *polar moment of inertia* of the circular cross section. Also, the *torsional shear stress* at the radial distance r from the axis of the shaft in a given cross section will be

$$\tau = \frac{Tr}{J} \tag{10.2.2}$$

which increases linearly as shown in Fig. 10.3b. Thus, the maximum shear stress occurs at $r = a$,

$$\tau_{max} = \frac{Ta}{J} \tag{10.2.3}$$

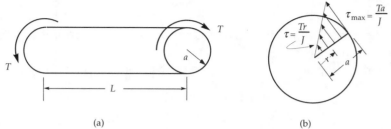

(a)   (b)

Figure 10.3 Circular shaft subject to a torque.

For a hollow shaft having an inner radius a_i and an outer a_o the above formulas are all valid, but with

$$J = \pi(a_o{}^4 - a_i{}^4)/2 \qquad\qquad \textbf{(10.2.4)}$$

Example 10.4

A 6 cm diameter, 2 m long magnesium ($G = 17 \times 10^9$ Pa) shaft is welded to a hollow ($c_o = 3$ cm and $c_i = 1.5$ cm) aluminum ($G = 27 \times 10^9$ Pa) shaft 1.2 m long. A moment of 2000 m·N is applied at end A. Determine the maximum torsional stress in each material and the angle of twist of end A relative to fixed end B.

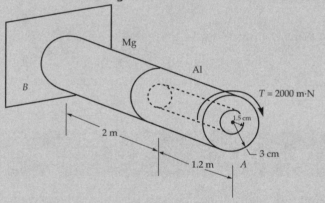

Solution. The polar moments of inertia are

$$J_{mg} = \pi a^4 / 2 = \pi(0.03)^4/2 = 1.272 \times 10^{-6} \text{ m}^4$$

$$J_{al} = \pi(a_o{}^4 - a_i{}^4)/2 = \pi(0.03^4 - 0.015^4)/2 = 1.193 \times 10^{-6} \text{ m}^4$$

From Eq. 10.2.3

$$\tau_{mg} = \frac{Ta}{J} = \frac{2000 \times 0.03}{1.272 \times 10^{-6}} = 47.17 \times 10^6 \text{ Pa}$$

$$\tau_{al} = \frac{2000 \times 0.03}{1.193 \times 10^{-6}} = 50.29 \times 10^6 \text{ Pa}$$

From Eq. 10.2.1 the angle of twist is

$$\phi = \phi_{mg} + \phi_{al} = \left(\frac{TL}{JG}\right)_{mg} + \left(\frac{TL}{JG}\right)_{al}$$

$$= \frac{2000 \times 2}{1.272 \times 10^{-6} \times 17 \times 10^9} + \frac{2000 \times 1.2}{1.193 \times 10^{-6} \times 27 \times 10^9}$$

$$= 0.1850 + 0.0745 = 0.2595 \text{ rad}$$

10.3 Beam Theory

The usual geometry of a beam is that of a member having the length much greater than the depth, with the forces applied perpendicular to this long dimension. The beams considered here have a longitudinal plane of symmetry in which the forces act and in which beam deflections occur. To illustrate, we consider a *T* shaped beam having the cross section shown in Fig. 10.4b, supported either as a cantilever beam, Fig. 10.4a, or as a simply-supported beam, Fig. 10.4c. The longitudinal axis of the beam (*x*-axis here) passes through the centroidal points of all cross sections. The *xy*-plane is the plane of symmetry. Any combination of concentrated and distributed loads may act on the beam.

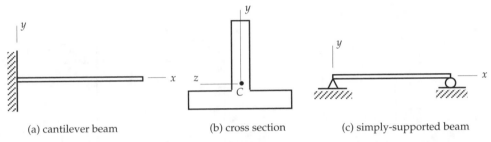

| (a) cantilever beam | (b) cross section | (c) simply-supported beam |

Figure 10.4 Beam geometry.

At the typical cross section of the loaded beam there is an internal force *V* called the *shear force*, and an internal moment *M* called the *bending moment*. Both *V* and *M* may be determined by a free-body diagram of the left hand portion of the beam, and are, in general, functions of *x* as shown in Fig. 10.5, where positive values of *V* and *M* are displayed. A plot of *V(x)* is called a *shear diagram* and a plot of *M(x)* is a *moment diagram*. At a given cross section where the moment has the value *M*, the (longitudinal) bending stress acting normal to the cross section is

$$\sigma_x = -\frac{My}{I} \tag{10.3.1}$$

where *I* is the plane moment of inertia of the cross sectional area relative to the centroidal axis. The minus sign is needed to assure a compressive stress for positive *y* values when the moment *M* is positive. The stress is a linear function of *y* as is shown in Fig. 10.6b, with the maximum compression occurring at the top of the beam, and the maximum tension (a *tensile stress*) at the bottom for the positive *M*. The bending stress is zero at *y* = 0, the so-called *neutral axis*.

🔑 Bending stress is a linear function of *y* with the maximum compression occurring at the top of the beam, and the maximum tension at the bottom for the positive *M*.

• For a beam with rectangular cross section the vertical shear stress is parabolic.

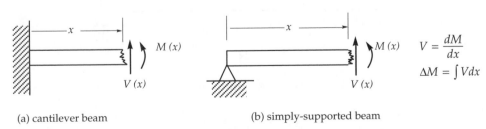

| (a) cantilever beam | (b) simply-supported beam |

$$V = \frac{dM}{dx}$$

$$\Delta M = \int V dx$$

Figure 10.5 Internal shear force and bending moment.

The stress due to the shear force V is a vertical shear stress

$$\tau_{xy} = \frac{VQ}{Ib} \qquad \textbf{(10.3.2)}$$

where b is breadth, or thickness of the beam at the position (y coordinate) at which the shear stress is calculated. The symbol Q stands for the first moment about the neutral axis of the area between the position of τ_{xy} and the top of the beam. For a rectangular beam τ_{xy} is parabolic. For the T beam it has the shape shown in Fig. 10.6c. In both cases the maximum shear stress occurs at the neutral axis (centroidal position).

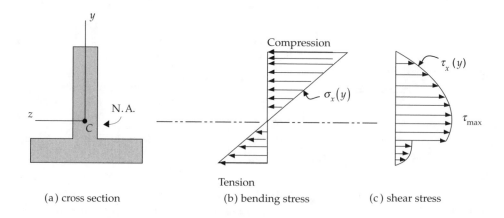

(a) cross section   (b) bending stress   (c) shear stress

Figure 10.6 Beam stresses for positive M.

The vertical displacement of the x-axis of a loaded beam measures the beam deflection. The curve of this deflection $v = v(x)$ is called the *equation of the elastic line*, shown in Figure 10.7. Also, the slope $\theta = \theta(x) = dv / dx$ of the deflection curve is an important quantity in beam theory. Table 10.2 lists some useful formulas for basic beams.

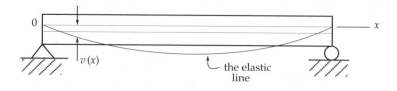

Figure 10.7 Beam deflection.

TABLE 10.2 Beam Formulas

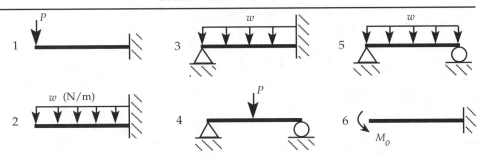

Number	Max Shear	Max Moment	Max Deflection	Max Slope
1	P	PL	$PL^3/3EI$	$PL^2/2EI$
2	wL	$wL^2/2$	$wL^4/8EI$	$wL^3/6EI$
3	$5wL/8$	$wL^2/8$	$wL^4/185EI$	
4	$P/2$	$PL/4$	$PL^3/48EI$	$PL^2/16EI$
5	$wL/2$	$wL^2/8$	$5wL^4/384EI$	$wL^3/24EI$
6		M_o	$M_oL^2/2EI$	M_oL/EI

Example 10.5

Sketch the shear and moment diagrams for the beam shown.

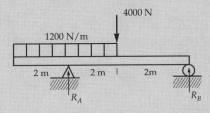

Solution.

First, determine the support reactions R_A and R_B:

$$\sum M_B = 4R_A - 4000(2) - 4(1200)4 = 0$$

$$\therefore R_A = 6800 \text{ N}$$

$$\sum M_A = 4R_B - 4000(2) = 0$$

$$\therefore R_B = 2000 \text{ N}$$

The values of V and M as functions of x are shown in the sketches; V is the resultant of all forces actin n the portion of the beam to the left of the x-location. The change in moment is the area under the shear diagram, $\Delta M = \int V dx$. Note from the diagrams that the maximum positive and negative moments occur at locations where the shear plot crosses the x-axis; the values of −2400 and 4000 are simply the appropriate areas under the shear diagram. Note that $M = 0$ at both ends and $V = 0$ at the left end.

Example 10.6

If the beam of Example 10.5 has the cross section shown below, determine the maximum tensile and compressive stresses, and the maximum shear stress.

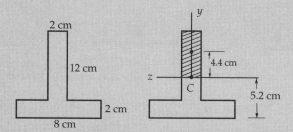

Solution. First, we locate the neutral axis by determining C relative to the bottom of the beam, as shown above:

$$\bar{y} = \frac{\sum y_i A_i}{\sum A_i} = \frac{16(1) + 24(8)}{16 + 24} = 5.2 \text{ cm}$$

The moment of inertia is (use $I = \bar{I} + Ad^2$)

$$I = \frac{8(2^3)}{12} + 16(4.2)^2 + \frac{2(12)^3}{12} + 24(2.8)^2$$

$$= 763.7 \text{ cm}^4$$

The maximum positive M is 4000 N · m at $x = 4$, so the maximum compressive stress is (intuitively, we can visualize compression in the top fibers under the 4000 N force)

$$\left(\sigma_c\right)_{max} = \frac{My}{I} = \frac{4000(0.088)}{764 \times 10^{-8}} = 46.1 \times 10^6 \text{ Pa}$$

The maximum negative M is 2400 N · m at $x = 2$, so the maximum tensile stress is (intuitively, we know that tension occurs in the top fibers to the left of R_A)

$$\left(\sigma_t\right)_{max} = \frac{My}{I} = \frac{2400(0.088)}{764 \times 10^{-8}} = 27.6 \times 10^6 \text{ Pa}$$

The maximum V is 4400 N. The moment of the cross-hatched area with respect to the neutral axis is Q. Therefore,

$$Q = \bar{y}A = 0.044 \times (0.02 \times 0.088) = 7.744 \times 10^{-5} \text{ m}^3$$

Since $b = 0.02$ at $y = 0$, the maximum shear stress is

$$\tau_{max} = \frac{VQ}{Ib} = \frac{4400 \times 7.744 \times 10^{-5}}{764 \times 10^{-8} \times 0.02} = 2.23 \times 10^6 \text{ Pa}$$

Example 10.7

Determine the maximum deflection of a 3 cm × 24 cm rectangular aluminum beam, 5 m long, if a concentrated load of 800 N acts downward at its mid-point.

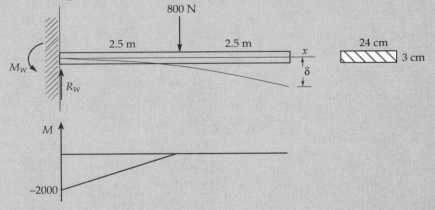

Solution. As the moment diagram shows, M is zero for the right-hand half of the beam. The right-hand half remains straight, but is inclined at the slope of the beam at mid-point. The left hand half is a simple end-loaded cantilever. From Table 10.2 with $L = 2.5$ m,

$$\delta = \delta_{\text{middle}} + \theta L = \frac{PL^3}{3EI} + \frac{PL^2}{2EI}(L) = \frac{5PL^3}{6EI}$$

$$= \frac{5(800)(2.5)^3}{6 \times (70 \times 10^9)(0.24)0.03^3/12} = 0.276 \text{ m}$$

10.4 Combined Stress

It often happens that structural members are simultaneously subjected to some combination of axial, torsional and bending loads. In such cases the state of stress at points on the surface of the member consists of both normal and shear components, and is called *combined stress*. At any given point of interest on the surface we introduce a local set of coordinate axes and focus attention on the stresses acting on a very small rectangular element of material at the same point P as shown by Fig. 10.8a. For an element aligned with a rotated set of $x'y'$-axes at the same point, located by the c.c.w. angle θ, shown in Fig. 10.8b, the primed stresses will differ from the original unprimed stresses, the relationship being a function of θ. At a certain angle θ_p, with which we associate the axes x^* and y^*, Fig. 10.8c, the normal stresses will reach their maximum (x^*-direction) and minimum (y^*-direction) values, while the shear stresses vanish. These axes are called *principal axes of stress*, and the values σ_1 and σ_2 are called the *principal stresses*. It turns out that

$$\sigma_1 = \sigma_{\max} = \frac{\sigma_x + \sigma_y}{2} + \sqrt{\left(\frac{\sigma_x - \sigma_y}{2}\right)^2 + \tau_{xy}^2} \qquad \textbf{(10.4.1a)}$$

$$\sigma_2 = \sigma_{\min} = \frac{\sigma_x + \sigma_y}{2} - \sqrt{\left(\frac{\sigma_x - \sigma_y}{2}\right)^2 + \tau_{xy}^2} \qquad \textbf{(10.4.1b)}$$

When structural members are subjected to axial, torsional and bending loads, the state of stress at points on the surface of the member consists of both normal and shear components, and is called *combined stress*.

10-MECHANICS

and the angle θ_p at which they occur is calculated from

$$\tan 2\theta_p = \frac{2\tau_{xy}}{\sigma_x - \sigma_y} \tag{10.4.2}$$

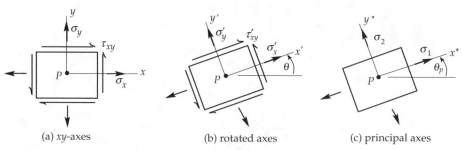

(a) *xy*-axes   (b) rotated axes   (c) principal axes

Figure 10.8 State of stress.

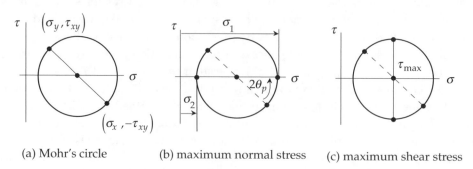

Mohr's circle is sketched by locating both ends of a diameter, whose center is always on the horizontal axis, the diameter ends being $\left(\sigma_x, -\tau_{xy}\right)$ and $\left(\sigma_y, \tau_{xy}\right)$.

• Rather than refer to the formulas, we can simply sketch Mohr's circle and easily find τ_{max} and σ_1.

As stated, relative to the *x*y**-axes the shear stresses are zero. The maximum shear stress occurs with respect to axes rotated 45° relative to the principal axes; its value is

$$\tau_{max} = \frac{\sigma_1 - \sigma_2}{2} = \sqrt{\left(\frac{\sigma_x - \sigma_y}{2}\right)^2 + \tau_{xy}^2} \tag{10.4.3}$$

A graphical method is often used when obtaining stresses on a particular plane; it utilizes *Mohr's circle*. Mohr's circle is sketched by locating both ends of a diameter, whose center is always on the horizontal axis. For the stress state of Fig. 10.8a, which shows positive stresses, we plot the diameter ends as $\left(\sigma_x, -\tau_{xy}\right)$ and $\left(\sigma_y, \tau_{xy}\right)$. The stresses on any plane, oriented at an angle θ with respect to the stresses on any known plane, are then the coordinates of a point on Mohr's circle located an angle 2θ from the known point. Once Mohr's circle is sketched, it is relatively obvious that the maximum shear stress is the circle's

(a) Mohr's circle   (b) maximum normal stress   (c) maximum shear stress

Figure. 10.9 Mohr's circle and maximum stresses.

radius, and the maximum normal stress is the circle's radius plus $\left(\sigma_x + \sigma_y\right)/2$, as observed in Fig. 10.9a. These are, in fact, equivalent to the formulas in the above equations. Rather than refer to the formulas, we can simply sketch Mohr's circle and easily find τ_{max} and σ_1, the quantities often of interest, since they may lead to failure.

Example 10.8

A solid circular shaft of radius 5 cm and length 3 m has a 2 m rigid bar welded to end A, and is "built in" to the vertical wall at B. A load of 8 kN acts at end C, and an axial force of 80 kN compresses the shaft as shown. Determine the maximum normal, and maximum shear stress at point P on the top of the shaft, midway between A and B.

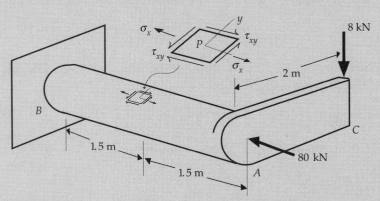

Solution. The torque on the shaft is $T = (8000)(2) = 16\,000$ N·m. The torsional shear stress on the element at P is

$$\tau_{xy} = \frac{Tr}{J} = \frac{16\,000(0.05)}{\pi(0.05)^4/2} = 81.5 \times 10^6 \text{ Pa} \quad \text{or} \quad 81.5 \text{ MPa}$$

The axial compressive stress is

$$\sigma_x = \frac{F}{A} = \frac{-80\,000}{\pi(0.05)^2} = -10.2 \times 10^6 \text{ Pa} \quad \text{or} \quad -10.2 \text{ MPa}$$

The tensile bending stress on the element at P (also a σ_x stress) is

$$\sigma_x = \frac{My}{I} = \frac{8000(1.5)(0.05)}{\pi(0.05)^4/4} = 122.2 \times 10^6 \text{ Pa} \quad \text{or} \quad 122.2 \text{ MPa}$$

Mohr's circle:

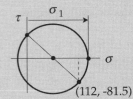

$$\text{radius} = \sqrt{(112/2)^2 + 81.5^2}$$
$$= 98.9 = \tau_{max}$$

$$\sigma_1 = \text{radius} + 112/2$$
$$= 154.9$$

Thus, the stress components on the element at P (in MPa) are

$$\sigma_x = 122.2 - 10.2 = 112, \quad \sigma_y = 0, \quad \tau_{xy} = 81.5$$

so that from Eq. 10.4.1a the maximum normal stress is

$$\sigma_{max} = \frac{112 + 0}{2} + \sqrt{\left(\frac{112 - 0}{2}\right)^2 + (81.5)^2} = 155 \text{ MPa}$$

From Eq. 10.4.3 the maximum shear stress is

$$\tau_{max} = \sqrt{\left(\frac{112 - 0}{2}\right)^2 + (81.5)^2} = 98.9 \text{ MPa}$$

As another case illustrating the ideas of combined stress, let us consider a cylindrical vessel of inside diameter D and wall thickness t (with $t/D << 0.05$) containing a fluid under a pressure p, and subjected to a torque T as shown in Fig. 10.10. We consider the stresses acting upon a small element of the wall having sides parallel and perpendicular, respectively, to the axis of the cylinder. By sectioning the cylinder perpendicular to its axis at the element, we find from axial equilibrium that the *longitudinal stress*, also called *axial stress*, in the wall is

$$\sigma_a = \frac{pD}{4t} \qquad\qquad \textbf{(10.4.4)}$$

Similarly by sectioning lengthwise through the axis, radial equilibrium requires the *circumferential stress*, also called *hoop stress*, to be

$$\sigma_t = \frac{pD}{2t} \qquad\qquad \textbf{(10.4.5)}$$

And finally, from torsional equilibrium about the vessel's axis, the shear stress in the wall is

$$\tau = \frac{Tr}{J} \qquad\qquad \textbf{(10.4.6)}$$

where $J = 2\pi r^3 t$, the approximate polar moment of inertia. From these formulas we may calculate the maximum normal and shear stresses as a problem in combined stress.

> 🔑 In a cyclindrical vessel the axial stress is σ_a, and the circumferential stress is σ_t.

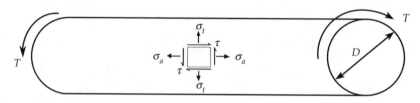

Figure 10.10 Pressurized cylinder under torque.

Finally, we note that in the absence of the torque T in Fig. 10.10, the maximum tensile stress is σ_t, the minimum tensile stress is σ_a, and the maximum shear stress is

$$\tau_{max} = \frac{\sigma_t - \sigma_a}{2} \qquad\qquad \textbf{(10.4.7)}$$

Also, for a thin-walled spherical container under pressure p the normal stress in the wall is

$$\sigma = \frac{pD}{4t} \qquad\qquad \textbf{(10.4.8)}$$

in every direction, and the shear stress in the wall is zero everywhere.

Example 10.9

A cylindrical tank of radius 40 cm and wall thickness 3 mm is subjected to an internal pressure of 2 MPa, and a torque of 0.5 MN · m. Determine the maximum normal and shear stresses in the cylinder wall.

Solution. From Eq. 10.4.4 the longitudinal stress is

$$\sigma_a = \frac{pr}{2t} = \frac{2(0.4)}{2(0.003)} = 133 \text{ MPa}$$

<u>Mohr's circle</u>

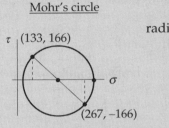

$$\text{radius} = \left[\left(\frac{267 - 133}{2}\right)^2 + 166^2\right]^{1/2}$$
$$= 179 \text{ MPa} = \tau_{max}$$

$$\sigma_1 = \text{radius} + (267 + 133)/2$$
$$= 379 \text{ MPa}$$

From Eq. 10.4.5 the circumferential stress is

$$\sigma_t = \frac{pr}{t} = \frac{(2)(0.4)}{(0.003)} = 267 \text{ MPa}$$

From Eq. 10.4.6 the shear stress is

$$\tau_{xy} = \frac{Tr}{J} = \frac{(0.5)(0.4)}{2\pi(0.4)^3(0.003)} = 166 \text{ MPa}$$

Thus, from Eq. 10.4.1a

$$\sigma_{max} = \frac{133 + 267}{2} + \sqrt{\left(\frac{133 - 267}{2}\right)^2 + (166)^2} = 379 \text{ MPa}$$

and from Eq. 10.4.3

$$\tau_{max} = \sqrt{\left(\frac{133 - 267}{2}\right)^2 + (166)^2} = 179 \text{ MPa}$$

10.5 Composite Bars and Beams

(Might not be tested.)

> A composite member is composed of several parallel portions, each of a particular material, securely bonded together and loaded axially.

Consider a member composed of several parallel portions, each of a particular material, securely bonded together and loaded axially. As an example, we show in Fig. 10.11 a composite bar of three materials subjected through rigid and parallel end plates to an axial force P. Let the portion of the bar have cross-sectional areas A_1, A_2 and A_3, as well as moduli of elasticity E_1, E_2, and E_3, respectively. Furthermore, let $E_1 \leq E_2 \leq E_3$ and form the ratios

$$m = E_2/E_1 \quad \text{and} \quad n = E_3/E_1 \tag{10.5.1}$$

Since the axial deformation is the same for each material, Hooke's law requires

$$\sigma_2 = m\sigma_1 \quad \text{and} \quad \sigma_3 = n\sigma_1 \tag{10.5.2}$$

and also that $\sigma_1 = P/A_T$ where A_T is the "transformed area" such that

$$\sigma_1 = \frac{P}{A_T} = \frac{P}{A_1 + mA_2 + nA_3} \tag{10.5.3}$$

The generalization to a bar of any number of materials is obvious.

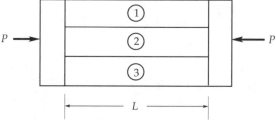

Figure 10.11 Composite bar.

Example 10.10

Let a composite bar made of aluminum, steel, and brass be subjected to an axial load of 500 kN. Determine the stress in each material if $E_{al} = 70$ GPa, $E_{st} = 210$ GPa, and $E_{br} = 105$ GPa, together with $A_{al} = 0.04$ m^2, $A_{st} = 0.006$ m^2, and $A_{br} = 0.08$ m^2.

Solution. From Eq. 10.5.1, with reference to Fig. 10.11,

$$m = \frac{E_{br}}{E_{al}} = \frac{105}{70} = 1.5$$

$$n = \frac{E_{st}}{E_{al}} = \frac{210}{70} = 3.0$$

From Eq. 10.5.3 we have

$$\sigma_{al} = \frac{P}{A_1 + mA_2 + nA_3} = \frac{500 \times 10^3}{0.04 + 1.5(0.08) + 3(0.006)} = 2.8 \text{ MPa}$$

From Eq. 10.5.2 there results

$$\sigma_{br} = m\sigma_1 = 1.5(2.8) = 4.2 \text{ MPa}$$

$$\sigma_{st} = n\sigma_1 = 3.0(2.8) = 8.4 \text{ MPa}$$

For a beam having a composite section and subjected to a bending moment M we again determine the ratios $E_2/E_1 = m$, $E_3/E_1 = n$, etc., and from them construct a "transformed cross section" by multiplying the width of each material by the corresponding ratio. We then determine the centroid of the transformed cross section, and calculate the moment of inertia I_T about the neutral axis of the transformed section. Thus,

$$\sigma_1 = -\frac{My}{I_T} \tag{10.5.4}$$

with $\sigma_2 = m\sigma_1$ and $\sigma_3 = n\sigma_1$, etc. An example illustrates the method.

Example 10.11

Let a composite steel and aluminum beam having the cross section shown be subjected to a positive bending moment of $90 \text{ N} \cdot \text{m}$. Determine the maximum bending stress in each material.

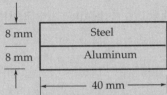

Solution. Here $m = E_s/E_a = 210/70 = 3$ so that the area has the geometry shown below with the neutral axis (N.A.) calculated to be 10 mm from the bottom.

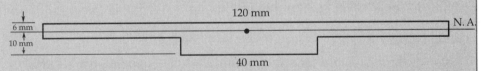

The moment of inertia about the N.A. is

$$I_T = \frac{(0.12)(0.006)^3}{3} + \frac{(0.04)(0.01)^3}{3} + \frac{(0.08)(0.002)^3}{3}$$

$$= 22 \times 10^{-9} \text{ m}^4$$

Thus, the maximum bending stress in the aluminum is

$$\left(\sigma_{al}\right)_{\max} = -\frac{My}{I_T} = -\frac{90(-0.01)}{22 \times 10^{-9}} = 41 \text{ MPa}$$

and the maximum bending stress in the steel is

$$\left(\sigma_{st}\right)_{\max} = -\frac{My}{I_T} = -3\left(\frac{90(0.006)}{22 \times 10^{-9}}\right) = -74 \text{ MPa}$$

🔑 For a beam having a composite section we construct a "transformed cross section" by multiplying the width of each material by a corresponding ratio.

10.6 Columns

Long slender members loaded axially in compression are referred to as *columns*. Such members frequently fail by *buckling* (excessive lateral deflection) rather than by crushing. Buckling onset depends not only on the material properties but also the geometry and type of end supports of the column. The axial load at the onset of buckling is called the *critical load*.

If the *slenderness ratio* of the column, defined as L/r (length divided by least radius of gyration r where $r = \sqrt{I/A}$), is greater than 120 (it can be as low as 60) the critical load for a column is the Euler load

$$P_{cr} = \pi^2 EI / k^2 L^2 \tag{10.6.1}$$

Values of k, with end supports shown in parentheses, are given as:

$$
\begin{aligned}
k &= 1 && \text{(pinned - pinned)} \\
k &= 0.5 && \text{(fixed - fixed)} \\
k &= 0.7 && \text{(pinned - fixed)} \\
k &= 2 && \text{(free - fixed)}
\end{aligned}
\tag{10.6.2}
$$

Intermediate columns are those whose slenderness ratios are less than 120 but greater than that at which failure occurs by crushing. For these, empirical formulas have been developed to predict buckling.

> **Buckling onset depends not only on the material properties but also the geometry and type of end supports of the column.**
>
> • Intermediate columns are those whose slenderness ratios are less than 120 but greater than that at which failure occurs by crushing.

Example 10.12

Determine the critical load for a square steel ($E = 210$ GPa) strut 8 cm $\times$ 8 cm if its length is 6 m under (a) pinned ends, (b) fixed ends.

Solution. The moment of inertia is

$$I = bh^3 / 12 = (0.08)(0.08)^3 / 12 = 3.4 \times 10^{-6} \text{ m}^4$$

a) The critical load for pinned ends is

$$P_{cr} = \frac{\pi^2 EI}{L^2} = \frac{\pi^2 (210 \times 10^9)(3.4 \times 10^{-6})}{6^2} = 195\ 000 \text{ N}$$

The normal stress, which must not exceed the yield stress, is

$$\sigma = \frac{F}{A} = \frac{195 \times 10^3}{0.0064} = 30.5 \times 10^6 \text{ Pa}$$

This is substantially less than the yield stress for all steels.

b) The critical load for fixed ends is

$$P_{cr} = \frac{\pi^2 (210 \times 10^9)(3.4 \times 10^{-6})}{0.5^2 \times 6^2} = 780\ 000 \text{ N}$$

The normal stress for this case is

$$\sigma = \frac{780 \times 10^3}{0.0064} = 122 \times 10^6 \text{ Pa}$$

Practice Problems

(If you choose to work only a few problems, select those with a star.)

Stress and Strain

*10.1   A structural member with the same material properties in all directions at any particular point is

    a) homogeneous

    b) isotropic

    c) isentropic

    d) holomorphic

*10.2   The amount of lateral strain in a tension member can be calculated using

    a) the bulk modulus

    b) Poisson's ratio

    c) the yield stress

    d) Hooke's law

10.3   Wood has grain resulting in material properties quite different normal to the grain compared with properties parallel to the grain. Such a material is

    a) nonhomogeneous

    b) nonholomorphic

    c) nonorthotropic

    d) nonisotropic

*10.4   Find the allowable load, in kN, on a 2-cm-dia, 1-m-long, steel rod if its maximum elongation cannot exceed 0.1 cm.

    a) 35   b) 45   c) 55   d) 66

10.5   An elevator is suspended by a 2-cm-dia, 30-m-long steel cable. Twenty people, with a total weight of 14 000 N, enter. How far, in millimeters, does the elevator drop?

    a) 3.5   b) 4.5   c) 5.5   d) 6.4

10.6   A hole, one meter from the end of a structural steel member fixed at one end, is 0.8 mm shy of matching another hole for possible connection. What force, in kN, is necessary to stretch it for connection? The cross section is 25 mm × 3 mm.

    a) 12.6   b) 13.6   c) 14.7   d) 15.8

10.7   As the load is applied, edge $A\,B$ moves 0.03 mm to the right. Determine the shear modulus, in MPa.

    a) 50 300   c) 38 600

    b) 41 700   d) 32 500

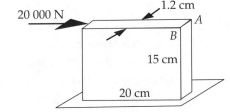

10.8   A 5-cm-dia steel shaft is subjected to an axial tensile force of 600 kN. What is the diameter, in cm, after the force is applied? Use $v = 0.28$.

a) 4.998   b) 4.996   c) 4.994   d) 4.992

*10.9   An aluminum cylinder carries an axial compressive load of 1500 kN. Its diameter measures exactly 12.015 cm and its height 19.311 cm. What was its original diameter, in cm?

a) 12.010   b) 12.008   c) 12.006   d) 12.004

Thermal Stress

10.10   A tensile stress of 100 MPa exists in a 2-cm-dia steel rod that is fastened securely between two rigid walls. If the temperature increases by 30° C, determine the final stress, in MPa in the rod.

a) 46.7   b) 41.2   c) 36.9   d) 26.2

*10.11   A steel bridge span is normally 300 m long. What is the difference in length, in cm, between January (–35° C) and August (40° C)?

a) 26   b) 28   c) 30   d) 32

10.12   An aluminum bar at 30° C is inserted between two rigid stationary walls by inducing a compressive stress of 70MPa. At what temperature, in ° C, will the bar drop out?

a) 10   b) 0   c) –8   d) –14

*10.13   Brass could not be used to reinforce concrete because

a) its density is too large.

b) its density is too low.

c) it is too expensive.

d) its coefficient of thermal expansion is not right.

Torsion

*10.14   The maximum shearing stress, in MPa, that exists in a 6-cm-dia shaft subjected to a 200 N · m torque is

a) 4.72   b) 5.83   c) 7.29   d) 8.91

10.15   The shaft of Prob. 10.14 is replaced with a 6-cm-outside diameter, 5-cm inside diameter hollow shaft. What is the maximum shearing stress, in MPa?

a) 5.5   b) 6.4   c) 7.3   d) 9.1

10.16   The maximum allowable shear stress in a 10-cm-dia shaft is 140 MPa. What maximum torque, in N · m, can be applied?

a) 27 500   b) 21 400   c) 19 300   d) 17 100

10.17   A builder uses a 50-cm-long, 1-cm-dia steel drill. If two opposite forces of 200 N are applied normal to the shaft, each with a moment arm of 15 cm, what angle of twist, in degrees, occurs in the drill?

a) 29.3   b) 24.6   c) 22.8   d) 21.1

10.18　A solid circular shaft, 8 cm in diameter, transmits a torque of 1200 N·m. Calculate the maximum normal stress in the shaft.

　　　a) 24 MPa　　　b) 18 MPa　　　c) 14 MPa　　　d) 12 MPa

Bending Moments

10.19　The maximum bending stress at a given cross section of an I-beam occurs

　　　a) where the shearing stress is maximum.

　　　b) at the outermost fiber.

　　　c) at the joint of the web and the flange.

　　　d) at the neutral axis.

10.20　The moment diagram for a simply-supported beam with a load at the midpoint is a

　　　a) triangle　　　b) parabola　　　c) trapezoid　　　d) rectangle

10.21　Find the bending moment, in N·m, at A.

　　　a) 12 000　　　c) 16 000

　　　b) 14 000　　　d) 18 000

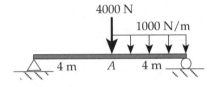

*10.22　What is the bending moment, in N·m, at A?

　　　a) 26 000　　　c) 22 000

　　　b) 24 000　　　d) 20 000

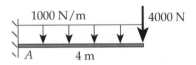

Stresses in Beams

*10.23　Find the maximum tensile stress, in MPa.

　　　a) 94

　　　b) 86

　　　c) 82

　　　d) 76

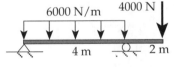

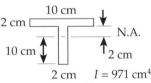

*10.24　What is the maximum compressive stress, in MPa, in the beam of Prob. 10.23?

　　　a) 96　　　b) 90　　　c) 82　　　d) 76

*10.25　What is the maximum shearing stress, in MPa, in the beam of Prob. 10.23?

　　　a) 7.2　　　b) 8.2　　　c) 9.6　　　d) 11.3

*10.26　The shearing stress distribution $\tau = VQ/Ib$ on the cross section of the T-beam in Prob. 10.23 most resembles which sketch?

a) 　　b) 　　c) 　　d)

10.27 If the allowable bending stress is 140 MPa in the beam of Prob. 10.22, calculate the *section modulus* defined by I/y, in cm^3.

a) 196   b) 184   c) 171   d) 162

10.28 Find the maximum bending stress, in MPa, if the 10-cm-wide beam is 5 cm deep.

a) 200   c) 160

b) 180   d) 140

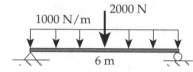

10.29 If the beam of Prob. 10.28 were 5 cm wide and 10 cm deep, find the maximum bending stress, in MPa.

a) 80   b) 90   c) 110   d) 120

10.30 Find the maximum shearing stress, in MPa, of a simply supported, 6-m-long beam with a 5 cm × 5 cm cross section if it has a 2000 N load at the mid point.

a) 0.6   b) 0.9   c) 1.2   d) 1.6

Deflection of Beams

*10.31 What is the maximum deflection, in cm, of a simply supported, 6-m-long steel beam with a 5 cm × 5 cm cross-section if it has a 2000 N load at the midpoint?

a) 6.35   b) 7.02   c) 7.63   d) 8.23

10.32 Find the maximum deflection, in cm, for the steel beam of Prob. 10.28.

a) 39.7   b) 32.4   c) 28.3   d) 11.8

10.33 If the deflection of the right end of the 5-cm-dia steel beam is 10 cm, what is the load P, in N?

a) 403

b) 523

c) 768

d) 872

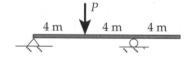

Combined Stresses

*10.34 Find the maximum shearing stress, in MPa.

a) 80

b) 70

c) 60

d) 50

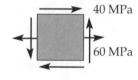

10.35 What is the maximum tensile stress, in MPa?

a) 40

b) 30

c) 20

d) 10

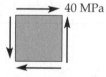

10.36 Determine the maximum shearing stress, in MPa.

a) 80   c) 50

b) 60   d) 40

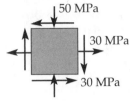

*10.37 Find the maximum shearing stress, in MPa, in the shaft.

a) 29.5   c) 27.5

b) 28.5   d) 26.5

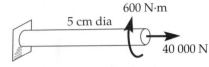

10.38 The maximum normal stress, in MPa, in the shaft of Prob. 10.37 is

a) 52.8   b) 41.7   c) 36.7   d) 30.1

10.39 The normal stress, in MPa, at pt. *A* is

a) 263   c) 228

b) 241   d) 213

10.40 The maximum shearing stress, in MPa, at pt. *A* in Prob. 10.39 is

a) 140   b) 130   c) 120   d) 110

10.41 The maximum shearing stress, in MPa, in the circular shaft is

a) 171   c) 154

b) 167   d) 142

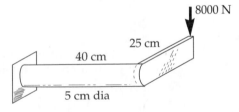

10.42 The maximum tensile stress, in MPa, in the circular shaft of Prob. 10.41 is

a) 284   b) 248   c) 223   d) 212

Thin-Walled Pressure Vessels

10.43 The allowable tensile stress for a pressurized cylinder is 180 MPa. What maximum pressure, in kPa, is allowed if the 80-cm-dia cylinder is made of 0.5 cm thick material?

a) 2400   b) 2250   c) 2150   d) 2050

10.44 The maximum normal stress that can occur in a 120-cm-dia steel sphere is 200 MPa. If it is to contain a pressure of 8000 kPa, what must be the minimum thickness, in cm?

a) 1.6   b) 1.4   c) 1.2   d) 1.0

10.45 What is the maximum shearing stress, in MPa, in the sphere of Prob. 10.44?

a) 0   b) 50   c) 100   d) 150

Composite Sections

10.46   A compression member, composed of 1.2-cm-thick steel pipe with 25-cm-inside diameter, is filled with concrete. Find the stress, in MPa, in the steel if the load is 2000 kN.

a) 137

b) 145

c) 155

d) 165

10.47   If the flanges are aluminum and the rib is steel, find the maximum tensile stress, in MPa, in the beam.

a) 7.89

b) 6.31

c) 5.72

d) 8.73

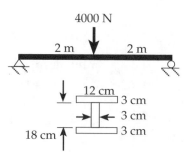

10.48   If the flanges of the I-beam of Prob. 10.47 are steel and the rib is aluminum, what is the maximum tensile stress, in MPa, in the beam?

a) 7.89

b) 6.31

c) 5.67

d) 4.91

Columns

10.49   What is the minimum length, in meters, for which a 10 cm × 10 cm wooden post can be considered a long column? Assume a maximum slenderness ratio of 60.

a) 4.03   b) 3.12   c) 2.24   d) 1.73

*10.50 A free-standing platform, holding 2000 N, is to be supported by a 10-cm-dia vertical aluminum strut. How long, in meters, can it be if a safety factor of 2 is used?

a) 18.3   b) 16.6   c) 14.6   d) 12.2

10.51   What increase in temperature, in °C, is necessary to cause a 2-cm-dia, 4-m-long, steel rod with fixed ends to buckle? There is no initial stress.

a) 4.63   b) 5.27   c) 6.34   d) 7.12

10.52   A column with both ends fixed buckles when subjected to a force of 30 000 N. One end is then allowed to be free. At what force, in newtons, will it buckle?

a) 2025   b) 1875   c) 1725   d) 1650

Questions 10.53–10.57

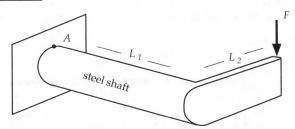

rectangular beam — 2 cm × 5 cm

shaft — 5 cm diameter

$F = 2000$ N

$L_1 = 2$ m

$L_2 = 1$ m

$E = 210 \times 10^9$ Pa

10.53 The maximum normal stress in the rectangular beam is, in MPa,

   a) 120

   b) 180

   c) 240

   d) 360

10.54 The maximum vertical shearing stress in the rectangular beam is, in kPa,

   a) 1200

   b) 1800

   c) 2400

   d) 3000

10.55 The stress situation at pt. A is described by which element? (Point A is at the top.)

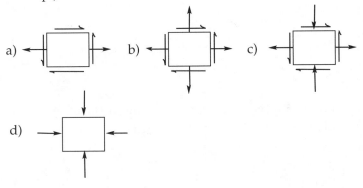

10.56 The maximum normal stress in the shaft is, in MPa,

   a) 392   b) 345   c) 326   d) 247

10.57 The maximum deflection of the shaft is, in cm,

   a) 3.9   b) 5.1   c) 6.6   d) 8.3

Questions 10.58 – 10.62

A steel pressure vessel with concave ends is held between two rigid walls, as shown.

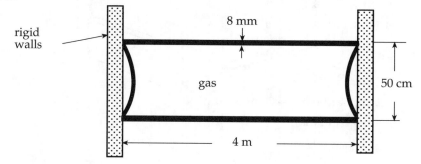

8 mm

rigid walls

gas

50 cm

4 m

10.58 What is the maximum pressure in the gas that would result in a hoop stress of 80 MPa?

   a)   1280 kPa
   b)   2560 kPa
   c)   3840 kPa
   d)   5120 kPa

10.59 The compressive force exerted by the rigid walls that would result in an axial stress of 60 MPa when the gas pressure is 2 MPa is nearest

   a)   360 kN
   b)   240 kN
   c)   120 kN
   d)   60 kN

10.60 The pressure vessel just touches the rigid walls when the gas pressure is 2 MPa. The temperature increase needed to result in a zero axial stress is nearest

   a)   126°C
   b)   47°C
   c)   21°C
   d)   13°C

10.61 For the situation of Problem 10.60, the maximum shearing stress in the pressure vessel is nearest

   a)   0 MPA
   b)   16 MPA
   c)   31 MPa
   d)   74 MPa

10.62 If a torque of 400 kN·m were superposed on the situation of Problem 10.60, the maximum normal stress would be nearest

   a)   250 MPa   b)   160 MPa   c)   130 MPa   d)   90 MPa

Questions 10.63 – 10.67

The beam is level before the distributed load is applied.

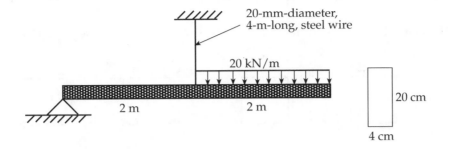

10.63   The axial stress in the steel wire is nearest

   a)   190 MPa
   b)   95 MPA
   c)   47 MPa
   d)   23 MPa

10.64   The force needed at the left end to hold the beam in equilibrium is nearest

   a)   100 kN
   b)   60 kN
   c)   40 kN
   d)   20 kN

10.65   The maximum normal stress in the beam is nearest

   a)   150 MPa
   b)   30 MPa
   c)   15 MPa
   d)   7.5 MPa

10.66   The maximum vertical shear stress in the beam is nearest

   a)   150 MPa
   b)   30 MPa
   c)   15 MPa
   d)   7.5 MPa

10.67   The deflection of the right end of the beam is nearest

   a)   4.2 mm
   b)   7.4 mm
   c)   15.6 mm
   d)   67.2 mm

10-MECHANICS

Questions 10.68 – 10.72

A 6-cm-diameter, 12-m-long, aluminum shaft is subject to a compressive force of 60 kN and a torque of 750 N·m. No other loads act on the shaft. Use $\alpha_{al} = 23 \times 10^{-6}°\text{C}^{-1}$.

10.68   Select the stress condition that exists on an outer-most fiber away from the ends.

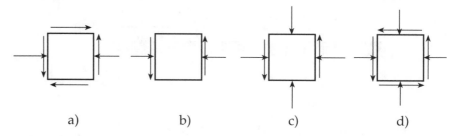

     a)   b)   c)   d)

10.69   The radius marked on the end of the unloaded shaft will rotate through how many degrees after it is loaded?

    a) 31.2°

    b) 14.5°

    c) 2.5°

    d) 0.25°

10.70   The larger principle stress (magnitude only) is nearest

    a) 11 MPa

    b) 21 MPa

    c) 31 MPa

    d) 41 MPa

10.71   The angle that a principle stress makes with the axis of the shaft is nearest

    a) 10°

    b) 20°

    c) 30°

    d) 40°

10.72   If the unloaded shaft with rounded ends (similar to pinned ends) is placed between two rigid barriers, the temperature rise that would cause buckling is nearest

    a) 10°C

    b) 7°C

    c) 3°C

    d) 1°C

Questions 10.73 – 10.75 refers to the steel beam shown.

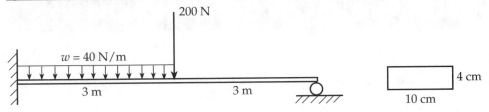

10.73 If the right end support is removed, the deflection of the right end of the beam is nearest

  a) 2 cm

  b) 3 cm

  c) 4 cm

  d) 5 cm

10.74 The maximum shear force in the beam is nearest

  a) 170 N

  b) 150 N

  c) 110 N

  d) 50 N

10.75 The maximum moment in the beam is nearest

  a) 150 N·m

  b) 300 N·m

  c) 450 N·m

  d) 600 N·m

Solutions to Practice Problems

10.1 **b)** Isotropic

10.2 **b)** Poisson's Ratio

10.3 **d)**

10.4 **d)** $\sigma = E\delta/L = P/\pi r^2$

$\therefore P = E\,\delta\pi r^2/L = 210 \times 10^9 \times 0.001 \times \pi \times 0.01^2/1 = 66\,000$ N

10.5 **d)** $\dfrac{P}{\pi r^2} = E\dfrac{\delta}{L}.$ $\therefore \delta = \dfrac{14\,000 \times 30}{\pi \times 0.01^2 \times 210 \times 10^9} = 0.0064$ m

10.6 **a)** $\dfrac{P}{A} = E\dfrac{\delta}{L}.$ $\therefore P = \dfrac{AE\delta}{L} = 0.025 \times 0.003 \times \left(210 \times 10^9\right) \times \dfrac{0.0008}{1} = 12\,600$ N

10.7 **b)** $\dfrac{P}{A} = G\dfrac{\delta}{L}.$ $\therefore G = \dfrac{PL}{A\delta} = \dfrac{20\,000 \times 0.15}{0.012 \times 0.2 \times 0.00003} = 41.7 \times 10^9$ Pa

10.8 **a)** $P/A = E\varepsilon.$ $\varepsilon = \dfrac{600\,000}{\pi \times 0.025^2 \times 210 \times 10^9} = 0.001455$

$\Delta d = v\varepsilon d = 0.28 \times 0.001455 \times 5 = 0.00204$ cm

$d = d - \Delta d = 5 - 0.00204 = 4.9980$ cm

10.9 **b)** $P/A = E\varepsilon.$ $\varepsilon = \dfrac{1\,500\,000}{\pi \times 0.06^2 \times 70 \times 10^9} = 0.00190$

$\Delta d = v\varepsilon d = 0.33 \times 0.0019 \times 12.015 = 0.0075$ cm

$d = d - \Delta d = 12.015 - 0.0075 = 12.008$ cm

10.10 **d)** $\sigma = E\delta/L.$ $100 \times 10^6 = 210 \times 10^9 (\delta/L).$ $\therefore \delta = 4.76 \times 10^{-4} L$

$\delta_T = \alpha L\Delta T = 11.7 \times 10^{-6} \times 30L = 3.51 \times 10^{-4}L.$ $\delta_{final} = \delta - \delta_T = 1.25 \times 10^{-4}L$

$\therefore \sigma = \left(210 \times 10^9\right) \times \left(1.25 \times 10^{-4}\right) = 26.2 \times 10^6$ Pa

10.11 **a)** $\delta = \alpha L\Delta T = \left(11.7 \times 10^{-6}\right) \times 300 \times 75 = 0.263$ m

10.12 **d)** $\dfrac{\delta}{L} = \dfrac{\sigma}{E} = \alpha\Delta T.$ $\dfrac{70 \times 10^6}{70 \times 10^9} = 23 \times 10^{-6}(30 - T).$ $\therefore T = -13.5°C$

10.13 **d)** It expands at a different rate.

10.14 **a)** $\tau = \dfrac{Tr}{J} = \dfrac{200 \times 0.03}{\pi \times 0.06^4/32} = 4.72 \times 10^6$ Pa

10.15 **d)** $J = \pi\left(a_1^4 - a_2^4\right)/2 = \pi\left(0.03^4 - .025^4\right)/2 = 65.9 \times 10^{-8}$

$\tau = \dfrac{Tr}{J} = \dfrac{200 \times 0.03}{65.9 \times 10^{-8}} = 9.10 \times 10^6$ Pa

10.16 **a)** $T = \dfrac{\tau J}{r} = \dfrac{\left(140 \times 10^6\right) \times \pi \times .05^4/2}{0.05} = 27\,500 \text{ N} \cdot \text{m}$

10.17 **d)** $\theta = \dfrac{TL}{JG} = \dfrac{200 \times 0.3 \times 0.5}{\left(83 \times 10^9\right) \times \pi \times .05^4/2} = 0.368 \text{ rad or } 21.1°$

10.18 **d)** $\tau_{\max} = \dfrac{Tr}{J} = \dfrac{1200 \times 0.04}{\pi \times 0.04^4/2} = 11.9 \times 10^6 \text{ Pa.}$

$\therefore \sigma_{\max} = 11.9 \times 10^6 \text{ Pa.}$

10.19 **b)** $\sigma = My/I.$ $\sigma_{\max}$ occurs at $y = y_{\max}$

10.20 **a)** A triangle.

10.21 **a)** $\sum M_{right} = 0.$ $\therefore 8F_{left} = 4000 \times 4 + 4000 \times 2.$ $\therefore F = 3000.$

$M_A = 3000 \times 4 = 12\,000 \text{ N} \cdot \text{m}$

10.22 **b)** $M_A = 4000 \times 4 + 4000 \times 2 = 24\,000 \text{ N} \cdot \text{m}$

10.23 **b)** $4F_{right} = 24\,000 \times 2 + 4000 \times 6.$ $\therefore F_{right} = 18\,000 \text{ N.}$ $4F_{left} = 24\,000 \times 2 - 4000 \times 2.$

$\therefore F_{left} = 10\,000 \text{ N.}$ $M_{\max} = \text{area under diagram} = 10\,000 \times 1.667/2 = 8330 \text{ N} \cdot \text{m.}$

$\sigma = \dfrac{My}{I} = \dfrac{8330 \times 0.1}{971 \times 10^{-8}} = 85.8 \times 10^6 \text{ Pa}$

10.24 **c)** Compression occurs in bottom fibers over right support.

There, $M = 4000 \times 2 = 8000 \text{ N} \cdot \text{m.}$ $\sigma = \dfrac{My}{I} = \dfrac{8000 \times 0.1}{971 \times 10^{-8}} = 82.4 \times 10^6 \text{ Pa}$

10.25 **a)** $\tau_{\max} = \dfrac{VQ}{Ib} = \dfrac{14\,000(0.002 \times 0.05)}{\left(971 \times 10^{-8}\right) \times 0.02} = 7.21 \times 10^6 \text{ Pa}$

10.26 **c)** $\tau_{\max}$ occurs on the N.A. with a sudden decrease when b goes from 2 to 16 cm.

Also, it is a parabolic distribution.

10.27 **c)** $\sigma = \dfrac{My}{I}.$ $\dfrac{I}{y} = \dfrac{M}{\sigma} = \dfrac{24\,000}{140 \times 10^6} = 171 \times 10^{-6} \text{ m}^3$

10.28 **b)** Using the area under the curve: $M_{\max} = 1000 \times 3 + 3000 \times 3/2 = 7500 \text{ N} \cdot \text{m}$

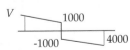

$\sigma_{\max} = \dfrac{My}{I} = \dfrac{7500 \times 0.025}{0.1 \times 0.05^3/12} = 180 \times 10^6 \text{ Pa}$

10.29 b) $\sigma_{max} = \dfrac{My}{I} = \dfrac{7500 \times 0.05}{0.05 \times 0.1^3 / 12} = 90 \times 10^6$ Pa

10.30 a) $V_{max} = 1000.$ $\tau_{max} = \dfrac{VQ}{Ib} = \dfrac{1000(0.025 \times 0.05 \times 0.0125)}{\left(0.05 \times 0.05^3 / 12\right) \times 0.05} = 600 \times 10^3$ Pa

10.31 d) $\delta = \dfrac{PL^3}{48EI} = \dfrac{2000 \times 6^3}{48 \times \left(210 \times 10^9\right) \times 0.05^4 / 12} = 0.0823$ m

10.32 d) $\delta = \dfrac{PL^3}{48EI} + \dfrac{5wL^4}{384EI}.$ $I = \dfrac{bh^3}{12} = \dfrac{0.1 \times 0.05^3}{12} = 1.04 \times 10^{-6}$

$= \dfrac{2000 \times 6^3}{48 \times \left(210 \times 10^9\right) \times 1.04 \times 10^{-6}} + \dfrac{1000 \times 5 \times 6^4}{384 \times \left(210 \times 10^9\right) \times 1.04 \times 10^{-6}} = 0.118$ m

10.33 a) $\delta = \theta L_2 = \dfrac{PL^2}{16EI} \times 4.$ $0.1 = \dfrac{P \times 8^2 \times 4}{16 \times \left(210 \times 10^9\right) \pi \times .025^4 / 4}.$ $\therefore P = 403$ N

10.34 d) $\tau_{max} = \dfrac{1}{2} \sqrt{\left(\sigma_x - \sigma_y\right)^2 + 4\tau^2} = \dfrac{1}{2} \sqrt{60^2 + 4 \times 40^2} = 50$ MPa

10.35 a) $\sigma_{max} = \dfrac{1}{2}\left(\sigma_x + \sigma_y\right) + \tau_{max} = 0 + 40 = 40$ MPa

10.36 c) $\tau_{max} = \dfrac{1}{2} \sqrt{(30 + 50)^2 + 4 \times 30^2} = 50$ MPa

10.37 d) $\tau = Tr/J = 600 \times 0.025 \Big/ \dfrac{\pi \times .025^4}{2} = 24.45 \times 10^6$ Pa

$\sigma = P/A = 40\,000 \Big/ \pi \times 0.025^2 = 20.37 \times 10^6$ Pa

$\therefore \tau_{max} = \dfrac{1}{2} \sqrt{20.37^2 + 4 \times 24.45^2} = 26.5 \times 10^6$ Pa

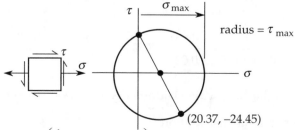

10.38 c) $\sigma_{max} = \left(\dfrac{1}{2} \times 20.37 + 26.5\right) \times 10^6 = 36.7 \times 10^6$ Pa

10.39 b) $My/I = 3\,200 \times 0.025 \Big/ \dfrac{\pi \times .025^4}{4} = 261 \times 10^6$ comp.

$P/A = 40\,000 \Big/ \pi \times 0.025^2 = 20.4 \times 10^6$ Pa tension.

$\sigma_A = (261 - 20.4) \times 10^6 = 241 \times 10^6$ Pa

10.40 c) $\tau_{max} = \sigma/2 = 120 \times 10^6$ Pa. $VQ/Ib = 0$ on outer fibers.

10.41 c) $\tau = \dfrac{Tr}{J} = \dfrac{8\,000 \times 0.25 \times 0.025}{\pi \times .025^4/2} = 81.5 \times 10^6$ Pa

$\sigma = \dfrac{My}{I} = \dfrac{8\,000 \times 0.4 \times 0.025}{\pi \times .025^4/4} = 261 \times 10^6$ Pa

$\tau_{max} = \dfrac{1}{2}\sqrt{261^2 + 4 \times 81.5^2} \times 10^6 = 154 \times 10^6$ Pa

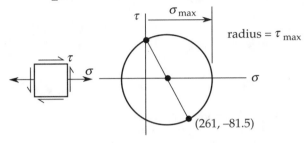

10.42 a) $\sigma_{max} = \left(\dfrac{1}{2} \times 261 + 154\right) \times 10^6 = 284 \times 10^6$ Pa

10.43 b) $\sigma_t = pD/2t. \quad \therefore p = 180 \times 10^6 \times 2 \times 0.005/0.8 = 2250 \times 10^3$ Pa

10.44 c) $\sigma_a = pD/4t. \quad \therefore t = \dfrac{8000 \times 10^3 \times 1.2}{4 \times 200 \times 10^6} = 0.012$ m

10.45 a) $\tau_{max} = \dfrac{1}{2}\sqrt{(200 - 200) + 0 \times 4} = 0$

10.46 a) $\left(\dfrac{\Delta L}{L}\right)_s = \left(\dfrac{\Delta L}{L}\right)_c. \quad \therefore \varepsilon_s = \varepsilon_c. \quad \therefore \sigma_s = \dfrac{E_s}{E_c}\sigma_c = 10.5\,\sigma_c.$

$F_s + F_c = 2\,000\,000 \quad \text{or} \quad A_s\sigma_s + A_c\sigma_c = 2\,000\,000.$

$\sigma_s\left[\pi\left(0.137^2 - 0.125^2\right) + \pi \times \dfrac{0.125^2}{10.5}\right] = 2 \times 10^6. \quad \therefore \sigma_s = 137 \times 10^6$ Pa.

10.47 d) $n = E/E_{min} = 3.$ The area is transformed:

$I_t = \dfrac{0.12 \times 0.24^3}{12} - \dfrac{0.03 \times 0.18^3}{12} = 1.237 \times 10^{-4}$ m^4.

$\therefore \sigma_{al} = \dfrac{My}{I} = \dfrac{2000 \times 2 \times 0.12}{1.237 \times 10^{-4}} = 3.88 \times 10^6$ Pa,

$\sigma_s = \dfrac{nMy}{I} = \dfrac{3 \times 2000 \times 2 \times 0.09}{1.237 \times 10^{-4}} = 8.73 \times 10^6$ Pa

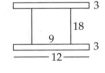

10.48 c) $n = E/E_{min} = 3.$ The area is transformed :

$I_t = \dfrac{0.36 \times 0.24^3}{12} - \dfrac{0.33 \times 0.18^3}{12} = 2.54 \times 10^{-4}$ m^4.

$\therefore \sigma_s = \dfrac{nMy}{I} = \dfrac{3 \times 4000 \times 0.12}{2.54 \times 10^{-4}} = 5.67 \times 10^6$ Pa

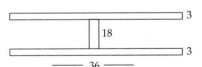

10.49 d) $60 = \dfrac{L}{r} = \dfrac{L}{\sqrt{I/A}} = \dfrac{L}{\sqrt{0.1 \times \left(0.1^3/12\right)/0.01}}$. $\quad \therefore L = 1.73$ m

10.50 c) Assume $P = 4000$ N using a factor of safety of 2.

$$4000 = \dfrac{\pi^2 \times 70 \times 10^9 \times \pi \times \left(0.1^4/64\right)}{4L^2}. \quad \therefore L = 14.55 \text{ m}$$

10.51 b) $P_{cr} = 4\pi^2 EI/L^2 = \alpha \Delta T E A.$ $\quad \Delta T = \dfrac{4\pi^2 I}{\alpha A L^2} = \dfrac{4\pi^2 \times \pi \times \left(0.02^4/64\right)}{11.7 \times 10^{-6} \times \pi \times 0.01^2 \times 4^2} = 5.27\,°C$

10.52 b) $P_{cr} = 4\pi^2 EI/L^2 = 30\,000.$ $\;\therefore \pi^2 EI/L^2 = 7500.$ $\;\therefore P_{cr} = \pi^2 EI/4L^2 = 7500/4 = 1875$ N

10.53 c) $M_{max} = FL_2 = 2000 \times 1 = 2000$ N·m.

$$\sigma = \dfrac{My}{I} = \dfrac{2000 \times 0.025}{0.02 \times 0.05^3/12} = 240 \times 10^6 \text{ Pa.}$$

10.54 d) $\dfrac{VQ}{Ib} = \dfrac{2000 \times \left(0.02 \times 0.025\right) \times 0.0125}{\left(0.02 \times 0.05^3/12\right) \times 0.02} = 3 \times 10^6$ Pa.

10.55 a) The force F provides a torque of 2000 N·m and a force of 2000 N acting on the end of the steel shaft. This is best described by (a) since the top fibers experience tension. There is no normal stress in the circumferential direction, ruling out (b), (c) and (d).

10.56 b) $\sigma = \dfrac{My}{I} = \dfrac{(2000 \times 2) \times 0.025}{\pi \times 0.025^4/4} = 326 \times 10^6$ Pa.

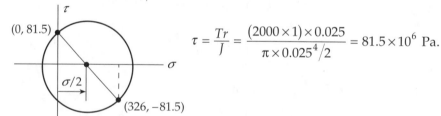

$\tau = \dfrac{Tr}{J} = \dfrac{(2000 \times 1) \times 0.025}{\pi \times 0.025^4/2} = 81.5 \times 10^6$ Pa.

$$\therefore \sigma_{max} = 163 + \left[163^2 + 81.5^2\right]^{1/2}$$

$$= 345 \text{ MPa.}$$

10.57 d) $\delta = \dfrac{PL^3}{3EI} = \dfrac{2000 \times 2^3}{3 \times 210 \times 10^9 \times \pi \times 0.025^4/4} = 0.0828$ m.

10.58 b) $\sigma_t = \dfrac{pD}{2t}.$ $\quad 80\,000 = \dfrac{p \times 0.5}{2 \times 0.008}.$ $\quad \therefore p = 2560$ kPa

10.59 a) $\sigma_a = \dfrac{F}{A} + \dfrac{pD}{4t}.$ $\quad 60\,000 = \dfrac{F}{\pi \times 0.5 \times 0.008} + \dfrac{2000 \times 0.5}{4 \times 0.008}.$ $\quad \therefore F = 361$ kN

10.60 d) $\sigma_a = \dfrac{pD}{4t} - \dfrac{\delta E}{L} = \dfrac{pD}{4t} - \dfrac{\alpha L \Delta T E}{L}$

$$0 = \frac{2000 \times 0.5}{4 \times 0.008} - 11.7 \times 10^{-6} \Delta T \times 207 \times 10^6. \quad \therefore \Delta T = 12.9°C$$

10.61 c)   Neglect the radial normal stress of 2 MPa due to the pressure acting in the radial direction:

$$\sigma_a = 0, \quad \sigma_t = \frac{pD}{2t} = \frac{2000 \times 0.5}{2 \times 0.008} = 62\,500 \text{ kPa}$$

$$\tau_{max} = \frac{\sigma_t}{2} = 31,500 \text{ kPa (obvious from Mohr's circle)}$$

10.62 b)   Find the normal stress (neglect the normal stress in the radial direction) and the shear stress, then use Mohr's circle:

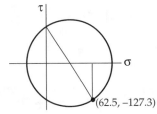

$$\sigma_a = 0, \quad \sigma_t = \frac{pD}{2t} = \frac{2000 \times 0.5}{2 \times 0.008} = 62\,500 \text{ kPa,}$$

$$\tau_{xy} = \frac{Tr}{J} = \frac{400 \times 0.25}{2\pi 0.25^3 \times 0.008} = 127\,300 \text{ kPa}$$

$$\therefore \sigma_{max} = \sqrt{127.3^2 + 31.25^2} + 31.25 = 162 \text{ MPa}$$

We have used the polar moment J to be

$$J = \pi(a^4 - b^4)/2 = \pi(a^2 - b^2)(a^2 + b^2) \cong \pi(a - b)(a + b)2R^2 \cong 4\pi t R^3$$

where R is the radius of the pressure vessel.

10.63 a)   Sum moments about the left end to find the force F in the wire:

$$2F = 3 \times (20 \times 2). \quad \therefore F = 60 \text{ kN}$$

$$\sigma = \frac{P}{A} = \frac{60}{\pi \times 0.01^2} = 1.91 \times 10^5 \text{ kPa}$$

10.64 d)   Since F was found to be 60 kN in Problem 10.63, we sum forces in the vertical direction to find

$$F_{end} = F - w \times L = 60 - 20 \times 2 = 20 \text{ kN acting down}$$

10.65 a)   The normal stress is found as follows:

$$\sigma = \frac{Mc}{I} = \frac{40 \times 0.1}{0.04 \times 0.2^3 / 12} = 150\,000 \text{ kPa}$$

10.66 d)   The vertical shear stress is found as follows:

$$\tau_{xy} = \frac{VQ}{Ib} = \frac{40 \times (0.1 \times 0.04) \times 0.05}{(0.04 \times 0.2^3 / 12) \times 0.04} = 7500 \text{ kPa}$$

10.67 b)   Add the wire elongation, the slope at the wire times the length and the deflection due to the distributed load:

$$\delta = \delta_{wire} + \frac{\delta_{wire}}{L} \times L + \delta_{load} = 2\frac{PL}{AE} + \frac{wL^4}{8EI}$$

$$= \left[2 \times \frac{60 \times 2}{0.04 \times 0.2} + \frac{20 \times 2^4}{8 \times 0.04 \times 0.2^3 / 12} \right] \frac{1}{207 \times 10^6} = 0.00739 \text{ m}$$

10.68 a)   Shear stress always exists on all four faces.

10.69 b) $\phi = \dfrac{TL}{JG} = \dfrac{750 \times 12}{28 \times 10^9 \times \pi \times 0.03^4 / 2} = 0.253$ rad or $14.5°$

10.70 c) Find the normal and shear stresses and use Mohr's circle:

$$\sigma_a = \frac{P}{A} = \frac{-60}{\pi \times 0.03^2} = -21\,220 \text{ kPa}$$

$$\tau_{\phi z} = \frac{Tr}{J} = \frac{750 \times 0.03}{\pi \times 0.03^4 / 2} = 17.68 \times 10^6 \text{ Pa}$$

$$\therefore \sigma_{\max} = \sqrt{17.68^2 + 10.6^2} + 10.6 = 31.2 \text{ MPa}$$

10.71 b) The angle on Mohr's circle is twice the angle on the actual shaft:

$$\tan 2\theta = \frac{\tau_{\phi z}}{\sigma_a / 2} = \frac{17.68}{21.2 / 2} = 1.67. \quad \therefore \theta = 29.5°$$

10.72 d) The temperature rise that causes buckling is found as follows (refer to the Civil Engineering section of the NCEES Handbook):

$$P_{cr} = \frac{\pi^2 EI}{k^2 L^2} . \quad \frac{\delta A E}{L} = \frac{\pi^2 EI}{k^2 L^2} . \quad \alpha L \Delta T \times \pi r^2 = \frac{\pi^2 (\pi r^4 / 4)}{k^2 L}$$

$$\therefore \Delta T = \frac{\pi^2 \times 0.03^2 / 4}{23 \times 10^{-6} \times 1^2 \times 12^2} = 0.67°C$$

10.73 d) Sum the deflections from the distributed load and the concentrated load (we use $L = 3$ m):

$$\delta = \frac{wL^4}{8EI} + \frac{wL^3}{6EI} \times L + \frac{PL^2}{6EI}(6L - L) = \frac{7wL^4}{24EI} + \frac{5PL^3}{6EI}$$

$$= \left(\frac{7 \times 40 \times 3^4}{24} + \frac{5 \times 200 \times 3^3}{6} \right) \bigg/ \left(207 \times 10^9 \times 0.1 \times 0.04^3 / 12 \right) = 0.0493 \text{ m}$$

10.74 a) Add a concentrated load at the right end to raise the beam to the original position, i.e., to raise the beam 0.0493 m:

$$F_{right\ end} = \frac{PL^3}{6EI} = \frac{P \times 6^3}{6 \times 207 \times 10^9 \times 0.1 \times 0.04^3 / 12} = 0.0493. \quad \therefore P = 151.2 \text{ N}$$

A free-body diagram of the beam gives

$$F_{left\ end} = 168.8 \text{ N}$$

10.75 c) A moment diagram provides the solution:

$$M_{left\ end} = 151.2 \times 6 - 200 \times 3 - 120 \times 1.5 = 127.2 \text{ N} \cdot \text{m}$$

The maximum moment occurs under the 200-N load:

$$M = 151.2 \times 3 = 453.6 \text{ N} \cdot \text{m}$$

Fluid Mechanics

by Merle C. Potter

Chapter 11

Strategic Study Note

If you're planning a short review and you're outlining the NCEES Handbook, omit reviewing the following Handbook subjects since they are not expected to be tested in the FE/EIT exam:

- Surface Tension and Capillarity
- Multipath Pipeline Problems
- Orifices
- Jet Propulsion
- Hazen-Williams Equation

Introduction

Fluid Mechanics deals with the statics, kinematics and dynamics of fluids, including both gases and liquids. Most fluid flows can be assumed to be incompressible (constant density); such flows include liquid flows as well as low speed gas flows (with velocities less than about 100 m/s). In addition, particular flows are either viscous or inviscid. Viscous effects dominate internal flows—such as flow in a pipe—and must be included near the boundaries of external flows (flow near the surface of an airfoil). Viscous flows are laminar if well-behaved, or turbulent if chaotic and highly fluctuating. Inviscid flows occur primarily as external flows outside the boundary layers that contain viscous effects. This review will focus on *Newtonian fluids*, that is, fluids which exhibit linear stress-strain-rate relationships; Newtonian fluids include air, water, oil, gasoline and tar. Please note that we have used upper case P for pressure in thermo, whereas in fluids we use lower case p; that's simply conventional.

We have used metric (SI) units only, since those are the units used in the actual exam. Make sure you are familiar with SI units. We have given some quantities in both sets of units since this book is also often used as a general reference.

Incompressible flows include low speed gas flows with velocities less than about 100 m/s.

- Inviscid flows occur primarily as external flows outside the boundary layers.

11.1 Fluid Properties

Some of the more common fluid properties are defined below and listed in Tables 11.1 and 11.2 for water and air at standard conditions.

density $\qquad \rho = \dfrac{M}{\rlap{\diagup}V}$ **(11.1.1)**

specific weight $\qquad \gamma = \rho g = \dfrac{W}{\rlap{\diagup}V}$ **(11.1.2)**

viscosity $\qquad \mu = \dfrac{\tau}{du/dy}$ **(11.1.3)**

kinematic viscosity $\qquad \nu = \dfrac{\mu}{\rho}$ **(11.1.4)**

specific gravity $\qquad SG = \dfrac{\rho_x}{\rho_{H_2O}}$ **(11.1.5)**

bulk modulus $\qquad K = -\rlap{\diagup}V \dfrac{\Delta p}{\Delta \rlap{\diagup}V}$ **(11.1.6)**

speed of sound $\qquad c_{liquid} = \sqrt{K/\rho} \qquad c_{gas} = \sqrt{kRT} \qquad (k_{air} = 1.4)$ **(11.1.7)**

TABLE 11.1 Properties

Property	Symbol	Definition	Water (20°C)	Air (STP)
density	ρ	$\dfrac{\text{mass}}{\text{volume}}$	$1000 \ \text{kg}/\text{m}^3$	$1.23 \ \text{kg}/\text{m}^3$
viscosity	μ	$\dfrac{\text{shear stress}}{\text{velocity gradient}}$	$10^{-3} \ \text{N·s}/\text{m}^2$	$2.0 \times 10^{-5} \ \text{N·s}/\text{m}^2$
kinematic viscosity	ν	$\dfrac{\text{viscosity}}{\text{density}}$	$10^{-6} \ \text{m}^2/\text{s}$	$1.6 \times 10^{-5} \ \text{m}^2/\text{s}$
speed of sound	c	velocity of propagation of a small wave	$1480 \ \text{m/s}$	$343 \ \text{m/s}$
specific weight	γ	$\dfrac{\text{weight}}{\text{volume}}$	$9800 \ \text{N}/\text{m}^3$	$12 \ \text{N}/\text{m}^3$
surface tension	σ	stored energy per unit area	$0.073 \ \text{J}/\text{m}^2$	
bulk modulus	K	$-\text{volume} \dfrac{\Delta \text{ pressure}}{\Delta \text{ volume}}$	$220 \times 10^4 \ \text{kPa}$	
vapor pressure	p_v	pressure at which liquid & vapor are in equilibrium	$2.45 \ \text{kPa}$	

Notes: • Kinematic viscosity is used because the ratio μ/ρ occurs frequently.
• Surface tension is used primarily for calculating capillary rise.
• Vapor pressure is used to predict *cavitation* which exists whenever the local pressure falls below the vapor pressure (for water at standard temperatures, the vapor pressure is close to absolute zero).

Vapor pressure is used to predict *cavitation* which exists whenever the local pressure falls below the vapor pressure.

TABLE 11.2 Properties of Water and Air (English Units)

Properties of Water (English)

Temperature °F	Density slugs/ft³	Viscosity lb-sec/ft²	Surface Tension lb/ft	Vapor Pressure lb/in²	Bulk Modulus lb/in²
32	1.94	3.75×10^{-5}	0.518×10^{-2}	0.089	293,000
40	1.94	3.23×10^{-5}	0.514×10^{-2}	0.122	294,000
50	1.94	2.74×10^{-5}	0.509×10^{-2}	0.178	305,000
60	1.94	2.36×10^{-5}	0.504×10^{-2}	0.256	311,000
70	1.94	2.05×10^{-5}	0.500×10^{-2}	0.340	320,000
80	1.93	1.80×10^{-5}	0.492×10^{-2}	0.507	322,000
90	1.93	1.60×10^{-5}	0.486×10^{-2}	0.698	323,000
100	1.93	1.42×10^{-5}	0.480×10^{-2}	0.949	327,000
120	1.92	1.17×10^{-5}	0.465×10^{-2}	1.69	333,000
140	1.91	0.98×10^{-5}	0.454×10^{-2}	2.89	330,000
160	1.90	0.84×10^{-5}	0.441×10^{-2}	4.74	326,000
180	1.88	0.73×10^{-5}	0.426×10^{-2}	7.51	318,000
200	1.87	0.64×10^{-5}	0.412×10^{-2}	11.53	308,000
212	1.86	0.59×10^{-5}	0.404×10^{-2}	14.7	300,000

Properties of Air at Standard Pressure (English)

Temperature °F	Density slugs/ft³	Viscosity lb-sec/ft²	Kinematic Viscosity ft²/sec
0	0.00268	3.28×10^{-7}	12.6×10^{-5}
20	0.00257	3.50×10^{-7}	13.6×10^{-5}
40	0.00247	3.62×10^{-7}	14.6×10^{-5}
60	0.00237	3.74×10^{-7}	15.8×10^{-5}
68	0.00233	3.81×10^{-7}	16.0×10^{-5}
80	0.00228	3.85×10^{-7}	16.9×10^{-5}
100	0.00220	3.96×10^{-7}	18.0×10^{-5}
120	0.00215	4.07×10^{-7}	18.9×10^{-5}

Properties of the Atmosphere (English)

Altitude ft	Temperature °F	Pressure lb/ft²	Density slugs/ft³	Kinematic Viscosity ft²/sec	Velocity of Sound ft/sec
0	59.0	2116	0.00237	1.56×10^{-4}	1117
1,000	55.4	2041	0.00231	1.60×10^{-4}	1113
2,000	51.9	1968	0.00224	1.64×10^{-4}	1109
5,000	41.2	1760	0.00205	1.77×10^{-4}	1098
10,000	23.4	1455	0.00176	2.00×10^{-4}	1078
15,000	5.54	1194	0.00150	2.28×10^{-4}	1058
20,000	−12.3	973	0.00127	2.61×10^{-4}	1037
25,000	−30.1	785	0.00107	3.00×10^{-4}	1016
30,000	−48.0	628	0.000890	3.47×10^{-4}	995
35,000	−65.8	498	0.000737	4.04×10^{-4}	973
36,000	−67.6	475	0.000709	4.18×10^{-4}	971
40,000	−67.6	392	0.000586	5.06×10^{-4}	971
50,000	−67.6	242	0.000362	8.18×10^{-4}	971
100,000	−67.6	22.4	3.31×10^{-5}	89.5×10^{-4}	971
110,000	−47.4	13.9	1.97×10^{-5}	1.57×10^{-6}	996
150,000	113.5	3.00	3.05×10^{-6}	13.2×10^{-6}	1174
200,000	160.0	0.665	6.20×10^{-7}	68.4×10^{-6}	1220

11·FLUIDS

TABLE 11.2 M Properties of Water and Air (Metric Units)

Properties of Water (Metric)

Temperature °C	Density kg/m³	Viscosity N·s/m²	Kinematic Viscosity m²/s	Bulk Modulus kPa	Surface Tension N/m	Vapor Pressure kPa
0	999.9	1.792×10^{-3}	1.792×10^{-6}	204×10^4	7.62×10^{-2}	0.588
5	1000.0	1.519×10^{-3}	1.519×10^{-6}	206×10^4	7.54×10^{-2}	0.882
10	999.7	1.308×10^{-3}	1.308×10^{-6}	211×10^4	7.48×10^{-2}	1.176
15	999.1	1.140×10^{-3}	1.141×10^{-6}	214×10^4	7.41×10^{-2}	1.666
20	998.2	1.005×10^{-3}	1.007×10^{-6}	220×10^4	7.36×10^{-2}	2.447
30	995.7	0.801×10^{-3}	0.804×10^{-6}	223×10^4	7.18×10^{-2}	4.297
40	992.2	0.656×10^{-3}	0.661×10^{-6}	227×10^4	7.01×10^{-2}	7.400
50	988.1	0.549×10^{-3}	0.556×10^{-6}	230×10^4	6.82×10^{-2}	12.220
60	983.2	0.469×10^{-3}	0.477×10^{-6}	228×10^4	6.68×10^{-2}	19.600
70	977.8	0.406×10^{-3}	0.415×10^{-6}	225×10^4	6.50×10^{-2}	30.700
80	971.8	0.357×10^{-3}	0.367×10^{-6}	221×10^4	6.30×10^{-2}	46.400
90	965.3	0.317×10^{-3}	0.328×10^{-6}	216×10^4	6.12×10^{-2}	68.200
100	958.4	0.284×10^{-3}	0.296×10^{-6}	207×10^4	5.94×10^{-2}	97.500

Properties of Air at Standard Pressure (Metric)

Temperature	Density kg/m³	Specific Weight N/m³	Viscosity N·s/m²	Kinematic Viscosity m²/s
−20°C	1.39	13.6	1.56×10^{-5}	1.13×10^{-5}
−10°C	1.34	13.1	1.62×10^{-5}	1.21×10^{-5}
0°C	1.29	12.6	1.68×10^{-5}	1.30×10^{-5}
10°C	1.25	12.2	1.73×10^{-5}	1.39×10^{-5}
20°C	1.20	11.8	1.80×10^{-5}	1.49×10^{-5}
40°C	1.12	11.0	1.91×10^{-5}	1.70×10^{-5}
60°C	1.06	10.4	2.03×10^{-5}	1.92×10^{-5}
80°C	0.99	9.71	2.15×10^{-5}	2.17×10^{-5}
100°C	0.94	9.24	2.28×10^{-5}	2.45×10^{-5}

Properties of the Atmosphere (Metric)

Altitude m	Temperature K	p/p_0 (p_0=101 kPa)	ρ/ρ_0 (ρ_0=1.23 kg/m³)
0	288.2	1.000	1.000
1 000	281.7	0.8870	0.9075
2 000	275.2	0.7846	0.8217
4 000	262.2	0.6085	0.6689
6 000	249.2	0.4660	0.5389
8 000	236.2	0.3519	0.4292
10 000	223.3	0.2615	0.3376
12 000	216.7	0.1915	0.2546
14 000	216.7	0.1399	0.1860
16 000	216.7	0.1022	0.1359
18 000	216.7	0.07466	0.09930
20 000	216.7	0.05457	0.07258
22 000	218.6	0.03995	0.05266
26 000	222.5	0.02160	0.02797
30 000	226.5	0.01181	0.01503
40 000	250.4	0.2834×10^{-2}	0.3262×10^{-2}
50 000	270.7	0.7874×10^{-3}	0.8383×10^{-3}
60 000	255.8	0.2217×10^{-3}	0.2497×10^{-3}
70 000	219.7	0.5448×10^{-4}	0.7146×10^{-4}
80 000	180.7	0.1023×10^{-4}	0.1632×10^{-4}
90 000	180.7	0.1622×10^{-5}	0.2588×10^{-5}

Example 11.1

A velocity difference of 2.4 m/s is measured between radial points 2 mm apart in a pipe in which 20°C water is flowing. What is the shear stress?

Solution. Using Eq. 11.1.3 we find, with $\mu = 10^{-3}$ N·s/m^2 from Table 11.1,

$$\tau = \mu \frac{du}{dy} \cong \mu \frac{\Delta u}{\Delta y} = 10^{-3} \frac{2.4}{0.002} = 1.2 \text{ Pa}$$

Example 11.2

Find the speed of sound in air at an elevation of 1000 m.

Solution. From Table 11.2 we find $T = 281.7$ K. Using Eq. 11.1.7, with $R = 287$ J/kg·K, there results

$$c = \sqrt{kRT} = \sqrt{1.4 \times 287 \times 281.7} = 336.4 \text{ m/s}$$

Note: Temperature must be absolute.

11.2 Fluid Statics

Typical problems in fluid statics involve manometers, forces on plane and curved surfaces, and buoyancy. All of these problems are solved by using the pressure distribution derived from summing forces on an infinitesimal element of fluid; in differential form with h positive downward, it is

$$dp = \gamma \, dh \tag{11.2.1}$$

For constant specific weight, assuming $p = 0$ at $h = 0$, we have

$$p = \gamma h \tag{11.2.2}$$

Equation 11.2.2 can be used to interpret manometer readings directly. By summing forces on elements of a plane surface, we would find the magnitude and location of a force acting on one side (refer to Fig. 11.1) to be

$$F = \gamma h_c A \tag{11.2.3}$$

NCEES form

$$y_p = y_c + \frac{I_c}{y_c A} \qquad\qquad z^* = \frac{I}{A Z_c} \tag{11.2.4}$$

where y_c (Z_c in NCEES handbook) locates the centroid and I_c is the second moment[†] of the area about the centroidal axis.

[†]The second moment I_c (often symbolized by $\bar{I}$) of three common areas:

$$I_c = \frac{bh^3}{12}$$

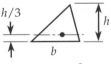

$$I_c = \frac{bh^3}{36}$$

$$I_c = \frac{\pi r^4}{4} = \frac{\pi d^4}{64}$$

> Typical problems in fluid statics involve manometers, forces on plane and curved surfaces, and buoyancy.

To solve problems involving curved surfaces, we simply draw a free-body diagram of the liquid contained above the curved surface and, using the above formulas, solve the problem.

To solve buoyancy-related problems we use Archimedes' principle which states: the buoyant force on a submerged object is equal to the weight of displaced liquid; that is,

$$F_b = \gamma V_{displaced} \tag{11.2.5}$$

To solve problems involving curved surfaces, we simply draw a free-body diagram of the liquid contained above the curved surface.

• To solve buoyancy-related problems we use Archimedes' principle.

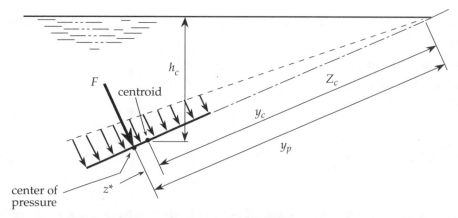

Figure 11.1 Force on a plane surface.

Example 11.3

Find the pressure difference between the air pipe and the water pipe.

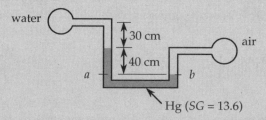

Solution. We first locate points "*a*" and "*b*" in the same fluid where $p_a = p_b$; then using Eq. 11.2.2

$$p_{water} + 9800 \times 0.3 + (9800 \times 13.6) \times 0.4 = p_{air} + \overset{neglect}{\cancel{\gamma_{air}}} \times 0.4$$

$$\therefore p_{air} - p_{water} = 56\,300\,\text{Pa} \quad \text{or} \quad 56.3\,\text{kPa}$$

Example 11.4

What is the pressure in pipe A?

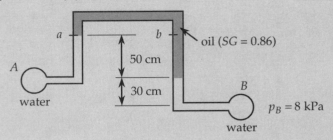

Solution. Locate points "a" and "b" so that $p_a = p_b$. Then, using Eq. 11.2.2 there results

$$p_A - 9800 \times 0.5 = 8000 - 9800 \times 0.3 - (9800 \times 0.86) \times 0.5$$

$$\therefore p_A = 5750 \text{ Pa} \quad \text{or} \quad 5.75 \text{ kPa}$$

Example 11.5

Find the force P needed to hold the 5-m-wide gate closed.

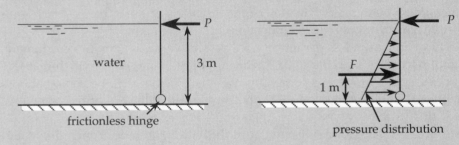

Solution. First, we note that the pressure distribution is triangular, as shown. Hence, the resultant force F acts 1/3 up from the hinge through the centroid of the triangular distribution. Summing moments about the hinge gives

$$F \times 1 = P \times 3$$

$$\therefore P = F/3 = \gamma h_c A/3$$

$$= 9800 \times \frac{3}{2} \times (5 \times 3)/3 = 73\,500 \text{ N}$$

Note: If the top of the gate were not at the free surface, we would find y_p using Eq. 11.2.4.

Example 11.6

A rectangular 4 m × 20 m vessel has a mass of 40 000 kg. How far will it sink in water when carrying a load of 100 000 kg?

Solution. The total weight of the loaded vessel must equal the weight of the displaced water. This is expressed as

$$W = \gamma \mathcal{V}$$

$$(40\ 000 + 100\ 000) \times 9.8 = 9800 \times 4 \times 20 \times h$$

$$\therefore h = 1.75\,\text{m}$$

11.3 Dimensionless Parameters and Similitude

> A dimensionless parameter involving several quantities is formed by combining the quantities so that the combination of quantities is dimensionless.

Information involving phenomena encountered in fluid mechanics is often presented in terms of dimensionless parameters. For example, the lift force F_L on a streamlined body can be represented by a lift coefficient C_L, a dimensionless parameter. Rather than plotting the lift force as a function of velocity, the lift coefficient could be plotted as a function of the Reynolds number, or the Mach number—two other dimensionless parameters.

To form dimensionless parameters, we first list various quantities encountered in fluid mechanics in Table 11.3. A dimensionless parameter involving several quantities is then formed by combining the quantities so that the combination of quantities is dimensionless. If all units are present in the quantities to be combined, this usually requires four quantities. For example, the four quantities power $\dot{W}$, flow rate Q, specific weight γ, and head H can be arranged as the dimensionless parameter $\dot{W}/\gamma QH$. Many dimensionless parameters have special significance; they are identified as follows:

$$\text{Reynolds number} = \frac{\text{inertial force}}{\text{viscous force}} \qquad \text{Re} = \frac{V\ell\rho}{\mu} = \frac{V\ell}{\nu}$$

$$\text{Froude number} = \frac{\text{inertial force}}{\text{gravity force}} \qquad \text{Fr} = \frac{V^2}{\ell g}$$

$$\text{Mach number} = \frac{\text{inertial force}}{\text{compressibility force}} \qquad \text{M} = \frac{V}{c}$$

$$\text{Weber number} = \frac{\text{inertial force}}{\text{surface tension force}} \qquad \text{We} = \frac{V^2\ell\rho}{\sigma}$$

$$\text{Pressure coefficient} = \frac{\text{pressure force}}{\text{inertial force}} \qquad C_p = \frac{\Delta p}{\frac{1}{2}\rho V^2}$$

$$\text{Drag coefficient} = \frac{\text{drag force}}{\text{inertial force}} \qquad C_D = \frac{\text{drag}}{\frac{1}{2}\rho V^2 A}$$

So, rather than writing the drag force on a cylinder as a function of length ℓ, diameter D, velocity V, viscosity μ, and density ρ, i.e.,

$$F_D = f(\ell, D, V, \mu, \rho) \qquad \text{(11.3.2)}$$

we express the relationship using dimensionless parameters as

$$C_D = f\left(\frac{V\rho D}{\mu}, \frac{\ell}{D}\right) \qquad \text{(11.3.3)}$$

The subject of similarity is encountered when attempting to use the results of a model study in predicting the performance of a prototype. We always assume *geometric similarity*, that is, the model is constructed to scale with the prototype; the length scale $\ell_p/\ell_m = \lambda$ is usually designated. The primary notion is simply stated: *Dimensionless quantities associated with the model are equal to corresponding dimensionless quantities associated with the prototype.* For example, if viscous effects dominate we would require

$$\text{Re}_m = \text{Re}_p \qquad \text{(11.3.4)}$$

Then if we are interested in, for example, the drag force, we would demand the dimensionless forces to be equal:

$$(F_D)^*_m = (F_D)^*_p \qquad \text{(11.3.5)}$$

where the asterisk * denotes a dimensionless quantity. Since force is pressure (ρV^2 from Bernoulli's equation) times area (ℓ^2), the above equation can be expressed in terms of dimensional quantities:

$$\frac{(F_D)_m}{\rho_m V_m^2 \ell_m^2} = \frac{(F_D)_p}{\rho_p V_p^2 \ell_p^2} \qquad \text{(11.3.6)}$$

This would allow us to predict the drag force expected on the prototype as

$$(F_D)_p = (F_D)_m \frac{\rho_p \ell_p^2 V_p^2}{\rho_m \ell_m^2 V_m^2} \qquad \text{(11.3.7)}$$

The same strategy is used for other quantities of interest.

> The subject of similarity is encountered when attempting to use the results of a model study to predict the performance of a prototype.

TABLE 11.3 Symbols and Dimensions of Quantities Used in Fluid Mechanics

Quantity	Symbol	Dimensions	Quantity	Symbol	Dimensions
Length	ℓ	L	Pressure	p	M/LT^2
Time	t	T	Stress	τ	M/LT^2
Mass	m	M	Density	ρ	M/L^3
Force	F	ML/T^2	Specific Weight	γ	M/L^2T^2
Velocity	V	L/T	Viscosity	μ	M/LT
Acceleration	a	L/T^2	Kinematic Viscosity	v	L^2/T
Frequency	ω	T^{-1}	Work	W	ML^2/T^2
Gravity	g	L/T^2	Power	$\dot{W}$	ML^2/T^3
Area	A	L^2	Heat Flux	$\dot{Q}$	ML^2/T^3
Flow Rate	Q	L^3/T	Surface Tension	σ	M/T^2
Mass Flux	$\dot{m}$	M/T	Bulk Modulus	K	M/LT^2

Example 11.7

Combine $\dot{W}$, Q, γ, and H as a dimensionless parameter.

Solution. First, let us note the dimensions on each variable:

$$\left[\dot{W}\right] = \frac{ML^2}{T^3} \qquad [Q] = \frac{L^3}{T} \qquad [\gamma] = \frac{M}{L^2 T^2} \qquad [H] = L$$

Now, by inspection we simply form the dimensionless parameter. Note that to eliminate the mass unit, $\dot{W}$ and γ must appear as the ratio, $\dot{W}/\gamma$. This puts an extra time unit in the denominator; hence, Q must appear with γ as $\dot{W}/\gamma Q$. Now, we inspect the length unit and find one length unit still in the numerator. This requires H in the denominator giving the dimensionless parameter as

$$\frac{\dot{W}}{\gamma Q H}$$

Example 11.8

If a flow rate of 0.2 m^3/s is measured over a 9-to-1 scale model of a weir, what flow rate can be expected on the prototype?

Solution. First, we recognize that gravity forces dominate (as they do in all problems involving weirs, dams, ships, and open channels), and demand that

$$\mathrm{Fr}_p = \mathrm{Fr}_m \qquad \text{or} \qquad \frac{V_p{}^2}{\ell_p g_p} = \frac{V_m{}^2}{\ell_m g_m}$$

$$\therefore \frac{V_p}{V_m} = \sqrt{\frac{\ell_p}{\ell_m}} = 3$$

The dimensionless flow rates are now equated:

$$Q_p{}^* = Q_m{}^*$$

$$\frac{Q_p}{V_p \ell_p{}^2} = \frac{Q_m}{V_m \ell_m{}^2}$$

recognizing that velocity times area ($V \times \ell^2$) give the flow rate. We have

$$Q_p = Q_m \frac{V_p \ell_p{}^2}{V_m \ell_m{}^2}$$

$$= 0.2 \times 3 \times 9^2 = 48.6 \ \mathrm{m^3/s}$$

11.4 Control Volume Equations

When solving problems in fluid dynamics, we are most often interested in volumes into which and from which fluid flows; such volumes are called *control volumes*. The control volume equations include the conservation of mass (the continuity equation), Newton's second law (the momentum equation), and the first law of thermodynamics (the energy equation). We will not derive the equations but simply state them and then apply them to some situations of interest. We will assume *steady, incompressible flow* with *uniform velocity profiles*. The equations take the following forms:

continuity: $A_1 V_1 = A_2 V_2$ **(11.4.1)**

momentum: $\sum \mathbf{F} = \rho Q (\mathbf{V}_2 - \mathbf{V}_1)$ **(11.4.2)**

energy $-\dfrac{\dot{W}_S}{\gamma Q} = \dfrac{V_2^2 - V_1^2}{2g} + \dfrac{p_2 - p_1}{\gamma} + z_2 - z_1 + h_f$ **(11.4.3)**

where

$Q = AV = $ flow rate **(11.4.4a)**

$\dot{W}_S = $ shaft work (positive for a turbine)

$h_f = $ head loss

$\dot{m} = \rho AV = $ mass flow rate (mass flux) **(11.4.4b)**

If there is no shaft work term $\dot{W}_S$ (due to a pump or turbine) between the two sections and the losses are zero, then the energy equation reduces to the *Bernoulli equation*, namely,

$$\dfrac{V_2^2}{2g} + \dfrac{p_2}{\gamma} + z_2 = \dfrac{V_1^2}{2g} + \dfrac{p_1}{\gamma} + z_1 \qquad \textbf{(11.4.5)}$$

We should note that for a turbulent flow the velocity profile is essentially uniform, so the above equations are valid for the vast majority of flows since most flows are turbulent. For a laminar flow, however, the velocity profile in a pipe or a channel is parabolic, so the above equations must be modified. Since laminar flows are of little engineering interest we do not concern ourselves with such modifications.

For flow in a pipe, the head loss can be related to the friction factor by the *Darcy-Weisbach equation*,

$$h_f = f \dfrac{L}{D} \dfrac{V^2}{2g} \qquad \textbf{(11.4.6)}$$

where the friction factor is related to the Reynolds number, Re $= VD/\nu$, and the relative roughness e/D by the Moody diagram, Fig. 11.2; the roughness e is given for various materials. Note that for completely turbulent flows (those in the "wholly rough" region of Fig. 11.2), the friction factor is constant so that the head loss varies with the square of the velocity. For laminar flow the friction factor is $f = 64/$Re so that the head loss is directly proportional to the velocity. We can then show that, for laminar flow in a horizontal pipe,

$$Q = \dfrac{\pi^4 \Delta p}{128 \mu L} \qquad \textbf{(11.4.7)}$$

If the pipe is on an angle simply replace Δp with $\Delta p - \gamma(z_2 - z_1)$.

Control volumes are volumes into which and/or from which fluid flows.

•For a turbulent flow the velocity profile is essentially uniform.

•For completely turbulent flows, the friction factor is constant so that the head loss varies with the square of the velocity.

11-FLUIDS

For sudden geometry changes, such as valves, elbows, and enlargements, the head loss (often called a *minor loss*) is determined by using a loss coefficient C; that is,

$$h_f = C \frac{V^2}{2g} \tag{11.4.8}$$

where V is the characteristic velocity associated with the device. Typical values are given in Table 11.4.

In engineering practice, the loss coefficient is often expressed as an *equivalent length* L_e of pipe; if that is done, the equivalent length is expressed as

$$L_e = C \frac{D}{f} \tag{11.4.9}$$

> 🔑 If the cross section is non-circular, a good approximation can be obtained by using the hydraulic radius.

The above analysis, using the Moody diagram and the loss coefficients on the following page, can be applied directly to only circular cross-section conduits; if the cross section is non-circular but fairly "open" (rectangular with aspect ratio less than four, oval, or triangular), a good approximation can be obtained by using the *hydraulic radius* defined by

$$R_H = A/P \tag{11.4.10}$$

where A is the cross sectional flow area and P is the *wetted perimeter* (that perimeter where the fluid is in contact with the solid boundary). Using this formula the diameter of a pipe is $D = 4R_H$. The Reynolds number then takes the form

$$\text{Re} = \frac{4VR_H}{\nu} \tag{11.4.11}$$

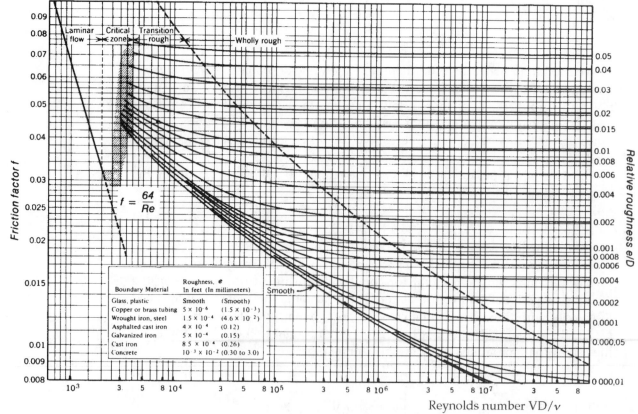

Figure 11.2 The Moody Diagram.

If the shape is not "open," such as flow in an anulus, the error in using the above relationships will be quite significant.

A final note in this article defines the energy grade line (*EGL*) and the hydraulic grade line (*HGL*). The distance $(z + p/\gamma)$ above the datum (the zero elevation line) locates the *HGL*, and the distance $(z + p/\gamma + V^2/2g)$ above the datum locates the *EGL*. These are shown in Fig. 11.3. Note that the pump head H_P is given by

$$H_P = -\frac{\dot{W}_P}{\gamma Q} \qquad \text{(11.4.12)}$$

The negative sign is necessary since the pump power $\dot{W}_P$ is negative.

> The hydraulic grade line is the distance $(z + p/\gamma)$ above the datum.

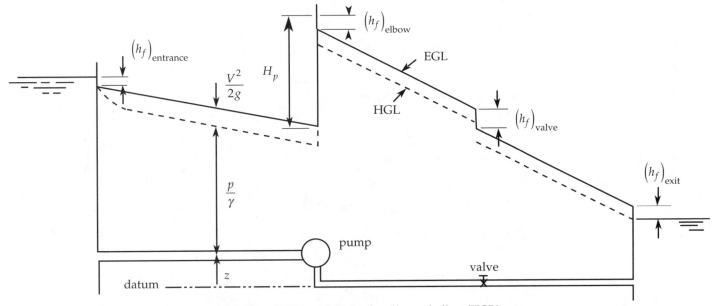

Figure 11.3 The energy grade line (*EGL*) and the hydraulic grade line (*HGL*).

TABLE 11.4 Loss Coefficients

Geometry	C	Geometry	C
Globe valve (fully open)	6.4	Reentrant entrance	0.8
(half open)	9.5	Well-rounded entrance	0.03++
Angle valve (fully open)	5.0	Pipe exit	1.0
Swing check valve		Sudden contraction (2 to 1)*	0.25++
(fully open)	2.5	(5 to 1)*	0.41++
Gate valve (fully open)	0.2	(10 to 1)*	0.46++
(half open)	5.6	Orifice plate (1.5 to 1)*	0.85
(one-quarter open)	24.0	(2 to 1)*	3.4
Close return bend	2.2	(4 to 1)*	29
Standard tee	1.8	Sudden enlargement+ $(1 - A_1/A_2)^2$	
Standard elbow	0.9	90° miter bend	
Medium sweep elbow	0.7	(without vanes)	1.1
Long sweep elbow	0.6	(with vanes)	0.2
45° elbow	0.4	General contraction	
Square-edged entrance	0.5	(30° included angle)	0.02
		(70° included angle)	0.07

*Area ratio +Based on V_1 ++Based on V_2

11-FLUIDS

Example 11.9

The velocity in a 2-cm-dia pipe is 10 m/s. If the pipe enlarges to 4-cm-dia, find the velocity and the flow rate.

Solution. The continuity equation is used as follows:

$$A_1 V_1 = A_2 V_2$$

$$\frac{\pi D_1^2}{4} V_1 = \frac{\pi D_2^2}{4} V_2$$

$$\therefore V_2 = V_1 \frac{D_1^2}{D_2^2} = 10 \times \frac{2^2}{4^2} = 2.5 \text{ m/s}$$

The flow rate is

$$Q = A_1 V_1$$

$$= \pi \times 0.01^2 \times 10 = 0.00314 \text{ m}^3/\text{s}$$

Example 11.10

What force is exerted on the joint if the flow rate of water is 0.01 m^3/s?

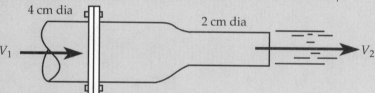

4 cm dia

2 cm dia

V_1

V_2

Solution. The velocities are found to be

$$V_1 = \frac{Q}{A_1} = \frac{0.01}{\pi \times 0.02^2} = 7.96 \text{ m/s}$$

$$V_2 = \frac{Q}{A_2} = \frac{0.01}{\pi \times 0.01^2} = 31.8 \text{ m/s}$$

Bernoulli's equation is used to find the pressure at section 1. There results, using $p_2 = 0$ (atmospheric pressure is zero gage),

$$\frac{V_1^2}{2g} + \frac{p_1}{\gamma} = \frac{V_2^2}{2g} + \frac{p_2}{\gamma}$$

$$\frac{7.96^2}{2 \times 9.8} + \frac{p_1}{9800} = \frac{31.8^2}{2 \times 9.8}. \qquad \therefore p_1 = 474\ 000 \text{ Pa}$$

Now, using the control volume shown, we can apply the momentum equation (11.4.2) in the x-direction:

$p_1 A_1 \longrightarrow \qquad F_j \longleftarrow \qquad$ ——— x

F_j = the force of the
contraction on the water

$$p_1 A_1 - F_j = \rho Q(V_2 - V_1)$$

$$474\ 000 \times \pi \times 0.02^2 - F_j = 1000 \times 0.01(31.8 - 7.96)$$

$$\therefore F_j = 357 \text{ N}$$

Note: Remember, all forces on the control volume must be included. Never forget the pressure force.

Example 11.11

What is the force F needed to hold the plate as shown?

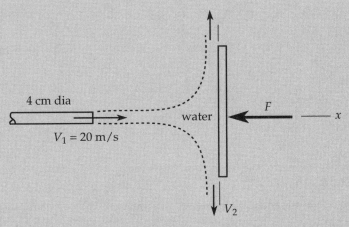

Solution. The momentum equation (11.4.2) is a vector equation; applying it in the x-direction results in

$$-F = \rho Q(\overset{0}{\cancel{V_{2x}}} - V_{1x}).$$

$$\therefore F = \rho A_1 V_1^2$$

$$= 1000 \times \pi \times 0.02^2 \times 20^2 = 503 \text{ N}.$$

Note: Since the water is open to the atmosphere, $p_2 = p_1$, and if we neglect elevation changes, Bernoulli's equation requires $V_2 = V_1$. However, here $V_{2x} = 0$ so V_2 was not necessary.

Example 11.12

Find the power produced by this blade. It's one of a series.

$V_1 = 100 \text{ m/s}$

$60°$

$v = 40 \text{ m/s}$

2 cm dia

Solution. The relative velocity of the water over the blade remains constant. It is $v_r = 100 - 40 = 60 \text{ m/s}$. Then

$$F_x = \rho Q\left[(v_{r2})_x - (v_{r1})_x\right] = 1000 \times \left(\pi \times .01^2 \times 100\right)[60\cos 60° - 60] = -942 \text{ N}.$$

The power is (only F_x produces power)

$$\dot{W} = F_x \times v = 942 \times 40 = 37\,700 \text{ W} \quad \text{or} \quad 37.7 \text{ kW}$$

Example 11.13

What is the pump power needed to increase the pressure by 600 kPa in a 8-cm-dia pipe transporting 0.04 m^3/s of water?

Solution. The energy equation (11.4.3) is used:

$$-\frac{\dot{W}_S}{\gamma Q} = \frac{V_2^2 - V_1^2}{2g}^{\,0} + \frac{p_2 - p_1}{\gamma} + z_2 - z_1^{\,0}$$

$$-\frac{-\dot{W}_P}{9800 \times 0.04} = \frac{600\ 000}{9800} \qquad \therefore \dot{W}_P = 24\ 000\ \text{W} \quad \text{or} \quad 24\ \text{kW}.$$

Example 11.14

A pitot tube is used to measure the velocity in the pipe. If $V = 15$ m/s, what is H?

Solution. Bernoulli's equation can be used to relate the pressure at pt. 2, which is just inside the tube, to the velocity V. It gives

$$\frac{V_2^2}{2g}^{\,0} + \frac{p_2}{\gamma} + z_2 = \frac{V_1^2}{2g} + \frac{p_1}{\gamma} + z_1$$

$$\therefore p_2 = p_1 + \gamma \frac{V_1^2}{2g}$$

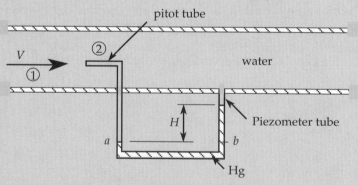

The manometer allows us to write

$$p_a = p_b$$

$$\gamma H + p_2 = \gamma_{Hg} H + p_1$$

where the distance from pt. 2 to the top of H balances on each side. Substituting for p_2 we have

$$\gamma H + p_1 + \gamma \frac{V_1^2}{2g} = \gamma_{Hg} H + p_1$$

$$\therefore H = \frac{\gamma}{\gamma_{Hg} - \gamma} \cdot \frac{V_1^2}{2g}$$

$$= \frac{9800}{13.6 \times 9800 - 9800} \cdot \frac{15^2}{2 \times 9.8} = 0.91\ \text{m}$$

Note: The piezometer tube on the right leg measures the pressure p_1 in the pipe.

Example 11.15

For a water flow rate of 0.02 m^3/s, find the turbine output if it is 80% efficient.

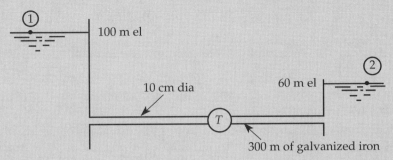

Solution. The energy equation (11.4.3) takes the form:

$$-\frac{\dot{W}_T}{\gamma Q} = \frac{V_2^2 - \cancelto{0}{V_1^2}}{2g} + \cancelto{0}{\frac{p_2 - p_1}{\gamma}} + z_2 - z_1 + \left(C_{inlet} + C_{exit} + f\frac{L}{D} \right)\frac{V^2}{2g}$$

where Eqs. 11.4.6 and 11.4.8 have been used for the head loss. To find f, using the Moody diagram, we need

$$V = \frac{0.02}{\pi \times 0.05^2} = 2.55 \text{ m/s}, \quad Re = \frac{2.55 \times 0.1}{10^{-6}} = 2.55 \times 10^5, \quad \frac{e}{D} = \frac{0.15}{100} = 0.0015$$

$$\therefore f = 0.022$$

Using the loss coefficients from Table 11.4 we have

$$-\frac{\dot{W}_T}{9800 \times 0.02} = 60 - 100 + \left(0.5 + 1.0 + 0.022 \frac{300}{0.1} \right)\frac{2.55^2}{2 \times 9.8}$$

$$\therefore \dot{W}_T = 3450 \text{ W} \quad \text{and} \quad \left(\dot{W}_T \right)_{actual} = 3450 \times 0.8 = 2760 \text{ W}$$

Example 11.16

The pressure drop over a 4-cm-dia, 300-m-long section of pipe is measured to be 120 kPa. If the elevation drops 25 m over that length of pipe and the flow rate of water is 0.003 m^3/s, calculate the friction factor and the power loss.

Solution. The velocity is found to be

$$V = \frac{Q}{A} = \frac{0.003}{\pi \times 0.02^2} = 2.39 \text{ m/s}$$

The energy equation (11.4.3) with Eq. 11.4.6 then gives

$$-\cancelto{0}{\frac{\dot{W}_S}{\gamma Q}} = \frac{V_2^2 - \cancelto{0}{V_1^2}}{2g} + \frac{p_2 - p_1}{\gamma} + z_2 - z_1 + f\frac{L}{D}\frac{V^2}{2g}$$

$$0 = -\frac{120\,000}{9800} - 25 + f\frac{300}{0.04}\frac{2.39^2}{2 \times 9.8}$$

$$\therefore f = 0.0170, \quad h_f = 37.2 \text{ m}$$

The power loss is

$$\dot{W}_{friction} = h_f \gamma Q$$
$$= 37.2 \times 9800 \times 0.003 = 1095 \text{ W}$$

where the head loss h_f is analogous to the pump head in Eq. 11.4.12.

Example 11.17

Estimate the loss coefficient for an orifice plate if $A_1/A_0 = 2$.

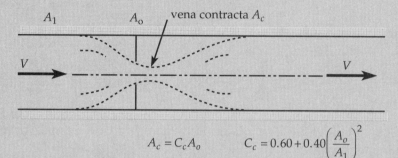

$$A_c = C_c A_o \qquad C_c = 0.60 + 0.40\left(\frac{A_o}{A_1}\right)^2$$

Solution. We approximate the flow situation shown as a gradual contraction up to A_c and a sudden enlargement from A_c back to A_1. The loss coefficient for the contraction is very small so it will be neglected. For the enlargement, we need to know A_c; it is

$$A_c = C_c A_0 = \left[0.6 + 0.4\left(\frac{A_0}{A_1}\right)^2\right]A_0 = \left[0.6 + 0.4\left(\frac{1}{2}\right)^2\right]\frac{A_1}{2} = 0.35 A_1$$

Using the loss coefficient for an enlargement from Table 11.4, there results

$$h_f = C\frac{V_c^2}{2g}$$

$$= \left(1 - \frac{A_c}{A_1}\right)^2\frac{V_c^2}{2g} = (1 - 0.35)^2\frac{1}{0.35^2}\frac{V_1^2}{2g} = 3.45\frac{V_1^2}{2g}$$

where the continuity equation $A_c V_c = A_1 V_1$ has been used. The loss coefficient for the orifice plate is thus

$$C = 3.4$$

Note: Two-place accuracy is assumed since C_c is known to only two significant figures.

11.5 Open Channel Flow

If liquid flows down a slope in an open channel at a constant depth, the energy equation (11.4.3) takes the form

$$-\frac{\dot{W}_s}{\gamma Q}^{\,0} = \frac{V_2^2 - V_1^2}{2g}^{\,0} + \frac{p_2 - p_1}{\gamma}^{\,0} + z_2 - z_1 + h_f \qquad \textbf{(11.5.1)}$$

which shows that the head loss is given by

$$h_f = z_1 - z_2 = LS \qquad \textbf{(11.5.2)}$$

where L is the length of the channel between the two sections and S is the slope. Since we normally have small angles, we can use $S = \tan\theta = \sin\theta = \theta$ where θ is the angle that the channel makes with the horizontal.

The *Chezy-Manning equation* is used to relate the flow rate to the slope and the cross section; it is

$$Q = \frac{1.0}{n} A R_H^{2/3} S^{1/2} \quad \text{(metric-SI)} \qquad \textbf{(11.5.3)}$$

where R_H is the hydraulic radius given by Eq. 11.4.9, A is the cross sectional area, and n is the Manning n, given in Table 11.5. The constant 1.0 must be replaced by 1.49 if English units are used. The most efficient cross section occurs when the width is twice the depth for a rectangular section, and when the sides are equal in length to the bottom width and make angles of 60° with the horizontal for a trapezoidal cross section.

The *Chezy-Manning equation* is used to relate the flow rate to the slope and the cross section.

TABLE 11.5 Average Values* of the Manning n

Wall Material	Manning n	Wall Material	Manning n
Planed wood	.012	Concrete pipe	.015
Unplaned wood	.013	Riveted steel	.017
Finished concrete	.012	Earth, straight	.022
Unfinished concrete	.014	Corrugated metal flumes	.025
Sewer Pipe	.013	Rubble	.03
Brick .016		Earth with stones and weeds	.035
Cast iron, wrought iron .015		Mountain streams	.05

*If $R_H > 3$ m, increase n by 15%.

Example 11.18

A 2-m-dia concrete pipe transports water at a depth of 0.8 m. What is the flow rate if the slope is 0.001?

Solution. Calculate the geometric properties:

$$\alpha = \sin^{-1}\frac{0.2}{1.0} = 11.54°$$

$$\therefore \theta = 156.9°$$

$$A = \pi \times 1^2 \times \frac{156.9}{360} - 0.2 \times \cos 11.54° \times \frac{1}{2} \times 2 = 1.174 \text{ m}^2$$

$$P = \pi \times 2 \times \frac{156.9}{360} = 2.738 \text{ m}$$

For concrete pipe, $n = 0.015$, so

$$Q = \frac{1.0}{n} A R_H^{2/3} S^{1/2} = \frac{1.0}{0.015} \times 1.174 \times \left(\frac{1.174}{2.738}\right)^{2/3} \times 0.001^{1/2} = 1.41 \text{ m}^3/\text{s}$$

11·FLUIDS

11.6 External Flow

Flows of engineering interest around a body are typically high-Reynolds-number flows. Most often separation occurs, except for a streamlined body such as the wings of an aircraft. Separation leads to relatively high drag but often it cannot be avoided; examples include flow of air around automobiles, golf balls, billboards and parachutes. The drag force F_D is calculated using the drag coefficient C_D:

$$F_D = \frac{1}{2} \rho V^2 A C_D \qquad (11.6.1)$$

where A represents the projected area of the body (for a sphere A would be the area of a circle, and for a cylinder A would be the area of a rectangle). The drag coefficient must be given for a particular body, or it can be read from Figure 11.4 for a sphere, cylinder or disk.

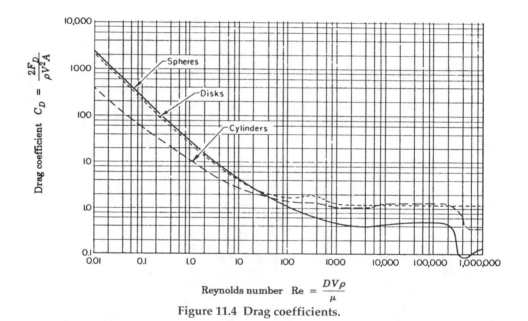

Reynolds number $\quad \text{Re} = \dfrac{DV\rho}{\mu}$

Figure 11.4 Drag coefficients.

Example 11.19

Estimate the maximum moment that must be resisted by the base of a 4m x 10m billboard due to a 80 km/hr wind. The billboard is supported by a 15-cm-diameter, 12-m-high pole. Assume:

$$\left(C_D\right)_{\text{rectangle}} = 1.2, \quad \rho_{\text{air}} = 1.2 \text{ kg/m}^3, \quad \text{and} \quad \nu_{\text{air}} = 1.5 \times 10^{-5} \text{ m}^2/\text{s}$$

Solution. We calculate the Reynolds number for the pole to be

$$\text{Re} = \frac{VD}{\nu} = \frac{(80 \times 1000/3600) \times 0.15}{1.5 \times 10^{-5}} = 2.22 \times 10^5$$

From Fig. 11.4 the drag coefficient is about 1.0. The forces on the pole and billboard are

$$(F_D)_{\text{pole}} = \frac{1}{2}\rho V^2 A C_D$$

$$= \frac{1}{2} \times 1.2 \times 22.22^2 (12 \times 0.15) \times 1.0 = 533 \text{ N}$$

$$(F_D)_{\text{billboard}} = \frac{1}{2}\rho V^2 A C_D$$

$$= \frac{1}{2} \times 1.2 \times 22.22^2 \times (4 \times 10) \times 1.2 = 14\ 220 \text{ N}$$

The moment to be resisted is then

$$M = (F_D)_{\text{pole}} \times \frac{H}{2} + (F_D)_{\text{billboard}} \times \left(h + \frac{h}{2}\right)$$

$$= 533 \times \frac{12}{2} + 14\ 220 \times \left(12 + \frac{4}{2}\right) = 202\ 000 \quad \text{N} \cdot \text{m}$$

11.7 Compressible Flow

A gas flow with a Mach number below 0.3 (at standard conditions this means velocities less than about 100 m/s) can be treated as an incompressible flow, as in previous articles. If the Mach number is greater than 0.3, the density variation must be accounted for. For such problems, we use the control volume equation as

continuity: $$\rho_1 A_1 V_1 = \rho_2 A_2 V_2 \qquad \textbf{(11.7.1)}$$

momentum (x-direction): $$\sum F = \dot{m}(V_2 - V_1) \qquad \textbf{(11.7.2)}$$

energy: $$\frac{\dot{Q} - \dot{W}_s}{\dot{m}} = \frac{V_2^2 - V_1^2}{2} + c_p(T_2 - T_1) \qquad \textbf{(11.7.3)}$$

where

$$\dot{m} = \rho A V = \text{mass flux} \qquad \textbf{(11.7.4)}$$

$$c_p = \text{constant pressure specific heat}$$

We often use the ideal gas relations (they become inaccurate at high pressure or low temperature)

$$p = \rho RT \qquad c_p = c_v + R \qquad k = c_p / c_v \qquad \textbf{(11.7.5)}$$

The energy equation for an ideal gas takes the form

$$\frac{\dot{Q} - \dot{W}_S}{\dot{m}} = \frac{V_2^2 - V_1^2}{2} + \frac{k}{k-1}\left(\frac{p_2}{\rho_2} - \frac{p_1}{\rho_1}\right) \qquad \textbf{(11.7.6)}$$

We recall that the speed of sound and Mach number are given by

$$c = \sqrt{kRT} \qquad \text{M} = V/c \qquad \textbf{(11.7.7)}$$

Subsonic flow occurs whenever M < 1 and supersonic flow whenever M > 1. In subsonic flows, losses are quite small and isentropic flows can usually be assumed; thus, we can relate the properties by the isentropic relations

$$\frac{T_2}{T_1} = \left(\frac{p_2}{p_1}\right)^{\frac{k-1}{k}} \qquad \frac{p_2}{p_1} = \left(\frac{\rho_2}{\rho_1}\right)^{k} \qquad \textbf{(11.7.8)}$$

🔑 If the Mach number is greater than 0.3, the density variation must be accounted for.

•In subsonic flows, losses are quite small and isentropic flows can usually be assumed.

11-FLUIDS

For air $k = 1.4$, $c_p = 1.00$ kJ/kg·K, $R = 0.287$ kJ/kg·K. The isentropic flow table (Table 11.6) can also be used.

For supersonic flows, shock waves are encountered; across a normal shock wave, Table 11.7 can be used with isentropic flow assumed before and after the shock. If the entropy change is desired, it is given by

> To obtain a supersonic flow, the flow must first accelerate through a converging section to a throat, then an enlarging section will allow it to reach supersonic speed.

$$\Delta s = c_p \ln \frac{T_2}{T_1} - R \ln \frac{p_2}{p_1} \qquad (11.7.9)$$

Supersonic flow behaves quite differently from subsonic flow; its velocity increases with increasing area and decreases with decreasing area. Hence, to obtain a supersonic flow from a reservoir, the flow must first accelerate through a converging section to a throat where M = 1; then an enlarging section will allow it to reach supersonic speed with M > 1. Supersonic flow cannot occur in a converging section only.

Example 11.20

Air is flowing from a 20°C reservoir to the atmosphere through the converging-diverging nozzle shown. What reservoir pressure will locate a normal shock wave at the exit? Also, find V_C and the mass flux.

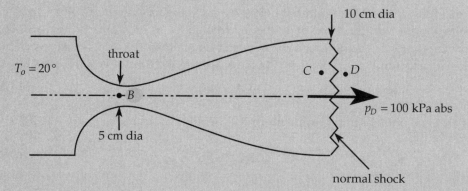

Solution. We know that at the throat the Mach number is unity. Such an area is the *critical area* and is designated A^* in the isentropic flow table. Between points B and C we have

$$\frac{A_C}{A_B} = \frac{A}{A^*} = \frac{\pi \times 5^2}{\pi \times 2.5^2} = 4$$

Using Table 11.6 we find

$$M_C = 2.94$$

Then from Table 11.7 we find, across the shock,

$$\frac{p_C}{p_D} = 9.92 \qquad \therefore p_C = 9.92 \times 100 = 992 \text{ kPa}$$

The isentropic flow Table 11.6 then gives, at M = 2.94,

$$\frac{p_C}{p_o} = 0.0298 \qquad \therefore p_o = \frac{992}{0.0298} = 33\,300 \text{ kPa}$$

To find V_C we must determine T_C. Using Table 11.6 at M = 2.94 we find

$$\frac{T_C}{T_o} = 0.3665 \qquad \therefore T_C = (273 + 20) \times 0.3665 = 107.4 \text{ K}$$

The velocity is then found to be

$$V_C = M_C \sqrt{kRT_C}$$
$$= 2.94\sqrt{1.4 \times 287 \times 107.4} = 611 \text{ m/s}$$

The mass flux is

$$\dot{m} = \rho_C A_C V_C$$
$$= \frac{p_C}{RT_C} A_C V_C = \frac{992\,000}{287 \times 107.4} \times \pi \times 0.05^2 \times 611 = 154 \text{ kg/s}$$

TABLE 11.6 Isentropic Flow (air, $k = 1.4$)

M_1	A/A^*	p/p_0	ρ/ρ_0	T/T_0	V/V^*
0.00	∞	1.000	1.000	1.000	0.000
0.05	11.591	0.998	0.999	1.000	0.055
0.10	5.822	0.993	0.995	0.998	0.109
0.15	3.910	0.984	0.989	0.996	0.164
0.20	2.964	0.972	0.980	0.992	0.218
0.25	2.403	0.957	0.969	0.988	0.272
0.30	2.035	0.939	0.956	0.982	0.326
0.35	1.778	0.919	0.941	0.976	0.379
0.40	1.590	0.896	0.924	0.969	0.431
0.45	1.449	0.870	0.906	0.961	0.483
0.50	1.340	0.843	0.885	0.952	0.535
0.55	1.255	0.814	0.863	0.943	0.585
0.60	1.188	0.784	0.840	0.933	0.635
0.65	1.136	0.753	0.816	0.922	0.684
0.70	1.094	0.721	0.792	0.911	0.732
0.75	1.062	0.689	0.766	0.899	0.779
0.80	1.038	0.656	0.740	0.887	0.825
0.85	1.021	0.624	0.714	0.874	0.870
0.90	1.009	0.591	0.687	0.861	0.915
0.95	1.002	0.559	0.660	0.847	0.958
1.00	1.000	0.528	0.634	0.833	1.000
1.10	1.008	0.468	0.582	0.805	1.081
1.20	1.030	0.412	0.531	0.776	1.158
1.30	1.066	0.361	0.483	0.747	1.231
1.40	1.115	0.314	0.437	0.718	1.300
1.50	1.176	0.272	0.395	0.690	1.365
1.60	1.250	0.235	0.356	0.661	1.425
1.70	1.338	0.203	0.320	0.634	1.482
1.80	1.439	0.174	0.287	0.607	1.536
1.90	1.555	0.149	0.257	0.581	1.586
2.00	1.687	0.128	0.230	0.556	1.633
2.10	1.837	0.109	0.206	0.531	1.677
2.20	2.005	0.094	0.184	0.508	1.718
2.30	2.193	0.080	0.165	0.486	1.756
2.40	2.403	0.068	0.147	0.465	1.792
2.50	2.637	0.059	0.132	0.444	1.826
2.60	2.896	0.050	0.118	0.425	1.857
2.70	3.183	0.043	0.106	0.407	1.887
2.80	3.500	0.037	0.085	0.389	1.914
2.90	3.850	0.032	0.085	0.373	1.940
3.00	4.235	0.027	0.076	0.357	1.964
3.50	6.790	0.013	0.045	0.290	2.064
4.00	10.719	0.007	0.028	0.238	2.138
4.50	16.562	0.003	0.017	0.198	2.194
5.00	25.000	0.002	0.011	0.167	2.236
5.50	36.869	0.001	0.008	0.142	2.269
6.00	53.180	0.001	0.005	0.122	2.295
6.50	75.134	0.000	0.004	0.106	2.316
7.00	104.143	0.000	0.003	0.093	2.333
7.50	141.842	0.000	0.002	0.082	2.347
8.00	190.110	0.000	0.001	0.072	2.359
8.50	251.086	0.000	0.001	0.065	2.369
8.00	327.189	0.000	0.001	0.058	2.377
9.50	421.130	0.000	0.001	0.052	2.384
10.00	535.936	0.000	0.000	0.048	2.390
∞	∞	0.000	0.000	0.000	∞

TABLE 11.7 Normal Shock Wave (air, $k = 1.4$)

M_1	M_2	p_2/p_1	T_2/T_1	ρ_2/ρ_1	p_{02}/p_{01}
1.00	1.000	1.000	1.000	1.000	1.000
1.05	0.953	1.120	1.033	1.084	1.000
1.10	0.912	1.245	1.065	1.169	0.999
1.15	0.875	1.376	1.097	1.255	0.997
1.20	0.842	1.513	1.128	1.342	0.993
1.25	0.813	1.656	1.159	1.429	0.987
1.30	0.786	1.805	1.191	1.516	0.979
1.35	0.762	1.960	1.223	1.603	0.970
1.40	0.740	2.120	1.255	1.690	0.958
1.45	0.720	2.286	1.287	1.776	0.945
1.50	0.701	2.458	1.320	1.862	0.930
1.55	0.684	2.636	1.354	1.947	0.913
1.60	0.668	2.820	1.388	2.032	0.895
1.65	0.654	3.010	1.423	2.115	0.876
1.70	0.641	3.205	1.458	2.198	0.856
1.75	0.628	3.406	1.495	2.279	0.835
1.80	0.617	3.613	1.532	2.359	0.813
1.85	0.606	3.826	1.569	2.438	0.790
1.90	0.596	4.045	1.608	2.516	0.767
1.95	0.586	4.270	1.647	2.592	0.744
2.00	0.577	4.500	1.687	2.667	0.721
2.05	0.569	4.736	1.729	2.740	0.698
2.10	0.561	4.978	1.770	2.812	0.674
2.15	0.554	5.226	1.813	2.882	0.651
2.20	0.547	5.480	1.857	2.951	0.628
2.25	0.541	5.740	1.901	3.019	0.606
2.30	0.534	6.005	1.947	3.085	0.583
2.35	0.529	6.276	1.993	3.149	0.561
2.40	0.523	6.553	2.040	3.212	0.540
2.45	0.518	6.836	2.088	3.273	0.519
2.50	0.513	7.125	2.137	3.333	0.499
2.55	0.508	7.420	2.187	3.392	0.479
2.60	0.504	7.720	2.238	3.449	0.460
2.65	0.500	8.026	2.290	3.505	0.442
2.70	0.496	8.338	2.343	3.559	0.424
2.75	0.492	8.656	2.397	3.612	0.406
2.80	0.488	8.980	2.451	3.664	0.389
2.85	0.485	9.310	2.507	3.714	0.373
2.90	0.481	9.645	2.563	3.763	0.358
2.95	0.478	9.986	2.621	3.811	0.343
3.00	0.475	10.333	2.679	3.857	0.328
3.50	0.451	14.125	3.315	4.261	0.213
4.00	0.435	18.500	4.047	4.571	0.139
4.50	0.424	23.458	4.875	4.812	0.092
5.00	0.415	29.000	5.800	5.000	0.062
5.50	0.409	35.125	6.822	5.149	0.042
6.00	0.404	41.833	7.941	5.268	0.030
6.50	0.400	49.125	9.156	5.365	0.021
7.00	0.397	57.000	10.469	5.444	0.015
7.50	0.395	65.458	11.879	5.510	0.011
8.00	0.393	74.500	13.387	5.565	0.008
8.50	0.391	84.125	14.991	5.612	0.006
9.00	0.390	94.333	16.693	5.651	0.005
9.50	0.389	105.125	18.492	5.685	0.004
10.00	0.388	116.500	20.387	5.714	0.003
∞	0.378	∞	∞	6.000	0.000

Practice Problems

(If you choose to work only a few problems, select those with an asterisk)

General

*11.1   A fluid is a substance that
  a) is essentially incompressible.
  b) always moves when subjected to a shearing stress.
  c) has a viscosity that always increases with temperature.
  d) has a viscosity that always decreases with temperature.

*11.2   Viscosity has dimensions of
  a) FT^2/L b) F/TL^2 c) M/LT^2 d) M/LT

*11.3   The viscosity of a fluid varies with
  a) temperature.   c) density.
  b) pressure.   d) temperature and pressure.

*11.4   In an isothermal atmosphere the pressure
  a) is constant with elevation.
  b) decreases exponentially with elevation.
  c) cannot be related to elevation.
  d) decreases near the surface but approaches a constant value.

11.5   If a fluid "fails" in a piping system, the "failure" is related to which of the following properties?
  a) surface tension   c) viscosity
  b) bulk modulus   d) vapor pressure

11.6   A strong wind blows against a window on a building. The force on the window can be approximated using:
  a) Bernoulli's equation
  b) the Moody diagram
  c) the Darcy equation
  d) the impulse-momentum principle

*11.7   A torque of 1.6 N·m is needed to rotate the cylinder at 1000 rad/s. Estimate the viscosity $(N·s/m^2)$.
  a) 0.1   c) 0.3
  b) 0.2   d) 0.4

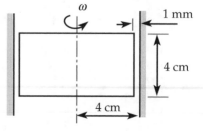

11.8   A pressure of 500 kPa applied to 2 m³ of liquid results in a volume change of 0.004 m³. The bulk modulus, in MPa, is
  a) 2.5   b) 25   c) 250   d) 2500

*11.9 Water at 20°C will rise, in a clean 1-mm-dia glass tube, a distance, in cm, of
   a) 1   b) 2   c) 3   d) 4

11.10 Water at 20°C flows in a piping system at a low velocity. At what pressure, in kPa abs, will cavitation result?
   a) 35.6   b) 20.1   c) 10.6   d) 2.45

11.11 A man is observed to strike an object and 1.2 s later the sound is heard. How far away, in meters, is the man?
   a) 220   b) 370   c) 410   d) 520

11.12 The viscosity of a fluid with specific gravity 1.3 is measured to be 0.0034 $N \cdot s/m^2$. Its kinematic viscosity, in m^2/s, is

   a) 2.6×10^{-6} b) 4.4×10^{-6} c) 5.8×10^{-6} d) 7.2×10^{-6}

Fluid Statics

11.13 Fresh water 2 m deep flows over the top of 4 m of salt water $(SG = 1.04)$. The pressure at the bottom, in kPa, is
   a) 60.4   b) 58.8   c) 55.2   d) 51.3

*11.14 What pressure, in kPa, is equivalent to 600 mm of Hg?
   a) 100   b) 95.2   c) 80.0   d) 55.2

11.15 What pressure, in MPa, must be maintained in a diving bell, at a depth of 1200 m, to keep out the ocean water $(SG = 1.03)$?
   a) 1.24   b) 5.16   c) 9.32   d) 12.1

11.16 Predict the pressure, in kPa, at an elevation of 2000 m in an isothermal atmosphere assuming $T = 20°C$. Assume $p_{atm} = 100$ kPa.
   a) 87
   b) 82
   c) 79
   d) 71

*11.17 The force F, in newtons, is
   a) 25
   b) 8.9
   c) 2.5
   d) 1.5

11.18 A U-tube manometer, attached to an air pipe, measures 20 cm of mercury. The pressure, in kPa, in the air pipe is
   a) 26.7   b) 32.4   c) 38.6   d) 42.5

*11.19 The pressure p, in kPa, is

 a) 37.0

 b) 40.0

 c) 45.2

 d) 48.0

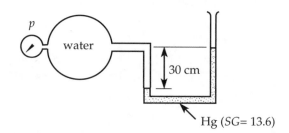

11.20 A 2-m-dia, 3-m-high, cylindrical water tank is pressurized such that the pressure at the top is 20 kPa. The force, in kN, acting on the bottom is

 a) 195

 b) 176

 c) 155

 d) 132

11.21 A manometer, utilizing a pitot probe, measures H mm of mercury. If the flow rate is desired in a pipe to which the manometer is attached, what additional information is needed?

 I.   The temperature of the water

 II.   The pressure in the pipe

 III. The density of the mercury

 IV. The diameter of the pipe

 a) I, II and III   b) I, II and IV   c) II, III and IV   d) I, III and IV

11.22 The force, in kN, acting on one of the 1.5-m sides of an open cubical water tank (which is full) is

 a) 18.2   b) 16.5

 c) 15.3   d) 12.1

*11.23 The force P, in kN, to hold the 3-m-wide gate in the position shown is

 a) 55

 b) 60

 c) 65

 d) 70

11.24 The force P, in kN, to just open the 4-m-wide gate is

 a) 710

 b) 762

 c) 831

 d) 983

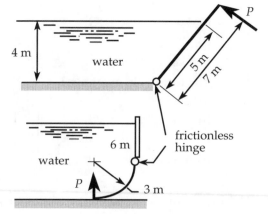

*11.25 The force P, in kN, on the 5-m-wide gate is

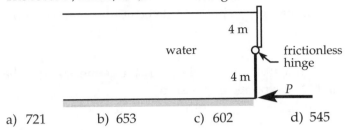

a) 721   b) 653   c) 602   d) 545

11.26 Four cars, with a mass of 1500 kg each, are loaded on a 6-m-wide, 12-m-long small-car ferry. How far, in cm, will it sink in the water?

a) 15.2   b) 11.5   c) 10.2   d) 8.3

*11.27 An object weighs 100 N in air and 25 N when submerged in water. Its specific gravity is

a) 1.11   b) 1.22   c) 1.33   d) 1.44

11.28 What pressure differential, in pascals, exists at the bottom of a 3 m vertical wall if the temperature inside is 20°C and outside it is –20°C? Assume equal pressures at the top.

a) 15   b) 12   c) 9   d) 6

Dimensionless Parameters

11.29 Arrange pressure p, flow rate Q, diameter D, and density ρ into a dimensionless group.

a) $pQ^2/\rho D^4$ b) $p/\rho Q^2 D^4$ c) $pD^4\rho/Q^2$ d) $pD^4/\rho Q^2$

*11.30 Combine surface tension σ, density ρ, diameter D, and velocity V into a dimensionless para-meter.

a) $\sigma/\rho V^2 D$ b) $\sigma D/\rho V$ c) $\sigma\rho/VD$ d) $\sigma V/\rho D$

*11.31 The Reynolds number is a ratio of
a) velocity effects to viscous effects.
b) inertial forces to viscous forces.
c) mass flux to viscosity.
d) flow rate to kinematic viscosity.

11.32 The Froude number is a ratio of
a) inertial forces to viscous forces.
b) body forces to viscous forces.
c) body forces to pressure forces.
d) inertial forces to body forces.

Similitude

*11.33 What flow rate, in m^3/s, is needed using a 20:1 scale model of a dam over which 4 m^3/s of water flows?

a) 0.010   b) 0.0068   c) 0.0047   d) 0.0022

11.34 It is proposed to model a submarine moving at 10 m/s by testing a 10:1 scale model. What velocity, in m/s, would be needed in the model study?

    a) 100   b) 80   c) 40   d) 1

11.35 The drag force on a 40:1 scale model of a ship is measured to be 10 N. What force, in kN, is expected on the ship?

    a) 640   b) 520   c) 320   d) 160

11.36 The power output of a 10:1 scale model of a water wheel is measured to be 20 W. The power output in kW expected from the prototype is

    a) 200   b) 150   c) 100   d) 63

Continuity

11.37 The velocity in a 2-cm-dia pipe is 20 m/s. If the pipe enlarges to 5-cm-dia, the velocity, in m/s, will be

    a) 8.0   b) 6.4   c) 3.2   d) 2.0

*11.38 A 2-cm-dia pipe transports water at 20 m/s. If it exits out 100 small 2-mm-dia holes, the exiting velocity, in m/s, will be

    a) 120   b) 80   c) 40   d) 20

11.39 Water flows through a 2-cm-dia pipe at 20 m/s. It then flows radially outward between two discs, 2 mm apart. When it reaches a radius of 40 cm, its velocity, in m/s, will be

    a) 1.00   b) 1.25   c) 2.25   d) 3.65

Bernoulli's Equation

11.40 Select the false statement for the Bernoulli equation.

    a) It can be used for an unsteady flow.
    b) It can be used along a streamline.
    c) It can be used in an inertial coordinate system.
    d) It can be used in an inviscid flow.

11.41 The pressure force, in newtons, on the 15-cm-dia headlight of an automobile traveling at 25 m/s is

    a) 10.4   b) 6.8   c) 5.6   d) 4.8

*11.42 The pressure inside a 4-cm-dia hose is 700 kPa. If the water exits through a 2-cm-dia nozzle, what velocity, in m/s, can be expected inside the hose?

    a) 20.4   b) 16.3   c) 12.4   d) 9.7

11.43 Calculate V, in m/s.

    a) 8
    b) 7
    c) 6
    d) 5

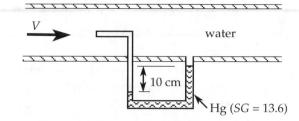

11.44 Water enters a turbine at 900 kPa with negligible velocity. What maximum speed, in m/s, can it reach before it enters the turbine rotor?
a) 52   b) 47   c) 45   d) 42

*11.45 If the density of the air is 1.2 kg/m^3, find F, in newtons.

a) 2.4
b) 3.6
c) 4.8
d) 7.6

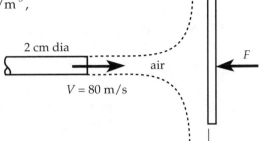

Momentum

2 cm dia

air

$V = 80$ m/s

F

11.46 If a single plate like the one of Prob. 11.45, but with $V = 20$ m/s, $\rho = 1000$ kg/m^3 and jet area $= 200$ cm^2, is to move at 10 m/s to the right the force F, in newtons, is
a) 1000   b) 2000   c) 3000   d) 4000

11.47 A rocket exits exhaust gases with $\rho = 0.5$ kg/m^3 out a 50-cm-dia nozzle at a velocity of 1200 m/s. Estimate the thrust, in kN.
a) 420   b) 280   c) 140   d) 90

11.48 A high-speed vehicle, traveling at 50 m/s, dips an 80-cm-wide scoop into water and deflects the water 180°. If it dips 5 cm deep, what force, in kN, is exerted on the scoop?
a) 200   b) 150   c) 100   d) 50

11.49 What force, in newtons, acts on the nozzle?

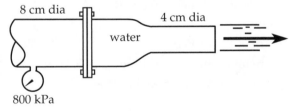

8 cm dia

4 cm dia

water

800 kPa

a) 4020   b) 3230   c) 2420   d) 1830

*11.50 The locus of elevations that water will rise in a series of pitot tubes is called

Energy

a) the hydraulic grade line.   c) the velocity head.
b) the energy grade line.   d) the pressure head.

11.51 The velocity head in a section of a pipe is given by
a) the difference between the *EGL* and the *HGL* at the section.
b) the elevation of the *EGL*.
c) the elevation of the *HGL*.
d) Bernoulli's equation applied from the inlet to the section.

*11.52 A pressure rise of 500 kPa is needed across a pump in a pipe transporting 0.2 m³/s of water. If the pump is 85% efficient , the power needed, in kW, would be

a) 118   b) 100   c) 85   d) 65

11.53 An 85% efficient turbine accepts 0.8 m³/s of water at a pressure of 600 kPa. What is the maximum power output, in kW if it exhausts to the atmosphere?

a) 320   b) 410   c) 560   d) 640

11.54 A liquid flows in a pipe at a Reynolds number of 5000.
a) The flow is laminar.
b) The flow is turbulent.
c) The flow is transitory, between laminar and turbulent.
d) The flow could be any of the above.

11.55 If the turbine is 88% efficient, the power output, in kW, is

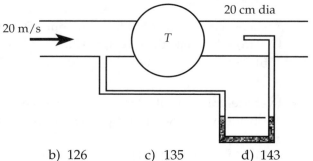

a) 111   b) 126   c) 135   d) 143

11.56 To determine the flow rate using a square-edged orifice, the pressure must be measured upstream of the orifice and
a) at the orifice.
b) just upstream of the orifice.
c) just downstream of the orifice at the vena contracta.
d) at least 10 diameters downstream of the orifice.

11.57 Freon flows through an expansion valve. Select the best statement.
a) The temperature increases.
b) The internal energy remains constant.
c) The pressure remains constant.
d) The enthalpy remains constant.

Losses

11.58 A laminar flow exists in a pipe flow. We know that
a) the velocity profile is linear.
b) the Reynolds number is less than 2000.
c) the shear stress distribution is linear.
d) the pipe is smooth.

*11.59 In a completely turbulent flow the head loss
   a) increases with the velocity.
   b) increases with the velocity squared.
   c) decreases with wall roughness.
   d) increases with diameter.

*11.60 The shear stress in a turbulent pipe flow
   a) varies parabolically with the radius.
   b) is constant over the pipe radius.
   c) varies according to the 1/7th power law.
   d) is zero at the center and increases linearly to the wall.

*11.61 The velocity distribution in a turbulent flow in a pipe is often assumed to
   a) vary parabolically.
   b) be zero at the wall and increase linearly to the center.
   c) vary according to the 1/7th power law.
   d) be unpredictable and is thus not used.

11.62 The velocity profile between parallel plates is calculated to be Vy/δ, where y is measured from the bottom plate and δ is the distance between plates. We know that:

   I. The flow is laminar. II. The flow is turbulent. III. The flow is steady.

   IV. One plate is stationary and the other is moving with velocity V.

   a) I, III, and IV only   c) I and III only
   b) II, III and IV only   d) II and IV only

*11.63 The Moody diagram is sketched. The friction factor for turbulent flow in a smooth pipe is given by curve
   a) *A*
   b) *B*
   c) *D*
   d) *E*

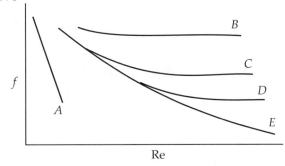

*11.64 For the Moody diagram given in Problem 11.60, the completely turbulent flow is best represented by curve
   a) *A*   b) *B*   c) *C*   d) *D*

*11.65 The pressure gradient $(\Delta p / \Delta x)$ in a developed turbulent flow in a horizontal constant diameter pipe
  a) is constant.
  b) varies linearly with axial distance.
  c) is zero.
  d) decrease exponentially.

*11.66 The head loss in a pipe flow can be calculated using
  a) the Bernoulli equation.   c) the Chezy-Manning equation.
  b) the Darcy-Weisbach equation. d) the Momentum equation.

*11.67 Minor losses in a piping system are
  a) less than the friction factor losses, $f \dfrac{L}{D} \dfrac{V^2}{2g}$.
  b) due to the viscous stresses.
  c) assumed to vary linearly with the velocity.
  d) found by using loss coefficients.

*11.68 In a turbulent flow in a pipe we know the
  a) Reynolds number is greater than 10 000.
  b) fluid particles move in straight lines.
  c) head loss varies linearly with the flow rate.
  d) shear stress varies linearly with radius.

*11.69 Water flows through a 10-cm-dia, 100-m-long pipe connecting two reservoirs with an elevation difference of 40 m. The average velocity is 6 m/s. Neglecting minor losses, the friction factor is
  a) 0.020   b) 0.022   c) 0.024   d) 0.026

*11.70 Find the power required, in kW, by the 85% efficient pump if $Q = 0.02\,\mathrm{m^3/s}$.

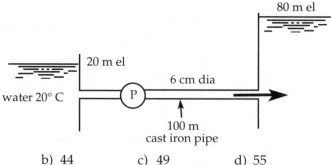

  a) 35   b) 44   c) 49   d) 55

11.71 The pressure at section A in a 4-cm-dia, wrought-iron, horizontal pipe is 510 kPa. A fully open globe valve, two elbows, and 50 meters of pipe connect section B. If $Q = 0.006\,\mathrm{m^3/s}$ of water, the pressure p_B, in kPa, is
  a) 300   b) 250   c) 200   d) 100

11.72 A golf ball has dimples to increase its flight distance. Select the best reason that accounts for the longer flight distance of a dimpled ball compared to that of a smooth ball.
a) The shearing stress is smaller on the dimpled ball.
b) The pressure on the front of the smooth ball is larger.
c) The wake on the dimpled ball is smaller.
d) The compressible air results in a lower drag.

11.73 A water system is to be installed in a community that is quite hilly. The design engineer must be certain that:
a) the hydraulic grade line must always be above the pipe line.
b) the energy grade line must always be above the pipe line.
c) the stagnation pressure must remain positive in the pipe line.
d) the cavitation number must not exceed unity.

11.74 Air at 20°C and 100 kPa abs is transported through 500 m of smooth, horizontal, $15 \text{ cm} \times 40 \text{ cm}$ rectangular duct with a flow rate of 0.3 m^3 / s. The pressure drop, in pascals, is
a) 800   b) 700   c) 600   d) 500

11.75 Estimate the loss coefficient C in a sudden contraction $A_1/A_2 = 2$ by neglecting the losses up to the vena contracta A_c. Assume that $A_c/A_2 = 0.62 + 0.38(A_2/A_1)^3$ and $h_f = CV_2^2/2g$.
a) 0.40   b) 0.35   c) 0.30   d) 0.25

11.76 An elbow exists in a 6-cm-dia galvanized iron pipe transporting 0.02 m^3/s of water. Find the equivalent length of the elbow, in meters.
a) 6.3   b) 4.5   c) 3.6   d) 2.2

Open Channel Flow

*11.77 The depth of water in a 3-m-wide, rectangular, finished concrete channel is 2 m. If the slope is 0.001, estimate the flow rate, in m^3/s.
a) 14   b) 13   c) 12   d) 11

11.78 At what depth, in meters, will 10 m^3/s of water flow in a 4-m-wide, rectangular, brick channel if the slope is 0.001?
a) 1.3   b) 1.4   c) 1.5   d) 1.6

11.79 A 2-m-dia, brick storm sewer transports 10 m^3/s when it's nearly full. Estimate the slope of the sewer.
a) 0.0070   b) 0.0065   c) 0.0060   d) 0.0055

Compressible Flow

*11.80 The pressure and temperature in air in a 10-cm-dia pipe are 500 kPa abs and 40°C, respectively. What is the mass flux, in kg/s, if the velocity is 100 m/s?
a) 6.63   b) 5.81   c) 4.37   d) 4.02

*11.81 Air in a reservoir at 20°C and 500 kPa abs exits a hole with a velocity, in m/s, of

a) 353   b) 333   c) 313   d) 273

11.82 A farmer uses 20°C nitrogen pressurized to 800 kPa abs . Estimate the temperature, in °C, in the nitrogen as it exits a short hose fitted to the tank.

a) –110   b) –90   c) –70   d) –50

11.83 Select the correct statement concerning a supersonic flow.

a) It occurs after a converging nozzle for sufficiently low receiver pressures.

b) In a converging nozzle the velocity increases.

c) It may occur in a converging-diverging nozzle attached to a reservoir.

d) In a diverging nozzle the temperature increases.

11.84 Estimate p_1 in kPa.

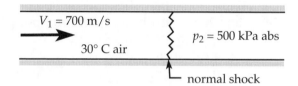

a) 110

b) 120

c) 130

d) 140

11.85 Air leaves a reservoir and accelerates until a shock wave is encountered at a diameter of 10 cm. If the throat diameter is 6 cm, what is the Mach number before the shock wave?

a) 2.03

b) 2.19

c) 2.56

d) 3.02

11.86 A supersonic aircraft flies at $M=2$ at an elevation of 1000 m. How long, in seconds, after it passes overhead is the aircraft heard?

a) 2.3

b) 2.5

c) 2.7

d) 2.9

11.87 Air at 20°C is to exit a nozzle from a reservoir. What maximum pressure, in kPa abs, can the reservoir have if compressibility effects can be neglected? $p_{atm} = 100$ kPa.

a) 115

b) 111

c) 109

d) 106

<u>Questions 11.88–11.92</u>

Water flows through the horizontal nozzle shown so that $V_1 = 4$ m/s. Neglect any losses through the nozzle and use $\gamma_{water} = 9800$ N/m^3, and $v = 10^{-6}$ m^2/s.

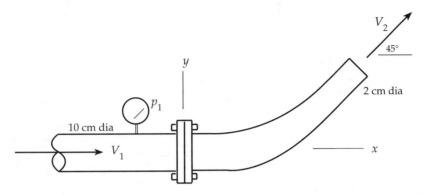

11.88 The pressure p_1 at the bolted joint is nearest
    a) 100 kPa
    b) 400kPa
    c) 3 MPa
    d) 5 MPa

11.89 Estimate the difference in pressure between the pressure at a section 100 meters upstream of the bolted joint and p_1. The cast iron section of pipe is horizontal.
    a) 190 kPa
    b) 210 kPa
    c) 290 kPa
    d) 420 kPa

11.90 If the pipe in Question 11.89 were plastic rather than cast iron, what would the pressure difference be?
    a) 100 kPa
    b) 160 kPa
    c) 210 kPa
    d) 360 kPa

11.91 The force exerted by the water on the bend in the x–direction is nearest
    a) 2.1 kN
    b) 16 kN
    c) 23 kN
    d) 37 kN

11.92 The force exerted by the water on the bend in the y–direction is nearest
    a) 2.2 kN   b) 17 kN   c) 24 kN   d) 38 kN

Questions 11.93–11.97

The pump provides 1.2 cubic meters of water each minute to the holding tank. The pump is 85% efficient and $p_{atm} = 100$ kPa. The cast iron pipe is 6 cm in diameter.

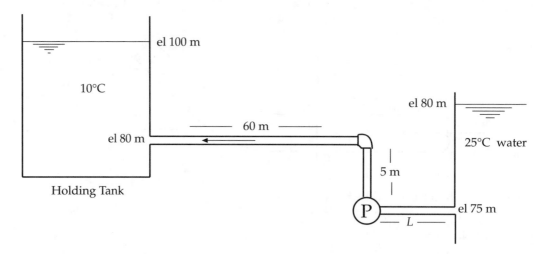

11.93 Prior to the pump being turned on, the pressure at the pump exit is nearest
a) 100 kPa   b) 196 kPa   c) 245 kPa   d) 315 kPa

11.94 If $L = 10$ m, the power requirement required to operate the pump is nearest
a) 6.2 kW   b) 13 kW   c) 18 kW   d) 26 kW

11.95 The maximum distance L that the pump can be located from the supply reservoir is nearest
a) 8 m   b) 13 m   c) 20 m   d) 28 m

11.96 The pump is removed and replaced with an elbow. The maximum possible flow rate is nearest

a) 2 m³/min b) 6 m³/min   b) 9 m³/min   d) 12 m³/min

11.97 If the pump is replaced with a 90%-efficient turbine and the flow rate reduces to 0.4 m³/min, estimate the power produced by the turbine.
a) 3 kW   b) 2 kW   c) 1 kW   d) 0.5 kW

Questions 11.98–11.103

An impulse turbine blade is sketched. There are four such jets acting on the turbine. Each jet produces a velocity of 100 m/s.

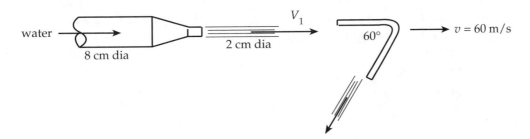

11.98   The flow rate of water from each jet is

   a) 1.4 m^3/min

   b) 1.2 m^3/min

   c) 0.9 m^3/min

   d) 0.03 m^3/min

11.99   The pressure just upstream of the nozzle in the supply line is nearest
   a) 5 kPa
   b) 50 kPa
   c) 500 kPa
   d) 5 MPa

11.100   The angle the water jet makes with the vector $\mathbf{V}_2$ after it leaves the blade is
   a) 20°   b) 30°   c) 40°   d) 50°

11.101   The average tangential component of force produced by each jet on one of the blades is nearest
   a) 32 N   b) 25 N   c) 19 N   d) 14 N

11.102   The power produced by this ideal impulse turbine is nearest
   a) 4.5 kW
   b) 3.4 kW
   c) 2.6 kW
   d) 1.1 kW

11.103   The blade speed that would produce the maximum turbine power is
   a) 40 m/s
   b) 45 m/s
   c) 50 m/s
   d) 55 m/s

Questions 11.104–11.107

A large spherical, 10-m-diameter balloon is to be propelled through the 10°C air at 10 m/s. For the air $v = 10^{-5}$ ft^2/s and $\rho = 1.2$ kg/m^3.

11.104 If a 50-cm-diameter model of the balloon is to be studied, what speed should be selected if a 20°C water channel is used?

    a) 2.2 m/s

    b) 8.7 m/s

    c) 10 m/s

    d) 14.3 m/s

11.105 The power needed to propel the balloon is nearest

    a) 10 hp

    b) 20 hp

    c) 30 hp

    d) 40 hp

11.106 If the balloon were extended to take the shape of a long dirigible, it's drag could be estimated to be that of a long, flat plate. Neglect the drag on the spherical nose and the rear where the power unit would be placed and estimate the power requirement if the airship is 150 meters long and travels at 10 m/s.

    a) 90 hp

    b) 42 hp

    c) 8 hp

    d) 5 hp

11.107 A pitot probe, placed in the nose of the balloon, would read a pressure of

    a) 6 Pa

    b) 60 Pa

    c) 160 Pa

    d) 106 Pa

Solutions to Practice Problems

11.1 **b)** a) is true for a liquid and low speed gas flows. c) is true of gases.
d) is true for a liquid.

11.2 **d)** $\tau = \mu\,du/dy$. $\therefore \mu = \tau/du/dy$. $[\mu] = \dfrac{F/L^2}{\dfrac{L}{T}/L} = \dfrac{FT}{L^2} = \dfrac{\left(ML/T^2\right)T}{L^2} = \dfrac{M}{LT}$

11.3 **a)** Viscosity μ varies with temperature only.

11.4 **b)** $dp = -\gamma dz = -\rho g dz$. $p = \rho RT$ (ideal gas)

$\therefore\ dp = -\dfrac{p}{RT}g dz\ \ \text{or}\ \ \dfrac{dp}{p} = -\dfrac{g}{RT}dz.$

$\int\dfrac{dp}{p} = -\dfrac{g}{RT}\int dz.$ $\therefore\ \ln p = -Cz.$ $\therefore\ p = e^{-Cz}.$

11.5 **d)**

11.6 **a)** Bernoulli's equation allows the pressure to be calculated. Multiply the
pressure by the area to find the force.

11.7 **a)** $T = \tau A r = \mu\dfrac{du}{dy}A r = \mu\dfrac{r\omega}{t}2\pi r L r.$

$1.6 = \mu\dfrac{0.04\times1000}{0.001}2\pi\times0.04\times0.04\times0.04.$ $\therefore \mu = 0.1\,\text{N}\cdot\text{s/m}^2$

11.8 **c)** $K = -\cancel{V}\dfrac{\Delta p}{\cancel{\Delta V}} = -2\dfrac{500}{-0.004} = 250\,000$ or $250\,\text{MPa}.$

11.9 **c)** $\sigma\,\pi D = \gamma\pi r^2 L$

$0.0736\times\pi\times0.001 = 9800\pi\times0.0005^2 L$

$\therefore L = 0.03\,\text{m}\ \ \text{or}\ \ 3\,\text{cm}.$

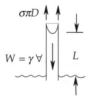

11.10 **d)** Cavitation occurs when the pressure reaches the vapor pressure = 2.45
kPa. (See Table 11.2.)

11.11 **c)** $L = V\Delta t = \sqrt{kRT}\,\Delta t = \sqrt{1.4\times287\times288}\times1.2 = 408\,\text{m}.$
Assume $T = 15°C$. T must be in absolute. $\therefore\ T = 288.$

11.12 **a)** $v = \dfrac{\mu}{\rho} = \dfrac{0.0034}{1.3\times1000} = 2.6\times10^{-6}.$

11.13 **a)** $p = \gamma_1\Delta h_1 + \gamma_2\Delta h_2$ where $\gamma_2 = SG\times\gamma_{H_2O}$
$= 9800\times2 + 1.04\times9800\times4 = 60\,400$ Pa or 60.4 kPa.

11-FLUIDS

11.14 **c)** $p = \gamma h$ where $\gamma_{Hg} = 13.6\, \gamma_{H_2O}$

$$= 13.6 \times 9800 \times 0.6 = 80\ 000 \text{ Pa}.$$

11.15 **d)** $p = \gamma h = 1.03 \times 9800 \times 1200 = 12.1 \times 10^6 \text{ Pa}$ or 12.1 MPa.

11.16 **c)** $dp = -\gamma dz = -\rho g dz = -p \dfrac{g}{RT} dz$ using $p = \rho RT$

$$\therefore \frac{dp}{p} = -\frac{g}{RT} dz. \quad \int_{100}^{p} dp/p = -\frac{g}{RT} \int_{0}^{2000} dz.$$

$$\therefore \ln \frac{p}{100} = -\frac{9.8}{287 \times 293} \times 2000. \quad \therefore p = 79.2 \text{ kPa}.$$

11.17 **c)** $F = pA. \quad p = \dfrac{1000}{\pi \times 0.05^2} + 0.86 \times 9800 \times 0.2 = 129\ 000 \text{ Pa}.$

$$\therefore F = 129\ 000 \times \pi \times 0.0025^2 = 2.53 \text{ N}.$$

11.18 **a)** $p = \gamma h = (13.6 \times 9800) \times 0.2 = 26\ 700 \text{ Pa}$ or 26.7 kPa.

11.19 **a)** $p + 9800 \times 0.3 = 13.6 \times 9800 \times 0.3. \quad \therefore p = 37\ 000 \text{ Pa}.$

11.20 **c)** $F = pA = (20\ 000 + 9800 \times 3)\pi \times 1^2 = 155\ 000 \text{ N}.$

11.21 **c)** Bernoulli's equation includes both pressure and velocity, so pressure is needed. To interpret the manometer, the density of mercury is needed. The pitot tube is sensitive to velocity, not flow rate, so the area is needed.

11.22 **b)** $F = p_c A = 9800 \times \dfrac{1.5}{2} \times 1.5^2 = 16\ 500 \text{ N}.$

11.23 **d)** $7P = \dfrac{5}{3} F = \dfrac{5}{3} \gamma h_c A. \quad \therefore P = \dfrac{5}{21} \times 9800 \times 2 \times 15 = 70\ 000 \text{ N}.$

11.24 **d)** All pressures on the curved section pass through the center. Moments about the hinge give

$$P = F_v = \gamma \times \text{Volume} = 9800 \times (9\pi/4) \times 4 + 9800 \times 6 \times 3 \times 4 = 983\ 000 \text{ N}.$$

11.25 **b)** $y_p = y_c + \dfrac{I_c}{Ay_c} = 6 + \dfrac{5 \times 4^3/12}{6 \times 20} = 6.22 \text{ m}.$

$$4P = F \times 2.22 = \gamma h_c A \times 2.22. \quad \therefore P = 9800 \times 6 \times 20 \times 2.22 / 4 = 653\ 000 \text{ N}.$$

11.26 **d)** $W = \gamma V. \quad 4 \times 1500 \times 9.8 = 9800 \times 6 \times 12 \times h. \quad \therefore h = 0.0833 \text{ m}.$

11.27 **c)** $25 = 100 - 9800V. \quad \therefore V = 0.00765 \text{ m}^3.$

$$100 = 9800(SG) \times 0.00765. \quad \therefore SG = 1.33.$$

11.28 **d)** $\Delta p = \Delta \gamma \times h = \left(\dfrac{1}{253} - \dfrac{1}{293} \right) \times \dfrac{100}{0.287} \times 3 \times 9.8 = 5.53 \text{ Pa}.$

11.29 d) $[p] = \dfrac{M}{LT^2}$ $[Q] = \dfrac{L^3}{T}$ $[D] = L$ $[\rho] = \dfrac{M}{L^3}$.

First, eliminate M, then T, then L:

$$\frac{M}{LT^2} \cdot \frac{L^3}{M} \cdot \frac{T^2}{L^6} \cdot L^4 = p \cdot \frac{1}{\rho} \cdot \frac{1}{Q^2} \cdot D^4 = \frac{pD^4}{\rho Q^2}.$$

11.30 a) $[\sigma] = \dfrac{M}{T^2}$ $[\rho] = \dfrac{M}{L^3}$ $[D] = L$ $[V] = \dfrac{L}{T}$.   Combine: $\dfrac{\sigma}{\rho} \dfrac{1}{V^2} \dfrac{1}{D}$

11.31 b) Inertial force to viscous forces.

11.32 d)

11.33 d) $(\text{Fr})_m = (\text{Fr})_p$. $\therefore \dfrac{V_m^2}{l_m g} = \dfrac{V_p^2}{l_p g}$. $\therefore \dfrac{V_m^2}{V_p^2} = \dfrac{1}{20}$.

$Q_m^* = Q_p^*$ or $\dfrac{Q_m}{V_m l_m^2} = \dfrac{Q_p}{V_p l_p^2}$. $\therefore Q_m = 4 \times \dfrac{1}{20^2} \times \dfrac{1}{\sqrt{20}} = 0.0022$.

11.34 a) $\text{Re}_m = \text{Re}_p$. $\left(\dfrac{Vl}{\nu}\right)_m = \left(\dfrac{Vl}{\nu}\right)_p$. $\therefore \dfrac{V_m}{V_p} = \dfrac{l_p}{l_m} = 10$.

$\therefore V_m = 10\, V_p = 10 \times 10 = 100$ m/s.

11.35 a) $\text{Fr}_m = \text{Fr}_p$. $\therefore \left(\dfrac{V^2}{lg}\right)_m = \left(\dfrac{V^2}{lg}\right)_p$. $\therefore \dfrac{V_p^2}{V_m^2} = \dfrac{\ell_p}{\ell_m}$.

$(F_D)_m^* = (F_D)_p^*$ or $\dfrac{(F_D)_m}{\rho_m V_m^2 l_m^2} = \dfrac{(F_D)_p}{\rho_p V_p^2 l_p^2}$. $\therefore (F_D)_p = 10\dfrac{\rho_p}{\rho_m}\dfrac{V_p^2}{V_m^2}\dfrac{l_p^2}{l_m^2} = 10\dfrac{l_p^3}{l_m^3}$.

$\therefore (F_D)_p = 10 \times 40^3 = 640\ 000$ N.

11.36 d) $\text{Fr}_m = \text{Fr}_p$. $\left(\dfrac{V^2}{lg}\right)_m = \left(\dfrac{V^2}{lg}\right)_p$. $\therefore \dfrac{V_p^2}{V_m^2} = 10$.

$\dot{W}_p^* = \dot{W}_m^*$. $\dfrac{\dot{W}_m}{\rho_m V_m^3 l_m^2} = \dfrac{\dot{W}_p}{\rho_p V_p^3 l_p^2}$.

$\therefore \dot{W}_p = \dfrac{V_p^3}{V_m^3}\dfrac{l_p^2}{l_m^2}\dot{W}_m = 10^3 \sqrt{10} \times 20 = 63\ 250$ W.

11.37 c) $V_2 = 20\pi \times 2^2 / \pi \times 5^2 = 3.2$ m/s.

11.38 d) $V_2 = 20\pi \times 1^2 / 100 \times \pi \times 0.1^2 = 20$ m/s.

11.39 b) $V_2 \times 2\pi \times 40 \times 0.2 = 20 \times \pi \times 1^2$. $\therefore V_2 = 1.25$ m/s.

11.40 **a)** Bernoulli's equation is only applicable in a steady, viscous, incompressible flow along a streamline in an inertial coordinate system. It must be modified to accommodate other effects, such as compressible viscous flow.

11.41 **b)** $p = \rho V^2/2 = 1.23 \times 25^2/2 = 384$ Pa. $F = pA = 384 \times \pi \times 0.075^2 = 6.79$ N.

11.42 **d)** $V_2 A_2 = V_1 A_1$. $\therefore V_2 = V_1 \times 4^2/2^2 = 4V_1$.

$$\frac{p_1}{\rho} + \frac{V_1^2}{2} = \cancelto{0}{\frac{p_2}{\rho}} + \frac{V_2^2}{2}. \quad \frac{700\,000}{1000} + \frac{V_1^2}{2} = \frac{16V_1^2}{2}. \quad \therefore V_1 = 9.66 \text{ m/s}$$

11.43 **d)** $p + \rho \dfrac{V^2}{2} + 9800 \times 0.1 = p + 13.6 \times 9800 \times 0.1.$

$\therefore V^2 = 12.6 \times 9800 \times 0.1 \times 2/1000.$ $\therefore V = 4.97$ m/s .

11.44 **c)** Cavitation results if $p_2 = -100$ kPa.

$$\frac{p_1}{\rho} + \cancelto{0}{\frac{V_1^2}{2}} = \frac{p_2}{\rho} + \frac{V_2^2}{2}. \quad 900\,000/1000 = -100\,000/1000 + V_2^2/2. \quad \therefore V_2 = 44.7 \text{ m/s.}$$

11.45 **a)** $F = \rho A V^2 = 1.2 \times \pi \times 0.01^2 \times 80^2 = 2.41.$

11.46 **b)** Momentum: $-F = \rho A v_r (v_{r2} - v_{r1})_x$. $F = 1000 \times 0.02 \times 10(10 - 0) = 2000$ N.

$(v_r$ is relative speed$)$

Note: With a single blade we must also use relative speed for $\dot{m} = \rho A V$ since not all of the fluid leaving the jet has its momentum changed.

11.47 **c)** $F = \rho A V^2 = .5 \times \pi \times 0.25^2 \times 1200^2 = 141\,000$ N.

11.48 **a)** $-F = \rho A V(-V - V)$. $\therefore F = 2\rho A V^2$.

$\therefore F = 2 \times 1000 \times 0.05 \times 0.8 \times 50^2 = 200\,000$ N.

11.49 **c)** $p_1 A_1 - F = \rho A_1 V_1 (V_2 - V_1)$. $V_2 = 4V_1$. $\dfrac{p_1}{\rho} + \dfrac{V_1^2}{2} = \cancelto{0}{\dfrac{p_2}{\rho}} + \dfrac{V_2^2}{2} = \dfrac{16V_1^2}{2}.$

$\therefore V_1 = \sqrt{\dfrac{800\,000}{1000} \times \dfrac{2}{15}} = 10.3.$ $V_2 = 41.2$.

$\therefore F = 800\,000 \times \pi \times 0.04^2 - 1000 \times \pi \times 0.04^2 \times 10.3 \times (41.2 - 10.3) = 2420$ N.

11.50 **b)** The energy grade line.

11.51 **a)** EGL has elevation $\dfrac{V^2}{2g} + \dfrac{p}{\gamma} + z$. The HGL has elevation $\dfrac{p}{\gamma} + z$.

11.52 **a)** $\dot{W}_P = \gamma Q \dfrac{\Delta p}{\gamma} \Big/ 0.85 = 0.2 \times 500 / 0.85 = 117.6$ kW .

11.53 b) $\dot{W}_T = \gamma Q \dfrac{\Delta p}{\gamma} \times 0.85 = 0.8 \times 600 \times 0.85 = 408 \text{ kW}.$

11.54 d) The flow could be laminar, turbulent or transitory depending on the conditions of the pipe (rough, smooth, vibrating) and the fluid (calm or full of fluctuations).

11.55 a) manometer: $p_1 = p_2 + \rho V_2^2 / 2.$ $-\dfrac{\dot{W}_T}{\gamma Q} = \dfrac{V_2^2}{2g} + \dfrac{p_2}{\gamma} - \dfrac{V_1^2}{2g} - \dfrac{p_1}{\gamma}$ (100% efficient)

$\therefore \dot{W}_T = Q\dfrac{V_2^2}{2}\rho\eta = \left(20 \times \pi \times 0.1^2\right)\dfrac{20^2}{2} \times 1000 \times .88 = 111\,000 \text{ W}.$

11.56 c) In an orifice, the minimum pressure (maximum velocity) occurs at the vena contracta. The loss coefficient is based on this minimum pressure.

11.57 d) The energy equation for a control volume, with no work or heat transfer demands that $\Delta h = 0$.

11.58 c) Laminar flow can occur in a pipe upwards of 40 000 Reynolds number. At low Reynolds number a laminar flow occurs in even a rough pipe. Viscous effects dominate in a laminar flow.

11.59 b) Increases with the velocity squared.

11.60 d) Increases linearly to the wall.

11.61 c) Vary as the 1/7th power law.

11.62 a) The flow is laminar and steady, and $v = V$ at $y = \delta$ and $v = 0$ at $y = 0$.

11.63 d) By curve E.

11.64 b) By curve B.

11.65 a) Pressure varies linearly. $\therefore \dfrac{\Delta p}{\Delta x} = \text{Const}.$

11.66 b) The Darcy-Weisbach equation.

11.67 d) Found by using loss coefficients.

11.68 d) Shear stress varies linearly with radius.

11.69 b) $h_f = f\dfrac{L}{D}\dfrac{V^2}{2g}.$ $\therefore f = 40\dfrac{0.1}{100}\dfrac{2 \times 9.8}{6^2} = 0.0218.$

11.70 b) $V = Q/A = \dfrac{0.02}{\pi \times 0.03^2} = 7.07 \text{ m/s}.$ $\text{Re} = \dfrac{VD}{\nu} = 7.07 \times 0.06/10^{-6} = 4.2 \times 10^5.$

$\dfrac{e}{D} = \dfrac{.26}{60} = .0043.$ From Fig. 11.2 $f = 0.03.$

$$\dot{W}_p = \frac{\gamma Q}{\eta}\left(\frac{\cancelto{0}{V_2^2}}{2g} + \frac{\cancelto{0}{p_2}}{\gamma} + z_2 - \frac{\cancelto{0}{V_1^2}}{2g} - \frac{\cancelto{0}{p_1}}{\gamma} - z_1 + f\frac{L}{D}\frac{V^2}{2g} + C\frac{V^2}{2g}\right)$$

$$= \frac{9800 \times 0.02}{0.85}\left[80 - 20 + \left(0.03\frac{100}{.06} + 1 + .5\right)\frac{7.07^2}{2 \times 9.8}\right] = 44\ 000\ \text{W}.$$

11.71 · **d)** $V = Q/A = \dfrac{0.006}{\pi \times 0.03^2} = 4.77\ \text{m/s}.$ $\text{Re} = \dfrac{VD}{\nu} = 4.77 \times .04 / 10^{-6} = 1.9 \times 10^5.$

$\dfrac{e}{D} = \dfrac{0.046}{40} = 0.0011$.   From Fig. 11.2 $f = 0.022.$ $0 = \dfrac{p_B - p_A}{\gamma} + f\dfrac{L}{D}\dfrac{V^2}{2g} + C\dfrac{V^2}{2g}.$

$\therefore p_B = 510\ 000 - \left(.022\dfrac{50}{.04} + 6.4 + 2 \times .9\right)\dfrac{4.77^2}{2 \times 9.8} \times 9800 = 104\ 000\ \text{Pa}.$

11.72 **c)**   The dimples induce turbulence in the boundary layer causing the separated region to move further to the rear of the ball resulting in a smaller wake.

11.73 **a)**   The pressure (the static pressure) must remain positive at all points in the pipe so a leak can not allow possible pollutants into the water.

11.74 **b)** $V = Q/A = 0.3/(.15 \times .4) = 5\ \text{m/s}.$ $R_H = \dfrac{40 \times 15}{110} = 5.45\ \text{cm}.$

$\text{Re} = \dfrac{5 \times 4 \times .0545}{1.5 \times 10^{-5}} = 7.2 \times 10^4.$ With $\dfrac{e}{D} = 0,$ $f = 0.02.$

$\Delta p = f\dfrac{L}{4R_H}\dfrac{V^2}{2g}\gamma = .02\dfrac{500}{4 \times .0545}\dfrac{5^2}{2} \times 1.19 = 682\ \text{Pa}.$

11.75 **d)** $A_c/A_2 = .62 + .38(.5)^3 = 0.668.$ $C_1 = (1 - .668)^2 = 0.11.$

$0.11\ V_c^2/2g = C\ V_2^2/2g.$ $\therefore C = 0.11\left(\dfrac{A_2}{A_c}\right)^2 = .11 \times \dfrac{1}{.668^2} = 0.25.$

11.76 **d)** $V = Q/A = 0.02/\pi \times .03^2 = 7.07\ \text{m/s}.$ $e/D = .15/60 = .0025$

$\text{Re} = \dfrac{7.07 \times .06}{10^{-6}} = 4.2 \times 10^5.$ $\therefore f = 0.024.$

$L_e = CD/f = 0.9 \times 0.06/0.025 = 2.16\ \text{m}.$

11.77 **a)** $Q = \dfrac{1}{n}AR_H^{2/3}S^{1/2} = \dfrac{1}{.012} \times 6 \times .86^{2/3} \times .001^{1/2} = 14.3$

where $R_H = 6/(3 + 4) = 0.86\ \text{m}.$

11.78 **b)** $Q = \dfrac{1}{n}AR_H^{2/3}S^{1/2} = \dfrac{1}{.016}4h\left(\dfrac{4h}{4 + 2h}\right)^{2/3} \times .001^{1/2} = 10.$

Trial - and - error : $h = 1.4\ \text{m}.$

11.79 **b)** $Q = \dfrac{1}{n}AR_H^{2/3}S^{1/2} = \dfrac{1}{.016}\pi \times 1^2 \times .5^{2/3}S^{1/2} = 10,$ where $R_H = \dfrac{A}{P} = \dfrac{\pi \times 1^2}{2\pi} = .5.$

$\therefore S = 0.00654.$

11.80 c) $\rho = p/RT = 500/.287 \times 313 = 5.57 \text{ kg/m}^3$

$\dot{m} = \rho AV = 5.57 \times \pi \times .05^2 \times 100 = 4.37 \text{ kg/s}$

11.81 d) $T_e = T_o(p_e/p_o)^{k-1/k} = 293\left(\dfrac{100}{500}\right)^{.286} = 185 \text{ K}.$

$V = Mc = 1\sqrt{1.4 \times 287 \times 185} = 273 \text{ m/s}.$

11.82 a) $T_e = T_o(p_e/p_o)^{k-1/k} = 293\left(\dfrac{100}{800}\right)^{.286} = 162 \text{ K}. \quad \therefore T_e = 162 - 273 = -111°\text{C}.$

11.83 c) To obtain supersonic flow from a reservoir the subsonic velocity must increase in a converging section until $m = 1$ at the throat and then continue to increase in the diverging section. As velocity increases, temperature (and enthalpy) decrease. Velocity decreases in a converging section if $M > 1$.

11.84 a) $M_1 = \dfrac{V_1}{c_1} = \dfrac{700}{\sqrt{1.4 \times 287 \times 303}} = 2.01 \quad \therefore \dfrac{p_2}{p_1} = 4.54 \quad \text{(from Normal Shock Table)}$

$\therefore p_1 = p_2 \ 4.54 = 500/4.54 = 110 \text{ kPa}$

11.85 c) $\dfrac{A}{A^*} = \dfrac{10^2}{6^2} = 2.78. \quad \therefore 2.5 < M_1 < 2.6 \quad \text{(Isentropic flow Table)}$

11.86 b) $\sin\phi = \dfrac{1}{M} = \dfrac{1}{2}. \quad \therefore \phi = 30°$

$\tan 30° = \dfrac{1000}{L}. \quad \therefore L = 1732 \text{ m}$

$\Delta t = \dfrac{L}{V} = \dfrac{1732}{2\sqrt{1.4 \times 287 \times 293}} = 2.52 \text{ sec}.$

11.87 d) Assume $M_e = 0.3$, the maximum if the density is assumed constant (i.e., $\rho_e = 0.97\rho_o$). $V_e = M_e c_e = 0.3\sqrt{1.4 \times 287 \, T_e}$.

$\therefore V_e^2 = 36.2 T_e. \quad \text{energy}: \quad 0 = \dfrac{V_e^2 - V_o^2}{2} + c_p(T_e - T_o).$

$36.2 T_e = 2 \times 1000(293 - T_e). \quad \therefore T_e = 287.8$

$p_o = p_e(T_o/T_e)^{\frac{k}{k-1}} = 100\left(\dfrac{293}{287.8}\right)^{\frac{1.4}{.4}} = 106.$

11.88 d) To use Bernoulli's equation we must find the velocity:

$V_2 = V_1\dfrac{A_1}{A_2} = 4\dfrac{10^2}{2^2} = 100 \text{ m/s}$

$\therefore \ p_1 = p_2 + \dfrac{V_2^2 - V_1^2}{2g}\gamma = 0 + \dfrac{100^2 - 4^2}{2 \times 9.8}9800 = 4.99 \times 10^6 \text{ Pa}$

11.89 b) Use Darcy's equation. Moody's diagram gives f:

11-FLUIDS

$$\Delta p = \gamma h_f = \gamma f \frac{L}{D} \frac{V^2}{2g}$$

$$\text{Re} = \frac{VD}{\nu} = \frac{4 \times 0.1}{10^{-6}} = 4 \times 10^5, \quad \frac{e}{D} = \frac{0.26}{100} = 0.0026. \quad \therefore f = 0.025$$

$$\therefore \Delta p = 9800 \times 0.025 \frac{100}{0.1} \frac{4^2}{2 \times 9.8} = 2.0 \times 10^5 \text{ Pa}$$

11.90 a)   The Moody diagram with $e = 0$ provides f:

$$\frac{e}{D} = 0 \text{ with } \text{Re} = 4 \times 10^5 \text{ provides } f = 0.013.$$

$$\therefore \Delta p = 9800 \times 0.013 \times \frac{100}{0.1} \frac{4^2}{2 \times 9.8} = 1.04 \times 10^5 \text{ Pa}$$

11.91 d)   The momentum equation provides the solution:

$$\Sigma F_x = \rho Q(V_{2x} - V_{1x})$$

$$p_1 A_1 - F_x = \rho A V(V_{2x} - V_{1x})$$

$$4.99 \times 10^6 \times \pi \times 0.05^2 - F_x = 1000 \times \pi \times 0.05^2 \times 4(100 \cos 45° - 4)$$

$$\therefore F_x = 37\ 000 \text{ N}$$

11.92 a)   The momentum equation in the y-direction gives

$$\Sigma F_y = \rho Q(V_{2y} - V_{1y})$$

$$F_y = \rho A V(V_{2y} - 0) = 1000 \times \pi \times 0.05^2 \times 4 \times 100 \sin 45° = 2220 \text{ N}$$

11.93 c) $p = \gamma h = 9800 \times 25 = 245\ 000 \text{ Pa}$

11.94 d)   The energy equation requires us to calculate the head loss:

$$V = \frac{Q}{A} = \frac{1.2/60}{\pi \times 0.03^2} = 7.07 \text{ m/s}, \quad \text{Re} = \frac{VD}{\nu} = \frac{7.07 \times 0.06}{0.9 \times 10^{-6}} = 4.7 \times 10^5$$

$$\frac{e}{D} = \frac{0.25}{60} = 0.0042. \quad \therefore \text{Moody's diagram gives } f = 0.029$$

Finally

$$\frac{p_1}{\gamma} + z_1 + \frac{V_1^2}{2g} = \frac{p_2}{\gamma} + z_2 + \frac{V_2^2}{2g} + \left[C_{entrance} + C_{elbow} + C_{exit} + f\frac{L}{D} \right] \frac{V^2}{2g} + \frac{\dot{W}_P}{Q\gamma} \eta$$

$$0 + 10 + 0 = 0 + 25 + 0 + \left[0.5 + 0.9 + 1.0 + 0.029\frac{75}{0.06} \right] \frac{7.07^2}{2 \times 9.8} + \frac{\dot{W}_P}{(1.2/60) \times 9800} \times 0.85$$

$$\therefore \dot{W}_P = -26\,200 \text{ W} \quad \text{or} \quad -26 \text{ kW}$$

11.95 b)   Follow the calculations of Problem 11.94 and find $f = 0.029$. Then let $p_2 = p_v = 3.2$ kPa abs. Apply the energy equation from the reservoir surface to the pump inlet:

$$\frac{p_1}{\gamma} + z_1 + \frac{V_1^2}{2g} = \frac{p_2}{\gamma} + z_2 + \frac{V_2^2}{2g} + \left[C_{entrance} + f\frac{L}{D} \right] \frac{V^2}{2g} + \frac{\dot{W}_P}{Q\gamma} \eta$$

$$0 + 10 + 0 = \frac{-96.8 \times 1000}{9800} + 0 + \frac{7.07^2}{2 \times 9.8} + \left[0.5 + 0.029\frac{L}{0.06} \right] \frac{7.07^2}{2 \times 9.8}. \quad \therefore L = 13 \text{ m}$$

11.96 d) The energy equation with no losses (for maximum flow rate) from the tank surface to the pipe outlet gives

$$\frac{p_1}{\gamma} + z_1 + \frac{V_1^2}{2g} = \frac{p_2}{\gamma} + z_2 + \frac{V_2^2}{2g}$$

$$0 + 25 + 0 = \frac{9800 \times 10}{9800} + \frac{V_2^2}{2 \times 9.8}. \quad \therefore V_2 = 17.1 \text{ m/s}$$

$$Q = AV = \pi \times 0.06^2 \times 17.1 = 0.193 \text{ m}^3/\text{s} \text{ or } 11.6 \text{ m}^3/\text{min}$$

11.97 d) Apply the energy equation from the tank surface to the reservoir surface:

$$V = \frac{Q}{A} = \frac{0.4}{\pi \times 0.03^2} = 2.36 \text{ m/s}. \quad \therefore \text{Re} = 1.6 \times 10^5, \frac{e}{D} = 0.0042 \text{ so that } f = 0.030$$

$$\frac{p_1}{\gamma} + z_1 + \frac{V_1^2}{2g} = \frac{p_2}{\gamma} + z_2 + \frac{V_2^2}{2g} + \left[C_{entrance} + C_{elbow} + C_{exit} + f\frac{L}{D} \right]\frac{V^2}{2g} + \frac{\dot{W}_T}{\eta Q \gamma}$$

$$0 + 100 + 0 = 0 + 80 + 0 + \left[0.5 + 0.9 + 1.0 + 0.03\frac{75}{0.06} \right]\frac{2.36^2}{2 \times 9.8} + \frac{\dot{W}_P}{0.9 \times (0.4/60) \times 9800}$$

$$\therefore \dot{W}_T = 509 \text{ W}$$

11.98 b) $Q = AV = \pi \times 0.01^2 \times 100 = 0.0314 \text{ m}^3/\text{s} \text{ or } 1.2 \text{ m}^3/\text{min}$

11.99 d) Bernoulli's equation with no losses gives

$$V = V_1\frac{A_1}{A} = 100\frac{0.01^2}{0.04^2} = 6.25 \text{ m/s}.$$

$$\frac{p}{\gamma} + \frac{V^2}{2g} = \frac{p_1}{\gamma} + \frac{V_1^2}{2g}. \quad \frac{p}{9800} + \frac{6.25^2}{2 \times 9.8} = 0 + \frac{100^2}{2 \times 9.8}. \quad \therefore p = 4.98 \times 10^6 \text{ Pa}$$

11.100 c) Sketch the velocity polygon first:

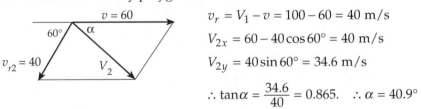

$$v_r = V_1 - v = 100 - 60 = 40 \text{ m/s}$$

$$V_{2x} = 60 - 40\cos 60° = 40 \text{ m/s}$$

$$V_{2y} = 40\sin 60° = 34.6 \text{ m/s}$$

$$\therefore \tan\alpha = \frac{34.6}{40} = 0.865. \quad \therefore \alpha = 40.9°$$

11.101 c) The x-component momentum equation provides

$$-F_x = \rho Q\left[(v_{r2})_x - (v_{r1})_x \right]$$

$$= 1000 \times \pi \times 0.01^2[-40\cos 60° - 40] = -18.8 \text{ N}$$

11.102 a) Power is force times velocity:

$$\dot{W} = 4F_x v$$

$$= 4 \times 18.8 \times 60 = 4510 \text{ W}$$

11.103 **c)** Equate the power to the maximum power from the NCEES Handbook:

$$\rho Q (V_1 - v)(1 - \cos \alpha)v = \rho Q \frac{V_1^2}{4}(1 - \cos \alpha)$$

$$\therefore (100 - v)v = \frac{100^2}{4} \quad \text{or} \quad v^2 - 100v + 2500 = 0$$

$$\therefore v = \frac{100 \pm \sqrt{100\,000 - 100\,000}}{2} = 50 \text{ m/s}$$

11.104 **d)** Use the notions of Similitude; Reynolds number is the required parameter:

$$\frac{V_m D_m}{v_m} = \frac{V_p D_p}{v_p}. \quad \therefore V_m = V_p \frac{D_p}{D_m} \frac{v_m}{v_p} = 10 \times 20 \times \frac{10^{-6}}{1.4 \times 10^{-5}} = 14.3 \text{ m/s}$$

11.105 **a)** First, estimate the force that resists motion using the drag coefficient for a sphere:

$$\text{Re} = \frac{VD}{v} = \frac{10 \times 10}{1.4 \times 10^{-5}} = 7 \times 10^6$$

$$F = \frac{1}{2}\rho V^2 A C_D = \frac{1}{2} \times 1.2 \times 10^2 \times \pi \times 5^2 \times 0.15 = 707 \text{ N}$$

$$\dot{W} = F \times V = 707 \times 10 = 7070 \text{ W} \quad \text{or} \quad \frac{7070}{746} = 9.5 \text{ Hp}$$

11.106 **c)** Assume the width of the plate is the circumference of the dirigible:

$$\text{Re} = \frac{VD}{v} = \frac{10 \times 150}{1.4 \times 10^{-5}} = 1.07 \times 10^8$$

$$C_D = 0.031 / \text{Re}^{1/7} = \frac{0.031}{(1.07 \times 10^8)^{1/7}} = 0.00221$$

$$\therefore F = \frac{1}{2}\rho V^2 A C_D = \frac{1}{2} \times 1.2 \times 10^2 \times \pi \times 10 \times 150 \times 0.00221 = 625 \text{ N}$$

$$\dot{W} = F \times V = 625 \times 10 = 6250 \text{ W} \quad \text{or} \quad \frac{6250}{746} = 8.4 \text{ Hp}$$

11.107 **b)** Bernoulli's equation says that the increase in pressure from the free-stream to the stagnation point on the nose is given by

$$\Delta p = \frac{1}{2}\rho V^2 = \frac{1}{2} \times 1.2 \times 10^2 = 60 \text{ Pa}$$

Engineering Ethics

by John B. Dilworth

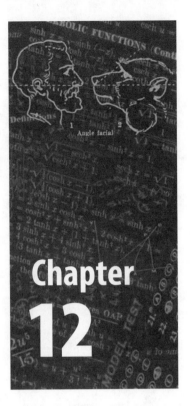

Chapter 12

12.1 Introduction

In addition to technical expertise and professionalism, engineers are also expected by society and by their profession to maintain high standards of ethical conduct in their professional lives. This chapter will cover the most important issues of ethics insofar as they are relevant to careers in the various engineering disciplines. A brief concluding section will also summarize the various legal guidelines and requirements with which engineers are expected to be familiar.

To begin, here is a summary of the basic areas and kinds of questions to be covered.

Summary

1. Since engineering ethics is a branch of ethics, we start with a clarification of the nature of ethics, and how ethical values and concerns differ from other kinds of values and concerns.

2. Next, the specific concerns of engineering ethics will be examined, and distinguished from other concerns about values which engineers may also have. Such non-ethical concerns include personal preferences, social or political values, and more technical professional values related to becoming and remaining an excellent engineer from a purely engineering or scientific point of view.

3. After the preliminary clarifications and distinctions above, we then examine the basic issues, concepts and special topics of engineering ethics. Most of these are also included in or assumed by the codes of ethics provided by various professional engineering societies.

It will be useful to examine one of these codes in more detail, namely the National Council of Examiners for Engineering and Surveying (NCEES) Model Rules of Professional Conduct. The study of this code will give engineers a good understanding of the kind of real-world requirements which professional engineering societies uphold for their members. The discussion will also be supplemented with some model answers to typical ethics questions, which provide a useful test of familiarity with and understanding of the ethical issues covered in such codes. In addition, more wide-ranging discussion and essay ethics questions are included to encourage more principled and independent thinking about ethical issues by engineers.

12.2 The Nature of Ethics

Ethical standards exist independently of any particular group of experts

Generally, ethics is concerned with standards, rules or guidelines for moral or socially approved conduct such as being honest or trustworthy, or acting in the best interest of a society.

Not all standards or values are ethical standards, though. For example, personal preferences and values such as individual choices of food or clothing aren't important enough to qualify as ethical values or choices. Generally speaking, ethical standards apply only to conduct which could have some significant effect on the lives of people in general.

Thus for an engineer, using a substandard grade of steel in the construction of a bridge would definitely violate ethical standards because of the potential for safety hazards for people in general. But on the other hand, using an inferior brand of ketchup on one's fries does not violate any ethical standards, since at worst it would only violate personal, non-ethical standards of what tastes good to oneself.

Ethics and ethical standards should also be distinguished from matters of legality and legal standards. Roughly speaking, the distinction is that legal standards are defined in legal documents by some properly appointed legal body, and those documents and legal experts determine what the law is and who should obey it.

In ethics, by contrast, it is instead assumed that ethical standards exist independently of any particular group of experts (being accessible to all through the exercise of their own thinking capacities), and that a codification or written-down form of the standards merely describes or summarizes what those pre-existing ethical standards are, rather than (as in the case of the law) defining their very nature.

For example, if there were a legal requirement that any load-bearing beam in a bridge must be able to bear five times the average real-world stress on the beam, then it is a simple matter of calculation to determine whether a beam meets the legal standard or not. However, an ethical standard for what would be an adequate safety factor in such a case is a very different matter, and it cannot be settled by calculation or appeal to a rule-book, since an ethically concerned engineer could convincingly argue that conventional or routine safety factors are really ethically inadequate and unacceptable. Such a person cannot be answered merely by appeal to some rule-book or to current legal standards for such matters.

Another vital point about ethics is that its standards are always more important than any other standards. Thus in the contrast between personal and ethical standards discussed above, if one's personal standards conflict with ethical standards, then one must suppress one's personal standards to resolve the conflict in favor of the ethical standards. For example, if one personally values finding the highest-paying job, but it turns out that the job in question involves some ethically wrong conduct, then it is one's ethical duty not to accept that job, but to take a lower-paying, more ethical job instead.

It is generally held that even legal standards must give way to ethical standards in the case of conflicts. For example, suppose that a law governing motor vehicles did not currently require a vehicle recall in the case when engineering defects were found in its construction. Nevertheless, if a good case could be made that this was an ethically unacceptable situation, then the law would have to be changed to conform to the ethical standard. So here too, other kinds of values or standards must be suppressed or adjusted in the case of a conflict with ethical standards, which are always of overriding importance.

> 🔑 Even legal standards must give way to ethical standards in the case of conflicts.

The Subject Matter of Ethics

The subject of ethics includes both theories about the nature of ethics (this part of ethics is sometimes called *meta-ethics*), and recommendations of appropriate standards or guidelines for morally right or good behavior by people (sometimes described as *normative ethics*). *Engineering ethics* mainly deals with such normative or ethical standards as to how responsible engineers should behave.

Three main varieties of meta-ethical theories are ethical skepticism, relativism, and absolutism. Skeptics believe that ethical beliefs and standards are merely a matter of subjective personal opinion or biased feelings, so that there really are not any justifiable, reliable ethical standards. However, we can ignore this theory here, since professionals in any field, including engineering, are required as part of their professional obligations to adhere to high ethical standards. So ethical skeptics should seek some other line of work than engineering or the other professions.

> 🔑 Ethical skeptics should seek some other line of work than engineering.

Ethical relativism claims that in some way ethical standards are relative to a society or culture. In contrast, *ethical absolutism* claims that the same ethical standards apply to all societies and cultures. Applied to engineering ethics, this would be a dispute about whether or not it would be acceptable for different societies to have different engineering ethics standards for their professional engineers.

Fortunately, we can avoid this dispute here, at least at the present introductory level, in a similar manner to that in which we avoided ethical skepticism. As already noted, professionals in any field, including engineering, are required as part of their professional obligations to adhere to high ethical standards. But inevitably those high standards in practice are those approved or debated within the specific society in which an engineers beginning their own professional lives. So for present purposes we can put aside as peripheral or irrelevant the question of whether or not other societies should adopt codes of engineering ethics similar to our own.

Normative Ethics

Returning to normative ethics, recall that it involves recommendations of appropriate standards or guidelines for morally right or good behavior by people, and that engineering ethics mainly deals with such normative or ethical standards as to how responsible engineers should behave. We will be examining these standards as applied to engineering in succeeding sections. But for the present, here is a brief summary of some standard approaches to normative ethics.

There are two main approaches to normative ethics. The first views the subject primarily in terms of rules or principles for right conduct, developed on various different bases such as that of intuition, reason or social tradition. Fortunately for us, in spite of the disagreements as to the basis or source of normative ethical principles, there is very general agreement on what the resulting rules should be—rules such as "Always tell the truth," "Keep your promises," "Protect innocent life," and so on.

The other main approach to normative ethics focuses instead on ethical behavior viewed as whatever actions will best promote the general welfare or benefit of all people. This is often called a *"utilitarian"* approach to normative ethics, and it can be summed up in the slogan "The greatest good for the greatest number." Another common description for this approach is as a *"consequentialist"* ethic, in that it morally judges an action in terms of whether or not it would have better consequences than any other action one could perform.

Conflicts in Ethics

Potentially at least, it seems there could be a conflict between the rule-based versus the utilitarian or consequentialist approaches to normative ethics. For example, following the principle "Always tell the truth" may apparently not have the best consequences in a particular case, while the action which does seem to have the best consequences (possibly a case of lying) may violate a moral principle.

However, fortunately, most utilitarians agree that a deeper analysis will almost always show that what their consequentialist ethic says is morally correct is substantially the same as what conforms to the ethical standards recommended by the rule-based ethical theories. So we will find that in practice both ethics in general and engineering ethics in particular contain elements from both approaches, which generally co-exist without any fundamental difficulty.

Another example of this practical convergence in spite of initial theoretical differences is found in the issue of intentions versus actions. Rule-based theories tell us that being ethical involves following a morally correct rule or principle, whatever the consequences of so doing.

However, the following concern could be raised: Since human beings are fallible and imperfect, the best they can do is to sincerely intend to follow a morally correct rule. So whatever happens as a result of their actions in doing so, no matter how bad it is, nevertheless they will be morally blameless because their intentions were good. (Example: a well-intentioned person tries to push a passerby out of the way of a speeding vehicle, but only succeeds in pushing him or her more directly into its path.)

On the other hand, from the utilitarian or consequentialist approach, a person's intentions are morally irrelevant; only the actual consequences of their actions are relevant to judging the morality of their actions. So as before, it initially looks as if there could be a fundamental conflict between the rule-based and utilitarian, consequence-based approaches.

Fortunately, though, here too a deeper analysis can resolve the apparent clash between these approaches. Though it is true that humans are imperfect, nevertheless we also have enough intelligence and rationality so that we can legitimately be held responsible for cases in which we actually fail to follow the ethically correct rule. Though mismatches between good intentions and good actions can occur, it is the responsibility of ethical persons to eliminate or avoid all potentially serious cases where such clashes might occur.

A standard example of this is driving while drunk. Even if a person sincerely did intend to drive well and not injure anyone while he/she was drunk, nevertheless they can be held responsible for any injuries they cause in spite of their good intentions. Since their moral duty is to always follow ethical rules such as "Cause no harm to innocent persons," they have a duty to avoid getting into situations of this kind where they know they may be unable to avoid breaking such rules. Thus they should either not drink before driving, or not drive after drinking, to ensure that they do not violate the moral rule.

Hence in practice, and on a deeper analysis, both the rule-based and consequence-based theories of ethics would agree that "good intentions are not enough" in ethics, and that ethical behavior requires actually doing what is right—sincere intentions or wishful thinking have no special ethical value, nor are they legitimate excuses for ethically bad behavior.

> Sincere intentions or wishful thinking have no special ethical value, nor are they legitimate excuses for ethically bad behavior.

Special Topics to Consider

Before concluding this section, a couple of special topics should be mentioned which do not fit easily into the standard classification of rule versus utilitarian approaches, but which are nevertheless generally regarded as being ethically important.

The first of these is the concept of *justice*. Intuitively, it is ethically wrong to treat people in unjust or unfair ways. People should be given what they deserve, and also all people should be treated equally. But it is difficult to reduce justice to a series of rules, and justice may even conflict sometimes with a utilitarian approach, since what is best for most may be unfair to minorities.

The second special topic is that of *human rights*. For example, the U.S. Constitution talks about the rights to life, liberty and the pursuit of happiness. As with justice, moral rights are not easily reducible to rules, and they may conflict with the greatest good for most people in some cases.

Descriptive Ethics

In addition to the term "ethics" being used to refer to meta-ethics or normative ethics, sometimes it is used more descriptively (as in "the ethics of a society") to refer to the actual ethical or moral customs or guidelines that people do follow in the given society. To some extent engineering ethics is also descriptive in this way, in that it includes the actual standards which professional engineers have adhered to and continue to adhere to as registered engineers.

Nevertheless, the standards of engineering ethics should always be viewed as having normative force as well—as part of normative ethics, not just descriptive ethics. Thus they should be viewed as standards which one is required to follow as a necessary guide to one's future conduct, not merely as standards which as a matter of fact engineers have followed up to now.

Example 12.1

A person's behavior is always ethical when one:

    A)   Does what is best for oneself

    B)   Has good intentions, no matter how things turn out

    C)   Does what is best for everyone

    D)   Does what is most profitable

Solution: Since ethics is concerned with standards (other than purely legal ones) for socially approved conduct and with promoting the general welfare, C is the only acceptable answer. The other three answers (doing what is best for oneself, acting with good intentions, and doing what is most profitable) may or may not involve socially approved conduct or promote the general welfare, depending on the individual case, and therefore they cannot guarantee ethical behavior.

Example 12.2

Which of the following ensure that behavior is ethical?

  I. Following the law

  II. Acting in the best interest of a society

  III. Following non-legal standards for socially approved conduct

    A)   All of the above

    B)   II and III only

    C)   None of the above

    D)   I only

Solution: Given that ethics is concerned with standards (other than purely legal ones) for socially approved conduct and with promoting the general welfare, the choices rate as follows: Following the law (I) cannot ensure ethical behavior, because a given law might itself be unethical (example: earlier laws legitimizing slavery.) But both II and III do ensure that behavior is ethical. Hence the correct option is B.

12.3 The Nature of Engineering Ethics

Much of engineering ethics is an applied or more specific form of what could be called "general ethics," that is, ethical standards which apply to any human activity or occupation. For example, ethical duties of honesty, fair dealing with other people, obeying the relevant laws of one's country or state, and so on apply in any situation. Thus some of the ethical obligations of engineers are of this general kind also found in many other occupations and activities.

Other kinds of standards found in engineering ethics are more specific but not unique to engineers, such as the principles governing the ethical activities of any professionals in their contacts with clients or customers. These too are an important part of engineering ethics, and they show up in the large overlap in the contents of many codes of ethics derived from many different professions (engineering, law, medicine, academia, etc.).

Then finally there are some standards applying primarily to the profession of engineering, such as those dealing with the proper, ethical manner of approval of designs or plans by managers which require them to have professional engineering qualifications and expertise. These standards are what make engineering ethics distinctive relative to other kinds of applied ethics, but they are only one small part of the whole of engineering ethics, and so should not be over-emphasized.

Now to the question of how ethical standards for engineers differ from other standards of value which engineers might use. This brief discussion will parallel that given above for ethics. The aim is to get clear on which of the choices an engineer might make are relevant to engineering ethics, as opposed to other choices which are instead based on other kinds of values or standards.

As with ethics in general, purely personal choices or values are not relevant to engineering ethics. For example, an engineer who is submitting a bid to a potential client on an engineering project might personally decide to factor in a somewhat higher rate of profit on the project for him/herself than is usual in such projects.

However, as long as there is an open bidding process (where others are free to submit possibly lower bids), and as long as the personal pricing would not affect the quality of the work which would be done, then the pricing level remains a purely personal or economic decision with no ethical implications.

On the other hand, if an engineer were to decide to maximize his/her profit in another way—by submitting a low bid, but then secretly drastically compromising on the quality of materials used so as to achieve maximum personal profit—that would be a violation of engineering ethics standards, which generally require the use of high-quality materials and construction methods acceptable to all parties signing the initial project agreement. This would be a case in which a conflict between personal standards (maximum profit) and engineering ethical standards (honoring the contract and using high-quality materials and methods) must be resolved in favor of supporting the relevant engineering ethics standards in this case.

These contrasts between personal versus ethical values apply also to the related contrast of corporate or economic values versus ethical values. Thus the examples just given of legitimate versus ethically illegitimate maximizing of profits

A conflict between personal standards and engineering ethical standards must be resolved in favor of supporting the relevant engineering ethics standards would apply just as well if the motivation were the interest of some corporation or economic group—it would be equally wrong for a corporation or engineering firm to seek profit at the risk of lower engineering quality of products or services. Thus it is the duty of an engineer to uphold engineering ethics standards even if (to take an extreme case) his/her job is at risk, such as when doing the ethically right action would conflict with the non-ethical interests of a boss or corporate structure.

The relation of engineering ethics issues to legal issues applying to engineers should also be discussed. Although (as we saw previously) legal and ethical values are basically different kinds of values which should be distinguished, nevertheless it is generally true that one has an ethical obligation to obey the prevailing laws in a given jurisdiction. Also, persons voluntarily entering the engineering profession agree to abide by codes of ethics which explicitly or implicitly require compliance with existing laws, so here too good engineering ethics standards will generally be is in close harmony with existing legal codes governing the practice of engineering.

Another area of close harmony between different kinds of values in engineering ethics is found in the case of technical or scientific values. Any scientific community dealing with pure sciences or applied sciences such as engineering will have technical values concerning the proper and correct ways to construct theories, carry out calculations, make statistically satisfactory estimates where exact results are not possible, and so on. These themselves are not ethical values (good science is not the same as good ethics). But nevertheless engineers do have an ethical obligation to use good scientific methods at all times, and so here too (as with the law) there is a close correlation between practicing good science and being an ethical engineer.

One other topic should be mentioned here. Naturally, most of engineering ethics concerns an engineer's behavior while engaged in professional engineering activities. But one should be aware that engineering ethics codes also generally include prohibitions on unethical behavior while off the job as well, if those activities would affect public perceptions of one's professional integrity or status. This would include activities such as gambling which might tend to bring the profession of engineering into disrepute, deceptive or other inappropriate forms of advertising of services, or any other activities suggesting a lack of integrity or trustworthiness in an engineer.

> 🔑 Engineering ethics codes also generally include prohibitions on unethical behavior while off the job as well.

Example 12.3

Engineers should follow their professional code of ethics because:

   A)   It helps them avoid legal problems, such as getting sued

   B)   It provides a clear definition of what the public has a right to expect from responsible engineers

   C)   It raises the image of the profession and hence gets engineers more pay

   D)   The public will trust engineers more once they know engineers have a code of ethics

Solution: These choices are a little harder than those in previous questions, because even the wrong choices do have some connection with ethics. But as long as you follow the initial instruction (choose the best and most relevant answer), you shouldn't have any difficulty answering it.

Choice A: Avoiding legal problems is generally a good thing, but it's not the most relevant reason why the code should be followed (and in some cases, strictly following the code might make it more likely that you'd get sued, e.g., by a disgruntled contractor if you refuse to certify shoddy workmanship).

Choice C: Raising the image of the profession is a good thing, but not for the reason of getting more pay; that would be to act from self-interest rather than ethical motivations.

Choice D: Increased public trust is generally a good thing, but the mere knowledge that there is such a code means little unless engineers actually follow it, and for the right reasons.

Choice B: The best and most relevant answer. The code of ethics is designed to promote the public welfare, and hence the public has a right to expect that responsible engineers will follow each of its provisions, as clearly defined by the code.

Example 12.4

Engineers should act ethically because:

 A) If they don't, they risk getting demoted or fired

 B) The boss wants them to

 C) It feels good

 D) That's the way responsible engineers behave

Solution: As with problem 12.1, some of the wrong answers here do have some connection with ethics, so as before the task is to pick the best and most relevant answer.

Choice A: Even though ethical behavior may usually improve one's job security, it's not the most relevant reason for being ethical.

Choice B: Doing what the boss wants is a self-interested reason for acting, not an ethical reason.

Choice C: Even though, hopefully, being ethical will make engineers feel good, it's not the main reason why they should be ethical.

Choice D: The right answer. There's a very close connection between acting in a responsible manner and acting ethically.

Example 12.5

The first and foremost obligation of registered professional engineers is to:

 A) The public welfare

 B) Their employer

 C) The government

 D) The engineering profession

Solution: As before, the best and most relevant answer should be chosen.

Choice B: Engineers do have ethical obligations to their employer, but it's not their foremost or primary obligation.

Choice C: As with the employer, engineers do have some obligations to the government, but again, not the first or primary one.

Choice D: Obligations to the engineering profession are probably even more important than those to employers or the government, but still they are not the foremost obligation.

Choice A: Correct. The foremost, primary obligation of engineers is to the public welfare.

Example 12.6

Registered professional engineers should undertake services for clients only when:

A) They really need the fees

B) Their own bid is the lowest one

C) They are fully technically competent to carry out the services

D) Carrying out the services wouldn't involve excessive time or effort

Solution: Choice A: Personal financial need is a matter of self-interest, not of ethics.

Choice B: The competitive status of a bid is a matter of economics, not ethics.

Choice D: The amount of time involved in carrying out services is also a matter of economics and self-interest, rather than of ethics.

Choice C: Correct. Ethical engineers will not undertake to provide services for clients unless they are fully technically competent to carry them out.

12.4 The Issues and Topics of Engineering Ethics

Now we will examine the basic issues, concepts, and special topics of engineering ethics. Recall that most of these are also included in or assumed by the codes of ethics provided by various professional engineering societies. Hence as noted in the Introduction, we will use the most relevant one—the NCEES Model Rules of Professional Conduct—as the basis for the discussion. Its study will provide a good understanding of the typical actual ethical requirements imposed by professional engineering societies on their members.

The Preamble

The Preamble (the Introductory section) to the Rules is important in that it describes their purpose, which is to safeguard life, health and property, to promote the public welfare, and to maintain a high standard of integrity and practice among engineers. Where it is helpful, we will slightly paraphrase the statements taken from the code so as to clarify their meaning.

This part of the code makes explicit its connection with general ethical concerns which all ethical persons should adhere to. We will examine each of the items covered in turn in this statement of the purpose of the code.

1.) First, normative ethical theories universally agree that it is ethically wrong to cause harm to people. This is why the Preamble mentions the purpose of "safeguarding" life, health and property. Thus ethical persons in general, including engineers, should avoid doing anything which would damage or adversely affect other people. More positively, one should also take measures which will safeguard or preserve people from possible future harm.

For engineers, the more positive measures would include such things as building devices with extra "fail-safe" features included which make harmful consequences of their use as unlikely as possible. Overall, then, ethical persons take great care not to cause harm to others, and they take whatever extra steps are necessary to minimize risks of potential harm to others as well.

2.) The second purpose of the code is to "...promote the public welfare." Here too, standard normative ethical theories fully support this rule. It states a duty or obligation not simply to act in a harmless or safe way (as previously discussed), but in addition to take active steps so that one's professional activities will result in definite benefits and improved conditions for the general public.

For example, as an engineer planning a new highway this rule would require one not only to plan and build it in a safe manner (as previously discussed), but also to do such things as choose the shortest feasible route between its endpoints, or to choose that route which would permit the most efficient road-construction techniques, hence maximizing the utility of the highway to the general public and minimizing its cost to them as well.

3.) The third and last purpose of the code, according to the Preamble, is ".. to maintain a high standard of integrity and practice among engineers." Thus the code also has the purpose of ensuring that engineers will continue to be honest and trustworthy, and to maintain high standards of professional conduct and scientific expertise in their work.

Note that this Preamble makes it explicit that the reason why engineers should adhere to the code isn't simply because it is ethical to do so, or because their professional organization tells them to do it. Instead, it emphasizes that there are vital practical benefits to society which can only be achieved by engineers committing themselves to rigorously follow the code at all times.

Other issues covered in the Preamble are as follows:

> *"Engineering registration is a privilege and not a right. This privilege demands that engineers responsibly represent themselves before the public in a truthful and objective manner."*

A privilege is a socially earned license to do something which is granted by society only under certain conditions. For example, a driving license requires the passing of a driving test and other requirements. Similarly, engineering registration must be earned by recipients (they do not automatically have a right to that status) and the granting of it requires them in return to adhere to ethical standards such as the stated one.

> *"Engineers must compete fairly with others and avoid all conflicts of interest while faithfully serving the legitimate needs and interests of their employers and clients."*

Engineers will be honest and trustworthy, and maintain high standards of professional conduct and scientific expertise in their work.

Other Issues

This statement sums up a range of ethical requirements which are more fully covered in the body of the code, so the various issues which it raises will be discussed along with those requirements below.

The Engineer's Obligation to Society

The first group of rules in the code address **the engineer's obligation to society**. As before, we will slightly paraphrase the statements taken from the code so as to clarify their meaning:

> 1.) *While performing services, the engineer's foremost responsibility is to the public welfare.*

This rule is also featured in a related form in the Preamble, as a duty to promote the public welfare. The idea here of responsibility to the public welfare includes the idea of safeguarding the public from harm, as more fully spelled out in the next rule:

> 2.) *Engineers shall approve only those designs that safeguard the life, health, welfare and property of the public while conforming to accepted engineering standards.*

These two rules together imply a much broader context of responsibility for engineers than those arising from any one task or project. Designs and materials that seem perfectly adequate and ethically acceptable within the bounds of a given project may nevertheless be unacceptable because of wider issues about the public interest.

For example, until recently a refrigeration engineer could have specified Freon (a chlorinated fluorocarbon or CFC product) as the prime refrigerating agent for use in a product, and defended it as an efficient, inexpensive refrigerant with no risks to the purchaser of the appliance. However, we now know that there are significant risks to the public at large from such chemicals because of the long-term damage to the environment they cause when they leak out, perhaps many years after the useful life of the product is over. Rules 1 and 2 tell engineers that they must always keep such wider, possibly longer-term issues in mind on every project they work on.

> 3.) *If an engineer's professional judgment is overruled resulting in danger to the life, health, welfare or property of the public, the engineer shall notify his/her employer or client and any authority that may be appropriate.*

An important rule, which may place the engineer in a difficult position if his/her employer or client is among those contributing to the problem. But the engineer's duty in such cases is clear: "..any authority that may be appropriate" must be notified, even if the employer/client tries to prevent it. (Cases of this kind are popularly referred to as "whistle blowing.")

> 4.) *Engineers shall be objective and truthful in professional reports, statements, or testimonies and provide all pertinent supporting information relating to such reports, statements, or testimonies.*

> 5.) *Engineers shall not express a professional opinion publicly unless it is based upon knowledge of the facts and a competent evaluation of the subject matter.*

🔑 Designs and materials may be unacceptable because of wider issues about the public interest.

🔑 The duty to be forthcoming about all pertinent or relevant information in reports, etc.

Rules 4 and 5 together implement the general ethical requirement that one ought to tell the truth in the specific context of an engineer's professional duties. Note that the duty as mentioned in Rule 4 is not simply to be truthful in what one says, but also to be forthcoming about all pertinent or relevant information in reports, etc.

Rule 4 also mentions being "objective," which adds the element of being unbiased and basing one's beliefs and reports only on objective, verifiable matters of fact or theory.

Rule 5 enlarges on the idea of being objective in one's reports—others should be able to rely upon one's professional opinion, and they can do this only if one knows all of the relevant facts and is completely competent to evaluate the matter being dealt with.

> 6.) *Engineers shall not express a professional opinion on subject matters for which they are motivated or paid, unless they explicitly identify the parties on whose behalf they are expressing the opinion, and reveal the interest the parties have in the matters.*

Rule 6 expresses what is sometimes called the duty of full disclosure. Even if one honestly seeks to be truthful and objective (as in Rules 4 and 5), still doubts might be raised about one's motivation or objectivity unless one reveals on whose behalf one is expressing an opinion, and the interests that such persons have in the case. This rule is also related to the issue of conflicts of interest (see Rules 6 and 8 in the second section, below).

> 7.) *Engineers shall not associate in business ventures with nor permit their names or their firms' names to be used by any person or firm which is engaging in dishonest, fraudulent, or illegal business practice.*

This might be called the "clean hands" rule (shake hands only with those whose hands are as ethically clean as your own). It isn't sufficient to be completely ethical in one's own (or one's own company's or firm's) practices; one must also ensure that others do not profit from one's own good name if their own activities are unethical in some way. This Rule 7 is clearly related to Rule 1 concerning the public welfare—one must promote this in one's external dealings just as much as in one's own activities.

> 8.) *Engineers who have knowledge of a possible violation of any of the rules listed in this and the following two parts shall provide pertinent information and assist the state board in reaching a final determination of the possible violation.*

Rule 8 generalizes Rule 3 (a duty of disclosure when one's professional judgment is overruled) to a duty of disclosure in the case of any of these rules, when one has knowledge of possible violations of them. In terms of the public welfare, it is very important that each profession regulates itself in this way, so as to minimize or eliminate future infringements of its rules. Strict adherence to this rule also will also lead to wider appreciation and respect for the profession of engineering because of its willingness to "clean its own house" in this way.

The Engineer's Obligation to Employers and Clients

A professional engineer must be trustworthy as well as honest, and being trusted not to reveal confidential information is an important kind of trust.

The second group of rules in the code address **the engineer's obligation to employers and clients.**

> 1.) *Engineers shall not undertake technical assignments for which they are not qualified by education or experience.*

> 2.) *Engineers shall approve or seal only those plans or designs that deal with subjects in which they are competent and which have been prepared under their direct control and supervision.*

Rules 1 and 2 require an engineer to be professionally competent, both in undertaking technical assignments and in approving plans or designs. Rule 2 in fact requires a double kind of knowledge, both technical competence in the matters to be approved and that one has had direct control and supervision over their preparation. Only thus can one be sure that one's approval is legitimate and warranted.

> 3.) *Engineers may coordinate an entire project provided that each design component is signed or sealed by the engineer responsible for that design component.*

Rule 3 in effect invokes Rule 2. As long as each component of a project is satisfactorily approved as per Rule 2, then it is permissible for an engineer to coordinate an entire project. This also underlines the importance of Rule 2, as project managers have to rely heavily on the validity of the approvals for each prior part of a project.

> 4.) *Engineers shall not reveal professional information without the prior consent of the employer or client except as authorized or required by law.*

This confidentiality requirement is the other side of the coin of duties to tell the truth (as in Rules 4 and 5 of the first Obligations to Society section). Just as one must not lie or misinform, so also must one restrict to whom one reveals professionally relevant information. A professional engineer must be trustworthy as well as honest, and being trusted not to reveal confidential information is an important kind of trust.

Confidentiality is a central factor in assuring employers and clients that one's professional services for them are indeed for them alone, and that they can rely upon one's discretion in not revealing to others any private information without their full consent. This rule is also related to Rules 5 through 8 below, in that any revealing of information to others would probably create conflicts of interest or other "serving more than one master" problems of those kinds.

> 5.) *Engineers shall not solicit or accept valuable considerations, financial or otherwise, directly or indirectly, from contractors, their agents, or other parties while performing work for employers or clients.*

This is the first of four rules dealing with problems of "conflicts of interest." These are cases where one has some primary professional interest or group of interests—generally, to carry out some project for an employer or client—but where other factors might enter into the picture which would activate other, non-professional interests one also has which would then conflict with the professional interests.

In the case of Rule 5, the concern is that soliciting or accepting such things as gifts, hospitality, or suggestions of possible future job offers for oneself would activate non-job-related, personal interests of yours (for additional pay, career advancement, etc.) which would then be in conflict with one's primary professional interests and duties concerning a current project.

Special attention should be paid to this and the other conflict-of-interest rules, and they should be strictly observed. People are sometimes tempted to think that breaking these rules is ethically harmless, on the grounds that if one has a strong enough character, then one will not actually be professionally influenced in a detrimental way by gifts, etc., and hence that accepting such inducements cannot do any harm.

However, it is important to realize that even the *appearance* of a conflict of interest (however careful one is to avoid actually undermining one's professional interests) can create serious ethical problems. One basic concern about this is the potential loss of trust it could cause in an employer or client. Just as clients need to know that the engineer will keep their information confidential (as in Rule 4), so also they need to know that the engineer is single-mindedly working with only their interests at heart.

Any doubts raised because of the appearance of a conflict of interest could be very damaging to the client/engineer professional relationship. This is why it is necessary for the professional engineer to avoid doing anything which would create conflicts of interest or even the appearance of them.

Further rules are necessary to deal with conflicts of interest, because unfortunately in some situations the appearance or possibility of conflicts of interest may be virtually unavoidable, no matter how ethically careful everyone is. However, fortunately at the same time there is a powerful method available for minimizing any ethically bad effects of such situations. This is the method of full disclosure of potential conflicts to all interested parties, and it is addressed in the following two rules:

> 6.) *Engineers shall disclose to their employers or clients potential conflicts of interest or any other circumstances that could influence or appear to influence their professional judgment or the quality of their service.*

> 7.) *An engineer shall not accept financial or other compensation from more than one party for services rendered on one project unless the details are fully disclosed and agreed to by all parties concerned.*

Both these rules address issues of full disclosure, or keeping all the relevant parties fully informed as to areas of potential conflict or potentially undue external influences. The basic idea behind full disclosure is that it can maintain trust and confidence between all parties in several important ways, as detailed below.

First, if engineer A informs other party B about a potential conflict or influence, then A has been honest with B about that matter, hence maintaining or reinforcing B's trust in A. Furthermore, if B is not further concerned about the matter once he/she knows about it, then the potential problem (namely, the apparent conflict or potentially bad influence on A's professional conduct) has been completely defused.

Suppose on the other hand that B is initially concerned about the issue even after it was honestly revealed to B by A. Even so, the problem is already lessened: at least A has honestly revealed the area of concern. Things would be much

Even the *appearance* of a conflict of interest can create serious ethical problems.

worse if B later discovered the problem for him/herself, in a case when A had not fully disclosed it—that would be very destructive of trust between A and B.

Furthermore, now that B knows about the area of concern, and knows that A is fully cooperating with him/her in disclosing the potential problem, both of them can proceed to work out mutually acceptable ways of minimizing or disposing of the problem to their joint satisfaction. Thus even if the full disclosure does lead to an initial problem which needs to be resolved, nevertheless it is one which does not break down the trust between A and B. In fact it may even reinforce trust, in that A's willingness to fully disclose a potential conflict/influence and negotiate with B about it is good evidence for B of A's professional honesty and sincerity.

> 8.) *To avoid conflicts of interest, engineers shall not solicit or accept a professional contract from a governmental body on which a principal or officer of their firm serves as a member. An engineer who is a principal or employee of a private firm and who serves as a member of a governmental body shall not participate in decisions relating to the professional services solicited or provided by the firm to the governmental body.*

Rule 8 deals with a special case of potential conflicts of interest, namely, when one of the interested parties is a governmental body. In such a case, a somewhat stricter rule is required than for the more usual cases involving only non-governmental agencies.

In non-governmental cases, it is ethically sufficient to fully disclose potential conflicts of interests to all parties, and then to negotiate with the other parties as to how to deal with the potential conflicts. For example, if one's engineering firm has an official who was also on the board of directors of a bank, it would be ethically acceptable to accept a professional contract from that bank, as long as all parties were fully informed about the official's joint appointment prior to the agreement, and also as long as they could come to agree that the joint appointment was not an impediment to their signing a contract.

Returning to the governmental case, the reason why the stricter Rule 8 is required when one of the parties is a governmental body is as follows: In the case of agreements among private persons or businesses, they themselves are the only parties having a legitimate interest in the negotiations, and hence whatever they freely decide among themselves (of course assuming that no other ethical rules or laws are being broken) is acceptable.

On the other hand, in the case when a governmental body is involved, there is another interested party which is not directly represented in negotiations, namely the electorate or citizens of the jurisdiction covered by that governmental body. The governmental body must act only in ways which fully respect the interests and concerns of the electorate. In such a case, it is impossible to ensure that full disclosure to all of the citizens of the electorate of the potential conflicts of interest would be made in a case such as that envisaged in Rule 8, and hence there is a need for the stricter rule which completely prohibits conflicts of interest of the kinds defined in Rule 8. Only then can public trust both in the engineering profession and in governmental bodies be preserved.

When a governmental body is involved, there is another interested party which is not directly represented in negotiations, namely the electorate.

The third group of rules in the code primarily address **an engineer's obligations to other engineers**. These rules can be considered as more precise specifications of various rules already introduced, when applied to the specific context of obligations to other engineering professionals. The first rule also covers obligations to potential employers (whether they are engineers or not) when one is seeking employment.

> 1.) *Engineers shall not misrepresent or permit misrepresentation of their or any of their associates' academic or professional qualifications. They shall not misrepresent their level of responsibility nor the complexity of prior assignments. Pertinent facts relating to employers, employees, associates, joint ventures or past accomplishment shall not be misrepresented when soliciting employment or business.*

This Rule 1 is an application or more specific form of Rules 4 and 5 of the first section (concerning an engineer's obligation to society), which require objectivity and truthfulness in all professional reports, statements and opinions.

Rule 1 requires one not to misrepresent one's own qualifications, or those of associates, which is a very important kind of truthfulness and objectivity. The rule further specifies that this duty not to misrepresent applies also to issues of prior levels of responsibility and to the complexity of previous assignments as well. The rule concludes with a statement about any and all pertinent facts in one's previous history, and it requires that they too should not be misrepresented.

It might be thought that this Rule 1 is unnecessary, since it simply applies some general ethical principles already in the code to special cases and circumstances centering around issues of employment and qualifications. However, as with issues of conflicts of interest, there are some special temptations in these areas which are best addressed by explicitly spelling out what is ethically required for dealing with such situations.

A typical temptation in this area might go something like this: Even a well-meaning, otherwise generally honest engineer might be tempted to make his/her qualifications seem more impressive to a potential employer. One might rationalize that one really would be the best person to do the required job, and that therefore one is doing the employer a favor by making one's qualifications seem more impressive and thereby inducing them to hire oneself, rather than some less-qualified person whose paper qualifications might misleadingly look as good as one's own.

Clearly there could be many variants on this manner of thinking. But all would involve rationalization (the inventing of dubious reasons for what one wants to believe anyway) and wishful thinking, rather than the objectivity and true rationality and truthfulness which are required of professional engineers. So Rule 1 serves a useful function in explicitly stating requirements which some might otherwise be tempted to ignore or overlook.

> 2.) *Engineers shall not directly or indirectly give, solicit, or receive any gift or commission, or other valuable consideration, in order to obtain work, and shall not make a contribution to any political body with the intent of influencing the award of a contract by a governmental body.*

Rule 2 continues the prohibitions against conflicts of interest which were found in Rules 5 through 8 in the previous section (rules covering the engineer's

An Engineer's Obligations to Other Engineers

🔑 This duty not to misrepresent applies also to issues of prior levels of responsibility and to the complexity of previous assignments.

obligations to employers and clients). Those previous rules mainly covered cases where an engineer was already employed, while Rule 2 here specifically applies to attempts to obtain future work, including the award of a contract by a governmental body.

This Rule 2 also emphasizes that it is just as wrong to attempt to unduly influence someone else (a potential employer, for instance) as it would be to allow others to unduly influence oneself. Thus the rule underlines that it is just as ethically unacceptable to try to cause conflicts of interest in others as it is to allow oneself to be enmeshed in improper conflicts of interest.

It should be noted that the second part of Rule 2, "... and shall not make a contribution to any political body with the intent of influencing the award of a contract by a governmental body," specifically mentions the intent of the person making the contribution. Contributions are not prohibited, only contributions with the wrong intent.

This part of the rule could be difficult to apply or enforce in practice, because it may be very hard to establish what an engineer's actual intent was in making a political contribution. Also, the freedom to make political contributions to organizations of one's own choice is generally viewed as an ethical right which should be limited as little as possible. So this part of the rule very much depends on and appeals to the ethical conscience of the individual engineer, who must judge his/her own intentions in such cases and avoid such contributions when their own intent would be self-interested in the manner prohibited by the rule.

Note also that the first part of Rule 2, "Engineers shall not directly or indirectly give, solicit, or receive any gift or commission, or other valuable consideration, in order to obtain work ...," also mentions the reason or intention behind giving or receiving gifts, etc., in the phrase "in order to obtain work." However, in practice it is much easier to judge when gift-giving is ethically unacceptable than when political contributions are unacceptable, since there are more behavioral and social tests for suspicious inducements to obtain work than there are for suspicious political support. So it is much easier to police and regulate infringements of this first part of Rule 2 than it is for the second part.

> 3.) *Engineers shall not attempt to injure, maliciously or falsely, directly or indirectly, the professional reputations, prospects, practice or employment of other engineers, nor indiscriminately criticize the work of other engineers.*

Rule 3 as it stands is somewhat unclear, so some discussion is required to bring out its ethically legitimate core.

First, how should the subordinate phrases "maliciously or falsely" and "directly or indirectly" be interpreted? On one possible interpretation, Rule 3 says outright that engineers should never attempt to injure in any way or for any reason the professional reputations of other engineers. On this interpretation those phrases just give examples of possible modes of injury which are prohibited, leaving unmentioned any other possible modes of injury which are nevertheless also assumed to be prohibited.

However, another interpretation is possible, according to which it is only certain kinds of injury which are prohibited by Rule 3, namely those spelled out by those same phrases interpreted so that the "directly or indirectly" part modifies the "maliciously or falsely" part. On this interpretation, Rule 3 prohibits only malicious or false attempts (whether carried out directly or indirectly) to injure the reputations of other engineers.

It is ethically unacceptable to try to cause conflicts of interest in others as it is to allow oneself to be enmeshed in improper conflicts of interest.

This second interpretation would ethically permit attempts to injure the reputations of other engineers, as long as the attempts were carried out in a non-malicious and honest, truthful way (and presumably with the public welfare in mind as well).

Some support for this second interpretation can be derived from the final clause of Rule 3, "nor indiscriminately criticize the work of other engineers." Clearly, in this case it is not all criticism of the work of other engineers which is being prohibited, but only indiscriminate criticism. Thus the last section of Rule 3 outlaws criticism which is over-emotional, biased, not well reasoned or factually inaccurate, and so on, but it does not prohibit well-reasoned, careful, accurate, factually-based criticisms of other engineers.

Thus in support of the second interpretation, it might be said that there too, it is not all attempts to injure reputations, which are being prohibited, but only those which are malicious, false, indiscriminate or otherwise highly ethically questionable in the methods they employ.

However, there is still something to be said in favor of the first interpretation as well (which, it will be recalled, involves a blanket condemnation of all attempts to injure reputations). Those defending it might do so as follows: It is arguable on general ethical grounds that any attempt to injure someone's reputation must be viewed as going too far and therefore becoming unethical. Even if one is convinced that someone else's work is shoddy, dishonest, and so on, at most (it could be argued) one has a duty to point out the problems and shortcomings in their work. It is a big leap from criticizing an engineer's actions, on the one hand, to condemning the engineer in a way designed to injure his/her reputation, on the other hand.

Thus (on this line of thinking) one should criticize an engineer only out of a disinterested desire to let the truth be known by all, not with the aim of injuring someone's reputation—it is for others to judge whether the truth of what one has pointed out will diminish the reputation and so on of the engineer in question.

Fortunately, it is not necessary to definitively decide between these different interpretations of Rule 3. What is important is to become sensitive to the ethical issues involved in each interpretation. And for the purposes of conforming to Rule 3, both sides can agree that if criticism of other engineers ever becomes necessary, it should be done in a very cautious and objective manner, and with all due respect for the professional status of the person being criticized.

> If criticism of other engineers ever becomes necessary, it should be done in a very cautious and objective manner, and with all due respect for the professional status of the person being criticized.

Example 12.7

With respect to the Moral Rules of Professional Conduct for engineers:

A) The rules are a bad thing because they encourage engineers to spy on and betray their colleagues

B) The rules are a useful legal defense in court, when engineers can demonstrate that they obeyed the rules

C) The rules enhance the image of the profession and hence its economic benefits to its members

D) The rules are important in providing a summary of what the public has a right to expect from responsible engineers

12-ETHICS

Solution: Remember here that the best/most relevant answer is to be chosen, because each answer has some truth to it, but only one has the most truth.

Choice A: It is true that the rules require those who have knowledge of violations of the rules to report such cases to the relevant State Board. And this could involve one in collecting more information on the possible infringements, and hence exposing those involved to the scrutiny of the State Board. However, the generally negative connotations of "spying" and "betraying colleagues" do not make the rules bad—the activities in question are a necessary part of responsible reporting of possible violations to the authorities, and hence are morally fully justified.

Choice B: It is true that proof in court that one has followed the rules may be a useful legal defense. However, this is only a secondary, indirect effect of the ethical value of the rules themselves, and so B does not provide the best answer.

Choice C: Again, it is true that the adoption of the rules by the engineering profession will enhance its image and economic benefits. But like B, this is only a secondary and derivative effect of the rules.

Choice D: The right answer. Since the basic function of the rules is to provide a guide for ethical conduct for engineers, the rules also provide a useful summary for the public of what they have a right to expect from responsible engineers.

Example 12.8

The Model Rules of Professional Conduct require registered engineers to conform to all but one of the following rules—which rule is not required?

    A) Do not charge excessive fees

    B) Do not compete unfairly with others

    C) Perform services only in the areas of their competence

    D) Avoid conflicts of interest

Solution: There may be one or two problems of this kind in the exam, which can be solved by memorizing the rules or by checking them directly to see which are or are not included. However, it is better to acquire a good understanding, the basic ethical concerns behind the rules, in which case the right answer here will be clear immediately.

Rule A is not required because fees are a matter of free negotiation between engineers and clients. Hence a fee which might seem excessive to some may be acceptable to others because of an interest in extra quality, or unusually quick delivery time, and so on. The other three rules are required.

Example 12.9

You are a quality control engineer, supervising the completion of a product whose specification includes using only U.S.-made parts. However, at a very late stage you notice that one of your sub-contractors has supplied you with a part having foreign-made bolts in it—but these aren't very noticeable, and would function identically to U.S.-made bolts. Your customer urgently needs delivery of the finished product—what should you do?

A) Say nothing and deliver the product with the foreign bolts included, hoping this fact won't be noticed by the customer

B) Find (or, if necessary, invent) some roughly equivalent violation of the contract or specifications for which the customer (rather than your company) is responsible—then tell them you'll ignore their violation if they ignore your company's violation

C) Tell the customer about the problem, and let them decide what they wish you to do next

D) Put all your efforts into finding legal loopholes in the original specifications, or in the way they were negotiated, to avoid your company's appearing to have violated the specifications

Solution: Choice A: This is wrong because it is dishonest—it violates the requirement of being objective and truthful in reports, etc.

Choice B: This is wrong because "two wrongs don't make a right." Negotiations with clients should always be done in an ethically acceptable manner.

Choice D: This would violate at least the spirit of the initial agreement. The ethical requirement of being objective and truthful includes an obligation not to distort the intent of any agreements with clients.

Choice C: The correct answer. Being honest with a client or customer about any production difficulties allows them to decide what is in their best interest given the new disclosures, and provides a basis for further good-faith negotiations between the parties.

Example 12.10

You are the engineer of record on a building project which is behind schedule and urgently needed by the clients. Your boss wants you to certify some roofing construction as properly completed even though you know some questionable installation techniques were used. Should you:

A) Certify it, and negotiate a raise from your boss as your price for doing so

B) Refuse to certify it

C) Tell the clients about the problem, saying that you'll certify it if they want you to

D) Certify it, but keep a close watch on the project in future in case any problems develop with it

Solution: There are some temptations and half-right elements in some of these, but they must be resisted as not being completely ethical.

Choice A: Even if one informs one's boss of the problems, and negotiates his/her consent to your certifying it, nevertheless it is always wrong to certify work which does not measure up to the highest professional standards.

Choice C: Wrong for the same reason as A. Even if one honestly reveals the problems to the clients, and gets their consent, nevertheless it is the professional duty of an engineer not to certify dubious work.

Choice D: The initial certification would be wrong, no matter how carefully one monitors future progress in the hope of minimizing any future problems.

12·ETHICS

Choice B: The right choice. Whether or not one's boss is happy with this, it is one's professional duty to refuse certification in such cases, even if as a result one is re-assigned or fired.

Example 12.11

You are an engineer and a manager at an aerospace company with an important government contract supplying parts for a space shuttle. As an engineer, you know that a projected launch would face unknown risks, because the equipment for which you are responsible would be operating outside its tested range of be-haviors. However, since you are also a manager you know how important it is to your company that the launch be carried out promptly. Should you:

A) Allow your judgment as a manager to override your judgment as an engi-neer, and so permit the launching

B) Toss a coin to decide, since one's engineering and managerial roles are equally important, so neither should take precedence over the other

C) Abstain from voting in any group decision in the matter, since as both a manager and an engineer one has a conflict of interest in this case

D) Allow your judgment as an engineer to override your judgment as a man-ager, and so do not permit the launching

Solution: Note that a real-life case similar to this problem occurred with the Chal-lenger space-shuttle disaster.

Choice A: Wrong, because engineers have special professional duties and ethical commitments which go beyond those of corporate managers.

Choice B: Wrong for same reason as A; ethically, engineering responsibilities are more important than managerial responsibilities.

Choice C: Wrong because one's duties as a professional engineer require appro-priate action even if other factors may seem to point in the opposite direction or toward abstention.

Choice D: The correct choice. Whatever other duties an engineer has, his/her pro-fessional engineering responsibilities must always be given first priority.

Example 12.12

Your company buys large quantities of parts from various suppliers in a very com-petitive market sector. As a professional engineer you often get to make critical decisions on which supplier should be used for which parts. A new supplier is very eager to get your company's business. Not only that, but you find they are very eager to provide you personally with many benefits—free meals at high-class restaurants and free vacation weekends for (supposedly) business meetings and demonstrations, and other more confidential things such as expensive gifts that arrive through the mail, club memberships and so on. What should you do?

A) Do not accept any of the gifts that go beyond legitimate business entertain-ing, even if your company would allow you to accept such gifts

B) Report all the gifts, etc., to your company, and let them decide whether or not you should accept them

C) Accept the gifts without telling your company, because you know that your professional judgment about the supplier will not be biased by the gifts

D) Tell other potential suppliers about the gifts, and ask them to provide you personally with similar benefits so you won't be biased in favor of any particular supplier

Solution: Choice B: Wrong, because even if one's company finds such gifts awkward, it is still one's duty as a professional engineer not to become involved in such conflicts of interest.

Choice C: Also wrong. It doesn't matter whether you believe you can remain unbiased, because you still have the conflict, and the possible perception by others that you might be biased by it also remains an ethical problem.

Choice D: Wrong. Remember, two wrongs don't make a right, and the same principle applies no matter how many wrong actions are involved.

Choice A: The right answer. As with the reasoning on choice B, it makes no difference whether others (having less demanding ethical standards than engineers) would find such things acceptable or not. You must not accept any gifts the acceptance of which would involve you in conflicts of interest.

12.5 Engineering Ethics and Legal Issues

This section will provide an introduction to the various ways in which the law regulates and affects the profession of engineering. The impact of laws and regulations on various engineering ethics issues will also be discussed.

Engineers, like any citizens, are of course expected to obey the general legal rules and regulations of the societies in which they live. But here we will concentrate on those laws and legal concepts which have special relevance to engineers and the engineering professions. Every engineer needs to have a good basic grasp of these legal matters.

First is a very important area of the law which is central not only to engineering but to many professions and businesses as well. It concerns the regulation of the basic transactions between professionals and their clients or customers.

A *contract* is a mutual agreement between two or more parties to engage in a transaction which provides benefits to each of them. Here is a breakdown of this concept into its elements, each of which is required for a valid contract to exist. For simplicity we will concentrate on two-party contracts.

Contract Law

1) Mutual consent. Each of the parties to a contract must consent to the contract and agree to be bound by its terms.

2) Offer and acceptance. There must be an offer of some kind by one of the parties (e.g., to manufacture some equipment or carry out some services), and acceptance of that offer by the other party.

3) Consideration. Each party must provide something of value to the other party.

The first two conditions, mutual consent and offer/acceptance, are needed because merely discussing a possible contract in provisional terms establishes no legally binding agreement. A contract exists only when each party has established that the other consents to it, and that one is offering something which the other has decided to accept. In other words, a legally enforceable agreement requires a definite promise by each party to do something specific; vague talk about possible actions by each is not sufficient.

The issue of consideration is also important, but in more complex ways. The idea behind it is that there cannot be a legally enforceable contract unless each side stands to benefit in some way from the contract, so that after the contract is fulfilled, each has received some benefit which they did not have prior to being fulfilled.

Without such evidence of definite benefits for each party, it would often be impossible to decide whether or not each party had fulfilled their side of the agreement. For example, if an engineer were to hire a relative to do some work, and paid them for doing it, but did not specify in any way exactly what the work would be, then the courts would likely rule that no valid contract existed and so the payments to his/her relative were illegal or invalid.

Another kind of example where lack of consideration raises legal and ethical questions is as follows: If an engineering firm provided certain services to a client, but never asks for nor receives any payment for them, there would be strong suspicion that the services provided were some kind of bribe or illegal payback for other hidden services or benefits rather than part of a valid contract between the parties.

Some cases involving the issue of consideration are less clear-cut. For example, if an engineer decides to undertake a difficult and complex project, yet does so at a very low rate of pay far below standard prices for such work, could such a contract later be held to be invalid because of the very inadequate reward provided to the engineer? Generally the courts have held that it is up to the parties to a contract themselves to decide what constitutes adequate consideration or reward, so the law will not provide protection to engineers against any possibly self-destructive intentions or other errors of judgment in which they may become involved.

On the other hand, issues about specific amounts of consideration or reward are often central in settling contractual disputes between parties; see the section on breach of contracts below.

It should be noted that a contract does not have to be in writing to be valid. For example, an engineer could make a contract over the phone with a client. But a written contract is always desirable for clarity, and it provides documentation should any questions about the terms and conditions of the contract arise later. So engineers are well advised to prepare specific documentation on any agreements they make as soon as possible after the agreements are finalized.

> 🔑 Without evidence of definite benefits for each party, it would often be impossible to decide whether or not each party had fulfilled their side of the agreement.

> 🔑 A contract does not have to be in writing to be valid.

One of the main values of having a legally enforceable system of contracts is that in the case of any disputes between the parties, the contract provides an independent check or test of the validity of the claims of each party to the dispute. For example, if a client orders some parts from an engineering firm, but later is dissatisfied with them and wants replacements or a refund of payments, then the issue can be resolved by checking in the contract to see whether the parts conform to what is specified for them in the contract. If the engineering firm has carried out its part of the contract by supplying parts as specified, then legally the client has no case against it. Each party to a contract must decide ahead of time whether they really want what they are agreeing to in a contract, and therefore they cannot blame the other party to the contract even if they are unhappy about the outcome of the agreement later.

In order for an actual breach of contract to occur, there must be some actual violation of the terms of the contract by one or both of the parties involved. For example, if specified items were not supplied, or were supplied but were of substandard quality, or if items were not supplied until long after a deadline had expired, then the other party could claim that a breach of contract had occurred and that they are entitled to compensation or termination of the contract.

Generally speaking, those suing for breach of contract will try to obtain sufficient damages or compensation to recover the value that they would have obtained under the contract had it not been violated. In other words, the other party is being required to provide an equivalent value to that which they had previously offered under the provisions of the contract.

One further distinction should be noted here: that between a material and an immaterial breach of a contract. Material breaches concern vital elements of the contract, the presence of which would justify termination of a contract and a suit for damages. But there may be less severe deviations from a contract (such as a contractor not cleaning up a site at the end of a day's work, or being a few days late in delivering a product) which would be handled differently. Usually immaterial breaches will require the offending party only to make reparations, or to accept a reduced fee for their work.

Often the distinction between a material versus immaterial breach of a contract will depend on issues about consideration (which is, you will recall, the value being received by each party to the contract). For example, suppose engineering firm A fails to supply client B with certain parts X as specified in a contract, but supplies substitute parts Y instead.

If the contract specified parts of X, then there has certainly been a breach of the contract. But whether it is a material or immaterial breach will depend on whether the substitute parts Y are similar enough in value to parts X so that client B should be willing to accept them as a substitute for parts X. Intuitively, if B is just as well off (or nearly so) with the parts Y as he would have been with parts X, then the breach of the contract would only be an immaterial one. However, if parts Y are substantially worse than parts X, there would be a material breach of the contract, requiring stronger legal action.

This material/immaterial distinction has ethical implications as well. Generally, any party to a contract who is unable to fulfill the exact provisions of the contract is under an ethical as well as a legal imperative to do everything possible to provide at least an equivalent value to the other party to a contract.

Breach of Contract

🔑 In order for an actual breach of contract to occur, there must be some actual violation of the terms of the contract.

🔑 We should try to "read between the lines" in terms of the intent of those documents as understood by those who formulated them.

The Letter versus the Spirit of the Law

This is an important distinction. It comes about because laws or contracts typically are not completely specific in their terms, and so are open to varying degrees and types of interpretation in problematic cases.

How should such interpretations, or attempts to "read between the lines," be carried out? A standard view is that we should try to do so in terms of the intent or desired interpretations of those documents as understood by those who formulated them.

In this way ethical standards enter as an important element in understanding the "spirit" of laws and contracts. Because typically, lawmakers or contracting parties wrote their rules or agreements with general ethical standards in mind as to what would constitute the best and most ethically acceptable laws or contracts, given the purposes they were trying to achieve. Thus basic issues of engineering ethics are relevant even in cases when legal documents are being dealt with, insofar as such documents leave any room at all for disputes about their proper interpretation.

Practice Problems

12.1 With respect to the Moral Rules of Professional Conduct for engineers:

a) The rules are a bad thing because they encourage engineers to spy on and betray their colleagues.

b) The rules are a useful legal defense in court, when engineers can demonstrate that they obeyed the rules.

c) The rules enhance the image of the profession and hence its economic benefits to its members.

d) The rules are important in providing a summary of what the public has a right to expect from responsible engineers.

12.2 The Model Rules of Professional Conduct require registered engineers to conform to all but one of the following rules. Which rule is not required?

a) Do not charge excessive fees.

b) Do not compete unfairly with others.

c) Perform services only in the areas of personal competence.

d) Avoid conflicts of interest.

12.3 Assume you are a quality control engineer, supervising the completion of a product whose specification includes using only US-made parts. However, at a very late stage you notice that one of your sub-contractors has supplied you with a part having foreign-made bolts in it—but these aren't very noticeable and would function identically to US-made bolts. Your customer urgently needs delivery of the finished product. What should you do?

a) Say nothing and deliver the product with the foreign bolts included, hoping this fact won't be noticed by the customer.

b) Find (or, if necessary, invent) some roughly equivalent violation of the contract or specifications for which the customer (rather than your company) is responsible—then tell them you'll ignore their violation if they ignore your company's violation.

c) Tell the customer about the problem, and let them decide what they wish you to do next.

d) Put all your efforts into finding legal loopholes in the original specifications, or in the way they were negotiated, to avoid your company appearing to have violated the specifications.

12.4   You are the engineer of record on a building project which is behind schedule and urgently needed by the clients. Your boss wants you to certify some roofing construction as properly completed even though you know some questionable installation techniques were used. Should you:

a)   Certify it, and negotiate a raise from your boss as your price for doing so.

b)   Refuse to certify it.

c)   Tell the clients about the problem, saying that you'll certify it if they want you to.

d)   Certify it, but keep a close watch on the project in the future in case any problems develop with it.

12.5   You are an engineer and a manager at an aerospace company with an important government contract supplying parts for a space shuttle. As an engineer, you know that a projected launch would face unknown risks because the equipment for which you are responsible would be operating outside its tested range of behaviors. However, since you are also a manager you know how important it is to your company that the launch be carried out promptly. Should you:

a)   Allow your judgment as a manager to override your judgment as an engineer, and so permit the launching.

b)   Toss a coin to decide, since one's engineering and managerial roles are equally important, so neither should take precedence over the other and engineers.

c)   Abstain from voting in any group decision in the matter, since as both a manager and an engineer one has a conflict of interest in this case.

d)   Allow your judgment as an engineer to override your judgment as a manager, and do not permit the launching.

12.6   Your company buys large quantities of parts from various suppliers in a very competitive market sector. As a professional engineer you often get to make critical decisions on which supplier should be used for which parts. A new supplier is very eager to get your company's business. Not only that, but you find they are very eager to provide you personally with many benefits—free meals at high-class restaurants and free vacation weekends for supposed business meetings and demonstrations, and other more confidential things such as expensive gifts that arrive through the mail, club memberships and so on. What should you do?

a)   Do not accept any of the gifts that go beyond legitimate business entertaining, even if your company would allow you to accept such gifts.

b)   Report all gifts, etc., to your company, and let them decide whether or not you should accept them.

c)   Accept the gifts without telling your company, because you know that your professional judgment about the supplier will not be biased by the gifts.

d)   Tell other potential suppliers about the gifts, and ask them to provide you personally with similar benefits so you won't be biased in favor of any particular supplier.

Solutions to Practice Problems

12.1 d) Remember here that the best/most relevant answer is to be chosen, because each answer has some truth to it, but only one has the most truth.

Choice (a): It is true that the rules require those who have knowledge of violations of the rules to report such cases to the relevant State Board. And this could involve one in collecting more information on the possible infringements, and hence exposing those involved to the scrutiny of the State Board. However, the generally negative connotations of "spying" and "betraying colleagues" do not make the rules bad—the activities in question are a necessary part of responsible reporting of possible violations to the authorities, and hence are morally fully justified.

Choice (b): It is true that proof in court that one has followed the rules may be a useful legal defense. However, this is only a secondary, indirect effect of the ethical value of the rules themselves, and so B does not provide the best answer.

Choice (c): Again, it is true that the adoption of the rules by the engineering profession will enhance its image and economic benefits. But like B, this is only a secondary and derivative effect of the rules.

Choice (d): The right answer. Since the basic function of the rules is to provide a guide for ethical conduct for engineers, the rules also provide a useful summary for the public of what they have a right to expect from responsible engineers.

12.2 a) There may be one or two problems of this kind in the exam which can be solved by memorizing the rules or by checking them directly to see which are or are not included. However, it is better to acquire a good understanding of the basic ethical concerns behind the rules, in which case the right answer here will be clear immediately.

Rule A is not required because fees are a matter of free negotiation between engineers and clients. Hence a fee which might seem excessive to some may be acceptable to others because of an interest in extra quality, or unusually quick delivery time, and so on. The other three rules are required.

12.3 c) Choice (a): This is wrong because it is dishonest—it violates the requirement of being objective and truthful in reports, etc.

Choice (b): This is wrong because "two wrongs don't make a right." Negotiations with clients should always be done in an ethically acceptable manner.

Choice (d): This would violate at least the spirit of the initial agreement. The ethical requirement of being objective and truthful includes an obligation not to distort the intent of any agreements with clients.

Choice (c): The correct answer. Being honest with a client or customer about any production difficulties allows them to decide what is in their best interest given the new disclosures, and provides a basis for further good-faith negotiations between the parties.

12.4 **b)** There are some temptations and half-right elements in some of these, but they must be resisted as not being completely ethical.

Choice (a): Even if one informs one's boss of the problems, and negotiates his/her consent to your certifying it, it is nevertheless always wrong to certify work which does not measure up to the highest professional standards.

Choice (c): Wrong for the same reason as A. Even if one honestly reveals the problems to the clients and gets their consent, nevertheless it is the professional duty of an engineer not to certify dubious work.

Choice (d): The initial certification would be wrong, no matter how carefully one monitors future progress in hope of minimizing any future problems.

Choice (b): The right choice. Whether or not one's boss is happy with this, it is one's professional duty to refuse certification in such cases, even if as a result one is reassigned or fired.

12.5 **d)** Note that a real-life case similar to this problem occurred with the Challenger space-shuttle disaster.

Choice (a): Wrong, because engineers have special professional duties and ethical commitments which go beyond those of corporate managers.

Choice (b): Wrong for same reason as A; ethically, engineering responsibilities are more important than managerial responsibilities.

Choice (c): Wrong, because one's duties as a professional engineer require appropriate action even if other factors may seem to point in the opposite direction or toward abstention.

Choice (d): The correct choice. Whatever other duties an engineer has, his/her professional engineering responsibilities must always be given first priority.

12.6 **a)** Choice (b): Wrong, because even if one's company finds such gifts unproblematic, it is still one's duty as a professional engineer not to become involved in such conflicts of interest.

Choice (c): Also wrong. It doesn't matter whether you believe you can remain unbiased, because you still have the conflict, and the possible perception by others that you might be biased by it also remains an ethical problem.

Choice (d): Wrong. Remember, two wrongs don't make a right, and the same principle applies no matter how many wrong actions are involved.

Choice (a): The right answer. As with the reasoning on choice B, it makes no difference whether others (having less demanding ethical standards than engineers) would find such things acceptable or not. You must not accept any gifts if their acceptance would involve you in conflicts of interest.

FE/EIT
Final Practice
Examination

Part
IV

This diagnostic exam is designed to indicate your areas of relative strength to help you prioritize your subsequent study. The morning session covers the same subjects for all test-takers. The afternoon sessions of both tests in this volume cover only the General DS subject area. To prepare for tests in other major DS areas, refer to our *FE/EIT Discipline Review* volume.

We at GLP have developed a CD that you may obtain at no charge by mailing in the reply card found at the back of this Review. It contains the same two exams that are found in this book presented in a lively, easy-to-use format which closely simulates the real testing experience. The CD will also provide you with a detailed score analysis of each exam via our Study-Director™ feature. Solutions with text references are also provided on the CD. If you are interested in the General Morning Session only, you can take and analyze that session only. The CD for our *"FE/EIT Discipline Review"* can be used for any afternoon Discipline test (except ChemE). So, if you plan on using the CD to take the exam, do not preview this Diagnostic Examination!

New! Interactive CD Exams with Study-Director™

Until you sit to take it, do not look or even glance at the material in this exam. To properly take this exam, spend at most four hours on each section. You may use only the Reference Handbook supplied by NCEES. One may be sent to you after you register for the exam or you may order a copy by calling Great Lakes Press at 1-800-837-0201. If you are studying without the NCEES Handbook, use the equation summaries provided at the end of this manual.

Taking the Diagnostic Exam

Battery-operated silent programmable calculators are allowed in nearly every state. Indicate your answers on the separate answer sheet. Be sure and answer all questions. Guess at those you do not have time to work through! Scratch paper is not allowed during the actual examination; large margins both here and on the test provide sufficient work space.

To score yourself, add your correct responses from the afternoon part to one-half of your correct responses from the morning part (a maximum score of 120). If you score less than 60 (50%) you may have difficulty with the actual examination. If your score is substantially greater than 60, you should be ready to pass!

The problems in the actual exam will be organized differently than in this exam.

FUNDAMENTALS OF ENGINEERING EXAM

Morning Session—Practice Exam

(Simulated answer form with topical breakout and scoring grid.)

BE SURE EACH MARK IS DARK AND COMPLETELY FILLS THE INTENDED SPACE AS ILLUSTRATED HERE:●.

MATH	MATERIALS	ECONOMICS	THERMODYNAMICS	DYNAMICS	FLUID MECHANICS
1 Ⓐ Ⓑ Ⓒ Ⓓ	31 Ⓐ Ⓑ Ⓒ Ⓓ	50 Ⓐ Ⓑ Ⓒ Ⓓ	67 Ⓐ Ⓑ Ⓒ Ⓓ	90 Ⓐ Ⓑ Ⓒ Ⓓ	108 Ⓐ Ⓑ Ⓒ Ⓓ
2 Ⓐ Ⓑ Ⓒ Ⓓ	32 Ⓐ Ⓑ Ⓒ Ⓓ	51 Ⓐ Ⓑ Ⓒ Ⓓ	68 Ⓐ Ⓑ Ⓒ Ⓓ	91 Ⓐ Ⓑ Ⓒ Ⓓ	109 Ⓐ Ⓑ Ⓒ Ⓓ
3 Ⓐ Ⓑ Ⓒ Ⓓ	33 Ⓐ Ⓑ Ⓒ Ⓓ	52 Ⓐ Ⓑ Ⓒ Ⓓ	69 Ⓐ Ⓑ Ⓒ Ⓓ	92 Ⓐ Ⓑ Ⓒ Ⓓ	110 Ⓐ Ⓑ Ⓒ Ⓓ
4 Ⓐ Ⓑ Ⓒ Ⓓ	34 Ⓐ Ⓑ Ⓒ Ⓓ	53 Ⓐ Ⓑ Ⓒ Ⓓ	70 Ⓐ Ⓑ Ⓒ Ⓓ	93 Ⓐ Ⓑ Ⓒ Ⓓ	111 Ⓐ Ⓑ Ⓒ Ⓓ
5 Ⓐ Ⓑ Ⓒ Ⓓ	35 Ⓐ Ⓑ Ⓒ Ⓓ	54 Ⓐ Ⓑ Ⓒ Ⓓ	71 Ⓐ Ⓑ Ⓒ Ⓓ	94 Ⓐ Ⓑ Ⓒ Ⓓ	112 Ⓐ Ⓑ Ⓒ Ⓓ
6 Ⓐ Ⓑ Ⓒ Ⓓ	36 Ⓐ Ⓑ Ⓒ Ⓓ		72 Ⓐ Ⓑ Ⓒ Ⓓ	95 Ⓐ Ⓑ Ⓒ Ⓓ	113 Ⓐ Ⓑ Ⓒ Ⓓ
7 Ⓐ Ⓑ Ⓒ Ⓓ	37 Ⓐ Ⓑ Ⓒ Ⓓ	Score: _____	73 Ⓐ Ⓑ Ⓒ Ⓓ	96 Ⓐ Ⓑ Ⓒ Ⓓ	114 Ⓐ Ⓑ Ⓒ Ⓓ
8 Ⓐ Ⓑ Ⓒ Ⓓ	38 Ⓐ Ⓑ Ⓒ Ⓓ		74 Ⓐ Ⓑ Ⓒ Ⓓ	97 Ⓐ Ⓑ Ⓒ Ⓓ	115 Ⓐ Ⓑ Ⓒ Ⓓ
9 Ⓐ Ⓑ Ⓒ Ⓓ		**ELECTRICAL**	75 Ⓐ Ⓑ Ⓒ Ⓓ	98 Ⓐ Ⓑ Ⓒ Ⓓ	
10 Ⓐ Ⓑ Ⓒ Ⓓ	Score: _____		76 Ⓐ Ⓑ Ⓒ Ⓓ	99 Ⓐ Ⓑ Ⓒ Ⓓ	Score: _____
11 Ⓐ Ⓑ Ⓒ Ⓓ		55 Ⓐ Ⓑ Ⓒ Ⓓ	77 Ⓐ Ⓑ Ⓒ Ⓓ		
12 Ⓐ Ⓑ Ⓒ Ⓓ		56 Ⓐ Ⓑ Ⓒ Ⓓ		Score: _____	**ETHICS**
13 Ⓐ Ⓑ Ⓒ Ⓓ	**CHEMISTRY**	57 Ⓐ Ⓑ Ⓒ Ⓓ	Score: _____		
14 Ⓐ Ⓑ Ⓒ Ⓓ	39 Ⓐ Ⓑ Ⓒ Ⓓ	58 Ⓐ Ⓑ Ⓒ Ⓓ		**MECHANICS**	116 Ⓐ Ⓑ Ⓒ Ⓓ
15 Ⓐ Ⓑ Ⓒ Ⓓ	40 Ⓐ Ⓑ Ⓒ Ⓓ	59 Ⓐ Ⓑ Ⓒ Ⓓ	**STATICS**		117 Ⓐ Ⓑ Ⓒ Ⓓ
16 Ⓐ Ⓑ Ⓒ Ⓓ	41 Ⓐ Ⓑ Ⓒ Ⓓ	60 Ⓐ Ⓑ Ⓒ Ⓓ		100 Ⓐ Ⓑ Ⓒ Ⓓ	118 Ⓐ Ⓑ Ⓒ Ⓓ
17 Ⓐ Ⓑ Ⓒ Ⓓ	42 Ⓐ Ⓑ Ⓒ Ⓓ	61 Ⓐ Ⓑ Ⓒ Ⓓ	78 Ⓐ Ⓑ Ⓒ Ⓓ	101 Ⓐ Ⓑ Ⓒ Ⓓ	119 Ⓐ Ⓑ Ⓒ Ⓓ
18 Ⓐ Ⓑ Ⓒ Ⓓ	43 Ⓐ Ⓑ Ⓒ Ⓓ	62 Ⓐ Ⓑ Ⓒ Ⓓ	79 Ⓐ Ⓑ Ⓒ Ⓓ	102 Ⓐ Ⓑ Ⓒ Ⓓ	120 Ⓐ Ⓑ Ⓒ Ⓓ
19 Ⓐ Ⓑ Ⓒ Ⓓ	44 Ⓐ Ⓑ Ⓒ Ⓓ	63 Ⓐ Ⓑ Ⓒ Ⓓ	80 Ⓐ Ⓑ Ⓒ Ⓓ	103 Ⓐ Ⓑ Ⓒ Ⓓ	
20 Ⓐ Ⓑ Ⓒ Ⓓ	45 Ⓐ Ⓑ Ⓒ Ⓓ	64 Ⓐ Ⓑ Ⓒ Ⓓ	81 Ⓐ Ⓑ Ⓒ Ⓓ	104 Ⓐ Ⓑ Ⓒ Ⓓ	Score: _____
21 Ⓐ Ⓑ Ⓒ Ⓓ	46 Ⓐ Ⓑ Ⓒ Ⓓ	65 Ⓐ Ⓑ Ⓒ Ⓓ	82 Ⓐ Ⓑ Ⓒ Ⓓ	105 Ⓐ Ⓑ Ⓒ Ⓓ	
22 Ⓐ Ⓑ Ⓒ Ⓓ	47 Ⓐ Ⓑ Ⓒ Ⓓ	66 Ⓐ Ⓑ Ⓒ Ⓓ	83 Ⓐ Ⓑ Ⓒ Ⓓ	106 Ⓐ Ⓑ Ⓒ Ⓓ	
23 Ⓐ Ⓑ Ⓒ Ⓓ	48 Ⓐ Ⓑ Ⓒ Ⓓ		84 Ⓐ Ⓑ Ⓒ Ⓓ	107 Ⓐ Ⓑ Ⓒ Ⓓ	
24 Ⓐ Ⓑ Ⓒ Ⓓ	49 Ⓐ Ⓑ Ⓒ Ⓓ	Score: _____	85 Ⓐ Ⓑ Ⓒ Ⓓ		
			86 Ⓐ Ⓑ Ⓒ Ⓓ	Score: _____	
Score: _____	Score: _____		87 Ⓐ Ⓑ Ⓒ Ⓓ		
			88 Ⓐ Ⓑ Ⓒ Ⓓ		
			89 Ⓐ Ⓑ Ⓒ Ⓓ		
COMPUTERS					
			Score: _____		
25 Ⓐ Ⓑ Ⓒ Ⓓ					
26 Ⓐ Ⓑ Ⓒ Ⓓ					
27 Ⓐ Ⓑ Ⓒ Ⓓ					
28 Ⓐ Ⓑ Ⓒ Ⓓ					
29 Ⓐ Ⓑ Ⓒ Ⓓ					
30 Ⓐ Ⓑ Ⓒ Ⓓ					
Score: _____					

Morning Session—Practice Exam

4 hours maximum

Each of the 120 problems is followed by four answers.
Select the response that is best and circle the corresponding letter on the answer sheet.

1. The equation of a straight line passing through $(1, 4)$ and $(4, 1)$ is
   (A) $x - y = 3$
   (B) $x + y = 5$
   (C) $x + y = 3$
   (D) $x - y = 5$

2. The radius of a circle whose equation is $x^2 - 6(x + y) + y^2 = -2$ is
   (A) 1
   (B) 2
   (C) 3
   (D) 4

3. Evaluate the determinant of this matrix: $\begin{bmatrix} 0 & 1 & 0 \\ 2 & 3 & 3 \\ 3 & 4 & 6 \end{bmatrix}$
   (A) 16
   (B) 8
   (C) 3
   (D) –3

4. Find the value of this limit: $\lim\limits_{x \to 0} \dfrac{\sin x}{x}$
   (A) 0
   (B) 1/2
   (C) 1
   (D) 2

5. The slope of the straight line $y = 4 - 3x$ is
   (A) –4
   (B) –3
   (C) 4/3
   (D) 3

EXAM 2

6. Find the intersection point B of the two curves $y = x^2$ and $y = 4 - 3x$.

   (A) $(2, 1)$

   (B) $(1, 1)$

   (C) $(1, 2)$

   (D) $(2, 3)$

7. Find the area bounded by $x = y^2$ and $y = x^2$.

   (A) $1/6$

   (B) $1/3$

   (C) $1/2$

   (D) 2

8. One of the roots of $i^{1/3}$ is given by

   (A) $-\dfrac{\sqrt{3}}{2} - \dfrac{1}{2}i$

   (B) $-\dfrac{1}{2} + \dfrac{\sqrt{3}}{2}i$

   (C) $\dfrac{\sqrt{3}}{2} + \dfrac{1}{2}i$

   (D) $\dfrac{1}{2} + \dfrac{\sqrt{3}}{2}i$

9. Find the value of x that results in a maximum value for y if $x^2 - 4x + y^2 + 4y = -2$.

   (A) 1

   (B) 2

   (C) 3

   (D) 4

10. Given: $\dot{y} + 4y = 0$, $y(0) = 2$. Find $y(t)$.

    (A) $2e^{-4t}$

    (B) $2e^{4t}$

    (C) $2 \sin 4t$

    (D) $2 \cos 4t$

11. The solution, as $t \to \infty$, of $\ddot{y} + 4\dot{y} + 4y = 20$ is

    (A) $y = 0$

    (B) $y = e^{-2t}$

    (C) $y = te^{-2t}$

    (D) $y = 5$

12. It takes Pigeon A 2 hours to fly straight home averaging 20 km/hr. It takes Pigeon B 2 hours and 20 minutes to fly straight home averaging 30 km/hr. If both pigeons start from the same spot but fly at an angle of 120° to each other, about how far apart do they live?

    (A) 96 km

    (B) 87 km

    (C) 80 km

    (D) 73 km

13. Evaluate $\int_0^{\pi/2} \sin 2\theta \cos^2\theta \, d\theta$.

    (A) $-1/2$

    (B) $-1/4$

    (C) $1/2$

    (D) $1/4$

14. Find the solution (x_1, x_2, x_3) of the following set of equations.

$$x_1 + x_2 \qquad = 3$$
$$x_2 + x_3 = 1$$
$$x_1 + x_2 + x_3 = 3$$

    (A) $(1, 2, -1)$

    (B) $(1, 2, 1)$

    (C) $(2, 1, 0)$

    (D) $(0, 3, -2)$

15. A matrix $\mathbf{A}$ has eigenvalues (characteristic values) λ found from which of the following equations?

    (A) $|\mathbf{A} - \lambda\mathbf{I}| = 0$

    (B) $\mathbf{AI} = \lambda\mathbf{x}$

    (C) $|\mathbf{A}| = \lambda$

    (D) $\mathbf{Ax} - \lambda\mathbf{I} = 0$

16. Find the projection of $\mathbf{A} = 10\mathbf{i} - 2\mathbf{j} + 8\mathbf{k}$ in the direction of $\mathbf{B} = 2\mathbf{i} - 6\mathbf{j} + 3\mathbf{k}$.

    (A) -6

    (B) 0

    (C) 4

    (D) 8

17. The divergence of the vector function $\mathbf{u} = xy\mathbf{i} + 2y^2\mathbf{j} - yz\mathbf{k}$ at the point $(0, 1, 1)$ is

    (A) -4

    (B) -1

    (C) 0

    (D) 4

Workspace Below

18. The centroid $\bar{y}$ of the area formed by the x-axis, $x^2 = y$, and the line $x = 2$ is
    (A) 1.4
    (B) 1.2
    (C) 1.1
    (D) 1.0

19. A paraboloid 4 units high is formed by rotating $x^2 = y$ about the y-axis. Its volume is
    (A) 4π
    (B) 6π
    (C) 8π
    (D) 10π

20. The Laplace transform of $e^{-2t} \sin 3t$ is given by
    (A) $3/\left(s^2 + 4s + 13\right)$
    (B) $2/\left(s^2 + 6s + 13\right)$
    (C) $2/\left(s^2 + 4s + 13\right)$
    (D) $3/\left(s^2 - 4s + 13\right)$

21. Write the product $(3 + 4i)(1 - 2i)$ in polar form.
    (A) $5.39 \angle -158°$
    (B) $11.18 \angle 79.7°$
    (C) $11.18 \angle 100.3°$
    (D) $5.39 \angle -21.8°$

22. Select the only linear differential equation.
    (A) $\ddot{y} + x\dot{y} + \sin y = 0$
    (B) $\ddot{y} + \dot{y}\sin x + y = 0$
    (C) $x\ddot{y} + y\dot{y} + 10y = 3x$
    (D) $\ddot{y} + \dot{y}\sin y + xy = 3\sin x$

23. How many times out of 100 attempts are you likely to select a red ball first and a black ball second from a bucket of balls containing 40 red balls, 25 black balls, and 35 white balls? (The first ball is to be reinserted.)
    (A) 14
    (B) 12
    (C) 10
    (D) 8

24. Find the sample standard deviation of 5, 2, 6, 3.

    (A) 0.80

    (B) 1.83

    (C) 2.54

    (D) 3.26

25. What is the base 16 equivalent of the base 10 number 739?

    (A) 739

    (B) 397

    (C) 2143

    (D) 2E3

26. A spread sheet is set up as follows:

Cell	Entry
A1	4
B1	1
C1	–5
D1	=sqrt(B1*B1–4*A1*C1)
E1	=–(B1–D1)/(2*A1)
F1	=–(B1+D1)/(2*A1)

    The values in cells E1 and F1 are, respectively,

    (A) 1, –1.25

    (B) 1, 1.25

    (C) –1, –1.25

    (D) –1, 1.25

27. The Boolean equation and DON'T CARE condition

    $$Y = AC + \overline{A}\,\overline{B}\,\overline{C}D + ABC; \quad \overline{B}\,\overline{C}D + \overline{B}\,\overline{C}\,\overline{D} = 0$$

    simplify to

    (A) $Y = AC + \overline{A}\,\overline{C}D$

    (B) $Y = AC + \overline{A}B\overline{C}D + \overline{A}\,\overline{B}\,\overline{C}$

    (C) $Y = A\overline{B}\,\overline{C}$

    (D) $Y = \overline{A}D$

28. Consider the following program segment:

$$X = 0$$
$$Y = 0$$
$$Z = 0$$
$$\text{FOR } K = 1 \text{ TO } 3$$
$$X = X + 1$$
$$Z = Z + (X * Y)$$
$$Y = Y + 1$$
$$\text{NEXT K}$$

This program segment produces what final values for X, Y, and Z?

(A) 3, 3, 8

(B) 3, 4, 8

(C) 2, 3, 8

(D) 3, 3, 16

29. The logic expression $f(w, x, y, z) = \Sigma m$ (4-8, 13, 15) has how many prime implicants?

(A) 7

(B) 4

(C) 3

(D) 16

30. A given CPU takes 4 cycles to execute an average instruction. Approximately how many instructions can be executed in 1 second if the CPU is running at 133 Mhz? Express the answer in MIPS.

(A) 532×10^{-6}

(B) 532

(C) 0.3325

(D) 33

31. The development of the mass spectrometer provided the first evidence of

(A) isotopes

(B) neutrons

(C) deuterons

(D) isobars

32. The non-linear portion of an engineering stress-strain diagram represents

(A) ultimate tensile strength.

(B) reversible deformation.

(C) plastic deformation.

(D) engineering modulus.

33. The 0.2% offset yield stress is the
    (A) stress at 0.2% elastic strain.
    (B) yield point of a carbon steel.
    (C) stress recovery after plastic deformation.
    (D) stress at the intersection point of a line drawn parallel to the elastic portion of the stress-strain diagram at a total strain of 0.2%.

34. Upper and lower yield points are observed in
    (A) all pure metals.
    (B) carbon steels.
    (C) brittle metals.
    (D) an alpha-beta brass.

35. Creep failure occurs due to
    (A) gradual application of a load at ordinary temperatures.
    (B) a very rapid rate of loading at subzero temperatures.
    (C) formation of voids under a steady load at elevated temperatures.
    (D) excessive work hardening.

36. Which of the following statements regarding ductile-brittle transition is not true?
    (A) There is a sudden loss of ductility below a critical temperature.
    (B) There is a loss of toughness at lower temperatures.
    (C) Carbon steels are less susceptible to ductile-brittle transition.
    (D) Some pure metals, such as aluminum, copper, or nickel, do not exhibit a ductile-brittle transition.

37. Metal fatigue can be defined as
    (A) failure due to repeated application of stress higher than the ultimate tensile strength.
    (B) failure due to repeated cyclic stress below the endurance limit.
    (C) failure due to repeated cyclic stress after necking has just been observed.
    (D) failure due to repeated cyclic stress, even below the yield stress.

38. For a plain carbon steel, all of the following are true except:
    (A) a steel can be hardened without carburizing.
    (B) yield strength of a steel can be increased by cold rolling.
    (C) high carbon steel is less ductile than medium carbon steel.
    (D) larger grain size steel is stronger than small grain size steel.

39. Astatine (At, element no. 85) is in Group VIIA of the periodic table, as are chlorine and iodine. Which of the following is not characteristic of astatine?
    (A) It is a deeply colored, volatile substance.
    (B) It reacts with sodium vigorously to give $NaAt$.
    (C) It reacts with hydrogen to give H_2At.
    (D) It is less electronegative than chlorine.

40. Which of the following elements is least likely to form a negative ion?
    (A) chlorine (Cl, no. 17)
    (B) strontium (Sr, no. 38)
    (C) sulfur (S, no. 16)
    (D) phosphorous (P, no. 15)

41. In the electrolysis of an aqueous solution of potassium bromide, what species migrates towards the positive electrode (the anode)?
    (A) K^+
    (B) H_2O
    (C) H_2O^-
    (D) Br^-

42. In order to determine the number of moles of N_2 in 3.7 liters of the pure gas at STP, you would use
    (A) the law of definite proportions
    (B) Avogadro's Law
    (C) the equilibrium constant
    (D) the periodic table

43. The oxidation number (oxidation state of valence) of chlorine in potassium perchlorate, $KClO_4$, is
    (A) –4
    (B) 0
    (C) –1
    (D) +7

44. Fewer collisions between molecules of gases at lower temperature generally results in
    (A) a smaller equilibrium constant
    (B) a smaller rate constant
    (C) Boyle's law
    (D) a larger equilibrium constant

45. Which of the following would not increase the amount of the product in the given reaction?

$$CH_3OH + CH_3CO_2H \overset{HCl}{\underset{}{\rightleftharpoons}} CH_3CO_2CH_3 + H_2O$$

    (A) Addition of more CH_3OH
    (B) Addition of more CH_3CO_2H
    (C) Addition of more HCl
    (D) Removal of H_2O

46. If the endothermic reaction given were at equilibrium, which of the following would shift the equilibrium to the right?

$$\text{Heat} + Br_2(g) + 2Cl^- \rightleftharpoons Cl_2(g) + 2Br^-$$

    (A) Increasing P at constant T
    (B) Decreasing P at constant T
    (C) Increasing T at constant V
    (D) Decreasing T at constant V

47. Oxidation of propene with potassium permanganate proceeds as follows (not balanced):

$$CH_3CHCH_2 + KMnO_4 + H_2SO_4 \rightarrow CH_3CO_2H + CO_2(g) + K_2SO_4 + MnO_2 + H_2O$$

    In the balanced equation, how many liters of CO_2 would be formed from 1 mol of propene?
    (A) 1
    (B) 22.4
    (C) 44.0
    (D) 44.8

48. The product of the reaction of Mg (atomic number 12) with chlorine (atomic number 17) is
    (A) $MgCl$
    (B) $MgCl_2$
    (C) $MgCl_3$
    (D) Mg_2Cl

49. What is the equilibrium constant for the following reaction?

$$C(s) + 2Cl_2(g) = CCl_4(g)$$

(A) $[CCl_4]/[Cl_2]$

(B) $[CCl_4]/[Cl_2]^2$

(C) $[Cl_2]/[CCl_4]$

(D) $[Cl_2]^2/[CCl_4]$

50. An amount P is invested at interest rate i per compounding period. F is the account balance after n compounding periods. Select the formula that relates F to P.

(A) $F = P(1+i)^{n-1}$

(B) $F = P(1+i)^n$

(C) $F = P(1+i)^i$

(D) $F = P(1+i)^{-n}$

51. A truck is purchased for $20,000. At the end of its 5 year life its salvage value will be $2000. Using general straight line depreciation, compute the book value of the truck after 3 years.

(A) $0

(B) $3600

(C) $7200

(D) $9200

52. A machine costs $10,000, has an estimated life of 10 years and a scrap value of $1500. Assuming no inflation and an interest rate of 4%, what uniform annual amount must be invested at the end of each of the 10 years in order to replace the machine?

(A) $708

(B) $850

(C) $1000

(D) $1152

53. An investment has infinite life and annual costs of $3000 for the first 5 years and $1600 per year thereafter. Using 6% interest per annum, compute the present worth of the annual disbursements.

(A) $15,000

(B) $25,000

(C) $32,600

(D) $50,200

54. Interest on a debt is 12% per year compounded monthly. Compute the effective annual interest rate.

    (A) 1%

    (B) 12%

    (C) 12.7%

    (D) 13.2%

55. The current through the battery in the circuit shown is

    (A) 1.5 A

    (B) 2.0 A

    (C) 2.5 A

    (D) 3.0 A

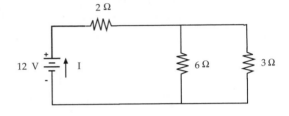

56. The equivalent resistance between points a and b is

    (A) 4 Ω

    (B) 6 Ω

    (C) 8 Ω

    (D) 10 Ω

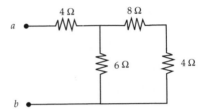

57. If $v(t) = 100 \sin 377t$, the magnitude of the rms voltage across the 20 ohm resistor is

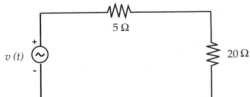

    (A) 4.0 V

    (B) 14.1 V

    (C) 35.0 V

    (D) 56.6 V

58. With a sinusoidal voltage of 100 volts rms, find the capacitive reactance X_C so that the source current is in phase with the source voltage.

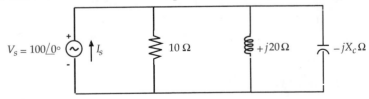

    (A) 0.05 Ω

    (B) 0.10 Ω

    (C) 10 Ω

    (D) 20 Ω

Workspace Below

59. If $X_C = 25$ ohms in Prob. 58, what is the power delivered to the 10 ohm resistor?

(A) 10 W

(B) 100 W

(C) 200 W

(D) 1000 W

60. The square-wave voltage is measured with a true rms reading voltmeter. The voltmeter would read

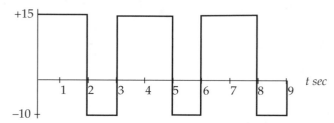

(A) 12.25

(B) 13.54

(C) 15.0

(D) 20.00

61. If $v(t) = 141.1 \sin 377t$, find R so that the capacitor's maximum voltage rating of 50 volts rms is not exceeded.

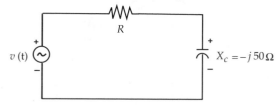

(A) 50.0 Ω

(B) 86.6 Ω

(C) 92.1 Ω

(D) 100 Ω

62. In a series RLC network the applied voltage is $v(t) = 70.7 \sin 377t$ and the circuit current is $i(t) = 5.1 \sin(377t + 0.16)$. The power delivered to the network at $t = 10^{-3}$ seconds is

(A) 67.9 W

(B) 83.3 W

(C) 95.6 W

(D) 180.3 W

63. If the initial current is zero and the switch is closed at $t = 0$, find the current at $t = 10^{-6}$ sec.

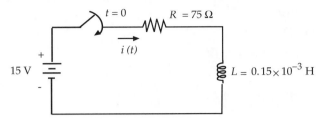

(A) 0.079 A

(B) 0.099 A

(C) 0.126 A

(D) 0.151 A

64. A 2-cm-dia., 10-cm-long air-core solenoid is used to create a DC magnetic flux density of 0.05 tesla. How many turns must be on the solenoid if the power supply can deliver only 2.5 amperes?

(A) 682

(B) 975

(C) 1590

(D) 2170

65. Calculate the magnitude and direction of the force, in newtons, on an electron placed between the parallel plates shown.

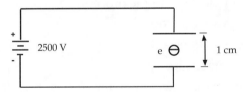

(A) 4×10^{-14} down

(B) 4×10^{-14} up

(C) 4×10^{-17} down

(D) 4×10^{-17} up

66. Two parallel conductors (a transmission line), 3 m apart in air, are oppositely charged to a charge density of 5.6×10^{-6} coulombs/m. Find the electrical force of attraction between the conductors.

(A) 1.88×10^{-5} N/m

(B) 0.19 N/m

(C) 0.336 N/m

(D) 7.95 N/m

Workspace Below

67. A thermodynamic system, contained in a rigid vessel with a paddle wheel, undergoes an adiabatic process. Select the correct equation if kinetic and potential energy changes are negligible. (The energy equation is $Q - W = \Delta U$.)

(A) $Q = \Delta U$

(B) $W = (P_2 - P_1)V$

(C) $-W = \Delta U$

(D) $U = mc_p \Delta T$

68. A container contains half liquid water and half vapor by volume. Select the best estimate of the quality if the pressure is atmospheric and $T = 100°C$.

(A) $x = 0$

(B) $x = 0.0006$

(C) $x = 0.1$

(D) $x = 0.5$

69. The reversible work done during an adiabatic process in a rigid container is equal to

(A) 0

(B) $(P_2 - P_1)V$

(C) $c_p \Delta T$

(D) $T\Delta S$

70. During an ideal isentropic process

(A) the work is zero

(B) the heat transfer is zero

(C) the entropy increases

(D) the internal energy remains constant

71. If both the volume and the pressure of an ideal gas contained in a cylinder are doubled, the temperature is

(A) constant

(B) doubled

(C) quadrupled

(D) halved

72. Select the correct statement about a Carnot cycle.

(A) It has four isentropic processes.

(B) It has two isentropic processes and two isothermal processes.

(C) It has two reversible processes and two irreversible processes.

(D) It has all irreversible processes.

73. An inventor proposes to produce energy from 90 kg/s of geothermal water at 100° C. Calculate the maximum possible energy output of a control volume device if $T_{atm} = 20°$ C. $(c_p)_{water} = 4.18$ kJ/kg·°C .

    (A) 1.2 MW

    (B) 3.6 MW

    (C) 5.8 MW

    (D) 30 MW

74. 40 J of work is done on a system in a rigid container while the internal energy increases by 20 J. The heat transfer is

    (A) 20 J

    (B) –20 J

    (C) 60 J

    (D) –60 J

75. An ideal gas undergoes an isothermal expansion in a cylinder. Select the true statement. $(Q - W = \Delta U)$

    (A) $W = (P_2 - P_1)V$

    (B) $W = 0$

    (C) $W = -\Delta U$

    (D) $W = Q$

76. The net entropy change in the universe during an adiabatic, irreversible process is

    (A) positive

    (B) negative

    (C) zero

    (D) $\int \frac{dQ}{T}$

77. Refrigerant-134a is heated from –40° C until it is completely vaporized while the pressure is held constant at 200 kPa. The heat transfer is

    (A) 400 kJ/kg

    (B) 360 kJ/kg

    (C) 320 kJ/kg

    (D) 240 kJ/kg

78. The moment about the x-axis produced by the force $\mathbf{F} = 10\mathbf{i} - 20\mathbf{j} + 40\mathbf{k}$ acting at the point $(2, 1, 1)$ is

    (A) 30

    (B) 40

    (C) 50

    (D) 60

Workspace Below

79. The reaction at A is

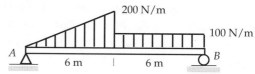

(A) 450 N

(B) 550 N

(C) 650 N

(D) 750 N

80. The force in link AB is

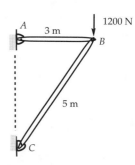

(A) 800 N

(B) 900 N

(C) 1000 N

(D) 1100 N

81. Determine the tension in cable AB.

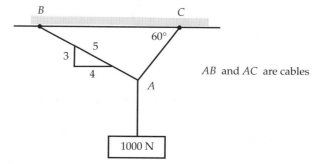

AB and *AC* are cables

(A) 392 N

(B) 451 N

(C) 482 N

(D) 504 N

82. Find the force in link BF. (All members are of equal length.)

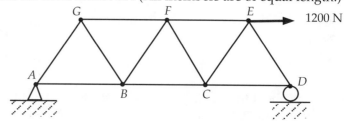

(A) 400 N

(B) 500 N

(C) 600 N

(D) 700 N

83. A block will slide down a 30° incline if the coefficient of friction is less than
    (A) 0.577
    (B) 0.591
    (C) 0.625
    (D) 0.674

84. What force *F* is needed for equilibrium? Neglect friction.
    (A) $W/4$
    (B) $W/5$
    (C) $W/6$
    (D) $W/7$

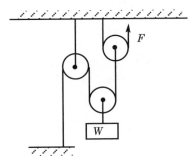

85. The scalar product of $\mathbf{F} = 2\mathbf{i} - 3\mathbf{j} + \mathbf{k}$ and $\mathbf{d} = \mathbf{i} + 2\mathbf{j} - \mathbf{k}$ is
    (A) $2\mathbf{i} - 6\mathbf{j} - \mathbf{k}$
    (B) $\mathbf{i} + 3\mathbf{j} + 7\mathbf{k}$
    (C) 5
    (D) –5

86. The maximum moment in the beam is
    (A) 4200 N·m
    (B) 5600 N·m
    (C) 6400 N·m
    (D) 6800 N·m

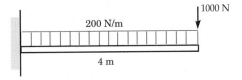

87. One complete revolution of a rope about a post is used to hold a boat. What maximum force by the boat can be resisted if the holder provides a force of 100 N? The coefficient of friction is 0.5.
    (A) 200 N
    (B) 900 N
    (C) 1800 N
    (D) 2300 N

88. Find the *y*-coordinate of the centroid.
    (A) 2
    (B) 2.25
    (C) 2.5
    (D) 2.75

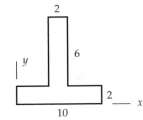

89. The moment of inertia about the x-axis is 320 cm⁴. What is the moment of inertia about the x'-axis?

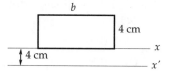

(A) 1220 cm⁴

(B) 1760 cm⁴

(C) 1920 cm⁴

(D) 2240 cm⁴

90. An object experiences the velocity shown. How far will it move in 6 seconds?

(A) 40 m

(B) 60 m

(C) 80 m

(D) 100 m

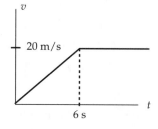

91. A wheel rotates at 20 rad/s. How many total revolutions will it rotate in 4 s, after it begins to decelerate at 10 rad/s²?

(A) 3.18

(B) 4.25

(C) 5.91

(D) 6.37

92. An object is accelerating to the right along a straight path at 2 m/s². The object begins with a velocity of 10 m/s to the left. How far does it travel (total distance) in 15 seconds?

(A) 125

(B) 115

(C) 105

(D) 90

93. A cannon can make a maximum angle of 30° with the horizon. What is the minimum speed of a cannon ball if it must clear a 10-m-high obstacle 30 m away?

(A) 28.0 m/s

(B) 30.5 m/s

(C) 32.8 m/s

(D) 34.1 m/s

94. Find ω_{AB} if V_C is 20 m/s to the right.
    (A) 20 rad/s
    (B) 30 rad/s
    (C) 40 rad/s
    (D) 50 rad/s

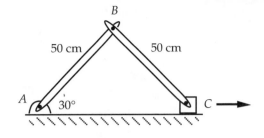

95. Find the angular acceleration of link AB in Prob. 94 if $a_C = 0$ and $\omega_{AB} = 40$ rad/s.
    (A) 120 rad/s²
    (B) 620 rad/s²
    (C) 980 rad/s²
    (D) 2770 rad/s²

96. Find the tension in the string which is wrapped around the 50 kg cylinder. $I_{cylinder} = \frac{1}{2}mr^2$.
    (A) 80 N
    (B) 100 N
    (C) 110 N
    (D) 140 N

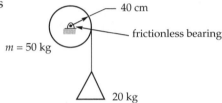

97. Find the maximum acceleration of a mass at the end of a 2-m-long string. It swings like a pendulum with a maximum angle from the vertical of 30°.
    (A) 4.9 m/s²
    (B) 5.6 m/s²
    (C) 6.2 m/s²
    (D) 7.5 m/s²

98. The 50 kg object strikes the unstretched spring. Find the maximum deflection.

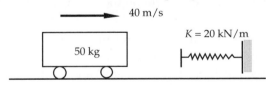

    (A) 1 m
    (B) 2 m
    (C) 3 m
    (D) 4 m

Workspace Below

99. A ball strikes a wall as shown. If the coefficient of restitution is 0.8, find θ.

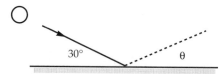

(A) 16°
(B) 19°
(C) 22°
(D) 25°

100. What is the maximum normal stress?

(A) 3 MPa
(B) 4 MPa
(C) 6 MPa
(D) 8 MPa

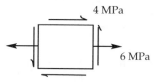

101. A steel rod just fits into position. What stress is induced if $\Delta T_{rod} = +40°C$? $E = 210 \times 10^6$ kPa, $\alpha = 11.7 \times 10^{-6°}$ C^{-1}.

(A) 28 MPa
(B) 41 MPa
(C) 59 MPa
(D) 98 MPa

102. The maximum vertical shearing stress due to VQ/Ib in a beam with a rectangular cross section

(A) occurs where the normal stress is a maximum.
(B) occurs at the neutral axis.
(C) occurs at the outermost fiber.
(D) is linearly dependent on the distance from the neutral axis.

103. The ratio of the maximum normal stress to the maximum vertical shearing stress in a cantilever beam of length L with rectangular cross section $h \times b$ (h is the height) and loaded at the end is given by

(A) L/h
(B) $2 L/h$
(C) $4 L/h$
(D) $2 L/b$

104. Find the maximum vertical shear in the beam if $w = P/L$.

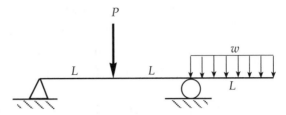

(A) $P/4$

(B) $P/2$

(C) $3P/4$

(D) P

105. The maximum bending moment in the beam of Prob. 104 is

(A) $PL/4$

(B) $13PL/8$

(C) $PL/2$

(D) $5PL/8$

106. A man climbs to the top of a 20-m-high, 6-cm-dia steel flag pole. His maximum weight (with a factor of safety of 2) should be at most ($E = 210 \times 10^6$ kPa)

(A) 1126 N

(B) 982 N

(C) 824 N

(D) 412 N

107. A 4-cm-dia, 20-cm-long, horizontal cantilevered shaft is subjected to a torque of 500 N·m and a vertical load of 2000 N at the free end. What is the maximum shearing stress in the shaft?

(A) 50.9 MPa

(B) 48.2 MPa

(C) 41.1 MPa

(D) 39.8 MPa

108. Flow through a sudden contraction in a pipe

(A) is usually laminar.

(B) results in a significant energy loss.

(C) can be analyzed using Bernoulli's equation.

(D) has a relatively small loss coefficient.

109. The force P required per meter of gate width (into the paper) is

(A) 29 kN

(B) 33 kN

(C) 35 kN

(D) 102 kN

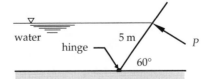

Workspace Below

110. In a turbulent pipe flow the
     (A) shear forces dominate inertial forces.
     (B) inertial forces dominate shear forces.
     (C) pressure forces dominate inertial forces.
     (D) body forces dominate inertial forces.

111. Which of the following ratios of velocity V, diameter D, power $\dot{W}$, and density ρ is dimensionless?

     (A) $\dfrac{\dot{W}D}{\rho V^2}$

     (B) $\dfrac{\dot{W}}{\rho V^3 D^2}$

     (C) $\dfrac{\dot{W}\rho}{V^3 D^2}$

     (D) $\dfrac{V\dot{W}}{\rho D^3}$

112. The pressure loss due to friction in a horizontal section of constant diameter pipe is usually determined using the
     (A) Darcy equation
     (B) Chezy-Manning equation
     (C) Bernoulli's equation
     (D) Navier-Stokes equation

113. Flow over a 27-m-high dam is to be studied in a lab with a 3-m-high model. If the river has a flow rate of 74 m³/s, the model flow rate should be
     (A) 30 m³/s
     (B) 3 m³/s
     (C) 0.3 m³/s
     (D) 9 m³/s

Questions 114-115 relate to the following figure.

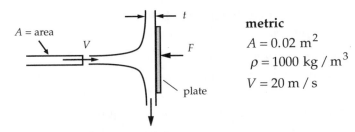

metric

$A = 0.02 \text{ m}^2$

$\rho = 1000 \text{ kg} / \text{m}^3$

$V = 20 \text{ m} / \text{s}$

114. At a plate radius of 20 cm t is about
   (A) 8 mm
   (B) 16 mm
   (C) 30 mm
   (D) 52 mm

115. For a stationary plate the force F is
   (A) 4000 N
   (B) 6000 N
   (C) 8000 N
   (D) 10 000 N

116. People behave ethically when they:
   (A) Do what they most feel like doing
   (B) Do what their parents or other older people tell them to do
   (C) Do what will most benefit people in general
   (D) Do what will most advance their own careers

117. With respect to the Moral Rules of Professional Conduct for engineers:
   (A) The rules are a bad thing because they encourage engineers to spy on and betray their colleagues
   (B) The rules are a useful legal defense in court, when engineers can demonstrate that they obeyed the rules
   (C) Their main use is in making the engineering profession look respectable to federal, state and local officials
   (D) The rules are important in providing a summary of what the public has a right to expect from responsible engineers

Workspace Below

118. Engineers should behave in an ethical manner because:
   (A)   It's required of them as responsible engineers
   (B)   If their colleagues perceive them as behaving ethically, then their career prospects will be enhanced
   (C)   Their lives will be made happier by it
   (D)   Their employers will reward it

119. Registered professional engineers are ethically required to:
   (A)   Do what is best for their own profession, even if it conflicts with the public welfare
   (B)   Work to advance the public welfare, and maintain a high standard of integrity and practice in doing so
   (C)   Advance their own careers whenever possible
   (D)   Serve the interests of their employer, even if they conflict with the public interest

120. The Model Rules of Professional Conduct require registered engineers to conform to all but one of the following rules—which rule is not required?
   (A)   Represent themselves before the public in an objective and truthful manner
   (B)   Perform services only in the areas of their competence
   (C)   Avoid conflicts of interest
   (D)   Do not charge excessive fees

STOP!

•The Afternoon Session is Next•

If you finish before 4 hours is up, you may return to any of the problems in the morning session. <u>Do not look</u> at the afternoon session problems. Take a 1 hour break and then continue with the afternoon session.

FUNDAMENTALS OF ENGINEERING EXAM

Afternoon Session—Practice Exam

(Simulated answer form with topical breakout and scoring grid.)

BE SURE EACH MARK IS DARK AND COMPLETELY FILLS THE INTENDED SPACE AS ILLUSTRATED HERE: ● .

MATH

1 Ⓐ Ⓑ Ⓒ Ⓓ
2 Ⓐ Ⓑ Ⓒ Ⓓ
3 Ⓐ Ⓑ Ⓒ Ⓓ
4 Ⓐ Ⓑ Ⓒ Ⓓ
5 Ⓐ Ⓑ Ⓒ Ⓓ
6 Ⓐ Ⓑ Ⓒ Ⓓ
7 Ⓐ Ⓑ Ⓒ Ⓓ
8 Ⓐ Ⓑ Ⓒ Ⓓ
9 Ⓐ Ⓑ Ⓒ Ⓓ
10 Ⓐ Ⓑ Ⓒ Ⓓ
11 Ⓐ Ⓑ Ⓒ Ⓓ
12 Ⓐ Ⓑ Ⓒ Ⓓ

Score: _____

COMPUTERS

13 Ⓐ Ⓑ Ⓒ Ⓓ
14 Ⓐ Ⓑ Ⓒ Ⓓ
15 Ⓐ Ⓑ Ⓒ Ⓓ

Score: _____

MATERIALS

16 Ⓐ Ⓑ Ⓒ Ⓓ
17 Ⓐ Ⓑ Ⓒ Ⓓ
18 Ⓐ Ⓑ Ⓒ Ⓓ

Score: _____

CHEMISTRY

19 Ⓐ Ⓑ Ⓒ Ⓓ
20 Ⓐ Ⓑ Ⓒ Ⓓ
21 Ⓐ Ⓑ Ⓒ Ⓓ
22 Ⓐ Ⓑ Ⓒ Ⓓ

Score: _____

STATICS

23 Ⓐ Ⓑ Ⓒ Ⓓ
24 Ⓐ Ⓑ Ⓒ Ⓓ
25 Ⓐ Ⓑ Ⓒ Ⓓ
26 Ⓐ Ⓑ Ⓒ Ⓓ
27 Ⓐ Ⓑ Ⓒ Ⓓ
28 Ⓐ Ⓑ Ⓒ Ⓓ

Score: _____

DYNAMICS

29 Ⓐ Ⓑ Ⓒ Ⓓ
30 Ⓐ Ⓑ Ⓒ Ⓓ
31 Ⓐ Ⓑ Ⓒ Ⓓ
32 Ⓐ Ⓑ Ⓒ Ⓓ

Score: _____

MECHANICS

33 Ⓐ Ⓑ Ⓒ Ⓓ
34 Ⓐ Ⓑ Ⓒ Ⓓ
35 Ⓐ Ⓑ Ⓒ Ⓓ
36 Ⓐ Ⓑ Ⓒ Ⓓ
37 Ⓐ Ⓑ Ⓒ Ⓓ

Score: _____

ELECTRICAL

38 Ⓐ Ⓑ Ⓒ Ⓓ
39 Ⓐ Ⓑ Ⓒ Ⓓ
40 Ⓐ Ⓑ Ⓒ Ⓓ
41 Ⓐ Ⓑ Ⓒ Ⓓ
42 Ⓐ Ⓑ Ⓒ Ⓓ
43 Ⓐ Ⓑ Ⓒ Ⓓ

Score: _____

THERMO/FLUIDS

44 Ⓐ Ⓑ Ⓒ Ⓓ
45 Ⓐ Ⓑ Ⓒ Ⓓ
46 Ⓐ Ⓑ Ⓒ Ⓓ
47 Ⓐ Ⓑ Ⓒ Ⓓ
48 Ⓐ Ⓑ Ⓒ Ⓓ
49 Ⓐ Ⓑ Ⓒ Ⓓ
50 Ⓐ Ⓑ Ⓒ Ⓓ
51 Ⓐ Ⓑ Ⓒ Ⓓ
52 Ⓐ Ⓑ Ⓒ Ⓓ
53 Ⓐ Ⓑ Ⓒ Ⓓ
54 Ⓐ Ⓑ Ⓒ Ⓓ

Score: _____

ECONOMICS

55 Ⓐ Ⓑ Ⓒ Ⓓ
56 Ⓐ Ⓑ Ⓒ Ⓓ
57 Ⓐ Ⓑ Ⓒ Ⓓ

Score: _____

ETHICS

58 Ⓐ Ⓑ Ⓒ Ⓓ
59 Ⓐ Ⓑ Ⓒ Ⓓ
60 Ⓐ Ⓑ Ⓒ Ⓓ

Score: _____

cut here!

Workspace Below

Afternoon Session—Practice Exam

4 hours maximum

Each of the 60 problems is followed by four answers.
Select the response that is best and circle the corresponding letter on the answer sheet.

Questions 1-4

Four vectors are given in Cartesian coordinates as

$$A = 3i + 2j + 2k, \quad B = j - k,$$
$$C = 2i + 2j + k, \quad D = x^2i + xyj + z^2k$$

1. The angle between vectors **A** and **B** is
    (A) 0°
    (B) 45°
    (C) 90°
    (D) 135°

2. The vector product (cross product) **B** × **C** is
    (A) $3i - 2j - 2k$
    (B) $3i - 4j - 2k$
    (C) $3i + 4j - 2k$
    (D) $5i - 4j + 2k$

3. Determine $\nabla \cdot D$ at the point (1, 0, –1).

    Use $\nabla = \frac{\partial}{\partial x}i + \frac{\partial}{\partial y}j + \frac{\partial}{\partial z}k$.

    (A) $2i + j + 2k$
    (B) $2i + 2k$
    (C) 0
    (D) 1

4. The area of a parallelogram with sides **B** and **C** is
    (A) 4.12
    (B) 3.24
    (C) 3
    (D) 2.08

Questions 5-8

The motion of an undamped spring acted upon by a force
$F(t) = 16 \sin \omega t$ is described by

$$\ddot{y} + 25y = 16 \sin \omega t$$

where y is the displacement and t is the time. The initial conditions are $y(0) = 0$ and $\dot{y}(0) = 8$.

5. The general solution of the homogeneous equation is

   (A) $c_1 e^{5t} + c_2 e^{-5t}$

   (B) $c_1 \sin 5t$

   (C) $c_1 \cos 5t$

   (D) $c_1 \cos 5t + c_2 \sin 5t$

6. If $\omega = 3$ the particular solution is

   (A) $c_3 \sin 3t$

   (B) $\sin 3t$

   (C) $c_1 \sin 3t + c_2 \cos 5t$

   (D) $c_1 \cos 5t + c_2 \sin 5t$

7. Resonance occurs if ω is

   (A) 1

   (B) 2

   (C) 3

   (D) 5

8. If a damping term $8\dot{y}$ were added to the original differential equation with $\omega = 5$ the steady-state solution would have an amplitude of

   (A) 0.5

   (B) 0.4

   (C) 0.3

   (D) 0.2

Questions 9-12

Given the set of equations represented by $[a_{ij}] [x_j] = [r_i]$:

$$2x_1 + 3x_2 = 12$$
$$2x_1 + x_2 = 2$$

9. What is the adjoint matrix $[a_{ij}]^+$?

(A) $\begin{bmatrix} 1 & -3 \\ -2 & 2 \end{bmatrix}$

(B) $\begin{bmatrix} 1 & -1 \\ -3 & 2 \end{bmatrix}$

(C) $\begin{bmatrix} 1 & 1 \\ 3 & 2 \end{bmatrix}$

(D) $\begin{bmatrix} 1 & 3 \\ 1 & 2 \end{bmatrix}$

10. What is the inverse matrix $[a_{ij}]^{-1}$?

(A) $\begin{bmatrix} -1 & -3 \\ -1 & -2 \end{bmatrix}$

(B) $\dfrac{1}{4}\begin{bmatrix} -1 & 3 \\ 2 & -2 \end{bmatrix}$

(C) $\dfrac{1}{2}\begin{bmatrix} 1 & -1 \\ -3 & 2 \end{bmatrix}$

(D) $\dfrac{1}{5}\begin{bmatrix} 1 & -3 \\ -1 & 2 \end{bmatrix}$

11. When using Cramer's rule, x_2 can be found by evaluating a determinant $|b_{ij}|$ and then dividing by the determinant $|a_{ij}|$. What is $|b_{ij}|$ for x_2?

(A) 20

(B) 4

(C) 0

(D) –20

12. What are the eigenvalues (characteristic values) associated with the matrix $[a_{ij}]$?

(A) 2, 6

(B) 5, 0

(C) 0, 4

(D) 4, –1

Workspace Below

13. Find the logic expression which implements $f(x,y,z) = \bar{x}\,\bar{y}\,\bar{z} + y\,\bar{z} + xyz$ using a minimum number of NAND gates in a hazard-free circuit.

   (A) $(\bar{x}\,\bar{z})\,(xy)$

   (B) $\overline{\overline{(\bar{x}\,\bar{z})}\;\overline{(y\,\bar{z})}\;\overline{(xy)}}$

   (C) $\overline{\overline{(\bar{x}\,\bar{z})}\;\overline{(xy)}}$

   (D) $(\bar{x}\,\bar{z}) + (y\,\bar{z}) + (xy)$

14. How wide, in bits, must an address bus be to access 8K different bytes of information?

   (A) 4096

   (B) 8

   (C) 16

   (D) 13

15. In a standard spreadsheet format cells B3 through B7 contain the values 5, 6, 7, 8, and 9, respectively. Cell B8 contains the formula (+B3*3)+@SUM(B4..B7). The value in cell B8 is then most nearly:

   (A) 19

   (B) 45

   (C) 50

   (D) 218

16. All of the following conditions strengthen metals and alloys except:

   (A) presence of second phase precipitates

   (B) presence of dispersed fibers or particles

   (C) presence of martensite phase in steel

   (D) annealing of cold worked metal above its recrystallization temperature

17. A plain carbon steel containing 0.18 wt.% carbon (SAE 1018 steel) is heated to 1100° C and then slow cooled to room temperature. Metallographic examination of this steel will show:

   (A) Ferrite + Pearlite.

   (B) Bainite + Martensite

   (C) Cementite + Ferrite.

   (D) Martensite + Cementite.

Workspace Below

18. A peritectoid reaction is one in which:

   (A) a solid phase reacts with a liquid phase to form a different solid phase.

   (B) a solid phase reacts with a second solid phase to form a third solid phase.

   (C) a liquid phase reacts with a second liquid phase to form a new solid phase.

   (D) a solid phase decomposes to two different solid phases.

19. Iron reacts with copper sulfate according to the following unbalanced equation:

$$Fe + CuSO_4 \rightarrow Fe_2(SO_4)_3 + Cu$$

   Atomic weights are $Fe = 56$, $Cu = 63.5$, $S = 32$, $O = 16$. How much copper will be formed from reaction of one gram-atom of iron with excess copper sulfate?

   (A) 0.5 g-atom

   (B) 1.0 g-atom

   (C) 127 g

   (D) 95 g

20. The valence electron configuration of Sulfur (atomic number 16) is

   (A) $1s(2), 2s(2), 2p_x(2), 2p_y(2), 2p_z(2), 3s(2), 3p_x(2), 3p_y(1), 3p_z(1)$.

   (B) $2s(2), 2p_x(2), 2p_y(1), 2p_z(1)$.

   (C) $3s(2), 3p_x(2), 3p_y(1), 3p_z(1)$.

   (D) $3s(2), 3p_x(1), 3p_y(1)$.

21. The type of bond present in ethane, C_2H_6, is

   (A) metallic

   (B) ionic

   (C) Van der Waals

   (D) covalent

22. Which of the following statements is false?

   (A) An exothermic reaction always goes faster than an endothermic reaction.

   (B) A catalyst provides a different route by which the reaction can occur.

   (C) Some reactions may never reach completion (100% products).

   (D) The rate of a reaction depends upon the height of the energy barrier (energy of activation).

Questions 23-27

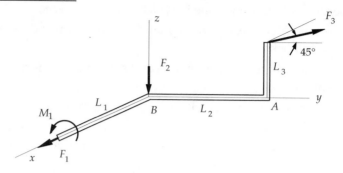

$L_1 = 20$ cm	$F_1 = 60$ N	$M_1 = 10$ N·m
$L_2 = 15$ cm	$F_2 = 20$ N	
$L_3 = 10$ cm	$F_3 = 40$ N — has no z-component	

23. The system of forces is
    (A) 3-D
    (B) concurrent
    (C) parallel
    (D) 2-D

24. If the rigid assembly is held in equilibrium with a support at A, a force at A must have magnitude
    (A) 47 N
    (B) 52 N
    (C) 58 N
    (D) 61 N

25. If the rigid assembly is held in equilibrium with a support at A, a moment at A must have magnitude
    (A) 10 N·m
    (B) 14 N·m
    (C) 20 N·m
    (D) 26 N·m

26. If F_1 were moved to point B, it would be replaced by a
    (A) force only
    (B) force and a clockwise moment
    (C) clockwise moment only
    (D) force and a counterclockwise moment

27. If F_1 and M_1 were moved to point A, the resulting moment would have magnitude
    (A) 9.4 N·m
    (B) 11.2 N·m
    (C) 13.4 N·m
    (D) 15.2 N·m

Questions 28-32

$L_1 = 30$ cm $\omega_1 = 10$ rad / s

$L_2 = 50$ cm $\alpha_1 = 0$

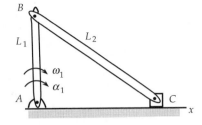

28. The angular velocity of link BC is

    (A) 0

    (B) 5 rad/s

    (C) 10 rad/s

    (D) 15 rad/s

29. The velocity of the slider at C is

    (A) 1 m/s

    (B) 2 m/s

    (C) 3 m/s

    (D) 4 m/s

30. The angular acceleration of link BC is

    (A) 0

    (B) 25 rad/s^2

    (C) 50 rad/s^2

    (D) 75 rad/s^2

31. The acceleration of C is

    (A) 15 m/s^2

    (B) 17.5 m/s^2

    (C) 20 m/s^2

    (D) 22.5 m/s^2

32. If a bead slides down link AB at a constant velocity of 2 m/s, what is the magnitude of its acceleration when it is halfway between A and B ?

    (A) 24 m/s^2

    (B) 30 m/s^2

    (C) 40 m/s^2

    (D) 43 m/s^2

Workspace Below

Questions 33-37

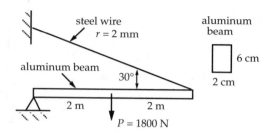

33. Assuming the weightless beam to be rigid, the right end will drop a distance of
    (A) 0.4 mm
    (B) 2.6 mm
    (C) 6.3 mm
    (D) 17.3 mm

34. The maximum tensile stress in the weightless beam is
    (A) 24 MPa
    (B) 56 MPa
    (C) 92 MPa
    (D) 150 MPa

35. The maximum shear stress in the weightless beam, due to the vertical shear, is
    (A) 1.12 MPa
    (B) 240 kPa
    (C) 520 kPa
    (D) 890 kPa

36. The maximum shear stress in the wire is
    (A) 72 MPa
    (B) 24 MPa
    (C) 48 MPa
    (D) 64 MPa

37. The bending moment diagram resembles a
    (A) circle
    (B) rectangle
    (C) triangle
    (D) parabola

Questions 38-40

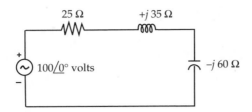

38. Using the source voltage 100 $\underline{/0°}$ rms as the reference, what is the voltage across the +j 35 ohm inductor?

    (A) 35$\underline{/90°}$

    (B) 99.0$\underline{/135°}$

    (C) 170$\underline{/-45°}$

    (D) 2.83$\underline{/45°}$

39. What is the total average real power delivered to the network?

    (A) 280 W

    (B) 200 W

    (C) 170 W

    (D) 120 W

40. What is the power factor for this network?

    (A) 0.38

    (B) 0.42

    (C) 0.58

    (D) 0.71

Workspace Below

Questions 41-43

41. The voltage V_{An} in magnitude and phase is

    (A) $120\underline{/0°}$

    (B) $120\underline{/30°}$

    (C) $120\underline{/-30°}$

    (D) $208\underline{/-120°}$

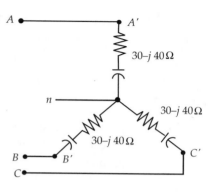

42. The current, in magnitude and phase, in the line CC' is

    (A) $2.4\underline{/36.9°}$

    (B) $2.4\underline{/53.1°}$

    (C) $2.4\underline{/173.1°}$

    (D) $4.16\underline{/67°}$

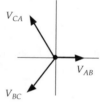

43. The total real power delivered to the wye connected load is

    (A) 518 W

    (B) 691 W

    (C) 1557 W

    (D) 2077 W

Questions 44-49

$P(\text{high}) = 6\,\text{MPa}$
$P(\text{low}) = 10\,\text{kPa}$
$T_3 = 600°\,\text{C}$
$\dot{m} = 5\,\text{kg/s}$
$\rho\,(\text{water}) = 1000\,\text{kg/m}^3$

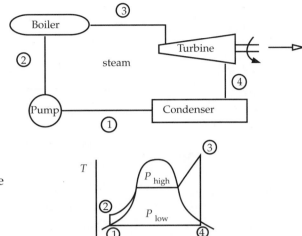

44. The quality of the steam leaving the turbine is

(A) 0.83
(B) 0.85
(C) 0.87
(D) 0.89

45. The maximum output for the turbine is closest to

(A) 4 MW
(B) 5 MW
(C) 6 MW
(D) 7 MW

46. The minimum pump power input is

(A) 20 kW
(B) 30 kW
(C) 50 kW
(D) 75 kW

47. The energy requirement by the boiler is

(A) 14.1 MJ/s
(B) 17.3 MJ/s
(C) 22.3 MJ/s
(D) 31.0 MJ/s

48. The efficiency of this Rankine cycle is

(A) 25%
(B) 30%
(C) 35%
(D) 40%

49. The maximum efficiency that could be realized by any cycle operating between the limits of this cycle is approximately

(A) 76%
(B) 68%
(C) 63%
(D) 59%

Workspace Below

Questions 50-54

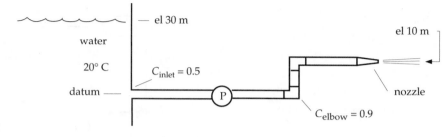

pipe material	= cast iron
pipe diameter	= 5 cm
pipe length	= 200 m
nozzle exit dia	= 2 cm
density of water	= 1000 kg/m³
flow rate	= 0.02 m³/s

50. The velocity in the pipe is
    (A) 6 m/s
    (B) 8 m/s
    (C) 10 m/s
    (D) 12 m/s

51. The pressure just upstream of the nozzle is
    (A) 520 kPa
    (B) 720 kPa
    (C) 930 kPa
    (D) 1980 kPa

52. What is the maximum distance the pump can be located from the reservoir inlet to avoid cavitation?
    (A) 4 m
    (B) 6 m
    (C) 10 m
    (D) 16 m

53. Using the pump energy requirement of 157 Hp, find the maximum pressure rise across the pump. (1 Hp = 746 W.)
    (A) 2100 kPa
    (B) 4300 kPa
    (C) 5900 kPa
    (D) 8100 kPa

54. What force is needed to hold the nozzle onto the pipe?
    (A) 1200 N
    (B) 2820 N
    (C) 4600 N
    (D) 6200 N

Questions 55-57

The City of Sprawl operates a public transportation system. Because the system is a government entity, it pays no taxes and can procure capital by selling bonds which pay 6% annual interest on par value.

55. A fleet of vehicles is needed for the city's new dial-a-ride service. Two models are being considered. Cost estimates are:

	Guppy	Shark
First cost	$25,500	$42,000
Annual maintenance	$ 1200	$ 1800
Life (years)	3	6
Salvage value	$ 900	$ 1500

What is the annual advantage of selecting the Guppy?
    (A) –$16,500
    (B) –$850
    (C) –$600
    (D) –$330

56. If interest on the bonds were paid semi-annually rather than annually, what would be the effective annual rate?
    (A) 6.1%
    (B) 6.25%
    (C) 16%
    (D) 106%

57. A Sprawl Transportation Authority bond has par value of $5000 and term of 10 years. The bond pays 5% nominal annual interest on par value. Estimate the selling price of the bond if the market interest rate is 6%.
    (A) $4632
    (B) $5000
    (C) $7500
    (D) $8000

58. You are a quality control engineer, supervising the completion of a product whose specification includes using only US-made parts. However, at a very late stage you notice one of your sub-contractors has supplied you with a part having foreign-made bolts in it—but these aren't very noticeable, and would function identically to US-made bolts. Your customer urgently needs delivery of the finished product. What should you do?

(A) Say nothing and deliver the product with the foreign bolts included, hoping this fact won't be noticed by the customer.

(B) Tell the customer that the product is currently unavailable, and sue the sub-contractor who included the foreign-made bolts for the amount you would have made upon successful delivery of the product .

(C) Put all your efforts into finding legal loopholes in the original specifications, or in the way they were negotiated, to avoid your company appearing to have violated the specifications.

(D) Tell the customer about the problem, and let them decide what they wish you to do next.

59. You are the engineer responsible for approving the safety of any design changes in new automobiles at your car company. The designers have come up with a simpler and much cheaper bracket for attaching the gas tank to the rear axle and bumper on a new model—but tests have shown this is more vulnerable to rear-end collisions than previous designs (hence, more potential deaths or injuries in accidents.) However, the new bracket is legal by current government standards, and no more unsafe than designs competitors are planning to use. Further, company accountants estimate that potential lawsuit costs (from accident victims) for the new design would be much less than the cost of continuing to use the older, more expensive bracket design. What is your best course of action?

(A) Tell your bosses about the increased safety risks of the new design, but let them decide whether or not to cancel or improve it.

(B) Ignore the problem, since the accountants have shown that overall it's the cheapest solution for the company.

(C) Do not approve the new design under any conditions, even if it costs you your job, or even if you have to "blow the whistle" on the dangers of the new design to the press or the government.

(D) Since you might be blamed if the increased safety risk is found, approve the new design so as to safeguard your job, but cleverly alter the test data so that the new design no longer seems less safe.

60. Your company buys large quantities of parts from various suppliers in a very competitive market sector. As a professional engineer you often get to make critical decisions on which supplier should be used for which parts. A new supplier is very eager to get your company's business. Not only that, but you find they are very eager to provide you personally with many benefits—free meals at high-class restaurants and free vacation weekends for (supposedly) business meetings and demonstrations, and other more confidential things such as expensive gifts that arrive through the mail, club memberships, and so on. What should you do?

(A) Report the gifts to your company, and let them decide whether or not you should accept the gifts.

(B) Accept the gifts without telling your company, because you know that your professional judgment about the supplier will not be biased by the gifts.

(C) Do not accept any of the gifts that go beyond legitimate business entertaining, even if your company would allow you to accept such gifts.

(D) Pressure the supplier to give you even more gifts—tell them you'll report previous gifts to your company if they don't agree to your requests.

STOP!
•You are finished with the Practice Exam!•

If you finish before 4 hours have elapsed, you may return to any of the problems in the afternoon session. You may not return to the morning session.

Workspace Below

FUNDAMENTALS OF ENGINEERING EXAM

ANSWER KEY—Morning—Practice Exam

(Answers with topical breakout and scoring grid.)

cut here!

BE SURE EACH MARK IS DARK AND COMPLETELY FILLS THE INTENDED SPACE AS ILLUSTRATED HERE: ●.

MATH

#	A	B	C	D
1		●		
2				●
3				●
4			●	
5		●		
6		●		
7		●		
8			●	
9		●		
10	●			
11				●
12	●			
13			●	
14			●	
15	●			
16				●
17				●
18		●		
19			●	
20	●			
21			●	
22		●		
23			●	
24		●		

Score: _____

COMPUTERS

#	A	B	C	D
25				●
26	●			
27	●			
28	●			
29			●	
30				●

Score: _____

MATERIALS

#	A	B	C	D
31	●			
32			●	
33				●
34		●		
35			●	
36		●		
37				●
38				●

Score: _____

CHEMISTRY

#	A	B	C	D
39			●	
40		●		
41				●
42		●		
43				●
44		●		
45			●	
45			●	
47			●	
48		●		
49		●		

Score: _____

ECONOMICS

#	A	B	C	D
50		●		
51				●
52	●			
53			●	
54			●	

Score: _____

ELECTRICAL

#	A	B	C	D
55				●
56			●	
57				●
58				●
59				●
60		●		
61		●		
62	●			
63	●			
64			●	
65		●		
66		●		

Score: _____

THERMODYNAMICS

#	A	B	C	D
67			●	
68		●		
69	●			
70		●		
71			●	
72		●		
73				●
74		●		
75				●
76	●			
77				●

Score: _____

STATICS

#	A	B	C	D
78				●
79		●		
80		●		
81				●
82	●			
83	●			
84			●	
85				●
86		●		
87				●
88			●	
89				●

Score: _____

DYNAMICS

#	A	B	C	D
90		●		
91				●
92	●			
93	●			
94			●	
95				●
96			●	
97	●			
98		●		
99				●

Score: _____

MECHANICS

#	A	B	C	D
100				●
101				●
102		●		
103			●	
104				●
105			●	
106				●
107	●			

Score: _____

FLUID MECHANICS

#	A	B	C	D
108		●		
109			●	
110		●		
111		●		
112	●			
113			●	
114		●		
115			●	

Score: _____

ETHICS

#	A	B	C	D
116			●	
117				●
118	●			
119		●		
120				●

Score: _____

Practice Exam Solutions—Morning

1. **B** The point (1, 4) must satisfy the equation. Only (B) does this.

    $m = (1-4)/(4-1) = -1.$ $y - 4 = -1(x-1)$ or $x + y = 5.$

2. **D** $(x-3)^2 + (y-3)^2 = 16.$ $r^2 = 16.$ $\therefore r = 4.$

3. **D** $0 + 9 + 0 - 0 - 0 - 12 = -3.$

4. **C** $\dfrac{\cos 0}{1} = 1.$ (We differentiated both numerator and denominator.)

5. **B** $y = mx + b = -3x + 4.$ $\therefore m = -3.$

6. **B** $y = 4 - 3x = x^2.$ $x^2 + 3x - 4 = 0.$ $x = \dfrac{-3 \pm \sqrt{9+16}}{2} = \dfrac{-3 \pm 5}{2} = 1$ or $-4.$

    $\therefore$ Use $x = 1.$ $\therefore y = 1^2 = 1.$

7. **B** The curves intersect at the origin and at (1, 1). Using a horizontal strip.

    $\text{Area} = \int (x_2 - x_1)dy = \int_0^1 (\sqrt{y} - y^2)dy = \dfrac{2}{3}(1) - \dfrac{1}{3} = \dfrac{1}{3}.$

8. **C** $i = e^{\pi i/2}.$ $\therefore i^{1/3} = e^{\pi i/6} = \cos\dfrac{\pi}{6} + i\sin\dfrac{\pi}{6} = \dfrac{\sqrt{3}}{2} + \dfrac{1}{2}i.$

9. **B** $2x - 4 + 2y\dfrac{dy}{dx} + 4\dfrac{dy}{dx} = 0.$ $\therefore \dfrac{dy}{dx} = \dfrac{2-x}{y+2} = 0.$ $\therefore x = 2.$

10. **A** $\dfrac{dy}{dt} = -4y.$ $\dfrac{dy}{y} = -4dt.$ $\therefore \ln y = -4t + \ln C.$ $\therefore \dfrac{y}{C} = e^{-4t}.$

    $y(0) = 2.$ $\therefore C = 2.$ $\therefore y(t) = 2e^{-4t}.$

11. **D** $y_p = A.$ $4A = 20.$ $\therefore A = 5.$ $\therefore y_p = 5.$ Note: $y_h(\infty) = 0.$

12. **A** $d^2 = a^2 + b^2 - 2ab\cos\theta$

    $= 40^2 + 70^2 - 2(40)(70)\cos 120°$

    $= 9300.$ $\therefore d = 96.4$ km

13. **C** Let $\cos\theta = y.$ Then $dy = -\sin\theta d\theta.$ Let $\sin 2\theta = 2\sin\theta\cos\theta.$ Then

    $2\int_0^{\pi/2} \sin\theta\cos\theta\cos^2\theta d\theta$

    $= -2\int_0^{\pi/2} \cos^3\theta(-\sin\theta d\theta)$

    $= -2\int y^3 dy = -2\dfrac{y^4}{4}$

    $= -2\dfrac{\cos^4\theta}{4}\Big|_0^{\pi/2} = \dfrac{-2}{4}(0-1)$

    $= \dfrac{1}{2}$

14. **C** $x_1 - x_3 = 2$ and $x_3 = 0$. $\therefore x_1 = 2$ and $x_2 = 1$.

15. **A** $\mathbf{Ax} = \lambda\mathbf{x}$ or $(\mathbf{A} - \lambda\mathbf{I})\mathbf{x} = \mathbf{0}$. This is true if $|\mathbf{A} - \lambda\mathbf{I}| = 0$.

16. **D** $\mathbf{A} \cdot \mathbf{i}_B = (10\mathbf{i} - 2\mathbf{j} + 8\mathbf{k}) \cdot \dfrac{2\mathbf{i} - 6\mathbf{j} + 3\mathbf{k}}{\sqrt{4 + 36 + 9}} = \dfrac{1}{7}(20 + 12 + 24) = 8$.

17. **D** $\nabla \cdot \mathbf{u} = \dfrac{\partial}{\partial x}(xy) + \dfrac{\partial}{\partial y}(2y^2) + \dfrac{\partial}{\partial z}(-yz) = y + 4y - y = 4(1) = 4$.

18. **B** $\bar{y} = \dfrac{\int \left(\dfrac{y}{2}\right) y\, dx}{\int y\, dx} = \dfrac{\dfrac{1}{2}\displaystyle\int_0^2 x^4\, dx}{\displaystyle\int_0^2 x^2\, dx} = \dfrac{1}{2} \times \dfrac{32/5}{8/3} = \dfrac{6}{5} = 1.2$.

Note: A vertical strip was used. The centroid of this vertical strip is at $y/2$

19. **C** $V = \displaystyle\int_0^4 \pi x^2\, dy = \pi\displaystyle\int_0^4 y\, dy = \pi\dfrac{4^2}{2} = 8\pi$.

20. **A** $F(s) = \dfrac{3}{(s+2)^2 + 3^2} = \dfrac{3}{s^2 + 4s + 13}$

21. **C** $(3 + 4i)(1 - 2i) = 3 + 8 + 4i - 6i = 11 - 2i$.

$= \sqrt{11^2 + 2^2}\ \big/\!\underline{\tan^{-1}\tfrac{-2}{11}}$

$= 11.18\ \big/\!\underline{100.3°}$

22. **B** See above Eq. 1.7.1.

23. **C** $P(\text{red})P(\text{black}) = \dfrac{40}{100} \times \dfrac{25}{100} = 0.4 \times 0.25 = 0.1$. $0.1 \times 100 = 10$.

24. **B** $\sigma = \left[\dfrac{(5-4)^2 + (2-4)^2 + (6-4)^2 + (3-4)^2}{3}\right]^{1/2}$

$= \left(\dfrac{1 + 4 + 4 + 1}{3}\right)^{1/2} = \sqrt{\dfrac{10}{3}} = 1.826$.

25. **D** $16^2 x + 16y + 16^0 z = 739$.

Let $x = 2$. $16^2 \times 2 = 512$. $739 - 512 = 227$.
Let $y = 14 = \mathrm{E}$. $16 \times 14 = 224$. $739 - 736 = 3$.
Let $z = 3$. $\therefore (2\mathrm{E}3)_{16} = (739)_{10}$.

26. **A**

27. **A**

28. **A**

	X	Y	Z
K=1	1	1	0
K=2	2	2	2
K=3	3	3	8

29. **C**

WX \ YZ	00	01	11	10
00	0	4	12	8
01	1	5	13	9
11	3	7	15	11
10	2	6	14	10

$\overline{w}\,x, \ x\,z, \ w\,\overline{x}\,\overline{y}\,\overline{z}$ are the 3 prime implicants

30. **D** $\dfrac{133 \times 10^6 \text{ cycles}}{\text{sec}} \times \dfrac{1 \text{ instr.}}{4 \text{ cycles}} = 33.25 \times 10^6 \dfrac{\text{instrs.}}{\text{sec}} \approx 33 \text{ MIPS}$

31. **A**

32. **C** Beyond the region of linear stress-strain response, plastic deformation begins, and strain is no longer a linear function of stress.

33. **D** The onset of plastic flow or the point at which nonlinear stress-strain behavior begins is often difficult to ascertain. Thus, as a convention, the stress corresponding to the point of intersection of a straight line parallel to the linear position of the stress-strain curve, and at a total strain of 0.002, is defined as the 0.2% yield stress.

34. **B** The occurrence of upper- and lower-yield points is a phenomenon associated with the barrier to dislocation motion posed by impurity or solute atoms. In mild steel, the carbon atoms produce such a barrier. A higher stress (upper-yield point) is needed to "break loose" the dislocations from these barriers; once freed they can move at a lower stress (lower yield-point).

35. **C** At an elevated temperature, and at a constant load even much lower than the load necessary for yielding, metals and alloys fail due to the nucleation and growth of voids.

36. **C** The ductility of carbon steel is very sensitive to temperature, and brittle fracture occurs at a temperature below the ductile-brittle transition temperature. This temperature increases as the carbon content increases.

37. **D** The reason fatigue failure is so treacherous is because it can occur well below the yield stress of a metal or alloy. Failure of an airplane wing section due to repeated vibration is a drastic example.

38. **D** The presence of grain boundaries strengthens steel. Also small non-elongated grains give rise to a more isotropic deformation behavior. Grain refinement often is a technique to increase strength of steel.

39. **C** If you know that Cl and I are monovalent and form HCl and HI, then At, in the same group (VIIA) will also form HAt, not H_2At. Alterna-

tively, you could examine the electron configuration and discover that At is one electron short of Rn (86), and is therefore monovalent.

40. **B**   Look at the periodic table. Sr is the furthest to the left, therefore the least electronegative, therefore the least likely to form a negative ion.

41. **D**   Negative ions migrate toward the positive anode. Br^- is the only negative ion present (H_2O^- is not a stable ion).

42. **B**   See Avogadro's Law: You therefore know that 3.7 l of N_2 contains the same number of molecules (or moles) as 3.7 l of He, i.e., $3.7/22.4$.

43. **D**   If you know that the oxidation number of K is +1 and O is –2, then Cl must be +7 to give a net of 0 ($+1 - 2(4) + 7 = 0$).

44. **B**   From the collision theory of reaction rate it is intuitive that more collisions result in a faster rate and fewer result in a slower rate.

45. **C**   Since HCl is written over the arrows, it is most likely a catalyst. Note that it does not appear in the reactants or products. Catalysts do not normally alter the equilibrium constant.

46. **C**   Since the moles of gas are the same on both sides of the equilibrium, the volume of gas is unchanged. Therefore, changing P will not affect the equilibrium. Since heat is input on the left, increasing T will shift the equilibrium to the right (Le Chatelier principle).

47. **B**   It is sufficient to recognize that one molecule of propene (3 carbon atoms) gives one molecule of CH_3CO_2H (2 carbon atoms) and one of CO_2 (1 carbon atom). Therefore one mole of propene gives one mole of $CO_2 = 22.4$ l.

48. **B**   If you know that Mg is in the same group as Cu and Be (group IIA) and therefore divalent, and Cl is in group VIIA (F, Br, I) and therefore monovalent, then the answer clearly is $MgCl_2$. You could also see from the periodic table that Mg (atomic number = 12) contains 2 more electrons than the noble gas neon (atomic number = 10) and is therefore divalent. Cl (atomic number = 17) has one less electron than the noble gas At (atomic number = 18) and is therefore monovalent.

49. **B**   Carbon, a solid, does not enter into the equilibrium constant expression since its concentration is a constant. Cl_2 enters as $(Cl_2)^2$ since there are 2 moles of Cl_2 formed from every mole of CCl_4.

50. **B**   By inspection.

51. **D** $D = (20,000 - 2,000)/5 = 3600$. $V_3 = 20,000 - 3 \times 3600 = \$9200$.

52. **A** $A = (10,000 - 1,500)(A/F)_{10}^4 = \$708$.

53. **C** $P = 1600(P/A)_\infty^6 + 1400(P/A)_5^6 = \$32,600$.

54. **C** $i = \frac{12\%}{12} = 1\%.$ $i_e = 1.01^{12} - 1 = 0.127.$ $\therefore i_e = 12.7\%.$

55. **D**   Reduce the circuit using equivalent resistances. $I = \frac{V}{R} = \frac{12}{4} = 3$ amp.

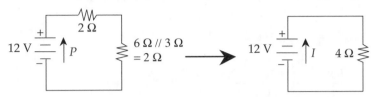

56. **C** $8 + 4 = 12\,\Omega.$ $\dfrac{1}{\dfrac{1}{6} + \dfrac{1}{12}} = \dfrac{72}{18} = 4\,\Omega.$ $\therefore 4 + 4 = 8\,\Omega.$

57. **D**   The rms source voltage is $V_s = \dfrac{V_{max}}{\sqrt{2}} = \dfrac{100}{1.414} = 70.7$ V. The voltage

across the $20\,\Omega$ resistor is $V_{20} = \dfrac{20}{20+5}\,V_s = \dfrac{4}{5} \times 70.7 = 56.6$ V.

58. **D**   In order for V_S and I_S to be in phase, the circuit must be resonant. This requires that the inductor and capacitor have equal values of susceptance.

$Y_L + Y_C = 0,$ $\dfrac{1}{j20} + \dfrac{1}{-jX_C} = 0,$ $-j\dfrac{1}{20} + j\dfrac{1}{X_C} = 0,$ $X_C = 20\ \Omega.$

59. **D**   Note that the voltage across the $10\,\Omega$ resistor does not change as X_C

changes. It remains at $V_S = 100\angle 0°$ V. $\therefore P_{10} = \dfrac{V_S^{\,2}}{R} = \dfrac{100^2}{10} = 1000$ W.

60. **B**   Compute the rms value of the square wave. Plot $v^2(t)$ for one period:

$$V_{rms} = \sqrt{\frac{1}{T}\int_0^T v^2(t)\,dt}$$

$$V_{rms}^2 = \frac{1}{3}[2 \times 225 + 1 \times 100]$$

$$V_{rms} = \sqrt{\frac{550}{3}} = \sqrt{183.3} = 13.54 \text{ V}$$

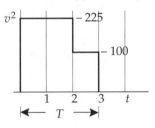

61. **B**   The rms source voltage is $V_S = \dfrac{V_{max}}{\sqrt{2}} = \dfrac{141.4}{\sqrt{2}} = 100$

$|V_C| = |I||X_C| \le 50$

$|I|\,50 \le 50,$ $|I| \le 1,$ $I = \dfrac{100}{R - j50}$

$|I| = \dfrac{100}{\sqrt{R^2 + 2500}} \le 1,$ $10\,000 \le R^2 + 2500,$ $R^2 \ge 7500.$ $\therefore R \ge 86.6\,\Omega.$

62. **A** $p(t) = v(t)i(t) = 70.7\sin(377t) \times 5.1\sin(377t + 0.16)$
$p(0.001) = 70.7\sin(0.377) \times 5.1\sin(0.377 + 0.16) = 67.9$ W.

63. **A** $I(t) = I_\infty + (I_0 - I_\infty)e^{-\frac{t}{T}}$. The current through the inductor cannot change instantly. $\therefore I_0 = 0$. The inductor has zero resistance.

$\therefore I_\infty = \dfrac{15}{75} = 0.2$, $T = \dfrac{L}{R} = \dfrac{0.15 \times 10^{-3}}{75} = 2 \times 10^{-6}$ and

$I(10^{-6}) = 0.2 + (0 - 0.2)e^{-\frac{10^{-6}}{2 \times 10^{-6}}} = 0.079$ A.

64. **C** $B = \dfrac{\mu N I}{\ell} = \dfrac{4\pi \times 10^{-7} N 2.5}{0.1} = 0.05$ Tesla. Solve for N:

$N = \dfrac{5 \times 10^{-3}}{\pi \times 10^{-6}} = 1591$ turns.

65. **B** $\mathbf{F} = q\mathbf{E}$, $E = \dfrac{V}{d} \rightarrow F = \dfrac{qV}{d} = \dfrac{1.6 \times 10^{-19} \times 2500}{0.01} = 4 \times 10^{-14}$ N, toward the positive plate.

66. **B**   The E field created by one line of charge is $E = \dfrac{\rho_L}{2\pi\varepsilon r} \dfrac{\text{volts}}{\text{meter}}\left(\dfrac{\text{newtons}}{\text{coulomb}}\right)$.

The force on a dq in the other line of charge is $df = dqE = \dfrac{\rho_L dq}{2\pi\varepsilon r}$. Sum the differential forces to get the total force on a 1 meter length. Use $dq = \rho_L dx$.

$F = \int_0^1 df = \int_0^1 \dfrac{\rho_L dx \rho_L}{2\pi\varepsilon(3)} = \dfrac{\rho_L{}^2(1)}{2\pi\varepsilon(3)} = \dfrac{\left(5.6 \times 10^{-6}\right)^2}{2\pi \times 3 \times 8.85 \times 10^{-12}} = 0.19$ N .

67. **C**   Adiabatic $\Rightarrow Q = 0$.   Paddle wheel $\Rightarrow W \neq 0$. $\therefore -W = \Delta U$.
Note: $W \neq \int P dV$ since the process is not in quasiequilibrium.

68. **B** $x = \dfrac{m_g}{m_f + m_g} = \dfrac{\dfrac{V}{v_g}}{\dfrac{V}{v_f} + \dfrac{V}{v_g}} = \dfrac{\dfrac{1}{1.673}}{\dfrac{1}{0.00104} + \dfrac{1}{1.673}} = 0.000621$ (using metric units).

The mass of liquid is much, much greater than the mass of vapor. So $x = .0006$ is probably the answer. Check by using the saturated pressure table. We also use mass = Volume/specific volume.

69. **A**   Rigid $\Rightarrow W = 0$ (reversible work only).

70. **B**   The heat transfer is zero since for an ideal (reversible) isentropic process $ds = \dfrac{\delta Q}{T} = 0$.

71. **C** $P_1 V_1 = mRT_1$. $(2P_1)(2V_1) = mRT_2$. $\therefore T_2 = \dfrac{4P_1 V_1}{mR} = 4T_1$.

72. **B**   All processes in a Carnot cycle are reversible.

73. **D** $\dot{W} = \dot{m}\Delta h = 90 \times 4.18(100 - 20) = 30096$ kW   or   30 MW

74. **B**   Work done by a system is positive. Work done on a system is negative.
$Q - W = \Delta U$. $Q = 20 + (-40) = -20$ J

75. **D** $\Delta U = mc_v \Delta T = 0$ since $\Delta T = 0$ (isothermal).

76. **A**   If the process is reversible $\Delta S_{net} = 0$. If irreversible $\Delta S_{net} > 0$.

77. **D**   Use Fig. 7.9: $Q = \Delta h = 390 - 150 = 240$ kJ/kg.

78. **D** $\mathbf{M} = \mathbf{F} \times \mathbf{r} = (10\mathbf{i} - 20\mathbf{j} + 40\mathbf{k}) \times (2\mathbf{i} + \mathbf{j} + \mathbf{k}) = (-40 - 20)\mathbf{i} + \underline{\quad}\mathbf{j} + \underline{\quad}\mathbf{k}$.

       $\therefore M_x = 60$ N·m.

79. **B**   Moments about $B : \sum M_B :$ $12F_A = 600 \times 3 + 600 \times 8.$ $\therefore F_A = 550$ N.
       Note: The force that replaces the triangular distribution acts through the centroid of the triangle; i.e., 4 m from A.

80. **B**   Sketch the force triangle.
       $\sum M_C :$ $1200 \times 3 = F_{AB} \times 4.$ $\therefore F_{AB} = 900$ N.

81. **D** $\left.\begin{array}{l} \dfrac{4}{5}F_{AB} = \dfrac{1}{2}F_{AC} \\[2mm] \dfrac{3}{5}F_{AB} + 0.866F_{AC} = 1000 \end{array}\right\}F_{AB} = 504$ N.   Forces act at point A as shown.

       $F_{AB} \swarrow$ $\searrow F_{AC}$ $\downarrow 1000$

82. **A**   Moments about $D : \sum M_D :$ $1200 \times 0.866L = F_A \times 3L.$ $\therefore F_A = 346$ N.

       Cut links GF, BF, and BC.

       $\sum F_y :$ $0.866\,F_{BF} = 346.$ $\therefore F_{BF} = 400$ N.

83. **A**   If the component of the weight acting down the plane exceeds the friction force μF, motion results.

       $\sum F_n :$ $N = 0.866$ W.

       $\sum F_t :$ $F = 0.5W = \mu N = \mu \times 0.866W.$ $\therefore \mu = \dfrac{0.5}{0.866} = 0.577.$

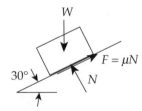

84. **A**   The top right pulley:

       $2F + 2F = W.$ $\therefore F = \dfrac{W}{4}$

85. **D** $(2\mathbf{i} - 3\mathbf{j} + \mathbf{k}) \cdot (\mathbf{i} + 2\mathbf{j} - \mathbf{k}) = 2 - 6 - 1 = -5.$

86. **B**   The maximum moment occurs at the wall:
$M_{\text{max}} = 1000 \times 4 + 800 \times 2 = 5600 \text{ N} \cdot \text{m}.$

87. **D** $F = 100e^{0.5(2\pi)} = 2314 \text{ N}.$

88. **C** $\bar{y} = \dfrac{12(5) + 20(1)}{12 + 20} = 2.5.$

89. **D** $320 = \dfrac{b \times 4^3}{3}. \quad \therefore b = 15. \quad I_x = I_c + Ad^2 = \dfrac{15 \times 4^3}{12} + 60 \times 6^2 = 2240.$

90. **B** $v = \dfrac{ds}{dt}. \quad \Delta s = \int v\,dt = \int_0^6 \dfrac{20}{6} t\,dt = \dfrac{10}{3} \times \dfrac{6^2}{2} = 60 \text{ m}.$

91. **D**

$\omega = \omega_0 + \alpha t$	$\omega^2 = \omega_0^2 + 2\alpha(\theta - \theta_0)$	
$0 = 20 - 10t$	$0 = 20^2 - 2(10)\theta$	When $t = 4$ sec, $\theta = -20$ rad
$\therefore t = 2$ when $\omega = 0.$	$\therefore \theta = 20$ rad at $t = 2$ sec.	$\therefore \theta_{\text{total}} = 40$ rad, or 6.37 rev

92. **A**

$v = v_0 + at$	$v^2 = v_0^2 + 2a(s - s_0)$	$s = s_0 + v_0 t + \frac{1}{2}at^2$
$0 = -10 + 2t$	$0 = 10^2 + 2(2)s$	$= \frac{1}{2} \times 2 \times 10^2 = 100$ m
$\therefore t = 5$ when $v = 0.$	$\therefore s = -25$ m at $t = 5$ sec.	$\therefore s_{\text{total}} = 100 + 25 = 125$ m.

93. **A** $\left.\begin{array}{l} 30 = v_0 t \times 0.866 \\[2mm] 10 = v_0 t \times 0.5 - \dfrac{1}{2} \times 9.8 t^2 \end{array}\right\} \quad \begin{array}{l} v_0 t = 34.64 \\[2mm] 10 = 34.64 \times 0.5 - \dfrac{1}{2} \times 9.8 t^2 \end{array}$

$\therefore t = 1.222$ sec. $\therefore v_0 = 28.3 \text{ m/s}.$

94. **C** $\mathbf{v}_C = \mathbf{v}_B + \mathbf{v}_{C/B}. \quad v_B = r\omega_{AB} = 0.5\omega_{AB}. \quad v_{C/B} = 0.5\omega_{BC}.$
The velocity polygon with $\mathbf{v}_B \perp \mathbf{r}_{AB}$ and $\mathbf{v}_{C/B} \perp \mathbf{r}_{BC}$ is an
equilateral triangle with all sides equal.
$\therefore v_C = 20 = 0.5\omega_{AB}. \quad \therefore \omega_{AB} = 40 \text{ rad/s}.$

95. **D** $\mathbf{a}_C = \mathbf{a}_B + \mathbf{a}_{C/B}. \quad (a_B)_n = r\omega_{AB}^2. \quad (a_B)_t = r\alpha_{AB}.$
$(a_{C/B})_n = r\omega_{CB}^2. \quad (a_{C/B})_t = r\alpha_{CB}.$ From symmetry of the
velocity polygon of No. 94, $\omega_{CB} = \omega_{AB} = 40 \text{ rad/s}.$
Draw the acceleration polygon:
$(0.5\alpha_{AB}) \times 0.5 = (0.5 \times 40^2) \times 0.866. \quad \therefore \alpha_{AB} = 2771 \text{ rad/s}^2.$

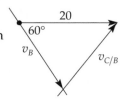

96. **C** $\left.\begin{array}{l} \sum M = I\alpha. \quad 0.4T = \dfrac{1}{2} \times 50 \times 0.4^2 (a/0.4) \\[3mm] \sum F = ma. \quad 20 \times 9.8 - T = 20a \end{array}\right\} \quad \therefore T = 109 \text{ N}.$

97. **A**   At the extreme position the velocity is zero and the acceleration is maximum. Draw a free-body at the 30° position. Forces in the tangential direction provide:

$$\sum F_t = ma_t$$

$$mg\cos 60° = ma_t. \quad \therefore a_t = 9.8 \times 0.5 = 4.9 \text{ m/s}^2.$$

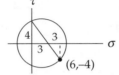

98. **B** $\frac{1}{2}mv^2 = \frac{1}{2}Kx^2. \quad \frac{1}{2}\times 50 \times 40^2 = \frac{1}{2}\times 20\,000 x^2. \quad \therefore x = 2 \text{ m.}$

99. **D** $e = -\dfrac{\text{separation velocity}}{\text{approach velocity}}. \quad 0.8 = \dfrac{v'\sin\theta}{v\sin 30°} = \dfrac{v\cos 30°\sin\theta}{v\sin 30°\cos\theta}.$

$\tan\theta = 0.8\dfrac{\sin 30°}{\cos 30°} = 0.462. \quad \therefore \theta = 24.8°.$

Note: $v\cos 30° = v'\cos\theta$ in the tangential direction.

100. **D** $\sigma_{\max} = \dfrac{6+0}{2} + \left[(6-0)^2/4 + 4^2\right] = 8 \text{ kPa.}$

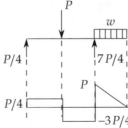

101. **D** $\delta_t = \alpha(T - T_0)L = \dfrac{PL}{AE} = \sigma\dfrac{L}{E}.$

$11.7\times 10^{-6}\times 40 = \dfrac{\sigma}{210\times 10^9}. \quad \therefore \sigma = 98.3\times 10^6 \text{ Pa}$

102. **B**   The vertical shear stress varies parabolically over the area.

103. **C** $M = PL$ and $V = P.$ $\dfrac{\sigma}{\tau} = \dfrac{My/I}{VQ/Ib} = \dfrac{Myb}{VQ} = \dfrac{PL(h/2)b}{P(hb/2)(h/4)} = 4\dfrac{L}{h}.$

104. **D**   Find the reactive forces. (Draw the shear diagram. The maximum shear is P.) $R_{\text{left}}\times 2L = PL - P\dfrac{L}{2}. \quad \therefore R_{\text{left}} = P/4$ and $R_{\text{right}} = 7P/4.$

$\therefore V_{\max} = P$ at right support.

105. **C**   The moment is the area under the shear diagram.

$M_{\max} = PL/2$ over right support.

106. **D** $P_{\text{cr}} = \dfrac{\pi^2 EI}{k^2 L^2} = \dfrac{\pi^2 \times 210\times 10^9 \times \pi\times 0.03^4/4}{2^2\times 20^2} = 824 \text{ N.} \quad \therefore P_{\text{actual}} = 412 \text{ N.}$

107. **A** $\sigma = \dfrac{My}{I} = \dfrac{2000\times 0.2\times 0.02}{\pi\times 0.02^4/4} = 63.7\times 10^6 \text{ Pa.} \quad \tau = \dfrac{Tr}{J} = \dfrac{500\times 0.02}{\pi\times 0.02^4/2} = 39.8\times 10^6 \text{ Pa.}$

$\therefore \tau_{\max} = 50.9 \text{ MPa}$ using Mohr's circle (or the equations).

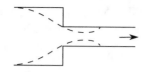

108. **B**   The flow separates upstream and downstream of the contraction with relatively large losses.

109. **C**   The pressure distribution is triangular ($p = 0$ at the surface and $p = \gamma h$ at the hinge.) The force of the water on the gate acts through the centroid of the triangular distribution; i.e., $5/3$ m from the hinge. Moments about the hinge gives:
$$F = \gamma h_c A = 9800 \times (5 \times 0.866/2) \times (5 \times 1) = 106\,000 \text{ N}. \quad \therefore P = F/3 = 35.3 \text{ kN}.$$

110. **B**   Shear forces result from viscosity which dominates in a laminar flow. The turbulent stress due to $\overline{u'v'}$ is an inertial effect.

111. **B** $[V] = L/T$, $[D] = L$, $[\dot{W}] = [\text{force} \times \text{velocity}] = M\dfrac{L}{T^2} \times \dfrac{L}{T} = ML^2/T^3$,
$[\rho] = M/L^3$. To cancel T, we must have $\dot{W}/V^3$. To cancel M, we divide by ρ: $\dot{W}/V^3\rho$. To cancel L we have $\dot{W}/V^3\rho D^2$.

112. **A**   Darcy's equation is $h_L = f\dfrac{L}{D}\dfrac{V^2}{2g}$ and is $\dfrac{\Delta p}{\gamma}$ for a horizontal section.

113. **C**   For free surface flows (dams, ships, open channels, etc.) the Froude number governs. Hence:
$$(Fr)_m = (Fr)_p. \quad \frac{V_m^2}{L_m g_m} = \frac{V_p^2}{L_p g_p}. \quad \therefore \frac{V_m}{V_p} = \sqrt{\frac{L_m}{L_p}} = \frac{1}{3}.$$
$$Q_m^* = Q_p^*. \quad \frac{Q_m}{V_m L_m^2} = \frac{Q_p}{V_p L_p^2}. \quad \therefore Q_m = Q_p \frac{V_m}{V_p} \frac{L_m^2}{L_p^2} = 80 \times \frac{1}{3} \times \left(\frac{1}{9}\right)^2 = 0.329 \text{ m}^3 \text{ s}.$$

114. **B** $A_1 V_1 = A_2 V_2$. $0.02 \times 20 = 2\pi \times 0.2t \times 20$. $\therefore t = 0.0159$ m or 16 mm.
Note: $V_2 = V$ since Bernoulli's eq. demands that if $p_1 = p_2$.

115. **C**   Momentum: $-F = \rho A V(V_{2x} - V_{1x})$. $F = 1000 \times 0.02 \times 20(20 - 0) = 8000$ N.

116. **C**

117. **D**

118. **A**

119. **B**

120. **D**

FUNDAMENTALS OF ENGINEERING EXAM

ANSWER KEY—Afternoon—Practice Exam

(Answers with topical breakout and scoring grid.)

BE SURE EACH MARK IS DARK AND COMPLETELY FILLS THE INTENDED SPACE AS ILLUSTRATED HERE: ●.

MATH

1. Ⓐ Ⓑ ● Ⓓ
2. ● Ⓑ Ⓒ Ⓓ
3. Ⓐ Ⓑ Ⓒ ●
4. ● Ⓑ Ⓒ Ⓓ
5. Ⓐ Ⓑ Ⓒ ●
6. Ⓐ ● Ⓒ Ⓓ
7. Ⓐ Ⓑ Ⓒ ●
8. Ⓐ ● Ⓒ Ⓓ
9. ● Ⓑ Ⓒ Ⓓ
10. Ⓐ ● Ⓒ Ⓓ
11. Ⓐ Ⓑ Ⓒ ●
12. Ⓐ Ⓑ Ⓒ ●

Score: _____

COMPUTERS

13. Ⓐ ● Ⓒ Ⓓ
14. Ⓐ Ⓑ Ⓒ ●
15. Ⓐ ● Ⓒ Ⓓ

Score: _____

MATERIALS

16. Ⓐ Ⓑ Ⓒ ●
17. ● Ⓑ Ⓒ Ⓓ
18. Ⓐ ● Ⓒ Ⓓ

Score: _____

CHEMISTRY

19. Ⓐ Ⓑ Ⓒ ●
20. Ⓐ Ⓑ ● Ⓓ
21. Ⓐ Ⓑ Ⓒ ●
22. ● Ⓑ Ⓒ Ⓓ

Score: _____

STATICS

23. ● Ⓑ Ⓒ Ⓓ
24. ● Ⓑ Ⓒ Ⓓ
25. Ⓐ ● Ⓒ Ⓓ
26. ● Ⓑ Ⓒ Ⓓ
27. Ⓐ Ⓑ ● Ⓓ
28. ● Ⓑ Ⓒ Ⓓ

Score: _____

DYNAMICS

29. Ⓐ Ⓑ ● Ⓓ
30. Ⓐ Ⓑ Ⓒ ●
31. Ⓐ Ⓑ Ⓒ ●
32. Ⓐ Ⓑ Ⓒ ●

Score: _____

MECHANICS

33. Ⓐ Ⓑ ● Ⓓ
34. Ⓐ Ⓑ Ⓒ ●
35. ● Ⓑ Ⓒ Ⓓ
36. ● Ⓑ Ⓒ Ⓓ
37. Ⓐ Ⓑ ● Ⓓ

Score: _____

ELECTRICAL

38. Ⓐ ● Ⓒ Ⓓ
39. Ⓐ ● Ⓒ Ⓓ
40. Ⓐ Ⓑ Ⓒ ●
41. Ⓐ Ⓑ ● Ⓓ
42. Ⓐ Ⓑ ● Ⓓ
43. ● Ⓑ Ⓒ Ⓓ

Score: _____

THERMO/FLUIDS

44. Ⓐ Ⓑ ● Ⓓ
45. Ⓐ Ⓑ Ⓒ ●
46. Ⓐ ● Ⓒ Ⓓ
47. Ⓐ ● Ⓒ Ⓓ
48. Ⓐ Ⓑ Ⓒ ●
49. Ⓐ Ⓑ ● Ⓓ
50. Ⓐ Ⓑ ● Ⓓ
51. Ⓐ Ⓑ Ⓒ ●
52. Ⓐ Ⓑ ● Ⓓ
53. Ⓐ Ⓑ ● Ⓓ
54. Ⓐ ● Ⓒ Ⓓ

Score: _____

ECONOMICS

55. Ⓐ Ⓑ Ⓒ ●
56. ● Ⓑ Ⓒ Ⓓ
57. ● Ⓑ Ⓒ Ⓓ

Score: _____

ETHICS

58. Ⓐ Ⓑ Ⓒ ●
59. Ⓐ Ⓑ ● Ⓓ
60. Ⓐ Ⓑ ● Ⓓ

Score: _____

Practice Exam Solutions—Afternoon

1. **C** $\mathbf{A} \cdot \mathbf{B} = AB \cos \theta.$ $(3\mathbf{i} + 2\mathbf{j} + 2\mathbf{k}) \cdot (\mathbf{j} - \mathbf{k}) = \sqrt{9 + 4 + 4}\sqrt{1 + 1} \cos \theta.$

    $\therefore 0 = \cos \theta.$ $\therefore \theta = 90°.$

2. **A** $\mathbf{B} \cdot \mathbf{C} = \begin{vmatrix} 0 & 1 & -1 \\ 2 & 2 & 1 \\ \mathbf{i} & \mathbf{j} & \mathbf{k} \end{vmatrix} = (1 + 2)\mathbf{i} + (-2 - 0)\mathbf{j} + (0 - 2)\mathbf{k} = 3\mathbf{i} - 2\mathbf{j} - 2\mathbf{k}.$

3. **D** $\nabla \cdot \mathbf{D} = \left(\dfrac{\partial}{\partial x}\mathbf{i} + \dfrac{\partial}{\partial y}\mathbf{j} + \dfrac{\partial}{\partial z}\mathbf{k} \right) \cdot \left(x^2\mathbf{i} + xy\mathbf{j} + z^2\mathbf{k} \right) = 2x + x + 2z = 3 - 2 = 1.$

4. **A** $|\mathbf{B} \times \mathbf{C}| = |(\mathbf{j} - \mathbf{k}) \times (2\mathbf{i} + 2\mathbf{j} + \mathbf{k})| = |3\mathbf{i} - 2\mathbf{j} - 2\mathbf{k}| = 4.12$

5. **D** $\ddot{y} + 25y = 0.$ $r^2 + 25 = 0.$ $\therefore r = \pm 5i.$ $\therefore y_h(t) = C_1 e^{5it} + C_2 e^{-5it} = A \cos 5t + B \sin 5t.$

6. **B** $y_p = A \sin 3t.$ $-9A + 25A = 16.$ $\therefore A = 1.$ $\therefore y_p(t) = \sin 3t.$

7. **D**   The natural frequency is the coefficient of t in the homogeneous solution: $\omega_n = 5$ rad/s . (See No. 5).

8. **B**   Steady state is the particular solution. (Damping always drives the homogeneous solution to zero for large time.) Note: Substitute into the differential equation.

    $y_p = A \sin 5t + B \cos 5t.$

    $-25A \sin 5t - 25B \cos 5t + 40A \cos 5t - 40B \sin 5t + 25A \sin 5t + 25B \cos 5t = 16 \sin 5t.$

    $\left. \begin{array}{l} \sin 5t: \quad -40B = 16. \quad \therefore B = -0.4 \\ \cos 5t: \quad 40A = 0. \quad \therefore A = 0 \end{array} \right\} \therefore y_p(t) = y_{\text{steady-state}} = -0.4 \cos 5t. \quad \text{Amp} = 0.4.$

9. **A** $\begin{bmatrix} 2 & 3 \\ 2 & 1 \end{bmatrix}^+ = \text{adj}\,\mathbf{A} = \begin{bmatrix} 1 & -3 \\ -2 & 2 \end{bmatrix}.$ The adjoint is the transpose of the matrix whose elements are the respective cofactors of the elements of the given matrix.

10. **B** $\mathbf{A}^{-1} = \dfrac{\text{adj}\,\mathbf{A}}{|\mathbf{A}|} = -\dfrac{1}{4}\begin{bmatrix} 1 & -3 \\ -2 & 2 \end{bmatrix} = \dfrac{1}{4}\begin{bmatrix} -1 & 3 \\ 2 & -2 \end{bmatrix}.$

11. **D** $|b_{ij}| = \begin{vmatrix} 2 & 12 \\ 2 & 2 \end{vmatrix} = 4 - 24 = -20.$

12. **D** $\begin{vmatrix} 2-\lambda & 3 \\ 2 & 1-\lambda \end{vmatrix} = (2-\lambda)(1-\lambda) - 6 = \lambda^2 - 3\lambda - 4 = 0 = (\lambda - 4)(\lambda + 1).$

$\therefore \lambda = 4, -1.$

13. **B** $f\min = \dfrac{\bar{x}\,\bar{z} + y\,\bar{z} + xy}{(\bar{x}\,\bar{z}) + (y\,\bar{z}) + (x\,y)}$

	XY			
Z	00	01	11	10
0	1	1	1	
1			1	

Expansion: $\bar{x}\,\bar{y}\,\bar{z} + y\,\bar{z}(x + \bar{x}) + x\,y\,z$

$= \bar{x}\,\bar{y}\,\bar{z} + x\,y\,\bar{z} + \bar{x}\,y\,\bar{z} + x\,y\,z$

$= M_0 + M_6 + M_2 + M_7$

$= \Sigma M(0,2,6,7)$

14. **D** $8K = 8192$

$\log_2 8192 = 13$

15. **B** The formula calculates $(5*3) + (6+7+8+9) = 45$

16. **D** Annealing of cold worked metals or alloys produces recrystallization and grain growth. Associated with this process is the loss of cold-worked hardness or strength.

17. **A** See the Fe-C phase diagram. At 1100°C, a 0.18% C sample is 100 austenite (γ-phase). On cooling first the γ + Fe_3C phase field is crossed, and then at temperatures below 723°C the sample is in the ferrite + pearlite phase field.

18. **B** Note the difference between the terms ending in *tic* and *toid* (eutectic, eutectoid, peritectic, peritectoid, etc.). Eutec*tic* is the reaction between two liquids to form a solid. Eutec*toid* is the reaction between two solids to form a third solid.

19. **D** First you must balance the equation:

$$2\,Fe + 3\,CuSO_4 = Fe_2(SO_4)_3 + 3Cu$$

Then it is clear that 2 gram-atoms of Fe gives 3 gram-atoms of Cu and one gram-atom of Fe gives 1.5 gram-atom or 1.5(63.5) = 95 g of Cu.

20. **C** The valence electronic configuration is that of the outermost shell of an atom, i.e. the 3 level in sulfur.

21. **D** Ethane, a non-polar organic molecule, is held together by covalent bonds, as is the norm for compounds of carbon and hydrogen.

22. **A** An exothermic reaction has a favorable equibrium constant, but the rate depends on the activation energy.

23. **A**

24. **A** $\sum F = 0$. $F_A - 20\mathbf{k} + 60\mathbf{i} - 0.707(40)\mathbf{i} - 0.707(40)\mathbf{j} = 0$.

$\therefore F_A = -31.7\mathbf{i} - 28.3\mathbf{j} + 20\mathbf{k}$. $F_A = 47$ N.

25. **B** $\sum M_A = 0$.

$M_A + 10\mathbf{i} + (20 \times 0.15)\mathbf{i} + (60 \times 0.15)\mathbf{k} - (28.3 \times 0.1)\mathbf{i} - (28.3 \times 0.1)\mathbf{j} = 0$.

$\therefore M_A = -10.2\mathbf{i} - 2.83\mathbf{j} + 9\mathbf{k}$. $M_A = \sqrt{10.2^2 + 2.83^2 + 9^2} = 13.9$ N·m.

26. **A**

27. **C** $\mathbf{M} = 10\mathbf{i} + (60 \times 0.15)\mathbf{k} = 10\mathbf{i} + 9\mathbf{k}$. $M = \sqrt{100 + 81} = 13.45$ N·m.

28. **A** $\mathbf{v}_C = \mathbf{v}_B + \mathbf{v}_{C/B}$. A velocity polygon shows that $\mathbf{v}_B = \mathbf{v}_C$ so that $\omega_{BC} = 0$.

29. **C** $v_C = v_B = r\omega = 0.3 \times 10 = 3$ m/s.

30. **D** Draw an acceleration polygon. $\mathbf{a}_C = \mathbf{a}_B + \mathbf{a}_{C/B}$. $\mathbf{a}_B$ is in

y-direction, $\mathbf{a}_C$ is in x-direction, and $\mathbf{a}_{C/B}$ is $\perp \mathbf{r}_{BC}$. Using

$a_B = 30$, $a_{C/B} = 30 \times \dfrac{5}{4} = 37.5 = 0.5\alpha_{BC}$. $\therefore \alpha_{BC} = 75$ rad/s^2.

31. **D** From the acceleration polygon above, $a_C = 30 \times \dfrac{3}{4} = 22.5$ m/s^2.

32. **D** $a_{\text{Coriolis}} = 2\omega v = 2 \times 10 \times 2 = 40$ m/s^2.

$a_{\text{normal}} = r\omega^2 = 0.15 \times 10^2 = 15$ m/s^2. $\Bigg\}$ $a = \sqrt{1600 + 225} = 42.7$ m/s^2.

Note: The Coriolis acceleration is normal to the direction of **v**, normal to the arm.

33. **C** $T \sin 30° \times 2L = PL$. $\therefore T = 1800$ N. $\delta = \dfrac{1800 \times 4/0.866}{\pi \times 0.002^2 \times 210 \times 10^9} = 3.15 \times 10^{-3}$ m.

Note: The end drops straight down, but the wire stretches in the direction of the wire. $\therefore$ The end drops $3.15/\sin 30° = 6.3$ mm.

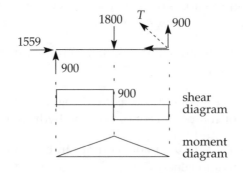

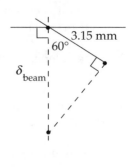

34. **D** The maximum tensile stress occurs at the outer fiber on the bottom of the beam where the moment is largest (i.e., under P).

$$\sigma_{max} = \frac{My}{I} = \frac{(P/2 \times L)h/2}{ah^3/12} = \frac{3PL}{ah^2} = \frac{3 \times 1800 \times 2}{0.02 \times 0.06^2} = 150 \times 10^6 \text{ Pa}.$$

35. **A** $\tau = \dfrac{VQ}{Ib} = \dfrac{(P/2)(ah/2)(h/4)}{(ah^3/12)a} = \dfrac{3P}{4ah} = \dfrac{3 \times 1800}{4 \times 0.02 \times 0.06} = 1.125 \times 10^6 \text{ Pa}.$

Refer to Example 10.6 for the calculation of Q.

36. **A** $\tau_{max} = \dfrac{\sigma}{2} = \dfrac{P/A}{2} = \dfrac{1800}{2\pi \times 0.002^2} = 71.6 \times 10^6 \text{ Pa}.$ (Think of Mohr's circle.)

37. **C** The moment diagram results from integrating the shear diagram.

38. **B** Find the current, then the voltage across the inductor is $V_L = Iz$.

$$Iz = \frac{100\angle 0°}{25 + j35 - j60} = 2.83\angle 45° \text{ A}$$

$$V_L = (2.83\angle 45°)(j35) = (2.83\angle 45°)(35\angle 90°) = 99\angle 135° \text{ volts}$$

39. **B** $P = I^2R = (2.83)^2 25 = 200 \text{ W}.$

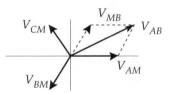

40. **D** power factor $= \cos\theta.$ $pf = \cos 45° = 0.707 \approx 0.71.$

41. **C** Note that the phase sequence is V_{AM}, V_{BM}, V_{CM}, or ABC. Also: $V_{AB} = V_{AM} + V_{MB}$. In the problem statement V_{AB} is shown at 0°, thus V_{AM} will be at –30°. Since $V_{ph} = \dfrac{V_{line}}{\sqrt{3}}$, $V_{AM} = \dfrac{208}{\sqrt{3}} \angle -30° = 120\angle -30° \text{ V}.$

42. **C** From Problem 41: $V_{CM} = 120\angle 120°.$

$$I_{CC'} = \frac{V_{CM}}{30 - j40} = \frac{120\angle 120°}{5\angle -53.1°} = 2.4\angle 173.1° \text{ amp}.$$

43. **A** Since this is a balanced 3ϕ load, $P_T = 3P_{ph}.$

$$P_T = 3(I_{ph})^2 R_{ph} = 3(2.4)^2 30 = 518.4 \text{ W}.$$

44. **C** $s_3 = s_4 = 7.1677 = 0.6491 + x_4(7.5019).$ $\therefore x_4 = 0.869.$

45. **D** $\dot{W}_T = \dot{m}(h_3 - h_4) = 5(3658.4 - 2271) = 6940 \text{ kW}.$
$h_4 = 191.8 + 0.869 \times 2392.8 = 2271$ where x_4 is from Problem 44.

46. **B** Use the energy equation (thermo or fluids):

$$\dot{Q} - \dot{W} = \dot{m}\left[\frac{p_2 - p_1}{\rho} + \frac{V_2^2 - V_1^2}{2} + g(z_2 - z_1)\right].$$

$$\dot{W}_P = \dot{m}\frac{p_2 - p_1}{\rho} = 5\frac{6000 - 10}{1000} = 30 \text{ kW}.$$

47. **B** $\dot{Q}_B = \dot{m}(h_3 - h_2) = 5(3658.4 - 191.8) = 17\,330$ kJ/s.

48. **D** $\eta = \dfrac{\dot{W}_T}{\dot{Q}_B} = \dfrac{6940}{17330} = 0.400$.

49. **C** $\eta_{\max} = 1 - \dfrac{T_{\text{low}}}{T_{\text{high}}} = 1 - \dfrac{318.8}{873} = 0.635$

50. **C** $V = \dfrac{Q}{A} = \dfrac{0.02}{\pi \times 0.025^2} = 10.2$ m/s.

51. **D** $V_{\text{exit}} = V \dfrac{A}{A_{\text{exit}}} = 10.2 \dfrac{5^2}{2^2} = 63.8$ m/s.

Bernoulli:

$\dfrac{10.2^2}{2 \times 9.8} + \dfrac{p}{9800} = \dfrac{63.8^2}{2 \times 9.8} + \dfrac{0}{9800}$. $\therefore p = 198.3 \times 10^4$ Pa or 1983 kPa.

52. **C**   Energy (surface to inlet): Use

$\text{Re} = \dfrac{VD}{\nu} = \dfrac{10.2 \times 0.05}{10^{-6}} = 5.1 \times 10^5$. $\dfrac{e}{D} = \dfrac{0.26}{50} = 0.0052$. $\therefore f = 0.03$.

$30 = \dfrac{10.2^2}{2 \times 9.8} + \dfrac{-100\,000}{9800} + \left(0.03 \dfrac{L}{0.05} + 0.5\right) \dfrac{10.2^2}{2 \times 9.8}$. $\therefore L = 10.1$ m.

53. **C** $\dot{W}_p = Q\Delta p = 0.02\Delta p = 157 \times 0.746$. $\therefore \Delta p = 5860$ kPa.

54. **B** $\sum F = \rho Q (V_2 - V_1)$. $p_1 A_1 - F = \rho Q (V_2 - V_1)$.

$1983\,000 \times \pi \times 0.025^2 - F = 1000 \times 0.02(63.8 - 10.2)$. $\therefore F = 2820$ N.

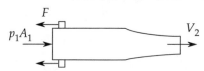

55. **D** $\text{ANEV} = \left[-25,500(A/P)_3^6 - 1200 + 900(A/F)_3^6\right]$

$- \left[-42,000(A/P)_6^6 - 1800 + 1500(A/F)_6^6\right] = -\$330$.

56. **A** $i = \dfrac{6\%}{2} = 3\%$; $i_e = (1.03)^2 - 1 = 0.061$; $i_e = 6.1\%$.

57. **A** $0.05 \times 5000 = \$250$

$P = 250(P/A)_{10}^6 + 5000(P/F)_{10}^6 = \$4632$.

58. **D**

59. **C**

60. **C**

Equation Summaries

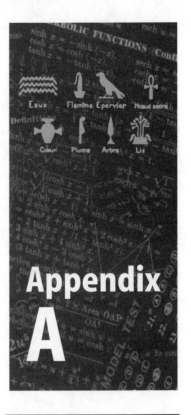

Appendix A

The following pages are Equation Summary Sheets of the FE/EIT subjects which rely most on equations. They are intended to be used for quick overviews, handy problem-solving—and as part of a special strategy for preparing for the exam in its present format.

The selected equations are presented in the same format and nomenclature as is to be found in the NCEES Reference Handbook, a booklet which is given to all exam applicants. Be prepared! You may find some of the nomenclature to be different from what you are used to using, as the NCEES has apparently obtained some of it from older or obscure texts.

These summaries are useful for study

The current edition of the NCEES Reference Handbook has many extraneous equations which will in all likelihood be of little aid in solving exam problems. As discussed earlier, an excellent exam preparation strategy is to identify the equations you find to be most useful, then highlight them and become acquainted with their position in the Handbook so that you may quickly access them in the "clean" Handbook during the exam itself. This strategy should maximize your ability to perform as well as possible, given the present exam format.

Summaries can help you anticipate and prepare for NCEES obstacles

You may pre-program any programmable calculator to solve many of the problems on the FE exam, e.g., problems involving matrices, permutations, standard deviations, Mohr's circle problems, etc. Or you may choose to buy the HP 48G, which has hundreds of equations and constants preprogrammed. (We offer this superior calculator at a significant discount. See page 9 or catalog pages at back.) One or two states might not allow the use of the HP 48G, so be sure you check with your state board.

Calculators are a good way to access equations during the exam

Mathematics
—Selected Equations from the NCEES Reference Handbook—

Straight Line: $y = mx + b$ (slope - intercept form) $m = \dfrac{y_2 - y_1}{x_2 - x_1}$ (slope)

$y - y_1 = m(x - x_1)$ (point - slope form) $m_1 = -\dfrac{1}{m_2}$ (two perpendicular lines)

Quadratic Equation: $ax^2 + bx + c = 0$ roots $= \dfrac{-b \pm \sqrt{b^2 - 4ac}}{2a}$

Conic Sections:

	General Form	$h = k = 0$
Parabola:	$(y - k)^2 = 2p(x - h)$	$y^2 = 2px$ Focus: $(p/2, 0)$ Directrix: $x = -p/2$
Ellipse:	$\dfrac{(x - h)^2}{a^2} + \dfrac{(y - k)^2}{b^2} = 1$	$\dfrac{x^2}{a^2} + \dfrac{y^2}{b^2} = 1$ Focus: $\left(\sqrt{a^2 - b^2},\ 0 \right)$
Hyperbola:	$\dfrac{(x - h)^2}{a^2} - \dfrac{(y - k)^2}{b^2} = 1$	$\dfrac{x^2}{a^2} - \dfrac{y^2}{b^2} = 1$ Focus: $\left(\sqrt{a^2 + b^2},\ 0 \right)$
Circle:	$(x - h)^2 + (y - k)^2 = r^2$	$x^2 + y^2 = r^2$

Logarithms:

$\ln x = 2.3026 \ \log x$ $\log xy = \log x + \log y$ $\log x/y = \log x - \log y$

$\log_b b^n = n$ $\log_b b = 1$

$\log x^c = c \log x$ $\log 1 = 0$ If $b^c = x$, then $\log_b x = c$

Trigonometry:

$\sin \theta = y / r$ $\cos \theta = x / r$

$\tan \theta = y / x$ $\cot \theta = x / y$

$\csc \theta = r / y$ $\sec \theta = r / x$

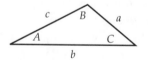

Law of Sines: $\dfrac{a}{\sin A} = \dfrac{b}{\sin B} = \dfrac{c}{\sin C}$

Law of Cosines: $a^2 = b^2 + c^2 - 2bc \cos A$

Identities:

$\tan \theta = \sin \theta / \cos \theta$ $\sin 2\alpha = 2 \sin \alpha \cos \alpha$

$\sin^2 \theta + \cos^2 \theta = 1$ $\cos 2\alpha = \cos^2 \alpha - \sin^2 \alpha$

$\sin(\alpha + \beta) = \sin \alpha \cos \beta + \cos \alpha \sin \beta$ $= 2 \cos^2 \alpha - 1$

$\cos(\alpha + \beta) = \cos \alpha \cos \beta - \sin \alpha \sin \beta$ $= 1 - 2 \sin^2 \alpha$

Complex Numbers:

$$i = \sqrt{-1} \qquad\qquad x + iy = re^{i\theta} \qquad\qquad \cos\theta = \frac{e^{i\theta} + e^{-i\theta}}{2}$$

$$r = \sqrt{x^2 + y^2} \qquad\qquad e^{i\theta} = \cos\theta + i\sin\theta \qquad\qquad \sin\theta = \frac{e^{i\theta} - e^{-i\theta}}{2i}$$

$$(x + iy)^n = r^n(\cos n\theta + i\sin n\theta)$$

Matrices:

Transpose: $\quad \mathbf{B} = \mathbf{A}^T \quad$ if $\quad b_{ji} = a_{ij}$

Inverse: $\quad \mathbf{A}^{-1} = \dfrac{\text{adj}(\mathbf{A})}{|\mathbf{A}|}$

Adjoint: $\quad \text{adj}(\mathbf{A}) = $ matrix formed by replacing $\mathbf{A}^T$ elements with their cofactors

Cofactor: $\quad \text{cofactor} = \text{minor} \times (-1)^{h+k} \quad$ where $h = $ column, $k = $ row

Minor: $\quad \text{minor} = $ determinant that remains after the common row and column are struck out

Vectors:

$$\mathbf{A} \cdot \mathbf{B} = a_x b_x + a_y b_y + a_z b_z \qquad \mathbf{A} \times \mathbf{B} = \begin{vmatrix} \mathbf{i} & \mathbf{j} & \mathbf{k} \\ a_x & a_y & a_z \\ b_x & b_y & b_z \end{vmatrix}$$

$$= |\mathbf{A}||\mathbf{B}|\cos\theta = \mathbf{B} \cdot \mathbf{A}$$

$$= |\mathbf{A}||\mathbf{B}|\mathbf{n}\sin\theta = -\mathbf{B} \times \mathbf{A} \quad \text{where } \mathbf{n} \text{ is } \perp \text{ plane of } \mathbf{A} \text{ and } \mathbf{B}$$

$$\mathbf{i} \cdot \mathbf{i} = \mathbf{j} \cdot \mathbf{j} = \mathbf{k} \cdot \mathbf{k} = 1 \qquad \mathbf{i} \times \mathbf{j} = \mathbf{k}, \quad \mathbf{j} \times \mathbf{k} = \mathbf{i}, \quad \mathbf{k} \times \mathbf{i} = \mathbf{j}$$

Taylor Series:

$$f(x) = f(a) + \frac{f'(a)}{1!}(x - a) + \frac{f''(a)}{2!}(x - a)^2 + \cdots$$

Maclaurin Series: $\quad$ a Taylor series with $a = 0$

Probability and Statistics:

$$P(n, r) = \frac{n!}{(n - r)!} \qquad \text{(permutation of } n \text{ things taken } r \text{ at a time)}$$

$$C(n, r) = \frac{P(n, r)}{r!} = \frac{n!}{r!(n - r)!} \qquad \text{(combination of } n \text{ things taken } r \text{ at a time)}$$

$$\bar{x} = \frac{x_1 + x_2 + \cdots + x_n}{n} \qquad \text{(arithmetic mean)}$$

$$\sigma^2 = \frac{\sum(x_i - \bar{x})^2}{n - 1} \qquad \text{(variance)}$$

$$\sigma = \sqrt{\text{variance}} \qquad \text{(sample standard deviation)}$$

$$\text{median} = \begin{cases} \text{middle value if odd number of items} \\ \frac{1}{2}(\text{sum of middle two values}) \text{ if even number of items} \end{cases}$$

$$\text{mode} = \text{value that occurs most often}$$

Calculus: $f'(x) = 0 \begin{cases} \text{maximum} & \text{if } f''(x) < 0 \\ \text{minimum} & \text{if } f''(x) > 0 \end{cases}$

L'Hospital's Rule: $\displaystyle \lim_{x \to a} \frac{f(x)}{g(x)} = \lim_{x \to a} \frac{f'(x)}{g'(x)}$ if $\dfrac{f(a)}{g(a)} = \dfrac{0}{0}$ or $\dfrac{\infty}{\infty}$

$\dfrac{d}{dx}(uv) = u\dfrac{dv}{dx} + v\dfrac{du}{dx}$ $\dfrac{d}{dx}(\ln u) = \dfrac{1}{u}\dfrac{du}{dx}$ $\dfrac{d}{dx}(\sin u) = \cos u \dfrac{du}{dx}$

$\dfrac{d}{dx}\left(\dfrac{u}{v}\right) = \dfrac{v\,du/dx - u\,dv/dx}{v^2}$ $\dfrac{d}{dx}\left(e^u\right) = e^u \dfrac{du}{dx}$ $\dfrac{d}{dx}(\cos u) = -\sin u \dfrac{du}{dx}$

$\dfrac{d}{dx}\left(u^n\right) = nu^{n-1}\dfrac{du}{dx}$

$\displaystyle \int x^n dx = \frac{x^{n+1}}{n+1} \qquad n \neq -1$ $\displaystyle \int \sin x\, dx = -\cos x$ $\displaystyle \int \sin^2 x\, dx = \frac{x}{2} - \frac{\sin 2x}{4}$

$\displaystyle \int \frac{dx}{ax+b} = \frac{1}{a}\ln|ax+b|$ $\displaystyle \int \cos x\, dx = \sin x$ $\displaystyle \int \cos^2 x\, dx = \frac{x}{2} + \frac{\sin 2x}{4}$

$\displaystyle \int e^{ax} dx = \frac{1}{a}e^{ax}$

Differential Equations: $y'' + 2ay' + by = f(x)$ (linear, 2nd order, constant coefficient, nonhomogeneous)

Homogeneous solution: $y_h(x) = C_1 e^{r_1 x} + C_2 e^{r_2 x}$ if $r_1 \neq r_2$ where $r^2 + 2ar + b = 0$

$\qquad\qquad\qquad\qquad = \left(C_1 + C_2 x\right)e^{r_1 x}$ if $r_1 = r_2$

$\qquad\qquad\qquad\qquad = e^{-ax}\left(C_1 \cos \beta x + C_2 \sin \beta x\right)$ if $a^2 < b$. $\beta = \sqrt{b - a^2}$

Particular solution: $y_p = B$ if $f(x) = A$

$\qquad\qquad\qquad = Be^{\alpha x}$ if $f(x) = Ae^{\alpha x}$

$\qquad\qquad\qquad = B_1 \sin \omega x + B_2 \cos \omega x$ if $f(x) = A_1 \sin \omega x + A_2 \cos \omega x$

General solution: $y(x) = y_h(x) + y_p(x)$

Mechanics of Materials
—Selected equations from the NCEES Reference Handbook—

Definitions:

$$\sigma = \varepsilon E$$

$$\tau = \gamma G$$

$$E = 2G(1 + v)$$

$$v = -\frac{\varepsilon_{lateral}}{\varepsilon_{longitudinal}}$$

E = modulus of elasticity

G = shear modulus

σ and τ = normal and shear stress

ε and γ = normal and shear strain

v = Poisson's ratio

Uniaxial Loading:

$$\left.\begin{array}{c} \sigma = \dfrac{P}{A} \\[2ex] \varepsilon = \dfrac{\delta}{L} \end{array}\right\} \quad \delta = \dfrac{PL}{AE}$$

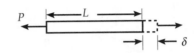

Thermal Deformation: $\quad \delta_t = \alpha L\left(T - T_o\right)$

α = coefficient of thermal expansion

Thin-walled Pressure Vessel: $\quad \sigma_t = \dfrac{pD}{2t} \quad$ hoop (circumferential) stress

$$\sigma_a = \dfrac{pD}{4t} \quad \text{axial (longitudinal) stress}$$

t = cylinder thickness
D = cylinder diameter
p = pressure

Stress and Strain:

Stress Condition

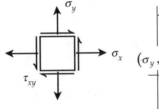

Mohr's Circle

(σ_y, τ_{xy})

$(\sigma_x, -\tau_{xy})$

2θ

Maximum and Minimum Stresses

$$\sigma_1 = \sigma_{max} = \frac{\sigma_x + \sigma_y}{2} + \left[\left(\sigma_x - \sigma_y\right)^2 \Big/ 4 + \tau_{xy}^2\right]^{1/2}$$

$$\sigma_2 = \sigma_{min} = \frac{\sigma_x + \sigma_y}{2} - \left[\left(\sigma_x - \sigma_y\right)^2 \Big/ 4 + \tau_{xy}^2\right]^{1/2}$$

$$\tau_{max} = \frac{\sigma_1 - \sigma_2}{2} = \text{radius of Mohr's circle}$$

3-D Strain: $\quad \varepsilon_x = \dfrac{1}{E}\left[\sigma_x - v\left(\sigma_y + \sigma_z\right)\right]$

$$\gamma_{xy} = \frac{\tau_{xy}}{G}$$

Torsion: $\quad \tau = \dfrac{Tr}{J} \quad$ (shear stress)

$$\phi = \frac{TL}{JG} \quad \text{(angle of twist)}$$

J = polar moment of inertia
$\quad = \pi r^4 / 2 \;$ for a circle

Beams: $\quad V = \dfrac{dM}{dx}$

$$\sigma = -\frac{My}{I}$$

$$\tau = \frac{VQ}{Ib}$$

$$EIy'' = M$$

V = vertical shear force,

I = centroidal moment of inertia
$\quad = bh^3/12 \;$ for a rectangle
$\quad = \pi r^4/4 \;$ for a circle

Q = moment of area between
$\quad y$ - position and top or bottom

differential equation of deflection curve

M = bending moment

y = distance from neutral axis

Columns: $\quad P_{cr} = \dfrac{\pi^2 EI}{k^2 L^2} \qquad k = \begin{cases} 1 & \text{ends pinned} \\ 0.5 & \text{ends fixed} \\ 0.7 & \text{one pinned, one fixed} \\ 2 & \text{one fixed, one free} \end{cases}$

Dynamics
—Selected equations from the NCEES Reference Handbook—

Kinematics (motion only)

Tangential and Normal Components:

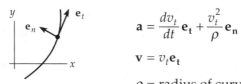

$$\mathbf{a} = \frac{dv_t}{dt}\mathbf{e_t} + \frac{v_t^2}{\rho}\mathbf{e_n}$$

$$\mathbf{v} = v_t\mathbf{e_t}$$

ρ = radius of curvature

Plane Circular Motion:

$$\mathbf{e_r} = -\mathbf{e_n}$$
$$\mathbf{e_\theta} = \mathbf{e_t}$$

$$\omega = \dot\theta = \frac{v_t}{r}$$

$$a_t = r\alpha$$

$$\alpha = \dot\omega = \ddot\theta = \frac{a_t}{r}$$

$$a_n = \frac{v_t^2}{r} = r\omega^2$$

$$v_t = r\omega$$

$$s = r\theta$$

Straight Line Motion:

$$s = s_0 + v_0 t + a_0 t^2/2$$
$$v = v_0 + a_0 t$$
$$v^2 = v_0^2 + 2a_0(s - s_0)$$

Projectile Motion:

$$a_x = 0, \quad a_y = -g$$
$$v_x = v_0\cos\theta$$
$$v_y = v_0\sin\theta - gt$$

$$x = v_0 t\cos\theta$$
$$y = v_0 t\sin\theta - \tfrac{1}{2}gt^2$$

Kinematics (forces and motion)

$$\sum\mathbf{F} = \frac{d}{dt}(m\mathbf{v}), \quad \sum F_t = ma_t = m\frac{dv_t}{dt}, \quad \sum F_n = ma_n = m\frac{v_t^2}{\rho}$$

Impulse and Momentum:

$$m[v_x(t) - v_x(0)] = \int_0^t F_x(t)\,dt \quad \text{or} \quad \text{change in momentum = impulse}$$

Work and Energy:

$$PE_1 + KE_1 + W_{1\to2} = PE_2 + KE_2 \quad \text{where}$$

$$KE = \tfrac{1}{2}mv^2$$
$$PE = mgh \quad \text{(gravity)}$$
$$= \tfrac{1}{2}kx^2 \quad \text{(spring)}$$
$$W_{1\to2} = \text{friction force work}$$

Impact:

$$m_1 v_1 + m_2 v_2 = m_1 v_1' + m_2 v_2'$$

$$e = -\frac{v_{1n}' - v_{2n}'}{v_{1n} - v_{2n}} = \begin{cases}1 & \text{elastic}\\ 0 & \text{plastic}\end{cases}$$

v_1, v_2 = velocities before impact
v_1', v_2' = velocities after impact

Rotation:

$$I_o\alpha = \sum M_o \quad \text{where} \quad I_o = \int(x^2 + y^2)\,dm, \text{ rotation about } O.$$

constant M:

$$\alpha = \frac{M}{I}$$
$$\omega = \omega_o + \frac{M}{I}t$$
$$\theta = \theta_o + \omega_o t + \frac{M}{2I}t^2$$

work and energy:

$$I_o\frac{\omega^2}{2} - I_o\frac{\omega_o^2}{2} = \int_{\theta_o}^{\theta} M\,d\theta$$

Banking of Curves:

$$\tan\theta = \frac{v^2}{rg} \quad \text{where} \quad r = \text{radius of curvature}$$
$$\theta = \text{angle between surface and horizontal}$$

Electric Circuits
—Selected Equations from the NCEES Reference Handbook—

Electrostatics: $F_2 = \dfrac{Q_1 Q_2}{4\pi\varepsilon r^2}$ (force on charge 2 due to charge 1) ε = permittivity — $C^2/N \cdot m^2$ = F/m

$$= 8.85 \times 10^{-12} \text{ for air or free space}$$

$E = \dfrac{Q}{4\pi\varepsilon r^2}$ (electric field intensity due to point charge Q — C)

$E_L = \dfrac{\rho_L}{2\pi\varepsilon r}$ (radial field due to line charge ρ_L — C/m)

$E_s = \dfrac{\rho_s}{2\varepsilon}$ (plane field due to sheet charge ρ_s — C/m^2)

$Q = \oint \varepsilon \mathbf{E} \cdot d\mathbf{A}$ (enclosed charge — C)

$E = \dfrac{V}{d}$ (electric field between plates with potential difference V separated by the distance d)

$H = \dfrac{I}{2\pi r}$ (magnetic field strength due to current in long wire)

$B = \mu H$ (magnetic flux density)

$\mathbf{F} = I\mathbf{L} \times \mathbf{B}$ (force on conductor) $\mathbf{L}$ = length vector of conductor

DC Circuits: *Resistors:* $V = IR$ (Ohm's law) $R_T = R_1 + R_2 + \cdots$ (series)

$P = VI = \dfrac{V^2}{R} = I^2 R$ (power) $R_T = \left[\frac{1}{R_1} + \frac{1}{R_2} + \cdots\right]^{-1}$ (parallel)

Capacitors: $i = C\dfrac{dv}{dt}$ $\underset{\text{stored}}{energy} = \frac{1}{2}Cv^2$ $C_{eq} = C_1 + C_2 + \cdots$ (parallel)

$v = \dfrac{1}{C}\int i\,dt$ $C_{eq} = \left[\frac{1}{C_1} + \frac{1}{C_2} + \cdots\right]^{-1}$ (series)

Inductors: $i = \dfrac{1}{L}\int v\,dt$ $\underset{\text{stored}}{energy} = \frac{1}{2}Li^2$ $L_{eq} = L_1 + L_2 + \cdots$ (series)

$v = L\dfrac{di}{dt}$ $L_{eq} = \left[\frac{1}{L_1} + \frac{1}{L_2} + \cdots\right]^{-1}$ (parallel)

Kirchhoff's Voltage Law (KVL): $\sum V_{rises} = \sum V_{drops} = 0$

Kirchhoff's Current Law (KCL): $\sum I_{in} = \sum I_{out}$

Thévenin equivalent circuit:

$R_{eq} = \dfrac{V_{eq}}{I_{sc}}$ I_{sc} = short circuit current

V_{eq} = open circuit voltage

RC Transients:

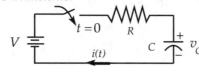

$$v_C(t) = v_C(0)e^{-t/RC} + V\left(1 - e^{-t/RC}\right)$$

$$i(t) = \left\{[V - v_C(0)]/R\right\}e^{-t/RC}$$

RL Transients:

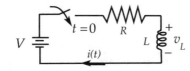

$$v_L(t) = -i(0)Re^{-Rt/L} + Ve^{-Rt/L}$$

$$i(t) = i(0)e^{-Rt/L} + \frac{V}{R}\left(1 - e^{-Rt/L}\right)$$

Operational Amplifiers:

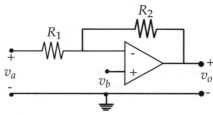

$$v_o = -\frac{R_2}{R_1}v_a + \left(1 + \frac{R_2}{R_1}\right)v_b$$

inverting if $v_b = 0$

non - inverting if $v_a = 0$

AC Circuits: (single phase)

$$f = \frac{1}{T} = \frac{\omega}{2\pi}$$

f = frequency (Hz)
T = period (sec)
ω = angular frequency (rad / s)

$$V_{avg} = \frac{2}{\pi}V_{max}$$ (full-wave rectified sine wave)

$$V_{avg} = \frac{1}{\pi}V_{max}$$ (half-wave rectified sine wave)

$$V_{rms} = \frac{1}{\sqrt{2}}V_{max}$$ (full-wave rectified sine wave)

$$V_{rms} = \frac{1}{2}V_{max}$$ (half-wave rectified sine wave)

Resistor: $Z = R$ Z = Impedance = V / I

Capacitor: $Z = -\dfrac{j}{\omega C} = -jX$ X = Reactance

Inductor: $Z = j\omega L = jX$

Complex Power: $V = IZ$

$$P = \tfrac{1}{2}V_{max}I_{max}\cos\theta = V_{rms}I_{rms}\cos\theta$$ (real power)   ($\theta = 0$ for resistors)

$$Q = \tfrac{1}{2}V_{max}I_{max}\sin\theta = V_{rms}I_{rms}\sin\theta$$ (reactive power)

$$\text{p.f.} = \cos\theta$$ (power factor)

Resonance: $$f = \frac{1}{2\pi\sqrt{LC}}$$ (resonant frequency for series and parallel circuits)

Fluid Mechanics
—Selected Equations from the NCEES Reference Handbook—

Properties: $\rho = \dfrac{m}{V}$ (density) $\tau_n = -p$ (normal stress)

$\gamma = \rho g$ (specific weight) $\tau_t = \mu \dfrac{dv}{dy}$ (tangential stress)

$v = \dfrac{\mu}{\rho}$ (kinematic viscosity) μ = dynamic viscosity

Statics: $p_2 - p_1 = -\gamma h$ (h is vertical upward) $F = \gamma h_C A$

$F_{\text{buoyant}} = \gamma V_{\text{displaced}}$ (Archimedes' principle) $z^* = \dfrac{I_C}{A Z_C}$

One-Dimensional Flows: $A_1 V_1 = A_2 V_2$ (continuity equation)

$Q = AV$ (flow rate)

$\dot{m} = \rho A V$ (mass flow rate)

$-\dfrac{\dot{W}_S}{\gamma Q} + \dfrac{p_1}{\gamma} + \dfrac{V_1^2}{2g} + z_1 = \dfrac{p_2}{\gamma} + \dfrac{V_2^2}{2g} + z_2 + h_f$ (Energy Equation — if $h_f = \dot{W}_s = 0$, then Bernoulli Eq.)

$h_f = f \dfrac{L}{D} \dfrac{V^2}{2g}$ (Darcy's Equation — find f on Moody Diagram)

$\text{Re} = \dfrac{VD\rho}{\mu}$ (Reynolds Number)

$h_{f,\,\text{fitting}} = C \dfrac{V^2}{2g}$ (minor losses — C is loss coefficient)

$\sum F = \rho Q (V_2 - V_1)$ (Momentum equation)

Perfect Gas: $p = \rho R T$ (perfect gas law)

$c = \sqrt{kRT}$ (speed of sound)

$M = \dfrac{V}{c}$ (Mach number)

Similitude: If viscous effects dominate (internal flows) then Reynolds numbers on prototype and model are equated:

$(\text{Re})_p = (\text{Re})_m$ or $\left(\dfrac{V \ell \rho}{\mu} \right)_p = \left(\dfrac{V \ell \rho}{\mu} \right)_m$

If gravity dominates (dams, weirs, ships) then Froude numbers are equated:

$(\text{Fr})_p = (\text{Fr})_m$ or $\left(\dfrac{V^2}{\ell g} \right)_p = \left(\dfrac{V^2}{\ell g} \right)_m$

Open Channel: $Q = \dfrac{C}{n} A R^{2/3} S^{1/2}$ where $R = \dfrac{A}{P_{\text{wetted}}}$

$C = \begin{cases} 1.0 & \text{metric} \\ 1.49 & \text{english} \end{cases}$

Thermodynamics
—Selected Equations from the NCEES Reference Handbook—

Properties:

P (absolute pressure, kPa or lbf/in^2)

$v = \dfrac{V}{m}$ (specific volume, m^3/kg or ft^3/lbm)

u (internal energy, kJ/kg or Btu/lbm)

$h = u + Pv$ (enthalpy, kJ/kg or Btu/lbm)

s (entropy, kJ/kg·K or Btu/lbm-°R)

c_p (constant pressure specific heat, kJ/kg·K or Btu/lbm-°R)

c_v (constant volume specific heat, kJ/kg·K or Btu/lbm-°R)

$x = \dfrac{m_v}{m_{total}}$ (quality)

Two phase system:

$v = v_f + x v_{fg}$ where $v_{fg} = v_g - v_f$ v_f = saturated liquid value

$h = h_f + x h_{fg}$ v_g = saturated vapor value

Ideal gas:

$Pv = RT, \quad PV = mRT$ where $R = \dfrac{\overline{R}}{M}, \quad \overline{R} = 8.314 \dfrac{kJ}{kmol \cdot K}$ or $1545 \dfrac{ft\text{-}lbf}{lbmol\text{-}°R}$

$\Delta u = c_v \Delta T, \quad\quad\quad\quad\quad \Delta h = c_p \Delta T$

$\Delta s = c_p \ln \dfrac{T_2}{T_1} - R \ln \dfrac{P_2}{P_1} = c_v \ln \dfrac{T_2}{T_1} + R \ln \dfrac{v_2}{v_1}$

$\left. \begin{array}{c} \dfrac{T_2}{T_1} = \left(\dfrac{P_2}{P_1}\right)^{\frac{k-1}{k}} = \left(\dfrac{v_1}{v_2}\right)^{k-1}, \quad\quad P_2 v_2^k = P_1 v_1^k \\[2mm] k = c_p/c_v \end{array} \right\}$ (constant entropy process)

First law (system): $q - w = \Delta u$ where $w = \int P dv$

$$= RT \ln \dfrac{v_2}{v_1} = RT \ln \dfrac{P_1}{P_2} \quad \text{(isothermal process with ideal gas)}$$

First law (control volume):

$h_i + V_i^2/2 = h_e + V_e^2/2$ (nozzles, diffusers) i = inlet

$h_i = h_e + w$ (turbine, compressor) e = exit

$h_i = h_e$ (throttling device, valve)

$h_i + q = h_e$ (boilers, condensers, evaporators)

Cycles: $\eta = \dfrac{W}{Q_H} = \dfrac{Q_H - Q_L}{Q_H}$ (efficiency) $\text{COP} = \dfrac{Q_H}{W}$ (heat pump)

$\qquad\qquad = 1 - \dfrac{T_L}{T_H}$ (Carnot cycle) $= \dfrac{Q_L}{W}$ (refrigerator)

Second Law: No engine can produce work while transferring heat with a single reservoir. (Kelvin-Planck)

No refrigerator can operate without a work input. (Clausius)

$\Delta S \geq \displaystyle\int \dfrac{\delta Q}{T}$ $\Delta S = \dfrac{Q}{T}$ (reservoir or T = const)

$\Delta S_{total} = \Delta S_{surr} + \Delta S_{system} \geq 0$ $\Delta S = C_p \ln \dfrac{T_2}{T_1}$ (solid or liquid)

Heat Transfer: $\dot{Q} = -kA \dfrac{dT}{dx}$ (conduction) $k = \text{conductivity}$

$\qquad\qquad = -kA \dfrac{T_2 - T_1}{L}$ (through a wall) $R = \dfrac{L}{kA}$ (resistance factor)

$\dot{Q} = hA(T_1 - T_2)$ (convection) $R = \dfrac{1}{hA}$ (resistance factor)

$\qquad\qquad = \varepsilon\sigma A\left(T_1^4 - T_2^4\right)F_{12}$ (radiation) $h = \text{convection coefficient}$

$\varepsilon = 1$ for black body   (emissivity)

$\sigma = 5.67 \times 10^{-8} \ \dfrac{W}{m^2 \cdot K^4}$ (Stefan - Boltzmann constant)

$F_{12} = 1$ if one body encloses the other   (shape factor)

English and SI Units

The following tables present the SI (Systems International) units and the conversion of English units to SI units, along with some of the more common conversion factors.

SI Prefixes

Multiplication Factor	Prefix	Symbol
10^{15}	peta	P
10^{12}	tera	T
10^{9}	giga	G
10^{6}	mega	M
10^{3}	kilo	k
10^{-1}	deci	d
10^{-2}	centi	c
10^{-3}	mili	m
10^{-6}	micro	μ
10^{-9}	nano	n
10^{-12}	pico	p
10^{-15}	femto	f

SI Base Units

Quantity	Name	Symbol
length	meter	m
mass	kilogram	kg
time	second	s
electric current	ampere	A
temperature	kelvin	K
amount of substance	mole	mol
luminous intensity	candela	cd

SI Derived Units

Quantity	Name	Symbol	In Terms of Other Units
area	square meter		m^2
volume	cubic meter		m^3
velocity	meter per second		m/s
acceleration	meter per second squared		m/s^2
density	kilogram per cubic meter		kg/m^3
specific volume	cubic meter per kilogram		m^3/kg
frequency	hertz	Hz	s^{-1}
force	newton	N	$m \cdot kg/s^2$
pressure, stress	pascal	Pa	$kg/(m \cdot s^2)$
energy, work, heat	joule	J	$N \cdot m$
power	watt	W	J/s
electric charge	coulomb	C	$A \cdot s$
electric potential	volt	V	W/A
capacitance	farad	F	C/V
electric resistance	ohm	Ω	V/A
conductance	siemens	S	A/V
magnetic flux	weber	Wb	$V \cdot s$
inductance	henry	H	Wb/A
viscosity	pascal second		$Pa \cdot s$
moment (torque)	meter newton		$N \cdot m$
heat flux	watt per square meter		W/m^2
entropy	joule per kelvin		J/K
specific heat	joule per kilogram-kelvin		$J/(kg \cdot K)$
conductivity	watt per meter-kelvin		$W/(m \cdot K)$

Conversion Factors to SI Units

English	SI	SI Symbol	To Convert from English to SI Multiply by
Area			
square inch	square centimeter	cm2	6.452
square foot	square meter	m2	0.09290
acre	hectare	ha	0.4047
Length			
inch	centimeter	cm	2.54
foot	meter	m	0.3048
mile	kilometer	km	1.6093
Volume			
cubic inch	cubic centimeter	cm^3	16.387
cubic foot	cubic meter	m^3	0.02832
gallon	cubic meter	m^3	0.003785
gallon	liter	L	3.785
Mass			
pound mass	kilogram	kg	0.4536
slug	kilogram	kg	14.59
Force			
pound	newton	N	4.448
kip(1000 lb)	newton	N	4448
Density			
pound/cubic foot	kilogram/cubic meter	kg/m^3	16.02
pound/cubic foot	grams/liter	g/L	16.02
Work, Energy, Heat			
foot-pound	joule	J	1.356
Btu	joule	J	1055
Btu	kilowatt-hour	kWh	0.000293
therm	kilowatt-hour	kWh	29.3

Conversion Factors to SI Units (continued)

English	SI	SI Symbol	To Convert from English to SI Multiply by
Power, Heat, Rate			
horsepower	watt	W	745.7
foot pound/sec	watt	W	1.356
Btu/hour	watt	W	0.2931
Btu/hour-ft²-°F	watt/meter squared-°C	$W/m^2 \cdot {}^\circ C$	5.678
tons of refrig.	kilowatts	kW	3.517
Pressure			
pound/square inch	kilopascal	kPa	6.895
pound/square foot	kilopascal	kPa	0.04788
inches of H_2O	kilopascal	kPa	0.2486
inches of Hg	kilopascal	kPa	3.374
one atmosphere	kilopascal	kPa	101.3
Temperature			
Fahrenheit	Celsius	°C	$5\,(^\circ F - 32)/9$
Fahrenheit	kelvin	K	$5\,(^\circ F + 460)/9$
Velocity			
foot/second	meter/second	m/s	0.3048
mile/hour	meter/second	m/s	0.4470
mile/hour	kilometer/hour	km/h	1.609
Acceleration			
foot/second squared	meter/second squared	m/s^2	0.3048
Torque			
pound-foot	newton-meter	$N \cdot m$	1.356
pound-inch	newton-meter	$N \cdot m$	0.1130
Viscosity, Kinematic Viscosity			
pound-sec/square foot	newton-sec/square meter	$N \cdot s/m^2$	47.88
square foot/second	square meter/second	m^2/s	0.09290
Flow Rate			
cubic foot/minute	cubic meter/second	m^3/s	0.0004719
cubic foot/minute	liter/second	L/s	0.4719
Frequency			
cycles/second	hertz	Hz	1.00

Conversion Factors

Length

1 cm	= 0.3937 in
1 m	= 3.281 ft
1 yd	= 3 ft
1 mi	= 5280 ft
1 mi	= 1760 yd
1 km	= 3281 ft

Area

1 cm^2	= 0.155 in^2
1 m^2	= 10.76 ft^2
1 ha	= 10^4 m^2
1 acre	= 100 m^2
1 acre	= 4047 m^2
1 acre	= 43,560 ft^2

Volume

1 ft^3	= 28.32 L
1 L	= 0.03531 ft^3
1 L	= 0.2642 gal
1 m^3	= 264.2 gal
1 ft^3	= 7.481 gal
1 m^3	= 35.31 ft^3
1 acre-ft	= 43,560 ft^3
1 m^3	= 1000 L

Velocity

1 m/s	= 3.281 ft/s
1 mph	= 1.467 ft/s
1 mph	= 0.8684 knot
1 knot	= 1.688 ft/s
1 km/h	= 0.2778 m/s
1 km/h	= 0.6214 mph

Force

1 lb	= 4.448×10^5 dyne
1 lb	= 32.17 pdl
1 lb	= 0.4536 kg
1 N	= 10^5 dyne
1 N	= 0.2248 lb
1 kip	= 1000 lb

Mass

1 oz	= 28.35 g
1 lb	= 0.4536 kg
1 kg	= 2.205 lb
1 slug	= 14.59 kg
1 slug	= 32.17 lb

Work and Heat

1 Btu	= 778.2 ft-lb
1 Btu	= 1055 J
1 Cal	= 3.088 ft-lb
1 J	= 10^7 ergs
1 kJ	= 0.9478 ft-lb
1 Btu	= 0.2929 W · hr
1 ton	= 12,000 Btu/hr
1 kWh	= 3414 Btu
1 quad	= 10^{15} Btu
1 therm	= 10^5 Btu

Power

1 Hp	= 550 ft-lb/s
1 HP	= 33,000 ft-lb/min
1 Hp	= 0.7067 Btu/s
1 Hp	= 2545 Btu/hr
1 Hp	= 745.7 W
1 W	= 3.414 Btu/hr
1 kW	= 1.341 Hp
1 ton	= 12,000 Btu/hr

Volume Flow Rate

1 cfm	= 7.481 gal/min
1 cfm	= 0.4719 L/s
1 m^3/s	= 35.31 ft^3/s
1 m^3/s	= 2119 cfm
1 gal/min	= 0.1337 cfm

Torque

1 N · m	= 10^7 dyne · cm
1 N · m	= 0.7376 lb-ft
1 N · m	= 10 197 g · cm
1 lb-ft	= 1.356 N · m

Viscosity

1 lb-s/ft^2	= 478 poise
1 poise	= 1 g/cm · s
1 N · s/m^2	= 0.02089 lb-s/ft^2

Pressure

1 atm	= 14.7 psi
1 atm	= 29.92 in Hg
1 atm	= 33.93 ft H_2O
1 atm	= 1.013 bar
1 atm	= 1.033 kg/cm^2
1 atm	= 101.3 kPa
1 psi	= 2.036 in Hg
1 psi	= 6.895 kPa
1 psi	= 68 950 dyne/cm^2
1 ft H_2O	= 0.4331 psi
1 kPa	= 0.145 psi

Index

READER REMARKS & REWARDS SURVEY

Your suggestions help us to improve this review continuously. As a way of saying thanks, we'll send you a FREE FE/EIT exams CD ($29.95 value) when you fill out and return this card. (Please include $5 shipping/handling.)

ABOUT YOU

Name _____

Address _____

City / State / ZIP _____

Phone / E–mail _____

Field / Position _____

❑ "You can tell them I said so!"   ❑ "Hey, send me that free CD!"
($5 ship/hndl, incl. check or CC#)

COMMENTS

_____

_____

_____

_____

Any content we missed? _____

_____

QUICK SURVEY

1) Your review? (F/G) (F/CE) (F/ME) (F/EE) (F/IE) (F/ChE) (P/CE) (P/ME) (P/EE)

2) Overall, this book is:
   A   Too sketchy
   B   Just about right
   C   Too much material

3) The problems in this book are:
   A   Too easy
   B   Just about right
   C   Too difficult

4) The solutions are:
   A   Too sketchy
   B   Just about right
   C   Too much explanation

5) Did you participate in a review course?
   A   YES, Course location/name _____
   B   NO

6) Did you use other material in your preparation?
   Please list_____

7) How long since your undergraduate college graduation:
   _____ years   _____ haven't yet

8) Rank factors in order of influence on your initial appraisal of this book (1 being most important):
   _____ Price   _____ Reputation
   _____ Written by professors _____ Presentation of material
   _____ Depth / Amount of material
   _____ Other _____

REWARDS FOR ERRATA!   *(Attach separate sheet if desired.)*

Think you found a mistake? We happily offer up to $3 for each error that has not already been discovered, depending on relevance

Error _____ Proposed Correction_____

Page Number_____ Problem or Example Number_____

SEND INFO TO A FRIEND, COLLEAGUE, OR COMPANY MANAGER

The following people would appreciate a *one–time* mailing of a catalog of your FE & PE resources.

Name_____   Name_____   Name_____

Address_____   Address_____   Address_____

_____   _____   _____

City _____   City _____   City _____

State / ZIP _____   State / ZIP _____   State / ZIP _____

❑ Civil ❑ Mechanical   ❑ Civil ❑ Mechanical   ❑ Civil ❑ Mechanical
❑ Electrical ❑ Other   ❑ Electrical ❑ Other   ❑ Electrical ❑ Other

TO RECEIVE *FREE* CD ...a $29.95 value!...fill out post-paid form, return with credit card info or check payable to "Great Lakes Press," for $5 shipping/handling.

Credit card #: _____ Exp. Date: _____

CC Billing Address:_____

Cut along this line, then fold, tape and mail

5/2001

Hey! Send me my FREE FE Exams CD!

 Check this box, fill out entire form on reverse side... ...then tear, fold and send in this whole postpaid card!

(please allow 2 weeks for delivery)

• CD includes 6 solved exams, Study-Director™ ...and much more!

Fold here second ↓

Just fill out, fold, tape & drop this survey card into any mailbox!

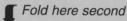

BUSINESS REPLY MAIL
FIRST-CLASS MAIL   PERMIT NO 71   GROVER, MO

POSTAGE WILL BE PAID BY ADDRESSEE

**GREAT LAKES PRESS
PO BOX 550
WILDWOOD, MO 63040-9913**

Fold here first ↑

Cut along this line, then fold, tape and mail